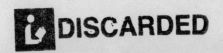

A SHORT HISTORY OF
MODERN EUROPE

THE MACMILLAN COMPANY
NEW YORK · BOSTON · CHICAGO · DALLAS
ATLANTA · SAN FRANCISCO

MACMILLAN & CO., Limited
LONDON · BOMBAY · CALCUTTA
MELBOURNE

**THE MACMILLAN COMPANY
OF CANADA, Limited**
TORONTO

ALPHONSVS CARDINALIS
ARCHIEPVS. LVGDVN

C. Mellan Gall' del. et f.   Roma Sup. per.
1 6 5 6

CARDINAL RICHELIEU

A SHORT HISTORY *of*
MODERN
EUROPE

BY T. W. RIKER

PROFESSOR OF MODERN EUROPEAN HISTORY AT THE
UNIVERSITY OF TEXAS. CORRESPONDING MEMBER OF THE
ACADÉMIE ROUMAIN. AUTHOR OF "THE MAKING OF
ROUMANIA," ETC., ETC.

1935

THE MACMILLAN COMPANY

NEW YORK

Published July, 1935.

SET UP AND ELECTROTYPED BY T. MOREY & SON

PRINTED IN THE UNITED STATES OF AMERICA

TO THE MEMORY OF
MY MOTHER,
WHO WAS
ALWAYS MY GREATEST INSPIRATION

PREFACE

History is both a drama and a process of evolution. It is the former which gives vitality to the latter; it is the latter which enables us to comprehend the struggle of man with his environment—a struggle which has brought us our present society.

How much of this struggle in the making of contemporary Europe should be pressed into a single volume is a problem that can find no single solution. The relative importance of this factor or that is a subject on which there can be no general agreement. It is inevitable that some phases should have to be slighted in this volume, and I have felt it necessary, wisely or otherwise, to give relatively little attention to arts and letters, the progress of science, the conduct of wars, and the place of tastes, habits, and religion in modern life, not because they are not all to be considered history, but because the inevitable demands of space required the unhappy task of compression. It has been my purpose also to deal with England more as an integral part of Europe than as a country which passed through various internal vicissitudes—a study more pertinent, it seemed to me, to a course on English history. It is, in general, my assumption that if the thread of development is clear, the teacher may diverge at any point and utilize some of the supplementary references; and as this book is intended primarily for the underclassman, I decided, after some hesitation, to confine them to works in English. Contrary to the usual practice, I have not begun at any arbitrary date. The story of the making of Modern Europe seemed to me to require an excursion far back into the Middle Ages, but as an elaborate description of the setting was hardly practicable, the introduction assumes that the student has taken a course in medieval history. I have divided the field into "eras," here again finding it impossible to settle on any specific dates; but a perusal of the subject matter will easily show approximately the block of history covered in each case. My main task has been to show how institutions evolved, then changed, and sometimes passed—all under the impact of man and time. Such procedure often required a critical attitude, else it might fail to be clear why man has not retained

his heritage in full. But the history of Europe is a drama without
a finale. We must needs break off while humanity is still in the
process of struggle—it knows not whither.

To my friends, Messrs. E. R. Adair, F. L. Nussbaum, and
M. R. Gutsch, all of whom read portions of the manuscript in the
highly critical spirit that I desired, I owe an immense debt of
gratitude. Messrs. W. T. Morgan, Franklin E. Palm, Calvin B.
Hoover, J. W. Swain, and Louis Gottschalk graciously supplied
me with information on matters in which they were specialists;
Mr. Frank Burr Marsh and Mr. Clarence Perkins gave me freely
of their time in discussing certain aspects of medieval history; and
some suggestions of Mr. R. E. Turner proved very useful. In
Mr. Hoover's admirable book, *Germany Enters the Third Reich*, I
found the clearest guide to the study of conditions which formed
the complicated background of Hitler's advent to power. To my
wife I am deeply grateful for help in verifying the index, and to
Messrs. Frederick T. Sutphen and A. V. V. Raymond of The
Macmillan Company for that genuine spirit of co-operation which
always means so much to an author. It is my hope that the course
of modern European history has been correctly presented, and that
my efforts at interpretation will not too often run counter to the
teacher's own judgment.

                                                      T. W. R.

AUSTIN, TEXAS
April, 1935

CONTENTS

ILLUSTRATIONS

MAPS

I. THE COMING OF THE MODERN AGE

1. THE EMERGENCE OF THE INDIVIDUAL

The individual in history; The individual in the early Middle Ages; Rôle of the Church; The preliminary renaissance; The Renaissance: its meaning and origins, its fruits; The Reformation: its causes, its beginnings and progress, its scope, explanation of its success, its fruits.

2. THE EMERGENCE OF THE MIDDLE CLASS

Meaning of the middle class; Rise of the towns; Coming of a money economy; Rise of capitalism; The expansion of trade; Growing political importance of the middle class; Influence of the explorations.

3. THE EMERGENCE OF THE MODERN STATE

A. INTERNAL ASPECTS

The feudal state as the antecedent of the modern state; The germ of the modern state; Evolution of the modern state: political aspects, economic aspects; Influence of the Renaissance; Influence of the Reformation.

B. EXTERNAL ASPECTS—THE FABRIC OF EUROPE

The Roman ideal of universal empire; The Church as an exponent of the imperial idea; The Holy Roman Empire as an exponent of the imperial idea; Basic weakness of the two; Causes of the collapse of the imperial idea; The "national" state; Influence of the Renaissance; Influence of the Reformation; The Catholic Reaction: origins, instruments; The Wars of Religion; A new fabric of Europe.

The term, "modern," is so relative that even an approximate date for the beginning of the Modern Age is very misleading. The shading of the Middle Ages into the Modern Age was a long and gradual process. As an historian has well expressed it, "The trend of recent historical research leads one to doubt the very conception of any very definite medieval period. The evolution of modern European society has been continuous." The purpose of this introduction is therefore to show the development of certain forces, which, battling with what has come to be thought of as essentially "medieval," produced by the seventeenth century a mental outlook very different from that of the age when, let us say, the papacy and feudalism were at their height. We are, in other words, concerned with a period of transition. First of all, however, it may be well to consider for a moment the geographical setting.

To classify Europe as a separate continent is from the strictly geographical standpoint somewhat arbitrary. Though the Mediterranean Sea detaches it definitely from Africa, and though the Black and Caspian Seas and the Caucasus Mountains partially separate it from Asia, the Ural Mountains form only an approximate boundary to the east, and it was the gap to the south of these mountains, the low, marshy waste that intervenes between the Urals and the Caspian Sea, that let in the hordes from Asia; and, furthermore, the country to the east of the Urals is in no way dissimilar to that on the west.[1] There is some point, therefore, in saying that Europe is just an appendage of Asia. Even in the matter of human geography the accepted boundaries of Europe may be challenged; for the peoples of the Barbary Coast, to the north of the Sahara Desert, are of the same racial stock as the peoples of southern Europe, while the Turks, on the other hand, seem rather to belong to Asia than to Europe. Our demarcation of Europe is even from the standpoint of history comparatively recent, if we take into consideration the whole period of civilized man. Civilization for many centuries had its principal center in the Mediterranean basin, and not only Italy and Greece but Egypt and Asia Minor belonged at certain periods to that same miniature world which drew so much of its life from the great interior sea. Similarly, there has always been the same level of culture on both sides of the Urals, and if we look at the continent of Europe as a map of civilization, we might imagine a gradual slope from the Oder and the upper Danube to the Volga, and from there on a dead level. Yet the steady cultural decline of the eastern shores of the Mediterranean, the subjection of northern Africa to Islam, and the eventual incursion of Russia into the European family provide us with something of a justification for definitely marking off a separate continent—the accepted boundary being purely one of convenience.

But close attachment to Asia and proximity at one point to Africa has had an impressive effect on Europe's past. The Arabs

[1] Dr. H. J. Fleure, the British geographer, points out that climatically the Pripet Marshes form a natural dividing line. Europe to the west of these marshes seldom suffers excessive heat and its winters are rarely severe; while "the Russian plain beyond the Pripet Marshes is, on the other hand, subject to painful extremes which seriously limit man's efficiency in both summer and winter and leave him but short periods in spring and autumn for effective freshness and enterprise." The tendency of the Russians to alternating periods of extreme lassitude and an almost ferocious energy is sometimes explained on the score of climate.

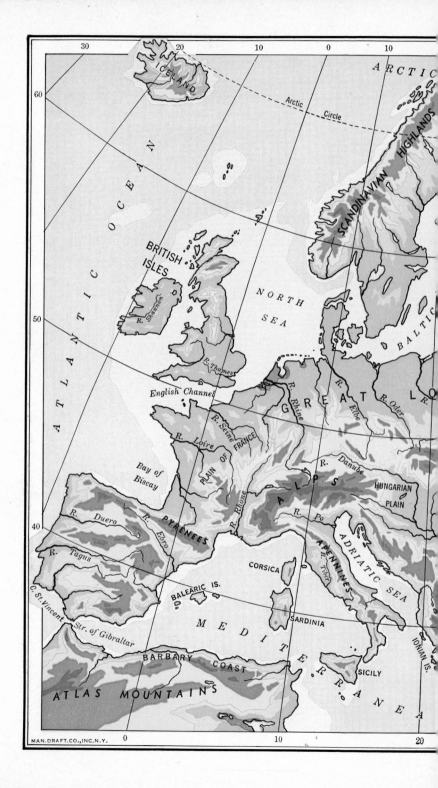

ARCTIC

SCANDINAVIAN HIGHLANDS

Arctic Circle

60

ICELAND

ATLANTIC OCEAN

BRITISH
ISLES

NORTH
SEA

BALTIC

50

R. Shannon

R. Thames

English Channel

GREAT

R. Rhine

R. Elbe

R. Oder

R.

R. Seine

R. Loire

PLAIN OF FRANCE

Bay of
Biscay

R. Rhone

A L P S

R. Danube

HUNGARIAN
PLAIN

40

R. Duero

R. Ebro

PYRENEES

R. Po

APENNINES

ADRIATIC SEA

R. Tagus

CORSICA

R. Tiber

C. St. Vincent

BALEARIC IS.

SARDINIA

Str. of Gibraltar

M E D I T E R

IONIAN IS.

BARBARY COAST

SICILY

R A N E A

ATLAS MOUNTAINS

MAN. DRAFT. CO., INC. N.Y.

30   20   10   0   10

0   10   20

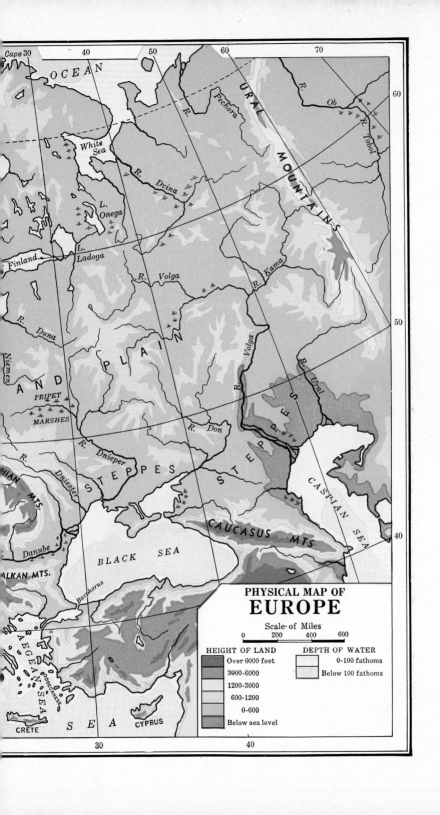

OCEAN

URAL

White
Sea

R.

R. Pechora

Ob

R.

R. Tobol

60

R. Dvina

L.
Onega

Finland

L.
Ladoga

R. Volga

R. Kama

50

Niemen

R. Duna

P L A I N

Volga

R. Ural

PRIPET
MARSHES

R. Don

S T E P P E S

CASPIAN SEA

R. Dnieper

R.

Dniester

S T E P P E S

CAUCASUS MTS.

40

HIAN MTS.

Danube

BLACK   SEA

BALKAN MTS.

Bosphorus

AEGEAN SEA

DODECANESE

PHYSICAL MAP OF
EUROPE

Scale of Miles

0   200   400   600

CRETE

CYPRUS

SEA

HEIGHT OF LAND	DEPTH OF WATER
Over 6000 feet	0-100 fathoms
3000-6000	Below 100 fathoms
1200-3000	
600-1200	
0-600	
Below sea level	

passed into Spain, the Turks crossed the Dardanelles and entered the Balkan Peninsula, and, earlier than these incursions, countless Asiatic tribes had swept clear across the Russian steppes, some to settle permanently in Europe, others merely to plunder and return to Mother Asia. It was only after Europe became fairly well peopled and states began to be formed that such inundations ceased. Europe, becoming civilized, began to defend herself. Indeed the Arabs, after apparently earning the right to remain in Spain, were finally thrown out, and in our own day the Turks have been all but extruded from their choice spot on the Bosphorus. It is not our purpose to trace the mysterious origins of Europe's peoples—a task that would take us back to a period anterior to these migrations. Their differences in language and physiognomy are a fact, but the causes we shall leave to the ethnologists to settle. It may perhaps be fitting, however, to mention some at least of the reasons why a continent, so much smaller than its neighbors, has far and away surpassed them in cultural attainments.

In its land surface, in the character of its soil, and in its climate Europe has much the advantage over both Asia and Africa. There are no great stretches of desert, no impassable mountain ranges (as in Asia), and, west of the Pripet Marshes, there are few regions to be found where either cold or heat is intense. It is remarkably homogeneous in its geographical character. In no other continent does so large an area receive sufficient rainfall at every season of the year. It has also abundant storms, which produce those changes of temperature that make for human vigor. It is fortunate, too, that so large an expanse of itself is bathed by the warm currents of the Gulf Stream, and the gentle, moderating effects of the west winds are felt as far to the east as Lake Ladoga. In the productivity of its soil and its supply of mineral deposits it is likewise unusually favored; and its long and broken sea-front make it easy for at least half the continent to reach the outside world. Culturally Russia has lagged behind the rest of Europe, for there the monotonous immensity of her seemingly boundless plains tended to produce a fairly uniform type of person, who also, as the result of historical circumstances, lived his life for the most part aloof from the rest of Europe. But Russia is at best a mere blending of Europe and Asia; the cultural center of the continent lies further west. In the words of the American geographer, Huntington, "The energetic area of western and central Europe has been the

great center of civilization for a thousand years. From it has gone
forth more new ideas than from all the rest of the world combined.
Its manufactures have flooded all parts of the earth. Politically it
dominates about sixty per cent of the earth's surface. Socially its
domination is still greater. . . . Wherever one turns, one feels the
tentacles of the great European center of civilization reaching out
and vivifying the life of the whole world." It is our task to see how
the people of Europe, building on the heritage of an earlier period,
the Middle Ages, shaped the Modern Europe of today.

Europe of the seventeenth century was a Europe bringing order
out of chaos, a Europe that was coming to fix more clearly its
standards, and a Europe that was founding its offshoots across
the seas. But first we must trace the emergence of those three
predominant factors that contributed the human power behind
our present civilization.

The Emergence of the Individual

The individual in history

Perhaps there is nothing on which the march of civilization so
much depends as upon the position of the individual. It was the
individualism of the Greeks that gave their civilization its free
play and varied flavor, and it was the individualism of the more
practical and disciplined Romans that enabled them to found a
great empire and adapt to their own uses the culture of the Greeks.
While it is true that excess of freedom may come to require some
restraint for the benefit of society as a whole, it is generally the
emergence of the individual from the mass that makes possible the
cutting of new roads of progress. In a sense all history is the
fitting of countless human beings into a mold that insures a certain
continuity and stability in human affairs and at the same time
enables the individual to express his personality within its range.

The individual in the early Middle Ages

Yet that mold of which we speak was in the early Middle Ages
of so tough and narrow a texture that the individual was all but
completely lost to view. If he were a peasant, he held a fixed position in the medieval land system; if he were a craftsman, he was
under the rigid tutelage of his gild; if he essayed to think, he was
under the all-embracing authority of the Church, which regulated
in every particular his moral, religious, and intellectual life. It was
not, however, that such bondage was intended to make slaves of
human beings but rather that an age which was struggling to keep
its scraps of civilization required a corporate life to enable it to

subsist. The peasant must have protection while he fed himself and his family and the lord who defended him; the craftsman needed the protective weight of the gild to defend him against the dishonest worker within the gates and the marauder on the threshold; and the individual Christian, if he had any hopes of Heaven, must look to the all-knowing, ever-vigilant authority of the Church to defend him against the Devil or the sower of false beliefs. Indeed it was the Church which had saved what was left from the wreck of civilization and had given a crude society a consciousness of unity for a single lofty purpose. None the less, speaking generally, the individual was merged in that huge, ungainly mass which was medieval society in the Dark Ages. Those few more dominating personalities who were able through their position to make their voices heard in human affairs seemed to utilize their faculties to confirm existing tradition and to fortify an order of which they were themselves the servants as well as the champions. The dominant note in the Middle Ages was obedience to authority. Ideally—and for a long time actually—the individual was but a part, and a very obscure part of a whole. He was but a cog in an enthralling and intricate machine.

With the ever-present need of tempering violence or defending oneself against it, this static civilization seemed, in a sense, a refuge from a world threatened with anarchy. Much of the scientific knowledge which the Ancients had contributed had been lost, and the spirit of learning had seemed to depart with it. Turning in disgust from a decadent society amid the glory that once was Rome, the early Christians had looked heavenward and sought in religion a means of living in the hope of a better world. Thus gradually the Christian Church, which represented the only stable force in a decaying social order, came to be the rallying-point for all the ignorant masses and the torch which alone could light the way of knowledge. And this knowledge, as was natural, was subordinated to religion, while religion was the key to eternal life. Born in sin (through the effects of Adam's fall), and sinful again on his own account, it was only through the ministrations of the Church (so men were taught) that the individual could be purified and prepared to attain salvation. In the conception of the Church this temporal life was only the *via dolorosa*, the painful way to the hereafter—that world beyond which alone was worthy of contemplation. So exclusive and absorbing, indeed,

The rôle of the Church

was this attitude of mind that there was no room for observation or experience. The universe and all its mysteries were explainable by Holy Writ.[1] The marvels of nature were of less consequence than the miracles which saints were supposed to perform. Nothing, in fact, in this temporal life mattered. It was in such a spirit that monasticism was founded, and it was that same spirit that sent men into the wilderness to flee from the temptations of this world and fit themselves to win eternal bliss by stifling every bodily impulse while they contemplated the Divine. When St. Augustine, greatest of the Church fathers, specified what things should be studied, whether history, or rhetoric, or logic, or the animals, plants, minerals, and places mentioned in the Bible, it was that Scripture might be better comprehended, and not for any better understanding of these subjects. Thus Scripture, together with its interpretation by the Church fathers, soon to become a body of doctrine, was alone worthy of the attention of the learned, while for the common man faith or respect for his superiors sufficed. It was no wonder that the age believed in miracles. It was only less strange that Churchmen did. Since Scripture itself abounds in the supernatural and since even people as worldly as the Greeks had had their mysteries, one can well understand the existing concept of a miracle-working Deity. "That the great facts of the Christian creed were beyond the proof or disproof of reason was a principle definitely accepted by the Fathers." It was likewise assumed that morality was the handmaid of religion. No holiness was possible outside the bonds of the Church. Conscience and intellect were equally in harness.

Thus if we go back to the earlier Middle Ages (a strict division of time is almost impossible), we find that only the clergy (with a few negligible exceptions) were really educated, and knowledge was cultivated and utilized only to expound certain precepts all of which had the prime aim of gaining for man salvation. Deriving the little knowledge it had from the storehouse of the past and converting it to one end, the Church held the human mentality in a straightjacket, while it decried the appeal of the flesh as the promptings of the Evil One. The fact that it was inevitable and perhaps necessary that authority should have been unquestioned

---

[1] There were some rather insignificant mathematical treatises during the Dark Ages and a rudimentary encyclopedia, full of fancies as well as facts, but showing a little trace of Greek influences.

must not blind us to the fact that it was so. Only within a certain narrow radius was there room for speculation and it did not penetrate to fundamentals. When scholasticism developed in course of time with its purpose of proving the verity of certain traditions by means of logic—the method which the discovery of certain works of the Greek philosopher, Aristotle, had rendered popular—we reach the greatest achievement of the medieval intellect. There was no thought of searching out new truths. It was "rather the contemplation of a truth, static, fixed, complete, and perfect for all eternity." But if the affairs of God and man were as simple as then imagined, human society might have looked through a peephole indefinitely.

But mankind cannot fortify itself against all change, for there is always the unexpected in human affairs. When the Arabs, more advanced in the realm of knowledge than Europeans, established an empire in Spain in the eighth century, it was almost inevitable that eventually the results of their researches would find their way to the minds of Christian Europe. Again, when the Crusades, so typically medieval in their blending of the barbaric with missionary zeal, brought men to countries they had never seen before and civilizations they had never known (Saracen or Byzantine), the broadening influence of such contacts was bound to bring results. Further it must be realized that towns had sprung up within the shell of feudalism, and that, gradually outgrowing the confines of the local market and profiting in some cases by trade with the East, they became the logical exponents of a new and more mundane outlook on life. In truth the Italian towns had never wholly ceased to possess a certain individuality, and we have record of certain of their schools taught by laymen as early as the seventh century. When a university was established at Bologna toward the end of the eleventh century, it became the greatest center for that purely secular study, Roman law. It was the Arabic influence in Spain, the Crusades, the revival of trade, and the founding of universities—phenomena which made themselves decisively felt in the twelfth century—that paved the way for what we may call the twelfth and thirteenth century renaissance. Already the static medieval world was beginning to throb with a new life.

Though it is obvious that the economic order was becoming slightly less compressing to the individual (the peasants, for example, were beginning to be emancipated from serfdom), it was

The preliminary renaissance

the blows dealt the moral and intellectual authority of the Church
that most claim our present attention to this formative epoch.
The individual seemed to be tugging at his fetters and beginning to
look at the world about him. Something of the new spirit was
manifested by the Troubadours, those singers of southern France
in the twelfth century, who found such exquisite joy in earthly
things; and we may also recall in the same period that half-roman-
tic, half-practical figure, Frederick II, who accepted the holy call
of the Crusades, yet stooped to negotiate a profitable peace with
the Infidel—surely a precursor of Francis I, the future ally of the
Sultan. The individual was pitting his strength against the medieval conscience, and sometimes—at least for a time—he might
succeed. After all, the world was broadening. When an Arab was
commissioned by a prince of Sicily to set forth in a book the existing
knowledge of geography, we may be sure that in the twelfth century
the Church had ceased to be the sole fount of learning; and if the
Church did use Aristotle to fortify Christian doctrine, other writings of the same philosopher, become better known through Arabic
influence, led many to wonder if after all the works of ancient
writers might not hold some hidden truths about this world which
they inhabited. It was probably due to the Arabs that the mariner's
compass and gunpowder, as well as paper, (all of Asiatic origin) came to be known in the twelfth century; while the making of mechanical clocks—at least as early as the thirteenth—
showed some technological advance, besides beginning to give the
world a more general and more accurate sense of time. Even
spectacles made their appearance before the end of the thirteenth
century—a marvelous boon to the aging scholar of some generations later. More and more, indeed, was the human mind stretching out to the unknown. How much might it not discover? The
passionate desire of the monk, Abelard, in the twelfth century,
to understand in order to believe showed a spirit of unwillingness to leave all mysteries to the realm of the supernatural. Still
more of a departure was the position of Roger Bacon, probably
the greatest intellect of the century following. Though he held the
conventional view that knowledge should serve the ends of theology
alone, he boldly proclaimed the importance of learning things by
observation instead of merely evolving theories from philosophical
deductions. And for Bacon, as well as others, experimentation
seemed the prime key to invention. Faintly, then, we see the in-

dividual mind asserting itself. Even while the Church's ascendancy in religion was practically unchallenged, its intellectual eminence was being shaken. The bases of knowledge were being scrutinized; learning was already beginning to take on a secular tinge; and in Italy, where relics of the past could not fail to serve as something of an inspiration, the Latin writers, Cicero and Virgil, were beginning to be praised for their own worth and men were turning back to an age whence more and more knowledge could be derived. It was indeed the love of the classics that ushered in the period of the Renaissance.

The Renaissance was primarily a revival of learning for its own *The Renais-* sake or for what men might derive therefrom, and it began with a *sance: its meaning and* rediscovery of the classics. In its broader aspects, however, the *origins* movement signified a gradual evolution through which society passed in the fourteenth and fifteenth centuries, causing men to weaken and (in some cases) to burst the fetters with which medievalism with its exalted uniformity had hedged them in, and thus releasing to a great extent the individual mind. Its fundamental spirit was that of inquiry. It emphasized the fact (already perceived in the twelfth century) that civilization was not static but a moving panorama which opened up an infinite fund of possibilities. It partly caused, partly comprised the discovery of a new world, the cultivation of learning for its own intrinsic value, the founding of new sciences, the flowering of a more expressive art, and an essentially critical spirit, even to the turning of a searchlight on religion. It was essentially a layman's movement, though it came to involve even the Church in its all-pervasive influence. Though historically the movement may be said to have begun with an assiduous search for the writings of the ancient world (a door which the Italian scholar, Petrarch, had been first to open); yet, as there are no sharp turns in history, one may readily infer that the seeds of the so-called Renaissance had been sown during that earlier period of awakening we have discussed.

What is known as humanism (the study of the *litteræ humaniores* or classics) had its birth in Italy, for it was there that inspiration could be gleaned from the stately relics of the past and it was there also that urban life had come to demand a greater luxury of self-expression. On the side of the ancient languages humanism required a studied accuracy; on the side of content it meant the pursuit of a wider knowledge and deeper appreciation of the

classics and hence an eager desire to know Greek—first taught in
Italy toward the end of the fourteenth century. We shall not take
time to renew our acquaintance with the writers who first embodied
the new spirit or remind ourselves of the artists who constituted
the glory of fifteenth century Italy. It may be well, however, to
realize that the wealth of her petty despots had much to do with
the promotion of this art, giving talent all the greater opportunity for expression. While the architects of the great cathe-
drals which were the crowning glory of the Middle Ages had
so effaced themselves in the corporate life to which they belonged
that even their names are unknown to us, the painters and sculptors
of the Renaissance belonged rather to the period when personal
ambition as well as the lure of the infinite had come to inspire
genius. It is true that the artist's talent was generally displayed
in sacred themes; yet Raphael painted the portrait of a pope and
Cellini carved the figure of a pagan god. In any case the spirit was
released from the spell of Heaven and soared above the leveling
habits of medievalism.

Its fruits   In no field of endeavor was the new freedom of the individual
more plainly shown than in that of science. In no other field were
the preconceptions of the Middle Ages so rudely shattered. The
sciences of physics, chemistry, anatomy, zoology, and botany
came definitely into being—foundations laid for future centuries
of research. Medicine had already come to attain the importance
of a science (much in the first place having been learned from the
Arabs), and surgery soon took its place beside it, operations being
performed on certain parts of the body with alcoholics to deaden
the pain. Servetus, the Spaniard, whom Calvin later put to death,
discovered the circulation of the blood through the lungs, though
it was not till the seventeenth century that Harvey learned the
whole functioning of the heart in this connection. Nor should one
forget historical criticism with its pioneer, Lorenzo Valla, who
showed that certain documents on which the Church had laid great
store were clumsy forgeries. Here the critical spirit of the Renaissance was interestingly exemplified. It was when science directly
countered its cherished beliefs that the Church was liable to show
a stubborn resistance, and it was perhaps the field of astronomy
that by reason of its fascination for the medievalists held always
the chief perils for the investigator. When the Polish scholar,
Copernicus, found convincing proof for the view that the sun, not

the earth, was the center of the universe, the matter of giving it publicity required the utmost caution,[1] and when his follower, in the seventeenth century, Galileo, confirmed his position, he was brought to bar by the Church and forced, under threat of torture, to retract his views. Yet even the Church did not discourage the actual fact of investigation. It was clearly impossible to turn the hands of the clock backward, now that time and man had opened new doors of knowledge. The art of navigation, revolutionized by the mariner's compass and other inventions, led to longer and longer voyages, which, culminating in the circumnavigation of the globe, confirmed existing belief that the earth was not flat but round. But more important, perhaps, than all other forces for change was the invention of printing. This great achievement of German artisans led at once to the multiplication of books and, in consequence, to a far greater spread of human knowledge. Through its capacity for the spread of ideas it made the Reformation possible.

Yet one cannot but feel some misgivings for the price which the individual sometimes paid to view the world in his own way. In its emphasis on other-worldliness the Church had tried to make society humble and not self-seeking. The very fact of its patronage of the gilds with their stern morality, its denunciation of usury as implying extortion, and its plea for a "just price," showed a fatherly care for its flock that denoted to a certain extent the existence of a species of social control. The medieval monk had been an agent of homely instruction as well as material relief. Poverty, indeed, was not an evil in the conception of the Church, and charity, as a means, not of removing it, but of expressing a spirit of love, was probably more genuine and effective in the Middle Ages than was the case after the Church's influence waned. The spirit of the Renaissance, with its stress on the temporal life, brought self-interest more to the foreground than that common love of humanity which the Church had long expressed; and even the Church itself had had to view the amassing of wealth as a natural phenomenon. When the individual, profiting by the spirit of a changing world, sought to accumulate "treasures on earth" (more than ever after the great explorations of the fifteenth cen-

[1] It should be noted that the Lutherans were at first more enraged than the Catholic Church by this discovery, though they were, of course, quite powerless in the matter.

tury), expecting as his right the fullest profit from his enterprise, Christian morality seemed to be forced to adopt less rigid standards.[1] The banker could not feel that the taking of interest was a sin, or the merchant, that the price which he could obtain was reprehensible. Thus the restless spirit of the age broke through the regulations which the Church had lovingly devised for the protection of society.

In the changing world of the Renaissance the cloister and the hermitage had largely lost their appeal. Life was too rich now to be despised as a condition of irksome waiting. Indeed it was upon the monks and nuns, whose life seemed so useless in many eyes, that the new critics of society trained their first guns. By the pen of Rabelais, the jovial fabulist, who made the French court rock with laughter, and by that of the Dutchman, Erasmus, the greatest scholar of his day, the monks were equally held up to ridicule. The temporal life, while still a stepping-stone to Heaven, had come to be a place where men should mingle freely with one another and find much that was worthy of inspection and delight. Sinful though he might be, man was interesting—even in the eyes of Montaigne, the cheerful skeptic of the Renaissance in France, who delighted in showing up his limitations. In Italy, indeed, the love of ancient models and the lessening of the old respect for things invisible had led to a riot of paganism, the body being enthroned with little regard for the soul, while art and letters took with many the place formerly accorded to religion. Too romantic to care for theology and too individualistic to set up a new dogmatic system to replace the old, the Italians had no part in the shaping of the new Christendom and even lacked the moral strength to keep their liberties safe. That is why Italy, the cradle of the Renaissance, succumbed to internal quarrels and its spirit became finally broken under foreign rule and intellectual tyranny.

But with some of the northern peoples the Renaissance displayed a more earnest side. With them the shift of interest from God to man was less profound. That spirit of inquiry which sent Italians to the classics turned scholars north of the Alps to a study of the Scriptures. The searching scholarship of Erasmus showed that the standard version of the Bible was seriously inaccurate; other

[1] In the thirteenth century the fate of the Church's campaign against usury showed that their opposition was, as Professor Clapham, the British economist says, a "forlorn hope." Yet even in the sixteenth century one finds business men worried over the influence of such teachings upon their creditors.

scholars, Wyclif in England and (later) Lefèvre in France, translated the Bible (or part of it) into the vernacular, thus bringing it—at least by word of mouth—to the common man. These scholars were among the precursors of the Reformation. In such men, moreover, the liberal spirit of the Renaissance was embodied. The medieval emphasis on authority, so typical of the men who were to lead the Reformation, was usually quite foreign to their spirit. Perhaps if the Protestant Revolt had not assumed a dogmatic turn, perhaps if it had not been as constructive as it was destructive, its success would have been doubtful. But it was not the way of Erasmus. The fact that he was so keen a critic seemed to unfit him for the work of a reformer. It was both a narrower mind and a more courageous spirit that history cast for the leadership of the Religious Revolution.

While the Church's intellectual ascendancy was shattered by the Renaissance, this movement left her religious domination unimpaired. Even the skepticism that manifested itself in Italy or elsewhere did not break outwardly with the Church. Yet none the less the Renaissance paved the way for the Reformation. The individual emancipated from feudalism or going to a new world in quest of gain or using his wits to find new truths was potentially a person that was ready to release himself from a system which still held the human conscience in subjection. If this was to be the last-attained phase of the passing of medievalism, it was perhaps because in no other sphere of human interest was tradition so strong and in no other sphere was human error so perilous. Man might defy temporal authority and lose his life, but, if man defied the will of God, he might also lose his soul.

We shall not enter in detail into the causes of the Religious Revolution, since to do so would demand an exhaustive study of the Church, more appropriate to a book dealing primarily with the Middle Ages. The movement we are discussing is commonly called the "Reformation" because its whole effect was to heal certain abuses and, on the part of certain communities, to re-form the structure of religious life. That movement, which by involving a secession from the Universal Church brought about these results is also called the Protestant Revolt. But its effects were so far-reaching and of such significance to a later period that it was rather a "revolution"—a religious revolution, giving the individual ultimately if not immediately the right to follow in religion the

The Reformation:
its causes

dictates of his heart or mind. This revolution had its origin, like all revolutions, in certain conditions in the existing order coupled with a wave of enlightenment which seemed to show them up as false or in certain ways unsatisfying.

The misfortune of the Church was that it had to perform the mission of Christ on earth and yet was made up of fallible human beings. Such was the paradox unavoidable in human affairs, and even some of the Apostles had strayed from the Master's ways. In the very nature of things subsequent Churchmen—at least those with the greatest authority—did not live in the simple environment that surrounded Jesus and the Twelve. The Church was an institution which became rich through the pious bequests of the faithful or the tempting facility with which it could exploit them, and it also came to possess temporal power, that is territorial power, through the need of defending itself in an age of violence. Wealth might be expended in luxury or in misdirected efforts such as wars against the heathen. Power might be interpreted to imply a right to dictate to men in all things for their good—a practice which would inevitably rouse antagonism on the part of·princes who had also tasted power. At all times during the Middle Ages the Church had paid the price of such blunders, and sometimes it realized, or was made to realize, the dangers of wealth or power. Nearly every monastic order—the institution which of all the products of the Church was most intended to emulate poverty and holy living— had succumbed to excess of wealth and been forced to reform, only to suffer the same experience again. The attempt to force its will upon kings, the failure to find a practical boundary between things temporal and things spiritual, had brought the Church in conflict with forces that had more brute strength at their command, with a consequent weakening of the Church not only in power but in authority and prestige. Much of the trouble that beset the Church had, of course, been due to lack of wisdom on the part of certain popes, for the Church, if we consider one side, was an absolute monarchy with all the inherent evils that absolute monarchy can possess, together with one misfortune to which an hereditary absolutism is not subject—namely, a periodic occasion for a political squabble to obtain a post of exceptional influence and wealth. Since Italians were adept at political intrigue and since most of the college of cardinals which elected the popes were Italians, the popes were usually of Italian extraction, many during the Renaissance coming of powerful Italian families. Hence, as the world became more secular, the modern state more self-sufficient and self-assertive, and the pope's immediate neighbors less respectful and more acquisitive, the papacy became more and more Italian in its character, less and less universal in its outlook and spirit. No greater attack upon the dignity of the Church had ever been dealt it than when the popes had been forced to leave the Eternal City for that virtual exile in Avignon where they gave the world the impression of being tools of the French kings. The sight of two and sometimes three popes wrangling for the mantle of St. Peter was an even greater scandal. Even when the Church righted itself—that is, when Church councils brought peace and unity once more and the papacy was restored to Rome—the effect of that baneful period was not effaced. Within the ranks of the clergy themselves had arisen the question whether the pope or a general council (the sum total of the higher clergy) was the rightfully dominant body in the Church. Thus the Church was threatened with the loss of the strategic value of absolute monarchy and was at the same time torn with a strife which left it divided against itself. It was in the day of the Church's deepest humiliation—that is, the fourteenth century—that the Renaissance came to weaken men's faith in its omniscience. More than that, after the papacy's return to Italy, the subtle influence of the Renaissance, with its incentive to worldly splendor, caught the popes themselves in its toils. Thus Leo X, the pope whom history selected to pit his strength against Luther, cared for little beyond his manuscripts and art treasures. Worse than that, the Renaissance popes had fallen into the vices so prevalent in Italian society. While it is probably true that the moral tone of the Church, in general, had greatly improved after the return from Avignon, nevertheless the conduct of the popes themselves—or at least most of them—was enough to shock the conscience of every pious Christian. There were, indeed, many devoted Churchmen—not all of them humanists by any means—who had honestly deplored the corruption which they saw in the Avignon days, and the demand for a "reformation in head and members" had been a solemn issue at the councils of the fifteenth century. But the conciliar movement of reform had suffered by the political recovery of the papacy, and it took the storms of revolt to bring it again to life.

But it was not alone the moral prestige of the Church which

had suffered during this period of upheaval. Some of the Church's traditions had received assault. In the fifteenth century Lorenzo Valla had exposed the spurious character of one of the documents on which the papacy had built up its claims. The lesson was obvious enough. If the Church could err in some of its cherished traditions, why not in others? Already heretics like John Huss had gone so far as to deny that the Church was confined to the clergy; rather was it the whole body of the faithful, of which Christ, not the pope, was the head; and for this position the Bohemian reformer had paid with his life. Though it was true, of course, that Wyclif and his follower, Huss, had taken an extreme position which few were willing to countenance, nevertheless it is clear that the Church, before the storms that were soon to beset her, was liberal enough to allow a certain degree of theological discussion, and hence the majority of the humanists were content to let the truth, as they saw it, reveal itself, as it were, instead of waging war directly on the institution itself. They preferred in other words to remain within the Church and try, rather, to adapt it to the new learning. Nevertheless the whole spirit of the northern humanists was to cut through the elaborate doctrines which the medieval scholars had devised and the emphasis on externals which in a primitive and credulous society had been natural and perhaps necessary and to find the source of religion in the Bible itself. Somewhat the same in spirit were the mystics who sought and felt that they had found a direct communion with God, and it was this group, more than the humanists with their "rationalism," that gave Luther his subsequent slant. And finally, in noting those forces that were undermining the position of the Church we should include the vigorous self-interest which manifested itself in the rising modern state and in a self-centered and ambitious middle class. These two factors which we shall consider as contributive to the passing of the Middle Ages were essentially out of harmony with an institution which drew its strength and inspiration from the past, and the Church's claims to material support from all the faithful touched a spot that was certainly becoming more and more tender—namely, the purse. Just as the kings of France and England in the fourteenth century had not only refused to allow the Church sole competence over the crimes of Churchmen but also had checked the flow of money in taxes to Rome, so in the fifteenth century the middle class of Germany were beginning to resent the exactions of what they regarded as an Italian autocracy.

Thus it may be seen that the streams which flowed into the torrent of revolution were various. One was religious and moral, looking for a higher level of religious life. Another was intellectual, striking at least in spirit at some of the doctrines of the Church. Another was political, and still another, economic, the first two being closely blended and having little to do with the others. None of them alone possessed enough strength to produce a torrent. None of these forces, when viewed in the large, was deliberately aimed to overthrow the religious ascendancy of the Church. But in one way or another they lent themselves irresistibly to that end. All, in fact, being, broadly speaking, aspects of what we call the Renaissance, converged to produce a revolution. Medievalism was to make its last stand against the arrogance of the individual.

We can relate only briefly the story of the Protestant Revolt. *Its beginnings and progress* Cases of heresy were not unusual in the Middle Ages but they had had no lasting significance. There had been a distinct foretaste of the coming revolt in the career of John Wyclif, the English reformer of the fourteenth century, who denied the authority of the pope and many of the Church's doctrines. Later in the century, a disciple of Wyclif, the Bohemian, John Huss, had many followers, and it is not improbable that if the printing press had then been invented, enabling such a movement to spread rapidly, Huss, rather than Luther, would have been the standard-bearer of the Religious Revolution. One of the leading causes of disaffection was papal extortion, as the difficulties in getting money from the better organized nations of the West had led the pope to throw a disproportionate burden on the German people, who possessed no powerful prince to protect their interests. It was Luther, indeed, who provided the unifying element, which, in default of a sovereign, was needed by this spirit of protest if it were to lead to open defiance. The spark which lighted the conflagration was the affair of the indulgences in 1517. An easy way by which the papacy raised money was by the granting of what was known as an indulgence, a cancellation, conditional on repentance, of some of the punishment imposed by divine justice upon the sinner after his guilt had been forgiven through the priestly absolution; and a common means of escaping such temporal punishments was that of giving a sum of money for a sacred end. A *plenary* indulgence—

the type that was widely offered at this time—signified "the removal of the entire punishment due to sin so that no expiation in purgatory was necessary," and it could be obtained either for oneself or for one of the departed. To the masses, who were impressed by the weight of their sins and by the teaching that even a forgiving God demanded the performance of penance, it seemed a cheap way of getting out of future agonies. It was natural, however, that the procurer of an indulgence should think not of the object for which money was sought [1] but the mere fact that he was purchasing

Wood cut by Hans Brosamer

MARTIN LUTHER

an act of grace; and it is equally clear that many who sold these indulgences often grossly misrepresented them in an effort to promote their sale. We shall not dwell on the doctrine (which was not very old) or the rather sordid features of this particular sale. It happened that when a hawker of these commodities began to sell them in the neighborhood of Saxony,[2] a certain monk, Martin Luther, who was also professor of theology at the University of Wittenberg, raised his voice in denunciation. Luther dealt rather gently with the doctrine itself, but it galled him to see a gullible people paying what they could not afford in order to rid themselves of punishment which undoubtedly they deserved; repentance for one's sins, he felt, should suffice as consolation; and anyway why did not the pope empty purgatory for charity's sake? Originally placarded for discussion by his colleagues, this diatribe was printed and rapidly circulated; and naturally it struck a responsive cord. Was it not, after all, another case of this Italian potentate endeavoring to bleed the simple-minded Germans? Almost before

[1] In this case it was the building of St. Peter's at Rome.
[2] He was prohibited by the elector of Saxony from entering his dominions.

he knew it Luther found himself the head of a party and a movement. Since he had already come to believe that what he called "faith" made men righteous rather than the efficacy of those Sacraments concerned with salvation, it was clear that he was already in thought a heretic; and the skillful maneuvers of the Church, roused at last from its lethargy by the ruin of the sale of indulgences, together with his own rather obstinate and violent disposition, was soon to reveal him one in fact. When he was placed by his questioners in the position of denying first the authority of the pope and then that of a general council of the Church, he accepted the result as final, burned the papal bull of condemnation (of course, amid great applause), and wrote three pamphlets which impugned five of the seven sacraments of the Church, excoriated the papacy, and insisted on the efficacy of faith as against external rites and acts. While not, perhaps, aware of creating a schism, Luther was definitely establishing the bases of a new theology.

But matters were hastening to a crisis. Since the Church, while condemning a heretic, was obliged (even if it had been able to apprehend Luther) to depend upon a secular authority to consign him to the flames, the pope tried, though without success, to win over Luther's prince, the elector of Saxony, and the latter's overlord, the new emperor, Charles V. Although Charles and most of the princes were unfavorable to Luther, being repelled by his extreme position, yet none of them was especially sympathetic with the pope, Charles, because he had recently been at odds with him in Italy and because he felt that the Church really needed some reform, and the princes, because they had their own grudges against the papacy and did not like the idea of its browbeating a German. It was therefore decided to compromise; and Luther was summoned for a hearing—in a sense, a trial—before the imperial diet, then meeting at Worms. Although not knowing whether his safe-conduct would be respected (for Huss had been given one, and it had not saved him from the stake), Luther's courage did not fail him, and it was doubtless encouraged by the ovation which he received from the knights—the humbler nobles—as he rode to the place of meeting. We shall not dwell upon his momentary qualms or his subsequent unflinching courage and resolution. The immediate outcome was, in effect, indecisive; though even a negative victory for the heretic was momentous. Luther and his writings were formally condemned, though he was permitted in accordance with his safe-conduct to take his leave, and he was immediately given shelter in a castle of his friendly patron, the Elector of Saxony. Charles, for his part, soon left Germany for Spain, and little effort was made to give effect to the imperial edict. Indeed, the emperor's position in Germany was so weak (his vassals, the princes being practically independent) that if Charles, a foreigner by blood, had tried to enforce the edict, he would probably have strengthened Luther. The one way in which he could have had some hope of crushing the heretic was by insisting on the calling of a general council to reform the Church. But Charles was young, as well as engrossed in political problems; and perhaps, too, he underestimated the crisis. At all events, the Diet of Worms (1521) was something of a turning-point in history.

The failure of the Diet of Worms and the publicity which Luther's case had acquired on that occasion gave a great stimulus to the revolt, and the number of adherents rapidly increased, especially in the towns. There was also a general unrest which bode ill for all authority. The peasants rose in revolt and were cruelly repressed, Luther himself urging the princes to the utmost severity. Not himself interested in political and social questions, he did not wish to risk the impression that his own movement was dangerous to the existing social order; and more and more, as he required political support, he seemed to attach his movement to the interests of the princes, the pillars of order in Germany. Some time previously some religious fanatics had threatened to bring his movement into contempt, but Luther had succeeded in restoring order; and in 1530 his friend, Melancthon, formulated the Lutheran creed in what was known as the "Augsburg Confession," and this shaping of a platform, as it were, gave the movement greater unity.

Its scope   Meanwhile revolt from the Church had widened considerably in scope. In Switzerland it had begun at about the same time as in Germany, some of the cantons soon going so far as to renounce the authority of the Church. In England, while humanism had bred some cases of heresy, the revolt had its beginning in a political quarrel between the king, Henry VIII, and the pope, leading finally to a secession of the English church from Rome. But in Henry's time there was little change in doctrine, though it was significant that the Bible in English was brought direct to the masses. During the short reign of his successor, Edward VI, the tenets of the Anglican Church (somewhat similar to those of Lutheranism) were put into definite form, and after a brief Catholic reaction under his successor, Mary I, a final settlement of Anglican belief, the so-called Thirty-nine Articles, was framed in the reign of Elizabeth, and became the doctrinal basis of the Established Church of England. The divergence of the Anglican faith from that of the Catholic was not so great but that most of the population could gradually accept the change, though there still remained some Catholics, and most of Henry's clergy had refused to sever their ties with the ancient Church. It has been argued that the success of the Revolution in obtaining the allegiance of the great majority of the English people was due to an active minority, including a large number of nobles, many of whom had shared the fruits of Henry's pillage of the monasteries, a middle class whose mind was receptive to change, and a vigorous group of popular writers who undertook to "enlighten" public opinion. But Anglicanism, being State-ridden, produced no really great constructive thinkers. It was the Swiss revolt which contributed the greatest Protestant theologian and organizer. John Calvin, a French scholar who had fled from persecution in France, wrote his conception of the Christian religion with such clear and logical deduction from his premises that his theories readily furnished the doctrinal basis of Swiss Protestantism; and later, establishing himself at Geneva, he worked out a sort of fusion of Church and State under a régime so arbitrary that his enemies rightly called him "the pope of Geneva." Calvinism was mainly characterized by three things. In the first place, in contradistinction to the old Church, it emphasized the omnipotence of God, denying (as Luther also did) the free will of man, and holding that salvation was a gift of God to those alone to whom he chose to impart his grace. In other words some were predestined or "elected" to be saved, while others were correspondingly damned. This fatalistic theology, drawn from St. Augustine's interpretation of St. Paul, may largely explain the historic tenacity of the Calvinists, who felt that God's plan for man was strictly foreordained and that the godly—and the divine grace was supposed to reveal itself to the godly—must seek their chosen aims in life unswervingly. In the second place, as distinguished from Lutheranism, which had placed itself under the protection of the State, Calvinism stood for a democratic form of

Church government—a fact which made it the better suited to religious minorities on the defensive and rendered it especially acceptable to the middle classes. Thirdly and finally, Calvinism, taking the Bible literally (especially the moral code of the Jews) and gaining its inspiration from its austere and pitiless founder, prescribed strictly the moral conduct of its followers, and frowned on worldly pleasures in a manner reminiscent of the asceticism of the early monks. Apart from the principal Protestant sects, there were some offshoots which emphasized certain practices not countenanced by the others and a few free-thinkers like Servetus whom Calvin put to death. Just as Lutheranism spread to Poland and the Scandinavian countries, Calvinism took root in Scotland, England, France, the Netherlands, and Hungary as well as here and there in Germany. In both England and France, however, Calvinism was an illicit religion; for every well-organized state subjected all its subjects to one exclusive faith.

Explanation of its success　　It was during this expansive period that the fate of the Protestant Revolt was also decided. In Germany, where it had received its original impetus from resentment against the papacy, suppression of the revolt would probably have doomed the movement as a whole; hence the importance of the immunity which it enjoyed after the Diet of Worms. While it was formulating its creed, it gained a large number of princes, most of whom were doubtless attracted by the opportunity afforded them of seizing the Church lands in their dominions. Thus arose the secularization issue, destined to disturb the peace of Germany in a later generation. But the chief cause of the survival of Protestantism during these crucial years was probably negative. Charles V not only lacked the power as emperor to execute the Edict of Worms but also was too preoccupied with wars against France and the Turks to give heresy much attention. In short, the Catholic world was sundered, the Emperor and the King of France being most of the time at war; while as yet the Church had not bestirred itself to organize resistance. When at last the harassed emperor formed the plan, on the one hand, of forcing the pope to call a general council, while he undertook, on the other hand, to force the Protestants as rebellious subjects to make submission (preparatory to the meeting of a general council), a brief civil war ensued, characterized at first by imperial success, then followed by a futile compromise, and finally by a general uprising of the German princes against Charles, who was suspected of pursuing the political object of making himself their master. Thus politics again saved the Protestant Revolt. The King of France had even been in league with the Protestant princes against his fellow-Catholic, the Emperor. The outcome of the imbroglio was a compromise in 1555, known as the Peace of Augsburg, the principal feature of which was that each prince might choose between the Catholic faith and the Augsburg Confession, his choice being incumbent upon his subjects, who, if they then refused to conform, had no other course than to seek some other abode. The peace was thus only a very limited measure of toleration, since, apart from imperial towns, where both religions might persist, only princes had the right of choice, and their choice was narrowly restricted. Yet it gave heresy a legal standing in the empire, and the immunity which it gained allowed time for its consolidation in other countries. The revolt was beyond a doubt a revolution.

Yet secession from the Church had not meant general toleration; *Its fruits* it had not brought (or was even expected to bring) religious liberty. The whole movement was a reformation in the sense that the religious life of Christendom was somewhat elevated as a result, for the Church reformed itself, as we shall notice later, while in Protestant countries many clerical abuses were brought to an end. The whole movement led also to greater stress upon an educated clergy, and some of the reformers, like Luther, were prominent in advocating popular education, that men might read the Bible for themselves. It also deepened the secular influence in society in certain ways. In Protestant countries not only education but various philanthropic institutions became more and more the province of the State, though in Catholic countries this transition was yet to be accomplished. And in this connection it should be noted that the passing of the Church's monopoly in caring for the individual (especially the less fortunate individual) left this task to an institution (the modern state), which has been more generally concerned with protecting the propertied than of looking after the property-less. The social viewpoint which the Church had once expressed has only been partially realized in recent times. Such, in fact, was part of the cost of the Reformation—a fact which will become more evident later on. Of the more immediate cost—the accentuation of bigotry—we have already spoken. As far as Calvinism was concerned, the effect of its stern morality was noticeably felt at least among Anglo-Saxons, while the practice of self-government in Calvinist churches seems to have made that sect less satisfied with absolutism in politics and fostered the growth of democratic ideas. But in matters of belief and conscience the importance of the Religious Revolution was not in its immediate results, for, indeed, it seemed to repress the individual, setting up several masters instead of one. It lay rather in the fact that the shattering of the Church's monopoly in prescribing religious beliefs must lead eventually to a general relaxation in that sphere. The door was at least ajar if not actually open; for the lesson of the Religious Revolution was that men dared to question what had been taught them as the only means of salvation. To question this again would become increasingly easier as civilization advanced and the world became more worldly. That same dignity which the Renaissance had accorded the man of culture would eventually become extended to the common man. It is in the ultimate results of the upheaval that one finds it a revolution.

Thus the individual was emerging from the fetters of medievalism. Full political, economic, and religious freedom would come only in the Modern Era. In the meantime, the class which had become the greatest force in modernizing society had made its appearance.

THE EMERGENCE OF THE MIDDLE CLASS

Meaning of the middle class

By the middle class, or bourgeoisie, we mean especially the class which devotes itself to business as a livelihood, whether trade, or manufacturing, or finance. The fact that its social position was not supposed to be as high as that of the landed aristocracy and yet not so low as that of the peasantry will account for the term; it stood midway in the social scale (which was a matter of tradition) between the upper and lower strata of a society founded originally on the land. It is, however, a loose term, for it seems to have included even the proletariat or working class prior to the Industrial Revolution, as well as laymen who followed a profession, such as lawyers, teachers, authors, artists, etc. In tracing their contribution to the making of the Modern Age, these intellectuals have been treated to some extent in the previous section. We are concerned at this point with the people who made the towns and who were the founders and promoters of an industrial and commercial economy, the natural correlative of an agricultural econ-

omy. Since their rôle was more materially constructive than either
the fighting class or the praying class into which the aristocracy
was divided, while at the same time they possessed more economic
freedom than the peasantry, and since concentration in towns in
which there were active spirits who had seen something of the
world made for a greater mental quickening than the static life
of the country, the middle class as a rule became the most active
of all agents for the advance of civilization.

The existence of towns and urban life was, of course, no new *Rise of the*
phenomenon, as anyone knows who has read anything of ancient *towns*
history. Research has seemed to show that most of the towns of
the Roman Empire had managed to survive the barbarian invasions that produced the Dark Ages and that it was the Saracens,
rather, who, making the Mediterranean a closed sea, brought for
most of them strangulation and final ruin. A purely agricultural
economy was then evolved, which soon became a basis of what is
known as the feudal system—a régime we shall review in another
place. Suffice it to say here that the so-called manor—a peasant
village with its lord as pillar of security—was, in general, the
economic unit, and society seemed for a time to need no other.
Gradually, however, communities developed, more mercantile
than agrarian—in other words, the towns. How they emerged
has been a matter of long controversy among historians, and it is
possible that the same origins cannot be cited for all localities.
But, in general, it would seem that towns developed as a means of
supplying the needs of a feudal lord, or of one of his garrisoned
posts, or, in some cases, of a monastery. Its citizens were recruited
from roving merchants who saw the profit to be derived from
such needs and who sought the protection which some lord was
willing to give them. At the same time the attractive force of this
little group—outside the castle walls—drew the primitive village
artisans (the smiths and cobblers and so on) into the selfsame
community. There were always, however, towns, situated on
favorable sites for trade, which pre-dated the Dark Ages and were
now more a symptom of trade revival than a new phenomenon.
In any case the towns in most localities were drawn into the feudal
system. They wished protection and they got it, though, of course,
they had to pay for it. Some of them suffered greatly, it would
seem, from the lords' exactions, but when charters came to be
granted, as the result of bargaining with the lords, they acquired

considerable freedom. No doubt, in the weary period of political disintegration to which the empire of Charlemagne had succumbed, the presence of the feudal system, based as it was on military power, brought a certain measure of stability to society without which the towns themselves might possibly have been unable to withstand the armed despoiler. Yet, even so, it had its evil side. When commerce finally developed, it was often much disturbed by constant strife among the nobles, or hampered by a multitude of petty tolls in an age when the world politically was cut up into small fragments; and if a town happened to be isolated, as in certain parts of Germany, it was always liable to be harried by petty nobles who for all their titles were little more than freebooters. Not, of course, until the rise of the modern state was commerce ever really secure. The towns had partly, in a sense, grown out of feudalism, but they also quickly outgrew it.

The middle class, which inhabited the towns, was roughly divided into two groups, artisans and merchants; and each was similarly organized. It was characteristic of the Middle Ages that each was bound by strict regulations incumbent upon its members. The craft gild standardized the manner of making whatever was its specialty and also sponsored the training of apprentices to assist, and perhaps eventually to succeed, the master-artisans. The merchant gild [1] took measures for the common safety of its members; and in a sense the leagues of towns which banded together to defend their trade were leagues of merchant gilds. The very existence of towns meant the reaching out to something more than the local market which had characterized the village, and exchanges between towns were largely carried on through fairs, most of which were held annually, though some, indeed, more frequently. Exchange transactions were generally, at first, a matter of barter; for money in most of Europe for a time became practically extinct. Indeed, when the sole economic unit had been the manor, there was scarcely need of money. The village smith could be paid for his services with a measure of wheat; the lord drew from his tenants manual labor or payment in kind. In other words, the manor had been practically self-sufficient. And even for the towns at first the market was limited to a very narrow radius. But what of the surplus wheat and wine that the lord could usually command? Such

---

[1] Not to be confounded with the so-called "gild merchant" in England, which was a local association designed to control the town market.

commodities might be readily exchanged for industrial products—even for luxuries from distant lands as soon as maritime trade had revived. What was needed was a symbol by which value might be measured. The towns in widening the market soon demanded better facilities. Obviously much cartage was required by barter, just as, later, after the reintroduction of money, the cartage of specie itself became so difficult and dangerous that instruments of credit came into play. It was not until money became the common medium of exchange that a great field of opportunity was opened to the middle class.

The precious metals as mediums of exchange never passed entirely out of use in western Europe; but coinage practically ceased for several centuries. In the sixth century it seems to have reappeared,[1] though it was probably not until the thirteenth that it came into general use. At any rate the device of a prince's seal to give specie a certain ready and recognizable validity was a natural transition; and coins came to be minted by princes, nobles, and even towns, with the natural accompaniment of money-changers, whose position as embryonic bankers and financial experts was of no little importance. Despite the fact that there was not enough of the precious metals to meet the demand, we may consider that in the twelfth and thirteenth centuries western Europe, at least, passed to a money economy. *The coming of a money economy*

The use of money vastly simplified exchange. It enabled the landlord soon to exact money instead of produce from his serfs, and incidentally this innovation compelled the peasants to sell their surplus. And naturally town and country could more readily come to terms. Moreover, the use of money suggested some further expedients for facilitating exchange, more especially because the conveyance of large sums of money was highly dangerous. Thus, quite early, bills of exchange came into use, first (apparently) in Italy, then in other countries, and very commonly at fairs, where so many merchants came from the same place that the balance between creditors and debtors could be easily adjusted, comparatively little if any shipment of specie being required. Incidentally, these instruments of credit lightened the burden on the small stock of money in circulation, and led naturally to a great expansion of business. Perhaps, too, they involved a degree *The rise of capitalism*

---

[1] Silver and copper were employed at first, gold not being minted till the thirteenth century.

of mutual confidence, which lies at the basis of credit. Much less of this virtue, however, was present in money-lending, as evidenced by the excessive interest rates charged—higher even than would be warranted by the actual scarcity of money. At first in the hands of the Jews (because such traffic was frowned upon by the Church), money-lending became so profitable that Italians came to engage in it, and (regardless of Christian scruples) even the later Crusades seem to have been financed by this means. From the money-lender developed, in turn, the banker. Apart from the loaning of money, the medieval banker began his calling very simply as a mere custodian of funds left in his care for safe-keeping, for which service the depositor paid a certain sum. Then he became a sort of clearing house for the transfer of money from one of his depositors to another in the event of one of them incurring a debt to another. Finally the banker loaned out some of his deposits at interest, and by the close of the thirteenth century large sums of money were invested in the promotion of trade. The Florentines (generally known in financial circles by the broader term of "Lombards") made immense fortunes in banking. As early as the thirteenth century the banking houses of Florence had agents far and wide; they collected the revenues of the pope, financed the English wool trade, and frequently lent to needy monarchs on condition of certain "concessions." The profitable use of money as capital—that is, the means of providing the wherewithal for meeting current expenses—was an important stage in Europe's economic education.

The rise of capitalism had, in fact, been the most important direct result of the development of a money economy. We have already mentioned the bill of exchange, which obviated the need of shipping large sums of money—a rôle which the Knights Templars with armed escorts had so frequently played. In the later Middle Ages bills payable to order or at a stated time and promissory notes also came into use, as well as improved methods of bookkeeping. It was capitalism, operating in such forms, that, more than anything else, opened out the limited horizon of the towns and gave them a wider market. Such a movement was, of course, only gradual, the average merchant having little with which to launch on big undertakings. Sometimes it was a lord, or even a monastery that used its surplus revenues from land to serve as capital. Probably shipping—in which the Italian seaport towns were especially interested—had been the first field of enterprise promoted by the use of capital. We also know that as far back as the twelfth century (especially in Italy) merchants began to control the production of some of the gilds, a certain merchant, for example, furnishing a cloth-maker with wool and paying him eventually for the finished product, which he himself would then dispatch to the intended market. Commerce in the Middle Ages being more highly developed than industry, one finds that commercial capital dominated industry much more than industrial capital promoted commerce. Sometimes, with the better understanding of what could be actually achieved with money, the capital of one man allied itself with the commercial activities of another and the result was often the evolution of a business house with wide ramifications. The selling of stock in such an enterprise was only a step farther.[1]

Yet, notwithstanding its obvious advantages, it was not without some difficulties that capitalism had made its way. The risks involved were great, though it is certainly a proof of the strides that capitalism was making that commercial insurance, grounded on regular payment of premiums, was in existence at the beginning of the fourteenth century. Then, the Church, as we have noticed, had condemned loaning at interest (the practice known as usury), and it was this business which had made the Jews unpopular— sometimes deservedly so. When it seemed both impracticable and impossible to combat the movement successfully, Christian morality came to ignore it through certain subterfuges like the theory that the labor in transmitting money deserved some recompense. The theory of the "just price" (an effort of the Church to protect the consumer) had also to be combated in certain quarters where men who became rich were viewed with suspicion in an age that had been taught by the Church that poverty was a social virtue. No doubt, too, in a society that was just becoming initiated into the mysteries of a money economy the temptation to be dishonest was almost irresistible. While kings debased the currency, there was much cheating among money-changers; and the natural fluctuation in rates of exchange must indeed have puzzled mentalities which could then conceive of silver only as silver with nothing

---

[1] Professor J. W. Thompson tells us that the first stocks were government bonds. But the joint-stock company seems to have been a very gradual evolution and was not common even in the fourteenth century.

but an intrinsic value. Moreover, speculation followed naturally in the wake of capitalism, and the eventual establishment of bourses afforded easy opportunities for gambling. Yet those bourses themselves marked an important step forward. To meet and dabble in securities that represented goods, instead of handling the goods themselves, obviously simplified the technique of commerce. It also led to the decay of fairs as business gravitated towards towns, like Frankfort and Antwerp, which served as permanent centers of trade. Thus the development of capitalism was a stabilizing influence in the economic world, while at the same time it led to greater fluidity of wealth.

The expansion of trade

To a large extent the circulation of goods throughout Europe was stimulated by the over-sea trade, in which the seaport towns of Italy, profiting by their geographical position, had come to take the leading share. Since the Italian towns had never wholly succumbed to the barbarian waves which had submerged the Roman Empire, and had maintained their independence against all external authorities (Italy had never been feudalized to the extent of other lands), they were able to enjoy a slow but continuous growth, eke profit from the expanding needs of an improved civilization, and avail themselves of the knowledge brought to Europe by the Crusades. Just as Florence founded her prosperity on wool and banking and Milan put her energies into manufacturing arms, other towns, notably Genoa and Venice, made their fortunes out of tapping the resources of the East. Little, of course, was known of the lands whence flowed these marvelous treasures. Only the most intrepid merchants, or explorers like Marco Polo, had come into direct contact with that civilized world of Asia, lying beyond the vast stretch of mountain and desert land over which fierce nomad tribes roamed at will. Yet this almost impassable barrier was partly flanked by water, and after contacts had been made with the Saracens of the Levant, a sort of bridge had been opened which, linking East and West, had enabled the products of the East to percolate freely into Europe. By the beginning of the fourteenth century Venice had practically a monopoly of this traffic, the spices, gems, brocades, and other commodities of the East being brought by Arab shippers across Egypt or Mesopotamia to the Mediterranean coast where Venetian merchants shipped them to the wharves of Venice; thence they were sent by land or sea to Bruges or Antwerp, which became the distributing centers for northern Europe. Towns like Augsburg and Nuremberg on the land route to the Netherlands owed much of their importance to this trade; while, farther north, the Hanseatic towns, which brought the products of the Baltic region—furs, flax, timber, etc.—to London to be exchanged for woolen goods, also brought them to Bruges and Antwerp to exchange for pepper and cinnamon. So highly were spices prized at a time when the diet of Europe possessed but little variety that no article of trade brought so ready or so lucrative a market, and on occasions they were even used as mediums of exchange—hence the use of the same word in France (*épices*) to signify court fees. By the beginning of the fourteenth century Europe was spanned from end to end by a network of trade routes, producing, in a sense, an immense economic unit—an index of the thriving activity of the middle class.

One can readily understand that the economic importance of this class would come to be reflected in its political status and influence. Most of the towns, strictly speaking, had a place in the feudal system, the nature of their obligations (generally money payments) being often fixed in the charter granted to them by the lord to whom they owed a nominal allegiance; while in Germany, as time went on, these obligations were so indefinite that the imperial towns—those holding allegiance of the emperor—merely voted occasional supplies for imperial defense. In the Baltic world the Hanseatic League, a group of towns extending from the Netherlands to Novgorod in Russia, became a power of the first importance. Meanwhile, the towns of Spain and France, as well as those in central Europe, became at least self-governing bodies, those in northern France—the so-called "communes"—receiving charters from the crown, with whom they were naturally in alliance against the nobles. Already, too, members of the middle class were beginning to hold office in the king's service, especially those who had a knowledge of Roman law, on which the royal power was being founded. The economic value of this class to the rising monarchies is evidenced by the introduction of representatives of the towns into the feudal estates or diets and their participation with the nobles in the English parliament. Obviously, from the towns, much more than from the barons, the prince could derive the money power, essential to his objects. The strange career of Jacques Cœur, who made his fortune in trade, then extended his

Growing political importance of the middle class

activities to include mining and manufacturing, and was able to loan a French king money enough to recover Normandy and Guienne, interestingly illustrates the importance of capitalism in politics. Yet it was dangerous to serve princes, as the Florentines found when an English king repudiated his debts, and as Jacques Cœur himself discovered before his death. Would it be long before kings would seek to appropriate for themselves a more direct share of the wealth of their subjects by organizing and controlling the economic life of their states? To this historic change we shall devote another section. It is sufficient to note here the growing importance of the middle class and the realization of the strength which the money power imparted.

Influence of the explorations But the greatest boon which fortune had yet offered to the middle class was the discovery of a new world. Even in that age when capitalism had come to make definite strides the scarcity of specie had been a serious handicap. Happily, the discovery of new silver mines in Europe during the fifteenth century had greatly added to the store of precious metals in circulation, but this fortunate gift of nature was not to be compared with the gold mines which the navigators discovered. Moreover, the opening of a water route to the East,[1] breaking down the monopoly of Venice and giving the merchants of the West direct access to the markets of the East increased the volume of trade and thereby immensely increased the number of merchants. Meanwhile the rise of prices, occasioned by the vast influx of precious metals, was an added incentive to the artisan and the merchant. Landlords also profited in some countries insofar as manorial services became transformed into money payments, and such tenants as had early commuted these services now obviously gained from having cheaper money with which to discharge them. Only the lot of the class which furnished the labor for industrial production was worse than it had been before, since wages failed to keep pace with prices, and the rigid organization of the gilds made it all but impossible for a workman to market his labor. The evolution of a rich bourgeoisie had its ugly reverse side—an unhappy proletariat of the towns,[2] depressed by the abnormal cost of living, and outside

---

[1] There was a close connection between the successful pioneering in the West and the greatly increased volume of trade with the East; for India demanded silver (not Western products) in return for her wares.

[2] The only compensation to a member of the proletariat for low wages and little chance to rise was the substantial security of his job and an assurance against

of England (where the wage-scale was somewhat regulated), without even the capricious aid of benevolent despotism. Pity for the poor—so common in the Middle Ages—was one of the benefits lost with the waning influence of the Church. Though it was this element which in many places was attracted to Calvinism and even to more radical sects, salvation through revolt for so small and weak a class was utterly impossible. Another example of the declining influence of the Church has already been noted. Changing moral standards, forced by the acquisitive spirit of the age, gave full freedom to the middle class to shape its own code of business. If Calvinists preached the virtues of thrift and industry, they simply reflected the temper of the class from which they sprang.

The possession of material wealth, whether in capital or land, was the key to the comfortable life. The middle class was not yet—in most of Europe—invading the cherished preserves of the aristocracy, but it had fully and definitely established itself as an indispensable element in modern society. And already this class had demonstrated that it, rather than the nobles, could provide the sinews of strength for the modern state. Individual enterprise was making the middle class, and the middle class was providing much of the money as well as the brains that put the power of kings and princes on a firm foundation. It is to this rising political phenomenon, the modern state, that we must now give our attention.

THE EMERGENCE OF THE MODERN STATE

Human relationships are disorderly and susceptible to constant violence until they are regulated by laws or by customs which have the force of law. When a community has come to be banded together under a régime of law which it recognizes and to which, in general, it adheres, we have the essence of a state. And, strictly speaking, a state implies a fixity of position, or, in other words, a territorial basis. It was the state, as fashioned by the Romans, with its compact organization and definite frontiers that gave men their clearest conception of the institution and served as a convenient model for a later age. Yet the state of the Romans was

excessive exploitation, thanks to the ancient rules of the gilds. As Professor Pirenne has said, "The gild system must be recognized as the only source of protection for the worker before the period of social legislation in the nineteenth century." Much of the poor of the towns was made up of those who had never been apprentices, and, of course, the professional beggars.

in the end an unwieldy thing, its population becoming dangerously heterogeneous, whereas the modern state, much narrower in its territorial range, was much more closely identified with a single people. We must trace the evolution of the modern state, and then try to discern its position in the world. We shall study this institution first in its internal, then in its external aspects—the latter subject raising the question whether for Europe as a whole there has been any practical substitute for universal empire.

Internal Aspects

The feudal state as the antecedent of the modern state

Between the Roman Empire and the modern (approximating a national) state there was a chronological gap. In that period of transition which we call the "Dark Ages" men lacked the benefits of the old order without as yet devising anything better to take its place. Yet as society must somehow be held together if it were not to go back to migratory habits and chronic anarchy, the institution known as feudalism was evolved.[1] It was this curious invention of human need, this form of a state—if state it can be called— out of whose shell emerged that permanent institution, the modern state.

The feudal system (or, if one chooses, the feudal-manorial system[2]) was in its essence a means of providing protection through a kind of relationship established between various military chiefs, or lords (as we may better call them), as political and economic entities, and between the lords themselves and the men who fed them. In a society which was at first almost wholly agricultural it was necessary that the peasants should receive at least enough protection to enable them to till the land they occupied. As occupancy of the land was theirs only by favor of some lord (though it came to be regarded as inalienable and hereditary), it was this lord who was able, and in his own interest was ready, to accord them protection; while for this occupancy, which at least by implication included protection, they paid by certain services such

[1] It may also be recalled that with the virtual disappearance of money a prince was naturally led to reward services by bestowing lands. The result was a distribution of responsibility in the task of holding society together. It is not that the landed chieftain consciously embodied the "social viewpoint" but rather that he had the vital need of protecting himself in an age of violence.

[2] The manorial system is treated here as an integral part of feudalism (even though it antedated it), for the two came to be inseparable. As Professor Lynn Thorndike says, "In a broader sense it (feudalism) covers the life of the subjugated peasantry upon the land dominated by the warriors." Feudalism, being tied up with land, rested on agrarian foundations.

as working for a fixed number of days on the lord's estate. At first peasants were serfs, and thus bound to the land which they held, but though such a condition seemed to invite exploitation, the lord, inasmuch as he required his lands to be tilled, could not afford to drive his peasants into flight. Moreover, tenure of the land was at least in effect hereditary, not subject to confiscation. The relations between lord and serf were not, however, solely economic; they were also political. When feudalism was at its height, police and judicial rights over his serfs were also vested in the lord. This politico-economic unit was known as the "manor." In course of time serfdom declined, either through voluntary act of the lord or through purchase of freedom by the serfs; later on, the obligation to work for the lord was often commuted into payments in money or kind; and finally, as we shall see, political jurisdiction became generally obsolete. Yet we are speaking only of tendencies, more especially in certain countries; and even in France, where transformation was relatively rapid, the economic bondage implicit in the manorial tie was not finally abolished until the French Revolution.

The other side of feudalism—and indeed the primary purpose of the institution—was concerned with the relations of the several lords with one another. From this standpoint a manor or group of manors usually constituted what was known as a "fief," a tract of land held by one lord as vassal of another, to whom, in return, he owed certain customary services, such as the obligation to fight for him on certain occasions; while it was equally understood that this overlord or "suzerain" owed his vassal special protection. We shall not enter into the complexities of the system (which in England presented certain exceptions to the form on the Continent), but must note that this contractual relationship between lord and vassal might be duplicated in an ascending scale of lords until we reach the apex of the pyramid, which is usually the man called "king." Viewed broadly, such a scheme provided a horde of big and little policemen, without whose occasional devotion to their feudal oath no man's life or property would have been safe. Primarily the relationship was military, designed to enable a man to possess a retinue who would fight for him, since fighting was the chief sport and occupation of these favored few. Yet, as we have implied, there were other obligations which the feudal vassal owed his lord; he was required on certain occasions to pay him a sum of money (the so-called *aide*), and he was to assist him with counsel, and also help him mete out justice. Each lord and his several vassals thus constituted a rudimentary principality, but the ties which held it together were based on contract [1] and unalterable. The complete governing power, what we understand by sovereignty, did not repose in the suzerain—did not in fact repose anywhere—and his vassals were not his subjects. The jurisdiction of the king himself (who was little more than first among equals)[2] was limited to the peasants on his domains and the vassals who owed him services, and in the case of his vassals his authority was definitely restricted by the terms of the unwritten contract which custom had rendered sacred. Such was the feudal monarchy. If it can be regarded as a state, it was of a very loose and rudimentary type.

Yet the feudal system—which is usually identified with Europe, though it had almost exact parallels on other continents—was a fortunate phenomenon in that crude society in which it developed. The feudal castle was a refuge for the peasants in time of danger. Moreover, slight as were the services which the king received from his vassals, they gave him some means of building up that power whereby he was eventually able to form the modern state at the expense of feudalism. The feudal system became general throughout Europe, though in most of Italy it early disappeared, and in Russia it took a somewhat different form. It was one of the most curious inventions born of human ingenuity to cope with human frailties.

Yet, just as human nature may pervert the best of governments, so it manifested its seamy side—and quite readily too—in feudalism. Indeed one is apt to forget the evils which the institution allayed because of those which it held in itself, when viewed at close range. Since the lord was primarily a warrior, he must needs consume much of his time in fighting; and the right of private warfare was a cherished feudal custom. While the protection afforded

---

[1] The tie between lord and vassal had been consecrated by the ceremony of homage when the vassal received his fief, and in feudal conception the fief itself was not hereditary but rather the vassalage. The obligations of a serf to his lord, on the other hand, were not primarily personal but explicitly attached to the land. A peasant on inheriting his land paid to his lord a sum of money known as a "relief."

[2] Much of his prestige in France was of a somewhat personal character; he was a sort of *paterfamilias*, for whom some of his vassals performed certain services in his household.

by armor prevented a heavy mortality among these fighters, such a
sport was a grievous nuisance to the towns and particularly to the
peasants, whose fields were often devastated. Theoretically the
tie between vassal and lord should have tended to prevent wars;
actually there was nothing more precarious. Even though a vassal
might plead at the suzerain's court against some fellow-vassal, the
danger of such a journey, which left his family exposed to attack,
was sufficient to discourage recourse to such a method, particularly
as settling the matter by the sword was consecrated by custom.
Without ignoring its evident elements of restraint, feudalism only
tempered anarchy, it did not cure it, and in the last analysis it was
force that still ruled.

It was through the stronger arm of the king, when the superior *The germ*
force was his, that feudalism itself would yield to control and a *of the*
better system be gradually evolved. If the king had a domain, he *modern state*
had at least the nucleus of territorial power, and though his
vassals, the greater nobles, had precisely the same advantages,
judicial, fiscal, administrative, and military, nevertheless the
suzerain of suzerains was the king, and something could be made
of such a title in bold hands. The French kings, fortunate in being
atop the feudal pyramid, had also a domain of their own; and it
was a rare stroke of fortune that for eleven generations there was
always a son to succeed, and that even the founder of the Valois
line, Philip VI (1328–50), was a cousin of the preceding king. In
Germany, on the contrary, the frequent changes of dynasty prevented the establishment of a continuous royal domain. Moreover
the lords had steadily gained at the expense of the crown, and the
kingdom fell into permanent disruption. In France, Spain, and
England, on the other hand, the royal power grew and became the
matrix of the modern state.

In France, which we may study as typical of the latter process, *The*
the kings, especially from the twelfth century, seized every op- *evolution of the modern*
portunity they had of extending and consolidating their power. We *state:*
have already mentioned the limitations which had normally hedged *(1) Political aspects*
it in. Not only was the exercise of his power shared with his
vassals but a feudal king could not reach the vassals of his vassals
or even their serfs, and in many cases he had explicitly granted the
greater nobles "immunity"—freedom from all exercise of the
royal authority on their estates. Yet from the close of the twelfth
century we find the king using every occasion for stretching his

prerogative, encroaching on his vassals by a ceaseless process of attrition. Sometimes, as the result of negotiation, his laws were accepted on the domains of these greater nobles; sometimes he usurped the right of sending his officials to collect the feudal *aide* directly from their tenants; sometimes, appealing to Roman law, he interfered with his vassals' judicial competence, classifying certain cases, such as crimes against his person or his honor, as "royal cases," justiciable only before his own court. In the later Middle Ages the kind of cases so denominated steadily multiplied till the nobles were practically confined merely to cases involving their serfs. It was, in fact, on Roman law that the king founded his claim to sovereignty. While at first this meant little in practice outside the royal domain, such a position, when constantly reiterated, especially when the extension of the royal domain gave the king a greater power than any of his vassals, was not without its weight. The fact that the royal sovereignty was a pregnant and virile force is interestingly illustrated by the attitude of the French kings toward private war. In the thirteenth century the crown invented what was known as an "assurance." When one of the parties in a quarrel requested an assurance from his enemy that he would not attack him, the king ruled that it must be given. During the same century private war was forbidden at times when the king himself was at war, and in the fourteenth century it was prohibited altogether. Naturally this wholesome object was not completely attained, but we know that private war did decline, and it is obvious that those nobles who dwelt nearest to the king were in general more susceptible to his action. As early as the eleventh century the crown had begun the practice of hiring professional soldiers (mercenary troops), which undoubtedly enabled it to give more effect to its will. It is interesting to realize that the royal power had emerged as a new element of order, a stabilizing force in a social system which had proved its limitations.

In its long struggle with feudalism the crown got valuable assistance, whether in the form of money or of expert knowledge, from a vigorous middle class, who were its natural allies in checking the violence of the nobles. In France many towns, which had managed to obtain self-government but still owed a measure of allegiance to feudal lords, were granted new charters directly by the king. In Spain the towns were given every encouragement to resist the nobles, and it was through that alliance of king and burghers that

the power of the Spanish grandees was eventually broken. In
Spain of the twelfth century representatives of the towns took
their place in the feudal assembly, the cortes; and in the fourteenth
century occurred the first meeting of the estates general in France
—deputations from the towns being summoned by the king as
chief suzerain,[1] to sit beside the landed feudal classes. It was from
such bodies—which under other names soon prevailed throughout
Europe—that the crown solicited money, and it was doubtless
because of the wealth of the burgher element that they had been
merged into a separate order on a par with the feudal classes.
Thus the money power—already a prominent factor in European
society—was contributing to enhance the royal power. Naturally
it was from the middle class, paid by money instead of by lands
that the king recruited the bulk of the personnel of his administration;[2] they were better educated than the nobles, and the circumstances of their position made them infinitely more loyal.
While it is true that the Valois kings established governorships in
the provinces, which because of their military character were conferred upon noblemen, nevertheless the judges, the fiscal agents,
and often the most intimate counselors were drawn from the middle
class—a practice dating back at least to the eleventh century.
Yet from the time of Philip the Fair (in the early fourteenth century), when the middle class won a species of recognition in the estates general, began also the gradual abasement of the towns. As
the royal power expanded, one notes a growing interference with
liberties—culminating in a wholesale revoking of charters and the
stifling of autonomy. It was only in less degree that the upper
classes were subjected to the selfsame pressure. While it is true
that until royal taxation became an established practice the estates
general and the provincial estates (similarly constituted) were still
of financial importance, the crown never allowed these institutions
to follow the precedent of the English parliament, which came in
time to hold the purse-strings. It was undoubtedly the expanding
needs of the royal treasury which account for much of the attack on
vested interests. Philip the Fair did not scruple to invade clerical
immunities from taxation. To the nobles he allowed the privilege

---

[1] It will be recalled that the towns had been drawn into the feudal system.
See page 25.

[2] Public offices, when held by nobles, had often been regarded as hereditary fiefs.
The middle class received salaries and in course of time many were encouraged
to buy their posts.

of commuting their military service if they wished—a practice which had already been employed in England. Though such taxes were by custom extraordinary (for the feudal service itself was that), they had the effect of weakening feudalism in its most basic aspect. We have already noted the employment of mercenaries. Such troops, in contradistinction to the feudal levies, were much more willing to serve on a long campaign, and were certainly more capable of an undivided attachment. Thus the military dependence of the crown upon its vassals was fast becoming obsolete. It was, indeed, through its superior military power,[1] more than by any other means, that it was able to buttress its power and gradually extend it.

The Hundred Years' War, though it abased the power of the crown for a time, had the ultimate result of greatly increasing it, and thereby molding France still more into a modern state. In the first place, it took a heavy toll of lives from among the nobility, and discredited their methods of warfare. In the second place, something like a national spirit was developed through the exploits of Jeanne Darc, and this spirit rallied to the king as liberator of the land; more than ever before, whatever their place in the feudal scale, the French people looked to the crown as the symbol of order and the defender of the common weal. In the third place—and this was of supreme importance—the crown came more and more to adopt the practice of levying direct taxes without waiting for the assent of the estates general. Under Charles VII the so-called *taille*—originally requiring its consent as a special subsidy in time of war—became permanent, and the crown determined its amount (augmenting it if it chose) by dint of its own power. A French historian of the reign considers that from 1440 "the financial rôle of the estates general was terminated." But the royal right of taxation, while it had evolved from custom and various emergencies, was clearly an attribute of the royal power according to Roman law, and, now that the king was able to bring this right into permanent practice, the royal sovereignty was indeed an established fact. It was but a natural corollary to this reform that the same right was expressly withheld from the nobles. Thus France was not to be a congeries of sovereign principalities but an organized whole under the sovereignty of the king. Naturally there was some resistance to such arbitrary action, but it must

---

[1] The invention of gunpowder also gave the crown a decided advantage over the traditional weapons of feudalism as well as a means of destroying its strongholds.

always be borne in mind that the meeting of an estates general
was arduous and expensive for its members in a day when the
roads were bad and disorders not infrequent, and extraordinary
taxes had become so frequent that continuous royal taxation
was probably accepted as a matter of habit. Fourthly and finally,
it was from the fruit of this tax, the *taille*, that Charles VII (fol-

Painting in the Royal Library of Belgium, reproduced from Magoffin and Duncalf,
Ancient and Medieval History, *published by Silver, Burdett and Company*

THE TAKING OF A FEUDAL CASTLE BY ARTILLERY

lowing temporary devices of some of his predecessors) established
a standing army. The ability to dispense with the military aid of
the nobles in time of war through the maintenance of an army of
hired soldiers gave the king the power of the sword—or shall we
say artillery?—which enabled him the better to hold his people in
subjection as well as to pursue a strong policy abroad. Thus the
royal sovereignty, realized in a judicial sense, and attempted with
some success in legislation, was now established in those matters
of chief importance to the crown—namely, war and taxation. It
would be too much to say that France was as yet an absolute
monarchy, for the nobles who governed the provinces were not
very amenable to control, and the enforcement of laws was hap-

hazard at best; yet the growth of the crown was such that, generally speaking, one finds an active central government functioning in all spheres of public activity. The feudal state had not wholly disappeared, but its lines had become dimmed in proportion as those of the modern state had become clear and impressive.

What we have, in short, is the modern state appearing in the form of an hereditary monarchy, which is gradually becoming absolute. It was apparently in Spain that the king's power first attained that stage of being, in fact if not in theory, most nearly unlimited. While the configuration of the Iberian Peninsula, crossed as it was by numerous mountain ranges, does not readily make for national unity, most of the states which had emerged out of the collapse of the Moorish power had become amalgamated in one way or another, and the union of Castile and Aragon by the marriage of Ferdinand and Isabella in 1469 brought most of the peninsula under the rule of one or other of these sovereigns. When the Emperor Charles V (called Charles I in Spain) inherited both Castile and Aragon, the rulership of Spain was concentrated in a single hand. Charles was able to depress the towns as Ferdinand had crushed the nobles, and his son Philip II, made the authority of the crown, exercised as it was through a numerous corps of officials, more effective than that in any other European state. Moreover, the long struggle with the Moors had availed to make the Spanish kings the champions of the faith as well as the rulers of the land, and thus the influence of the Church was always exerted on the side of the crown. Little bothered by his cortes, Philip II taxed his subjects as he pleased; and his military power, based on a paid soldiery rather than on irregular feudal levies, gave him a power over his people that was only once challenged.

France and Spain, indeed, furnish us with our example of the modern state evolving as an absolute monarchy—a pattern which all the other great Continental powers were to follow. But we must note that the making of England did not proceed along quite the same lines, but gives us instead an exception that was to have an important bearing on the position of the individual in English society. In England there existed from the time of the Norman Conquest the same feudal institutions we have noticed on the Continent; they were introduced, in fact, by William the Conqueror, who, as duke of Normandy, was a vassal of the French king, and knew no other system of maintaining order. But in distributing the lands of the conquered natives among his followers he was fortunate in two respects. Most of the fiefs which he granted were widely scattered, and no one of these could readily become a menace to the royal power. Moreover, he kept the lion's share himself, and was thus less dependent on his vassals for financial aid, while he also inherited from his Anglo-Saxon predecessors the duty of protecting commerce and the consequent privilege of levying duties on foreign trade. It happened also that intermittently at least the crown was represented by strong kings, who were able through their own officials to build up a machinery of justice under the royal supervision. Even when the royal power temporarily broke down under John and Henry III in the thirteenth century the feudal barons made no attempt to grasp at independence but merely tried—and not successfully—to operate the government themselves. By that time the need of a strong central power, able to maintain order, was becoming more and more recognized not only by the baronage but by the middle class as well, both of whom had financial interest in the wool trade—the barons as sheep-raisers and the merchants as dealers in fabrics. It was this union of barons and burghers that created the English parliament, which in its continuous vigor became the bulwark of the limited monarchy—a monarchy not less active because it was limited. Thus England remained an organic unit without requiring the tie of absolute monarchy to prevent disruption.

But elsewhere it was through the simpler concept of the development and extension of the royal authority that the various political units were welded into one. Yet in France, for example, if the concept itself was simple, the process of carrying it out had obviously been difficult. Undermining the power of the nobles had been a long and ceaseless struggle, not unbroken at times by periods of apparent defeat. The elimination of the greater nobles through the extension of the royal domain, though the process had been slow, was, perhaps, the most effective means of consolidating the royal power. Through a failure of heirs a vassal dukedom would customarily pass to the crown, and this without any offense to feudal principles. Marriage was another means of acquiring such a fief; still another was conquest (justified sometimes by treason, which was a "royal case"). From the twelfth through the fifteenth century the royal domain grew at intervals until it coincided with the whole kingdom of France. It was then that royal officials were resident throughout the land. Insofar as the people of France came to recognize one law, the king's law, France had become a modern state.

(2) Economic aspects

It is important to notice that this process of political amalgamation had also its economic side. The arbitrary conduct of the medieval towns, freed substantially from feudal control, had often stood in the way of the economic interest of larger areas, giving precedence rather to local considerations. Neighboring towns were as jealous of each other as nations later became; outsiders, viewed as "foreigners," were seldom allowed the privileges which citizens themselves enjoyed; and often the rural population, less organized than the town, was quite at the latter's mercy when it brought its wheat or wool to be exchanged for industrial products.[1] In Germany one finds a constant struggle between various leagues of towns and neighboring princes until in most instances the monopolies exercised by the towns, the diversion of trade in their own interest, and, in short, the stubbornness of a local economy had to give way more and more to the territorial power of a rising state. Some towns managed to preserve their political freedom for many centuries, but their economic independence was gradually shattered.[2] In France, where the king soon saw in the export trade a source of revenue and hence wanted commodities to move as freely as possible, the political subordination of the towns was perhaps inevitable. This process has been noted. After a time the king arrogated to himself the right to allow or prohibit fairs, often using their lucrative trade as a source of taxation, and there were many royal ordinances directly affecting industry and commerce. Side by side with this invasion of town autonomy went attacks on the coining rights of the great nobles. Louis IX had been fairly successful in giving the royal coins a greater currency than that of his vassals; and several kings aimed at a common coinage as well as a uniform system of weights and measures, but apparently the royal power was unable to surmount the force of local resistance. Along other lines the crown was more successful. From the thirteenth century on it often drew revenue from taxes on exports[3] as

---

[1] One gathers, however, from Professor Gras (*An Introduction to Economic History*) that this was much less true of western than of central Europe, where the German scholar, Schmoller, has laid great emphasis on the friction between town and country.

[2] The gradual decay of the Hanseatic League furnishes an excellent example.

[3] The general substitution of a tax on imports for one on exports only took place when the force of international competition made itself felt. At least by the reign

well as from other levies on commerce. Some kings prohibited the export of the precious metals in order to conserve the small supply that was then available. After the issue of the Hundred Years' War had been decided the crown could give more attention to its broader economic interests. Charles VII was very active in the promotion of commerce, tried to improve some of the ports, and made a point of giving protection to French merchants in foreign countries. His successor, Louis XI, not only established the silk industry in France but promoted trade with the East by decreeing that wares from the Levant might be imported only in French vessels. Yet, in general, the French seaports conducted their commerce as they saw fit without the government's help or hindrance; for commercial policy was still primarily municipal rather than national. Indeed, it was not till the French Revolution—and in some cases even later—that the towns were entirely assimilated to a national economy.

The events which led the modern state to a more direct interest in commerce were the great discoveries, which, as we have seen, were a phase of the Renaissance. It was but natural that the lucrative trade of Venice with the East should have spurred the ambition of princes to realize some of this wealth. When it appeared that gold could be found in distant lands, there was an additional incentive for pioneering, for the scarcity of precious metals, aggravated by the fact that there was a constant drain of specie to the East to pay for its products, had greatly hampered the conduct of business transactions.[1] We shall not tell at length the familiar story of the explorations. The Portuguese, after discovering gold in Africa, eventually rounded the Cape of Good Hope, and opened the water route to India. The products of the East, hitherto so expensive because of monopoly prices as well as by reason of the pillage of caravans or the even greater cost of placating the native chiefs in Egypt, were now procurable in the West in greater quantities and at much less cost—a fact which naturally inspired other countries to follow in the wake of Portugal. The Spaniards sailed west for the same objective, and found, to their astonishment, a new world. While the Dutch trailed the

Influence of the Renaissance

of Louis XI the idea of national self-sufficiency had found expression, and the trend of commercial opinion seems to show that by the end of the sixteenth century France was ready for the protectionist (mercantilist) attitude of the seventeenth.

[1] This does not argue, of course, that gold was not mainly sought for its own intrinsic value and peculiar attractiveness.

Portuguese, the English and French sought India by the northwest passage, and later opened the continent of North America. The halcyon days of Venice were now permanently at an end. Commerce had ceased to be primarily municipal; it had come to be once for all national. The scope of the modern state had thereby become enlarged, for over-sea trade, soon to become colonial trade, had now become an interest of national governments.

There were other ways, however, by which the Renaissance—if we use the term broadly—promoted the development of the modern state. The printing of books in the vernacular developed more easily a national culture with its unifying influence; while in external affairs the influence of the Renaissance also had its effect, as will be noted.

Influence
of the
Reformation
And finally we must point out that the Religious Revolution had an important political result. Apart from the relations of different monarchs with the papacy, which we shall consider presently, the ecclesiastical organization in many Protestant states was placed under the headship of the crown. Thus, in general, to the Protestant princes was ascribed a new prerogative: that of determining their subjects' religion. And in all states there was a tendency to regard one uniform faith as necessary to autocratic rule. The union of Church and State, wherever it occurred, meant, in effect, a further enlargement of the scope of the modern state. Church matters came within its purview to a certain extent along with political and economic affairs.

Yet there is little doubt that the religious question, producing as it did a schism in Christendom, did much more to weaken the modern state than strengthen it. Indeed, religious hatred, allying itself with feudalism, challenged, in some cases, the work of several centuries of plodding development. The details of this crisis we shall leave to the next section, not because it logically belongs there, but rather because the Wars of Religion are important in another connection and the story can best be told as one continuous drama. It was not until the seventeenth century that France was able to build anew her shattered political edifice.

Thus far we have been concerned with the making of the modern state as an institution with the exclusive right of ordering the lives of its subjects, this exclusive right or sovereignty being vested as a rule in a monarch. But there were a number of these organisms, and their number ran counter to another type of polity against which they claimed sovereignty. It is thus to the external relations of the modern state that we must now turn.

External Aspects—The Fabric of Europe

The incorporation of all men under a law that will secure peace among them is an idea to conjure with. Its nearest approximation has been the empire of Rome, which comprised almost all of the civilized world, and nearly all the *terra cognita,* that is, the land known to the Romans. Within this vast domain, governed by the Roman emperor through his functionaries, every man was a Roman citizen; and for many centuries the *pax Romana,* the Roman peace, kept order within its midst. Such an ideal of universal empire was not, perhaps, inherently impracticable at that time, for there was but one main fount of civilization, and while there doubtless were materials for making different nations, they lacked the breath of life which could only come from a civilization inherent in themselves. At all events, after the Roman Empire had succumbed to the barbarian invasions, there emerged out of its wreckage potential nationalities, the Spaniards, French, English, etc., though it was long before these different elements could be really called self-conscious, and the crude kingdoms of the Middle Ages did not even follow a definite linguistic pattern, being largely the creations of circumstance. On the other hand, there rose an institution, claiming a species of universality on the lines of the Roman Empire. This was the Universal Church.

The Roman ideal of universal empire

If feudalism produced a state more indigenous to the Middle Ages in the sense that it was peculiar to that age, the Church, though a replica of a more ancient institution, was decidedly the most vigorous organism of that age. It was through its influence the one really unifying element in Christendom, and it gave the western world a degree of unity it had not enjoyed since the fall of Rome. To begin with, it employed one language, Latin, the sole medium for the written word as long as Churchmen alone were literate. It was through that common language of learning that men from all corners of the relatively civilized world could communicate with one another, and thus may be explained the cosmopolitan character of the medieval universities. Moreover, a man of the lowest estate was able then to acquire within the kindly folds of the Church the best education of his day. Incidentally it is interesting to note that such a man might rise to the

The Church as an exponent of the imperial idea

position of highest eminence; for, even though the Church became largely Italian in policy, it remained (and still remains) a socially democratic institution, and, as such, was quite unique in the Middle Ages. But the Medieval Church was not only—nor was it primarily—the center of Western culture. It shaped men's religious beliefs and it gave them moral instruction. For many centuries its religious monopoly was hardly questioned; while the extent of its moral influence is well illustrated by the "Truce of God"— that experiment by which feudal nobles were persuaded to abstain from fighting at certain intervals. The Church had also much of the character of a state, for it was composed of a vast hierarchy of officials, collecting taxes, judging offenses, and even organizing armies. While it had direct authority only over the clergy, it ruled in many matters touching the laity, since questions concerning marriage (which was a sacrament) and wills were within the cognizance of the ecclesiastical courts. There was therefore intellectual, religious, moral, and even a certain degree of political unity under the Church. It produced no counterpart of the *pax Romana*, but it was nevertheless a means of holding Christendom together. There is no more impressive example of the potent influence of the Church than its ability to send the worldly monarchs of the West on a series of crusades to fight the enemies of the faith.

The Holy Roman Empire as an exponent of the imperial idea

But the Church was not the only representative of the Roman ideal of universal empire. As there reigned until 1453 a successor to the Roman emperors at Constantinople, it was but natural that the idea of restoring the Empire of the West should appeal to the imagination of the western world. For this and various other reasons Charlemagne, king of the Franks, was crowned emperor by the pope in the year 800. He had been a good friend of the papacy, like his father before him, and he was expected in his new rôle to be defender of the Church. There was the spiritual head and the temporal head, and the temporal sword was supposed to defend things spiritual in this temporal world. It may be added that Charlemagne's realm was so vast that his title seemed really justified by the actual extent of his power. Yet with the disintegration of this empire under his successors this first experiment of a temporal overlordship came to an end. The honor of being emperor was bandied about among petty Italian princes and was consequently so cheapened that it lost all real significance. Finally in the tenth century a king of Germany (one of the divisions into which Charlemagne's empire had fallen) aspired to restore the empire in his person, and in 962 was crowned emperor by the pope. This ruler, who bore the name of Otto I, thus founded the Holy Roman Empire, destined to last for nearly nine hundred years.

It is an interesting fact that this secular revival of empire came at a time when the papacy itself had fallen into dishonor. The fact that the pope had long been chosen by the clergy and people of Rome had naturally led to its becoming a political shuttle, and often the worst characters were able to snatch the mantle of St. Peter. Even a great pope like Gregory VII found his position as head of an august and universal church greatly hampered by the chronic turmoil at Rome, and though the institution of the college of cardinals in the eleventh century took the right of electing the pope out of the hands of the Roman mob, the papacy never became wholly free of local politics. It was primarily in self-defense that it came to devote so much attention to its territorial power and to subordinate its spiritual rôle to that of an Italian prince. On the other hand, the "holy Roman emperors," with all their solemn pretensions, had hardly a more solid basis for their own power. The Empire was already feudalized; its ruler was elected by a group of the greater nobles; he had no imperial domain; and he never came to exercise the full rights of sovereignty. Moreover, his imperial authority was not recognized even nominally outside of Germany and Italy.

Yet the conception of universal empire proved wonderfully tenacious. The medieval mind liked to think of the kingdom of God on earth being administered by two vicegerents, divinely authorized to play their respective rôles, one as head of the Church, the other as head of the State. It was the supreme example of how theology was mixed up with politics as with everything else in the Middle Ages. But the test of such a polity was whether it could work. In the first place, could the dual leadership function harmoniously and effectively? In the second place, could it exercise its authority in Christendom at large?

It is obvious that there must have been questions of disputed jurisdiction between these two lords of Christendom. Where did the spiritual prerogatives end, and the temporal prerogatives begin? The question of who should have the patronage of ecclesiastical offices, which under the feudal system had come to include

The basic weakness of the two

Causes of the collapse of the imperial

land held as fiefs of a temporal prince, was the chief rock on which
the dual leadership came to grief. We shall not review the famous
investiture controversy. Suffice it to say that the struggle prevented any stable co-operation between Church and State and in
the end was damaging to both. In the thick of the quarrel the
question of who by moral right was superior—pope or emperor—
seems singularly futile. The papal contention that it held the
Empire of the West by virtue of the gift of the Emperor Constantine (the famous "Donation of Constantine") was not then known
to rest upon a forgery, but there were plenty of biblical passages to
support the imperial claims of ruling by divine right. Such a
theory, while it had been first advanced by the popes in respect to
their own authority, was too impressive a pretension not to be
grasped at by the emperors. In any case it was the emperors who
first were compelled to succumb to the weight of realities. Though
usually crowned by the popes (the last instance was in 1536), the
emperors never effectively established their hold upon Italy, and,
by chasing this glittering bauble, they steadily lost ground even in
Germany. In vain the great poet, Dante, looked to this universal
sovereign, the emperor, ruling by Roman law, as the symbol and
embodiment of law and justice in the world—and incidentally
as the cure for Italy's woes; it was long before his day that the
imperial power was doomed. Yet the papacy itself was not much
more fortunate. Though the career of Innocent III in the thirteenth century brought its political influence to its height, the
rôle of dictating to monarchs by fighting them with spiritual
weapons,[1] and that of receiving whole kingdoms as fiefs of papal
Rome, were chiefly due to the ability of a single pope and the
relative weakness of the secular princes of his day. In any case the
pope's claim to temporal overlordship could not long endure in the
face of the rise of the modern state. It was this new force which
was to shatter the dreams of universal empire. The Renaissance
and Reformation completed the process of its extinction.

It was the question of the extent of its jurisdiction that brought
the papacy into conflict with the monarchies of the West. The
English kings of the eleventh and twelfth centuries had insisted
upon controlling the appointments of the higher clergy and had
vigorously combated the power of the Church courts with their
handling of appeals to Rome. In France these same questions

---

[1] Such as excommunication and the interdict.

arose much later (after the power of the papacy had been humbled);
and when relations with the papacy did actually become acute,
the issue was financial. It was but natural that needy monarchs,
held back by feudal custom from exercising unlimited taxing
power, should cast their greedy eyes on the vast wealth of the
Church. In the last decade of the thirteenth century both Edward I
of England and Philip the Fair of France determined to lay imposts
on the clergy despite their traditional immunity. Sometimes, it is
true, the pope had allowed the clergy to be taxed when support of a
crusade was required, but such a precedent was not supposed to
mean the right to continue the practice. In response to these royal
encroachments, mentioned above, Pope Boniface VIII issued his
bull *Clericis Laicos,* forbidding the imposition of lay assessments of
any sort on the persons and property of the clergy. Edward I, to
whom the bull was also addressed, replied by proclaiming the
clergy outside the law, with the result that Church property was so
badly plundered that the papacy was forced to yield. Philip, for
his part, not only held his point but forbade his clergy to pay any
taxes to Rome. The struggle became increasingly bitter till in
1302 the bull *Unam Sanctam* defined the position of the Church in
an extreme form, alleging that the temporal power was subject
to the spiritual and that the spiritual was accountable to God
alone. "We declare, assert, define, and pronounce it necessary,"
declared the Pope, "for the salvation of every human being that he
must yield obedience to the Roman pontiff." The final outcome
was the arrest of the aged pope by an emissary of Philip's with the
help of some of the former's rebellious vassals, and he died soon
afterward probably as a result of the shock. Then followed the
removal of the papacy to Avignon, a possession on the border of
France, where it was sometimes no more than an instrument of the
French king. At all events, with Boniface VIII the medieval idea
of the papacy exercising a universal authority was definitely
exploded.

For the modern state, with its pretension to supreme power,
this was a notable triumph. It is true that the papacy did not lose
its right to collect money from all the clergy, and that the immunity
of the clergy from taxation was usually respected, though the
French crown often solicited and received subsidies from time to
time; but in most countries the existence of the Church as a state
within a state (*imperium in imperio*) was steadily undermined.

In France (and in England as well) more and more cases which had been reserved to the ecclesiastical courts were transferred to the royal tribunals or at least subjected to their interference. Practical questions growing out of marriage and inheritance were brought within the competence of the royal courts, and even cases of clerical crime, with the exception of minor offenses, came to be judged by the king's tribunals. In both England and France, and to a large extent in Spain also, the national Church became administratively independent of the papacy. Indeed in France this process was aided by the attitude of the clergy themselves, who, usually giving their primary allegiance to the crown, came to be known as the "Gallican Church"—the product of resentment against papal interference. Had certain circumstances been otherwise, it might have been quite easy for the Church of France to parallel that of England and completely sever its bonds with papal authority.

The "national" state

Have we not, then, some evidence of a new spirit gradually permeating the modern state? It is interesting to observe that when Philip called an estates general to back him in his struggle with the pope, this moral approval was heartily given. Making all due allowance for the effects of royal coercion, have we not, after all, an exhibition of a national spirit, a manifestation of nationalism? Are we not justified in speaking of a "national" state, defending the dignity of its ruler in a struggle with an outside power? Yes, vaguely the state was in the process of becoming national in the sense of beginning to feel a self-reliance that was based on common interests and common customs, just as vaguely it was becoming "modern" in the sense that it was being brought under one law. Largely the two went hand in hand. While the annexation of Toulouse to the French crown meant the incorporation of a people with quite a distinct culture, its assimilation to the "French type" quickly followed on its political amalgamation. It is undoubtedly true that class spirit was still stronger than national spirit; yet Englishmen considered themselves quite superior to Frenchmen and looked upon them as aliens, and the French came to feel a spontaneous longing to rid their soil of the English. Nationalism as an emotion was only in its faint beginnings; generally it was dormant; but in times of stress a people could be awakened to a sense of its birthright and determined to defend it. Such, indeed, was the case of the Scotch, who developed a national feeling in their resistance to English invasions. Sometimes one is reminded of a family whose members, possessed of different temperaments, often quarrel among themselves, yet stand as one against an enemy outside. So it was with the Spaniards, broken up into different compartments by the character of their country and sometimes differing in language, yet welded into a nation by the long and bitter struggle with the Moors. Even among a people as disorganized as the Germans a national feeling asserted itself in Luther's struggle with the papacy. In the English people, living as they did on an island, and working out institutions that were peculiar to themselves, a feeling of proud contempt for other nations was early manifested.

The Renaissance did much to develop the potentialities of nationalism, and insofar as it weakened the unity of the Church, intellectual and moral, it redounded to the advantage of the State—whether we look upon the State as the embodiment of a nation or the instrument of a monarch for his private ends. The very fact that a king of France ("eldest daughter of the Church," as she was fondly called) would form an alliance with a prince of Islam, against which the Church had once dispatched the leading princes of Christendom, including, indeed, several kings of France, well demonstrated the change in spiritual values that had taken place in three centuries. One must, however, guard against the impulse to exaggerate. In the sixteenth century the papacy, by reason of its theoretical detachment, had still considerable prestige. Now and then it held the scales between contending monarchs; its arbitration was sometimes sought in political quarrels; and its partition of the world between Spain and Portugal—which was seriously respected by these rivals—showed that even after it had degenerated into a normally unaggressive Italian power, the papacy could still loom high in public affairs. But the Renaissance, in placing the temporal above the spiritual, was sharpening the moral division of Christendom, and shifting the center of gravity from Rome to other centers of political life. Nowhere does one find a more eloquent example of the political trend than in Machiavelli's *The Prince.* For this famous Italian theorist, the State, typified by the prince, should dominate society. The plain spirit of his teaching was that anything that served the interest of the State was justifiable. Since the Christian religion taught meekness and generosity as cardinal virtues, it was dangerous to the power, and

Influence of the Renaissance

hence inimical to the progress, of the State. For the ruler, at least, morality was nought else but "reasons of state." Intended merely to promote the unity of Italy under a single head, *The Prince* became the gospel of unscrupulous sovereigns, already prompted by the individualistic spirit of the Renaissance, and conscious of their power. Furthermore, the art of diplomacy, long practiced so successfully by the Italians, became a model for western Europe with the spread of Italian culture. Spain under Ferdinand the Catholic, France under Francis I, and England under the Tudors organized ministries of foreign affairs and sent resident ambassadors to foreign courts after the manner practiced by Venice. But there were also ways in which the influence of the Renaissance touched more directly what we have called the "national state." The printing of books and other writings in the vernacular not only had the effect of reducing provincial differences by the creation in some countries of an official language, but also, as we have said, gave rise to a national culture, which sometimes, as in the case of Shakespeare, became a conscious vehicle of patriotism. And so, although class interests remained predominant and kings generally followed their personal whims and most of the people were still illiterate, yet we have something more than the germs of national states. We have forces strong enough to assert themselves effectively against any claim to universal dominion.

Influence of the Reformation

If, then, the Church was no longer able to exercise political control and had only a partial allegiance from its own caste; if it no longer enjoyed intellectual or spiritual ascendancy; little remained but the monopoly of religious belief to suggest its claims to universal empire. This at least gave it still some political influence, and was the one remaining element which tied Christendom together. It was this one remaining tie which the Reformation snapped.

The Catholic Reaction: Origins

We may recall how the Church stood on the defensive in the early stages of the Religious Revolution. Many of its leading prelates had been well aware that a reformation was needed, and we know that the efforts of general councils to bring about reform "both in head and members" had largely foundered on the quarrels of national monarchs, whose clergy were often intractable—another evidence of the weakening of the Church by the new forces. Parallel with the Lutheran struggle in Germany there was much discussion of the question of holding another general council (it was the favorite dream of the Emperor Charles V), and numerous efforts were made—three in Germany and one in France—to find a common ground whereon the Protestants might come back to Mother Church. The ravages of schism were, however, far too deep to make it possible to reinforce a tottering structure. When the Council of Trent finally met (about the middle of the sixteenth century), it was in no spirit of compromise, but rather to accept the schism as a fact, and to heal it—if it could be healed—either by making the Church itself a clear and incisive force, morally reformed, and better able to revive once more the loyalty of the lost or indifferent, or else, if preaching and example should fail, by trying the expedient of force. Such was the purpose and such the spirit of the so-called Counter-Reformation.

Because reformation was but one instrument in this crusade, the term, Counter-Reformation is less historically suitable than Catholic Reaction. There is no reason to doubt the sincerity of the reformation aspect as an object in itself, but it seems to merge in the larger effort to roll back the tide of Protestantism. The Catholic Reaction was a movement to turn the pendulum back and recover the lost ground. Its spirit came from Spain, that country least affected by the Renaissance, most given to mystical fancies and chivalrous devotion, most zealous for the raising of moral standards among the clergy, and, perhaps because of the long struggles for the faith, most loyal to the teachings of the Church. It was a medieval spirit in a sense, unbending in its attitude toward the critical spirit of the day, yet showing much of that selfless, unworldly temper that was so charming a characteristic of the Middle Ages. It was perhaps best exemplified in Cardinal Caraffa, who, though of Neapolitan birth and oddly enough a hater of Spain (because of her hold on southern Italy), was nevertheless impressed by the success of a monastic revival which he had witnessed himself in Spain. When he later became pope as Paul IV, he represented both aspects of the movement—the rooting out of clerical abuses and the extirpation of heresy. The spiritual leadership of the movement was to be vested in a reformed and refortified papacy, the first exponent of which—though a weaker character—had been Paul III, who began his pontificate in 1536 and was the pope who was induced to call a general council. But the influence of Spain, whose ruler, Charles V, had forced this convocation, was the really dominant factor. And it was this influence that was personified in the Society or Company of Jesus —otherwise known as the Jesuits.

Instruments The Jesuits were the most potent agents of the Catholic Reaction. Founded by an able Spanish zealot, who had once been a knight, Ignatius Loyola, this order received the sanction of Pope Paul III in 1542, and, bound by a special oath of obedience to the pope, came to be known as the "militia of the holy see." They were prepared, indeed, to go wherever he sent them "at once, unconditionally, without question, and without reward." Organized like an army, rigorously trained both morally and intellectually for their task, and carrying the virtue of devotion to the point of self-abnegation, they went about their labors, teaching, preaching, and winning the hearts of thousands through the intimacy of the confessional; and to them may be ascribed the chief triumphs of the Catholic Reaction. They won back for the faith a large part of southern Germany, as well as Poland, and the very hatred which they incurred from their enemies was an evidence of their capacity. As instruments of the Catholic Reaction, they were far more effective than the inquisition, first revived in Spain, and later in Rome (by Paul III), which obviously had little to do in countries where heresy had taken no root. The other weapon of force, the armies of a secular prince, was somewhat more effective, but, as we shall presently see, did little more than set a limit on Protestant success. The platform of the movement was to be found in the decrees of the Council of Trent, which not only provided for a better disciplined and better educated clergy and stigmatized certain abuses, but reasserted in definite form the theological position of the Church, and reaffirmed, in effect,[1] the sovereign position of the pope in its governance. Thus the Church —Roman now, much more than universal—was morally and materially consolidated. Despite some quarreling between the popes and the leading secular leaders of the movement, the Catholic Reaction showed remarkable zeal and unity of purpose.

The Wars of Religion It was the Catholic Reaction, brought into collision with the Protestant Revolt, which produced the so-called Wars of Religion —a struggle which engulfed most of Christendom, and pursued its weary course until human nature seemed almost to turn from

---

[1] The pope was given the sole right of interpreting the Tridentine decrees (the decrees of the Council of Trent). A general council of the Church did not meet again until 1869.

religion itself as the source of spiritual guidance, and political
interests, coming more and more to the fore, made capital out of the
struggle for their own ends. In some places this wracking conflict
threatened to disrupt the modern state. In France the Calvinist
or "Huguenot" [1] nobility used the religious question as a means
of weakening the royal power in an effort to bring back the feudal
state—an eventuality which seemed only too imminent as the
last of the Valois kings were notoriously weak. The Religious
Wars in France, which began in 1562 and lasted intermittently
till 1598, brought the country to the verge of ruin. It was in vain
that a "national" party, the so-called "Politiques," had tried to
end the struggle by provoking a war with Spain; most of the nobles
still gratified their taste for private war; and after the heretic
Henry of Navarre became the legitimate ruler of France, the
Catholic nobility, aided from without by the Catholic Reaction,
represented the cause of feudalism as the Huguenot nobles had
done. It was to prevent the possible accession of a heretic to the
throne—which in those days would presumably have meant a
heretic France—that Philip II of Spain had intervened. Already
this prince had tried to dethrone the English queen, Elizabeth; and,
if we consider the many plots against her throne as well as the
existence of a large Catholic minority in her realm, it seems almost a miracle that England came through this stormy period
without a civil war. Spain herself was also a victim of the struggle,
for the Dutch, under the enlightened leadership of William of
Orange, and with timely aid from Elizabeth, successfully won their
independence. Here again religion was not the only factor; for
the Dutch revolt was a nationalist uprising against an alien ruler,
Philip of Spain.

Philip II was one of the most tragic failures in history. Pains-
taking to the point of meticulousness, tenacious to the point of not
knowing when he was beaten, inflexibly devoted to the Church,
but morose, secretive, and suspicious of all his ablest servants, he
was an impossible man for an impossible task—the exercise of
Spain's supremacy in Europe for the recovery of western Europe
for the Church. Even the wealth of the new world provided only an
inflated greatness, for Spain had few industries, and fanaticism
soon extirpated her most industrious element—the Moriscos of

---

[1] The name "Huguenots" was probably a French corruption of the German
word, *Eidgenossen* (confederates), used of the Swiss Protestants.

Andalusia. The only tangible success to Philip's credit—and it belongs more to his general, Alexander of Parma—was the recovery of the southern provinces of the Netherlands, which had joined the northern provinces in revolt. Elsewhere he merely squandered the resources of his country to no purpose. He lost the northern provinces of the Netherlands to the revolting Dutch; the great fleet which he sent against England was scattered or sunk; and he was powerless to keep the tolerant Henry of Navarre from the French throne. He is an interesting example of a mediocre man, called upon by circumstances to play a rôle which was inherently impossible of success.

But the disruptive character of the religious wars was not confined to western Europe. They involved the Holy Roman Empire, and revealed to the fullest extent the impotence of that ruler who theoretically aspired to universal dominion. We may recall that even in Germany the emperor had never been anything but a feudal overlord, and even as such his power had steadily diminished. The Hapsburg emperors, who had successively worn the imperial crown since 1372, drew all their actual strength from their hereditary possessions, such as Austria and other states which they held as fiefs of the empire. As emperor, the Hapsburg ruler was wholly dependent upon his vassals, who, meeting periodically in the diet, occasionally voted money or raised contingents for imperial defense, but more often refused to do either. Left without any really effective central government, the empire lapsed into chronic anarchy. The only elements of order were certain princes, lay or ecclesiastical, who, though theoretically vassals of the emperor, were practically independent. Nowhere was the right of private warfare so freely indulged in; and it was a proof of the hollowness of the empire that the common means of defending the peace was a league of towns and princes, which functioned quite outside the imperial machinery to protect itself against the prevailing disorders. In a country, already aflame the religious question added just so much more fuel to the fire. In Luther's day, as we have noticed, a formidable uprising of the peasants took place—a terrible proof of the impotence of a feudal state. Yet the least thing that the princes desired was an increase in the imperial power. When the Emperor Charles V was suspected of trying, with the aid of Spanish troops, to make himself a sovereign, all princes, whether Catholic or Protestant, combined against him, and the result was that famous compromise, the Peace of Augsburg.

The Peace of Augsburg (1555) was supposed to solve the religious question—not because anyone believed in toleration (with few exceptions, such as Montaigne, no one in that age believed in freedom of conscience as a matter of principle), but rather because political considerations seemed to the German princes more important than religious. It was the same spirit which had animated the Politiques, and the same also which had moved William the Silent in his efforts to bind all Netherlanders, whatever their faith, in a common resistance to Spain. Viewed as a pacific solution, the Peace of Augsburg rested on a kind of religious balance. The strength of the Catholic and Lutheran princes was then about equal. Yet, since according to the terms of the Peace a prince might change his religion and carry his subjects with him, the balance was at best precarious, especially as the ecclesiastical principalities were in their nature not hereditary, and there were no really adequate means for preventing Protestant influences from capturing the cathedral chapters which chose these bishops or archbishops.[1] By 1570 a number of these important states had become secularized, while in many of the secular Catholic principalities heresy had taken root, largely through the indifference of the Catholic princes during a period of comparative peace. Finally, it must be recalled that the imperial government had no machinery with which to enforce the Peace of Augsburg when either side violated it. The failure of the religious peace was everywhere manifest.

Such was the situation when the Catholic Reaction entered Germany. For a militant movement such as this the opportunity was peculiarly favorable. The strength of the Protestant cause had lain very largely in its ability to make capital out of the abuses in the Church; now, however, the Church was at last reformed; and,

[1] The secularization of Church lands within a prince's dominions was supposed to have been ended by the Peace of Augsburg. The secularization of the ecclesiastical principalities was supposed to have been prevented by the Ecclesiastical Reservation (a supplement to the Peace), which required a bishop or archbishop who held of the emperor to resign if he became a Protestant. Unhappily for the Catholic cause, no provision had been made for insuring that a cathedral chapter should remain Catholic, and if it chose a Protestant as bishop, the latter, having no right to perform ecclesiastical functions, became simply and solely an hereditary secular prince. Christian IV of Denmark had his son chosen "bishop" in a number of ecclesiastical principalities, and the electors of Brandenburg were also very active in this process.

in general, its theology was hardly less intelligible to the common man than the dogmas which Luther had taught, while the beauty of the Catholic ritual had all its old appeal. Moreover, there were quarrels among the Protestants themselves, especially between Lutherans and Calvinists (the latter having no standing under the Peace), which glaringly contrasted with that unity of spirit displayed by the Catholic Reaction. More and more, as the result of conversions—in which the Jesuits played their part—or of evictions, the Catholic princes recovered their hold on the religious life of their states. It would only be a question of time when the forces of reaction would be turned against the Protestant despoilers of the Church lands. Several times Germany narrowly escaped the outbreak of religious war, as the contending parties fought for control of an imperial town or a principality. Finally in 1618 the Bohemians, who were Lutheran in leanings, raised the standard of revolt against their king, who was none other than the Emperor himself; and thus began the greatest and most terrible of the religious struggles—the Thirty Years' War. After the fires of religious war had burned themselves out in the rest of Europe, they had become enkindled in that country which had long been a tinder box of hatred, greed, and anarchy.

We shall give but little space to the complicated story of this struggle. Begun as a local sedition, it soon became a civil war, and finally became European in scope. Though the religious factor was very strong at first, especially as regards the Calvinists, who were outlaws under the provisions of the Peace, the Thirty Years' War was predominantly a political struggle. Since the Hapsburgs had numerous and scattered dominions, all their enemies, whether Catholic or Protestant, were soon arrayed against them. The Lutheran princes were chiefly concerned with keeping their secularized lands and bought neutrality (for a time) from the Emperor while he and his allies turned their guns upon the Calvinists. Foreign princes, like the kings of Denmark and Sweden, were mostly concerned with aggrandizing themselves at the expense of a land which had apparently lost all means of defense. All Germany was engulfed before the war was finally ended, and in some places, such as Bohemia, the Catholic Reaction was very severe. Once indeed it looked as if the Emperor might, with the aid of his accomplished general, Wallenstein, make himself a sovereign by virtue of the army at his disposal. But Ferdinand II was unequal

EUROPE

AFTER THE
PEACE OF WESTPHALIA
1648

Scale of Miles
0   100   200   300

Brandenburg-Prussia
Church Lands
Spain
Austria
Sweden
Boundary of the
Holy Roman
Empire

NORDEN

NORTH SEA

SCOTLAND

Edinburgh

IRELAND
Dublin

I. OF MAN

WALES

ENGLAND

London

Amsterdam
The Hague

UNITED PROVINCES

Antwerp

Münster

Cologne

HESS

Fra

THE

Dunkirk

Brussels

SPANISH NETHERLANDS

Calais

Luxemburg

Worms

PALA-TINATE

CHANNEL IS.

Rocroy

Verdun

Metz

Nord

Strass

R. Seine

Paris

Reims

Tou

FRANCHE COMTÉ

Basle

Con

stan

Nantes

R. Loire

F R A N C E

La Rochelle

Geneva

SWITZERLA

Lyons

SAVOY

DUTCHY OF
SAVOY

PIED-MONT

MILANES

Pa

Genoa

Montauban

LANGUEDOC

Orange

Avignon

Toulouse

Pinerolo

PYRENEES

NAVARRE

Marseilles

Nice

R. Ebro

ARAGON

ROUSSILLON

CORSICA
(To Genoa)

PORTUGAL

R. Douro

CATALONIA

Barcelona

Madrid

R. Tagus

SARDINIA
(To Sp.)

Lisbon

S P A I N

BALEARIC IS.

Seville

M E D I T E

Tangier

ATLANTIC OCEAN

MAN DRAFT.CO.,INC.N.Y.

to so bold a conception (in fact, he always looked upon the struggle as primarily religious), and in the end he gave way to the jealous fears of the Catholic princes, who insisted on the downfall of his instrument. Yet the character of Wallenstein himself is such a puzzle that one cannot be certain that with all his political acumen and religious tolerance he would ever have shown the capacity for making a united imperial Germany. Judging him by contrast with other leaders, he deserves credit for having organized a fairly well disciplined army, supporting itself largely by requisitions. Much of the fighting, unhappily, was carried on by mercenary bands, caring for nothing at all but plunder and ravaging everything in sight. It was for this reason chiefly that the Thirty Years' War ranks probably as the most devastating conflict in modern history.

Politically the Thirty Years' War was, to all intents and purposes, the finishing blow to the Holy Roman Empire. Though that *A new fabric of Europe* organism lasted in theory down to Napoleon, its feeble elements of authority were completely paralyzed by the struggle and the German princes were now independent in all but name. Religiously the war had ended in a compromise. The right of the prince to choose his religion (Calvinism being now added to the range of selection) was confirmed by the Peace of Westphalia (1648), and geographically that was to mean that north Germany remained Protestant and south Germany Catholic. In a larger significance it meant, of course, that the fruits of the Religious Revolution were not lost. But the chief result of the Thirty Years' War from the political standpoint was the final dissolution of Christendom, conceived as a moral unit. Henceforth there would be national states which acknowledged no allegiance to the pope and would not even look to his influence to settle their numerous differences. Europe had lost her last species of solidarity. From now on the peace of Europe must rest on what has been called a sovereign state system. Various national states had gained in territory and power as a result of the struggle. They were sovereign in the sense that they owned no superior. Would they work out a new fabric of Europe, more effective than any form of universal empire, to keep the world at peace?

It is interesting to notice that during the Thirty Years' War lived and wrote the man who has been called the father of international law. Hugo Grotius was a Dutchman who had become learned in jurisprudence and also knew something of politics from personal experience. The argument of his great work, *Concerning War and Peace* (1625) was that society has an essential solidarity based on the innate sociability of man, and that this concept of "natural law" should direct the conduct of all nations. Though he specified the kinds of war which in his opinion were justifiable, he also discussed some practicable means of avoiding war. But he did not limit the sovereignty of the state or suggest any coercive power for enforcing the world's peace, and the merit of his work lies chiefly in an abstract ideal. Unfortunately his teachings—the direct antithesis of Machiavelli's—merely constituted a conception, on which the World has been slow to act. The only basis on which the statesmen of Europe endeavored to avert war, or at least to prevent any power from becoming strong enough to realize the dream of universal empire (which in itself might have prevented war) was the idea, long practiced among the squabbling states of Italy, namely the balance of power. The essence of this doctrine was that no one state should become so formidable as to endanger the independence of the others. If one threatened to become so strong, the others would have reason to combine against it. On the basis of this principle of an equilibrium of Europe the national states might try by diplomacy to adjust their differences, and the treaties which they made were supposed, at least in theory, to be binding on their signatories. But it is clear that international law was only in its beginnings; and the very triumph of the national state, sovereign within and without, as the basic political conception of society, would make anything like a super-state, standing for peace and justice for them all, more difficult than ever of realization. In this respect the modern world has something to learn in principle from the Middle Ages.

But most of the things we associate with the Middle Ages were doomed by the aggressive, pushful advance of human strength and human intellect. The three threads of progress which we have followed give us the approach to the modern world. In some ways they were interrelated. The rising self-confidence of the individual was at bottom the cause of the growth of the middle class, and the middle class assisted the evolution of the modern state, which became strong enough to puncture the dream of universal empire. It is a mistake, however, to portray the middle class, as some recent historians do, as running the modern state and exploiting it in their interest. Kings still generally chose their advisers from the upper classes, and while they depended to some extent on the middle class to operate their governmental machinery, and while they realized the importance of economic interests and endeavored to promote them, the initiative in policy did not rest with the men of the towns. With negligible exceptions the modern state first evolves as an absolute monarchy, and most of its acts, good or bad, are attributable to kings and noblemen. Of all the forces of transition, that collective force, the state, will achieve the most striking triumphs of the seventeenth century, but, looking to the distant future, the genius of the individual in science, business, and politics has most to do with making our present society.

FOR FURTHER READING OR STUDY

Emerton, E., *The Beginnings of Modern Europe;* Thompson, J. W., *Economic and Social History of the Later Middle Ages;* Randall, J. H., *The Making of the Modern Mind;* Thorndyke, L., *A Short History of Civilization;* Usher, A. L., *A History of Mechanical Invention;* Day, C., *History of Commerce,* chaps. v–xv; Knight, M. M., *Economic History of Europe to the End of the Middle Ages,* esp. chap. vi; Gras, N. S. B., *An Introduction to Economic History,* chap. iv; Nussbaum, F. L., *A History of the Economic Institutions of Modern Europe,* parts 1 and 2; Hobson, J. A., *The Evolution of Modern Capitalism,* chaps i and ii; Green, A. S., *Town Life in the Fifteenth Century;* Robertson, H. M., *Rise of Economic Individualism;* MacIver, R. M., *The Modern State;* Seignobos, C., *Evolution of the French People,* chaps. iv–xiii; Guignebert, C., *A Short History of the French People,* vol. i, chaps xi–xvii; Tilley, A., *Medieval France,* chaps. i, ii (esp. pp. 60–77), and v; Chapman, E., *History of Spain,* chaps. i–xxiv; Davis, H. W. C., *England under the Normans and Angevins;* Muir, R., *Nationalism and Internationalism,* part 2, chaps. i and ii and part 3, chap. i; Figgis, J. N., *The Divine Right of Kings;* Rose, J. H., *Nationality in Modern History,* chap. i; Hayes, C. J. H., *A Political and Cultural History of Modern Europe,* vol. i, chaps. i–vi; Hyma, A., *Europe from the Renaissance to 1815,* chaps. i–viii (a very useful survey); Gillespie, J. E., *A History of Europe, 1500–1815,* part i, chaps. i–iii; Higby, C. P., *European History, 1492–1815,* chaps. i–v; Abbott, W. C., *The Expansion of Europe,* vol. i, chap. iii; Hulme, E. M., *Renaissance and Reformation;* Lucas, H. S., *The Renaissance and the Reformation;* Smith, P., *The Era of the Reformation* and *Erasmus;* Murray, R. H., *Erasmus and Luther;* Armstrong, E., *The Emperor Charles V,* 2 vols., and *The French Wars of Religion* (three essays); Grant, A. J., *The French Monarchy,* vol. i, chaps. iii–v (on the Wars of Religion); Geyl, P., *The Revolt of the Netherlands;* Putnam, R., *William the Silent;* Hume, M. J. S., *Philip II;* Henderson, E. F., *A Short History of Germany;* Wakeman, H. O., *European History, 1598–1715,* chaps. iii–v (on the Thirty Years' War); Fletcher, G. R. L., *Gustavus Adolphus;* Vreeland, H., *Hugo Grotius;* Hayes, C. J. H., "Significance of the Reformation in the Light of

Contemporary Scholarship," *Catholic Historical Review*, vol. xvii, p. 395 ff. There is, as yet, no satisfactory study of the Catholic Reaction.

The Cambridge Modern History, 14 vols. (including index volume and atlas), covering the period from the Renaissance to about 1900, is a co-operative work by a large staff of specialists and very useful for reference, though often too detailed to be interesting reading; vols. i–iv carry the reader through the Thirty Years' War. For ready reference *The Encyclopedia Britannica* and *The Encyclopedia of the Social Sciences* are invaluable; and Shepherd's *Historical Atlas* is an important aid. Useful hand-books for geography are Bogardus, J. F., *Europe: A Geographical Survey* and Lyde, L. W., *The Continent of Europe*.

THE ERA OF NATIONAL CONSOLIDATION

II. THE RISE OF BOURBON FRANCE

1. THE WORK OF HENRY IV

Conditions on the accession of Henry IV; Character of Henry IV; Work of restoration: (1) political, (2) economic; Foreign policy; Henry IV as the formulator of Bourbon policy.

2. THE WORK OF RICHELIEU

Importance of Richelieu; Accession to power; Character and methods; Repression of the Huguenots; Suppression of the nobles; Minor activities; Foreign policy: (1) objects and preliminary measures, (2) intervention in the Thirty Years' War.

3. THE WORK OF MAZARIN

Importance of Mazarin; Accession to power and character; The Fronde; Mazarin's foreign policy.

4. THE ZENITH OF THE BOURBON MONARCHY UNDER LOUIS XIV

A. THE CHARACTER OF THE MONARCHY

Royalty as a system: (1) political aspects, (2) economic aspects, (3) cultural aspects; Royalty as an art; The seamy side.

B. THE FRAMEWORK OF THE MONARCHY

The bureaucracy; The king's council; The legislative power; The executive power: (1) The central administration, (2) the provincial administration, (3) the financial administration; The judicial power; The nobles of the robe.

C. THE POSITION OF FRANCE IN EUROPE

Foreign policy of Louis XIV; The ascent; The decline; Death of Louis XIV.

D. AFTERMATH OF THE REIGN OF LOUIS XIV

The Regency; Rule of Louis XV.

The welding together of the weak and disjointed France of the Valois régime into a strong and compact state was the work of the Bourbon monarchy. Insofar as this was due to the vision and statesmanship of its directing minds, the achievement may be ascribed to Henry IV (first of the Bourbon kings) and to Richelieu, with some finishing touches to the structure by Mazarin and Louis XIV. This process of national development is of considerable

historical importance not only because it explains the ascendancy
of France in Europe, but also because it reveals France of the
seventeenth century as the great exemplar of the modern state,
and, to that extent, a beacon light of civilization.

THE WORK OF HENRY IV

*Conditions
on the
accession of
Henry IV*

The task which confronted Henry IV on his accession [1] was one
that might well have staggered the most courageous and resourceful of sovereigns. More than thirty years of intermittent civil war

Painting by Goltzius
HENRY IV

had sapped the vitality of the
nation to an extent that many
must have despaired of better
things. The country was impoverished; industry was at a
standstill; much of the land
was untilled; bandits roamed
the countryside; and the government was not only hopelessly in debt and living from
hand to mouth but burdened
with a horde of financial officials who were only too ready
to sacrifice public honesty to
private gain. Such was the
economic side of the picture.
But the political was no
brighter. The king had little
beyond his own personality to enforce respect; most of the nobility
were in league with the foreign enemy; the Spanish invaders were
still occupying parts of the country; and the religious question,
which had rent France in twain, was still unsolved. Apparently
the first problem was to gain adhesion to the king's leadership.
Then a policy of pacification and reform might be calculated to
put the ruined nation on its feet.

*Character of
Henry IV*

There is little denying that Henry IV was peculiarly qualified
for this difficult task. Long inured to fighting, he was a man of
simple tastes and a certain inborn camaraderie which endeared

[1] Henry IV was king by hereditary right when the last Valois king, Henry III,
was murdered in 1589. But his right to the throne was disputed, and it was not till
1593 that he was crowned and became really *de facto* king.

him to his followers and speedily won the sympathy and the confidence of his subjects. He could enjoy his pleasures with perfect abandon, and was possibly more dissolute than most of the princes of his time; but he was firm enough, when necessary, to inspire confidence, and was too astute a politician not to know how much was possible of achievement. His very sense of humor saved him from discouragement, and personal ambition kept his eye always fixed on some distant goal. He was, in short, the ideal physician for the ills of France.

Henry's initial task was the restoration of his country to normal health. It embraced two features, as we have implied, political and economic. On the political side he accomplished three things. First, he won over the disaffected nobility by offering them honors and positions if they would transfer their allegiance to the crown. It is no doubt an evidence of weakness that he used political arts instead of force to insure obedience, but in truth the crown was hardly strong enough to do otherwise than feel its way, and Henry was shrewd enough to try the method of conciliation first. Such a policy was well suited to the Catholic nobles, who, with the collapse of Spanish arms, were only too eager to seek their fortunes in the rival camp. Secondly, Henry made peace with Spain, and so removed the foreign invader from the soil of France. And finally, he issued the Edict of Nantes, 1598, which brought about religious— and thus furthered political—peace.

The work of restoration: (1) political

It was in handling the religious question that Henry had most displayed his political acumen. A Calvinist by inheritance but never a religious man, he had had no compunction about changing his religion—a maneuver which had opened the gates of Paris and helped greatly to consolidate his throne. Now that the official religion was to remain Catholic—the religion of the great majority of Frenchmen—it was easy for him to grant concessions to the Calvinists which both expediency and loyalty demanded. By the Edict of Nantes (called, ironically enough, "perpetual and irrevocable") the "so-called Reformed Religion" was accorded a legal status within certain prescribed conditions. Freedom of conscience was granted, and freedom of worship in certain localities— enough, it was thought, to fulfill the needs of a small minority— while, at the same time, the bestowal of civil rights meant that Calvinists might legally be appointed to any office. As a special guarantee to protect them against attack by the stronger party, they were allowed the right to garrison (in some cases at the king's expense) more than a hundred [1] walled towns. Here in such places as La Rochelle they might freely hold their assemblies (explicitly for religious purposes), and no officer of the crown had the right to enter. It is easy to perceive that the Huguenot party might in course of time become a source of danger to the royal authority—a sort of state within a state; but, as in his treatment of the nobles, Henry's aim was to attain unity by satisfying or protecting all elements in the population. The religious settlement was essentially a compromise, designed to secure religious peace. France remained a Catholic state but granted a limited toleration to one of the other religious communions. It was not the result of any lofty principle but rather an act of political expediency. And if we recall the Protestant alliances of the Valois kings and the religious breadth of the Politiques we may realize that such statesmanship on his part was far from revolutionary in France, though it is true that he put politics above religion in a more important and comprehensive way than any of his predecessors. The flaw in the scheme—the constitution of a separate political power in the heart of the body politic—may not seriously detract from the King's sagacity, since the gravity of the crisis demanded extraordinary measures to secure peace.

(2) Economic

The securing of political peace and the recognition that there was one law and one authority for France had much to do with the economic revival of the kingdom. Lawlessness did not wholly cease, but Henry tried to protect the peasants from depredations by stopping irregular warfare and interposing a check on the rapacity of financial officials. One of his first acts was to appoint an old companion-at-arms, the Duke of Sully as superintendent of the finances. Sully was a cold and gruff person, like most treasury watch-dogs, but he fully answered to the requisites of his post. The old crowd of dishonest officials was dismissed and replaced by men more calculated to act in the true spirit of the new régime. Sully then imposed honesty in the collection of the taxes and economy in the expenditure of the revenue. Realizing too that there would be more money for the king's purse if the country were

[1] This privilege, accorded originally for eight years, seems to have continued for some time after this period had elapsed; but most of the towns were taken away by the crown after a Huguenot rising in 1621-2 (during the next reign) and according to Richelieu himself (though his veracity has been disputed) there were only two left at the time when the privilege was finally withdrawn.

to develop its natural resources, he undertook some direct aid to agriculture by draining marshes, constructing a canal between the Loire and the Seine, and improving the public highways. Henry even went further and gave direct encouragement to industry, especially the manufacture of luxuries, such as silks, china, and glass. Also, in order to facilitate industrial revival he adopted the mercantilist theory of a protective tariff—proceeding on the notion that a country must always sell more than it bought. While it has been amply proved that this "favorable balance of trade" is not a real index to prosperity, the policy is important as marking a direction which his successors were to follow, and it undoubtedly did help France to enjoy a virtual monopoly of the trade in articles of luxury. Henry also promoted commerce by such measures as the development of a merchant marine, and he encouraged the colonization of the lands which France was opening in North America and which led to the founding of Louisburg and Quebec—the beginning of France's empire in the new world. Looking at the problem from the government's angle, the nation was able to bear a greater burden of taxation, while from the standpoint of the taxpayer the increased profits from his labor enabled him to reserve for his own use more than had been possible for a generation. With extraordinary rapidity the country recovered its normal prosperity and enjoyed a security and contentment it had not known for half a century.

But Henry IV was by natural taste a warrior, and, despite his surly and economical superintendent, he meant that much of the treasure thus amassed should be spent on rehabilitating France's position among the nations. The old rivalry between France and the house of Hapsburg only slumbered, and a wise king had to look to the national defenses. The weakest point on the frontier was in the east, where the Duke of Savoy, always a potential ally of the Hapsburgs, held some districts which stretched as far as the river Saône, thus permitting him to dispatch an army through the passes of the Vosges into the very heart of France. To get these districts was, therefore, Henry's first project in foreign policy after the signing of his peace with Spain; and it would seem that Savoy's possession of Saluzzo (a district on the Italian side of the Alps, seized from France during the anarchy of the religious wars) might offer the possibility of an adjustment. When patient negotiation seemed to promise little result, Henry at length resorted to

Foreign policy

force, and brought the duke to terms. The coveted districts were ceded to France while Savoy retained Saluzzo. This settlement, the Treaty of Lyons (1601), was negatively important as confirming France's abandonment of the old adventurous policy of seeking land in Italy, and positively it was a striking achievement in strengthening her frontier at its most vulnerable point.

The King was criticized by one of his friends for bargaining like a merchant. But such procedure was characteristic of his cautious wisdom. While fully impressed with the menace of Hapsburg power on three sides, he confined himself for some years to embarrassing them by indirect attacks upon their interests such as sending subsidies to the Dutch in their struggle with Spain, gaining from Switzerland the right to use the passes over the Alps, and entering into close relations with various Italian states. More important from the standpoint of a future war was his renewal of a Valois contract with the Swiss government to furnish him with mercenaries for his army. It was still uncertain whether Henry would find himself strong enough to challenge both Austria and Spain when an incident occurred which shows that great events often hang on trivial affairs. Henry had fallen in love with the beautiful wife of one of his noblemen, the Prince of Condé, and was so assiduous in his attentions that the prince took his wife and fled to Brussels where he claimed and received the protection of the Spanish governor of the Netherlands. Furious at this rebuff, Henry talked openly of revenge, and immediately prepared for war. A dispute over the succession to the imperial duchies, Cleve and Jülich, which had instigated the emperor to send a force to occupy Jülich (not far from the French frontier), gave him a more suitable pretext for action. Henry made an alliance with the Calvinist Union in Germany, and set in readiness three armies to hurl against Austria and Spain. But fate intervened in a tragic way. The King was riding through the streets of Paris on May 14, 1610, when he was stabbed to death by a madman.

Henry IV as the formulator of Bourbon policy

It was probably fortunate for his country that Henry met his end when he did, since it is to be doubted whether France was really strong enough as yet to wage war on three fronts. But it is unfortunate that the work of national upbuilding could not have gone on under so wise and forceful a monarch. Nevertheless Henry had done enough to set a standard for his successors. He had made the absolute monarchy seem a reality. In spite of sporadic rebel-

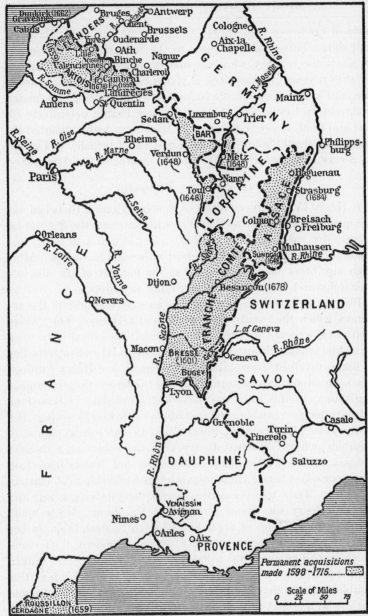

Dunkirk (1662)
Gravelines
Calais
Bruges
Ghent
Antwerp
Cologne
R. Scheldt
FLANDERS
R. Lys
Aix-la-Chapelle
R. Rhine
Ypres
Oudenarde
(1678)
Lille
Ath
Namur
Binche
(1668)
Valenciennes
Charleroi
GERMANY
ARTOIS
Cambrai
Mainz
(1678)
(1659)
R. Somme
Landrecies
R. Moselle
Amiens
St. Quentin
Sedan
Luxemburg
Trier
Philippsburg
R. Seine
R. Oise
Rheims
BAR
Verdun (1648)
Metz (1648)
R. Marne
Haguenau
Nancy
Paris
R. Seine
Toul (1648)
LORRAINE
Strasburg (1684)
ALSACE
Colmar
Breisach
Freiburg
Orleans
R. Yonne
R. Loire
Dijon
Mulhausen
R. Saône
SUNDGAU (1648)
R. Rhine
Nevers
Besançon (1678)
FRANCHE COMTÉ
SWITZERLAND
F R A N C E
R. Saône
L. of Geneva
Macon
BRESSE (1601)
R. Rhône
BUGEY
Geneva
Lyon
SAVOY
R. Rhône
Grenoble
Turin
Casale
Pinerolo
DAUPHINÉ
Saluzzo
VENAISSIN
Nimes
Avignon
Arles
Aix
PROVENCE

Permanent acquisitions
made 1598–1715 ....

Scale of Miles
0   25   50   75

ROUSSILLON
CERDAGNE   (1659)

Adapted from Ogg, Europe in the 17th Century, *A. & C. Black*

THE EXPANSION OF FRANCE IN THE SEVENTEENTH CENTURY

lions of noblemen who abused the power he had given them, he had shown himself always equal to the emergency, always ready to show the nobility who was master of France. His reign of seventeen years [1] had resulted in giving his country a new lease of life, and a chance once more to look forward. Even in his foreign policy he had done something to prepare France defensively for war and in his desire to humble the Hapsburgs he had pointed the course she should follow to reach a position of primacy in Europe. In a very real sense Henry IV was the creator of Bourbon policy.

THE WORK OF RICHELIEU

Importance of Richelieu

If Henry IV was the architect of Bourbon France, Richelieu was the master-mason. It was Richelieu who, catching the spirit of his predecessor, made the king absolute in fact as well as in theory and made the kingdom he ruled the most influential in Europe. More than any other man, Richelieu was the founder of the absolute monarchy and the ascendancy of France in Europe.

Accession to power

But the task of Richelieu was not an easy one despite the advances which the country had made under Henry. The sudden death of the occupant of the throne had left the crown to be worn by a child of eight, Henry's oldest son, Louis XIII. This, according to usage, involved the installation of a regent, and Henry's widow, Marie de' Medici, was naturally the one to exercise these functions. Unfortunately this lady was exceedingly indolent, possessed no capacity for government, and was always ruled by favorites. For many years there was an interruption in the logical course of Bourbon policy. Whereas Henry kept the nobles at a discreet distance, Marie loaded them with favors and always leaned on their counsels; whereas Henry assumed the leadership in all matters of policy, Marie was persuaded to call the estates general; and whereas Henry was about to fight the Hapsburgs, Marie made friends with the court of Spain and picked a Spanish bride for her son. To the dismay of Sully, now in sullen retirement, the fortune which he had amassed was squandered to no purpose, and France seemed headed for a return to Valois days. But the events of this troubled period offered some experience to an ecclesiastic of noble birth, who had first forged to the front during the meeting of the estates general. Armand de Plessis, Bishop of Luçon, who was honored with the cardinal's hat in 1622 and henceforth known as

[1] See note on page 68.

Cardinal Richelieu, had managed by assiduous wire-pulling to gain in 1616 the office of secretary of state. Six months later, on the king's assumption of power, Richelieu followed the Queen Mother into retirement, but after several years of floundering Louis called him back to office in 1624, and in office he remained till the end of his days. Not possessing good health or much energy, Louis XIII had nevertheless a large measure of his father's good judgment and common sense, and to his honor and patriotism it may be said that he never allowed his personal dislike of the Cardinal or any natural feeling of jealousy to stand in the way of giving him full authority to govern France. Thus, through the King's self-effacement, Richelieu shaped Bourbon policy for the remainder of the reign.

Richelieu is one of those characters who by force of personality *Character and methods* etch themselves in clear, bold strokes on the canvass of history. It was not given to his contemporaries to see any traces of weakness. He was the strength of the crown personified; the "embodiment of intellect and will." This meant that he could be relentless in the handling of a foe, and that he allowed no scruple to affect his attaining an end; while, coupled with a cold and ruthless energy was a vision that saw the primal needs of France. No doubt much of his harshness and irrascibility was due to the state of his health which was always frail; and his natural reserve was deepened by a studious detachment which he felt to be necessary as the instrument of the "Lord's annointed." Moreover, with enemies on every side, he had always to be on his guard, and whenever circumstances compelled his separation from the King (which he avoided as little as possible), he saw to it that Louis was surrounded by persons whom he could trust. There was little indeed that Richelieu's spies did not discover, and, in filling positions of trust with none but obsequious satellites, he created a sort of machine, subservient to his will. One could hardly conceive of a government more relentlessly impersonal; for if he compelled others to sacrifice themselves to the public interest, he at least never spared himself; nor did his iron will ever relax as long as life remained in his body. It is no wonder that such a man was very generally feared and hated. Most persons are, after all, very subjective, and none but the Cardinal himself envisaged the France that he was fashioning. But historical perspective gives Richelieu his true position. He is the statesman *par excellence* of that period when the modern state was being evolved into its present unified pattern. If he did not see the social imperfections that lurked beneath the imposing edifice he was building, it was that men of the seventeenth century were moved by another purpose. Richelieu partly made and partly typified his age.

Repression of the Huguenots

We have remarked upon the privileges of the Huguenots, which gave them the position of a state within a state. Such privileges could be easily abused if there were reason to believe that the crown was not quite loyal to the Edict of Nantes. Doubtless, too, the Huguenots were often led astray by the noblemen in their ranks, who used these special privileges for personal ends. Three uprisings convinced Richelieu that he must wrest from them their strongholds and leave them no longer the status of a separate political entity. After the siege and capture of La Rochelle—which the Cardinal himself directed—the crown granted (1629) what was known as the Peace of Grace.[1] With a statesmanship that surely does him credit Richelieu allowed the Huguenots to retain the religious privileges which they had enjoyed under the Edict but abolished those special guarantees which had impaired the unity of France. No longer religious conflicts disturbed the peace of the realm.

Suppression of the nobles

The repression of the Huguenots was one method, as we have implied, of striking at the power of the nobles, who were always ready to conspire against the crown. But Richelieu went further. With a contempt for the feudal right of private warfare, long since condemned by the crown, he had decrees enacted against duelling, and by dealing out summary punishment for infraction of these edicts, he made a public example of all offenders. There were frequent rebellions, but Richelieu not only put them down but razed the castles of the nobles and thus deprived them of their last refuge of defense. Times had obviously changed since the day when the only way to remove a dangerous nobleman was to hire an assassin. Richelieu's victims felt the majesty of the king's law, and the number of prominent noblemen sent to the scaffold was proof that the crown no longer had any mercy for feudal disorder. Not content with demonstrating his power over the nobles, Richelieu kept them under a systematic surveillance. By sending officials, known as intendants (chosen from the middle class), to various points throughout France, he placed his reliance on a group of men equipped with exceptionally wide powers while at the same time

[1] See page 70. The Peace of Grace is otherwise known as the Peace of Alais.

acting as instruments of the crown. These intendants, more and more tending to become permanent officials, were the chief means of consolidating the realm. The system was not perfected till the time of Louis XIV, but it was already sufficiently effective to enable the crown to make its authority constantly felt. If Richelieu did not break feudal power, he provided the means of dooming it to extinction.

But the Cardinal did not limit his activities to the major task before him. He encouraged commerce, gave the government's patronage to colonization (not with conspicuous success), and created a navy. In the field of letters he founded the Academy of France, which promoted the standardization of the French language. His economic policy followed the lines laid down by Henry, though it was characteristic of the Cardinal that he exercised a more rigid control of industry, and, faithful to the same principle, he centralized the postal and courier service. Even in the administration of the finances he was disposed to make some changes, but, generally speaking, his record as an administrator ranks below his other achievements, and the national revenue was much less capably handled than in Henry's day. But much of the Cardinal's energies were necessarily expended in watching and to a large extent influencing the course of events in Europe. *Minor activities*

Richelieu's determination to make France the greatest power in Europe might be deemed a dynastic conception, not differing fundamentally from the adventurous policy of the Valois. Yet insofar as he aimed to make his country defensible, Richelieu's policy was national and rational. The France which he aspired to exalt was peculiarly open to attack. At the south Spain still possessed territory (Roussillon and Cerdagne) on the French side of the Pyrenees; on the northeast the Spanish Netherlands brought the frontier of this rival power within a hundred miles of Paris; while further to the south on the eastern boundary lay a cluster of principalities belonging nominally to the Holy Roman Empire, some being actual possessions of the Hapsburgs like Franche Comté (an appanage of Spain) and Alsace, on the Rhine (a possession of Austria), while others such as Lorraine, Savoy, and Genoa were more than likely, owing to fear of their powerful neighbor, to promote the Hapsburg interests. A wise statesman must see the need of establishing the natural frontiers: the Rhine, the Pyrenees, and the Alps; for the fact indeed that Spain had given support to *Foreign policy: (1) Objects and preliminary measures* the rebellious Huguenots showed the ever-constant danger. It was more than traditional dislike that enrolled this crafty statesman against the Hapsburgs.

Yet Richelieu, like Henry, proceeded with a caution bred of a knowledge of the real condition of France. The most that he was at first able to do was to embarrass the enemies of France wherever an opportunity offered. One of his first acts was to take under his protection some Protestant Swiss who held an important pass of the Alps, thus cutting (for the moment at least) [1] a main artery by which the two Hapsburg powers were wont to co-operate. Efforts to restrict their influence in Italy—producing a brief war with Spain— were stopped by a Huguenot rising, and there was reason for the Cardinal's warning to Louis that he could not hope to play a great part in Europe until disorders in his realm had been suppressed. After the Peace of Grace the Cardinal could deal with his problem with a somewhat firmer hand.

The situation in Germany was, indeed, an opportunity which this arch-enemy of the Hapsburgs could hardly overlook. Already the Thirty Years' War had been raging for eight years when Richelieu took office, and he was far too keen a diplomatist not to make up his mind to mingle in this bitter and complex struggle. Staunch Catholic though he was, he had no hesitation whatever in throwing support to the Protestants in their resistance to the Hapsburgs, and in so doing he was merely following the policy of Henry IV and the Valois before him. Besides sending money to the Dutch in their renewed struggle with Spain, he looked for some powerful instrument to launch against the emperor. Such an instrument he found in Gustavus Adolphus, King of Sweden, who had already fought successful wars with Denmark and Russia and was now involved in a long and arduous conflict with Catholic Poland. By timely diplomacy Richelieu mediated peace between Sweden and Poland, and after some futile efforts to dictate the Swedish king's policy he reached an understanding with him in 1631 after Gustavus' landing in Germany. By this treaty of alliance Richelieu pledged France to aid Gustavus with subsidies for a period of five years. The same year he secured an alliance with the Catholic League, which had fallen out with the Emperor over the position of Wallenstein and had brought about his dis-

[1] This advantage was only temporary, as embarrassments at home forced him to allow the Hapsburgs to recover the pass.

missal. It is not impossible that Richelieu himself had helped to foment this bitter feud, though we have no evidence that he did more than oppose in general the Emperor's policy. In the meantime, simultaneous with his operations in Germany, he reached a fairly successful agreement in Italy, whereby Savoy, the ally of the Hapsburgs, had been forced to cede to France Pinerolo, a strong position on the Italian side of the Alps. The only serious difficulty was the conduct of his allies, Gustavus Adolphus and the League, who came to blows, as might be expected, over the religious issue. But Gustavus fell in battle in 1632; then Wallenstein, who had been recalled by the Emperor, was murdered two years later; and finally in the same year, 1634, the Hapsburg forces won the decisive Battle of Nördlingen, recovering south Germany for the Catholics, and, with the aid of Lorraine, threatening France herself with invasion.

It was now that Richelieu saw that the time had come for France to play a more active rôle in the struggle. True, he had not by this time completely vanquished the nobles, but, after all, it was foreign war that afforded this element the chance to gratify its tastes, while at the same time actually pressed them into the service of the State. Moreover, France had fresh troops to pit against the war-worn armies of the Hapsburgs, and there was still the possibility of finding useful allies. In any event, France could not wisely allow the Hapsburg bonds to tighten on her frontiers. So in 1635 Richelieu brought France as a principal into the war, and armies were launched simultaneously against Austria and Spain. These thrusts were not immediately successful—for the rawness of the French troops was an obstacle to be overcome—but understandings were reached with Sweden and with various Protestant states in Germany, as well as with the Portuguese and Catalans who profited by this occasion to seek their independence. By 1642 the French were on the Ebro and had crossed the Rhine. And in that year, ill and worn out by his efforts, the great cardinal passed from the scene. Three months later the king himself followed his minister to the grave. It was the belief that France had won her long struggle and had come within sight of her goal [1] that cheered

(2) Intervention in the Thirty Years' War

---

[1] There is some reason to think that Richelieu might have made peace with Spain in 1640 but for the intrigues of a fascinating woman, the Duchess of Chevreuse, who, hating Richelieu, is said to have persuaded the court of Spain that the death of the Cardinal would soon occur and that therefore by waiting better terms might be obtained.

these stalwart patriots on their death-bed. There was now the mere problem of garnering the harvest.

The Work of Mazarin

Importance of Mazarin

The passing of Richelieu left the work of the Bourbon monarchy to be carried on by the third statesman of the trio, his friend and political pupil, Cardinal Mazarin. In foreign relations Mazarin must rank as the continuator of Richelieu, the one to dictate the terms of a triumphant peace.

Accession to power and character

But history often plays us curious tricks, and, as events were soon to prove, all the patient achievements of Richelieu were threatened with disaster. The death of Louis XIII, leading to the accession of his son, a child of five, placed the government once more in the hands of a regent—the late king's widow, Anne of Austria. True, Anne was not a woman of the type of Marie de' Medici, but her position, at best rather weak, had been deliberately rendered more so by a husband who had never liked her. Restricted in the exercise of her power by a council imposed by the conditions of Louis' will, she accordingly took the step of persuading the parlement of Paris [1] to annul the royal testament and give her plenary power. It is questionable whether the parlement had this right, but it gave a coup d'état a semblance of legality. Meanwhile Anne took as her counselor Cardinal Mazarini, or Mazarin, as he was commonly called in France. This statesman, whose intellect was now to govern France, had been one of the many clergymen whom Richelieu had employed on diplomatic missions, and is said to have been the Cardinal's own choice as his successor. A gifted diplomatist and a typical Italian of his day in his suave manners and literary tastes, he was at the same time a person of tortuous methods and dubious personal honesty. He had, moreover, the unenviable fortune of being a newcomer on the

The Fronde

scene. Some fresh exactions of money, the like of which from Richelieu had been borne as a matter of habit, seemed utterly intolerable when coming from an Italian, chosen to govern France by an inexperienced woman, a foreigner like himself. It was not Mazarin's fault that the finances were in disorder or that he had to augment the taxes to pay for the war, but his methods were quite needlessly unscrupulous and exasperating. An explosion, long brewing, was finally produced in Paris. Curiously enough it

[1] The parlement of Paris was a sovereign court which registered all royal acts.

was the middle class, generally the powerful adjunct of the crown, from whom the attack proceeded. The parlement had done the Regent a favor, and was now prepared to profit by her weakness. In short, it demanded rather peremptorily a share in the government. A high-spirited woman, Anne rejected its demands and arrested its president. Barricades were then raised in the city and something like a rebellion was in the offing. There was little chance, however, that seventeenth century Paris would carry off a political revolution. The danger was from quite another quarter.

Quick to profit by the Regency's embarrassments, a large section of the nobility joined the forces of revolt. They justified their stand on the ground that they aimed to liberate the crown from evil counsels. To some extent they were inspired, no doubt, by hatred of Mazarin. But the principal motive force which prompted their sudden action was the hope of regaining the power which Richelieu had taken from them. It was feudalism's last stand against the absolute monarchy. It is interesting, indeed, to observe how in this period of transition there is still an element which puts class interest above the unity of the nation as typified by the crown. France was at war with Spain; yet two of her leading marshals, Turenne and Condé, did not scruple to fight in the service of the king of Spain against their country. Fortunately for France, the feudal nobles had little capacity for such a struggle. "The Fronde," as the rebellion was called because of its essential frivolity (the word was derived from a name given the street-gamins of Paris) was a failure, partly because of divisions among the nobles, partly because Turenne, disgusted with the vanity of Condé, was won over to the court, and partly because the Regent and Mazarin were ready to take advantage of every sign of weakness exhibited by their enemies. When the Cardinal fled into exile, the ostensible object of the revolt had apparently ceased to exist. Actually, when the government had gained the upper hand, Mazarin quietly returned, and his position was unassailable. The nobles had had their lesson, and never again did they try to break the ever-tightening grip of the absolute monarchy.

The reaction of this crisis on the course of the war can well be guessed. Before the Fronde France had won notable victories and peace at last had been forced upon the Emperor. Then, with the Fronde, Spain had not only won back the ground she had lost but had invaded France at two points. When domestic peace was re-

Mazarin's foreign policy

stored, Mazarin had patiently to go to work organizing new armies and repeating the campaigns which Richelieu had waged. But happily he was equal to the emergency and his diplomatic skill was admirably demonstrated. By forming the League of the Rhine in 1658 he held the Emperor in check, and by a timely alliance with England (then under the Protector Cromwell, who saw a chance to seize some Spanish colonies) he was able at last to bring Spain to her knees. The long war was finally ended.

The result was a triumph for Bourbon policy. By the Peace of Westphalia, signed with the emperor in 1648, France had acquired most of Alsace (Strasburg explicitly excepted), the emperor's recognition to the detachment of Metz, Toul, and Verdun from the empire,[1] and the retention of certain points which gave her the strategic advantage in any future conflict with the Hapsburgs. By the Peace of the Pyrenees with Spain, 1659, France acquired Cerdagne and Roussillon as well as territorial acquisitions in the northeast which widened the distance between Paris and the Spanish Netherlands. Possession of Alsace brought the French frontier to the Rhine, while in the south the Pyrenees now formed an unbroken wall. Only in his futile effort to get Savoy and Nice had Mazarin fallen short of fulfilling his hopes. Nevertheless he had ably carried on his predecessor's work, and the ideal of "natural boundaries" had to a great extent been realized. All this paved the way for the ascendancy of Louis XIV.

Mazarin survived the Peace by only two years, dying in 1661. Already the young king had attained his majority, and on the Cardinal's death he definitely took the reins of power in his hand. We are on the threshold of the personal rule of Louis XIV.

The Zenith of the Bourbon Monarchy under Louis XIV

The reign of Louis XIV was the culmination of the national development we have traced. The absolute monarchy now revealed its full strength, and for some time draped itself in gorgeous plumage. The ascendancy of France in Europe became an irrefutable fact, which other powers must countenance if they did not always relish. For a time at least it was truly the "Age of Louis XIV." The court and government of France were the pattern for all others. France was the most civilized country of

---

[1] France had seized these three bishoprics during the war with Spain which had closed in the reign of Henry IV.

Europe, as civilization was then interpreted. Her kingdom was the most carefully ordered, her public service the most efficient, her armies and navies the best equipped and commanded, her manufactures the most delicately wrought, her court the most artistic. System ruled, and system can at least be very impressive. If we find in it moral flaws, they were not at all apparent to contemporaries—at least not until the sun had definitely set. But judged by the standard of a seventeenth century statesman, such as Richelieu for example, the Bourbon monarchy at its height had one fatal limitation. The king who was the personification of it all lacked the judgment to see the limit of its capacity. Absolute monarchy requires infinite wisdom of the monarch, for it is not easy to be rid of him unless he is a fool or a scoundrel. And Louis was neither. He was, in some respects, a great king. If he was not quite great enough, that was France's and his own misfortune.

The monarchy which Richelieu had fashioned out of the materials which had come down to him reached its acme of efficiency under Louis XIV. But here too, in a sense, it was Richelieu's hand at work. Louis XIV would have no prime minister ("I resolved at all costs," he wrote in his memoirs, "to have no prime minister"), but the ministers who governed the kingdom under his constant supervision, Colbert, the head of the finances, Lionne, the principal secretary for foreign affairs, and Louvois, the war minister, had all been trained in the service of Mazarin, the chief of Richelieu's pupils. It was to Louis' credit—or perhaps it was just chance—that he picked the right instruments for his purpose. But in all their activities the king was present, himself, in spirit—and often in the flesh. His ministers knew that his heart and his attention were directed to everything they did. Every day the king met his council, received reports, approved or made suggestions; probably no one toiled more conscientiously than he, and certain it is that no one felt an equal responsibility. There was an inspiration in working for such a man, especially when every one idolized him. The loyalty of the bureaucracy was as keen, indeed, as any that might be cultivated in a commonwealth. If its object was, indeed, kingship, that does not alter the fact of its existence or its intensity.

The pattern of the monarchy has already been described. For hardening its lines, for giving it proper nourishment, for finding the needed materials for polishing it—such was Colbert's task. This man, who played a sort of steward's part for the great king's

The Character of the Monarchy

Royalty as a system: (1) political aspects

(2) Economic aspects

vast estate, was the son of a manufacturer and the product of a system which gave capable members of the middle class a chance to receive rewards somewhat commensurate to their merits. Sullen and unamiable, not above utilizing his position to advance his relatives and enrich himself (albeit by conventionally honest methods), Colbert atoned for many of his shortcomings by his wholehearted devotion to his work. As head of the finances, he performed a feat analogous to that of Sully—straightening out the tangles which war, incompetence, and dishonesty had produced, and devising ways of furthering the national prosperity, thereby adding ultimately to the proceeds of the treasury. Unlike Sully, his interest embraced and in fact chiefly concerned industrial production, though there was really no part of the national economy that Colbert did not take into consideration. Adopting the mercantilist doctrines of his predecessors but giving them a more vigorous application (corresponding to the greater authority behind him and the greater claims upon the national capacity), Colbert sought to direct the economic life of the country as rigidly as its political life was ordered. France must be self-sufficient (this was a logical parallel to the need of defensible frontiers); France must be also in a position to outclass her business rivals (this, again, corresponded to the process of political aggrandizement). Mercantilism was the economic analogue of absolute monarchy, and just as absolute monarchy received its highest development under Louis XIV, so mercantilism was applied to a fuller extent than ever before—or since. While the gild organization of industry was not new, Colbert brought its operations under the strict control of the government. It was determined what establishments should produce and how they should produce. There must be no wasteful competition within, while the success of competition without should be guaranteed by elaborate rules for keeping up the standard of the product. While, on the one side, Colbert stimulated agriculture by increasing and bettering the means of communication, on the other side he imposed embargoes on foodstuffs whenever there was danger that the country might run short. While, on the one hand, he restricted imports by high tariffs (especially when fostering infant industries) and by trying to keep his artisans from going to other countries, on the other hand he stimulated production by royal subsidies, by importing skilled workers, and by encouraging new fashions. It is hardly to be doubted that the manufacture of luxuries for the king's glory had also the motive of giving other monarchs an appetite for these things and thus opening up for France a lucrative foreign market. By all such methods Colbert intended that, France being a successful seller, more money should flow into the kingdom than flow out; and this balance was not only (in Colbert's reasoning) an index of her prosperity but should provide Louis with money for his army (Colbert himself would vastly have preferred more money-making investments) and to enhance the national greatness. It was natural for him to believe that Spain's period of greatness had been due to the prodigious influx of precious metals, but his shrewd judgment told him that the main reason for Spain's decline had been the lack of industrial development that might have put this treasure to use. Unfortunately the vice of a paternalism is that the protected parties tend to lean too much on government help and fail to develop that fighting spirit which means so much in business. Besides, the monopolies he created—his giving, for example, to chartered companies the exclusive privilege of trading in a special sphere—tended to make them satisfied with a moderate amount of profit. Moreover, the monopoly of colonial trade was a real detriment to the colonies, which could produce more commodities than the homeland could assimilate. Yet Colbert was not to blame if the weakness of his system (which will be discussed more generally elsewhere) was not apparent to him or to his age. It was due in great part to him that the quality of French manufactured goods was superior, in general, to that found elsewhere, and it was due to him that the consuming capacity of the court was kept constantly and variously fed—a condition which promoted internal trade and thus provided work for innumerable hands. For this stimulus of production the King's own conception of his position, as one of unparalleled grandeur, may be said to have been primarily responsible. Thus the economic side of royalty as a system reaches the same logical climax as the political.

Finally we note in the sphere of culture that same culmination of a development. Under the patronage of Richelieu literature had flourished and, catching the spirit of the age, writers gave and continued to give their chief attention to form. Not only was the French language purified in vocabulary, not only did it acquire greater precision, but the chief ideal of writers was to compose their lines in elegant and rhythmical phraseology. It suited that

(3) Cultural aspects

sense of order which was so fundamental a characteristic of Bourbon France. This school of literature, known as classicism, reached its height in the tragedies of Racine, the comedies of Molière, and the fables of La Fontaine, as well as in the works of other great writers of this golden age. It is also true that such writers, in spite of certain defects which come of an age when even thinking was largely standardized, showed unusual literary charm as well as craftsmanship. La Fontaine's talking animals have a homely appreciation of the good and bad impulses of mankind and set them forth with delightful humor; Molière satirizes human weaknesses with equal skill; and the serious Racine depicts his characters and their fate with tender fidelity. If there was greater literary genius during this period, it was largely because it was encouraged and often even subsidized by a king who thoroughly appreciated the importance of cultural output as contributive to his greatness. All the arts were patronized. Music received the special attention of the king, and operas were sung for his and the court's enjoyment. Architecture was important because there were new palaces to be built; and sculpture was indispensable for their adornment. The weaving of tapestries (the famous house of Gobelins was established in 1667), the collecting of paintings and all manner of curios, the casting of bronzes and medals to depict the greatness of the reign—all such occupations advanced the development of the arts. In this field it was Colbert who was the omnipresent stage-manager, providing the talent to embellish the king's surroundings. It was his organizing gifts that brought into being a series of academies, one of painting, one of music, one of architecture, to act as experts to advise him in the promotion of the arts; while the existing Academy of France, which concerned itself with letters, had never toiled so hard as when Colbert set it to work. It was characteristic that this body, of whom Boileau was the leading luminary, became a board of censors, developing and conserving the best literary standards as the age understood them. But even humbler men contributed to the reign of culture. It was the French artisan, who under Colbert's patient supervision fashioned the *articles de luxe*, whether tapestries or carriages or snuff-boxes or what-not, that perhaps contributed most to the royal magnificence. Thus arts and letters reach a definite peak in Louis' reign, attaining a perfection of form and revealing an inner excellence that nothing in the earlier models had displayed.

And the one to profit by all this was France, but France was *Royalty as an art* personified by her king. Of limited education and not, apparently, blessed with a great intellect, kept from making many mistakes more through caution and dignity than through any real gift of penetration, but a man of essentially orderly habits and excellent taste, Louis XIV, with all his palpable limitations, fitted the pattern which his predecessors had made, and which his own inspiration was able so well to embellish. Royalty to him was more than a system; it was an art. In the elaborate etiquette of the Court of Versailles (which one historian has attributed to his half-Spanish extraction) he was consciously impressing his subjects with the majesty of kingship. One had to get used to his presence, so a chronicler of the court has confessed, in order to avoid embarrassment. Tall, graceful, and of stately bearing, Louis reminded everyone instantly and constantly that he was king. If he never forgot himself, it was perhaps because his manners had become habitual. And around him was a grandeur of which everyone was conscious. The palace of Versailles, built at so much cost of lives and money, was the stage on which the great king practiced his chosen art. Here the Muses cast their treasures at his feet; here the arts were displayed in all their polished magnificence. And the nobles who made up this court gave royalty its proper setting. It was to this position that the foes of absolute monarchy had sunk—that of pensioners to wait upon the king, mere instruments to reflect an added luster to his splendor. There was no longer any chance of feudal uprisings. The king made them toe the mark and noted every absence. The abasement of the nobility was complete. Everyone, indeed, saw the king as the source of social, no less than political, favor and gratifications. Louis' emblem was the rising sun; and to be warmed by its rays was the acme of social ambition. One needed only to add, for its spiritual value, the fiction that the king was Heaven's instrument on earth. The "divine right of kings"—already expounded by Richelieu—was the halo which alone royalty needed to give it the finishing touch. When Louis attended mass, his court formed a semi-circle about him, kneeling and gazing at him, while he himself faced the altar, looking to God. Such was the king-worship which Louis' conception of monarchy produced. But with nothing but adoration, is it possible for a human being fitly to measure himself?

It was probably Louis' vanity that accounts for most of his

Etching by Mourey, from Le Livre des Fêtes Françaises

PRESENTATION OF THE OPERA ALCESTE AT VERSAILLES

mistakes, especially in his later years when the ablest of his ministers were no more. A precept that he laid down to his son is not without relevancy here. "To deliberate at leisure on all important matters and to take the advice of different people thereon is not (as the foolish imagine) an indication of weakness or dependence on others but rather of prudence and steadfastness." Unhappily Louis himself was not always able to penetrate bad counsel, and too often he was blinded by his own self-conceit. His attitude in religion sufficiently illustrates this trait—plus a certain latent piety, which took an unfortunate direction. Inspired by the belief that his subjects should adhere to the king's religion, continually pressed by the clergy, whose voluntary subsidies were naturally much desired, and perhaps influenced by his morganatic wife, Madame de Maintenon, Louis authorized against the Huguenots a campaign of intrigue and persecution which finally culminated in the revocation of the Edict of Nantes (1685). There is not a better example of the lengths to which autocracy may go when its precepts are unsound. "One king, one law, one faith" was the adage which Louis fulfilled literally. The danger of absolute monarchy lies principally in the limited outlook which it allows the individual. Louis' bigotry in religion, the reverse of the wise policy of his predecessors, was no doubt the accentuation of the spirit of his system. But the evil may be seen in other ways. It has been intimated that absolute monarchy when powerful, may overtax its strength, and such was Louis' sin when he embarked on his later wars. It is also evident that this royalty, so carefully systemized, so artistically embellished, was blasting in its spirit to all germs of originality. Genius cannot follow a pattern and be true to itself. With all the brilliance of the culture that glorified this reign, the mind was really fettered. It could not speculate on the how and why of politics because the existing system must be taken as axiomatic. It could not really experiment in science, art, or letters because, apart from the deadening influence of an atmosphere of convention, certain definite standards were rigorously enforced. Thus intellectual output followed stereotyped lines. It was generally artificial, unimaginative, and fundamentally uncritical. Such was the inherent weakness of a régime that dazzled its age, but which over-exalted authority as the basis of the modern state.

Yet absolute monarchy must have its fling, and when one compares, as one must, its orderly habits with the feudal chaos that went before, one must admit that it had a place in the progress of civilization. Perhaps a hasty glimpse at its organization may enable us the better to understand it.

The Framework of the Monarchy

We have noted the bases of the royal power and its consolidation. Manifestly the king himself exercised little of the power that reposed in him; for with the steady growth of the realm he had been forced more and more to delegate the business of governing and administering it to his instruments. Thus had emerged what is called a bureaucracy—a corps of functionaries whose duty it was to make laws, see to their execution, and dispense justice, all in the king's name and subject to a greater or less extent to his direct control, but functioning in general as responsible officials. It will not be feasible in this sketch to mention any but the more important organs and agents of government, but it should be born in mind that there were thousands of persons under commission to perform certain duties in the public service. Aside from important exceptions we shall mention, all office holders were nominees of the crown and removable by the crown. This, of course, afforded room for the king's personal influence; and there were other ways (to be noted presently) by which he exercised his power on occasions. But in general he allowed the machinery of state to function without interference, satisfied that the centralized administration was sufficient to enforce his will or that of the special advisers in whom he reposed his confidence.

The bureaucracy

The king's council

The pivot of this governmental machinery was the king's council. The time had passed when these counselors were members by vested right; they were all the king's nominees and served during his pleasure. It was, however, a rather unwieldy body, and the expansion of business had necessitated its breaking up into inner divisions. The council of state had direction of foreign affairs and other matters—especially questions of major importance—in which the crown was especially interested. The king himself usually presided over its meetings, and from it emanated the most important legislation. There was also a council of dispatches, concerned with provincial business and dating from the time of Richelieu, whose reliance upon the intendants seemed to require such an organ to discuss matters of police and the enforcement of the laws. Then there was a council of finance whose business was to devise ways and means and to see to the apportionment of the revenue. And finally there was the council of parties or privy council, a section primarily judicial. Evidently the competence of the king's council covered a wide and varied range. It was a deliberative and administrative council in the sense that it advised the king in matter of policy and supervised the general work of administration; it was legislative in that it made the necessary laws; and it was judicial insofar as it had a general supervision over the administration of justice as well as handled certain cases in which the king was specially interested. All this proves that the chief functions of government were not then carefully distinguished and sorted out as in a state of the present day.

We have intimated that it was the task of the king's council to make the necessary laws, the more important ones having their origin in the council of state, while most of those concerned with routine matters were framed in the council of dispatches, and the augmentation of a tax would naturally be the task of the council of finance. Possibly the work of one of the sections was reviewed by the council as a whole before the project of a royal act was finally approved. Then, to become valid, it required the king's sanction—through the process of stamping it with the great seal, which was always in the custody of the chancellor. Since, moreover, the chancellor himself was supposed to examine, and if necessary raise technical objections to, all proposed legislation, he was traditionally the "keeper of the king's conscience." After the royal sanction had been given, the council's project became a law; and it is clear that just as the king could have acted on his own initiative and inspired the preparation of a law in the beginning (as Henry IV had inspired the Edict of Nantes), so he might, if he chose, refuse to sanction a projected law, in other words, might interpose a veto. Thus a king could and sometimes did play a direct part in the process of legislation. Finally, when the royal seal had been affixed, the law was sent to the parlement of Paris for registration. This inscribing of the law on the registers of the parlement was merely for convenience, and registration was not in any sense a voluntary duty. The eventual claim of a right to refuse registration was not, of course, in harmony with the acknowledged principle of the royal sovereignty.

The legislative power

Under a régime in which all power was derived from the crown it is clear that the old feudal assemblies, the notables, the estates general, and the provincial estates, had no logical place. Henry IV had convoked an assembly of notables [1] in 1596 and told them that, unlike his predecessors, he called them not to learn the royal will but to give him counsel. This, however, was during the period when Henry felt forced to conciliate the nobles, and it is not improbable that it was also a subtle means of shelving the estates general, which during his predecessor's reign had greatly embarrassed the government. The notables met only rarely during the early Bourbon period and never during the heyday of the absolute monarchy. The estates general met once during the period, as we have already noticed—called in 1614 by the regent, Marie de' Medici under pressure from the nobility. Fortunately for the crown, however, the large preponderance of office holders in the third estate and constant quarrels between the different orders prevented a united front, and the assemblage was dissolved without making so much as a dent in the royal power. Class divisions were evidently too deep in France to admit of the estates general playing the rôle of the English parliament. In any event the Bourbons felt no need of such a body; and besides being disinclined to give the nobles a chance to recover their solidarity, they had other and more direct means of feeling the pulse of the nation; so it was not again called till the eve of the French Revolution. Some of the provincial estates still lingered, though they were reduced to the mechanical duty of voting the money required by the crown, and some were even suppressed—three by Richelieu and one by Louis XIV. Thus by this time feudal assemblies had clearly become obsolete. It was a uniform Bourbon principle that all initiative reposed in the crown.

The executive power: (1) the central administration   The executive power, like the legislative, was wielded by the instruments of the crown. It may be considered under three heads: the central administration, the provincial administration, and the financial administration. Apart from the supervisory functions of the king's council, the central administration consisted of the ministers, a category that comprised the chancellor, the superintendent (or comptroller) of the finances, and the so-called ministers or secretaries of state. The chancellor was by tradition the king's legal adviser, kept his seal, and presided over his council in his absence. He also enjoyed the nominal headship of the judiciary. He was not, however, an administrative head in the sense of the superintendent of the finances, who had an important de-

[1] Composed of dignitaries from the upper classes nominated by the crown.

partment under his direct supervision. The secretaries of state, once called the secretaries of the king's commands because they executed specific commissions for the king, had become responsible functionaries toward the end of the sixteenth century, acting henceforth on their own initiative in the king's name. During the early Bourbon period there were four with that title, and their overlapping spheres are another example of the strange confusion of powers during the Old Régime. Under Louis XIV, however, their competence became a little more precise,[1] and they concerned themselves respectively with foreign affairs, the army, the navy, and domestic affairs. But there was no prime minister responsible for them all, each one reporting directly to the king. If Richelieu acted the rôle of a premier, it was not because he held such a position by actual title but only because he engrossed the king's favor. Louis XIV, going further, would allow no minister a position of pre-eminence.

While the secretary of state for foreign affairs corresponded with ambassadors, the secretary of state for the king's household (a sort of secretary of the interior) drafted most of the instructions to the intendants as well as received their reports. The intendants were, perhaps more than any other officials, the pillars of the monarchy. We have noticed how formidable had been the governors of the provinces. Richelieu deliberately ignored them by employing officials more directly responsible to the crown. Since royal commissioners had often performed a useful service in restoring order for the crown during the period when the nobles were still untamed, Richelieu continued the practice, sending them into all parts of the realm. It was, finally, Colbert who made them permanent working institutions. For the intendants, as these officials came to be called, a new administrative division was created, known as the generality, of which there were seventeen in the beginning, though later the number was increased. The title which each bore, "intendant of justice, police, and finance," gives some notion of their functions. They were the crown's chief dependence for raising the national revenue and for keeping the country in order—the chief practical objects for knitting the kingdom closely with the crown. In his financial rôle the intendant supervised the collection of taxes, and, unless there were provincial estates, he also

(2) The provincial administration

---

[1] But it was never entirely so. Louvois, for example, received the direction of fine arts after the death of Colbert.

took part in their assessment. In the sphere of justice he saw to it
that courts and judges did their duty, and he took direct cognizance of crimes against the State, such as treason, counterfeiting,
and smuggling. As a police official he was responsible for order,
issuing ordinances when necessary, and levying and utilizing the
local militia. But even these duties do not suggest all his manifold
functions. He took charge of the upkeep of the highways, dispensed appropriations, supervised the courier service, and exercised a rigid control over all the towns and villages within his
jurisdiction. Even parlements and governors were made to feel
subservience. The extent of the intendants' power was left in-
tentionally vague in order that they might wield a discretionary
authority. Yet they were all amenable to the royal will, instruments of the central government to see that the law was enforced
and that the taxes were duly raised. The kingdom might be compared to a machine, wherein the power, generated and operated
from the center, radiated to all parts of its intricate mechanism to
make an efficient whole.

*(3) The
financial
administra-
tion*

The system of handling the finances had none of the simplicity
of the provincial administration, since the former, unlike the latter,
was not a deliberate creation but, rather, evolved to a great extent
out of feudal institutions. The principal direct tax, the *taille*, had
originally been the impost which feudal lords paid to their suzerain
on extraordinary occasions, and which, like the earlier *aides*, had
been shifted to their tenants and collected by royal officials. Levied
sometimes on land though more often on all sources of income, it
fell exclusively on commoners, and since many of the middle class
were able to purchase exemption, it was predominantly a peasant's
tax. Every year the amount of the *taille* was determined—presumably by the council of finances at the instance of the comptroller. Where there were no assemblies to vote and assess the tax,
the burden was distributed among the various generalities in
accordance with their relative wealth; then in each generality the
intendant fixed the quota for its subdivisions, the *élections*, as well
as for the several parishes in each *élection;* finally a parish committee,[1] elected by the taxpayers themselves, assessed it among
individuals. The revenue thus raised passed through several hands
on its way to the royal treasury, some of it being deducted by royal

---

[1] These collectors were (until 1775) personally responsible for the quota of their
parish, and were therefore notoriously harsh in performing their duties.

order for local needs. As time went on, other direct taxes, generally on income, were instituted, and from the time of Sully the so-called *corvée*, a levy on the peasant's time for work on the public highways. There were also indirect taxes, such as taxes on the sale of wine, customs duties or tariffs, tolls on provincial frontiers, and the so-called *gabelle*, a tax on salt which took the form of an arbitrary price fixed by the government (which held a monopoly of the sale) and which involved the obligation of every householder to purchase a certain amount. Most of the indirect taxes were farmed out to individuals who were obliged to pay into the treasury only a specified proportion of the revenues they raised. There were, however, other sources of revenue beside the taxes. The crown still collected dues on its own estates;[1] it sold offices and emoluments; and received voluntary subsidies from the Church. The head of the administration was the superintendent, later the comptroller, of the finances, who had the oversight of expenditures as well as collections, and sometimes, as in the case of Colbert, exercised a sort of regulative power over the economic life of the whole realm.

The judicial administration, like the financial, was somewhat complex, and it had certain unique features. While there were still *The judicial power* feudal courts in operation, most of their rights had been steadily appropriated by the crown, and all the king's subjects were for most cases amenable to the royal courts. The ordinary local judge was the prevost, though appeal from his verdict might be made to the court of the bailiff. Probably as a means of selling honors to aid the treasury the presidial seat had been instituted by Henry II in several of the larger towns, and this had cognizance over cases in which property of a certain value was involved. The supreme courts of appeal—called frequently sovereign courts because their judgments were supposed to be final—existed in the shape of the parlements, one in each province and an additional one in Paris. Most of the posts in the judiciary were bought and held for life, while a seat in the parlement of Paris became from the time of Henry IV the property of the incumbent, who might bequeath it to his heir or sell it to another. This practice (which was not confined to judicial posts), while it often led to certain abuses, had

---

[1] The king's private estates, acquired by purchase, legacy, or donation, are to be distinguished from the royal domain which had come to be identified with the whole kingdom.

the good result of making for judicial independence; for by tradition at least a judge was irremovable, as long as an annual tax was paid to the crown (graded in proportion to the price of his seat), and he was thus able to dispense justice without any fear of dismissal.

It was perhaps because the tribunals of justice were less amenable to royal control that the king often took a direct hand in the administration of justice. Such cases were known as "reserved justice," and the royal pardon may be cited as an example. Most often the practice was applied in cases of treason, for handling which the local tribunals were often lacking in sufficient moral independence. It was for this purpose that the privy council, referred to above, had been brought into being. Such cases were "evoked" before this council, which would generally examine the evidence and, if satisfied, would appoint special commissioners to try the offender in question. Since these special tribunals were instruments of the crown, specially selected to reflect the royal wishes, it was as though the king himself were actually judging the case; and it need hardly be added that the verdict was nearly always a conviction. This was the practice so frequently employed by Richelieu in his efforts to break the power of the nobles. A still more arbitrary form of reserved justice was employed by Louis XIV who issued what was known as *lettres de cachet*, a sealed warrant for the arrest and punishment of the person whose name was under the seal; in this case the victim was not tried by law at all.

Such is a fragmentary picture of the judiciary of the old monarchy. There were numerous other courts (taxation courts, courts martial, etc.), but they need not detain us. The judicial rôle of the intendant (already mentioned) and that of the council and special commissioners constituted a direct interference with the administration of justice, from which even the parlements were not exempt, though theoretically the system was designed to enforce the reign of justice, the source of which was held to be the crown.

The nobles of the robe Save on a few rare occasions all the posts in the bureaucracy except those of the ministers and ambassadors and a few seats, chiefly honorary, in the parlement of Paris, were filled by men of the middle class, most of the members of the judiciary being lawyers. A great many offices, especially in the judiciary, carried with them not only ownership (as has been noted) but patents of nobility and even immunity from the *taille*. Thus was constituted (originally in Valois days but greatly developed by the Bourbons) a new nobility, known as the "nobility of the robe." While they might in course of time become formidable to the crown, their positions were so tied up with the monarchy which had created them that under a powerful master they were only efficient tools. When later their efficiency and discipline declined, the reason may be sought in other circumstances.

It remains now to consider the position of France in Europe under Louis XIV. What was this climax of national development to signify in France's relations with other powers? It was natural that a monarch with so exalted an opinion of himself and with such power at his command should make his influence felt in every part of Europe. In his sending of a contingent to fight the Turks he amused himself with thinking that "His Most Christian Majesty" was fulfilling his proper rôle of crusading against the Infidel—so far did Louis go back of the secular policy of his Valois predecessors; it was natural, too, that he should lord it over every other potentate, the papacy not excluded; and he nearly caused a breach with Spain by insisting upon the precedence of his ambassador over Spain's at an English court ceremonial. When finally he came to formulate a definite foreign policy, we may observe that it was often essentially reactionary. Imbued with the medieval fiction of universal dominion, he twice tried by bribing the electors to get himself chosen holy Roman emperor. While in seeking to extend his territories to the Rhine he seemed, to be sure, to be following a national policy, it may be doubted if he thought of practical objects as much as the chance of using his power to despoil his neighbors. It was Spain, the occupant of the Netherlands, whose weakness most readily tempted attack; and throughout his foreign adventures Louis always had a number of powers angling for his favor or greedily accepting subsidies. Admiration for *le Grand Monarque* and the lure of his gold were powerful factors in obtaining allies. And Louis meant that all Europe should cower before his throne or feel the force of his will.

The Position of France in Europe

Foreign policy of Louis XIV

We shall not relate his wars in much detail. Making an unprovoked aggression under a legal subterfuge, he began war with Spain in 1667, and his armies invaded the Netherlands and Franche Comté. As Spain had no longer any power of resistance, there was nothing apparently to stay the advance of Louis' well-trained armies. Holland, however, became alarmed at the conquest

The ascent

of the Netherlands, fearing the loss of a buffer state; and when she induced England and Sweden to join her in a threat of intervention, Louis wisely paused for the moment and decided (1668) to fall back upon his diplomatic skill. At least he had slightly pushed back the boundary of the Netherlands by acquiring several fortresses on the frontier. Meanwhile, by skillful use of diplomacy, backed by money, he broke up the Triple Alliance and isolated Holland. Wounded pride then demanded that the Dutch should be soundly punished for having dared to arrest his march. The Dutch, for their part, having lost considerable business as the result of Colbert's tariffs, were not disposed to show a chastened spirit. War finally broke out in 1672, and again a large French army swept into the Netherlands, with Holland as the objective. The beleaguered Dutch, ready now to have peace at almost any price, offered terms that would have given France the Rhine as part of her boundary. But Louis was a prey to his own arrogance, and his demands were so insulting that his little opponents preferred to trust their fate to further resistance. After France had lost a chance to take Amsterdam by a swift advance, the men of Holland, having pluckily cut their dikes to flood the enemy's line of approach, and then rallied to the leadership of another William of Orange, successfully held their ground against the invaders. France's only ally, England, having pulled out of the war, and another coalition having formed to oppose him, Louis discreetly made peace in 1678, gaining nothing from Holland, but forcing Spain to yield to him Franche Comté. The next ten years were an interval of nominal peace. Yet, taking advantage of a sudden advance of the Turks on the emperor's capital, he had seized on various pretexts several districts and towns that bordered his eastern frontier, notably Luxemburg and Strasburg (the former capital of Alsace). When in 1684 his possession of all these spoils was recognized by treaty, we reach the zenith of Bourbon power.

The decline   The very next year may equally mark the beginning of its decline. The revocation of the Edict of Nantes not only drove from France some of her most skillful artisans (many of whom went to the countries that were soon to be her enemies) but it shocked the Protestant world and stiffened that resistance of which Europe had given evidence. The League of Augsburg was formed to defend the Empire, and it was hoped that Holland—and England too if William should supplant her unpopular king—would soon

join it. Though he knew that revolution was gathering about
James II and that William was only delaying his invasion of England because the Dutch feared another French blow at the Netherlands, Louis made the strategic mistake of leveling his attack on
the Empire, laying claim to the Rhenish Palatinate whose crown
was in dispute. Hence William was free to sail at once for England.
The resultant downfall of James in the Revolution of 1688 and
the accession of England under William III as well as Holland to
the League of Augsburg were more serious checks of fortune than
he had ever experienced before. The course of the war was devoid
of brilliance on either side, but France was the first to feel exhaustion, and in 1697 Louis signed the Treaty of Ryswick, making no
gains, and actually relinquishing Luxemburg. For the first time
in the Bourbon period France had been forced to step back a pace.

The final struggle to arrest the power of Bourbon France was
the War of the Spanish Succession (1702–13). The king of Spain,
Charles II, was an imbecile and childless, and the Spanish nation
itself was in a state of progressive decay, though some of its numerous possessions (the Spanish Netherlands, the Milanese, and
the colonial empire in particular) were rich spoils to tempt the
aggressor. For thirty years the succession to these vast domains
had been an object of intrigue between Bourbons and Hapsburgs,
both of whom had a candidate for the inheritance. When Charles
at length died in 1700 and it was found that in his will Louis'
grandson, Philip of Anjou, had been designated his heir, French
policy seemed to have won a unique triumph. Louis naturally
accepted the proffered crown in the name of his grandson, and the
rest of Europe prepared to resist this new aggression, as they regarded it. More, indeed, was involved than the old question of
the balance of power, since France might now enjoy the privilege
of trading with the Spanish colonies, with which, in spite of Spain's
prohibitions, the English and Dutch had long been carrying on a
lucrative traffic. For England, moreover, the revival of the old
danger of a strong power in possession of the Netherlands, was
sufficient to provoke alarm. Before William's death (in 1702) the
Grand Alliance had been formed, including England, Holland,
Austria, and later Brandenburg; and the greatest of Louis' wars
was fought in a number of theaters, on sea as well as on land.
After the failure of a French advance on Vienna (the Battle of
Blenheim [1704] was the first time an army of Bourbon France had

met with decisive defeat in the field of battle) France was thrown back entirely on the defensive, and not only did she lose her hold on Italy, but thanks to the brilliant generalship of the Duke of Marlborough, the chief commander on the side of the Allies, she was forced to give up the Netherlands as well. Exhausted and yet unable to win honorable terms of peace, Louis humbled his pride and appealed to his people, now faced with all the perils of invasion. The consequent display of a better morale on the part of the French, together with the fall of Marlborough and the war party in Great Britain, as well as quarrels among the Allies, contributed to end the war, which was closed by the Utrecht Settlement (1713–5). Philip retained the throne of Spain, though with the stipulation that the two crowns should never be united, and he was forced to cede the Netherlands and the Milanese to Austria. The Dutch got a fortified barrier (the right to garrison certain towns of the Austrian Netherlands on the border of France) and Great Britain (as we may call England since the union with Scotland in 1707) bagged important gains in America, as well as the stronghold of Gibraltar, guarding the entrance to the Mediterranean.

Under the circumstances, and thanks largely to the fact that Louis had brought the British to a separate peace without waiting for their allies, France had come off remarkably well after so many serious reverses. But the sun of Bourbon France had unquestionably set. And the great king himself did not long survive this last disastrous struggle. After most of his immediate family had been stricken by fatal diseases, thus casting an additional *Death of* cloud over his last years, Louis XIV died in 1715 at the age of *Louis XIV* seventy-seven after the unprecedentedly long reign of seventy-two years.

Aftermath The throne now passed in an instant from an old man to a child *of the Reign* of four—a great-grandson of the late king. During the minority *of Louis XIV* of Louis XV the royal prerogatives were wielded by a nephew of Louis XIV, Philip, Duke of Orleans. Though the most famous of *The Regency* all the regencies in French history, the period is not one of great historical importance, and is chiefly notable for its reaction against the sedate and formal manners of the previous reign. Probably never before had society been more reckless or vices more open. Yet with all his shameless debauchery the Regent was a man of ability, and in foreign affairs his government commanded respect.

The chief issue in western Europe was the maintenance of the balance of power secured at Utrecht, though there were a few slight modifications of this settlement, and the duke of Savoy was allowed in 1720 to assume the title of king of Sardinia. Later in the century (1738) a prince of the Spanish branch of the house of Bourbon acquired Naples and Sicily, known as the " kingdom of the Two Sicilies." Meanwhile, the so-called "Family Compact" united in a constant policy the two Bourbon governments of France and Spain—a logical outcome of the War of the Spanish Succession.

The rule of Louis XV

Louis XV began his personal rule in 1723, and, thanks to the counsels of Cardinal Fleury, whom he made his chief minister [1] in 1726, France enjoyed for a time a period of real prosperity. Foreign trade almost quadrupled; the merchant marine was steadily developed; and so strict was the Cardinal's economy that the budget was regularly balanced, and hence the government's credit was greatly improved. As the result of the War of the Polish Succession in which France participated (but under Fleury's leadership expended her efforts very judiciously) the reversion [2] of the duchy of Lorraine was secured, annexation being effected in 1767. "Thanks to the Cardinal," wrote an over-zealous admirer, "the King is master and arbiter of Europe." But Fleury's wise and cautious policy was upset by young courtiers who obtained an influence over the king through one or another of his mistresses. The War of the Austrian Succession (1741–8) [3] was a questionable venture and brought no compensation for the loss of blood and treasure. More disastrous still was the Seven Years' War (1755–63), which cost France the loss of most of her colonies. Louis XV spent his time in a riot of self-indulgence and left his policy as a rule to the caprices of a mistress. His court was a faint replica of that of Louis XIV. There was much the same addiction to ceremonial and there were sumptuous fêtes at times, but Louis XV was not the one to attract "king-worship," and such was the royal inertia that the courtiers were almost constantly intriguing, while favorites like Madame de Pompadour squandered the national resources and lowered the

---

[1] Fleury did not, however, bear the title of prime minister.

[2] Lorraine became the possession of the Polish ex-king, the father-in-law of Louis XV, and it was stipulated that on his death it should pass to the crown of France.

[3] For the circumstances see chap. iii. Fleury died in 1743 in the course of the war.

status of royalty itself. The Bourbon monarchy, which had once made France the greatest power in Europe, was now heading her fast toward an abyss.

FOR FURTHER READING OR STUDY

Robinson, J. H. and Beard, C. A., *Readings in Modern European History*, vol. i, chaps. i–iii; Reddaway, W. F., *Select Documents of European History*, vol. ii, nos. 65–7, 75–7, 88–9, 95–112; Louis XIV, *A King's Lessons in State-craft* (ed. Lorgnon, J.); Callières, *On the Matter of negotiating with Princes;* St. Simon, L de R. duc de, *Memoirs*, 3 vols.; Duclos, P., *Secret Memoirs of the Regency.*

Clark, C. N., *The Seventeenth Century* (a study of aspects of the seventeenth century as a whole, topical rather than chronological); Ogg, D., *The Seventeenth Century*, chap. i (society and institutions), chap. ii (Henry IV), chap. v (Richelieu and Mazarin), chaps. vi–viii (Louis XIV); Wakeman, H. O., *European History, 1598–1715* (not always reliable but excellent for pen portraits), chap. ii (Henry IV), vi–vii (Richelieu and Mazarin), and ix–xii, xiv–xv (Louis XIV); Gillespie, J. E., *A History of Europe, 1500–1815*, chaps. xiv (early Bourbon period) and xv (Louis XIV and Louis XV); Hayes, C. J. H., *A Political and Cultural History of Modern Europe*, vol. i, chap. vi; Grant, A. J., *The French Monarchy*, vol. i, chap. vi (Henry IV), chaps. vii and ix (Richelieu and Mazarin), vol. ii, chaps. x–xv (Louis XIV) and xvi–xviii (Louis XV); Seignobos, C., *The Evolution of the French People*, chaps. xiv–xv (good); Guignebert, C., *A Short History of the French People*, vol. ii, chaps. xx–xxiii; *Modern France* (ed. Tilley, A.), chaps. ii (seventeenth century) and iii (eighteenth century); Bainville, J., *A History of France* (penetrating work by a French publicist); Boulenger, J., *The Seventeenth Century* (readable semi-popular history of the reigns of Louis XIII and Louis XIV, giving excellent description of the Fronde and of the court of Louis XIV).

Willert, P. F., *Henry of Navarre;* Lodge, R., *Richelieu;* Federn, K., *Richelieu;* Perkins, J. B., *Richelieu and France under Mazarin*, 2 vols. (interesting chapters on social conditions); Hassall, A., *Mazarin;* Sargent, A. J., *The Economic Policy of Colbert;* Baird, R. H., *The Huguenots and the Revocation of the Edict of Nantes;* Hugon, C., *Social Life in the Seventeenth Century;* Atkinson, C. T., *Marlborough and the Rise of the British Army;* Churchill, W. S., *Marlborough, His Life and Times;* Head, F. S., *The Fallen Stuarts* (how Louis XIV used the dethroned house of Stuart as an instrument against England); Guérard, A. L., *The Life and Death of an Ideal* (in praise of the régime of order); Bradby, G. F., *The Great Days of Versailles;* Stryienski, C., *The Eighteenth Century* (popular, but gives good account of the Regency); Perkins, J. B., *France under the Regency* and *France under Louis XV*, 2 vols.; Palm, F. C., "Mercantilism as a Factor in Richelieu's Policy of National Interests," *Political Science Quarterly*, xxxix, 650 ff.

III. THE EMERGENCE OF GREAT POWERS IN CENTRAL EUROPE

1. THE RISE OF PRUSSIA

A. ORIGINS OF PRUSSIA

Brandenburg as a base; Prussia as a base; Early years of Brandenburg-Prussia.

B. THE MAKING OF THE MODERN STATE OF PRUSSIA UNDER THE GREAT ELECTOR

Condition of Brandenburg-Prussia on the accession of the Great Elector; Character of the Great Elector; Work of the Great Elector; Establishment of the kingdom of Prussia under Frederick I.

C. PRUSSIA *vs.* AUSTRIA—THE AGGRANDIZEMENT OF PRUSSIA

Frederick William I: his character, work, and importance; Accession and character of Frederick the Great; Prussia *vs.* Austria; Frederick's wars; Estimate of Frederick's statesmanship.

2. THE REMAKING OF AUSTRIA

Obstacles to Austria's progress; Character and work of Maria Theresa; Character and policy of Joseph II

The disintegration of the Holy Roman Empire into a collection of states which exercised not nominal but actual sovereignty has already been pointed out. The helplessness of the empire had already been demonstrated when France occupied and acquired from Spain the three bishoprics, Metz, Toul, and Verdun, and the Thirty Years' War had seemed to show that Germany must fall a victim to the aggressive modern states outside her borders. Not so long as peace had to depend on petty princes, often moreover in league with a foreign power, could anything but anarchy prevail in central Europe. Since the authority of the emperor had slumped past hope of recovery, the only chance of filling up this hollow spot in Europe lay in the emergence of a modern state within the empire, compact enough and strong enough not only to defend its own territories but to reach out, as it were, and bring more and more of the other German states within its orbit. Not one but two such states actually emerged out of the wreckage of the empire. It was because there were two instead of one that Germany became

103

divided into two rival camps. Yet, even so, there came about a certain integration which might serve to withstand the foreigner and eventually result in the creation of a German nation. The first of the two to attain the status of a modern state was Prussia.

THE RISE OF PRUSSIA

Origins of Prussia

The rise of Prussia is a remarkable historical phenomenon. This state had its origin in extraordinarily inauspicious conditions, and was, in fact, a rather artificial creation. But it had the advantage during the early days of its development of being situated somewhat on the fringe of Europe, and when it reached the point of struggling for a brighter future, it owed its success to the fusion of two factors: opportunism and force. The former was the salient quality of the dynasty that made Prussia, while the military traditions which gave that quality both its scope and its chance of success were the gift of her landed nobility. But this union of the two did not occur until the seventeenth century. We must go back to these two bases before we erect this singular state.

Brandenburg as a base

The Hohenzollerns, the family which made Prussia what she became, were originally petty princes of southern Germany. They managed to make themselves useful to the holy Roman emperors; and eventually, in return for some support to the Emperor Sigismund, one, Frederick von Hohenzollern, was rewarded in 1415 with the principality of Brandenburg. This little "march," as it was called, had been a frontier appanage of the German crown, designed as a sort of dam to hold back the Slavs and Lithuanians from inundating the empire. After two centuries of skillful management it had fallen into decay under a new dynasty, and was not, perhaps, a very promising prize when it came to the lot of the Hohenzollerns. Yet this family has seldom missed a chance of grabbing territory, and its prestige was much enhanced by the conferment upon its chief of the dignity of an elector of the empire. During the following two centuries the little state managed to acquire more elbow room, and out of the Cleve-Jülich affair (which has been noted in another connection),[1] it got a footing on the Rhine—far removed, however, from the center of the elector's power. Its greatest good fortune came in 1618 when Brandenburg acquired Prussia; and this now leads us to consider the other base of this awkward political structure.

[1] See page 72.

The military strain which has run through most of the history of *Prussia as* Prussia and later manifested itself so clearly in Imperial Germany *a base* may perhaps be traced back to a band of German knights. These knights were the members of the so-called Teutonic Order, founded in 1190, and, as in the case of most crusading orders, intended for service in the Holy Land. Since, however, crusades against the Infidel had quite gone out of fashion, and since there was missionary work to be done on the shores of the Baltic by way of taming the heathen tribes beyond the borders of the empire, the grand master desired to move the order thither, and hence early in the thirteenth century the papacy authorized it to enter the marshy wilderness east of the Oder, convert the natives of that region, a people of Lithuanian stock known as the Prussians, and carve out an ecclesiastical state. The precedent had already been set by another knightly order, the Sword Bearers or Livonian Knights, who had occupied for similar purposes Livonia and Esthonia, further up on the Baltic littoral. The Teutonic Knights—mostly Germans, as their name indicates, though there were later recruits from other peoples—had all the roughness of pioneers combined with the zeal of crusaders, and, garbed in their white robes, each of which was surmounted by a huge black cross, they commenced in 1231 their holy war of conquest.

It was not, as it turned out, an easy task. The Prussians resisted these intruders with a bravery akin to desperation, and it was half a century before they were finally subdued. They were then promptly Christianized by the sword and also reduced to serfdom. Most of the knights became landed proprietors, but other Germans came who were permitted to settle as merchants and founded thriving towns which took a brisk share of the Baltic trade. Hence the order maintained a navy as well as an army. Though the land itself was only rich in spots, there were not many to possess it, and marshes and forests provided a fairly defensible frontier. At the height of the order in the fourteenth century its military power was formidable, and it successfully held back both Poles and Lithuanians from access to the sea. But the problem of a small contingent of some two thousand men holding the supreme power was one that required continuous skill, and the order became a prey to inner dissensions which sapped its strength. In the fifteenth century it lost the famous Battle of Tannenberg to the Poles, and had to accept the suzerainty of the king of Poland as well as to cede to

him West Prussia. A century later the state became secularized
when the order, whose religious fervor had long since declined,
became converted to Lutheranism—a step which resulted in the
conversion of the knights into hereditary nobles, while the grand
master of the order became hereditary duke of Prussia. This
duke, as it happened (though it was due much less to chance than
to successful politics), was a Hohenzollern, and it was he who had
successfully carried through the transformation of the order, solely,
of course, to aggrandize himself and his family. Seeing the opportunity thus presented, the Elector of Brandenburg drew closer
to his kinsman, linked his house by marriage with that of the
duke, and finally in 1569, after much bargaining with the King of
Poland, he acquired the succession to the duchy for the crown of
Brandenburg. On the death of the last duke of the original line in
1618 the elector succeeded to the title.

*The early
years of
Branden-
burg-
Prussia*

The union of Brandenburg and Prussia was a stride in the advancement of the Hohenzollern fortunes. The Prussian nobility,
descendants of the knights, were excellent fighting material if they
could ever be tamed, and the state had been considerably enlarged.
During the Thirty Years' War, which had commenced the same
year, Brandenburg-Prussia had to pass through a critical period,
but by following as far as possible a cautious neutrality, she kept
the lands she had been shrewd enough to secularize, and when
finally forced by Sweden to enter the war, she expended no more
effort than was necessary. Apart from timidity and greed, the
elector George William found it constitutionally difficult to make
up his mind—perhaps because he had little mind to make up. He
had no scruple about changing sides, and in the end the electorate
was pretty badly pillaged. In 1640 his son and successor, Frederick
William (1640–88), definitely withdrew from the war, and hus-
banded his resources till the final peace. By the Treaties of Westphalia Brandenburg-Prussia became the recognized possessor of
all the gains she had made since 1610 including Farther Pomerania,
which brought the electorate of Brandenburg to the sea. Fortune
had certainly blown her way; but not the least cause of her growth
had been the steady refusal to place the cause of German Protestantism above her own particularist interests. Nothing ever took
second place to them.

But if we go back to 1640, the outlook had been far from promising. The task which confronted the Great Elector on his acces-

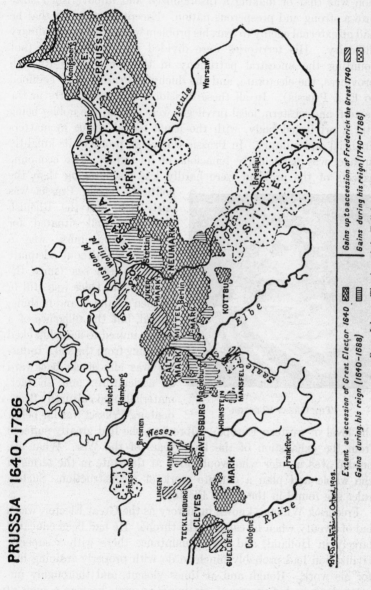

PRUSSIA 1640-1786

Gains up to accession of Frederick the Great 1740
Gains during his reign (1740-1786)
Extent at accession of Great Elector 1640
Gains during his reign (1640-1688)

From Johnson, The Age of the Enlightened Despot, 1660–1789, Methuen & Co., Ltd.

B.V. Darbishire, Oxford, 1903.

107

The Making of the Modern State of Prussia under the Great Elector

sion was that of making a disorganized and impoverished state into a strong and prosperous nation. Except for the fact that he had no external enemy to fear, his problem was one of extraordinary difficulty. His territories were divided into three groups (not counting the ancestral patrimony in the south): the Rhenish provinces, the electorate, and the duchy of Prussia (now confined

Condition of Brandenburg-Prussia on the accession of the Great Elector

to East Prussia). In all these divisions, but particularly in the eastern and western, local privileges were strong, the nobles being still a privileged body, with the usual feudal status in matters financial and military. In Prussia this class, proud of its knightly lineage, was particularly tenacious of its rights. The economic aspects of the problem were hardly less discouraging than the

Statue by Andreas Schlüter

THE GREAT ELECTOR

political. While Prussia was fairly rich, and the Rhenish provinces well situated for trade, Brandenburg was a sandy waste without adequate outlet to the sea (since the mouth of the Oder was still in Sweden's hands), and nothing, indeed, but the diligence of a people inured to hardship eked anything from the soil. Industry was almost as backward as agriculture; and, in fact, materially and culturally Brandenburg-Prussia was far below

the level of western Europe. Moreover, she had greatly suffered from the exhaustion of the later years of the War. What she needed was a ruler who would look at the state in the terms of the whole and plan a definite work of reconstruction. Such a ruler she found in the Great Elector.

Character of the Great Elector

Frederick William, known in history as the Great Elector, was a lad of twenty when he came to the throne. He had been educated largely in Holland, and his acquaintance there with a superior civilization had probably much to do with properly training him for his work. Rough and at times violent, and thoroughly unscrupulous in his means of attaining an end, he was a man of shrewd judgment, tireless energy, and inflexible will. Perhaps the fact that he was a Calvinist by conviction partly accounts for his patience under difficulties and his iron determination. He was, moreover, extraordinarily tolerant. He got along with his Lutheran subjects, and neither Catholic nor Protestant was hampered in his religion or debarred from the public service. He was, in short, a practical statesman, ready enough to learn from others, and equally ready to employ any visible expedient for accomplishing whatever object he had in view.

Such a man, therefore, was equal to the problem, and since he had also the good fortune of a long reign of forty-eight years, he achieved a great work of reconstruction. Instead of following it chronologically, we shall summarize his work.

Work of the Great Elector

In the first place, the Great Elector not only enabled Brandenburg-Prussia to recover from the devastation of the Thirty Years' War; he developed her resources and gained for her a real prosperity. To enable his people to know better methods of farming he encouraged the Dutch to settle in his dominions and found colonies, which, as he properly reasoned, might serve as an object lesson for his people in farming and gardening. What the Dutch did for agriculture French Huguenots did for manufactures. Old industries prospered and new ones were created. Mercantilist like all other rulers of his age, he adopted a protective tariff and severely regulated industry. For the development of commerce he cut a canal between the Spree and the Oder (thus giving Berlin, his capital, access to the sea), got privileges of navigation on the Elbe, and dredged the ports of Prussia. He even fitted out a company to trade with the African coast, and though this enterprise failed, the expanding commerce of his state was evidence of the measure of his success.

In the second place the Great Elector so developed and added to the existing organs of government that he created a fairly workable bureaucracy and made the power of the crown supreme throughout the realm. When he encountered opposition in East Prussia, he did not hesitate to deal it crushing blows. Three Prussian nobles were put to death and others made to feel the force of his will. He may be said to have tamed the Prussian nobles and pressed them into the service of the crown. In reorganizing the government he made the secret council of state (usually meeting in his presence) the working center, while ministers undertook the work of administration—not divided, however, according to the various departments of business but following strictly geographical lines. In the provinces he ignored or bullied the local diets and vested the chief responsibility in stadtholders, chosen by himself and responsible to the council of state. It is not improbable that, like Sweden, he employed the French government as his model, and some of the taxes, such as the *gabelle* and the excise, were interestingly reminiscent of France; but he went even further than the French crown in encroaching on the privileged immunity of the nobles. In 1688, at the time of his death, the revenue raised was seven times what it had been in 1640—a fact eloquent of good management as well as the increased prosperity of the country. But the greatest result of his statecraft was the welding of these disharmonious provinces of his realm into a fairly compact unit. He made Prussia a modern state.

In the third place, the Great Elector may be said to have founded the military power of Prussia. For the customary local militias and irregular levies he substituted a standing army. By the end of his reign it had been trebled, being about 30,000 strong. For its training and management he had the invaluable aid of the "junkers" (the Prussian nobility) whose military traditions provided standards that eventually conferred on the state an almost unique reputation. Perhaps also they were responsible for the harsh discipline enforced in the army, though the men of Brandenburg-Prussia, schooled by their long and tedious struggle with the land, were good material for the molding of such a machine. The support of the army (poorly as it was paid) and the care of the national defenses constituted the greatest claim on the budget and was always a grievous burden. But there is little doubt that the reputation of these troops had much to do with Brandenburg-Prussia's improved standing in the world.

In the fourth place, the Great Elector not only made Brandenburg-Prussia the strongest state in Germany; he gave her a prestige that precluded her any longer from being regarded solely as a German power. Indeed, no previous ruler of his state had played so important a rôle in European affairs. Very slippery and astute in his foreign relations, he was sometimes the enemy of France, sometimes her subsidized friend. He failed to win the coveted mouth of the Oder through a war with Sweden, since Louis XIV insisted on his giving up his conquests, but his victory over the Swedes demonstrated the superiority of his army over soldiers who had hitherto been looked upon as supreme; and by playing off

Sweden and Poland against each other he acquired from the Polish king full sovereignty over Prussia. Save for his honorary vassalage, as elector, to the emperor, he could lift his head as proudly as the King of France. All that seemed to be needed for the national dignity was the elevation of his dominions to the status of a kingdom.

The son of the Great Elector was, in general, unlike his father. The Great Elector had been a man of simple habits, and his little court, far from emulating Versailles, was, as one historian puts it, more like a family circle. Frederick, his son (1688–1713), on the contrary, had great love for the trappings of power. He was extravagantly fond of ceremony and delighted in gorgeous liveries. Unlike his father, too, Frederick (who had been an invalid in his youth) had no tastes for anything military, and, if he augmented his army, it was probably more in order to enhance his personal dignity than for any practical purpose. Though he did appreciate science and founded an academy for its encouragement, he can hardly be said to have revealed a domestic policy, added little to the development of institutions, and put his state deeply in debt by his extravagance. *Establishment of the kingdom of Prussia under Frederick I*

Yet Frederick had some of the Hohenzollern astuteness. By bargaining with the Emperor, who wanted the support of his army in the War of the Spanish Succession, Frederick got for himself and his house a royal title. While this raising of Prussia to the dignity of a kingdom may seem but a paltry achievement, it emphasized the fact that Prussia had an importance quite apart from her position in Germany, and fittingly crowned the work of the Great Elector. The time must come when she would snatch equality with Austria and come to be classed, like the Hapsburg state, as a "great power."

Frederick William (1713–40), the son and successor of Frederick I, had all the coarseness and hardness of one who cared for nothing but the army and lacked the intellect to perceive any rôle for a Prussian king but that of a military chief. Ready now to take her place among the powers of first rank, Prussia was still a land practically devoid of any culture, with no horizon beyond the severely material duty of living her life. Frederick William had nothing but contempt for art and letters, and when he found that his promising son (the future Frederick the Great) had literary tastes, he never rested till he was content that he had finally *Prussia vs. Austria— the Aggrandizement of Prussia*

Frederick William I: his character, work, and importance

pounded them out of his heart and crushed his youthful longings. With a single thought in mind he made his home seem like a barrack and his kingdom an armed camp. Crusty in disposition and boorish in his manners, he was at all times a martinet, and the fear which he inspired is well illustrated by the story of the officer who had the wrong man executed rather than face his sovereign's displeasure for executing no one at all. Frederick William had, in fact, the Hohenzollern traits carried to the point where virtues become vices. He was strong-willed to the point of obstinacy, economical to the point of parsimony, and—though he must be credited with great fortitude when suffering physical pain—cautious to the point of timidity. Probably much of his brutality is to be ascribed to his physical condition, for he was often tortured with gout and not infrequently intoxicated. Yet it is seldom that he showed a spark of human feeling and even the sincerity of his religion hardly atones for the uglier features of his character.

Indeed Frederick William typified Prussia at her worst. Everyone lived for the maintenance and improvement of the army. The ranks were steadily filled by the rigors of conscription, while everyone, not a soldier, was made to feel acutely the burden on his resources. The King himself was used to skimping, for even as a boy he had kept a strict account of every penny saved, and what he did not spend on the equipment of his soldiers he hoarded in the treasury. And yet this royal drillmaster had no desire to fight. His rôle in foreign politics, though sometimes treacherous, was also often obsequious—especially toward Austria. Only once did he use his army—when Charles XII of Sweden, broken by his terrific struggle with Russia, stood at bay against a coalition of powers; then Frederick William espied an easy victory and added to his kingdom part of Swedish Pomerania, gaining at last for Prussia the coveted mouth of the Oder. But generally he was content with watching his soldiers drill, holding elaborate parades, and shaping a code of discipline unparalleled in its severity. It was as though this fine army were a work of art that might be spoiled if it were plunged into the hurly-burly of battle. The army was, in short, his hobby—not better illustrated than by the efforts which he made to secure the tallest specimens for his service.

And yet, with all his limitations, Frederick William played a part in the upbuilding of Prussia. In obtaining a port for Brandenburg, he added something of really solid and positive value. With his ingrained sense of order he somewhat improved the bureaucratic machine, giving unity to the military and financial administration. Perhaps his greatest achievement was his enactment that elementary schooling, where possible, should be compulsory; and with all his parsimony he established more than a thousand rural schools.[1] If he melted down the sumptuous plate and sold many of the treasures of his father, he at all events kept abundant money in his coffers; and it was this well-filled treasury and his well-trained army that made possible the achievements of his son. Military to the core, Prussia was ready to cross swords with other powers, with every reason for confidence in the outcome.

It is idle, perhaps, to speculate what Frederick the Great might have been if he had not been subjected in his youth to the brutalities of such a father. When his attempt at flight had failed and he was compelled to witness the execution of his dearest friend, the companion of his escapade, Frederick learned to become expert in deceit, keeping up his literary pursuits in secret, while ostensibly learning the details of administration under his father's relentless eye. When he came to the throne in 1740, he was a man without any softness of any kind. His heart was of steel; his mind was that of the cynic who sees only the frailties of humanity and does not scruple to make use of them; he had no code of honor save a steadfastness to the one objective which he sought—the welfare of the State. Yet he kept his taste for letters, and he had too fine an intellect to satisfy himself with paltry things. He also appreciated merit, and, while he was irrascible and exacting like the typical Hohenzollern, he had the knack of inspiring his subjects with devotion as well as respect. He was truly unfortunate in never having experienced—what meant so much to the average German —the joys and solace of family life. He ignored his wife (who had been foisted on him for political reasons by his father) and after the deaths of his mother and sister to whom he was sincerely attached, no creature save his faithful dogs ever really got close to his heart. Yet he was too much of a philosopher to let his warped soul make

Accession and character of Frederick the Great

---

[1] Frederick William made attendance compulsory where schools existed. His son, Frederick the Great, continued his policy, and decreed that if parents could not meet the cost of tuition, it should be paid by the Church or from the poor funds. In 1787—a year before his death—the management of schools was transferred from the Church to a government council of education. A few of the smaller German states (Weimar, first of all), under the influence of Luther's stress on education, had enacted compulsory elementary education in the seventeenth century, but the law was often difficult to enforce for lack of schools or teachers.

him miserable, and doubtless he found a certain measure of happiness in his reading, his reflections, and his absorption in his work. Duty was enthroned as never before in Prussia. Whether or not his application of this virtue was well conceived, whether or not he always knew what was best for Prussia may well be questioned. But at least he put the interest of Prussia, as he conceived it, above all other considerations. It was not his fault that his age imposed the whole responsibility on the monarch.

Prussia vs. Austria

Methodical as he was and in some ways narrow-minded, Frederick the Great was the one Hohenzollern who dared to strike boldly and put his power to the hazard—though, even so, it must be admitted that his youth and the play of accident had something to do with his action. In the very year of his accession, 1740, when he was only twenty-eight, occurred the fateful death of the Emperor Charles VI, leaving a daughter, Maria Theresa, to succeed to the Hapsburg lands. One may wonder, if the opportunity had not presented itself of taking advantage of an inexperienced woman, beset with manifold difficulties, whether Frederick would deliberately have embarked on a war of aggression. At all events he did not hesitate. He made up his mind to have Silesia. Appropriation of this province seemed geographically justified, since, situated as it was in the upper valley of the Oder, it was a natural appendage to his dominions, and in Prussia's possession would afford her an extension of her natural frontier on the Austrian side. Finally it may be suspected that he yearned to match his power with that of Austria and to gain for Prussia in the eyes of the world a recognition of equality with the more venerable German state. Some musty claims to Silesia were easily found in the Prussian archives (for no monarch of the modern world began war, however aggressive, without some specious pretext), and it was also true enough that Austria had not fulfilled her bargain when Frederick William had agreed to endorse the Pragmatic Sanction—that instrument which had provided for the Austrian succession and for the preservation of which Charles VI has spent most of his reign in purchasing the assent of the Powers. Certainly it was no one's but Austria's business who was chosen to rule her territories, and the rights of other claimants had been long ago renounced. The sum and substance of it was that Frederick wanted Silesia and intended to filch it in one way or another.

Having resolved to plunder his rival, he offered her two alternatives—either an alliance against her other enemies if she would cede Silesia to him peacefully or war if she refused. Since Maria Theresa treated such a proposal as it deserved, Frederick forthwith invaded Silesia and thus precipitated a European war.

Though Silesia was the stake, it was a test of strength between the two chief German states. Looking at the situation broadly, we can see that all the advantages were on the side of Prussia. Austria was still largely disorganized—hardly yet a modern state, while Prussia had a fairly efficient bureaucracy and an unquestionably superior army, not to mention the unknown military gifts of her sovereign. In addition to this Austria had to face not one but a host of enemies, since Prussia was not the only one to disregard her pledges. Apart from some meager subsidies from Great Britain, Maria Theresa got no aid from beyond her borders.

The War of the Austrian Succession, which began in 1741, was a *Frederick's* complicated struggle in which the fortunes of war often varied but *wars* never long deserted Frederick. He did not scruple to leave his allies, France and Bavaria, in the lurch by twice withdrawing from the war; and a re-entry into the struggle, after he had got Silesia by treaty, was a second act of aggression, prompted, it seems, by the fear that Austria, then victorious, would succeed in redressing the balance. In the end he kept Silesia, and though the war dragged on till 1748, it had closed for Frederick himself three years earlier.

It is sometimes the case, however, that duplicity wins a measure of retribution. Prussia had no friends after the war was over, and the enmity of Maria Theresa was only cooling until she found a favorable occasion for recovering the province she had lost. No doubt also the contempt which Frederick expressed for all women, and for three women in particular, Maria Theresa, the Czarina Elizabeth, and Madame de Pompadour, had something to do with forming a new coalition against him. In the Seven Years' War, which began in 1756 he had Austria in front of him, Russia on one flank, France on the other, and even (for a time) Sweden in the rear. By a timely blow in anticipation of his enemies he had prevented his neighbor, Saxony, from adding her strength to the league, and an alliance with England gave him at least financial aid. Yet in spite of his marvelous generalship and a fortitude that had to endure even the sacking of his capital, Frederick the Great would certainly have succumbed to defeat but for an extraordinary piece of luck. In 1761 the death of the Czarina was followed by the accession of the mad czar, Peter III, who so far reversed the policy of his predecessor that he restored East Prussia which had been won by Russian arms and even entered into an alliance with the late enemy of his country. Though his deposition in 1762 put an end to Russian participation, the war ended as it began with no gains for any of the belligerents. Frederick kept Silesia but at a frightful cost.

And he had had his fill of fighting. Indeed he took extreme precautions to prevent being drawn into another struggle; for, though he was fortunate enough to obtain a slice of Poland, this was rather the kind of easy and cheap aggrandizement in which the Hohenzollerns were most adept. But he kept his energies to the end, proving himself a monarch of peace as well as of war, and died in 1786 at the age of seventy-four.

Estimate of Frederick's statesmanship   In seeking to take the measure of Frederick's statesmanship we must now take a survey of his work. What were his contributions to the forward march of Prussia? They were mostly in external policy. In the first place, he strengthened Prussia's frontiers by the acquisition of Silesia and widened the distance between his capital and the Austrian frontier. He also acquired what was most important, the province of West Prussia (obtained by the First Partition of Poland in 1772), which, by connecting East Prussia with Brandenburg, gave his kingdom that territorial unity which she had sadly lacked. In the second place, by the excellence of his army and the display of his own genius as a tactician in many victorious battles he won for Prussia a position of first rank among the powers. She would now be considered a great power along with Austria, and her word would count powerfully in European politics. That was perhaps the most striking significance of his career. As one writer has expressed it, "The Prussian state no less than the Prussian army had cast its spell over the mind of Europe." Thirdly and finally, Frederick improved his country somewhat along various lines of internal development. It was important that she should stand the strain of war and it was hence necessary to sharpen her efficiency. Just as he augmented and improved his army (raised ultimately to 150,000 on a peace footing with a potential increase to 200,000), so he brought about a greater co-ordination in the civil administration—the more necessary as he never ceased personally to direct it. He also continued the work of his predecessors in encouraging both industry and commerce; he connected the Elbe and Vistula by a series of canals; and he continued and carried to a greater extent than ever before the policy of internal colonization. Immigrants were attracted from all parts of Germany to settle in his dominions, and he gave especial attention to his new province of West Prussia, planting German colonists among the Poles to raise the native level of civilization and directly assisting the peasants by subsidies and other means. A learned historian has estimated that at the end of the eighteenth century a third of the population of Prussia was composed of immigrants or sons of immigrants. Such, moreover, is an illustration of the essential continuity of Hohenzollern policy.

Yet Frederick's statesmanship, marked as it was, is not wholly free from criticism. It may be questioned whether Silesia was worth the hatred which his country had to incur through the circumstances of its seizure or worth the hardships that had to be endured in order to keep it. Well did Mirabeau say, "Prussia is not a people that has an army but an army that has a people." From the Great Elector down the size and cost of the army were out of proportion to the population or its resources and the burden must have been crushing to the spirit as well as the body. Inured to militarism, the Prussians became over-disciplined—to the cost of imagination and initiative. Moreover, Frederick's very competence turned out to be an obstacle to the development of his people. "The first servant of the State," as he called himself, he engrossed so much responsibility, supervising even the smallest details of administration, that he left too little to the discretion of his subordinates. He did not even bother to train his heir; much less did he fit his public servants to carry on when he had gone; so that even his wonderful army became after his death little more than a pretentious but rusty machine. Finally, with all his study and enlightenment Frederick made hardly a dent in the existing social system, which was actually so stratified in Prussia that members of one class were debarred from acquiring land from those of another, and each class was carefully restricted to its traditional pursuits. Though it is true that he carefully purged the criminal code of its worst features, he did little to relieve the crushing burdens of the peasantry, which, indeed, had been increased by the rigors of conscription. He had the intelligence to anticipate much of the work of the French Revolution, but he lacked the soul of the innovator, or else perhaps he was too much of a patriot (in a narrow sense) to run the risk of weakening the structure of the state.

None the less Frederick the Great was a dominating figure in his age, and the rôle he played was in some degree at least a testimony of the qualities of his house. Four generations of Hohenzollerns had contributed each in turn to rear a solid structure that even later disasters could not wholly bring to ruin. Certain it is that Prussia could now hold her own with Austria and match her for the hegemony of Germany.

The Remaking of Austria

Obstacles to Austria's progress

Somewhat parallel with the development of a new state, Prussia, occurred the recasting of an old one, Austria. The rivalry between the two in the eighteenth century could never have been foreseen in the sixteenth, for the ruler of the Holy Roman Empire was one of the greatest monarchs at a time when Prussia, or rather Brandenburg, was a struggling little electorate. But while possession of the imperial crown gave Austria her chief distinction, it was also an element of weakness. Championship of the Catholic cause in the Thirty Years' War and the attempt to control the course of German politics had only served to waste her opportunities. When the Peace of Westphalia finally dispelled the dream of Catholic ascendency in Europe and imperial sovereignty in the Holy Roman Empire, there was a chance at last that the Hapsburg emperors would follow a national policy. The heart of their strength lay in their hereditary dominions, Austria and its appendages, Styria, Carniola, Carinthia, Hungary, and Bohemia. Here, on and near the Danube, were the materials for the founding of a strong state. The reconquest of Hungary from the Turks—undertaken toward the close of the seventeenth century—had seemed to show that the Hapsburg rulers had at last become disillusioned as to the worth of the imperial claims.

But the emperors were not yet through with dynastic dreams. The question of the Spanish succession had fatally reopened the old question of uniting the thrones of Vienna and Madrid, and the result of the subsequent war was to saddle them at least with strange and remote possessions, the Netherlands and the Milanese. Moreover, an effect of the Thirty Years' War and the wars of Louis XIV had been to divert the Hapsburg rulers from the more important problem of internal development. There were, it is true, the meager foundations of a bureaucracy. Ferdinand II had established a central council; and a corps of officials, financial and judicial, combatted with indifferent success the political chaos of an essentially feudal state. But the kingdom of Hungary had its own separate diet as well as the traditions of political self-sufficiency; Bohemia also had her provincial estates as also did every province of Austria proper; and in the Netherlands particularism was too strong to admit of any interference. To get money to run the government or to wage war the emperors had to bargain with a multitude of interests. It was not until the time of Maria Theresa that serious effort was made to give this living skeleton a body to make it move.

Maria Theresa, who began to rule this scattered empire in 1740, was a woman who combined a fervent patriotism with a fine judgment of what was essential to her success. Endowed with *Character and work of Maria Theresa*

Painting by Pencini

MARIA THERESA

common sense rather than originality, religious to the point of bigotry, but possessed of a warm heart and a steadfast soul, she set herself to the task of developing in her subjects an allegiance capable of unified action under the crown. But she was aware not only of her country's limitations but of her own. Too loyal to faithful service to dismiss the aged counselors of her father, she waited until they died; then she picked such men as Kaunitz who were in sympathy with her policy and could give her valuable advice. Meanwhile the tremendous ordeal which she had had to face almost from the moment of her accession—the War of the Austrian Succession—had had two notable effects. It showed her that the various peoples of different languages and traditions who made up the population of her realm were capable of a personal loyalty to the crown—something, indeed, on which she could build. And secondly it was borne upon her that she could not hope to recover

Silesia until her house was set in order. The new counselors she chose were relied upon to tell how to do this.

It is obvious that for this scattered and polyglot realm to become a modern state was a harder task than for any other European power. The fact that Maria Theresa developed a better-working bureaucracy; that she was able to put into the field an army of over 100,000; that, above all, she was able to encroach on the immunity of the nobles from taxation and levy taxes on Church property attests well to the resolution and capacity of the sovereign and her ministers. She never ventured to suppress the various diets, and she failed to persuade the Hungarians to bear their proper share of the national burdens, but, as in the case of the Bourbon monarchy, she forced the local diets to vote what subsidies she pleased (usually for a ten-year period); she also limited municipal autonomy, unified the judicial administration (with Hungary excepted), promulgated uniform codes of law, and furthered unity by building a fine system of highways. When she died in 1780, it might be said that Austria proper and Bohemia were subjected to the direct control of the government. Imperfect as it might be in some respects, so much of Austria might be called a modern state.

Character and policy of Joseph II It might have been well if her successor had built more slowly on this groundwork. The assimilation of regions like Hungary and the Netherlands, entrenched as they were in long-established privileges that antedated Hapsburg rule, was a problem better solved by time than by efforts at coercion. Unfortunately Joseph II was a headstrong idealist, who, thoroughly versed in the rationalism imbibed from the French philosophers, set out to achieve a complete renovation of his realm, failing totally to comprehend the latent force with which human nature with its essential conservatism and self-interest can resist the impatient reformer. Doubtless, if there is such a thing as taking one's duty too seriously, that charge could be made against Joseph. Deprived by sudden death of a wife to whom he was tenderly attached, he sought his whole solace in his work, seldom allowing his natural charm to filter through the earnest gravity of his demeanor. Naturally kind-hearted, he reasoned that kindness had best be imparted wholesale through thoroughgoing reforms. His sense of justice demanded that all his subjects should be equal before the law and equally amenable to the crown according to their capacity. A stickler for order and efficiency, he determined to have a uniform

administration. Solicitous for Austria's future, he hoped to give
her a more compact and defensible position. He would have been
too wise to achieve success in a democratic commonwealth; as a
despot he might have succeeded—provided he had been strong
enough to force his way to the end.

The recounting of the more important of Joseph's reforms will
suffice to show his policy. He reorganized his dominions by the
creation of thirteen new administrative divisions at the head of
each of which was a magistrate whose business it was to see that
the laws were enforced and that the peasant was protected from
any injustice on the part of his lord. Such an arbitrary arrangement
took no account of provincial boundaries or even the peculiar status
of the Netherlands and Hungary. Obviously the local diets were
deprived of all authority, and practically ceased to function. He
took steps also to make German the official language of Hungary,
though it is clear that he did not, as the Hungarians feared, intend
to supplant the native officials by Germans. He levied taxes on
land without regard to privileged interests, the nobility and the
Church being forced to contribute their share, and he sought to
make Hungary raise her proper quota of the national revenue.
His social reforms were no less radical. Anxious to undermine
feudal institutions and put his subjects more nearly on a level, he
abolished serfdom, allowed the peasant to commute the *corvée*
into a money payment, and made it legally possible for him to
become a landed proprietor. Besides appropriating for the crown
the appointment of the higher clergy, he established seminaries
under State auspices for the better training of priests, established
the civil marriage, legalized divorce, and allowed non-Catholics
religious freedom as well as eligibility to office. For the better
enlightenment of his realm he instituted a system of free, public,
and compulsory education. Aside from his program of reform, his
activities deserve attention. Following mercantilist ideas, he
established almost prohibitive tariffs on many foreign commodities.
In his foreign policy he tried to get a longer coast-line on the
Adriatic, and he grasped at an opportunity of exchanging the
Netherlands for Bavaria—a plan which was frustrated by a coalition of German states engineered by Frederick the Great. It was
another instance of the old rivalry between Prussia and Austria.

Unfortunately few of Joseph's reforms survived him. It was
obvious that class privileges and interests as well as national and

local traditions had been drastically attacked, and the result was profound and widespread dissatisfaction culminating in open resistance on the part of Hungary and the Netherlands. He might well have succeeded with many of his reforms, but, as was said of him by a contemporary, "he never took the first step before he had taken the second." It was the irony of his good intentions that even the peasants seemed not to appreciate what he had done for them; they failed to understand the limits of their freedom, and in some cases rose in arms against their landlords. As he lay dying in 1790 he realized how completely and tragically he had failed. The Low Countries were lost; Hungary was in ferment; from no quarter was gratitude or sympathy extended. His epitaph, he said, should be: "Here lies the man who never succeeded in anything that he attempted." His brother, Leopold II, who succeeded him, was compelled to reverse his policy completely, thus recovering the allegiance of Hungary and the Netherlands, and pacifying the realm of privilege. Only the abolition of serfdom in some of the Austrian dominions remained out of the wreck of Joseph's program.

Joseph II was the statesman *par excellence* of the age of reason. He failed because, human nature being as it is, a statesman must, if he is to succeed, be also an expert politician and, like Henry IV of France, appreciate the extent of his power. In many ways he belonged to the nineteenth century rather than the eighteenth, and history does not move with as rapid strides as he had ordained.

FOR FURTHER READING OR STUDY

Robinson, J. H., and Beard, C. A., *Readings in Modern European History*, vol. i, nos. 29–40, 101–2 and vol. ii, nos. 1–17; Reddaway, W. F., *Select Documents of European History*, vol. ii, nos. 113–6, chap. x (*passim*); Catt, H. A. de, *Frederick the Great: Memoirs of His Reader*, 2 vols.

Gillespie, J. E., *Modern Europe, 1500–1815*, chap. xx (*passim*); Marriott, J. A. R., and Robertson, C. G., *The Evolution of Prussia* (interesting brief account), chaps. i–iv; Schevill, F., *The Making of Modern Germany*, lects. i–ii; Ogg, D., *The Seventeenth Century*, pp. 441–4 (on the Great Elector); Wakeman, H. O., *European History, 1598–1715*, pp. 290–7 (the Great Elector), 308–9 (Frederick I) (*passim*); Whitman, S., *Austria;* Leger, L., *A History of Austria-Hungary.*

Reddaway, W. F., *Frederick the Great;* Bright, J. F., *Maria Theresa;* Bright, J. F., *Joseph II;* Bruun, G., *The Enlightened Despots* (for Joseph II); Padover, S. K., *The Revolutionary Emperor;* Marczali, H., *Hungary in the Eighteenth Century;* Dorn, W., "Prussian Bureaucracy in the Eighteenth Century," *Political Science Quarterly*, xlvi, 403 ff., xlvii, 75 ff.

IV. THE RISE OF RUSSIA

1. THE EVOLUTION OF RUSSIA

A. The Rise of Kiev and the Dispersion of the Russian People
   The early Russians; Formation of a state; Influence of Byzantium; Hegemony and decline of Kiev—growing disruption of Russia; The Tatar conquest.

B. The Unification of Russia under the Hegemony of Muscovy
   Rise and hegemony of Muscovy; Ivan the Great and his neighbors— strengthening of Muscovy's hegemony; Ivan's position; Liberation from the Tatars; Muscovy as the state of the Great Russians; Foreign relations of Ivan—renewed contact with the West; Evolution of society under Ivan the Great; Importance of Ivan the Great; Work of Basil III.

C. Civil Strife, Stagnation, and Revival
   Rise of a disaffected aristocracy; Accession and character of Ivan the Terrible; Foreign policy; Domestic policy; The "Time of Troubles"; National revival; Russia at the accession of Peter the Great: (1) geographical position, (2) social conditions, (3) political conditions.

2. RUSSIA BECOMES A GREAT EUROPEAN POWER UNDER PETER THE GREAT

Accession and character of Peter the Great; Fundamental policy; Military measures; Political reforms; Economic policy; Social reforms; The inrush of the West; Importance of Peter the Great and estimate of his statesmanship.

3. THE ALLIANCE OF THE NOBILITY AND THE CROWN

A. An Interlude of Arrested Development
   The post-Petrine reaction; The régime of favorites; Hardening of social conditions.

B. Continued Europeanization of Russia under Catherine the Great
   Accession and character of Catherine the Great; Importance of Catherine the Great and estimate of her statesmanship.

4. THE AGGRANDIZEMENT OF RUSSIA AND THE RISE OF THE EASTERN QUESTION

A. Motives of Russian Expansion

B. Expansion to the West—the Conflict with Sweden
   Position of Sweden; The Northern War.

C. Expansion to the West and South—The First Partition of Poland and the Treaty of Kutchuk Kainardji
   Condition of Poland; Condition of Turkey; The designs on Poland The Polish imbroglio; Catherine's first war with Turkey and interven-

tion of Frederick the Great; First Partition of Poland; Treaty of Kutchuk Kainardji.

D. THE EASTERN QUESTION AS THE STAKE OF INTERNATIONAL RIVALRIES
   Catherine's second war with Turkey; The British intervention.

E. EXPANSION TO THE EAST

———————

Immensity and flatness are the most striking impressions one has of Russia. Except for swamps in the west and deep forests in the north it has practically no natural barriers within, and from far back in history it has been the principal highway from Asia into Europe. Hence from earliest times it was overrun by many peoples, and among those who settled the land there was no doubt a good deal of intermingling of stocks. While the group known as the Finns (probably a people of Mongol origin) sought the region to the far north and the Letts and Lithuanians (two peoples closely akin) settled the stretches along the Baltic, it was a portion of that great linguistic group, known as the Slavs, that spread into the interior. This group (whatever may have been their remote origins) fell into three main divisions: the southern Slavs (Slovenes, Serbo-Croats, and Bulgarians), the western Slavs (Czechs, Slovaks, and Poles), and the eastern Slavs or Russians. It was to the Russians (differing among themselves to some extent as they mingled with other peoples) that the land to be known as Russia came to belong—a fact chiefly due to numerical predominance; but no people has been more shaped by conditions of geography and history, and it is now our task to trace their varying fortunes. Russia was in a sense a sort of step-child of Europe. She seems in many respects to belong to Asia; yet she forced her way into the European family, and henceforth had to be regarded as a factor of great importance in the history of modern Europe. To understand this fully one needs to trace the story of Russia's national evolution.

THE EVOLUTION OF RUSSIA

The Rise of Kiev and the Dispersion of the Russian People

The people who formed the nucleus of Russia's population were, as already noted, a branch of that linguistic group known as the Slavs. They were not, of course, the earliest people that roamed over the country that we now know as Russia, but, as they were the ones to become the molders of the Russian nation, we shall go no farther back. These Slavs who peopled Russia seem to have come from the northern slopes of the Carpathian Mountains, *The early Russians* and as early as the ninth century they occupied the land stretching roughly from the Gulf of Finland to the shores of the Black Sea and extending eastward as far as the river Oka, not far from where Moscow now stands. Originally these Slavs were in the tribal state. They hunted or tilled the land, and, as fast as they exhausted the fertility of the soil they occupied, they moved on and tilled other land, for there was plenty of room to roam, and they often felt the pressure of other wandering tribes. Since they were essentially nomads, they had no sense of a settled existence. Each tribe seemed to have a chief or prince, but his authority was seldom strong, and the tribe naturally spread out into scattered family units, the recognized primacy of the head of the family giving the whole system—if one could call it a system—a patriarchal character. In each tribe these elders met when occasion required in an assembly called the *veche*, which discussed and voted orally on any question that concerned the tribe. It was thus a patriarchal régime, not precisely democratic but certainly not autocratic, though a prince had doubtless the influence that always belongs to a leader. Even the prince himself was chosen by the *veche*.

But the general want of economic stability and the restlessness *The formation of a state* which comes from a nomadic life often led to internal strife as well as inter-tribal disputes. It was a happy accident, therefore, that the Varangians, who apparently haled from Scandinavia, and represented a higher grade of civilization, began to make forays from the north. These Varangians seem also to have been called "Russ," meaning "oarsmen," [1] by the Finns, a people of Mongolian origin to the north of the Slavs, and the name came to be applied to the Slavs themselves, after the Varangians mingled with them. The scantiness of the records make it difficult to fix the date of the coming of these northmen, but it seems to have been somewhere about the middle of the ninth century. Whether we may believe that they had been engaged to protect the commerce of the "Russ" or Russians (for some of the tribes had come to settle themselves in towns for the trade in furs), or whether the story of the ancient chronicle is true that these "Russ" appealed to the newcomers for a prince, the fact of the new leadership is the really important thing. The working of this vigorous influence, the weakening of tribal divisions, the concentration of life more and

[1] As in the case of a good many names, however, the origin is by no means settled.

more in commercial centers (for many of the Varangians were traders), and the enhancement of the authority of the prince whom the northmen provided—all this leads us to the fact that Russia became a state, with a definite capital, Kiev, and fairly definite frontiers. Such was the first important stage in the national development.

The state thus founded was not then known as Russia but as the grand duchy of Kiev. Its patriarchal form was not changed, but the rule of the prince tended to become absolute, and his subjects gradually accustomed themselves to settled habitations. Kiev, the capital, was the center of the commercial as well as the political life of the state, but other towns, such as Novgorod in the north, were of some importance, and these more remote towns were strongly fortified so as to resist any attacks from outside foes. More often, however, the Russians themselves were the aggressors in those days. Even before the coming of the Varangians we know that they had made frequent raids on the Byzantine Empire, and *Influence of* it is probable that the adventurous spirit of the northmen was *Byzantium* responsible for the growing number of these expeditions. One may observe from a glance at the map that the Dnieper flows into the Black Sea and forms a natural highway to the south. Relations with the Eastern Empire were therefore to be expected, and, though often checked by wars, a brisk trade developed, the Russians sending chiefly furs and slaves, and receiving in return silks, gold, wine, and fruit. But contact with this power had greater importance than any material gains. It was from Byzantium that the Russians received Christianity (characteristically enough, a prince of Kiev, having adopted it himself, forced it wholesale on his people), and it was in Byzantium that they got their first glimpse of a highly developed state whose emperor claimed to rule by divine right and whose laws and institution gave an impression of durability. From the Church, indeed, the Russians received their first code of law, with its recognition of private as distinguished from tribal or communal property, and, due also to the Church, the institution of marriage came to follow definite rules and restrictions. Such influences readily grew out of the establishment of a religious hierarchy under the headship of the metropolitan of Kiev. It may also be remarked that the veiling of women and their isolation in the *terem* or women's quarters were probably borrowings from Byzantium. With all its peculiarities and imperfections, the infiltration of what we may call Byzantine civilization marked the second important stage in the national development of Russia.

But a good many trials and vicissitudes were destined to intervene before the third important advance. For more than two centuries Kiev flourished. It was on the great avenue of trade between the Baltic and Black seas; it possessed a certain culture and even a literary efflorescence; and the fact that it was known to the West is proved by a marriage between a king of France and a daughter of the prince of Kiev. But the political system which the state had developed under its Varangian rulers held the seeds of its dissolution. Scattered communities in a sparsely settled country had naturally their local rulers, and the state was really a group of principalities held together by a certain allegiance (partly due to kinship, partly to be explained by economic dependence) to the prince who reigned at Kiev. It was always the oldest of the dynasty, who ruled at the capital city, while the next in line ruled the second most important political unit, and so on down, the number of principalities being eventually more than eighty. Whenever death created a vacancy at Kiev, there was a general shift, and it can easily be seen that such an upheaval was naturally fraught with danger. Lack of precision in the status of different generations and the natural instinct of the strong to profit by the weak led to frequent and bitter struggles. On occasions a powerful incumbent of the throne at Kiev would set the realm in order, but more often discord prevailed. Then external struggles further sapped the strength of Kiev. Being close to the frontier, it was often raided by the tribes to the west and south; while to the east lay the great stretch of steppe, the treeless plain, over which Asiatic tribes poured in frequent forays, forcing the men of Kiev to be ever on the watch and ready for defense. A third and final cause of its decline was the migration (partly induced by these hostile incursions, and partly by the quest of more land) of more and more Russians to the northeast, where they found abundant land, the soil of which could be made arable by burning the forests and using the ashes for fertilization. Thus it was that in course of time the political center shifted from Kiev to the region of the upper Volga. In the twelfth century Suzdal, with its capital at Vladimir, wrested the leadership from Kiev. Here at Vladimir the prince for the first time became a stationary ruler, refusing to

Hegemony and decline of Kiev— the growing disruption of Russia

exchange his throne for any other.[1] Here in the north also the Russians came in contact with large numbers of Finns, docile people whom they easily assimilated. But Suzdal had no sooner humbled Kiev than she declined, herself. A policy of conferring portions of the state as appanages upon kinsmen resulted in progressive disruption, especially as the population was more scattered than ever. Thus, by the end of the twelfth century, Russia was a vast agglomeration of political units, in no way capable of defending themselves against a powerful attack.

The Tatar conquest
Such was the situation when the Tatar tempest smote Russia. The Tatars were another of those migratory peoples whose lust for adventure brought its impress on European history. Unlike the Varangians, however, they came as marauding conquerors, were always alien in spirit to the masses whom they subjugated, and tended to lower rather than raise the level of culture in the countries they subdued. The Tatars who invaded Russia were subjects of Genghis Khan, whose court was in Mongolia; they had swept over much of Asia during the twelfth century; and by 1200 their advance columns had reached the Volga. The Russians called them the Golden Horde because of their yellow faces. They were, in fact, Mongolians, and still in that primitive state of nomadism from which their distant kinsmen, the Bulgars and Magyars, had long since emerged.

Whether it is true or not that emissaries from the Tatar khan had first offered peace to a Russian prince who straightway put them to death, the doom of the country was sealed. The Russians were no match for the invaders in unity, leadership, or even numbers—since only the upper classes were bred to arms. All Russia save Novgorod and the forested lands to the north fell under the Tatar sway. Indeed, the Mongol wave did not recede till it reached the Danube, and even the West trembled. In submerged Russia death and destruction were to be seen on every hand. The once-proud city of Kiev was reduced to a straggling village, and most of those Russians able to survive the ravaging of their lands fled far to the northeast.

Though the Mongol period lasted about a century and a half, its imprint upon Russia's internal life seems to have been slight. This may be explained partly by the fact that the Tatars had little to

---

[1] The *veche* seems also to have died out during this period of migration, though it was still retained in the city state of Novgorod.

give and partly from the circumstance that conquest was not, in general, followed by colonization. Only the vast, unoccupied steppes to the south and east were held in actual possession, and those for grazing purposes to support a conquering host. All that the khans required of the Russian princes were homage, tribute, and on some occasions military contingents. None the less, the Mongol conquest is of importance, negatively as holding Russia aloof from the rest of Europe, and positively as aiding in the development of a new political entity, namely Muscovy.

The principality of Muscovy was one of those appanages derived from the disruptive policy of Suzdal. Its chief city, Moscow, is first known to us a little before the middle of the twelfth century—then as a halting place for the traveler from Vladimir to Kiev. That Muscovy came in time to gain pre-eminence over Suzdal and ultimately over all Russia was due partly to its central position, partly to the patient extension of its power by a line of princes, who, while not at all brilliant, were imbued with a dynastic tradition of a continuous policy, and partly to its treatment by the khan. Though Moscow had been burned by the Tatars, and though Muscovy had been laid waste like other principalities, its revival was sufficiently rapid to enable it to bribe the khan to leave it in comparative peace. Finally its growing importance was actually utilized to the profit of the conquerors. For many years, it seems, the annual tribute, collected from every Russian state, had been farmed out to certain merchants. Then the more convenient method was devised of getting the prince of Muscovy to play this rôle; and so it was he who was ultimately required to collect tribute from all Russia and send it on to the khan.[1] At any rate, this fact, more than anything else, gave Muscovy a primacy among the multiple principalities. Henceforth Moscow has been the core of Russia—at times the political and always the spiritual center of the Russian nation. We may well mark the hegemony of Muscovy as the third stage in the national development.

The course of development in virtue of which Muscovy's rule was gradually consolidated and extended to the rest of Russia was largely the work of certain of her princes, who, perhaps more than

The Unification of Russia under the Hegemony of Muscovy

Rise and hegemony of Muscovy

---

[1] According to Pokrovsky, the Tatars also made a special point of cultivating the Russian Church, the clergy being exempted from all levies including tribute to the khan.

Ivan the Great and his neigh-bors— strengthen-ing of Muscovy's hegemony

any of their predecessors, were the builders of the Russian state. One of the most illustrious was Ivan the Great, who came to the

Estes and Lauriat, Boston

IVAN THE GREAT

throne in 1462. In general he may be said to have been a typical Muscovite ruler; his patient oppor- tunism, his cunning, and his cruelty were character- istic of his house but more conspicuous in him in pro- portion as he was a stronger character than the rest. When he struck, it was a terrible, almost ma- niacal blow, though, in general, he preferred to circumvent an enemy than crush him, and he was be- lieved at times to be ac- tually guilty of cowardice —not extraordinary, after all, if we remember how the Muscovite princes

cringed to the Tatar khans. None the less, Ivan patiently went to work to extend the scope of his princely rule, and he held a more exalted view of his position than any previous Muscovite ruler.

Thanks to the strengthening of the princely authority, Ivan never encountered serious opposition at home; but abroad he had plenty of enemies. To the north the city state of Novgorod (now grown to prodigious size), fearing absorption by the rising power of Muscovy, agreed to a certain vassalage to Lithuania in return for military protection, and now it showed toward Muscovy an atti- tude of arrogance. Not far to the west was Lithuania herself, a kingdom swollen by the conquests she had secured when the Rus- sian states in the west, broken by the Mongol wave, had been unable to defend themselves. Between Muscovy and Lithu- ania lay a debatable ground: former dependencies of Kiev which had survived the Lithuanian incursion and various appanages of Suzdal whose allegiance to Muscovy was hardly more than nominal. Finally to the east and south was the Tatar horde.

Fortunately for the position of Muscovy the power of the khan was now perceptibly on the decline; some of his lieutenants had carved out independent khanates (Kazan in the northeast and Astrakhan and the Crimea in the south); and much of the fear of the Tatars had already been eliminated by a beating which the Russians had given them in the open field. In 1380 Dmitri, a predecessor of Ivan's, had won the Battle of Kulikovo, which proved to the Russians at last that the Tatars were not invincible. This victory had, moreover, strengthened the hegemony of Muscovy, since under her banner, it was believed, deliverance would come. The prestige of Ivan's state was also enhanced by the shifting of the religious center of Russia from Kiev and Vladimir to Moscow; for the metropolitan of Kiev had transferred his seat to the place of greatest security and influence. The attainment of the spiritual headship of Russia was doubtless a powerful aid in the promotion of the later task of political unification. When in 1452 Constantinople (or, as the Russians called it, "Czargrad") was captured by the Infidel, Muscovy emerged as the leading Orthodox power and the defender of the faith. It now remained for Ivan and his dynasty to prove that Muscovy could play the rôle for which she had been cast.

Ivan was undoubtedly fully imbued with the importance which his position gave him. In 1472 he married Sophia Paleologus, niece of the last Byzantine emperor, and from then on the Muscovite princes regarded themselves as heirs to that empire whose ruler had been called by the Byzantine Church "lord and governor of the inhabited world." To such an exalted potentate the traditional Kremlin seemed too mean, and Ivan built another palace more adapted to his grandeur. Under him also one finds the beginning of a court with its accompanying ceremonial—a proper halo for a capital with a 100,000 souls.[1] It is no wonder that he conceived himself as ruling by divine right—an easy variant of the oriental conception of a temporal viceroy of Heaven. But Ivan's position lay on more solid and legal grounds. An appanage had always been considered both as an estate and as a principality. He was both the owner of his subjects' land and entitled to their obedience. Only one thing seemed incongruous in all this show of majesty, and that was his connection with the Tatars. It

Ivan's position

[1] This may be a fair estimate if Pokrovsky's figure, 200,000 souls, is correct for less than a century later.

was ridiculous for the heir of the Cæsars to be vassal of another prince.

Liberation from the Tatars

Ivan felt no doubt that the time had come to shake off this hateful yoke. He had already intrigued with the Khan of the Crimea against the Khan of the Golden Horde, and even refused to pay further tribute. In 1480 the Khan of the Golden Horde commenced an invasion to enforce his rights. After much hesitation—which many ascribed to cowardice—Ivan finally made a stand, and the amusing upshot of the affair was that both commanders were frightened, the Russians, it was said, retreating faster than their enemies. Nevertheless the Khan seemed impressed by the strength of the Muscovite state, and no more tribute was exacted. The emancipation of Russia had been won.

Muscovy as the state of the Great Russians

Ivan showed more resolution in his dealings with other powers. He faithfully continued the policy of his predecessors, steadily gathering in the neighboring appanage principalities; he conquered and annexed those, like Suzdal, which claimed to be suzerain states. He was especially determined to bring Novgorod to submission, for her vassalage to Catholic Lithuania seemed not only an act of defiance but treason to the Orthodox faith. This proud state, which had long preserved what may be called a voluntary dependence, was now forced to make submission, and its great bell—which had summoned the local *veche* to its meetings—was carried to Moscow in triumph. The effect of Ivan's conquests was to amalgamate nearly all the people known as the Great Russians —that mixture of Russians and Finns which had peopled the northern forests. It was the Great Russians who had built up the Muscovite state and who became in time the most numerous element in the population of Russia. A mysterious folk they were, essentially oriental, but very largely a product of their environment. Struggles with the forest made them at once restless and yet rugged and tenacious. The shortness of the summer season made them the more grasping of the moment before the time of comparative idleness. Thus the Great Russian is a paradox—capable of ferocious energy and of equally conspicuous apathy and resignation. It is no wonder that they created—and also endured—the most cold-blooded and ruthless autocracy in Europe.

To the southwest, the Russians of Kiev—distinguished from the Great Russians as Little Russians, slightly differing from the former in language and physiognomy—had fallen a prey, as we have seen,

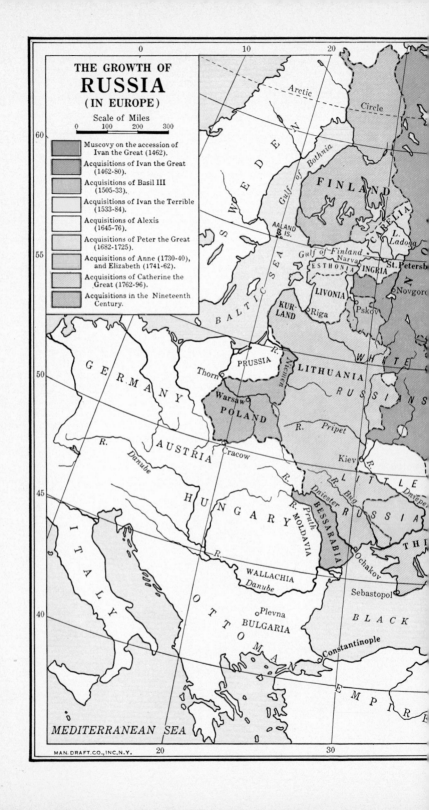

THE GROWTH OF
RUSSIA
(IN EUROPE)

Scale of Miles
0   100   200   300

Muscovy on the accession of
Ivan the Great (1462).

Acquisitions of Ivan the Great
(1462-80).

Acquisitions of Basil III
(1505-33).

Acquisitions of Ivan the Terrible
(1533-84).

Acquisitions of Alexis
(1645-76).

Acquisitions of Peter the Great
(1682-1725).

Acquisitions of Anne (1730-40),
and Elizabeth (1741-62).

Acquisitions of Catherine the
Great (1762-96).

Acquisitions in the Nineteenth
Century.

MAN. DRAFT.CO., INC., N.Y.

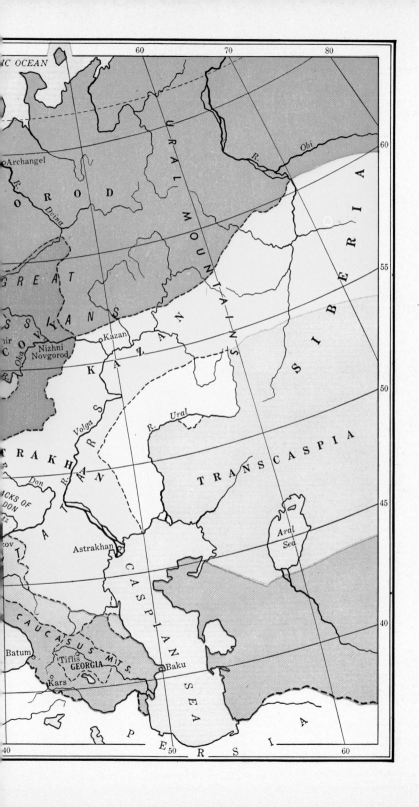

to the aggressions of Lithuania.[1] It was almost inevitable that a *Foreign relations of Ivan—renewed contact with the West* collision should occur between Muscovy and Lithuania; but as yet they were too closely matched for either to become the victor, and Ivan's war with his neighbor was one of a long series of conflicts, that was not to reach its climax for many generations. But it can at least be said that the prince of Muscovy held his own and that Lithuania was glad of a respite, while his fortunate neighbors, the Tatar khans, soon sank to a rôle of subservience. Moreover, by extending his influence Ivan had been able to bring his state into contact with Europe. When Sweden joined Lithuania, Ivan responded by an alliance with Denmark. He carried on negotiations with the holy Roman emperor, and there was talk of a marriage alliance. His reduction of Novgorod brought him a commercial outlet in the west, and the circumstances of his marriage—arranged by the pope with the futile hope of a union of the two churches—led to the coming of many Italian visitors to Russia. After four centuries of complete isolation Russia began to turn her face once more to the west.

Parallel with the political changes we have observed there were *Evolution of society under Ivan the Great* certain social changes which we must now take time to consider. The social divisions of the Russian states—the suzerain states and their appanages—had followed for the most part a fairly uniform pattern, and in some respects came to approximate Western feudalism. The upper crust of society was a class known as the *boyars*— originally compounded of Varangian knights and the older Slavic nobility. These were the "prince's men" and constituted his fighting forces. From about the eleventh century, when it appears that tilling of the land came to be looked upon as more profitable than trade, the *boyars* generally became landowners, and their slaves—who formed the mass of the population—became less and less a commodity of commerce and instead were definitely settled upon the land. This process had probably the sanction of the prince, though it does not appear that the fact of ownership of an estate carried with it any military obligation—the latter being still a personal matter. It is also to be observed that originally a *boyar* might transfer his allegiance to another prince (probably an evidence of the vagrant strain one finds in the early Russians), but

---

[1] A large block of the Little Russians, intermarrying with the Lithuanians, produced a people known as the "White Russians," though their language but little differed from that of the Little Russians.

when the Grand duke of Muscovy took the position that all land was lawfully his,[1] this custom was of necessity curtailed. Indeed the tendency of Muscovy was to make the *boyars* amenable to State control—else the State would have soon been at their mercy. When Moscow became a capital of greater splendor than even Kiev in its palmiest days, it became a focus of attraction for *boyars* from far and wide. Doubtless many believed that the prince of Muscovy was in a position to grant them larger estates than any they were holding in an appanage of a lesser prince—a hope that was not, in general, unfulfilled. Then, besides this shifting of allegiance was the exodus of those deposed princes themselves, along with their own subject *boyars*, who had no other course than to tread the way to Moscow. It was these newer *boyars* who developed a kind of code according to which their official positions should depend upon the quality of their pedigree. As one writer has expressed it, "it was a sort of trade union founded on genealogical principles." Feeling naturally the pressure of such a group, Ivan placed his chief dependence either upon the old Muscovite *boyars* or upon men of lowlier station—a kind of official nobility upon whom he conferred lands during the duration of their service. But even the newly subjected *boyars* (the ex-princes and the like) held lands on condition of performing military service—since Muscovy's frequent wars called for a heavy toll of warriors. The idea of land in exchange for service [2]—natural enough in a country where money was scarce—presents us obviously with an analogy to feudalism, but it was not till Ivan the Terrible in the sixteenth century that all such estates came to be regarded as hereditary.

While *boyars* or other nobles formed the responsible class in official and military matters, the merchants and peasants were the taxpayers. The peasantry was made up partly of slaves, more often, however, of freemen, who entered into contracts with the lords, and, theoretically at least, were free to seek other masters when their bargains had been fulfilled. Usually in the contract was a

---

[1] This claim of sovereignty conveying land ownership has been commonly attributed to Tatar influence, but a recent Slavic writer, V. Miakotine, points out that it was common among the Turks and is disposed to think that it was borrowed directly or indirectly from Byzantium.

[2] The czar also farmed out to certain nobles the collection of revenues as well as police duties. These emoluments were commonly known as "feedings" and the holders seem to have fed themselves most generously out of the spoil. The Russian historian, Pokrowsky, remarks that the more crimes in his district, the greater the "feeder's" personal profit; and such extortion came to be a very great burden on the peasantry.

compulsion to fight, when called upon, for the lord, since pressure from the Tatars had necessitated larger armies and the *boyars* were supposed to supply the czar with contingents. On the whole, the free-holding peasants were not as yet seriously depressed, though, as the czar was in theory owner of all the land, he could expropriate peasant proprietors in favor of some of his *boyars,* and there appears to be evidence that he sometimes did so. It was not till the sixteenth century, however, that the peasantry lost most of its economic independence—a change we shall notice later.

Russian society seems to have been conspicuous for violence and vice, if the reports of foreign sojourners are to be credited. "The whole country," wrote one traveler, "is filled with rapine and murder; they make [*sic*] no account of the life of a man." Another declared the Russians "great talkers and liars without any faith or trust in their words, flatterers and dissemblers"; and more than one was impressed with the revolting vices to be met with on every hand. It is interesting to find Westerners of the sixteenth century noting Russian society as far below the levels with which they themselves were familiar.

Ivan's government, too, was crude, but it seems to have fulfilled the needs of a backward and remote society. To make use of the *boyars* and yet hold them in check was the prince's preoccupation, and Ivan himself was undeniably an autocrat. Perhaps neither he nor the *boyars* saw very definitely a path of divergence—the more remarkable in that the prince's right of succession was somewhat vague. Ivan never adopted the principle of primogeniture in its entirety, merely reserving the accustomed right of picking his successor (it is interesting to note that he had his son crowned in his lifetime like the early Capetians in France), and he even continued the dangerous practice of granting appanages, reduced, however, in size and insuring the supremacy of the suzerain prince at Moscow. It would probably be incorrect to regard him as a conscious innovator. He was a man of exceptional force who took the natural course dictated by tradition or geographical factors. But he must rank, nevertheless, as one of the greatest of Russia's builders. He was the final liberator of Russia and the leading contributor to her unification; he made his state known to the West; and he not only left a tradition of princely majesty that greatly strengthened autocracy but through his fortuitous marriage left a policy in the Near East as a legacy to his successors. Not

Importance of Ivan the Great

without reason he styled himself "czar of all the Russians." [1] Though the western branches of the Russians were yet to be emancipated, it may not be amiss now to drop the designation, "Muscovy" and henceforth write of "Russia."

Work of Basil III

It was fortunate for Russia that Ivan III was succeeded by a son who was able to carry on his work. Basil III (1505-33) was not quite so colorful a character as his father, as he was much more reserved (perhaps an inheritance from his Byzantine mother) and not readily accessible to his people, but he had the same autocratic disposition and the same lofty conception of his position. "He has unlimited control over life and property," wrote a foreign visitor. "None dare to differ with him. The will of the prince is the will of God." Following his father's lead Basil cultivated closer relations with the West, and had diplomatic representatives in every important country but France and England. He intrigued in the affairs of the Tatar khanates and continued the struggle with Lithuania. But his chief service was the virtual completion of Ivan's work of unifying "Great Russia." Yet these years of amalgamation form also a turning point in Russian history, for it is then that one may also note the portents of the coming period of disruption.

Civil Strife, Stagnation, and Revival

Rise of a disaffected aristocracy

We have noted the concentration of the *boyars* at Moscow, the result in some cases of the czardom's attractive force and in some cases of the dispossession of princes who had no other refuge. These ex-princes were naturally from the first a disaffected element, bitter over their downfall, resentful over the favors shown to the earlier Muscovite *boyars*. The presence of such an element was something like an infection which spread to other members of the class. Ivan the Great himself had sometimes chafed against the arrogance of these newcomers—so different from that fine tradition of loyalty which the earlier *boyars* had shown. Under Basil, less disposed to treat them civilly, they were still more factious and turbulent; but Basil never gave them any quarter. He ignored his *duma*—a council made up exclusively of *boyars*—and punished with death a number of the malcontents. Yet it is obvious that autocracy, depending so much on the personal qualities of the czar, was facing a very serious domestic problem.

---

[1] The Russian historian, Kluchevsky, finds a public act as early as 1480—the year of the emancipation from the Tatar yoke—in which this title was used. It was the Slavonic form of "Cæsar".

When Basil's death left a child of nine, Ivan IV, to succeed him, *Accession* the disaffected element among the *boyars* saw their chance. Since *and character of* provision had never been made for government during a minority, *Ivan the Terrible* the ruling power became nothing but a spoil for which certain factions in the *boyarie* contended. No one cared about the young prince who was often without the necessities of life and continually forced to witness these orgies of greed and crime. Not until he had reached the age of sixteen did he finally break his fetters and assume his sovereign rights. One of his first acts was to have some of his persecutors torn to pieces by wild dogs.

Ivan the Terrible is a man whose lurid career has furnished abundant material for the dramatically inclined. It is perhaps more interesting to inquire into the causes of his singular character. In some ways his conduct was typical of his time and his race, and both his father and grandfather had exhibited those strong passions which are characteristic of the Great Russians, particularly at this earlier period. Then, too, much of his well-known baseness, his cunning, his cruelty, his morbidly sensitive nature were in part the product of his unhappy and neglected boyhood. It is also probable that his violence was somewhat sadistic in character, and in his later years he was certainly a paranoiac. Whether insane or not, he was at least a nervous, impulsive person who never learned the least self-control, and from his early days had become habituated to an attitude of self-defense. Such a character had none of the calm sagacity of the statesman, and all his acts seem to have been prompted by the circumstances of the moment. In most respects, therefore, his reign was negative and even destructive, though certain of his achievements had consequences that are too important to pass over.

The more progressive features of Ivan's reign were on the side *Foreign* of foreign policy. Always restless, the Czar flung himself into a *policy* war with a crusading order, the Knights of Livonia, as well as undertook the conquest of two of the Tatar khanates. As a matter of fact, both of these projects seemed to meet a national need. The Livonian Knights, egged on by Sweden, had interfered with the trade through Narva (Novgorod's port on the Gulf of Finland), and the merchants of Moscow were not only anxious to protect this port but eager indeed to better their opportunities by obtaining a foothold on the Baltic. Likewise the wars with the Tatar khans coincided with the longing of some of the nobles to exchange their existing estates for the more fertile lands to the south; while, again, the merchants saw a chance of intercourse with Persia by reaching the Caspian Sea via the Volga, and with Turkey by the route of the river Don to the Black Sea. It is true that Ivan was only partially successful. He not only failed to reach the Baltic but he even lost Narva, since, with the break-up of the Livonian Order, Sweden and Poland were strong enough to bar his way. He also failed to get the Crimea, whose khan placed himself under the protection of his fellow-Mossulman, the sultan of Turkey. But the Czar was able to conquer Kazan and then Astrakhan, thus opening the road to the East. Moreover, he brought about closer relations with the West than ever before. When the northern stretches of Russia came to be colonized, Muscovy founded the port of Archangel on the White Sea, and it was by virtue of an expedition, wrecked off the northern coast, that the English "discovered" Ivan, and that trade relations were opened between the two countries. With a panting for thrills that was natural to his emotional temperament Ivan eagerly encouraged foreigners to come to Moscow, and hoped thereby to raise the material level of his state. But the soul of a savage was always in him. If the Italian physicians whom he lured to Russia failed to cure their patients' maladies, they were liable to lose their heads. None the less, Ivan had continued the tradition of intercourse with the West.

Domestic policy   It was on the domestic side that Ivan failed so conspicuously. Hating and fearing the *boyars,* some of whom had made his life so wretched in his youth, and with most of whom he was at odds in his later years, he determined to scotch their power at its roots. Confiscating right and left their estates, he divided them among a group of land-hungry nobles, who became thereby his special retainers, and provided him with a picked body of footmen, the so-called Streltsi, who now constituted the buttress of his power. Simultaneously he ignored the old *duma,* composed as it was of arrogant *boyars,* and called into being a more intimate council, made up solely of the new favorites. Yet the results of this policy were most unhappy for Russia. These newly aggrandized nobles exploited the peasants to such an extent that this fact, coupled with a devastating Tatar raid in 1571, led to a steady depopulation of the lands in the Moscow area, the fugitives preferring the poorer lands and the forests to the north; and this was the movement, incidentally, which brought the boundary of Muscovy to the shores of the White Sea. Moreover, the aristocracy itself was not broken by these acts, but rather it was a case of the lower layer supplanting the upper. After Ivan's death it was very largely this new nobility which threatened the Muscovite state with permanent disruption. Thus, in trying to cure one evil, he had really created a greater one.

On the whole Ivan failed in his chief task as national builder. He was an autocrat because he was subtle enough and terrible enough to impose his will upon his subjects; but he failed to rear a structure that would long survive his death, failed to remove the danger that was sapping the foundations of his state. He even alienated the Church, which had always been the dynasty's staunch ally. He quarreled with the Metropolitan and summarily put him to death. He also wreaked his fury on Novgorod, massacring thousands of its citizens—then held a requiem mass for the repose of their souls! In the orgies of his last years his intellect was completely under the mastery of his emotions. When he killed his own son in a fit of rage, he not only dealt his dynasty a mortal blow [1] but gave the finishing touch to his long-drawn-out work of national destruction. Two years later, on his death-bed, he realized himself that his policy had been a failure.

With Ivan's death in 1584 began a period when the crown was perilously insecure, and Russia drifted into what has been commonly called the "Time of Troubles." It was a period of "feudal" anarchy, foreign war, and economic and political paralysis. Different factions of the nobility contended for the mastery, and various puppet czars were raised to the shaky throne. A prominent rôle during this period was played by the Cossacks,[2] bands of freelance warriors, who dwelt on the southern steppes, and, actuated by the hope of plunder, lent their aid to first one and then another of the pretenders to the Russian throne. The climax of the "troubles" was reached when the Poles captured Moscow and a prince of that country essayed to rule as czar of Muscovy. It was this crowning humiliation which roused the people of Moscow to rise in fierce revolt and shake off in its beginnings this foreign domina-

The "Time of Troubles"

[1] Ivan, it is true, was succeeded by a younger son, but the new czar, unlike his brother, was totally incompetent, and power passed into the hands of a capable nobleman, Boris Godunov, who was chosen czar when Ivan's son died. Boris' son and successor was murdered a few months after his accession, and the czardom became the spoil of contending factions. The so-called Time of Troubles extended from 1598 to 1613.

[2] Probably originally runaway slaves, they eventually played a useful rôle for the czars as frontier guards.

tion. A *zemski sobor*, a body composed of appointed members of different classes (somewhat analogous to the feudal diets of western Europe), met and chose a member of one of the older *boyar* families, which, perhaps because of kinship to the Ivans, had managed to escape the vengeful hand of the "terrible czar." This youth, who proved to be the founder of a new dynasty, was Michael Romanov. His election in 1613 ended a half-century of discord and misery. Now the work of national upbuilding could be resumed.

National revival

In the national rehabilitation it was evident that both sides— crown and nobility—had gained, but, instead of a renewal of the struggle, of which each was heartily sick, a sort of tacit understanding was achieved. Under Michael and his son Alexis the nobles seemed reasonably content with the new economic security which the evolution of serfdom had given them. At the same time the crown began patiently to develop a more simplified bureaucracy, recruited, it is true, in the main, from the aristocracy but gradually subjected to the routine work of governing for the czar. Both of these changes will receive fuller treatment farther on. It is important to note here that the reign of Michael and especially that of Alexis formed a period of renewed activity. The Czar Alexis, after a long struggle with Poland, and largely owing to the revolt of the Polish Cossacks, succeeded in acquiring "White Russia"[1] and also "Little Russia" to the river Dnieper, as well as Kiev on the farther bank. Thus was the work of unifying the Russians under one rule virtually completed. It was also during this period that some attempt was made to borrow from the experience of the West. Michael had started the precedent of hiring mercenaries to aid him in a war with Sweden; and the easygoing but far-seeing Alexis made successful efforts to attract foreign capital. Not only material things, such as Western clothes and furniture were imported in greater quantities, but even some of the artistic output of the West became known to Russia. Perhaps greater progress would have been made but for the prejudices of the *boyars*.[2] On the whole this czar was a worthy predecessor of his son. It was as though Russia, having recovered from a long period of paralyzing illness, was now ready to face about again and seek her logical destiny. This "coming of the West" and all it

---

[1] See page 133.
[2] Alexis' chief adviser, Nashchokin, called by the German historian, Stählin, "the first modern man in Russia," was contemptuously spoken of as "the foreigner."

implied, soon to become expressed in the changes which took
place under Peter the Great, brings us to the fourth important
stage in the national development of Russia.

In order the better to understand Peter's position and task, it *Russia at*
may be well to take a brief survey of the situation of Russia at the *the accession*
of Peter the
time of his accession. The empire was of considerable size, extend- *Great: (1)*
ing from the Arctic Ocean to the Caspian Sea and from the Gulf of *ical*
geograph-
Obi to Kiev. Some lands in the west, peopled by Little Russians, *position*
were still in the possession of Poland, which, together with Sweden,
barred the way to the coveted Baltic. To the south lay the khanate
of the Crimea under the suzerainty of Turkey, preventing access
to the Black Sea. The only approach to the open seas was by the
frozen north, where the straggling port of Archangel was free of
ice for barely a quarter of the year. Under such circumstances trade
with the West was necessarily limited, and Western influence had
hardly more than touched a few of the towns. Russia was isolated,
and, partly because of her isolation, was far below the European
standard of civilization.

The middle class was still of relatively little importance. The *(2) Social*
conditions
bulk of the population was agricultural and roughly divided into
two classes, nobles and peasants. The former, though possessed of
little unity as a class, thanks to personal jealousies and the size of
the country, were nevertheless a powerful element, holding all the
chief offices, civil and military, and owning most of the land. In
proportion as their fortunes rose, those of the peasants were degraded. Up to the sixteenth century the peasantry had the recognized right of shifting its base. When the *boyars* had moved to new
tracts, the peasants had gone with them; also they voluntarily
settled on the estates which the crown had given the *boyars*. While
it is true that, in general, the peasant was in economic dependence
on his lord, the relationship was grounded on a contract, the lord
loaning the peasant the capital he required—seed, stock, implements, etc.—and receiving in return either a specified rent in kind
or a certain amount of free labor. Under this régime the landlord
could not evict a tenant before the harvest was ripe, nor, on the
other hand, could the peasant leave the estate until his dues had
been paid the landlord. It is obvious that his relationship with his
lord was theoretically of mutual convenience; he was not only not
bound to the lord; he was not bound to the soil, which he might
leave, for example, to become a merchant or artisan. In a primi-

tive way the peasants even managed their own affairs in the village community known as the *mir*.

Yet gradually but relentlessly a combination of circumstances changed the position of the free peasant into that of a serf, and finally relegated him to a condition little better than that of a slave. A general cause of this transition was the fact of economic dependence, already mentioned. It was seldom that a peasant could readily repay the loans made by his lord, and the new nobility of Ivan the Terrible had made the conditions increasingly onerous. But apart from this factor (which need not alone have led to this result), the establishment of serfdom may be attributed to three causes. In the first place, agricultural depression during the reign of Ivan the Terrible and still more during the "Time of Troubles" had led to a dearth of labor. Countless peasants were fleeing to the forests or else seeking better conditions under other landlords; in this pass the landlords were constantly stealing peasants from one another; and the stability of the landed nobility was seriously shaken. This class, accordingly, used its influence in the state to curtail and finally abolish the peasants' free right of "removal." In the second place, the fiscal obligations of the peasant tended more and more to tie him to the land he occupied. Not only did the *mir* insist that he stay and share the collective responsibility, but the State for fiscal reasons wished to fix the peasant where he could easily be reached. In the third place the ancient custom of transferring slaves from domestic to agricultural service [1] and of inducing peasants on various occasions to serve in the household had resulted in the gradual lowering of the peasant to the status of a slave [2] insofar as the slave was legally inseparable from the lord. In the reign of Alexis the influence of the nobles was sufficient to bring about a legal determination of the peasant's relations with his lord with the object and result of converting him and his family to the position of serfs, who could not legally sever the tie with their lord. [3] It is true that he was not yet a chattel, obliged to obey his

[1] The tendency had been accentuated by the dearth of labor during the Time of Troubles.

[2] There were numerous cases also where serfs voluntarily sold themselves into slavery in order to cancel their debts and free themselves from the obligation of paying taxes to the State.

[3] New contracts made in 1627 had been the first to bind peasants to their lords. Under Alexis a further step was taken toward legalizing serfdom by allowing a lord to reclaim a fugitive tenant without any regard to the length of time he had been absent.

lord in everything; but there was no law to protect him from progressive exploitation.

With the peasantry now stationary and completely inarticulate (3) Political conditions there was nothing to disturb the dreary serenity of Russian society but occasional disagreements between the crown and the nobility or the clergy; though it should be noted, in passing, that in 1589 the office of patriarch [1] had been founded as head of the Russian Church. Such, however, was the ignorance of the clergy that with the exception of a few of the leading prelates the relations of the Church with the crown or with the people are not matters of much importance. On the nobility, however, the government continued largely to rest. As a central council the *duma* still functioned as an advisory body for the czar. For the administration of the various public services, whether political, financial, military, or ceremonial, a multitude of bureaus has been created which dated from the time of the Ivans. They were heterogeneous affairs with little unity or definiteness and no strong tradition of service, but they constituted the rudiments of a bureaucracy. Under the first Romanovs an effort was made to co-ordinate some of these boards and place them under a single directive council. Connected with this central administration were the provincial officials, known as *voivodes*, who possessed a vague authority somewhat analogous to the French intendants, and it was through these instruments—made universal in the time of Michael—that the self-governing *mir* was attached to the autocracy. Although the landlords collected taxes from their serfs, over whom they exercised powers of police and justice, this responsibility was supervised by the *voivodes*, who even at times dealt directly with the *mir* to the extent of relieving the landlord of all political functions. Apart from their other political duties, the nobles owed military service to the czar and had to raise contingents of soldiers to that end. On the whole, the political structure of the state was crude and incoherent, with little guarantee of justice or efficiency. It was left for the disturbing hand of Peter to give it a greater precision.

Russia Becomes a Great Power under Peter the Great

An unimportant interlude followed the death of Alexis in 1676. His son and successor, Theodore II, was sickly and ruled for only

[1] This institution (suggested long ago by the fall of Constantinople) was due to Boris Goduvov; and the patriarch, in turn, had used his influence with the *zemski sober* to get Boris elected czar.

six years. Then, as the principle of primogeniture had never been adopted for Russian dynasties, and as Alexis had left no will, it was a question which of two other sons should succeed to the throne. Since both had political backers, a compromise was reached whereby both were proclaimed czars, but the government was really usurped by their sister, Sophia, with the support of some of the reactionary elements. Meanwhile the younger czar, Peter, played with soldiers and bided his time. As he grew older he formed a body of knights, equipped and drilled by himself, and in 1689, at the age of seventeen, he struck a successful blow for independence. Sophia was sent to a convent; and seven years later, on the death of his invalid brother, Peter gave up his martial diversions and began his personal rule.

Peter the Great has always remained one of the most picturesque sovereigns who ever occupied a throne. He was nearly seven feet tall, large of frame, and of great muscular strength; and temper and will seemed to correspond to these massive proportions. He was a strange mixture of good and bad, strength and weakness. In his boorishness and ferocity he fairly well exemplified his people of that age. He had almost as little self-control as Ivan the Terrible, and seemed utterly impervious to the sensibilities of others. Yet he differed from most of his predecessors, notably the Ivans, in his frank and open methods, his essential straightforwardness, his inborn camaraderie. If he lacked all sense of the dignity that became a sovereign of the seventeenth century, it was because he was too innately a Russian to see the importance of kingly manners, and in any case was too impulsive to school his personal deportment. He had something of the simplicity of a child, and for him conventions did not exist. He took for his second wife the daughter of a peasant who had been the mistress of several officers and then of the czar himself, since she was gross enough and vulgar enough to appeal to his sensual fancies. He was never so much at home as when he toiled with an axe in hand in a shipyard, or when he fraternized with workmen. His sense of humor was violent and clownish— well illustrated by his fondness for compelling people to do the things that were most repugnant, such as forcing an ecclesiastic to become drunk or a young woman to marry a suitor whom she loathed. His greatest idea of fun was to play a practical joke, and he did nothing in moderation. A typical Great Russian in many respects, he worked hard, played hard, did everything hard. Anyone who crossed him did so at his peril. Always dangerous even when sober, he was capable of any violence when engaged in one of his orgies. He never stopped for reflection; he was perpetually in action. Yet it can at least be said of Peter, as of Richelieu, that if he never spared his people, he never spared himself in the cause which he consciously served; and that cause was the good of Russia as he saw it. Indeed, he was so completely lacking in vanity that he was always ready to learn, always eager to see and profit by his mistakes, honest with himself as with his fellow men. Without exceptional intellect he dominated his country by his extraordinary personality and his overmastering will. With his determination to make a new Russia, radically different from the old, and his power of enforcing his will, he was like a sudden hurricane, let loose upon a dull and placid countryside. To Russia he was a shock. And she was both too sluggish and too utterly dazed to understand him. But she cowered at his feet.

The fundamental policy of Peter was to make Russia a European power. He found her isolated, relatively stagnant, content to live on in her old groove, but little touched as yet by influences from without. Peter was resolved to change all that. He meant that she should be drawn closer to the West by giving her a seaboard on the Baltic, and then, by virtue of the intercourse thus afforded, as well as by other ways, she should gain the practical knowledge that would raise her to the level of Western civilization. The methods by which he sought to bring in the light were his foreign conquests, his journeys of observation (as well as those of others whom he sent abroad), his employment of foreigners in his service, and his change of capital. These methods will be mentioned again in the course of the subsequent narrative. *Fundamental policy*

Of all the means of bringing Russia closer to the West, there was none more obvious than that of obtaining a frontage on the Baltic —the line which Ivan the Terrible had followed to no purpose. Such a policy involved a struggle with Sweden, which held the fringe of territories (Esthonia and Livonia) that separated Russia from her natural geographical objective. We shall reserve for another place an account of Peter's wars, only observing here that by seeking outlets to the west, south, and east, Peter definitely initiated that long and patient struggle to reach the open seas, and thus to obtain for Russia a more favorable position. In his first clash with Sweden he was decisively defeated. Peter's forces *Military measures* had been hastily raised, and poorly drilled and commanded; he had to learn what it meant to encounter a Western army, and nothing better proved to him the backwardness of Russia. But Peter profited by his experience. He forced his nobles to serve in the army as a civic obligation; he established periodic levies not only to fill the depleted ranks but to provide him with reserves; and he bent every effort to provide his armies with adequate equipment, as well as to raise the requisite funds for their support. While it can never be said that his armies were the equal of those of the West, the unremitting effort to raise their standard and the accumulated experience of twenty-five years of warfare finally hammered the Russian army into a fairly orderly body, quite able to atone for its earlier disgrace. Moreover, Peter's unflagging energies were not limited to his military establishments. Before he had actually reached the Baltic he began the building of a navy, sufficient to protect his commerce on the sea he was about to sail. It was evident to the West that a new power had arisen out of the East to form an integral part of the fabric of old Europe.

Political reforms   Peter's wars had more than the result we mentioned of making Russia respected by the nations of the West. They had an immediate effect upon her internal development. Peter was forced not only to rebuild his army but to bring the processes of his government to a far greater efficiency. The most elemental need was money without which his country could not have borne the strain of the struggle. In his various expedients Peter followed no settled plan, no carefully thought-out program. He merely conjured up ways to produce revenue, and thereupon strove vigorously to apply them. By the establishment of a poll tax he made every peasant household bear a share of the national burden. By dividing the country into ten large administrative divisions, each under a governor (largely superseding the *voivode* [1]), he made that official responsible for sending regular subsidies to the government. From the nobility he exacted not money but service. Every nobleman was forced to serve the State either in a civil or in a military capacity. The code by which certain grades of nobles occupied certain posts had been abolished under his predecessor; and under Peter commoners were often ennobled and placed in high positions, the essential key to office—theoretically at least—being fitness for the place. And the official machinery itself was thoroughly over-

---

[1] The *voivode* lost his fiscal and military functions and became a local judge.

hauled. Since the old organs of government were faultily constructed and often, as in the case of the *duma*, too addicted to a slow pace and an obsolete routine, Peter reorganized the governmental system on the pattern he learned from Sweden after the conquest of Livonia. To replace the *duma*, where vested interests reigned, he constituted a senate, composed of a few persons, not all of noble birth, selected by himself. In place of the old boards, whose functions had so often overlapped, he instituted ten new ones, the so-called "colleges," each with a directing head and each in charge of some department of the administration. Since the Church was found to be hostile to his reforms, he abolished the patriarchate and established a so-called synod as an advisory council to himself as head of the Church. In all these matters Peter reserved for himself complete authority. While the senate was at first chiefly concerned with administering the government during his absence, it was never allowed to develop more than supervisory functions. It had no initiative in legislation, its chief function in this regard being to clarify and promulgate the czar's numerous decrees. Peter had machinery, such as it was, to impress his wishes upon the nation, but he never ceased, himself, to push the lever.

Much of his procedure was no doubt derived from personal contact with the West. It was from the West that he borrowed the current idea that the wealth of a country was measured by its exports. Much of his time and attention was given to the prodigious task of making Russia an industrial and commercial power. Partly by inducing foreigners to establish factories in Russia, partly by direct government patronage of industries (in some cases the government itself went into business), partly by teaching Russian craftsmen the superior methods of the West, he sought to elevate his country to Western standards, and, following mercantilist doctrines, tried to make her self-sufficient and relatively prosperous. To provide the labor for factories he levied upon the serfs, and thus forced them into a new kind of bondage. Even merchants were permitted to buy serfs for the handling of their traffic. By obtaining access to the Baltic he greatly promoted trade, and the creation of a navy was designed to give it security. *Economic policy*

In such measures one can discern Peter's practical turn of mind; but in his social reforms he followed rather his whims than any idea of practical benefit. Determined that his people should be *Social reforms* remolded on the European pattern, he decreed that beards should be shaved off; that the long trailing robes should be curtailed; and that women should come out of their seclusion and mingle freely with men. Himself a devotee of dancing (since he enjoyed anything active), he forced people to dance, and was often, himself, their instructor. It was these efforts to change the habits of his people that met the most strenuous opposition. People argued that the loss of their beards and the curtailment of their garments were dangerous in a country of rigorous winters; and, curiously enough, the women did not care to leave the *terem*. But Peter was obdurate. He cut beards himself on some occasions, and decreed heavy penalties for failing to obey his edicts. When the Streltsi rose in revolt, he treated them with great harshness and abolished them as a body. His own son, Alexis, was executed by his orders because he had dared an insurrection against his policy.

The inrush of the West

Through all his hectic reign Peter was striving to educate himself and his people. He made two long trips to the West, one occupying more than a year, and on his return he introduced, and sometimes personally applied, the knowledge he had acquired. He even presumed to be a surgeon; and, again, having acquired a dentist's implements, he proceeded to pull teeth. Anything of a practical or scientific nature found him immediately responsive. In Holland he spent his time in learning to build ships; and carpentering was one of his favorite hobbies. Naturally he sent young Russians to learn the ways of the West; he established technical schools; and he forced the nobles to acquire at least the rudiments of an education. He showed great favor to foreigners, some of whom he even employed in his "colleges," while others undertook to instruct the Russian artisan. No better example of what an autocrat could do—even better perhaps than his arbitrary changing of the calendar—was his building of a new capital. Since Moscow represented the traditions of the old school, and since Russia was now to face west, he founded a new capital on the Neva, named partly in his honor,[1] St. Petersburg. The fact that it was built on marshes, in a deadly climate, and far from the geographical center of Russia deterred him not in the least. He compelled his court to reside there, and by sheer force of his will he made it a great city, destined, indeed, to remain the political center of Russia for more

---

[1] The name seems to have been derived partly from a fortress, named after Peter, and partly from the cathedral of Saints Peter and Paul, which Peter founded.

than two hundred years. By the effacement of Moscow he seemed to be tearing up Russia from the very roots.

And yet the historian knows that no people can be completely made over by the power of a single despot or the accomplishments of one generation. In judging the statesmanship of Peter we are forced to measure it not by what he sought or seemed to do but by what he actually achieved. On the credit side his accomplish- *Importance of Peter the Great and estimate of his statesmanship*

Engraved for The Eclectic *by Perine & Giles, N. Y.*

PETER THE GREAT

ments were, in truth, conspicuous. He created a navy and greatly improved his army, though neither was as yet up to European standards. He somewhat improved the bureaucracy, but, like everything else he did, his new creations were hastily, one might say sloppily, put together, and failed to work harmoniously. He always took too much upon himself, and the measure of responsibility he delegated was often misunderstood because of the clumsiness and vagueness of the institutions he founded. *Voivodes* were not suppressed; yet neither were they made amenable to the governors; and the governors themselves were only indirectly accountable to the central government. True, some of Peter's difficulty lay in the qualities of the people on whom he had to depend; he frequently upbraided the senate for their incompetence (he even appointed a special officer to watch them), and he was constantly degrading and replacing. But this is just one evidence of the fact that Peter could not educate his people with sufficient speed to make them really efficient. Even his economic policy was often misdirected. He made his weavers use larger looms, but did not see that their houses were too small to provide the necessary space. He protected industries that were too weak to profit by his efforts. The cost of his wars was so exhausting that he left his country, in general, much poorer than he had found it. While he undoubtedly brought much knowledge to his people, it must be realized that this was only of the practical sort; of real culture he had no conception, and, always to the last a barbarian himself, he could not raise his people above his own impoverished level. The customs which he introduced, never extensively applied outside his immediate circle, were merely outward signs of Western influence; they were never really rooted in the life of the Russian people. Peter could not change their feelings or make them innately different. None the less, he contributed something to the material development of Russia; he improved her military and created her naval power; he made her government a little more efficient; and he not only won for her a seaboard and gave to her foreign policy a definite direction, but he may fairly be said to have made Russia a Great Power. Thanks to his intimacy with the West and the window he secured on the Baltic, Russia was eligible to be accepted into the European family.

So much for this orgy of energy which made in some respects a new Russia. But what of the aftermath? What of the guiding force after the grip of the formidable czar was no longer felt? It was after Peter's death in 1725 that the foundations of his autocracy were tested and found wanting. The nobility who had served the State had done so under the stimulus or the lash of a stronger character. There were no traditions of loyalty to the sovereign as sovereign; no strong, disinterested bureaucracy, as in France, to enforce the sovereign's will. That is why the rats could gnaw deep into the body politic; and by the rats we mean the landed aristocracy.

THE ALLIANCE OF THE NOBILITY AND THE CROWN

It was something of a test of the reformer's work that the subsequent period of misgovernment did not alter the position of

Russia in the eyes of the world. But the spirit of his reforms was quite lost sight of in the general scramble for power which began from the moment when the great czar breathed his last. Autocracy had become in certain ways so oppressive that for a while the dominant thought was to set limits to its power. Sometimes such limits were definitely inscribed and then imposed upon the ruler, but the jealousy and self-interest of individual nobles contending for personal power precluded any sort of constitutional régime. Thus autocracy was preserved—but an autocracy no less onerous than it had been in the days of Peter; for it was an autocracy of caprice, in other words a despotism. Generally speaking, this period—that is, up to the year 1762—was one of arrested development. All the machinery which Peter had created remained in force, but it was like a new building, not very strong at best, that is gradually allowed to fall into disrepair. There was almost continuous misgovernment, unbroken by any appreciable signs of progress.

An Interlude of Arrested Development

The post-Petrine reaction

It was the régime of court favorites. Czardom seemed to have broken with the death of Peter, and it was long before its pieces were put together again. In a very limited sense Peter was himself responsible, since he had enacted no law of succession for the imperial crown, and dreading the thought of death (his vices had carried him off at the age of fifty-five), he had left no provision for an heir. Thus was suffered to continue the old tradition that the crown was something to be gambled for. Yet in any case the dynasty was lamentably weak. All the ostensible candidates for the succession during this period were either sickly youths or vicious women, the last of this wretched series being the mad Czar, Peter III. We shall not take space to chronicle these reigns. Every czar or czarina lived, politically speaking, from hand to mouth, and the three czarinas, whose reigns were longer than those of the czars, were invariably ruled by favorites. The sorriest period was the reign of Anne, whose coarseness, buffoonery, and heartless cruelty recall both Peter the Great and Ivan the Terrible at their worst. It was under her that Germans from the Baltic provinces entered the public service and made themselves deservedly unpopular. One of them even had the effrontery to speak of his adopted countrymen as "you Russians." Fortunately death put an end to this species of foreign rule, but ignorance and extravagance still reigned in government circles, and no one seemed able

The régime of favorites

or even willing to promote the national good. Indeed, Russia was simply living on the resources of the moment and took no thought for the morrow. It is nearly always so when the aristocracy rule the state.

Hardening of social conditions   This period (if one includes also the reign of Catherine which followed) was a sort of heyday of the Russian nobles, even though only a few of them were fortunate enough to gain a sovereign's favor and privately enrich themselves. The law by which Peter had forced a sort of conscription on the nobility was first modified by exemptions and then finally repealed. At the same time their power over their serfs was immeasurably strengthened. Since much of the countryside was being depopulated by the exodus of peasants to the southern steppes, especially to the khanate of the Crimea, the government made every landowner responsible for the taxes owed by his serfs, and at the same time it granted him the right to mete out punishments for all offenses saving brigandage and murder. Such a policy simply made the landed nobility the agents of the government and gave serfdom itself the character of political bondage as well as economic. It is true that the lord, in his turn, was obligated to feed his serfs in famine years, and he was even expressly prohibited from ruining them by over-exploitation; yet there was no court of law to which the peasants might appeal, nor could they even complain to the authorities under penalty of the knout or of banishment to the mines of Siberia. Hence, while three days of work each week was legally due the lord, it was not uncommon for this time to be extended to four or five. The law even allowed the lord to separate a serf from the land itself and to sell him, as one might, a piece of merchandise. "Thus," as a writer has expressed it, "for all practical purposes the bound people were in person and in property at their masters' disposition." They were, in short, chattels. There is, therefore, no great wonder that thousands sought refuge in flight or that despair finally climaxed in the fearful peasant rising of 1773, which wrought tremendous havoc before it was finally suppressed. It was not the first but it was the last important *jacquerie* prior to the twentieth century.

Such, we may say, were the firstfruits of the alliance between the crown and the nobility. The material promise of the country was not appreciably affected by this hardening of serfdom, but the landed aristocracy was somewhat in danger of lapsing into its former insularity. What was needed was a vigorous national leadership—a sovereign to resuscitate the Petrine traditions. In this period of history the crown alone could point the way to progress. It was perhaps a stroke of fortune that the last of these adventurers who streaked across the history of eighteenth century Russia was capable of restoring political stability.

Catherine the Great had been an obscure German princess who at the suggestion of Frederick the Great became the wife of Peter III, grandson of Peter the Great. When she as well as the court had become thoroughly weary of her husband's brutal idiocy, a plot for his dethronement was concocted between the Empress herself and some of the nobles, including officers of the imperial guards, and successfully accomplished its object. A few days later the dethroned czar, while under arrest, was murdered in a drunken brawl. Meanwhile Catherine had mounted the throne. The fact that she did so at the expense of an ex-czar still living (though imprisoned and shortly afterward done to death) and with the blood, we might say, of her own husband on her hands did not worry that lady a particle. Her accession was the more extraordinary in that she was a German without a single drop of Russian blood in her veins. By right her son, Paul, then a child of ten, should, rather, have succeeded, but Paul was speedily banished into inconspicuous exile. In the sense that Catherine had long planned to possess the throne and had known how by her tact and captivating charms to attract an important following and had been at the right place at the right time, she may be considered a self-made monarch, and perhaps deserved her fortune.

Continued Europeani- zation of Russia under Catherine the Great

Accession and character of Catherine the Great

In some respects Catherine displayed the color of her surroundings. She was dissolute and capricious, and never quite ceased to be an adventuress. She was quite as unscrupulous as her predecessors but far more clever than most of them, not excepting Peter the Great, and she was the first ruler of Russia who may be said to have been really educated. While Peter had worked but read little and never thought, Catherine did all three. Being much more civilized than her subjects, she contrasted with most of her predecessors in keeping her temper within bounds and not indulging in senseless cruelty. But her benevolence seldom reached beyond the objects of her affection, and though in a sense she became a good Russian, she never seriously exerted herself to relieve the social injustices about her. Catherine was something of a philosopher and meant to enjoy life to the full, though without undue effort. "I used to say to myself," she remarks in her memoirs, "that happiness and misery depend on ourselves; if you feel unhappy, raise yourself above your misery, and so act that your happiness may be independent of all accidents. To such a disposition I naturally joined great sensibility and a face, to say the least of it interesting —one which pleased at first sight without art or effort. . . . If I may be allowed the expression, I venture to assert in my own behalf that I was a *true gentleman*—one whose cast of mind was more male than female; and yet I was anything but masculine, for, joined to the mind and character of a man, I possessed the charms of a very agreeable woman." We may concede to Catherine all that she ascribed to herself. Yet, with all her keen intelligence and learning, she was not a conspicuous innovator; and it has been said that if Peter had made his epoch, it was rather her epoch that made Catherine. Nevertheless she achieved something. Not her least service, indeed, was to restore respect for the crown.

Importance of Catherine the Great and estimate of her statesmanship

Catherine may be regarded as the continuer of Peter's work. She resumed his foreign policy with the object of pushing Russia westward and finding further outlets to the south. This work—which constitutes her sole title to greatness—will be described in another place. But she was also a follower of Peter in eagerly importing the enlightenment of the West—not, however, its aids to material advancement but, rather, more strictly speaking, its culture. She corresponded with Voltaire, welcomed Diderot to her court, and implanted in remote St. Petersburg a taste for art and letters. While it can hardly be said that her intellectual coterie had wide ramifications, nevertheless the Russian court began to acquire polish, and seed was sown that was destined to blossom later. Thirdly and finally, Catherine made Peter's machinery of government more workable, and, on the whole, ruled a better-ordered state than he had done. She also instituted—though it was hardly more than a gesture—a very limited system of public education.

Since Catherine had many schemes for the betterment of society, such as a new and more humane code of laws, it was clearly a misfortune—if we believe in her sincerity—that her sole dependence in the government was on the nobles. The alliance of crown and nobility was in itself sufficient to preclude any thought of ameliorating the position of the peasants. The spirit of reform which Catherine had imbibed from her broader outlook had little deeper effect than Peter's earlier efforts to revolutionize dress. Lacking a virile middle class, Russia lacked that requisite of progress that meant so much in the West. The privileges of the nobles (such as immunity from taxation) were now recognized by law, and it was in their hands that she even lodged the government of the provinces. She seems to have been usually successful in her choice of counselors—a fact that somewhat atoned for certain flaws in the central government; but it was not till the reign of her grandson, Alexander I, that Peter's awkward "colleges" were replaced by single ministers, each with his own department and responsible to the czar. Catherine was really more of a philosopher than a statesman and was not endowed with great creative talent. Most of her store of energy (and she was naturally rather indolent) seems to have flowed into foreign affairs.

THE AGGRANDIZEMENT OF RUSSIA AND THE RISE OF THE EASTERN QUESTION

The aggrandizement of Russia is the study of a giant, long asleep, who has suddenly awakened and come in time to know his strength. The clue to Russia's policy we must find in her geography. Icebound except for three months of the year when the White Sea was open to navigation, she needed to burst the fetters with which other powers were binding her and to obtain—in Peter's picturesque language "a port on a hot sea." Hence the need of reaching the Baltic and, better still, the Black Sea, with a chance of gaining access through the Straits to the Mediterranean. But if such was an economic motive, there was also a political. By expanding to the west she might hope to become a factor of great importance in the affairs of Europe. By stretching toward the Balkans, she might expect in course of time to acquire Constantinople and thus obtain a position strategically unrivaled in the world. To the accomplishment of this end the thousands of Orthodox Christians under Ottoman subjection, long attached to the Russian czars by the bonds of a common religion, were both an incentive to intervention and, potentially at least, the instruments of the process. Then too the heritage of Byzantium, the old historic right of ruling in the capital of the Cæsars was a further spur to rouse the zeal of a sentimental people. Such were the potent forces, geographical and historical, which combined to push Russia on a quest for a grandiose future. In the path of westward expansion lay Sweden and Poland;

Motives of Russian Expansion

to the south lay the Ottoman Empire; to the east, separating Russia from the waters of the Pacific, lay the vast plains of Siberia, inhabited by nomad tribes. In these three directions Peter's energies turned, following in a measure the feeble attempts of his predecessors but enjoying a power of action which they had never developed. And the first real test of that power was made against Sweden.

The position of Sweden at the close of the seventeenth century was the visible expression of the prowess of her dynasty. The house of Vasa had commenced its rule when Gustavus Vasa, a Swedish nobleman, had succeeded in 1523 in liberating his country from Danish rule. Yet in those days and for long afterward Denmark was the strongest power of the Baltic. Flanked as she was by two

seas and possessing Norway as well as two provinces, Halland and Scania, across the Sound, she all but completely shut off Sweden from the North Sea, and by her spanning of the Sound was able to levy tolls on all vessels that passed through it. It was to avoid these exactions, incidentally, that the Dutch had rounded the North Cape to trade with Russia at Archangel. But the Baltic trade netted Denmark a large revenue, for most of the materials for ship-building, timber, flax, hemp, and tar were derived from that region. Yet Denmark owed her position less to her power than to the accident of geography; and she had no rulers to equal in ability those of her neighbor, Sweden. Touching the sea at only one point on the west, Sweden was nevertheless master of Finland, whose location seemed for a time to point the direction in which to expand. Gustavus I, while he had given his country its start as an independent power, had not sought to extend her territories; but his immediate successors, taking advantage of the decay of the Order of Sword Bearers (the crusading knights who had ruled a stretch of the Baltic littoral since early in the twelfth century) conquered Esthonia and commenced to dispute the possession of Livonia, both on the eastern shore of the Baltic. Then came the heroic figure, Gustavus Adolphus, who waged four wars, and whose exploits resulted in the conquest of Ingria and Karelia (to the east of Finland), Livonia and Pomerania on the Baltic, and Bremen and Verden on the North Sea. His armies had won victories in the heart of Europe, and Sweden had become in a few generations the leading force in the Baltic world and a power of the first rank. Under Gustavus' daughter, Christine, Sweden forced her troublesome neighbor to grant her exemption from the Sound tolls, and under her warlike successor, Charles X, she conquered Halland and Scania, thus gaining the coveted coast line on the west. The zenith of Sweden's power may be said to have been reached at the time of his death in 1661.

Yet it must be confessed that Sweden's greatness was very artificial. A country with a small population and meager resources, she had been carried beyond her strength by the brilliance of her rulers. Her empire was hollow and scattered, difficult to govern, and still more difficult to defend. Moreover, while the absolutism of her sovereigns had been recognized in theory and a bureaucratic government had been developed to give it backing, the power of the nobles had never been broken as in France, and they were only held in leash by strong and resolute rulers who, in general, kept them occupied in military adventures. It was under these circumstances that in 1697 Charles XII came to the throne, and he had no sooner done so than he was attacked by a coalition of Sweden's neighbors, Denmark, Poland, and Russia, who were ready now to challenge her supremacy in the Baltic. Thus commenced, with Sweden on the defensive, the so-called Northern War.

War with Sweden was a temptation which Peter the Great could not resist, especially as he had already—though after some difficulty—come out triumphant in a short struggle with Turkey. It was characteristic of Peter with his intense love of the sea that one of his first acts had been an attack on the port of Azov, situated on the sea of that name, and hence affording him a ready access to the trade of the Black Sea. Peter's glee at opening a window to the south can well be imagined, and he at once began the building of a fleet of boats. Two years later, in 1699, he was induced to join in the concerted attack upon Sweden. But, unhappily for Peter's optimism, Charles XII was an unusually formidable adversary. There was nothing on earth that he enjoyed so much as fighting; it was said that he relished its very hardships. With a swiftness of movement for which he was always famous he fell upon each member of the coalition in turn and thrust it back in headlong retreat. Peter had been the second to receive the onset, his attack upon Narva being converted into ignominious defeat. Charles, having then whipped Poland and set up a new ruler, advanced into the heart of Germany where he soon became involved in a dispute with the Emperor Leopold. Since Europe was then engulfed in

The Northern War

another struggle, the War of the Spanish Succession, there was a prospect that Charles, in search for more adventures, would side with Louis XIV against the emperor and become, in short, the arbiter of Europe.

But however much the crisis of 1706 may appeal to the imagination, it does not appear that Charles ever seriously considered a French alliance. The Duke of Marlborough, who was sufficiently worried to make a hurried pilgrimage to Charles' camp, was finally persuaded that the Swede had other objects. In fact, Charles' advance into Germany had been a fatal mistake, for he allowed the Russian colossus the time to scamble to his feet. Peter had profited by his lesson and was now ready for another bout. The result was a renewal of war, and ultimately Charles invaded Russia with the object of entering Moscow. At best it was a hazardous maneuver, and Charles, who was conspicuously lacking in judgment as well as in a sense of strategy, gave Peter all the advantage that he could hope for. Though his army was superior in quality to the Russians, it was not only exhausted but considerably outnumbered when the decisive moment arrived, and the Battle of Poltava (1709) proved a decisive victory for Russia. Charles fled to Turkey which he succeeded eventually in embroiling with Russia, and he got a certain revenge when the Turks recovered Azov. But the Swedish empire collapsed as a result of Poltava. The trans-Baltic provinces were overrun by the armies of a new coalition, while the Swedish nobles, restive in the absence of their ruler, plunged the homeland into turmoil. Charles' return did not help matters, and he finally met a soldier's death in 1718. All Sweden's outlying provinces save Finland and part of Pomerania were lost. For Russia it meant the attainment of a Baltic seaboard.

The external history of Russia from Peter's death in 1725 to Catherine's accession in 1762 was comparatively unimportant even though Russia was occasionally involved in wars with certain of her neighbors. Catherine closed the Seven Years' War, as far as Russia was concerned, in 1762, and turned her attention to more promising undertakings. The real successor of Peter, she aimed to bring Russia nearer to the heart of Europe, and also to find some outlets to the south—a frontage on the Black Sea, and commercial, if not also political, access to the Mediterranean. Here, as we have said, there were weak states in the way—Poland to the west and Turkey to the south.

Poland was a country, which, like Spain, had known a glorious past, but had fallen into impotence and decay. The Poles, like the Russians, were a Slavic people, but possessed of less patient endurance than the Russians and more naturally impulsive and effervescent. The kingdom which they had founded in the tenth century lay between Lithuania and the Holy Roman Empire, and extended from the Baltic to the edge of the steppe which skirted the Black Sea. Into their constant wars with their neighbors we have no space to enter here. The Poles could boast of many martial heroes, and during their golden age they developed a notable culture. The size of the kingdom was much enlarged by union with Lithuania under the Lithuanian dynasty of Jagello in the fourteenth century, and this huge and unwieldy state was kept intact by a line of capable kings. Unhappily the throne had always been in theory elective, and, while it had been customary to elect the eldest son of a deceased Jagello, the extinction of this line in 1570 led to serious results. It was from then on that the Polish crown became a stake among foreign powers, each seeking the election of its chosen candidate, and injecting into the national life the virus of political corruption. Also, as another result of this national misfortune, more and more concessions were wrung from these puppet kings until the monarchy was left but a republic in disguise, all sovereignty being vested in a diet made up of nobles, most of whom were in the pay of foreign powers.

Yet there is a third reason (beside the accidental ending of a strong dynasty and the intervention of foreign powers) to account for Poland's collapse. The Polish nobles were a turbulent, undisciplined class, which, no longer held in check by a strong government, was only too ready to follow its personal impulses. Socially these nobles had long possessed ascendancy, having reduced the peasants to serfdom, hardly inseparable from slavery. There was a middle class of German extraction in Danzig and other towns but hardly of sufficient size to lessen the cleavage between a tyrannical nobility and a downtrodden peasantry. Equally dominant politically, they ruled through the national diet, and the last touch was added to an unworkable constitution when in the seventeenth century the so-called *liberum veto* was adopted. On the theory that all nobles were absolutely equal in political rights, any member of the diet could rise before his seat and, pronouncing the words, "I object," could prevent any bill from passing the assem-

Expansion to the West and South— the First Partition of Poland and the Treaty of Kutchuk Kainardji

Condition of Poland

bly. More than that, any member had the right of "exploding" the diet—that is, forcing a dissolution, involving, moreover, the annulment of all acts which it had passed. Since it is hard enough for any body of men to be unanimous, one can judge how impossible it must have been in an assembly composed of men without patriotism or any sense of unity or discipline. Sovereignty had come to rest not so much with an assembly or with a class as with each individual noble. Thus in legal form was sealed the prevailing anarchy. No wonder the French philosopher, Rousseau, expressed the view that whenever Poland moved, she had a fit of apoplexy. Yet political impotence, though the worst, was not the only, element of weakness. Out of a population of 11,500,000 in the eighteenth century about a million were "Dissidents"—belonging not to the national religion, the Roman Catholic, but professing either the Lutheran or Orthodox faith; and, thanks to religious fanaticism, these minorities were without political rights or complete religious freedom. It is true that these Dissidents were, generally speaking, inferior in culture to the rest of the population, and were not, as a matter of fact, a seditious element; but they were a tempting wedge for foreign interference, already fatally exerted through the corruption of the nobility. Finally, except for the Carpathians, which divided her from Austria, Poland had no natural boundaries to aid in her defense. She was a weak and defenseless state, placed by the accident of geography between strong and expansive neighbors. Nothing better illustrates the fact that the medieval polity, characterized as it was by aristocratic anarchy, was now in the eighteenth century hopelessly obsolete and unable to maintain its existence in the face of the modern state. Since she could not now reform—for a small progressive minority was hopeless against the dominance of the rest—Poland was doomed.

Condition of Turkey

The other power, whose fate was curiously entwined with that of Poland, was Turkey, otherwise known as the Ottoman Empire. Like Poland, she had had her period of greatness, commencing, of course, when she forced her way into Europe in the fourteenth century and climaxing in the reign of Solyman the Magnificent when the Ottoman Empire extended from the Euphrates to the Danube and from north of the Black Sea to the frontier of Morocco. Under the leadership of the greatest of her sultans the Turks had twice advanced on Vienna, and once it was only with the greatest effort that Christendom had been saved. But Turkey had had her apogee and her decline had already set in. A third advance on Vienna was repulsed before its gates in 1683 largely through the heroism of a Polish king, John Sobieski, and that historic year marked, as it happens, a definite turning-point in the history of eastern Europe. Turkey was henceforth thrown upon the defensive, and what has since become known as the Eastern Question had arisen to torment the diplomats of Europe. Roughly speaking, the Eastern Question was: what was to become of Turkey? For her position in Europe was immensely tempting to her neighbors, and she was not any longer able to defend it.

The greatness of Turkey had, in fact, been built on a false foundation. It had been due almost entirely to the ability of a few successive sultans; for neither morally nor politically had the empire any strength. The Turks had no political capacity and for governing their conquests had to depend largely on the services of the conquered, whose loyalty naturally was in question. With the passing of her strong rulers Turkey's hollowness became revealed. The government was run in haphazard fashion by favorites of the palace; the pashas who governed the various provinces were all but independent; and corruption (in which the enslaved Christians who held office were pastmasters) was corroding the whole administration. Unlike Poland, she had something in the way of national barriers—the Danube and the Balkan Mountains —but she was even weaker in one respect than Poland, for the great mass of her population were unwilling subjects, professing another faith, and hating their rulers as an alien and oppressive yoke. Nothing but fear and the long habit of subjection kept them from rising in rebellion. In truth, the Turks, in spite of their lack of leadership, were excellent warriors still, and could easily have held their own unless attacked by outside powers. But unhappily for Turkey, as for Poland, it was the time when growing nations were seeking their logical boundaries, and no weak state could hope to arrest their march.

Into these first wars of aggression we cannot enter in detail here. Austria was the leader in this long crusade of reprisal. By early in the eighteenth century the Hapsburgs had recovered Hungary, and at one time an Austrian army had occupied Belgrade, the citadel of Turkey on the Danube. In these earlier struggles Austria had sometimes the aid of Russia (we have noted the adventures of Peter) and of Venice, who was struggling to maintain what was left of her scattered empire. But it was Russia, when her power was fully able to be displayed, that menaced the very existence of the Ottoman power in Europe.

The designs on Poland

We have pointed out the underlying geographical and historical factors that doomed Poland to destruction. More specifically, her three powerful neighbors, Austria, Prussia, and Russia were bound to regard her as ripe for conquest. While Prussia wanted that portion of Polish territory known as West Prussia to connect the two main divisions of her realm, Russia thought of Poland as a future acquisition to make herself that much more of a European power. Austria, alone of the three, had no immediate design on Polish territory and was content with the status quo as long as the electors of Saxony, Austrian tools, were safely in possession of the Polish throne. But she might, of course, be pushed into some aggression by jealousy of her rivals.

The partition of Poland had been long ago forecast. As early as the sixteenth century the subject had been discussed between an emperor and a czar. Charles X thought of it, and Peter the Great had discussed the possibility with Frederick I of Prussia. Then the struggles in central Europe delayed further consideration until peace was signed between Austria and Prussia in 1763, and the following year the Saxon king of Poland died without leaving any heir to traffic for the succession. This at once raised the Polish question in acute form, for Catherine and Frederick the Great were quick to see their opportunity, and no distractions in other directions prevented their taking action. It is true that Russia wanted not to snatch a piece of Poland but to dominate the whole, whereas Frederick must by some turn of fortune obtain West Prussia. But for the present each was satisfied to keep Poland weak, and something might be gained by joint action.

The Polish imbroglio

With Frederick's concurrence Catherine chose their common candidate for the Polish throne. It was Stanislas Poniatowski, a Polish nobleman, who had been one of Catherine's innumerable lovers, and had actually sought her support. The Czarina said that she loved him for "his pensive face and his expressive eyes." More likely she saw in him a docile tool who would amply support her interests, for, in spite of Stanislas' nobility of character, he was not a man of much stability, and even a stronger man might easily have succumbed.

But the choice of the ruler was not the only feature of the bargain between these crowned vultures. They entered into a defensive alliance for eight years (each to aid the other financially if attacked) and likewise agreed as regards Poland that the *liberum veto* should be maintained and that Dissidents should be accorded equal rights with Roman Catholics. When these demands were put to the diet, it refused to listen and Catherine found it desirable to punctuate her arguments with troops. Poor Stanislas was helpless; he wanted his country reformed, but he knew that his only strength was in his foreign protectress, and there was no possible resistance to Catherine's Cossacks. So Poland, squirming, yielded to compulsion. The result, however, was civil war. Bands of "Patriots," as they called themselves, who resented both foreign influence and religious toleration, rose in revolt against their government, and, of course, had to deal not so much with Polish troops as with Russia's invading forces. After a devastating struggle of several months the "Patriots" were forced to flee, and Catherine's Cossacks pursued them across the frontier into Turkey. It was this encroachment on Ottoman territory that speedily involved Turkey in the imbroglio.

It was at this juncture that France played a temporary but decisive rôle in the ugly drama. Choiseul, minister of Louis XV, had followed the usual policy of his government in patronizing the weaker powers of Europe to harass the stronger ones, and had already expended money on behalf of the Polish rebels, who might be said on this occasion to represent the cause of Polish independence. He now saw an opportunity of pitting Turkey against Russia. Such balancing of forces would keep the East in turmoil while he concentrated his thoughts on his coming struggle with England. Through the French ambassador at Constantinople, the Count of Vergennes, he persuaded the Sultan to resent the violation of his neutrality by Russian troops, knowing full well that Russia herself would be more than willing to accept the challenge. Since obviously the question was not susceptible to discussion, the Sultan finally took the step of arresting the Russian minister and imprisoning him in the Castle of the Seven Towers. This was the conventional Turkish mode of declaring war. Thus began in 1768 Catherine's first war with Turkey—an opportunity of future gain which she must certainly have welcomed, though it is true that her hands were partly tied.

Catherine's first war with Turkey and intervention of Frederick the Great

The outbreak of the Turkish war led at once to international complications. After some months of getting ready the Russians occupied the Danubian Principalities, Moldavia and Wallachia, and eventually held the line of the river Danube. Both Prussia and Austria were naturally dismayed, Prussia because of her obligation to assist an ally (Frederick managed to get out of this by haggling over the terms) and Austria because she could not bear to see Russia biting off chunks of the "eastern cake," as Frederick called Turkey, unless she should also get her share. Catherine, for her part, seeing that France, Prussia, and Austria were all viewing her with suspicion, talked very modestly of what she expected as a result of the war. Yet no one could doubt that she meant to get what she could, and that might mean Constantinople, or at the very least, the Principalities. If only some equivalent could be found that might avail to arrest the Czarina's march! Well, there was one place where every one might seek such compensation and maintain the balance of power, and that was Poland. Frederick's resourceful mind thus hit upon the idea of joint partition.

For a time Catherine steadily resisted this tempting lure. She was willing to limit her conquests but she must have a protectorate over the Danubian Principalities and another over the Crimea which she had occupied as well. But Austria was beginning by this time to make some serious threats (bluffing, as it turned out, for Maria Theresa would not hear of war), and Catherine knew that in event of actual war with Austria she could not count on Frederick, who was showing an unwonted intimacy with Vienna. In the summer of 1770 she decided that it might be well to sound her ally, and thus invited Frederick's brother, Prince Henry, to visit St. Petersburg as her guest. "You understand, my dear brother," wrote Frederick, "what skillful handling that woman will need. . . . You will please make the Empress the most flattering compliments from me, and you will say everything you can of the admiration which she inspires in every one—in fact, all that is necessary." It was some time indeed before Catherine fully appreciated the risky game she was then playing, but Austria and Prussia had both been encroaching on Polish territory (a precautionary measure, of course!), and finally she said to Henry, "Well, why should not everyone take something too?" After a year of haggling on Catherine's part and of duplicity and haggling on Frederick's a bargain was finally struck. Russia and Prussia should each take a specified slice of Poland.

It remained now to induce Vienna to participate. Neither Frederick nor Catherine wanted Austria to be in a position to feed her jealousy by intriguing with the Poles and rendering their own situation more difficult. She must therefore be invited, nay even pressed, to join in this act of banditry—in the name of the balance of power! At first Maria Theresa would have none of it. Her conscience forbade her to pillage a friendly neighbor: "Let us rather be held weaklings," she said, "than knaves." Unfortunately for her scruples Austrian diplomacy had over-reached itself. While it had held Russia on the Danube by the threat of intervention, it had sought to get Dalmatia as "compensation" for Russia's possession of the Principalities, and after a good deal of bluster about war Maria Theresa had confessed (in a channel that reached Frederick) that she really had no intention of resorting to arms. Now if other powers were

Medallion from The Connoisseur
CATHERINE THE GREAT

getting territory all this scheming was not only futile but seemed to render her position rather ridiculous. So, after much pressure from Joseph and Kaunitz and with many tears, Maria Theresa gave in. And the more she wept over Poland, the more she actually took, and she got in the end the best piece.

A three-cornered agreement was finally reached and signed in July, 1772. Prussia acquired West Prussia except the towns of Danzig and Thorn. Russia received a slice on the east, peopled largely by Lithuanians and Little Russians. Austria obtained Galicia on the other side of the Carpathians. Prussia's share included 600,000 people; Russia's, 1,600,000; Austria's, 2,600,000. For Poland the affair was serious indeed. The loss of West Prussia meant the cutting off of her natural access to the Baltic, and Galicia had been the richest of her provinces. Moreover, diplomatic surgery is an ominous experiment. The victim, enfeebled by a first operation, might have to submit to another.

The First Partition of Poland

Meanwhile Catherine had still her Turkish war to dispose of.

Treaty of
Kutchuk
Kainardji

Frederick had called the war a contest between the blind and one-eyed, and Russia—the "one-eyed"—found it apparently impossible to dislodge the Turks from their positions beyond the Danube. She was willing to relinquish the Danubian Principalities (to that extent Austrian policy had been successful), and though the Moldo-Wallachians had welcomed liberation, a plot to incite the Greeks to insurrection had proved a sorry failure. Distracted by the peasant uprising of 1773 and the danger of a war with Sweden (she rightly suspected Frederick of complicity), Catherine wisely decided to make peace. A Russian victory south of the Danube finally brought the Turks to terms, and the result was the Treaty of Kutchuk Kainardji.

By this famous treaty, signed in July, 1774, Russia gained a solid footing on the Black Sea, the right to send her merchantmen through the Straits into the Mediterranean, and the independence of the Tatar khanate of the Crimea—manifestly a step toward its eventual incorporation in the Russian Empire. Apart from this, by various clauses, the phraseology of which was purposely vague, she procured the right to intercede on behalf of the Danubian Principalities as well as the Greek Church of Constantinople. The right of offering "representations" was later translated into a right to intervene in the domestic affairs of the Ottoman Empire. The transaction had hardly been completed when Austria seized the Bukovina (the northern tip of Moldavia), while Frederick grabbed a hundred villages in Poland. Thus again was the equilibrium preserved. Perhaps also they realized that Catherine had not said her last word.

The Eastern
Question as
the Stake of
Interna-
tional
Rivalries

The Treaty of Kutchuk Kainardji proved, in fact, no more than a milestone in Russia's triumphal advance. Annexation of the Crimea was its logical sequel. The security of Russia from Tatar raids, the shutting off of a refuge for fugitive serfs, and the value of a longer coast line on the Black Sea—all these motives served to inspire a seizure of the khanate. After cultivating the friendship of Joseph—which soon ripened into an informal alliance—Catherine proclaimed in 1783 the annexation of the Crimea. Isolated and friendless, Turkey recognized the change. Soon afterward the naval station of Sebastopol was established on the peninsula to which the name, the Crimea, is customarily applied. In 1787 Catherine and Joseph toured together the new provinces, and at one place she led him underneath a triumphal arch, bearing the significant inscription, "The road to Constantinople."

Catherine's
second war
with Turkey

Whether if Frederick the Great had not died in 1786 Russian policy might have slackened its pace is a matter of speculation. In any event it suited Joseph to plan with Catherine a partition of the Ottoman Empire, and there was apparently no prospect of external interference. While Austria hoped for Dalmatia to extend her Adriatic littoral (this was to be ceded by Venice in exchange for the Morea), Catherine dreamed not only of a protectorate over the Danubian Principalities but of a new Byzantine empire with its capital at Constantinople, to be ruled by one of her grandsons, appropriately christened Constantine. France should have Egypt, if she wished it, and that might avail to keep her from making trouble. When Turkey foolishly provoked a second conflict, the way seemed open for the destruction of the Ottoman Empire.

Yet the issue of Catherine's second war with Turkey (1787-92) was very disappointing. A sudden war with Sweden was at once a source of embarrassment; then Austria, her ally, was distracted by revolts at home, while Russia herself was annoyed by a sudden reform movement in Poland; finally a coalition of powers, Great Britain, Holland, and Prussia, seemed about to threaten Austria with armed intervention; and when Joseph II died in February, 1790, his successor, Leopold II, rather than risk a war with Prussia, made a hasty peace with the Turks. Deserted by her ally, Catherine saw that she, too, must soon make peace; and though her armies had by this time pounded out some striking victories, the Triple Alliance resolved that Russia, no less than Austria, should respect the balance of power. Catherine, nevertheless, determined *The British* to make sure of Ochakov, a port on the Black Sea that was prac- *intervention* tically free of ice throughout the year. For some reason William Pitt, who was then prime minister of England, was ready to make its seizure a *casus belli*, and only the vigorous opposition in cabinet and parliament prevented armed intervention to arrest the Russian advance. Catherine kept Ochakov, but only slightly extended her seacoast by the Treaty of Jassy (1792), which ended the war.

Great Britain's threatened participation in the war was an interesting portent. It showed clearly enough that the Eastern Question was now a bone of contention between the powers, and it foreshadowed the long rivalry of Russia and Great Britain in the Near East. Henceforth Great Britain was usually the foremost champion of the integrity of the Ottoman Empire.

Expansion to the East   For Russia, her objective, Constantinople, was still a long way off. Yet the tentacles of the great empire were reaching out far and wide. And while she now faced Europe, she was still able to take a look at Asia over her shoulder.

As far back as the reign of Ivan the Terrible some Cossacks had penetrated Siberia, and fortified posts had been established on the river Obi. Bleak and covered with forests, the land we know as Siberia was then traversed by nomad tribes of the Mongol race. During the reign of Alexis settlements were founded on the Amur and there was much desultory fighting with the Chinese, but it was left to Peter the Great to plant the Russian eagles on the shores of the Pacific Ocean and even to establish treaty relations with China. He it was also who dispatched an expedition, commanded by a Danish navigator, Bering, to determine whether Asia was joined to America, and Bering eventually discovered Alaska. It was originally the fur trade which had prompted this expansion in Asia, though it is obvious that the thought of a new sea sufficed to rouse the energies of Peter. Meanwhile a plan to conquer the Transcaspian region and open up trade relations with India had proved abortive.

Catherine paid less attention to Siberia and the Pacific, but she successfully extended her frontiers on the southeast. In 1780 she accepted a protectorate over Georgia, a Christian principality in the heart of the Caucasus Mountains, and this was finally annexed to Russia early in the nineteenth century. With Persia Russia had been occasionally at war but without appreciable results. But it is interesting to observe that Russia had become in part at least once more an Asiatic power. Moreover, the eastward wave of expansiôn gives us additional light on the direction of Russian foreign policy.

FOR FURTHER READING OR STUDY

Robinson, J. H., and Beard, C. A., *Readings in Modern European History*, vol. i, nos. 25–8, 41–4; and chap. vi, sec. 15; Reddaway, W. F., and Butterfield, H., *Select Documents of European History*, vol. ii, nos. 117–9 and vol. iii, nos. 18–27, 84–6; Korb, J. C., *Scenes from the Court of Peter the Great* (extracts from a diary); Catherine II, *Memoirs*.

Nowak, F., *Russia and the Rise of Slavdom* (a brief survey); Gillespie, J. E., *Modern Europe, 1500–1815*, chap. xxi; Platonov, S. F., *History of Russia* (convenient manual by a Russian), chaps. i–viii; Pares, B., *A History of Russia*, chaps. i–xv; Beazley, R., Forbes, N., and Birkett, G. A., *Russia from the*

Varangians to the Bolsheviks, books i and ii; Rambaud, A., *History of Russia,* 3 vols. (interesting though somewhat out of date); Vernadsky, G., *A History of Russia* (a trifle dull); Mavor, J., *An Economic History of Russia,* vol. i, esp. book i.

Kovalewski, M., *Russian Political Institutions,* chaps. i–v; Robinson, G. T., *Rural Russia under the Old Régime,* chaps. i and ii; Graham, S., *Ivan the Terrible* (popular); Waliszewski, K., *Peter the Great* (a fascinating biography by a Polish scholar); Bain, R. N., *Peter III, Emperor of Russia: the Story of a Crisis and a Crime;* Waliszewski, K., *The Story of a Throne: Catherine the Great;* Stomberg, A. A., *A History of Sweden;* Bain, R. N., *Scandinavia,* chaps. iii–x (Denmark and the rise of Sweden); Wakeman, H. O., *European History, 1598–1715* (entertaining on period of Swedish expansion); Gade, J. A., *Charles the Twelfth;* Bain, R. N., *Charles XII;* Hill, D. J., *History of Diplomacy,* vol. iii, pp. 290–302 (Charles XII and Europe); Orvis, J. S., *A Brief History of Poland;* Bain, R. N., *The Last Polish King and His Contemporaries;* Schevill, F., *The History of the Balkan Peninsula,* esp. chaps. xiv–xvii; Lybyer, A. H., *The Government of the Ottoman Empire in the Time of Suleiman the Magnificent;* Sorel, A., *The Eastern Question in the Eighteenth Century;* Golder, F. A., *Russian Expansion on the Pacific, 1641–1850.*

V. THE EVOLUTION OF ENGLAND AS A CONSTITUTIONAL MONARCHY

1. THE POLITICAL HERITAGE OF THE SEVENTEENTH CENTURY

Rise of the constitution; The limited monarchy; Peculiar case of the Tudors.

2. THE STRUGGLE FOR SOVEREIGNTY BETWEEN CROWN AND PARLIAMENT AND THE REVOLUTION OF 1688

A. THE FIRST PERIOD OF THE STRUGGLE

Accession of the house of Stuart; General causes of the struggle; Course of the struggle; The Civil War; Fall of the monarchy; The Commonwealth; The Restoration.

B. THE SECOND PERIOD OF THE STRUGGLE

Spirit of the Restoration; Character of Charles II; Political importance of the Restoration; Rise of political parties; Menace of absolutism: (1) under Charles II, (2) under James II; The Revolution—Solution of the question of sovereignty.

3. THE RULE OF THE LANDED ARISTOCRACY AND THE RISE OF CABINET GOVERNMENT

Character of the ruling class; Evolution of ministerial responsibility; Prevalence of corruption in political life; Rise of the cabinet; National policy in the eighteenth century.

4. THE EVOLUTION OF "GREAT BRITAIN AND IRELAND"

Régime of personal union with Scotland; The Act of Union; Conquest and exploitation of Ireland; Union with Ireland.

We have already noticed that England, in emerging from feudalism into the form of a modern state, was able to dispense with the all-pervasive will of an autocratic monarch. She was, indeed, the unique exception of a nation sustaining its unity under a limited monarchy—limited, we may add, not by feudal survivals but in the more modern sense, by the play of institutions more or less representative of the nation. And yet, during the course of the seventeenth century, when absolute monarchy on the Continent was being perfected, it would have been strange if some attempt had not been made by the English kings to follow the conventional pattern of this period. Whether the constitutional liberties of the English people were strongly enough entrenched to withstand the test, whether the royal supremacy, already a fact under the house of Tudor, was to make itself impregnable—such was to be the predominant issue in this crucial period of English history. We may note incidentally that England was particularly fortunate in her geography. She enjoyed a greater security than Continental states like France or Prussia, and after the loss of Calais in 1558 she was not tempted by the lure of conquest into challenging the military power of her Continental rivals. A greater concentration on matters of more direct personal interest to her people had the effect of developing in England a more vigorous national sentiment than anywhere else in Europe. And perhaps we may urge that underlying this sentiment was the Englishman's stubborn insistence on managing his own affairs—a national quality that was perhaps largely an Anglo-Saxon inheritance. To appreciate the force of this historic individualism we should look back for a moment to the growth of the constitution. It was a slow and rather painful growth, rather the product of struggle and trial than of the propounding of abstract theories (for which the English mind has little fondness), but with all its incompleteness even as late as the eighteenth century it may be said nevertheless to have prepared the way for that robust political freedom which Englishmen enjoy today.

THE POLITICAL HERITAGE OF THE SEVENTEENTH CENTURY

There is nothing on the Continent analogous to the English constitution. It is a compound of certain immemorial usages and rules of procedure (together known as the "common law"),[1] certain charters, customs, parliamentary statutes, and judicial interpretations. Part of it is written, but much of it is not; there has never been an attempt to compile it in its entirety; and it is easily altered or amended. Even in its crude beginnings—long before any of its features came to be supplied to it by parliaments—it received a certain reverence from kings and nobles alike. Local self-government, for example, which had been a legacy of the Anglo-Saxon period, was fostered and developed under the Normans; and

Rise of the constitution

---

[1] The common law, as Professor W. B. Munro says, is judge-made law in contradistinction to statutes, that is, acts passed by parliament. Originally a body of usages "common" to the realm, it "grew by decision and by record, not by enactment."

it was by virtue of the common law that the individual was protected in many of his rights. When protection was insufficient, he had also the privilege of appealing to the crown, which had its special machinery for dealing with defects in the common law. But the crown was not always the protector of the common good; for the Norman king was a feudal monarch, and his position as such was often beset with difficulty. Naturally enough these aspirants to sovereignty strained at their fetters, especially when it was a question of obtaining money, and that is why the Charter of 1100, voluntarily granted by Henry I, and the more famous Magna Charta, extorted from King John in 1215, are highly significant. While the prescriptions subscribed to in these charters were mainly feudal, their acceptance by the crown—in the second case a forced acceptance—implied the existence of a contract, according to which the king must respect his obligations. Hence, after feudalism had lost its political importance, there still remained the tradition that the crown was subject to the law.

The limited monarchy
The barons who drew up Magna Charta intended that the "great council," in the presence of which the king legislated, should be a safeguard against further encroachments by the crown. Such encroachments were likely to be in matters relating to money, since a kingdom frequently at war had clearly outgrown the principle that the king had sufficient resources in the existing feudal dues and other customary revenues, and it became increasingly necessary to ask for occasional subsidies from his council. It was also plain that the middle class could not be reached by feudal exactions and yet were a tempting source of wealth for the royal treasury. Gradually the great council came to be evolved into what was known as "parliament," recruited not only from the nobles and the clergy but from the middle class as well; and originally it was understood that the consent of each estate was needed for any levy on its members.[1] Though for a short time, indeed, parliament met as three estates, after the Continental fashion, it eventually divided permanently into a "house of lords" and a "house of commons." In the reign of Edward I (toward the close of the thirteenth century) parliament may be said to have acquired an established position, for this king, having been called upon to confirm Magna Charta, was made to under-

---

[1] In the later Middle Ages separate taxation of each estate by its own representatives was gradually abandoned, and parliament acted for all.

stand, and he acknowledged the fact, that all new taxes were dependent on a previous grant from parliament; and it was generally understood that such grants were only to be expected in an emergency. Generally speaking, the house of lords was, prior to the seventeenth century, the more important body, though it was customary from as early as 1407 for grants of money to be first made in the commons (as the more representative body) and then passed by the lords. Naturally, too, there were grievances that the crown was expected to redress; and little by little it came to be customary for parliaments to attach conditions to the granting of supplies. Sometimes also, as for instance in the reign of Edward III, parliament granted money for a specific purpose, such as war with Scotland, thus foreshadowing the system of legislative appropriations. Partly owing to the Hundred Years' War, which required heavier grants than had been customary, and especially due to the weakness of Henry VI, the crown during the time of the Lancastrian kings became especially dependent on parliament. It was in that period that members of parliament acquired from the king the recognition of their freedom from arrest and freedom of debate during a session.

In the matter of acquiring the right to share the legislative power with the king progress was not so rapid. At first parliament merely presented petitions to the crown, to which the latter might or might not accede. Since, however, it met only at the royal summons, it was easy for a king to forget his promise or enact legislation that inadequately met the need. At all events, by the middle of the fifteenth century we find parliament making many statutes itself, though the royal sanction was, of course, necessary to complete the operation. Then it was that the "bill" replaced the petition. The least progress was made in the exercise of control over the initiative of the crown. A body known as the privy council (an offshoot of the former great council) constituted the king's body of advisers, and some of them served as his ministers. During the reign of Edward III the commons devised the means known as "impeachment" for getting rid of an unpopular minister. The commons placed its charges before the lords who then decided the case; and if the offender were found guilty, his removal (not to mention other penalties) was assured. But this was very different from direct participation of the legislature in governmental policy—a privilege that must await the direct subordination of ministers to parliament.

Meanwhile the individual subject found his protection in the common law. In England there were no *lettres de cachet*, and, theoretically at least (though actually the law was capable of much evasion),[1] a person indicted for crime could not be kept in prison indefinitely without a trial. Moreover, any officer of the crown who violated the rights of the individual, as understood in the common law, was liable to be sued before a jury. Thus in the fifteenth century a famous English jurist, Sir John Fortescue, could say, "The king of England cannot alter nor change the laws of the realm according to his pleasure." England had traveled in a different direction from those Continental countries governed by Roman law, according to which the king's pleasure had the force of law. Yet one must not suppose that parliament was really the sole source of the legislative power. Kings had a practice of issuing what were known as proclamations (based on the old right of issuing ordinances in the original great council), which, though they were not supposed to contravene an existing statute or the common law, often did curtail the liberty of a subject. Sometimes, moreover, the crown suspended the operation of a law by the application of the so-called dispensing power, destined, as we shall see, to make trouble for the house of Stuart in the seventeenth century.

The peculiar case of the Tudors   In fact, in spite of the spirit and sometimes the letter of the constitution, some of the sovereigns of the house of Tudor [2] did govern "according to their pleasure." The Wars of the Roses had something to do with this curious revival of the royal power, not, of course, in the same degree as the Hundred Years' War had operated in France, but as giving the Tudor sovereigns a chance to replenish the nobility with men of their own creation of whose loyalty they were assured; and further, the century of civil war which Englishmen had had to endure made them willing to accept a strong monarchy for the sake of having protection for their economic interests. The same feeling was manifested during the struggles that ensued with the papacy and Spain. The separation of the English Church from

[1] See Taswell-Langmead, *English Constitutional History*, pp. 572-3, for defects in the law, not materially remedied till the Habeas Corpus Act of 1679. Nevertheless the principle that the prisoner had a right to secure a warrant issued to his jailer bidding the latter present him (hence the term, *habeas corpus*, "Have the body"), together with a statement of the cause of detention, before a court or judge for a hearing of the case was an instrument that could be used in fighting any attempt at judicial despotism.

[2] There were five sovereigns: Henry VII (1485–1509), Henry VIII (1509–47), Edward VI (1547–53), Mary I (1553–8), and Elizabeth (1558–1603).

Rome, while the initial circumstances had grated somewhat on popular sensibilities, won eventual approval as the repudiation of an external authority in the sphere of religion; and England's early-developed sense of nationality showed all its inherent strength in this struggle, particularly when Elizabeth came to be threatened with dethronement by the Rome-inspired forces of the Catholic Reaction. Another important aspect of the Religious Revolution was the confiscation of the monasteries, much of which spoil came into private hands and had the same effect in attaching the beneficiaries to the crown as the confiscation of the Church lands during the French Revolution was to make those who acquired this wealth staunch supporters of the Revolution. Though all of them were forceful personalities, it may be questioned whether the Tudors were endowed with great statesmanship, and the chief merit of Elizabeth lay in the choice of some of her counselors. But they did not give the impression of wanting to set up absolute monarchy, and they seem to have had the knack of winning the sympathies of their subjects. Yet inasmuch as elections to the commons were sometimes manipulated by the crown and parliament occasionally cudgeled into submission one may gather that the strength of the Tudor monarchy lay in forces rather deeper than personal popularity. Tudor policy had, in general, co-incided with the national interest, as the nation viewed it. Yet before the period closed there were unmistakable signs that parliament had begun to outgrow the royal tutelage. And it was always borne in mind that thanks to England's constitutional traditions the monarchy was limited in theory, whatever it was in practice; hence it ill behooved the crown to contest that theory. Such was the lesson to be learned by the house of Stuart.

The Struggle for Sovereignty between Crown and Parliament and the Revolution of 1688

On the death of Elizabeth in 1603 her cousin, James VI of Scotland of the house of Stuart became king of England as James I and united in his person the two kingdoms. His mother had been the ill-fated [1] "Mary, Queen of Scots," who had been executed by Elizabeth in 1587, and his reign even from childhood had been one of constant struggle either with turbulent nobles or with domineer-

The First Period of the Struggle

Accession of the house of Stuart

---

[1] Mary Stuart, after a long captivity in England, had been executed by Elizabeth in 1587 because of her supposed complicity in designs on the English throne.

ing parsons. Essentially a lover of peace, James had generally managed by keeping his enemies at odds with one another to avoid any serious trouble. But he was used to a people of rougher mold than the English and also less united. Between the two nations there were memories of long enmities and little sympathy, and to the English James was a stranger and almost a foreigner. Yet the fatal unpopularity of the house of Stuart had little to do with its Scottish extraction. Unlike its counterpart in Scotland, the English parliament took itself very seriously; and the causes of its breach with the first two kings of the house of Stuart may be summarized as fourfold.

General causes of the struggle

In the first place, there was an important negative cause of the monarchy's troubles. There was no longer felt that need of unity in the face of peril, which had kept Englishmen loyal and even subservient to Elizabeth. Conspiracies against the throne had finally ceased; the Armada had come to grief; the Catholic Reaction had spent itself, as far as England was concerned. When James made peace with Spain in 1604 a period had closed. Domestic policies would now come to the front, and the crown would now be viewed with a far more critical eye.

A second reason for the political struggle was the growth of Puritanism. During the reign of Elizabeth, when Calvinism or (to use its English equivalent) Presbyterianism had come to be the dominant creed of Scotland, a large majority of the English Protestants had come to desire a more simplified system of worship than that generally adopted and at least a reduction (they came in time to demand abolition) of the authority of the bishops. Aside from these Puritans, as they came to be called, others, more extreme, asked, rather, for toleration outside the Church and were known as "Independents" or "Congregationalists," but the great majority, disapproving of an earlier movement to force Calvinism upon England, preferred to stay within the Established Church, provided that certain rites were altered and that congregations were practically self-governing. In this way they could proceed— quite in the spirit of Geneva—to divorce art from religion, enforce a godly Sunday, and regulate popular morals. One might feel that such a body might better have left the fold and set up a church of its own making, but it must be realized that toleration was not yet an accepted principle, and not to be of the king's religion was to court outlawry and persecution. James, for his part, had no quarrel with Calvinist doctrines, but he knew only too well the meddlesome proclivities of these folk and he looked upon the cult as dangerous on political grounds. Accordingly, to any suggestion of making changes in the Anglican Church he responded with asperity, and as this element was strong in parliament, the resistance which he encountered on other questions may be partly ascribed to this cause. Unfortunately, too, his policy in other respects was calculated to widen the breach. The Puritan strength was largely in the middle class, which missed its war with Spain and the chance of plundering Spanish galleons; while prejudice as well as interest was involved when it became known that James was seeking a marriage alliance with the Spanish court. While it is true that such a policy was open to criticism on many grounds, there is little doubt that James was less insular than most of his subjects, and, thanks partly to his learning, less intolerant. With much reason on his side he no longer classed as dangerous the English Catholics, who were still in theory subjected to certain penal laws, which Elizabeth had held as a warning over their heads, somewhat as the guillotine was to be used in the French Revolution to frighten confirmed royalists into obedience. James was as tolerant to Catholics as he dared to be, and so was his son, Charles, whose wife, a sister of Louis XIII of France, was a Catholic. Religious bitterness was much more aggravated under Charles I, who swung almost as far to the right as the Puritans did to the left, and who by trying to bring the Anglican Church into greater resemblance to the Catholic, drove most of the Puritans to demand the entire supplanting of the Anglican faith by unadulterated Presbyterianism. The attempt to impose Anglicanism upon Scotland was Charles's supreme folly, and led indirectly to his downfall.

A third cause of the trouble was the personality of the rulers. That parliament would have tried a saint's patience may be readily admitted, and kings of the seventeenth century were very far from saints. But neither James nor Charles seemed to possess a grain of tact. Early in his reign James expounded the doctrine of the divine right of kings, and claimed by right the power which the Tudors had tacitly exercised but never discussed. An Englishman, while often forbearing, resents being told that he must obey as an obligation, and has ordinarily a supreme contempt for theories. It was but natural that such pronouncements—which were not nearly so dangerous as they sounded—were looked upon as a declaration of war against his liberties. But Charles was more than tactless. Naturally very shy, and drawn to very few people through his affections, he was cold and aloof in his manner—a quality that discouraged confidence and made his inveterate stubbornness particularly exasperating. When he came to show in course of time that his word was not to be trusted, his reserve seemed to imply a deeper meaning. Neither was a good judge of men or understood the temper of the people whom they ruled. As Professor Trevelyan has said, James knew Scotland but not England, and Charles knew neither.

But a fourth reason for the coming struggle was perhaps the most important of all, and that was the failure of the English parliament to comprehend the financial needs of the crown. The ordinary revenues which were expected to support the government and meet the king's personal requirements had been inadequate even in Tudor days, and James I faced a deficit from the beginning of his reign. Perhaps the principal explanation may be found in the soaring prices of all commodities—a condition which began in the sixteenth century and became increasingly more serious in the seventeenth. Yet parliament seemed to feel that only in the event of war should it be expected to make supplementary grants, and even on such an occasion it never voted enough to meet requirements.[1] The king "must live of his own," as contemporaries were fond of saying. Since parliament was apparently incapable of viewing this question broadly, the crown was driven to expedients for raising money that either went beyond its constitutional rights or at least might be so represented. It is undoubtedly true that James I was extravagant and exasperating, but much of his financial difficulty was due to circumstances that were altogether beyond him, and parliament always viewed the question purely as a personal matter. Doubtless a basic cause of much of this lack of co-operation was the sharp separation of the executive and legislative organs. Not unless the crown could control parliament or parliament could become responsible for the government was there much chance of mutual understanding. It was, after all, the penalty of a divided sovereignty, and it is hard to believe that even the Tudors could have long avoided this

[1] The desire to support the Protestant cause in the Thirty Years' War without providing sufficient means for making such intervention effectual displays parliamentary stupidity in glaring light. After a time English policy came to be taken for what it was worth, and the national prestige was accordingly lowered.

issue. With the Stuarts, less endowed with a clear sense of what was possible, and beset with certain new domestic problems, the gap grew rapidly wider and more fatal.

The struggle between crown and parliament was generally over *Course of* money, though it came to involve a defense of parliament's *the struggle* privileges against attack.   Parliament would grant but little money to James, and there was much wrangling over the nature of the royal prerogative. Under Charles the struggle became acute. His first parliament was soon dissolved because he would not tolerate criticism of his government, and the second fared no better, since it refused to grant any money until an unpopular minister was removed. After a still more stormy experience with his third parliament Charles resolved to get along without this fractious body. In the intervals during which no parliament met (and none at all met from 1629 to 1640) the king used different expedients for raising money, some of which were plainly obsolete and most of which were constitutionally questionable. When, on one occasion, taxpayers rebelled, he threw them into prison. Thrice on different grounds he imprisoned certain members of the house of commons, one of whom eventually died in the Tower rather than try to purchase release by making submission. Every time parliament had met, it had reiterated its privileges, and in the famous Petition of Right (1628) it extorted the royal sanction to a condemnation of arbitrary imprisonment and punishment by martial law. And so the struggle for political supremacy went on. On some occasions the house of commons exceeded its own rights, as when it once refused to adjourn at the royal command (really an act of revolution!); but more often it was the king who stretched his prerogative, and he could generally trust the judges to uphold him, since their tenure rested entirely on the royal favor. Charles, for his part, never looked upon himself as anything but an autocrat, somewhat compelled, it is true, to recognize a constitution, but none the less an autocrat. When he dismissed his third parliament with the warning that if it would not give him money he would raise it himself, he declared to the astonished members, "Take not this as a threatening, for I scorn to threaten any but my equals." Yet the men he was thus despising were the most respected people in England, most of them members of the landed aristocracy whose great-grandfathers Henry VIII had enriched with the spoils of the Church. Whether they were Puritans or

Anglicans, they were equally opposed to any abuse of the royal power. But few of them understood that what they were really fighting for was the supremacy of parliament. Sovereignty must lie somewhere. There must—at least in a crisis—be some supreme control. The English constitution had not yet worked this out, since the financial check was supposed to preclude misgovernment. That it had not always done so had been proved by certain palace revolutions. Perhaps, therefore, this struggle was indispensable to put the constitution itself on a clear and rational basis.

But it should have been obvious to the King of England, as it was to Continental sovereigns, that unless he could corrupt his enemies (in this case by packing the house of commons), he could not hope to become absolute without an army, and England had no standing army. When Charles got into his foolish quarrel with Scotland, he was forced to call a parliament to end a foreign invasion. The canny Scots had invaded the northern counties and demanded to be bought off; and since Charles could not drive them off, it was necessary to get the required indemnity from parliament. This parliament, known as the "Long Parliament," proceeded to attack the royal policy along a wide front,[1] and after the king had vainly tried to arrest some of its leaders, perceiving the temper of the London populace, he fled to the north of England, and civil war began.

The Civil War

We shall not dwell on the events of the "Great Rebellion." The crown was loyally supported by most of the nobility, too royalist to take up arms against their king; but the majority of the active elements in the nation were ready for armed revolt. The parliamentary forces had also the advantage of superior resources, since not only was London on their side, but they could count on the revenues collectable at English ports; and they later got the timely aid of the Scots by a promise to deliver the Church over to Calvinism. Moreover, the rebels produced a man of organizing ability, Oliver Cromwell, whose "New Model Army" was able in the end to vanquish the king's forces and make Charles a prisoner.

But, as so often occurs in revolutions, the victors split over the

---

[1] Some of the Long Parliament's legislation was of considerable importance and was explicitly retained at the Restoration. The crown was precluded in unmistakable terms from raising money without parliamentary consent. Above all, special courts of justice by which the crown had been able directly to intervene in the administration of justice or to tyrannize over the Church were formally abolished.

task of reconstruction. While parliament, mainly Presbyterian, *Fall of the* *monarchy* had committed the nation to Calvinism, Cromwell and most of the army leaders were Independents, and wanted toleration for all Protestant creeds except Anglicanism. The fact that parliament established the Presbyterian Church and imposed penalties for not conforming to it aroused their worst fears, and they, accordingly, resolved to act with a strong hand. The Presbyterians were expelled from the house of commons by force, and as a fifth of this body had already absented itself to fight for the king, there was only the so-called "Rump" left to give the new leaders constituent authority. Determination of the form of government was therefore to be the work of a minority—and, as a matter of fact, largely the result of circumstances. Cromwell would fain have kept the monarchy, but he found after patient negotiation that Charles was not to be trusted, and it seemed the simplest solution to end it altogether. It is interesting to observe that the Rump declared itself as having "the supreme power in the nation" on the ground of "representing the people," who were "the original of all just power." But such a claim of popular sovereignty was novel and premature, and it did not fit the facts, since the Rump was obviously not representative, and England was now really under a military dictatorship. There was also no legal precedent for convicting Charles of treason against the *nation.* Manifestly his trial and execution in January, 1649, were acts of revolution, whatever the moral or practical justification.

And it was a revolutionary régime that followed. A sort of re- *The Com-* public was set up, known as the Commonwealth, but as it rested *monwealth* on the army, of which Cromwell was still head, it was actually, as we have said, a military dictatorship. It hardly changed its character when a constitution [1] was finally put into force, establishing what was known as the Protectorate with large executive powers vested in Cromwell as lord protector. Though he refused the title of king, the Protector was a sovereign in all but name, and more of an autocrat than the Stuarts, for he had behind him a standing army. Oliver was a man of strong will and a good deal of ingenuity in meeting problems as they arose. A certain ruthless strain in his character was combined with a conviction, clearly derived from his Puritan background, that when he had taken a resolution,

---

[1] The one example, in England, of a written constitution. It came to an end, of course, with the régime which created it.

it was God's own will; and it was in God's name as well as in England's that he extended his sturdy rule over the British Isles. But the Protectorate was doomed when Oliver died in 1658, for it was much too sudden an innovation to satisfy a people as fond of their traditions as the English, and the presence of a large army was liable to become a menace as well as a security. When the Protector's son proved unequal to the emergency, this illegitimate monarchy came to an end. Very fortunately, after a period of intolerable anarchy, one of the army leaders, General Monk, sprang into the breach and secured the election of a "free parliament," which proceeded to call back the house of Stuart to the throne.

The Restoration

Charles II, eldest son of the late king, assumed his duties in the month of May, 1660. The parliament which had called him (known as a convention parliament because it had not been summoned by royal writs) gave way to a second parliament after the crown had begun to function, and by 1661 the constitution had recovered its normal character.

The Second Period of the Struggle

The Restoration had been the work of no single religious group, and many of the Presbyterians had become royalist through hatred of all that had happened in recent years. None the less, Presbyterianism as a political factor was doomed. The new parliament was overwhelmingly Anglican, and all who professed otherwise were placed under religious and political disabilities. At the outset, however, harmony had prevailed. The Restoration was hailed with evident relief and even joy. Most people were still too staunchly royalist in the traditional sense to approve of the dictatorship of an upstart, and the execution of a king had profoundly shocked them. They had also looked upon the Protectorate as a species of military rule, which an Englishman instinctively dislikes; and though the national prestige had been restored after a period of weak policy or isolation, Oliver's rule, nevertheless, had been a heavy expense. Finally, there was a revulsion against Puritanism with its austere view of religion and its attempt to regulate morals. There was a general feeling in 1660 that an era of good feeling had begun. And this spirit seemed typified in the new king.

The spirit of the Restoration

Character of Charles II

Charles II, the ablest of the Stuarts, resembled in some respects his maternal grandfather, Henry of Navarre. He loved his leisure and his vices, delighted his companions by his wit, and was quite too hardened a skeptic not to be aware of both his own and other people's limitations—a trait that made him tolerant in disposition. Above all, he had the knack of measuring correctly his own position. When he tried to obtain relief for Catholics and Dissenters and found his parliament unwilling to grant it, he dropped the project for the moment, though secretly intending to gain this boon for Catholics in another way. Having spent fourteen years in exile, he did not propose to risk a return of the experience, and consequently he meant to avoid his father's mistake of making an enemy of the house of commons. "I hope," he was reported as saying to a friend, "that the friends I have in the house will stick to me, and those that do I will requite them, and those that do otherwise I shall find time to cry quits with." A wary politician, Charles kept a keener eye on public affairs than his subjects realized, with the result that they paid rather heavily for their mistake.

In any case, it was difficult to avoid the basic question as to which was supreme—the crown or parliament. All the numerous privileges which parliament had managed to preserve and even to extend during the earlier Stuart period up to the time of the civil war were still valid, and Charles had promised before he came to England that to parliament should be left the religious settlement. On the surface it might seem that perhaps a margin of victory lay with the crown, since Charles had been called to the throne under but few positive conditions; but the moral strength of parliament, compared to its position under the Tudors, had certainly been enhanced, and it was hardly likely to forget that it had made, as well as unmade, a king. In fact, the struggle may be said to have ended in something like a draw, which means that political supremacy was still the issue. Politically the Restoration had achieved, or perhaps we may say, restored, a kind of balance between crown and parliament. The king could still veto legislation or dissolve parliament when he chose, but it was parliament that held the purse-strings and initiated legislation. It was practically inevitable that this balance would be tilted one way or the other. It is an interesting fact that in one of the Dutch Wars the commons insisted upon some accounting of the sums appropriated—a step in the direction of controlling the executive. The crown, however, enjoyed the advantage of large customs receipts, owing to the thriving condition of trade, while parliament's comparative goodwill (in spite of an occasional "pettish mood," as Samuel Pepys

Political importance of the Restoration

expressed it) may have been due in some measure to a period of
general prosperity, bringing among other boons, an increase in
land values. In any case Charles found a way of getting around its
carping niggardliness. Louis XIV was willing to pay him generous
subsidies in the hope that he (Charles) might manage to restore
Catholicism in England, and with the assurance of English aid in
reducing Holland. Having no real antagonism for his cousin, and
aware that Holland was a natural enemy on commercial grounds,
Charles probably did not feel that he was selling his policy to a
foreign power, though in any case he might have been willing to
do so in order to insure, if possible, his independence of parliament.
But it is interesting to note that many members of parliament
itself were also in French pay, and many of Charles's ministers
were intermittently bribed. It was an evidence of the low political
morals of this period—to be explained, perhaps, as a feature of the
reaction from the moral and political earnestness of Puritanism as
well as an outgrowth of the years of wandering and exile which
many of these young royalists had had to endure.

*Rise of
political
parties*

Yet in contrast to the blighting of political life by sordid practices, interest in public affairs did not wane but rather increased
under the influence of a cleavage between two groups on certain
fundamental questions. One of the king's ministers, the Earl of
Danby, became the founder of a party which in general stood for
persecution of Dissenters and a broad interpretation of the royal
prerogative, even going so far as to preach the new doctrine of
non-resistance—that is, non-resistance to a king who even exceeded his prerogatives. An opposing group, whose leader was the
Earl of Shaftesbury, patronized the Dissenters, harried the Roman
Catholics, and was jealous of any extension of the royal prerogative. These two parties, known as "Tories" and "Whigs" respectively, were laying the foundations of the party government
which later became so important a feature of the political life of
England.

*The menace
of
absolutism:
(1) under
Charles II*

But the early history of these parties was far from creditable.
If the Tories owed their temporary dominance partly to corruption,
the Whigs resorted to demagogic methods—capitalizing to the
full a faked Roman Catholic plot against the King, and even going
so far as to try to obtain the exclusion of the King's brother from
the succession on the ground that he was a Catholic. Charles let
them overreach themselves, even stoop to conspiracy, and then.

dissolving parliament, which was at that time in the hands of the Whigs, he struck at them with a force that paralyzed them as a party. He was now in a position to consolidate his authority. In the last four years of his reign he met no parliament, determined to wait until he was sure of having one that was filled with his satellites, and for that period he depended in the main on Louis' gold. In the meantime he proceeded by questionable means to place the Tories in possession of all boroughs which were then under control of the Whigs. Since the boroughs had much to do with electing the house of commons, he had reason to expect that future parliaments would let him enjoy his leisure and hold to the Tory slogan of non-resistance. Had anything gone wrong, he had a small standing army (allowed him by his first parliament), which he might use to quell revolt. But there was one important safeguard against arbitrary power. The Act of Habeas Corpus, which parliament had passed in 1679, made it possible for an offender against the laws to be assured a speedy trial instead of languishing in prison at the pleasure of the king.

But whatever the impending danger to English liberties, Charles died, rather suddenly, in 1685, and the test of his plans was to come under his crossgrained successor. James II possessed none of his brother's tact, and seemed to believe that he could attain his ends by the force of his personal will. His first parliament, packed according to the scheme which Charles had put into force, was subservient enough to have given a shrewd monarch a chance of establishing an autocracy very difficult to overthrow. But James was not shrewd; he was downright stupid; and he subordinated everything to securing reparation for his Catholic subjects, who were still under the old religious disabilities and had in effect been excluded from both parliament and public office during his predecessor's reign. Deeply religious and a fervent Catholic, he may perhaps have intended ultimately to make the Catholic faith the exclusive religion in his kingdom, and it is important to remember that the year of his accession was the year of the revocation of the Edict of Nantes. At all events, without regard to existing laws, he appointed Catholics to office, and even gave them Church preferments. Then in 1687, in virtue of the dispensing power, he suspended the penal laws against both Catholics and Dissenters—the latter being included in order to give people the illusion of a policy of toleration. The danger of a sovereign over-

(2) Under James II

riding the laws of the land was the greater from the fact that there
was a standing army—recently raised to 16,000 men—which
James deliberately used to influence parliamentary elections, as
well as to overawe London when a mob had tried to suppress some
Catholic worshipers.

But we know that of all issues the position of Catholics was the
one on which the English people, as a whole, were most sensitive.
Symptoms of disapproval should have warned him, but James
was invariably headstrong, and even mild opposition to his policy
was ignored or browbeaten. After two years of his rule there was
pretty general discontent. Only the thought that the two daughters
of the King by his first wife were Protestant gave the nation any
hope of a brighter future.

*The Revo-
lution—
solution of
the question
of
sovereignty*

But the hope was soon dissolved. Early in 1688 James' Catholic
queen bore a son and heir to the throne; and the English people
could thus imagine an indefinite line of despotic and Catholic
sovereigns. Hence a group of prominent nobles, convinced of the
strength of the public outcry against James, invited William of
Orange, who happened to be a grandson of James I as well as the
husband of James' daughter, Mary, to come to England and head
an uprising against the king. It was an interesting case of a foreign
invasion, instigated and welcomed by the people of the country
invaded. In fact, everything went favorably for the enterprise.
Louis, who could have prevented it, did not do so. James' army,
which might have been expected to resist, was so mutinous that
he saw that it could not avail him. And James himself had neither
the wit nor the courage to stay on his throne and appeal to his
people. All his enemies wanted was for him to take his departure,
and this he obligingly did. In December, 1688, he fled to France
and the protection of his cousin, Louis XIV. As there had
been no movement in his favor, there had been no civil war, no
bloodshed. And yet it was all a most momentous occurrence.
For the new king owed his position to the men who looked
upon him as the symbol and guardian of their constitutional
liberties; and the idea of absolute monarchy was forever shattered. No wonder the English have called it their "Glorious
Revolution."

The chief significance of the Revolution of 1688 lay in the fact
that it placed sovereignty definitely into the hands of parliament.
Now, at last, the outcome of the struggle had been reached. The

new parliament [1] that met (called by an irregularly constituted gathering of Charles II's parliaments) acclaimed William and Mary [2] as sovereigns but only after they had formally accepted a "declaration of rights" as a gage of their fidelity to the new régime. With some additions this statement was converted into a statute. By the so-called Bill of Rights (1689) all the various abuses of which the country had complained (suspending or dispensing with the laws and so on) were formally denounced, and it was held that without parliamentary consent a standing army, quartered in England, was illegal. As an historian has well said, "The Bill of Rights decided in favour of the people and against the king all the principal questions which had been contested throughout the Stuart period." An additional safeguard that the king should not rule without parliament was afforded by the Mutiny Act (1690), which made the army dependent upon legislative grant voted for one year's duration, and since a small force was obviously necessary for colonial defense, the king could not dispense with annual meetings of his parliament. Later, by the Act of Settlement judges were made removable only upon the request of both houses—a measure which effectually freed the bench from royal control. The legal position of Catholics was unchanged by the Revolution, but Dissenters naturally profited by the calling of a Calvinist king. By the Act of Toleration (1689) all Dissenters save Unitarians were accorded religious freedom. Catholics were not included in this act, but the penal laws against them were seldom rigidly enforced.[3] The cause of religious freedom had measurably advanced, but only Anglicans were able to enjoy full political rights,[4] and thus religious equality was still to come.

The new king was entirely faithful to the Revolution. William was a strong personality, cold and taciturn in his manner and never very popular in England, but his chief interest lay always in

[1] It was a "convention" parliament because William had not as yet the right, strictly speaking, to call it, and the usual forms could not be observed. After it had duly offered the crown to William and Mary and the offer had been accepted, it declared itself a valid parliament.

[2] The accession of Mary as co-sovereign was a slight gesture of respect for the principle of legitimacy, and interestingly illustrates the national disinclination to sharp changes.

[3] The last of these penal laws were repealed in 1791.

[4] The sacramental test, designed to exclude Catholics from parliament and public office, had the effect of excluding all conscientious Dissenters as well; but from 1729 annual bills of indemnity were passed by parliament, removing the penalties for Dissenters who declined to take communion according to the rites of the Church of England. The "tests" themselves were not abolished till 1826.

foreign affairs,[1] and in order to have as free a hand as possible in that sphere, he had let his subjects whittle the royal prerogative without demur. Much of his time at first was spent in consolidating his position. Scotland was brought to accept the Revolutionary Settlement without much difficulty, but force alone availed to bring Ireland around. In 1690 the Irish rose at James' call, and when James came over to head them, William crossed to Ireland, defeated his rival in the Battle of the Boyne, and speedily put down the rising. James could only take flight again, and though "Jacobites" were numerous enough in Scotland, the chance that the Catholic branch of the house of Stuart would recover the throne became increasingly slight as time went on. In 1701 by the Act of Settlement the succession was declared to extend, after the Princess Anne, to Sophia, Electress of Hanover (a grand-daughter of James I) and her heirs, the male line of the house of Stuart being thus definitely excluded from the throne. That body which had called a legitimist king to the throne in 1660, and then, having deposed one, had made a new king in 1689, now regulated the succession. The English nation had definitely escaped a régime of autocracy, enlightened or otherwise. Instead, it had come to be ruled by an oligarchy, which, having interests that co-incided with those of the nation, was more likely to be consistently enlightened.

The Rule of the Landed Aristocracy and the Rise of Cabinet Government

Character of the ruling class

If politically the Revolution of 1688 established the supremacy of parliament, socially, for that very reason, it inaugurated the rule of the landed aristocracy, who had long dominated both houses of parliament, it is true, but had now no longer to cope with a power-ful monarch. Judged from the standpoint of political morals, these aristocrats were rather less admirable than the members of the class who had figured in the early Stuart period. They were less narrow in their outlook, it is true, and much less bigoted—partly for the reason that the religious question had ceased to enjoy its former vogue and acidity; but they lacked that quality of stark sincerity, which seemed to atone for the kinks in the Puritan temperament, as well as for that obstinate loyalty of the men who had fought for their king. Perhaps because the reaction against

---

[1] The struggle with Louis XIV occupied most of William's reign and that of his successor, Anne (1702-14).

Puritanism had settled deep in the national consciousness, perhaps because they no longer had to test their mettle in a life and death struggle for political rights and could now give more attention to selfish interests, the ruling class which came into power in 1688 were very generally men of elastic principles, and often openly sordid methods. The standard of political morality had, on the whole, become lowered. Hence, the gradual emergence of a political machine, embracing parliament and government—a phenomenon which we shall presently discuss. But it is also true that the men of parliament, in coming to assume a greater responsibility, acquired a knowledge of the world which made their policy intelligently constructive. However seamy the political background of these men, many of them showed a practical statesmanship that goes far to explain the solid greatness of imperial Britain. But in 1688, despite their triumph over the crown, they had, first of all, to consolidate their rule.

The sovereignty of parliament implied something more than *Evolution of* the exercise of legislative power or the ability to check the power *ministerial* of the executive through the withholding of supplies. The crown *responsibility* must be held through its ministers more directly accountable to the house of commons. We have noticed the method of impeachment employed against an unpopular minister, but this was a negative method of exercising influence, and did not insure the appointment of ministers who really had the confidence of parliament. There was an interesting portent of ministerial responsibility in a speech of Pym, one of the leaders of the opposition to Charles I, when he had said that ministers should be "such as the parliament may have cause to confide in." Of course, the convenience of having ministers and parliament in accord might work both ways: it should smooth out things for the king as well as for his commons; and it is noticeable that Charles II sometimes picked as his chief minister a prominent leader of parliament and also that he was apt to dismiss him if parliament withdrew its confidence. With the division of politics into two groups, Whigs and Tories, one of whom always controlled the commons, it should have been easy to solve this problem. But William III, who was a skillful politician and did not wish to alienate either of the parties, much preferred to pick his ministers from both. Only once did he, and only twice did his successor Anne, possess a ministry of one party, and the Tory ministry of Anne during the last years of her reign was the

result of personal feeling. But after the disruption of the Tories
(the result of a conspiracy to undo the Act of Settlement in favor
of the dethroned house of Stuart) the first Hanoverian king,[1]
George I, had no choice but to pick his ministers from the Whigs,
since there were only a handful of Tories left in parliament, and all
ministries down to 1762 were composed exclusively of Whigs. Yet
with one party in full control there were almost inevitably squabbles within its ranks and the picking of Whigs for ministers did not
necessarily in itself mean ministerial responsibility. When in 1746
George II attempted to form a ministry that would be personally
agreeable to him, he found that he could not do so, for the nominees
selected were unable to count on the backing of the house of commons. This case was significant evidence that ministerial responsibility—quite without deliberate planning—had come into actual
practice; and more and more it came to be accepted as a feature
of the constitution. The notion of a prime minister, picking his
colleagues and holding them all to a common policy, was rather
more vague, though because of his strong leadership, Sir Robert
Walpole was for twenty-one years (1721–42) premier in all but
name. In general, during the period of Whig ascendancy the
crown simply leaned on the politician who was able through a
political machine to command a safe majority in the house of
commons.

Prevalence
of corruption
in political
life

The system of choosing members of the house of commons was
particularly susceptible to manipulation. The size of the electorate
was, to begin with, very small in proportion to the entire population, for qualification rested upon landed property. Moreover,
there had been no reapportionment of seats in accordance with
the shifting of population, and in general both counties and boroughs (the two parallel electoral units) were either overrepresented
or underrepresented. The former evil applied particularly to the
boroughs, many of which had decayed since their early establishment, and many more of which had been deliberately created
prior to the Revolution for the express purpose of furnishing support to the crown. In some of the boroughs (the so-called "rotton
boroughs") the number of electors were so few that they were
all-too-easily controlled by some local magnate or by the crown.

---

[1] The monarchs of the house of Hanover were George I (1714–27), George II
(1727–60), George III (1760–1820), George IV (1820–30), William IV (1830–7),
and Victoria (1837–1901).

In 1780 it has been estimated that a majority of the house was chosen by as few as 6,000 voters, and that 457 out of 658 members were virtually nominees of the ministry. Sir Robert Walpole was so far successful in controlling the nomination of members of the commons and also in bribing them with various honors and emoluments at the disposal of the crown that for twenty years his mastery of parliament was beyond all question. One of his lieutenants, the Duke of Newcastle, came to exercise a similar patronage, while Henry Fox, at times a colleague of Newcastle's and later a satellite of George III, did most of the dirty work of "tickling the palm," as he expressed it. So excellently did the system serve the Whigs that George III through his Tory minister, Lord North, pursued the same methods, and parliament was packed in the king's interest during much of the period when England was fighting the American colonies. When finally even this purchased majority fell to pieces and a commons was elected which opposed the King's wishes, George intrigued against his ministers, and regardless of the principle of ministerial responsibility, gave the premiership to William Pitt in the face of a hostile commons. Since, however, the general election sustained Pitt, the principle was again applied. From this time on parliaments were less corrupt; and Pitt by virtue of his personality long enjoyed both the favor of the king on the one hand and that of the commons on the other. The Tories gained a position analogous to that of the Whigs in the early Hanoverian period, but they owed their long ascendancy chiefly to the fact that they happened to be the party which conducted the war with Revolutionary France, and hence the policy which they adopted had the approval of the nation. It is noticeable that for about forty years George III had played a part as king very different from the negative rôle of his two predecessors, but only once had he deliberately pitted his strength against that of parliament, and under his successors there was never any questioning the gradually established principle of ministerial responsibility.

Parallel with the shifting of control from executive to legislature one must note the transfer of leadership from the king to one or more of his ministers. William III allowed no one to shape foreign policy but himself, and George III by virtue of his personality dominated some of his ministers, but the other monarchs who ruled England since 1688 left the initiative almost wholly in the hands of their ministers, who with rare exceptions, had the back-

ing of parliament, and usually resigned when they ceased to have
it. In the meantime, it was not the ministry, strictly speaking,
that initiated policy but the cabinet—the body which more and
more became the pivot of the government.

Rise of the
cabinet

From early times certain privy councilors (usually ministers
also) who happened to command the king's favor, had formed a
small council, at first secret, which the king was wont to consult on
matters he held to be of special importance. There was such a
body (at this time, a committee of the privy council) with whom
James I secretly discussed his plan of a Spanish marriage for the
prince of Wales. During the reign of Charles II it seems to have
been generally recognized that the king possessed an informal
advisory body, and the term, "cabinet" or "cabinet council"
came to be frequently employed. But the personnel of the group
depended entirely upon the royal favor; its membership was not
always known; it had no legal position as such; and it left no
records. After the Revolution of 1688 such a body (composed, as a
rule, of the principal ministers) came to be much more important,
being used by William to ascertain the strength of his parliamentary support and sometimes to procure it. It was still primarily an instrument of the king, though, now that ministries
were virtually responsible to the house of commons, it could
easily become a means of bringing the policy of the king into
line with parliament's wishes. In William's time it always met
in his presence, and it was supposed to do the same under Anne,
but we hear of its meeting privately without her—an indication that it felt unanimity to be desirable before meeting her,
and also an omen of its future independence. It was under the
first Hanoverian king that it secured an independent position and
became much more the mind of the legislature than that of the
crown. George I had little interest in England and was furthermore handicapped by his inability to speak English. Hence he
ceased to attend the meetings of the cabinet, leaving to it entirely,
the formulation of policy; and this precedent (if we except some
occasional dictation from George III) has generally been followed
ever since. Since it met without the king, it prepared a brief
minute of its proceedings for his perusal. It is worth while to
note, however, that the cabinet became so large that in the second
half of the eighteenth century we find policy being initiated in an
inner circle of the cabinet, of variable personnel (depending upon

the judgment of the cabinet's leading member), and often popularly spoken of as the "conciliabulum." In any event, the cabinet had long since superseded the privy council, which came to have little more than an honorary position; and from early in the nineteenth century it was the cabinet (generally composed of the chief ministers and perhaps a few others) which prompted the resignation of a ministry when it ceased to have the support of the house of commons, or of the public in a general election.

It was thus through the gradual development of cabinet government that executive and legislature became merged under the control of the legislature, or more properly speaking, of the house of commons. Manifestly, the practice of impeachment had long since fallen into disuse as unnecessary. If the king chose his ministers from prominent members of parliament, especially of the house of commons, there was an easier method of getting rid of an unpopular minister: he would automatically resign under fire. The king's veto of legislation became also obsolete, once the executive policy was shaped by ministers who held their position on the basis of parliamentary approval; and the last exercise of such legislative power by the crown was in 1706. Even the choice of the cabinet was actually, if not nominally, the privilege of the king's leading minister, though it was not till the nineteenth century that the members of the government collectively resigned when it lost the support of the commons.

Much progress in England has been due to the rivalry of the two great parties for the approval of the electorate, but throughout most of the eighteenth century either Whigs or Tories had so completely dominated parliament that the ardent struggles of earlier days were almost forgotten; and most of the legislative output of the period was comparatively insignificant. The greatest advance, in fact, was made in empire-building. After Walpole's placid and prosperous rule the British nation soon drifted into the struggle which made it the leading colonial power of the world; thus the main problems were imperial, involving chiefly the relations of England with her American colonies and India. There was, however, a mild movement for parliamentary reform (that is, making for a more representative house of commons), sponsored chiefly by William Pitt, who was George III's chief minister during most of the period from 1785 to 1806; and it was due to a more ardent reformer, Charles Fox, the leader of the more radical

National policy in the eighteenth century

Whigs, that the traffic in African slaves was eventually prohibited. But, as far as liberal policies in general were concerned, the French Revolution had acted as a deterrent, and reform was put in storage for a generation. Pitt himself parted completely with his earlier desire for parliamentary reform, and played on the prevalent fear of a revolutionary outbreak in England to put through some repressive measures, suspending the Habeas Corpus Act as well as placing restrictions on the press and public meetings. It was perhaps not unnatural that even the relatively enlightened English aristocracy should feel alarmed at the plight of aristocracy in France and at the rise of social forces which had seldom seriously disturbed the usual calm of English politics. Only later would the value of England's contribution to Continental polity—the principle of ministerial responsibility—be fully appreciated.

It remains to say a word of Scotland and Ireland—the two neighbor-lands of England, which for various reasons were needed to become an integral part of her kingdom.

THE EVOLUTION OF "GREAT BRITAIN AND IRELAND"

The régime of personal union with Scotland

It was a happy accident that a king of Scotland was called to the throne of England, for it made much easier the fusion of the smaller kingdom with the larger. Memories of bitter struggles between the two and the interventions of France on the side of Scotland made it seem of great practical importance to England to acquire Scotland. When James came to London, he desired a close union between the countries, and it was with great annoyance that he discovered the weight of English prejudice. He could not prevail upon parliament to grant even freedom of trade to his Scottish subjects. Later, as we noticed, the Scots played an important part in the struggle with Charles I, but they were royalists by conviction, and Oliver found it necessary to enforce his rule in the border kingdom. Throughout the reigns of the Restored Stuarts Scotland returned to her normal state of factional quarrels, and it was not till the reign of Anne that the Scottish question was settled.

The Act of Union

In 1707 after long negotiation the union of England and Scotland was effected. The Scottish parliament was abolished, and representation was granted to the Scottish nobles and people in the English parliament at Westminster. The loss of Edinburgh as a capital was something of a blow to the Scots, but they rejoiced in the continued ascendancy of the Presbyterian Church and in

sharing the commercial advantages of England. Devotion to their
religion and to their pocket-books were, in short, decisive arguments. For England the union seemed especially urgent in view
of foreign war and the danger that the Jacobites would gain an
ascendancy in Scotland. The union of England and Scotland
brought into being the so-called "Kingdom of Great Britain."

Relations with Ireland were very much stormier than those with *The conquest*
Scotland. The Irish, divided as they were into clans, and a prey to *and exploitation*
constant feuds, were hardly to be called a nation, and having *of Ireland*
largely lost their ancient culture in the ravages of foreign invasion,
they had fallen to a low stage of civilization. England's foothold
in Ireland dates from the twelfth century when a settlement centering in Dublin was established, called the "Pale"; and some
time later a parliament emerged there, as in England, but only
for the inhabitants of the Pale. Since, however, these English
settlers had become rapidly assimilated, an effort was made under
Henry VII to obtain a firmer grip, and by "Poyning's Law," as
it was called, the Irish parliament was made subordinate to the
English government.[1] During Elizabeth's reign Spain tried to
utilize Ireland as a basis for attacks upon England, and hence
the Queen undertook a partial conquest of the island. The affair
was a dark and bloody chapter of English history. The cruelties
perpetrated on the Irish seem to the historian, Lecky, to require
"the widest stretch of historic charity," even allowing for the
standards of the sixteenth century. But Ireland remained in discord; the Irish resented the attempts to force them into the Anglican Church, and conceived, as Trevelyan says, a zealous devotion
for the Catholic faith, which they identified with passionate hatred
for the English. In the Elizabethan conquest one may say that
Irish nationalism was born.

From the English standpoint the problem was still far from
solved. Much of the land, it is true, was confiscated, and in
James I's time the Ulster plantation was established in the north,
made up largely of Scottish Presbyterians. But discord and
turbulence continued. When Cromwell had to enforce his strange
régime over the British Isles, he undertook the conquest of all
Ireland by fire and sword, and left in that country a name that is
still thought of with grim horror. Cromwell continued the expropriation of the natives, three quarters of the island (a contem-

[1] More definitely, to the privy council.

porary put it, "four-fifths") becoming the property of English or
Scottish landlords, while the natives sank to the position of indigent tenants on their estates. Still more confiscations followed
the rising of the Irish under the ex-King James II to which we
have already alluded. Yet it is worthy of note that the Ulster
Dissenters, dominant as they were in Ireland, were not included
in the benefits of the Act of Toleration, and this accounts in a
large measure for the migrations of so many of them to foreign
lands.

There was, of course, no grace for the Catholic Irish. Strong in
their position and monopolizing the Irish parliament (from which
Catholics were excluded), the foreign settlers in Ireland proceeded
to fasten on the natives a machinery of oppression so grinding
that it has probably no parallel in western Europe. The penal
laws against the Catholic religion, introduced by Elizabeth and
since elaborated, were not very effective, for it is virtually impossible to destroy the faith of the majority in any land; but the educational and economic disabilities later included in the code had
the effect of degrading the natives to ignorance and poverty. A
Scottish traveler in Ireland, Arthur Young, expressed his conviction that the laws were really not so much directed against Catholicism as "against the industry and property of whoever professes
that religion." How truly, indeed, was Ireland the victim of exploitation is evidenced by the prohibitive tariffs established in
England, which deprived the Irish of their market for live stock
and ruined the thriving industries which had developed in the
Irish towns. In the latter case it was the Protestant Irish who
chiefly suffered.

Union with Ireland

During much of the eighteenth century Ireland lay prone under
the heel of the conqueror, for most of her sturdiest sons had emigrated, many of them entering the service of the French. But
when the French Revolution broke out, it stirred the old embers of
unrest, and Pitt came to the conclusion that the only way to solve
the Irish question was organic union with England. After the
Irish parliament had been duly bribed to abolish itself, the Irish
were granted representation in the British parliament, though as
Catholics were still excluded from that body, the Act of Union
was of advantage to only a small minority. At all events, in
1800 was established the "United Kingdom of Great Britain and
Ireland."

FOR FURTHER READING OR STUDY

Cheyney, E. P., *Readings in English History*, especially chaps. xiv–xvi; Prothero, E. W., *Statutes and Constitutional Documents, 1558–1625;* Gardiner, S. R., *Constitutional Documents of the Puritan Revolution, 1625–60;* Robertson, C. G., *Select Statutes, 1660–1832;* Whitelock, B., *Memoirs* (for early Stuart period and Commonwealth); Stone, T. G., *England under the Restoration;* Grimblot, P., *Letters of William III and Louis XIV;* Walpole, H., *Memoirs of the Reign of George II*, 2 vols.

Gillespie, J. E., *History of Europe, 1500–1815*, chap. xvii (excellent survey); Hayes, C. J. H., *A Political and Cultural History of Modern Europe*, vol. i, chap. x; Lunt, W. E., *History of England* (very useful text), esp. chaps. xxii–xxviii; Cross, A. L., *A Shorter History of England and Greater Britain* (more detailed than Lunt), esp. chaps. xxvii–xl, xlii–xlv; Trevelyan, G. M., *History of England*, book iv and book v *(passim)*; Adams, E. B., *Constitutional History of England*, esp. chaps. xi–xvi; Taswell-Langmead, T. P., *English Constitutional History;* Wingfield-Stratford, E., *History of British Civilization*, 2 vols. (chatty and interesting though not always convincing); Trevelyan, G. M., *England under the Stuarts* (vivid and entertaining); Leadam, I. S., *A Political History of England, 1702–60 (passim);* Hunt, W., *A Political History of England, 1760–1801 (passim)*; Clark, C. N., *The Later Stuarts, 1660–1714* (a volume of *The Oxford History of England*, an excellent treatment).

Pollard, A. F., *The Evolution of Parliament;* Gooch, G. P., *English Democratic Ideas in the Seventeenth Century;* Notestein, W., *The Winning of the Initiative by the House of Commons* (an important study); Dietz, F. C., *English Public Finance, 1558–1641* (part i interesting on the conflicts with parliament over money); Jenks, E., *Constitutional Experiments of the Commonwealth;* Williams, C., *James I;* Firth, C. H., *Oliver Cromwell* (most scholarly study); Taylor, G. R. S., *Cromwell;* Buchan, J., *Oliver Cromwell* (most recent work); Hertz, G. B., *English Public Opinion after the Restoration;* Airy, O., *Charles II* (excellent); Bryant, *King Charles II* (partial to Charles); Ogg, O., *England in the Reign of Charles II*, 2 vols.; Turberville, A. S., "The House of Lords under Charles II," *Eng. Hist. Rev.*, xliv, 400 ff., xlv, 58 ff.; Abbott, W. C., "The Origins of English Political Parties," *Amer. Hist. Rev.*, xxiv, 578 ff.; Traill, H. D., *Shaftesbury;* Groce, C. L., "Louis XIV's Financial Relations with Charles II and the English Parliament," *Jour. Mod. Hist.*, i., 177 ff.; Trevelyan, G. M., *England under Queen Anne;* Morgan, W. T., *English Political Parties and Leaders in the Reign of Queen Anne* (scholarly monograph in brief compass); Traill, H. D., *William III* (brief sketch); Blauvelt, M. T., *The Development of Cabinet Government* (brief sketch); Turner, E. R., "The Development of the Cabinet," *Amer. Hist. Rev.*, xviii, 127 ff.; Temperley, H. W. V., "A Note on Inner and Outer Cabinets," *Eng. Hist. Rev.*, xxxi, 291 ff.; Morley, J., *Walpole;* Porritt, E., *The Unreformed House of Commons*, 2 vols. (standard work on the subject); Riker, T. W., *Henry Fox, First Lord Holland*, 2 vols. (somewhat tedious picture of political methods under the unreformed house of commons); Trevelyan, J. O., *The Early History of Charles James Fox* (interesting on the ways of the landed aristocracy in the eighteenth century); Hammond, J. L., *Charles James Fox* (an appreciation rather than a biography);

Rosebery, Lord, *Pitt* (interesting); Matthieson, W. L., *Scotland and the Union;*
Lecky, W. E. H., *History of Ireland in the Eighteenth Century,* 5 vols. (part
of his monumental *History of England in the Eighteenth Century*); Murray,
A. E., *Commercial and Financial Relations between England and Ireland;* Brown,
L. F., *The First Earl of Shaftesbury* (just published).

VI. IMPERIALISM, MERCANTILISM, AND WORLD CONFLICT

1. EVOLUTION OF THE FIRST ERA OF WORLD POLITICS

Ascendancy of Spain and Portugal: (1) its character, (2) its collapse; Motives of imperialism; Imperialist organization: (1) the chartered companies, (2) mercantilism; Results of imperialism: (1) economic—the development of capitalism, (2) social, (3) political.

2. THE MARITIME ASCENDANCY OF HOLLAND AND ITS COLLAPSE

Foundations and aspects of Dutch ascendancy; The "golden age" of Holland; Causes of collapse; Collapse of Dutch ascendancy; Decline of Holland.

3. THE ANGLO-FRENCH STRUGGLE—THE TRIUMPH OF BRITISH IMPERIALISM

Origins of the struggle; Theaters of the struggle; Comparison of the contestants; Evolution and course of the struggle; Significance of the struggle.

4. WORLD POLITICS IN UPHEAVAL

Causes of the American Revolution; Intervention of France; Passing of mercantilism.

We have observed that one of the incidents of the transition from the Middle Ages to the Modern Era was the widening of Europe's interest to include other continents. While we are not interested here in the meaning which this had for a new world, the effect of such a movement upon European society and upon the interrelationship of the expanding nations must receive a little attention. The vision of men penetrated to new theaters of opportunity, and the objects of their endeavors were of sufficient importance to produce heavy sacrifices and often acute rivalries. We are, in fact, entering upon the first era of world politics in modern history.

Evolution of the First Era of World Politics

The first epoch of world politics may be said to have begun in 1494 when Spain and Portugal signed the Treaty of Tordesillas, accepting the results of the papal arbitrament, which had allotted to Spain all discoveries west of the fiftieth meridian and to Portugal

The ascendancy of Spain and Portugal: (1) its character

199

all that lay east of that line. Spain's interest lay chiefly in the Americas, while the Portuguese viewed as their own the coast of Africa from the Mediterranean around to the Red Sea, the lands skirting the Indian Ocean, the East Indies, and (in the Western Hemisphere) Brazil. Before the seventeenth century Spain had established military occupation in Mexico, Peru, the West Indies, and the Philippines, and ruled these countries with an iron hand through governor generals. The Portuguese established fortified posts at various points in Asia and the East Indies, and governed their conquests in similar fashion. The closest economic ties paralleled the political. Spaniards and Portuguese were the sole purveyors of the riches of their respective colonies, and, according to the doctrine of the closed sea which they propounded, the ships of all other nations were prohibited from their waters. The economic policy thus adopted by the first imperialist powers of the Modern Era served to some extent as a model for other powers. While a monopoly of the open seas could hardly have been maintained—even if Spanish and Portuguese sea power had been greater than it was—the firm linking of the colonies to the mother country and the control which the State exercised directly over trade were destined to become the basic features of the mercantile system.

(2) Its collapse

But not only was the monopoly exercised by Spain and Portugal impossible to maintain; even their pre-eminence as colonial powers was relatively short-lived. The chief cause of the decline of Spain was the want of enough industries to absorb the precious metals which had given her for a time a certain inflated prosperity. Since Spaniards had to go to foreign markets to satisfy most of their wants, the bullion which flowed into the country speedily flowed out again—into the pockets of their enemies, the English and the Dutch. Moreover, even had the Spaniards been inclined toward commerce, the government's restriction of the colonial trade to a single port, Seville, the strict regulations imposed, and the heavy taxes exacted from the traffic were sufficient to dwarf it from the outset; and such industries as existed were throttled by Philip II, whose fanaticism eventually drove the Moriscos to revolt (they were expelled under his successor), and whose wars had involved a constant drain on limited resources. One cannot but reach the conclusion that the Spanish colonial power was an impossible growth—an empire erected upon quicksands. As an historian has well said (in contrasting it with the English) "While Spain exploited her colonies for the advantage of the royal treasury, officials, and priests, England administered her colonies for the advantage of the mercantile classes." Unfortunately the mercantile classes were in Spain also exploited. It is also to be observed that the more vigorous of Spanish manhood passed into the Church or into the army instead of giving its life to more productive national pursuits. Though not, at best, a rich country, Spain sacrificed her chances as a great imperial power to ignorance of economic factors. In falling from her high estate, she dragged down Portugal with her, for the latter had been annexed by Philip II in 1580. Yet Portugal, too, was already on the decline. She was too weak a nation to administer successfully her immensely scattered empire; corruption had eaten deep into her very vitals; and when new competitors rose, she lacked the strength to combat them. Inevitably the arena of world politics broadened out to include other and more vigorous nations.

Aside from English "buccaneers," the Dutch were the first to challenge the privileged position of Spain and Portugal. As soon as their liberation from Spain was fairly well assured, they began to take advantage of the Portuguese explorations, determined to seek themselves the all-water route to the East. When in 1580 a short-sighted edict of Spain prohibited them from trading any longer at Lisbon, they had no other alternative than to go direct to the Spice Islands themselves. Moreover, now that they were no longer subject to Spain, and were, in fact, usually fighting her, they had no compunction, of course, about attacking the trade of the Portuguese and wresting from them several of their possessions. The second period of the struggle which Holland waged against Spain was colonial, not one of self-defense; it was an offensive war, fought for colonies and commerce. But the Dutch were not alone in this profitable prospecting. The doctrine of the free sea which they espoused and on which their great jurist, Grotius, wrote a learned disquisition, might accrue to the advantage of others. Just as English sailors had "ridden the Spanish main" and plundered Spanish galleons, so English merchants, too, began to seek the coveted riches of the East. The stage was being set for the appearance of new rivalries.

The motives of this pushing of national interest beyond the *Motives of* portals of Europe were various—political, religious, and economic *imperialism* being among the most conspicuous. The political motives were hardly separable from the economic. Nations were not then obsessed by the passion for area which meant so much in the later period of world politics, but insofar as national governments sought opportunities of enrichment in order to support standing armies and thereby augment their power in Europe the inspiration was political. Such was certainly one of Spain's considerations. Religious motives also played a certain part, though secondary no doubt, at the Spanish and Portuguese courts. While the Spaniards hoped to bring the true faith and the hope of Heaven to the heathen, the Portuguese sought to rescue the fabled kingdom of Prester John—that Christian state supposed to be submerged somewhere in the Moslem world—and they were ever eager to destroy the Mohammedans whom they encountered. Later on, the hope of freedom from persecution led certain elements (French and English), to seek an asylum across the seas; but such was not, of course, a factor of government policy, the Huguenots, in fact, seeking the refuge of the English colonies, as the colonies of their own country were barred to them. Beyond a doubt the predominant motive impelling all the imperialist powers was economic. It was to get direct control of the treasures of the East, particularly spices, that national monarchs sent exploring expeditions in all directions. When by the accident of discovery a new world was opened up, the quest of gold and silver began to take the most prominent place. Then, as the various resources of the newly discovered lands came to be more definitely known, commodities such as tea, coffee, sugar, tobacco, and furs, as well as raw materials for manufacture such as cotton and wool became the leading objects of attention. The mercantile system, which we shall presently discuss, gave added zest to the planting of colonies. Governments were interested not only because the traffic contributed to the prosperity of their subjects but also because they saw in it new openings for taxation. Also those in power (as well as people in general) promoted the movement because it enabled them to gratify their taste for new or cheaper luxuries. This may be described as a social motive. In any case the opening up of new fields for exploitation meant an immediate expansion of trade, and governments, like individuals—and sometimes no doubt under pressure from individuals—are always subject to captivation by the lure of easy money. The risk of life involved was the affair of individuals; risk of capital (such as ships fitted out by Spain) was

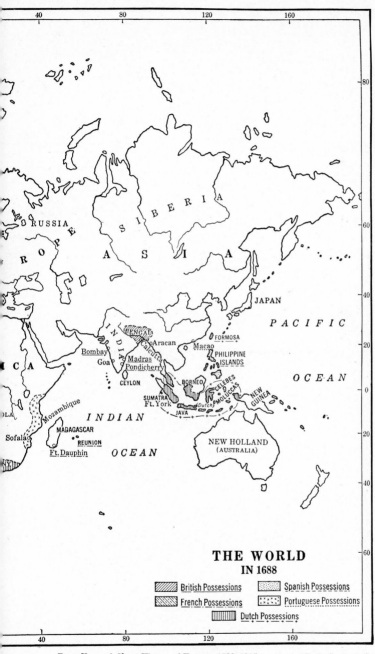

THE WORLD
IN 1688

British Possessions Spanish Possessions
French Possessions Portuguese Possessions
Dutch Possessions

From *Hyma*, A Short History of Europe, 1500–1815, *courtesy of F. S. Crofts & Co.*

at first, in part at least, an affair of governments; but even here the risk was soon to be shifted more and more to those private agencies, the chartered companies.

If there is one thing in particular that the English merchants had learned, it was that in trading with distant points or relatively backward countries it was necessary to bind themselves into a company for the purpose of distributing the risk as well as for providing adequate means of protecting their stations and their ships. Such, for example, was the so-called Merchant Adventurers, which dated from early in the fifteenth century. It received a charter from the crown, conferring upon it a monopoly of trade within a certain area, and it kept a common fund for joint expenses. The idea of a monopoly was, of course, not new. Even as far back as the Emperor Frederick II in the twelfth century we find a sovereign claiming a monopoly of certain industries, and the efforts of the gilds (themselves a monopoly) had always been in the direction of engrossing the local market.[1] In the case of the Merchant Adventurers and other "regulated" companies (so called because of certain self-imposed regulations after the manner of the gilds), any member, while enjoying the advantages of the company (for which he paid by contributions to its funds) was free to carry on his trade as an independent merchant. Parallel, however, with the regulated company, was a type which gradually supplanted it, known as the joint-stock company, which traded as a corporate body and whose members owned a part of the common stock and shared all profits or losses. The most famous examples of this type[2] were the English East India Company, founded in 1600, the Dutch East India Company (formed by the amalgamation of a number of smaller companies), founded in 1602, and the French East India Company, founded in 1664.

While some differences might be noted between the various charters which authorized these companies, nearly all had certain features in common. They were given a monopoly as against other merchants of the same country in a specified zone; they were empowered to acquire land, establish colonies or trading posts, and even to make laws in such regions under their sway and punish offenders against those laws; and by implication at least they

Imperial organization: (1) the chartered companies

---

[1] For the growth of monopoly practices to control the market in the sixteenth and seventeenth centuries see Gillespie, *A History of Europe, 1550–1815*, pp. 89–90.

[2] The Dutch East India Company became a joint-stock company in 1612, the British East India Company in 1614.

might make treaties with native princes and even wage war. It is evident from the powers conferred upon them that they exercised sovereign rights in the name of the government to whose allegiance they belonged. It goes without saying that their vessels were heavily armed for self-protection, or (as was sometimes the case with the Dutch) supplied with warships by the government. Unlike the Spanish and Portuguese merchants, most of the chartered companies enjoyed very large initiative, the government merely retaining the right to alter their status if it chose or to tax them as it pleased or to requisition their vessels for naval purposes if necessary. Some of the Continental companies, especially the French, were heavily subsidized by the government, but, in general, there was little difficulty in getting capital either through the selling of shares (transferable and generally divisible) or by raising loans. Most of them, for a time, were exceedingly lucrative speculations.

While for most countries the chartered company was the favorite method of commercial pioneering and trade with the East was destined to be so conducted for a long period, the rôle of the companies which had been formed to trade with the West proved less enduring. Whereas the countries in the East or in the tropics, characterized as they were by a dense population or an unhealthful climate, were not adapted to colonization, most of North America was but thinly peopled by natives and afforded abundant room for European settlement. As settlers in the English colonies gradually grew in number, they became less amenable to the control of a board of directors whose headquarters were in London. After failing in certain cases to protect the monopoly accorded the companies, the crown finally took the step of revoking their charters altogether (the only exception being the Plymouth Company, whose stock was bought out by the settlers themselves), and new methods were devised for administering the colonies. The North American colonies of Great Britain were something of an administrative experiment, and no uniform system of handling them was ever adopted. But this is, after all, rather typical of the British mind.

(2) Mer-cantilism

The growing importance of the chartered company, especially the evolution of the newer type, the joint-stock company, was one of those ways by which the self-conscious nations of Europe adapted themselves to the tremendous opportunities presented by the opening of vast new stores of wealth. Another means of meeting this shock of fortune was what became known as "mercantilism." As an economic conception it included first of all the notion of national self-sufficiency, and such an idea is readily enough explained by the emergence of the modern state itself, conscious of its unity, and determined to hold its own among its fellows. For the State to intervene to regulate industry and commerce on behalf of its larger interests had been a very early phenomenon, as we have noticed, and such a practice had been inherited from the towns. But mercantilism developed into something more aggressive than this idea of economic self-defense, as it were. It came to mean commercial aggression deliberately waged at the expense of one's neighbors. We have noted already the keenness of the competition for the trade of the East. The quantities of gold and silver which flowed from the West—at first through Spanish hands—seemed to dazzle an age which had already become used to a money economy but was as yet not wholly aware of the potential wealth concealed in credit. Hence it came to be generally believed that the accumulated stock of bullion was the index of a nation's wealth (the sudden greatness of Spain was regarded as proof of this fact), and therefore it became the policy of all governments to prevent all exportation of the precious metals [1] (an effort which quickly proved impracticable) and, above all, to attract as much of it as possible to their own dominions. This latter object was to be obtained [2] by securing what was known as a "favorable balance of trade." Each nation must sell to another more than it bought from it, it being assumed that the balance would be paid in specie. Hence, while colonies and other areas of exploitation furnished an abundance of raw materials, skilled artisans were pushed to turn out the finished product, and diplomacy did its best to widen the market for the export trade. Viewed in its natural historical setting, this quest of self-dependence and the effort to get the best of a commercial rival were a logical parallel to that process of political consolidation and territorial aggrandizement that formed the very keynote of the seventeenth century. And the object of all this was power. Mercantilism was inherent in the spirit of the age.

[1] Embargoes on money were, of course, not novel. They had been frequent in the Middle Ages because of the scarcity of gold and silver.

[2] A secondary method pursued by England was the plunder of the Spanish treasure-ships.

The part that colonies played in the system was of great importance. No longer viewed as limitless stores of gold (the mistaken lure of some of the earlier chartered companies), they were nevertheless to supply the mother country with things that would dispense her from buying elsewhere (England, for example, being able to get naval stores from America rather than having to buy them any longer from the Baltic lands), and, above all, to send her the raw materials that were needed for manufactures. The colony was, of course, not to be permitted to manufacture anything that might compete with any of the industries of the mother country, since it was also to provide an outlet for manufactured goods that could not readily be disposed of nearer home. Thus a cardinal feature of mercantilism was that the resources of the colonies were exclusively reserved to the mother country. Metropolis and colonies were together to form one economic unit—the colonies practically closed to the rest of the world,[1] the metropolis only opened to a certain extent under necessity and generally difficult to reach over a high tariff wall.

Besides the attainment of economic independence, partly through the possession of colonies, mercantilism strove for supremacy in commercial competition. This involved four things: the establishment of protective tariffs, designed not only to protect home industries but to discourage and sometimes even to prohibit the importation of foreign goods; the artificial stimulation of industry by government subsidies and other privileges, such as monopolies; the maintenance of high standards of quality for manufactured goods (enforced largely through the gilds, where this was practicable); and the securing of commercial treaties which would open markets on favorable terms for industrial products. The goal of all this endeavor was to force the foreigner to buy more than he sold, the balance being generally paid in specie. It was by the Methuen Treaty with Portugal in 1703 that Great Britain secured a monopoly of the Portuguese market for her goods and thus obtained a steady flow of gold from the mines of Brazil. Yet one must observe that, as time went on, the mercantilists—especially in England—gave much less weight to the purely monetary aspects of their doctrines. The unfavorable balance of trade which

[1] England did allow her colonies to trade with foreign countries in commodities she did not herself need. Thus some of Newfoundland's fish was transported to the Mediterranean. But the colonial policy of Spain was strictly exclusionist, and that of France and Holland also until well after the middle of the eighteenth century.

England had suffered in her relations with France was largely counterbalanced by the influx of Huguenot refugees who brought both their capital and technical skill to England's shores; and, as capitalism developed, the investments possessed by one people in the country of another tended often to bridge the gap between visible exports and imports. In any case, governmental regulation was designed to father and foster the native industries and enable them to get the best of foreign competitors.

If such were the main features of mercantilism,[1] we should note that there were some differences in scope or application. English mercantilist policy paid great attention to shipping, and the Navigation Acts, restricting more and more the list of commodities that could be imported in any but English ships, was one of the most rigorous applications of the mercantile system. It is noticeable also that in England, where the gilds were so nearly defunct that efforts to revive them signally failed, government control of industry was inevitably more direct, but, partly because of opposition to the Stuarts, it was only tolerably effective, whereas in France where the gilds formed a convenient economic unit, and where the crown built up large industries itself, government control was relatively easy. Finally we may note that Dutch tariffs were normally rather low—never prohibitive except when a tariff war happened to be raging—for the simple reason that Holland, whose life depended on her carrying trade, required the free flow of imports from all quarters. Mercantilism was not a formulated program. It had a general character and certain general objects but its application varied according to conditions. It may be observed that Prussia was in a sense the most mercantilist country of all since agriculture also was brought within its orbit.

Insofar as mercantilism was something of a planned economy and put a nation's prosperity above the interest of the individual or of a class, the concept held at bottom much that was sound. The business element was deemed to be selfish and to consider nothing else but personal profit. But such a policy of government control was carried to considerable lengths when Elizabeth forced

[1] The term is used here broadly as comprehending a general system of policy pursued by governments, susceptible, of course, to modification, as time went on. The mercantilist *writers* of the period so differed in their views that one cannot find in them a uniform body of doctrine. Moreover, many represented certain business interests and hence their sincerity is open to question. Mercantilism is therefore better understood by following the acts of the governing bodies of this period.

her subjects to eat fish on certain days in order to promote the
fishing industry and when James I tried to compel his people to
wear only clothes made from English fabrics. Acts for regulating
consumption, reminiscent of the sumptuary edicts of the Middle
Ages, became more and more unpopular, and the better alternative of achieving the same end by controlled and protected production proved much more efficacious, since the consumer had then
to take what he could get. But whatever its practical features,
mercantilism, as it was applied, often defeated its own ends. Raw
materials from abroad were sometimes thoughtlessly debarred
when certain industries needed them. The English Navigation
Acts often prevented the native shipper from getting the cargoes
he needed, and he pointed sometimes with envy to the more liberal
policy of the Dutch. Mercantilism also took too little account of
the fact that trade itself was broadly international and that hence
an unfavorable balance with one country might be more than made
up by a favorable balance with another. Not only did this truth
come to be realized in course of time but also the fact that prohibiting imports from a country had the effect of discouraging
that country from buying the stuff that produced exports—a
policy which thus reacted upon the prohibiter. Moreover, the
system led too frequently to commercial warfare, which, in turn,
led sometimes to actual war. When James I, in the interest of the
dyers, forbade the exportation of English cloth until it had first
been dyed and finished, the Dutch closed their ports to English
cloths of all sorts, and England was finally forced to recede, though
not until after both countries had suffered. In France under Colbert's guidance British goods were almost debarred, so high were
his tariffs; and during most of the eighteenth century England
similarly treated France [1] —acts which certainly contributed in a
measure to embitter relations. Louis XIV's war with Holland was
partly, as we have noted, the result of Colbert's tariffs. It is also
fairly evident that industry when fathered so much by a government (as in France) came to feel a spirit of dependence that inevitably discouraged enterprise. And finally—what Colbert, the
prince of mercantilists, did not realize—industries as narrowed
as the gild system required could not turn out the volume of goods
that capitalism was able more and more to render possible.

The joint stock company and the evolution of mercantilism

[1] Smuggling, of course, flourished on both sides.

were among the immediate results of the new imperialism, but both (to the extent they were applied) turned out to be transitory phenomena and may be regarded as experiments of national policy. The accumulation of wealth which came to Europe was something of more durable significance. The customs dues in England in 1660 amounted to £400,000 as against £36,000 in 1603, and a very large proportion of this growth must be accounted for by the over-sea trade. The finding of new commodities in distant lands was paralleled by the opening of new markets for Europe's manufactures. Moreover the rise of prices and the lowering of interest rates, both due to the increase of money in circulation, had a stimulating effect upon business. New avenues of investment were opened up, and many an emigrant to the new world made his fortune as a planter and then returned to his native home to enjoy its fruits. The French had profited less than the English and Dutch, for though a uniform coinage had finally been adopted, internal trade was still distracted by tolls, and people in France preferred to invest their savings in government bonds (*rentes*) than in productive business enterprises. Yet there is no doubt that France prospered, as the growth of her foreign trade distinctly showed.

Results of imperialism: (1) economic—the development of capitalism

But the most solid economic result of the new imperialism was the impetus given to capitalism in the economic life of Europe. No doubt the great influx of gold and silver from America, more than trebling the world's supply, had much to do with this. There was now more money in circulation and consequently more persons anxious to put it to profitable use. Hence the increased importance of banking, already made so profitable by the Fuggers, who, as soon as Spain had opened up the treasures of the new world, gained a direct share in the traffic in return for a generous loan to the Spanish crown. Even more striking as an example of a credit institution was the bourse or stock exchange of Antwerp where large stores of capital were accumulated and loaned out. The universal employment of standing armies, a conspicuous feature of the modern state, greatly encouraged the development of a money market from which loans could be readily obtained. When Antwerp declined, as a result of the Religious Wars, the center of the financial world shifted to Amsterdam, the Dutch having become the greatest capitalists of Europe by the end of the seventeenth century. In 1608 the Bank of Amsterdam had been founded—not only a place where money could be deposited and a clearing house of exchange (issuing drafts for sums of money sent from one country to another) but also a reservoir of capital which might be invested in profitable undertakings, such as one of the chartered companies. Banking was becoming more and more a corporate, less and less an individual or family affair. In 1694 the Bank of England had been founded, the original purpose of which was to issue paper money on the strength of the government's credit. Thanks also to increase of capital, interest rates were lowered and it is an evidence of the greater volume of business that prices became more stable, and less the result of bargain, as had been usual in pre-capitalistic Europe. The usual form of capitalistic organization was the "firm," whose personnel was variable and which possessed a legal status with collective obligations for all its debts. Joint-stock companies, though not numerous (at least before the end of the eighteenth century), were to be found not only in commerce but in industry as well. Due to a speculative mania in the early eighteenth century, this form of business organization (made possible by the practice of a more systematic accounting) came somewhat into disfavor for a time, but the very fact of this wild speculation showed the progress which capitalism had made.

Indeed, capitalism was making itself felt in all spheres of economic activity. Since the great commercial companies required a greater quantity of manufactured goods than industry organized under the gild system was able to produce, it became more and more customary for the capitalist to hand the raw material directly to a number of persons working in their homes (hence the term, the "domestic system"), who then turned it into the finished product. In France the government itself promoted capitalistic enterprises, some of the kings offering exemptions from taxation to persons who would promote large-scale production (*la grande industrie*), and the nobles were not only permitted but (actually) encouraged to lend their capital in such directions. Thus many of the leading magnates patronized mining or manufacturing; and there were some cases, indeed, where the government itself went into business.[1] On the whole capitalism in France had a slower development than in either England or Holland partly because

---

[1] For example Richelieu founded the royal printing press, and under Louis XIV the Gobelins tapestries became a government establishment. In Prussia and Russia there were also royal industries.

of the very fact that it was government-driven and less spontaneous and partly because, as we have said, the French investor preferred less venturesome forms of investment, such as an administrative post or government bonds. Yet a good deal of capital went into the purchase and development of landed estates, for, apart from the social motive, the greater profusion of money had led, in general, to the transformation of payments in kind owed by the peasant into what was equivalent to rent—a fact which tended to make agriculture an attractive field of investment. In England, as far back as the sixteenth century, much of the common land had been "enclosed"—that is, fenced in for grazing purposes, since sheep-raising had proved more profitable than farming. In the eighteenth century, however, agriculture revived through the use of capital, and another period of "enclosures" was the result. For a time, it may be added that while the volume of wealth had been greatly increased, it had also become more concentrated. It was the wealthy middle class that provided the luxuries of civilization, and thus made possible their enjoyment by kings and courts—not to mention, the wealthy aristocrat who made his annual pilgrimage to the capital for the "season."

The new imperialism, in fact, promoted many social changes. *(2) Social* The middle class were enriched, as never before, and veritable captains of industry, already noticeable in the sixteenth century, steadily multiplied. It is to be noted that an increasing number became ennobled. In England the buying of marks of heraldry became an increasing practice, and in France under Louis XIV as many as five hundred patents of nobility were purchased from the crown, while others were conferred through the buying of feudal estates. Perhaps it was the infusion of this new element into the French aristocracy that partly explains the decline of feudal enmity to the crown. And even the old aristocracy had not proved entirely immune against the pervading influence of capitalism. In England the survival of this class (destined to be extirpated in France) may have been due not only to its enjoyment of political functions but to the fact that "during the sixteenth and seventeenth centuries it was rapidly becoming an aristocracy of wealth,"[1]

---

[1] The American economist, Professor J. U. Nef, here quoted, has ascertained that a great many of this class were financially interested in the coal industry, and thinks that that helped to break down the old prejudice against having anything to do with business. His interesting discussion may be read in *The Rise of the British Coal Industry*, vol. iii, part 4, chap. iii.

and certainly this was more true in the eighteenth century when investment in over-sea trade had already made many fortunes. The nobleman's contempt for trade had at least no bearing on the use which he made of his capital. The money power had definitely invaded society, and courts were not the only centers of prodigal display. That the middle class itself attained a higher cultural level may perhaps be doubted. The plutocrats of Holland, perhaps because it flattered their sense of importance, did much for art and letters, but in England, if we are to believe the British historian of the middle class, this element showed lamentably little interest in such pursuits and preferred a country estate or a public career. The retired merchant became a baronet and hunted fox or game like the class whose ways he emulated.

At all events, the middle class grew noticeably in importance—a fact that we must remember when we come to discuss the origins of the French and Industrial Revolutions. The classes that profited least were the peasants who at times were exploited more than they had been of old, and the industrial proletariat, whose wages had not kept pace with the cost of living and who had no means of bettering their condition. Generally speaking, among the masses the standard of living was but little improved by these events, but for those who could afford the good things of life the material benefits accruing from this economic boom were without precedent in history. Coaches and carriages had come into use; windows were now glassed; knives, spoons, and forks made eating more agreeable; clocks and watches were fairly common; the diet was extended to include tea, coffee, and cocoa, not to mention gin and rum; sugar vied with spices for flavoring, while spices themselves had become cheaper and were no longer the monopoly of the very rich; and though certain tropical fruits could hardly survive the over-sea voyage, lemons and oranges came in profusion, and even some new vegetables, like the potato and the tomato. The pleasant pastime of smoking was also a direct result of the contact with the new world, though tobacco in the form of snuff was more usual in upper circles until the end of the eighteenth century. Many of the new conveniences, such as watches, pitchers, needles, and wire, were a product of that spirit of invention which, like the explorations, had been an important aspect of the Renaissance; and it is interesting to note the appearance of the umbrella—a welcome adaptation of the oriental parasol. The finest canes were made of wood which also came from the Far East, and the substitution of the walking-stick for the sword as part of the accouterment of the gentleman is an interesting illustration of the passing of the feudal influence in society. Dress was naturally much affected by the growth of manufactures and the cheapening of its output. Silk and velvet and (to some extent) wool were giving place to cotton and linen, and even among the masses the wearing of underclothing, as well as the use of bedding, became fairly general. Also noticeable was the greater variety of household effects, such as upholstered furniture and wall-paper (the latter, of Chinese origin). Such were but a few of the tangible effects upon society of this broadening of man's horizon.

The political results of the new imperialism were the founding *(3) Political* of colonial empires and the emergence of what we have called "world politics." Quarrels between different nations, ordinarily over exclusively European stakes, were little by little extending their scope to include a wider field. The fact that the transition was rather gradual may be ascribed partly to the tenacity of the old orientation, partly to the delegation of political responsibility to private companies, and partly to the vastness of the undeveloped area and the feeble resistance of those pioneer world powers, Spain and Portugal. For nearly two centuries after the great explorations the vultures which fed upon the carcasses of the Spanish and Portuguese empires found enough to keep them preoccupied without becoming seriously involved with one another. Yet such clashes as occasionally occurred were premonitions of the more acute rivalry to come, and showed the continuity of world politics. In the East, where the spoils of Portugal were an object of contention between English and Dutch, the English became firmly established in India, but they were pushed out of the East Indies by their rivals, who stained their record by the "massacre of Amboyna." The rôle of the Dutch in the seventeenth century was of such transcendent importance as to deserve some special attention.

The Maritime Ascendancy of Holland and Its Collapse

The maritime ascendancy which the Dutch enjoyed in the first *Founda-* half of the seventeenth century affords an example of what a *tions and aspects of* shrewd and energetic people can accomplish when confronted *Dutch* with a marvelous opportunity. Even before the great explorations *ascendancy* and the launching of imperialism the Dutch had shown themselves the most enterprising people in all Europe. Living in a country largely reclaimed from the sea by dikes and pumps and having little room to expand, they had small incentive to develop agriculture (though they raised enough food for their own needs) and gave their chief attention to fishing and trading. One has only to recall that they supplied a goodly portion of Catholic Europe with fish, that they became the chief purveyors of the spices brought by the Portuguese to Europe, and that they had gradually wrested from the Hanse towns the commercial supremacy of the Baltic. They had almost a monopoly of the transport trade of Europe, for their freight charges were lower than those of any competitor. When the circumstances we have noted sent them direct to the East, they were qualified to become the heirs to Portugal's fortune. In seamanship, commercial experience, and business capacity, as well as in the size of their merchant marine and the quality of their navy they easily outclassed all rivals. England under James I was hesitant and vacillating and under Charles I was drawn into the maelstrom of civil war. France, the other possible competitor, was still seeking natural frontiers or absorbed in the final struggles between the nobility and the crown. At the time when Fortune offered men her greatest store of opportunity and in an age when competition always held the germs of war it was assuredly for the Dutch a second stroke of luck that their powerful neighbors were still but half awake to the situation.

We have already indicated that the Dutch appropriated the East Indies and by so doing got a monopoly of the spice trade. Since some of the islands, notably Java, were also rich in coffee, they had a most lucrative trade in that commodity as well. While they made no special effort to establish themselves in India, they got a foothold on the rich island of Ceylon, and were the only ones to set up a station in Japan. Moreover, the ease with which they acquired their tropical possessions, in short, the cheapness of their conquests, gave them a distinct advantage. They had only savages to subdue, and, as a rule, there was no need to establish settlements. Only in New Amsterdam, where it was necessary to keep open the route of the Hudson for the traffic in furs did the Dutch deliberately colonize what they had taken, and the fact that some of their number did settle at the Cape of Good Hope was rather an accident than the result of deliberate policy; the Cape, like Ceylon, served as a coaling station, and was originally acquired for that

DUTCH MERCHANTMEN OF THE SEVENTEENTH CENTURY

Engraving by Zeeman

215

purpose. For a considerable period there was no empire so intelligently administered as Holland's, no companies so well organized as hers or which received such wholehearted national backing. The companies were required to report each year to the national assembly, the estates general, and its books were open to government inspection; and while it is true that only a limited number of persons were directly involved, nevertheless these companies—and especially the East India Company—represented a large share of the accumulated capital of the nation. Since, moreover, the trade with the East was the most lucrative trade in the world, one may easily account for the rise of stupendous fortunes.

Yet it would be a mistake in studying the maritime ascendancy of the Dutch to place undue emphasis on the East Indian trade. Most of the coastal trade of Europe was in their hands—which, of course, meant most of the sea-borne freight. Moreover their trade in the North and Baltic Seas is believed to have represented a greater number of ships and more volume than all the rest of their commerce put together. While it is true that the tribute which Denmark levied on merchantmen entering the Baltic had led the Dutch to open a way into Russia from the north, they were shrewd enough to give their support to Denmark against Sweden and thereby secured a reduction of these tolls. Though it was secondary to fishing and maritime trade, Holland was active also in manufacturing. Her cloth and linen industries were flourishing institutions, and in printing and book-making she left all competitors far behind. Her damp soil was also well adapted to market gardening, and the raising of choice plants became a hobby of the wealthy. Finally, we may recall that Holland was during her heyday the banking center of Europe, and capital became so plentiful that in no country was the interest so low—often five or four per cent. It would be a mistake to assume that everyone was wealthy—there were poor workmen in the factories and poor peasants who barely made a living—but there was less poverty in proportion to the population then in any other land and more governmental agencies for public welfare.

The "golden age" of Holland   The rôle of Venice in the Middle Ages has shown that where there is great wealth there is also splendor, and during her halcyon days Holland's position as a center of culture was quite unrivaled. It was characteristic of a practical people that religious freedom should be allowed. Though only Calvinists could hold public office (and the real political plums were a monopoly of the few), the Dutch took their Calvinism lightly, many of them being actually free-thinkers; and for practical purposes it behooved them to welcome refugees from other lands. Thus certain great philosophers pursued their studies unhindered in Holland, and it was from a Dutch printing-press that the most famous work of the great radical, Rousseau, saw the light. Naturally, the Dutch themselves provided writers, one of whom, Hugo Grotius, was undoubtedly one of the most learned men of his day. Rembrandt was merely one of the many geniuses who honored the Dutch school of art and whose paintings adorned the comfortable homes of opulent burghers. Many of them travelers in distant lands, the Dutch were the most enlightened and probably the most interesting people of this age. Their period of prosperity was in great degree a tribute to their intelligence. But the clouds were not far distant.

With all the ability of the Dutch they could not in the nature *Causes of* of things perpetuate their good fortune. In the first place, their *collapse* government was weak and unable readily to meet a national emergency. The Republic of the United Provinces, as it was called, was a loose federation of seven sovereign states. For common affairs there was an estates general, composed of delegates from each of these provinces, who were bound by instructions and whose transactions were therefore subject to intolerable delays. There was also an executive body, the council of state, likewise representative, but it was quite overshadowed by the estates general, which had the direction of foreign affairs and even military and naval matters. Yet on all important questions unanimity was required— a condition which made it possible for any province to prevent action. Such elements of unity as existed in this land lay, rather, outside the constitution. Each province had a *stadhouder* or chief executive, and it was customary for the leading member of the house of Orange to be chosen by most of the provinces, though after the abortive effort of one of the family to turn his position into that of an hereditary monarch of the whole state the office was abolished in five of the provinces, and the Orange party for a while suffered eclipse. A more effective element of unity was the predominance of the middle class whose interests centered in Holland, a province so far surpassing the others in wealth and population that its name was commonly given to the nation as a whole. Yet here again we discern an element of weakness. The very wealth of these prosperous burghers had an enervating effect; becoming a leisure class, they were all too easily lulled to a false security. Moreover, the privileged position of this narrow plutocracy, which monopolized most of the offices, excited jealousy among those whose wealth was unequal to buying favors; while the partisans of the house of Orange, who represented monarchical as against republican principles, had the natural temptation to take every advantage of a national crisis in order to undermine the rule of the merchant princes.

And secondly—and what is more important—Holland was too small a country to defend itself against great powers like England and France, should they ever care to challenge her position or threaten her independence. It was only a question of time when envy and dislike of this fortunate nation would bring on that test of strength to which the Dutch were intrinsically unequal. The first to strike them a blow were the English.

Collapse of Dutch ascendancy

When the Stuart régime gave way temporarily to the Commonwealth, England in the person of Oliver Cromwell resumed a policy more in keeping with the national interest. Impressed by the dominance which the Dutch enjoyed in shipping (even most of England's sugar trade with the West Indies was carried in Dutch ships), the English parliament passed the famous Navigation Act of 1651, which forbade the importation of foreign goods into English ports except in English vessels or in those of the countries which had produced the goods. The act was obviously aimed at the Dutch. While it is too much to say that it dealt their carrying trade a mortal blow, their activities were certainly limited to a marked degree. Naturally they were thrown into consternation, for thousands of their ships were compelled to lie idle, and acute economic depression at once set in. Negotiations between the countries seemed only to envenom the English government, which set out to enforce its claim to the sovereignty of neighboring seas (which it designated as "English waters") by insisting that every Dutch captain lower his flag and fire a salute on meeting an English ship. The seizure of Dutch ships to search for contraband proved the last straw, and a collision between the navies soon followed. This proved to be the first of three wars between the two nations growing out of commercial interests. While the Dutch put up a gallant resistance and sometimes worsted their adversaries, they came out, in general, the losers; and, besides the compulsion to cede New Amsterdam, they were greatly exhausted by the loss of trade occasioned by the struggle. In fact, considering that their vessels normally dotted the seas, Dutch trade was particularly vulnerable, and England had little to lose and everything to gain by such a struggle. In the third war—the second to be fought under the Stuart restoration—Holland was forced to face not only England but France of Louis XIV. We have elsewhere [1] dealt with this war, and observed what a close call she had. We need only mention here that Colbert, like Cromwell, had been anxious to free his country from commercial dependence on the Dutch, and regardless of the fact that the French merchant marine was inadequate to provide the necessary facilities to French trade, the Dutch had been excluded from all trade with the French West Indies, and mercantilism was thus given a conspicuous demonstration.

It was long before Holland recovered from these catastrophic events, and her former commercial ascendancy was never regained. During the eighteenth century her decline was in proportion to England's gain, and Frederick the Great put it pithily when he said that she was a little boat in the wake of a great ship. Indeed, the old quality of putting up a fight against great odds had seemingly been crushed under the blessings she had long enjoyed; and now the national fiber was sapped by internal jealousies and political corruption, as well as by reckless speculation—often the desperate recourse of the weak. London succeeded Amsterdam as the financial capital of the world, and when the Bank of Amsterdam, that former symbol of honest credit, collapsed with the ruin of the East India Company, the Dutch may be said to have drunk their cup of bitterness to its dregs. Even as imperialists they had not been above reproach, for they had shown too great a disposition to make their fortunes quickly, and the destruction of the spice trees in the East Indies had not only alienated the natives but seriously impaired the value of these colonies. Yet Holland had not given up her eminence without a struggle, and if she had not, in defeat, shown sufficient dignity or vigor, it yet remains true that the chief cause of her downfall was the inexorable fact that in politics as in other things the victory is to the strong.

Decline of Holland

The elimination of Holland brought the French and English face to face.

[1] See page 98.

THE ANGLO-FRENCH STRUGGLE—THE TRIUMPH OF BRITISH IMPERIALISM

Origins of the struggle
The general explanation of the Anglo-French struggle for colonial supremacy is to be found in the value of the lands opened by exploration and the readiness with which men will fight for lucre unless properly restrained. Perhaps the most interesting fact in the evolution of the struggle is that the inception came much more from companies and colonies than from the home governments themselves. The very logic which had underlain the chartered company was that it took from the mother country the major responsibility in empire-building. Whether it made war or not in pursuit of its ends was, generally speaking, its own affair, and there were occasions—for example, the Anglo-Dutch struggles in the Far East and the Anglo-French fighting in Canada during the Thirty Years' War—when the home governments studiously avoided being embroiled. Yet if such conflicts became chronic or seriously acute, it would be difficult for the mother countries to stand aloof. The fact that some English had been murdered by the Dutch on the Island of Amboyna had been one of the contributive causes of the feud between England and Holland. Perhaps, indeed, the companies would find such problems more than they could handle—a circumstance that would tend to throw responsibility back to its original source. It is obvious that the stakes were too great to be appropriated by any power without a struggle, and neither France nor Great Britain was prepared to yield primacy to the other. Then, apart from the underlying causes of conflict, there was, of course, the fact that boundary lines between their respective empires had never been clearly determined. Did possession depend on exploration or settlement? What was the meaning of this or that treaty stipulation, when precise geographical knowledge was really not at hand? In the case of India—by what right did such and such a potentate make a concession instead of some rival claimant to the throne? Such, however, were rather pretexts for war than causes. In an age when mercantilism was basic of all commercial policy and colonies considered as reservoirs of wealth, such a thing as peaceful competition or a colonial "equilibrium" was almost beyond conception. Moreover, in the case of the English and French we have the example of two people who had always felt mutually alien if not hostile, and

during the reign of Louis XIV had been twice at war with each
other.

Looking forward apace to the struggle, it was to be fought in
three arenas: North America, the West Indies, and India. In North
America the French had explored the Mississippi country, the
basin of the Great Lakes, and the St. Lawrence valley, and had
established themselves on Newfoundland and Nova Scotia, as
well as at New Orleans, near the mouth of the Mississippi. The
fur trade with the Indians was the chief lure in Canada, and the
Atlantic fisheries formed the attraction to Newfoundland and
Nova Scotia. The English colonists also had a taste of the fur
trade, especially after the acquisition of New Amsterdam—which
linked, by the way, the northern group of colonies with the southern; they were also tempted to cross the Alleghenies, a natural
barrier between the rival zones, but in so doing they deliberately
encroached on a sphere that France already looked upon as hers.
On the whole, we may judge that the English were the aggressors,
though it could be urged that a few isolated forts and trading posts
were hardly a reasonable basis for the French claim over half a
continent. In the Caribbean area the English possessed the greatest number of islands, including the Bahamas, the Barbados, the
Leewards, and Jamaica; but the French islands, Martinique,
Guadaloupe, and San Domingo were incomparably, the richer,
chiefly because of their sugar. Both people traded in African slaves,
since both needed them for labor in their semi-tropical colonies.
While this demonstrates that the commercial and to some extent
the industrial economy of Europe was based largely upon slave
labor, the moral obloquy of this practice must not be overemphasized. These negroes were often already slaves in Africa where the
traffic had long been flourishing, and since it was an age when most
peasants in Europe were serfs and little distinguishable in their
status from slaves, it cannot be thought strange that the conscience
of the seventeenth century was not shocked by such a traffic.

The chief theater of the struggle was, of course, to be India.
Here, unlike the Western Hemisphere, was a fairly dense population, certain elements of which possessed a civilization from which
the West had something to learn. Politically India was until early
in the eighteenth century under a single rule, the Mogul dynasty,
but this rule was never consolidated, and with the collapse of the
central power, the formerly subject princes became independent

*Theaters of
the struggle*

sovereigns. This condition of decay and disruption laid India readily open to European encroachment. It also rendered the Indian problem peculiarly complex, for it gave rival trading companies the opportunity to back different princes or—as was frequently the case—pretenders to the thrones of certain princes. Of the enormous value of India there was no question. While it is true that the development of the silk industry in Europe had somewhat reduced the demand for Indian silks, it was still the source of the choicest fabrics as well as gems, perfumes, pepper, and many articles of oriental art. Especially valuable to industrial countries was the raw cotton which was easily grown there. Its pepper was all the more prized by the English since the other spices had become a monopoly of the Dutch—though when sugar came to be imported, the spice trade faced a competitor which somewhat diminished its former pre-eminence. One of the problems of the English trade with India was to find the precious metals to pay for her produce—for, such, in general, was all that the natives were willing to take; and it was on this ground largely that the traffic in slaves, paid for by the Spaniards in gold, was to England of such transcendent importance. It was the English, more than the Dutch, that had shattered the position of Portugal in India, where she was finally reduced to a few precarious footholds (though still the only power which possessed a station in China). Gaining the favor of the mogul, the English had established their first emporium at Surat in 1612 (for which they paid an annual sum), but later they moved their western mart to Bombay, which they acquired from Portugal in 1661. On the eastern side they established themselves at points near the modern towns of Madras and Calcutta, and these establishments, being fortified, were a step toward the future conquest of the peninsula. While the Dutch, after some efforts at penetration, had come to confine themselves to Ceylon and the East Indies, the French under Colbert's leadership became the strongest competitor in the field. Undaunted by the failure of three earlier Indian companies (Richelieu's had foundered, so to speak, on Madagascar), Colbert founded a new company in 1664, which dealt directly with the mogul, and established its headquarters at Pondicherry on the east coast. Later other "factories," as trading posts were called, were established at various points. On the whole, however, in spite of the cleverness of the French governors, the trade with India did not prosper, and the company was bankrupt by the close of the seventeenth century. Had not the government intervened, and reorganized it in 1723, the French would most likely have dropped out of India. As it was, the lease of life which they renewed prepared them to meet their rivals on more than equal terms, and the contest for India was destined to be the most dramatic chapter of the Anglo-French duel.

In forecasting this struggle between France and Great Britain for colonial supremacy it may be well to compare their capacity as world powers; for the result of such a scrutiny may explain the ultimate outcome. *Comparison of the contestants*

In the first place, Great Britain was better able to give concentrated attention to colonial development. Being an island and having no need to seek better frontiers or to defend what she had—except by naval superiority in the Channel—she did not have to carry the burden of Continental struggles (her subsidies and a small army being a relatively slight investment), and her policy could, accordingly be directed outside of Europe. It was the Continental distraction which had kept France from taking an active part in the explorations—though this fact, it may be remembered, was rather due to the ineptitude of the Valois kings than to any practical element in their policy of aggrandizement. Under the first two Bourbon kings France showed a real desire to carve out an empire and actually inaugurated such a movement, but the need of making herself defensible in Europe naturally forbade any great activity in colonization, and hence it was not till the time of Louis XIV and Colbert that a real foundation was laid for French power across the seas. Yet the impetus was not maintained, for Louis' later wars and the subsidies paid to his allies (not to mention an expensive court) so completely absorbed her resources that the colonies received but scant attention.

In the second place, the English people were much more interested than the French in over-sea commerce and colonization. Probably part of this explanation is temperamental—a factor attributable partly to geography and partly to history. The English, an island people, were more naturally drawn to the sea for their livelihood; they were thus quick to avail themselves of new opportunities offered (we have but to remember how they eked profit out of the long feud with Spain), and, taking them as a whole, they were probably more adventurous than the French.

Besides, manufacturing, which is essentially calculated to profit from imperialism, had an early start in England, and her merchants were always looking for new openings; France, on the other hand, was more essentially agricultural. Satisfied in the long run with smaller returns, the French peasant was hard to transplant; while the French merchant preferred less risky enterprises nearer home. Whereas the younger scions of the English nobility, having no hope of inheriting anything, were only too glad to try their fortunes across the seas, this class in France—until special enactments of Louis XIV—was excluded by tradition from having anything to do with commerce. Many of the landed aristocracy in England were directly interested in commercial enterprises, whereas in France, where every noble inherited some land, it practically limited its interest to agriculture, plus, sometimes, a royal pension. Thus English colonial policy was spontaneous; that of France was, generally speaking, artificial—prompted and stimulated by a government which had to bribe and almost dragoon its subjects into participation. Due chiefly to differences in temperament and environment, this difference in spirit may also be explained by the contrast in the character of the two governments. After getting rid of autocratic rule in the Revolution of 1688 and developing cabinet government during the Hanoverian period the English aristocracy, which controlled parliament and government, was able to secure the support of commercial enterprises which their own interest dictated. The French, on the other hand, had never ceased to be morally subjected to a paternalism (even to some extent to the deadening influence of the gilds), and economic initiative was therefore rather discouraged and bound to be a slower growth. Imperialism was never a national issue with the French as with the English.

Since imperialism had much less interest for the French, it was difficult to attract them to the colonies. Louis XIV, as will be remembered, debarred Huguenots from his colonies, whereas England, in spite of official intolerance at home, allowed dissenters, whether Catholic or Protestant, to find asylums in America. If we also recall that the English charters allowed the English colonies a measure of self-government, while the French colonies were subjected to bureaucratic control, we can see an additional reason for a more rapid and perhaps we might add, more wholesome colonial development among the English than among the

French. It is an interesting paradox that among the French who rose to leadership in colonial development there were greater flashes of ability displayed than among the English. The former had a much greater knack of getting on with the Indians, for example, and there are few names in British colonial annals to be compared with those of the great explorers, Champlain and La Salle or such colonial governors as Martin, Frontenac, Duquesne, Montcalm, and Dupleix. Yet the more solid qualities of the English colonists as a whole were more contributive to success than the brilliance of a Montcalm or a Dupleix. Then, too, generally speaking, the French who did participate in colonization were too anxious, like the Dutch, to make their fortunes quickly. In America they were largely traders with the Indians rather than settlers. The English, on the other hand, made homes for themselves and became a stable and enduring force. British imperialism was not so humane, it is true, for whereas the French made efforts to convert the Indian, and win his sympathy, the English treated him as a nuisance and cheated him out of his lands, but the greed of the English settlers was not as a rule to their detriment, since the Indians were not united and were not equipped to resist them. It was a steady, pushful tenacity underlying a genuine spirit of enterprise, unscrupulous or otherwise, that made the English the superior force in their rivalry with the French.

In the third place, France, in the exhausting pursuit of her land objects, had let her navy, like her colonies, languish. The English navy, on the other hand, was steadily developed and augmented. If ever the two powers came to blows, the English had the superior weapon with which to decide the issue.

Finally it might be added that when the crucial test came, Great Britain found a man of genius (the elder Pitt) to display the leadership and driving power necessary to success, while France in the nerveless hands of Louis XV, who squandered the national revenues on a Pompadour, was in no wise equipped to make the most of her resources. Probably by the eighteenth century she would have lost the battle for the other reasons we have mentioned, but the incapacity of the government will easily explain the extent of her disasters.

While the struggle between these rivals was long foreshadowed, *Evolution* it was some time before either government was fully aroused, and *and course* indeed one may say that they were pushed into the struggle by *of the* *struggle* force of circumstances. The wars of Louis XIV had, of course, had their echoes across the seas. While the East India companies really preferred to keep out of the quarrel, the British government forced the issue, and the French lost Pondicherry to the Dutch, who, however, returned it at the Peace of Ryswick. In North America there was a parallel struggle between English and French colonists with varying success. It was more because of France's reverses in Europe that Great Britain made a distinct stride forward. By the Utrecht Settlement she not only got the exclusive contract to supply the Spanish colonies with slaves (a right previously extorted by the French), but also got the Hudson Bay territory (long in dispute), Nova Scotia, and Newfoundland. Thus New France was hemmed in on two sides, while the vagueness of the boundary lines between the opposing empires gave ground for future trouble. After another interval of peace there was another war both in America and India, corresponding to the War of the Austrian Succession, and this, again, was indecisive. Finally in the 'fifties the rivalry of colonists in America reached a crisis which brought the whole issue of imperialism into the foreground, and led on the part of Great Britain to active intervention.

The news of the defeat of a small force of English colonials at the hands of French and Indians in 1754 led an active party in British politics, of whom the king's son, the Duke of Cumberland and Henry Fox were prime-movers, to instigate the sending of a force of British regulars under Edward Braddock to avenge the disaster. While there was still nominal peace between the two governments the War Party in London was ready now to challenge France; and a French squadron *en route* to Quebec was attacked by a British fleet in July, 1755. Even so the pusillanimous government of Louis XV tried to avoid formal hostilities—the more so as it was being drawn into the Seven Years' War—but the rush of events was too much for it. Some initial defeats of the British— including the loss of Braddock's army—led meanwhile to a change of ministries at London, and William Pitt, afterwards Earl of Chatham, became the consuming force which swept the British to victory both on sea and on land, and led to a decisive issue both in Canada and in India. The participation of Spain in the war on the side of France had only served to make British success the more decisive. More than anything else, it had been British sea power that had given the victory to Great Britain.

In India the course of the struggle was peculiar, one side having at first distinctly the advantage, and then when it lost, it lost completely. Borrowing the idea from the Portuguese, the French had early adopted the practice of mixing in native politics. Moreover, they had grasped the fact that the native troops, or "Sepoys," as they were called, when trained and officered by Europeans, became an exceedingly effective means of defending and even extending the company's interests. Under Joseph Dupleix, who became governor general in 1739, the French company revealed a definite policy. Dupleix saw well enough that commercially the French could not compete with the English. It was, therefore, his policy to ingratiate himself with the more powerful princes, and by building up a political power based on military strength and native favor, to drive the English out of India. Since he could expect but little support from the government at home, he had to place his chief dependence on native troops, and in carrying the heavy expenses of his program he soon ran his company heavily into debt. Dupleix was a daring and patriotic gambler, but neither his daring nor his patiotism was appreciated by the government of Louis XV. Though the advent of Robert Clive to defend the interests of the English company naturally intensified the struggle (for Clive was a worthy opponent of the Frenchman and quick to copy his methods), no support was sent to Dupleix; and when the company had denounced his policy and it appeared from the complaints of the British that his activities were disturbing the "peace" between the two companies, his government recalled him. This was in 1754, just on the eve of the decisive conflict. Since France had now thrown away her best instrument, the success of Clive was assured. After some striking victories over the French and their native allies the British conquered Bengal, which was to constitute a base for their future empire in India. As France was only permitted to retain her factories on condition that she would not raise native troops, she was powerless further to challenge British predominance in India.

Thus the struggle for colonial supremacy had ended in the decisive victory of the British. It was a struggle that cost even the victors considerable sacrifice. High prices for the consumer and temporary losses to trade through the profitable privateering of the French had taxed the national patience, even if they did not produce misgivings. But, possessed now of the largest colonial

Significance of the struggle

empire and a volume of maritime trade that left her competitors far behind, Great Britain had emerged from the conflict the richest and probably also the most powerful of the European nations. And her greatest rival had been humbled. Of all the French possessions there remained only a few holdings on the African coast, French Guiana, some of the West Indies, a few factories in India, two small islands off the coast of Newfoundland (for fishing purposes), and two islands in the Indian Ocean near Madagascar. Henceforth British imperialism—for more than a century at least—became the dominant force in world politics. Yet the French were not yet reconciled to defeat, and the contest was scarcely over when the British Empire was shaken by a formidable convulsion.

WORLD POLITICS IN UPHEAVAL

Causes of the American Revolution

The fundamental cause of the American Revolution was the rise of a nationality, in the making of which geography and temperament were the decisive factors. The distance of the American colonies from the mother country and the boundless space which they occupied made them feel a detachment and self-confidence that tended toward independence. The fact also that they were Englishmen made them peculiarly sensitive to dictation, and the habit of initiative which had been bred in the colonies by the circumstances of their origin, the self-reliance of the companies, and the degree of self-government conferred upon the settlers, accentuated this attitude. As soon as the French had been expelled from Canada, they ceased to need, as they supposed, the military aid of the home government, while the degree of economic control exercised by the mother country seemed to them simply an outworn and irksome form of bondage.

As a triumph of the spirit of nationalism or the vindication of popular rights the American Revolution had a political significance which was perhaps more American than European. But as a protest against mercantilism it had an economic importance that was destined to be far-reaching. Mercantilism, as relating to the English colonies, had been given a definite application by the Navigation Act of 1660 during the reign of Charles II when imperial policy had been largely reformulated. By this act certain colonial products, including cotton, sugar, hides, tobacco, and masts, could be exported only to Great Britain, and imports to the colonies from foreign countries might come to them only through or from Great Britain. The colonies were also prohibited from manufacturing anything that would compete with the industries of the mother country. Port duties in the colonies were collected in the colonies, not so much as a source of revenue as a means of seeing that these regulations were observed and that no trade with foreign countries might be possible. At the same time the colonies had certain reciprocal advantages. A series of "drawbacks" on foreign goods which had been taxed in British ports made such articles actually cheaper in the colonies than in England. Moreover, certain colonial products, though confined to the British market, were allowed a monopoly of that market, and were sometimes further aided by government bounties. As a matter of fact the regulations which might have cramped the colonies had not been well enforced, and the New Englanders had long been carrying on a thriving contraband trade with the French West Indies. When shortly after the accession of George III in 1760 the regulations became more rigidly applied, there was a natural irritation. The political grievances of the colonists were not serious before 1765, though the colonial governors, generally [1] appointed by the crown, had in some cases failed to get along with a difficult people and been recalled.

The issue which really produced a breach between the colonies and the metropolis was the question of imperial taxation. The inability of the colonies to defend themselves against a sudden Indian attack—a fact demonstrated by Pontiac's rebellion in 1764 —had emphasized the need of a standing army of regular soldiers, while naval protection was at the same time required in the event that France should wage a war of retaliation. Heavily burdened with debt from the expensive armaments which had won the late war, the British government felt that the American colonies, requiring as they did both military and naval protection, should contribute something to the expense. It was perfectly willing that the colonists themselves should devise the means, but, as it happened, there was so much jealousy among the colonies themselves, so much fear on the part of each that it might be expected to bear more than its just share of the common burden, that it became

---

[1] The governor was in some cases chosen by the proprietor or group of proprietors to whom the charter had been granted. In Pennsylvania the proprietor himself filled the position analogous to that of governor.

manifest that no scheme sponsored by the colonies themselves was to be expected. The experiment of the famous Stamp Act of 1765 was the government's solution. It led to the cry of "no taxation without representation," and the colonies refused to allow the tax to be imposed. In other words there was open rebellion. Though the offensive measure was annulled and the government later tried to impose a light tax on tea and other commodities before being exported to the colonies—actually a lower tax than was paid by the English importer and consequently making tea cheaper in America than in England—the colonists again resisted, and consignments of tea were destroyed in Boston harbor. Certain penal measures followed, the home government having now determined to enforce respect for the crown, and bloodshed at Lexington and Concord in 1775 brought matters to a crisis. The War of American Independence had begun.

Intervention of France

We shall not follow the course of this weary struggle. The conduct of the war was grievously mismanaged by the British; yet the colonists would probably not have triumphed without foreign aid. It was not without reason that the British ministers had felt the need of defending the empire against French attack.

The accession of the Duke of Choiseul to office as secretary of state for foreign affairs in 1758 had brought a belated vigor into French policy before the end of the Seven Years' War. It was due to him that Spain had been brought into the war, and it was his dexterity that was partly responsible for saving his country certain losses at the Peace of Paris, which closed the struggle. Choiseul was an adept at intrigue and was something of an adventurer, but he was nevertheless a statesman of no small ability, and his sympathy with the more liberal tendencies of the day together with his fervent patriotism made him a refreshing contrast to the rest of the decrepit court of Louis XV. After the Seven Years' War he made it his business to improve France's position in Europe and to strengthen her in all respects for a renewal of the struggle. He cultivated close relations with Spain and Austria, and was responsible for the marriage of the dauphin, Louis, with the Archduchess Marie Antoinette—a union which proved to have a significance that he could never have foreseen. By an adroit use of his opportunities he carried through the purchase of Corsica from Genoa in 1768 in the teeth of British jealousy and opposition. He even dreamed of acquiring Egypt—a plan which later developed into an attempt, with Turkish consent, to reopen the short route to the East and thereby neutralize the advantages the British had won in India.[1] Above all, he was busy building up the military and naval power of France, looking forward to an eventual renewal of the struggle with Great Britain. When he fell in 1770 owing to a court intrigue, he bequeathed this policy of revenge to Vergennes, the secretary of state for foreign affairs under Louis XVI, who came to the throne in 1775.

It was the Count of Vergennes who took advantage of Great Britain's embroilment with America to deal his country's rival the long-intended blow. The Americans had already sought French aid, and not only was money loaned by the French government, but French officers, including that liberal nobleman, the Marquis of Lafayette, volunteered for the American service. In 1778 France, having signed a treaty of alliance with the Continental Congress, declared war against Great Britain; and the next year, her ally, Spain followed suit. When, two years later, a league of neutral powers was formed to defend their shipping against British interference in search of contraband, the plight of Great Britain seemed extreme. The independence of the American colonies, which meant the disruption of the British Empire, and the recovery of a few colonies by the Treaty of Versailles (1783) seemed to justify French policy. But it must not be supposed that France had eclipsed her rival. She had not even tried to recover Canada, and since she had ceded Louisiana to Spain in 1763 (the price of Spanish participation in the previous war), she was now without a foothold on the American continent. Moreover, the doorway to the East was barely opened. The dubious conduct of the Mamelukes [2] who ruled Egypt, the hesitation of the French crown to use coercion (since Egypt was a nominal dependency of Turkey), and a quarrel among groups of merchants for a monopoly of the trade prevented the enterprise from making any headway. It is chiefly important as a legacy to the Revolution and Bonaparte.

Yet companies and monopolies and in fact all the paraphenalia of the mercantile system were clearly doomed. The success of the American Revolution had demonstrated the practical dangers that were involved, and the rise of more liberal theories—a subject *The passing of mercantilism*

---

[1] Such designs go back at least to the time of Richelieu. Colbert had made an unsuccessful effort to reopen this route.

[2] Twenty-four beys who ruled various divisions of Egypt, and were almost independent of Turkey, the suzerain power.

that will concern us later—was a challenge to the very basis of the system. Already Choiseul had relaxed the regulations as applied to the French West Indies, allowing them to trade with the British colonies,[1] and the Wars of the French Revolution, which at times cut off the French colonies from all contact with the motherland, made it impossible ever to go back to the old tutelage. Only by tariffs would the European Powers seek any longer to absorb the trade of their colonies. The revolt of the South American colonies ended the system as applied by Spain, and the British government repealed the Navigation Acts before the middle of the nineteenth century. World politics were to continue, but the attempt to maintain a closed economic unit was apparently a thing of the past.

FOR FURTHER READING OR STUDY

Robinson and Beard, *Readings in Modern European History*, vol. i, chaps. vi and vii; Reddaway, W. F., *Select Documents of European History*, vol. ii, chap. iv; Cheyney, E. P., *Readings in English History*, chap. vi, esp. sec. v.

Hayes, C. J. H., *A Political and Cultural History of Modern Europe*, vol. i, 76–95 (excellent on the results of imperialism), chap. ix (rise of the British Empire), and pp. 469–95 (American Revolution); Gillespie, J. E., *A History of Europe, 1500–1815*, chaps. v (mercantilism and the companies), xvi (Holland), xviii (Anglo-French duel), and xix (American Revolution); Ogg, F. A., *Economic Development of Modern Europe*, chaps. i–iv; Day, C., *A History of Commerce*, part iii; Nussbaum, F. L., *A History of the Economic Institutions of Modern Europe* (based on a work of the German scholar, Sombart, and very suggestive and illuminating), parts ii and iii; Lunt, W. E., *History of England*, chap. xxx; Cross, A. L., *History of England and Greater Britain*, chaps. xli and xliii.

Abbott, W. C., *The Expansion of Europe*, 2 vols. (broader in scope than the title indicates and rather superficial); Muir, P., *The Expansion of Europe* (a brief sketch) chaps. i–iii; Cunningham, *An Essay on Western Civilization in Its Economic Aspects*, vol. ii, book v; Renard, C., and Weulersse, G., *Life and Work in Modern Europe* (interesting); Cheyney, E. P., *Economic Background of American History*, chaps. vii and viii (trading companies); Barnes, H. E., *World Politics in Modern Civilization* (clear and suggestive and on this earlier period very objective), chaps. ii–v; Linden, H. V., "Alexander VI and the Demarcation of the Maritime and Colonial Dominions of Spain and Portugal," *Amer. Hist. Rev.*, xxii, 1 ff.; Horrocks, J. W., *A Short History of Mercantilism* (interesting brief sketch), chaps. i–ix; Lipson, E., *The Economic History of England*, esp. vols. ii and iii (mercantilism); Cole, C. W., *French*

---

[1] The French West Indies were specifically allowed to import certain foods and other necessities which France herself could not supply. A decree of 1784 went much further than that of 1767, but the influence of French merchants, who feared American competition, held Vergennes back from opening the door completely.

Mercantilist Doctrines before Colbert; Castillo, A. V., *Spanish Mercantilism;* Biggar, H. P., *Early Trading Companies of New France;* Causton, G., and Keane, A. H., *The Early Chartered Companies,* esp. chaps. x–xii (Dutch colonization); Morris, H. C., *History of Colonization,* 2 vols. (good in spots but rather out of date); Knowles, L. C. A., *The Economic Development of the Overseas Empire;* Beer, G. L., *The Old Colonial System* (British); Unwin, G., *Industrial Organization in the Seventeenth and Eighteenth Centuries* (British); Hobson, J. A., *The Evolution of Modern Capitalism,* chaps. i and ii; Seé, H., *Modern Capitalism: Its Origins and Evolution,* chaps. iv–vii; Sombart, W., *The Quintessence of Capitalism* (largely on the middle class spirit); Gillespie, J. E., *A History of Geographical Discovery* (brief) and *The Influence of Oversea Expansion in England to 1700* (in Columbia Studies in History, etc., vol. 91); Botsford, J. E., *English Society in the Eighteenth Century as Influenced from Oversea;* Ogg, D., *The Seventeenth Century,* chap. x (Holland); Edmundson, G., *History of Holland;* Blok, P. J., *History of the People of the Netherlands,* 5 vols. (a standard work); Reichwein, A., *China and Europe in the Eighteenth Century;* Robinson, H., *The Development of the British Empire,* chaps. i–viii; Hertz, G. B., *British Imperialism in the Eighteenth Century;* Mahan, A. T., *The Influence of Sea Power upon History;* Andrews, C. M., "Anglo-French Commercial Rivalry," *Amer. Hist. Rev.,* v., 539 ff., 761 ff.; Hunter, W. W., *A Brief History of the Indian Peoples;* Dodwell, H., *Dupleix and Clive;* Corbett, J., *England in the Seven Years' War,* 2 vols.; Riker, T. W., *Henry Fox,* vol. i., chap. iv (Anglo-French rupture); Williams, B., *The Life of William Pitt, Earl of Chatham,* 2 vols.; Egerton, H. E., *The Causes and Character of the American Revolution;* Van Tyne, C. H., *The Causes of the War of Independence;* Soltau, C., *Choiseul;* Van Tyne, C. H., "French Aid before the Alliance of 1778," *Amer. Hist. Rev.,* vol. xxi, 20 ff.; Corwin, E. H., *French Policies and the American Alliance of 1778;* Adams, C. B., "The Influence of the American Revolution on England's Government of Her Colonies," *Amer. Hist. Rev.,* vol. i; Girault, C., *The Colonial Tariff Policy of France,* chap. i; Nussbaum, F. L., "The French Colonial Arrêt of 1784," *S. Atl. Qu.,* xxvii, 62 ff.

VII. EUROPE OF THE OLD RÉGIME—THE BACKGROUND AND ORIGINS OF THE FRENCH REVOLUTION

1. POLITICAL CONDITIONS ON THE EVE OF THE FRENCH REVOLUTION

Legal status of the modern state; International anarchy; Foreign policy in the eighteenth century; Absolute monarchy in principle and organization; Defects of the system in France: (1) moral, (2) practical.

2. SOCIAL AND ECONOMIC CONDITIONS ON THE EVE OF THE REVOLUTION

A. Conditions in Europe in general

The agricultural classes: (1) the clergy, (2) the nobles, (3) the peasantry; The mercantile classes: (1) the artisans, (2) the merchants.

B. Conditions in France in particular

Social contrasts; The clergy; The nobles; The peasantry; Range of the middle class; The artisans and the decay of the gilds; Position and temper of the middle class—the origins of the French Revolution.

3. THE INTELLECTUAL REVOLT AND THE SPIRITUAL AWAKENING

A. Rationalism and the Development of a Public Opinion as the Positive Cause of the French Revolution

Origins of rationalism: (1) revival of science and importance of Newton, (2) influence of the secular trend and reaction against dogmatism; Religious bigotry as the first target; Absolute monarchy and "privilege" under scrutiny; Leading exponents of rationalism: (1) Montesquieu, (2) the Encyclopedists and others, (3) the Economists, (4) Voltaire; Character and limitations of rationalism; Rousseau, the "lone wolf"; Evolution of a public opinion; The government and public opinion; Question of reform—"Benevolent despotism": (1) in Europe, (2) in France.

B. The Weakness of the Monarchy as the Negative Cause of the French Revolution

Causes of the monarchy's weakness; "Privilege" as the obstacle to reform.

C. The Financial Crisis and the Insurgence of the Nobility

"Privilege" on the offensive; Widening of the insurgence; Capitulation of the crown—the summons of an estates general.

The "Old Régime" is the term applied to the political and social relationships in Europe before the French Revolution began the work of transforming them. We have to examine this earlier period in order to perceive the origins of the movement and appreciate more fully its significance. To this end, we shall glance at Europe as a whole, but give more special attention to France, not because it was typical but because it was the land where revolution started.

POLITICAL CONDITIONS ON THE EVE OF THE FRENCH REVOLUTION

In a broad sense the Old Régime consisted politically of a collection of states large and small and indeed almost innumerable if we are to include the various political elements within the structure of the Holy Roman Empire. Whatever type of government it represented, whether an absolute monarchy, a limited monarchy, an obsolete feudal state like Poland, a confederacy like Switzerland, or a plutocratic republic like Holland or Venice, each state was considered legitimate in the public law of Europe, and its sovereignty was unchallengeable. The products of historical evolution were to that extent accepted as established facts. Most of the larger states had expanded as the result of marriage or conquest, and the limits of such a state were co-terminous with a sovereign's hereditary rights. In the great majority of cases most of the people whom he governed probably spoke his language and shared with him a sense of common nationality, but this was merely because the state had developed from a smaller nucleus which had formed with its ruler a cultural unit. Theoretically the state was not bound to comprehend a single nationality or to limit itself to such. Fundamentally it was dynastic rather than national (in that sense). Thus a state like Austria, though its core was German, comprehended within its limits a varied collection of peoples, all ruled by the house of Hapsburg on the principle of dynastic inheritance. There were no wars declared in the name of nationality, and indeed the dismemberment of Poland was a negation of such a principle. When a prince resolved to despoil a neighbor, he did it usually on the ground of some hereditary or treaty claim, thus cloaking with hypocrisy a sheer act of aggression. Sometimes, as in the case of Poland, no effort was made to gloss over the crime.

As in the past two centuries, the only idea which acted as a

Legal status of the modern state

Interna-
tional
anarchy
preventive of war was the doctrine of the balance of power. It was the application of this doctrine which had availed in a sense to save the Rhine lands and the Low Countries from becoming a part of France. But the eighteenth century found a vicious method of perverting it. While the conception might still offer protection to the larger states, the smaller ones might actually become victims of the principle. Through the invention of a sort of corollary of the balance of power, namely, joint partition by mutual agreement, a nation in a state of decay might be carved into a number of pieces, and by such an unscrupulous device the equilibrium among the despoilers be substantially maintained. Nothing, indeed, staid the hand of violence but fear—or that respect for a power or group of powers that was akin to fear. Each and every sovereign did what he dared to do. Reasons of state had become the guiding principle of monarchs—whether it seemed to prompt aggression or to restrain it on the part of others. To evade or ignore treaties was a common practice of the time. When Mazarin had planned the marriage between Louis XIV and the infanta of Spain, he spoke glibly of the prospect of annexing Spain no matter what renunciations might have to be made in the marriage treaty. Frederick the Great solemnly observed that for every sovereign fraud was sometimes a duty. Where there was so conspicuous an absence of international morality, it was not strange that international law was little better than a tissue of abstractions. The fabric of Europe was a flimsy structure at best. In practice, if not by right, it was a régime of international anarchy.

Foreign
policy in the
eighteenth
century
"He who gains nothing loses," said Catherine the Great. A policy of aggression was still the favorite preoccupation of most monarchs. Yet if we look back over the lapse of time, we can observe considerable change in the kind of objects pursued. The feudal king fought to control his vassals or to appropriate their domains in order to add them to his own. The king of the sixteenth century, less preoccupied by dangers at home, sought to extend his territories from motives of adventure or personal glory; it was what we have called a dynastic policy. In the seventeenth century we reach a period of transition. While a dynastic policy is still occasionally manifested (notably when Louis XIV tried to get the imperial crown, or when Sweden tried to span the Baltic), such statesmen as Richelieu and Peter the Great saw the need of more practical aims—in the case of the former, the quest of natural

EUROPE
IN 1789

SCALE OF MILES
0   50 100 150 200 250 300

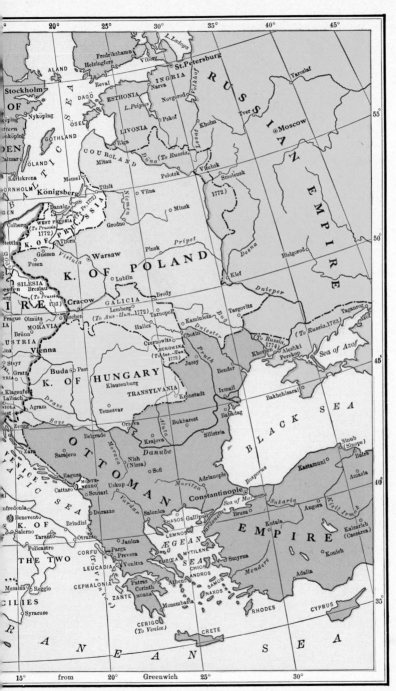

m Gottschalk, The Era of the French Revolution (1715–1815), *courtesy of Houghton Mifflin Company*

boundaries; in the case of the latter, the dream of reaching the open seas. Practical considerations were the motives in the eighteenth century. If we glance at the map, we may perceive the natural goals of expanding states. Hanover by acquiring Bremen and Verden pushed her way to the North Sea; Austria sought to extend her seaboard on the Adriatic; Russia wanted a solid footing on the Black Sea; Brandenburg-Prussia, having wrested from Sweden part of Pomerania, longed to possess the rest in order to increase her frontage on the Baltic. In getting Silesia Frederick the Great was able to extend his mountain frontier, and by seizing Polish Prussia, he gave his dominions a much-needed compactness; Joseph II had a similar object in trying to get Bavaria; and Russia's designs on Poland were prompted by the ambition to become more of a European power. For the most part each nation seemed to be shifting, or trying to shift, into its natural geographical position.

Absolute monarchy in principle and organization

. All the greater states except Great Britain (a limited monarchy under the sway of the landed aristocracy) were absolute monarchies. The sovereign, as we have observed, ruled, according to theory, by Roman law or divine right, though actually his power rested on force—a matter of historical development. All these states were so organized that the authority of the crown could permeate every corner of the realm. A defier of the royal will would have to reckon with the police and possibly with the military as well; and, with the exception of certain of the Hapsburg dominions, the force of local interest was powerless against the strength of the bureaucratic machine. Nevertheless it must be admitted that the smoothness of the system depended in large measure upon the character of the sovereign. Under a king like Louis XV, devoid of all sense of responsibility and too frequently surrounded by incompetent administrators, the machine often ran of its own momentum, and, lacking effective direction, each petty official had a chance to abuse his power. It is also true that even at best the system was fraught with much administrative confusion. It had sometimes been felt expedient to retain the institutions peculiar to a province which had been acquired—a lesson which Joseph II learned to his cost in the case of the Netherlands. Some parts of Prussia were much more rigidly governed than others. While the political power of feudalism had been broken, it had often enough authority to impede the administration. When provincial diets had to be consulted, their action, even if sometimes dictated, must have involved much delay. In France scarcely anything was ever formally abolished. Obsolete institutions were simply overshadowed by newer ones. Rather than run the risk of offending vested interests, and too indigent to redeem a multitude of purchased posts, the crown ordinarily let well enough alone, satisfied, apparently, with putting substantial control into the hands of its chosen instruments. It was a sort of system of checks and balances without such checks and balances being at all useful, but, rather, detrimental to an orderly and equitable administration. Thus jurisdictions often overlapped. It was not always clear before what tribunal a man with a suit to plead should bring his case. After he had acted to the best of his knowledge, judgment might be reversed by another court claiming competence. There was not even a uniform code of law, and it was often uncertain what code was properly applicable to a given community. It was similar with the financial administration. Some parts of France had to pay one price for salt; another, another; while still others were not bound to buy of the government at all. The *taille*, as we have noticed, was sometimes levied on land, and sometimes on all sources of income. There could be no justice in such a system—or lack of system. The kingdom of France had been built up by patches, and little effort had been made to weave it together into a smooth and seamless whole. Yet the same was true of Prussia or Spain, and even more true of Austria, while the administrative system of Russia was perhaps the clumsiest of all.

It was only through capable direction that such a system could work harmoniously, and since monarchy was unhappily hereditary, no continuity of capable rule could be guaranteed. Moreover, even at best, in a system wherein all authority is derived from the top, efficiency is pretty apt to filter out before it ever reaches the bottom. Centralized administration always tends toward a tedious routine. In France, where the towns and villages were closely tied to the central government it was sometimes five years before a village could get permission to repair a public building. The absolute monarchy of the Old Régime was essentially a paternalism. It was much more enlightened, it is true, in the eighteenth century than it had been in the seventeenth; it did not revel merely in splendor or give its chief attention, as in France, to the artistic side of royalty; it did not exist simply and solely for power, as the mecantilists had taught; it was really conscious of certain social problems urgently demanding attention, and it even achieved a little in that direction. Yet even "benevolent despotism" (which we shall study more fully later) took too much upon itself.[1] Generally fitful at best, it found it all too easy to follow traditional ways. And in politics as well as economics it left too little to the initiative of the governed.

In France the faults of the system were not more glaring than elsewhere, but it was there, as we shall observe, that they came under closest scrutiny, and it was there that the Old Régime was first to go to pieces. In general it may be said that the government was not deliberately oppressive, but that the system in operation was so full of faults and anomalies (we have mentioned a few) that it worked undue hardship on the people, while, from the practical standpoint it failed to solve the problem of meeting its needs. To revert for a moment to the moral defects—justice was expensive and difficult to obtain, for the judges, having bought or inherited their offices, had to support themselves in large part by fees in the performance of their functions. Not only were people unequal before the law (many degrading punishments, such as flogging, were exclusively reserved for commoners), but penalties tended to be too severe, many crimes, like petty thieving, being capital offenses. Procedure was always to the disadvantage of the defendant, who had to bear the presumption of guilt, and was not privileged to employ counsel. Sometimes—though this applied rather to the upper classes—men were arrested and punished without the formality of a trial, and it came to be fairly common for a courtier to obtain these *lettres de cachet* to satisfy a personal grudge. But it was the financial system that weighed most heavily on the people, since not only had the extravagance of kings led to greatly increased taxation but the virtual immunity of the upper classes from most of the taxes cast the burden upon those who could least afford it. And the burden was sometimes the heavier by reason of the method of collection. The farming of the indirect taxes to private individuals offered every incentive to extortion, and there was point in Sully's remark that the farmers of the taxes were the worst enemies of the State,—"more destructive

Defects of the system in France: (1) moral

---

[1] The very solicitude of a paternalistic government for the general interest was often unwisely manifested. The grain trade in France was always severely regulated for fear of famine, but a province possessing a surplus was often forbidden to export it.

to the kingdom" (so added another observer) "than armed invaders."

(2) Practical   It was this letting out of contracts to tax-farmers, or farmers-general, as they were called, that throws most lurid light on the decrepitude of the old monarchy—though the practice was by no means confined to France. At certain intervals (usually every six years) the government entered into contracts with a powerful financial group for the levying of the indirect taxes. These farmers-general, paid a stipulated sum to the government; but, as the surplus (usually about twenty per cent of the revenue obtained) went into their private pockets, it can readily be seen that the government gave up much of its available revenue. Such a device was obviously prompted by the need of cash in advance. The same sacrifice of the future to the present was shown by the constant creation of offices for the purpose of selling them, some four thousand of which conveyed immunity from direct taxation. Thus, for the sake of ready money, a taxpayer had been eliminated. Indeed, the government was often in such a quandary to raise money that it sold exemptions from certain taxes to towns and whole districts. Doubtless, moreover, among so large a corps of officials much money was wasted through careless accounting or sheer dishonesty; and the privilege of the king to tap the treasury as he chose—sometimes without leaving a record—led to further confusion and embarrassment. In the last days of the Bourbon monarchy the government was always anticipating revenues—that is, borrowing on them in advance; yet the deficit was constantly increasing, and even the mounting public debt was unable to keep pace with the government's expenditures. The only way by which France could have become solvent would have been to tax the privileged classes. Sometimes, indeed, this very device was tried, some of the income taxes being theoretically applicable to all classes alike, but the Church was always able to compound by paying a special subsidy, and most of the nobles had influence enough to keep their immunities safe. It was the old spirit of feudalism, still powerful enough to hamper the policy of the crown. Royal extravagance and feudal survivals combined to bring the monarchy to ruin. Financially France had never caught up after the reign of Louis XIV, and the reigns of his two successors only served to put her deeper into the mire.

To understand the strength of vested interests we must now take

a survey of social conditions on the eve of the Revolution. It is a
kind of paradox of history that after the political power of feudalism had been broken it had yet enough strength to hold the absolute monarchy at bay. Nevertheless, that instrument and buffer
of the crown, the middle class, was beginning to take the road to a
dominant position in society.

SOCIAL AND ECONOMIC CONDITIONS ON THE EVE OF THE FRENCH REVOLUTION

The social divisions on the Continent were still in general what *Conditions in Europe in general*
they had been in the Middle Ages, especially the cleavage between
the upper and lower classes. In most countries the clergy were the
first estate, the nobles, the second, while the third estate included
all the rest of the population except in Sweden where the peasants, *The agricultural classes:*
constituted a fourth estate, leaving the third to the middle class.

Both the nobles and the upper clergy were feudal lords, and except in a few countries where capitalism had made progress, these
classes held the chief sources of wealth, since Europe was still pre- *(1) The clergy*
dominantly agricultural. The rôle of the clergy in Catholic states
was, of course, of extreme importance, since they not only minis-
tered to the religious needs of the people but also provided most of
the schools and charitable agencies, such as hospitals and asylums
of one kind or another. Only in Germany had some of the eccle-
siastics become, through the weakness of the imperial authority,
territorial princes, possessing a political as well as a social and
economic importance. In all Continental monarchies the nobles *(2) The nobles*
monopolized the chief positions in the central government, the
leading diplomatic posts, and the commissions in the army and
navy; and with the exception of the first-named category the same
was true of England where the nobility still dominated parliament.
To this class belonged the exclusive profession of courtier—a rôle
that was indispensable in the current conception of monarchy. In
central and eastern Europe the nobles were much more strongly
entrenched than in France, where their class spirit had been broken
and where the middle class had assumed an important rôle. While
they were no longer able to limit the power of the sovereign or even *(3) The peasantry*
always able to preserve their fiscal immunities intact, they were
still much more the allies of the crown than its subordinates. We
have already noticed their formidable power in the Hapsburg
lands; in Prussia and Russia many of these magnates possessed

enormous estates and always a preponderant influence in the government. The status of the peasants varied. In the Rhine country most of them were now landowners, though saddled, of course, with the usual feudal burdens. East of the Elbe, however—notably in Bavaria, Austria, Prussia, Poland, and Russia—most of the peasants were serfs, and in many parts of Germany they held only a life occupancy of the land, while more often still they appeared as laborers on a lord's estate. But the lot of the Italian peasants was hardly better, and in the southern part of the peninsula their poverty was proverbial. Excepting France for the moment and perhaps England where conditions were peculiar, it was only in the kingdom of Sardinia, the Low Countries, and the Rhenish lands that the peasant was really able to eke out a decent living. In the British Isles, which once boasted of its sturdy yeomanry, the independent peasant was fast becoming extinct. The enclosure movement (already mentioned) had not only dispossessed large numbers of peasant proprietors but resulted in the creation of large farms, promoted by capital and even beginning to be developed by agricultural machinery. At the same time the rise of the factory system with its cheaper modes of production was fast depriving the English peasant of his chance to supplement his income by spinning or weaving on the side. In the face of such competitors the small holder could not possibly survive, and if we disregard the few who managed to rise to a higher position, he was soon to become a tenant on a large estate (farming with borrowed capital) or (more often) a member of the rural proletariat. Such was England's "Agricultural Revolution."

The mercantile classes: (1) the artisans

It was the fact that most of Europe was predominantly agricultural that gave the upper classes their great importance under the Old Régime. Certainly it was an evidence of the relative backwardness of industry that in most of Europe large towns were few; and, outside of England, France, and the Low Countries, the middle class was comparatively unimportant. On the Continent manufacturing was still as a rule conducted under the gild system of organization, wherein the master-artisan plied his craft with the aid of journeymen and apprentices and then sold the product to the consumer. Such a system, with its rules and regulations, had been designed primarily, as we have said, to maintain a rigid standard of quality, but it had the result (and partly the intention) of limiting competition both from within and from without. Backed by governments which were always trying to increase exports in accordance with mercantilist doctrines, and thus favored monopolistic organizations, the masters not only held to their standard methods of production, eschewing anything novel or experimental, but jealously guarded their limited membership, making it well nigh impossible for the journeymen (their wage-earning assistants) to enter their ranks. Some of the journeymen, as a matter of fact, had formed unions, and strikes were not uncommon, but such efforts had little chance of bettering conditions and had, in fact, only a symptomatic importance. In England, however, the gild system had lost all significance in the seventeenth century, and in its place had arisen the "domestic" or "putting-out" system. Merchants with capital "put out" the raw material to scattered workers (most of them were peasants) who then, working in their homes, turned out the finished product. Those who had formerly been masters under the gild system either became these capitalist merchants or, as was usually the case, sank to the position of cottage wage-earners. Then, in turn, the domestic system began to give way to the modern factory, a phenomenon we shall discuss in a subsequent chapter. In spite of the persistence of the gilds on the Continent (they were especially strong in Prussia) the domestic system had made its appearance during the eighteenth century (especially in the case of the textile industries), and for peasants who needed to supplement their meager incomes during the winter the flexibility of this newer system was a great benefit. Sometimes the "putting-out" merchant represented a company which trafficked with a wide market, but often he was merely a middleman who distributed his products to various tradesmen in the towns, with whose needs he kept in touch. The selling of goods on commission (generally at from two to five per cent of the value of the goods) had become an increasingly common practice. The growth of capitalism we have discussed in a previous chapter, and the beginnings of a machine economy we reserve for a later one.

If the manufacturer was limited in his profits by the limitations *(2) The merchants* of hand labor and in most cases by the conservatism and exclusiveness of the gilds, the merchant was not much better off. Internal trade had to cope with barriers both natural and artificial. Though France was usually acknowledged to be superior to other countries in the construction of her roads, it may be said that, generally speaking, most of the thoroughfares in eighteenth century Europe were quite unfit for commerce, and hence rivers and canals (of which since the sixteenth century there had been a rapid increase) comprised the principal arteries of transportation.[1] But on all canals and rivers in most Continental countries were numerous toll-stations, operating for revenue for towns along the route, and most of the provinces also imposed tariffs on their frontiers—relics of the day when provinces had been separate feudal entities. Thus merchandise shipped from Brittany to Provence had to pay a duty seven times *en route*. One may also bear in mind that transportation by oxen was painfully slow as compared with the better means provided by a later age. If oxen provided the motive power on land, the wind had to furnish it on sea. Voyages were long affairs. It was sometimes all of two years before a merchantman bound for the East returned with its cargo of fabrics and spices. And though brigands in much of Europe were now comparatively rare (thanks to the rise of the modern state), pirates abounded in distant waters both in the old world and the new. It is true that the chartered companies with their merchant fleets minimized such risks, but it helps us to understand the tremendous difficulties of the individual trader—not to mention the fact that usually he was an interloper challenging a monopoly, which, theoretically at least, enjoyed the backing of a government. Obviously the chartered companies played somewhat the same rôles that the gilds did in manufacturing —that of precluding competition, and in any case it was not until the British navy vanquished piracy—a long and patient process— that individual merchants drew much profit from the East. Also, in taking a glance at the numerous handicaps of the eighteenth century merchant, we should recall the obstructive machinery of the mercantile system; for whatever the hope of each and every nation to excel its commercial rival, foreign tariffs did assuredly restrict international trade. Likewise wars interrupted the flow of commerce between nations or in any case impeded it. Commerce, as J. A. Hobson has pointed out, was still overwhelmingly domestic. The export trade of England in 1712 was estimated at less than a sixth of the internal trade of that year, and all countries for the most part consumed, themselves, what they produced. On the whole, we may infer that while there were rich merchants as there

---

[1] The whole subject of transportation, travel, and communication is interestingly treated in Nussbaum, *A History of the Economic Institutions of Modern Europe*, pp. 168–83.

were also rich financiers (thanks to the opportunities of capitalism), the vast bulk of the middle class were still men of small incomes, considerably better off than the peasants, it is true, but by no means able to live a life of luxury.

Social conditions in France were, in general, rather better than on the rest of the Continent, though there were, of course, some glaring contrasts. The privileged position of the upper classes in direct taxation made, as we have noted, the burden all the heavier on the peasant. The fact also that much of this money flowed into pensions to the court nobility, who performed no useful service to the State, made the injustice of the system all the more patent. Moreover, in the ranks of the secular clergy there was a definite cleavage between the higher clergy who got revenues from land as well as most of the produce of the tithe (the tax paid by land-owners [1] to the Church) and the lower clergy, chiefly made up of parish priests, who were granted but a pittance, hardly sufficient to sustain life. It is no wonder that the lower clergy felt bitter toward their superiors. It was this class, sprung largely from the peasantry, that came closest to the people; and it could hardly be thought strange if common sufferings and mutual sympathies should lead eventually to common action against a régime that treated them so ill. Finally there was the contrast between the workman and his master—neither very affluent, yet the former at the mercy of the latter; this condition we shall presently discuss.

Conditions in France in particular

Social contrasts

The clergy or first estate, numbered in all over 100,000 persons. The proportion of land owned by the Church is a matter of some dispute, but there is no question but that its economic power was considerable, though the clergy counted less than two per cent of the population. Some of the bishops were immensely wealthy and spent much of their time at Versailles, deliberately neglecting their duties. Yet such cases in the nature of things attract the most attention, and it is not clear that French churchmen at this time were any more worldly than their position had always tended to make them. One thing which had long militated against the probity of the French Church had been the fact that ever since the Concordat of Bologna in the sixteenth century the higher clergy owed their positions in the first instance to the crown, which kept all benefices as a preserve for the nobility. The monastic orders, comprising what was known as the regular clergy, were in

The clergy

[1] It was at one time levied on industry as well.

a state of rapid decay, comparatively few concerning themselves with any tangible services to the people. Generally speaking, the Church did not serve society to an extent anything like proportionate to its wealth. Neither its educational nor its philanthropic work was more than a "drop in the bucket" of illiteracy and poverty. It did contribute voluntary subsidies to the government, but such were small sums in relation to its total wealth. More than two thirds of the clergy, however, belonged to the lower ranks and profited little by the privileged position of the order; and this was the group who furnished spiritual guidance to the mass of the people.

The nobles   While the clergy were hardly a moral unit, divided as they were along social and economic lines, they had at least a common calling and a hierarchical organization. The nobles, on the other hand, were not united by anything except the bond of "privilege." Speaking generally, it would be hard to find a group more irresponsible. A few were very rich and the envy of all the others, but even those with the greatest advantages showed little political capacity, and nearly all who had the means to enjoy a life of comparative ease left their estates in the charge of stewards. It was the court nobility that basked in the royal favor. They were the ones who got the important offices, commissions, and pensions. But the great majority of the second estate are to be classed as "country nobles," not because they were the only ones to possess estates but because they were too poor or too insignificant to go to Versailles. Nursing their bitterness in seclusion, many of them exacted the uttermost farthing from their tenants, for whom they took delight in vaunting their contempt. It was this class which searched the records for additional rights—a fact which partly explains the later uprisings against the châteaux. Apart from maritime trade and large industrial enterprises, the nobles were excluded from a business career, and since comparatively few could obtain bishoprics or commissions in the army, it is no wonder that they seemed a useless drag on society. They had even lost their ancient class feeling. So many members of the wealthy bourgeoisie had bought estates conveying titles of nobility that the integrity of the caste had been much diluted in the course of the centuries, and it was said that few nobles could trace their lineage back to feudal days. Taking them as a whole, the nobles were not rich; for their estates tended to diminish as a result of the laws of inheritance, and their purses were unequal to the demands of their position. That is why the royal pension was a godsend to the favored few.

Side by side with the feudal nobility were the official nobility, the nobles of the robe, never looked upon as equals by the others and belonging theoretically to the middle class, yet swelling the numbers of the privileged. A good many of this class had bought land, and many of the older nobility did not scruple to go to this element (and to the rich financiers as well) to find well-dowered matches for their sons. The political importance of the group—some four thousand in all—chiefly centered in the parlement of Paris, whose important rôle we have elsewhere noted, and whose struggles to thwart the crown finally induced Louis XV to abolish the institution altogether, though it was speedily restored under his amiable successor. These arrogant judges were the only ones to fight the monarchy openly,[1] but they were not progressive, for they were opposed to freedom of the press and to all reform, judicial, social, or economic. They enjoyed their immense prestige through daring to resist a king that was supposed to be all-powerful.

But the greatest offenders against the stability of the monarchy were the courtiers. They were a baneful influence in government circles, blocking the paths of progress, parasites who lived for the moment, largely supported by a bankrupt government whose resources they consumed in idle luxury. It was they who constituted the entourage of Louis XVI and his young and spendthrift queen, Marie Antoinette. The waste of the national resources can well be illustrated by the fact that the royal household numbered four thousand persons, and it was said that eighty persons were employed to wait on the king's daughter when she was but a year old. The number of equipages, the vast retinue of servants, the lavish expenditures on parties are all evidences of the prodigious cost of the court. It was, of course, the kings who had created this symbol of their magnificence, and to some extent Louis XVI was the victim of a tradition; yet, even if he had had the disposition to curtail expenses, it is doubtful if any monarch but a Peter the Great could have combated the powerful influence of the nobility. The absolute monarchy, in debasing the nobles to the level of courtiers, had wrapped itself in a mesh that was gradually but certainly smothering it to death.

[1] By holding up legislation which they were supposed to register. See page 91.

While the clergy numbered something over 100,000 and the nobles about 400,000, the third estate comprised the rest of the 25,000,000; but it was a comprehensive category and included persons as different in fortunes as the wealthy capitalist and the agricultural laborer, the master of the shop and his poor apprentice. The great mass of the third estate was, of course, made up of peasants, who constituted probably nine tenths of the population. Hardly a million were now serfs (a condition that contrasted with most of Europe), and most of the peasants are commonly regarded as having been owners of the land they tilled; but as almost all owed sundry feudal obligations, including an annual sum analogous to rent, it would be more correct to regard them as hereditary lease-holders. Since these various manorial services dated from a time when their peasant ancestors paid their lords largely for protection—a duty now monopolized by the State—it can be realized how obsolete and unjust were these surviving remnants of feudalism. While such obligations were not precisely uniform for all, there were some which were so common as to be almost universal. The old compulsion to work a certain number of days on the lord's estate had usually been commuted into a small money payment or a share (anywhere from a twelfth to a sixth) of the harvest;[1] but there were tolls which the lord collected on roads and bridges that intervened between the peasant and his market; and there was the obligation to send grapes to the lord's winepress, grain to the lord's oven, flour to the lord's bakery, and cattle to the lord's slaughterhouse. In each case a fee was charged, and as the business of grinding the wheat (like these other *banalités*) was in general farmed out to a private individual, it was frequently charged that the millers mixed lime with the flour; and one minister, who had reason to know, declared that three-fourths of the kingdom ate bad bread. There is no doubt that as a rule the peasant's position was pretty grave, burdened as he was by State taxes (including the *corvée*[2]) as well as by tithes and feudal exactions. Moreover, lots tended to be small, a fact which made an occasional drought especially ruinous. Comparatively few peasants were able to supplement their incomes by spinning or weaving during the winter; and most of them, indeed, were forced by their

[1] When land was sold or inherited the tax due the lord generally equaled about a year's produce.
[2] See page 95.

meager resources to lease some additional land from a lord, who provided the seed and stock and was repaid by half—sometimes even more—of the crop. Many of these *métayers*, as they were called, eked out but a bare existence. Saddest of all, however, was the case of the rural laborers, for their lots (when they had any at all) were too small to be life-sustaining, and employment— not always to be had—brought a pitifully low wage. Agriculture was also very backward, as the peasant had little capital, and there were few large estates with intensive cultivation as existed in England at this time. Nevertheless, in England the small proprietor was rapidly dying out. In France he was poor and rather hopeless; yet he was the progenitor of the free peasant proprietor of today.

The middle class or bourgeoisie embraced, as we know, most of *Range of the middle class* the intellectuals, the business element (whether commercial, industrial, or financial), and most of the government officials. They formed a very wide "middle," so to speak, since at the top we find a group who by reason of their fortunes were likely to become merged with the second estate, while at the bottom the tailor's apprentice or the courtier's lackey was hardly better off than the average tiller of the soil. The strength of such a class lay not in its unity (for it had none) but in that element possessing wealth— to which we must add in the eighteenth century a few intellectuals, who furnished the moral leadership.

But while the development of capitalism had affected both in- *The artisans and the decay of the gilds* dustry and commerce, the outlook of the mercantile element was really rather circumscribed. Industry was still under the deadening grip of the gilds, which, in turn, were held in the still more deadening grip of the government. Before the advent of machinery the master worked with his men, but an industrial household was by no means a happy community of workers under a sympathetic chief. The journeymen, or skilled worker, had little chance to become a master, who usually found means to give the succession to a son or son-in-law; and while his working day was long (often fifteen to eighteen hours), his wages were low in proportion to the cost of living. On the lowest scale in the shop was the apprentice, who, in order to learn a trade, bound himself to the master for a term of years (anywhere from four to eight) and received board and lodging as his sole remuneration. He was not supposed to leave the shop without permission, might be required to do anything, and was, in short, the butt of the establishment. He had, however, the prospect of becoming a journeyman if he made good. Yet there is irony in the fact that the artisans who were masters were not much better off than the men who served them. In very truth they had paid dearly through the years for the government's protection. Even Colbert, the greatest believer in the gilds, had bled them for the confirmation of their privileges (this was to help defray the cost of the Dutch War), and under Louis XV the license fees became so excessive that many of the gilds became bankrupt—another example of the readiness of a needy government to strike at the sources of wealth for the sake of some ready cash. Some of the masters were driven by penury to become no more than hired employees of a merchant, who regularly supplied them with raw materials, and compelled them for a fixed wage to work from early dawn till far into the night. This was the so-called "domestic system" (already mentioned), which even in France was beginning to undermine the gilds; and it is hardly strange that under the influence of new ideas the government finally in 1762 allowed persons outside of towns where gilds existed to engage in industrial production without belonging to a gild provided they conformed to certain general regulations. Meanwhile, already there had arisen, side by side with the small shops under gild regulation, some larger units, rudimentary factories, employing hundreds of workmen, and sometimes—in the case of certain establishments in northern France—making some use of machinery. It is clear that the classic system of production was slowly dying, and if the French Revolution were not to deal it a mortal blow, the Industrial Revolution would certainly do so.

Position and temper of the middle class—the origins of the French Revolution

While the artisans, encased in the gild system, had no chance of becoming affluent, many of the large producers had amassed considerable wealth, and capital was employed more widely in the eighteenth century than ever before. Still more wealthy were the farmers of the taxes, who were often the chief creditors of the crown. Then many merchants had enriched themselves from the over-sea trade. In the traffic with the Levant the French had quite outdistanced the British, and the volume of commerce with the French West Indies had increased at least tenfold since the beginning of the eighteenth century. Generally speaking, if we except the situation of most of the peasants (though even this is a disputable point), economic conditions in France had generally improved since the death of Louis XV, and as the peasants were not the class that was stirred into action, we cannot seek in economic distress the cause of the French Revolution. Rather it was because the upper layers of the bourgeoisie were discontented with their lot. Responsible as they were in large measure for the general prosperity, indispensable to a government that had to borrow in order to live, and holding innumerable positions in the administration, they felt that they should not be excluded from the highest political honors—still practically the preserve of an idle and ill-educated nobility. Despite the influence of certain philosophers (notably Montesquieu) to which some of its number undoubtedly succumbed, it is by no means an established fact that as a class the bourgeoisie disapproved of absolute monarchy in principle. When the crown tried to liberate trade from its shackles, many of this class were disposed to view it as an instrument of their own, and were ready to give it backing if it showed a real stability. But certainly the bourgeoisie wanted a monarchy shorn of its frills, that is, liberated from the influence of an arrogant and for the most part worthless privileged class. It felt that worth, rather than birth, should be the real test of social recognition. It was, moreover, especially galling that the nobles refused to treat them as social equals, and the experience of Madame Roland, who, when invited by a nobleman to dinner, found that she was to eat in the servants' quarters, was probably not exceptional. "What made the Revolution?" exclaimed Napoleon. "Vanity. Liberty was only the excuse." Yet in taking such a position, the bourgeoisie was not thinking of the common man. The Revolution was an outcome of a struggle between classes, of a movement for social equality by the bourgeoisie. And for waging such a struggle the middle class was prompted by the spirit of the times.

It was, in fact, an emotional reaction which came to France that accounts for the Revolution. The financial crisis we shall discuss was the occasion, but the origins lay deeper, and the storm had long been brewing. In other words, the conditions which called for drastic action—whether reform or revolution—were not new and were not, in general, worse then they had been (with the important exception of the state of the royal finances), but it was now in the second half of the eighteenth century that men were brought to realize the outworn character of many of the modes and institutions which constituted the Old Régime. Once this fact became clearly revealed by a systematic process of thought, the bourgeoisie could place its case on a higher level than class interest. This spiritual awakening was thus the outcome of an intellectual revolt.

THE INTELLECTUAL REVOLT AND THE SPIRITUAL AWAKENING

Rationalism and the Development of a Public Opinion as the Positive Cause of the French Revolution

Origins of rationalism: (1) the revival of science and the importance of Newton

To trace the sources of the intellectual revolt one must go back a considerable period. We have noticed that Roger Bacon had broken new paths with his emphasis on observation instead of the old method of logical deduction from dubious postulates. Science had to be released from the thralldom of tradition imposed upon it by the Church. Then the Renaissance, as we have noticed, questioned many of the existing sources of knowledge and encouraged the individual to do his own thinking. Most of the humanists, it is true, were interested much more in arts and letters than in science; to them the happiness of man was of far more importance than the secrets encased in nature. Yet that spirit of investigation which the Renaissance inculcated could hardly be limited to one field, as the great achievements of Copernicus and others so amply proved. If the age of Luther and Calvin produced so few discoveries and inventions, it was doubtless because the main stream of the Renaissance flowed for a time out of its course into the torrent of dogmatic theology. In the comparative quiet which followed the religious struggles and the English civil war men turned again to science, and before the seventeenth century had closed it produced its greatest figure in the field of learning, Isaac Newton. It was this English scientist, who, exploring the world of nature, as Copernicus had done before him, proved that the universe was a great machine, governed by natural laws, and interpretable by mathematical formulæ. Whilst Roger Bacon had collected his data by careful observation but knew not how to derive from them the proper conclusions, Newton's method (to quote Dr. J. H. Randall) was "by analysis of observed facts to arrive at some fundamental principle and finally by observation and experiment to prove that what follows logically from the principle is in agreement with experience." Speculative hypotheses were not, in his conception, the points to start with; rather should one begin with the phenomena themselves; hence, the ground of Newton's discoveries—such as the laws of gravitation. It was left for John Locke, his contemporary and compatriot, to give more special attention to man, and the effect of external phenomena upon his mind. We shall not take time to catalogue the various discoveries by which so many of the sciences took on a fresh momentum, but it may be well to note that physics, chemistry, bacteriology, and astronomy were given their solid foundations in the seventeenth century; while botany, physiology, and geology may be said to have followed in the eighteenth, and knowledge in the older sciences continued to

Portrait by van der Banck

Sir Isaac Newton

advance. It is not to be wondered that practical invention proceeded apace, and that the age gave rise to the Industrial Revolution.

But we are here specifically interested in the relation of this outburst of individualism to the political and social problems of the day. And here we must go back to Newton. The idea of a universe ordered on some rational plan led to the conviction that man himself was part of the rational order of things. The stupendous laws which governed his existence were the work of some mystic cause; let it be called God—such was the position of the Deists. But apart from the causal function and the probable existence of a "hereafter," the Deists admitted no divine intervention in human affairs. Once man was created, he was subject to the play of natural laws. But this was not all; he was also the product—as Locke had emphasized—of his experience. This was, indeed, harking back to the "law of nature," so common among the ancients, which, to quote an eminent jurist, "should signify the rules of conduct deducible by reason from the general conditions of society." Those conditions must manifestly be viewed and appraised in the light of human experience.

Hence we arrive at the conclusion that from observation and experience (taking of course, into consideration the play of natural forces) reason should develop; and reason must be the test of existing institutions. Those which did not play a socially useful function must therefore be cast aside. This phase of the intellectual awakening is sometimes known as rationalism, and it provided a criterion, namely reason, for estimating the value of human institutions. Taken even more broadly to include Rousseau (who interpreted what was "natural" from a somewhat different viewpoint) the whole movement is generally spoken of as the Enlightenment. It may be said to be the lens through which the Old Régime came to be viewed; and it might under certain conditions become the harbinger of revolution.

(2) The influence of the secular trend and the reaction against dogmatism

But while Newton's discovery and the reflections of empiricists like Locke seemed to provide a basis for rationalism, this manner of thinking went back for its inspiration to deeper causes. The modern state, which had come to order human relationships, was an essentially practical phenomenon. Reasons of state, whether political or economic, had found it possible to a certain extent to break through the crust of a rigid social order. We have noted that the Renaissance not only awakened the individual intellect but seemed to justify a secular outlook on life. Statesmen like Richelieu, the Great Elector, and Peter the Great viewed everything—even religion itself—from a coldly practical standpoint. If indeed they had not imbibed the actual spirit of the Renaissance, they had doubtless learned to be practical in the hard school of experience. And so, just as Richelieu and Mazarin left the Protestants their religious beliefs, the rulers of Russia and Prussia welcomed men of different creeds to their dominions, glad to utilize their talents in the service of the State. Moreover, the Reformation, in striking at the basis of religion as it had been taught for so many centuries, led, at least in certain quarters, to a disposition to give much less importance to religion in human affairs. The very intensity with which the Religious Revolution had been waged and the bitterness and carnage which it had engendered inevitably produced a reaction. The world was beginning to be weary of theology. Hence when Louis XIV went back to the outworn habit of strict orthodoxy and even revived the unhappy practice of religious persecution, that feeling of revulsion appeared with redoubled strength. It was this fact, besides the declining greatness of the monarchy itself, that may explain why France contributed so powerfully to the intellectual awakening.

It was religious bigotry which had first to meet the onslaughts of the post-Reformation period. We have mentioned Montaigne, the easy-going skeptic, whose philosophy of life had held no room for intolerance of any sort. Some of the earliest and most vehement proponents of religious toleration were Dutchmen who had imbibed the spirit of Erasmus; and it was in Holland, the land where business alone mattered, that men like Grotius could freely talk of the evils of intolerance. Of the seventeenth century group, which we may regard as the precursors of rationalism, none (unless we except Locke) was of such weight as Pierre Bayle, a French Huguenot who left his native country shortly before the Edict of Revocation and published his thoughts in the far safer refuge of Holland. Bayle insisted that religion was not an affair of the State, and that one could not humanly compel a man to believe otherwise than his conscience should dictate. In his trenchant and logical arguments against the tyranny of creeds, as well as his skeptical attitude of mind, he prepared the way for the more telling shafts of a later generation. *Religious bigotry as the first target*

While religious autocracy was courting the first attacks, would the secular institutions of the day escape scrutiny? As long as monarchy patronized learning and dazzled the world, it was hardly to be expected that even the best intellects would give deliberate thought to its possible limitations. And yet the seventeenth century is something of a turning-point, corresponding, after all, with the turn in Louis' fortunes. While Locke, the great apologist for the "Glorious Revolution" was busily expounding the merits of a limited monarchy under the auspices of the middle class, there were some in France who were coming to believe that somehow, in view of the tribulations which Louis' rule had brought to his *Absolute monarchy and "privilege" under scrutiny* subjects, absolute monarchy should be tempered. The good abbé, Fénelon, far from subscribing to the prevalent doctrine of the divine right of kings, deplored the fact that people must be ruled by one who was as human as themselves; and in a letter to Louis (which he never sent or published) he vented his feelings over the tragic destitution which he saw on every hand. "You are afraid to open your eyes; you are afraid of being induced to sacrifice something of your own glory. This glory which hardens your heart is dearer to you than justice, than your own peace of mind, than the preservation of your people, who are dying off daily through ill-nesses caused by famine. . . ." Somewhat the same spirit was ex-pressed by Vauban, the great military engineer, who, moved by the crushing burdens which Louis' disastrous policy had brought upon his people, expressed, at least by implication, his hope for a more just system of taxation. Such a position was, in effect, a criticism of "privilege"; and the king's own financiers, though they did not pen their views, doubtless longed to invade the immunities of the feudal aristocracy. In the main, however, the writers who thought of political reform were anxious for a return to a limited monarchy, somewhat molded on the feudal pattern, with a revival of the old importance of the estates general and the provincial estates. Such a view was no doubt reactionary, and would naturally enough be held by any nobleman who wrote of politics, but it was something that even "feudalism" was putting its case in writing. Later on the jurist, Montesquieu, subscribed to the same position. It was not till the eighteenth century that the intellectual revolt may be said to commence in earnest, but its sources are fairly apparent. The practical turn of the age, the revived activity in the field of science, the declining interest in religion, and the palpable shortcomings of certain institutions had all prepared the ground for rationalism.

Leading exponents of rationalism: (1) Montes- quieu

Of the earlier rationalists the most famous was Montesquieu. His earliest work, *The Persian Letters*, was a satire on French society in which, by taking the people of Persia as an imaginary model, he poked all manner of fun at a privileged aristocracy, the corruption of the court, and the folly of religious intolerance. Since the work appeared during the Regency—when much that might be danger-ous was condoned for a good laugh—its author went unscathed. In 1748 appeared his more famous work, *The Spirit of Laws*. While dealing gently with monarchy in the manner we have described, he used his knowledge of the British system (for he had paid a visit to England) to expound the virtues, as he thought, of a separation of powers. "There is no liberty," he remarked, "if the judicial power be not separated from the legislative and executive"; and he further demanded the separation of the executive from the legislative—a situation which he wrongly supposed was then existent across the Channel. Though Montesquieu was a true rationalist in seeing the need of certain reforms, he showed a deeper insight in arguing that laws were often the product of circumstance and that different environments and racial characteristics made it difficult to generalize on what is a good law for all peoples. But some things, such as the severity of the criminal law and religious intolerance, seemed to him fundamentally objectionable, even though he made no pretense of drafting new reforms. Though it is true that Montesquieu's work was subjected to much criticism by his own generation, his pointed strictures on despotism gave much cheer to the *parlementaires* who were obstructing the will of the crown (not always wisely) during the last years of Louis XV.

No doubt *The Spirit of Laws* gave considerable impetus to political and social discussion. Probably the most learned of all this series of *philosophes* was Denis Diderot, who, with the aid of a multitude of collaborators, published an encyclopedia, designed to contain the sum of human knowledge carefully strained and analyzed. It was also in some respects a vehicle of criticism, since by implication at least many existing abuses were denounced. As the work was twice stopped by the royal censor, nothing but Diderot's unflagging courage and patience (as well as, on one occasion, the timely intervention of Choiseul) made its completion possible. The work had also the effect of cementing closer ties between certain writers who were interested in the undertaking or actual contributors. The Enlightenment also spread to other countries. The Italian thinker, Beccaria, excoriated the rigor of the criminal codes in vogue, and there were several writers in Germany who penned denunciations of unrestrained absolutism. In England Jeremy Bentham showed the true spirit of rationalism in declaiming against the sanctity of existing institutions and advocating experiment as conducive to the general good.

(2) The Encyclopedists and others

Of paramount importance was a group of thinkers who sought to apply rationalism in the economic sphere. These writers, who called themselves the "Economists," [1] directed their blows at

(3) The Economists

---

[1] They were called at a later time the "Physiocrats," signifying "nature rulers."

every form of governmental regulation, and traced the "natural laws" by which wealth distributed itself if not checked or interfered with by governments. Laissez-faire (let alone) may be regarded as the watchword of this school. Belonging to the same general group but towering above them all was the Scottish writer, Adam Smith, whose great work, *The Wealth of Nations* (1776) was the most powerful indictment of mercantilism ever penned, and he is usually regarded as the greatest of all protagonists of free trade. Even before the Revolution, as we shall notice, the influence of these men was felt; and the first half of the nineteenth century was destined to become as truly the age of Smith as the second half of the eighteenth had been the age of Voltaire.

(4) Voltaire   Of this intellectual circle the most conspicuous and perhaps the most brilliant was Voltaire. An exceedingly prolific writer, he poured forth dramas, satirical poems, historical works, essays on various subjects, and even an exposition of Newton. He was also a rare combination of man of letters and business man, and his profitable speculations enabled him to live the life he chose without recourse to a patron. Yet he was not above wire-pulling, and he cultivated prominent people, like Choiseul, who might help him escape the rigors of the censorship. Voltaire's chief target was the Church. "Annihilate the infamous thing," he wrote, and what he meant was the spirit of bigotry and superstition. Even when he did not allege its pernicious influence, he seems to have looked upon the Church as a privileged nuisance. Marriage was to him primarily a social rather than a religious institution, and a civil contract, he felt, should be all that was necessary. He felt also that the wealth of the Church should bear its equitable share of taxation; and in one of his most forceful works, *The Letters on the English,* he pointed out among other things that the Church and nobility in England were not exempt from direct taxation. As a

because they grounded their theories on what they believed to be "natural law." They represented a sort of reaction against commerce and industry, with which mercantilism was chiefly concerned, considering them "sterile" because, as they argued, these involved merely exchange, which contributed nothing to wealth. They had no notion of utility or demand as a criterion of value. Their attitude of laissez-faire proceeded from contempt for industry rather than from reasoning, as in the case of Adam Smith. But while the Physiocrats believed only in taxing land (to them the source of all wealth), they were incensed against the unequal distribution of wealth and wanted to see the peasant relieved of his feudal burdens. Turgot (who differed from the rest of the school in not denying that industry and commerce were unproductive) had some chance to apply his views, and we shall find him trying to make an end of the government *corvée*.

reformer he plowed deeper than Montesquieu, for he did not hesitate to attack "privilege," and he once violently arraigned the parlement of Paris for condemning an author who had written against feudalism. Yet he avowed his disbelief in social equality, and accepted class divisions as final and inevitable. A practical intelligence, a keen sense of justice, and a kindly streak in his nature made this astute cynic a ready sympathizer with anyone who suffered from persecution or the inhumanity of the penal code, and he spared no effort to get justice for many a victim of the existing order. Thanks to his brilliant pen, he enjoyed a celebrity far greater than any of the other *philosophes*. For nearly two years he was the guest of Frederick the Great; he corresponded with Catherine II; and his home was a Mecca for hundreds who came to pay him homage. No man of his time was more read or fêted. No one perhaps enjoyed a greater publicity, though he was vain enough to be often piqued by criticism. He was an odd mixture of courage and timidity. Deist though he was, he occasionally partook of the mass to soften the government's wrath, and he definitely established his abode near the Swiss frontier so that he could easily seek refuge across the border. Yet in his slashing attacks on the Church and other pillars of the Old Régime he was something of a crusader, and everything he wrote was couched in the most exquisite wit—a fact which made his arrows all the more deadly. He was the prince of rationalists, and all the characteristics of the movement, its merits and defects, are displayed in his career.

The idea underlying rationalism, as we have said, was that everything should bear the test of reason. Let us mark now the manner of its application. It parted altogether with faith as an integral part of religion, and substituted for orthodox religion, as the guiding force in life, a morality concerned with social welfare. The critical attitude it assumed made it *a priori* rather hostile to existing conventions; at least they must prove their social worth. Being practical from that standpoint, it was naturally humanitarian. In punctuating his argument that the penalty should fit the crime, Voltaire cited the case of a servant who was condemned to death for stealing some linen from a mistress who actually owed her money. Doubtless "reason" followed the promptings of the heart more than the rationalists would have admitted. The heavy weight of taxation upon the peasant or the burdens placed upon

Character and limitations of rationalism

him by feudalism ran counter to their sense of justice, while at the same time they could argue against these things in a perfectly rational spirit. One naturally deduces from their reasoning that man's comfort and happiness were the things most to be sought for in this—almost sufficient—temporal world, but not many of them, like Holbach [1] and Jeremy Bentham, followed the dubious doctrine that seeking one's own interest would lead, as a matter of course, to the general good. Generally speaking, the virtue that was most extolled was that of human kindness. With their breadth of outlook, the rationalists naturally tended to cosmopolitanism. They entirely disapproved of national wars, and, rejoicing in a common learning which knew no national frontiers, they formed a sort of universal cult, the like of which had not been felt since the time of Erasmus. Perhaps a product of this spirit, the German poet, Goethe, who flourished a little later, prided himself on feeling no love of country, choosing rather to attach himself in spirit to any land (and it happened to be France) that represented to him the peak of culture. Pacifism was a natural accompaniment of cosmopolitanism, though there were many before Voltaire's day, who, like him, had exposed the folly of most wars. Yet, keen critics though they were, the rationalists were far from revolutionary. Most of them believed in absolute monarchy, and felt that the reforms they wanted could best come about from above. Thus Voltaire said that for his part he preferred to be ruled by one fine lion than by two hundred rats. [2] Most of them, on the whole, rather erred on the side of caution. With a wholesome respect for the censorship they often attacked by implication alone, and they frequently sought the shelter of anonymity. One gets the impression that they did not always dig as deeply as they would have wished. Nor were they, as a whole, constructive, and Montesquieu, who may be regarded as the sole important exception, was indeed somewhat reactionary, as we have noted. But the fundamental defect of the rationalists was the confidence which they placed in human reason. They seemed to believe that anyone should be able to know what was best for him, and that good laws were all that were needed to make men happy. They failed, almost as much as Rousseau and the romantic school, to realize the com-

[1] Holbach was a pronounced atheist and thereby incurred the disapproval of Voltaire and other Deists.

[2] Voltaire's statement was made in reference to the parlement of Paris, then at loggerheads with the king.

plexity of human nature. With the exception, moreover, of Montesquieu, they discounted the influence of the past in shaping human character and tendencies. Yet the historical importance of the rationalists was very great. They undermined respect for the Old Régime, and by their continuous barrage of criticism they made it easier for later thinkers to try their luck at really intelligent building. It is not certain that, but for the rationalists, there would ever have been a Rousseau.

It was in the last decade before the outbreak of the French *Rousseau,* Revolution that a somewhat different spirit seemed to captivate a *the "lone* society which had gorged itself on "reason." This change was *wolf"* due to the advent of a new figure in the public eye, Jean Jacques Rousseau. Of all the men who have made modern history, there is hardly one whose intellect was more warped by faults of character. A moral pervert, with an ego constantly aggravated by morbid introspection, and in his later years a victim of paranoia, Rousseau was probably a pathological case, and with all his flashes of genius, he was always strongly impelled by his emotions. Thus may we account for many of his contradictions. An ardent sympathizer with the masses, he lacked the ability to adapt himself to any social group. Profoundly interested in education, he, nevertheless, sent his own (illegitimate) children to a foundling asylum. Intolerant of restraint and often banned for his incendiary ideas, he nevertheless expounded religious views which opened the way for persecution.[1] A man of intense moral fervor, he committed almost every sin in the decalogue. Perhaps these curious kinks in his character are partly to be explained by his neglected childhood and by the vagabond life which he led in his youth; indeed he never quite ceased to be a vagabond, and though as often befriended as repulsed, he accepted kindness without gratitude just as he bore hardships with the feeling that his innocence was powerless to protect him against circumstance. It was a proof of the growing esteem for men with ideas that such a person as Rousseau, self-educated and always boorish in his manners, should have obtained en entrée by the back door, as one writer puts it, to the intellectual

[1] Perhaps because of his Genevan background, Rousseau was deeply religious, though not in the orthodox sense. He recommended a "civil religion," the "dogmas" of which were belief in God (according to the Deist conception), in immortality, in "the happiness of the just and the punishment of the wicked," and in the "sanctity of the social contract and the laws." But "if any one," he writes, "after publicly recognizing these dogmas, behaves as if he does not believe them, let him be punished by death." Yet in the next paragraph he denounces intolerance.

world of Paris, that charmingly witty society which looked upon itself as the censor of the age. But Rousseau could not find in it any affinity. Abnormally shy, completely devoid of a sense of humor, painfully lacking in self-control, and intolerant of all criticism, he could not live in peace with the other philosophers, who, even when they did not agree with him, fully recognized his worth, and were broad enough to give his sentiments a full hearing. Yet the very fact of his handicaps—his personality, his poverty, and the views that he held in an age that was moving slowly—must attest to his vigorous self-confidence and the brilliance of his often curiously distorted imagination.

Portrait by Allen Ramsay

JEAN JACQUES ROUSSEAU

In contradistinction to most of the rationalists, Rousseau was deliberately constructive. His vivid imagination pushed through the frequently shoddy and outworn accumulations of history and looked beyond to a new order. He could do this the more readily, moreover, because, unlike the rationalists, he did not bother to test his premises but allowed himself to be moved by his emotions.

Rousseau was at bottom a sentimentalist. His principal theory, stated in a nutshell, was that man was essentially good, but corrupted by civilization; take him back to a simpler existence and give him the advantage of a proper education and he might be expected to act wisely. Holding as he did this exalted view of mankind, he felt that it was in the people that sovereignty should properly rest. He imagined that in some remote age men had delegated their sovereignty to the community of which they were a part, that then a prince usurped this sovereignty, but that it still properly resided in the community, which might depose the prince if he failed to do his duty. Such was the basic theme of the *Social*

Contract, published in 1762, and destined to be the gospel of radical revolutionists. "From whatever side we approach our principle," he writes, "we reach the same conclusion: that the social contract sets up among the citizens an equality of such a kind that they all bind themselves to observe the same conditions and should therefore all enjoy the same rights." He laid great stress on what he termed the "general will," which may perhaps be understood as the freedom of the sovereign people operating as a sort of intuitive desire for the general welfare, but which in practice might not always display good judgment (it depended, he inferred, on the level of education), and which (alas for the "natural rights" of man!) must be interpreted by the majority. As Rousseau disapproved of parliaments ("the people cannot be represented"), we may presume that he would have approved of the referendum as the best device for eliciting the general will.

There is so much that is abstract and even sometimes contradictory in Rousseau that it is hard, indeed, to state his position precisely. There was little in his philosophy that was original (the compact theory, for instance, had often been expounded), and his views were neither scientific at bottom nor always logical in exposition. Out of sorts with himself and the world, he must have enjoyed to the full his tirade against civilization, and it was characteristic of the man that he did not qualify his criticisms. Despising as he did the government of Louis XV and the hollow and cynical society of his day, he looked to the suffering masses as the rightful possessors of sovereignty, and believing as he did in the essential goodness of man, he explicitly evoked the principle of equality. Yet Rousseau profoundly dreaded revolution, and now and then his caution was as amazing as it was futile. He frankly agreed with Montesquieu that the same form of government was not suited to all states; he admitted that popular sovereignty was only workable in a very small community and where men were approximately equal in rank and fortune; and he showed a profound respect for law and even for the rights of property, though he felt that man's original equality in property rights had perished when someone had begun to seize some land for his own enrichment. But it did not really matter what one thought of Rousseau's arguments. It was the spirit of his writings, more than the letter, that really counted. He wanted men to be natural. He wished the child to develop spontaneously, and in his plea for a less fettered and less stereotyped instruction, he is pointed to as the founder of modern methods of education. He was the champion of the simple life, the ardent lover of the beauties of nature, the promoter of romanticism—letting the spirit soar above the cold facts of reason. It seemed as if the very novelty of his preaching (his works included a romantic novel) had the effect of taking people out of themselves. Above all he inspired men to believe in democracy and equality, and seemed to open to the individual a new world.

Evolution of a public opinion

In a sense the exhilarating genius of Rousseau was like a breath of fresh air coming into an atmosphere redolent of decay and of an excess of the conventional and commonplace. But to minds already open to the idea of change the airing of radical views could hardly have been a shock. Not every bourgeois had yet become a rationalist, but so large a number was reading the works of Montesquieu and Voltaire (not to mention the lesser lights), that we may be justified in speaking of a public opinion—meaning by that a vigorous, restive attitude of dissent from many of the principles and practices of the Old Régime. The salons were, of course, a clearinghouse for the ideas of most of the philosophers, many of whom were regular *habitués*. Later discussion clubs—*sociétés de pensée* they were called—were formed not only in Paris but in many of the provincial centers. Then there were the Masonic lodges in some of the larger towns, where all the more radical theories received a vigorous airing. Many of the future orators of the Revolution belonged to these organizations, and doubtless had already acquired a local fame. Finally, an increasing number of brochures appeared from the pen of anonymous writers following up the writings of the greater lights, somewhat like the foamy trough that follows in the wake of a steamer. In the 'eighties, after the leading salons had ceased to be held, the homes of rich financiers were often a center for the gathering of intellectuals—the meeting-place for new and more radical opinions. By this time interest in Rousseau had almost superseded the earlier vogue of rationalism, and the triumph of the American Revolution had seemed to show that his ideas were capable of application.

Generally speaking, public opinion was the affair of the middle class, more particularly the lawyers, wealthy business men, and some of the government officials. Yet its range also included a few nobles like Lafayette, and, what was perhaps more interesting, it was beginning to include the masses. While it is true, of course, that the mass of the nation could not read (the number of primary schools was small in proportion to the total population), nevertheless there were plenty of people of humbler calling who had heard of the new ideas and discussed them on a street corner or in the public square. "Life overflowed in the eighteenth century street, and a funny story or daring idea flew from mouth to mouth." Even some of the parish priests are known to have been readers of the *Encyclopedia*, and the real import of their influence is still unknown. At all events, it seems evident that the number of centers for the generation of a public opinion were steadily multiplying, and that even the masses—at all events the urban proletariat—were coming to be articulate. There was no plotting of revolution, but there was undoubtedly a serious undercurrent of unrest.

It must not be supposed that Church and State were entirely unmoved by all this ferment. The occasional vigor of the censorship seemed to show that there was always a limit to the government's patience. But in general the king's ministers, especially those of Louis XVI, seemed disinclined to court unnecessary trouble. Somewhat earlier Pompadour and Choiseul had actually patronized the philosophers, but in Louis XVI's time it was rather more dangerous to play with fire. No doubt the fact that some of the ministers themselves were mildly permeated with the new ideas, and the fact that "society"—or at least its thoughtful elements—had given them something of a vogue had much to do with dampening the censor's ardor. Now and then, it is true, a pamphlet would be burned, but not till after the mischief had been done. Indeed the decrepit government of Louis XV had allowed the movement to gather too much strength in the beginning. Was it not conceivable, then, that the government of his successor might steal some of the thunder of the reformers and yield in some measure to the Enlightenment? Was it too late for absolute monarchy to save itself by reform? *The government and public opinion*

It is interesting to observe that throughout Europe various monarchs had been touched by the Enlightenment. Not only had many of them read the works of Voltaire and others but two of them, Frederick the Great and Catherine II, had come into direct contact with members of the philosophic group. Voltaire, as we have said, visited Frederick the Great, Diderot went on a *The question of reform—"Benevolent despotism": (1) in Europe* mission to St. Petersburg, and both these monarchs corresponded with certain of the philosophers. Both monarchs prided themselves on being patterns of the Enlightenment. Yet when it came to putting thoughts into action, neither Frederick nor Catherine was willing to proceed very far. With all due notice of a few reforms in Prussia it seems evident that with Frederick as with Catherine "enlightenment" was something of a pose. Only in Portugal, Spain, Denmark, Tuscany, and Austria was reform seriously attempted. In Joseph II benevolent despotism reached its highest level, but with him, for various reasons already mentioned, it met with complete disaster. But what of France— accustomed leader in the world of culture and classic home of the Enlightenment?

(2) In France

Of all nations France should have been the home of enlightened monarchy. Most of the *philosophes* themselves had cherished the belief that only through the crown should the reforms that they desired be achieved. It is a testimony of the influence of this cult that even in the days of Louis XV the government had earnestly tried to free the grain trade from its trammels,[1] and in the parallel sphere of industry it had undermined the gilds, as we have noted.[2] When Louis XVI came to the throne of his unmourned predecessor, a spontaneous feeling of hope seemed to spring from every heart. Moreover, the new king's ministers were certainly a good omen. With Turgot, the liberal economist, the experienced and successful intendant, as head of the finances, Louis seemed to have chosen the likeliest instrument for effecting a reformation in the disordered life of the monarchy. The King promised him his backing, and Turgot commenced his task. Though popular prejudice had thwarted the former attempts to free the grain trade, Turgot did not hesitate to resume the policy. He also went further than his predecessors and attempted to destroy the gilds. The explanation of his failure will be presently considered. It is important, however, to realize that Turgot's energy and enlightenment were by no means a unique example of the government's good intentions. Some of his successors were responsible for re-

[1] Grain might be shipped freely throughout France and even exported to foreign countries when a stable price was assured the home consumer. Unhappily bad harvests followed these edicts (1763–4) and it was popularly believed that speculators had cornered the market, causing the high cost of bread. There was so great an outcry that the government suspended its edicts. Later Turgot was to encounter much the same expérience.

[2] Page 250.

forms in an effort to do justice to various elements in the population or for the purpose of rendering the government more efficient. But when all has been said, the actual results of benevolent despotism were slight, and it became increasingly clear that the monarchy lacked the courage to take the steps that would have assured its own salvation.

In the first place, Louis XVI, with all his kindness of heart, had a sluggish mentality, and what was more, a weak will. Where the situation called for the boldness and tenacity of a Joseph II plus the finesse of a Catherine the Great, Louis had not even the latent capacity of his grandfather. The government which he headed seemed willing enough to bend to the Enlightenment, but, as in the previous reign, there was a lack of any reasoned, clean-cut policy. The monarchy alternately smiled and frowned on rationalism. It lacked the moral courage to fight on either side of the issue. In the second place, the state of the finances, which we have already described, was fast approaching bankruptcy. Mild measures of relief, which might have sufficed a century earlier, were now no longer practicable. The crown must attempt the heroic or would perish. One of two things, and possibly both, were necessary: either the government must drastically retrench, put a check on the court's extravagance, and curtail the long list of pensions, or it must tap new resources. But in either case—and here is the third cause of the monarchy's plight—the sacrifice must be borne by the privileged classes. The time had come when only by overriding the claims of feudal tradition could the monarchy find the revenues to go on. But realizing the opposition that must ensue, one can readily see how hopeless was this problem for a Louis XVI. Absolute monarchy was revealing its fatal flaw—the fact that sovereignty depended on the accident of heredity.

The Weakness of the Monarchy as the Negative Cause of the French Revolution

Causes of the monarchy's weakness

It was, in fact, the stifling influence of the upper classes, pressing constantly on a weak king and a frivolous queen, that blocked every avenue of escape from the dilemma. Turgot had tried manfully to put order into the finances; he had bravely imposed economies, and had been so far successful as to reduce the annual deficit by more than a third; then, in order to give the nation a better chance to exploit its resources, he had for the moment abolished the gilds as well as the *corvée* (that levy on the peasants' time), and had embarked on various measures to free internal

"Privilege" as the obstacle to reform

trade. But the minister soon saw, if he were not actually aware of it from the first, that he would have to encroach upon "privilege," and when he sought to put through a land tax, falling on all classes alike, the uproar which had been gathering from all the elements whose interests or prejudices had been attacked by the reckless minister now reached a fatal climax. Exerting their influence through the Queen, the courtiers persuaded Louis to dismiss him. Doubtless Turgot, like Joseph II, had attempted too much at one time, but it was hard for a man to be patient when he saw so much to be done, and there was something strangely prophetic in the warning he uttered to the King. "Do not forget, Sire," was the minister's parting comment, "that weakness cost Charles I his head." The crown had taken a suicidal step, for Turgot, perhaps alone among his contemporaries, might conceivably have saved the absolute monarchy. From now on the rickety government was headed for final collapse. Well might Voltaire say, when he heard of Turgot's fall: "I am as one dashed to the ground. Never can we console ourselves for having seen the golden age dawn and perish. My eyes see only death in front of me, now that Monsieur Turgot is gone."

The Financial Crisis and the Insurgence of the Nobility

In truth the absolute monarchy sounded its own death knell when Turgot was dismissed. His immediate successors, such as Necker (a banker called to the helm because he could borrow on his personal credit) were men of far inferior capacity and merely kept the government afloat by temporary expedients. Mostly it was by borrowing, and such was merely sinking deeper into the slough. Moreover, the War of American Independence was

"Privilege" on the offensive

a boomerang for the monarchy, not only because it popularized liberal ideas, but especially because it augmented the public debt by fifteen hundred million livres. But embarrassments only increased after Necker's fall. A subsequent comptroller of the finances, Calonne, allowed—and perhaps encouraged—a new outburst of extravagance, and both the debt and the deficit mounted to still higher levels. Reckless courtier though he was, Calonne saw that such a policy could not continue.

It became increasingly evident that a crash was close at hand. Calonne was forced to the conclusion that the only possible solution was to levy on "privilege." Since neither he nor the King, however, possessed sufficient courage to take so drastic a step by dint of the royal fiat, Calonne persuaded the King to call an assembly of notables. If only the privileged class, once they learned of the monarchy's plight, would signify their willingness to be taxed, then indeed the crisis might be passed and the monarchy might scramble to its feet. The meeting of the assembly of notables in 1787 was pregnant with possibilities. Instead, however, of leading to the rescue of the government, it marked the beginning of the insurgence of the privileged classes against the monarchy.

Calonne's concrete proposal was a land tax which should fall on all classes without distinction. Besides this, he revived many of Turgot's other measures—the abolition of tariffs on provincial frontiers, the freedom of the grain trade from government regulation, and the immediate reduction of the *taille*. There was at once, of course, objections to these proposals, more especially to the new tax. To put all classes on an equal footing "would," declared the notables, "destroy the [existing] hierarchy, necessary to the maintenance of the monarchy." Such was, of course, specious reasoning, but when the assembly attempted to learn the exact condition of the finances, it immediately put the minister on the defensive. When he finally confessed a deficit of 112,000,000 livres, the notables simply refused to be convinced and proceeded to demand proof. For some reason—probably because his books were in a muddle—Calonne refused, pleading that the king had accepted the figures and that was enough. In vain he appealed to the patriotism of the assemblage; the notables would have none of his new tax. The upshot of the episode was so fierce a storm of protest that Louis finally yielded, and dismissed Calonne from office.

If Calonne had found the notables intractable, it was not likely that his successor, Brienne, would find them any less so. In fact, after failing once more to get a full report on the finances, they declared themselves unable to give advice, and hypocritically bewailed the taxpayer's lot. There was, therefore, nothing left for the King to do but to dissolve them. But the meeting had held the germ of the French Revolution. One of the nobles present, the Marquis of Lafayette, whose adventurous soul had enjoyed the atmosphere of revolution across the seas, had dared to declare for the calling of an estates general.

The demand for an estates general—now for the first time raised as a national issue [1]—following as it did the refusal of the

[1] It had, however, been demanded by the parlement of Bordeaux in 1785.

notables to advise an attack on "privilege," seemed to indicate that the upper classes were determined to limit the power of the crown. The estates general was a much more august body than the notables, and though it would include representatives of the third estate, the fact that two orders were constituted of the upper classes would presumably insure their mastery of its proceedings. On the part of these magnates the whole movement was apparently reactionary—a revival of the old elements of opposition to the crown; but the fact of immediate importance was the moral collapse of the monarchy.

Widening of the insurgence

And meanwhile the movement was beginning to reach the other section of the nobility. Brienne, having decided to institute the proposed tax by royal enactment, was confronted with the resistance of the parlement of Paris. When requested to register the tax, the magistrates demanded the submission of a report on the finances, declaring also that "the nation alone, in an estates general assembled, can consent to a perpetual impost"; and on July 24, 1787 it formally demanded an estates general. Thus did the nobles of the robe join the nobles by birth in a deliberate movement to embarrass the crown and curtail its authority. For the moment the King showed fight and the parlement was ordered summarily into exile. But methods by which the crown had formerly coerced its judges were apparently futile now. Other tribunals took up the cause of the parlement and pronounced the tax illegal. Brienne then finally yielded and the parlement was recalled. But the government was no nearer to a solution of its problems. The parlement merely reiterated its demand for an estates general. One of the older members brought their case to the King himself: "Your ministers, Sire, wish to avoid the estates general because they fear its surveillance. But their hopes are vain. The needs of the State will force you to convoke it within two years."

Capitulation of the crown —the summons of an estates general

So frank an utterance but exemplifies the declining respect for the sovereign. It must be realized, too, that the parlement, notwithstanding the dubious character of its resistance (for its members were a selfish caste, mainly interested in showing their power), had seemed to excited citizens the veritable champions of all classes in a struggle with arrogant despotism. The increasing unpopularity of the Queen (who was usually blamed for everything) also fanned the public fury and reacted against the government. Hopeless to put through the tax, and for the moment only anxious for new loans to meet current expenses, the King finally consented to the calling of the estates general within five years. When further resistance developed—the parlement demanding an immediate convocation—the government took the desperate course of attempting a reorganization of the judiciary. But after the parlement had been forced to register this new decree, the provincial parlements joined the revolt. So great had become the public agitation by this time that the provincial estates of Dauphiny, long suppressed by royal action, now resumed its functions, and not only sent a petition to the king, demanding an estates general but took an oath to pay no taxes till the assembly was convoked.

The crown was at its wits' end. There was scarcely any money in the treasury; current interest on the government debt could not be met; and a loan could not be covered. Bankruptcy was at hand. Hence, on July 5, 1788 Louis XVI issued a call for an estates general, the elective representatives of the nation. The way was opened for revolution.

FOR FURTHER READING OR STUDY

Robinson and Beard, *Readings in Modern European History*, vol. i, chaps. viii–xi; *Transcripts and Reprints*, vol. vi (French philosophers of the eighteenth century); Butterfield H., *Select Documents of European History*, vol. iii, chaps. v and vi; Young, A., *Travels in France;* Montesquieu, *The Spirit of Laws* (ed. Nugent, T.), 2 vols.; Rousseau, *The Social Contract* (various editions); *Memoirs and Anecdotes of the Duc de Ségur.*

Hayes, C. J. H., *A Political and Cultural History of Modern Europe*, vol. i, pp. 496–596; Gillespie, J. E., *A History of Modern Europe, 1500–1815,* chaps. xxii–xxiii and pp. 483–98; Gershoy, L., *The French Revolution and Napoleon,* chaps. i–iv; Gottschalk, L., *The Era of the French Revolution,* part i, book i, chaps. i–iv; Grant, A. J., *The French Monarchy*, vol. ii, chaps. xix–xxi; Seignobos, C., *The Evolution of the French People,* chap. xvi; Guignebert, C., *A Short History of the French People,* vol. ii, chaps. xxiv and xxvii (a good brief survey); Tilley, A., *Modern France,* chaps. iv (*passim*) and v; Bourne, H. E., *The Revolutionary Period in Europe,* chaps. i (useful survey of Europe), ii–v and vii; Ogg, F. A., *The Economic Development of Modern Europe,* chap. iii (on the gilds); Day, C., *A History of Commerce,* chap. xxv (French economic policy); Madelin, L., *The French Revolution,* chaps. i–v (interesting but only a glance); Mathiez, A., *The French Revolution,* chaps. i–ii (useful summary of economic conditions in France); Flick, A. C., *Modern World History, 1776–1926,* chap. iv.

Lowell, E. J., *The Eve of the French Revolution* (somewhat out of date but still a fair survey of conditions in France); Funck-Brentano, F., *The Old Régime in France* (discursive but interesting); Ducros, L.. *French Society in the Eighteenth Century;* Seé, H., *Economic and Social Conditions in France in the Eighteenth Century* (a valuable study); *The Cambridge Modern History,* vol. viii, chap. ii (useful reference for conditions in France); Herbert, S., *The Fall of Feudalism in France,* chap. i; Richard, E., *History of German Civilization;* La Rocheterie, M. de, *The Life of Marie Antoinette;* Smith, P., *A History of Modern Culture,* 2 vols.; Mowat, R. B., *The Age of Reason* (interesting sidelight rather than a complete picture); Turberville, A. S., *English Men and Manners in Eighteenth Century;* Thorndike, *A Short History of Civilization,* chaps. xxxiv and xxxvii; Sedgwick, W. T., and Tyler, H. W., *A Short History of Science;* Shipley, A. E., *The Revival of Science in the Seventeenth Century;* Randall, H., *The Making of the Modern Mind,* book iii; Laski, H. L., *Political Thought in England from Locke to Bentham;* Hearnshaw, J. F. C., *Social and Political Ideas of Some Great Thinkers in the Seventeenth and Eighteenth Centuries;* Robinson, H., *Bayle, the Skeptic;* Mornet, D., *French Political Thought in the Eighteenth Century;* Martin, K., *French Liberal Thought in the Eighteenth Century* (interesting); Sorel, A., *Montesquieu;* Morley, J., *Voltaire;* Maurois, A., *Voltaire* (brief, popular); Morley, J., *Diderot and the Encyclopedists;* Morley, J., *Rousseau;* Josephson, M., *Jean-Jacques Rousseau* (sympathetic); Hendel, C., *Jean Jacques Rousseau, Moralist,* 2 vols.; Say, L., *Turgot;* Stephens, W. W., *Life and Writings of Turgot;* Hearnshaw, F. J. C., *The Social and Political Ideas of Some Great French Thinkers of the Age of Reason;* Schapiro, J. S., *Condorcet and the Rise of Liberalism;* Rocquain, F., *The Revolutionary Period Preceding the French Revolution* (rather overestimates the importance of the quarrels between the crown and parlement); Roustan, M., *The Pioneers of the French Revolution;* Clergue, H., *The Salon;* Bruun, G., *The Enlightened Despots;* Knowles, L., "New Light on the Economic Causes of the French Revolution," *Economic Journal,* xxix, 1 ff.

THE ERA OF REVOLUTION

VIII. THE FRENCH REVOLUTION

1. THE REGENERATION OF FRANCE

A. The Assumption of Leadership by the Middle Class and the Opening of the Revolutionary Drama

Immediate significance of the summons of an estates general; Question of organization; State of public opinion; Opening of the estates general; The deadlock; Outbreak of the Revolution; Triumph of the middle class and inauguration of the Constituent Assembly.

B. The Revolution as an Instrument of the Populace

(1) *The Revolution in Paris*

The July Riots; The October Riots; The King's opportunity.

(2) *The Revolution in the Provinces*

The "municipal revolution"; Uprising of the peasantry; Downfall of feudalism.

C. The Revolution as an Instrument of the Middle Class—The Establishment of the "Bourgeois Monarchy"

(1) *Character of the Constituent Assembly*

Merits of the assembly; Leading personalities in the assembly; Demerits of the assembly.

(2) *Work of the Constituent Assembly*

Question of fundamental rights; Destructive work of the assembly; Constructive work of the assembly: (1) organization of the constitutional monarchy, (2) immediate solution of the financial problem, (3) the Civil Constitution of the Clergy; Momentary ascendency of the middle class; Estimate of the work of the assembly.

2. THE CLIMAX OF THE REVOLUTION—THE FALL OF MONARCHY AND THE CLASH WITH EUROPE

A. The Doom of the "Bourgeois Monarchy"

Growth of popular unrest; Rôle of the Jacobin Club; Instability of the new régime and failure of Mirabeau; Disaffection of the army; Incapacity of the King; The "Flight to Varennes"; Popular intervention and its result; Last days of the Constituent Assembly.

B. The Legislative Assembly and the Outbreak of War

Opening and character of the Legislative Assembly; Parties in the Assembly—the leadership of the Girondins; The Girondins and the war issue.

C. The Supremacy of the Populace and the Downfall of the "Bour-
    geois Monarchy"

Intervention of the populace and the beginning of mob rule; Influence of
the national crisis; Downfall of the monarchy; The September Massacres; The
National Convention and the establishment of the First Republic; Girondins
vs. Jacobins; Fall of the Girondins—the eclipse of the middle class.

Since adequate reform in the Old Régime seemed slow and
almost impossible of attainment, it may be fortunate for the world
that revolution overtook society and thus accelerated the march
of civilization. The reason why this movement that was to revolutionize political and social relationships in Europe had its
beginnings in France has already been noted. Like most revolutions, it was not deliberately planned, but was precipitated by
the course of events; and it was some time, indeed, before people
realized that it was a revolution—still less that it was likely to
involve Europe. Naturally its influence in the broader sphere
would depend on the ultimate course of the movement in France.
It was in France that the absolute monarchy of the Old Régime
had broken down.

The Regeneration of France

We have noticed that the bankruptcy of the monarchy, together
with its lack of moral courage, had resulted in surrender to the
demand for an estates general. We have also noticed that it was
the privileged classes which had forced this surrender, not with
any idea of establishing a popular régime or civic equality, but
rather with a view of strengthening their own position. With a
blindness characteristic of a class that lived in the past, they did
not see that their own interests were really bound up with the
monarchy, and to attack absolutism was to expose the citadel of
"privilege" to a like assault. We can only think that they expected to dominate the coming estates general, and did not appreciate for the moment the extent of the moral upheaval.

Less active than the nobles at the outset, the members of the
middle class were, after all, the kernel of what we have called
"public opinion." It was they who had brought about the intellectual awakening; it was they who had circulated opinions throughout the land; and they who took the keenest interest in the coming
assembly. As has already been said, their chief enemy was "privilege." When Necker had published in 1781 what purported to be

an account of the state of the finances, it was the long pension list there disclosed, that seemed to aggravate the bitterness which this class already cherished against the monarchy as a protector of "privilege." That they had any rooted dislike of monarchy in principle may be doubted, but if it were necessary to limit monarchy in order to rid it of this fungus, then monarchy should be placed under some sort of shackles. But it is doubtful if at this point—that is, when the estates general was called—many of the bourgeoisie really knew exactly what they wanted. Some control over the finances—the determination of the sources of revenue and the manner in which it should be spent—was something on which the class was ready to insist; otherwise the meaning of a "constitution" was for the future to determine. But in any case the important immediate fact was that they and not the nobles were rapidly assuming command of the situation. We must now follow the course of events which opened the drama of revolution.

The Assumption of Leadership by the Middle Class and the Opening of the Revolutionary Drama

The decree of council of July 5, 1788, which had definitely called the estates general, followed by that of August 8, which summoned it to meet on May 1, 1789, was of tremendous moral significance. *Immediate significance of the summons of an estates general* Unquestionably it betokened a defeat for the monarchy and marked a definite shifting of the moral leadership from the crown to the nation as a whole. To the general public—for one may now use the term to include a very large constituency—the act seemed almost like a mystic "open-sesame." What might not this historic assemblage accomplish? No estates general had met for a period of one hundred and seventy-five years—none within the memory of any living man; nor could the oldest man in the kingdom have heard an account of the previous one from his great-grandfather. Naturally enough, it seemed that if this strange, bygone institution were now to be revived, great events must surely follow. France would be regenerated.

In fact so completely had this ancient institution passed out of men's calculations that the government itself had only a vague *The question of organization* idea of how it should be constituted. Hence it instituted a commission to search through the records, while it also invited anyone who could to furnish information. As a matter of political tactics such a move was probably unwise, for it encouraged speculation among all classes of society, and those who looked forward to controlling the assembly were encouraged to press their claims. The crucial question was whether the estates general should resolve itself into three separate chambers, as had been the case in 1614—in which case the first and second estates (comprising deputies of the privileged classes) would outvote the third—or whether they should meet and vote as one body. In the latter case, provided the third estate was given a preponderance in numbers, and provided some at least of the lower clergy would vote with them, the middle class might be expected to control the assembly. Naturally the privileged classes clamored for the first alternative, while a group of the middle class, who had organized for the campaign as the so-called "National Party," agitated for the second and more revolutionary device.

The crown was alone qualified to decide this question, but Louis seemed incapable of any decision, and the minister on whom he relied was ever a shifty opportunist. To succeed Brienne (whose position had become untenable) the King had recalled Necker, and it was to him that he had confided the intricate problem of getting together the estates general. Not wishing to offend the privileged classes, Necker delayed till the end of the year all positive instructions. In the meantime the parlement of Paris had shown its true colors by declaring for the former usage of separate meetings of the three orders—thus proving more clearly than ever how ridiculous had been the assumption that it was the champion of the people. Necker even called back the notables again, and they, as might be expected, declared for precisely the same solution. Convinced, nevertheless, that he must yield a point unless he were to lose that public esteem which he had done so little to deserve, he caused it to be announced toward the close of the year that the third estate should have as many deputies as both the other orders combined. But of the more important question, how the estates should meet, whether as one body or three, he said nothing. It was something, however, that the crown promised control of taxation by the estates general (was absolute monarchy really abdicating?), as well as other reforms. On the other hand, he explicitly upheld "privilege." Such a policy of trimming meant that Necker was wholly unequal to the task of enabling the crown to recover the leadership. The inevitable result was a struggle between the privileged and unprivileged for the control of the estates general. As one writer put it in January, 1789, "It is no longer but very secondarily a question of the king, of despotism, and of the constitution; it is a war between the third estate and the two other orders."

And the bourgeoisie was constantly gaining in moral power. *State of public opinion* Stimulated by the government's queries, a flood of pamphlets had appeared, and not only was the more democratic plan for the organization of the estates general widely circulated but public opinion was instructed as to the powers it should exercise and what it should demand. Agitation, moreover, redoubled, as the winter wore on, for a bad harvest had caused acute distress in the countryside, and brigandage was so rife that many provinces were terrorized. It was the beginning of the "Great Fear"—that terror of all sorts of enemies, real and unreal, which later racked a country already excited by revolution. In the towns, too, there was hardly less suffering, for a commercial treaty with England, which had given favored treatment to French wines but had allowed English textiles to come in and capture the market, had seriously depressed French industry and thrown thousands out of work. Rumor had it that there were a hundred thousand beggars in the city of Paris! It is no wonder that sporadic riots occurred. Yet, while grain was seized on some occasions by famished peasants, cases of actual bloodshed seem to have been rare. The government —perhaps wisely—allowed these fires to burn themselves out, and under the circumstances, considering the crisis which the country was passing through, the national temper was remarkably tranquil.

Perhaps one explanation is that, apart from those impelled by hunger, the public interest was focused on the elections. We shall not take time to describe the rather intricate arrangements prescribed by Necker. While the election of the deputies for the first and second estate was relatively simple, that of the third estate was indirect (sometimes very much so), and it is remarkable that in a country, unused to such an experience, the balloting took place with so few cases of violence, especially as the suffrage in the case of the third estate was practically universal. Most of the deputies chosen for the third estate were bourgeois, as might be expected; and though there were some prominent figures from the towns, there was a rather notable predominance of country lawyers. It was a very striking fact that the parish priests won a

majority of seats for the first estate, thus portending a breach in
one of the privileged orders. In the meantime, besides the election
of deputies, each order had the duty of preparing *cahiers* or
grievances, and there is nothing more instructive of the state of
mind in France at this critical moment. Except where they were
coerced, the lower clergy had their fling at their arrogant superiors.
The nobles' *cahiers*, while silent, of course, on the matter of "privilege," joined with those of the other orders in condemning absolutism; and thus it appeared that a limited monarchy of some
sort was very generally demanded. But, whereas the privileged
classes looked back to the days of the feudal monarchy, the third
estate wanted a more liberal constitution, and insisted that the
estates general, meeting as one body, should create one. In some
cases model *cahiers*, conveniently provided by the National Party,
had been followed almost word for word; yet there is no reason
to doubt the spontaneity of the grievances drafted, and such evils
as feudalism, tax-farming, court pensions, and judicial abuses
needed no guide to call them into expression. On the part of the
National Party, there was a very pronounced demand for a constitution, in default of which the deputies were to refuse on behalf
of the nation all payment of taxes; while most of the third estate
(in their minds at least) were bent on securing equality with the
nobles. Thus absolutism and "privilege" were now clearly on the
defensive. The Old Régime was passing under the minute scrutiny
of the people, and it seemed perchance that the "millenium" of the
philosophers was now at hand.

Opening of the estates general

The deputies began in May to pour into Versailles, where the
estates general was to be held, in various halls of the royal palace.
They must have been an odd assortment—gaily attired noblemen,
clergymen in their long robes, and the third estate clad in somber
black according to custom, and feeling, no doubt, very ill at ease
at their first visit to the court. On May 3 a reception was held
at the palace where the King officially greeted them. On the
4th—which was Sunday—they attended mass in the royal chapel.
On May 5 occurred the formal opening. They were first addressed
by the King, then by one of his ministers, finally by Necker, the
director-general of the finances. The King's speech, which he read
but most probably had not written, alluded to the immense debt
and the unequal burden of the taxes, which the first two orders
would lessen by their disposition to renounce their ancient immuni-

ties, and after promising retrenchments, it requested the estates general to "take means of re-establishing permanent order and of upholding the public credit"; beyond a warning against "exaggerated innovations" it gave no hint of any idea that a new régime was in the making. The speech of Necker, wholly concerned with the immediate problem of meeting a deficit, which with sudden timidity he deliberately minimized (it was actually 162,000,000 livres but he confessed only 56,000,000), was even less enlightening. As a French writer puts it, "he continued to believe himself face to face with a financial crisis when he was really confronted with revolution."

Though scarcely as yet contemplating revolution, the members of the third estate were much disappointed by the opening meeting. Nothing had been said as to the manner of meeting—whether in three orders or one. Nothing had been said as to the extent of their power or how much responsibility was to be placed on their shoulders. Why had they been summoned, they must have wondered. Perhaps the King and Necker wondered too. In some vague way the estates general was supposed to help the monarchy out of its financial embarrassments, but once more one is impressed with the fact that the crown seemed unable to grasp the leadership. *The deadlock*

This leadership was soon to be snatched not by the estates general but by the third estate. So far as one can determine, their deputies totaled 621 against 285 for the nobles and 308 for the clergy, giving the third estate a slight preponderance. If the lower clergy should side with them, a substantial liberal majority would be assured. The fundamental problem was to secure a meeting in one assembly—voting by individual (*par téte*) rather than by estate (*par ordre*). This would insure the ascendancy of the middle class. So, after deciding that they would not constitute themselves a separate chamber, they opened negotiations with the other orders, inviting them to join them to form one assembly. The lower clergy, much impressed, were almost ready to comply, but in the end the bishops managed to hold them back by a decision to give the proposals "serious examination." Several weeks were spent in futile communications—save that nineteen parish priests finally left their order and came over. And all the time the crown stood idly by and did nothing.

Finally, on June 17, the third estate took the bit in its teeth. If the crown would not solve the crucial question, then they would

Outbreak of the Revolution

solve it for themselves. Solemnly, and with full determination to accept the consequences of their acts, they passed a decree to the effect that, representing as they did ninety-six per cent of the nation, they and only they were qualified to voice its will; hence they constituted themselves "the National Assembly." It was, of course, a step which none but the king had the legal right to take. The third estate was taking the law into its own hands. They even went so far as to deny the king the right to veto their future acts. Such proceedings may be said to mark the outbreak of the Revolution.

Triumph of the middle class and inauguration of the Constituent Assembly

Would these intrepid deputies have to pay for their boldness? No, Louis XVI was too mild a man to treat lawlessness as most of his predecessors would have done. We do not even know his immediate reaction. But after the first estate decided by a close vote to add their numbers to the "National Assembly," the reactionary elements at court induced the King to assert his authority. He would lay down the law to the assembly and force it to meet as three bodies. For this purpose a royal session should be held in a few days. In the meantime sessions of all the estates were suspended, and the hall where the national assembly was accustomed to meet was closed and locked. Unfortunately for the King's plans, the third estate had not been informed in time of this decision, and gathered as usual on the 20th to begin its sitting. When the deputies found the doors of the assembly-room barred and even picketed by armed guards, they regarded it as a calculated insult. Repairing to the in-door tennis-court near by, they took an oath never to separate but to meet wherever circumstances might demand until they had made a constitution and established it on firm foundations. Thus the third estate had pledged itself to make France a constitutional monarchy. Not the arrogant privileged classes but the "enlightened" bourgeoisie were to shape the Revolution.

But again the crown was unequal to the situation. Louis XVI duly held the royal session, commanded the estates to meet henceforth in separate assemblies, and solemnly warned his hearers against tampering with the property and privileges of the upper orders. Once more the King had made his choice, and again had taken the side of "privilege." The concessions which he also promised—concessions which might have been a successful basis for co-operation a month ago—were heard in stony silence. After the first and second estates had filed from the hall, the third estate still lingered behind. "You have heard His Majesty's orders," said the master of ceremonies. "Know you," answered a thunderous voice (it was the voice of the redoubtable Mirabeau) that nothing but the bayonet will avail to disperse the commoners of France." Heartened by this defiance, the third estate held its ground. It had made itself the sovereign will of France, and it would not shirk the issue.

Even the King was willing now to yield. "Well, then, let them stay," he sighed. More than that, on June 26 he ordered the other two estates to join the third estate in forming one assembly. Thus the National Assembly had triumphed in the long initial battle. On July 6 a committee was appointed to draft a constitution. Henceforth we shall speak of the "Constituent Assembly." Yes, France was to be regenerated.

But was this pleasant work of regeneration to be the monopoly of the few? When a revolution is unchained, will it not reach out to other elements of society—like the ever-widening eddies that follow a stone thrown into a pool?

The Revolution as an Instrument of the Populace

When the middle class set out to make a constitution and shape a new France, it might have been doubted if they would be allowed to monopolize this task. There were other elements in the nation who had an interest in this work of transformation, and what the Revolution might appear to the tax-ridden peasant or to the ill-paid journeyman might be quite different from what it seemed to the average comfortably-off member of the bourgeoisie. It would be strange indeed if some incident did not bring this latent force, the populace, into the Revolution. Public excitement in a time of revolution is far-reaching. And Paris, in particular, was inflammable material. Here as always, was the throbbing pulse of the nation.

The Revolution in Paris

Paris was normally a town of about 600,000 inhabitants. At this time, however, it was greatly congested by tens of thousands of starving peasants who had come to beg the government for food. Some efforts had been made by the municipal authorities to distribute bread among the refugees, though the problem had been only partially solved. Besides these victims of drought and a bad harvest there were also armed bandits who frequently broke into the city, and, despite all precautions, man-

The July Riots

aged to accomplish considerable looting. One of the two regiments cantoned in the city, the French guards, was so infected by revolutionary excitement that it was felt to be quite incapable of keeping order. Hence the "electors" of Paris (the men who had elected the deputies of the third estate) formed themselves into a committee, which, in co-operation with the city authorities, tried to plan some better means of preserving peace. To this end they resolved (July 11) to petition the assembly to provide as soon as possible a "bourgeois guard." But as yet there was no divergence between the middle class and the populace. Was not the third estate the people's champion? It was only as the result of a sudden crisis that the populace showed its hand—and then it was as an ally of the bourgeois assembly.

The success which the third estate had achieved over the crown had been really too glorious to last. Again the reactionary influences at court worked their will upon the puzzled king, and Louis decided that to be master of his realm he must have at his hand some soldiers—not the mutinous French guards but Swiss and German mercenaries. Accordingly, on June 26 he called up 20,000 men and stationed them near Versailles. Whether he meant to intimidate the assembly or actually to dissolve it (which is not impossible), he certainly succeeded in giving it momentary qualms. Mirabeau carried a motion urging the King to recall the troops— to which Louis replied in substance that the troops were merely intended to prevent disorders, and that if the assembly felt uneasy at Versailles, it might retire to another town. Finally on July 11 the King took another step. He dismissed Necker, and formed a new ministry composed of men of reactionary views.

It was this news, together with hunger, midsummer heat, and rumors that bandits were about to break into the city, that brought about the July Riots. When on the 12th word reached the crowds who frequented the booths and shops in the gardens of the Palais Royal that the popular minister was ousted—the man whose presence in the government had been a sort of guarantee that the crown would keep faith with the Revolution—the excitement became intense. Thousands gathered in a moment. They must defend the assembly from this plot and the city from the bandits. A brush with a detachment of cavalry [1]—who wished to avoid

---

[1] The court seemed dazed, and the mercenary troops at Versailles were not ordered into the city.

bloodshed—did not prove a serious affair, but the mob resolved to have arms, and numerous gun-shops, not to mention the veterans' home, were pillaged for weapons. Some of them also burned the various "barriers" or toll-stations in order that food might come into the city free of the hated *octroi*. Also a great many bakeries were plundered by the hungry. On the 13th the national guard was finally organized and managed to keep order. But on the 14th a new mob was formed, which soon got out of hand, and

From an old engraving

THE BASTILLE

resolved to get hold of the arms contained in the old fortress, known as the Bastille, situated in the heart of the city. For some time the Bastille had been chiefly used as a prison, and as such seemed to many the symbol of oppressive despotism (though, as a matter of fact, there were then but seven inmates). The commandant was very anxious to avoid a bloody encounter, and after numerous parleys, some accidental scrimmage, and the agile feat of two men who managed to get into the inner court and lower the drawbridge, he found his Swiss soldiers so insubordinate (partly because food was short) that he capitulated "with the honors of war"—a pledge which was soon violated, as he and other officers were mercilessly butchered. Such, in a few words, was the "taking of the Bastille."

The results of this explosion were various and important. The King recalled Necker, dispersed the troops, and a few days later visited Paris, where he decked himself in a cockade of red, white, and blue [1]—that tricolor which became the badge of the Revolution. Thus the crown pledged new loyalty to the people. The court, however, was moved in another fashion, for several nobles, including the King's brother, the Count of Artois, scurried out of the country—the first of many emigrations of nobles. "The rats are leaving the sinking ship," remarked one of the revolutionary journals. The bourgeoisie, or more specifically the commission of "electors," warned by what might happen from a mob, reorganized the old city government, now to be known as the "commune," as well as completed the organization of the national guard, of which Lafayette, the nobleman of liberal sympathies, was made commandant. It was the first suggestion of the coming rift between the middle class and the populace. But for the present it must be confessed that the populace had rallied splendidly to the defense of the middle class. They had saved the assembly and perhaps the Revolution. For the first but not the last time the Revolution had become the instrument of the people. More than that, as we shall note again, the July Riots stirred the nation, and greatly sharpened insurgence in the provinces. Emphatically the Revolution was now a popular movement.

The October Riots

It was not strange that Paris found it difficult to settle down. Several murders occurred in the ensuing days, for Paris had tasted blood, and for the first time knew its power. Moreover public opinion—now a really dynamic force—was being molded in a radical direction. Hundreds of newspapers appeared—brief sheets, containing few news-items but many opinions, the most popular of which was known as *The Friend of the People*, written by a half-mad firebrand, Jean Paul Marat. Besides the gardens of the Palais Royal (which the Duke of Orleans had thrown open to the public) the cabarets or wine-shops were a nursery for the development of public opinion among the lower classes; while the bourgeoisie had its salons and also its clubs, the most famous of which, the Jacobin Club, became later, after it opened its meetings to the public, one of the greatest agencies for influencing the popular mind. It was no wonder, then, that Paris was in a ferment. And there were other reasons too. The King's cousin, the Duke of Orléans—"Philippe Égalité," as he called himself—was hoping to

---

[1] Red and blue were the colors of Paris; white stood for the lilies of France. So the combination symbolized the union of king and people.

profit by the monarchy's embarrassments to oust the King and get the crown for himself; and a party in his pay, which at one time included Mirabeau and the popular leader, Danton, had probably much to do with inciting the populace. Moreover, the King's hesitation to sanction certain decrees caused some of the radical agitators to believe that he ought to be brought permanently to Paris—especially after it was learned that a regiment of regulars had been ordered to Versailles. Finally misery stalked more than ever throughout the city. The traffic in luxuries had suffered greatly from the continuous emigrations of the nobles, and unemployment was on the increase. Every day long queues of women stood before the bakeries to get their ration of bread, which was poor, dear, and scarce. By the beginning of October Paris was primed for another explosion.

This time Versailles was the target. The news of an insult to the Revolution during an orgie at the palace, combined with the incendiary utterances of Marat and the more potent fact of hunger among the poorer element of Paris produced on October 5 a march of several thousand women to Versailles, bent at least on obtaining bread, and perhaps minded also to get the "royal baker" and bring him to Paris. Lafayette would fain have prevented this demonstration, but he found to his chagrin that many of his men were noisily abetting it, and, rather than risk his head, he let the women have their way, he and the national guard following the mob at a discreet distance. After the crowd had reached Versailles, a journey of eight miles, it was too tired at first to do more than heckle the assembly, but that night (or rather early in the morning) after some of the more turbulent elements had got drunk, there was an attack upon the palace and two of its guards were killed. At this juncture Lafayette, who had gone to an inn for a nap—"He slept against his king" was the way an enemy expressed it—turned up and ordered his guards to clear the palace. Then after the King, Queen, and Dauphin had shown themselves on a balcony to the assembled rabble, he persuaded Louis to assent to its demand that he go to Paris. "We have got the baker and the baker's wife and the baker's little boy!" so, according to legend, the rabble shouted. It was a weird procession—these six thousand "fishwives," accompanied by Lafayette and his guardsmen, and lugging some cart-loads of grain which they had commandeered, escorting the royal family to the Tuileries in Paris.

It has been appropriately called "the funeral march of the old monarchy."

It was the second occasion when the populace played an important rôle in the Revolution. And this time it displayed more strikingly its power over the crown. Moreover, the middle class was incidentally affected, since the assembly had to follow the king to Paris. Henceforth the monarchy was to rest in the bosom of the people. Would it survive so close an embrace?

The King's opportunity

"The King was a prisoner," writes the French historian, Sagnac, "but he was still revered. He could yet find an occasion to make himself popular, and perhaps to moderate the course of the Revolution. . . . All depended on his skill and courage." But to expect skillful leadership from Louis was simply to assume a quality that he did not have. Mirabeau secretly advised him to leave Paris for the provincial town of Rouen, and then, calling the assembly to him, to invoke the loyalty of the provinces to support him against Paris. The result of such a maneuver—if the King had had the hardihood to execute it—can only be conjectured. One may measure his political judgment, however, when he preferred to chide the assembly for not showing itself more gracious to the people. But, after all, were not the provinces themselves in a state of upheaval?

The Revolution in the Provinces

It was hardly to be expected that the provinces would remain quiet under the spell of these events. In Lyons at the beginning of July some unemployed artisans had burned the toll-gates in order to reduce the cost of living. But it was the news of the July Riots that set the countryside in motion. Again, as so often in the history of France, Paris led the way and the rest of the nation followed. Thus an immediate effect of the July days was the perpetration of similar disturbances in other towns. Fortunately none of these urban centers in the provinces held so large a mass of idle or hungry workmen, and the effect of these explosions was to induce the middle class to remodel municipal government and to organize national guards after the fashion of the one in Paris. This reconstitution of the towns as "communes" on a more or less democratic basis is what is commonly called the "municipal revolution." Since the authority of the intendants was paralyzed, it is evident that the bureaucracy, the pillar of the monarchy, was fast going to pieces.

The "municipal revolution"

But the provinces mean, of course, chiefly the peasantry. Now at last even these more sluggish members of humanity were going *Uprising of the peasantry* to assert themselves. For them, above all things, feudalism was the bane. And from the middle of July on through August occurred sporadic attacks upon the châteaux, partly because they symbolized a hateful yoke, partly because they sometimes held records of the peasants' servitude. But the feudal lords were not the only sufferers. Agents of the tax-farmers were sometimes beaten or killed, and the same fate befell those millers who had so often defrauded the peasants. The Revolution had become—even more than in Paris—a social upheaval.

When the tidings of these events reached the assembly, it was *Downfall of feudalism* at once realized that something must be done. Feudalism was doomed, though something, of course, might be salvaged from the wreck. In the session of August 4 such a wave of self-sacrifice swept over the deputies that nobles and clergy vied with each other in giving up their privileges. All vestiges of feudalism, all the ancient equalities were swept away in a single night, and the tired assembly wound up its labors by proclaiming the astonished king the restorer of liberty. Yet with all this orgy of enthusiasm there had been some calculation. For the forfeiting of manorial rights over the peasants the privileged classes expected some compensation; and it was not till some years later that the peasants' emancipation was complete.

In any case feudalism may be said to have perished. For, with negligible exceptions, the peasants no longer recognized these ancient obligations.[1] In the meantime the provinces continued in a state of agitation. The Great Fear—fear of bandits, fear of the landlords, fear of the unknown—swept through the countryside, producing still further excesses. It was partly to restore order in the countryside that national guards had been established, and the bourgeoisie, some of whom had had to forfeit some feudal rights on lands they had purchased, took energetic steps to protect property from further assault.

Yet the middle class must have felt a malignant delight in seeing the plight of its enemies, the upper classes. We have now to inquire how it was using the Revolution as an instrument in its own interest.

---

[1] Apart from feudal obligations, the case of the voluntary agreement which the *métayer* had entered into with a lord was, of course, somewhat different, but even he got relief later on not so much through legislation as through the decimation of the landed aristocracy.

*The Revolution as an Instrument of the Middle Class—The
Establishment of the "Bourgeois Monarchy"*

The period of the Constituent Assembly is the period of bourgeois ascendancy, exercised through the legislature and after a
time and to a lesser extent through the communes and national
guards. It is the period when this class attempted to control the
course of the Revolution—a class which because their interests
were bound up with business and even to some extent with land
were from the social point of view essentially conservative. Theoretically they had no quarrel with the nobles and the Church when
it was a question of political rights or economic power, but they
meant to end the privileged position of these classes; and, for
themselves, they did not choose to govern through court intrigue,
as the upper classes had done, but rather by so remodeling the
political institutions that they (outnumbering, of course, the
upper classes) might control the government directly. Yet they
had withal the difficult position of being face to face with enemies
both above them and below them in the social order, neither of
whom were in control of the political machinery but perhaps were
all the more dangerous because their schemes were under cover
and they were capable of sudden outbreaks. The conspiracy which
had led to the July Riots is an example of the danger from the
upper classes; the July Riots themselves, an example of the power
which the populace could wield. Unless the members of the bourgeoisie could steer their way successfully between this "Scylla
and Charybdis," their predominance and their work were plainly
doomed. For the time being at least they had their opportunity.
The work of the Constituent Assembly was the measure of their
statesmanship, the test of their practical skill. Looking at the
Revolution as a whole, one sees that this first period was the
beneficent period, when the evils of the Old Régime were swept
away. But such is always the easier task of a revolution. It is the
constructive work that tests its quality as a tonic for society.
Hence we have to inquire at some length into the stability of the
new régime. First, however, we should glance at the men entrusted with this task.

*Character
of the
Constituent
Assembly*

The body that set itself the task of making a new order for
France had, unlike the English parliament, no tradition of continuous activity. It was the creature of circumstance. Hence these

men of the middle class—products of revolution—had to learn
the business of law-making as best they could. But being fresh at *Merits of the assembly*
the task had a certain advantage. They were full of enthusiasm,
and for the most part honestly wished to justify their leadership.
It is not certain that they consciously put the interests of their
class above higher considerations. They were, on the whole, the
most enlightened element in the nation, and they knew it. If
they did not take a broader view of economic justice—that is,
give the working classes and poorer peasants new opportunities—
one must realize that the problem of a fair distribution of wealth
had not seriously entered the realm of reasoned opinion, and that
that problem is still unsolved in the twentieth century. This
bourgeoisie had at least a liberal philosophy, which, combined with
a deep and unswerving instinct for order, was calculated to make
a safe and sane revolution.

We have little space to become acquainted with the leading *Leading personalities in the assembly*
members of the assembly. Interestingly enough, the reactionaries
produced no capable leaders, but some of the ablest liberals were
of aristocratic rank. Among the bishops, Talleyrand, though an
unscrupulous opportunist, had one of the shrewdest minds in the
assembly. Lafayette was a sincere and courageous liberal, too vain
of his fame to be a successful politician and possibly a bit shallow,
yet broadened by his experience with revolution on two continents.
Mounier, who had instigated the "tennis-court oath" and presided over the drafting of the constitution, was a sober citizen who
thought everything out, a little egotistical to be sure, but not so
empty as to be impressed by popular clamor. Bailly, a leading
scientist (recently made mayor of Paris); Barnave, a keen thinker
and able debater, though rather volatile and impulsive; and
Robespierre, the little sour-faced lawyer on the extreme left, soon
to look beyond the hall of the assembly to the Jacobin Club where
he divined that power lay—such also were men who stood out
from among the mass. But easily the greatest figure of the assembly was Mirabeau. Pock-marked and blear-eyed, of ungainly
form and thunderous voice, he was a person to be noticed in any
crowd, and he once laughingly remarked that his ugliness was his
power. After a wild and reckless youth and a reputation for not
being always honorable in his dealings, he had been rejected by
his own order, the nobles, but had been chosen a deputy for the
third estate. Remarkably gifted as an orator—though his speeches

were often composed by others—he could sway the assembly as no other of its members. But he was no mere wind-bag. He had excellent judgment both in finance and in foreign affairs, a wealth of natural common sense, and a true statesman's grasp of realities. Unhappily he was too outspoken in his dislike or contempt for most of his fellows and too heedless of impressions to be a successful politician; hence his failure to enjoy the full influence his capacity deserved.

Demerits of the assembly

And it was sound leadership that this body most seriously needed. Along with the good points it had all the defects of pioneer reformers. These deputies had learned their principles from the philosophers, notably Rousseau, but they did not know any more than Rousseau, how to put them into practice. Experience is necessary to give balance, and balance, doubly necessary during a revolution, is doubly hard at such a time to attain. They wasted precious time defining their rights—always a pleasanter thought than prescribing duties—while the country lapsed into anarchy. Enjoying their taste of power, they would not adopt any strict parliamentary procedure, lest it should curb their love of debate; and the size of the assembly was always a hindrance to dispatch. Moreover, being human, they liked applause, and—especially after the removal of their sessions to Paris—many of them fell victims to the galleries, and deliberately played the demagogue. It was not unusual for an important subject under discussion to be suspended by the reception of a deputation from the "sovereign people"—perhaps a group of women or children. Yet one must always remember the difficult environment in which they worked, especially after the assembly had moved to Paris. On the whole it is less strange that they failed to accomplish more that was solid and good than that they accomplished as much as they did.

Work of the Constituent Assembly

The Constitution of 1791, as it has come to be called, was preceded by a preamble known as the "Declaration of the Rights of Man and Citizen." It was natural that the assembly should first begin with working out its fundamental ideas, and the French mind usually seems to prefer to work in that manner. It was also natural that men whose lives had been more or less at the disposal of a sovereign should now determine, in their newly won freedom, what they considered to be their "natural rights," and such was quite in keeping with the spirit of Rousseau. The Declaration

The question of fundamental rights

(which deserves to be read in full) definitely vested sovereignty in the people, this sovereignty being expressed in the law, "the expression of the general will," as they put it, following Rousseau. "Liberty" and "property" were declared to be "natural rights," and freedom from oppression was to be secured by the abolition of arbitrary arrest. Civic equality was guaranteed. "Men are born free and equal in rights" was the cardinal principle of the whole. It is regrettable that the assembly did not wait to see if it meant to realize this principle in practice. The practical Mirabeau felt that such views might be intoxicating to the people; it was, he said, lifting a veil too quickly. Another deputy objected that "men are more prone to insist on their rights than to fulfill their duties," and it is clear enough that this pleasant discussion drew the assembly's attention away from more vital problems. Yet the Declaration of the Rights of Man bespoke the confidence of its authors that they were founding a new era, and, as a charter of democracy, it was to prove a moral stimulus to generations to come. The failure to consider all its applications may be ascribed to the fact that in August when it was passed people were still in the ecstatic stage of the Revolution.

The beneficial work of the Constituent Assembly is to be found chiefly in its abolition of the inequalities and injustices of the Old Régime. Serfdom, feudal services (the matter of compensation being left over to another assembly), tithes to the Church, internal tariffs, and gilds, and all the financial and judicial abuses were swept away; and the destruction of "privilege" in its ancient form allowed the inauguration of a new principle—equality before the law. Indeed, the social evils of the Old Régime had always been the ones most provocative of discontent. Absolutism was ended too, but there had not been the same degree of dissatisfaction with the political system in vogue, and monarchy was retained, even though, as we shall see, it was placed under rigorous limitations. The destruction of the social order—that is, "privilege"—was precipitated, as we have seen, by the course of events, and took place before the new order was formulated. Hence there was some point in Mirabeau's warning that the peasants, relieved of their feudal obligations, might feel that now they had none even to the State. No doubt the fact of destroying wholesale before the work of construction could be well begun was a serious practical blunder. Yet it is difficult to see how the assembly could have avoided it.

Destructive work of the assembly

One of the most notable acts of that body was a general adhesion to the principle of religious toleration.

Constructive work: (1) *the organization of the constitutional monarchy*

The reorganization of the State meant first of all to these deputies the reconstitution of the position of the crown. To begin with, its dependence was assured by the confiscation of the royal estates and the adoption of a civil list—that is, an allowance for the support of the king and the royal family. The making of war and the signing of treaties were also made dependent on legislative approval. The crown was given no power of initiating laws, but it was allowed a "suspensive veto"—that is, the right to hold up a measure until it had been passed by three assemblies. The king was still allowed to appoint his ministers, but they were excluded from the assembly, and the placing of most offices on an elective basis not only reduced the royal power of appointment but created an administrative body in no way responsible to the central government. In place of the old provinces were established eighty-three departments of fairly equal size—a tribute to the French passion for logic and uniformity. All departmental bodies were now to be elected by the people. In place of the old judicial system, largely hereditary and self-supporting, the new judges were also to be elected, and paid salaries by the government. The abolition of the old bureaucracy meant the passing of the nobility of the robe (another leveling of "privilege"), though it was voted that they should be compensated for the offices they had owned.

The provisions touching the legislature were equally radical. It was decided after much debate and in spite of the recommendations of Mounier's committee that the legislature should consist of one chamber, elected by the people. It was in the manner of choosing it that the assembly took special precautions to insure it against ultra-radical tendencies. Not only was the suffrage to be indirect, but there was to be a property qualification for all voters, and a higher one still for deputies. Only such "active citizens" (as distinguished from "passive citizens") were privileged to vote. The result was that some three million citizens were disfranchised; while for election to the legislature itself not more than 35,000 were eligible. By so doing the Constituent Assembly deliberately violated the principle of the Declaration of the Rights of Man, which had proclaimed equality of rights. But it is easy to comprehend the reasons for this ostensible injustice. The bourgeoisie had experienced the power of the populace, and they did not propose to allow it to swamp the Revolution. Moreover they reasoned quite properly that the masses were as yet too ignorant to be given political rights.

Of all the problems confronting the Constituent Assembly the most acute had been the financial problem. It was this problem which had been the immediate cause of the Revolution and most earnestly demanded solution. After abolishing most of the taxes of the Old Régime the assembly had instituted some new direct taxes upon land and other sources of wealth. But it is an unfortunate feature of most revolutions that non-payment of taxes is one of the firstfruits of the general collapse of moral discipline, and comparatively little revenue was collected. Necker then asked for a "patriotic donation," but here again the revolutionary spirit proved unavailing. Finally, as a means of rescuing the State from bankruptcy, it was proposed by Talleyrand, a member of the higher clergy, that the vast wealth of the Church be taken over by the State. Such a proposal almost seemed an inspiration, and with Mirabeau's ardent support the measure was carried. On the basis of this new wealth paper notes, really interest-bearing bonds, known as *assignats*, were issued, and the holder of such a bond was entitled to demand its equivalent in land if he so desired. By such means, undoubtedly, a great many persons were bound by personal interest to the Revolution. But the measure had its difficulties, and the thought of disposing of all this land actually put Necker [1] to bed. Indeed, the fact of dumping so much real estate on the market at one time inevitably reduced its value. Hence the depreciation of the *assignats* began even before the blunder was committed of issuing too many.[2] But the financial problem was at least solved for the moment. Other important aspects of the measure were the resultant compulsion of the State to pay salaries to the clergy and to take over the bulk of the Church's educational and philanthropic work. Thus the State's sphere of activity was considerably enlarged.

(2) The immediate solution of the financial problem

But the Church not only suffered the loss of its tithes and its lands. Still more far-reaching was the so-called Civil Constitution of the Clergy, which regulated the relations of Church and State, and to which all clergy were later required to take the oath. By

(3) The Civil Constitution of the Clergy

[1] Necker resigned and left the country in September, 1790, and his retirement was hardly noticed. The Revolution had clearly outgrown him.

[2] The fact some of the Church lands were mortgaged had deterred some investors and contributed to the depreciation. Later *assignats* took the form of bank notes.

this instrument the number of dioceses was made to correspond with the number of departments, and all.the secular clergy were to be chosen by popular election, no papal confirmation being required. At the same time the clergy were henceforth to be paid by the State. The Catholic Church was, in effect, made a department of the State. Inasmuch as the crown for nearly two centuries had nominated the higher clergy (subject, of course, to papal confirmation), the act was not entirely radical in principle. But the Concordat of Bologna had been a bilateral affair, while the Civil Constitution was the act of one party alone, and an act which, moreover, ignored the traditional position of the papacy. A further objection from the clerical standpoint was the fact that non-Catholics might participate in the choice of the clergy, though it should be realized, on the other hand, that the Catholic Church was the one church subsidized by the State, and that hence its support rested on all taxpayers alike. Despite the objectionable features the lower clergy were easily placated by the fixing of salaries much higher than they had heretofore enjoyed and most of the higher clergy seemed willing to accept the measure, provided only that the Pope would give his approval. Unfortunately the papacy, notwithstanding its acquiescence in similar arbitrary action in Russian Poland, would not accept this solution. Dislike of the Declaration of the Rights of Man because of the freedom it proclaimed, dismay at the disaffection in his principality of Avignon, as well as the pressure of the *émigrés* and of the French ambassador at Rome induced the Pope to refuse his sanction and to prohibit the French clergy from taking the required oath. The result was to render the Civil Constitution of the Clergy a costly failure, giving rise as it did to one of the gravest problems of the Revolution.

Momentary ascendency of the middle class

Such was the work of bourgeois statesmanship. Probably many of the more radical measures were partly caused by the transfer of the assembly to Paris, where popular influences were much more easily felt. By many of such measures—which we shall recapitulate presently—the cautious bourgeoisie was undermining its own position, for with the fate of the constitutional monarchy, its creation, was its own fate inevitably entwined. But in the meantime it seemed to have well entrenched itself. Political power was in its hands both at Paris and in the provinces, and in that respect it was, in a sense, a new privileged class, based on property. Through the spoliation of the Church many of the class had been indirectly enriched, and its economic power seemed equally secure from below since, following close on an act which abolished the gilds, another measure, the Chapelier Law, prohibited all combinations of the industrial workers. But the course of a revolution depends upon public opinion, and public opinion was free; it remained to be seen whether it would adapt itself to the shortcomings of middle-class rule and indefinitely put up with it.

Surveying the work of the Constituent Assembly as a whole, *Estimate of the work of the assembly* we must realize that its formal abolition of all the patent evils of the Old Régime and its establishment of a régime that afforded at least a section of the citizenry participation in public affairs gave distinct promise of a better order of things. Unfortunately the assembly had made some serious blunders. Apart from the ill-advised motion of Robespierre to the effect that members of the Constituent Assembly were ineligible to sit in the new legislature, it may be doubted if the election of judges is calculated to make for a fearless and honest judiciary, and it was certainly proved by the course of events that a unicameral legislature, however justified in democratic theory, does not work out well in practice—especially in time of revolution. Still more serious was the over-issuance of *assignats*, which shook the national credit and ushered in a new financial crisis. But the most fatal acts of the Constituent Assembly were the weakness of the executive under the new constitution, the administrative decentralization, and the Civil Constitution of the Clergy. The sharp separation of executive and legislature, with the preponderance of power in the hands of the latter, was due partly to Montesquieu's teaching, partly to fear of the crown, and partly to the assembly's jealousy of Mirabeau, whose ambition to become one of the king's ministers was well known. It meant in effect that no understanding or co-operation between king and assembly was possible. The ministers could be called to account before the assembly for their proceedings and were constantly open to attack, especially as the royal veto was calculated to irritate the assembly and thwart its will. Not only had the crown no initiative but it was virtually isolated, and this at a time when its fidelity to the revolution was in question, and its conduct, at best, under suspicion. In the second place, the decentralization of the administration left the enforcement of the laws to officials who, elected by the people, had no responsibility to the central government. It was as though eighty-three separate republics had been erected in France, and the danger of the country falling asunder is obvious. In the third place, the Civil Constitution of the Clergy, since most of the clergy could not conscientiously accept it in face of the Pope's commands, alienated the lower clergy (the former allies of the middle class) from the Revolution, and caused a schism in the Church which profoundly disturbed the religious life of the nation. The assembly did not realize the strength of Catholic feeling especially among the masses. No amount of official encouragement or pressure could attach the majority of the people to the constitutional clergy; while the non-jurors (those who refused to take the oath) received outspoken approval. It was not long before violence was perpetrated by the partisans of both groups, and a train of hatred was left for future legislatures to face. Worse still, this questionable measure made an enemy of the King, and it thus reacted very seriously on the monarchy, as we shall see.

It is the compromising position in which the crown was placed that forms a connecting link between the period of the Constituent Assembly and the somewhat overlapping period which we are now to enter.

The Climax of the Revolution—the Fall of Monarchy and Clash with Europe

The period of the Revolution which we have just considered produced some solid results as far as France was concerned. The period we are about to enter is chiefly important for the contact of the Revolution with Europe; otherwise its results were largely ephemeral. It is always to be noticed that a revolution goes so far in its rampaging course that the pendulum has to swing back before the final outcome can be reached. Already in the first year of the Revolution we have a foretaste of the darker days to come. The populace, under the leadership of a sincere but ruthless minority, was soon to capture the Revolution and bring its work of destruction to a climax. The coming orgy was to mean anarchy at home and a clash with the old order abroad.

During this period the monarchy was the storm-center. The old social order had disappeared, but the monarchy, albeit limited in power, remained as a symbol of bygone days, and apparently, as events were to show, out of accord with the Revolution. With the constitutional monarchy were also associated, as we have said, the rule of the middle class. When the Revolution should plunge to the lowest class in the social scale, then the rule of the middle class would be scrapped along with the system which it had adopted.

The Doom of the "Bourgeois Monarchy"

The reasons for the doom of the "bourgeois monarchy" were chiefly three; the growing self-confidence and self-assertiveness of the populace, partly caused by economic distress which the Constituent Assembly had failed adequately to relieve, and later fed by radical clubs and the excitement of foreign invasion; an attempt at counter-revolution, which was largely inspired by the Civil Constitution of the Clergy; and the instability of the new régime, which became all the more accentuated when the Constitution of 1791 came finally to be applied.

The danger from the popular forces was measurably increased *Growth of popular unrest* by that all-important incident, the transfer of the seat of government from Versailles to Paris. This reacted on the existing régime in two ways. It made the King, as events were to prove, practically a captive in the hands of the Revolution; and it subjected the assembly itself to the constant pressure of the populace. This term, the populace, which we have used to cover all the lower classes, may now be employed to mean the turbulent elements in Paris,[1] viz.: the proletariat (including, of course, its women), the near-by peasants who had flocked into the city for food or work, some of the lower middle class (petty artisans and merchants) who were victims of loss of business or revolutionary excitement, and, last but not least, the perennial riff-raff of a great city. Now, indeed, that the populace had learned to know its power, it might in any case have strained it to the limit; but economic distress was always in the background and always a contributive factor to the popular unrest. This problem—to some extent an inheritance, like national bankruptcy from the Old Régime—was first met (though rather late) by distributions of rations among the hungry and the

---

[1] The size and composition of the populace has been a matter of much speculation. A German scholar who made a study of Paris during the Revolution considered that the elements of disorder could never have numbered much over 20,000 and he believed that 6,000 (more than half, foreigners) represented a more usual figure. Obviously nothing more then a very rough estimate is possible.

employment of several thousand persons in public workshops. Such action was in line with the assembly's principle that charity was a function of the State; and on this basis the Chapelier Law (June, 1791), denying the right of workmen to fight for their common interests, was logical enough. But the assembly was quite unequal to a program of social reform that might have reached to the core of the problem, and palliative measures proved miserably inadequate. Industry became more and more the prey of unsettled conditions; unemployment steadily increased; and finally distress was enhanced by the declining value of the *assignats*, which had correspondingly raised the cost of living. Hence the working class, deprived of their right to strike, were naturally tempted to seek an alternative outlet in acts of violence. Thus there existed a festering sore, which became steadily worse as time went on, and would only be probed when the rule of the middle class gave way to direct action by the populace or its leaders.

Rôle of the Jacobin Club   Another factor, which certainly capitalized popular unrest if it did not actually augment it was the Jacobin Club, already mentioned as an agency for the molding of public opinion. This society, which had its branches (almost seven thousand in all) in the provincial towns, carried on through newspapers and pamphlets a ceaseless propaganda (inculcating such doctrines as the sovereignty of the people), as well as actively engaged in electioneering—a practice in which its well-disciplined unity, no less than its occasional acts of violence, stood it in good stead. Out of this famous club (as well as other radical societies) was to emerge an important grouping, which may conveniently be called the "Jacobins" to distinguish them from the more moderate elements who in 1791 seceded from the club after it took on a radical hue. Socially the Jacobins were bourgeois,[1] but politically they tended to become, in the course of events, proletarian, though for most of them the proletariat was only a means to an end. The importance of the Jacobin Club lay in the fact that it provided this party with a political machine which later on enabled it in alliance with the Paris commune (whose strength was to lie in the mob) to play a dominant rôle in the Revolution. The fact that this party grew out of a club accounts in a measure for the emphasis placed on ritual and the molding of a kind of religion of the "pure in heart,"

---

[1] Hence they were, for the most part, thoroughly devoted, at least in principle, to the rights of property.

which later gave the Terror much of its masterful self-confidence. In 1791 the club was just beginning to exert a subversive influence.

Barring a real insight into the conditions underlying the temper of the people and disposing them to follow the lead of political demagogues, the only way to preserve the existing order was to strengthen the power of the crown. It was this fact which Mirabeau, the shrewdest statesman of the Revolution, readily grasped. He had tried in vain to prevent the weakening of the executive, centering his efforts in particular on the question of allowing the crown to choose its ministers from the legislature. It was his own ambition to become a minister, and as the leading member of the assembly, he would have been an ideal link between the crown and the legislature, but it was largely in order to thwart him, as we have said, that the assembly had excluded ministers from its membership. He would fain have allowed the principle to be adopted even if he himself were sacrificed. "Let the house simply vote that Monsieur de Mirabeau is to be excluded from the ministry," he exclaimed in impotent rage. Swallowing his disappointment, Mirabeau then tried to form an alliance with Lafayette—for a year the most popular man in France and also a partisan of a strong monarchy—and together they did at least try to keep the King from taking steps that might compromise his position. Unfortunately these two men, whose qualities were such that between them they might possibly have saved the monarchy, seemed unable to work together in any harmony; for Lafayette was too vain to follow the lead of a superior intellect, and Mirabeau's contempt for the Marquis had been only too often displayed. Mirabeau did succeed through a friend in establishing a connection with the court, but unfortunately the King would seldom follow his advice chiefly because the Queen would not overcome her repugnance for a man whom she regarded as an adventurer. There is much reason to believe that in paying him an allowance they simply had the idea of buying off an enemy; but the acceptance of the subsidy (though it was chiefly to pay his debts) was a mistake on Mirabeau's part, for when the fact became known, his influence in the assembly was naturally diminished. Few historians believe that he was a hireling of the court, but such disregard for appearances was fatal to his leadership. Finding the assembly bent on radical measures of which he violently disapproved, Mirabeau deliberately encouraged them in that direction with the hope of producing a conservative reac-

Instability of the new régime and the failure of Mirabeau

tion. Toward the close of his career his position seemed somewhat strengthened, but unhappily his health, long sapped by dissipation, finally succumbed to the strain of his labors. On April 2, 1791 the man who was perhaps best qualified to guide the Revolution passed from the scene. "I carry with me," he said during his last days, "the ruin of the monarchy. After my death factions will dispute about its fragments."

Disaffection of the army

The weakness of the constitutional monarchy would not perhaps have been fatal if the army could have been relied on. But it was because the army was thoroughly impregnated with revolution—and had been so from the beginning—that it could not be depended upon to put down any disorders. Far from trying to keep the army out of politics, the revolutionary leaders had made them the veritable center of the great celebration on July 14, 1790, the first anniversary of the fall of the Bastille. The very presence of the national guards beside the regiments of the line was enough to break down discipline completely. The sporadic mutinies that occurred were eloquent enough of the state of feeling in the army; and it was doubtful if even the regiments in Lorraine, supposedly the most loyal of the troops, would be willing to help the King recover his power.

Incapacity of the king

Considering the weakness of his position, the King had only the choice of being an astute politician; but here, as we have divined in his relations with Mirabeau, he was sadly wanting in insight and moral independence. It was not his fault perhaps but certainly his misfortune that he was totally miscast for the rôle he had to play. Thus the instability of the monarchy presents three chief aspects: the constitutional weakness of the executive, the disaffection of the custodians of order, and the personal limitations of the monarch.

The "flight to Varennes"

The King was, in fact, fast reaching the conclusion that he did not even wish to uphold his constitutional authority. Mirabeau, who had constantly warned him against the influence of the nobles, had once counseled him, as we have noticed, to leave his turbulent capital and throw himself wholeheartedly on the loyalty of the provinces—not, however, to destroy the Revolution but to sustain it. The idea recurred to the King, but not as Mirabeau intended it—as a means of saving the Revolution from excesses—but rather in order to destroy it. For Louis had come to feel that his position was intolerable. As early as the autumn of 1790, when he learned of the intention of the assembly to make the clergy take the oath to the Civil Constitution, he secretly sent an emissary to urge foreign monarchs to help him restore his authority. After he had accepted under pressure the decree itself—an act on his part which sorely troubled his conscience—he became an implacable enemy of the Revolution, and a much more ready conspirator. Moreover, the failure of his attempt to leave Paris for St. Cloud, where he was accustomed to attend mass at Easter, due to the blocking of his passage by crowds who suspected him of some design to escape from Paris, convinced him that he was a prisoner, and that only by breaking his bars would he be free. On June 20, after arranging with Marshal Bouillé, the commander of the troops in Lorraine, to meet him and furnish him with the means of putting down the Revolution, Louis and his family left Paris in disguise, and so far without discovery. But the plot in the end miscarried, partly because the King's carriage was so large as to attract attention, and partly because Bouillé's troops were so mutinous that the marshal could not reach the fugitives in time. At length the identity of the royal family was discovered, and, the assembly having been informed of the incident, they were escorted home by three of its deputies amid the scurrilous abuse of the villagers along the way. The King had lost his chance of obtaining freedom.

Instead, he won lasting ignominy. Despite the fact that the flight of the King had at first caused consternation among a people who could not conceive as yet of a nation without a king; despite the studied tolerance of the assembly, who, rather than hold the King guilty of treason and risk the failure of a constitution which they had been so long in making, adopted the fiction that he had been kidnaped, the monarchy had lost its last remnants of prestige when the King had been dragged back, a traitor beyond all question to the Revolution and to the constitution under which he reigned. From that time emerged a group, centering in a club known as the Cordeliers and led by such men as Danton, an astute and unscrupulous lawyer from the provinces, avowedly favoring the dethronement of the King and the establishment of a republic.

As a reply to the assembly's "suspension" of the King from his functions these radicals demanded his dethronement, and to that end prepared a petition which on July 17 was placed on the "altar of the nation," a huge structure in the Champs de Mars (an open field in Paris), erected in honor of the taking of the Bastille. The *Popular intervention and its result*

result of all this was an unforeseen tragedy. When the frenzy of some of the mob who had gathered to sign the petition led to the lynching of two men, suspected of plotting to blow up the altar, the assembly instructed Bailly, the mayor, and Lafayette, commandant of the national guard, to restore order. The outcome was a scrimmage in which about fifty persons were shot and killed by the guards. It was the first bloody collision between the middle class and the populace, and it deepened the rift between them.

Last days of the Constituent Assembly

The assembly had, indeed, quite lost the confidence of the masses. The monarchy which they had set up was now practically without a prop. In September a manifesto of the Emperor and the King of Prussia (the so-called Declaration of Pillnitz), which declared the cause of Louis XVI the cause of all monarchs, also reacted upon the monarchy, for it identified Louis XVI with foreign opponents of the Revolution. The Constituent Assembly in its last weeks seemed to cherish the feeling that its work had been in vain. Barnave, who with many others had left the Jacobin Club and founded another club, the Feuillants, to champion the preservation of the constitution, shifted back into the position which Mirabeau had once occupied and sought a revision of the constitution in a conservative direction. But the assembly had no heart for such a task, and little was accomplished. As a parting shot, and as if to try to recover its confidence, it passed a decree prohibiting any change in the constitution for a period of ten years—surely a satire on the future! Finally, on September 30, 1791, the constitution having been accepted by the King, the assembly ended its sessions. It was a sorry legacy indeed which it bequeathed to its successor.

The Legislative Assembly and the Outbreak of War

Opening and character of the Legislative Assembly

The Legislative Assembly—the legislature provided by the Constitution of 1791—had already been elected, and began its career on October 1; for it had been feared that if one day intervened without a legislature in session the court might in some way find the means to regain power. These new representatives—745 in number—were a younger group than their predecessors, and all of them new to their business; for by the passage of the doctrinaire Robespierre's resolution all the deputies of the old assembly, most of whom had perhaps learned something from experience, had been deliberately excluded from standing for re-election. The new deputies came to Paris in a naïve and bewildered spirit, and were for the most part highly susceptible to the currents of public opinion.

It is an interesting evidence of the downward course of the Revolution that the Feuillants who sat on the right in this assembly had been the radicals of the Constituent Assembly. The majority, sitting in the center, were not committed to any group, and likely to be swayed by the oratory of the moment. On the extreme left sat the Jacobins [1]—a broad term which may be used now to comprise all the radicals who sought the favor of the mob —and beside them the Girondins, an aggregation of young journalists and lawyers, who were only a shade less hostile to the monarchy, though too bourgeois in their feelings ever to cater to the populace. There were many eloquent orators among this number, and they gloried in the watchword, "Liberty, equality, fraternity," without, in general, showing the capacity for reasoned statesmanship. Their chief inspiration was Manon Roland, a woman of great vitality and charm, usually swayed by her emotions, and bitter and unreasonable in her hatreds.[2] It was in her salon that the Girondins held conclave.

Parties in the assembly —the leadership of the Girondins

The assembly as a whole never pretended to have respect for the King or his Feuillant ministers; and the defects of the constitution were becoming daily more apparent. When the King vetoed certain very natural measures directed against *émigrés* and non-jurors, hostility to the monarchy was naturally increased, and more and more radicals became avowedly republican. The Girondins, more anxious at this stage than any other group to ruin the monarchy, found a lever for that purpose in the issue of foreign war. We shall deal elsewhere on the origins of the struggle with Europe. Apart from their strictly personal interests, the Girondins saw in it two objects: the spread of liberty to the world outside and a means of forcing the King into the open. If he were forced to declare war on his brother-monarchs and break with his former friends, the *émigrés*, it would not be long, they reasoned, before they would convict him of the treachery they suspected.

The Girondins and the war issue

---

[1] Called in the Convention the "Mountaineers" from the high seats they occupied.

[2] No doubt the play of personality, always important in any democracy, is particularly in evidence during the turmoil of revolution, and the French, with all their fondness for ideas, are a people very prone to be moved by such psychological factors. The personality of the Girondins, as well as that of some of the Jacobins, had much to do with shaping the course of events, quite regardless of what reason or circumstances suggested.

In March their fiery eloquence brought the downfall of the ministry, and the King felt forced to pick its successor from the Girondins. Among the new ministers (necessarily chosen from outside the assembly) were Dumouriez, an adventurer who secretly longed for a dictatorship, and Roland, whose restless wife was now more than ever able to sway the party councils.

Strangely enough, the Right was also for war—for a reason quite opposite from that of the Girondins, namely the hope of strengthening the monarchy. Only Robespierre and certain other Jacobins outside the assembly opposed war as likely to increase the misery of the poor and postpone internal reforms. "The thing for us to do," declared Robespierre at the Jacobin Club, "is to set our own affairs in order and to acquire liberty for ourselves before offering it to others." But in the assembly the great majority were swept into war hysteria by the oratory of the Girondins, and when (after it became known that Dumouriez's provocative ultimatum to Austria had met with no reply) a declaration of war was moved in the assembly, only a handful of deputies cast their votes against it. On April 20, 1792, the King formally declared war against the Emperor—incidentally the Queen's nephew.

Thus began in a spirit of lightheartedness and frenzied enthusiasm a struggle that was to last for twenty-three years, leading France through anarchy and the Terror to military despotism and finally to "Waterloo." The more immediate sequel was the downfall of the monarchy.

The Supremacy of the Populace and the Downfall of the "Bourgeois Monarchy"

The final ruin of the monarchy did not come about exactly as the Girondins had expected, for no one as yet discovered the King's correspondence with foreign powers; but the war did lead to the actual accomplishment of their object (though in a way they would never have countenanced) through an insurgence of the popular elements.

Intervention of the populace and the beginning of mob rule

For the moment, indeed, the Girondins were thrust on the defensive. The armies at the front were in no condition to meet the enemy, and had Austria been prepared for the decisive victory she won in the beginning, the country would have been straightway invaded. While everyone in government circles was trying to put the blame on some one else, the King, never an adept at political tactics, enfuriated the Girondins by vetoing two decrees of somewhat dubious expediency. A violent quarrel followed, and the King took occasion to get rid of his unwelcome ministers. The Girondins, naturally furious, vowed vengeance in Manon's salon. But it was the populace which now resorted to action. On June 20 a mob broke into the Tuileries and tried to coerce the King into withdrawing his hateful vetoes. With a marvelous courage Louis held them at bay for more than an hour and firmly refused to yield. The episode is chiefly important as marking the beginning of a year of anarchy, wherein all the public authorities were subjected to the caprices of the lower elements of Paris.

There was just one slender chance for the King to extricate himself. Lafayette, now one of the commanders at the front, hurried to Paris and demanded the punishment of those guilty of the outrage of June 20, which he openly attributed to the scheming of the Jacobin Club. He also hoped by summoning certain of the loyal elements in the national guard, to strengthen the government's position. But the King and Queen seemed utterly unable to learn wisdom. The Queen said that she would rather perish than accept assistance from Lafayette, and complacently betrayed the general's plans. So Lafayette, perforce, returned to his post, and after one more futile effort to save the King, he succumbed to the course of events, which for him meant flight and imprisonment in an Austrian fortress. He was a man of unflinching courage, and had he been blessed with any political sagacity, might have exerted during the early years of the Revolution a more stabilizing influence.

But it would be too much to say that anyone, save perhaps the King himself, could have saved the monarchy now. And the King, for his part, could think of no other means of saving his throne than that of urging his fellow-monarchs to threaten the Revolution with destruction and trying to corrupt some of the popular leaders who, like Danton, for the most part took his money and betrayed their trust. Everything in the month of July seemed to be tending toward a crisis. On the one side, an undernourished populace was ready to be led to any work of destruction. On the other, the menace of invasion hung heavily over the land; and on July 11 the assembly declared the country in danger, all national guards being called to arms. On the 30th arrived a contingent of the national guard of Marseilles, singing the song that was to become the

Influence of the national crisis

anthem of the Revolution, the *Marseillaise;* and Paris immediately went wild with excitement. It was about this time that the bourgeois commune of Paris was replaced by a self-constituted council, composed of representatives of the forty-eight sections of the city; and it was this essentially proletarian body, the so-called "Insurrectionary Commune," which now inaugurated its dictatorship.[1] It was under its auspices that Paris carried on its régime of anarchy, and, dominating the Revolution, subjected the nation to its will.

Downfall of the monarchy

The materials for explosion being at hand, it was the Brunswick Manifesto, a product of Louis' intrigues, that finally brought it about. The proclamation of the Prussian commander, instigated by the Emperor and the King of Prussia, announced the impending invasion of France and threatened Paris with destruction if any harm should befall the royal family. Nothing could have been more calculated to goad the populace to fury. Even in the assembly voices had demanded the King's abdication, and the Commune made up its mind to force the issue. After due warning to the assembly, which seemed helpless to avert the crisis, the Commune on August 10 launched another attack on the Tuileries. Warned in time, the King and his family took refuge with the assembly, but most of the Swiss guard which defended the palace paid for their loyalty with their lives, and the palace itself was given over to plunder and carnage. Meanwhile a mob descended upon the assembly and forced that body to vote the suspension of the King. At last the throne had fallen. The royal family were now lodged in a prison known as the Temple where they awaited their tragic fate.

And along with the monarchy had ended the privileged position of the bourgeoisie, for the next assembly was to be chosen by practically universal suffrage. Evidently middle class rule was slipping.

The "September massacres"

France was now a *de facto* republic—the product of the anarchy of the Paris mob. But for the moment fear of invasion transcended every other consideration. One of the frontier towns fell before the invaders, and Paris was thrown into hysteria. Appearing before the assembly, Danton, lately chosen one of the members of the provisional government, electrified his hearers by his famous

---

[1] That formerly bourgeois and thoroughly reliable instrument, the national guard, had likewise become largely an agent of lawlessness.

exhortation, "Daring, more daring, and still more daring, and France is saved!" As a means of allaying the popular panic (or perhaps because it was itself the victim of it) the Commune had incarcerated several thousand persons who by reason of their calling or connections might be traitors in disguise; but frantic mobs insisted that these prisoners might break out and slay the wives and children of the soldiers at the front. Without any hindrance from the authorities they broke into the prisons and during four days (September 2–5) about eleven hundred persons were butchered in cold blood, sometimes under circumstances of the foulest savagery. It was a proof of the anarchy that existed that no authority, national or municipal, tried to stop the hideous outrage. It was perhaps the darkest chapter in the history of the Revolution, and is an interesting evidence of the excesses to which the lower element of a city population will stoop in time of excitement and when power is in its hands.

The National Convention and the establishment of the First Republic

Meanwhile the "suspension of the King" had been treated as equivalent to the termination of the Constitution of 1791, and it was decided to convoke a "convention," to be elected by universal suffrage, to determine the new régime. The demand had been made by Robespierre even before the episode of August 10, and the Girondins, whose strength lay in the departments, were not averse to such a measure. But since the elections took place during the September Massacres and when excitement was at its highest, it would seem that barely ten per cent of the electorate really exercised their rights. Fear, as well as perhaps a weariness of the Revolution, kept the great majority of citizens in their homes. When the Convention met on September 21, 1792, its first act was to proclaim the republic, then existing in all but name. As there were no monarchists in the assembly, there was not a dissenting vote, though there was also, it was said, a conspicuous lack of enthusiasm. The republic seemed to be accepted as something inevitable.

Girondins vs. Jacobins

The prime duty of the new régime was to repel invasion, and with this problem we shall concern ourselves later. A provisional government, of which Danton was the leading member, attempted to bridge the gap until the government could be definitely organized. But underlying all the incidents of the succeeding months was a struggle between two factions—a struggle for ascendancy which in time became so acute as to become a struggle for existence. The Girondins, who sat on the right (the conservative right!) of the assembly were the sworn enemies of the Jacobins, who sat on the left, and who under Robespierre's leadership had long been the passive allies and sometimes the abettors of the Commune. Except that they were both republicans and patriots the contrast between the two parties was very sharp. It was less a difference in principles than in methods and social outlook. The Girondins looked to the legislative body to shape the course of the Revolution, and relied upon arguments and oratory to carry their aims. The Jacobins, on the other hand, who had small influence in the assembly, depended on popular violence to achieve their objects. If the Girondins were doctrinaires, the Jacobins were essentially realists and men of action. Naturally the Girondins looked to the departments (electing the largest number of deputies) for their support; the Jacobins, to Paris, where their instruments, the mob and the Commune were always at hand. The Girondins tended perhaps to favor a decentralized republic, which would rob Paris of its dominance, while the Jacobins were soon to espouse the idea of a strong central government as a means of weathering the crisis. Finally, it should be noted that the Girondins, being well-to-do men of property (probably misled into radicalism by their devotion to Rousseau), wished to make sure that propertied interests were as little interfered with as possible; they disapproved of the heavy requisitions on wealth which seemed to be necessitated by the war and were opposed to a control of prices in the interest of the poor. The Jacobins, on the other hand, while at first equally staunch in their adherence to these liberal ideas (inherited from the *philosophes*), found it advisable, in order to provide for the national defense and in order to fortify their leadership of the populace, to go back to the idea, more typical of the Old Régime, of government regulation for social ends. It is obvious that the Girondins represented the bourgeoisie, and that the Jacobins, whatever their calling, were, temporarily at least, the champions of the proletariat. How the Jacobins finally broke the proletariat, while judiciously seeking their interests, was for later events to disclose; for the present their thought was only on expedients. Perhaps the Girondins, for their part, had really too much talent to become successful political leaders. They were individualist to the core. And the crisis called for self-discipline and self-sacrifice— for a hard and iron unity.

Strong in their position in the assembly, and ever short-sighted, the Girondins opened the attack upon their enemies. They wished naturally to protect themselves against the Commune, but they wasted their efforts as well as courted unnecessary danger by bitter attacks upon Robespierre and other popular leaders. The Jacobins, of course, gave them as good as they received, and in time the futile oratory of the Girondins lost them the support of the center, on which they counted in order to retain their hold on the assembly. But the issue on which the outcome of the struggle hung was the question of Louis' fate. The Girondins, not wanting to kill the King, strove to postpone this vexing question indefinitely. The Jacobins, on the other hand, fearing for their lives if ever the monarchy were restored at the end of the war, were determined that the King should die, Robespierre, for his part, wishing even to dispense with any trial. The Jacobins won the major point, and placed their rivals in the position of being open to the accusation of attachment to the monarchy. Such were the circumstances which underlay the King's trial, which began early in December. Though without any constitutional right to do so, the Convention constituted itself a jury, and as the voting on the case was oral and in the presence of galleries packed with a vociferous mob, one can readily divine that the outcome was never doubtful. The King (who was allowed the privilege of counsel) was unanimously pronounced guilty of conspiracy—a just conviction, as we know, though the Convention had no actual proof of guilt. But it was obviously not a moral question at all, but solely personal and political. When it came to fixing the sentence the Girondins were hopelessly divided, and this, as it turned out, proved fatal to the King, who was condemned to immediate [1] execution by a bare majority of one—in a house, let us remember, elected by a very small minority of the citizens of France. Clearly the King's death was not the expressed will of the nation. It was the work of a vigorous and cold-blooded minority, some of whom were simply actuated by fear. On January 21 Louis XVI met his death on the guillotine. A failure in life, he won general admiration by the stoical way in which he met his end. Like most of the people who were sacrificed to the Revolution, the King knew how to die.

The ruin of the Girondins was now practically assured. They had not done enough to save the King, but they had done enough

[1] Twenty-six, however, were for a postponed execution.

EXECUTION OF LOUIS XVI

From Tableaux Historiques de la Révolution Française

Place de la Révolution (afterwards Place de la Concorde), Paris

to compromise their standing with the rabble, and in an atmosphere of hatred and suspicion it was easy to brand them as royalists. Bitter recriminations were hurled back and forth by the two parties, but for the Girondins it was always a losing battle. Hugging their prejudices to the last, they had already spurned the friendly overtures of Danton (who had long been struggling for harmony), refusing to ally themselves with a man whose hands, they said, were stained with the blood of the Massacres of September,[1] and they finally made him one of their deadliest enemies. When the treason of Dumouriez put them on the defensive, it was Danton who took full advantage of their plight. Yet the Girondins never learned what it was to be silent. On the very eve of their downfall one of their number threatened Paris with destruction in the event of another popular demonstration. On May 31, 1792 the Commune, with the connivance of the Jacobin deputies, threw a mob into the assembly, and overthrew the provisional government, controlled by the Girondins. Two days later a similar maneuvre resulted in the complete subjection of the Convention, who obediently decreed the expulsion and arrest of thirty-one of its members, most of whom were prominent Girondins. It was the downfall of the party. After a demonstration of the departments in their favor the Girondins were all proscribed, some guillotined in Paris, others hunted down and driven to suicide or the guillotine, only a few being fortunate enough to escape. It had been a struggle for existence, and the Girondins had lost the fight. It was the temporary eclipse of the bourgeoisie.

Fall of the Girondins—the eclipse of the middle class

But already the party of violence, the outwardly proletarian party, had devised new methods for the government of France. And it was not to be a proletarian dictatorship. The Jacobins were now free to give their attention to the war and its requirements. In fact, the outbreak of the war had already been a turning-point in the Revolution, for national defense or national glory, their exigencies and consequences, were thenceforward to transcend every other consideration.

FOR FURTHER READING OR STUDY

Robinson, J. H., and Beard, C. A., *Readings in Modern European History*, chaps. xii and xiii (*passim*); Butterfield, H., *Select Documents of European History*, vol. iii, chap. vii; Anderson, F. M., *Constitutions and Documents:*

---

[1] Madame Roland had probably much to do with this repulse, as she loathed Danton as a "coarse and slovenly plebeian."

France, 1789–1901 (an extremely useful compilation); Rigby, E., *Letters from France;* Morris, G., *Letters and Diary,* 2 vols.; Biré, E., *Diary of a Citizen of Paris during the Terror,* vol. i, esp., chap. xxxix (on the king's trial).

Hazen, C. D., *The French Revolution* (an excellent text in two volumes), vol. i., chaps. vii–xix, xxi, xxiii, vol. ii, chaps. xxiv–xxviii, xxxi; Bourne, H. E., *The Revolutionary Era in Europe,*[1] chaps. vii–ix, xii (*passim*), (without literary charm but a generally reliable reference); Gottschalk, L., *The Era of the French Revolution,*[1] (excellently written text); book ii and book iii, chap. i, Gershoy, L., *The French Revolution and Napoleon,*[1] (very useful text), chaps. iv (*passim*), v–ix, x (*passim*), xi (*passim*); Bradby, E. D., *A Brief History of the French Revolution;* Madelin, L., *The French Revolution* (a brilliant depiction of the Revolution though somewhat hostile to it); Aulard, A. F., *The French Revolution: A Political History,* 4 vols. (political ideas and institutions); Mathiez, A., *The French Revolution* (chiefly valuable for social aspects, but written with obvious bias against all conservatives); Gillespie, J. E., *A History of Europe,* pp. 498–529; Hayes, C. J. H., *A Political and Cultural History of Modern Europe,*[1] vol. i, pp. 597–622; Seignobos, C., *The Evolution of the French People,* chap. xvii; Guignebert, C., *A Short History of the French People,* vol. ii, chaps. xxvii–xxviii.

Henderson, E. F., *Symbol and Satire of the French Revolution;* Brinton, C., *A Decade of Revolution, 1789–1799* (a scholarly essay with an excessive fondness for epigram) and *The Jacobins* (also an analytical essay); Herbert, S., *The Fall of Feudalism in France;* Witham, J. M., *A Biographical History of the French Revolution;* Thompson, J. M., *Leaders of the French Revolution* (excellent); Béraud, *Twelve Portraits of the French Revolution;* Willert, P. F., *Mirabeau;* Fling, F. M., *The Youth of Mirabeau* and *Mirabeau and the French Revolution,* 2 vols.; Gottschalk, *Jean Paul Marat: A Study in Radicalism;* Bradby, E. D., *Life of Barnave,* 2 vols.; Clémenceau-Jacquemart, *Life of Madame Roland,* 2 vols.; Young, C., *A Lady Who Loved Herself* (on Manon Roland); Ellery, E., *Brissot de Warville* (a study of a Girondin leader); Bourne, H. E., "Municipal Politics in Paris," *Amer. Hist. Rev.,* x, 263 ff. and 280 ff.

Would profit by a more itemized index.

IX. THE REVOLUTION'S CHALLENGE TO EUROPE

1. THE EVOLUTION OF THE CONFLICT WITH EUROPE

Attitude of Europe toward the Revolution; Attitude of the Revolution toward Europe; Fundamental causes of the war.

2. THE OBJECTS AND EXTENSION OF THE WAR

Objects of France; Nationalism as a new force; The First Coalition.

3. THE CRITICAL PERIOD OF THE REVOLUTION

A. THE FIRST CRISIS—THE REVOLUTION SAVED BY THE POLISH QUESTION

Condition of Revolutionary France as a belligerent; Revival of the Polish question; Valmy; The Second Partition of Poland.

B. THE SECOND CRISIS—THE REVOLUTION SAVED BY THE TERROR

(1) *The Evolution of the Terror*

External crisis—Neerwinden; Internal crisis—the Vendéan uprising; Germs of the Terror; The crisis deepens—the communal revolt; Conciliatory measures; Position and character of Danton.

(2) *The Character and Organization of the Terror*

Character and purpose of the Terror; Machinery of the Terror; Pedigree of the terrorists.

(3) *The Operation of the Terror*

Pacification of France; Secondary object of the Terror; Breaking of the Commune; Position and character of Robespierre; Breach in the Terror—Danton *vs.* Robespierre; End of Danton; The Terror at its height; End of the Terror in the Coup d'État of Thermidor.

4. REVOLUTIONARY FRANCE, TRIUMPHANT

Superiority of France over the First Coalition; A successful war of aggression.

If the French Revolution had merely remodeled the social and political order in France, it would have been an important movement, but its influence was far greater than that. We must now study its external relations and see how it came into collision with the outside world. We shall also notice incidentally the reaction of the war with Europe upon the situation in France. And it is the combination of the war and the simultaneous changes in France that furnished the setting and the occasion for the rise of Napoleon Bonaparte and the emergence of a military despotism out of the wreckage and the turmoil of the Revolution.

The Evolution of the Conflict with Europe

Superficially one might not have expected during the first year or so of the Revolution any conflict at all between France and the other monarchies of Europe; for these powers belittled the Revolution at that time, and the Revolution had too much on its hands, so to speak, to bother with Europe.

Attitude of Europe toward the Revolution Looking at the Revolution through the spectacles of Europe, we find that in the beginning it was completely misinterpreted and underrated by the autocracies of that time. There is perhaps nothing astonishing in this. Sedition was not an uncommon experience in the history of any monarchy—Russia herself had had a serious rebellion to face in 1773—and to suppose that this uprising in France was a really more grievous convulsion would have argued a most remarkable penetration. On the whole, foreign monarchs seem to have been pleased with this phenomenon. It simply meant that France, traditionally the strongest power in Europe, was for the first time unable to play her usually powerful rôle; her diplomacy was paralyzed. Thus if the old powers wished to pursue their aggressions somewhere, the hand of France would not deter them. When later they discovered their mistake—say after the "flight to Varennes"—they were still rather wary of provoking a quarrel. It was probably to appease the *émigrés*, who kept constantly nagging him to do something, that the Emperor consulted his fellow-sovereigns on the advisability of some concerted action, and the Declaration of Pillnitz was the result. But this pronouncement, which declared the plight of Louis "a matter of common interest," predicated any action on the assumption that all monarchs would agree—which the Emperor himself knew to be impossible. The powers, on the whole, still hugged the delusion that the Revolution was a local ebullition; they did not suppose that the pot would ever boil over on them. It was not until grievances against the Revolution steadily accumulated, and certain acts of the Revolution were construed as a sort of challenge that they prepared for war. Then, despite the disclaimer of self-interest, they meant to seize the opportunity to aggrandize themselves at the expense of France as well as to protect themselves from the infection she was spreading.

Equally pacific at first was the attitude of Revolutionary France toward foreign powers. When the revolting Netherlands solicited her aid against the Emperor, Mirabeau was able to prevent a *Attitude of the Revolution toward Europe* favorable response to this appeal. In the same year (1790) when Spain, in virtue of the Family Compact, expected French aid in a controversy with Great Britain, the Constituent Assembly refused to countenance the existing alliance, and to make matters doubly sure, deprived the king of all right to make war without legislative approval. And even after the petition of Avignon to be united with France put the pacifism of the Revolution to a much severer test, the assembly skillfully hedged on the question for nearly a year. So naïve was the new order that in April, 1791, Louis XVI was required to send a circular letter to foreign courts, explaining and justifying the Revolution, which he was made to include among his "titles to glory"; it was also stated that it was a "base calumny" that the King was "not free." Finally a provision was inserted in the Constitution of 1791 that "the French nation renounces the undertaking of any war with a view of making conquests, and will never employ its forces against the liberty of any people." (Nothing, of course, was said of the rights of sovereigns.)

But such a laudable attitude of minding one's own business became increasingly hard to live up to in practice. In 1791 Avignon was finally incorporated with France. The excuse was made that this was not territorial aggrandizement after the manner of the Old Régime; France simply could not refuse to receive a people who had come to her spontaneously. This was exalting a new principle—that of nationalism or nationalist self-determination.[1] But the danger of such action was well expressed by a friend of Mirabeau, when he declared, "It is evident that after such conduct France will be in a state of war with all governments; she will threaten them with domestic insurrection, and insurrection will lead to conquest." The real turning-point, however, came with the Legislative Assembly, when the Girondins welcomed a war, partly because they were born missionaries who wished to spread the principles of the Revolution to other lands—and certain decrees of the assembly were partly to that effect—and partly, as we have seen, as a means of discrediting monarchy at home. It is true that such differences as had arisen between France and the

---

[1] The holding of a plebiscite in Avignon on the question was perhaps the first illustration of a people voting its own disposition—in other words, nationalist self-determination.

old monarchies might perhaps have been peaceably adjusted despite the tie of kinship between the Queen of France and the Emperor, despite even the efforts of the *émigrés* to provoke war; but the heedless, provocative attitude of the Girondins drove straight to a rupture with Austria.

Fundamental causes of the war

But after all, if one views the question broadly, was not this war virtually inevitable? The Revolution was too victorious at home and too self-satisfied to contain itself within its own borders; and the old monarchies felt themselves seriously jeopardized by the triumphant principles of the Revolution. How were the peasants of central Europe to be held down while those in France were freed of all feudal obligations? How were the monarchs to deal with this propaganda in favor of political liberty? The principles of the Old Régime and those of Revolutionary France were too diametrically opposed to one another to make it possible, so it seemed, for both to exist on the same continent. The annexation of Avignon seemed to reveal the Revolution as an anarchical force, subversive of the rights of other monarchs and of the public law of Europe. It was fear as well as cupidity that inspired the old monarchies to fight. It was enthusiasm and scorn that moved the Revolution to challenge them. "Let us fling down to the kings the head of a king as gage of battle!" There was something terrifically final in Danton's resounding words.

But who could have foreseen the complexity of the struggle, its varied objects, and its curious personal twist before it was over?

THE OBJECTS AND EXTENSION OF THE WAR

The objects of France

And now that the clash had come—looking ahead a little, how did Revolutionary France fit the war to its idealism? How did these sons of Rousseau view the struggle? At the outset it was more than anything else a war of self-defense. Far from being able to chastise the enemies of liberty, the French were at first unable for a while to prevent invasion. When the danger lessened, one finds the pursuance of an aim already revealed. The French were to bring liberty and equality to all people who desired it. The Revolution was a militant force, a great crusade for the emancipation of the world. It was an evidence of this cosmopolitan spirit, this assumption that all men might live under the same enlightened principles, that certain foreign champions of liberty were invited to take seats in the National Convention. But it is also to be observed that hearkening to the honest appeals of other peoples for French help to remove their chains might only too easily lead to the assumption that France knew already what was best for other peoples, and that "the French nation" would "treat as enemies" those who, "refusing liberty and equality or renouncing them, may wish to . . . treat with the prince or the privileged classes." From this position, it was, of course, an easy step, albeit in a sense a step backward, to turn a war of liberation into a war of aggrandizement; and we may look ahead to record that the Austrian Netherlands, definitely freed by French arms in 1794 were annexed to France the following year. This was, of course going back to the manners of the Old Régime with a hypocrisy that had never characterized the Old Régime. And finally, the third object, revealed by the French in the war, was a direct inheritance from the past. The securing of "natural boundaries"—meaning in particular the Rhine and the Alps—was a veritable revival of Bourbon policy. Apparently reasons of state and no better code of international morals had captured the Revolution.

Yet in pursuing these practical ends Revolutionary France was true to a new principle—a selfish principle—which the Revolution itself had let loose. That principle of "fraternity," which might so much better have signified "humanity" had come to be narrowly construed as the united sentiment of the French people themselves against their enemies abroad. We have already observed nationalism in its meager beginnings. Nationalism was now a force of far greater power than ever before because it was inspired from below. The French nation moved no longer at the will of a monarch but of its own free will and with an enthusiasm impossible in earlier times. The days of the Terror (to be later described) revealed a people in a desperate struggle to defend all that had made them what they were. The *Marseillaise* was a hymn of national resistance to the danger of conquest and exploitation. When France was passing through this new ordeal by fire, something was burned into her soul which she would always preserve. It was this nationalism, which, passing from the stage of self-preservation to that of self-interest at the expense of other states, brought France to adopt the classic methods of the Old Régime. But the new spirit had much to do with explaining her later triumphs over states whose policies were not inherently less selfish.

As to the enemies of France, they did not pretend to pursue a

Nationalism as a new force

*The First
Coalition*

more enlightened policy than had been customary in international politics. After France broke with Great Britain in February, 1793 the First Coalition was formed, and its avowed, though secret, object was the dismemberment of France. The powers composing it were Austria, Prussia, Great Britain, Spain, and Sardinia. While the Continental powers provided most of the armies (though a few British forces were put into the field), the rôle of Great Britain in the war was chiefly twofold. She was paymaster of the coalition, and she used her navy to take French colonies and drive French commerce from the seas. Since the French navy was lamentably weak at this time, there is nothing, perhaps, which better illustrates the madness of French policy than the breach with Great Britain. It is true that the provocation had not been all on one side, but it had been particularly in France's interest to avoid any collision with the mistress of the seas.

In the meantime France had entered upon the most critical period of the Revolution. Assailed both from without and from within, the Revolution had to meet its most terrible test.

THE CRITICAL PERIOD OF THE REVOLUTION

At the outset of the war nothing but sheer luck saved the Revolution. In other words nothing prevented Revolutionary France from being crushed but the fact that another state in Europe was threatened with a similar fate, having the same incapacity to defend itself and some of the same enemies. One of these two—Poland or Revolutionary France—was certainly doomed. Which of the two would be saved would depend on which the more attracted their predatory neighbors.

The First Crisis—The Revolution Saved by the Polish Question

*Condition
of Revolu-
tionary
France as a
belligerent*

The French Revolutionists with all the simplicity of inexperience had plunged into an abyss of which they knew not the bottom. The first few weeks brought disillusion. The French army which had swept into the Netherlands was utterly routed. Happily the Austrians, as we have noted, were not prepared for so complete a victory, and were slow to press their advantage. Happily also Prussia had not yet joined the struggle; so the odds were not yet heavily against France. But it seemed as if when Prussia did decide to enter the war (she had already allied herself with Austria) that the outcome could hardly be doubtful. It would take some months to retrieve this initial disaster, and the Allies could easily crush so weak an enemy.

The initial helplessness of France to withstand invasion can be readily explained. In the first place, the French soldiers were for the most part insubordinate. The principle of equality can hardly be applied to an army, which if it is to fight with any success must obey orders without question. The murder of one of the generals by his own soldiers, when he was trying to check their retreat, showed the extent to which discipline had collapsed. In the second place, thousands of officers, being nobles, had emigrated, and the army was therefore sadly underofficered. In the third place, the government itself was incapable, inexperienced, and insecure. The minister of war was generally chosen for political considerations, and as a matter of fact the office frequently changed hands. For some time to come there was much friction between the civil government and the generals in the field, due partly to official meddling and partly to the insufficient equipment of which all the generals complained. It is manifest that Revolutionary France had to learn the art of war as well as the art of governing. Yet mobilization of the national energies was hardly possible while the country was in a state of anarchy. In the summer of 1792 the monarchy was breaking down and even the growing sense of peril did not enable the Revolutionists to put the nation into an adequate state of defense. The panic which seized Paris in September and helped to produce the September Massacres was a symptom of the moral collapse behind the lines, and it could hardly be expected that the army would be fitted to meet the crisis.

And yet, strange to say, the moral fiber of the Allies was also shaken. They had been attacked in the rear, so to speak, by the diplomacy of Russia.

By a curious stroke of fortune Catherine the Great, partly as a result of circumstances, partly as a result of deliberate calculation, had taken this time to raise the Polish question. While she was embroiled in her second Turkish war, the Poles had been shrewd enough to scrap their historic constitution which, as we have observed, had paralyzed them as a nation, and in 1791 had adopted a new one, establishing an hereditary dynasty with considerable executive power, an electorate broad enough to include the middle class, and even a guarantee of religious toleration. Of course, neither Russia nor Prussia was anxious to see a rejuvenated Poland.

Revival of the Polish question

Catherine realized only too keenly that this movement, if successful, would end all chance of Russian domination, which ever since
the partition of 1772, had been a settled feature of her policy.
The hitherto submissive Stanislas was evidently beginning to free
himself from her apron-strings. What should be done? It was
evident that she must act; and the present moment was peculiarly
auspicious. Now that Austria and Prussia had been so rash as to
become involved in a war with France, now that their backs were,
so to speak, obligingly turned to the Polish question, there could
hardly have been a better opportunity for intervention. Perhaps
she might bag the whole of Poland, or at any rate establish her
domination over the kingdom. She accordingly hastened to make
peace with Turkey, and gave her whole attention to the problem
at her door. The juxtaposition of events is rather interesting.
In April (1792) France had declared war against Austria. In May
Catherine marched her troops into Poland.

Valmy

The effect of Russia's policy on her two rivals, Austria and Prussia, can well be imagined. After labored preparations they had
got two armies into the field, the Austrians in the Netherlands, the
Prussians facing the eastern frontier of France; but neither power
had mobilized its full strength. The Austrians, in particular,
showed little disposition to co-operate in attack, and their forces
were much below the number they had promised for the campaign.
After the fall of some border fortresses the French finally made a
stand, facing the Prussian invaders at Valmy on September 20.
The Battle of Valmy was hardly more than an exchange of cannon
shots; yet it was singularly decisive. The Prussian army not only
retired but even re-crossed the Rhine. Their leader had blundered
badly when he allowed the French to occupy strong positions, and
his army, already decimated by disease, showed none of the traces
of Prussia's one-time military supremacy. But chiefly the fiasco
was due to official distraction. Neither Austria nor Prussia could
really put their heart into the campaign, while their common
interests in Poland were threatened by Catherine's action. Already Polish reform had been crushed under Russian bayonets.

*The Second
Partition
of Poland*

The sequel of these events can readily be guessed. While the
French were now emboldened to take the offensive, Prussia made a
hasty agreement with Russia, and in 1793 occurred the Second
Partition of Poland. Thanks to a French invasion of the Netherlands, Austria had not been in a position to support her claims; but

Prussia had marched an army into Poland, and Catherine had been obliged to divide the spoil. Meanwhile Revolutionary France had been providentially saved.

But one must admit that it was more good fortune than good management that Revolutionary France had held her own, and after this carving of Poland the Allies were able once more to look to the west. The French had therefore still to meet their fundamental problem.

The Second Crisis—The Revolution Saved by the Terror

The advance of the Revolutionary armies had at first accomplished great things. Belgium was "liberated," and Savoy and Nice, which had belonged to the King of Sardinia, had been occupied and annexed with the approval of at least a large section of the populations concerned. Since a French army also held the line of the Rhine, it appeared that the "natural boundaries" had been reached. But this success was only illusory, and for two reasons it was soon turned into disaster. In the first place, the "liberators," as we have intimated before, converted their policy into one of exploitation. Many requisitions were laid on the poor Belgians, while thoughtless confiscation of Church property offended a deeply religious people. All this was contrary to the policy of Dumouriez, who had hoped for Belgium support, and he berated the government soundly for this brutal indifference to the feelings of the Netherlanders. Moreover, his troops were insufficiently provided with clothing and even ammunition, and lack of provisions made it necessary to forage at the expense of the inhabitants. In the second place, the condition of the army was still, as may be gathered, greatly inferior to that of the Allies, who were now able to strengthen their forces considerably in the west. Thoroughly disgusted with his situation, Dumouriez planned after beating the Austrians to march with his victorious army on Paris and restore the monarchy in the person of Louis XVII, the young son of the late king, still a prisoner in the Temple. But, unfortunately for the cause of strong government, Dumouriez did not beat the Austrians. On March 28, 1793 he received a crushing defeat at Neerwinden, and finding his troops unwilling to carry out his design of marching to Paris, he deserted to the enemy. A little later the French army on the Rhine sustained defeat and was also forced to retreat. Again France was threatened with invasion.

Evolution of the Terror

External crisis— Neerwinden

Internal crisis—the Vendéan uprising

And at this moment she was even more broken and divided than she had been a year earlier. Early in March a serious revolt had broken out among the peasants of La Vendée, a department in the west in what had formerly been Brittany. Partly it was occasioned by an attempt to enforce conscription; but the fundamental cause of this explosion was religious, for these peasants were fervent Catholics, and they had looked upon the government's religious policy with a deep and growing resentment. Some initial successes of the insurgents seemed to presage a formidable civil war. Since many of the towns in southern France were highly indignant at the excesses of Paris and the policy of making the wealthier classes bear the expenses of the war, a sort of alliance was threatened between the middle class and peasantry for the purpose of ousting the mob-ridden government at Paris.

Germs of the Terror

With the dreadful prospect of civil war looming in the background, it was clear that nothing but extraordinary efforts could save the country from conquest and partition. The men at Paris —that is, all true patriots in the Convention—realized at last the mistake that had been made in whittling down the executive. Even now, it is true, they were not disposed to choose ministers from the legislature as Danton urged (and for the reason that Danton, like Mirabeau, was suspected of personal motives), but the Girondins carried through the project of creating what was known as the committee of public safety, a body of nine persons (eventually twelve), whose authority was placed over that of the ministers, and which was empowered to take what measures were required for the national defense. Oddly enough, the Girondins themselves did not dominate the committee, the outstanding member of which was Danton. It was he who had been largely responsible for the revolutionary tribunal to deal summarily with all cases of conspiracy. The evolution of a strong government with teeth marks the appearance of some of the machinery of what was to be known as the "Terror."

The crisis deepens— the communal revolt

But the gravity of the crisis deepened. Before the end of May the city of Lyons overthrew its radical government and was followed by other cities in an attitude of open defiance of the central government. The fall of the Girondins, whose strength, we may remember, lay in the departments, fanned the flames of revolt, and a number of provincial towns were soon involved. The decentralization of France had now, in truth, proved a disastrous blunder, for the country seemed on the verge of falling to pieces. And besides all this, there was acute economic distress.[1]

The crisis was so grave that the new government was wise enough to begin by making some conciliatory gestures as a means of arresting the spread of the revolt. To influence the peasantry the confiscated property of the *émigrés* was divided into small lots and offered for sale. The principle of compensation for the loss of feudal rights was also finally abolished. In order to appease the proletariat, a maximum price was placed on wheat—though such a policy was naturally harmful to the peasants and had eventually to be abandoned; also a minimum wage was enacted for a time. Simultaneously, in order to mollify the middle class, whose wealth had been conscripted for the national defense, some measures were now passed which lightened the burden of all but the most wealthy. Finally the Convention adopted a constitution which by favoring decentralization and providing for a referendum on all questions before the legislature was calculated to please the majority of the citizenry. This curious experiment in constitutionalism was subjected to a plebiscite—that is, a vote of the totality of the citizens; but after its passage (by a large majority) the project was promptly shelved; and indeed the whole affair was apparently a Jacobin ruse [2] to arrest the spread of the bourgeois rising before the government itself was ready to crush it.

Conciliatory measures

Even toward the national foe there was at first a spirit of temporizing. Danton seems to have wanted peace if honorable terms could be obtained, so that the Revolution might be "consolidated," as he expressed it. In April he had persuaded the Convention to renounce its former policy of intervention in other countries and a decree to that effect was intended not only to conciliate the Belgians but (in Danton's view) to open the way to a speedy termination of the war. Danton was a man of singular character. With a sagacity that few of his followers seemed to possess he realized the importance of strong leadership, and, while ready to exert force relentlessly when a crisis seemed to require it, he was equally convinced that tact and moderation were essential virtues in accomplishing public ends. Unfortunately, in the turmoil of revolution, when all the baser passions were let loose, Danton often

Position and character of Danton

---

[1] *The Recollections of Baron Frenilly* (pp. 129–30) gives a graphic description of the crisis as it affected the average Parisian.

[2] The Jacobins worked over a project of the Girondins.

played the demagogue with the object of furthering his personal
ambition. He was also avaricious and venal, swindling first the
king and then the government of the Republic. He was always
indeed an opportunist, intriguing with often mutually hostile
parties in order to insure his own safety, whatever the outcome.
But he was not a vindictive person, too careless and easy-going, in
fact, to cherish hatred; and he deplored the factional spirit as much
as he did the pitiless driving of an idea to an extreme. It was
because of a certain tendency to laziness, which had the effect of
slackening his energies, that he failed to keep steady watch on the
man who felt himself to be the country's sole reliance and who
never lost a chance of driving toward his ultimate goal. For this
reason, when it was decreed that the committee of public safety
should change its personnel Danton was not included, and shortly
afterward Robespierre became not only a member but its leading
spirit. All of this, of course, argues that Danton was not a man of
exceptional popularity.[1] Indeed his probity had long been under
suspicion, and though he still had a personal following, most of the
Jacobins turned rather to Robespierre for leadership. Yet insofar
as the Terror represented strong government, capable of putting
down with ferocity if necessary all discordant elements and uniting
with vigor against the foreign enemy, this system typified the
ideas of Danton more than those of any other revolutionary statesman.

*Character
and
Organiza-
tion of the
Terror*

The Terror was an emergency despotism—a "dictatorship of
distress," as one of its champions put it. It was founded on the
theory that only by establishing a despotism could civil war be
ended, unity restored, and the country put in a condition to defend
itself against the enemy at its doors. It was no light thing for
a country, torn by revolution and anarchy, to fight most of Europe.
The French nation must put more of its soul into the task. But

*Character
and purpose
of the
Terror*

since patriotism was not an easy sentiment to cultivate during the
dark hours of defeat and since in any case there were large elements of the population either actually disloyal or at least unwilling to discipline themselves to follow the government's lead, it
was deemed necessary to back this despotism by "terror." If
men would not fight from love or loyalty they must fight from fear;
hence, the machinery of capital punishment which the govern-

[1] Danton's popularity had been impaired by his peace policy, and he was also
believed by many to have been implicated in Dumouriez's plot against the Republic.

ment had at its hand to destroy all elements of opposition, all
traitors not only actual but potential, and which could be used as a
kind of whip brandished over the heads of the French nation.
Such will partly explain the regularity of the executions—daily
warnings of what might happen to any heart that was not true.
It must not be supposed, of course, that the great majority of the
people actually suffered under the Terror. Most people gave no
grounds for suspicion and went about their daily tasks as always,
though in Paris it was felt expedient to shun publicity as far as
possible. Certainly, the joy of life was not abolished by the Terror.
The theaters were well attended; even a little prosperity returned.
But the majority of the middle class did well to keep out of politics.
For there was always a weapon in reserve that could be used against
them, and it behooved every man and every woman to avoid
suspicion.

It was obviously an abnormal régime, but the times themselves
were abnormal. It was an unconstitutional régime; for it was felt
that the government's hand must not be fettered by a constitution,
and it would have been hardly possible, indeed, to expect the
majority of citizens to realize the gravity of the crisis and vote
spontaneously for autocratic rule. For the time being the French
people had to put their liberties in storage and forget the principles
of the Revolution in order that those very principles might triumph
in the end. One does not deny the fact that it was an unwholesome
régime and that many were far from happy in an atmosphere of
suspicion. It must be admitted, too, that there were many persons
unjustly killed, many persons who suffered merely for belonging
to a certain class or on insufficient evidence of treason. Yet it is
difficult to see how without the Terror France could have pulled
herself out of anarchy and civil war and mobilized the strength
to beat back the foreign foe. It was, in short, a marvelous product
of practical statesmanship. And it saved France.

The cornerstone and indeed the very soul of the Terror was the
committee of public safety. There were ministers, it is true, but
they were hardly more than clerks of the great committee. There
was a legislature too, the Convention,[1] which in theory at least
possessed the supreme power, but in actual fact was a mere crea-

The machinery of the Terror

---

[1] While its part in the Terror has given the Convention its chief historical importance, this body occupied itself with many other things. It freed the slaves in
the colonies, adopted the metric system of weights and measures, and drafted
schemes for a system of popular education and the codification of the law.

ture of the body it had created. Though the members of the committee were elected for one month, they were almost always reelected, and in course of time the Convention came to fear its own creation. Under orders from the committee were the deputies on mission, members of the Convention chosen by twos to go to every department and to every army in the field. They were the long arm of the government, invested with power to enforce loyalty in the country and at the front. They wielded despotic power, though, like the intendants of old, they were responsible to the government. Thus it may be observed that France was centralized once more. A nation which had fallen apart was now restored to unity.

The system of terror which emanated from the government was wielded by various committees and tribunals. Throughout France was established a network of "revolutionary committees" whose chief business was to enforce the Law of Suspects—a terrible law which rendered suspect all persons who might in any way be identified with the Old Régime; it might even be applied to anyone who could not show a positive service to the Revolution, the record of each citizen being inscribed on a "card of security," which was a sort of passport that everyone was supposed to have in his keeping. In Paris a central committee, known as the committee of general security, examined cases of suspicion, and decided who should be haled before the revolutionary tribunal. Since, however, this central court was unable to handle all the many cases, courts of much the same character were established in the country at large. There were even regular panels of jurymen to judge these cases, but it was quite impossible, of course, to expect them to be impartial. For most of the persons brought before these courts the guillotine was in store.

Such were the principal organs of the Terror, though it was even more elaborate than we have described. Some of its machinery— the committee of public safety, the revolutionary tribunal, and the deputies on mission—had come into being before the system was fully evolved. By September, 1793, the "Reign of Terror" was supposed officially to begin. It was not, at all events, more terrible than the reign of anarchy that preceded it when the populace had taken the law into its own hands and occasionally perpetrated massacres. As Danton said, "Let us be terrible in order to dispense the people from being terrible." It was organized terror as a contrast to the promiscuous terror of the mob. And it could be

used against the mob itself if it ever disturbed the even tenor of
the new régime. One may remark in connection with the Terror,
as with certain other episodes of the Revolution, that men who in
private life were gentleness itself did not shrink from any atrocity
in the pursuit of an ideal. "Terrorism" had something of the
flavor of a religion.

Another curious aspect of the Terror was the fact that, in gen- *The pedigree*
eral, the very men who had patronized and in some cases insti- *of the*
gated the recent orgies in anarchy and who had talked loudest *terrorists*
about liberty were now among the champions of autocracy. It
was a strange perversion of Jacobinism, the metamorphosis of a
demagogue into a patriot. It is an interesting evidence of the fact
that democracy must usually yield to nationalism, curtailing
freedom of opinion and exacting unusual sacrifices from the citizen when a nation is at war. And at least the bloodthirstiness of
the Terror was natural enough to men who had been using such
methods through the hands of mobs to repress the conservatives
in the earlier days of the Revolution. They were no longer leaders
of the populace, but they used the methods of the populace to
make impossible even an effort at resistance. It was Marat who
had said, "We must establish the despotism of liberty in order to
suppress the despotism of kings." It is an interesting fact that
Danton, Marat, and Dumouriez had all judged that some dictatorship was a necessary outcome of the Revolution; and incidentally,
Edmund Burke, a bitter critic of the Revolution, had even fore-
told the ultimate appearance of the dictator in uniform.

The first activities of the Terror (while it was still in a state of *Operation*
evolution) were directed against internal uprisings. The Vendéan *of the*
revolt was put down with ruthless severity, a particularly brutal *Terror*
deputy having been given the supervision of this work, which
resulted in the burning of villages and the butchery of some two
thousand people. Further atrocities accompanied the suppression *The*
of the revolting towns. Meanwhile, in June there was a harvest *pacification*
of executions in Paris, including Bailly, Barnave, "Philippe Égal- *of France*
ité," and a score or more Girondins. We may recall Madame
Roland's famous words on the way to the scaffold: "Liberty, how
many crimes are committed in thy name!" In October the woman
whom she had hated, Marie Antoinette, also went to the guillotine.
It was a ghastly responsibility that these men of the Terror had
assumed.

The
secondary
object of
the Terror

But it should be realized that there was one group among the Jacobins who had an ulterior motive in establishing the Terror. It was a small group too, but it was led by the little man whose quiet, wary tactics had made him the most powerful member of the great committee—namely, Robespierre. This group intended that the Terror should go on until the Republic should be founded on an entirely new pattern. It should be a régime, inspired by "civic virtue," sufficiently broad in its humanity to intervene directly in the interests of the poorer classes—a policy eminently practicable on the part of a government as despotic as that of the Terror. The regulative policy, necessitated by the war, should now be supplemented by measures in the interest of reform. It is not improbable that Robespierre had all along been looking to this goal. With the downward plunge of the Revolution, lopping off first the reactionaries, then the liberal nobles and royalist bourgeois, and finally the republican bourgeois, the populace, as the lower layer, had at last been reached, and with it the popular leaders, the Jacobins and their henchmen of the Commune. Such was the turn of fortune which had given power to Danton and Robespierre. But while the war had forced these two into the rôle of patriots, the Commune was still untamed; and here were found the fanatics whose coarse polemics, blatant atheism, and clamors for the nationalization of industry profoundly jarred the bourgeois sensibilities of Robespierre. The sending of most of this element to the guillotine in March, 1794 put the Commune into immediate eclipse. Thus was the Terror setting its seal on the period of the disorders. But Robespierre, for his own purposes, had still one obstacle before him. There was Danton.

The breaking
of the
Commune

Position and
character of
Robespierre

Robespierre and Danton were two men of such mutually contradictory qualities that any co-operation at this juncture was inconceivable. A practically minded but easy-going libertine, Danton was anathema to a person of Robespierre's temperament and principles. Austere in his private life and rigidly honest ("the incorruptible," he was called), Robespierre was a man of fixed ideas, who never bent to realities and seldom temporized. He owed his popularity with the masses to the confidence which they placed in his sincerity, and it can hardly be said that such confidence was misplaced. But while he had learned by experience to become an impressive speaker, Robespierre had none of those human qualities which could endear him to a person at close range,

He was cold, aloof, habitually grave, and without a spark of humor. He was more of an oracle than a statesman. He had something of the mystic quality of the medieval monk, turned crusader, and his processes of thinking seldom delved below the abstract. With two exceptions, his colleagues on the committee did not take him over-seriously, and if he seemed to sway the Terror for the present, it was partly because a certain popularization of its objects had some value in their eyes and partly because some of them, like Carnot at the war office, were preoccupied with details of administration, while others—the sordid element—needed the Terror to protect their own dubious records. But there were some in the Convention who grew restive under the Terror and whose grumbling revealed what might be the beginning of a reaction. Would Danton, lately maneuvered out of the committee, be able to recover his leadership?

The issue was clearly drawn. Danton declared that the Terror *The* must be relaxed. The country was pacified, the invader had been *breach in the Terror—* beaten back, peace with honor was possible, and it was now time *Danton vs.* to end a system which had demonstrably done its work. Doubt- *Robespierre* less personal feelings added strength to his convictions. Of a highly impressionable temperament, his soul had begun to revolt against the interminable executions, and besides, he wanted the return of normal times in order to enjoy the fortune he had amassed from the Revolution. His position was now the more formidable because of its ready appeal to the cowering bourgeois throughout the country. Certain decrees of the Convention (the famous Ventôse [1] decrees), instigated by the Robespierre faction, sequestering all property of suspects with a view of enriching the poor, was quite enough to frighten the bourgeois out of their wits. Such, then, was the spirit of the "Indulgents," as they were called; and, unless this movement were quashed, the dreams of Robespierre were vain.

It was evident to Danton himself that the blow was soon to *The end* descend; for several of his friends, whose peculations, more easily *of Danton* proved than his, gave their enemies a target, were openly attacked in the Convention. Yet it was characteristic of the man that he shrugged his shoulders at danger and scorned to fight or to flee.

---

[1] Ventôse (like Prairial, Thermidor, Vendémiaire, and Brumaire) was a month in the Revolutionary calendar. The "year I" was held to have begun on September 22, 1792, the birthday of the First Republic.

Finally, in April, 1794, he and his followers were arrested, hastily tried on trumped-up charges, and met their fate on the guillotine. "Show my head to the people," Danton had said to his executioner; "it is worth it."

The Terror at its height   The arrest of Danton had produced a great sensation but his death really made but little impression—an interesting testimony of the fact that if a tribune of the people slows his pace, he soon ceases to be an idol. The elimination of Danton and the "Indulgents" left Robespierre to all appearances supreme. Now at last he was in a position to usher in his "reign of virtue." But, as always, his ideas were quite nebulous. He prated about the need of civic virtue; he held an elaborate religious festival (inaugurating the religion of Rousseau [1]); he looked forward, in the manner of Rousseau, to a fairer distribution of wealth, some steps being taken for giving effect to the decrees of sequestration; but when it came to a comprehensive policy of social reform, the leadership of Robespierre was evidently bankrupt. How, then, could the Terror be justified? [2] The answer was merely a stiffening of the system. By the Law of the 22nd Prairial (drafted by Robespierre himself), the Terror was so intensified that any sort of evidence was admitted in trials, and judgments were explicitly left to the "conscience" of the jurors. No wonder the number of executions multiplied. And yet the great victory of Fleurus on June 26—one of the decisive battles of the war—seemed to prove beyond a doubt that the Terror was no longer needed.

End of the Terror in the Coup d'État of Thermidor   But fortunately Robespierre had overreached himself. By a provision of the act of Prairial even a member of the Convention might be sent before the revolutionary tribunal. Was anyone now safe from the power of this fanatic? Were even his own colleagues safe? Did not the Terror dangle over every head? Some of them knew only too well that their conduct was not so pure as to suit the Incorruptible; and it was this fear of the unrighteous for the self-righteous which promoted a new reaction against the Terror. Aware of the movement against him, yet confident of his hold over the Convention, Robespierre had made the tactical mistake of

---

[1] See page 261, note.

[2] According to his admirer, Mathiez, he wished the Terror to continue until the rich had been finally deprived of their wealth for the benefit of the poor (the Ventôse decrees), and in that way achieve that ideal of economic equality which Rousseau had preached. It was characteristic of the man that having made up his mind that a certain course was right, he took little account of the insuperable difficulties.

absenting himself for several weeks from meetings of the committee. When finally, emerging from retirement, he made a speech in the Convention, full of denunciation of the enemies of the Republic, yet refusing to mention names, he was sealing his own doom. It was desperation, born of mortal fear, that brought revolt finally to a head. The Terror, in very truth, was crashing of its own weight.

We shall not recount the story of the "tyrant's" fall. An effort of the Commune to effect his escape having been frustrated, he and his followers were outlawed by the Convention, and they were guillotined on the 10th of Thermidor, July 28, 1794. The Terror had come to an end in the blood of its principal champion.

The critical period of the Revolution was not yet ended—for the reaction which now set in threatened for a short time to end in a return to monarchy; but thanks to the Terror, the most acute dangers were past. If France accepted a king, at least it would not be because he would be forced upon her by the First Coalition. The tide had too definitely turned.

REVOLUTIONARY FRANCE, TRIUMPHANT

The Allies did not take immediate advantage of the French defeats in the spring of 1793; and in a few months it was a new France which confronted them—a France, armed to the teeth, and ready, indeed, to face the united strength of five powers.

When we remember the condition of the French army at the outset of the war, the transformation which took place seems almost a miracle—a marvelous proof, certainly, of the vitality of the French nation. Neither materially nor morally was the First Coalition a match for the France which the Terror created. Much of this great achievement was due to the labors and organizing genius of that member of the committee of public safety who had general charge of the conduct of the war, Lazarre Carnot. This "organizer of victory" systematically overhauled and renovated every department of the service. On the basis of the *levée en masse* (August, 1793), which rendered every able-bodied citizen liable for service, thirteen armies were placed in the field, totaling 750,000 men. Never in modern history had so large a fighting force been mobilized for service. The combined strength of the First Coalition was not inferior in point of numbers, but in organization and equipment it was no longer a match for France. Like

The superiority of France over the First Coalition

all coalitions, it was unwieldy and unharmonious and seemingly incapable of any unified strategy. In fighting spirit, too, the French far surpassed their more experienced adversaries. Whereas the armies of the Allies were fighting simply because they were forced to fight, the French soldier was something more than a conscript; he realized that he was fighting for a France that belonged to *him*—the France of the Revolution. No greater effusion of patriotism has ever been shown than this patriotism of the Terror, with its twofold basis, defense of country and defense of the Revolution. It was characteristic of the Terror that the generals knew they must win, else they would probably pay for defeat upon the scaffold; and several of the French commanders were tried and sent to the guillotine simply because of reverses in the field. In place of the claims of birth which had prevailed in the king's army and still prevailed in those of the First Coalition, every soldier under the tricolor knew that he had at least a chance to rise from the ranks and possibly to become the commander of an army. It was during this period that many of Napoleon's marshals—some of them, men of the humblest extraction—won their spurs. The principle of equality—meaning equality of opportunity—did much for the morale of the French. And when at last victory crowned their efforts, they felt a new enthusiasm. A war of triumphant aggression had been launched. Going into battle, singing the *Marseillaise*, the French armies were irresistible.

A successful war of aggression

We shall not detail the campaigns. The forces of the Allies were beaten back till once more the French had won the natural boundaries. Even Holland was conquered. And when Prussia, deserting her allies, made peace with France, the First Coalition received a staggering blow. Spain's defection shortly followed. The year

The Third Partition of Poland

1795, which witnessed the extinction of Poland, was a year of triumph for the newly invigorated nation of the West. Instead of dismembering France, Austria had lost the Netherlands, and Prussia, her territories on the Rhine. Indeed by the Treaty of Basel (1795) Prussia recognized, in effect, the principle of the natural boundaries. And all this transpired before the coming of Napoleon Bonaparte.

FOR FURTHER READING OR STUDY

Robinson, J. H., and Beard, C. A., *Readings in Modern European History*, vol. i, chap. xiii (*passim*); Anderson, F. M., *Constitutions and Documents:*

France, 1789–1901; Biré, C., *Diary of a Citizen of France during the Terror,* vol. ii; *Recollections of Baron de Frenilly;* Mercier, L. S., *The Picture of Paris before and after the Revolution.*

Hazen, C. D., *The French Revolution,* vol. i., chaps. xx and xxii, vol. ii., chaps. xxix–xxx, xxxii–xxxix; Bourne, H. E., *The Revolutionary Era in Europe,* esp. chaps. xi, xii (*passim*) and xiii; Gottschalk, L., *The Era of the French Revolution,* book iii, chap. ii (the Reign of Terror); Gershoy, L., *The French Revolution and Napoleon,* chaps. ix–xi; Bradby, E. D., *The French Revolution;* Madelin, L., *The French Revolution* (always entertaining, but very hostile to the Terror); Mathiez, A., *The French Revolution* (idealizing Robespierre); Gillespie, J. E., *A History of Europe, 1500–1815,* pp. 529–38; Hayes, C. J. H., *A Political and Cultural History of Modern Europe,* vol. i, pp. 622–39; Guignebert, C., *A Short History of the French People,* vol. ii, chaps. xxix–xxx (*passim*) and xxxii.

Brinton, C., *A Decade of Revolution* (dissenting from Mathiez's apotheosis of Robespierre); Clapham, J. H., *The Causes of the War of 1792;* Phipps, R. W., *The Armies of the First French Republic,* 3 vols.; Mahan, A. T., *The Influence of Sea Power upon the French Revolution and Empire,* 2 vols.; Kerr, W. B., *The Reign of Terror* (by a disciple of Mathiez); Mathews, S., *The French Revolution,* chaps. xvii–xix (very convenient description of the Terror); Madelin, L., *Danton* (a readable but rather uncritical biography, less convincing than Mathiez's strictures on Danton); Bain, R. N., *The Last King of Poland and His Contemporaries;* Lord, R. H., *The Second Partition of Poland;* Rose, J. H., *Nationality in Modern History,* chap. ii.

X. THE PURGING AND CONSOLIDATION OF THE REVOLUTION UNDER NAPOLEON

1. THE OPPORTUNITY AND RISE OF NAPOLEON BONAPARTE

A. THE YOUTH AND TRAINING OF NAPOLEON BONAPARTE
Early interests; A critical moment.

B THE EXPERIMENT OF THE "BOURGEOIS REPUBLIC"
The Thermidorean Reaction; Establishment of the Directory; Rising of the 13th Vendémiaire; Character of the Directory; Society under the Directory; Rule of the Directory.

C. THE SHADOW OF MILITARY DESPOTISM

2. THE RISE OF THE FIRST EMPIRE

Bonaparte's opportunity—the Coup d'État of Brumaire; Establishment of the Consulate; Establishment of the Life Consulate; Establishment of the Empire; Character of the Empire—Napoleon as a politician; Explanation of the return to absolutism; Foundations of Napoleon's greatness: genius, will, and work.

3. THE REORGANIZATION OF FRANCE

Napoleon's motives as a reformer; Reorganization of the state; Various activities; Reorganization of the Church; Napoleon and the Revolution.

4. NAPOLEON, LORD OF EUROPE

Napoleon and the art of war; Napoleon as a diplomatist; Napoleon as a conqueror; Napoleon as an imperialist.

5. "TILSIT"—THE ZENITH OF NAPOLEON'S POWER

Duping of Alexander I; Humiliation of Prussia; The Franco-Russian alliance; Importance of "Tilsit."

6. THE COLLAPSE OF FRENCH DOMINATION OVER EUROPE

A. GENERAL CAUSES
Napoleon's overconfidence; Precariousness of his position; The Continental System: (1) its genesis and evolution, (2) its operation, (3) its failure; The nationalist uprising: (1) in Spain, (2) in Germany; Invasion of Russia: (1) its causes, (2) its failure, (3) significance of its outcome.

B. THE WAR OF LIBERATION
Prussia assumes the leadership; Formation of the Last Coalition; Reasons for the Allies' success; Leipzig and the downfall of Napoleon's empire in Europe; The first abdication.

C. The Last Phase

   Napoleon's opportunity and return; The last stand—Waterloo; The final
abdication, exile, and death; Historical importance of Napoleon.

The French Revolution through its leveling process had unified
the French nation as never before, and, thanks to that revolution,
drawing so deeply from the capacity of a people who had arisen
to the emergencies that beset them, France had become once more
the greatest power of Europe. This new spirit was to permeate
the whole of Europe through the organizing genius of a man who
was able to show up in glaring fashion the inefficiency of the old
order as represented by the old monarchies. But France herself
was to show that she was not ready to change her habits completely. The Revolution had gone too far in some respects, and
the pendulum must swing back. In the year following the Terror
the French people were ready to take an account of stock and
search for a middle ground. It was their failure then to find a
solution of this kind, together with the war, which provided the
best field of opportunity for talent, that opened the way for
Napoleon Bonaparte.

The Opportunity and Rise of Napoleon Bonaparte

Napoleon Bonaparte was born August 15, 1769 on the island of *The Youth and*
Corsica about a year after it had been acquired by France. It had *Training of*
been called the "isle of unrest," for it had long been in a state of *Napoleon Bonaparte*
rebellion against the republic of Genoa to which it belonged, and
that decadent little republic had sold it to France for a mere song.
No one could then have realized what that sale was to mean to
France, but Rousseau had once written, "I have a presentiment
that this little island will some day astonish Europe." One of
those who continued the unrest after the transfer of the country
to France was the father of Napoleon Bonaparte, but he was also
one of the first to make his peace with the new master.

Napoleon's family was of noble extraction but far from well- *Early*
to-do. His father was fortunate enough to obtain for him a scholar- *interests*
ship in a military school in France, where officers were made; and
after several years of training young Bonaparte emerged as a
sub-lieutenant of artillery. As a child he had been cross-grained
and very difficult to manage; as a school-boy he had been surly
and taciturn and not always very diligent in his studies unless

they happened to arouse his interest. But he had early shown a taste for martial sports; and whenever his military duties permitted it, he spent much of his time in reading. In some respects, no doubt, the works of the *philosophes* affected some of his later viewpoints, but most of his ideas were probably the product of experience and observation. At this time he was impressionable, and his youthful energy clamored for outlets. His first aspiration was to free his native island from France, and he engaged in active intrigues to that end despite the fact that he owed his living to his commission as a French officer. But as these efforts were not successful, he finally, in 1793, definitely gave up his hope of liberating Corsica, and made up his mind to serve his government for what he could get out of it. He was promoted steadily, sometimes, it is true, because of the shortage of officers, but once certainly because he showed to timely advantage his gift of strategy,[1] and for this service he was promoted to the command of a brigade. Soon after this he became involved in the disgrace of the Robespierre faction with whom he had been playing politics (after the fashion of all the revolutionary generals), but he was too valuable an officer to send to the guillotine, and he suffered nothing worse than an eight-day imprisonment.

A critical moment

So far this opportunist had managed to show his natural ability; yet he was lucky in having been able to escape some pitfalls. The greatest demand that he made of Dame Fortune was in the summer of 1795 when he refused to accept an assignment in the Army of the West because he felt himself to be worthy of something better. For this insubordination he was suspended from rank, and it seemed for a moment as though his career had reached an untimely end. But by sheer luck he got the chance to redeem himself in the incident of the 13th Vendémiaire—the circumstances of which must now lead us back to the period of transition which followed the Terror.

The Experiment of the "Bourgeois Republic"

The Thermidorean Reaction

The reaction which followed the Reign of Terror is historically known as the Thermidorean Reaction. The Convention was so glad to be rid of the "monster" it had created that the committee of public safety together with all the machinery of the Terror was abolished. The Jacobins showed some fight, of course, but the odds were heavily against them. Some of the ex-Terrorists were themselves fed to the guillotine which they had used so ruthlessly against

[1] At the recapture of Toulon from the British in 1795.

others; and it was clear enough that the Convention, now directed by a moderate majority, was determined to break at least with the immediate past. Would the reaction go so far as to restore the monarchy? There were, no doubt, plenty of royalists in France (Professor Parisset thinks royalism was not so much spontaneous as induced by British gold), but the legitimate king, Louis XVII, perished in the Temple in June, 1795, and his uncle, the Count of Provence, an exile since 1789, was not a person calculated to inspire a large following. Moreover, one could not be sure that the *émigrés* would accept the leveling work of the Revolution. So, in spite of much intriguing in the background and an epidemic of massacres of radicals by conservatives (the so-called "White Terror"), the path of compromise was chosen. The general run of the bourgeoisie, which was now able to return to politics and to dominate public opinion, decided to stick to the republic as the lesser of two evils, and it was this class which impressed its character on the new régime.

The so-called Constitution of the Year III was framed and promulgated during the summer of 1795. Its framers felt that they were profiting by experience when they established a property qualification for suffrage (election was also to be indirect) and a two-chambered legislature (the council of ancients and the council of five hundred); but these sons of the Revolution had yet to learn the practical value of executive leadership resting on legislative support. The new executive, known as the directory, a body of five to be chosen (one each year) for a term of five years by the legislature, had no initiative in legislation, and was, on the whole, a rather weak organ. The administration of the country at large was a compromise between the centralization of the Old Régime and the decentralization of the constitutional monarchy. There were to be resident commissioners in each department appointed by the central government to see to the enforcement of the laws, though the local authorities continued to be elective. In its electoral requirements and its weak executive the new policy resembled the Constitutional Monarchy. Also, like the Constitution of 1791, it put political power into the hands of the middle class. The former régime was the bourgeois monarchy; this one was the bourgeois republic.

Establishment of the Directory

This new republican experiment, which is commonly known as the "Directory," probably well expressed the national desire for an order stable enough to preclude any violent changes. Besides the electoral arrangements and a bicameral legislature the Convention took the further precaution of decreeing that two-thirds of its membership should hold over to the new legislature. Since most of this body were regicides (men who had voted for a king's death), they were deliberately guarding against a royalist reaction which might conceivably cost them their heads. The "Thermidorians" had always the problem of pursuing a middle course, proof against Jacobinism on the left and Bourbonism on the right. But the policy of "middle-grounders" is always a difficult one, since their policy is apt to be negative; and this was one of the essential weaknesses of the new régime.

The rising of the 13th Vendémiaire

At this juncture the policy met with a direct challenge. While the constitution, referred to a plebiscite, was accepted—in a light vote—by a very large majority, the supplementary decrees encountered a spirited opposition in Paris, and an effort was made to oust the Convention by force. This uprising is what is known as the incident of the 13th Vendémiaire (October 5, 1795). Since it was necessary to command the approaches to the Tuileries with guns, the services of a capable artillery officer were needed, and the choice was General Bonaparte. While the insurgents were foolishly delaying their attack, Bonaparte was planting his cannon, and when finally they were ready to advance, it was to charge into the cannon's mouth. The rising was crushed and the Convention was thus sustained. And—what is still more important—Bonaparte had retrieved his shattered fortunes and had good hope of winning some tangible recognition of his service.

The character of the Directory

The following month the new régime began to operate. The rule of the Directory, though it lasted four years, proved to be one of the most vicious governments that France has ever endured. The bourgeois politicians who now guided the nation were, in general, a group of corrupt and self-seeking time-servers. Many of them were speculators and profiteers who seemed to care for nothing but the enjoyment of power and wealth. With a brazenry that was the more cruel because of the sufferings of the poor these bourgeois flaunted their ill-gotten wealth and plunged into the most reckless dissipation. Doubtless the peculiar tone of society was

Society under the Directory

partly due to the moral reaction which naturally followed the harsh discipline and dangers of the Terror. The "victim balls," to which persons were invited who could claim that they had lost a relative on the guillotine, are an interesting evidence of the cynicism that prevailed. People who had been through the strain of the preceding years felt that they had a right to enjoy life to the full without any need to think at all of private virtue or public duty. It was this vapid and dissolute society into which young Bonaparte awkwardly plunged, and it was one of its typical figures, Joséphine de Beauharnais, with whom he fell in love, and whom he married. But Bonaparte had the advantage of being a sojourner, as it were. His talents belonged to the army for the present, though his casual observation of politicians may have proved a useful experience.

The misgovernment of the Directory was chiefly the result of the peculiar factors we have mentioned. It was, however, aggravated by the faults of the constitution. Since the executive was not responsible to the legislature, and had to confront the public in periodic elections, it deliberately tried to control these by bribery or intimidation. There was every evidence that the nation was becoming increasingly estranged, and that only by crooked measures could this clique of politicians succeed in retaining power. The continued issuance of paper money had plunged the government once more into financial ruin and the country into the misery of unstable prices; the people of wealth who were not fortunate enough to be in power were exploited by forced loans; and the poor were almost driven to desperation. There was not even external peace, for the Directory needed the war to enable it to bleed conquered countries and thus to rescue it from bankruptcy. Besides, there was danger lest, if the army should come home, it would not tolerate so despicable a government. *The rule of the Directory*

One may feel indeed that, roughly speaking, the best element in France was now in the army. Would it be long before the army would assert itself and end this rickety government? Conditions in France were becoming ripe for a military dictatorship. *The Shadow of Military Despotism*

The public dissatisfaction with the Directory was an asset for Bonaparte as soon as his political ambition was awakened; but it was the war which, in the meantime, gave him a chance to display his genius and to capture the public imagination. We shall not follow his career in any detail. But we may note that after "Vendémiaire" he received what he had long desired, the command of the Army of Italy. The appointment was due to Carnot, who had seen a plan which Bonaparte had once drawn up for the conquest of Italy, and who recognized the general's unusual gifts. During the year 1796–7 Bonaparte won a series of striking victories, which ended the First Coalition, and brought peace with all the powers but Great Britain. No commander in the field had acquired so distinguished a reputation.

But Bonaparte was something more than a successful general. He had arrogated to himself the right to direct negotiations, even fixing the terms of peace to be imposed on France's enemies. In response to their disapproval on one occasion, he calmly declared, "The army has approved." Once indeed the directors had tried to make him share the command with another officer, but Bonaparte would not countenance it for a moment, and the directors had to give way. For one thing, they needed the spoils which Bonaparte sent from Italy to lift them out of bankruptcy. Then on one occasion they also required his assistance to prop up their shaky positions. In 1797 he had sent one of his generals, the bluff Augereau, to support them in a movement against the councils. It is clear that the Directory was too dependent on the military to assert its independence. And Bonaparte was under no illusions about the power that he held. "Do you suppose," he said to a friend, "that I am gaining my victories in Italy in order to advance the lawyers of the Directory. . . . The victories we have gained have given the French soldier his true character. I owe everything to him. Let the Directory attempt to deprive me of my command, and they will see who is master." He had sensed the situation correctly. Already the civil government was completely overshadowed by the military.

"And I am only," Bonaparte had said, "at the beginning of my career." It was true enough. Of military glory he had had but a tempting taste; and his political career was yet before him. After the peace he took up his quarters in a beautiful château near Milan where he received the homage of Italy. Would he now return at the head of his host and claim his reward? No—he said that the pear was not yet ripe. But if it was not yet ripe, it was ripening.

THE RISE OF THE FIRST EMPIRE

It was once said of Napoleon Bonaparte that he would never stop short of mounting either the scaffold or the throne. For a person of his genius and his daring a commonplace destiny was unthinkable.

But for the present Bonaparte's thoughts were on the war. *Bonaparte's* There was still Great Britain to be fought, and Bonaparte always *opportunity* regarded her as France's principal enemy. The Directory them- *d'État of* selves had probably more fear of him. It was far from comfortable *Brumaire* having so popular a general in their midst (for after the Peace Bonaparte had been summoned back to Paris), and it was charac- teristic of the Directory that they planned an invasion of England partly, one may suspect, because it would be hazardous and not improbably end in failure and the eclipse of the national hero. Bonaparte seems to have divined their intentions, and he finally persuaded them to send him to Egypt instead. This, too, was a dubious project, and, as a matter of fact, met with failure—though it was not Bonaparte's fault that the requisite for success, namely, sea power, was not at his disposal. In the meantime, the Directory had begun a series of aggressions in Europe, which gave rise to the formation of the Second Coalition (Russia, Austria, and Great Britain). Without the genius of Bonaparte the French forces were quite unable to meet such odds. Once again, it seemed, opportunity knocked at his door.

Bonaparte returned from Egypt in October, 1799. It was a puzzled and dejected France that received him. The radicals had managed to turn tables on the moderates and had now the control of the government; but the new directors had only deepened the public discontent, first by their policy of bleeding the rich (thus alienating the wealthier middle class) and secondly by the Law of Hostages which compelled each department to give hostages to the government for its loyalty. Abroad French armies had sustained defeat, and though the tide had turned before Bonaparte came back to "save France," all the conquests which he had won were now lost. Public opinion was so dissatisfied that already a plot was on foot to invoke the aid of the army and reorganize the State under some military leader. This conspiracy was engineered by the Abbé Sieyès, one of the directors, in collusion with the moderates in the council of ancients. It was not so much an attempt to return to the old do-nothing régime. Rather it hastened the trend toward military despotism.

Bonaparte carefully took soundings of the situation, and after gaining numerous adherents, plunged heartily into the conspiracy, and became both its instrument and its leader. Made commander of the troops in Paris (to guard against a radical uprising), he delivered a public speech which might be regarded as a challenge to the present régime. The Directory speedily broke up, three of its members being accomplices in the plot and the other two arrested. The chief obstacle was the council of five hundred, in which the radicals held a majority. Wisely enough, the councils were meeting at St. Cloud rather than at Paris where the populace might have been encouraged to take a hand; but Bonaparte's efforts to over-awe the ancients by virtue of his presence (he was nothing of an orator) were singularly futile, and when he tried to harangue the council of five hundred, he was not only compelled to retire but he barely escaped the ignoble fate of Robespierre. Luckily Lucien, his brother, was president of the five hundred, and he managed during the din to fetch some soldiers, who were persuaded that their general had been maltreated, and forthwith invaded the hall. The outcome was the expulsion of the deputies by armed force. Thus was executed the Coup d'État of the 18th Brumaire (November 9, 1799).

*Establish-
ment of the
Consulate*

The cards were now in Bonaparte's hands and he was free to play them. A fraction of the councils, hastily gotten together, adopted under Bonaparte's auspices the Constitution of the Year VIII, which established what came to be known as the Consulate. The executive was composed of three consuls, but practically all its power was vested in the first consul, who was Bonaparte himself, named in the constitution for that office. The legislature was to be so split up—one body to propose the laws, another to discuss them, a third to pass on them, and a fourth (the senate) to test their constitutionality—that no opposition to the will of Bonaparte need be feared. Soon afterward (that is, in 1800) the government was completely centralized in the manner of the Old Régime. Bonaparte was now assuredly master of France—an absolute ruler in actual fact if not in name. The new arrangements were submitted to a plebiscite and ratified by an overwhelming majority. On December 15, 1799, a proclamation was issued in these words: "Citizens, the Revolution is established upon the principles which were its origin. It is at an end."

*Establish-
ment of the
Life
Consulate*

In the sense that the Revolution stood for the principle of equality of opportunity it appeared to have finished its work. Bonaparte represented and safeguarded the new social order. Even the principle of liberty was not, of course, to be permanently buried, but it was at present in eclipse, and its destroyer was to mount yet

higher. Under the existing constitution Bonaparte enjoyed but a
ten-year term as first consul, and he had, besides, to share the
honors with two colleagues. Such a position could hardly accord
with his ambition. After he had achieved new glories for France—
recovered the lost conquests, crushed the Second Coalition, effected
a general peace (which even included Great Britain), and restored
religious tranquility—he was awarded in 1802 with the position of
consul for life. This new constitution made him the sole executive.
In position he was now more of a monarch than the head of the
republic, and henceforth, like other monarchs, he signed all documents by his Christian name—"Napoleon."

But even this second rung on the ladder was not enough. His *Establish-*
vanity demanded the trappings and grandeur of power. Nothing *ment of the Empire*
but an essentially monarchical title (that of consul was of clearly
republican origin) and hereditary rule were left to complete his
progress to the pinnacle. Should he take the title of king? No,
that would have been an affront to the traditions of the Revolution. The one title which seemed to fit his greatness was that of
"emperor"; he should be hailed a new Charlemagne. After a
royalist plot in 1803,[1] it was alleged that the country would not
be safe against a reaction unless a dynasty were established. If
Napoleon should be murdered (and such had been the object of
numerous plots), there would then be an heir to keep alive Napoleonic traditions. On May 18, 1804 he was, accordingly, proclaimed "emperor of the French," his rule being made hereditary
under a new constitution, and, as before, approved by the people
in a plebiscite. Even the pope was summoned to crown him, though
in the end Napoleon snatched the crown himself and placed it upon
his own head. The act was logical enough. Napoleon Bonaparte
was a self-made monarch, and such strength as he required was
implied in his new title, "emperor of the *French*." [2]

The Establishment of the Empire meant the revival of a court.
Since Napoleon's family and intimates were sprung from relatively

[1] It was a consequence of this plot that Napoleon had a young member of a
collateral branch of the house of Bourbon, the Duke of Enghien, kidnapped on
neutral territory, brought to Paris, and shot after a military trial. Enghien had been
in the pay of the British government, and had been designated for a leading part
in the intended invasion of France. Napoleon seems to have intended his death as a
warning to the royalists. For a defense of his action see Kircheisen, *Napoleon*,
pp. 255–8.

[2] The holding of a plebiscite, as in the case of the Life Consulate, was another
democratic gesture.

Character of the empire —Napoleon as a politician humble beginnings, it was found desirable to employ some of the former figures of the Bourbon court to teach these newly empurpled personages how to act in their new capacity. Etiquette and ceremony returned, though it must be added that Napoleon himself cared little for pomp, and ceremonies he felt to be a waste of valuable time. He merely thought himself entitled to the grandeur that went with monarchy, and he believed that the people had really missed these baubles and would be glad to see them back. Like the adroit politician he always was, he had an eye for scenic effects. While about him were gorgeous costumes and much parading of gold and green, he himself would often appear in somber dress—perhaps in uniform. No doubt he was consciously conveying the impression that while politically he was master, with all the setting that properly befitted an emperor, socially he was still "Citizen Bonaparte." The new régime was not, at any rate, one of privilege. While noble titles came back into vogue, they were only awarded for definite merit. In 1802 was constituted the Legion of Honor in which men were enrolled who had performed conspicuous service for the State. All that was demanded of a subject was devotion. Even the *émigrés*, though their lands were not restored, were welcomed back to the fold, and some of them were glad to obtain employment from a Bonaparte. Thus Napoleon was emphatically a national leader.

Much of his success was due to the fact of understanding so well the temperament of the French. Himself an Italian, he could view them always with a certain calm detachment. He realized their vanity as a people ("Give them glory," he once said, "and you can lead them anywhere"); he knew their fondness for pageantry and anything that pleased the senses (hence, the value of a court, and hence too, the treasures taken from Italy to make Paris the shrine of an adoring Europe); he understood their thrift and their somewhat stolid spirit of enterprise (hence he gave them a well-ordered administration); and he knew that like most people they yearned to gratify their religious instincts (hence the ending of religious turmoil). Above all, he respected the principle of equality. Did he not himself personify that principle? "I am the Revolution," he once declared.

Explanation of the return to absolutism But he said on another occasion, "I destroyed the Revolution," and this was equally correct. After a whirligig of political experiments France had come back in 1804 to hereditary absolutism.

After turning full circle she was back to where she had been when the Revolution began. How shall we explain this paradox? How was it that the French, after enjoying the boon of political liberty, should be willing to surrender it and to accept without a murmur a return to the rule of a monarch with all that that implied? The explanation is threefold. The French had wearied of the political features of the Revolution. They had been through so many vicissitudes, so much dreary experimentation that they wanted a stable government, and this Napoleon Bonaparte seemed able to insure. Public opinion was tired of political agitation, tired of the endless elections, tired of the disorders which had throttled the nation's economic life; and it was now a comfortable change to place responsibility in the hands of a single person who, as a soldier, would have a true sense of order. In the second place, Napoleon, as a strong ruler, was able to protect the more valued fruits of the Revolution. His power was a guarantee that the nobles of the Old Régime would never recover their lands or their former privileged position. The men who had gained in property or prominence from the Revolution, as well as the men who had shed the blood of a legitimate monarch, looked upon the Consulate and the Empire as a safeguard. And finally we may recall the extraordinary lure of Napoleon's own personality. "There burnt in him," writes Holland Rose, "the flame of genius. It defies analysis; it baffles description; but generals and troops felt the spell. Civilians who sought to control the young warrior found themselves in the meshes of an all-controlling will—why, they knew not; but one after another they succumbed." If this was true in the beginning, it was truer as time went on, when that genius had been displayed. No soldier of France had ever wrought such wonders. And then, as we have said, he understood his people, and gave them for the moment what they wanted. "My policy," he said, "consists in governing men as they wish to be governed. That, I think, is the way of recognizing the sovereignty of the people." To that end, he looked always for men of capacity to be his instruments; and, in general, he was not deceived.

If we consider the fact of his skill not only in war and diplomacy but in the art of government with all that that implies, one is bound to be impressed by his marvelous versatility. But while one admits his talent, it is important to realize also that Napoleon's achievements were only made possible by hard and incessant work. Every

Foundations of Napoleon's greatness: genius, will, and work

waking moment his brain was active. "I am always working," he once declared; "I work when I am dining, I work at the theater; in the middle of the night I wake up and work . . . When I am meditating, I am in a state of extremely painful agitation. . . . I am like a woman in travail." Some of his success, no doubt, he owed to his unbounded confidence in himself; " 'Impossible,' " he is alleged to have said, "is not a French word." But he did not pretend to be naturally omniscient. His part in a conversation was that of asking endless questions; he craved to know all facts that

Engraving by Mme. Fournier

NAPOLEON

might prove serviceable to his ends; he was displaying his sense of thoroughness. He was seldom, indeed, obliged to make snap judgments, for he carefully foresaw all calculable contingencies. "He kept his eyes on the board," writes a biographer, "and long before a piece had to be moved, he had marked its place." It was a proof of his great mentality, indeed, that he saw the importance of details without ever allowing them to get in the way of his vision. He was the hardest of taskmasters; indeed he literally worked some of his subjects to death; and it is doubtful if, outside of his family circle, he ever felt affection for any creature; he was too impersonal to regard men as anything but instruments to be used as long as they continued to be of service. For, to him, after all, nothing counted but success, and what mattered the shortness of life, if in the end it spelled achievement? No doubt his callous ambition was largely forgiven in the light of what he was able to do for France. Yet admiration for his capacity does not alone account for the devotion which he received. Though he was ready to take any unscrupulous advantage over an enemy, one may concede that in normal affairs he, generally speaking, "played fair." He was adamant when punishment seemed to be needed, but he was equally just in rewarding devoted service. He had a ferocious temper, but he seldom allowed it the mastery of his brain, and it was this remarkable self-command in those moments of passion that made him the more formidable as an enemy. Yet he had a certain respect for the courage of one who refuted him. "With his keen sense of personal honor," writes Holland Rose, "he could not but respect the same sentiment in those whom he annoyed." So great an egotist could afford to be magnanimous with petty offenses. He did not ask for love but only that kind of loyalty that springs from respect—or sometimes, fear. At all events, love from his soldiers at least, he did get, perhaps because they knew that he shared their hardships; he was "one of them." It is related that during the return from Moscow, when men were freezing to death, some of the soldiers handed some faggots, which they had gathered for their campfire, to one of Napoleon's servants, bidding him, "Take them to the Emperor." And to all his subjects, soldiers and citizens alike, Napoleon seemed to impart a measure of that overpowering confidence which he always felt in himself.

The popularity which he enjoyed at the time of the Consulate—it was as first consul that he began his rôle of autocrat—was not only enhanced by the victorious peace which he secured but also by the products of his statesmanship. In other words he consolidated his position by the reforms which he enacted; and to these we must now turn.

THE REORGANIZATION OF FRANCE

The motives for Napoleon's reforms were perhaps three. He wished the gratitude of the nation, thereby to strengthen himself. He had, secondly, a practical mind, which required the institution of an orderly, stable government. He had, thirdly, a steady care for his own fame. "I hope," he said, "to leave to posterity a renown that may serve as an example or as a reproach to my successors." *Napoleon's motives as a reformer*

A reorganization of the State along new lines had already been foreshadowed by the autocratic rule implicit in the Consulate. In general, the principle of election was replaced by that of appointment. The general structure of the judiciary remained, but judges were now appointed by the first consul (later by the emperor). Similarly the division into departments was retained, but over each was placed a prefect, appointed by the first consul. Thus after the experiment of decentralization under the Constitutional *Reorganization of the State*

Monarchy and the half-centralization of the Directory we return to the rigid centralization of the Old Régime. But there was now a more systematic procedure—for example, the departments of fairly equal size which the Revolution had bequeathed. In many cases we notice that Napoleon carried through or rounded out work planned or actually begun by the revolutionary assemblies. The Convention had made some provision for public instruction, but its achievements had gone little beyond its paper decrees; Napoleon provided such a system, centralized, of course, like all other public services. The unification and codification of the laws—a matter studied by the various assemblies [1]—was finally made a fact under Napoleon. This monumental achievement was primarily the work of a commission of jurists; yet all its plans had been supervised by the emperor himself, who, though he knew little law, was able by his keen perception and practical turn of mind to make important contributions. The finances were set in order for the first time in a decade. Napoleon strove to make his people understand that payment of taxes was a public duty and must not be shirked. Few new taxes were instituted, but the old ones were carefully supervised and collected, and all the revenue was economically administered. It was but a short time before the national credit was restored, and France enjoyed a degree of stability that she had never known before. One of the Napoleonic creations was a national bank, the Bank of France, designed to give manufacturers the benefit of loans at a low interest. Indeed Napoleon made every effort to rebuild the shattered industrial life of his country, and won a large measure of success. He also constructed the finest thoroughfares in Europe largely in order to promote internal trade. In his attitude toward culture Napoleon could hardly be called well-rounded. Though deeply interested in science, and fond of the theater and opera, he took but a passing interest in the arts; and literature did not thrive during his reign—perhaps through fear of bureaucratic vigilance. The purpose of the schools he felt to be the rearing of devoted citizens, taught by men with "fixed principles," as he put it. He was, in fact, too much of an autocrat to countenance anything likely to lead to a demand for political change. It was for that reason that he maintained a censorship. However much he might satisfy public opinion, he did not

Various activities

---

[1] The work of a committee of the Convention was of considerable value to Napoleon's jurists.

choose to allow it any chance to cause him embarrassment. Inasmuch as opposition is sometimes wholesome, it was perhaps unfortunate that the Revolution had killed off most of the men of conspicuous talent, leaving trimmers or competent subalterns to take their place.

It was partly because it taught respect for authority that Napoleon valued the Catholic Church, and as soon as he began as first consul to adopt a program of reform, he gave his attention to the healing of the religious schism. Only through reconciliation with the papacy could religious unity be restored and the religious wants of the nation be satisfied. Agreement was reached as the result of negotiation, and the result was the famous Concordat of 1801. By this instrument the higher clergy, though appointed by the State, must receive the confirmation of the pope; the lower clergy were to be appointed by the bishops, with the sanction of the government; and all were to be paid by the State, in compensation for the Church's renunciation of the confiscated lands. It might seem that a wiser policy would have been sharp separation of Church and State, but Napoleon was a firm believer in concentration as a principle of statecraft, and he probably wanted the Church to be in a position of dependence. At any rate he restored religious peace. *Reorganization of the Church*

By his work of reorganization Napoleon purged the Revolution of the features which seemed to make for chaos, and retained those which might be calculated to bring out merit and to render the State a more efficient machine. In that sense he harnessed the Revolution to the chariot of autocracy. But Napoleon also capitalized the patriotism, born of the Revolution, to lead his soldiers on a path of territorial aggrandizement. It was here that self-interest and vanity came to mar the soundness of his judgment and to push him into a course that was harmful not only to Europe but to the French nation as well. *Napoleon and the Revolution*

NAPOLEON, LORD OF EUROPE

Napoleon as national leader stood on solid ground. Napoleon as lord of Europe stood majestically on an artificial structure held aloft by bayonets. It was the misfortune of France that this great statesman was first of all a soldier—possessed of an uncanny skill for circumventing his enemies and of an inordinate ambition. The first wars that he waged were not of his own making, but from *Napoleon and the art of war*

1806 on Napoleon's policy meant struggles to dominate Europe and bend it to his will. We shall not follow the story of his campaigns or trace the steady growth of the Napoleonic empire. We saw the end of the First Coalition. The Second Coalition was shattered by Napoleon's triumph at Marengo, supplemented by Moreau's decisive victory at Hohenlinden. Peace with Austria followed in 1801; peace with Great Britain in 1802. But war with Great Britain was renewed in 1803, and with British encouragement the Third Coalition was formed (Austria, Russia, and Great Britain). Emperor now, and with the Grand Army composed of seasoned veterans, Napoleon won the Battle of Austerlitz in December, 1805, and forced a third peace on Austria (the Treaty of Pressburg). The following year Prussia took Austria's place in the coalition, but was overwhelmed in the twin battles of Jena and Auerstädt; and Russia after a prolonged resistance was vanquished at the Battle of Friedland in June, 1807. With the Peace of Tilsit, which followed, a landmark was reached in Napoleon's career the significance of which we shall discuss presently. We have given only a summary of these achievements because we think it more important to dwell on the methods of Napoleon and the varied aspects of his rôle in the world at large.

To Napoleon the art of war was a favorite study and pastime, and few if any conquerors in history have so thoroughly comprehended it. In the first place, he gave a great deal of attention to the "psychology" of his army. He often set before his soldiers the love of glory and hope of material gain. "I will lead you," he told the Army of Italy when he assumed command, "into the most fertile plains in the world. Rich provinces, great cities will be in your power. There you will find honor, glory, and wealth. Soldiers of the Army of Italy, shall you be lacking in courage and perseverance." But much as he encouraged valor on the part of his troops, he rated discipline even higher. "The great qualities of the soldier," he said, "are constancy and obedience; valor is secondary." Napoleon's armies were highly efficient machines; and though his maxim was to "make war support war" (as was usual with commanders), this was done rather by subsidies and requisitions than by indiscriminate plunder. He was not naturally cruel, and he did not burn and pillage as he went.

In the planning of a campaign Napoleon always strove to have numerical superiority when he should strike the decisive blow, and he was ever on the watch to catch the enemy when its forces were divided. Like many another strategist, he appreciated the importance of turning the enemy's flank. Thus he won Milan without a pitched battle in 1796 by marching to the north of the Austrians and threatening to cut off their communications. He performed the same feat against the Austrian general, Mack, at Ulm in 1805 and compelled his capitulation. In this case, as in many others, he had made a feint as though he intended to march along another route and then concentrated the bulk of his troops for the real offensive. When compelled to fight in general on the defensive, he nearly always snatched the offensive, as illustrated in his campaign in France in 1814 when he had to give attention to several invading armies. The assailant has always the advantage (as he and others have reasoned) of choosing the time and place for giving battle. At Austerlitz in 1805, finding himself outnumbered and the enemy anxious to fight, he tried the opposite course of entrenching himself, luring the enemy to attack him at a certain point until its lines were thinned at the center, and then by quick concentration he leveled a furious attack at this weakened center and crashed through the enemy's lines. It was at Austerlitz that Napoleon displayed most brilliantly his qualities as a tactician.

Much of Napoleon's unusual skill in strategy was due to his study of topography and his understanding of the terrain on which a campaign was to be fought. He was quick to catch the enemy with a river at its back as at Friedland. In planning his first Italian campaign in 1796 he perceived that the roads which the Austrians and Sardinians were respectively holding followed two river valleys, and that they diverged, one in the direction of Turin, the other in the direction of Milan. Since each army was protecting the approach to its respective capital, Napoleon saw that by striking a blow at either one at the correct angle, he would force them both to retire, and the further they retreated, the further they would be separated, and that he could then defeat them singly. He later pursued much the same plan against the Prussians and British at Waterloo. He pierced the Austrian flank in 1800 by performing the unexpected feat of crossing the Alps, and the Austrians had to fight the Battle of Marengo to save their line of retreat. But it must be realized that the preliminary planning of a campaign was not always rigorously followed, for the movements of an enemy were an unknown quantity, and Napoleon had to adapt his policy accordingly. Though marvelously quick to size up a situation, he was sometimes guilty of an error in judgment, and later in life (after having fought with many incompetent commanders) he tended to underestimate his adversary. The marvelous mobility of his armies, the speed with which they marched often took the enemy quite unawares and enabled Napoleon to snatch a victory before his opponent was ready to face him. This largely explains the crushing defeat of Prussia in 1806. Summing up his advantages, he won his victories chiefly because he possessed a deeper grasp than his opponents of the opportunities offered by natural features, handled his army with extraordinary facility, and was ever on the alert to catch his enemy in a false move that laid it open to an overwhelming blow. It is quite true that he was often pitted against inferior intellects; yet the capacity of some of his opponents is too easily belittled by impression of the outcome, and it must not be forgotten that he outgeneraled Wellington and Blücher in the preliminaries of Waterloo and might easily have won the battle but for a half-day of physical collapse and a fatal miscalculation.

Napoleon as a diplomatist   The same skill in maneuver that he employed in war was also exhibited in his diplomacy. Just as he studied the enemy he was to meet in battle, so he studied the personalities he had to deal with in foreign relations. When the Czar Paul (who had succeeded to the Russian throne on the death of Catherine in 1796) broke with his allies of the Second Coalition, Napoleon made a business of cultivating his friendship. As Paul had been made grand master of the Knights of St. John, the crusading order which Napoleon had ousted from Malta on his way to Egypt, Napoleon was prepared to hand over to him the island, especially as it was being beleaguered by a British fleet and Napoleon knew that he could not expect to hold it. Such "generosity" made a great impression on the flighty czar, and he became so furious with the British when Malta capitulated that he formed a league of neutral powers (the Second League of Armed Neutrality) to defend neutral shipping against the harshness of the British fleets in their search for contraband goods. Subsequently Napoleon amused the Czar by planning with him a joint attack upon India; and the murder of Paul in 1801 as the result of a palace revolution was one of the few reverses which led Napoleon to display emotion. But the adroitness with which he outgeneraled British diplomats and made the prof-

itable Peace of Amiens may well have moderated his disappointment. Just as he took advantage of the Czar Paul's unbalanced
mentality, so Napoleon eked profit from the cupidity of the
Hohenzollern king, Frederick William III. He offered Prussia the
electorate of Hanover, which he had taken from the King of England, and thereby held Frederick William to an alliance until he
was ready to doff the mask and commence war. Just as he frequently defeated an enemy by falling upon its army in detach-
ments, so he often prevented a combination from forming against
him by raising an issue between them. In 1800 he had effectually
driven a wedge between Russia and England over the question
of Malta. In 1806 he alienated England from Prussia over Hanover, and a British fleet actually blockaded Prussia's ports. In
1806 also, he kept Russia, Austria, and Great Britain all diverted
in the East by his Turkish intrigues while he forced Prussia to face
him single-handed. Perhaps his greatest diplomatic achievement
was the conversion of the Czar Alexander I (who had succeeded
his father, Paul) from an enemy into an ally, and this triumph was
simply due to his understanding of the Czar's impressionable nature
and the way to appeal to his vanity and greed.

What did Napoleon's domination mean to Europe? How did *Napoleon*
Napoleon treat his conquests? His work in Italy before he was first *as a*
conqueror
consul well illustrates his policy. To the Italians in Austrian
Lombardy he posed in the first place as a liberator. This province
of the Hapsburgs was reorganized as the Cisalpine Republic with
a constitution like that of France. But Napoleon made the Italians
here and elsewhere pay for their freedom. There were heavy requisitions of food and money, especially in the case of princes like
the Pope and the Grandduke of Tuscany who were allowed to retain their independence. Such rulers had not only to pay indemnities but even to give up some of their art treasures. Later,
after he became, himself, the government of France, Napoleon
raised contingents for his armies in the lands which had come
under his sway, and if they happened to be on the seacoast, they
had to close their ports to British trade.

Germany, like Italy, was divided into different states, only
they were much more numerous. At the Peace of Basel (already
mentioned) [1] it had been agreed that Prussia should receive compensation for her losses on the left bank of the Rhine by obtaining

[1] Page 334.

territories across the river. Thus had been foreshadowed a territorial reconstitution of Germany; and it was left for Napoleon to carry the plan into effect. Generally speaking, his policy was to hand over the smaller states, including the ecclesiastical principalities and imperial towns, to the larger ones. By such an arrangement he insured recognition of the natural boundaries from Austria as well as Prussia, and he also built up a party in his interest, made up of states which he had aggrandized, like Bavaria, Würtemberg, and Saxony. Such juggling of territory was an interesting commentary on the futility of the old empire, and when in July, 1806, Napoleon formed the Confederation of the Rhine—an organization of states south of the river Main which provided him with 63,000 soldiers—the position of the Hapsburg emperor was so obviously stultified that several of the German states announced their separation from the empire, and the logical climax was reached when Napoleon himself in August, 1806, proclaimed the Holy Roman Empire at an end. The dethroned emperor did not protest, and shortly afterward assumed the title of emperor of Austria. Thus a touch of Napoleon's realism finally disposed of an outworn relic of the Middle Ages.

The Napoleonic régime in Europe had meanwhile quite lost its republican character. The Cisalpine Republic became the kingdom of Italy with Napoleon as its sovereign. Later he founded kingdoms for some of his brothers; and his step-son, Eugene, became King of Italy. His hold over dependent states was often consolidated by the enthronement of one of his family or a marriage between one of his family and a member of a ruling dynasty. But the exigencies of the Continental System, which we shall consider in another place, led to outright annexation of many dependencies, and the empire reached its territorial height about 1810. It was strongest, however, in 1807 when the Italians and Germans by dint of force or favor lay in the hollow of his hand. By his grip on central Europe Napoleon became the most powerful sovereign since the days of Charlemagne. It is doubtful if anyone else in modern history would have dared to imprison a pope.[1]

---

[1] It was a long-drawn-cut quarrel over many things, and Napoleon treated the Pope in the most domineering fashion, even at one time occupying a part of the Papal States. When he learned that the Pope had at last determined to defy him and was preparing a bull of excommunication, Napoleon had him arrested and imprisoned in France. In its later stages the quarrel had been over the Continental System, and in 1809 the Papal States were annexed to France.

But the scope of Napoleon's policy was not confined to Europe. *Napoleon as an imperialist* So great an emperor wished to extend his sway to remote continents and to erect a colonial empire second to none in the world. This meant necessarily a challenge to British colonial supremacy. Napoleon's enmity to Great Britain was, of course, inherited, but it became in course of time the most dominant force in his policy. As far back as when he went to Egypt, his object was to ruin British trade, for he reasoned that by opening up the short route to the East he could strike at what he believed to be the main source of British wealth—namely India. Unhappily for Napoleon, he could not retain Egypt without sea power. Nelson destroyed his fleet at the Battle of the Nile, and henceforth Egypt was definitely lost. His designs on the Mediterranean were hardly more successful. We have noted his failure to keep Malta—a port of great strategic importance because of its command of the old trade route to the East. In 1806 he ousted the Bourbons from the throne of Naples with the hope of getting Sicily, and he told his brother Joseph whom he made king of the Two Sicilies that the Mediterranean was the most important object of his policy; yet an attempt to take Sicily was frustrated by the British; and he was not much more successful in his designs on the Ionian Islands. His policy also embraced the new world—though with much the same result. He squandered lives relentlessly in trying to put down a native revolt in San Domingo, and admitted later that his expedition to that fever-ridden island was the greatest folly of his career. In 1801 he secured Louisiana from Spain, but two years later, when he was drifting into a renewal of war with Great Britain, he realized that he could not keep it, and so sold it to the United States. It is curious that a man of his clear perception could not have seen that without a superior navy his colonial dreams were vain. Nelson's great victory at Trafalgar in 1806 practically destroyed what sea power he had. But almost to the end of his reign his vivid imagination reached out to distant lands. He sent exploring expeditions to the Far East, and even intrigued with some of the native princes of India. Meanwhile, inability to cope with that "nation of shop-keepers" on the sea had driven him relentlessly into the alternative policy of trying to close the Continent to British trade.

Yet if war on British commerce was unlikely to achieve its object, it is equally true that so far British money and British diplomacy had been unable to check Napoleon's progress in Europe; so that up to 1807 there was still a deadlock between the mistress of the seas and the dominant power on land. And it remained to be seen whether the humiliation of Russia would avail to break that deadlock. Alexander had sued for peace; and the result was "Tilsit."

TILSIT—THE ZENITH OF NAPOLEON'S POWER

Duping of Alexander I

By arrangement Napoleon met the Czar on a raft in the river Niemen which flowed between the opposing camps. The interview lasted an hour and a half, and as there was no one else present, we can only guess the tenor of the conversation. But we know that Alexander was completely captivated. "I never," he said afterward, "had more prejudices against any man than against *him;* but after three quarters of an hour of conversation they disappeared like a dream"; and again, "Would that I had known him sooner! The veil is torn aside and the time of error is passed." Apparently the basis of an alliance was agreed upon, as well as the terms to be handed the Prussian king, who waited on the out-

Humiliation of Prussia

skirts to be summoned to learn his fate. The Treaties of Tilsit followed. The one between France and Prussia forced Prussia to hand over to France all her territory west of the Elbe (most of which was made into the kingdom of Westphalia for Jerome Bonaparte); to cede her Polish provinces to Saxony (whose ruler became grandduke of Warsaw), save that a small strip to the east was annexed to Russia, her former ally; to harbor a French army of occupation pending the payment of an indemnity; and to close her ports to British trade. By a subsequent convention she was forced to agree to an alliance and even to reduce her army to 42,000 men. Treaties had already been signed between France

The Franco-Russian alliance

and Russia. By the published treaty the Czar recognized the political changes that Napoleon had made and accepted French mediation in his Turkish war, but his expectation of Napoleon's consent to the cession of lands in the Near East was hardly borne out by anything in writing. In a secret treaty, signed on the same day (July 7, 1807), a defensive alliance was contracted between the two powers. Napoleon should join Russia against Turkey if his mediation were not accepted by the Porte, and in that case an agreement was to be reached for the cession by Turkey of certain provinces, though the treaty did not specify that Russia herself should have them. The Czar, in return, agreed to offer his mediation in the war between France and Great Britain, and if this were refused, he would close his ports to British commerce and join France in forcing certain neutral powers, Sweden, Denmark, and Portugal to do likewise. The Czar was won to this curious bargain partly by the hope of filching Finland from Sweden.

It is often said that at Tilsit Napoleon reached the height of his power. Central Europe lay at his feet, and Russia was doing his bidding. Possession of the Netherlands as well as these other gains meant that in British eyes he had completely shattered the balance of power, and for his policy of commercial warfare he had now the co-operation of the Czar. Yet this alliance which promised so much was of dubious strength, since no alliance can last unless it is of mutual advantage, and for Russia disillusionment was bound to come. Moreover, Tilsit led Napoleon into further adventures, as we shall notice, which ended in disaster. Thus Tilsit was, in a sense, the turning-point of his fortunes. *Importance of " Tilsit "*

THE COLLAPSE OF FRENCH DOMINATION OVER EUROPE

The liberation of Europe from Napoleon's domination was long in coming. The great emperor was to win many victories after Tilsit, and the territorial height of his empire was not reached till 1810. But the maintenace of so vast a domain depended on unerring skill, and like many another conqueror Napoleon came at last to lose his mental balance. He acquired the fixed idea that he could master any problem, vanquish any adversary. Now it is quite true that he had been able through force or favor to dictate to a multitude of princes, but if either of these methods should cease to be effective, then this artificial domination over Europe would begin to crack, and if the fissures became wide enough, the whole unwieldy edifice would fall to pieces like a house of cards. For, after all, beneath the princes whom he manipulated were their subjects, and these subjects might tire of his exactions and be driven by desperation to sweep their wavering princes into open hostility. It was certainly not inconceivable that that spirit which the French had shown in resisting foreign invasion might be born in other peoples who chafed against the tyranny of a foreign power. Given therefore the conqueror's untempered ambition and the latent resentment of millions of people, it only needed *General Causes*

Napoleon's overconfidence

Precariousness of his position

some fatal blunders in judgment to produce the complete collapse of his great empire.

The three blunders which combined to ruin Napoleon were the Continental System, the Spanish intrigue, and the invasion of Russia. The first was not in itself fatal but it had much to do with leading him directly into the second and was not unconnected with the third.

The Continental System: (1) its genesis and evolution

The Continental System was the plan, already stated, of closing all the ports on the Continent to British trade. This method of fighting Great Britain through commercial warfare had its genesis partly in the mercantile system, which had made war by tariffs a normal feature of the relations between nations, and partly in the more drastic measures which the Directory had taken against British trade. Not only had British imports been excluded from France but even certain commodities, like cotton and woolen goods, which bore the presumption of British manufacture (even though brought in by neutral shippers) had been excluded from the French market. When Napoleon's own influence came to be exerted on French policy, we must add the fact that he himself believed that Great Britain derived her chief wealth from her maritime trade and that to deprive her of her markets would mean that she would slowly bleed to death. Yet his motive was not wholly military. As the Continent possessed few industries, Napoleon cherished the hope of getting the whole of this market for French manufactured products, as one of the means of making France the leading industrial power. In pursuit of such an end, a struggle with England was inevitable. Already—before the inception of this policy—the Pope had been forced as early as 1797 to close his ports to British trade, and after the renewal of war with Great Britain in 1803 France made strenuous efforts to control the entire seaboard from Otranto in southern Italy all the way round to Hamburg on the North Sea. Finally, as we have noticed before, the disaster of Trafalgar had forced Napoleon to throw his chief emphasis on commercial war. Hence the decision (which we have noted) to bar the ports of Prussia to British goods. Such were the chief factors in the evolution of the Continental System. The fact that the British engaged in counter-measures, such as blockading the French coasts and preventing even neutral powers from trading by sea with France, naturally aggravated the struggle. In his famous Berlin decree, November 11, 1806, Napoleon forbade all access to the Continent to British goods, making such goods liable to seizure, and even ordered the arrest of all British subjects in countries under his sway. We shall not detail the story of the battle of decrees and orders [1] which followed. The Continental System had been inaugurated, and it became a continuous if not also the most dominant of Napoleon's policies.

The alliance with Russia, concluded at Tilsit, seemed to give Napoleon his greatest opportunity of success. Most of the Continent was already theoretically closed to British commerce, and now Russia was added to the list of exponents of the system, while the neutral powers, Denmark, Sweden, and Portugal were to be forced to follow suit. Denmark, as a matter of fact, required no coercion, as she was willing to form an alliance with Napoleon.[2] Sweden was forced into compliance by Russia, who took Finland as payment for her trouble. Portugal, seeing the danger of refusal (especially as Spain seemed to be in collusion with France against her), did not dare to reject the Emperor's demand, though her compliance did not avail to save her from worse to come. But—if we may leave this fateful chain of events for the moment—let us note the important fact that the Continental System quite failed to attain its object. It is true enough that Great Britain suffered, but she was far from being ruined. It was never possible, in fact, to seal up the whole Continent. In the first place the Ottoman Empire was outside the range of French activity, and much merchandise was shipped into Europe at Saloniki. It is often said that a chain is as strong as its weakest link, and here was even a missing link. In the second place, it was literally impossible to prevent smuggling. It was the difficulty of keeping his dependencies loyal to a policy that was economically ruinous to them that induced Napoleon to annex more and more of the seaboard states until, indeed, some two thousand miles of coast were under the direct control of French officials. Not only were the Papal States annexed (and the Pope for a time imprisoned) but even the maritime provinces of Austria. Yet even then it was never possible to prevent illicit trading—there were too many fortunes to be made in that way; and the Emperor himself sometimes connived at the infraction of his own decrees when he needed British

(2) Its operation

(3) Its failure

---

[1] The British retaliated by a strict blockade and other measures.

[2] Apprised of the impending alliance, the British bombarded Copenhagen and sailed off with the Danish fleet. It is no wonder that Denmark became Napoleon's staunchest ally.

boots for his soldiers. Moreover, the reduction of the volume of trade with Great Britain, which supplied so many articles of manufacture, was one of the grievances of those states which for other reasons had become restive under the demands of Napoleon's policy.

The
nationalist
uprising:
(1) in Spain

But economic injuries to a people do not cause so sharp a resentment as an insult to its pride. And it was here that Napoleon made his fatal blunder. It was soon evident that his quarrel with Portugal, which resulted in the sending of an army of 35,000 across Spain to invade that country, was really aimed not at the government of Lisbon but at that of Madrid. The right of transit across Spain was accorded through the influence of the prime minister, Prince Godoy, who was to receive a portion of Portugal as his reward. But Napoleon never intended to keep the bargain. He merely wanted to make sure of getting an army into Spain; and by the beginning of 1808 the French soldiers south of the Pyrenees numbered 100,000. It is no wonder that the Spanish royal family sought to follow the example of the Portuguese and flee to America. But Napoleon was on the watch, and his cruisers blocked his victims' chance of escape. Already Spain was in his iron grip.

While one may hazard a guess at the reasons for Napoleon's plot against Spain, it is rather hard to see its justification. Spain had been one of those powers which had for many years been promoting his policy. In his service she had squandered money, troops, and ships, and had closed her doors to British goods. The Bourbon king of Spain, Charles IV, was a feeble creature, whose queen lived in guilty relations with the prime minister, Godoy, and it was he (Godoy) who, to keep himself in power despite popular resentment, had sold his country's policy to Napoleon. Once Godoy had wavered in his subservience, and in 1806 had made an appeal to the Spanish people to rise in arms; but the victory of Jena followed, and Godoy quickly lapsed into docility—even to conniving at the annihilation of Portugal. But this was not to save Godoy or Spain. Perhaps Napoleon felt that a purchased sycophant could never be trusted.[1] Perhaps he felt that, now that the Bourbons had lost their thrones at Paris and Naples, he might as well make a clean sweep and oust them from Madrid as well.

---

[1] Kircheisen makes the point that Napoleon would have been wiser if he had struck down Godoy and married Ferdinand to a princess of the imperial house. "Had he done so," he thinks, "the whole of Spain would have saluted him as their country's benefactor."

Perhaps he longed to free the Spaniards from an oppressive and ignoble rule and to attach them through gratitude to their deliverer. Perhaps he simply enjoyed the experience of using his matchless skill to add a new throne to his plentiful store. Such may account for his tortuous policy in Spain.

At any rate, whether or not he had formed a settled design, circumstances played into his hands. The crown prince, Ferdinand, hated his parents and their favorite, and though fully as contemptible as they, he was regarded as a hero by the people of Madrid. In March, 1808, a mob gathered about the royal palace and clamored for Godoy's head. Ferdinand, importuned by his mother, saved her favorite's life, but he had done so on condition that his father should abdicate, and this condition was perforce fulfilled. This, of course, made Ferdinand king. Now was the chance for a national leader to head the popular movement and liberate Spain from a foreign yoke.

But Ferdinand was just as ready as his father and Godoy to bend the knee to France, and he was anxious that the Emperor should award him the hand of one of his nieces. Napoleon saw that the moment had come for closing his net about this wretched family. Ferdinand was accordingly lured over the mountains to Bayonne, whither the ex-King, his wife, and even Godoy followed. It was a nice little family party that the Emperor had on his hands. And as Charles was insisting that the crown had been wrested from him by force, Napoleon was now to decide the fate of the Spanish kingdom. Arbiter of the crown of Spain, he forthwith decided that neither father nor son should have it. After forcing a renunciation from them both, he called his brother Joseph from Naples to Madrid to become king of Spain. Such was the outcome of the intrigue which compassed the downfall of the Bourbons. It was the same old game of making fools of princes. But Napoleon had seen no further than this. He had reckoned without the people of Spain.

And nemesis was speedily to come. Joseph had not been on the throne of Madrid two weeks before he found himself in the midst of a nationalist uprising the like of which Europe had never seen. All over Spain local *juntas* or councils were formed; appeal was made to Great Britain, who sent a small army of auxiliaries; and Joseph soon found it necessary to retire behind the Ebro. Napoleon saw that he was in for something he had never anticipated. After making sure of the Czar's friendship (though this time he had to consent to Russia's wresting from Turkey the Danubian Principalities), he came down to Spain at the head of an army, expelled the British forces, and to all appearances stifled the revolt. It was then that Joseph, under his brother's direction, carried out some useful reforms. But not even by good government were the Spaniards reconciled to foreign rule. They would rather be oppressed than be benefited by a prince foisted upon them from without. After Napoleon's withdrawal the insurrection broke out more fiercely than ever, and what was known as the "Peninsular War," dragging on for many years, was destined to sap the resources of France until it contributed in large measure to the collapse of her power in Europe. No wonder Napoleon remarked later, "It was the Spanish ulcer that ruined me."

Indeed the most serious result of the Spanish uprising was its effect upon other countries. Its significance lay in the fact that it was the beginning of a nationalist movement of resistance, not confined to Spain but embracing other peoples. Napoleon had known nationalism only so far as the fighting spirit of France was a hang-over from the days of the Revolution, and in this way he had capitalized nationalism in his own interest. But as a force that might be turned against him it was a new and painful experience. This oversight was hardly strange, however, in view of the customary inertia of peoples held down by absolute monarchs.

(2) *In Germany* There was, of course, still a chance that the contagion might be stopped if the Emperor acted in time. But it should be added that the origins of this nationalist movement were not to be found wholly in Spain. Paradoxically enough, it was the spirit of the French Revolution itself, expressed in its obvious lessons of efficiency, that had induced Prussia in her grief and desperation to reform, and it was through reform that she attained to a spiritual fervor comparable to that of Spain's. Indeed Prussia's reaction to Napoleonic tyranny had come somewhat earlier than in Spain. Shortly after Tilsit, under the leadership of the patriot minister, Stein, Prussia rid herself of serfdom, leveled out many of the existing differences between classes, and established local self-government. People, no matter to what class they belonged, felt that they had now at last an interest in being Prussians. Thus a spirit of unity was achieved. It was no wonder that Napoleon forced

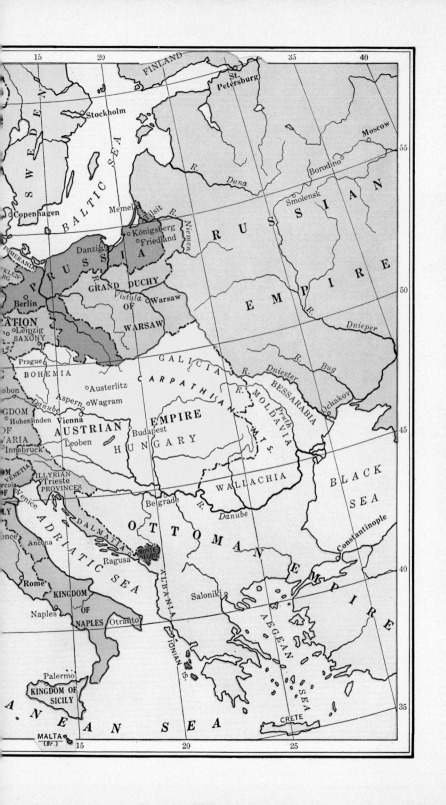

Stein's dismissal. But he overlooked another dauntless patriot, the Austrian foreign minister, Stadion. The regenerative work in Prussia, the ardent appeals of patriots like Fichte, the Saxon professor, and the sporadic outbreaks of violence in Jerome's misgoverned kingdom led Stadion and the Austrian emperor's able son, the Archduke Charles, to believe that the German people were ripe for a general rising. Judging by results, it would have been better if Austria had waited for the movement to grow a pace. But the temptation to strike a blow while Napoleon was engrossed in Spain was too cogent to resist. On August 6, 1809 the Archduke Charles issued a proclamation to his army, which was really meant as a clarion-call to Germany: "The freedom of Europe has sought refuge beneath your banners." Alone, but full of hope, Austria drew the sword once more.

But the bolt was premature. The Germans did not rise, and the Prussian King was too fearful of the Czar to make a move. And in the meantime, with his usual remarkable speed Napoleon mobilized an army, flung himself on the Austrian forces before they were ready, and brought a hard-fought campaign to a successful issue. The terms of peace were severe, and, as might be expected, Stadion paid for his zeal by an enforced resignation. But not the least of Napoleon's triumphs was his subsequent marriage with the Emperor's daughter, Mary Louise. It seems odd that Austria, four times humbled, should thus demean herself to gratify her conqueror; but the new Austrian foreign minister, Prince Metternich, was anxious, above all, to neutralize the Franco-Russian alliance, and he hoped that Austria's recovery would be rendered the more certain if she were free to plot and arm under the guise of ostensible friendship. Napoleon's motives were more transparent. To expect that so vast an empire should not descend to a son would have been to refute the logic of his career. Josephine had borne him no children, and must therefore be divorced. And while the need of an heir thus impelled him to seek another wife, the gratification of winning a bride from one of the oldest dynasties in Europe would naturally have its appeal to this Corsican adventurer, this self-enthroned son of the Revolution. When in 1811 a son was born—the "King of Rome"—it almost seemed as if Napoleon's dearest wish had been fulfilled. Yet in view of the muffled undercurrent of disaffection in much of Europe the Emperor Napoleon may be imagined as stalking majestically over thin ice; the least

misstep, indeed, and he was liable to crash through. This misstep
was the invasion of Russia in 1812.

Invasion of Russia: (1) its causes

The breach with Russia was so palpably unnecessary that it is
difficult to find a clue to it in anything but Napoleon's inflated
pride and his desire to humble the one remaining rival on the Continent. We shall not recount the circumstances by which he steadily goaded Alexander into war. The dupe of Tilsit had at last come
to see that he had been deluded; and distrust and resentment now
dominated his policy. Though Napoleon might have conciliated
him, he did not choose to do so, and his patronage of the Poles
seemed deliberately aimed at Russia. When Alexander allowed
British trade to enter his ports under neutral flags, war became
practically certain. For nearly a year Napoleon had been making
his preparations, both diplomatic and military; and by the summer of 1811 he had marshaled the largest host (over 600,000 men)
ever mobilized for one campaign. It was a titanic effort. But the
titan himself was no longer of his former vigor. Though only
forty-three, Napoleon had already begun to break, both mentally
and physically. He continually allowed his presumptions to over-
cloud his judgment, and he seemed to feel that his will, almost
alone, was sufficient to accomplish any purpose. Above all, his
health was far from good; on the march he was a frequent sufferer
from various ills, and he no longer had the capacity to rebound
from exceptional hardships. These factors do much to explain his
numerous blunders in the Russian campaign—a more than ordinary test of a man's nerves and of his endurance.

(2) Its failure

But Napoleon had never anticipated what was to come. What
he seems to have expected was a smashing victory like Friedland,
which should bring the Czar speedily to terms. Instead, he was
beguiled into a difficult march of more than eight hundred miles
with Moscow as the objective. The Russians, in short, had balked
him by simply avoiding a battle. Only once—at Borodino—did
they make a determined stand, and as that was near Moscow,
and as Napoleon's exhausted army was unequal to a decisive victory, the battle had come too late. When Napoleon reached the
old Russian capital, he had little more than a fourth of his army
left. Fighting, disease, and desertion had reduced its total to 130,-
000. Yet the Emperor had the fixed idea that if only he had Moscow in his hands, Alexander would certainly sue for peace.

But worse—far worse—was to come. The horrors of the Russian

campaign have so often been depicted that we shall not take space to recount them here. When Moscow had at last been reached, it was found to be practically deserted, and was for a time rendered untenable by a fire which consumed most of the city. About a month was spent in Moscow—precious time, for if the army had to go back, it would not now be able to escape a Russian winter. Since the Czar would not treat, and since most of the Russian army was out of reach, there was nothing for Napoleon to do but order a retreat. Divining his purpose, the Russians blocked his effort to pick a more southerly route that would have enabled the retreating army to find provisions; and the baffled host, numbering now a hundred thousand men, were forced to choose the route by which they had come—the devastated line of march. And all the time they had the Russians at their heels. Famished, and exhausted by forced marches (to avoid the Russians), and eventually overtaken by the rigors of a Russian winter, the remnant of the Grand Army pursued its ghastly retreat until, after it had at last crossed the Niemen, there were less than 10,000 of the enormous host which Napoleon had marshaled for the humbling of Russia. "Only about 1,000 of the guards remained in order; the rest roamed over the country, singly or in small bands, mostly unarmed and in rags." It is almost incredible to think of an army of 450,000 (the actual number engaged in the invasion) practically wiped out in a single campaign.

The significance of the Russian fiasco was momentous. It gave new heart to the enemies of Napoleon. Though something of the truth had filtered through to central Europe during the year 1812, it was only when the wasted remnants of the Grand Army began to pass through Germany that men realized the magnitude of the disaster. Everyone knew now that Napoleon was not a superman; he had been thoroughly and decisively beaten. Henceforth he was thrown upon the defensive, compelled to fight for the retention of his control over central Europe, and with forces that were not, in general, the equal of the army he had lost in Russia. But the chief significance of the Emperor's blunder was the moral effect that it had upon Europe. The nationalist movement of resistance, begun in Spain, was soon to envelop him in Germany. We are on the threshold of the War of Liberation. *(3) Significance of its outcome*

As soon as Napoleon had reached Germany, he rushed to France to raise new forces and in a few months he was back in Germany *The War of Liberation* with an army of over 200,000 men. But in the meantime important events had taken place. Austria had signed a secret truce with Russia, and the commander of the Prussian contingent which had been an auxiliary of the Grand Army did likewise, acting on his own responsibility.

Prussia assumes the leadership

The decisive rôle in this turning-point in Europe's fortunes was played by Prussia. We have already noted the patient laying of the foundations of a new social order in this state. The social reforms, begun in 1807, were being extended still further, the peasants being allowed to redeem their feudal rights by handing over a third of their holdings to their lords and retaining the remainder in full ownership. Of more immediate practical importance, Prussia had deliberately got around the limitation of her army to 42,000 men by constantly passing a stream of new recruits through the ranks, so that the bulk of the nation's manhood might acquire military training. Then, as soon as Prussia was free of foreign occupation, her army was completely reorganized, and a decree was issued, requiring service with the colors as a civic obligation. There seemed little doubt now that Prussia was ready to throw down the gauntlet to Napoleon. Yet for a long time her king hesitated (Frederick William deserved much credit for his choice of ministers but his nature was timid and vacillating), and it was really the force of popular pressure that swept him off his feet. In April, 1813, Prussia and Russia formed an alliance for the

Formation of the Last Coalition

liberation of Germany. It was the germ of the Last Coalition. Sweden and Great Britain are also to be included, but the Swedes did very little, and British operations were confined to Spain. Austria under Metternich still played a waiting game.

It was evident that Napoleon was facing a difficult problem. There were still no signs of disaffection in Italy, and the Confederation of the Rhine, which had gained so much from his favor, was not prepared as yet to desert their patron. But Prussia, thanks to the needless retreat of the French commander (before Napoleon's arrival) had recovered all her territory east of the Elbe, and the armies of Russia and Prussia were able to act as a unit. After a campaign which yielded nothing to either side the opposing enemies signed a truce. It has been said that Napoleon in his earlier days would never have made this serious blunder. Though he needed the truce for sound military reasons, the condition of his enemies demanded it far more. Besides, Austria was watching the struggle with the keenest interest. Believing that Napoleon was facing a losing fight, Metternich made up his mind to assume the rôle of arbiter. He offered Napoleon terms which would have practically meant the end of his sway in Germany, and these the Emperor indignantly refused. When the news came of Wellington's victory in Spain in the Battle of Vittoria, the die was cast. On August 12, 1813 Austria definitely joined the Last Coalition.

It can readily be judged that the great emperor was fighting a losing game and that the stake was the control of central Europe. *Reasons for the Allies' success* In other words he was threatened with the collapse of his empire. The causes of this collapse are easy to figure out. In the first place he was greatly outnumbered. On the accession of Austria to the Coalition the disparity was more than two to one. It was largely this disadvantage that made the campaign for Napoleon so essentially defensive. This meant, of course, that he had a long line to defend and that he had often to depend upon his marshals for important maneuvers. But the Emperor had always engrossed responsibility so completely himself that his subalterns were unequal to the task. When he won the Battle of Dresden, his marshals lost its fruits. It is also worthy of note that owing to the shortage of horses (due, of course, to the Russian campaign) Napoleon lacked sufficient cavalry to follow up a victory. And then, of course, there was the drain of the Peninsular War. A large force had to hold the line of the Pyrenees, and thanks partly to frequent quarrels between the marshals and partly to the superior generalship of Wellington, the French were gradually being pressed back into France. The second of the broad reasons for Napoleon's failure was the contrast in the quality of the two opposing armies. Napoleon's army was made up largely of young conscripts, thoroughly inexperienced and not too eager to fight; while his marshals, generally speaking, were weary of the war and anxious for a time of leisure to enjoy their honors. Generalship on the side of the Allies was not, it is true, superior, but the armies of the Coalition were imbued with the spirit of nationalism, and that superiority in morale which had meant so much to Napoleon in his earlier days had now shifted to the armies of his enemies. Moreover, the desire to be on the winning side, which had accounted for the subservience of so many German princes, was now ready to operate against the French.

The decisive battle was fought at Leipzig, October 14–16, 1813.

Leipzig and the downfall of Napoleon's empire in Europe

It was a hard fight, and the outcome, thanks to Napoleon's superior skill, was long in doubt. But the defection of the Saxons on the field of battle decided the issue. On November 2 Napoleon crossed the Rhine in full retreat. With the loss of Germany the Napoleonic empire in Europe collapsed. It was no longer possible

Painting by Braun

NAPOLEON IN RETREAT FROM LEIPZIG

even to retain Italy, which the Austrians were steadily recovering. The War of Liberation had been won.

The first abdication

"The Emperor Napoleon must become king of France." So Talleyrand had said, and after Napoleon's retirement to French territory the great captain was more than ever on the defensive. Yet the Allies were divided as to whether they really wanted to invade France, and they took the extraordinary step of making proposals to their vanquished enemy. These terms would have left to Napoleon the "natural boundaries"—in other words, the conquests which he had inherited from the Revolution. But he still refused to swallow the discomfiture of defeat, and gave an evasive answer. Hence the Allies crossed the Rhine.

We shall not dwell on the incidents of the campaign of 1814 save to note that Napoleon with an army reduced now to 70,000 performed extraordinary feats against the scattered but numerically superior strength of the Coalition. It should also be added that his troops fought valiantly in defense of their native land— inspired, indeed, by a very different feeling from that of trying to uphold the imperial policy in Europe. The end, however, could never be in doubt. While Napoleon sought to lure away the Austrians (who had been hanging back, not too anxious to press the campaign), and to cut his enemies' communications, the Allies united their forces and entered Paris. Even then the harassed emperor was unwilling to admit defeat, but since the enemy was in his capital and even the senate had decided against him, there was nothing to do but surrender to the inevitable. On April 4, 1814 Napoleon signed his abdication, and according to the terms that were dictated by the Allies, he repaired at once to Elba, a little island off the west coast of Italy. In taking leave of the Old Guard, he declared, "I abdicate; I yield nothing." It was the germ of the "return" and the "Hundred Days."

Napoleon stayed about ten months on the island of Elba. All the time he had been observing the situation in Europe, waiting for the opportunity to come back; and such an opportunity eventually arose from two causes. In the first place the powers assembled at Vienna were quarreling vigorously over the spoils, and Napoleon believed that these rifts would work in his favor; he even said later that he had heard that the Congress had broken up. In the second place, the Bourbons, restored to the throne of France, soon contrived to make themselves unpopular. Louis XVIII had granted a constitution (more liberal at least than any of Napoleon's), and he had recognized the property rights obtained from the Revolution; yet the airs of the returning *émigrés*, who behaved as though the Revolution had never happened, gave great offense to the new nobility of service, now plainly out of favor. Then thousands of soldiers, returning now from the war, found it hard to settle down, and after an interval of rest, they craved the excitement of battle and the thrill of Napoleon's leadership. Many a peasant family felt itself almost exalted by the fact of having a

The Last Phase

Napoleon's opportunity and return

veteran in its household, and for most of the common people Napoleon was still a hero. While it can hardly be said that the middle class or even the peasantry longed for Napoleon's return, they looked upon the Bourbons with a good deal of suspicion, wondering, after all, if the new social order, born of the Revolution, would be quite safe in their hands.

It was, accordingly, in the belief that he would be welcome that Napoleon returned to France. And he was not mistaken. While the mass of the population may have been somewhat apathetic—perhaps dazed by the very boldness of the stroke—his journey to Paris was none other than a series of ovations. The day after the Bourbons had taken flight the great adventurer re-entered his capital. It was his last great thrust for the recovery of his power.

The last stand— Waterloo But Napoleon's situation was undeniably critical. It is true that apart from a rising in La Vendée royalism caused him little trouble; but he had to grant a constitution, which gave the liberal elements a power that would be difficult to hold in leash. Worse than this was the external situation. As soon as they heard of his coming, the powers had ceased their brawls, and had agreed upon denouncing him as an outlaw. Napoleon had, therefore, to face a united Europe. Naturally, then, his only hope was to attack his enemies before they were ready. After detailing some troops to guard the Pyrenees and others to deal with La Vendée, he could spare barely 125,000 men, though they were mostly veterans, and there was certainly no question of their loyalty. Napoleon knew that he must attack the British and Prussian armies (together numbering over 200,000 men) quartered in Belgium before the Austrians and Russians were ready to re-enforce them; and he proposed as usual to catch his enemy unprepared. In fact, he marched his army so quickly to the attack that neither Wellington nor Blücher had his army concentrated or was ready to act with the other. Napoleon's aim was to strike at a point between them, and, taking advantage of the direction of the roads, throw them back in different directions. The plan of campaign was masterly, but he made some fatal blunders in its execution. Though he defeated the main body of the Prussians and drove back the advance posts of the British, he failed to take sufficient precautions for keeping the two armies from coming together. In the meantime, he wasted a whole day by slow marching, though some of this delay was certainly due to physical exhaustion. The result of all this was that the Battle of Waterloo was lost before it began. While Napoleon was pounding at Wellington's position and had a fair chance of snatching a victory in the end, the Prussians arrived in time to decide the issue. The Battle of Waterloo (June 18, 1815) was then followed by an Allied advance upon Paris.

No battle in history has perhaps more spectacular features than the Battle of Waterloo; no battle was more nearly won by the vanquished, or has created so much critical speculation; but even had Napoleon won the day, it is doubtful if he could have triumphed over all his many enemies.

The final abdication, exile, and death

A rapid flight to Paris was soon followed by abdication; and this time, in order to make sure that he would never trouble the peace of Europe again, he was sent to the little island of St. Helena in the south Atlantic Ocean, far from the coast of Africa. Here under the custody of a British governor—for the island belonged to Great Britain—Napoleon spent the remaining years of his life. Though he stated that he should have fallen on the battlefield of Waterloo, the fact of this great conqueror, "chained to a barren rock," has something of a dramatic touch, and was certainly eloquent proof of the dread with which his enemies regarded him. Though not exactly happy in his exile, he found abundant resources with which to while away his time, and it was characteristic of the man that he gave his major attention to following a definite plan—that of arranging his "martyrdom." When a fatal illness finally smote him, he bore his sufferings with the greatest fortitude, and died May 5, 1821 when not yet fifty-three years of age.

Historical importance of Napoleon

The chief importance of these years of exile was the task that he had imposed upon himself. It was then that he undertook to present his case to posterity; he was the friend of peace (for wars were only forced upon him!) and the champion of the principles of the Revolution. By this pose—which is known as the "Napoleonic Legend"—he hoped that some future Bonaparte (and he always thought of his son [1]) might construct a new stage and re-enact the drama of Napoleonic rule. It is a tribute to his vision and to his knowledge of the French people that his plan was to bear fruit. Whatever may be said in criticism of Napoleon, he was

[1] The Duke of Reichstadt ("Napoleon II"), known in romance as *L'Aiglon*, died in Vienna in 1831.

without doubt a commanding genius. His indomitable ambition must cloud our admiration for him as a man; yet, withal, he was a practical statesman who achieved much that was good, and even his wars, though they were hardly worth the price, brought many permanent benefits to Europe. Historically he embodied a period of transition. The last of a series of benevolent despots, he was at the same time one of the first of great modern statesmen. Napoleon valued ability and hated shams. He was undoubtedly too much of an egotist and too military to have a respect for public opinion, but he nevertheless gave the individual a chance to prove his worth.

FOR FURTHER READING OR STUDY

Robinson, J. H., and Beard, C. A., *Readings in Modern European History*, vol. i, chaps. xiv–xv; Anderson, R. M., *Constitutions and Documents: France, 1789–1901;* Butterfield, H., *Select Documents of European History*, chap. viii; Bourienne, *Memoirs of Napoleon Bonaparte*, 4 vols.; Coignet, *Narrative* (extracts from the diary of a Napoleonic soldier); Johnston, R. M., *The Corsican: A Diary of Napoleon's Life in His Own Words;* Kircheisen, F. M., *Napoleon's Autobiography* (similar); Funck, F. von, *In the Wake of Napoleon.*

Gillespie, J. E., *A History of Modern Europe, 1500–1815*, pp. 538–49 and chap. xxvi; Hayes, C. J. H., *A Political and Cultural History of Modern Europe*, vol. i, pp. 639–717; Gottschalk, L., *The Era of the French Revolution*, part i, book iii, chap. iv and part ii; Gershoy, L., *The French Revolution and Napoleon*, chaps. xiii–xxi; Bourne, H. E., *The Revolutionary Period in Europe*, chaps. xv–xxii, xxiv–xxvii; Fisher, H. A. L., *Napoleon* (very brief); Fournier, A., *Napoleon I*, 2 vols. (objective without being dull); Rose, J. H., *The Life of Napoleon I*, 2 vols. (interesting and scholarly but too British in viewpoint); Johnston, R. M., *Napoleon: A Short Biography* (chiefly military); Kircheisen, F. M. (interesting portraiture by the author of an exhaustive work in German); Bainville, J., *Napoleon* (a suggestive essay); *Cambridge Modern History*, vol. ix (useful for reference.)

Madelin, L., *The French Revolution*, chaps. xxv–xliv (through Brumaire) and epilogue; Hazen, C. D., *The French Revolution*, vol. ii, chaps. xl–lii (through Brumaire); Seignobos, C., *The Evolution of the French People*, pp. 288–95; Guignebert, C., *A Short History of the French People;* chaps. xxxii (*passim*), xxxiii–xxxiv; Mathiez, A., *After Robespierre: The Thermidorean Reaction;* Lokke, C., "French Dreams of Colonial Empire under the Directory and the Consulate," *Jour. Mod. Hist.*, ii, 237 ff.; Rose, J. H., *The Personality of Napoleon* (an interesting and enlightening little study); Levy, A., *The Private Life of Napoleon;* Geer, W., *Napoleon and His Family*, 3 vols.; Dodge, T. A., *Napoleon: A History of the Art of War;* Mowat, R. B., *The Diplomacy of Napoleon;* Rose, J. H., *Napoleonic Studies;* Fisher, H. A. L., *Napoleonic Statesmanship: Germany;* Wilkinson, S., *The Rise of General Bonaparte;* McClellan, G. B., *Venice and Bonaparte;* Coquelle, P., *Napoleon and England;* Elgood, P. G., *Bonaparte's Adventures in Egypt;* Mahan, A. T., *The Influence of Sea Power* on the *French Revolution and Empire*, 2 vols.; Deutsch, H. C., "Napoleonic Policy and the Project of a Descent upon England," *Jour. Mod. Hist.*, ii, 541 ff.; Shupp, P., *The European Powers and the Near Eastern Question, 1806–8;* Butterfield, H., *Peace Treaties of Napoleon, 1806–8;* Heckscher, E. F., *The Continental System;* Ford, G. S., *Stein and the Era of Reform in Prussia;* Langsam, W. C., *The Napoleonic Wars and German Nationalism in Austria;* Rosebery, Lord, *Napoleon: The Last Phase;* Ropes, J. C., *The Campaign of Waterloo;* Guérard, A. L., *Reflections on the Napoleonic Legend;* Scott, F. D., "Bernadotte and the Throne of France, 1814," *Jour. Mod. Hist.*, v, 465 ff.

XI. THE INFLUENCE AND AFTERMATH OF THE FRENCH REVOLUTION

1. THE RESULTS OF THE REVOLUTION

A. In France

Moral effect; Political results; Social and economic results.

B. Outside France

Residuum of Napoleonic reform; Undercurrent of hope.

C. The French Revolution and the Individual

2. THE PARIS–VIENNA SETTLEMENT—RECONSTRUCTION AND REACTION

A. The Treaties of Paris

The First Treaty; The Second Treaty.

B. The Vienna Settlement

Preparations for the Congress of Vienna—position of France; Character and setting of the Congress of Vienna; Territorial settlement; Underlying considerations; Fundamental defect of the settlement.

C. The Concert of Europe and the Organization of Reaction

Safeguards against France: (1) internal, (2) external; The Quadruple Alliance or Concert of Europe; Rôle of Alexander I; Metternich and his "system"; The Concert of Europe under Metternich's leadership; Collapse of the Concert of Europe

3. THE BEGINNING OF REFORM IN GREAT BRITAIN

Background of British reform; Early reform movement of the nineteenth century; The reform movement in abeyance; Foreign policy under Palmerston; The British vs. the Continental method of reform.

4. THE REVOLUTIONARY UNREST

A. The Rise of Nationalism in the Balkans

Case of the Bulgars; Case of the Greeks; Case of the Serbs; Case of the Roumans.

B. The Revolution of 1830 and Its Echoes

Causes of the Revolution of 1830; The Revolution of 1830; Liberation of Belgium; Echoes elsewhere.

C. The Revolution of 1848 and Its Echoes

Causes of the Revolution of 1848; The Revolution of 1848; The Second Republic and its failure; Establishment of the Second Empire; Revolution in central Europe—the crisis for Austria; The "March Revolution" in Austria; Collapse and recovery; Results of the upheaval.

The importance of the French Revolution, like that of all revolutions, could be measured only with time. If one looks for concrete changes, especially in Europe outside of France, comparatively few may challenge attention in 1815 after the great storm had spent itself. Politically and socially much of Europe was still the same as it had been in the days of the Enlightened Despots. Yet the principles of the Revolution had displayed their dynamic force in so memorable a fashion that the generation which had witnessed this demonstration was only too well aware that those principles must signify an eternal challenge. In other words, forces were let loose that could not be more than momentarily chained. The Revolution left a heritage of progress for unnumbered generations.

The quality of that heritage we must now take time to analyze.

The Results of the Revolution

While the inspirational value of the Revolution was the same whether in France or in the rest of Europe, the intensity with which the movement was felt depended for a time on the distance from its geographical source. Naturally France received the deepest imprint.

Liberty, equality, fraternity—these ideals of the Revolution *In France* entered into the consciousness of the French people and remained. Actually they emerged in only limited application in 1815 after *Moral effect* France had quieted down. Only a measure of political liberty was allowed by the Restored Bourbons. Some of the middle class were wealthy enough to be included in the suffrage, but this class could *Political* not be said to enjoy the dominant political influence. There was *results* no guarantee of freedom of the press or even of freedom of association. But it was something that henceforth, no matter what the nature of her government, France would possess a precise description of the governmental power—in other words a written constitution. The precision which had marked the thought of the philosophers, and which had displayed itself so often in constitutional experiments, had found a definite anchorage. No longer was monarchy absolute in theory and this fact was displayed on paper. And the wave of romantic reaction,[1] which inspired some of the conservative intellectuals and seemed in France as elsewhere to give the aging generation of pre-Revolutionary autocrats a moral

[1] "Romanticism" had its chief importance in literature rather than in politics.

basis for their organized resistance, had only a very temporary importance. Strengthened by experience and soon to be enriched by the Industrial Revolution, the bourgeoisie was to take again the center of the stage and bring society nearer to the goal of popular government. Democracy would have to proceed slowly—for the French had had enough of political orgies—but in course of time its merits would outweigh the national caution.

Social and economic results

But the greatest triumph of the spirit of the Enlightenment (the mother of the Revolution) was the attainment of religious toleration. Here rationalism won a success that was not to be overturned. Though the Catholic Church might still enjoy a peculiar prestige, the members of every other cult or of no cult at all had an equal right to believe as they chose and to demonstrate that belief or not as they pleased.

But this, after all, is a social result; and socially the Revolution had wrought, at the outset at least, its most striking achievement. "Privilege" was not entirely at an end while the suffrage was restricted and while workmen were unable to make headway in the economic world; but the old system of "privilege" had lost most of its strength with the loss of those lands and emoluments derived at least primarily from the accident of birth. Henceforth everyone was equal before the law, and the principle of equality of opportunity had no longer the barrier of birth to clamber over. The virtue of efficiency, which Napoleonic rule had sanctified, could not be wholly ignored even in a period of reaction. This efficiency, moreover, was indelibly expressed in many of the institutions which his statesmanship had wrought. The centralized administrative system, based on the simplified pattern of the Revolution, was destined to endure; so also in their fundamentals the Napoleonic Code, the educational system, and the Bank of France with its scope for the development of credit. One of the greatest gifts of the Revolution to France was uniformity of institutions for all her people. France was at last a political and economic unit, with a common administrative system, a unified body of law, a uniform metric system,[1] and an absence of economic barriers within. Thanks again to the Enlightenment, the gilds were all but dead,[2] and competition was free of all such artificial trammels. And

---

[1] This was the work of the Convention.

[2] A few gilds lingered on for some decades, but, having no special privileges, they were practically defunct.

finally, the redistribution of property, in particular the emergence of a free, landowning peasantry, was a permanent result of the Revolution. Many of the bourgeoisie had also acquired land, and in the size of their estates replaced in a certain sense the old feudal aristocracy, but wealth, rather than birth, would be the new passport to power. As for the peasantry, feudalism was dead, and the only exactions henceforth were those imposed by the state. Moreover, the number of peasant proprietors had increased and their holdings tended to be larger, though the law requiring a division of inheritances (one of the Revolutionary enactments) led naturally to some subsequent diminution. All these changes do not mean of course, that economic freedom was entirely complete, but most of the safeguards needed at this time, before the Industrial Revolution brought to France its own inherent problems, were now assured. If the proletariat was still a defenseless class, it was as yet a negligible element in the population.

In Europe outside of France we must distinguish between the immediate concrete changes produced by the Revolution and its ultimate results. In the former aspect we find Napoleon as the purveyor of institutions which France had already tested—institutions which had emerged from his conception of the Revolution. As to the latter aspect, Europe was inevitably impressed by the example of what a people had achieved when it swept away with a few strokes of the pen the entire Old Régime, and the lesson was not to be lost on future generations. *Outside France*

Had Napoleon's empire lasted, it is hardly to be doubted that reforms of a practical nature—social, economic, administrative, and educational—would have been spread broadcast. As it was, most of the countries that came into closest contact with him felt his transforming hand. In some, it is true, the results were not enduring; but in the Low Countries, some of the states along the Rhine, those of southern Germany, and the kingdom of Naples feudalism gave way to civic equality, and in many quarters religious toleration remained in force, the Napoleonic Code continued in most of its fundamentals, and better systems of administration showed the strength of the emperor's influence. Even the regeneration of Prussia, which we have noted, was indubitably the result of the same forces. As an eminent scholar has fitly expressed it, "No country that had been touched by French influence became ever again quite what it had been before." *The residuum of Napoleonic reform*

Sometimes, too, Napoleon wrought where he had hardly intended. The erection of a kingdom of Italy and the revival of a part of Poland did much respectively for Italian and Polish nationalism; and the uprising of the German people in their war of liberation was a manifestation of nationalism, quite as impressive as that of the French in the Reign of Terror. Political liberty which could not in its nature have been the gift of Napoleon was—with the exception of Poland—hardly anywhere to be found in 1815. But the idealism of the Revolution had definitely penetrated the European mind. There was a nucleus of intellectuals in almost every country, ready to fight for the principles of democracy and nationalism, and this undercurrent of hope was destined to make itself felt in subsequent revolutions—all inspired by that movement which had shaken the Old Régime and left it permanently vulnerable. It is in fact in the ultimate results of the Revolution that we realize its importance.

*The French
Revolution
and the
Individual*
And finally we must appreciate that the individual had come to the dawn of a new era. In France especially he had already become socially, economically, and spiritually a new being; but even in Europe as a whole his horizon had become broader. The great upheaval through which men had struggled during this period had the natural and inevitable effect of accustoming the mind to the idea of change. For the thinking individual the future was full of promise.

Thus the calm which followed the great upheaval was an illusory calm. The strength of historical forces was too mighty to be mastered by men who rested their case on mere outworn authority. But this lesson had to be learned, and this was part of the Revolution's "aftermath." To the champions of the old order who had fought Napoleon it seemed that with his defeat they had also vanquished the Revolution, and it was now their task to repair the breaches in the fabric of Europe and re-establish in all its strength the Old Régime. The settlement which they devised had two main features—one which directly concerned France and the other which involved a reconstruction of Europe.

THE PARIS-VIENNA SETTLEMENT—RECONSTRUCTION AND REACTION

*The Treaties
of Paris*
The First Treaty of Paris was signed on May 30, 1814 between France and the powers who had fought in the last war with Na-

poleon. The area of France was limited to the frontiers she had possessed before the Revolutionary War save for some minor additions in the northeast and southeast. The terms were not immoderate, and if we except the vengeful spirit of the Prussians, the attitude of the victors was marvelously restrained—a fact no doubt due to the sagacity of governments and the absence of an effective public opinion. Yet, even as it was, France had lost the "natural boundaries," which had crowned the martial exploits of the armies of the Revolution. *The First Treaty*

But she was soon to lose something more. The renewal of war in the "Hundred Days" required a new treaty after Napoleon's final expulsion, and this time the Powers meted out some additional punishment. By the Second Treaty of Paris, signed November 20, 1815 France was all but limited to the frontiers of 1790, Avignon being almost the only conquest retained. Had Prussia had her way, she would certainly have lost Alsace and much more. But the Czar had always contended, with one of his occasional flashes of wisdom, that if the Bourbons were to remain in France, the vanity of their subjects must not be too deeply wounded; and Great Britain after some hesitation came to the opinion that to wrest from France any of the lands which Louis XIV had won would only serve to make her the more dangerous to the peace. The most humiliating terms were, in fact, only provisional. She was to pay an indemnity of 700,000,000 francs within five years and to harbor an Allied army of occupation until the sum was paid. She was also compelled during this interval to accept the advice of a sort of council of vigilance, composed of the several ambassadors of the Allies resident in Paris. *The Second Treaty*

The Powers had also to deal with the territories which Napoleon had relinquished, and it had been decided as early as January, 1814, and later stipulated in the First Treaty of Paris that a congress "of all the powers" should be held at Vienna to conduct this work of territorial reconstruction. But many of its decisions had already been anticipated in the negotiations which had already been going on; and though there was some pretense of giving all eight powers who had signed the Treaty of Paris the honor of composing the Congress, the number was soon reduced to six and then to four, Austria, Prussia, Russia, and Great Britain. But they had reckoned without Talleyrand, the French minister of foreign affairs. This clever and unscrupulous adventurer, who had risen to prom- *The Vienna Settlement*

Preparations for the Congress of Vienna— the position of France

inence during the Revolution as a renegade cleric, had later made
his talent for diplomacy indispensable to Napoleon, and had recently engineered the return of the Bourbons, now proposed
to match his wits against the arrogance of the great Four. He
had already taken pains to cultivate Castelreagh, the British
foreign secretary, who saw in him an ally for curbing Russian
ambition; and he now made the capital point that France, as
one of the signatories of the Treaty of Paris, could not properly be
excluded from the coming deliberations.   Deliberately raising
embarrassing questions, he went so far as to remind the diplomats
that the treaty had stipulated a "general congress" representing
"all the powers." As the mighty Four did not want a congress at
all, and certainly not one composed of delegates of the minor powers, they finally yielded to Talleyrand and made room for France
in the inner council. Thus the Four became the Five. All in all it
was a notable triumph for a power so recently humbled; and one
can well understand her minister's exultation when he wrote, "I
was able to write to Paris that the house of Bourbon, which had
only returned to France five months ago, and France herself, who
had been conquered five months previously, found themselves
already put back into their proper place in Europe, and had
regained that influence that belonged to them in the most important deliberations of the Congress." In any case the whole question
was simplified. The Great Powers had firmly resolved that they
alone should make the settlement, and the minor powers would
simply have to abide by their decisions. Presumably the Congress
of Vienna was to be a cut-and-dried affair.

*Character
and setting
of the
Congress
of Vienna*

    In fact, strictly speaking, there was no congress at all. A score
or more of representatives from petty princes came to add their
piping voices to this European chorus, but they were only allowed
the privilege of forming the background. The foreign ministers
of the five great powers were the Congress. Behind this group of
professional diplomats there were, of course, the sovereigns of
these powers, three of whom, the Czar Alexander, the Emperor
Francis of Austria, King Frederick William of Prussia were present
at Vienna, though only the Czar took an important part in influencing proceedings. Certain other princes, like the kings of Würtemberg and Bavaria were also present but seldom consulted. Undoubtedly there was much intriguing in the background (it was
whispered that certain women often influenced important de-

cisions), and probably some of the disputes were aggravated by meddling of this sort; yet the self-interest of the victor powers was so ingrained that no ulterior influences could really affect their objects. Then, too, the leading personages had plenty of relaxation for their nerves. The court of Vienna had been lavish in its welcome, and the period of the sojourn of these diplomats was a constant round of festivities. "The Congress does not advance; it dances," observed a nobleman of the time. Dances, pageants, tournaments—it is estimated that it cost a bankrupt government about sixteen million dollars to uphold its prestige by furnishing these entertainments.

Yet all was not harmony by any means. Considering the greed of the powers who suddenly found on their hands so much territory to be distributed it is a wonder that any agreement at all was possible. When the diplomats gathered, it was well known that Russia had designs on practically all of what had once been the kingdom of Poland, and that Prussia was equally determined to incorporate the whole of Saxony; and that, in fact, the two powers were in secret collusion. So belligerent was Prussia that Austria, France, and Great Britain signed a secret defensive alliance, Talleyrand thus playing the pivotal rôle. But Prussia in the end backed down, and Russia, not willing to be isolated, obligingly followed suit. It was a hard-won victory for Castelreagh (always thinking of the balance of power), but Talleyrand might perhaps have scored more heavily by playing on the other side, for if Prussia had been allowed to swallow Saxony, she might have yielded to the king of that country some of her Rhenish possessions, and it would have been much more to France's interest to have a weaker neighbor on the Rhine. But at least he appeased French vanity by restoring the national prestige. No longer was France a pariah among the nations. One wonders what might have happened if Germany had possessed a Talleyrand in 1919.

The scope of the Congress' work was narrowed to the extent that Great Britain had insisted that colonies should not be discussed and that the Czar was equally averse to having the Eastern Question included. Yet the work of reconstruction involved most of Europe. Russia acquired the lion's share of "Poland," and maintained her hold upon Bessarabia (gained in 1812 from the war with Turkey) and upon Finland, which she had taken from Sweden in 1809, and for which Sweden was compensated by obtaining the

The territorial settlement

cession of Norway from Denmark. Prussia retained a portion of her Polish gains, and acquired about two fifths of Saxony as well as Swedish Pomerania and large extensions of territory in the west. Austria abandoned the Netherlands and received in compensation Lombardy-Venetia and Dalmatia, while she also retained such gains as Salzburg (a secularized archbishopric) and that part of her Polish lands known as Galicia. The Polish city of Cracow, an apple of discord, was made into the nucleus of a little independent republic, neutralized and placed under the protection of Austria, Prussia, and Russia. Many of the smaller powers were given a share of the spoils, if their conduct had been "correct" during the War of Liberation. Great Britain as usual added to her store of colonies—Ceylon, Mauritius, the Cape of Good Hope, Malta, and three of the West Indies, as well as the island of Heligoland, ceded by Denmark. All these bargains and more besides, duly registered in a collection of treaties, was finally incorporated in what was known as the Final Act of the Congress of Vienna, June 9, 1815. The last squabbling had been terminated by the news of Napoleon's return, and it is to be observed that the final treaty was signed more than a week before the decisive battle of Waterloo.

Underlying considerations

In making the above adjustments it can hardly be said that the diplomats troubled themselves much with principles. They did not consistently apply even the principle of dynasticism or legitimacy, for though the infamous Ferdinand was allowed to return to Madrid, and most of the Italian princes recovered their possessions, there was no reinstating of the numerous German princes whom Napoleon had expropriated for the good reason that these possessions had been seized by their larger neighbors. To the spoil, too, were added that portion of Saxony that went to Prussia and also Norway which went to Sweden. Republics having naturally no standing, neither Venice nor Genoa was revived, the former going to Austria, the latter to Sardinia. The victor powers naturally aggrandized themselves as "compensation" for the losses they had suffered during the Napoleonic upheaval, and as they were all, of course, jealous of one another, they subscribed to some extent to the doctrine of the balance of power. Thus the ambition of Russia and Prussia was somewhat arrested, and safeguards were built up against France—a point which we shall discuss presently. On the basis of what Castelreagh called a "just equilibrium" they hoped to establish an enduring peace. To a limited extent, more-

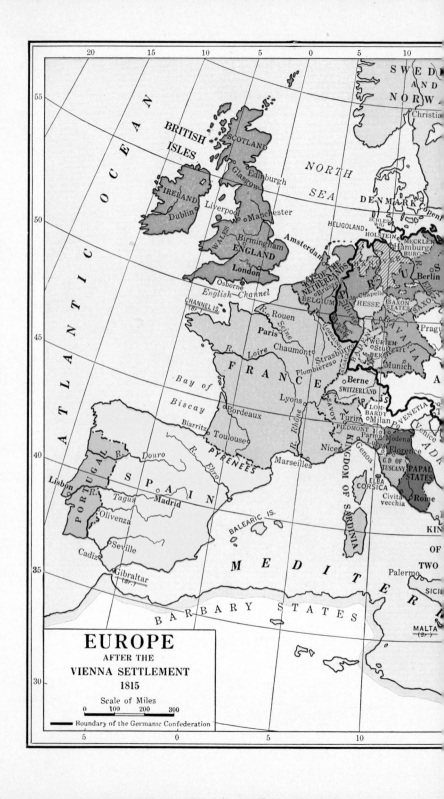

EUROPE

AFTER THE

VIENNA SETTLEMENT

1815

Scale of Miles

0   100   200   300

—— Boundary of the Germanic Confederation

over, they represented a species of internationalism. Through the
formation of the Concert of Europe (albeit this meant a dictatorship of the Great Powers) they gave Europe for a time a certain
solidarity; and the fact that they recognized some matters of common interest is shown by the principle adopted that the navigation
of international rivers should be free (it was specifically applied to
the Rhine) and by the general condemnation of the maritime traffic
in slaves—a concession extorted by Great Britain; but in neither
case was any machinery devised for enforcement. Another achievement of the Congress was the neutralization of Switzerland, which
thus became a principle of the public law of Europe.

But if internationalism had gained a little, there was a flagrant *Funda-*
disregard for nationalism. Belgium was united with Holland and *mental
defect of the*
Norway with Sweden much against the wishes of the peoples *settlement*
sacrificed. And to the great disappointment of German nationalists the reorganization of Germany took the old and obsolete form
of a loose federation of princes under Austrian hegemony. This
dubious creation was consecrated in what was known as the Act
of Federation and was the work of the Great Powers in concert with
some of the larger German states. The Italians faired even worse,
for they were not given even a federal organization. Indeed, the
only concession to nationalism (made quite outside the Congress)
was the constitution of Russian Poland into a kingdom, of which,
however, the Czar himself, its benevolent founder, was sovereign.
It is natural enough that the statesmen of 1815 should pay no heed
to the philosophy of the Revolution, natural that they should
underrate the strength of this new force, but in so doing the makers
of the Vienna Settlement weakened the whole structure they were
so diligently erecting. They deluded themselves with the idea that
the French Revolution had been nothing but a passing storm, and
that if the fabric of Europe were rebuilt a little stronger on the old
foundations, it could resist such storms in future. It is here that
one marks the chief significance of the new internationalism. If
for nearly forty years there was to be no general European war, it
was because most of the powers who had made the Vienna Settlement were severally or collectively combating revolution.

Anxious as they were to make their work enduring, the statesmen *The Concert
of Europe*
of 1815 gave some measure of attention to what they deemed to be *and the*
the fundamental dangers to Europe's peace. Experience with *Organization
of Reaction*
Napoleon had seemed to show that French ambition was not to be

trusted. Unreconciled to defeat, she might "break out" again and face Europe with another war. Then there was the danger of revolution, with which the French were fond of plaguing the rest of mankind. How deeply had this insidious influence really penetrated the countries outside of France? It was necessary, it seemed, to protect the public law of Europe against France. It was likewise necessary to fortify the restored Old Régime against the virus of revolution.

Safeguards against France: (1) internal   Against France safeguards were erected, both internal and external. The restoration of the Bourbons seemed a reasonable guarantee that France would not meddle with the affairs of her neighbors, and there was nothing about Louis XVIII to suggest a Louis XIV. Then for at least the initial years of this new régime the presence of an army of occupation and of an inter-allied council of advice might well provide the security needed to satisfy Europe. Indeed, the reaction which soon set in under the Bourbons pleased the Powers rather too well, and Great Britain had to warn the French king that the revolutionary elements might be roused to new efforts by dint of exasperation.

(2) External   Meanwhile further assurance was gained by raising barriers of defense. The enlarged kingdom of Holland in the north (this was a British idea) and the enlarged kingdom of Sardinia in the south constituted buffer states at either end of the line. Between was a neutralized Switzerland and a Germanic federation, which if rather ineffective in the main, was responsible for the garrisoning of certain border towns. In any case Prussia was now a strong Rhenish power, and it was a Prussian garrison which occupied the important town of Luxemburg, the capital of the little duchy of that name which had been given to the kingdom of Holland. Finally the great powers which had humbled France formed the Quadruple Alliance, explicitly directed against their recent foe. They were thus prepared to meet any aggression.

The Quadruple Alliance or Concert of Europe   This league had been an outgrowth of the Last Coalition. During the campaign of 1813 the four great powers at war with France had reached an agreement under the influence of Castelreagh, whereby they pledged themselves after the conclusion of peace with France to guarantee its permanence, and to supply a specified contingent to meet any future attack by France. This Treaty of Chaumont, as it was called, was to remain in force for twenty years. In spite, however, of this provision it was hastily renewed when the Powers learned of Napoleon's return from Elba. Then on

November 20, 1815 the treaty was signed which formed the Quadruple Alliance, confirming the previous arrangements, providing also for the exclusion of Napoleon and his family from the throne of France, and further stipulating that the signatory powers were to "renew their meetings at fixed periods . . . for the purpose of consulting upon their common interests and for the consideration of those measures which at each of those periods shall be considered the most salutary for the repose and prosperity of nations and for the maintenance of the peace of Europe." It may be gathered that this was more than an instrument designed to protect Europe against France; it was to be a means of stabilizing the whole status quo. And this was not all. It assumed "common interests," which could be regulated by common action. We have, in short, the birth of the Concert of Europe and the inauguration of an actual experiment in internationalism.

The pioneer and, without doubt, the most sincere of the internationalists was the Czar Alexander I. This sovereign was something like two photographs, one of the old, one of the new, taken on the same lens. Perhaps in that way he was a more rational product of his time than the hard-shelled doctrinaires who always looked back to the Old Régime. In his youth he had been nurtured on revolutionary doctrines, due to the influence of a French tutor who was a disciple of Rousseau, and all his life he was torn between a romantic attachment to liberal ideas and a morbid fear of their consequences. He was persuaded to give Poland a constitution— the one concession outside of France to the spirit of democracy— and, alone among the statesmen of the time, he was an avowed believer in "homogeneous nations," which was another way of subscribing to the principle of nationality. Finally, he had long been the champion of an active internationalism, capable of binding together the nations of Europe in an organization strong enough to safeguard international peace. Yet the means of attaining his ends was exceedingly shadowy in his mind. He was the author of the "Holy Alliance," a compact of princes to "treat one another as brothers," lending one another assistance when necessary, and to regard themselves toward their subjects as "fathers of families"; all, indeed, should be "members of one and the same Christian nation" and should "protect religion, justice, and peace." This famous instrument, constituting a kind of league of benevolent despots, which Metternich called "verbiage" and Castel-

*The rôle of
Alexander I*

reagh dubbed "a piece of sublime mysticism and nonsense," is somewhat hard to classify, for its conception of a single Christian state savors of cosmopolitanism, while the presumption of a number of sovereigns working together has the flavor of internationalism. It was, no doubt, the product of a confused mentality. Religious to the point of mysticism, Alexander looked no further or deeper than the spirit of his own benevolence. When he acted in any concrete fashion, it was usually on impulse, and he was always exceedingly susceptible both to the influence of circumstances and to a stronger personality than his own. By the time the Quadruple Alliance was under discussion he had already repented of his youthful liberalism and wished a clause inserted in the treaty, providing for armed intervention to deal with any cases of "revolutionary madness"—in combating which Castelreagh showed the first symptom of the later British policy of non-interference. Yet it was Alexander who really tried to make internationalism effective; for the original draft of the treaty seems to have been his, and hence it was he who sponsored the idea of international congresses. In short, Alexander was a man whose naturally generous impulses and chivalrous nature should have been supplemented by qualities of stability and common sense. Castelreagh had those qualities, but he was too insular in viewpoint to lend a ready sympathy to internationalism or to try to make it wisely constructive. Metternich also had those qualities in a measure, but his viewpoint too was national, and, worse than that, he was an inveterate reactionary. Hence it was that Metternich, as artful as the Czar was the reverse, was able soon to pervert this hopeful movement into an instrument for buttressing the old order.

Metternich and his "system"   Prince Metternich, the Austrian minister of foreign affairs, was a man of broad culture, an experienced and remarkably astute politician, and a cynic in everything except his own limitations. There was never a greater egotist, for it is doubtful if he ever altered any of his convictions, and to the end of his days he was firmly convinced of his own infallibility. After his career had been crowned by failure he was still able to say, "My mind has never entertained error." In his outlook he not only typified the Old Régime (at its worst!); he accurately expressed the needs of the Austrian Empire as he viewed them. For of all the countries in Europe this was the one whose foundations were most precarious, and it was no wonder, perhaps, that a sluggish and autocratic government was backed by one of the most stupid and deadening censorships ever devised. "Govern and change nothing," he told his imperial master. To Austria the spirit of nationalism might well have spelled destruction. Hence her subjects must be lulled to sleep lest they be tempted to think and assert themselves. Hence also the world outside must be rid of all contagion; for it is hard to keep immune if one's neighbor is somewhat infected! To watch the Pope abolish street-lighting in Rome because the French had happened to introduce it, to learn of the other follies of the reaction that swept over Europe in the years following the Peace, might perhaps have amused this statesman, had he possessed a sense of humor—but his mind was quite too wooden to plumb the personal equation. Metternich's ideal was a reactionary Europe bolstered and kept firm under Austrian hegemony. At the Congress of Vienna he saw to it that Italy was divided as of old into a number of petty states and that Germany was made into a federation of princes most of whom could be depended upon to follow Austria's lead. With her position of vantage in Lombardy Austria could see that the Italians meekly obeyed their rulers, and one of these rulers, the Bourbon King of the Two Sicilies, had secretly pledged himself to make no changes in his government incompatible with Austrian institutions. In Germany he made use of the federal diet, made up of representatives of the princes, to suppress intellectual freedom, and in this policy he had even the co-operation of Prussia, usually the rival of Austria, but now following obediently in the wake of Vienna. It was a doctrine of immobility that Metternich espoused, and through Austria's ascendency in central Europe he might hope to see it prevail for an indefinite period.

Yet Metternich saw also the value of concerted action by the Powers, and it was to get them all to unite in upholding the status quo that he proposed to make use of Alexander's embryonic internationalism. His success, of course, would depend on getting a personal hold on Alexander himself—a feat that might not be difficult in the latter's state of mind. At the next congress held— that of Aix-la-Chapelle in 1818—the Czar was the most conspicuous personage and for a time seemed to dominate its proceedings. Metternich, for his part, kept rather in the background, watching the course of events and particularly the Czar, whose volatile temperament he greatly distrusted. It was largely fear of a possible Franco-Russian rapprochement (a fear that was hardly justified) that influenced his attitude toward France. Despite some recent liberal tendencies in that country and a precautionary renewal of the Quadruple Alliance, it was decided that France was no longer a source of danger, and she was not only relieved of the army of occupation but actually admitted to the Concert of Europe— chiefly as a means of discouraging her from making other alignments. On the whole, it was at the Congress of Aix-la-Chapelle that the Concert displayed its most varied activity. It decided some German disputes and even admonished the King of Sweden. Like its future progeny, the League of Nations, it was most effective in dealing with small powers! It also discussed the problem of putting down piracy in the Mediterranean, though as this might have entailed the presence of a Russian fleet, the British deliberately prevented any action—as they also did in the case of the revolting colonies of Spain. One might easily discern a rift in the Concert of Europe, and this rift became all the clearer when Alexander proposed its extension into a universal alliance to guarantee all existing dynasties and territories. It is often a mistake for an idealist to press his logic too closely. The treaty which had created the Quadruple Alliance had contemplated measures that might conduce to the "repose and prosperity" of nations, but Great Britain did not really want commitments that might force her into a struggle to uphold some rickety dynasty. Hence Castelreagh made the statement that "the problem of a universal alliance for the peace and happiness of the world has always been one of speculation and hope, but it has never yet been reduced to practice, and if any opinion may be hazarded from its difficulty, it never can." He likewise opposed a Prussian proposal of an international force, quartered at Brussels, as likely to be irritating to France. The final protocol of the Congress confirmed the plan of holding congresses, but nothing was said of their object beyond the discussion of national "interests." Internationalism, promising to be oppressive, was foundering on the rock of British suspicion. Thus already had appeared that cleavage in the Concert of Europe, which was destined soon to wreck it.

The Concert of Europe under Metternich's leadership

Metternich was no doubt greatly pleased at the Czar's change of heart toward liberal movements. Yet he was often disturbed by the thought of Russia's power; the Czar's statement that his army was "at the disposal of Europe" might be sound internationalism and yet rather disquieting withal; and when in 1820 Alexander proposed that the Concert intervene in Spain (whose ruler had just been forced to grant a radical constitution), Metternich refused assent, fearing that the Czar would insist on dispatching a Russian army across Europe. In the policy of intervention Metternich meant that Austria should lead and that the other powers should follow. At all events, circumstances were playing into his hands. Alexander, exasperated by some troubles with the Poles and alarmed by various revolutionary rumors, soon yielded completely to Metternich the leadership of the Concert. "You have correctly judged the state of affairs," he said to the Prince on the eve of the next congress. . . . "Tell me what you wish and I will do it."

Three more congresses were held, prompted by actual revolutions. In the next two, at Troppau and Laibach respectively, Great Britain and France were represented only by "observers with limited powers." We have explained the British attitude. Bourbon France, seeing that internationalism was becoming a mask for national interest and that the Concert of Europe was simply an adjunct of the Metternich system, was too suspicious of Austrian policy in Italy to be willing to abet the Hapsburgs. Thus the three eastern powers acted alone. At Troppau Russia, Prussia, and Austria definitely proclaimed the right to intervene in any state to prevent a change of government; and Austria, as a self-appointed mandatory for the Concert, then put down revolutions in Naples and Sardinia. From the protocol of Troppau Great Britain and France had dissented and they viewed these actions with outspoken disapproval. But in 1821 trouble broke out afresh. The Greeks had just revolted against Turkey, and Alexander was strongly tempted to send them aid, though, true to his internationalism, he said he would not do so without the Concert's assent. More serious perhaps was the revolution in Spain, since France, fearing that history might repeat itself for a Bourbon, was anxious to intervene. The Congress of Verona met in 1822 to consider both these questions, and this time both France and Great Britain sent plenipotentiaries. But the Concert was quite unable to reach an agreement, and nothing was done. When, moreover, it was proposed that the powers should join with Spain in putting down her revolting colonies (Alexander had already wished to stretch his internationalism to cover "the interests of the universe"), Great Britain responded by recognizing their independ-

Collapse of the Concert of Europe

ence.[1] This action, inspired by George Canning, the British foreign secretary, practically marked the collapse of the Concert of Europe in its present character. On some occasions the three eastern powers continued to act together, led after Alexander's death in 1825 by his sterner successor, Nicholas I, but three powers hardly made a confederation, and the policy of intervention to put down revolution was henceforth applied only by powers acting separately when their interests seemed to be threatened and not because of any collective responsibility for the "repose and prosperity" of Europe. The wise course which internationalism might have followed was unhappily precluded by the policy of using it as an engine of repression.

But on the theoretical question of the right of intervention in the affairs of other countries the British were hardly consistent. Canning and later Palmerston were adepts at interference, though it was always, be it said, on the side of revolution. Where Castlereagh was neutral (and even on some occasions rather sympathetic with absolutism), these later statesmen made the policy of their country actively liberal. But Castlereagh, after all, was one of the men of 1815, and Great Britain, when true to herself, gave evidence of a liberality of outlook, not manifest on the Continent during the period we are considering. The trend of English politics during these years therefore deserves some brief analysis.

THE BEGINNING OF REFORM IN GREAT BRITAIN

The background of British reform

By the "beginning of reform" in Great Britain we should explain that this does not mean to imply that no reform had taken place previously. But we are thinking of that reform movement which was doubtless inspired in part [2] by the great upheavals on

[1] Alexander had claimed for Russia all the coast line of North America as far south as fifty-one degrees north latitude, and it was perhaps Russian ambition, more than the question of the Spanish colonies, that produced the famous "Monroe Doctrine," enunciated December 2, 1823. The substance of this pronouncement was that no European power should intervene in American affairs or use the Western Hemisphere as a field for colonization, the United States reciprocally promising not to meddle in the affairs of Europe. The enunciation of this policy proceeded after much discussion with Canning, and it is obvious that it was British supremacy on the seas that gave it real effect.

[2] It might be urged that to a certain extent this movement had been initiated by Pitt and especially Fox, and that it had been merely suspended during the long struggle with France (see page 193). Pitt's progressive views, even though later abandoned, served as a model for a liberal group of Tories, notably Canning, Huskisson, and Peel in the political generation which emerged after the Napoleonic struggle. But the continuity of the movement—if the demands of a small and impotent minority of Whigs could constitute a movement—was chiefly a legacy

the Continent. The English were not, however, a people given to revolution, and they had already dethroned autocracy and long since parted with feudalism. They were not, like the French, disposed to follow theories to a logical extreme, but, rather, a people who attained their ends through trial and deduction. They preferred to proceed slowly and cautiously, as is their wont, giving heed to agitation when it was loud enough, or listening to an enlightened leader, or perhaps finding the process of change in the hurly-burly of politics. And yet, with all the reputed common sense of the average Britisher, it must be realized that no people is more fond of its traditions, and that sometimes during this period reform was wrung from a sense of fear of having to face a more serious alternative. The danger of civil war in Ireland produced "Catholic emancipation" and the fear of a popular uprising finally clinched the First Reform Bill. Perhaps the most important phenomenon during this period of English history was the evolution of a healthy and vigorous public opinion. The press played its part, especially after the reduction of the tax on newspapers. The operations of propagandist associations, the most famous of which was the Anti-Corn-Law League, had often great weight. And besides these means of bringing parliament into contact with the public mind, the innovation of "lobbying" its members by bringing witnesses to furnish concrete testimony on a problem must also be included. But such innovations do not, of course, go back to the period of inertia which immediately followed the struggle with Napoleon.

On the whole, if we except factory conditions, which were probably worse than any coincident evils on the Continent, Great Britain in 1815 had a better-ordered society than existed anywhere else. The landed aristocracy which ruled the country were men who prized very deeply the privilege of serving their country in a political capacity. They were, on the whole, a benevolent aristocracy, not democratic but having the deep-rooted British sense of justice. In contrast to most Continental countries there was here unrestricted freedom of opinion, and a man might be punished only in accordance with the law. There was no judiciary in Europe comparable to the British in honesty and integrity.

of Fox, consistent champion of parliamentary reform, Catholic emancipation, and more liberal colonial and Irish policies. These two factions of Tories and Whigs respectively were responsible for the revival of reform in the 'twenties.

Yet there were plenty of limitations on human freedom in Great Britain; and she, too, had felt the spirit of reaction which had swept over the Continent after the Napoleonic era. When economic depression led to riots, they were sternly repressed without at first any efforts to remove the cause. Fortunately the English, as we have said, are a people who learn by experience. The high cost of living which had entailed so much misery led eventually—after famine in Ireland—to the removal of the tariff on foreign wheat, the Corn [1] Laws being repealed in 1846. The experience of losing the American colonies led eventually to a reaction against the Navigation Acts, and these were finally repealed in 1849. With these went a multitude of duties, and by the middle of the century England had definitely adopted free trade. It was argued that she could better sell her manufactured goods if she imported food in exchange. Another effect of her colonial experience was the granting of a measure of autonomy to the Canadians—an autonomy greatly broadened, as time went on. Among the reforms during the 'twenties were the reform of the criminal code (abolishing capital punishment for more than a hundred offenses) and the admission of Roman Catholics to parliament and public office. Most of these reforms were the work of the Tories, of whom Sir Robert Peel was the leading spirit. They did not go far enough, however, to meet the demands of the Whigs, who for nearly half a century (saving one brief interval) had constituted the party of opposition. And it was this party that was more susceptible to the currents of public opinion.

The Whigs forced their way into power by advocating parliamentary reform, and the fact that they were able to do so shows that even under the old corrupt and narrow political system with an electorate of less than a million out of a population of nearly twenty million, there was by 1830 a real reform spirit in the air. The Whigs were not advocates of universal suffrage, but they wished at least to extend the ballot to the upper middle class, many of whose members were close friends of the Whig nobles. Moreover, the fact that this element had just gained power in France by the Revolution of 1830 gave force to the demand in England for a more liberal franchise. In 1832, after a hard struggle, the First Reform Bill passed parliament, and the property qualifications were so modified that the upper middle class was included in the

---

[1] "Corn" is the usual English equivalent for wheat.

electorate. It is a mistake, of course, to assume that this element now controlled parliament and hence the government, but its influence was such that it often possessed the decisive voice. Soon after the Reform Bill local government was placed on a somewhat more democratic basis. The period of the 'thirties was prolific in reform. It was then that slavery was abolished in the colonies; it was then that the first important factory acts were passed, that the Poor Laws were revised, and that the tax on newspapers was reduced from fourpence to a penny, thus bringing the press within reach of most of the masses. The condition of the working class was much relieved in the late 'forties, and it was then that occurred the economic reforms already noted. We may mention also, in passing, that in 1837 the long reign of Victoria had begun—a period, for the most part, of unprecedented prosperity.

The reform movement slowed down about the middle of the century. For one thing the Revolutions of 1848 in Europe led many to fear that Great Britain too might be similarly affected. A movement of the proletariat, known as Chartism,[1] which had long been advocating universal suffrage, was unable to make headway against the sober caution of the governing classes. But in any case the reduction of the cost of living with the extension of free trade and the revival of employment with the growth of British industries had a quieting effect upon the unenfranchised elements. Then, too, most of the Whigs had come to the conclusion that reform had probably advanced far enough. Lord Palmerston, their leader, was the most conspicuous figure during the late 'forties and 'fifties, and he was implacably opposed to further extension of the suffrage. Until the working class could come into parliament, it was unlikely that their further needs would be met. In the meantime the national energy seemed to turn in another direction.

The reform movement in abeyance

Whatever his principles at home, in foreign policy Palmerston was liberal, and his avowed sympathies with revolutionary movements won him the fear and detestation of the Continental governments. He was partly moved, no doubt, by love of diplomatic maneuvering; he achieved nothing really constructive for European freedom; but his daring thrusts and arbitrary handling of foreign nations earned for him in England a tremendous popularity. It

Foreign policy under Palmerston

[1] So called from a document known as the People's Charter, which embodied the program of the movement.

was a priceless advantage to Great Britain that she was an island, and could therefore worry her rivals without fear of retaliation. Though not disposed to make any alliances, Palmerston often engaged with other powers in pursuit of some definite policy. In supporting the balance of power he was faithful to British traditions. He led the Concert of Europe in putting through the neutralization of Belgium to prevent its absorption by France, and he strove by various means to strengthen Turkey as a counterpoise to Russia. When he helped to make the Crimean War in 1853, he not only struck at the power of Russia, but also catered to a national sentiment bitterly hostile to autocracy. Undoubtedly Palmerston did much for British prestige, and his popularity with the public had somewhat the effect of neutralizing his negative policy at home.

The British vs. the Continental method of reform

No doubt British progress was spasmodic, and, in the course of half a century, rather slow. But where there are not revolutions, there are not the reactions that always follow. British progress was slow perhaps, but solid. In Great Britain the general election, often producing a political turn-over, with a different party in power and perhaps a new program of reform, had often the significance of a revolution, though it was orderly and bloodless and seldom bred animosities. It was otherwise on the Continent where popular or nationalist rights were in more or less chronic peril. Hence, in most of Europe—since the days of the French Revolution—a spirit of unrest.

THE REVOLUTIONARY UNREST

The disruption of the Concert of Europe ended anything like a concerted effort to stamp out revolution. Such outbreaks as took place in southern Europe had been easily put down, but even Metternich did not suppose that trouble would not recur, and for him and the Czar Nicholas vigilance was ever needed. The fabric of Europe was something like a structure which to all appearances seemed strong, yet underneath was a train of gunpowder, the influence of the French Revolution, which only required a match to start a series of explosions. The revolutionary forces, democracy and nationalism,[1] were trying constantly to break through this

---

[1] In course of time the idea of equality also came to the fore, chiefly as an inspiration to the workers and underlying the philosophy of socialism. This aspect of the revolutionary unrest will be discussed in the next chapter.

veneer that held them down. Even to the Near East—beyond what was generally thought of as Europe—the French Revolution had brought its message.

We have already noted the perennial weakness of the Ottoman Empire. The government was corrupt and decentralized, and no one in authority seemed to care at all what happened. The fatalistic Moslem felt that it was "all as Allah willed." Such a situation was serious because it invited attack from Turkey's powerful neighbors. But now a new danger arose. The spirit of nationality began to arouse those Christian peoples who had long lain inert under the military rule of the Turk. *The Rise of Nationalism in the Balkans*

If we except the Albanians, who were a hardy mountain folk, never quite subjugated but living still in a very primitive civilization, those peoples of the Balkans who were beginning to dream of freedom were four in number, the Greeks, the Bulgars, the Serbs, and the Roumans. The Bulgars, a Slavonic people of part-Finnish extraction and racially akin to the Magyars, were probably the most oppressed of the sultan's subjects, as most of them, stretched between the Danube and the Ægean Sea, lived in closest proximity to the Turkish capital. They were largely peasants and herdsmen, and most of them were quite unmindful of the days, many centuries ago, when a Bulgar prince had ruled over most of the Balkan Peninsula. Yet there were signs that even this rather sluggish people was beginning gradually to awaken. A few who had acquired some scholarship did something in the way of developing the written language, and in course of time some schools were founded. There was also a growing demand that the liturgy of their church should be written in Bulgar instead of Greek. Thus the Bulgars were at least a nationality in the making. *Case of the Bulgars*

Very different were the Greeks, a fairly enlightened people, who had frequently provided Turkey with her officials, and the head of whose Church, the patriarch, had a recognized authority over all the Balkan Christians. Though they were heavily taxed like most of the Balkan peoples, the Greeks were not greatly oppressed, and their condition was certainly no worse than it had been for several centuries. In fact, the Greeks, like the French bourgeoisie of the eighteenth century, were restless because they were prosperous. While those who dwelt in the country lived a humble pastoral life, many who dwelt in the cities or on the islands of the Ægean had made their fortunes in maritime trade—likewise an agency for *Case of the Greeks* coming into contact with Western influences. Naturally enough the philosophy of the French Revolution had stirred these people, and some cultured Greeks began to dream of the glory of ancient Greece and to carry on a movement to nurture Greek nationalism. History, language, and religion alike differentiated these people from the Turks and constituted the materials from which nationalism was generated. When an Albanian revolt suddenly revealed the hollowness of the Ottoman Empire, the Greeks tried an uprising themselves, and frightful massacres were perpetrated by the Turks in retaliation. There was some romance, no doubt, in the Greek Revolution, but there was also much brutality on both sides.

It is probable that, left to itself, the revolt would have soon flared out, but Russia had great sympathy for the Christians of the Balkans, and she saw likewise a chance of using them, now that they seemed strong enough for actual insurrection, as instruments of her policy. It seemed so certain that the Czar Nicholas would finally intervene that it was to forestall his acting alone and reaping the advantage thereof that Great Britain and France united with Russia in trying—though without success—to bring the belligerents to terms. British policy was at that time shaped by Canning, who, apart from the reason mentioned, had undoubtedly a sympathy for oppressed nationalities, and also thought of British commercial interests as well as some bankers who had partially financed the revolution. Though Russia was finally drawn into war, which brought the Turks to terms in the Treaty of Adrianople (1829), the settlement was really the work of all three powers. Thanks to British concern for Turkey, not more than two thirds of the Greeks actually won their freedom, but this at least was better than the Russian plan of autonomy. In 1830 the kingdom of Greece was founded under the guarantee of Great Britain, France, and Russia. It was a striking triumph of nationalism.

Case of the Serbs   To the north of the Greeks, in the western part of the Balkan Peninsula, and extending even across the Danube into Austria, were the Serbs, another Slavonic people, less naturally industrious and plodding than the Bulgars, but excellent fighters. They were a simple folk, most of them being engaged in raising goats and pigs, while each herdsman had also a plot of land for the subsistence of himself and his family. Like the Bulgars, the Serbs had once had their days of greatness, but for the last four centuries and more most of them had lain in complete subjection to the Turks—the only exceptions being the little group in Montenegro who maintained a precarious freedom in their mountain fastnesses, and the citizens of the tiny republic of Ragusa which eventually lost its independence to Napoleon and later became a possession of Austria. While the Serbs were used to oppression, the rapacity of the Turkish soldiery (for Belgrade was an outpost of defense) drove them to desperation, and they rose in revolt in 1807 under the leadership of a swineherd, Kara George. They succeeded with Russia's help in holding the Turks at bay for a time but were eventually put down. Then in 1815 they rose again under another swineherd, Milosh Obrenovich, and this time, fearing Russian intervention, Turkey granted a limited autonomy (including a national church and an hereditary dynasty) to most of the Serbs then living to the south of the Danube. This concession was confirmed in the Treaty of Adrianople (1829), and hence was formed the principality of Serbia. But the position of the new state was somewhat anomalous, for while tributary to the Porte [1] and still harboring Turkish garrisons in her fortresses, she was likewise under a vague protectorship of Russia, acknowledged by Turkey herself in 1826. Unhappily Russia did not always look after her charge, and Turkey frequently encroached on Serbian autonomy. Yet Serb nationalism, though still a vague thing, had had its birth, and a semi-independent state had come into being in the heart of the Balkan Peninsula.

To the northeast of the Serbs and north of the Danube were the Roumans, most of whom were subject to Turkey, though there *Case of the Roumans* were some across the mountains in Transylvania and still others were in Russian Bessarabia. They were a people of part-Roman extraction (more Roman, perhaps, than the modern Greek is Greek), and their language was of Roman origin. Those who lived in Turkey were fortunate in their distance from Constantinople, for though forced for three centuries to send supplies of grain to the Turkish capital, they had always retained a certain individuality, divided though they were between two little principalities, Moldavia and Wallachia. For a long period each principality had been ruled by a prince or "hospodar," chosen by the Porte, and usually a Greek, who together with his henchmen, always regarded

---

[1] The "Sublime Porte" was a name commonly given to the Turkish government. It signifies "high gate" and was reminiscent of days when official business was transacted at the palace gate.

the Principalities as political and economic spoils. In that way most of the land was held by men of Greek extraction, who had come to form a kind of aristocracy, and exploited the masses of the people, who were peasants. There was as yet little nationalist consciousness among the Roumans, but the interventions of Russia in the Near East had won for the Principalities a recognized autonomy, and in 1826 along with Serbia they were acknowledged as being under her special protection. By the Treaty of Adrianople (1829) Turkey was debarred from all military occupation of the Principalities; her right of intervention was subject to Russia's veto; and, in effect, she was really limited to the reception of annual tribute; also, for the first time, the Roumans were free to trade directly with the West. Soon afterward Russia provided the Principalities with a constitution, but, needless to say, it was not very liberal, and though she did much to improve their material condition, she also made them realize their dependence. When at last a nationalist flurry occurred in 1848, it was directed more against Russia than against Turkey.

At all events, nationalism had reared its head in the Balkans. By 1830 most of the Greeks were free, and a large proportion of the Serbs and Roumans were enjoying a fair autonomy. To what extent Balkan nationalism would become harnessed to Russian aggression was for the future to disclose.

As with the case of Russia, powers are often inconsistent when their principles and their interests happen to clash. Bourbon France had also concerned herself with the Greeks, and Bourbon France was certainly reactionary to the core. Already in 1830 the eyes of Europe were focused once more on Paris.

The Revolution of 1830 and its Echoes

The régime of the restored Bourbons had never much chance of long duration. Their return had been originally managed by Talleyrand in collusion with the Allied Powers, and after Napoleon's final overthrow they had come back into power as a matter of course. In France they were accepted without enthusiasm by a people tired of war and anxious chiefly for the resumption of settled conditions. But they never managed to become popular, and the peculiar circumstances under which they had been restored were a handicap from the start. As one wag expressed it, "They came back in the baggage of the Allies."

Causes of the Revolution of 1830

But the Bourbons themselves were largely to blame for the troubles in store for them. Louis XVIII, it is true, was an easy-going sovereign; he had a natural desire to avoid anything that would force him to "resume his travels"; and he talked with probable sincerity of "fusing the old and the new." But he surrounded himself, as was natural, with the men who had shared his exile, and these men seemed never to realize that the France to which they returned was a very different France from the one from which they had fled. It was a France, tired of revolution, it is true, but a France which had parted definitely with "privilege" and which had had a certain schooling in liberal ideas. The existence of a constitution was something of a safeguard (this much the Czar had required as the price of the Restoration), but time was to show that this safeguard could be easily evaded and even broken. An aggressive group of reactionaries, led by the King's brother, Charles of Artois, was determined upon a reaction, and dragged the King in their train. So vengeful was their conduct that the King himself in time became alarmed, and after the butchery of several Bonapartists more moderate counsels prevailed. But only for a time. By manipulating the electoral law, by establishing a rigid censorship of the press, and by taking steps toward restoring education into the hands of the Church the reactionaries hoped to consolidate their position and make all liberal opposition impossible. The Church and the aristocracy were now the dominant elements in politics, and the trend was only too evidently back toward absolutism and "privilege." It was no great wonder that the possessors of the confiscated lands began to tremble for their titles.

The climax was reached after Louis had been succeeded in 1820 by his stupid and aggressive brother, Charles X. It was now that the émigrés were given a money payment as compensation for the lands which they had lost, and although in a sense this cleared the titles of the present owners, the middle class was furious that the money had been derived from a reduction of the interest on government bonds, of which many of the class were holders. When finally the King arbitrarily tightened the censorship and still further limited the suffrage,[1] discontent came to a head. A revolt of some of the turbulent elements of Paris, inspired by certain journalists who were outraged by the gagging of the press, and assisted at least passively by the national guard and the troops quartered near Paris, led to the sudden abdication of the king; and the crown

The Revolution of 1830

[1] Features of the so-called "Four Ordinances."

was then offered to Louis Philippe, a son of the "Philippe Égalité," who had played so despicable a rôle in the Revolution. With a great show of democratic principles Louis Philippe accepted the crown, and for a time was chiefly advised by Lafayette. The new king was a Bourbon but he was at least the product of a revolution and was expected to remember the circumstances of his origin. Such was the Revolution of 1830.

Liberation of Belgium

It immediately had its echo in other lands. If France could strike a blow in defense of liberalism, other peoples might rise in behalf of nationalism. The explosion in Paris was felt almost immediately in the Netherlands. For various reasons the Belgians had long been discontented with Dutch rule, and they now felt inspired to throw it off. As this, however, involved one of the pillars of the Vienna Settlement, the powers were naturally disturbed, especially as it was suspected that France herself—following the precedent of 1792—had designs on Belgium. To avoid the greater evil, they recognized the independence of Belgium (1831), and for added security, affirmed her a "perpetually neutral state" with a pledge to respect and uphold her neutrality. Louis Philippe had been shrewd enough to see when he was beaten, and indeed our friend Talleyrand (now serving another régime) claims actually to have been the one to suggest this solution, though there is more reason to believe that the idea was British in origin. In any case, the successful revolt of the Belgians was a striking victory for nationalism, and it was the first breach in the Treaty of Vienna.

Echoes elsewhere

The other quarter immediately affected was Poland. Long anxious to be independent of Russia and restive under the misrule of the czar's representative at Warsaw, the Poles in 1831 resorted to insurrection. As, however, Nicholas I was a stern and relentless ruler, the movement was certainly precarious, and it was easily put down. The Poles then lost their separate status as a kingdom as well as their constitution. Poland was simply merged with the Russian Empire. Naturally there was also ferment in Germany, especially in the university centers, but nothing that could be called an insurrection. Italy, on the other hand, staged some new revolts, though they were easily put down by Austrian troops. In Germany, by way of special precaution, the federal diet forbade the existence of any political society and prohibited public meetings.

By the second half of the 'thirties Europe quieted down again, and the forces of reaction quite recovered their old complacency. But there was plenty of evidence, if one really wished to look, that the revolutionary elements were growing. Italians were secretly plotting their liberation from autocratic rule and Austrian domination; and Germans were quietly laying their plans for unity. Even in Austria herself there were signs of an awakening among some of her nationalities. There the language question was all-important, for this in Austria was the basic fact that determined nationality. In Hungary some Magyar patriots induced the diet to replace Latin by Magyar as the official language, and there was much talk of wringing further concessions from Vienna. The Czechs and Croats were meanwhile developing their literature, and the Poles, instigated by agitators from Cracow, were in 1846 on the verge of revolt. In self-defense the government at Vienna roused the Ruthenian peasants against their hated Polish landlords, promising to abolish their feudal obligations, though after the affray was over the promise was not observed. Then with the concurrence of Russia and Prussia Austria annexed the free state of Cracow—the second breach in the Vienna Settlement, and this time by one of its sponsors. But conditions were rather wearing on autocrats, and no wonder Metternich observed that "the world is very sick." All things considered, it was not impossible that a second signal from France might produce a greater upheaval.

And the signal at last came.

The July Monarchy—as the government of Louis Philippe was called because the Revolution of 1830 had taken place in July— was only a shade better than its predecessor. Though the King was an astute politician and knew the value of wearing the tricolor and dressing in citizen's clothes like the bourgeois king he was, his government was very far from liberal, and while the number of voters was now increased from 100,000 to 200,000, the change was not impressive seeing that the population of France was over 30,000,-000. Power had merely shifted from the landless aristocracy to the rich bourgeoisie. For the country as a whole it was a period of prosperity, to be sure, for it was natural that such a régime would show considerable interest in industry and commerce. But, generally speaking, the policy of the July Monarchy was negative. It did nothing to relieve the workers of the evil conditions which had come in with the Industrial Revolution; it was governed in its later years by a political machine whose corruption was flagrant

The Revolution of 1848 and its Echoes

Causes of the Revolution of 1848

and shameless; and its foreign policy was negative and humiliating. It is true that it accomplished the conquest of Algeria, though this was largely an accident, as the Algerian adventure had been a last *coup de théâtre* of the late Bourbon monarchy. In generally toadying to Great Britain, it lost the respect of all French patriots, and when it tried in its last days to pursue a stronger policy, it singularly bungled. The French will forgive anything of a government that gives them glory. Conversely, loss of prestige is a government's worst sin. As Lamartine, one of the liberals, acutely observed, "France is bored."

Opposition to the July Monarchy developed from three directions. The liberals, representing the intellectuals, the lower bourgeoisie, and some from the upper ranks of the latter class who were wearied of a humdrum rule, endeavored in spite of the fettering of the press to create a public opinion in support of a wider suffrage. Some of this element were secretly republican. A second group of malcontents were the socialists who represented the cause of the exploited proletariat. A third element looked hopefully abroad to the head of the house of Bonaparte, Louis Napoleon, nephew of the late emperor. The idea that a political movement might possibly be in the making never touched the imagination of a sluggish and complacent government. By bringing the remains of Napoleon I to Paris and erecting a mausoleum to do them honor the King had thought to win some popularity; likewise one of his ministers, Adolphe Thiers, wrote a eulogistic history of Napoleonic exploits. But such efforts were really a boomerang. An immense number of Frenchmen revered the great emperor's memory, and sons of the old veterans of those bygone days had been wont to look upon him almost as a god. The sordid commonplaceness of this plutocratic rule was all the more disgusting in their eyes. Profiting by this feeling, Louis Napoleon twice raised the standard of revolt, but his maneuvers were poorly planned and proved abortive. Yet they were not without a certain moral success. This intrepid pretender, who had barely escaped making himself ridiculous, took advantage of a public trial (another folly of a decrepit government) to make a dramatic appearance, and it was then that he offered the nation the "Napoleonic Legend." "I represent to you," he said, "a principle, a cause, a defeat. The principle is that of the sovereignty of the people; the cause, that of the Empire; the defeat, Waterloo. The principle you have recognized; the cause you have served; the defeat you wish to avenge." Subjected to a not uncomfortable imprisonment (the government had at least the sense not to make him a martyr), he escaped after six years and watched the death-throes of the July Monarchy from the close proximity of England. How much strength his cause had gained no one realized until, like his illustrious uncle, he was able to take advantage of a revolution.

The revolution which most people seemed to want but no one seemed to expect finally occurred. In February, 1848, economic stress combined with political agitation easily overthew a régime that in the end proved singularly hollow, and the King, like his unlamented predecessor, took the road to exile. As few seemed to want his infant grandson, a republic was proclaimed. *The Revolution of 1848*

The Revolution of 1848 was wholly the work of Paris, though the country at large seemed tacitly acquiescent. After a successful struggle with socialism the Second Republic turned out to be a moderate liberal régime, and its chief contribution was universal manhood suffrage. It failed, however, to endure because it lacked any roots in France outside of Paris, because it was weak in both leadership and organization, and because ultimately it had to meet a formidable enemy which had the backing of the nation. In April a constituent assembly provided the new republic with a constitution that proved to be its undoing. Most of the mistakes of 1791 had been repeated, and also the germ of a popularly supported monarchy had been planted. There was but one chamber provided, and there was to be no organic connection between executive and legislature. At the same time the president was to be elected by popular vote, and, thus constituted, would be able to appeal directly to the people against their chosen representatives. When the voters chose as president Louis Napoleon Bonaparte, the republic was clearly stultified. Out of the petty squabbles that soon ensued Louis Napoleon made ready capital. He was an adroit politician; he took pains to cultivate the Catholics and to appeal to the man in uniform; and he knew how to reach the hearts of the people and how to discredit his opponents. When the legislature, which was royalist (another symptom of the failure of the republic) passed a law which in effect deprived the working class of the suffrage, the president promptly championed the element thus excluded. While Paris, it is true, was still republican at heart, the rest of the country was monarchist in feeling, and strongly inclined to favor a new Bonaparte. *The Second Republic and its failure*

Establish-
ment of the
Second
Empire

A crisis approached in 1851. As the "Prince President" (for so he called himself!) was ineligible to re-election, and as his ambition would not countenance stepping down, there was no alternative but a coup d'état. On December 2, 1851, the anniversary of the coronation of Napoleon I, Louis Napoleon by a skillfully executed plot dispersed the assembly, clapped most of its members into prison, and assumed the power of an absolute sovereign. There had been some fighting in Paris (and consequent bloodshed), but it had been easily put down. Then the nation was asked to vote in a plebiscite to confer upon Louis Bonaparte constituent authority; and by an overwhelming vote he was sustained. It was the provinces' reply to Paris. The Second Republic lingered on for nearly a year in the guise of a dictatorship. Finally, in 1852, Louis Napoleon assumed the title of emperor of the French; and once more the result was ratified by plebiscite. Now France was no longer "bored"!

Revolution
in central
Europe—
the crisis
for Austria

We must now turn back to the immediate effects of the February Revolution—the Revolution of 1848 in France. The danger that the Powers, inspired by sinister memories of a republic, would intervene, was soon dispelled by the mere fact that they themselves were caught in the maelstrom of revolution. Starting with a revolution in Sicily and gathering its chief momentum from the February Revolution in France, the storm shook central Europe and swept even as far as the Danubian Principalities. The fact that it was much fiercer than the convulsion of 1830 shows how much the strength of nationalism had grown since that earlier upheaval. Perhaps also the construction of railways and the generally improved methods of communication made revolutionary ideas spread more rapidly than of old. Finally, we may note that the Industrial Revolution had begun to reach central Europe. In Vienna there was a needy proletariat, thrown out of work by the introduction of machinery into the factories.

The "March
Revolution"
in Austria

Oddly enough, the effect of the February Revolution was first felt in Austria. Nationalist hopes had long been stirring in the Hapsburg realm, and it was the Magyars, always proud and difficult to rule, who led the attack on the German ascendancy in the empire. Louis Kossuth, an impassioned orator, declaimed before the assembled Hungarian diet against the "pestilential air" that "breathes upon us" from the "charnel house" of Vienna. The effect of the speech was electrical. The Magyars proceeded without more ado to put their state in order (abolishing feudalism, enacting a new constitution, and adopting the fullest autonomy); other nationalities likewise asserted themselves; and in Vienna itself a riot broke out, which, directed largely against Metternich, soon drove the old statesman into retirement. Nothing better shows the force of the convulsion than the downfall of the man who had upheld a tottering system for so many years. But this was only the beginning. The emperor not only granted a constitution but soon afterward signed his abdication, leaving the throne to his young nephew, Francis Joseph. But the country was so badly shaken that the new emperor was hardly safe in his own capital. In May the government was terrorized by a mob led by university students and swelled by masses of peasants—that element which Austria had shamelessly betrayed in 1846.

Meanwhile, the empire itself was crumbling under the onslaughts of nationalism. The Magyars, while not renouncing allegiance to the dynasty, made themselves otherwise independent. The Czechs were likewise in revolt; while the Croats, on their side, were trying to win their freedom from Magyar rule. Down in Italy it was the same. The Italians of Lombardy-Venetia had risen and invoked the help of neighboring Sardinia. When Charles Albert, King of Sardinia, responded to this appeal, other Italian rulers were forced to join the movement. Italy from end to end was swept into the current. And, needless to say, Germany was affected. Princes were hurriedly granting constitutions, hoping by such means to save their tottering thrones. At Berlin there was a formidable riot, and the King of Prussia was forced again to promise a constitution; while in Germany as a whole the nationalist movement had brought into being a national assembly, meeting at Frankfort, whose purpose was to create at one stroke a liberal and unified Germany. It was all a spontaneous movement from below. The autocratic princelings in Italy and Germany had been forced to run to cover when the leadership of Vienna had failed them in the crisis.

Collapse and recovery

And yet, with all the odds against her, Austria managed to pull through, and to beat the forces of revolt on every hand. The explanation is varied. In the first place, the army, mostly German, was loyal and efficient. In the second place, the government let the Magyars alone and parlied with the Czechs while it concentrated on Italy. There Radetzky, the Austrian commander, defeated

Charles Albert and recovered Lombardy and Venetia. In the third place, though the capital was in uproar and even a republic was threatened while the army was absent in Italy, the government wisely abolished feudal services and in that way broke the resistance of the peasants. In the fourth place, Austria successfully played one nationality off against another. She took advantage of the discord between Czechs and Germans in Bohemia, and after winning decisively in Italy she put down the Czech revolt without much trouble. She meanwhile encouraged the Croats in their struggle with the Magyars, with whom she was now ready to come to conclusions. Yet the Magyars, who had by this time established a republic, would probably have held their own but for the fifth and final cause of Austria's recovery, the timely help of Russia. The Czar Nicholas did not choose to have a republic across his frontier, and when he poured 200,000 soldiers into Hungary, the issue was decided. The Maygar republic was crushed. The integrity of the Austrian Empire was preserved. And with the collapse of the nationalist movement in Germany her ascendancy in Germany as well as Italy was restored. Everywhere reaction was the order of the day.

Results of the upheaval   There were few tangible results of the mid-century upheaval. Sardinia managed to keep her constitution but only on suffrance; Prussia also got hers, though it was very illiberal; and feudalism was at last at an end in the Hapsburg empire. That is about all, for in most states autocracy was once more enthroned, and German and Italian hopes were seemingly quashed. Badly battered but triumphant, Austria had placed her heel on nationalism; and it must have seemed to progressive elements that her power was impregnable. Yet morally the elements of resistance were probably strengthened by the experience. The nationalists on the Danube had awakened to new life, and emancipation for them, as for the Italians, could only be a matter of time. 1849 was a dismal year, but 1852 was coming.

Two incidents in 1852 foreshadowed important events. The Second Empire was proclaimed, with Napoleon III as emperor; and Cavour became the premier of Sardinia. Europe was on the eve of another great upheaval.

Time, indeed, was on the side of the revolutionary elements. While it might seem, as one looks back on the period of struggle since 1815, that scant return had come from so much desperate effort, there yet remained a growing sentiment for adequate realization of the principles of the great Revolution. And it was about the middle of the century that the middle class on the Continent began perceptibly to enjoy the benefits of new sources of wealth and that the states of central Europe came to acquire a material power which they had never known before. Such power in the hands of progressive leaders would mean much; in short, the streams which flowed from the French Revolution were soon to gain new force from that other great convulsion, the Industrial Revolution.

FOR FURTHER READING OR STUDY

Robinson, J. W., and Beard, C. A., *Readings in Modern European History*, vol. i, chap. xvi and vol. ii, chaps. xvii, xix and xx; Scott, J. F., and Baltzly, A., *Readings in European History since 1814*, chaps. i–ii, v; Oakes, A. A., and Mowat, R. B., *The Great European Treaties of the Nineteenth Century;* Talleyrand, *Memoirs*, 5 vols.; Metternich, *Memoirs*, 3 vols.; Cheney, E. P., *Readings in English History*, chap. xxix (*passim*); Robertson, C. B., *Select Statutes, 1660–1832.*

Hayes, C. J. H., *A Political and Cultural History of Modern Europe*,[1] vol. i, pp. 696–717 (spread of the principles of the Revolution) and chap. xiv (through 1830); Hayes, *A Political and Social History of Modern Europe*, vol. ii, pp. 100–57; Hazen, C. D., *Europe since 1815* (admirably clear and interesting text for political history, the more attractive original edition being here cited), chaps. i–ix; Schapiro, J. S., *Modern and Contemporary European History* (a standard text), chaps. i, iv–xii; Higby, C. P., *History of Modern Europe*, chaps. i–iii, v–ix; Palm, F. C., and Graham, F. E., *Europe since Napoleon*, chaps. iii–vi, xiii–xiv; Andrews, C. M., *The Historical Development of Modern Europe*, vol. i, chaps. iii–x; Phillips., W. A., *Modern Europe*, chaps. i–xiii, (interesting but almost purely diplomatic) chaps. i–xiii; Fueter, E., *World History* (a suggestive essay rather than a narrative), chaps. vii–xiv, xxi; Croce, B., *History of Europe in the Nineteenth Century* (philosophical); Bourne, H. E., *The Revolutionary Period, in Europe*, chaps. xxiii and xxvii; Gottschalk, L., *The Era of the French Revolution*, part ii, book ii, chap. iii (post-Napoleonic settlement); Gershoy, L., *The French Revolution and Napoleon*, chap. xxi (post-Napoleonic settlement).

Brinton, C., *A Decade of Revolution* (presenting a masterly discussion of the influence of the French Revolution); Artz, F. B., *Reaction and Revolution, 1814–32* (covers the ground admirably); May, A., *The Age of Metternich* (excellently written brief study); Rose, J. H., *Nationality in Modern Europe*, lects. i–iv; Gooch, G. P., *Germany and the French Revolution;* Muir, R., *Nationalism and Internationalism*, part iii, chaps. i–iii; Webster, C. K., *The Congress of Vienna;* Cresson, W. P., *The Holy Alliance;* Phillips, W. A., *The Confederation of Europe* (excellent); Woodward, E. L., *Three Studies in European Conservatism* (includes able study of Metternich); Webster, C. K., *The Foreign Policy*

[1] The second volume of this work was not published when this book went to press.

of Castelreagh; Temperley, H. W. V., *The Foreign Policy of Canning;* Corti, E. C., *The Rise of the House of Rothschild* (financial dealings of the Great Powers); Fisher, H. A. L., *The Republican Tradition in Europe;* Seignobos, C., *The Evolution of the French People,* chaps. xviii–xix (through Napoleon III); Guignebert, C., *A Short History of the French People,* vol. ii, chaps. xxxv–xxxvii; Guérard, A. L., *French Civilization in the Nineteenth Century* (a brilliant sketch); Elton, G., *The Revolutionary Idea in France, 1789–1871;* Artz, F. B., *France under the Bourbon Restoration;* Lucar-Dubreton, J., *The Restoration and the July Monarchy;* Allison, J. S. C., *Thiers* (interesting for the July Monarchy); Whitehouse, H. R., *Life of Lamartine,* 2 vols.; Fisher, H. A. L., *Bonapartism* (keen essay on the fruitage of the Napoleonic Legend); Simpson, F. A., *The Rise of Louis Napoleon;* Schevill, F., *The Making of Modern Germany,* lect. 4; Leger, L., *The History of Austria-Hungary;* Miller, W., *The Ottoman Empire;* Forbes, N., *The Balkans* (contributions of varying merit); Schevill, F., *The History of the Balkan Peninsula,* chaps. xix–xxi; Waring, L. F., *Serbia* (brief but good); Lingelbach, W. E., "Belgian Neutrality; its Origin and Interpretation," *Amer. Hist. Rev.,* xxxix, 48 ff.; Lunt, W. E., *History of England,* chaps. xxxiv–xxxvi; Cross, A. L., *A History of England and Greater Britain,* chaps. xlviii–lii; Trevelyan, G. M., *British History in the Nineteenth Century;* Wingfield-Stratford, C., *A History of British Civilization,* vol. ii (largely interpretive); Halévy, E., *A History of the English People* (three volumes so far translated cover period 1815–41, very detailed and scholarly); Mathison, W. L., *England in Transition* (stops at 1832); Morley, J., *Life of Richard Cobden;* Thursfield, J. R., *Peel;* Strachey, G. L., *Queen Victoria* (a fascinating book); Cole, G. D. H., *The Life of William Cobbett* (on an English radical); Guedalla, P., *Palmerston* (scenic); Ward, A. W., and Gooch, G. P., *The History of British Foreign Policy,* vol. i.

XII. THE INDUSTRIAL REVOLUTION AND THE RISE OF THE MODERN PROLETARIAT

1. THE CAUSES AND EARLY COURSE OF THE INDUSTRIAL REVOLUTION

Meaning of the Industrial Revolution; Causes of the Industrial Revolution; England as the prime mover of the Industrial Revolution; Premonitions of the Industrial Revolution; Transformation of the textile industries; Advent of steam; Revolution in transportation; Immediate results of the Industrial Revolution; "The Reign of Terror" of the Industrial Revolution.

2. THE INFLUENCE OF LAISSEZ-FAIRE

A. ORIGINS AND MEANING OF LAISSEZ-FAIRE

B. ASPECTS OF LAISSEZ-FAIRE

(1) Economic: (a) in England, (b) on the Continent; (2) Social: (a) the workers under laissez-faire, (b) beginnings of State intervention, (c) tightening of laissez-faire under depression.

3. THE INDUSTRIAL REVOLUTION ON THE CONTINENT

In France; In Germany; Elsewhere.

4. THE AWAKENING OF THE PROLETARIAT

A. THE SETTING OF THE PROBLEM

Early signs of an awakening; Rule of the middle class.

B. THE WEAPONS OF THE PROLETARIAT

Trade-unionism: (1) in England, (2) on the Continent; Political agitation; Revolution: (1) antecedents of socialism, (2) rise of socialism, (3) attempt at social revolution.

5. KARL MARX AND A WORLD CREED FOR THE PROLETARIAT

Character and training of Marx; Assumption of leadership of the proletariat; Ideas and importance; A divided following.

6. THE EMERGENCE OF THE SOCIAL STATE

Just as the French Revolution transformed the moral outlook of the individual, proclaiming an innate right to a more unfettered life and an equality of opportunity to enjoy it, the Industrial Revolution profoundly changed his material situation. The latter movement had its beginnings before the former but did not become

411

European in scope until the former had run its course. Just as the French Revolution was the gift of France, the Industrial Revolution may be regarded as the greatest of all Great Britain's contributions to civilization. Later the two were to become associated in a sense through the enhanced importance of the middle class; but perhaps the most significant phenomenon arising directly from the Industrial Revolution was the emergence of an immense proletariat whose condition was vitally different in many ways from that of its prototype in the days of cottage industries and gilds.

THE CAUSES AND EARLY COURSE OF THE INDUSTRIAL REVOLUTION

Meaning of the Industrial Revolution

The Industrial Revolution was the transformation in the methods of production and transportation through the general substitution of power-driven machinery for hand labor. The actual period which the movement may be said to cover is a question on which there has been much variety of opinion, and one's judgment partly hinges on what is meant by the term, "revolution." Applying the meaning we have adopted (more or less sanctioned by tradition), one must nevertheless realize that the operation of the movement was very gradual even in England, and that the various immediate results, to be presently discussed, were by no means general even there till a century had passed after the movement may be said to have begun. As late as 1850 hand-labor was still employed in many industries in England and in no English industry was transformation complete. Many economists go so far as to doubt the very value of such a term as the "Industrial Revolution," pointing also to the fact that the sporadic use of machinery in production as well as the existence of the factory system of organization long antedated the period when machinery and the use of steam came radically to transform the textile industries. Certainly the suddenness and rapidity, once commonly ascribed to the Industrial Revolution, can no longer be credited. The movement not only was long in becoming general but had been long in preparation. "The great inventors and discoverers whose names are known," remarks a recent writer, "often built on foundations laid by scores of obscure men; their work was merely an improvement or refinement upon that of others and in turn needed still further improvement before it became really satisfactory." But, when all due weight has been given to centuries of patient experimenting (sometimes successful, sometimes otherwise) with the problem of making machines, and with due appreciation of the organizing achievements of capitalism in the past, the process of industrial transformation was immensely intensified in England during the late eighteenth century, and it was then that English society began to show some of the profound effects of the movement. Whether or not the earlier activities should be viewed as the initial stage of the revolution, or whether or not the whole movement was too gradual properly to be called a revolution, is perhaps after all a matter of definition. But the fact is certainly clear that the world which Palmerston saw after the middle of the nineteenth century was a very different world from that of Walpole or Frederick the Great.

The Industrial Revolution was due to a variety of causes, but which for convenience may perhaps be reduced to two. In the first place, the expansion of commerce which resulted from what we have called imperialism created a greater demand for manufactured goods to exchange for the commodities produced by colonies or other distant lands. At the same time, the growing accumulations of capital, as well as the increased store of raw materials which new areas of exploitation had opened up, broadened the opportunities for output on a large scale. The world was getting too big to revolve any longer on the axis of handicraft production. The expansion of commerce and with it the growth of commercial capitalism accelerated industry and demanded from it a greater return. In the second place, there had been, as we have noticed, a significant revival of science in the seventeenth century, and much of the value of that scientific study had lain in showing the essential orderliness of Nature, developing a confidence that her secrets could be fathomed, and demonstrating the need of accuracy and precision in the search for new discoveries. While it is true that the first machines were much more the result of practical experimentation and demonstration than of a knowledge of what science had disclosed, nevertheless the application of steam to industry was due in very large part to a study of pure science. *Causes of the Industrial Revolution*

Some, at least, of the reasons why the movement began in England rather than in a Continental country are fairly obvious. In England of the eighteenth century the man of business enjoyed a much greater initiative than his counterpart on the Continent. That part of the Netherlands, which had once loomed so large in *England as the prime mover of the Industrial Revolution* industrial history, had never quite recovered from the depressing effects of wars in which their status had been a stake.[1] In France, which we may regard as typical of the Continental monarchies, there was, thanks to the strength of mercantilism, much more official regulation, and the gilds, which had no wish for innovations, were protected by the government. In England, as we may remember, the gilds had, for the most part, given way to the domestic system; and because England, for reasons we have discussed, had become the leading commercial power, there was there a greater surplus capital to be utilized than in any other country. Capital in France was more often employed in the manufacture of armaments and luxuries, whereas in England greater attention had long been given to the more staple commodities like cloth, in the making of which less technical skill was required; and it was industries such as these that were more adapted to machine production. Perhaps, all in all, the Continental artisan was more of an artist than his British counterpart. The domestic system, into which the English workers were readily drawn, bespoke, no doubt, a less interesting existence, but, on the other hand, it offered employment to an increasing number of persons; and the decimation of the peasant proprietors—the outstanding feature of the Agricultural Revolution—threw on the market an immense and growing supply of labor. When we remember that in England there were also abundant supplies of coal and iron (and in close proximity to each other), we may conclude that in this land the materials for the development of modern industry were especially available. With these facts before us it hardly seems strange that in England should be found the strongest pressure for inventions. The coal industry was fast reaching its limits because water prevented the plumbing of the lower levels, and there was need of more powerful engines to pump it out. Similarly, the iron industry suffered actual decline because the process of smelting with charcoal required supplies of timber that were not available. Moreover, the cotton industry was pushed to meet the demand for cotton fabrics. Capitalism needed greater resources at its disposal. Hence in England appeared that galaxy of inventors, which may be viewed as the immediate cause of the Industrial Revolution.

As intimated already, this great transforming movement had long been foreshadowed. It is interesting to note that even before

[1] The port of Antwerp had been closed to commerce by the Peace of Westphalia.

the domestic system had come into general vogue a certain proto- *Premoni-* type of the modern factory system may be found in the presence *tions of the* in England during the sixteenth and seventeenth centuries of large *Revolution* workshops where a hundred or so workmen were engaged in spinning and weaving, and mention has already been made of large-scale production, financed by capital, in mining and other industries. An example of mass production had been furnished by the armament industry, while printing had afforded an example of a division of labor, printing, type-setting, binding, and other functions being performed in the same establishment. For arms-making the pressure of military demand had required something like factory organization; it also stimulated invention. The use of iron for making armor and later artillery produced in the fourteenth century the first blast furnace of which we have record, and the process of smelting was improved and perfected in the fifteenth and sixteenth centuries, though use had still to be made of charcoal, which was wasteful of the forests. For the every day business of living, the use of watermills and windmills for grinding corn or pumping water displayed the ingenuity with which mankind could utilize sources of power. But with only such power as man, horses, wind, or water could supply the development of industrial production was necessarily slow. The importance of these years lies in man's unconscious struggle toward goals which he could not perceive. A spirit of inventiveness had, of course, been an aspect of the Renaissance, though there were evidences of it earlier, largely due, as we have suggested, to the influence of the Arabs. The importance of the printing-press has already been noted. The sixteenth and seventeenth centuries were full of practical inventions. While the telescope, barometer, thermometer, and pendulum clock had little relation to industry, they amply attest to the progress which technology was making. In mining and manufacturing crude machines of various kinds were not unknown. Forge-hammers, worked by water-wheels, were used in the iron industry. The spinning-wheel had early come into western Europe from India, and its operation had been improved by Leonardo da Vinci, quite as much an inventor as he was an artist. Italian machines for throwing silk existed at least as far back as 1300, though they were apparently not copied in England till 1718. The invention of the stocking frame (by an Englishman in 1589) ended the need of knitting by hand, and heralded (as Paul Mantoux, a standard authority on the Industrial Revolution, points out), if it did not begin the Industrial Revolution. About the same time various men were battling with the problem of a steam-engine. This discovery of a new source of power that might be applicable to industry was of paramount significance, and was certainly one of the immediate premonitions of what was to come. Then in 1733 began that series of inventions which revolutionized the making of cotton cloth. Mantoux is probably right in emphasizing the major importance of the transformation of the textile industries, leading directly, as it did, to the rise of the modern factory. Just when one chooses to begin what we have called the Industrial Revolution is no doubt largely a matter of convenience. But it is important at least to realize that the movement was well under way in the second half of the eighteenth century.

The transformation of the textile industries

We shall not take space to describe the construction of the various mechanical devices which replaced the old-fashioned methods of weaving and spinning. Though the woolen industry was much older than the cotton (in 1701 woolen goods formed a fourth of the export trade), it was cotton that received the first momentum from this outburst of invention—largely due to the fact that, Indian fabrics having been prohibited through the influence of the wool merchants, there was all the more incentive for making cotton goods in England to meet the increasing demands of fashionable circles. The new machines, with which the names of Crompton, Cartwright, and many others are associated, raised the cotton and woolen industries to a productive capacity quite beyond the wildest dreams of a century ago. Richard Arkwright, who had a knack of exploiting other people's inventions, became a veritable captain of industry, owning and operating several factories. Since the first spinning-machines were run by water-power, it was necessary for mills to be established among the hills in the north of England where the rivers could provide the necessary force. Soon, however, the coming of steam made it practicable to plant factories over a much wider area, though they would naturally be thicker where coal was to be found.

The advent of steam

The application of steam to industry furnished the generative power needed to propel machinery, and thus opened up a limitless range of opportunity. The first steam-engines had been pumps and were used to advantage in ridding coal mines of water, thus enabling them to be worked to a greater depth. It was James Watt who brought the steam-engine directly into the service of the textile industries; and it was only a question of time when not only production but transportation would profit by its use. Meanwhile, the discovery of a process of smelting iron by coal (succeeding charcoal which had been expensive and wasteful of the forests) led to much greater use of iron; while the process of making steel

From the Scientific American

MILL ENGINE DESIGNED BY WATT

from iron soon underwent such notable improvement that the metal could be turned out in greater and cheaper quantities than ever before. Thus was facilitated the making of machinery itself, as well as other things such as bridges, vessels, etc., which required a harder and smoother metal than crude iron. If we also recall that the running of machinery required extensive supplies of fuel, we can understand the basic importance of coal, as well as iron, to modern industry.

But the growth of large-scale production would have been seriously limited without better means of transportation. An inland town like Manchester was at first greatly handicapped by being unable readily to obtain its raw materials or to dispose of its immense volume of goods. It is said that so congested were the three canals which connected it with Liverpool that it took a month

The Revolution in transportation

for cotton to cover the distance of thirty miles to reach the sea. Canals and turnpikes were, of course, the great arteries of transportation at the end of the eighteenth century, but while the process of macadamization soon revolutionized the latter, the problem of hauling goods in large bulk required speed as well as space. Here, as in production, coal, iron, and steam, united with the spirit of invention, supplied the need. First tramways, long in use for conveying coal, were run on iron rails; then the application of steam as a motor power produced the railroad. It is interesting to observe that when the railroad was first inaugurated—early in the nineteenth century—it was open to any company to use the tracks to convey passengers or merchandise; but considerations of safety soon persuaded governments and parliaments to fix the management of a railroad in the hands of a single company, and incidentally this gave rise to greater industrial concentration and a more rapid spread of railroads. Corresponding improvement in the means of water transportation went hand in hand with the improvement of roads and the construction of railways. The use of iron or steel, instead of wood, for the construction of vessels and the utilization of steam for propelling them made for swifter and safer crossings of the seas. Thus transportation as well as production was revolutionized. Easy access to markets vastly increased the demand for industrial products, while the materials with which commodities were made could come from China or Egypt or elsewhere in vastly increased quantities.

We have, indeed, now to consider some of the more striking aspects of the great transformation accomplished by the power-driven machine. What were the immediate results of the Industrial Revolution?

Immediate results of the Industrial Revolution

The first result to mention is that object which had primarily been sought. Manufactured goods could now be turned out in so much greater quantities than under the old handicraft system that demands could be more quickly and easily supplied—with the ultimate result that a higher standard of living was obtained and an infinitely greater number of persons came to enjoy the conveniences of life. Naturally as an outcome of large-scale production and the parallel improvement in methods of transportation commerce grew by leaps and bounds. Whereas under the old system the market had at best been rather limited—often enough merely local in its range—now things were made more generally without knowledge of the actual consumer, and output was limited only by the judgment of the producer. It was but a step farther to develop the art of advertising, and thus still more to stimulate the demand. If we may look beyond the years of squalor and misery through which the working classes passed before they made their power felt, the great majority of the people of the civilized world eventually enjoyed the benefits of a machine-made civilization. The modern newspaper, the automobile, and the radio have brought new funds of enjoyment even to many of the workers in factories. All manner of things that were once the luxuries of the few are now deemed almost necessities. And now that it has been proved possible to reconcile profit with shorter hours for the working classes, there is much more leisure time to enjoy the fruits of others' labor. Whatever the immediate cost, the Industrial Revolution opened the way to a new world.

In fact, the increased volume of production led to many impressive changes. Thanks partly to the enhanced productivity of land and industry, population greatly increased. There were also certain social and political results of this marvelous expansion of industry. With the greater mobility of persons as well as goods, due to the revolution in methods of transportation, the world for many persons had widened out, and travel as well as closer commercial relations greatly stimulated social intercourse, enhancing the unity of nations and leading perhaps to a little more international understanding. Even the relative position of nations came to be somewhat affected. Industrial Germany, for example, came to overshadow France, still predominantly agricultural. Backward countries were also to be opened to western capital, and imperialism would soon enjoy a powerful revival. But this, again, is dealing rather with ultimate than with immediate results of the Industrial Revolution.

A second immediate result was the predominance of the factory system in the organization of industry. The shops or cottages in which workers had formerly turned out their pottery or fabrics or what-not were not adapted to the harboring of machines; nor were the workers themselves able to bear the expense of buying them. Moreover, machines required not skill so much as patient application best attained by the concentrations of groups of workers under a single directing mind. The domestic system was not adaptable to the new order. Thus workers had now to assemble under one roof that all might play their part in the running of the machine and subject themselves to the discipline of the shop. By such means the capitalist achieved the most profitable results.

Closely connected with the rise of the factory system we may note as the third result the shifting of population from country to town—a process rendered all the easier in England by the decay of peasant proprietorship. Great towns now sprang up—the direct result of the establishment of factories, as thither flocked thousands of workers who had become uprooted from the domestic system. By 1851 half of England's population had become urban. In the new economic order the factory played somewhat the same rôle as the château had done in an earlier society. As the peasants who had lived on the domain of a lord had gone forth to till his fields, so the industrial workers now poured forth from their hovels at the sound of the factory whistle to begin their day's work for a modern industrial lord. It was a bare living that they got, and yet the decline of agriculture had driven many of them already into the transitional domestic system, whence they were finally absorbed into the factories. But apart from changes in land-holding which had squeezed out the peasants, the enhanced importance of industry had completely upset the balance between manufacturing and agriculture. While it is true that agriculture itself was becoming more profitable (through the changes already noted [1]) the tremendous field of opportunity to satisfy the more varied and less primal wants than eating and drinking had the result of making society more and more predominantly industrial, where it had formerly been chiefly agricultural. This tendency, so marked in England, was later to become apparent on the Continent as well.

A fourth feature of the new order was the sharp cleavage between employers and employed—between capital and labor. Whereas formerly under the gilds the artisan had generally worked with his men and journeymen at least had usually owned their own tools; whereas under the domestic system the employer brought the raw materials to the worker to turn into finished products for which he later returned, and the workers themselves often possessed the spindles and the looms; now under the régime of the factory system the employer seldom saw his men (usually he was represented by a foreman or superintendent) and much of the capital that was invested in the factory was owned by people who never saw the

[1] Page 242.

factory at all; while the tools, that is, the machinery, were part of the direct expense of the owner or the investors. The old personal relationship between master and journeymen, even the less frequent contact between merchant and cottagers, was gone. Despite their common interest a seemingly unbridgeable gulf divided the new industrial masters and their men.

And a fifth result was the changed moral attitude on the part of the workers toward their work. In the old days work had been more personal. The man who made a shoe was himself concerned with the making of every part of it. He could see it grow to completion in his hands, and there was a chance to employ his individual skill. After the coming of machine production all the processes which had anything to do with making an article were rigidly distributed. The worker performed but one function in the process of making a shoe, and that one function was purely mechanical. He was merely a "hand." The workers in the modern factory had but to push a lever or press a button or turn a crank the whole day long. Work was changed by the Industrial Revolution into a singularly monotonous and deadening affair. Since technical efficiency was furnished by the machine, the unskilled laborer had largely replaced the skilled. Even the presence of the employer in the old handicraft days had lent an element of interest to the workman's toil. Now labor was essentially impersonal.

A sixth result was a further depression of the working class. There was plenty of labor to be had, and the workers had to accept whatever conditions were dictated. Hence, for many a day, the long and grinding toil (fourteen to sixteen hours—even in some cases eighteen), the low wages, and the employment of an increasing number of women and children, which, being cheaper, still further depressed wages. It is now generally admitted that neither under the gild nor under the domestic system had working conditions been ideal. The cottages, or rather hovels, where a man and his wife and children had woven or spun were often hardly habitable, and the remuneration they received was generally so pitifully small that they were forced to labor far into the night. Yet in most cases these pre-Revolutionary workers consumed some of their day in farming or gardening, and thus the conditions under which they toiled were not so generally injurious as those which came to be associated with the factory system. Moreover, while it is too much to say that "their time was their own" if they had to labor incessantly to eke out a living, these cottage workmen were at least spared the ever-grinding pressure of factory discipline. Unquestionably, the houses in which the new proletariat lived were generally crowded and unsanitary, some of its members actually spending their nights in cellars, which were so damp and so unventilated as to be veritable dens of disease. And over all hung the fear of unemployment, for production had naturally its ups and downs with the opening of a world market and the frequent recurrence of war, and for unskilled labor there was little chance for the abler man to rise to a better position through competition. To be without work or to be unfit for work meant nothing less than to become a public charge; and inasmuch as in England each parish had the expense of maintaining its paupers, any chance for an indigent workman to seek work in another locality was obviously impossible; no other parish would harbor him. Worst of all were those offsprings of the Poor Laws, the workhouses, where paupers' children toiled—without a single soul even to notice their existence.

"The Reign of Terror" of the Industrial Revolution

It was the children who bore the greatest sufferings during the Industrial Revolution. Many thousands of paupers' children were supplied to the factories [1] by the parishes, who sought thereby to lessen their own expenses. These bonded children were given sometimes a trifling wage, sometimes only board and lodging. Even the length of the working day. was largely determined by the foreman, who might drive his little charges until they dropped from sheer exhaustion. Not infrequently they fell into the machinery to be killed or maimed for life. The brutality with which they were treated in order to keep them steadily at work is almost unbelievable. "Of course," writes Mantoux, "not all factories witnessed such scenes, but they were less rare than their incredible horror would lead us to suppose. Even if they had not been ill-treated, excessive labor, lack of sleep, and the nature of the work forced on children during the critical period of their growth would have been quite enough to ruin their health." Often, too, the food was both bad and insufficient; many of the factories were entirely without ventilation; and the workers were not infrequently victims of certain diseases traceable to the character of their work. Even making allowance for different conditions in different factories, there are few pages in history more ghastly than those years

---

[1] The practice began to become common when factories were located for the sake of water power in rather remote districts where labor was relatively scarce.

of adjustment to a machine economy. They may be called the "Reign of Terror" of the Industrial Revolution. And the thousands of puny, undersized members of the British proletariat today bear the marks of this tragic period.

Yet relief was long in coming, for manufacturers were in the heyday of sudden and enormous profits, and to buttress their position they had a certain philosophy of their own—ideas commonly known as "laissez-faire."

THE INFLUENCE OF LAISSEZ-FAIRE

We have already mentioned the working of rationalism in the economic sphere and the rise of that school of economists of whom Adam Smith was not the earliest but the most famous.[1] It is interesting to reflect that the intellectual awakening of the eighteenth century led not only to the French Revolution with its undermining of arbitrary power in the political world but also to the triumph of laissez-faire with its shattering of the same principle in the economic sphere. Yet this doctrine was merely the formulation of a sentiment which had been growing for some time more articulate—especially among the English middle class. Merchants had come to chafe under the many restrictions of the mercantile system and to resent all species of State intervention. Already in England the principle of wage regulation—an inheritance from the fourteenth century—had become practically inoperative, and as far as labor conditions were concerned, the English manufacturers had little cause to complain of official action. When finally the Industrial Revolution brought such problems into the foreground, they hailed the new idea of laissez-faire as particularly applicable to their interests. Laissez-faire, as it came to be expounded, involved two things: unfettered relations (1) between seller and buyer and (2) between employer and employee. No tariff or any other artificial regulation should control the market. No action by State or workers' organizations should be allowed to invade the principle of freedom of contract. The price of goods and the price of labor should follow simply the law of supply and demand. Fundamental among civic rights was that of owning property, which must be broadly construed as the right of employing one's capital as one chose, and it was the duty of the State to protect, not to interfere with this right. Thus the middle class, in obtaining

Origins and Meaning of Laissez-Faire

[1] Page 258.

liberty, made a point of guarding its interests as it conceived them. With the propertyless proletariat, possessed of nothing but its labor, liberty was hardly more than an illusion. Smith himself, though persuaded that in a "majority of cases" the general interest was properly served by the seeking of private interest, nevertheless admitted that in bargaining power labor was distinctly at a disadvantage. But Smith's teachings were meant to apply to the production of wealth and not to its distribution. The kernel of his scheme was the principle of free competition. He leveled, of course, his chief attack upon mercantilism, especially the old colonial system, which, as we have noted, was breaking down under the stress of world events as well as theories. But laissez-faire, as we have indicated, included two things: freedom from interference in the economic-commercial sphere, the complete fulfillment of which would be "free trade," and freedom of interference in the social-industrial sphere, the enjoyment of which would allow the capitalist to hire his labor as he chose without any check from above or from below.

Aspects of Laissez-Faire

(1) Economic (a) in England

The weakening of mercantilism was apparent in the eighteenth century, if not before. Capitalism had outgrown it, and the steady decline of the gilds in England and France had been the proof— quite apart from the contributive influence of laissez-faire. In 1786 William Pitt, under the influence of Adam Smith, had negotiated a commercial treaty with France, opening wide the French market for British manufactured goods, with the result of trebling the export trade with France for the next few years. Though he was not successful in achieving free trade with Ireland, it is probable that his policy would have continued but for the long struggle with France which followed in the train of the French Revolution. This struggle, as we have seen, led to a reaction in favor of tariffs and prohibitions. But after the war was over the drift toward free trade was soon resumed, chiefly under the leadership of James Huskisson and (later) Sir Robert Peel. Several factors were contributive to this trend. Many British industries, having come to acquire a fairly secure pre-eminence in the world market, needed no further protection, and the manufacturing interests were anxious for a freer inflow of raw materials. It was at the same time believed that cheaper food would reconcile the workers to low wages (let the landed elements bear the burden of relief by losing the tariff on their wheat), and, besides, would give industry a chance to balance its exports by food and raw materials from foreign countries. Curiously enough, it was under the Tories, the party of the landed aristocracy that the old economic system received its death-blows, though it was to mean a greatly reduced price for wheat and the additional burden of the income tax to take the place of the customs. Perhaps the full import of the movement was not at first foreseen. At the instance of Huskisson not only were several prohibitions removed and duties reduced but reciprocity treaties were concluded with foreign powers, allowing them a share in the colonial trade, thus virtually suspending the Navigation Acts. When Peel became premier (for the second time) in 1841, he was persuaded to sweep away a number of duties, making up for any immediate loss of revenue by substituting an income tax.[1] Meanwhile, as has been elsewhere noted, a bitter fight was being waged by two manufacturers, Richard Cobden and John Bright, against the Corn Laws, which still gave protection, "amounting to prohibition," to the home-grown wheat. As the Whigs, then in opposition, seemed to be favoring abolition, and under the influence of the Irish famine of 1845–6,[2] Peel carried through the repeal of these famous laws, and foreign wheat was admitted free. Three years later (1849) the Navigation Acts were repealed. More and more it had come to be regarded as a veritable axiom that free trade was to the best interest of Great Britain, since in becoming an industrial nation, it behooved her to look outside for the bulk of her food, and that by buying food from the Continent and colonial areas, she would be able in exchange to find an increasing market for her manufactures. Such became the position of the middle class, and, but for a few insignificant duties (preserved for revenue only), Great Britain committed herself to free trade. Thanks to being the pioneer in a machine economy and to the adoption of free trade, Great Britain became the workshop of the world, and her marvelous commercial supremacy was not only practically unchallenged for half a century but never till recent days has been seriously threatened.

Progress on the Continent toward free trade was much slower. It is true that in France internal tariffs disappeared with the

---

[1] Not ordinarily employed in England except in time of war. It now, however, became permanent. What the landed element was to lose through the liberation of wheat was made up to them as consumers through the reduced cost of living resulting from the adoption of free trade.

[2] Page 563.

Revolution (before that England was the only country blessed with internal free trade); it is also true that the gilds had lost their monopoly, as we have seen, and that competition was freer than ever before; but during the war with England mercantilism came back in all its glory, and Napoleon carried it so far as to try to close the whole of the Continent to British trade. Moreover, even within the immense zone under his sway, he sought a favored position for French goods, and, though not completely successful, he was able by tariff juggling to get a virtual monopoly of the Italian market. With Napoleon's fall was ended the struggle for economic conquest, and commercial policy followed less grandiose objects. But France, as well as the rest of the Continent, felt the need of many things, especially machinery, that the British alone could supply. Under the influence of such facts as well as the doctrine of laissez-faire France definitely changed her policy, and by a treaty of 1860 the tariffs on British goods were materially lowered. More than that, the policy led other countries to follow suit. If France's Continental neighbors were to compete with British goods in the French market, it was obviously impossible to do so unless they entered into similar agreements with France. Gradually, too, restrictions on shipping disappeared, and larger economic units were created, as tariff barriers were leveled between Russia and Poland, Austria and Hungary, Sweden and Norway, Wallachia and Moldavia, and also between most of the German states (the Zollverein). Primarily, no doubt, Great Britain's change of policy was responsible for this movement; yet it was France that was still looked up to as Europe's leading power, and it was France (under Napoleon III) who directly inspired this transformation. In general, the result of the leveling of tariff walls was a great expansion of trade, apparently justifying Smith's statement that no one is the loser by free exchanges and that on the contrary everyone gains. Prices were naturally lowered during this period, but any slight margin of loss to the manufacturer was more than made up by his gain as a consumer. But for the Franco-Prussian War, which brought into being a united Germany, on an intense wave of nationalism, it is not improbable that the trend of Europe toward free trade would have continued. In any event, commercial relations were much more the subject of bargain than had been the case a century ago, and the most-favored-nation clause (meaning that a power obtaining it had the same tariffs to meet as other nations) became a conventional practice in making commercial treaties between nations.

If laissez-faire, as applied in commerce, brought much material good to the consumer, such gains were more than offset for the working class by the way in which it operated in the sphere of industry. To secure their labor as cheaply as possible and to squeeze out of it all that it would bear was for manufacturers a sacred privilege. Labor was seemingly devoid of a human aspect; it was viewed simply as a commodity, in the same sense as machinery or raw material. It was partly this view which forbade the workers to organize in their interests; in the economic world they had no human rights—save the very inadequate right of selling their labor in the open market. For some time it was generally believed that the working class could never hope to better its condition. The clerical scholar, Malthus, urged that growth of population would proportionately limit the supply of available food, and the economist, Ricardo, held that all such growth, caused by a rise in wages during better times, would result in a superfluity of workers and a consequent lowering of wages—a view that was known as the "iron law of wages." There was even a feeling that work, however hard, was good discipline, and perhaps intended by Providence. Such was part of the moral background of laissez-faire, or economic individualism. Actually it was the power of the strong over the weak—which had its counterpart in the right of the majority to tyrannize over the minority in a democratic society. How could it be expected that a state so controlled would ever intervene?

The beginnings of State intervention for the relief of the working classes may be ascribed to two main causes. In the first place, there was some fear after the outbreak of war with Revolutionary France that unemployment as well as the increased cost of food and the existence of certain workers' organizations (there had already been some riots) might produce an epidemic of sedition. It was for this reason that the Poor Laws were revised. Even earlier than the Revolutionary crisis, that is, in 1782, an act of parliament had compelled parishes to find work on the farms for all able-bodied paupers, the workhouse being reserved for cripples and children. Another act, in 1793, forbade a parish to send a laborer back to his home parish unless he were plainly without any means of subsistence. A few years later, after some food riots, the principle

(2) Social

(a) The workers under laissez-faire

(b) Beginnings of State intervention

was generally adopted that all persons were entitled to a minimum
amount of subsistence and that the parish must, if necessary, supplement their wages—a laudable reform in principle but unfortunate, as it turned out, in practice, since it led manufacturers
deliberately to lower wages, and thus it worked to the actual detriment of the people it was supposed to help. Doubtless these cases
of public action in the interest of the working class were only a
timid beginning. How converted England was to laissez-faire is
shown by the fact that in 1799 an act was passed against workers'
organizations—an echo, it almost seemed, of the Chapelier Law
in France, which had emanated, of course, from the same philosophy. Even the old act which had permitted justices of the peace
to regulate wages was in 1813 repealed. Whatever reforms were
enacted must be handed out spontaneously by the State.

A second cause of the beginnings of State intervention was the
development of a more humanitarian spirit, a movement which
probably emanated from eighteenth century rationalism and which
expressed itself in politics through William Wilberforce's efforts to
secure the abolition of the slave trade, as well as the interest
which began to be shown in the moral welfare of workers' children.[1]
The legislation to protect the little chimney sweep was no doubt
actuated by this philanthropic spirit, from which, incidentally,
some manufacturers themselves were not exempt. Before the end
of the century there was some notable pressure put on parliament
to enact some measures of relief,[2] and it was the elder Peel, a
factory owner, who carried through in 1802 the first factory act.
It was a really ambitious measure but was unfortunately so worded
as to be easily evaded, and the stress of the Napoleonic struggle
diverted the public attention from social reform. But it was something that the government had really taken upon itself the duty of
imparting direct social relief. At least the tyranny of laissez-faire
was beginning to be challenged.

[1] Because of interest in their moral welfare a few schools were founded by private
associations to teach them to read the Bible, to spell, and to write. In some cases
older children were utilized to assist in teaching the younger ones (the so-called
monitor system). But an effort in 1807 to get parliamentary support for two years'
free schooling for poor children definitely raised the question "whether it was
proper that education should be diffused among the lower classes," and the measure,
though passed by the commons, was rejected in the lords. Even the philanthropists
were not in favor of popular education as a means of enabling the lower classes to
raise themselves socially but only to render them less an offense to respectability
and less liable to lawlessness and sedition.

[2] An effort was made in 1795 and again in 1800 to secure a wage for farm laborers
commensurate to the price of wheat.

Yet this tendency must not be overemphasized. The closing of (c) The tightening of laissez-faire under depression the struggle with France in 1815, and with it, an end of munitioning Continental armies caused a material falling off in British exports to the Continent. The result of this lowered demand for British goods was a sharp decline of production, in consequence of which 100,000 persons were immediately thrown out of work, and at a time when an army of 400,000 had somehow to be re-absorbed into economic life. It was no wonder that labor was cheap; and recovery was so slow that only the re-employment of the unemployed could be looked upon as an advance in the general condition of the workers. From 1815 to 1840 Great Britain faced a period of depression, which, though lightening as time went on, was responsible for the conviction that nothing should be done that would lessen to any degree the cheapness of production. Thus heightening of labor costs was steadily frowned upon—the more so as competition was keen among manufacturers. While it is true that some factory reforms were passed in the 'thirties, as well as a new Poor Law (1834), allowing a pauper if he were to escape the workhouse to migrate in search of a job, the general principle remained that manufacturers were justified in seeking their own interest with a minimum of State interference. Few as yet had come to believe that the workers as such had fundamental rights.

All such problems were but slightly raised on the Continent; yet the great revolution in England did eventually cross the Channel, and we must now give attention to this widening of the movement.

The Industrial Revolution on the Continent

In France the movement toward large-scale production and a *In France* machine economy was rudely interrupted by the French Revolution. From a decade of financial disorder and economic depression no relief was found till France went back once more to autocratic government. Then it was that Napoleon, anxious above all to get the markets of the Continent away from England and to flood them as far as possible with French goods, made a determined effort to revive French industry and spared neither money nor pains to attain that end. He established technical schools; he rewarded invention; he helped out manufacturers by government loans. Though it could hardly be said that the Industrial Revolution made much progress as yet in France, Napoleon tried to introduce weaving by machinery, and many of the mechanical devices invented in England were, notwithstanding British precautions, coming gradually to be known in France. Though conquest in the economic sphere had even smaller chance than in the political, and though he did not quite restore France herself to her former prosperity, Napoleon did stage a magnificent revival. It remained to be seen whether succeeding governments would gradually build on his work, and whether a period of peace would quicken the Industrial Revolution. Progress did, in fact, take place, though it was undeniably slow. One of the greatest handicaps in France was her scarcity of coal; and it was not till the middle of the century that her largest beds (those in the northeast) were appreciably tapped. During the same period Belgium, with her large coal deposits and her much greater relative interest in manufacturing was able to show a very much greater advance. Moreover, the French, in general were wedded to small establishments run with small capital, most of the labor (chiefly for the making of luxury articles) being still done by hand; while it is also to be remembered that the overwhelming majority still got their entire living from the land. Nevertheless, during the period of the July Monarchy we can fairly say that the Industrial Revolution was making headway, and the French were beginning to make their own machines. In 1832 railway construction commenced (promoted, of course, by the government), and became noticeably rapid before the middle of the nineteenth century. No doubt the fact that the Bank of France was very liberal in supplying credit may account for some of the progress made in developing a machine economy. The rate of progress remained substantially the same under Napoleon III, and up to 1870 it was still true that France was second only to Great Britain in the export of industrial products.

In Germany   In Germany the Industrial Revolution was bound to be slow, divided as she was into so many states, some of which were very backward. Outside of Prussia and the lands which had come under Napoleonic control, the gild system died hard, and it was not till nearly the middle of the nineteenth century that capitalism began to open the way to large-scale production. Up to that time, and, indeed until well afterward, the woolen and cotton industries still depended upon hand labor, and it is to be noticed that the peasants, having lost some of their holdings when they acquired proprietary rights, clung to weaving and spinning as by-industries as long as they found it possible. Yet spinning-machines, run by power, had already come into general use, especially in Prussia, and after the notable progress of the late 'sixties (when unity was half attained) the English found in Germany a serious competitor in the cotton industry. By this time steam had come to be extensively applied in the textile industries and the factory system had fairly begun. What progress there was is chiefly to be attributed to Prussia. It was she who had instigated the forming of the Zollverein, widening the market for German goods, and she who began the process of political amalgamation—a fact which certainly accounts for the rapid development after 1866.

Though in some particulars geography was none too favorable to the Germans, it is nevertheless equally true that they rejoiced in certain important natural advantages, such as a fairly central position, a number of navigable rivers, and fairly abundant supplies of coal and iron. In the 'forties the smelting of iron by coal made notable progress, and the utilization of coal and iron, made possible by railroad construction, which brought them together, as it were, greatly contributed to the progress we have noted. Obviously the Zollverein, which leveled tariff frontiers in Germany, raised at once the question of devising better means of transportation; and just as Prussia had taken the lead in tariff reform as well as in iron-mining, smelting, and the adoption of machinery, so it was Prussian capital that built the first railway. By 1850 there were approximately 3,000 miles of railroad in Germany; and already steam-navigation had appeared on many of the rivers. Yet even though German industry could count, as in France, upon State encouragement (a contrast, of course, to laissez-faire England), one can hardly say that the Germans caught up with the French before the founding of the German Empire. It was, therefore, for reasons that we shall later consider that Germany outdistanced France after 1870 and became the leading producer on the Continent.

Outside of Belgium, France, and Germany the Continent showed *Elsewhere* still by the end of the 'sixties little manifestation of the transformation which had begun in western Europe. The Industrial Revolution reached Austria and Italy comparatively late, and Russia was almost untouched until near the end of the century.

All this work of industrial development had availed to bring new wealth to the middle class; but what of the proletariat? What of the reverse side of the picture. We have already noted conditions which violate one's notions of justice. Was there to be no redress? Was the working class to accept indefinitely the "tyranny of the machine"?

THE AWAKENING OF THE PROLETARIAT

The Setting of the Problem

By the term, "awakening of the proletariat," it must not be assumed that all members of the working class at any time accepted their hard lot as inevitable or that they showed no spirit of revolt against a system which had turned them into slaves of a machine. Even before the Industrial Revolution there was enough class consciousness among journeymen to produce occasional strikes and even the destruction of tools, though the workers were then too small a class and too ill-organized to make much impression. After the Industrial Revolution had led to more concentration of population as well as more onerous conditions, such disturbances became more frequent. In many instances cottage workers attacked machines for their pitiless competition. After the Napoleonic struggle when England suffered from a depression due to the cessation of an abnormal market (the providing of her numerous allies with munitions), an epidemic of rioting pervaded the industrial regions, and many factories were sacked or burned by men who had been thrown out of work. Yet the State's only answer was repression; and a semi-prohibitive tariff on foreign wheat, by keeping up the price of bread, only made the lot of the poorer classes more grievous. On the part of the government there was little disposition to strike at the roots of the problem.

Early signs of an awakening

The rule of the middle class

We have already examined the position of the proletariat; it was the victim of historic forces. Its insecurity and weakness were possible because the middle class was the immediate beneficiary— moral and material—of both the French and Industrial Revolutions. The Industrial Revolution had given this class the power of dictating the terms under which labor was employed, since now, more than ever, capital was king. Meanwhile, the French Revolution had emphasized the rights of the individual, but in actual application these rights had opened the way to the exceptional individual, and it was to him that the "career open to talents" afforded a wider freedom. Then, too, the principle of laissez-faire lent a certain moral strength to the rising capitalist whose fortune was being made by the Industrial Revolution and whose power was coming to be felt more and more in the sphere of politics—in

France with the accession of the July Monarchy, in Great Britain since the Reform Bill of 1832. The proletariat on the other hand, a weak minority, excluded from the suffrage and often enough ignored by public opinion, was left without security in the new order. It was not enough to possess certain theoretical political rights; with this class it was the more pressing and vital problem of subsistence. Not till later on would the moral question be raised of a fairer remuneration for the share which the workers themselves took in the spread of material comforts through the Industrial Revolution.

It was a long pull ahead, and the prime necessity was to awaken to a sense of inherent power. The idea of a class consciousness which might move the workers to unite and wage a campaign in their own interest was but gradually developed; yet it portended immense changes. In seeking to promote their cause, they grasped at various instruments.

The two main agencies employed by the proletariat were trade-unionism and political agitation, the latter being intended to develop a public opinion that would force the ruling classes to grant it the rights of suffrage, thus opening the way to remedial legislation. Such means were more characteristic of Great Britain than the Continent, since the British proletariat was much less susceptible to the appeal of social revolution, and it was in Great Britain that a public opinion was more easily generated. A third instrument, more typical of the Continent, was insurrection, and this was where socialism was able to provide both a creed and an inspiration. *The Weapons of the Proletariat*

Trade-unionism was not altogether new with the Industrial Revolution, for there had been organizations of journeymen in the old handicraft days, as we have noticed; and though in general, these had been rather crude affairs, and in England usually temporary expedients, there were some cases at least, where the masters had been obliged to yield to pressure. The fact that statutory regulation of wages (and other matters) had ceased to be enforced any longer partly accounts for the movement in England; and when in time the skilled worker came to lose his exclusive position in the labor market (as soon as the Industrial Revolution began to operate), it was clear that the old industrial order was passing while the new one as yet could furnish no security. Yet to resist exploitation in the face of the growing power of laissez-faire clearly *Trade-unionism*

(1) In England

demanded more than isolated efforts. Workers under the domestic system were certainly too dispersed to combine readily, and, not meeting in large numbers, they were unable to compare their wrongs and to arrive at common grievances. Only when the factory came to take the place of the cottage did the workers perceive the strength that lay in numbers. It was toward the end of the eighteenth century, after the Industrial Revolution had begun to complicate a situation already aggravated by the high cost of food, that one notes a rapid increase of workers' societies and even some occasional riots. This new proletarian weapon came to be considered a serious menace, especially when the principles of the French Revolution had spread abroad, and, accordingly, in 1799, was passed by the British parliament the act, already mentioned, whereby workmen were forbidden to combine for the purpose of securing higher wages or shorter hours or for putting any form of pressure upon employers. While the penalty for infraction of this law was three months' imprisonment or two months' hard labor, it was possible under an earlier law to classify a strike as a conspiracy and to impose still heavier penalties. The terms of the act of 1799 were in some respects so sweeping that two workmen could not safely discuss with each other even the conditions of their employment. Thus laissez-faire was completely triumphant; and we have only to recall that eight years earlier similar action had been taken by the Constituent Assembly in France.

As a precaution against possible sedition the act of 1799 had a basis in reason, but there had really been little danger, as represented, that the workers would have the means of extorting unreasonable conditions, for most of them belonged in the ranks of the unskilled, and their places could only too easily be filled. In spite of the law numerous trade unions continued to exist, though there were many prosecutions, and public opinion itself was not as yet on the side of the workmen. At last in 1824–5 the law of 1799 was superseded by acts which permitted combinations of workmen, though violence was still prohibited, and even a strike might still be treated as conspiracy. Under such conditions the trade union was singularly ineffective as an instrument, though its importance in promoting class solidarity cannot be ignored. Meanwhile the consumers' co-operative stores, which served their customers on a non-profit basis, were an outgrowth of the growing habit on the part of the workers to meet in groups to discuss their common interests. This consumers' co-operative movement, which had its origins in England, has been one of the sanest instruments for protecting the masses from exploitation, and its progress has been notable throughout Europe. During the 'thirties, although there were some efforts to amalgamate some of the unions and even to hold an annual congress, trade-unionism seems to have made but little progress, and the proletariat seemed rather to place its hope in political action; it was not till after the Reform Bill of 1867, which gave the great majority of workers the ballot, that trade unions in England were finally relieved of all restrictions—a fact to be noted later.

On the Continent trade-unionism was for long time less important, since the proletariat itself was much less numerous. In France "societies of resistance," as they were called, existed *sub rosa*, and perhaps because the question was not very acute the government was rather lax in enforcing the Chapelier Law.[1] Under Napoleon III, who was an avowed friend of the workers, trade-unionism was deliberately tolerated, though it was not till later that it obtained legal recognition. In Germany the strength of the gild system, not to mention the disciplinary habits of most Germans, long retarded the growth of trade-unionism, and the earliest unions in Prussia appear to have been established as late as 1868. In Germany the socialist parties came to provide the proletariat with the germs of organization, and even such unions as existed were divided along political lines. As the economist, Birnie, has said, "The connection of trade-unionism with politics has always been much closer in Germany than in other countries." For that reason, perhaps, it has been a less effective weapon in itself. *(2) On the Continent*

In England, as we have said, trade-unionism played an important rôle in the development of class consciousness. Moreover, with the extension of railways and the cheapening of the postal system more avenues of intercommunication were opened to the workers. Also it should be realized that political organizations had been formed among this class, and that an able propagandist, William Cobbett, had placed his "tuppenny" journal within its reach. Proletarian agitation had much to do with the passage of the First Reform Bill. Finally, the stupid ruthlessness with which the government had treated well-founded discontent, had whetted a spirit of resistance among the workers. When in 1819 a peaceful *Political agitation*

[1] See page 300.

demonstration had been broken up with such severity that several casualties occurred (the so-called "Peterloo Massacre"), the impression was bound to penetrate far and wide. When it became manifest that the First Reform Bill did nothing, after all, for the proletariat, political agitation renewed its vigor, and for nearly two decades the program known as "Chartism" (mentioned in the previous chapter) became the most prominent phase of the working-class movement. Economic evils, it seemed to be felt, must be met by political action. Much of the discontent which fed the movement was due to the newly enacted Poor Law of 1834, which, while it abolished the wasteful system of outdoor relief, forced all paupers into the workhouse; and it was explicitly intended that their lot should be less comfortable than that of the independent worker, lest people who could help themselves might be tempted to become public charges. The Chartist program, which included universal suffrage, annual parliaments, and the secret ballot, could hardly be labeled subversive, though Great Britain had never gone the length of France in the direction of democracy. Unfortunately for the proletariat, Chartism revealed no strong leader like William Cobbett, the man who had lent so much zest to the agitation before the Reform Bill, and by the time it had got well under way, economic distress had become much relieved. The repeal of the Corn Laws in 1846 greatly reduced the price of food; while the general adoption of free trade lowered the cost of other commodities. From the late 'forties onward through two decades and more British industry enjoyed a period of perhaps unparalleled prosperity, and partly also because capital was more easily obtained [1] and a smaller share of the earnings of an enterprise were needed for its promotion, a higher wage-scale became general. Meanwhile the granting of the ten-hour day for women and "young persons" in the textile mills (1847) seemed to show that the workers' movement was gaining ground. In the words of an eminent economist, "to the hungry 'forties succeeded the sleek and prosperous 'fifties." Perhaps it was the improved position of the workers that made certain members of parliament see the folly of excluding so large and important body from the suffrage. At any rate parliamentary reform became an issue again in the 'fifties, and, gathering force in the 'sixties, led finally in 1867 to the Second Reform Bill, granting the right of suffrage to most of the pro-

[1] Due to an act of 1858 limiting the liability of stock-holders in a company.

letariat. In the concluding years of the agitation the workers had again organized societies to press their cause, and seem to have contributed powerfully to the final outcome. Whether their economic grievances were now to be solved by the ballot was yet to be seen. But in any case the British proletariat had fully awakened, and for fifty years, with varying intensity, had carried on a class struggle. And on the whole they got more recognition than their co-workers in France had obtained by insurrection.

On the Continent social problems were much later to become acute, since the Industrial Revolution made slower headway there. *Revolution: (1) the antecedents of socialism* Nevertheless the course which the labor movement would take on the Continent was perhaps prefigured by the French Revolution. The power that could be wielded by a minority in a revolution suggested that violence might be used for social ends, while the pastime of theorizing in quest of better conditions was likely to become a habit with the disciples of the *philosophes*. Attempts to fix prices and wages during the Terror have been noted as a concession to a frenzied proletariat, but its numbers were then too small to wield an influence for very long, and its friends among the Terrorists had only the vaguest notions of social regeneration. While it is true that certain thinkers from time immemorial had preached the idea of common ownership of property, and that a few of the minor *philosophes* had espoused such doctrines, such theories had always been looked upon as Utopian and had aroused little attention. When in 1796 a young journalist of peasant extraction, François Babeuf, attempted a conspiracy with the program of pooling all profits and distributing them through a governmental agency, it was quickly and easily put down and soon forgotten. The historical importance of this episode lies chiefly in its evidence that socialistic movements were not, after all, an innovation of the nineteenth century.

It is, of course, obvious that the Industrial Revolution brought social problems into the foreground. Now that the working class *(2) Rise of socialism* were gaining in numbers if not in misery, the grounds for seeking some panacea of relief were obvious enough. While trade-unionism battled for some immediate measures of relief, certain thoughtful men were envisaging a new order. In England of the 'thirties Robert Owen, a wealthy mill-owner, proposed a system of self-sufficing communities which should work in common and share equitably the fruits of all their labors. Contemporary with Owen, the French aristocrat, St. Simon, expounded views of somewhat the same nature. The State, thought St. Simon, should assume control of production and distribution, and use its wealth as capital to be loaned to communities working on a co-operative plan. Somewhat later another Frenchman, Charles Fourier, advocated a plan similar to Owen's. He did not look to the State but rather to smaller units, in which the workers should carry on a self-sufficient existence, sharing their toil and its fruits. Fourier thought, however, that ultimately these communities might be slightly amalgamated with a directing center at Constantinople!

These earlier "socialists" (the term came to be used first in the 'twenties) are commonly known as the "Utopians"—an epithet coined at their expense by that different kind of socialist, Karl Marx. They had but a very limited influence for the simple reason that they did not organize an active propaganda and consequently did not reach the hearts of the masses themselves. It was socialism (of a sort), propounded for the people but not actually accepted or promoted by the people. The Utopians strove mainly to teach by example. Owen and Fourier founded model communities which aimed to apply their respective ideas; but most of these laboratory demonstrations of socialism were badly conducted and met with failure. All the Utopians seem to have accepted Rousseau's premise of the innate goodness of man. "All that God made is good," said Fourier. They imagined, like the rationalists, that people could change their habits completely in an instant if only proper relationships were devised. They did not perceive that society was a matter of evolution.

A more practical socialist and a sort of transitional figure between the Utopians and Marx was the Frenchman, Louis Blanc, an aristocrat by birth and of slender resources, but distinguished by the brilliancy of his writings. Blanc was somewhat like the Utopians in expecting great things to be achieved in a relatively short time and he had like St. Simon the quixotic notion that everyone should be remunerated according to his needs ("From each according to his ability, to each according to his needs"), but he was more practical than the Utopians in that he was ready to use existing machinery to put his ideas into effect and he urged the importance of putting the State on a democratic basis in order to give it the moral right to supervise production. He proposed that national workshops should be established and endowed by the State, and the competition offered by such establishments, he believed, would ultimately bring to an end all private enterprise. At first the State itself should appoint the persons to direct each shop, but ultimately, after individual capacities were better known, the directors should be chosen only by the body of workers concerned. This idea of small self-governing industrial units (Blanc would have allied trades, like masons, carpenters, etc., in the same shop) lay at the basis of a movement (later to be examined) known as syndicalism. But insofar as Blanc would have the democratic state put its financial power behind the business of production, it was only one more step to make the public authority directly operate industry.

Little by little these earlier socialists were building up the philosophy or creed now known as "socialism." Socialism signifies the conduct of all the processes of production and distribution by society itself organized on a democratic basis. It would abolish all private capital and all private ownership of land. There would theoretically be an end of all exploitation of man by man, since every man would be a wage-earner and thus a member of the proletariat. It does not necessarily mean the elimination of all private property or the leveling of all individuals to the same wage, though some socialists have advanced these propositions. Generally speaking, it recognizes differences in capacity and would reward then accordingly, but it places the main emphasis upon service. "Genius," said Louis Blanc, "shall assert its legitimate empire not by the amount of tribute which it shall levy on society but by the greatness of the services it will render."

As an agitator Louis Blanc had much to do with bringing about the Revolution of 1848. His work, *The History of Ten Years*, was a scathing indictment of the July Monarchy, while his principle of the "right to work"—the right of everyone to expect the State to guarantee him employment—became a watchword of the proletariat of France. In the Revolution of 1830, which overthrew the restored Bourbon régime, the Paris workers had actually furnished the violence that had made the revolution possible. But in the eyes of the bourgeoisie, who quickly got control of the movement, they were something like a "jack-in-the-box," produced to scare the Bourbons out of power, but to be put out of sight as soon as the crisis was over. Indeed the July Monarchy came to be the government of the richer bourgeoisie, and from such a régime, operating

(3) Attempt at social revolution

as it did on the principle of laissez-faire, no amelioration of working-class conditions could be expected. It is true that the situation of the workers was not so bad as in England, and French scholars affirm that it was rather less terrible in France than it had been before the French Revolution. But the normal working day was fifteen hours; wages had failed to keep up with prices; and there were the familiar evils of congestion and unsanitary quarters. In September, 1830, there was some rioting in Paris and destruction of machinery; but it was in the silk mills of Lyons that conditions were probably worst. There men toiled for eighteen hours (some for as little as a sou an hour), and it is not to be wondered that they were driven by desperation to methods of violence. In 1831 efforts of the prefect to bring about a rise in wages foundered on the opposition of the manufacturers who were suffering from the depression which had followed the Revolution of 1830 as well as from foreign competition. When the government intervened to reprimand the prefect, a serious riot broke out, which was quelled with much difficulty and bloodshed. Three years later an attempt to reduce wages in the silk industry led to a general strike, which forced the manufacturers to recede; but many of the workers, infected by socialist doctrines, attempted a revolution with the slogan, "Live working or die fighting," and many of them did die; but the movement (more formidable than that of 1831) was savagely repressed. In general (for these strikes were only the most conspicuous among a great many at this time) manufacturers were able to break the force of resistance by utilizing more labor-saving devices. Yet class consciousness among the proletariat was certainly becoming aroused (in Paris and Lyons the workers were forming political organizations), and when Blanc talked as though the workers had some rights that society itself should recognize, there was inspiration enough to gather together the rudiments of a party, which was prepared, indeed, to assert itself if ever the time came. In 1848 at last struck the hour of revolution. We have elsewhere mentioned the overthrow of the July Monarchy. An economic crisis, which had thrown large numbers of men out of employment while it raised the cost of living to a prodigious height, roused a section of the working class of Paris (led, it appears by printers' employees and certain intellectuals) to join with some of the middle class in ending the July Monarchy, and it was hardly strange if they remembered Blanc's doctrine of the "right to work." True, when it came to giving shape to the new régime, it was an element of the bourgeoisie that took command. But the socialists were not so easily put aside. They demanded and received representation in the provisional government. In contradistinction to the moderates, like Lamartine, who wished to regard the existing régime as provisional until France had definitely spoken through an assembly, the socialists wanted to commit the nation at once to a socialist republic.

It was now that Blanc's opportunity seemed to have come. He was a member of the provisional government, and it was recognized that he had the masses behind him. Though it is true that he was unable to persuade his colleagues to set up a ministry of labor, he was for the time being mollified by the creation of a commission to study social questions and to make recommendations. This commission, which swelled in numbers until it was really an assembly, was composed for the most part of socialists, and proceeded to recommend certain reforms such as the eight-hour day and the minimum wage. As a labor parliament it took its duties very seriously and some of its proposals bore temporary fruit. Meanwhile national workshops had been opened, and throngs of the unemployed or underpaid gathered to reap the benefit of the new doctrine, the "right to work." Was Blanc to realize his dream?

No, it seems abundantly clear that the moderate element—these men of the middle class—had never proposed to allow any actual trend toward a socialist republic. They intended to provide work but only in order to keep the workers out of mischief and only so long as they might possibly prove dangerous. Instead of allowing Blanc to carry out his plan systematically, they provided essentially unproductive work such as digging up the streets. Blanc even believed that they were striving actually to wean away the workers from the cause which they had espoused. There is little doubt that the workshops as constituted were intended to discredit Blanc and socialism as well. "The real truth," he wrote, "is that they were created for no other purpose than that of placing at the orders of the official adversaries of socialism an army, which, if necessary, they might oppose to it." The fact that men received a franc a day even when there was no work (and there were soon more workers than work) had the natural result of weakening their energies. The additional fact that they were drawn from the industries to which they were accustomed and set to work with a pick was especially absurd in Blanc's eyes; and it is no wonder that he called the national workshops a "rabble of paupers" and a "premium upon idleness." His well-reasoned plans had sunk to a policy of dissipating the public funds as a matter of political tactics.

But, in any event, the innate weakness of the socialist movement was that it did not represent France. When the government found it necessary to raise taxes and when it became clear that the number of unemployed was increasing, due to the industrial depression which had followed the Revolution, it was too much to expect the people of the provinces to approve a system which meant the squandering of their money in public doles. Since universal suffrage had been declared, the nation had its weapon. Though the socialists had managed to have the elections to the Constituent Assembly postponed for some weeks, the final results of the balloting were no less eloquent of public sentiment. By an overwhelming vote France repudiated socialism. Blanc, in order to save something from the wreck, insisted that he did not propose that the State should confiscate all industries but that it "should intervene between the weak and the strong to protect the weak"— a fair enunciation of the idea of the "social state," which we shall see adopted by the capitalists themselves. But he and his party knew that they were fast losing ground, and some popular demonstrations did not help them. Finally the government felt sufficiently encouraged to take the offensive. The labor parliament perished; the national workshops were closed. Driven to despair, the socialists precipitated some bloody street riots in Paris—the famous "June Days"—which were sternly repressed. The idea of a socialist republic was plainly a chimera.

Thus insurrection had failed as a weapon of the proletariat. It was tried again in 1871 during the dark days of the Franco-Prussian War when the famous "Commune" occurred—an insurrection in which socialism reared its head again, but which failed even more disastrously than the movement which had been inspired by Louis Blanc. The idea of creating a new order by violence seemed futile. Socialism, availing itself of universal suffrage, was soon to enter politics, and the proletariat in France was to resort only to the violence that became associated with syndicalism—which was not insurrection. Yet the Revolution of 1848 had undoubtedly contributed to the awakening of the proletariat. Of even greater significance were the personality and teachings of a new leader, Karl Marx.

KARL MARX AND A WORLD CREED FOR THE PROLETARIAT

Karl Marx was a German Jew whose parents had been converted to the Christian religion. He studied law at two German universities but found that his tastes lay rather in philosophy and history, and he gleaned much inspiration from the German philosopher, Hegel, who conceived of history as a struggle between opposing elements leading to constant change. Debarred from holding a professorship because his advanced ideas incurred the suspicion of the Prussian government, he launched into a career as a journalist. Marx was a born agitator, and when by reading and reflection he had converted himself to socialism, he consecrated himself to the service of the proletariat. Since his editorial career had been shipwrecked on the government's dislike of his views (for caution was not in his make-up), and since he felt that he must know more of the social philosophy of his time, he resolved to go to Paris to study socialism at its source. It was the natural impulse of a scholar. Marx was a profound thinker, though not of the cloistered type; he was essentially a man of action. Dogmatic, overbearing, sometimes bitterly unjust, he nevertheless enjoyed immense respect and often devotion from his followers, who looked upon him as one inspired. Though irrascible at times (often due, no doubt, to poverty and overwork), he was naturally kind-hearted and affectionate, patient under a life of extraordinary hardship, and unswerving in his devotion to his ideals. Once when his poverty was extreme he was given an opportunity of bettering his fortunes by editing a journal that demanded conservative views, but self-respect would never allow him to bargain with his principles.

Character and training of Marx

It was when Marx went to Paris in 1843 that he began his long and fruitful exile. There he met the French socialists and no doubt both gave and received much useful inspiration.[1] Expelled from France by the action of the government at the instance of Prussia, he then went to Brussels, where with the aid of a friend of similar views, Friedrich Engels, he helped to promote the Communist

Assumption of leadership of the proletariat

---

[1] Dr. Shadwell attributes to one of the early French socialists, Pierre Leroux, Marx's division of society into bourgeoisie and proletariat, though Leroux had not gone so far as to preach class war.

League, made up largely of English socialists, to work by voice and pen for the overthrow of capitalism. In London in 1847 he produced in collaboration with Engels his famous work, *The Communist Manifesto*, which has been called "both a firebrand and a formulary." This work, as an eminent scholar, Harold Laski, has pointed out, "gave direction and philosophy to what had been before little more than an inchoate protest against injustice . . . It destroyed at a stroke both the belief that socialism could triumph without long preparation, and the hope that any form of economic organization was possible save that which was implicit in the facts of the time." It has often been pointed out that Marx's ideas were not original, but at least he presented a synthesis of various and sundry views which, taken together, might form a platform for the proletariat. *The Communist Manifesto* was his own exposition of socialism as well as an exhortation to all workers throughout the world to enroll under its banner. He preferred the term, "communist" to "socialist," since the Utopians had called themselves "socialists," and Marx had a different scheme in mind for the proletariat. In 1867 his more famous work, *Capital*, appeared—a scathing indictment of the economic order, but a rather ponderous work, which had less immediate influence than *The Communist Manifesto*. Marx spent most of the remainder of his life in London where he passed his time in study and writing until his death in 1883.

Ideas and importance

The importance of Marx lies not so much in his theories as in his inspiration. Many of his ideas are now considered to be untenable. His doctrine of surplus value, according to which the true value of a commodity, is measured by the amount and character of labor expended on it and the amount of labor over and above what was actually paid for in the form of wages was that "surplus value" representing exploitation by the capitalist, quite ignores the fact that commodities being of unlike utility (and the market demand must settle that point), labor cannot be the sole standard of value. His materialistic conception of history, according to which all changes have proceeded from economic causes, is also to be questioned, for, though the economic factors in history had certainly been insufficiently appreciated, man is too much a victim of his emotions to be actuated by only practical considerations. Finally, Marx was a faulty prophet in that he predicted that the rich would become richer and the poor, poorer, until the gulf would

become so wide that the very few wealthy capitalists at the top of
the social structure would no longer be able to stand against the
pressure of the multitude, and then would emerge quite naturally
a proletarian world. It is obvious that the proletariat has not

Photograph by Mayall, London

KARL MARX

become progressively impoverished, and that while concentration
of wealth in a few hands has been a steady tendency, the small
shop-keeper has still hung on with amazing vigor and, as far as the
peasantry is concerned, the whole trend in most countries has been
toward landownership. Marx himself admitted that the peasantry

was a tough problem, for their sturdy individualism has usually been harder to bend in the direction of socialism than even the benighted middle class itself.

But insofar as Marx predicted socialism as inevitable, he gave the proletariat something to hope for—a goal which it must ever keep in sight. Not that he felt that man should wait patiently for what this realistic fatalism ordained. The end should be hastened by proletarian effort. In contrast to the easy optimism of the Utopians Marx was almost a pessimist, for he believed that man would only gradually become regenerated. Unlike the Utopians also, he believed that the working class must win its own redemption. To arrive at better conditions, to reach the various milestones on the road to socialism, the workers must wage an unending conflict. This doctrine of the class struggle—a struggle which he traced through all history—was the feature of Marx's teachings that has most influenced his followers. It is the truer side of the practical or "scientific" socialism which he claimed to teach.

But Marx not only furnished the proletariat with inspiration and a working creed. He made socialism an international movement. "Workingmen of all countries, unite!" he had exclaimed in *The Communist Manifesto*. "The proletarians have nothing to lose but their chains, and a world to gain." True to his own conception of socialism as a class movement, having no regard for national lines, Marx became the guiding spirit of that organization known as the "International," formally inaugurated in 1864. Congresses were to be held from time to time, to which workers of all nations were to send representatives, and which should review the position of the proletariat and formulate platforms of reform. For various reasons the International met with no lasting success. A group of extreme individualists, known as anarchists, who wanted no authority in political or social affairs, created much discord until, discountenanced by Marx, they seceded from the organization. Then the English workers were much more interested in trade-unionism as a weapon than in a movement looking toward revolution. We know, too, that Marx was not always just in his estimate of men, and, always inclined to be dogmatic, he lacked the suppleness of a skillful political leader. Finally, national lines were still too sharp to be bridged by an international movement. French and German socialists were arrayed against each other in the Franco-Prussian War, and it became also increasingly difficult for workers in different countries to agree on program and methods. Marx himself had failed to foresee the tremendous power of revivified nationalism, which had the effect of sharpening national, in contradistinction to class, lines, and herding the workers themselves under its banner. Nevertheless, the idea that the proletariat belongs to a world movement and thereby subscribes to a uniform creed gained undoubtedly some momentum through the career of the International. The revival of the institution in 1889,[1] though in a limited form, attested to the strength of the idea.

It was on the question of how to interpret the class struggle that socialists have been divided ever since. Marx did not altogether eschew methods of violence; in *The Communist Manifesto* he (or Engels) wrote of a "forceable overthrow of all existing social conditions"; and once, toward the close of his life, he seemed to favor the "dictatorship of the proletariat." [2] Yet where practicable Marx seems to have preferred more peaceful methods, such as obtaining social reforms through parliamentary action. It was because he had satisfied himself after the mid-century upheaval that revolution as a weapon was premature that he had broken with the Communist League. Many wars must be fought, he admitted, and many changes occur before the proletariat was fitted for domination. Pressure in parliament upon the bourgeoisie might, indeed, have been construed as a mild form of the "class war." Late in life his friend, Engels, acknowledged that he and Marx had expected the "revolution" to come much sooner than it was likely to occur. "The fighting methods of 1848 are today [1895] obsolete in every respect." The prodigious development of capitalism since then had shown, he felt, its great expansive capacity, and he believed that the proletariat should place its main reliance on political action. It was in following such a view that socialism became a force in European politics.

It is, indeed, an evidence of the influence of Marx that socialist parties were rapidly formed in several countries, for now the workers knew that their movement was their own. Yet it soon became apparent that socialists could differ even violently on precepts and methods. The chief cleavage was usually one of method. There

A divided following

---

[1] This has been called the Second International.

[2] In 1875 Marx went so far as to assert that it might be necessary for the proletariat to seize power in order to effect the transition from capitalism to socialism. He had also defended the Commune, but it is also important to remember that he tried to prevent it.

were the moderates (sometimes called the "revisionists" because they dissented from some of Marx's opinions) who, in view of the fact that the inevitable goal was evidently very remote, emphasized the need of working for present reforms. This element was quite ready to work with the middle class and secure whatever compromises it could. It also regarded democracy as an absolute prerequisite to socialism. As opposed to these opportunists, however, there were various groups who took the class war more seriously and who were anxious to hasten by violence the dictatorship of the proletariat, no matter how small its numbers. In France the syndicalists were anxious by strikes, particularly a general strike, to force the existing order to capitulate. In Germany the revolutionary element was too German to be very violent in its methods, but in Russia there were forces which ultimately produced a social revolution and a type of social order of which Marx would probably have approved.

It was long before socialism came to exert an influence in politics or to lead the workers to class war that a measure of relief came to the proletariat—at least in England. This relief came, indeed, rather from above than from below. And it involved a changing conception of the State.

THE EMERGENCE OF THE SOCIAL STATE

The democratic or liberal state, coming to mean as it did Rousseau's rule of the majority, and usually in the interest of that majority, was no solution for the wrongs of a class which constituted the minority; and in the first half of the nineteenth century it was not even democratic to that extent. Moreover, the analogue of democracy in the economic world, the principle of laissez-faire, placed the working class at the mercy of the few who controlled business and who protected their own interests through governments and parliaments. Nevertheless scholars had begun to wonder if the boasted theory of laissez-faire had not some practical limitations. Gradually in England a public opinion came to be roused against the evils of the factory system. The act of 1802 had been, as we have seen, a deliberate action on the part of the State to challenge the brutal ascendancy of laissez-faire. This hopeful experiment, suspended during the second war with Napoleon, was revived immediately afterward, and in 1816 a parliamentary committee investigated the conditions of child labor. The result was the prohibition (in 1819) of the employment of children below nine in the cotton mills and the limiting of the employment of children between nine and sixteen to twelve hours a day. It was only a question of time when this salutary reform would be extended to other industries.

No doubt the publicity given the committee's report had something to do with creating a public opinion sympathetic with the working class. It cannot be said that trade-unionism had much to do with provoking these concessions. The humanity of certain Englishmen had been touched when they learned of the real facts, and though there was opposition from many of the factory owners,[1] the unremitting zeal of a young nobleman, Lord Ashley, afterwards Earl of Shaftesbury, was gradually able to wear down all resistance. Perhaps also the philosophy of Bentham, who had long ago stressed the greatest happiness of the greatest number, and of John Stuart Mill, who denounced the idea of laissez-faire as holding the capital wealth of a country more important than its just distribution had something to do with the success of these reformers. Then, too, the movement to abolish slavery in the colonies had led to the repeated assertion that there was a slavery in the mills and factories of England far worse than anything in the colonies. Little by little the hours of child workers were further reduced and the minimum age still further raised. Of special importance, moreover, was the appointment of government inspectors (by the Factory Act of 1833) which for the first time made factory reform really effective. Later the range of this protective legislation was made to include the mines, the employment of women and children underground being strictly prohibited by parliament in 1842. In the meantime, not only were factory owners compelled to take reasonable precautions against accidents to their workmen and provide more sanitary conditions in their factories [2] but some provision was also made for the education of working children. In 1847 after a long struggle the ten-hour day for the textile mills was adopted for all women and "young persons." Though adult men were not brought under the benefits of this

---

[1] Some of the factory-owners, however, were so anxious to obtain *entrée* into the best society that they were moved to end the scandal of having factories where humanity was so degraded.

[2] The importance of the establishment of a board of health in 1842 and the subsequent adoption of a drainage system (product of sanitary engineering) had a great deal to do with safeguarding the health of the factory workers. For the first time it became possible to live in crowded cities without jeopardizing one's health.

act, the effect was practically to standardize the English working day.

We have, in fact, the emergence of what may be called, for lack of a better term, the "social state."[1] England, where conditions had been worst, was now well on the road toward an enlightened attitude toward social problems and setting an example to other countries. The peculiar nature of the existing economic order required the direct interference of the State for the better protection of the working class. Partly it was a matter of social justice. Partly and perhaps mainly it was a recognition, born of fear, that the proletariat, already resorting to agitation, was beginning to become aware of its inherent power.[2] But partly also it proceeded from the practical view that the proper safeguarding of the working capacity of the workers would redound to the advantage of society as a whole. In a sense it was a reversion to the seventeenth century system of an authoritative state actively functioning in economic affairs. But the end was now more social than economic in that the State deliberately reached down to the masses.

Yet one must guard against the impression that laissez-faire was at an end, or that the social state was more than in its vague beginnings, even in England, during the greater part of the century. On the Continent, where industrialization proceeded at a slower pace, it was not till long after the middle of the century that social reforms were definitely inaugurated. But under Bismarck, as we shall see, the social state emerged in clear relief, and came to win in Europe general acceptance. Such measures by no means realized all the ideals of the proletariat. But the new policy of the State, controlled as it was by the landed or capitalistic elements, represented a new and interesting concession to the claims of that class which had borne the brunt of the Industrial Revolution. In a sense the nineteenth century is a long and painful period of adjustment, and the process has not yet arrived at anything like completion.

FOR FURTHER READING OR STUDY

Robinson, J. H., and Beard, C. A., *Readings in Modern European History*, vol. ii, chaps. xviii, xxvi (*passim*) and sec. 1909 (no. 394 is an extract from *The Communist Manifesto*); Cheyney, E. P., *Readings in English History*,

---

[1] The term has been coined by Professor Schapiro in his *Modern and Contemporary European History*. "Welfare state" has also been suggested.

[2] But for the concessions which had been made England too might have had a taste of revolution during 1848.

chap. xviii, sec. 2; Bland, B. E., Brown, M. A., and Tawney, R. H., *English Economic History: Select Documents*, secs. iii (factory reforms), iv (trade-unionism), and v (poor relief); Ryazanoff, D., *Karl Marx* (containing impressions of contemporaries).

Hayes, C. J. H., *A Political and Social History of Modern Europe*, vol. ii, pp. 100–23, 214–9, 252–71; Higby, C. P., *A History of Modern Europe*, chaps. iv and viii, secs. 1 and 6; Schapiro, J. S., *Modern and Contemporary European History*, chaps. iii, ix (*passim*), and xxviii; Gillespie, J. E., *A History of Europe, 1500–1815*, pp. 469–73; Palm, F. C., and Graham, F. E., *Europe since Napoleon*, chap. xvi (rise of the proletariat); Fueter, E., *World History, 1815–1920*, chaps. iii, xxi, and xxiii; Ogg, F. A., *Economic Development of Modern Europe*, parts i–iii; Day, C., *Economic Development in Modern Europe*, chaps. i–ii, (for England); Flick, A. C., *World History, 1776–1926*, esp. chaps. ix and xii; Lunt, W. E., *History of England*, chaps. xxxi and xxxiv (*passim*); Cross, A. L., *A Shorter History of England and Greater Britain*, chap. xliv; Barnes, H. E., *World Politics in Modern Civilization*, pp. 93–8, 119–22 (free trade); Birnie, A., *An Economic History of Europe* (unusually readable).

Dietz, F. C., *The Industrial Revolution* (brief sketch); Knowles, L. C. A., *The Industrial and Commercial Revolutions in Great Britain in the Nineteenth Century* and *Economic Development in the Nineteenth Century* (admirably clear and informing); Clapham, J. H., *An Economic History of Modern Britain*, 2 vols. (begins at 1815) and *The Economic Development of France and Germany* (*passim*); Cheyney, E. P., *An Introduction to the Industrial and Social History of England*, chap. viii (good elementary survey); Usher, A. L., *The Industrial History of England* (good); Slater, G., *The Making of Modern England* (chiefly social); Moffit, L. W., *England on the Eve of the Industrial Revolution;* Mantoux, P., *The Industrial Revolution in the Eighteenth Century* (standard work for the Industrial Revolution in England); George, M. D., *England in Transition* (interesting on social changes); Duer, M. C., *Health, Wealth, and Population in the Early Days of the Industrial Revolution;* White, L. W., and Shanahan, E. W., *The Industrial Revolution and the Modern World Today* (short and readable), part i; Mumford, L., *Technics and Civilization* (a challenging book); Hammond, J. L., and B., *The Skilled Laborer, The Town Laborer, The Rise of Modern Industry*, and *Lord Shaftesbury* (delightfully written works); Lord, J., *Capitalism and Steam Power;* Ashton, T. S., *Iron and Steel in the Industrial Revolution;* Kirkaldy, A. W., and Evans, A. D., *The History and Economics of Transport;* Randall, J. H., *The Making of the Modern Mind*, chap. xvii; Gide, C., and Rist, C., *A History of Economic Doctrines;* Fay, C. R., *Great Britain from Adam Smith to the Present Day* and *Corn Laws and Social England* (both informing but rather dull); Morley, J., *Life of Richard Cobden;* Dunham, A. L., *The Anglo-French History of Commerce of 1860 and the Progress of the Industrial Revolution in France* (a scholarly monograph); Cole, G. D. H., *A Short History of the British Working Class Movement*, vol. i, and *Life of William Cobbett;* Shadwell, A., *The Socialist Movement, 1824–1924*, vol. i; Marriott, J. A. R., *The Revolution of 1848 in its Economic Aspects;* Markham, S. F., *A History of Socialism* (popular); Sombart, W., *Socialism and the Social Movement* (good); Laidler, H. T., *A History of Socialist Thought* (useful though rather dull); Hearnshaw, F. J. C., *A Study of Socialism, Historical, Analytical, and Critical;* Bernstein, E.,

Revolutionary Socialism (by a revisionist); Skelton, O. D., *Socialism, a Critical Analysis;* Salter, F. R., *Karl Marx and Modern Socialism* (unsympathetic); Ruehle, O., *Karl Marx* (sympathetic and semi-popular); Stekloff, G. M., *History of the First International;* Orth, S. D., *Socialism and Democracy in Europe;* Hayes, C. J. H., "The History of German Socialism Reconsidered,"*Amer. Hist. Rev.*, xxiii, 62 ff.; Estey, J. A., *Revolutionary Syndicalism;* Dobb, M., *Business Enterprise and Social Reform;* Hutchins, B. L., and Harrison, A., *A History of Factory Legislation;* Webb, S., and B., *English Poor Law Policy.*

XIII. THE GREAT NATIONALIST UPHEAVAL— THE REMAKING OF CENTRAL EUROPE

1. NAPOLEON III AND THE PRINCIPLE OF NATIONALITY

A. CHARACTER AND ORGANIZATION OF THE SECOND EMPIRE

Character and position of Napoleon III; General character of the empire; Internal aspects of the empire: (1) political, (2) economic and social; External aspects of the empire.

B. THE CRIMEAN WAR AND THE MAKING OF ROUMANIA

Genesis of the war; Course of the war; The Treaty of Paris and the zenith of the Second Empire; The Treaty of Paris and Rouman nationalism; Crisis of 1857; Triumph of Rouman nationalism; Reorganization of "Roumania"; Later triumphs of nationalism in the Balkans—the Treaty of Berlin.

2. THE MAKING OF A NEW ITALY

A. PRELIMINARIES AND PREPARATIONS—THE LEADERSHIP OF SARDINIA

Italy in decay and disruption; Influence of the French Revolution and Napoleon; Agencies of revolution—the work of Mazzini; Uprising of 1848 and its failure; Hegemony of Sardinia.

B. CAVOUR AND THE LEADERSHIP OF SARDINIA

Cavour's qualifications and leadership; Preparatory phase of Cavour's policy: (1) internal, (2) external.

C. CAVOUR AND THE INTERVENTION OF NAPOLEON III—THE WAR OF INDEPENDENCE

Question of French aid; The Pact of Plombières; The War of Independence; Napoleon's defection.

D. THE ITALIAN REVOLUTION AND THE CONSUMMATION OF ITALIAN UNITY

Italy in revolution; Cession of Savoy and Nice and winning of central Italy; Conquest of the Two Sicilies; The Roman crisis and the conquest of central Italy; Popular aspect of Italian unity; Establishment of the kingdom of Italy; Completion of Italian unity; Comparison of the movements in Italy and Germany.

3. THE MAKING OF A NEW GERMANY

A. PRELIMINARIES—THE QUESTION OF PRUSSIA'S LEADERSHIP

Rise of German nationalism in the War of Liberation; The economic factor—the Zollverein; Moral factors—growth of democracy and nationalism and the episode of the Frankfort Parliament; Question of Prussia's fitness for leadership: (1) moral, (2) material.

453

B. BISMARCK AND PRUSSIA'S LEADERSHIP—THE PREPARATORY PHASE OF HIS
   POLICY

   Qualifications and methods of Bismarck; Bismarck's fundamental policy;
   Sharpening of his weapon.

C. BISMARCK *vs.* AUSTRIA—THE SEVEN WEEKS' WAR

   The Schleswig-Holstein question and the war with Denmark; Bismarck's
   preparations for war: (1) the sounding of Napoleon, (2) the alliance with
   Italy, (3) the question of a *casus belli;* The Seven Weeks' War; Bismarck's
   moderation and its causes; Results of the war—the North German Confederation; The duping of France and the conciliation of the south German
   states.

D. BISMARCK *vs.* FRANCE—THE FRANCO-PRUSSIAN WAR AND THE COMPLETION
   OF GERMAN UNITY

   Causes of the Franco-Prussian War: (1) the psychology of the Second
   Empire, (2) Bismarck's policy—the Hohenzollern intrigue; France's unreadiness for war; The Franco-Prussian War; Results of the war—the
   establishment of the German Empire.

4. THE MAKING OF AUSTRIA-HUNGARY

A. THE EVOLUTION OF THE DUAL MONARCHY

   Rôle of Deák; Austria's change of heart; Rise of dualism.

B. THE ORGANIZATION OF THE DUAL MONARCHY

   Character of the *Ausgleich;* Effects of the *Ausgleich.*

In the struggle against the influence of the French Revolution
the old order had been losing gradually but steadily. The principle of equality had gained ground when feudalism perished in
Austria. Liberty and fraternity (or nationalism) had, it is true,
made but few strides, but the proof of their strength had lain in
the extent and intensity of the struggle in central Europe before
the old order had managed to regain its footing. And it was now
after the middle of the century that some new factors were beginning to appear. The middle class was at last becoming a force in
central Europe, and some extraordinarily gifted men emerged to
lead the elements of progress. It was these geniuses who were to
bring Italians, Germans, and Magyars across a "red" sea to the
promised land. In this drama of regeneration the Second Empire
was curiously destined to play a part, and we may as well begin our
story by an inspection of its position.

NAPOLEON III AND THE PRINCIPLE OF NATIONALITY

Louis Napoleon Bonaparte, otherwise known as Napoleon III,
emperor of the French, is a man to whom both history and his-

torians have done scant justice. History pitted him against the greatest diplomatist of his day, the redoubtable Bismarck, at a time when his physical health was failing and when his position at home was passing through a process of transformation. Historians have rather too easily allowed themselves to be influenced by the detractions of some of his contemporaries and the fact of his final failure. The statement that "he was a man of one idea, and that when this was accomplished, he was without one" is a delicious epigram, but unfortunately not true. Napoleon had, of course, believed with absolute conviction that he would one day be emperor of the French, and he had worked unswervingly toward that one end. But he had plenty of ideas to execute as emperor— perhaps too many rather than too few—and it is certainly not generally believed that his striking achievements are chiefly attributable to any of his ministers. He was a strong personality, and both his services and his mistakes were his own.

Character and Organization of the Second Empire

Character and position of Napoleon III

Napoleon III was not, it is true, a man of exceptional ability. He lacked the foresight that would have saved him from some of his blunders, and he lacked the insight that would have enabled him to discern the merits and failings of others. He was also exceedingly reserved—a quality that gave the impression that he was fundamentally tricky—and he was somewhat irresolute for the reason, perhaps, that he was wont to view a problem from all sides. But he was a man of imagination and of an inborn generosity, which made him desirous of benefiting his people quite apart from the political expediency of so doing. He was magnanimous and not naturally vindictive. He was like Napoleon I in wishing to attract to his service all elements in the population. His courage was shown by his visit to the sick during a scourge of cholera, and by pursuing an unpopular object when he felt it to be wise. In his rise to power he had shown himself a dexterous politician, and he often displayed this quality in his diplomacy. But on attaining power, he sometimes misconceived his own strength, and he lacked that flashy brilliance, which to the French is more important in a leader than more sane and solid attainments. Indeed, in spite of his clever tactics, he had owed his rise not to himself so much as to his name. He was the product of circumstance, and he was never able to outgrow its grim exactions. He was somewhat like a man who has committed a crime which he is never able to live down. In short, his youthful dreams, his long exile, his patient and sometimes ill-starred efforts to attain to power, and his main reliance on the heritage from his uncle had made him something of an adventurer; and something of an adventurer he always was. And for that reason he was too prone to gamble when the stakes were too high and the odds were heavily against him. He was too much, sometimes, the victim of his own imagination.

General character of the empire

In fact, the Second Empire was itself an adventure. It was an attempt to revive benevolent despotism on a Napoleonic pattern, an attempt to impress the world—and especially France herself— with Napoleonic triumphs. The Second Empire would never have arisen but for the fact that the French people wished—or thought they wished—a repetition of the past. They had tried two brands of monarchy which had failed. They had tried a republic which had only meant squabbling and vacillation. They wanted above all else to see the national prestige rehabilitated. They wanted that glory of which they had been cheated under Louis Philippe. With rather impolitic candor the Emperor told a British ambassador that he knew that the instincts of France were military and domineering and that he was resolved to gratify them. He believed that he covered the wishes of the French people when he had said in 1849: "The name, Napoleon, is a complete program in itself; it stands for order, authority, religion, the welfare of the people within; without for national dignity." Yet lest some suppose that he meant to wage a series of wars (for no one wished to repeat the exhaustion of France in 1814), he declared when he became emperor that the Empire did not mean war—"The Empire is peace!": there were economic conquests to be gained, and the French were to be his soldiers for that purpose—soldiers, we may add, under a new captain of industry. It was perhaps a wise assurance, and it was also a clever appeal to the desire for material gain, so conspicuous in his day; but obviously Napoleon could never prevent the Empire from meaning war. If the French were willing once more to put their liberties in their pocket, he must justify the power he had usurped in the only way that he could do it. He must give them glory. By instinct a man of peace, and not a soldier like his celebrated uncle—he must nevertheless wage war. In a sense the Second Empire was a tragic historical paradox.

The Second Empire, then, was largely to be a replica of the First, and would be measured by that standard. Such was its greatest strength and also its greatest weakness.

The organization of the Empire was somewhat patterned after *Internal aspects of the Empire: (1) political* that of the Consulate, to which the Emperor specifically referred. Ministers were appointed by the emperor and responsible only to him. The laws were made by a council of state, also appointed by the emperor, and then subject to approval or rejection by a legislature elected by universal suffrage. But since the suffrage was carefully manipulated so as to insure a government majority; since laws could only be passed or rejected, and even the budget could be voted only *en bloc;* and since no publicity was allowed debates, such a legislature was singularly ineffective and never could become a focus for public opinion. There was a strict supervision of the press and careful restrictions upon public meeting. Worse than that, there was a very active secret police, which made a deadening atmosphere for all liberal tendencies; while the control of education was handed over to the Church. A writer has well said, that "he [Napoleon] paralyzed all those active national forces which tend to create the public spirit of a people, such as parliament, universal suffrage, the press, education, and associations." Napoleon III rested his position on public sentiment, but he did not wish it to be voluble. And in the period in which he lived one cannot say that experience should have taught him any differently. Whether it is true that he seriously intended, as he had promised, and as he professed to believe had been the intention of Napoleon I, to "crown despotism with liberty" as soon as the French were ready for the change, is not susceptible to proof. The fact that he eventually tried to do this does not prove or disprove his sincerity.

The Emperor, being a benevolent despot, was not the head of a *(2) Economic and social* faction like the other sovereigns who had ruled since 1814. His concern was the material welfare of all classes by making the State the promoter (though not the regulator) of the nation's economic life; and he gave France an unrivaled period of prosperity. In this respect his policy was calculated to please the middle class. The railway mileage increased almost fivefold; steamer lines stretched out to different quarters of the globe; and trade was further promoted by allowing colonial products to be imported in foreign ships. One of the greatest contributions of the Second Empire was the *Crédit foncier*, a national mortgage bank, at first subsidized by the State, which loaned money to peasants on the security of their land; and the steady inflow of capital into agriculture was naturally of the highest importance in an agricultural country. Having genuinely sympathized with the workingman during the days when he strove for power, Napoleon naturally gave him thought when he became emperor, though it must be confessed that he was more a believer in laissez-faire than of the principle of the "social state." He did something to improve the living conditions of the working class, and his policy of constructing boulevards in Paris as well as other public works gave employment to many thousands, but the bad conditions in the factories were hardly lessened, and though late in the reign the Emperor took a tolerant attitude toward unions, the change was probably the result of political expediency. Napoleon seems rather to have tried to benefit the country in the large. Being a convinced free-trader, he carried through a reciprocity treaty with Great Britain, which, while superficially harmful to French manufactures by allowing the competition of British goods, actually made it easier for raw materials to come in, and lowered the cost of living for the consumer. This so-called Cobden Treaty (1860) was the model of later agreements with other powers, and showed a sort of trend toward "economic internationalism"—until the making of new nations in central Europe led eventually to a mercantilistic reaction. Under the stimulus of the government and secure against the danger of political turmoil, capitalism developed many large industrial enterprises, and there is an element of daring in the business life of the Second Empire (sometimes conducive to speculation of the grosser sort) that has never been witnessed in France before or since.

External aspects of the empire   In close touch with bankers and industrial magnates, Napoleon was always on the lookout for commercial opportunities, and one of the greatest achievements of his reign was the digging of the Suez Canal—a project successfully carried out by a French engineer, Ferdinand de Lesseps and backed by the Emperor in the teeth of British opposition. Being a Bonaparte, he was naturally an imperialist. He extended France's colonial holdings, joined Great Britain in a war with China to get better protection for merchants, intervened to protect Christians in northern Syria (the result was the granting of some special privileges to the Christians of the Lebanon), and he tried, though without success, to get a foothold in the new world—the fatal Mexican expedition, which we shall later discuss more fully. There is little doubt but that he made

France for a time the most distinguished power in Europe. In short, the Second Empire was a very active régime, not always successful, but very often so, and chiefly important for its economic achievements and for its deliberate promotion of nationalism in Europe.

Napoleon III was one of the first statesmen of his time to believe thoroughly in the principle of nationality. "The great fault committed by the Congress of Vienna," he said in 1856, "was that the interests of the sovereigns were consulted, while the interests of their subjects were only neglected." As the legatee of Napoleonic traditions, he longed to see the complete collapse of the Vienna Settlement (of course, his very position on the French throne was a defiance of the arrangements of 1815), and he liked to imagine a Europe divided into states on a basis of nationality. Such was the Europe that somehow he hoped to fashion—a feat so tremendous that it would have been worthy of Napoleon I himself. Meanwhile the chance to win prestige for his dynasty and himself, the chance to rehabilitate France and gratify the national vanity was afforded by a crisis in the Near East.

It is doubtful if there was ever a more unnecessary war than the Crimean War, and the dreadful sufferings from cold and cholera which added to its horrors are a commentary on the lightness with which diplomats play with crises. A petty quarrel between Russia and Turkey over the question of guarding some sanctuaries in Palestine was settled after much bickering, and recent research has shown that Great Britain had already discussed with Russia an eventual partition of the Ottoman Empire. Hence Russia's aggressive policy, while a cause of the war, was not an inevitable cause; and even after Nicholas had made some peremptory demands—especially the acknowledgment of a protectorship over the Christians of the Ottoman Empire—Great Britain, France, and Austria managed to persuade him to recede, and it only required Turkish adhesion to a quite innocuous basis for negotiation to dispel completely the clouds of war—that is, provided the Czar kept his temper. But the Porte unexpectedly balked at the critical moment. That Turkey rejected the efforts of her friends seems to have been due to the British ambassador at Constantinople, Stratford Canning, who had a private grudge against Nicholas. The British government distrusted Canning and should have recalled him, but Palmerston, who had been originally responsible

The Crimean War and the Making of Roumania

Genesis of the war

for Canning's quarrel with the Czar, was a member of the ministry, and had sufficient influence to "prevent the preventing" of war. Russia thereupon occupied the Danubian Principalities, and Turkey promptly crossed the Danube and attacked the Russian army. Thus, in October, 1853, began the Crimean War.

Yet, clear as it is that the war may be ascribed to the caprice of diplomats, it is undoubtedly true that Palmerston and Canning reflected the general sentiment in England, which was hostile to Russia not only because of rivalry in the Near East but also because Nicholas seemed to the British the very quintessence of an outworn autocracy trying to hold the whole Continent in subjection. It is an interesting example of the fact that public opinion *Course of* cannot be trusted to prevent a war. As for Napoleon, recent re-*the war* search has shown that he had not wanted war, but, that once .Great Britain had decided upon strong measures, he decided to participate. It was, after all, a chance—and it seemed an easy chance—of winning the desired prestige for France. Later Sardinia joined—for reasons to be noted later. Austria was wobbly. She could not well fight the power which had so recently saved her existence, but she wanted to have an influence over the outcome, and she ultimately threatened to come into the war if Russia did not withdraw from the Principalities. When Russia did so, Austria promptly occupied them herself, promising to withdraw at the end of the war, but meanwhile trying to secure railway concessions that might ultimately mean economic conquest. Into the story of the campaigns we shall not enter. After a very hard struggle, mostly centering in the Black Sea about Sebastopol in the Crimea, Russia was beaten, and the Czar Alexander II, who had succeeded his father during the war, was anxious for peace. After some preliminary conditions had been accepted, a congress met at Paris to arrange the definitive treaty.

The Treaty By the Treaty of Paris (1856) Russia was compelled to give up *of Paris and* that portion of Bessarabia she had taken in 1812 and to agree to the *the zenith of* neutralization of the Black Sea (which meant that no Russian *the Second* fleets could be kept there), and to relinquish her protectorate over *Empire* Serbia and the Danubian Principalities. It was for Russia a reverse that she would not be likely to stomach for long. For Napoleon the war was heralded as a triumph. Though his commanders had not been very competent, the French soldiers had fought well, and his government's conduct of the war was at least not as bad

as that of the British. The Congress had also met in his capital—
another feather in the imperial eagle! And by bringing the war to
an end more quickly than suited Palmerston he won the gratitude
of the vanquished. The following year, after composing a quarrel
with Great Britain over the Danubian Principalities, Napoleon
and the Czar met at Stuttgart and agreed to pursue their eastern
policies in common. Napoleon was now actually the friend of all
the powers, and it seemed that in 1857 the Second Empire was the
pivot of European politics. Its position was essentially "Napoleonic."

All this seems very hollow—the familiar tale of diplomatic shuf- *The Treaty*
fling and "prestige." But there was one progressive feature of the *of Paris and*
Rouman
Treaty of Paris—in most respects a very stupid settlement. The *nationalism*
people of Moldavia and Wallachia, released from the Russian
protectorate, were to be allowed to elect assemblies, or "divans,"
as they were called, which should express their wishes as to the
question of their reorganization. The plan was a compromise
between the Austrian contention that they did not want to be
united and the French insistence that they did. The Powers were
not bound, however, to accept the sentiments of the Moldo-
Wallachians; they would review the question at another conference
to be called later. The important fact is that nationalism had
acquired so much esteem—thanks largely to the influence of
Napoleon III—that it was to be allowed now to express itself in a
plebiscite, and thus was given a certain standing in the public law
of Europe. In the meantime it was understood that Turkey could
not interfere with either Serbia or the Danubian Principalities
without the concurrence of the Powers who had signed the Treaty
of Paris. The protectorate which had formerly been wielded by
Russia was now assumed by the Concert of Europe.

The mass of the Moldo-Wallachians, being peasants, probably
cared but little how they were governed so long as they were not
too greatly exploited by their landlords—the class known as the
boyards. But many of the *boyards*, together with the intellectuals
and the citizens of the two capitals, had developed of late a genuine
nationalism; and though they did not aspire to sever their tie
with Turkey (the limited authority of the sultan may best be
described as "suzerainty"), they clamored much for union and a
foreign prince. Some of their leaders had hung on the outskirts
of the Congress of Paris, and sought to evoke the sympathies of

France; and while they were told that a foreign prince was not now practicable, the question of union became an issue of the Congress, as we have noted.

Crisis of 1857

Unhappily, despite the treaty, the Powers were divided on this question. Great Britain had stood with France at the Congress of Paris, then changed her mind and disapproved of the idea, though she could not well discountenance the plebiscite that was to be held. Turkey, assisted by Austria, proceeded to pack the coming divans so as to insure a vote against union, and though France had been working hard through her consuls at Bucharest and Jassy to strengthen the unionist cause, she thereby provoked Great Britain, who now gave much covert encouragement to the Turks. Stratford, once more the evil genius of the Near East, had kept his government dark in regard to the frauds, hoping that the Austro-Turkish policy would succeed in the end; and the elections to the Moldavian divan did roll up a majority against union. But Napoleon, who had long determined to help the Roumans despite the disapproval of his ambassadors, finally forced a crisis by demanding, on threat of a diplomatic rupture, that the Moldavian elections should be annulled and that preparations be made for a fair and honest plebiscite. When the Porte, backed by Austria and Great Britain, rejected this demand, France severed all relations with the Porte, and Russia, Prussia, and Sardinia immediately followed suit. Thus in the summer of 1857 the Treaty of Paris was apparently quite stultified. The Rouman question had brought on an international crisis, and the Concert of Europe was split into two camps.

Triumph of Rouman nationalism

But Napoleon felt that if he could reach Great Britain direct, the breach might be easily healed. He accordingly paid a hurried visit to England, and the result was the Pact of Osborne, by which it was apparently agreed (though the agreement was not in writing) that Napoleon should relinquish the idea of union (though this matter should be kept a secret [1]) and new elections should be held in the Principalities. Superficially the Pact of Osborne was a compromise. But actually it was a reverse for Palmerston and a triumph for Napoleon; for the new elections resulted in an overwhelming victory for the unionists, and the effect of this demons-

---

[1] Napoleon did not want it to become known to his recent allies that he had seemingly reversed his position behind their backs. He was, himself, confident that new elections would result in divans favorable to union and that the Powers would eventually have to heed the moral strength of Rouman nationalism.

tration could not but strengthen the cause of nationalism, and insure its eventual triumph. When the Powers met in another conference in 1858 and decided, in the spirit of Osborne, to confirm the separation of the two provinces, only allowing them a few minor things in common, the Principalities replied (1859) by each electing the same person as hospodar, a Moldavian named Couza, who had shown himself a vigorous friend of union. It was a striking retort of nationalism to an international protectorate that had tried to keep it in leading strings.

France was, of course, delighted, and as Austria was being drawn into an Italian war, there was for Great Britain nothing to do but make the best of it. The Porte was therefore persuaded to accept this act of revolution. But this was only the beginning of complications. Couza found that he could not govern with two legislatures and two ministries, especially as he was involved in constant friction with the *boyards*, who disliked him as a man of humbler extraction than themselves and also feared his liberal views. The Prince felt that he must strengthen his position, and this could only be done by the establishment of union—not simply personal union but the creation of one legislature, one ministry, one administration. To this end he presented his case to the suzerain power and directly appealed to Napoleon. And again Napoleon responded to his call; and after much negotiation with the Powers organic union was granted. But the *boyards* were less pleased. They had wanted union too, but they wanted Couza to proclaim it simply of his own accord, thinking in that way to discredit him with the Powers and precipitate his downfall. For Couza it had taken the most skillful maneuvering to hold them at bay while he brought the Powers around. In January, 1862 the first assembly met for the United Principalities. Officially it was not "Roumania," but actually "Roumania" had been made.

But Couza's difficulties were not over. *The boyards* were still able to paralyze his government and it was only by evasions of the constitution that he was able to get the money to run the government. More and more to the forefront came the demand for a foreign prince, for Couza, though a forceful and enlightened man in many respects, was never able to make his government honest or efficient, and corruption, class interest, and political inexperience were vices of long standing in the Principalities. Though the Prince, with French encouragement, was able in 1864 to make

Reorganization of "Roumania"

himself a dictator with a constitution modeled on that of the Second Empire, and though he enacted some excellent reforms, which brought his country nearer to the level of a Western state, the *boyards* never ceased to conspire again him, and in February, 1866, they were able to accomplish his overthrow. Now at last it seemed that the Moldo-Wallachians were to have their further wish—a foreign prince.

It was another test of the efficacy of the Concert of Europe and of a protectorate which had thus far proved brittle at every thrust. A conference, called at Paris, proceeded solemnly to deal with the question, and lectured the Roumans soundly for wanting a foreign prince. Russia would have liked to break up the union. But Napoleon was again their friend, and with his connivance the Moldo-Wallachians chose a prince from a collateral branch of the house of Hohenzollern, the dynasty that ruled at Berlin. With the secret approval of Prussia (for Bismarck wanted a Hohenzollern on the other side of Austria) the young Prince Charles accepted the offer and hurried to Bucharest to receive his crown. Six months later, after long negotiations, the Powers and the Porte duly recognized his position (1867).

Later triumphs of nationalism in the Balkans— the Treaty of Berlin

There is no doubt that Napoleon was chiefly responsible for the success of Rouman nationalism. Without his assistance the Roumans could hardly have withstood the combination of Turkey and Austria. He showed a similar sympathy with the Serbs, and when the Prince of Serbia, Michael Obrenovich, made up his mind to end the Turkish occupation (1867), it was France who most eagerly espoused his cause and enabled him to succeed. Some years after Napoleon's day the Porte lost even its right to tribute from the Roumans and the Serbs. In the Treaty of Berlin (1878) Roumania, Serbia, and Montenegro received the recognition of independence, and even most of the Bulgars, after some widely advertised massacres by the Turks, secured a limited autonomy—all this after another Balkan upheaval, and chiefly due to Russia. But the pact which France and Russia had made in 1857 had soon foundered on Napoleon's avowed sympathy for the Poles. Here he was not successful; for he could not, of course, think of deliberately fighting Russia, and his remonstrance with the Czar's stern repression of the Poles brought him only a sharp rebuff. It was a case where Napoleon's idealism had badly clouded his judgment.

But the most famous of all his achievements in the cause of nationality was concerned with the making of Italy.

The Making of a New Italy

It was the fate of the Italian people after giving the World the Renaissance to sink into an apathy which leads us to forget them for nearly three centuries. The Counter-Reformation and foreign domination had seemed to crush out that lively spirit which had blossomed so freely in the individual; the development of a modern state hardly seemed possible in a land in which the papacy occupied the central position; and the shifting of the commercial center from the Mediterranean towns to northern and western Europe had left the Italian people a prey to slow decay. In truth there was no "Italian people," but only various groups, under several governments, speaking a variation of the same tongue; and only a few intellectuals looked back to a happier past. In 1815 there were seven political entities in Italy: Lombardy-Venetia under Austria, the kingdom of Sardinia (embracing Savoy, Piedmont, and the island of Sardinia) in the northwest corner, Tuscany and three little duchies, Parma, Modena, and Lucca [1] south of Lombardy, the Papal States further south and extending across the peninsula, and finally the kingdom of the Two Sicilies, comprising the southern end of the peninsula and the island of Sicily. Italy was, in Metternich's words, just a "geographical expression."

Prelimina- ries and Prepara- tions—the Leadership of Sardinia

Italy in decay and description

Yet Italy had awakened. She had been stirred from end to end by the French Revolution. At one time or another all the Italians had been given a taste of democratic principles, and feudalism, where it had lingered had been stamped out for good. What is more important, Italians had come at last to develop an incipient nationalist feeling. Napoleon had brought together most of the northern half of the peninsula into a kingdom of Italy, and for the first time northern Italians had acquired a sense of unity as a people. Such a spirit, implicit in the French Revolution, must inevitably involve the other Italians. It was a dynamic age. Italy was on the eve of her resurrection—the "Risorgimento," as the Italians call it.

Influence of the French Revolution and Napoleon

The years following the Congress of Vienna were years of an uphill struggle in pursuit of aspirations. The Italians—or more correctly, an active minority—yearned for liberty and unity.

---

[1] Lucca was acquired by Tuscany in 1847.

*Agencies of
revolution—
the work of
Mazzini*
"Liberty" meant freedom from the oppressive rule of petty tyrants, and "unity" carried with it the expulsion of the Austrians.
The chief weapon in the cause was insurrection, plotted by secret
societies, first the "Carbonari," then later "Young Italy." None
of these insurrections was successful, for Austria was ever present,
and her strength lay behind the princes—her forces ever ready to
stamp out "revolution." Yet Young Italy had been something
besides an agency of violence. Its founder, Giuseppe Mazzini, was
a man of great spiritual power. Nervous, irrascible, too visionary
to be practical, he made a very poor conspirator, but he had all the
faith of a prophet and the courage of a crusader. How deeply he
and his followers felt their mission may be judged from the oath
prescribed for each member of Young Italy: "In the name of God
and Italy. In the name of all the martyrs of the holy Italian cause
who have fallen beneath foreign and domestic tyranny. . . . By
the blush that rises to my brow when I stand before citizens of
other lands, to know that I have no rights of citizenship, no country, and no national flag. . . . By the tears of Italian mothers for
their sons dead on the scaffold, in prison, or in exile. . . . By the
memory of our former greatness and the sense of our present
degradation. . . . By the sufferings of the millions I swear to
dedicate myself wholly and forever to strive to constitute Italy one
free, independent, republican nation." Mazzini believed what
most Italians thought impossible—that Italy *could* be free and
indivisible. There is no doubt but that his faith won thousands
of followers, and that he burnt into the very soul of those followers
an unflinching love of the cause. It was the kind of spirit that
produced a Garibaldi. Mazzini ranks as the second great contributor to Italian unity. Above all other persons, he laid the moral
foundations.

*The
uprising of
1848 and
its failure*
By 1848 the movement had grown apace, for now, instead of
sporadic insurrections, directed first against one, then against
another, of the Italian princes, revolt came to engulf the whole
peninsula. Pius IX, a liberal pope, had seemed to set the pace in
1846. Then in 1847 occurred the Milanese "tobacco riots," occasioned by the resolution of the people of that city to cease smoking
tobacco because it was a source of government revenue—a proceeding which roused the resentment of the Austrian authorities.
Then in January, 1848, a revolution broke out in Sicily, and the
infamous King Ferdinand granted a constitution in haste, to be

followed two months later by the king of Sardinia, Charles Albert, an absolutist at heart, but at least as it turned out, a champion of the Risorgimento. Finally came the news of the March Revolution in Vienna, and all Italy took fire.

The leadership was grasped by the wobbly Charles Albert, who happened to be the only prince who wanted to fight Austria. To serve under his leadership was not altogether agreeable to the Mazzinians, for their leader was an intense republican and he had good reason to distrust the King of Sardinia. But for the moment all believed that the hour of redemption was at hand. The Venetians and the Milanese threw off the Austrian yoke, and Charles Albert with an army responded promptly to their call. The Pope and the Grandduke of Tuscany were forced by their subjects to send their forces to join him, and even the King of the Two Sicilies had to mobilize an army. Revolution had become general.

Yet it failed, as we have seen; for Charles Albert, for all his bravery, was a poor commander, the Italians had none of the training that was vouchsafed to the Austrians, and there was no unity of command; moreover, there was a strange decline of enthusiasm after the war had once begun—showing perhaps that the nationalist cause was not yet a popular movement. Badly beaten, Charles Albert was forced to give up the struggle. In the desperation of defeat the Romans expelled the pope and the Tuscans their grandduke, each setting up a short-lived republic, as Venice had done. But reaction had set in, and nothing remained from the wreck but the Sardinian constitution, the retention of which was bought at the price of a heavy indemnity to Austria. Meanwhile there was an end of republics. The Austrians overthrew the ones at Venice and Florence; the French Republic, to please the Catholics, disposed of the one at Rome. And when the Pope returned, a contingent of French remained to make sure that he was safe; while an Austrian force still lingered in Romagna (one of the divisions of the Papal States). But there was one service France had rendered the Italian cause, thanks to Louis Napoleon, then president of the French Republic. By threatening intervention he prevented Austria from wiping out Sardinia as she had planned. As F. A. Simpson, his biographer, observes, "Had he not been Piedmont's shield in 1849, he could not in 1859 have been her sword."

The lesson of 1848—though Mazzini would not admit it—was that the Italians with all their fervor could not hope to contend

*The
hegemony
of Sardinia*
against Austria unaided. There was need of some foreign ally; and hence, diplomacy, quite as much as revolution, was required to solve this problem. And that, of course, premised some Italian government, loyal enough and capable enough to undertake this task. But the problem had its internal as well as external aspect. There must be one Italian state, around which as nucleus the others might rally; and Sardinia, despite her recent failure was the logical one. She was the most modern of them all; the one with the greatest inherent strength; and the only one devoted to the cause. She had now a new king, Victor Emmanuel II (for Charles Albert had followed defeat by abdication), and she had the good fortune to possess a minister who had the requisite talent for leading the Italian people to their goal. This man was Cavour.

*Cavour and
the
Leadership
of Sardinia*
Count Camillo di Cavour was a nobleman, who, like his contemporary, Bismarck, had also a practical business head. He had entered politics through the door of journalism, and later became a deputy of the Sardinian assembly, where he soon proved a power in debate. He was by conviction a staunch monarchist, and had no
*Cavour's
qualifica-
tions for
leadership*
sympathy with Mazzini's violent republicanism, but he was an earnest and aggressive liberal, and it was his belief that Italian unity must proceed under the leadership of the liberal house of Savoy. "Italy," he said, "must make herself by freedom, or we must give up trying to make her." [1] An extraordinarily clear-sighted statesman, an indefatigable worker, a skillful and daring opportunist, he was the man whom the Risorgimento needed. The fact that as a genius he was inclined to be dictatorial and did not always work well with others had made him many enemies at the outset of his career, but he gained the esteem of the King if not his affection, and his honesty and skill eventually won for him the wholehearted confidence of his countrymen.

*Preparatory
phase of
Cavour's
policy:
(1) internal*
Cavour's first thought was to make Sardinia worthy, both materially and morally, for the cause she had before her. The material problem was that of making her strong enough to hazard another war. Though faced with an enormous debt, Cavour dared to make his state embark on immense expenditures, knowing that its enhanced productivity would more than repay the cost; and in so doing he enjoyed the backing of the middle class, which also shared

---

[1] Apparently Cavour did not at first work consciously for Italian unity, which he even wrote of as "tomfoolery," but rather for Italy's liberation from Austria. The issue of union came to be forced upon him, however, by the spread of the Italian Revolution.

his liberal political views. Thus, under his inspiration as finance minister, Sardinia promoted the Industrial Revolution, completed her railway system, and negotiated a number of commercial treaties on a basis of free trade. He did not hesitate to increase enormously the burden of taxation, and with the proceeds raised an army of 70,000 men. At the same time, assuming for Sardinia a moral leadership in Italy, he made her a pattern of liberalism—not only as an example to the Italians but as a means of impressing Europe. Every little reform that Sardinia enacted was heralded to the world, for at publicity Cavour, the experienced journalist, was exceptionally adept; and the fact of Sardinia's liberalism made all the more glaring the notorious misgovernment of the Two Sicilies and the Papal States. In his determination to take from the Church certain privileges which had long since vanished in France and to confiscate the wealth of the monastic orders he was drawn into a struggle with Rome, but the

CAVOUR

sympathies of western Europe were on his side. And so far, though subjected to great provocation, he was careful not to pick a quarrel with Austria. With so heavy a task before her Sardinia must walk very straight in the eyes of Europe, especially of France and England. But why so much solicitude for the esteem of the Western Powers?

Cavour was convinced that to win Italian freedom Sardinia *(2) External* must have an ally. Italy was not to be freed by popular uprisings, as Mazzini still supposed. There was need of a large and well-trained army to cope with a power like Austria, and Sardinia's troops, though excellently trained, were obviously insufficient. It must be his task, then, to win the active support of either France or Great Britain. He was well known in both Paris and London, having visited both capitals more than once, and he felt a close affinity with the English, whose constitution he extravagantly admired. He had also met Napoleon and taken pains to reassure him that he was not a revolutionary like Mazzini. His chance to enlist Great Britain lay in her natural liberal sympathies—if only she would renounce her insularity. His chance to win France lay in Napoleon's avowed championship of nationalism—a championship which had once in his youthful days led him, apparently, to participate in an Italian insurrection. Both powers knew the petty tyranny that wracked most of the Italian states, and both knew the blighting influence of Austria on the peninsula. But it was no light thing to get either of these powers to carry sympathy with the Italians to the point of breaking with a great power and engaging it in a European war. How could Cavour hope to make so small a state as Sardinia the magnet of a great power like France for the liberation of a people that could only repay her with thanks?

The solution of this dilemma was provided by chance. In 1853 began the Crimean War, and Cavour resolved that Sardinia should contrive to enter the struggle. By fighting on the side of Great Britain and France (and he hoped that Austria would remain neutral) he reasoned that Sardinia would strengthen her bonds of intimacy with these countries as well as raise her own standing as a power. If little Sardinia could march with the big fellows, her interests would seem worthier of notice. But to many this policy seemed nothing but a gambler's throw. Why send Italians to perish in the cholera-ridden Crimea? It was pointed out—and wisely— that Sardinia, instead of squandering men and money in a cause in which she had absolutely no interest, might better husband her resources for the coming struggle with Austria. Cavour's difficulty was the greater because he could not avow openly the reasons for pushing this policy; the most that he could say was that Europe should be shown that "the sons of Italy know how to fight." And then there was the question of financing the exploit, for Sardinians would not want to engage as mercenaries; Cavour insisted that the army should be independently organized (it should not be used simply to fill up gaps in the Allied lines), and he proposed to find its support from a British loan. These conditions he was able to obtain. But only after a hard fight, and by dint of the confidence he had won for his magic skill, did he finally obtain the consent of the Sardinian parliament.

So a treaty was signed, and Sardinia entered the war. But the days of suspense were not over. Sardinia's allies were not acutely interested in this exploit, and Cavour did not know for certain that these 17,000 men would ever reach the front. It was with inexpressible relief that he learned that they had done so, and that they had acquitted themselves well. In most respects this little army was handled better than either the French or the British, and it made a good impression. How good was its morale may be judged from the observation of a Sardinian soldier, who was struggling in the slough of the trenches before Sebastopol. "Never mind," he said. "Of this mud Italy will be made."

Indeed, the gambler was winning his stake. As the result of the war Sardinia was awarded a seat at the Congress of Paris, and it was Cavour himself who occupied it. When the question of the Principalities came up before the diplomats, Cavour supported union with all his might. It was helping out a sister-nationality; there was also the possibility of giving it an Italian prince and by some shift like this gain something for Italian unity; above all, he was espousing a cause that was near to the heart of Napoleon. His craftiest stroke, however, was to get the condition of Italy before the Congress in the teeth of Austrian opposition; and though nothing was actually done beyond airing the question, the maneuver gave it a publicity which at the time was particularly valuable. After the Congress Cavour visited England, where he found a cordial welcome but no disposition to aid him. As a recent historian has shrewdly observed, "Cavour's point of view was never fully understood in England, who persisted in believing that a little goodwill on both sides was all that was required to re-establish friendly relations between Austria and Piedmont." With all his limitations Napoleon III had a breadth of view that was singularly wanting in Palmerston. It has been contended by Napoleon's recent biographer that, regardless of the Crimean War and Cavour's efforts, the Emperor would have come to the aid of Italy; but Cavour could, of course, not know the ultimate plans of that human sphynx, and in any case he had eloquently forced the issue. Before the Congress had met, Napoleon had asked him to state what he (Napoleon) could do for Italy, and Cavour, not sure of his ground, had made but a feeble response. Since then, however, Cavour's hopes had risen, and he confidently believed that he had got his needed ally. All things considered, the Congress of Paris was for Cavour a big success. He could feel that Sardinia would never again be looked upon as a petty Italian state; she had sud-

Cavour and the Intervention of Napoleon —the War of Independence

The question of French aid

denly risen to the stature of a European power. And he had focused at least the interest of Napoleon.

But in 1856 nothing was absolutely settled, and circumstances might quite easily have spoiled Cavour's game. When Austria picked a quarrel with Sardinia, and diplomatic relations were severed for a time, public opinion in England and France reacted in Sardinia's favor; yet if war had taken place at this time, it might have been fatal to the Italian cause. When, early in 1858, an attempt was made on Napoleon's life by an Italian, Cavour could not but be anxious over the effect. Napoleon, furious at the unmerited indignity, stormed at the King of Sardinia, and demanded that he take stringent measures to restrain the inflammatory utterances of his press—a demand which drew from the King a dignified refusal. Fortunately Napoleon was not a small man, and he seemed really to admire little Victor Emmanuel's spunk. Soon afterward he let it be known to Cavour that he was ready to talk business, and he proposed that the two should meet "by accident" at Plombières, a watering place in the Vosges, in July, 1858. So much depended on the interview that Cavour was exceedingly nervous. "The drama approaches conclusion," he wrote to a confidant; "pray Heaven that I do not blunder at that supreme moment!" Napoleon had taken no one into his confidence, and the part which the two played was for all the world like that of conspirators—and they were, indeed, conspirators against the peace of Europe. There were two interviews in all—one in the Emperor's cabinet, the other in his phaëton, which Napoleon himself drove for several hours in the mountains. There was apparently no bickering; for a sovereign was stating his terms. Napoleon promised to aid Sardinia against Austria and to free Italy "from the Alps to the Appenines" on certain conditions. While Lombardy, Venetia, and perhaps Parma, Modena, and part of the Papal States should belong to Sardinia outright, Italy as a whole should be formed into a confederation under the presidency of the pope, and France was to get as reward for her services Savoy and possibly Nice— possessions which would give France her natural boundaries on the southeast. Moreover, Napoleon stipulated that in bringing on war with Austria, Cavour must make sure that the responsibility could be placed squarely on Austria: France must have a respectable *casus belli!* To all of these conditions Cavour agreed, and though the pact was only oral, he was confident that Napoleon would keep it. After his return to Turin Cavour took a bolder tone. He wanted now to irritate Austria and force her to an indiscretion. In the meantime, the National Society, which he had founded in 1856 was working to encourage Italians to look to Sardinia for leadership and to dare anything for the cause. In central Italy the society was soon to steal Mazzini's cherished weapon of revolution.

By the beginning of 1859 it was evident enough to Europe that a crisis was impending. Both Austria and Sardinia were arming, and it was generally suspected that Sardinia had an understanding with France. In February Napoleon tried a device he was very fond of, the publication of a brochure, written by himself or by someone under his inspiration, to test public opinion at home and abroad. The present brochure—*The Emperor Napoleon and Italy* —was an able defense of the principle of nationality and the idea of a federated Italy, which Europe under the inspiration of France should now establish. A war of intervention was not suggested, but it was certainly an appeal to Europe to countenance changes in Italy, and was, in effect, an attack on the Vienna Settlement. The pamphlet produced a sensation, and Napoleon was made to realize how greatly many of his subjects, particularly the bankers and the Catholic faction (who feared for the pope) were opposed to war; but at least he had ascertained how everyone stood, and there is no evidence that he flinched from his resolution. But Europe, apart from the three powers immediately concerned, certainly did not want war, and Russia and Great Britain tried repeatedly by various proposals—mainly the idea of a European congress—to preclude its necessity. Great Britain would have preferred that Italy should not be united if it had to be accomplished with French help, and did not believe Napoleon when he denied that he had made an agreement with Sardinia. To Cavour the suspense of these days was so wearing that his friends were afraid that he might actually lose his mind. And when Great Britain proposed that Austria and Sardinia should both disarm, even Napoleon could not refuse to endorse the request. But fortunately Austria, who refused to descend to parity with Sardinia, did everything calculated to injure her own cause; and when she finally sent Sardinia an unreasonable ultimatum, Cavour saw that his chance had come. At last he was to have his war.

The War of Independence began in April, 1859, and lasted less than three months. True to his word, Napoleon sent an army into

The War of Independence

Italy, and together the French and Sardinian forces defeated the Austrians at Magenta and Solferino and drove them out of Lombardy. The effect on the Italians was electrical. Once more the people of Modena, Parma, Tuscany, and Romagna revolted against their rulers, and central Italy was prepared to profit by the war and join Sardinia. Tuscany, the one hesitant member of the group, had been brought into line by a patriot, hardly less staunch than Cavour himself—the Tuscan statesman, Ricasoli. The Italian Revolution had more than commenced; it was rapidly spreading. And then, to the consternation of all patriots (though Victor Emmanuel had been forewarned), Napoleon abandoned the war and made a separate peace with Austria.

Napoleon's defection

The reasons for Napoleon's action were various. He had wanted an enlarged Sardinia as a convenient buffer state against Austria— one that would be small enough, however, to remain a satellite of France. When it came to the making of a nation which by revolution might soon comprise the whole of the peninsula, Napoleon was dubious; and the strong Catholic faction, which had hated the war because it seemed to endanger the pope, had never ceased to clamor for its termination. It was also clear to Napoleon that his victories had not really crushed the Austrian strength and that to enter Venetia would be exceedingly hazardous, whereas if he withdrew from the war now, he could do so at a time when France had covered herself with glory. The Italians would feel outraged, but, after all, the Emperor had some reason to be disappointed at the scant welcome his troops had received in Lombardy (for benevolence likes appreciation!) and at the failure of the Tuscans to send recruits; and, moreover, being a man of gentle mold, he was convinced, as never before, of the brutality of war—which he had seen at close range. But, above all, he was greatly disquieted at the threatening conduct of Prussia on the Rhine. It is true that Prussia was still dickering with Austria on the conditions of her support, but Napoleon only saw the obvious danger that a possible defeat would bring on his head disastrous consequences. Yet he had not fulfilled his promise, and consequently could not exact his stipulated reward. Hence he told the king to think no more of ceding Savoy and Nice. Palmerston had declared that he ought to have offered his aid out of philanthropy alone. But one may question whether he or any Britisher would have done that; and, furthermore, Great Britain had kept her neutrality throughout this critical phase of the Revolution. In any event, Napoleon had thus far gained nothing but "glory."

He certainly did not get gratitude. When Cavour learned of the terms of the prospective treaty of peace, he saw only too clearly that Austria was still left dominant in the peninsula, and, furious at the King for submitting to the inevitable, he threw up his office in disgust. His impulsive outburst was no doubt due to nervous strain, but at least his resignation made him a national figure, as nothing else previously had done. No wonder the Revolution proceeded. By plebiscites Parma, Modena, Tuscany, and Romagna now voted annexation to Sardinia. But Victor Emmanuel knew that his hands were tied, and that he could not accept them. By the Treaty of Zürich Austria ceded Lombardy (saving two fortresses) to Sardinia, and it was agreed that the petty sovereigns who had been dethroned should be restored. Yet, who was to restore them? All depended now on the attitude of Napoleon; and while the Emperor would not allow Austria to restore the dethroned monarchs and even scandalized the Pope by suggesting that he should part with some of his territories, he did not propose to allow any further aggrandizement of Sardinia unless he were paid his price. It was not for nothing that he had warned Austria not to tamper with the Revolution. His army had sheathed its sword but his diplomacy was still active. Was he not now entitled to Savoy and Nice?

The Italian Revolution and the Consummation of Italian Unity

Italy in revolution

There seemed to be no one capable of guiding his country through this dilemma but Cavour, and in January, 1860, he returned to office. Satisfied that central Italy was worth the price, he persuaded Victor Emmanuel to assent to the cession of Savoy and Nice. Plebiscites were held in the regions in question, and they voted by large majorities for annexation to France. Savoy was French in feeling and there never had been any doubt of her wish to belong to France; presumably Nice, though strongly Italian, did not wish to be severed from Savoy. Thus the natural boundary—the prize which Mazarin had sought, and which the Revolution had won and lost, was now, at last, the gift of the Second Empire. But the plebiscite was something of a farce, for the deal had already been made, and had not been made conditional on the outcome of the vote. Napoleon, for his part, consented to the incorporation of the territories desired by Sardinia; and thus had closed another phase in the work of unification. Neither

Cession of Savoy and Nice and the winning of central Italy

Austria nor Russia showed a burning desire to uphold the Vienna Settlement, and Great Britain, though furious at the cession of Savoy and Nice (it was partly to mollify her that Napoleon signed the Cobden Treaty), showed from now on an enthusiastic approval of the Revolution. In spite of occasional talk of a congress, the Concert of Europe was only a specter in the background of this drama.

Venetia, Rome, and the Two Sicilies—half the peninsula was yet to be gained. Cavour felt that Venetia was for the present beyond his reach. He had tried during the late war to weaken Austria by enrolling the Hungarian Legion, a group of Magyar *émigrés* who were anxious to deal their enemy another blow; and it had been planned with Napoleon's help to dispatch some arms into Hungary through the Danubian Principalities. But after Napoleon's withdrawal from the war the maneuver came to nothing. Couza, with whose representative Sardinia signed a secret treaty, connived at the sending of arms into Moldavia, but their presence being discovered, they were sequestered by the Porte; and without any weapons the Magyars lacked the materials for revolution. In any case it is doubtful if Austria would have been so weakened that Venetia would have fallen from her grasp. Cavour now gave his chief attention to the question of the Papal States, for it was expected that Napoleon would soon recall his garrison, and the outlying regions were seething with revolt. Once this ground was won, Naples lay just beyond; for, as Cavour planned it, the Revolution should proceed from north to south. But here events transpired which gave the Revolution the opposite course. It is now that Garibaldi made his picturesque appearance.

Conquest of the Two Sicilies

Garibaldi, the warrior, was to share with Cavour, the diplomat, the chief honors in the making of Italy. A native of Nice and a seasoned revolutionary, Garibaldi had already won the affection of his countrymen by his daring, and during the War of Independence he had enrolled under his leadership a band of volunteers—a plan initiated by Cavour as a means of attracting recruits from outside Sardinia. After the cession of Nice to France (an act for which he never forgave Cavour) he was strongly inclined to attempt its recovery, but happily the one stable element in Garibaldi's temperament was his loyalty to his king. Then in April, 1860, came the news of an incipient revolution in Sicily, and while Cavour was debating the question of sending someone to guide it, Garibaldi was invited by the insurgents to come to their aid and head the movement. After some hesitation he accepted. Garibaldi was an honest, simple-minded egoist, a hater of the ways of politicians, and confident in the merits of the sword, a dauntless warrior and a loyal spirit. To the cause of Italy he had consecrated his life. And to lead his "redshirts" to the conquest of a kingdom was an exploit for which his talents were peculiarly fitted.

The ground had been prepared for Garibaldi's exploit by Mazzini, who was as adept in manufacturing revolutions as Bismarck was later in manufacturing wars. But there was nothing artificial about the Sicilian revolution, for the rule of the king was so bad that his subjects had been in a chronic state of incipient insurrection. Cavour could not openly support this present maneuver, for the King of Sardinia had no direct quarrel with the Neapolitan king and the attitude of Europe was bound to be opposed to intervention; but he connived at the expedition, and only hoped and prayed that it would keep clear of Rome. On May 3, 1860 Garibaldi sailed with his famous "Thousand," and entered the realm of romance as well as history. The feat of conquering a kingdom of 11,000,000 people with 1,150 men seems at first almost incredible, but the army he had to fight was badly led and mutinous, and most of the population were on the side of the invaders. After cleaning up Sicily, Garibaldi crossed to the mainland, and in a few days he had entered Naples. Possessed now of the whole kingdom of the Two Sicilies, Garibaldi announced his plan of marching on Rome.

It was at this juncture that Cavour felt it necessary to intervene. *Roman crisis and the conquest of central Italy* An attack on Rome would mean an encounter with Napoleon's force, still garrisoned in the city, and though the result of such an incident could only be conjectured, Cavour knew that Napoleon was capable of being turned immediately into an enemy of Italian unity—with consequences not at all pleasant to contemplate. It was a serious crisis, and the only way it could be surmounted was for Victor Emmanuel to lead an army into the Papal States and head off Garibaldi. Fortunately the hero had met with a slight reverse, which delayed his plans. Victor Emmanuel's army meanwhile defeated a papal force, and then entered Neapolitan territory. Napoleon made a fuss but it was only for Catholic consumption, and immediately left for Algeria to avoid embarrassing questions. Sardinia was now in possession of the papal territories to the east of Rome, but Rome was left unscathed.

Popular aspect of Italian unity

There was still, of course, the danger that Garibaldi, dictator in his new possession, and possibly a convert to Mazzini's views, might establish a republic and thus split Italy in two. But at the pinch Garibaldi proved loyal to Victor Emmanuel; duly handed over his conquests to his master, and then passed into honorable retirement. Then the conquests were sanctified by popular consent. Plebiscites were held in the Two Sicilies as well as in the outlying provinces of Rome (Umbria and the Marches) and by tremendous majorities annexation to Sardinia was voted. The holding of plebiscites was a new instrument of politics—Napoleonic in origin—and in no more eloquent fashion could the new importance of nationalism have been manifested. It seemed to prove in the case of Italy that union was the real will of her people.

Establishment of the kingdom of Italy

It only remained now to give the work its proper signification; and on February 18, 1861 an Italian parliament met, and Victor Emmanuel II was proclaimed "by the grace of God and the will of the nation king of Italy." The little state of Sardinia was no more. She had worked only for Italy and had merged her identity with it.

Cavour's work was drawing to a close. His last official act was to get the Italian parliament, then meeting at Florence, to vote Rome the prospective capital. The geographical center of Italy and the hearth of its greatest traditions, the "eternal city," was the only fitting capital for Italy. On June 6, 1861 Cavour died at the age of fifty-one, worn out by his long exertions. "We have made Italy" he murmured in his last moments. It was an extraordinary achievement, in which Cavour himself had been the leading personal factor and to a large extent the brains that made it possible. "A people," as one observer expressed it, "who had seemed dead, had arisen to new and vigorous life, breaking the spell which bound it, and showing itself worthy of a new and splendid destiny."

The completion of Italian unity

There were Venetia and Rome still to be won, and we shall soon notice the circumstances which gave them both to Italy. Venetia was acquired as the result of the Seven Weeks' War in 1866 and Rome was taken when the French withdrew their garrison in 1870. After that there were only a few scattered territories peopled by Italians that were not yet a part of Italy, and these were acquired by the Great War of 1914–8.

It is in connection with Venetia that the movement toward

German unity came in touch with its counterpart in Italy. The two movements had gone on coincidently, but the Germans had to wait longer for a state to place itself at their head, and the movement proceeded more placidly than in Italy—perhaps an index of the difference in temperament between the two peoples. In each arena Austria played the chief obstructive rôle, but as she was herself a German power, there was not among the Germans that intense moral issue that had ranged a whole people against alien domination. We shall not observe the people playing so dominant a part in the making of the German nation.

Comparison of the movements in Italy and Germany

The Making of a New Germany

German nationalism may be said to have begun with the War of Liberation. It is true that Germans had felt a certain sense of nationality during Luther's quarrel with Rome, but divided as they were among so many princes, who were more often than otherwise in league with an outside power, there was nothing calculated to keep alive that spirit of self-defense out of which nationalism is born, and so there was little in the way of a trend toward unity before the nineteenth century. In the war to free Germany from Napoleon not only were most of the princes willingly enrolled but their subjects had felt an enthusiasm that amounted to a real awakening. It was a fairly spontaneous movement of redemption, and as Prussia had led the way, it seemed as though Prussia should assume the leadership after the war, utilizing this spiritual movement to create a German nation. Unfortunately the Hohenzollerns were too narrow in their outlook, too incurably timid, to grasp this opportunity. Unity under Prussia would have threatened to mean the sacrifice of more then thirty princes, and it would certainly have meant an end of the hegemony of Austria, now resumed after the downfall of Napoleon. Metternich saw the issue and met it; and since public opinion was mute, he triumphed without difficulty. Hence the disappointment of German nationalists over the decisions at Vienna. Germany was to be another federation—nothing more—involving simply an alliance between particularism (the sectional spirit of the princes) and dynasticism (the historic authority of the princes together with the old pretension of Austria to wield a permanent influence in Germany— and anywhere else she could!).

Prelimina- ries—the Question of Prussia's Leadership

Rise of German nationalism in the War of Liberation

The three decades which followed the Vienna Settlement were,

The economic factor—the Zollverein

in fact, dreary years for Germany, but one important movement stands out. Prussia, as we have noticed, established, little by little, a *Zollverein*, which by 1842 included all the German states but Austria. This phenomenon of economic policy was important in two ways. In the first place, it taught the German states the merits of close relations; for in place of the multitude of tariffs which divided thirty-six states from one another, merchandise was now able to circulate freely from one end of Germany to the other. This development of material bonds of mutual benefit eventually led Germans more easily to prepare their minds for a common government. Economic union foreshadowed political union. In the second place, seeing that Prussia excluded Austria from membership in the Zollverein, it tended to draw the Germans toward the leadership of Prussia. As yet Prussia took no advantage of her position, for the Hohenzollerns allowed themselves to be dominated by Metternich, but if ever the break should come between Austria and Prussia, some of the German states would rally to Prussia's leadership.

Moral factors—the growth of democracy and nationalism and the episode of the Frankfort Parliament

The third stage in the progress of German nationalism was partly a result of the March Revolution and of the general upsetting of the political order in 1848. As the episode of the Frankfort Parliament showed the strength of the nationalist movement and also the development of liberal ideas, we must note the moral growth which Germans had come to experience, without which this incident could not have occurred. Shortly after the Congress of Vienna constitutions had been granted by some of the south German princes (it is in south Germany that one always found the most evidence of liberalism), but Prussia had done nothing but revive some of the powers of the old provincial diets and outside of a few quarters the middle class was quite excluded from politics. Public opinion was shackled in most of the states, and liberals, especially in Prussia, were victims of much petty persecution. The fact that democracy was a slow growth in Germany may perhaps be attributed to the slow development of the middle class, which is the element that ordinarily promotes it; yet, for all that, there were some members of that class, aspiring to political rights in proportion as their material wealth increased; and there were also liberal spirits in the universities. There was a thin liberal track which led to "Frankfort." Much deeper and wider was the nationalist or unitary trend, though the two were usually merged. The idea of unity was definitely propagated in two ways. There were student societies, like the Burschenschaft, which clamored for German unity and wore the colors red, black, and gold, as symbolic of this idea, but these societies soon succumbed to the Metternich system, and they played a less active rôle than the secret societies of Italy. More important were the teachings and writings of university professors, who expounded German history with special emphasis on Prussia's capacity for leadership and on the unhappy disintegration of Germany in a world of modern states. The plea for a common sentiment of unity especially against France, the historic foe, and for love of a fatherland which still existed only in patriotic dreams was reflected in the composing of martial songs, *Die Wacht am Rhein* (1840) and *Deutschland, Deutschland über alles* (1841). There was undoubtedly a quickening of the nationalist soul—especially in the 'forties. The intellectuals, bound more and more to unity through the working of these spiritual forces, corresponded to the merchants who saw unity as a matter of material advantage. In 1847 some active spirits planned an informal "national assembly" for the purpose of working out some scheme of political union—perhaps of a federal character (which need not entail the destruction of all the princes) but at all events a much more solid union than then existed. When, indeed, the March Revolution caused slumbering fires to be kindled anew, the movement received such ardent popular support that the princes themselves felt forced to give it their backing, and it was actually the old diet which called together a national assembly, to be elected by universal suffrage, to meet by its side at Frankfort in May, 1848. Such was the famous "Frankfort Parliament."

It was a momentous occasion for the German people. Now a constitution was framed on a liberal basis for a united Germany. For the governing power, there could be but one choice—namely Prussia. But here is where this hopeful movement foundered; for instead of deliberately assuming sovereign power, the Frankfort Parliament staked all on Prussia's leadership, and all such hopes were vain. The Hohenzollern king could never bring himself to accept a crown as a gift of the people (he would not "pick up a crown from the gutter," as he expressed it); he preferred to rule a smaller state by divine right and the power of the sword than to govern all Germany with a national parliament. Moreover, Austria was opposed to union,[1] and when Austria recovered her grip on central Europe, it would be necessary, perhaps, to meet her challenge—which might well mean war, not only with Austria herself but with many of the lesser states, at heart opposed to union. Frederick William was clearly not the man for a big conception or an heroic risk. Thus Prussia shirked the issue which Sardinia had just seized. And the significance of this decision was considerable. It did not mean that Prussia would not some day assume the leadership of German unity. But it did mean that Germans lost their chance to become united on a democratic basis. Liberalism was not to march with nationalism, as in Italy.

Question of Prussia's fitness for leadership: (1) moral

The reaction which swept over Germany in 1849 finished not only the Frankfort Parliament but also the institutions which, as we saw, had been hastily granted during the crisis. The King of Prussia, who had had to face a riot in his capital, had promised a constitution establishing universal suffrage, but when in 1850 the constitution was promulgated, it was seen how wantonly he had tricked his people. The popular chamber (much less important than the upper chamber whose members were nominated by the king) was to be chosen by universal suffrage, it is true, but this suffrage was so devised that the voters being divided into three classes on the basis of property and each class having an equal right to choose delegates to the chamber, the men of wealth could easily dominate the assembly. Of democracy of that sort the Hohenzollerns need have no fear. Moreover, the press was rigidly controlled; public meetings were closely watched and at the least pretext dissolved; and arbitrary arrest and imprisonment were not infrequent. Men supposed to be liberals were treated almost like outlaws, for all professions were virtually closed to them, and they could seldom hope to get justice in the courts. Prussia was practically an autocracy, in which the king and his allies, the junkers, ruled the land. With the question of German unity, on the other hand, Frederick William had some sympathy; but he merely envisaged a federation of princes looking to Prussian rather than Austrian hegemony; and to this, of course, Austria would not submit. When he started to found such an organization, Austria forced him to give it up in an agreement signed at Olmütz; and the old Germanic Confederation, which had virtually gone to pieces during

---

[1] Austria was free to become a member-state if only her German provinces were included, but to this she naturally would not consent.

the mid-century upheaval, was revived "in all its glory." The "humiliation of Olmütz," as Prussians called this episode, seemed more than ever to prove the moral unfitness of Prussia for leadership.

And yet, withal, Prussia was the one state capable of leading Germans to their goal; for Austria, only part-German and unalterably opposed to unity, was out of the question, and since the policy might readily involve a war, Prussia alone had the physical strength for the purpose. It was during the 'fifties, as we have noticed, that the Industrial Revolution came to Prussia and modern capitalism founded an enduring structure. Banks multiplied, railway mileage increased, and the electric telegraph was now for the first time pressed into the service of business. Hundreds of new enterprises were launched (those founded in 1856 alone represented a capital of over $100,000,000), and such establishments as the dye works of Berlin and the steel foundry of Albert Krupp became internationally famous. Even the junkers transformed their large estates into industrialized farms. A state as large as Prussia, and now blessed with unwonted prosperity, should be able to raise and equip a large army—for it was by such means in particular that autocratic Prussia would unify Germany. "Germany," said Bismarck, "does not look to Prussia's liberalism but to her power. . . . Not by speeches and majority votes are the great questions of the day to be decided (therein lay the blunder of 1848 and 1849), but by blood and iron." All that apparently was needed was a man to guide the policy, and such a man Prussia produced—Otto von Bismarck.

(2) Material

Bismarck was a wealthy junker. Like many of this class, he had held a post in the Prussian bureaucracy, and was even for a time a delegate of Prussia to the federal diet. Later he served as ambassador to St. Petersburg and Paris, and thus acquired a useful knowledge of two important countries with whom he was ultimately to deal. In politics he was by conviction a hide-bound conservative, though he did not scruple to play on the other side of the fence if it served his purpose. His acquaintance with the federal diet convinced him as nothing else of the utter futility of the existing political system in Germany, though he was not at first an enemy of Austria; rather, he looked upon her an an ally against "revolution." When, however, central Europe settled down, he shifted to the conviction that Austria was Prussia's inevitable foe,

Bismarck and Prussia's Leadership—the Preparatory Phase of his Policy

Qualifications and methods of Bismarck

and that sooner or later they must fight. He had all his life the sagacity to subordinate the lesser question to the greater. He never allowed himself to be tangled in some diplomatic web that would hamper his freedom of action, and he had no ideal but Prussia's greatness. "The healthiest basis of a state," he said, "is national selfishness . . . and it is unworthy of a state to strive for

Painting by von Lenbach

BISMARCK

anything that does not concern it." One reads with a smile the importance that he had already ascribed to Prussia in his memoirs, for, truth to tell, Prussian policy up to 1862 had been pitifully negative; yet, withal, Bismarck's confidence in Prussia had probably much to do with his overmastering confidence in himself. He merged Prussia with himself, and was almost as much of an autocrat as Frederick the Great had been.

But he was worthy of his presumption. A less engaging figure than Cavour, he had all the latter's dexterous opportunism, and perhaps more than the latter's daring. But Cavour had had to reason with a parliament as well as a king, and to keep an eye on public opinion. Bismarck had to convince a king, but he never paid much deference either to parliament or public opinion, and he broke through opposition by a disarming audacity. Boisterously genial when he chose, and of a frankness which sometimes amazed an adversary, he preserved in spite of excessive nervousness (often bordering on irritability) a studied tact and an unruffled judgment, and it is doubtful if he ever took a step without carefully considering its probable effect. When he had thoroughly prepared the ground and had gauged the sentiment of every capital in Europe, then he was ready to deal one of his sledge-hammer thrusts. Bismarck was one of those dominating personalities that have shaped the course of history to suit their ends, and it was his luck that he belonged to an age when he did not have to wrestle with the caprices of public opinion.

Bismarck was forty-seven when he was called to power in 1862 as minister-president of Prussia. It was his good fortune that he owed his appointment to the influence of Albrecht von Roon, the minister of war, who being a military man, was able to keep the army subservient to the government's policy even when it did not always understand or approve of it. For to Bismarck, skillful diplomatist that he was, the army was just one instrument to be used in the fulfillment of his schemes. Bismarck's policy was the unification of Germany for the aggrandizement of Prussia. It was to entail three wars, and all the "blood and iron" he had prophesied. It was also to demand an exceptional genius. During these years Bismarck appeared at his best; for, like Napoleon I, he did not seriously err until new forces entered history whose strength he could not fathom. *Bismarck's fundamental policy*

Bismarck's first care was to get for his future use the army that he required. By a law of 1814 Prussia had adopted universal service, but during the long period of peace appropriations for military purposes had been quite inadequate for keeping an army on such an ambitious footing. Whereas its size (on a war footing) should have been 450,000, it was only 215,000—more than half being absent from the rolls. When Bismarck took office, King William (who had succeeded to the throne of his brother in 1861) had been unable to induce the popular chamber to vote the budget required. *Sharpening of his weapon*

The wealthier middle class which composed this body was anxious to show its power and professed to believe that a larger army was simply desired to serve an autocrat's purpose. Bismarck accordingly got the King to call the situation an emergency and to raise the army required without regard to the popular chamber. It amounted to setting aside the constitution—and, in so doing, the government risked a revolution. But Bismarck knew his countrymen, knew how readily they bent to militarism, and he was prepared to take the risk. By 1863 he had his army—his main instrument for the achievement of German unity.

Bismarck vs. Prussia —the Seven Weeks' War

Having enhanced the strength of Prussia, Bismarck glanced at his traditional rival in German affairs. Whatever enemies he must meet on the road to German unity he knew that Austria was one that he could certainly reckon on. She would never willingly allow her leadership in Germany to pass to Prussia. She was the champion of the status quo—the old Confederation with its more than thirty princes, the interests of most of whom were linked with her own. Particularism was an enemy Bismarck would also have to face, but the arch-foe was its strong protectress, Austria. In 1863 he could hardly have foreseen how this war was to come about; but whenever it should come, he must manage, like Cavour, that the enemy should appear the aggressor. The tortuous road that he was to tread was opened in this year by the Schleswig-Holstein question.

The Schleswig-Holstein question and the war with Denmark

Schleswig and Holstein were two duchies attached to the kingdom of Denmark by a purely personal union—that is, the tie of a common sovereign and no more. There had been a good deal of trouble over their relations to Denmark, since the duchies were mostly German, and wished to be ruled by the Duke of Augustenburg, who had legally a better claim than the King of Denmark, and was besides a German; but in 1852 the Concert of Europe, including, of course, Austria and Prussia, had signed the Protocol of London, guaranteeing Danish rule on the basis of a personal union. Thus matters rested for some time. Then in 1863 the Danish parliament precipitated a crisis by adopting a new constitution, incorporating Schleswig as an integral part of Denmark. The act at once aroused an outcry in Germany. Schleswig was two-thirds German and was being forced under the Danish yoke! Yet, as Schleswig, unlike Holstein, was not a member of the Germanic Confederation, and as the Confederation itself had not been a party to the Protocol, this body had no case for interference. Nevertheless it meant to interfere, and a federal army was mobilized for action.

Bismarck at once determined to fish in these troubled waters. He had no intention that the duchies should be won by the Confederation and become the spoil of the Duke of Augustenburg. He was resolved that Prussia should have them; especially he coveted Holstein with its important position between the North and Baltic seas and the excellent harbor of Kiel. Doubtless also he saw a chance of quarreling with Austria over the question. In any case he intended that in the solution of an important German question Prussia and not the unwieldy conclave of princes should take the lead. Instead, however, of defying the whole Confederation including Austria, he proposed that Prussia and Austria should jointly intervene. They were to constitute themselves the self-appointed mandatories of Europe to uphold the Protocol of London. Austria, for her part, offended by the Confederation's flouting of the Protocol (for it had wanted both duchies for Augustenburg), was nothing loath. But the situation was one that required the most delicate handling; for the Danes might back down, instead of fighting, as Bismarck wanted; the federal army might get in the way and produce an unfortunate "incident"; and outside powers might interfere. Fortunately for Bismarck, he knew that his great Baltic neighbor was his friend, for he had stood ostentatiously on the side of Russia when the other powers had bothered her on the Polish question, and the two powers had, in fact, been bound by a common fear of the rebellious Poles. Of Napoleon he was less certain, for, true to the principle of nationality, the Emperor wanted neither Germans coerced by Danes nor Danes coerced by Germans; but he had already entangled himself in the Mexican expedition, and hence would not act without Great Britain; and the latter, hating him unjustifiably for the annexation of Savoy and Nice, refused his project of a congress, while she unintentionally helped Bismarck by making the Danes think that she would come to their aid. Sure of the international situation, it only remained for Bismarck to give Denmark terms that she would certainly reject, and to head off the federal army. He knew that German opinion was against him, but with Austria on his side he did not care. Yet there was no time to be lost. And if the Danes should back down, his plan was ruined.

Bismarck felt certain that they would not. Prussia and Austria demanded a withdrawal of the new constitution within forty-eight hours, and since only a parliament could do that and since the present parliament had just been dissolved, preparatory to the election of a new one, assent was literally impossible. It might have behooved the Danes to parley and appeal to Europe, but they seem to have trusted entirely to British support, which utterly failed them. Everything, therefore, turned out beautifully for Bismarck. War was declared; the invaders were naturally successful; and only Great Britain blustered. By the Treaty of Vienna (1864) Denmark handed over Schleswig and Holstein to Austria and Prussia to dispose of as they pleased. It was in the uncertainty of this settlement—the assumption that these two rivals could agree on the disposal of the duchies—that one might have found the germ of the Seven Weeks' War.

Nothing better showed the hollowness of public law in Europe than the Danish affair. Austria and Prussia, intervening on its behalf, had finally changed it to suit themselves. But a joint administration, or condominium, over the duchies could have but one result. Austria and Prussia were soon quarreling, and, but for William's reluctance to fight a German power, war might have broken out in 1865. Instead was signed the Convention of Gastein. The duchies were divided, Austria administering Holstein, Prussia, Schleswig, but nothing was said of their permanent disposition, and Augustenburg was doing all that he could, with Austria's backing, to get possession of them. "We have," said Bismarck, "just papered over the cracks."

Bismarck's preparations for war: (1) the sounding of Napoleon From the time of the Convention of Gastein Bismarck prepared for war. The army was, of course, in readiness, but he had to pay heed to Europe, for whenever there was a struggle between *great* powers, outsiders always felt that they should be paid for keeping quiet. With Italy he intended, if possible, to make an alliance, but hardly less important was the neutrality of France; hence, the famous interview of Biarritz, at the termination of which Bismarck was satisfied that Napoleon would not bother him. It has always been something of an enigma why the Emperor did not demand his "pound of flesh"; but the reasons seem fairly clear. In the first place he wanted the war between Austria and Prussia to take place, for he hoped in the final results to get the left bank of the Rhine (what a unique way of smashing what was left of the Vienna Settlement!), but he was apparently afraid that by being too grasping now he might drive Bismarck to patch up his differences with Austria—so little did he read Bismarck's policy! In the second place Napoleon was in no position at this moment to risk the chance of a possible check and of being drawn into war himself, for he had foolishly embarked on a project outside of Europe which not only involved his prestige but had seriously depleted his military resources. Anxious to pull off a spectacular triumph and influenced (perhaps unknowingly) by men who had been dealing in shady speculations, he had converted an effort to collect debts from the Mexican republic into a veritable war of conquest, setting up as emperor of Mexico, Francis Joseph's brother, Maximilian, presumably as a sort of dependent of Imperial France. Napoleon was therefore somewhat in the position of a man who cannot pay his legitimate debts because his money is tied up in stocks. But these were not the only reasons for slighting his country's interests and failing to score over Bismarck. As Grant Robertson has pointed out, Napoleon was already suffering from the malady which eventually carried him off. It is perfectly obvious that the Napoleon of Biarritz was not the Napoleon of Plombières. But, apart from his mental sluggishness at this time, there is one blunder that convicts Napoleon of extraordinary want of perception. Like British statesmen of the same period, he had failed to take accurate measure of Prussia. He believed that Austria would win, and that it was with Vienna that he must traffic. And Austria was willing to pay him for his neutrality by promising to cede Venetia to Italy—a return to the Emperor's flair for nationalities. It is a curious fact that Napoleon and Bismarck each despised the other. Which one was justified was very soon to be shown.

With Italy Bismarck made an alliance, with Venetia, of course, as the bait. When Austria finally offered Italy what she wanted in return for her neutrality (once Italy had offered military support in return for this prize but had been turned down), it was too late. And now that Bismarck had Italy to attack his enemy in the rear, he was not afraid of having to fight the south German princes. *(2) The alliance with Italy*

But Bismarck did not propose to give the impression that Prussia was so sordid as to go to war with Austria for the possession of the duchies—a natural inference since the two were quarreling again. Hence he raised the question of a reform of the Germanic Confederation. The question had long been pending, and Bavaria *(3) The question of a casus belli*

had shown a disposition to draw away from Austria by forming a
south German federation on an equality with Austria and Prussia.
According to the scheme which Bismarck now laid before the diet,
the assembly of the Confederation should be henceforth chosen
by universal suffrage, and he allowed the inference that Austria
was not to be included in the organization. As a possible device for
winning the south German liberals the measure was clever but
hardly successful, for no one believed that Bismarck's devotion to
"1848" could be genuine. Nor did it immediately produce war,
though Austria and most of the princes were certainly shocked by
so radical a plan. But it did undoubtedly exasperate Austria, and
it enabled Bismarck to mask the tangible cause of the coming
conflict. Without entering into the details it may simply be
stated that Bismarck used the Schleswig-Holstein question to
goad Austria into war. There was a moment, it is true, when a
congress—a favorite Napoleonic resource—might have blocked
all his scheming, as it had nearly blocked Cavour's, but as in 1859,
so in 1866 Austrian diplomacy was singularly stupid, and "hence
matters reached a crisis." On June 11 Austria pressed the diet for
federal action against Prussia, and the proposal was carried. Prussia then declared the Confederation at an end. Declarations of
war soon followed. Prussia, together with a few of her smaller
neighbors and Italy, faced Austria and most of the other German
states. From one point of view the Seven Weeks' War was a civil
war (that is why William had backed Bismarck with great reluctance), and it is nothing short of marvelous that the German blood
spilled in 1866 did not make the attainment of unity impossible—
at least for a generation.

*The Seven
Weeks' War*   The Seven Weeks' War was won by Prussia because Austria
had to fight on two fronts, because she had to face disaffection at
home, and because Prussia was incomparably the superior in
military technique and directing skill—Hellmuth von Moltke,
her chief of staff, being one of the greatest strategists of the nineteenth century. With a speed that startled the world and amply
proved the vaunted efficiency of her military machine, Prussia
fell upon her neighbors, Saxony, Hanover, and Hesse, and soon
put them out of action. Austria was successful against Italy, but
she suffered a crushing defeat at the hands of Prussia in the Battle
of Königgrätz or Sadowa—and this defeat was decisive. The
south German states were, meanwhile, also worsted, and soon after

Königgrätz sued for peace. Moltke with an army flushed with victory resolved to crown his triumph with the capture of Vienna.

But here is where Bismarck intervened. War was but one— albeit the most important one—of his instruments, and he knew both when to use it and when to lay it aside. Thus, much to the disgust of the army and against the inclination of the King, he insisted upon peace, even going so far as to threaten resignation if the King refused his wish; and in the end, though he was ill under the strain, Bismarck triumphed. The reasons for his moderation were threefold. In the first place, Bismarck knew that he had accomplished the purpose of the war—there would be no longer any question of the elimination of Austria from Germany—and he did not wish to make a bitter and vengeful enemy. For that reason by the Treaty of Prague Austria was not required to cede an inch of territory to Prussia but only to pay a small indemnity. Prussia satisfied herself with various annexations—Hanover, Hesse, Schleswig, Holstein, etc., and with the stipulation that Austria should exclude herself from all German federations. To Italy, by the way, went Venetia, and, to please Napoleon, the Danes of north Schleswig were to be allowed to vote their own disposition—though this provision was never fulfilled. In the second place, Bismarck did not wish too utterly to alienate the south German states whose inclusion, of course, would be needed for a united German nation. They, accordingly got off with small indemnities, and were actually allowed, if they chose, to form their own federation. A third reason for Bismarck's policy was Napoleon. The Emperor had offered his mediation, and might if he chose have attacked Prussia, if his terms were not accepted. When Bismarck, rejecting his terms (which will be noted again presently), bluffed Napoleon into thinking that he might throw his army against France, he was taking a tremendous risk, for this was before the armistice, and Prussia was not in a condition to fight another enemy. But Napoleon did not call his bluff, and was ostensibly contented with the honor of mediation on terms already outlined by Bismarck. Still one can well understand why Bismarck was anxious to end the war before the Emperor should fully awaken to its consequences.

Bismarck's moderation and its causes

Let us now survey the results of this momentous war. Prussia had aggrandized herself territorially; and incidentally we may note that the people of the territories annexed were not at all consulted as to their fate. Above all, Austria was thrust out of Germany (it

Results of the war— the North German Confederation

would mean eventually a new orientation of Austrian policy), and Prussia was able to form of her own free will the North German Confederation, embracing the German states north of the river Main. The constitution of this organization, which arranged for a bicameral legislature and which placed the controlling power in the hands of Prussia, became the model of the constitution for the future German Empire. The southern states were, for the present, not included, but we shall note that they soon became military allies. There was no question but that Prussia's hegemony in Germany was established. It is obvious, too, that Germany's unity was half won. The war also resulted in the furtherance of Italian unity, since Italy acquired Venetia. Finally, it led, as we shall see later, to a reconstitution of the Hapsburg monarchy. There never had been such an upheaval in central Europe, and henceforth, though Austria remained a Great Power, there was no question but that the center of political gravity in central Europe had shifted from Vienna to Berlin.

The duping of France and the conciliation of the south German states

Perhaps another result of the war was the discomfiture of France. It is clear enough that Napoleon's calculations had been upset. He had thought to receive a titbit on the Rhine from an exhausted victor, whom he had expected to be Austria. But now, after Königgrätz, common sense should have told him that he could not exact anything. Unfortunately the Emperor was suffering so acutely from nephritis that he hardly knew what he was doing, and surrounded, as he was, by second-rate advisers (largely, of course, his own fault), he was liable to resort to the refuge of the sick, and consent to almost anything if only to be left in peace. When, accordingly, he asked among other things for a large slice of the Rhineland, it is no wonder that Bismarck remarked that he was talking as though Prussia had been beaten. When, *after* the armistice Napoleon renewed his demand, his ambassador made the mistake of putting it into writing. Bismarck, of course, declined it, but pocketed the document. Later Benedetti, the French ambassador, asked for Belgium, and the same procedure followed except that Bismarck simply gave an evasive answer, leaving open a lure which Napoleon might later follow. Whether the story be true that he extracted the written demand from a wastebasket after the interview was over, it at least sounds plausible, and is an interesting proof of the maxim that whenever you sup with the Devil you need a long spoon. At all events, the important thing is that Bismarck had in his hand some damning evidence against France which he could use as he saw fit. It was his chief and immediate problem to conciliate the south German states, paving the way for their inclusion in a German empire under Prussia; and he knew that they were likely to turn to France, their historic protector. But now, by sheer luck, France had played into his hands. He proceeded, then, to publish the French demand for territory on the Rhine (which included, as a matter of fact, a province of Bavaria); and now the south German states could see only too clearly that their Gallic friend had betrayed them. After that it was not difficult for the North German Confederation to sign a series of treaties with the south German states which put their respective armies under Prussia's military control. Now, in the event that Napoleon made war, he would face a united Germany.

And now for Bismarck there was the problem of completing German unity. And he reasoned that this could be done only by marshaling all Germans in a war with an outside power, and that, of course, meant France. Only by creating unity of sentiment, gained through having to fight a common foe, would the south German states be prepared for organic unity. Moreover, he realized that France would never willingly permit the incorporation of these states; he had already pushed her just as far as French pride would permit. Thus the issue was clearly drawn. Bismarck had triumphed over liberalism, particularism, and Austrian dynasticism; he had now to leap the one remaining barrier—the balance of power. It was his problem, therefore, to bring about war with France, and to do it in such a way that France would be isolated, and also made to wield the actual challenge. The Franco-Prussian War proceeded from two general causes: the settled policy of Bismarck, which required it as a means of unifying Germany, and the moral position of the Second Empire. It is to this latter that we must now give our attention.

Bismarck vs. France —the Franco-Prussian War and the Completion of German Unity

Causes of the Franco-Prussian War

The decline of Napoleon III is so extraordinary that it may require a pathologist—perhaps even a psychoanalist—to provide a satisfactory explanation. His rise to his uncle's position was a brilliant performance; his foreign policy up to 1861 was a striking success. He had made France the arbiter of Europe, he had made possible the unification of Roumania and Italy, he had gained two coveted territories for France, and he had raised the national prestige both in the Near and Far East. Of more moment, perhaps,

(1) The psychology of the Second Empire

he had given his country an unprecedented prosperity. Yet from 1861 began the period of the Mexican expedition, of the foolish tampering with Poland, of the bungling policy toward German unity, and of the abysmal disaster of 1870. Napoleon was not a wizard, and he committed some sorry blunders during his prime, but it is hard to understand the growing unsteadiness of his hand. Perhaps a clue to his later failures may be found in the state of his health. His mentality, as well as his spirit, was undoubtedly affected by acute physical suffering. Yet we know also that the Emperor was too easy-going to be an accomplished autocrat (he lacked the flinty hardness of his uncle); he was too liable to be turned in a wrong direction; and some of his later misfortunes were due to early mistakes, which, like the proverbial "chickens," "came home to roost."

A second problem which faces us is why the French people, fed by national triumphs and gorged, so to speak, by material gains, should have turned more and more against him. Perhaps it was this very fact of being prosperous that began to make men critical. Such had been the case in 1789. No doubt the liberals had wanted order, and most of them had found the taste of a republic much too rancid; but, on the other hand, they did not wholly relish being relegated to the background; and Napoleon's henchmen as a rule were crafty adventurers like himself. Then, too, the French, having experienced so many vicissitudes, and having no longer that respect for the kingly office which at one time had covered a multitude of sins, were bound to put their sovereign under a very searching test. The very fact that Napoleon III was a usurper was, in a sense, an eternal challenge. There were always some keen intellects which had refused to accept Napoleon, and had never forgiven the Coup d'État. This revived liberalism did not make any great stir until the 'sixties, but when the Emperor's policy, as for instance his commercial treaties, gave a handle for criticism, some of the liberals eagerly grasped it. Furthermore Napoleon had broken with the so-called Ultramontanes (the intensely Catholic faction of the old legitimist royalists, whose favor he had once purchased),[1] and he thus felt that he had to turn to the other

---

[1] The influence of this faction had run like a red thread through all his foreign policy. He had turned his back on Italy partly because of this influence; its hand is also to be noted in his support of the Christians in the Near East and in his patronage of the Catholic Poles; and even his Mexican exploit had a slightly clerical aspect, since the Mexicans had confiscated the property of the Church. The strang-

political pole, the liberal element, for support. Hence began the
fulfillment of his dream of a "liberal empire." In 1860 he allowed
the chamber to reply to the address from the throne, thus enabling
it to criticize the government's policy, and also gave it a limited
publicity in debates; in 1861 he allowed it to examine the budget
clause by clause; in 1867 he granted the right of interpellation
(i.e. the right of a deputy to question any of the ministers); in 1868
he allowed considerable freedom of press and association; finally in
1870 he granted a responsible ministry. These concessions were
too gradual to be appreciated, though, but for a national crisis,
they might have prolonged for a time the life of the Empire. But, in
the meantime, discontent had given impetus to republicanism, even
socialism; and Napoleon had to grant virtual freedom to trade-
unionism in the hope of keeping the proletariat loyal. But by 1866
the Empire had worn itself threadbare, and masquerading in new
clothes hardly helped it to recover respect. The defeat of a French
army in Mexico erased all the memory of Solferino. The victories
of Prussia had quite eclipsed the heir of Napoleon the Great. One
saw only a sovereign prematurely old, an over-prominent clergy, an
artificial and intriguing court, a corrupt bureaucracy, and an army
that lived mainly on its past. If Napoleon had only found a really
talented statesman to guide his faltering hand, he might yet have
saved the Empire. But, as it was, his ministers were always quarreling—a symptom of the autocrat's own decline—and, save for
some jerky plunges, his policy became one of drift. The Paris
exposition of 1867 was the Empire's last splurge. The news of the
execution of Maximilian, which came to becloud its festivities, was
the shadow of the Emperor's own doom.

There was no way to save the Empire from rotting away but to
find some sort of elixir that would inject into it new life. Public
opinion was deeply sensitive over the snubbing France had received after Sadowa. "The whole country," wrote the Austrian
ambassador, "is animated by a single feeling, and that is hatred of
Prussia. Everywhere people are conscious of the mistakes that

est part of the affair is that this party never forgave him for his show of independence when he had come to the aid of Italy in 1859, and though he continued—to the
detriment of both his principles and his interests—to protect the pope, he never
regained its loyalty. Napoleon, at heart a free thinker, should better, if he felt that
he needed some active champions, have made a bid for the liberals at the beginning
of his reign. This, however, would have entailed a limitation on his own authority,
and he was too distrustful of liberalism to take such a risk. Probably his initial
mistake had been in believing that he needed the backing of any faction at all.

have been made and of the opportunity that will never return. They yearn for a spectacular revenge." At the very least they must have something as "compensation." Hence, Napoleon's unlucky plunges—and proportionately great losses. In 1867 he nearly got Luxemburg (which Holland was willing to sell), but German opinion was roused, and Napoleon, not wanting a war,[1] beat a rather ungraceful retreat. Then began some parleying with Austria over an alliance that would somehow get for France the left bank of the Rhine. Conscious of moral bankruptcy, the government was clutching at straws. Such was the national psychology during these years following Sadowa that another affront from Bismarck was certain to produce an explosion.

(2) Bismarck's policy—the Hohenzollern intrigue

And such was the France whom Bismarck intended to harry into war. His opportunity came with the "Hohenzollern candidacy." Spain, having a vacant throne to fill, offered it to young Leopold of Sigmaringen, a Hohenzollern cousin of the King of Prussia. Since France, on learning of the affair, made plain her disapproval, and since William did not want to be embroiled over family interests, Leopold, who was bound by strict family discipline to the head of the family, declined the honor—declined, in fact, three times. But Bismarck had seen his chance. If he could only get a Hohenzollern on the throne of Spain, it would mean to hem in France on two sides, or if, as was probable, she should object, it would mean war. He found it difficult to win over the King, but he finally succeeded; then he prompted another invitation to Leopold, and this time the prince accepted. As might be expected, public opinion in France at once blew up. Realizing, however, that there was justice in its indignation, William was glad when the prince once more declined the throne. It was for France, of course, a diplomatic triumph. Bismarck was so depressed at losing his war that he wrote in his memoirs, "My first idea was to retire from the service, because . . . I perceived in this extorted submission a humiliation of Germany for which I did not desire to be responsible." All should then have been well, but the fools who swayed the decrepit emperor were bent on "rubbing it in." Benedetti was sent to Ems, where the King was taking the waters, to extract from him the promise that he would pledge himself never to allow the

---

[1] The French writer, Joseph Reinach, considered that even now Napoleon's devotion to the principle of nationality made him complaisant toward German nationalism. At all events, it seems clear that he himself did not want war.

candidacy to be renewed. William would, of course, not grant so foolish a demand, and hence he told Benedetti that he regarded the incident as closed, and he later sent word to the Ambassador (who was expecting another interview) that he had nothing further to say. He then telegraphed to Bismarck the substance of the affair, and authorized him to publish the message if he chose. Moltke and Roon were dining with Bismarck when the message was brought in. They were all in the deepest gloom and the telegram only added to it. Then Bismarck suddenly saw his opportunity. Without changing the actual meaning of the telegram, he condensed it in such a manner as to make it appear that the King had given the Ambassador a sharp rebuff. "You have turned a retreat into an offensive," cried Moltke in high glee. Bismarck then sent the garbled version to the press. Paris at once went wild. There were shouts of "*Vive la guerre!*" on the boulevards, and at the opera that night the *Marseillaise* was sung—the first time since the founding of the Second Empire. For a moment the government hesitated, for it was by no means apparent that public opinion, in general, wanted war. But the hot-heads eventually triumphed. On July 19, 1870 France declared war on Prussia.

France's unreadiness for war

The Franco-Prussian War was, on France's part, a case of political suicide. The French army had nothing in its favor but its optimism. Its equipment was defective, for the liberals when they got control of the budget had refused to make it good. The minister of war had said that the army was "ready down to the last button"; it was nearer the truth to say that it had no buttons at all. Militarily unprepared, France was no more ready for war diplomatically. Bismarck had squared the Russian foreign minister by promising to connive at Russia's repudiation of the Treaty of Paris—a favor of which Gorchakov very soon availed himself. Austria was friendly to France, but no alliance had been made, and Italy was still smarting from a French frustration of a Garibaldean attack on Rome. Great Britain was not even benevolently neutral when Bismarck had sent to the *London Times* the proof of Napoleon's designs on Belgium. Thus France was isolated, and to all appearances was responsible for the war.

The Franco-Prussian War

The Franco-Prussian War was one of the most one-sided conflicts in history. In numbers,[1] generalship, and military organization and equipment Prussia had an overwhelming supremacy.

[1] Prussia could command, in round numbers, 450,000 against France's 300,000.

The confusion which prevailed in the French army when forced to resist invasion almost passed belief. The invaders drove one French force into Metz where it was effectually bottled up, while the other was speedily routed in the Battle of Sedan. When this army capitulated, Napoleon himself was taken prisoner along with more than 80,000 men. No one was surprised when Paris proclaimed a republic, September 4, 1870. The Second Empire had collapsed ingloriously in a national crisis.

A second period of the war, however, now commenced, and under the organizing genius of a committee of national defense and the patriotic leadership of Gambetta (a vigorous opponent of the Empire in its later years) the French put up an heroic resistance against insurmountable odds. The Prussians marched on Paris, and the new French levies battered vainly against the impenetrable iron ring which beset the city. Paris finally capitulated after a siege of nearly four months; the preliminaries of peace were ratified by a national assembly; and the definitive Treaty of Frankfort was signed on February 26, 1871. France surrendered Alsace (save the fortified town of Belfort) and most of Lorraine; she also agreed to pay within five years an indemnity of a billion dollars, pending which a German army was to occupy the country. Few had any thought now of Napoleon, who with the Empress had passed into exile in England, where he died two years later.

Results of the war— the establishment of the German Empire

As Bismarck had intended, the unity of Germany was consummated by the war. On January 18, 1871, in the Hall of Mirrors in the famous palace of Versailles William I was proclaimed German emperor. There was not a murmur in the general acclamation with which Germans now accepted the leadership of Prussia. And since in the enlarged federation Prussia would continue to hold the dominant position, the German nation would soon adopt the Prussian standard of a militarized and paternalistic state. Germany was not only unified but Prussianized. Italy also completed her unification, for when France had withdrawn her garrison from Rome to aid in the national defense, the Italians entered Rome without difficulty and made it their capital. Another result of the war was the emergence in international politics of the question of Alsace-Lorraine. Without sympathizing unduly with France for the loss of the provinces which supplied most of her minerals and for the gaping wound which it tore in her side, one must note that the seizure of these provinces was in flagrant violation of the new principle of nationality, for even the Alsatians, Germans as they were by race and language, had for the most part been assimilated to France in the two centuries of French rule; and furthermore (judging this action now from a practical standpoint also) to a proud people like the French, whatever their responsibility for the war, a punishment like this was bound to affect the general peace of Europe. Finally, a result of the war was the disturbance of the balance of power. The German Empire was so powerful that without a makeweight her position in Europe, especially under the military traditions of Prussia, was ominous for the future.

And on the other side of Germany a future ally was setting her house in order.

THE MAKING OF AUSTRIA-HUNGARY

The fundamental weakness of the Hapsburg monarchy had been clearly enough revealed during the mid-century upheaval. Yet Austria tried to delude herself by going back to the old system of autocracy, even making it, as far as Hungary was concerned, more rigid than ever. For more than a decade after her defeat in 1849 Hungary was nothing more than a fragment of the Austrian Empire, autocratically governed from Vienna.

The Evolution of the Dual Monarchy

But the Magyars were fortunate in that their extremists—men like Kossuth—had been broken by defeat, and that most of them were in exile. A more moderate party buoyed up the national hopes—a party that was prepared to extort concessions by peaceful means, and believed also in maintaining the integrity of the empire. The leader of this group was Francis Deák, a man of great personal popularity. Deák was a Magyar nobleman, a lawyer by profession, and a politician by force of circumstances. He was not an impressive debater but exerted an influence through his power in conversation and the impression of sincerity and rugged common sense which he invariably inspired. He managed to keep entirely free of conspiracy, and his patience and intelligence were always a great asset in dealing with the rather stupid bureaucrats who managed things at Vienna.

The rôle of Deák

But in the furtherance of their cause the Magyars were particularly lucky in the misfortunes which befell the dynasty. Austria's defeats in the War of Italian Independence operated to their advantage in two ways. In the first place it drew the Hapsburgs away from trying to maintain their power at a distance from the

Austria's change of heart

center of their dominions, and in the second place it proved to Francis Joseph that Austria could not retain the position of a Great Power as long as she was a prey to internal discord. The Magyars had not been loyal during this crisis, and had either of her wars lasted longer, Austria would probably have had to face another revolution. Fortunately Francis Joseph, though not endowed with great talent, was a person who could learn by experience, and he had a certain forbearance which made it possible for him to deal with different racial temperaments and complicated problems. It was after the Italian War that he resolved to change a system that had worked only injury to his dynasty and his realm.

Rise of dualism

At first it seemed that there were two alternative schemes by which the Hapsburg empire could be reconstituted. One—which seemed to accord best with a country composed of eleven nationalities—was a system of federalism, the essence of which was home rule for each of the nationalities and a general parliament for imperial concerns. The other was the retention of the centralist or unitary system with the qualification that representation in a common parliament should be based on population without regard to nationalist lines. Each of these schemes was tried, but neither was successful, partly because of faults in their working out, but mainly because of Magyar opposition. Hungary repudiated both experiments because neither would give her an influence greater than that of any one of the other nationalities, and she had been accustomed to regard her Croats, Slovaks, and Roumans as inferiors. Deák then proposed in 1865 a third scheme—the principle of dualism. The ancient kingdom of Hungary should recover its separate existence and individuality and even acquire an enhanced importance, but at the same time should be bound to the rest of the empire—that is, Austria—by ties that would enable the common ruler to stand for a united nation in the world at large. The negotiations between Vienna and Budapest were interrupted by the Seven Weeks' War, but when Austria met with decisive defeat at Sadowa, the Emperor without hesitation surrendered to Hungary's demands. The result was the establishment of the Dual Monarchy.

The Organization of the Dual Monarchy

The *Ausgleich* or Compromise of 1867 represented a system of government quite unique in the history of politics. It created a tie almost as loose as a personal union, but not quite, for it provided a machinery that was intended to promote a measure of co-operation, though substantially the two pillars of the system, Austria and *Character of the Ausgleich* Hungary, were two independent states. Each had its own consti- tution, ministry, parliament, administration, and postal and mone- tary systems, but under the common sovereign was an imperial ministry; and the acts of this ministry were supervised (not con- troled) by two bodies known as the delegations, one Austrian, one Hungarian, each meeting separately and conferring with the other by parallel communications, one in the German, the other in the Magyar language. Though by virtue of such conferences a certain accord might be reached in general policy, the initiative really reposed in the foreign minister (the only important member of the common ministry), who was appointed by and responsible to the emperor-king. Finally some important matters lay entirely outside the scope of the imperial machinery. Questions of an economic nature, such as the tariff, were settled at ten-year in- tervals by direct negotiation between the two states. Since the apportionment of the burden of national defense had thus to be regulated, it was every ten years a matter of considerable friction; while actual sums to be voted by each parliament for common needs were generally settled by parleys between the two premiers— a procedure quite outside the imperial constitution. Thus the de- fect of the system was the want of sufficient unity to make for harmony. The chief bond was, in fact, the sovereign—emperor in Austria and king in Hungary, and crowned in both countries. Subject to certain limitations, his power was practically that of an autocrat still.

It is obvious that such a system was fair only to the Germans *Effects of the Ausgleich* and the Magyars, the other nationalities having no separate recog- nition. The Croats were, however, so important that Hungary felt compelled to grant them a measure of autonomy in the Com- promise of 1868. The disappointment of the Czechs was manifested by a demand for a separate state on a par with Austria and Hun- gary, and though Francis Joseph consented to their demand, such a stir was made by the Magyars, who feared for the effect on their own nationalities, that the Emperor retracted his promise. Since the new constitution of Hungary gave the Magyars a much greater ascendancy in Hungary than the new constitution of Austria gave the Germans in Austria, there was a growing tendency for Hungary (who certainly bore a less equitable share in the common financial burdens) to become the more powerful partner in the Dual Monarchy. The Magyars not only freed themselves from German rule; they became slightly the dominant people of the Hapsburg realm.

FOR FURTHER READING OR STUDY

Robinson, J. H., and Beard, C. A., *Readings in Modern European History*, vol. ii, chaps. xxi–xxii; Scott, J. F., and Baltzly, A., *Readings in European History since 1814*, chap. vii; *Letters and Recollections of Mazzini* (ed. King); *Mazzini's Letters to an English Family*, 3 vols. (ed. Richards, E. F.); Della Rocca, E., *Autobiography of a Veteran; Bismarck, the Man and the Statesman*, 2 vols. (his memoirs); Busch, M., *Bismark: Some Secret Pages from His History; Correspondence of William III and Bismark*, 3 vols.; Hauterive, E. d'; *The Second Empire and Its Downfall* (from Bonaparte's private papers); Oakes, A. A., and Mowat, R. B., *op. cit.*, or Holland, T. E., *The Concert of Europe in the Eastern Question* (for the treaties of Paris and Berlin).

Hazen, C. D., *Europe since 1815*, chaps. x–xiii and xvii; Schapiro, J. S., *Modern and Contemporary European History*, chaps. xii–xv, xxi (the older edition treats Italy, 1815–71 and Germany, 1815–71 in single chapters); Hayes, C. J. H., *A Political and Social History of Modern Europe*, vol. ii, pp. 158–206, 426–34; Higby, C. P., *A History of Modern Europe*, part ii; Palm, F. C., and Graham, F. E., *Europe since Napoleon*, chaps. vii–ix; Andrews, C. M., *Historical Development of Modern Europe*, vol. ii, chaps. i–vii; Fueter, E., *World History*, chaps. xxii, xxv–xxvii; Croce, B., *History of Europe in the Nineteenth Century*, chaps. vii–viii; Phillips, W. A., *Modern Europe*, chaps. xiv–xviii.

Rose, J. H., *Nationality in Modern History*, lects. v and vi; Guignebert, C., *A Short History of the French People*, vol. ii, chap. xxxviii; Guedalla, P., *The Second Empire* (picturesque but superficial); Guerard, A. L., *French Civilization in the Nineteenth Century;* Simpson, F. A., *Louis Napoleon and the Recovery of France* (scholarly and interesting); Schevill, F., *The History of the Balkan Peninsula*, chaps. xxii–xxv; Puryear, V. J., *England, Russia, and the Straits Question;* Martin, K., *The Triumph of Lord Palmerston;* Temperley, H. W. V., "Stratford de Redcliffe and the Origins of the Crimean War," *Eng. Hist. Rev.*, xlviii, 656 ff.; East, F. M., *The Union of Moldavia and Wallachia;* Riker, T. W., *The Making of Roumania* (fullest account and traces connection [chap. ix] with Italian Revolution); Wambaugh, S., *A Monograph on Plebiscites;* Solmi, A., *The Making of Modern Italy;* Villari, L., *Italy*, chaps. i–iv (interpretive); King, B., *A History of Italian Unity*, 2 vols.; King, B., *Joseph Mazzini* (only fair); Holland, R. S., *Builders of United Italy;* Greenfield, K. R., *Economics and Liberalism in the Risorgimento* (confined to Lombardy); Martinengo-Cesaresco, E. L. H., *Cavour* (charming); Thayer, W. R., *The Life and Times of Cavour*, 2 vols. (a standard work, though rather partisan); White, A. J. B., *The Early Life and Letters of Cavour;* White, A. J. B., *The Political Life and Letters of Cavour;* Sumner, B. H., "The Secret Franco–Russian Treaty of 3 March, 1859," *Eng. Hist. Rev.*, xlviii, 48 ff.; Trevelyan, G. M., *Garibaldi and the Defense of the Roman Republic, Garibaldi and the Thousand*, and *Garibaldi and the Making of Italy;* Gay, M. W., "Garibaldi's Sicilian Campaign as Described by an American Diplomat," *Amer. Hist. Rev.*, xxix, 24 ff.; Marriot, J. A. R., and Robertson, C. G., *The Evolution of Prussia*, chaps. v–x, xi–xii; Smith, M.,

Bismarck and German Unity (a brief sketch); Headlam, J. W., *Bismarck;* Robertson, C. G., *Bismarck* (a brilliant study); Lord, R. N., "Bismarck and Russia in 1863," *Amer. Hist. Rev.*, xxix, 24 ff.; Steefel, L. D., *The Schleswig-Holstein Question;* Whitton, F. E., *Moltke;* Clark, C. W., *Franz Joseph and Bismarck before 1866;* Oncken, H., *Napoleon III and the Rhine;* Ollivier, E., *The Franco-Prussian War and Its Hidden Causes* (reflections of a minister of Napoleon III); Lord, R. H., *Origins of the War of 1870;* Raymond, D. N., *British Policy and Opinion during the Franco-Prussian War;* Carroll, E. M., "French Public Opinion on War with Prussia in 1870," *Amer. Hist. Rev.*, xxxi, 679 ff.; Leger, L., *The History of Austria-Hungary;* Redlich, J., *The Emperor Francis Joseph* (a penetrating biography); Corti, E. C., *The Reign of the House of Rothschild;* Riker, T. W., "Michael of Serbia and the Turkish Occupation," *Slavonic Rev.*, xii, 133 ff., 409 ff., 646 ff.; Medlicott, W. N., "The Recognition of Roumanian Independence" (an admirable study), *ibid.*, xi, 354 ff., 372.

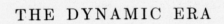

THE DYNAMIC ERA

XIV. EUROPE IN TRANSITION—SOCIAL, ECO-NOMIC, AND POLITICAL FORCES IN THE DYNAMIC AGE

1. THE SCIENTIFIC REVOLUTION AND THE RECASTING OF THE ECONOMIC ORDER

Nature and origins of the Scientific Revolution; Basic discoveries in the natural sciences; Progress in medical science; Progress in the physical sciences; New sources of power; Science and the economic order; The problem of economic reorganization; Rationalization and its results: (1) economic, (2) social.

2. THE EVOLUTION OF PUBLIC OPINION

Nature of public opinion; Early manifestations; Causes of growth; Significance.

3. POLITICAL REFORM

A. DEMOCRACY IN GENERAL

Basis and defects; Its practical expediency.

B. IN GREAT BRITAIN

The party system; Parliamentary reform; Abasement of the house of lords; Democracy in practice.

C. IN FRANCE

Evolution of the Third Republic; Organization of the republic; Consolidation of the republic; Conservation of the republic; Separation of Church and State; Democracy in practice.

D. IN ITALY

Problem of unity; Relations with the papacy; Democracy in practice.

E. IN OTHER COUNTRIES

The Scandinavian countries; The Netherlands and Belgium; Switzerland; Spain and Portugal.

4. SOCIAL REFORM

A. IN GERMANY

Bismarck and the "social state"; Position of the peasantry.

B. IN GREAT BRITAIN

Progress of trade-unionism; Rise of the Labor Party; Program of social reform: (1) causes, (2) content.

C. IN FRANCE

The proletariat; The peasantry.

507

D. IN ITALY

    The proletariat; The peasantry.

E. POSITION OF THE "SOCIAL STATE"

    Measure of the social state; Question of birth control.

    5. NATIONALISM AND THE SUBMERGED NATIONALITIES

      Some preliminary distinctions; Meaning of nationalism; Objects of nationalism; Nationalism in subjection: (1) case of the Poles, (2) case of the Irish, (3) other cases; Psychology of nationalism.

In the growing complexity of civilization in the Dynamic Age there stand out certain forces which have profoundly affected human relationships. Science has enlightened the world as never before and has revolutionized industry to an extent never dreamed of in the days which immediately followed the Industrial Revolution. The world of business has come to rest on a firmer basis and even the modern state has grown in strength—though not with a corresponding breadth of outlook on the world. The masses have become more thoroughly self-conscious, and the principle of the social state has come into general adoption. Also the gradual lessening of physical labor through the steady development of machine production and the moral liberation of the masses from the grip of the upper strata of society have released a new factor in human affairs—public opinion. The operation of these forces has given rise to new problems, new experiments, new dangers. The Dynamic Age is an age of adjustment, and in the end it may turn out to be more revolutionary than any previous age. We are here suggesting some of the vital changes that have taken place, though problems are left unsolved for subsequent generations. Later we shall discuss the great catastrophe which befell civilization—the Great War—and the effects which it has seemed to produce. But even this colossal disaster has not seriously interrupted the period of transition we have called the Dynamic Age.

THE SCIENTIFIC REVOLUTION AND THE RECASTING OF THE ECONOMIC ORDER

Nature and origins of the Scientific Revolution   It is always a question when the term "revolution" should be applied; and in the field of science it may be recalled that the discoveries of Copernicus, Newton, and others were revolutionary in their influence on preconceived theories. When the Church had

been shorn of its reputation for omniscience, the mind was at last
released to do its own thinking. Perhaps this phase of the Renaissance, which we have already discussed, was the greatest intellectual revolution. But the marvelous discoveries of the nineteenth
century have altered so completely man's conception of himself
and the world about him that one may properly use the term, the
"Scientific Revolution." And it is a revolution that under modern
conditions may be expected to go on as long as there is a human
mind to function. We shall here differentiate between those basic
discoveries which revamped or augmented the old sciences, with
all the significance which they seemed to have for man, and the
great continuous rush of mechanical inventions that has had a
direct bearing on his economic life.

The origins of what we have called the Scientific Revolution
may doubtless be found in that general stimulation of mental
effort which embraced both the French and Industrial Revolutions.
The generation which lived after these profound changes would
naturally be spurred to greater exertions. The struggling scientist
had now a greater confidence in the outcome of his labors as well as
a more appreciative world in which to work. Then it should be
added that the advances already made in the technique of production suggested further elaboration and new devices for turning out
goods more cheaply and more quickly than could be done by hand.
But the initial phase of the revolution (which began before what
we have called the "Dynamic Era") had not so much a practical
end in view as a desire simply to know the truth about nature,
man, and the universe.

With the further advance of science the biblical account of creation as a direct and instantaneous act of the Divine Creator was
one of the concepts first impeached. As far back as 1755 the French
scientist, Laplace, had propounded the theory that the earth,
like other planets, was the result of the compression of some of the
gaseous nebula of which the solar system was found to be composed.
The objections to the theory are of less importance than the fact
that Science was feeling her way to a sounder view of the great
and eternal "Cause." Hence, to bridge the span of time from the
birthday of the earth to the period of human activity became a
fascinating field for geologists, and forty years after Laplace's
treatise a Scotsman, James Hutton, contended that the present
form of the earth was the result of a gradual process and that of

*The basic
discoveries
in the
natural
sciences*

its beginnings he found "no trace." The ways in which gradual changes had occurred through thousands of millions of years was set forth at length by an English geologist, Sir Charles Lyell, in 1830–3. The very fact that sea-shells were found at great distance from the sea and even at high altitudes, and that human and animal fossils were found deeply embedded in rock were evidence, it seemed, of the great vistas of time that had preceded the dawn of history. The great antiquity of the earth seemed now established.

As the science of geology was revolutionized, so also, in course of time, was that of biology. As the earth had grown gradually to its present state, so had animals and plants come gradually to assume their present forms. In the latter part of the eighteenth century the French naturalist, Buffon, had reasoned that man had evolved from a lower species, and another Frenchman, Lamarck, advanced the theory that the whole animal world had developed from lower forms. Lyell's work gave new impetus to the study of this problem, and in the middle of the nineteenth century Alfred Wallace and Charles Darwin, working independently, arrived at what is known as the theory of evolution. Man and other animals and likewise plants have come up through various forms from crude beginnings, a surviving species having in each case a variant which had enabled it to surmount the dangers and accidents of life. It was the theory of the "survival of the fittest," as Wallace expressed it. Many of Darwin's conclusions had been reached during a visit to South America where he found the fossils of many extinct animals and where he was able to note also the conditions that had produced the degeneration or gradual extinction of certain species. Everywhere he was struck with the struggle between men and plants and the struggle of both with nature. Though some of Darwin's views, as expounded in his *Origin of Species* (1859), have since been disputed, his main thesis has been held by scientists ever since; and even the world of religion, though bitterly hostile at first, has gradually come to accept its basic truth. Incidentally, the notion of historical evolution came to have a greater significance, and the idea that our present conceptions and institutions were derived from an earlier stage of civilization tended to give the modern scholar a broader and more tolerant outlook on society. Subsequent to this startling revelation in biology emerged the new science of psychology, examining and explaining human behavior.

Among the greatest strides in the nineteenth century were those in the field of medicine, using the term broadly. The discovery of microscopic animal organisms called germs or bacteria explained the source of many diseases, and building on this knowledge, scientists were able by experiment to utilize the so-called anti-toxins, which the toxins or poisons arising from the activities of the bacteria had produced. This led to the study of preventive medicine, already foreshad-owed before the germ theory by Jenner's discovery of the vaccine to combat smallpox. Soon diphtheria, tetanus, ty-phoid fever, and other dis-eases yielded to treatment by serums. One of the pioneers in this field was the French chemist, Louis Pasteur, who by experimentation found the method of averting hydropho-bia and also eradicated the scourge that was infesting the silk worms of southern France and threatening the silk in-dustry with ruin. A study of dietetics also enriched the science of medicine, which came to depend less and less on the efficacy of drugs to cure

Progress in medical science

LORD LISTER

disease. Meanwhile diagnosis had been aided by the invention of the X-ray and other explorative devices, and surgery had similarly progressed. The use of anesthetics about the middle of the century proved one of the greatest blessings to human-ity. And in 1876 a British physician, Joseph Lister, gave the world the knowledge of antisepsis—methods of guarding wounds from attack by virulent bacteria and thus lessening the chances of infection. It goes without saying that these discoveries not only materially reduced suffering but greatly lowered the death rate. Life was longer in the aggregate and considerably more painless than it had been a century ago. As a great physician, Sir William Osler, has well said "Measure as we may the progress of the world—materially in the advantages of steam, electricity, and the mechanical appliances; intellectually in the diffusion of education; morally in the possibly higher standard of ethics—there is no one measure that can compare with the decrease of physical suffering in man, woman, and child when stricken by disease or accident. This is the one fact of supreme personal import to every one of us. This is the Promethean gift of the century to man."

Progress in the physical sciences   We can hardly take space to record the marvels of astronomy during this period, though it may be remarked that the immensity of the universe as compared with the tiny planet on which we live is more staggering to the comprehension than the billion or more years that the earth has run. Of much more direct importance has been the revolution in the physical sciences—in particular in physics. Early in the nineteenth century the so-called atomic theory was advanced by John Dalton, an English chemist, and has since been generally accepted. It is believed that matter is not inert, as it appears, but is made up of countless atoms; and for a long time it was thought that the atom was the smallest particle into which matter was divided. In 1897 Pierre and Marie Curie in discovering a new element, radium, paved the way for the discovery that smaller than the atom was the "electron," as it is called, which, as physicists have ascertained, revolves about the core of the atom, known as the nucleus. These electrons are negative charges of electricity, and they prove that matter is perpetually in motion. Thus the seemingly inanimate rock is in a constant state of activity. It is by the combining of different atoms that chemists have been able to make different substances, such as alcohol, indigo, and numerous dyes, which were once derived only from vegetation. Phosphorus and diamonds may also be made, and artificial manures are commonly used for fertilization of the soil. In learning the nature of heat, light, and sound, physics kept pace with chemistry in adding to our knowledge. Moreover, that mysterious force we call electricity was finally made applicable

New sources of power   to human use. In 1831 an English physicist, Michael Faraday, worked out the principle of the dynamo by which electric energy may be generated; and, after long experimenting, it gave rise to the electric motor, which runs trolleys, elevators, and even sometimes trains. The transmission of electricity by means of wires rendered it possible for a factory using this particular kind of power to be located without reference to the mines; and the value of water

power in generating electricity brought about in many cases a
return to the sites where mills used to be found in the early days
of the Industrial Revolution. Meanwhile coal came to find a competitor in oil, and the invention, or rather the perfecting, of the
internal combustion en-
gine (1895) opened the
way for a cheaper form
of motive power—cheaper
because it requires less
in bulk to provide the
needed power. It is this
engine that is used to
propel automobiles and
airplanes. Interestingly
enough, too, the increas-
ing use of oil, especially
in transportation, led to
the building up of one of
the greatest industries in
the world, and demand
for oil has widened the
scope of international rivalry. It is worth while
also to recall that meth-
ods of illumination under-

Painting by Phillips

MICHAEL FARADAY

went vast change within the memory of a generation—first ker-
osene, then gas, then electricity; though, obviously, much of Europe has yet to experience the complete evolution.

Meanwhile, parallel with the discovery of a new means of fur- *Science and*
nishing power one must bear in mind the continual flow of new *the economic*
machines and the improvement of old ones. The improved print- *order*
ing-press, the sewing-machine, photography (which goes back to
the 'twenties), the machine for making matches, the Bessemer
process of smelting, and modern methods of refrigeration are only
a few of the marvels of the period. The adapting of rubber to commercial uses (thanks initially to the experiments of Charles Good-
year in 1839) not only furnished water-proof articles of many sorts,
but provided one of the foundations of the automobile industry;
and the rubber industry is now one of the greatest in the world.
In every phase of society invention showed its mark. Business

was facilitated by the typewriter, the adding machine, and even the phonograph. Agriculture was made simpler and more profitable by the reaping machine and the tractor, and chemical fertilization made possible a more intensive cultivation of the soil. Punishment of crime was facilitated by the dictograph and by the scientific study of finger-prints. Even new amusements were eventually found through the cinema and the radio, both of which also have an educational value. And naturally enough, the capacity of industry was many times augmented by new and better machines.

Simultaneous with the progress of production was that of transportation. As the century wore on, Europe had become covered with a network of railways, and the work of canal construction had also proceeded. Of immense importance to world trade have been the Suez Canal, opened in 1869, and the Panama Canal, which was completed in 1914. The speed and safety of sea travel were also greatly enhanced. As late as 1870 most of the merchant fleets of the world were sailing-vessels, but from that time on the steamer has rapidly displaced them, and already iron had taken the place of wood in ship-construction. Before the Great War tremendous liners—great floating hotels—were traversing the seas. Meanwhile, just as the trolley (known in England as the "tram") had made for easier and more rapid communication between a city and its suburbs, so the automobile, which came into practical use toward the close of the century, brought the country nearer to the towns, and rapidly became a medium for the circulation of goods. About the same time aviation became a basis of experiment, and since the War it has offered the quickest service for travelers between the larger towns of Europe, though for commercial purposes it is still limited for the most part to carrying mail. It is confidently predicted that a still more rapid service will be possible in the so-called "stratosphere"—that aërial zone ten miles above the earth which the Swiss scientist, Piccard, first penetrated in 1931.

The improvement in methods of communication is notable in other ways than quicker means of travel. During the middle of the nineteenth century the electric telegraph appeared, and in 1866 the first cable was laid between Europe and America. Then in the 'seventies came the telephone, and in the last decade of the century, wireless telegraphy, made practicable by the work of the Italian inventor, Marconi. This discovery led to others—the

wireless telephone, the radio, television, and even the photograph-
ing (by wireless) of objects at a distance. The printing-press has
also marched with the times. By invention of the linotype the
process of composition was able to keep pace with that of production, and the great modern presses provide even for the cutting
and folding of paper by machinery. It has been said than an hour
after an important event has happened, the newsboy is shouting
it on the streets.

The effect of all these changes has been to make the world in
effect much smaller, and civilization more diffused. Nothing happens in any corner of the world that is not known in another corner
of it in a short space of time. Business transactions can be made
with great rapidity through the telegraph or telephone. Capital
was so easily and so profusely invested in foreign lands and the
world had become so inter-dependent for the satisfaction of its
needs that in 1900 one might have felt that a great war was inconceivable. Close communications were also, to all appearances,
making for mutual sympathy and understanding. The greater
strength of that counter-force, aggressive nationalism, will furnish
us with one of the clues to the basic instability of the economic
order.

It may be said that the steady stream of inventions was both *The problem*
a cause and an effect of the development of a more scientific man- *of economic*
agement in business. It was a result in that need of quicker and *reorganiza-*
cheaper service had stimulated invention and required a more *tion*
scientific management of enterprises. It was the cause insofar as
it enabled and instigated competent men in business to achieve
this quicker and cheaper service. Certainly the means which
chemistry discovered of utilizing mineral supplies greatly aided
the promotion of industry. But the organizing skill which has so
ably recast the economic order proceeded fundamentally from the
limitless possibilities opened long ago by the Industrial Revolution.
The inauguration of large-scale production suggested at once the
widening of the market. The remarkable growth of population in
the nineteenth century (which we have already noted) meant the
creation of more workers and more consumers. A more immediate
cause of this rationalization of industry was the realization that
competition limited profits and involved needless waste of energy
and capital. The old saying that "competition is the life of trade"
had a sound element of truth, for it often spurred the manufacturer

to the greatest possible care in turning out his product and it inspired the merchant to give the best possible service to his customer. But competition often meant the possession of so little capital on the part of the producer that the consumer was not really as well served as he would have been, had competition yielded in a measure to co-operation—for the larger the business, generally speaking the better able it is to exact a small profit on the particular article sold. It was also difficult for the producer for a wide competitive market to know how much to produce; the extent of the competition was always an unknown quality, to be guessed at best; and the consequent tendency was overproduction, with resultant ruin or at least depression. Moreover, under the competitive system there has often been an undue risk in starting an establishment. A depression in England during the 'thirties was ascribed by a contemporary solely to the fact that "British manufacturers have gone far beyond their rivals abroad in the rashness with which factories have been multiplied." Finally, competition often led to destructive underselling. It was to prevent this cut-throat competition that informal price-agreements became common among large industrial concerns—the first step toward the emergence of the "cartel," which we shall note as the loosest form of trust.

Rationalization and its results   It is obvious that individualism in business had to yield in a measure to some sort of industrial concentration. The economic reorganization which was devised in order to get the most value out of an expanding market and insure the maximum profit has come to be known by the term, "rationalization." It involved the rise of what is known as the "corporation," which insured a greater supply of capital and the possession of more and more capital as needed; a tendency to dominate the market by the creation of some species of monopoly; the employment of experts to reduce costs and in general to make a study of the problems of production and consumption; and the establishment of bureaus of research to develop mechanical devices that would facilitate production. Not all these aspects of rationalization are found everywhere present, for circumstances often prevent its complete realization, but all these aspects made themselves felt toward the close of the nineteenth century. It is these aspects which we must now take time to consider.

The corporation had the advantage over the traditional stock

company in that liability was limited to the proportional investment of each of the share-holders. Thus the risk involved was less.
It had a still more obvious advantage over the individual producer
in that it could more readily attract capital from without, its
managing personnel could more easily change, and it facilitated a
linking with other enterprises—in other words the creation of a
trust. It may be added that the rise of the corporation dating from
about the middle of the century, is not always included by scholars
as part of the process of rationalization (a term which has come
into use since the Great War), but it was at least a necessary step
to scientific organization. There was rationalization of a sort before
the term came into use.

Schemes for regulating the market through some form of monopoly also appeared during the period, and the tendency has been
growing ever since. It is thus that we have the rise of the so-called
"trust," which implies, as Hobson says, "a consolidation of capital
within a trade that is large enough and strong enough to control to
an appreciable extent the supply and the selling-price of the articles
with which it deals." Trusts or combinations are divided fundamentally into two kinds—the vertical and the horizontal. The
former signifies consolidation under a single management of different industries which in some way contribute to produce a certain
commodity. The cost of paper induced a British press organization
(of which Lord Northcliffe was the leading spirit) to erect mills in
Newfoundland for the manufacture of cellulose and paper. The
latter and more common type (the horizontal) is a combination of
different firms in the same industry for the control of the market.
The horizontal trust may take the form of complete amalgamation
through interlocking directorates or through the control of the
greater proportion of the stock of one company by another or
simply through agreements between independent companies in
the matter of the standard of goods, the extent of the output, the
geographical division of the market, and (above all) the prices to
be charged. This latter type, which assumes the independence of
the different companies, is known as the "cartel," and is commonest in Germany. As a result of agreement between some of the
larger coal companies in Germany each company was limited in its
production according to the size of its pits and the amount of capital invested, and prices were determined respectively for competitive zones, for non-competitive zones, and for foreign markets.

There were also international agreements such as those which produced the International Steel Cartel in 1926, and the price of all the important raw materials have come to be regulated in this way. By 1928 the Swedish Match Trust came to control eighty per cent of the world's production of matches. In France, as distinguished from most European countries, the independent producer is still predominant, and where there are corporations agreements have been mainly for the purpose of general policy. In England also the movement toward concentration has been slow, for as long as her manufacturers had the benefit of free trade they got most of their raw materials from abroad at small expense; and there has always been considerable popular prejudice against trusts, the consumer fearing that the cost of living would thereby be raised. It is, of course, true that monopoly of the market may lead to the charging of exorbitant prices, but unless the market is international, the trust has always to consider the point where it may be undersold by a foreign competitor. The British trusts, which are more favorable to a common management (though there are some agreements between independent companies) have a dominating position in the market for several industries, such as thread, salt, soda, whisky, tobacco, and locomotives. One might mention as other examples of the general movement toward industrial consolidation during the period the rail and bank mergers and what is known as the chain store. Another way of restricting competition, though not of necessity implying any monopoly, was through the rise of the now-familiar "department store."

The development of scientific management, through the employment of technical experts, who study severally the productive capacity of the enterprise, its problem of reducing costs, and the best way of capturing the market, is the very essence of rationalization. Besides the salaried directing board (representing the combination of manufacturers and financiers) we now find the technical expert, who is nowadays versed in the "science of management." It was an American expert, trained by practical experience, F. W. Taylor by name, who made a special study of the means of getting the greatest productivity from labor. Taylor began life as a common laborer but rose to be an engineer in a great steel foundry. In 1913 he published a book on the science of management, and his thesis was that every kind of work, however simple, could be made more effective through scientific study.

The time that every act should take should, in his opinion, be carefully measured. Assuming that the ordinary workman was slow and indifferent and that it was possible to "speed him up," he suggested several means by which this end could be secured. He believed that each worker should have a definite task to perform within a given time and should be remunerated according to the quantity of his output rather than the length of time expended, and that the accuracy of his work should also be proportionately rewarded. Not only the psychology of the workman but also his environment was carefully considered by those who followed in Taylor's footsteps. It is said that improvement in lighting alone increased the productivity of workmen in certain factories by forty per cent. Some of Taylor's methods are now deemed obsolete, as more and more labor has come to be absorbed by mechanical agencies; yet his fundamental ideas have held their ground. Another and more important method of insuring greater profits is the common device, known as "mass production." This experiment (which is obviously not new but has now become more general, through American inspiration), signifies turning out identical articles in great bulk—a method which greatly simplifies the problem of machine capacity. When a number of independent firms agree on the same type of article, the element of competition in variety or quality is thereby removed. According to a recent writer, "from the point of view of production the most direct advantage of standardization is that it enables articles to be manufactured continuously. The production in large quantities of articles of uniform pattern obviates the necessity of continuous changes in the set-up of machines and economies in the use of capital equipment." Another aspect of industrial technique is the study of the market, and here is where sales psychology has proved of great service. At a time when problems of public health attract a good deal of attention it is found useful to represent a soap as "life-giving" or a cigarette as not producing a cough. The public is very susceptible to propaganda of all kinds. It is also often captivated through the senses—hence the device of decorating shop windows or providing attractive containers for commodities for sale. Such devices may actually add to the cost of an article but produce a greater demand in spite of the fact. While forecasting the market always plays an important part in determining the volume of production, it is nevertheless deemed important to "create demand"; and advertising is a science in itself—a sort of branch of social psychology. Many of its manifestations are experimental and sometimes foolish, but there is a general belief that "advertising pays."

Finally, some firms have gone so far as to establish laboratories as part of their capital equipment. Here men of inventive ability may study new ways of using chemistry to promote the industry or specialists in engineering may experiment with a view of simplifying or perfecting machinery in operation. No longer is it deemed sufficient to wait for the individual inventor or for the chance results of university research. One might almost say that men are now required to invent by order. And even if a firm does not itself finance research, it may employ specialists to advise the management on the relation of its particular problems to the discoveries made available by public institutions.

(1)
Economic

Some of the economic results of this rationalization of industry have been indicated. Greater profits have been obtained through the reduction of costs, a study of the market, and (in some cases) the elimination of competition. Some enterprises have grown to a prodigious size. In place of the factory has arisen that huge economic unit known as the "plant," covering acres of ground, with machinery operated by an army of workmen, and capitalized by hundreds of thousands of dollars. We can easily understand the multiplication of millionaires, though it should be noted that the increase of labor costs (as the result of trade unions and other factors) and the policy of putting more and more of the earnings back into the business have tended to prevent the stock-holders from reaping the full measure of their harvest. In the new economy the banks play a central rôle. Thanks to the checking system and the clearing house little specie needs to be shipped and by making use of a certain proportion of private deposits a great expansion of credit has been possible, thus providing capital in quantities which in the earlier, less elastic economic régime had never been possible. Some of the results of this period of evolution or revolution can hardly yet be gauged. Will the automobile, which has already condemned the trolley to early extinction, have a similar effect on the railroad? So far it would seem that for long distances on land the railroad has as yet no adequate substitute, and for short journeys competition has at least had the excellent effect of forcing the railroads to improve the quality of their service.

Rationalization—or, as some prefer to call it, the "New Industrial Revolution," has largely recast the economic order. "The extreme individualism of the nineteenth century," writes a British author, "has been modified to such an extent that in practice perfectly free competition between business units rarely exists." Even independent producers have come to see the folly of cutthroat competition, and the whole tendency has been in the direction of market agreements. Rationalization undoubtedly simplifies most problems for the producer, and often it has led to lower prices than was possible under the old system of small-scale production on a competitive basis. But the consumer has not always gained, for in countries enjoying high protective tariffs international competition cannot take the place of domestic competition as a means of safeguarding his interests, and often enough he pays a monopoly price. There is even the chance, where competition has practically disappeared, that qualitative standards may be lowered. Also the greater the concentration of productive power, the more danger of overproduction on a large scale, with the usual consequence of widespread depression—a point that will receive our attention in a later chapter. And, finally, the larger the enterprise the more chance of stock-manipulation and other questionable practices which react so gravely on the small investor. The problem of protecting society as consumers and investors is one of the most difficult and one of the least considered of the problems of today. It would mean an enormous widening of the sphere of the social state.

The social results of rationalization are difficult as yet to meas- *(2) Social* ure, and no one can fortell the possible adjustments that may be made to an historic movement so profound in its effects upon civilization. Some of the immediate results are, however, fairly evident. The growth of rationalization has naturally led to a great increase of the managerial and technical staff in proportion to the number of workmen. It is also evident that the man who tends to the machine is very largely supplanting both the skilled and unskilled worker. Organization, system, and machinery have depersonalized industry to a remarkable degree. The army of stock-holders has little or nothing to do with the policy of the company whose capital it has provided, and few companies really depend on the life of any of their executives. In certain ways, no doubt, the cleavage between capital and labor is still very sharp.

Unequal distribution of wealth has come to be more conspicuous than ever before, and consequently has been a contributive cause of industrial unrest. The very fact that the working class has obtained the suffrage has made it more resentful of exploitation and more conscious of social barriers. On the other hand, in some respects the line between labor and capital has come to be less pronounced, directors and workers being both on the company pay-roll, and workers sometimes owning stock in the company. But one of the greatest levelers of the age has been the fact of mass production. In many cases the same standard of goods is used by high or low, since no other is obtainable; and since the masses furnish the bulk of consumption, there has been a tendency to turn out cheaper and flimsier articles instead of the better-made stuff that will stand the test of time. This tendency, it is true, is bound up with changes of style, which may be viewed as an effort to stimulate the market. Yet it is manifest enough that machine production under the system of rationalization offers very little variety and less and less scope to the individual taste. Mass production tends to lead to the "mass man." The fact that amusements, have, in general, become cheaper or more popular in their reach has tended to standardize taste as well as to level social barriers. "The radio, the cinema, and the modern press, by the transmission of the same news and the same entertainments simultaneously over the world, have been the chief agents in the international standardization of thought, of habit, and of outlook on life."

Along with the equalizing process between classes one may note the growing fusion of town and country due to the automobile. The development of 'bus lines from urban centers to distant parts of the country bring the peasants more readily to share the life of the towns and to emulate their ways. Conversely, urban dwellers are tending to find the country, which they can now more easily reach, more desirable for residence. There is, in a sense, a sort of "flight to the country," as a contrast to the earlier "flight to the towns," though it is noticeable in this connection that the development of readier means of communication has drawn a good deal of business away from the village or smaller town to the nearest industrial center where a greater and perhaps cheaper stock of commodities can be found. The tedium of isolation has departed, as also its charm. The world has been greatly contracted, and its mysteries laid bare.

The spiritual effect of this changing world on the individual is a matter of much discussion. That life and work in the average are less hard can scarcely be disputed. Labor-saving devices have lessened the worker's physical effort (provided he has a job); shorter hours have given him greater leisure to follow his fancies; and there are forms of entertainment at his disposal that his grandfather never knew. Looking back from the time of the Great War to the previous generation, the standard of living had risen in the aggregate, and the steady decline of the birth rate in western Europe was at least in a measure related to the demand for more luxuries for the few. Yet, in diffusing culture more widely through the medium of mass production, the present age has possibly lowered its quality. The legitimate stage can no longer compete with the machine-made cinema; and one wonders now if the radio will not soon displace the opera. As a musician once remarked, "Nobody who could be aesthetically satisfied with the turning of a disc would go out in the rain to a music hall." Canned music and canned plays, being cheaper, have an unanswerable appeal. Moreover, machinery saves one time as well as money. The art of cooking seems to be rendered less important by the "miracles" of canning. Things that are worth while almost invariably take time—why bother when the machine can spare the effort? Sometimes, too, one can "make believe" that one has something "just as good" as the best. Cheap substitutes, like artificial silk, and paste, instead of jewelry, have won a recognition even in fashionable circles. It may be argued, however, that taste is of really no value in itself and that its standardization on a new and lower plane is not of necessity harmful. This, of course, is a matter of opinion.

Is there a "shoddiness" in the present age that former periods of history seldom knew? Some observers, perhaps a bit more cynical than is justified, seem to feel that money and its display are becoming recognized, even in Europe, as the chief criterion of worth—much as one would expect in a middle-class social order. "The test of success," writes the British sociologist, Christopher Dawson, "is quantitative, not qualitative. A man is judged not by the character of his work, but by the money that he makes. Society has become an economic organism which judges its members by economic standards. The ideal has its apparent justification in the material prosperity that it produces. The life of the ordinary man has become more enjoyable and richer in material circumstances than it has ever been in the past. But it also involves a sacrifice of individual freedom and a certain lowering of cultural ideals. In order to realize the full possibilities of the new machine civilization, man has had to subject himself to its laws, to become himself the servant, if not the slave, of the machine. Corresponding to the economic mass we have the social mass, ruled despotically by the crowd spirit. The mental life of the mass depends not on the intensive intellectual culture of the individual members as was the case with the old leisured class but in standardized ways of life and thought." There is undoubtedly a serious danger that in a "machine-made" civilization man may sink to the level of a stereotype, a creature who thinks and acts as one of the mass. Fashion, indeed, has always moved the world, but now we are much closer to our fellows and much more prone to drift along with the dizzy crowd. The individual mind may well become dwarfed by the rule of system. The enterprising middle class may find itself a Frankenstein. This, however, is to speak of tendencies which may or may not be history in the making. Whether the ideal of equality means elevating or leveling is something for the future to disclose.

In any case that trait of individualism, product of four centuries, is quite too hardy a plant to die quickly, as anyone must realize who knows the Latin temperament. It is worthy of remark that of all the peoples of Europe (at all events, west of the Balkans) the French have probably been, on the whole, the least affected by these kaleidoscopic changes. Outside the tourist area in Paris, one finds but little evidence of the ultra-modern conveniences and of the standardized products which the Dynamic Age has given us. The French are a people who are, in the main, content with little (nowhere, incidentally, is the distribution of wealth less uneven than in France), and with all their proverbial thrift (approximating sometimes to meanness), they are not interested as a rule in the things that wealth can buy. The most self-centered people in Europe, they pursue the selfsame pastimes that their kind have been accustomed to for generations; they enjoy wit and they appreciate beauty; they insist upon quality in everything, however insignificant; and whatever they do, they put themselves into— the best that is in them. While it is true that an Englishman's taste for his garden, his dog, and his sports still persists, the quality of British goods has, generally speaking, become appreciably coarsened as well as cheapened. In France for the French, quality still resists the advance of standardization. One of the most interesting problems of the age is the question whether materialistic values are to conquer the peoples of Europe. In Russia, where a people with a peasant culture are being pressed into a single pattern, the solution is all too easy. But western civilization is still, in large part, a bounteous heritage, and he who knows history knows that the tastes and habits of men only gradually change.

At the outset of the Dynamic Age—say prior to the twentieth century—the social effects of rationalization were but dimly visible. But the political liberation of the masses, which we shall sketch, was largely the result of the awakening, which, as we saw, was a direct result of the Industrial Revolution. Thus democracy, when it came, was grounded on an economic basis. We shall first note the rise of the popular interest in politics. The political significance of this awakening was embodied to a great extent in that phenomenon: public opinion.

The Evolution of Public Opinion

Public opinion is an elusive factor.[1] It never at any time represents everyone; it does not always comprise the majority; but it may and must include a large articulate body of persons. Yet "large" is, of course, a relative term and cannot really be measured. Perhaps we can speak of "public opinion" when we refer to opinion manifested so strongly and so widely that it *appears* to be predominant, and has the character of a sort of psychological upheaval. It came to be a common and recognized factor in the society which emerged from the French and Industrial Revolutions. It was possible when people had become aware of their inherent power and had the legal right to express themselves or the temerity to fight for that privilege. Public opinion does not always, however, denote a rational public. The susceptibility of people to act collectively or in crowds often makes their manifestations of opinion largely a reflex of collective habits or a product, in part at least, of the emotions.

Nature of public opinion

In Europe, as a whole, before the French Revolution the classic

[1] One needs to be apologetic in trying to define public opinion, for definitions are legion and there is the greatest disparity among them. Obviously public opinion is not confined to the sphere of politics, though it is with its importance as a political phenomenon that we are concerned here.

Early mani-
festations manifestations of public opinion were peasants' revolts. Most of the masses were then peasants, and when roused by certain agitators to rise against oppression, they resorted to mob violence. Some cases have been noted in Germany and Russia, and there were a few of these *jacqueries*, as they were called, in France and England. During the religious controversies of the sixteenth century it might be urged that a public opinion existed against the minority religion, whether Catholic or Protestant, though this was hardly directed against the government, which generally favored the dominant creed. In an age when people as a rule were too dispersed and too inert to express themselves there was a certain prototype of public opinion in the occasional tumults breaking out in crowded cities.[1] Given certain grievances, it is not difficult in such an environment to produce a mob; and though hardly to be instanced as an example of public opinion in any broad sense, such episodes did reveal its nature under certain conditions, and were sometimes quite as effective in an earlier day as a widespread agitation would be now. Perhaps we may say that before the general intellectual awakening which did so much to produce the French and Industrial Revolutions public opinion, like nationalism (which, indeed, was one of its expressions) manifested itself occasionally, and always in a time of peculiar stress. It was naturally most common in England where political rights were greater and political struggles more frequent. When crown and parliament were at logger-heads during the early Stuart period, the country as a whole was deeply stirred, and in spite of the small size of the electorate one might feel that a really spontaneous public opinion had arisen against the crown. It may be suggested that public opinion was favorable to the Restoration and later approved the Revolution of 1688. But obviously we have no data for measuring even approximately the extent of this sentiment. Moreover, in the seventeenth and eighteenth centuries public opinion, when we are citing such examples, must be rather narrowly confined to the upper and middle classes. When we speak of such an agency producing the French Revolution, we are thinking of a large section

---

[1] An example was the outcry in London in 1734 against an excise tax devised by Walpole and passed by parliament, and which as the result of the popular clamor was rescinded. The "Lord George Gordon Riots" of 1780, inspired by a liberal act of parliament toward Catholics, was an exhibition of the worst side of the popular temper. It has been noted by a recent writer (Mr. Wingfield-Stratford) that an important factor in the degradation of the lower classes of eighteenth century England was cheap gin.

of the bourgeoisie, as well as a faction of the nobility, who agitated strongly enough to place a morally bankrupt monarchy at their mercy.

The French Revolution, of course, unloosed for a time a public *Causes of growth* opinion in France, though many of the acts of violence were neither prompted nor probably approved by the country as a whole and can hardly be cited as examples of public opinion. Moreover, popular government was such a novel phenomenon and the popular mind so unready for it that one hesitates to use the term in France after 1791 (that is, before the Third Republic), except insofar as it seemed to approve of the rise of Napoleon Bonaparte. The revolutions of 1830, 1848, and 1870 were all the work of minorities, tacitly accepted by the nation. In central Europe one can hardly feel that public opinion was yet educated up to an interest in public questions except where nationalist issues had been raised, and such movements, however strong, were purely regional, and thus not actions of the general public. But in England there was something very close to the realization of a public opinion in the pressure upon parliament for reform in 1832 and in the successful agitation for the repeal of the Corn Laws, and it seems very evident that it powerfully contributed to produce the Crimean War. If we look for an explanation of the growing importance of this force, we shall find it in the awakening of the proletariat, which resulted from the Industrial Revolution, together with the development of more rapid communications as well as conscious agencies of prop- aganda, and ultimately also in the rise of a popular press.[1] Mass opinion, however, as distinguished from upper- and middle-class opinion, was only possible when the proletariat became at least a contributive medium. It was this class which Bright and others mobilized for parliamentary reform, and it was the strength, or supposed strength of public opinion, that produced the widening of the suffrage in 1867. It was through universal suffrage that the masses expected to gain their economic ends. In France this had been granted in 1848. In other countries the boon came later. But *Significance* the importance of such a reform lies in the fact that political par- ties had henceforth to seek the vote of the masses. Viewed from the opposite angle, public opinion became the weapon of the elec-

---

[1] Various minor contributive agencies might be mentioned: reading or discussion clubs (the *sociétés de pensées* in France will be recalled) and journals of opinion, trade unions, and even schools, the quantity and quality of which were still, how- ever, in the middle of the nineteenth century far from impressive.

torate. Susceptible as it always is to leadership and even to unscrupulous manipulation, it nevertheless provides the moral background and sometimes the propelling force for democracy, nationalism, and social reorganization.

POLITICAL REFORM

Democracy in general

It was through democracy, as we have intimated, that public opinion promised to be effective. In conformity with the teachings of the eighteenth century philosophers man was assumed to be a rational being who could be calculated to know his own interest and pursue it. It was a democracy still confused in the nineteenth century with the idea of majority rule, though it should be noted that John Stuart Mill, one of the greatest champions of popular rights, strongly (though vainly) supported the idea of proportional representation—that is, representation of the minority in accordance with its numbers; and it was he also who with equal futility advocated woman suffrage. But it was not democracy entirely sold to the principle of laissez-faire, for the idea of social control won at least some triumphs in the factory acts; though a fundamental change in point of view was yet to come out. Democracy, as a creed, certainly arose from false assumptions. Man is, perhaps, as much a product of his emotions as of his intellect. He is not the rational being "seeking the happiness of the greatest number" which Jeremy Bentham, the English philosopher, had pictured him. The individual soon loses his identity in a group and is liable either to regard the governance of his country as something beyond his reach or to drift along with the tide under the sway of forceful leaders. Apathy or susceptibility—such were soon to prove basic vices of democracy, and a third was the lack of the proper training either for choosing the most efficient representatives or for judging of the merits of a public question. As Professor Randall (commenting on recent criticism) expresses it, "Men are not equal, the people are not intelligent, their voice is not God's, and far from being sovereign, they are everywhere the acquiescent prey of organized interests."

Basis and defects

Its practical expediency

Yet the period in which democracy began to be tried out was still a little prior to the time when civilization had become so complex that the man in the street was required to be a scholar; it was also before the time when social psychology vivisected man, as it were, and showed up his limitations. The long and short of it was that the masses, having developed a group consciousness, now demand the ballot, and it was cheaper and safer to have elections than revolutions. And popular rule (as it came to be applied) did bring about, as we shall see, a further development of the social state.

It was characteristic of England that her progress toward *In England* democracy was gradual, though, once a step forward was taken, there was no turning back. In political reforms the Liberals *Conserva-* (formerly known as the Whigs) were generally in the lead. The *tives and Liberals* Conservatives (successors of the Tories), on the other hand, were content as a rule with the political status quo, which they sought to "conserve," though they easily adapted themselves to the changes forced by their rivals and were never reactionary. They had the advantage over the Liberals insofar as they usually dominated the house of lords; while the Liberals, on their side, made more use of public opinion; they were the first to electioneer, and they often appealed direct to the unenfranchised masses, working up a sentiment in favor of their projects. After the Second Reform Bill (1867) one might figure out a rather rough division along social lines. The great majority of the Anglican clergy were Conservatives; so also were most of the aristocracy, the upper middle class, the tenant farmers, and the clerks in the cities (who thus felt that they had a link with the upper circle). A large minority of the aristocracy were Liberals, as well as most of the lower middle class and the industrial workers. Roman Catholics were naturally Conservatives; the Anglicans were divided but probably most of them were Conservatives; the Dissenters were nearly all Liberals. The Conservatives were strongest in the south of England; the Liberals strongest in the industrial region of the north and in Scotland and Wales. Looking ahead through the second half of the century, we find both parties favoring social reform, the Liberals taking the lead in parliamentary reform, the Conservatives trying to keep the Irish satisfied by economic concessions, while the Liberals came to advocate home rule, the Conservatives rather more inclined to champion imperial interests and to promote an imperialistic policy. Both parties were wedded at first to free trade, but later a large section of the Conservatives became protectionists under the leadership of Joseph Chamberlain.

The struggle between the parties was never more interesting than in the 'sixties and 'seventies when Gladstone was leader of the Liberals and Disraeli of the Conservatives. Gladstone was a man with an almost insatiable appetite for reform, and, once he had convinced himself that a certain reform was needed, he pushed it with all the earnestness of a crusader and the solemnity of a Cromwell. He was one of the greatest of political leaders, very skillful in handling his party, and always lucid and forceful in debate. Disraeli was a Jew, brilliant where Gladstone was more stolid and practical, unconventional where Gladstone was a model of propriety. His speeches were full of irony, and to listen to him was excellent entertainment, quite apart from whether his arguments were convincing. In politics he was something of an opportunist, and it was due to his political shrewdness that the Conservative Party became something more than a purely obstructive element in English politics. Gladstone had much the longer career, but left no followers in his party of first-rate ability unless we except Lloyd George, who is a remarkable politician. The Conservative leadership passed to such able men as Lord Salisbury, distinguished for his political skill and penetrating judgment, Joseph Chamberlain, an original and forceful personality, and A. J. Balfour, a man of great learning and considerable skill as a parliamentarian.

Parliamentary reform

The first political battle since the middle of the nineteenth century was fought over parliamentary reform. The Reform Bill of 1832 had left much to be desired, and there were a few Liberals who never ceased to clamor for a broader suffrage. When Palmerston died in 1865, Gladstone came rapidly to the front and introduced a bill the following year. Thanks to a combination of Conservatives and Palmerstonian Liberals, it met with defeat, and the Liberal ministry resigned, but Disraeli, who became premier soon after the Conservatives returned to power, had sensed the public demand for the reform, and having made up his mind that extension of the suffrage was practically inevitable, he determined that his party should get the credit for it. Hence it was actually under Conservative auspices that the Second Reform Bill was passed, so loosening the electoral requirements that the lower middle class, the tenant farmers, and most of the urban workmen were now accorded the suffrage. Mill's plea for the enfranchisement of women was only greeted with merriment, but two years later, in 1869, women received the right to vote in municipal elections, though the question of woman suffrage for general elections was not an important issue till the twentieth century.

The Conservatives did not immediately profit by Disraeli's timely maneuver, for the country rightly ascribed the reform to Gladstone (who had largely refashioned the bill in the course of its passage), and as the Liberals won decisively in the elections of 1868, Gladstone again became premier. His second ministry, sometimes known as the "Great Ministry," was signalized by great reforming activity. By the Forster Education Bill steps were taken to provide for a better-educated electorate [1]—a matter of special importance since so large a proportion of the masses had obtained the vote. Hardly less important was civil service reform—another product of Gladstone's second ministry. By an act of 1870 the various posts in the civil service were no longer to be the spoils of politicians but were opened to competitive examination. In 1872 the secret ballot was adopted for elections, thus safeguarding the voter from outside interference. Of the legalization of trade unions we shall speak in another place. Though Gladstone's program met with a check when he fell from power in 1874, it was resumed in his third ministry in 1884. In that year the Third Reform Bill was passed, still further extending the suffrage, which now included the miners and rural workmen. As this latter element was likely to be Conservative and somewhat offset the enfranchisement of the town workers, the Conservatives had not tried to defeat the bill, only insisting on a reapportionment of seats in the house of commons on the basis of population. This was the last reform bill until that of 1918 established practically universal suffrage for men and enfranchised women of thirty years of age or over. In 1928, by the so-called "Flapper Bill" women of twenty-one, like men of that age, received the suffrage; and there are now actually more women voters than men.

---

[1] Government aid to private schools had begun as early as 1833, and the subsidies were steadily increased from time to time, but the sums provided were still so inadequate that in 1870 less than half the children of the poor were to be found upon the registers, and in primary education Great Britain had sadly lagged behind France and Prussia. Much of Gladstone's political support, however, came from the middle and working classes, and these groups being largely Nonconformist, had pressed for a national system of education that would be free of the Anglicanism displayed in the State-aided schools. Forster's bill of 1870, while it continued the principle of State aid to private schools, provided also for schools maintained partly from local taxes, partly from government aid, and partly from children's fees, wherever it was found that private schools offered insufficient facilities. Elementary education was made compulsory in 1880 and free in 1891.

The abasement of the house of lords

There was another important aspect of the trend toward democracy, and that was the establishment of the supremacy of the house of commons in legislation. We have already noted that the sovereignty of parliament had been achieved by the Revolution of 1688, but it was still possible for the house of lords to override the will of the popular chamber, as they had done in the case of one of Gladstone's measures. The only way in which the lords could be coerced was by creating a sufficient number of new peers, as had been done (for the last time) in Anne's reign, and which had been threatened at the time of the First Reform Bill. When in 1909 the house of lords, contrary to custom, rejected the budget, the Liberal ministry, which had already suffered from obstruction in that quarter, determined to put through a bill that would end its power of veto. The Conservatives, who controlled the house of lords, professed to be willing to satisfy the wishes of the country as determined in a general election, and when the elections of 1910 showed a slight majority against them, the house of lords passed the budget. But this concession did not save it. In 1911 the Liberals presented it with a bill to the effect that any measure of the commons should become the law of the land after it had been passed in three successive sessions within two years, and also that any money bill passed by the commons should not require the sanction of the lords. When opposition to the bill developed among the peers, the ministry threatened the creation of as many as five hundred new peers; and, rather than have the blue blood of the chamber so diluted, the lords reluctantly yielded, and passed the bill. Henceforth the will of the commons has been supreme.

Democracy in practice

It would be too much to say that even now the English political system has reached its final development. A thoroughgoing scheme of proportional representation would undoubtedly make for greater democracy, and yet the British constitution is probably, on the whole, the most liberal in the world. A general election must be held at least every five years (since 1911[1]) or oftener if a cabinet, which introduces most of the legislation, is defeated on an important measure by the house of commons or if it loses in a "vote

---

[1] The limit of five years for any one parliament had been fixed by the Parliamentary Act of 1911, which had limited the powers of the house of lords. Since the power of the upper chamber had been curtailed, it seemed reasonable that the country should be consulted oftener than every seven years as had previously been the case.

of confidence." Thus at times the electorate becomes arbiter between executive and legislature. Recourse in that way to a referendum became exceedingly useful after the War when on two occasions no party had received a majority of the commons (this being due to the rise of the Laborites to compete with the older parties). Normally, however, there is complete harmony between executive and legislature, since by the nature of cabinet government the cabinet is an emanation of the legislature drawn from

THE BRITISH HOUSES OF PARLIAMENT

the party which controls the commons. Such a system makes for smoothness and efficiency; there is seldom the friction such as one finds between president and congress in the United States, where each may belong to a different party; and when a member of the cabinet seriously differs from the premier, he resigns. Politics in England is reasonably free from corruption. There have been occasions where wealthy men have been made peers as a reward for campaign contributions or in the expectation of getting them, and two newspaper magnates were raised to the peerage at the bidding of Lloyd George for obvious reasons, but it is not charged that many members of parliament consciously prostitute their position for business ends. The chief points of criticism brought against the commons are its size (it has 707 members) and, more especially its paucity of distinguished talent—a fact which is sometimes attributed to the growing number of members without cultural background and more often to the stringency of party discipline. Compared to an earlier day, there are perhaps fewer men of outstanding ability in the house of commons, though the statement is hardly susceptible to proof, and there are still in England, more than in any other country, certain families who have figured in politics for many generations, and stand for the highest traditions of public service. But, in general, it may be admitted that the party system does not develop talent of the highest order, and lessens rather than promotes real democracy—facts which may be ascribed to the development of the caucus. This institution was invented by some radicals (of whom Joseph Chamberlain was one) in Birmingham in 1867 after the passage of the Second Reform Bill. All Liberals in the borough, whether voters or not, were encouraged to join an organization, known as the Liberal Association, which elected a committee to formulate its sentiments; and to this platform any person standing for parliament for Birmingham must subscribe if he expected to be elected. After the overwhelming defeat of the Liberal Party in the elections of 1874 it was generally felt that some such plan of organization should have a wider range, and in 1877 the Liberal Association was extended to the rest of England, taking for its name the National Liberal Association. Such an institution did not mean, however, that the rank and file of Liberals controlled the party. While solicitous of the sentiment in their respective localities, the various leaders of the different branches of the Association really formulated the platform of the party, and to a large extent it was intended to line up a unanimous following for the leader of the party in parliament. His views, more or less influenced perhaps by those of his associates, were the will of the party, and the party machine (the Association) had the means of bearing down on all dissentients. Though the Conservative Party stood rather in less need of organization, since the landed elements from which they drew most of their strength included the subservient village and small-town folk, the defeat of the party in 1880 had the effect of bringing about an organization similar to that of the Liberals, called the Union of National Conservative Associations. Through this organization the Conservatives were able to mobilize and increase their strength in the towns and to offer serious competition to their rivals. Thanks to these organizations (and the Labor Party followed these examples), there is very active canvassing before every general election, and it is then that the strength of the machine is put to the test. For its practical purpose the caucus has proved effective, but its care to repress individual judgment both of the voter and of the candidate and its tendency to become static in its view of public questions have hardly made it a vehicle of democracy or a school of the highest statesmanship. Speaking in parliament in 1917, Lord Hugh Cecil, son of the late Lord Salisbury, declared that Gladstone, Disraeli, and Salisbury were too independent to have fitted into a parliament of the twentieth century. "Can any one doubt," he said, "that one great cause of danger to the house of commons is the exaggeration of the party system? . . . There is a tendency—I do not want to be thought attacking members of the house of commons—to exclude from this house any one who is not prepared to accept the full party doctrine, whatever it may be." It is easy, perhaps, to exaggerate the strength of the party discipline, but it is probably true that the cabinet, in order to be sure of its power, insists pretty rigorously on party uniformity.

But if public opinion is often molded in rather artificial fashion, there is nowhere where the citizen's right to be heard is more respected than in England. Save in a time of national peril anyone in England may speak his mind quite freely and openly—even to the extent of advocating anarchy, if he chooses. Even during the height of the Irish crisis when it was virtually an out-and-out struggle between two nations, excited Irishmen were permitted to deliver the bitterest invectives against the government in the public squares of London. The contempt which a Britisher feels for an opponent is so seldom expressed that it amounts, in effect, to tolerance. There is also that ingrained feeling that interfering with one's constitutional rights is not to be borne. Perhaps that quality of individualism, so often noted, may be reckoned on as discounting to a certain extent even the strength of party government, while an innate conservatism, at the same time, makes an Englishman suspicious of revolution. The stability of freedom-loving England is to be explained by the character of her people. She may not be as democratically governed as she thinks, but she plods ahead slowly, and that is what she likes. With the French there is much more talk of principle, but perhaps a slighter sense of public duty, as strong an individualism but perhaps less care in guarding it.

Political reform in France seemed likely to be achieved by spasmodic revolutions rather than by gradual evolution as in England, though we may remember that English history had had its ups and *In France* downs from the time of James I to the First Reform Bill. Though more inclined to theorize than the English, it is a mistake to regard the French as an inveterately fickle people because they have tr:ed so many experiments. As far as temperament is concerned, they are probably monarchist. They are prone to follow strong leadership; they are used to strongly centralized authority; they take an artistic delight in the pageantry that usually goes with monarchy. Every republic which they set up since 1789 was the act of a minority and much more the product of circumstance than the deep and genuine conviction of the nation as a whole. Had the monarchies which they tried been able to satisfy public sentiment, any one of them might have endured. But the Restored Bourbons had been rather too brusque with the idealism of the Revolution, the July Monarchy had failed to recognize the Industrial Revolution, and the Second Empire had disappointed the national vanity. Moreover, "1789" had still an intellectual appeal. It takes time, no doubt, to assimilate a revolution. Perhaps it took time to convince the French that they were not the kind of people to develop a liberal monarchy after the fashion of the English; the choice was between liberalism safeguarded by a republic or a semi-autocratic monarchy, of which they had had enough. Accident disposed of monarchy in 1870 and they were thrown, as twice before, to the other extreme. But that they were even yet prepared to adopt the principle of democracy was still a matter of doubt.

Hence for thirty years the issue of monarchism remained to distract French politics, though we shall see the issue fading more and more with the lapse of time. The initial crisis through which the country had to pass was the interval of uncertainty between the time when Paris had proclaimed the republic, September 4, 1870 and its definite organization in 1875. Born during the agony of a foreign war after the sudden collapse of the Empire, one might feel that the Third Republic had an extraordinarily inauspicious beginning. A national assembly, called to ratify peace with Germany, was monarchist largely for the reason that the republicans had been anxious to continue the war and France as a whole had wanted peace. In the following year, on the heels of this devastating struggle, there occurred what was known as the "Commune," that uprising of Paris against the government, which may chiefly be attributed to the overwrought nerves of a people who had had to endure the horrors and privations of a four months' siege. But, while there were many factors contributive to this explosion,[1] one of the most important was the suspicion that the assembly meant to undo the work of Paris and set aside the republic. After the "Commune" was suppressed one might have feared that the republic itself was likewise doomed. But the royalists did not want a monarchy sullied by the making of an unpopular peace; and though the assembly claimed constituent authority (that is, the authority to make a new constitution), it seemed in no hurry to use it. With some reluctance it conferred on Thiers, one of its number, the title of "president of the republic," regarding him solely as a stopgap, though it was only too glad to let him solve the immediate problem of pacifying France. When the country had settled down to normal conditions, these royalists meant to assert themselves. But from the point of view of their object they made a mistake. Time was on the side of the republic.

That the republic finally triumphed was mainly due to the fact that able and forceful leadership was to be found only in the ranks of the republicans. Whereas neither of the royalist candidates had the ability to exploit this opportunity, Thiers had the good sense to steer a middle course and stand for that moderate liberalism that was suited to the upper middle class. Though monarchist by conviction, he declared that a republic was "the form of government that divides us least." Meanwhile his handling of affairs was generally satisfactory. If he was harsh with the Paris workmen who had instigated the Commune, he had for that very reason won the approval of the bourgeoisie; moreover, the Germans were got rid of; the indemnity was paid with extraordinary rapidity; and the army reorganized. Would the royalists now feel that their time had come? True, it might seem that the republic itself was marking time, and that its merits were chiefly negative, but that active partisanship necessary to insure its lasting success was soon to appear. When Thiers fell from office in 1873, the moral leadership passed to the man best qualified for this second phase of the problem. Leon Gambetta, the gallant patriot and ardent republican, roused by voice and pen a vigorous public sentiment in favor of the republic. Aghast when not only the republicans gained in a by-election but even some avowed Bonapartists, the assembly took fright and passed the so-called Constitutional Laws, which definitely established the republic. It had been a republic in name

---

[1] The Commune had also a proletarian tinge, as we have noted (p. 442).

for five years; it was now a republic in law. The first crisis was over.

The organization of the Republic

By the constitution thus devised France was given a president chosen by the national assembly,[1] and declared to be irresponsible; in other words, executive power was wielded in his name by the ministers. The ministers were declared jointly and severally responsible to the chamber. The parliament was composed of two bodies, a chamber of deputies elected by universal suffrage and a senate, composed partly of nominees of the assembly (chosen for life) and partly by persons elected by various electoral colleges. The election of deputies was to take place every five years. The president was scarcely more than a ceremonial head. His importance lay in the fact that he might exercise some judgment as to what party leader in the chamber of deputies was likely to be able to form a cabinet that would command its support. The royalists of the Constituent Assembly, being legitimatists (that is, loyal to the Bourbon line) did not choose to have a president who might, if chosen by direct vote of the French people and endowed with considerable power, make himself a monarch after the fashion of Louis Napoleon. They still cherished the hope that a monarchy after their heart might be possible in the future. Only once is the term republic employed in the constitution, and even that amendment was passed by a bare majority of one. There was no declaration of individual rights, and the whole constitution had a sense of incompleteness—as though to be rounded off for a monarch later on. It was not even a highly original performance, and consequently quite un-French. The principle of ministerial responsibility was borrowed from the English. But it was a fortunate innovation, for parliamentary history had been a constant oscillation between a legislature dominated by the executive and an executive so isolated from the legislature that the two organs of government could not work together.

But it was not long before the republic had to pass through another ordeal. In 1875 a republican majority had been elected to the first house of deputies chosen under the constitution, but the senate was royalist and so was the president, Thiers' successor, Marshal MacMahon. In 1877 MacMahon took a step which would hardly have been possible if the constitution itself had not been lacking in precision. Refusing to tolerate a republican ministry

[1] A joint meeting of the two chambers.

which enjoyed the confidence of the chamber, he dissolved parliament (with the consent of the senate, as prescribed by the constitution) and called a new election. Much depended on the decision of the citizenry, for the principle of ministerial responsibility would have amounted to little if the president could flout the chamber in any such fashion. Viewed in another way, it was a question whether the president or the ministry should wield the executive leadership. In any event the republicans, after a spirited canvass, won a decisive victory. In 1879 MacMahon resigned and was succeeded by a staunch republican, and in the same year the senate became republican. There was no longer a house divided against itself.

During the next few years the republic was greatly strengthened. *Consolidation of the Republic* Freedom of the press and of association was granted with only reasonable limitations in the interest of the public welfare. In 1884 life senators were abolished. It is worthy of note that very few changes have been made in the constitution, and perhaps because of its very want of elaboration it has lasted. One of the most important reforms, as buttressing the republic, was the institution of a system of national education, free, secular, and compulsory between the ages of six and thirteen. The system was sponsored by Jules Ferry, one of the leading republican statesmen, not a man of fiery eloquence like Gambetta, but probably the ablest of the three men who laid the foundations of the republic. It is noticeable that during these years the republic became more definitely identified with the popular interest. Thanks to that grave but able statesman, Waldeck-Rousseau (whose heart was in painting rather than politics) trade unions were legalized in 1884, and thus one of the problems hanging over from the Industrial Revolution had been settled. Also much was done in the interest of the peasantry, and it is probable (though hardly susceptible to proof) that by 1885 most Frenchmen had become republican by conviction. If the interests of the peasantry were safeguarded by the republic, this would mean that an element which was still in the majority would be weaned away from the blandishments of the royalists. It should finally be added that the indemnity to Germany had been paid as the result of bonds in which the French themselves had invested, and the republic was thus, in a sense, a source of investment.

Yet storms continued to rage against the republic. A third

Conserva-
tion of the
Republic

crisis occurred in the late 'eighties when an adventurer, Captain Boulanger, taking advantage of some official scandals and petty squabbles in high places, attempted with royalist support to win popular favor and make himself a species of dictator. Fortunately he lacked the nerve to accomplish his purpose and the republicans had rallied quickly to the menaced government. In the 'nineties there was a similar slump, and another troubled period took place. When a certain Jewish officer, Captain Dreyfus, was wrongfully convicted of treason, the royalists made capital out of the prejudices of the republican statesmen and did all they could to embarrass the republic. It was the fourth crisis the republic had had to surmount, but the republican leaders were now ready to take the offensive.

The
separation
of Church
and State

The element in the royalist group which had been most active in its attack upon the republic were the clericals. They had never reconciled themselves to the passing of monarchy, which in France had usually patronized the Church and given it special advantages in the field of education. Gambetta's famous outburst, "Clericalism—there is the enemy" had been the slogan of the republicans in the '77 crisis. Later Ferry had dealt the clericals a blow when he instituted his public-schools system. Subsequent legislation was passed against the religious orders on the ground that they were nests of political intrigue. Finally, in 1899, in the midst of the Dreyfus affair most of the republican parties formed the so-called "Republican Bloc," pledged to continue the struggle with the Church. By this time the chief issue was the abrogation of the Concordat of 1801, in other words the separation of Church and State. The republican statesmen were opposed to a régime that gave any church a privileged position, and they felt that the Catholic Church was disloyal to the hand that fed it. Yet obviously the State, having confiscated the property of the Church, might still be deemed to owe it some support, and the papacy felt that the Concordat, being in the nature of a treaty, could not properly be altered without mutual consent. The controversy was long and bitter, and was not finally settled till 1907, though the Concordat had been repealed two years earlier. Henceforth the clergy had to depend on voluntary support, but Church edifices were placed at the disposal of the clergy. In the attitude of their government the French were but preserving their traditional policy of subordinating religious affairs to political. A very large proportion of Frenchmen are free-thinkers, though the women are as a rule fervent Catholics, and so, in general, is the peasantry.

It is noticeable that democracy through force of circumstances *Democracy* had been largely identified with anti-clericalism, and it is largely *in practice* because of the alleged influence of the priesthood over the women that woman suffrage has never been granted in France. But an experiment was once made with proportional representation,[1] and the public interest in politics, as evinced in the general elections every four years, compares favorably with that of other countries. The press also devotes a good deal of space to political matters. But it would be hardly correct to say that it molds opinion, for the French, while conservative as a people, are tenacious of their individual judgments and are not easily swayed by the opinions of others. Newspapers are much smaller than in England and are consequently more numerous, and the French are rather prone to read on all sides of a question.

There is one sense in which democracy has operated to a greater extent in France than in any other country. The chamber of deputies is the most powerful legislative body in Europe. Instead of being led by the executive (that is, the cabinet), as in England, it holds the executive power forever under the lash. The instability of the French ministries is, of course, proverbial, and is partly due to the fact that no party ever has a majority in the chamber; a ministry must always rest on a coalition, which may easily dissolve. Then the right of interpellation is often deliberately employed in the chamber to upset a ministry. Since a vote is taken immediately after an interpellation when feeling is running high, the result is frequently adverse to the ministry, which at once resigns. These ministerial crises often produce the unfortunate result of paralyzing government policy during an emergency. It is also evident that the efforts of a ministry to hold together by satisfying several parties has an enervating effect, and its legislative policy is liable to be halting and rather barren of results. Yet the downfall of a ministry is hardly more than a shake-up as a rule, most of the ministers generally returning under the newly chosen premier, and the result has usually been simply a slight veering to the right or to the left; it is only, as a rule, after a change in public sentiment, as shown in a general election, that an important change takes place in the complexion of a ministry. Moreover, the multi-

[1] In 1919. It proved to be a very faulty scheme, and was abandoned in 1934.

party system has its advantages. The Frenchman does not like to vote on a cut-and-dried platform, such as the parties in England offer the electorate; he is an "incorrigible individualist," and when he votes, he thinks rather of trends and principles than concrete issues. It should also be remembered that the departments of the public service are little affected by all these changes at the top. The real work of the administration (as in England) is in the hands of permanent secretaries, and nothing ever disturbs the even tenor of the bureaucracy. It is, perhaps, the combination of democracy and authority that makes their form of government so admirably suited to a people who have always been conspicuous for their contradictions.

In Italy

The problem of developing popular government in Italy was one that demanded time and patience before a practical solution could be reached. The first thing needed was to make Italy united in spirit as well as in law. It was one thing to unite for the purpose of a revolution, and another thing to stay united after the aim had been achieved; and there were differences within the Italian nation that were hard to bridge. These differences were temperamental, economic, and political. The north Italians, having something of a Teutonic blend in their composition, were industrious and enterprising, and it was in the north that the industrial life of the nation chiefly centered. The south Italians, compounded of divers races and tending to be indolent and unstable, were chiefly engaged in agriculture, and were both poorer than their compatriots of the north and had suffered much more from misgovernment in the past. Most of the illiterates—which totaled in 1861 some seventy per cent of the population—were found in the south, and it was there that disorder was most rife. Moreover, Italy had so long been divided into separate political divisions that most of her citizens thought regionally rather than nationally. They were Sicilians, or Venetians, or Florentines rather than Italians. To weld them into a really harmonious nation was, in fact, a prodigious problem.

The problem of unity

One of the best ways of insuring practical unity was the introduction (due to Ricasoli) of a centralized administrative system on the model of that of France, but this, except for the erasure of old frontiers, did little to make the Italians more united in feeling. The attainment of moral unity (as distinguished from organic unity) could come only with the process of time, when such binding factors as the extension of railways throughout the peninsula (leading to greater economic unity as well as more travel from one part of the country to another), the association of all manner of Italians in the army and navy, and the awakening of an interest in national affairs through the growth of literacy and the extension of the suffrage, had operated to make Italians perceive their common heritage and common interests. It is contended by some observers that spiritual unity has not yet been fully attained.

Relations with the papacy

Connected with the problem of properly unifying the nation was the obligation to compensate the papacy, which had been compelled to give up nearly all its temporal possessions. The Italian government was anxious to placate the Vatican, and by an act of the Italian parliament in 1871, called the Act of Papal Guarantees, the papacy was allowed complete sovereignty over a small precinct of the city of Rome, in which St. Peter's and the Vatican were located, as well as an indemnity amounting to 3,225,000 francs a year, and an almost complete separation of Church and State. But the pope was unwilling to accept the arrangement, and determined never to set foot on Italian soil, lest the act should be construed as recognizing the king of Italy, and he bade all faithful Catholics abstain from any part in Italian public affairs. Cavour's ideal of a "free church in a free state" was realized, but only through mutual forbearance. The pope himself voluntarily became "the prisoner of the Vatican"—a situation that lasted till 1928.

Democracy in practice

Hardly less serious than the lack of moral unity in 1861 was the lack of political experience. Only in Sardinia had there remained any liberal institutions. It was for that reason largely that the constitution of Sardinia had simply been extended to the kingdom of Italy. This meant the creation of a bicameral legislature and a responsible ministry. The upper house was constituted from various categories such as men who had distinguished themselves in the public service, the Church, or the sphere of letters, or who had paid a certain minimum of taxes. As in France, the lower house was much the more important. It is noticeable that the suffrage was still narrow. The founders of the kingdom seem to have realized that the great mass of the people was not ready for democracy.

Unfortunately the moderate liberals who gave Italy her start and guided her destinies for some fifteen years came gradually to lose power to the more radical element in the south. The suffrage was extended in 1882, and finally in 1912 it was made practically universal. From a study of domestic history during this period one may well conclude that democracy had marched too fast for the intellectual attainments of the people. The spirit of faction was strong in Italian public life; parties tended to group themselves about personalities, rather than issues; there were also frequent scandals in which some of the most prominent statesmen were implicated; graft and corruption were all-too-frequent; and the government launched into a policy of imperialism with a reckless disregard for the state of the finances. Politics in Italy were largely a game, in which certain men constructed political machines that enabled them to play for a number of years the rôle of dictator. One may remember this fact when the time comes to notice the setting up of a really stable dictatorship.

Evidently public opinion in Italy did not become habituated to parliamentary government. It expressed itself more readily in riots and demonstrations. Someone has said that the Italian is more ready to die for his country than to live for it—though this charge may, of course, be brought against many other peoples. It is also true that in what used to be the kingdom of Sardinia there was still a very genuine liberalism, and it is no doubt also true that there was a minority in public life that was really fitted to govern. Unfortunately it was a less scrupulous minority that, taking advantage of the ignorance of the sovereign people, used its power to advance its own interests.

In Other Countries

We have unfortunately little space to devote to the minor nations of Europe, though it should be realized that the Scandinavian countries and Belgium have contributed much to the world's culture and that Sweden and Denmark are among the best-governed countries in the world today, Denmark, in particular, having adopted a system of co-operative enterprise (especially in the dairy industry), which has placed the economic position of the country on an excellent foundation. Norway separated from Sweden in 1907 and set up a monarchy of her own, and it is rather remarkable that the dissolution of the union took place without any bloodshed. In the three Scandinavian countries, as well as in Holland and Belgium, the suffrage was at first limited, but after long agitation universal manhood suffrage was obtained in all except Holland. Woman suffrage was adopted in Norway in 1907, in Sweden in 1912, in Denmark in 1915; it does not yet exist in

The Scandinavian countries, the Netherlands, and Belgium

Belgium or the Netherlands. All these countries have bicameral parliaments and ministerial responsibility. Since Belgium is an industrial country she adopted an elaborate program of social legislation on the model of that of Germany.

Switzerland, because of its three different languages and the *Switzerland* traditional strength of the different cantons into which it is divided formed a federal type of government best suited for its purposes. The federal government is not strong, though possessed of sufficient authority to conduct the affairs of the republic. A parliamentary régime and universal manhood suffrage are features of the constitution, which also provides for the initiative and referendum.

Perhaps because the temperament of the people is different from *Spain and* that of the "northerners," above mentioned, the Iberian Peninsula *Portugal* has been a prey to much disorder ever since the time of Napoleon. Spain never recovered her position as a great power, and under the infamous Ferdinand VII suffered a great deal from oppression. After his death in 1833 a long period of unrest took place. Even the experiment of a republic was tried for a few years, but as this proved worse than royalist misgovernment, the monarchy was restored in 1875. In 1890 universal suffrage was instituted. But political life continued corrupt, and democracy, an illusion. The tendency for a party leader, as in Italy, to make himself a dictator by means of a political machine was finally to be the undoing of the monarchy itself, though it managed to endure till 1931. Portugal suffered from the same malignant evils as Spain, and in 1910 the monarchy was finally overthrown and replaced by a republic.

Social Reform

We have already noted social reform as a means on the part of *In Germany* the capitalistic classes to afford protection to the workers. A scheme of social insurance to that end was the experiment inaugurated by Bismarck in 1882. The scheme—which, as we shall notice, was generally adopted—was designed to protect the working class against poverty and other misfortunes only too liable to *Bismarck* befall those who normally were unable to sell their labor at a decent *and the* price and were hence unable themselves to take adequate care of *state"* the future. Bismarck, in presenting his program, spoke of it as "the further development of the modern state idea" [he meant, of course, the 'social state'], "the result of Christian ethics, according to which the State should discharge, besides the defensive duty of protecting existing rights, the positive duty of promoting the welfare of all its members and especially those who are weak." To this humanitarian motive could, of course, be added the practical consideration that a working class, thus protected, would in the long run repay the sacrifices of the capitalist class and make for a more efficient nation. But the prime purpose of the reform was hardly either the idea of social justice or that of the national welfare, broadly considered. Such a program had long been advocated by the German socialists, and it was to steal their thunder and thus weaken them as a party that Bismarck came to adopt it. "Give the workman the right to work as long as he is healthy," Bismarck told the reichstag, "assure him care when he is sick and maintenance when he is old . . . then the socialists will sing their swan song in vain and the workingmen will cease to swarm to their banner." It is a matter of historic fact that Bismarck's policy failed of its political object, but as the commencement of a social experiment it was one of the most important events of the age.

This program, the adoption of which began in 1883 and covered a number of enactments in succeeding years included compulsory insurance against accident and illness, old-age and survivors' pensions, and insurance for salaried employees, as well as compulsory treatment for tuberculosis in state sanitoria. The funds which provided compensation for accident were furnished entirely by the employers; in the case of sickness insurance and pensions workers and employers and (to a lesser extent) the State all bore a share in the cost of this scheme. These measures applied to persons earning less than 2,000 marks (about $500) a year. There was no insurance against unemployment until after the Great War (that is, in 1927), but most of the important towns as well as other agencies provided employment bureaus, and private organizations established lodging houses for workmen seeking a job, the only requirement being that they should work for their keep. This system of social insurance worked so well that paupers were rare in Germany before the War. Historically the experiment is chiefly significant in that it was copied in almost all European countries, and has been the highest expression of the social state.

Position of the peasantry   Generally speaking, the German peasants required no systematic policy of relief. As a general thing they owned their own land, as in France, though it was usually somewhat greater in extent.

The large estates were practically confined to East Prussia where junkers conducted farming with varying profit and were powerful enough to exploit the rural workers with impunity. Yet in time the general drift of the population to the towns forced these squires to import labor or raise wages. Moreover, as a means of furnishing relief to the rural laborer, the Prussian government bought some land, broke it into small holdings, and leased it to them.[1] Finally in 1911 agricultural laborers were brought within the scope of the insurance laws. Thanks to the influence of the junkers, agriculture, from the time of Bismarck, was protected by a tariff—the same thing, indeed, that Chamberlain sought in England but without success; for England had passed the period when agriculture was profitable enough to elicit the public interest.

It was in England, a country even more industrialized than Germany, that the social state had had its beginnings, as we have noticed, and though Germany was first responsible for its elaborate development, it was England who in the end went furthest in that direction. Socialism was not so strong in England as on the Continent, and until 1893 there was no "labor party" in politics; but trade-unionism was an exceedingly active force in pushing proletarian interests; and probably in no country was the proletariat so able to enlist the sympathy of public opinion. After most of the working class had got the vote in 1867 both parties (Conservatives and Liberals) saw the advantage of gratifying the workers, and in response to agitation the Gladstone ministry in 1871 granted to all trade unions full legal standing. As, however, the passage of the Criminal Law Amendment Act at the same time rendered them liable to prosecution for any coercive measures, satisfaction had hardly been granted, and it was left for Disraeli in 1875 to get the objectionable act repealed and thus to round out the work that Gladstone had begun. Disraeli had the idea of aligning the proletariat (whose vote he now sought) with the landed aristocracy against the powerful middle class. His "new Toryism," as it was called, presaged the later interest of the Conservatives in the cause of social reform. It is interesting, however, to note that if the proletariat was coming to be a power in politics, thanks to its possession of the ballot, it is also true that the aristocracy was being gradually pushed to the wall by the wealthy middle class.

In Great Britain

Progress of trade-unionism

[1] Much the same experiment was tried in England in 1882 in an effort of the Conservatives to rehabilitate the peasantry.

The hopeless decay of agriculture, made even more apparent by several years of depression at the end of the 'seventies, had led to more and more selling of estates to *nouveaux riches*, who prized them not as an investment but as a rung on the social ladder. Men like Joseph Chamberlain, a self-made manufacturer, were coming more and more to play a dominant rôle in politics. It was much more the mercantile element than the old landlords who had to meet the pressure of the workers. And the democratic state was still a little wary of the principle of social control.

And, as time went on, the labor leaders themselves became converts to laissez-faire and opposed to any action by the State. Moreover, trade-unionism was thus far a movement of the skilled workmen, and when the condition of this class had materially improved, its energies slackened. A socialist element, however, working through separate organizations, denounced this apathy, and agitated for a living wage for all workmen and a compulsory eight-hour day. Gradually in the 'eighties there developed what was known as the "New Unionism," which worked for certain practical reforms and especially for the organization of the unskilled workers into unions. The movement gained momentum when the condition of the London workers received publicity as the result of a careful survey. In 1888 a strike of the girls who made lucifer matches received so strong a public backing that it met with complete success. The following year witnessed a strike of dock-hands for a raise of wages, and as again public opinion supported the strikers, they won their case. More and more, trade-unionism was reaching to the submerged elements. By 1914 the total number of workmen enrolled in unions amounted to more than 4,000,000 or about twenty-five per cent of the proletariat. There was also a federation of trade unions.

Rise of the Labor Party The effort to enlist public opinion in an economic struggle had at times been marvelously effective, but the enactment of legislation in the direct interest of the working class could be greatly furthered by the entrance of "labor" into politics. In the general election of 1880 three independent candidates representing labor won seats in parliament, and the number was increased to ten by the elections of 1885 and to twelve in 1892. Finally, in 1893, after numerous vicissitudes, the Independent Labor Party was founded, with a platform pledged to socialism and including also such objects as the eight-hour day and State provision for the ill and the aged. In 1906 the party totaled twenty-nine members in parliament and in 1910 as many as forty. But it must be admitted that in many cases these victories were due to fusion with the Liberals, whose policy it was supposed to follow, and it was not till the collapse of the Liberal Party in 1918 that the Labor Party gained full independence. Yet, as we shall presently note, its influence had been strikingly successful.

Competing for the favor of the electorate, both the great parties had continued to interest themselves in labor questions. In 1880 during the second Gladstone ministry the principle of employer's liability for injuries to workmen was adopted, and an act passed under the ægis of Joseph Chamberlain in 1897 gave effect to this principle, though narrowing its application to the so-called "dangerous trades." [1] Both parties were interested in the problem of providing pensions for aged workers, and in 1905 during a Conservative ministry a commission was empowered to make a special study and report on the whole problem of the aged and infirm. It is an interesting fact that in the following year a resolution of a Labor member of parliament, proclaiming the principle that old-age pensions should be paid from public funds, was passed by the house of commons by a unanimous vote.

The prominence of social reform after the opening of the twentieth century, culminating in a great program of social insurance, had some important immediate causes. In the first place, public opinion was beginning to realize the gravity of the problem—not because of any danger of revolution but because it involved the competitive capacity of the nation. The physical tests for recruiting at the time of the Boer War had produced some appalling revelations. So many were discarded as unfit that it looked as if English society was decadent at the bottom. The children of the Industrial Revolution were proved to be seriously inefficient both physically and mentally. In the second place, official opinion was greatly impressed by the example of Germany. Relations between the two nations were none too friendly and might conceivably lead to war; now if Germany had found means of giving strength to her industrial population, it would certainly not do for Great Britain to lag behind. In the third place, the Liberals won a decisive victory in the elections of 1906, and while it is

The program of social reform

(1) Causes

---

[1] This included factory workers, however, as well as those in building, railroading, and mining.

probable that memories of the Boer War and public disapproval of Chamberlain's advocacy of tariff reform had much to do with achieving this result, the pronounced program of social reform on which the Liberals had made their fight (and which, of course, enabled them to fuse with the Laborites in most electoral districts) was certainly an added factor. Moreover, it may be noted that while they began their constructive program as soon as they got into power, much of their later activity was due to the party losses in the elections of 1910, which made them dependent on Labor support for the control of the house of commons. Hence, the importance of what came to be known as the "Lib-Lab Alliance."

(2) Content   The social program of the Asquith ministry, largely directed by David Lloyd George, the chancellor of the exchequer, was so far-reaching in scope as to amount almost to a social revolution. One of the most important enactments was the minimum wage, at first imposed[1] (1909) in certain so-called "sweated trades," such as tailoring, box-making, and lace-making, where working conditions were particularly bad, and which later (after a strike) was granted to miners (1912); while finally, in 1918 the minister of labor was empowered to extend it to other trades as he saw fit. Meanwhile various educational measures provided free meals, recreation grounds, and medical attendance for workers' children. Employers' liability for accidents was given a wider range by an act of 1906, which extended the benefits to all manual workers under contract. Compensation (amounting to half a week's wage up to a maximum of £1) was due all who were not hurt as the result of their own willful conduct and provided their injuries clearly disabled them for as much as a week. Employers were not compelled, as in Germany, to insure their men, but they have very generally felt forced to do so. Another important reform of the same year (though not to go into force until 1909) was an act granting an eight-hour day to coal miners—unquestionably the result of pressure from the Labor Party, as a parliamentary commission of inquiry had counseled strongly against it. Old-age pensions followed soon afterward, in 1908, entitling any worker of seventy, man or woman, who was not a criminal or an habitual

[1] The act was operated through trade boards, composed equally of representatives of employers and employees together with some appointees of the board of trade, and it was these trade boards that fixed the minimum wage. Over 3,000,000 workers in forty trades now benefit by this experiment.

loafer, to receive a pension—not large enough to carry with it complete support, else it might discourage thrift, but sufficient, if supplemented by some savings, to keep the individual out of the poorhouse. Unlike the similar measure in Germany, the State was to bear the whole expense.

Finally in 1911 the problems of illness and unemployment came to be treated in the so-called National Insurance Act. It included illness and unemployment insurance—both compulsory. The former was applied to every manual worker, and entitled him (or her) to claim a certain fixed amount in event of illness for twenty-six weeks, then a smaller figure as long as needed up to the age when he (or she) should be eligible to an old-age pension. The scheme also entitled the beneficiary to free medical attendance during illness.[1] The fund for its application was derived partly from the employer, partly from the employee,[2] and partly from the State. The problem of unemployment had already been dealt with by the Labor Exchange Bill of 1909, which opened labor exchanges throughout the kingdom for giving information where work could be found. Yet often no work was obtainable and here is where the insurance against unemployment, provided in the bill of 1912, was designed to secure relief, though, as an experiment, it was confined to two trades, building and engineering, where labor was seldom continuous. A stipend was to be paid the insured workman for a maximum period of fifteen weeks of unemployment. Here again the employer, the employee, and the State all contributed to the fund. The success of the experiment led parliament in 1920 to extend it to nearly all manual labor and to non-manual workers earning less than £250 a year. It was not till the after-war depression set in, about 1921, that the scheme was found inadequate; then it became a question not merely of tiding a workman over for a period of fifteen weeks but of supporting him perhaps permanently; and thus in 1924 Great Britain came to what has been popularly called "the dole"—a subject that will be considered in a later chapter. Since then there has been considerable legislation mainly concerned with enabling the State to carry this heavy load.

While Germany and Great Britain gave the idea of the social

---

[1] A special maternity benefit was also provided for women workers or the wives of insured men.

[2] Unless his wage fell below a certain figure.

In France

The proletariat

state its fullest development, almost all European countries have followed in the wake of Germany with similar measures. In France, besides an employer's liability law and legislative shortening of the working day, a measure was passed requiring compulsory insurance against illness, and another providing for old-age pensions; and as in England the State contributed to the operative fund. One of the greatest boons to the workers was the legal recognition accorded to trade unions in 1884. In 1900 was established a federation of unions, the *Confédération générale du Travail* (popularly known as the "C.G.T.")—an organization which was finally captured by the radical workmen, largely drawn from the unskilled, who had espoused the movement, already mentioned, known as syndicalism. The syndicalist [1] believed in what is called "direct action"; instead of seeking reforms through the channels of legislation (in other words, through political action); they strove, rather, to gain their ends by keeping the economic world in a constant state of turmoil, deliberately interfering with the process of production by damaging machinery or injuring the product (the methods known as "sabotage") [2] or by attempting a general strike. On the constructive side they are not sure that they believe in a state at all unless it might be conceived of as a loose federation of self-managing industrial unions. But the majority of French socialists have been opportunists, and have been glad to work with the "bourgeois" parties for social amelioration. In fact, only a minority of French workmen have become syndicalist, and perhaps because they hate to part with their cash, only a minority actually belong to unions at all. It should be remembered that France is a country where large-scale industries are few. A very large proportion of skilled workers make their own wares and sell them as well. The French artisan who works in his shop with perhaps an apprentice or two still persists even though the gild regulations have long since disappeared. And these artisans are in spirit much more to be classed with the bourgeoisie than with the proletariat. France is very largely a land of small shop-keepers and peasants—a fact which partially accounts for her conservatism.

Unlike England, agrarian conditions are of considerable impor-

---

[1] Derived from the French word for union, *syndicat*.

[2] "Sabotage" is supposed to be derived from the *sabot*, wooden shoe, which on one occasion some striking workmen threw into machinery in order to wreck it.

tance. In 1870 about two thirds of the population were peasants— *The peasantry* though the proportion gradually dwindled until now only a little more than half the French people get their living from the soil. The peasant, as a rule, owns his own land, which he and his family till with perhaps the aid of a few laborers. Large landowners are few, and so, on the other hand, are *métayers*, for France is supremely the land of the small proprietor. Narrow, of course, in viewpoint, the peasant is at the same time thrifty and hardworking, and even the hired laborer has as a rule his own little plot of land. Manifestly, the democratic republic had to serve so large a section of its citizenry, and it has done so in four chief ways. In the first place, the peasant was protected against foreign competition by a tariff on wine and wheat. In the second place, agricultural instruction was introduced into the curricula of the country schools and made compulsory. In the third place, agricultural societies were permitted in 1884 by the same law that legalized trade unions. Such organizations enabled the peasants to bargain the more easily for their needs, to market their produce on more favorable terms, and to learn of improved methods of agriculture. The farm laborers also formed unions, and when commodity prices generally rose early in the twentieth century, some strikes were attempted and usually won their object. In the fourth place, a great effort was made to provide the peasant with capital—not an easy matter, for it encountered a Frenchman's instinctive dislike for revealing the extent of his income. Though agriculture became capitalized to some extent during the period we are considering and better implements of farming came into use, it was still true that the land was not exploited to its full capacity. There is no question but that French agriculture is still an industry too little developed, but it furnishes much of the food and all of the wine for the population, and self-sufficiency has been the primary economic consideration.

In Italy, as in France, there had been social reform—chiefly *In Italy* during the period since 1880 while the more radical element in politics was in command. Trade unions were legalized, and a federation of unions organized, which, as in France, was captured *The proletariat* by the syndicalists. Owing to the influence of the politician, Giolitti, who, though not a socialist himself, made a practice of courting socialist support, a program of social legislation was enacted, which included old-age pensions, invalidity insurance, a workman's compensation act, and compulsory insurance against accident, as well as restrictions of the hours of work.

But the greatest need of Italy was relief for the peasants, who formed more than three quarters of the population in 1861, and is still about sixty per cent of the total. Unlike conditions in France, comparatively few peasants owned their own land. They were usually either *métayers* (tenants receiving some of their capital from a landlord with whom they shared their products in a stipulated proportion) or, as was the case in southern Italy, rural workers on large landed estates which were feudal in origin. In either case the Italian peasant lived always close to the borderline of subsistence—a fact partly due to the unfavorable character of the soil and partly due to his economic dependence. In case of a drought there was little to save him from starvation. Many of the peasants suffered from pellagra (a disease induced from eating bad corn) or from malaria if they lived in the swampy regions of middle Italy. In general it must be said that under the parliamentary régime the government failed to attack the rural problem in its fundamentals. It drained some marshes, launched a project of reforesting the mountains, undertook to check pellagra by furnishing instruction in dietetics, and provided a few land banks and agricultural schools, but nothing was done toward raising the peasant to a position of economic independence—such a step as Prussia took at great expense but with substantial results. Agriculture in Italy was backward and seemed likely to remain so. The fact that distress was chronic was evidenced by the steady stream of emigration. But with all his poverty the Italian peasant is at least a cheerful sufferer, and though usually rather ignorant and extremely superstitious, he is at any rate rendered industrious by force of circumstances.

Surveying the position of the common man during the period just treated, we may perhaps agree with the economist, Keynes, that the exceptional type was able to raise himself above his station and force his way into the ranks of the middle or upper classes. The rigid social stratification of the Old Régime had long since loosened (in France, indeed, had disappeared); rationalization had not yet extinguished the small independent producer; and the individual of promise had often a chance to better his condition. The late nineteenth century is sometimes thought of as the heyday of the "self-made man." Moreover, as illiteracy declined, knowledge was made more generally available—through newspapers at least. Yet such facts must not be overemphasized. For most of the toiling masses the handicaps were much too great to enable latent ability to assert itself. Inspiration requires background as a rule. The general standard of living among the workers was still too low to enable the average person in such a group to find his level. Only in skilled leadership was there seemingly a way out; and the instruments employed for pushing their cause, trade-unionism and active participation in politics, were necessarily slow in affecting the distribution of wealth. Moreover even the "social state" was capitalistic in its foundations, and, as an eminent scholar puts it, "an educational system which in most western countries ends at the age of fourteen is an insurance for capitalism against inconvenient attack." After all, capitalism, being so well entrenched, had only to defend. The argument of force, which trade-unionism implied did not receive general approval save when used with moderation. The "social state" was paternalistic, and only partially weaned from laissez-faire. Yet it is something that it was the product of an actual recognition of the importance of the proletariat in modern society. So much the pressure of the working class had accomplished. The question of really how near economic equality persons should approach who are mentally unequal is something perhaps for the biologists or psychologists to settle. But Science has not yet ordered society according to her own code of justice, and it is doubtful if she ever will.

In one way, however, applied science may help to solve the problem of ending poverty. Population, as we have noted, greatly increased, especially in England, as the result of the Industrial Revolution. Near the end of the eighteenth century Malthus presented his famous thesis that the growth of population, unless checked, would inevitably outstrip the means of subsistence, and he was especially concerned over the fecundity of the poor. Manifestly the problem of social relief is fundamentally aggravated by the excessive size of families which are unable to be self-dependent. With the development of medical science and a better knowledge of hygiene, both of which were gifts of the nineteenth century, the death rate was correspondingly lowered, and the problem became, if anything, more acute. Would the social state, in self-defense, let us say, adopt a reasoned attitude toward birth control? Fortunately or unfortunately (as one may view this problem), the religious

The question of birth control

mind of the period was in general thoroughly hostile to any interference with the course of nature. From about 1875 the fall of the
birth rate became general throughout western Europe but in most
countries it was the upper classes who deliberately restricted the
size of their families—chiefly, perhaps, as a means of enjoying a
higher standard of living for themselves and their children, and
partly because of the growing demand from women for a greater
sphere of activity outside of the home. Meanwhile the question
of bringing scientific knowledge of birth control before the masses
became—and still is—violently controversial. A well-known
author of a book on poverty has declared that "the greatest need
of mankind in his war against poverty is for such control and
regulation of his propagation as will result in a selective birth
rate." Certainly the size of families is intimately connected with
the standard of living, and if that standard is to be brought to a
decent level, prodigality in having children must be paid for by
some source—should it be paid for by society as a whole? Some
scholars go so far as to say that if the social state is to look after
the welfare of the masses, it has a right to expect the masses to
ease its burden in this regard. Nevertheless it is only in recent
years that private agencies for educative propaganda have begun
to win the sympathies of the public, and not only have governments in general shirked the problem but France and Italy have
recently passed legislation to obstruct such efforts. Apart from
religious influences (less inveterate than they once were), opposition to birth control has developed from a new angle. The new
Italy and the new Germany are doing what they can to promote
large families as a means of amassing man power. In other words,
the question is affected by nationalism—a spirit of so powerful a
nature that it needs to be examined in some detail.

Nationalism and the Submerged Nationalities

Some preliminary distinctions One may comprehend the psychology of nationalism by thinking
for the moment of patriotism, which is as familiar to us as de-
mocracy. While democracy is an inward force and has to do with
an individual's relations to the state of which he is a citizen,
patriotism, on the other hand, looks outward; the individual
envisages his country as a whole and looks out on other countries
with a sense of superiority or antagonism. Democracy and patriotism have nothing in common except that a democratic nation

is more articulate and hence may display a more vigorous patriotism. But patriotism is but a subdivision of the more general term, nationalism. Some people do not enjoy such a thing as a *patria* in the sense of a country which is theirs by choice. But patriotism has much the same character and is derived from the same origins as nationalism, and we shall deal with the latter as the more basic force. A group possessing the sentiment of nationalism is known as a nationality. The term, nation, commonly used by political scientists as synonymous with nationality, seems usually to imply independence and adherence to a common government.

Now what is nationalism? Being a psychological force and yet involving much that is tangible and real, it is hard to devise a completely adequate definition. Perhaps we may define it as the sense of unity and distinctiveness on the part of a people, coupled with the determination to defend and perhaps to promote those ideals and interests which hold it together as a group. There must always be something to bind such a people together, common traditions, common memories, common institutions, common ideals —all that go to make up a fairly uniform culture. But what, we may ask, goes to form a nationality in the beginning? How comes it that two peoples dwelling side by side may be of two distinct nationalities. The making of a nationality may be the result of a number of different factors. Language, religion, geography, or history (in the sense of a common experience in the past), or a combination of some of these factors may afford us our explanation. The Chinese lived in a natural geographical compartment and developed a language and institutions peculiar to themselves. Geography and language contributed powerfully to make the Italians a separate nationality, though there were enough inner differences to have kept them permanently divided, had not history stepped in and gradually developed a nationalist consciousness. Swiss nationalism has no common language as a basis and their country has little geographical unity, but they had once been bound together by common resistance to an alien yoke. Americans, on the other hand, speak the same language as the English; yet history and geography have made them a distinct nationality. In the case of the Croats and Serbs of Austria-Hungary the distinction was almost wholly one of religion, since their language was the same and some of them at least had shared the same historical

Meaning of nationalism

experience. Race has sometimes something to do with nationality, since the Russians and the Chinese are obviously of different race, but the races of Europe have so intermingled that in that continent nationalist distinctions are hardly along racial lines. Perhaps language was originally the most active determinant, for it was through its language, more than through anything else, that a people came to express its inmost self. We have already noted the rise of a national literature as contributive to the making of a national state.

We shall not review the history of a force, which as Gustave Le Bon has said, had its origin "at some undated period." There were evidences of it in the Middle Ages, as we have noted, though it was mostly latent then, since the masses lived for the most part in a static civilization, and, as Professor Pollard has said, "the absence of nationality is characteristic of all medieval institutions." When the spirit was aroused, it was usually in time of stress, as in France under Jeanne Darc. Except, perhaps, in England, where insularity early made for nationalist sentiment, nationalism was for the most part dormant during the Middle Ages [1] and hardly a vigorous force during the early Modern Era [2] though it should be noted that with the decline of feudal interests and religious antagonisms, loyalty to the crown developed the "national" point of view, as represented by the monarch and his ministers; moreover, mercantilism, though an affair chiefly of governments and the middle class, had been an exhibition of nationalism in a sense. So far as it may be said to exist during the Old Régime, it was an affair chiefly of the upper and middle classes, for the masses had hardly awakened to a nationalist consciousness. It was, in fact, the French Revolution, as we have noted, [3] that made it a really spontaneous and enduring force in European history. Its convulsive record in the nineteenth century prior to 1870 has already been discussed. Professor MacDougall, the social psychologist, rightly calls it "the most powerful factor in modern history."

Ever since the French Revolution had demonstrated the power

---

[1] See page 81.

[2] The precedence of religious over national interest was conspicuously displayed in the Wars of Religion when Catholics and Calvinists sometimes sided with enemies of their country. The Fronde (see page 81) furnished an interesting example of national interest sacrificed to class interest.

[3] Page 319.

of the self-reliant, self-propelled group, the various nationalities *Objects of* living under alien rule have naturally come to long for independence *nationalism* or, at the very least, autonomy. This desire is doubtless one of the most reasonable forms of nationalism, especially if the nationality in question is suffering from oppression or from an assault upon those qualities and traditions that have made it a nationality. Such an example of nationalism is comparable to the ideal of national defense, one of the manifestations of that spirit which an independent nation may be forced to display. For tracing other national objects we may even go back to the time when nationalism—in this case patriotism—was embodied largely in the sovereign or his small group of advisers who were able to look at the realm as a distinct unit. Among the commonest national objects as we have noticed, have been natural boundaries and the securing of an outlet on a sea, or, if an outlet is already possessed, the acquisition of territory that would provide a better position on a sea. It is obvious that strategic or commercial ends are here in view. After the French Revolution had made nationalism a popular force, most importance became attached to freeing the different members of a nationality still under foreign rule in order that all might be united under one flag and culture. This type of nationalism is irredentism, the aspiration to redeem the brothers in subjection; and as most states had grown up haphazardly, there were many such examples of nationalist elements coveted by an outside power. Manifestly irredentism was a highly subversive force, threatening the stability of many European states. Still another manifestation of nationalism is what we call imperialism, the demand for political or economic control of lands populated by relatively backward races. This type of nationalism—the most provocative of war during the period we are now considering—will be discussed in the next chapter.

There is also that phase of nationalism known as "economic nationalism," which may, as we shall notice, manifest itself as imperialism, but which may, on the other hand, appear as something more strictly defensive—the desire of a nation to protect its economic life from foreign competition. We have already noticed mercantilism as an aspect of the Era of National Consolidation. A sense of solidarity was promoted on the part of each nation by economic ties just as the mutual antagonism of nations was illustrated by economic barriers between them. In this manner the

Industrial Revolution in a sense promoted nationalism. Improved methods of communication, such as a network of railways, developed a more compact nation and placed the group feeling on a more solid and practical basis. As a complement to this development the erection of tariff walls had the effect of making each nation more of an economic unit, and as far as possible its ideal was that of national self-sufficiency. This has meant not only the capacity to feed itself but the assurance of having an abundance of raw materials for its industries—and such, as we shall point out later, was one of the motives for the revival of imperialism. Then, as a natural corollary, it was deemed necessary to protect home industries from foreign competition by means of tariffs. As a matter of fact, the trend during the first half of the nineteenth century had been rather in the opposite direction.[1] Under the influence of Adam Smith and on the basis of the reasoning that she must look outside for her food and facilitate its importation Great Britain, as we have seen, adopted what was practically free trade. Soon France under Napoleon III followed, in a measure, her example, and before long most of the Continental nations were bound together by treaties which provided for only low duties on imports and no prohibitive tariffs. It looked as if Europe had become converted to the idea of economic interdependence. But in the third quarter of the century—the period we are now considering—one witnessed a return to economic nationalism almost indeed as ironclad as in the days of mercantilism. The rise of new nations like Germany, the competition of American wheat, and the rapid industrial development of the Continent contributed to this change. Bismarck, though by conviction a free trader, responded to the demand of the junkers for a tariff on agricultural products, and Germany thus definitely adopted protection in 1879, extended later to manufactured articles. France soon followed Germany's example, and other nations followed in their wake. Only Great Britain still clung to free trade, but in the 'nineties the Conservative statesman, Joseph Chamberlain, raised the issue of "tariff reform," as a mild form of protection, made to include "imperial preference"—that is, allowing the British dominions a preferential treatment, and amounting, in effect, to the creation of an imperial *Zollverein*. Though his project met with no success, one might wonder how long the British would be able

[1] See page 426.

to remain the single exception in a world of protectionist nations. For the time when British goods flooded the markets of the Continent, insuring for Great Britain a period of unparalleled prosperity, had steadily drawn to a close, as industries on the Continent had developed.

Finally there is that species of nationalism which involves the attitude of a national government toward alien elements in the state when it undertakes a policy of assimilation. Such a policy is more in keeping with dynasticism—the idea that the people ruled by a government is a matter simply of dynastic inheritance and not concerned with nationalist differences. The process involved an attack upon another nationality—one that perhaps cherished the hope of becoming free. In the case of the Serbs of Austria-Hungary freedom meant the right to become incorporated with Serbia. The Alsatians and the Roumans of Hungary had similarly separatist aims. But with the Poles, the Irish, the Czechs, and the Finns there was at least no case of irredentism, since the whole nationality was subject to foreign rule.

An example of a nationality aspiring to freedom from subjection is furnished by the Poles. The kingdom of Poland, as will be remembered, was extinguished in the eighteenth century and its population divided between Austria, Prussia, and Russia. The Poles of Austria secured in the days of the Dual Monarchy a certain favored treatment and were not rebellious. Those in Russia had twice rebelled, and were held down since 1863 in a state of bitter subjection. The Russians hoped to extinguish Polish nationalism by confining the language of instruction to Russian in all schools; but in this purpose they were defeated, as the Poles preferred to remain in ignorance than be Russianized. Meanwhile Prussia was learning that even good treatment will not always avail to weaken nationalism. Frederick the Great, as we have noticed, had done much for the development of his Polish provinces, and the effect of the social reforms of the early nineteenth century was not only to free the Polish peasant from serfdom but to make him a landed proprietor. Even a certain amount of autonomy had been granted in the province of Posen. But the Poles were never content under Prussian rule. History, language, and (to a large extent) religion marked them out as a separate nationality, and they never forgave Prussia for her part in the destruction of the kingdom of Poland. Hence they revolted in

Nationalism in subjection: (1) case of the Poles

sympathy with the Russian Poles in 1831, and in consequence
the autonomy of Posen was withdrawn. During the 'fifties when
the Industrial Revolution made strides in Prussia a Polish middle
class was created—the one thing of which they had always stood
in need—and a sort of nationalist renascence was quietly promoted.
In 1863 there was another revolt in conjunction with that in
Russia. After the establishment of the German Empire Bismarck
made up his mind to solve this problem, so injurious to its integrity and security. In two ways he sought to depress Polish nationalism: by placing disabilities on the language of the Poles and
by weakening their ascendancy over the land. By certain acts of
legislation the Polish language was debarred from the elementary
schools as well as from public meetings of all sorts, including the
theater. Then he got the Prussian parliament to set aside a sum
of money to purchase land from the natives in order to sell it
to Germans. By this colonizing scheme he hoped to secure a German grip on the Polish provinces and undermine the unity of this
alien segment. But the scheme was a dismal failure. As the price
of land rose, many Poles made their fortunes in selling land
to these newcomers, and then proceeded to buy land in Silesia,
thus broadening the area of Polonism. Moreover, many of the
German settlers, finding the environment unfriendly, were willing to be assimilated, and became to all intents and purposes
Poles. Even the campaign against their language did not really
weaken the Poles but only served to embitter them. Bismarck,
like Napoleon, had failed to understand the strength of nationalism. After his day an effort was made to force the Poles to sell
land at a price fixed by the government, but this measure also
brought but little result. As J. H. Clapham, the British economist,
remarks, "The Poles continued to multiply and possess the earth.
If they were kept from it here and there, they went to the towns
and Polonized them." Generally speaking, Prussia's policy had
redounded not only to the material advantage of the Poles but
to their moral welfare as well. A people who had shown in times
past but little unity and self-reliance had come to acquire those
qualities in the stress of self-defense; and down to the outbreak of
the Great War the Poles were still a thorn in the side of Prussia.

(2) Case of the Irish

Another case of a submerged nationality which constituted a
vital problem for the governing power was that of the Irish. We
have already described the unhappy fortunes of this people under

British rule. Irish nationalism bore a striking analogy to Polish in that it was bred of differences of temperament and religion as well as the memory of historic wrongs. Unlike the Poles, however, most of the Irish had abandoned the use of their ancient tongue, and spoke the language of their rulers. Unlike the Poles also, the Irish population (and by this we mean Catholic Ireland, not Ulster) were in a state of abject poverty. Famine conditions in the 'forties (due to the failure of the potato crop) had caused the death of hundreds of thousands; and the despair which naturally ensued led to a stream of emigration. At the end of fifty years the population of Ireland had been reduced by almost half.

Economic instability was at the root of the Irish question. The land was tilled by a native tenantry of absentee landlords (generally of English extraction [1]) under conditions which even in normal times barely insured subsistence. Ireland, for one thing, is a country where the rainfall is over-abundant, and most of the land is boggy. The Irish peasant, who was not naturally thrifty or industrious, still employed antiquated methods of tillage, and had no capital, as a rule, with which to improve them. If perchance he should improve his holding, the usual result was a prompt increase of his rent, and in case he could not pay it, he was liable to be evicted with the loss of the little capital he had expended. Since, moreover, leases were short, tenure was at best precarious, and as there were more workers than tenancies, rent was unduly high owing to the large number of competitors for the land. Evictions for the non-payment of rent were the constantly recurring agony of Irish life, and the evil was on the increase. In the 'sixties there was a good deal of unrest, and the government had much cause to feel concern. It was partly because Disraeli had dodged the Irish question that Gladstone won the general election of 1868 and came into office pledged to secure some sort of amelioration for Ireland. One of his first measures was the disestablishment of the Anglican Church in that country, the Irish being no longer obliged to support an alien creed out of their meager resources.

Twice Gladstone attempted by legislation to solve the economic problem. On the second occasion (1881) he adopted the platform

---

[1] Descendants of the men who had profited by the confiscations of Tudor and Stuart times. As, according to Irish custom, the land had been held by clans rather than a few single landowners, expropriation had converted the status of a landowning class into one of tenantry.

of the Irish Land League (founded in 1879): fair rent, fixity of tenure (that is, so long as rent were paid) and free sale (that is, the right of a peasant to sell his tenancy and receive a compensation for any improvements that he had made); but these measures hardly reached the core of the problem, and Ireland was still unpacified. A large section of Irish opinion had come by this time to demand home rule, and a determined campaign was carried on by the Irish members of the house of commons who tried to force the issue by obstructing all legislative business. After the general election of 1885 Gladstone found himself without a working majority in the house unless he could count on the Irish members; so in 1886 he surrendered to the principle of home rule, and, accordingly, brought in his first measure to that effect. There was thus precipitated one of the most formidable political crises of the century. The bill was attacked by some on the ground that the Irish, if politically separated from England, would be a source of danger to the United Kingdom. Some, too, agreed with Salisbury that the Irish were incapable of self-government. But the most serious resistance was encountered from a group of Liberals, headed by Chamberlain, who, while believing in home rule, felt that the same status should also be granted to Ulster, which might otherwise be oppressed by the Catholic Irish. So strongly did this element feel that they seceded from the party, forming a new group, known as the Liberal Unionists, which eventually became absorbed in the Conservative Party. Thanks to their defection, the home rule bill failed to pass the house of commons, and Gladstone accordingly resigned. The sequel, of course, was another period of lawlessness and repression. In 1893, however, Gladstone returned to power (he was then in his eighty-fifth year), and he at once brought up a second bill, providing this time for the maintenance of Irish representation in the house of commons as a supplement to home rule. But this time it was the house of lords that rejected the bill, and Gladstone retired permanently from public life. Yet, the rival party, the Conservatives, who then came into power, were forced to apply some remedy to the Irish question. While putting down disorder with a heavy hand, they tried, as one of their opponents expressed it, to "kill home rule by kindness." By various legislative acts the State provided funds for buying out the landlords,[1] the peasants acquiring the land through loans

[1] Great financial inducements were made to the Irish landlords to sell, and

repaid to the State by annual payments over a long period of years. This policy (which, in principle, had first been suggested by the Liberal, John Bright) was designed to create a class of peasant proprietors as the most feasible method of solving the agrarian problem. So successful was the policy that by the end of British rule at least two thirds of the land had passed into the hands of the peasants in full ownership.

Unhappily the political problem was rendered no less acute because of better economic conditions. Home rule was still the object of Irish patriots. When in 1906 the Liberals recovered power, they gave their whole attention to social reform and had little thought for Ireland, but in the elections of 1910 they lost so many seats in the house of commons that the Asquith ministry found it necessary to look to the Irish nationalists for support for its social program. A sort of trade was arranged, and the result was the third home rule bill, similar to the lines of the second. Since by this time the veto power of the house of lords had been abolished, the passage of the bill was assured, but a sudden storm arose from an unexpected quarter. The Ulsterites resolved to revolt rather than be bound to a régime which they felt convinced would subject them to religious persecution and heavy taxation of Irish industries (mostly concentrated in Ulster); it was declared that home rule would mean "Rome rule," and with this position leading Conservatives in England openly sympathized. The Ulsterites proceeded to arm, and as the Catholic Irish did likewise, there was by 1914 every prospect of civil war. Nothing saved the situation but the coming of a European crisis and the outbreak of the Great War. As a truce was now imperative, the operation of the bill, recently passed, was now suspended for the duration of the War.

But if civil war was averted, the danger of an Irish rebellion was increased. For the Irish nationalists cared comparatively little for the European struggle and felt that their own cause had been betrayed. A more radical organization, known as Sinn Fein,[1] demanding not home rule but a republic, had been started some ten years back, and in 1917 it attempted an insurrection. The fact that many Irish were in collusion with Germany rendered the

finally some compulsion was legally applied—an unusual attack on the rights of property.

[1] Meaning in Irish "we ourselves."

situation doubly serious. The "Easter Rebellion," as it was called, was speedily put down (followed by the execution of some innocent members of Sinn Fein), and the ministry then revived the third home rule bill, though not applying it to Ulster, which had been far more loyal to the empire during the War and was still averse to union with the rest of Ireland. But conciliation was vain. Neither the Home-Rulers (the so-called Nationalists) nor the Sinn Feiners were as yet willing to consider the breaking up of Ireland, and it was felt that in making changes in the original bill the British government had been guilty of bad faith. In any case home rule was doomed. In the elections of 1918 the Home-Rulers were thoroughly beaten by the Sinn Feiners, and their erstwhile allies, the Liberals, were likewise routed. The Irish question was now to enter a new phase—a subject which we shall reserve to a later chapter.

(3) Other cases But excepting the Irish and the Catalans in Spain most of the subject nationalities were in central or eastern Europe. The Finns were not unreconciled to Russian rule as long as their constitution (which provided for autonomy and a personal union with Russia) was respected, but in 1906 the imperial government commenced an attack on Finnish nationalism; their constitution was abrogated, and it was only after a struggle that it was restored—not, however, without a reduction of Finland's rights. Mention has already been made of the Czechs of Austria,[1] whose stage of development certainly entitled them to autonomy at least. With the exception of the Serbo-Croats the rest of the subject peoples of the Dual Monarchy presented no serious problem, though it was doubtful if a state that was so clearly an offense to nationalism would manage to endure much longer in its existing form. A peculiarly harassing case was that of the people of Alsace-Lorraine, who much against their will had been handed over to Germany by the Treaty of Frankfort.[2] Treated with harshness under Bismarck and later with a certain studied effort at conciliation, they undoubtedly prospered in becoming subjects of industrial Germany; yet they were none the less unreconciled to German rule—fair evidence that nationalism is generally too strong to be purchased or beguiled. Exasperated because his efforts were not appreciated, the Emperor William II was quoted as saying, "She has felt my velvet glove; she

[1] See page 501.
[2] See pages 498–9.

will feel my iron one." Germany had failed to win the people of Alsace-Lorraine, just as Prussia had failed to win her Danes and Poles.

Manifestly nationalism, however we may regard it, is far too potent a force to be crushed. It is also obvious that civilization is all the richer for the cultural outflow of many different groups with their own particular outlook upon life. The policy of Germany and Russia in dealing with their subject nationalities was—to cite a famous epigram— "worse than a crime, it was a blunder." Even though the policy was not successful, it was always productive of hatred and a perpetual incentive to violence; and a nationality attacked is more likely to gain than lose in spiritual power.

Nationalism is essentially a phenomenon of social psychology. *The psychology of nationalism* It is often remarked that an individual will do, as a member of a group, many things that he would shrink from as an individual. The individual ego, in fact, yields in force to the collective ego, which accounts for that sense of unqualified superiority that one nation feels toward another. The Englishman *knows* that his institutions are the best; the Frenchman *knows* that his culture is supreme over all others; the Germans feel that they are the chosen people; the Americans with their boasted up-to-date-ness look on other peoples as hopelessly slow and stupid, not realizing, perhaps, that standards of value may differ. Of course we generally like what we are used to. The French and English as a rule abhor each other's cooking. The Frenchman who waits for a crowded omnibus until his number is called cannot comprehend how an American prefers to shove his way through a crowd. The average Englishman, with his innate sense of fair play, marvels that the German should need so many "forbidden" signs, and the German would not have it any other way and despises what he considers the unsystematic ways of the English. Through the centuries people have evolved the manners and institutions that are most adapted to their tastes, and it is the virtual uniformity of the group that gives us a nationality. There is little of reasoning about it. Nationalism is arrogantly self-satisfied; it has little of the power of introspection; it tyrannizes over its own. In time of war the individual is at once merged with the mass. He is not permitted, as a rule, to act according to his judgment, but is expected to serve his country "right or wrong." For him the law of the state—the nation-state—is the supreme law; his country's cause, the highest moral force that may be considered. It is thus assumed that individualism must always be sacrificed to nationalism. If not actually punished, the one who stands out and declines to go with the crowd is treated as a pariah. Nationalism has the qualities of a religion and is not readily amenable to reason. One knows also that the collective emotionalism of the group may carry an individual to the point where reason or conscience ceases to control his actions; and it is thus that the mob spirit is evolved. Of its very nature, nationalism is combative. Sensitive to outside currents, it is quick to resent insults. Viewing only its own objects as holy, it is quick to take advantage of the outsider. Nationalism, when reduced to its lowest terms, is collective vanity or collective selfishness. It is that force which has kept the world in a state of anarchy and is threatening civilization with destruction. Its nemesis will be viewed in the following chapters.

FOR FURTHER READING OR STUDY

Scott, J. F., and Baltzly, A., *Readings in European History*, chaps. vi and ix; Robinson, J. H., and Beard, C. A., *Readings in Modern European History*, vol. ii, chaps. xxiv–xxvi; Hayes, C. J. H., *British Social Politics* (extracts from pertinent matter); Gladstone, H. J., *After Thirty Years;* Asquith, H. H., *Fifty Years of British Parliament;* Giolitti, G , *My Memoirs;* Morley, J., *Recollections.*

Schapiro, J. S., *Modern and Contemporary European History*, xvi–xix, xx (pp. 395–8 for social reform in Germany), xxii, xxvi–xxvii (economic factors); Hayes, C. J. H., *Political and Social History of Modern Europe*, vol. ii, pp. 230–52 (science), 252–3 (the social state), chaps. xxii–xxiii; Higby, C. P., *History of Modern Europe*, chaps. xv, xviii, and xxi; Palm, F. C., and Graham, F. E., *Europe since Napoleon*, chaps. xiii, xvii–xviii; Fueter, E., *World History, 1815–1920*, chap. xxviii (new economic problems); Munro, W. B., *The Governments of Europe* (interesting and informing); Ogg, F. A., *European Governments and Politics*, part i (excellent for reference) and *The Economic Development of Modern Europe* (solid and serviceable); Day, C., *Economic Development in Modern Europe*, esp. chap. iv (English trade and manufactures); Birnie, D., *The Economic History of Europe*, esp. chap xiv (on social insurance); Thorndyke, L., *A Short History of Civilization*, chap. xxviii.

Randall, J. H., *The Making of the Modern Mind*, chaps. xviii–xix (excellent); Barnes, H. E., *Living in the Twentieth Century* (an admirably stimulating essay on the dynamic forces that have made the world of today); Bury, J. B., *The Idea of Progress;* Wallace, W. K., *The Trend of History;* Marvin, F. S., *The Century of Hope: A Sketch of Western Civilization from 1815 to the Great War;* Thomson, J. A., *An Introduction to Science;* Singer, C. A., *A Short History of Science;* Caldwell, O. W., and Slosson, E. E., *Science Remaking the World;*

Bettany, G. T., *Life of Charles Darwin;* Scott, W. B., *The Theory of Evolution;* Nussbaum, F. L., *A History of the Economic Institutions of Modern Europe,* part iv; Hobson, J. A., *The Evolution of Modern Capitalism;* White, L. W., and Shanahan, E. W., *The Industrial Revolution and the Economic World of Today,* part ii; Viljoen, S., *The Economic Tendencies of Today* (excellent); Jeffrey, E. C., *Coal and Civilization;* Veblen, T., *The Theory of Business Enterprise* and *The Theory of the Leisure Classes;* Taylor, F. W., *The Principles of Scientific Management;* Cooley, C. H., *Social Organization;* Schlichter, S. M., *Modern Economic Society;* Chase, S., *Men and Machines;* Freeman, R. A., *Social Decay and Regeneration;* Inge, W. R., *Outspoken Essays,* second series (chapters on the dilemma of civilization and the idea of progress); Lippmann, W., *Public Opinion;* Le Bon, G., *The Psychology of Crowds;* Laprade, W. E., "Public Opinion and the General Election of 1784," *Eng. Hist. Rev.,* xxxi, 224 ff.; Dicey, A. V., *Lectures on the Relations between Law and Public Opinion in England during the Nineteenth Century;* Hobhouse, L. T., *Liberalism;* Wingfield-Stratford, E., *The History of British Civilization,* vol. ii (interpretive history); Cross, A. L., *History of England and Greater Britain,* chaps. liii–lvi; Lunt, W. E., *History of England,* chaps. xxxvii–xxxix (foreign affairs included); Trevelyan, G. M., *British History in the Nineteenth Century* (interesting); Gretton, R. H., *A Modern History of the English People,* 2 vols. (begins at 1880); Adams, G. B., *Constitutional History of England,* chaps. xvii–xx; Usher, A. P., *An Industrial History of England,* esp. chaps. xix–xx; Muir, R., *How Britain Is Governed;* Dibelius, W., *England: Her Character and Her Genius* (profound and interesting analysis by a German); Blease, W. L., *A Short History of English Liberalism;* Halévy, E., *A History of the English People,* Epilogue, 2 vols., 1891–1915; Morley, J., *Life of William Ewert Gladstone,* 3 vols.; Monypenny, W. F., and Buckle, G. E., *The Life of Benjamin Disraeli, Earl of Beaconsfield,* 6 vols.; Maurois, A., *Disraeli: A Picture of the Victorian Age* (atmospheric and entertaining); Somervell, D. C., *Disraeli and Gladstone;* Cecil, G., *Life of Robert, Marquis of Salisbury,* 3 vols.; Garvin, J. L., *Life of Joseph Chamberlain,* 4 vols.; Raymond, E. T., *Life of Arthur James Balfour;* Seymour, C., *Electoral Reform in England and Wales;* Seignobos, C., *The Evolution of the French People,* chap. xx; Guignebert, C., *A Short History of the French People,* vol. ii, chap. xxxviii, sec. 4 and chap. xxxix; Wright, C. H. C., *The History of the Third Republic* (in brief compass); Vizetelly, E. A., *Republican France, 1870–1912* (chatty); Guérard, A. L., *French Civilization in the Nineteenth Century;* Huddleston, S., *France and the French;* Mason, E. S., *The Paris Commune;* Stannard, H., *Gambetta and the Foundation of the Third Republic;* Poincaré, R., *How France is Governed;* Middleton, W. L., *The French Political System* (excellent); Villari, L., *Italy,* chap. vi (pre-War political life); Groce, B., *A History of Italy, 1871–1915;* Solmi, A., *The Making of Modern Italy;* Coote, C. R., *Italian Town and Country Life* (charming); Pipkin, C. W., *Social Politics and Modern Democracies,* 2 vols. (confined to Great Britain and France); Clapham, J. H., *Economic Development of France and Germany;* Gillespie, F. E., *Labor and Politics in England, 1850–1867* (proletarian background of the Second Reform Bill); Tawney, R. H., *The British Labor Movement;* Cole, G. D. H., *A Short History of the British Working Class,* 3 vols.; Rayner, R. M., *The Story of Trade-Unionism* (popular but good); Hutchins, B. L., and Harrison, A., *A*

History of Factory Legislation; Dawson, W. H., *Bismarck and State Socialism and Social Insurance in Germany;* Estey, J. A., *Revolutionary Syndicalism;* Hayes, C. J. H., *Essays in Nationalism* (critical and spritely); Barker, E., *National Character and the Factors in its Formation;* Krehbiel, E., *Nationalism, War, and Society* (a syllabus with much fact and discussion); McDougall, W., *The Group Mind* (able analysis); Joseph, B., *Nationality, Its Nature and Problems* (by a Jew); Herbert, S., *Nationality and Its Problems;* Barker, E., *Ireland in the Last Fifty Years* (published in 1919); O'Connor, J., *History of Ireland, 1778–1924* (fair-minded Irish account); Turner, E. R., *Ireland and England* (stops at 1918); Phillips, W. A., *The Revolution in Ireland* (exhaustive and interesting but anti-Irish); Cerf, B., *Alsace-Lorraine since 1870;* Hayes, C. J. H., *France, A Nation of Patriots;* Boutmy, E., *The English People: A Study of Their Political Psychology.*

XV. MILITARISM, IMPERIALISM, AND IRRE-DENTISM—THE ORIGINS OF THE GREAT WAR

1. THE INTERNATIONAL SITUATION AFTER 1870—THE HEGEMONY OF GERMANY

A. The Organization of the German Empire

(1) *Political Aspects*

Dominance of Prussia; Organic strength of the government; Moral strength of the government.

(2) *Economic and Social Aspects*

Explanation of Germany's material strength; An era of prosperity; Germany as a paternalism.

B. Position of Germany in Europe—The Triple Alliance

Formation of the Triple Alliance; Formation of the Dual Alliance; A disturbance of the balance.

2. MILITARISM AND THE RACE OF ARMAMENTS

Militarism for defense; Race of naval armaments; The futile "Peace Movement"; Militarism for sport; Militarism and public opinion.

3. THE REVIVAL OF IMPERIALISM AND WORLD POLITICS

A. Causes and Significance

Minor factors; Economic motives; Political motives; Imperialism and the public.

B. The Leading World Powers

(1) *Great Britain*

The dominions; The crown colonies; India; Economic importance of the colonies.

(2) *France*

(3) *Italy*

(4) *Germany*

(5) *Russia*

C. The Areas of Exploitation—Imperialism at Work

(1) *Africa*

Opening of Africa; Partition of Africa; Remaining stakes.

(2) *The Far East*

Ancient states in Asia; China as a stake; The opening of China; The partition of China; Japanese imperialism and the Russo-Japanese War; Hegemony of Japan in the Far East; Financial imperialism in China.

(3) *The Near and Middle East*

Case of Persia; The Ottoman Empire: (1) its position, (2) its importance.

4. THE CLASH OF WORLD POWERS

A. ANGLO-FRENCH RIVALRY—THE EGYPTIAN QUESTION

Premonitions; Importance and plight of Egypt—the Anglo-French Condominium; Collapse of the Condominium and British occupation of Egypt; Divers quarrels; Struggle for the Nile—the Fashoda crisis.

B. GERMAN IMPERIALISM AND THE RISE OF THE TRIPLE ENTENTE

(1) *The Anglo-German Feud*

A new era of German imperialism; Question of South Africa and the Boer War; Continuous discords; Underlying factors.

(2) *The Entente Cordiale and the First Moroccan Crisis*

Formation and significance of the Entente Cordiale; Germany's intervention—the Moroccan crisis and settlement; Strengthening of the Entente Cordiale.

(3) *The Anglo-Russian Rapprochement and the Impenetrable Wall*

The Anglo-Russian Convention of 1907; From economic to political imperialism in Persia; Imperialistic encirclement.

(4) *The Equivocal Position of Italy*

C. THE EASTERN QUESTION AS THE HARBINGER OF WAR

(1) *The Rivalry for Supremacy in the Balkans—The Question of the Straits and the Bosnian Crisis*

The Treaty of Berlin and the recession of Russia; The Austro-German advance; Recovery of Russia; The Bosnian crisis and the intervention of Germany; Aftermath of the Bosnian crisis.

(2) *The Bagdad Railway Scheme*

Inception of the scheme; Attitude of Germany's rivals—difficulties and settlement.

(3) *The Growing Tension*

An illusory calm; The Agadir crisis; The Turco-Italian War; Renewal of Russian designs; The Balkan League and the First Balkan War; The Second Balkan War and the position of Constantinople; Serbia as the storm center of Europe.

5. AUSTRIAN DYNASTICISM *VS.* SERB IRREDENTISM

A. AUSTRIA-HUNGARY AND THE SOUTHERN SLAVS

Incongruity and instability of the Dual Monarchy; Sources of its strength; Position of the southern Slavs.

B. THE EVOLUTION OF PANSERBISM

Serbia and Balkan politics; Underlying causes of the Austro-Serbian feud; Growth of Serbian resentment—the question of the Adriatic; Stress of Austria's problem; The issue of panserbism.

6. PREPARATIONS FOR WAR

Tightening of the Triple Entente; Position of Poincaré; The gathering storm; Question of responsibility.

Our study of nationalism has enabled us to understand its inherent perils. Nationalism as imperialism was a dangerous force, magnified in proportion as the stakes were large, the fields remote, and the complications of a sort that could not readily be foreseen. Imperialism, allied with militarism, signified a predisposition to war as a means of attaining national objects. Nationalism as irredentism threatened the integrity of existing states and often embittered their relations. The existence of two armed camps to keep the balance of power and insure peace carried within itself the germs of its own destruction. The world did not want war; diplomats as a rule did not want war; but the fabric of Europe was no more firm, no more unified than it had been in the days of Grotius, and it was now, in the age of aggressive nationalism, much more liable to dissolution. Wars were no longer merely an affair of kings or ministers. An articulate and vigorous public opinion, with its care for an infinite number of personal interests, its ignorance of foreign affairs, and its collective emotionalism formed the background of the rivalries and feuds which came to fever heat in the year 1914. And because the nations of the world were self-conscious groups, with many inner groups, also self-conscious, a war involving all the great powers would be something more than a war. The Great War, or the World War, as it is also labeled, proved to be in many respects a revolution.

It was a long time coming, and one wonders just when its approach may be said to have begun. Perhaps it was foreshadowed as far back as 1870.

THE INTERNATIONAL SITUATION AFTER 1870—THE HEGEMONY OF GERMANY

When the German Empire was founded in 1871, such an achievement was important not only as the making of a nation; it marked the entrance into the family of nations of a very strong power—a power which, profiting by Bismarck's planning, was able to dominate foreign politics for more than thirty years. With France crushed and isolated, and Great Britain holding herself aloof from

the Continent or humoring her deeply rooted distrust of Russia,
it is not too much to say that Germany under Bismarck had upset
the balance of power. Should that newly acquired hegemony be
wisely exercised, Europe need not fear, but there is some logic
in the old theory that it is not well that any power in Europe should
become too formidable. Just how menacing Germany might be
would depend in a measure upon the international situation,
which we shall presently discuss. But it is equally important to
examine her inner structure. A contemporary writer was not far off
when he stated that Imperial Germany was "the most stupendous
fact in modern history."

The Organization of the German Empire

*Political
Aspects*

The constitution of the German Empire was chiefly Bismarck's
work, and it represented the quality of his statesmanship. It was
a medium though which the nation could express its energy under
strong leadership. Impressed with the necessity of conciliating
certain elements which caused him trouble during his work for

*Dominance
of Prussia*

German unity, he yielded to particularism to the extent of forming
the new Germany into a federation of autonomous states (a sort
of enlargement of the North German Confederation), and he
yielded to liberalism or democracy to the extent of providing for a
popular chamber, the reichstag, elected by universal manhood
suffrage. But with that subtle intuition that always marked his
statecraft Bismarck yielded actually nothing that would really
interfere with the strength of the imperial government. Prussia
was able in one way or another to dominate the empire. Her king
was German emperor; her population was large enough to insure a
Prussian predominance in the reichstag; her control of the upper
chamber, the bundesrath, though not assured by actual voting
strength (for Prussia had but seventeen votes out of fifty-eight),
was rendered fairly certain by her influence in several neighboring
states in north Germany; and finally the imperial constitution
could not be amended if fourteen adverse votes were cast in the
bundesrath—a provision which thus gave Prussia the opportunity
of thwarting any movement in a liberal direction. So close were
the interests of Prussia to those of Germany that the imperial
chancellor was generally premier of Prussia as well. At the same
time the concession to liberalism was nothing more than a gesture,
another consummate piece of political cynicism, for the reichstag

as a legislative body amounted to little, and was not even permanently representative, as no provision had been made for the redistribution of seats to accord with the growth of the urban population. Bismarck had nothing to lose by letting Bavaria or Würtemberg manage its local affairs or by letting the representatives of the people air their views in what has been called the "hall of echoes."

The German Empire, as constituted, was a semi-autocracy. *Organic strength of the government* The emperor was free to appoint his chancellor (the one important imperial minister) as he chose and to keep him as long as he chose. Much the more important branch of the legislature was the bundesrath, a body composed of appointees of the various governments which made up the federation, and since all but three of these governments were monarchical (the three exceptions being the free cities of Hamburg, Bremen, and Lübeck), and since these monarchical governments were not especially liberal, the upper chamber was bound to be conservative and on imperial (that is, national) questions was not likely to oppose Prussia. The reichstag was demonstrably weak, first because practically all legislation originated in the bundesrath, secondly because it did not have complete control over taxation (old taxes being collected without the need of its sanction, and certain appropriations, as for instance for the army, being voted for a term of years), and thirdly because ministerial responsibility was not recognized as a working feature of the constitution.[1] The reichstag could, indeed, reject a project presented to it by the bundesrath and could refuse to give its assent to a new appropriation, but its power was no more than simply restrictive, and if recalcitrant, it could be dissolved by the emperor with the sanction of the bundesrath. Then before a new parliament was called the government could employ its agencies for influencing the electorate with the good hope of obtaining one that was more dutiful. Thus the emperor controlled the chancellor, who controlled the bundesrath (of which he was president), which in turn completely overshadowed the reichstag.

In appreciating the weakness of the reichstag we must understand that it lacked what every popular chamber needs as a basis —a vigorous public opinion. There was, to begin with, neither

[1] The fact that the chancellor was supposed by the constitution to countersign all acts of the emperor and thus accept responsibility for them was of no practical importance whatever, as he was not accountable to the reichstag for anything he did.

*Moral
strength
of the
government*

complete freedom of the press nor unrestricted freedom of association. For there was nothing like a "declaration of rights" in the
constitution. While on matters of national prestige the public
mind was sometimes assertive, there was, generally speaking, little
interest in domestic questions, and the status of the reichstag was
not such as to invite it. Much of the press was government
controlled, for Bismarck had seen the importance of mobilizing
the intellect in the service of the government. The chairs in the
universities were filled by men whose politics were acceptable to
the government; and it goes without saying that no member of
the Social Democratic Party, which was the only really liberal
political party, could ever hope to hold either a professorship or
any high official position. One must also bear in mind that the
Germans, like the Italians, had had but little experience with
parliamentary institutions and that the habits of discipline in-
stilled into them in the army were not conducive to the development of a spirit of independence. Moreover, schools, pulpit, and
press were freely used to impart the duty of obedience. As ad-
duced by certain philosophers, the German theory of state leveled
the individual to nothing in comparison to the State, which was
exalted as the embodiment of power. But the individual reaped
abundant return for all his subservience. The governments, imperial or regional, which guided his destinies in rather autocratic
fashion, took ample care of those matters which seemed most
vital to every German. Hence our need of viewing the other side
of the shield.

*Economic
and Social
Aspects*

The solidity of Germany's political system was somewhat
duplicated in her economic affairs. The material strength of the
nation was attributable to various factors. In the first place

*Explanation
of
Germany's
material
strength*

geography was fairly kind to Germany. Though her position
would have been more favorable had she possessed the mouth of
the Rhine and faced the Atlantic (one may note the narrow sea-
front for that great industrial region traversed by the Rhine),
nevertheless in natural resources she was rather to be envied. She
had abundant coal, and the iron ore of Lorraine added greatly
to her industrial capacity—not the least of her benefits from the
war with France. In the second place Germany had those qualities
needed to take advantage of her assets and to utilize the opportunities which the Industrial Revolution had placed in her hands.
As regards Germans in general, they seemed to possess a wonderful

facility for adapting the discoveries of others to their own peculiar needs. It was the discovery of two Scotsmen of how to smelt the iron ore of Lorraine that enabled the Germans to exploit this wonderful natural resource. It was through the invention of another Britisher that the great aniline dye industry was started— an industry that has no peer in its field. It would be a mistake, however, to assume that the Germans have no inventive capacity, for their chemists have made wonderful discoveries, and no people have been more thorough in applying science to industry—with the result that articles of manufacture were often to be bought more cheaply in Germany than anywhere else, and the caption, "made in Germany" was read throughout the world. Besides, the German merchant studied the tastes of his customers, and gave them what they wanted. Such was, of course, an example of German enterprise. Moreover, the German worker was docile and easy to manage—qualities probably due to the habit of discipline ingrained in a nation that had always been military. Then the Germans also seemed to have a genius for organization— though whether it was a native trait or whether that too was acquired through military training can only be a matter for speculation. In any case the establishment of the empire made possible the co-ordination and concentration of the national energies.

The result was that the German government guided and fathered the nation's economic development. Railways were government-owned, and their rates made flexible enough to protect home industries against foreign competition. A marvelous merchant marine was developed, and subsidized by the government, steamer-lines connecting Germany with all parts of the world. The banks were also closely affiliated with the government. The interests of labor were cared for by social insurance and other measures which we have noticed, and, naturally enough, the investment which the German worker had placed in this scheme for his protection had the effect of discouraging him from emigration. For the agriculturalist and manufacturer the protective tariff was adopted —with the result, incidentally, of fostering the growth of trusts, thus bringing about a concentration of wealth. The coal syndicate practically dominated the domestic market, and it was commonly said that about fifty men directed Germany's economic life. But the guiding hand of the government made all this possible.

The result of all these factors was a material growth quite unprecedented in its rapidity. Germany's electrical and chemical industries left all foreign competitors far behind, and though in the making of textiles she never caught up with the British, her output of steel became nearly twice that of Great Britain, and in the manufacture of toys she led the world. The volume of her foreign trade increased by leaps and bounds, and between 1870 and 1912 Germany slid into second place among the commercial nations of the world. The same was true of her merchant marine, which by 1914 could boast of a net tonnage of over 3,000,-000. Hamburg had rapidly become the most thriving port on the Continent, not only as Germany's leading port, but, by virtue of the volume of goods re-exported to other nations, as a sort of distributing center for the Continent. But the point had been reached where an increasing supply of raw materials had regularly to be imported, and this will partly explain Germany's feverish demand for colonies, lest an unfavorable balance of trade, not to mention hostile tariffs, should hamper her steady growth. At all events, Germany was the workshop of the Continent, and such was her material prosperity that poverty hardly existed within her borders.

It is no great wonder that the majority of Germans were well content with a régime which in spite of its somewhat autocratic character, enabled them to maintain a comfortable living. A government which took such serious care of the working class would naturally perceive the vital importance of education. Every child was entitled to at least a common school education at the public cost, and for children between the ages of six and fourteen attendance at school was compulsory. Socially the German system was undemocratic (though the same might be said of the French and English systems). Members of the middle class did not send their children to the free schools if they could avoid it, and they, in turn, were unable to aspire to the schools of the aristocracy; while restrictions partly curricular and partly financial tended to keep the children of the masses from getting beyond the elementary grades. Excess of discipline was also a feature of the system; teachers were carefully chosen for conservative views; and in Prussia loyalty to the kaiser was carefully inculcated. Yet the aim was to furnish competent instruction, and care was taken of the physique as well as the mind of each pupil. "The ultimate aim, never lost to view," wrote an American scholar in 1912, "is that the boy shall be made a good soldier and a self-supporting and useful citizen, and the girl shall become a model *Hausfrau* and mother. The first requisite of national power is recognized to be sturdy, intelligent, thrifty men and women." Much was also done, especially in Prussia, to foster the loyalty of youth through the patronage of various youth organizations, amalgamated in 1911 as the Young German League, which had as one of its objects preparation for military training.[1] Prussia expended a considerable sum on welfare work among her youth. It goes without saying that German towns were models of cleanliness and efficient administration. Also they were thoroughly policed. No one was allowed to become a nuisance to his neighbor, and if "FORBIDDEN" signs were prevalent everywhere, it was because the social viewpoint had precedence over individual impulses or interests. The police as the custodians of order and of the general interest could at times be very meddlesome and domineering, but Germans felt, in general, that the benefit was worth the price. They found no charm in the Anglo-Saxon or Latin exaltation of the individual. To them the degree of liberty enjoyed by the French and English spelled chaos and extravagance. They preferred a more thoroughly developed "social state," grounded as it was on the public welfare and functioning with organized efficiency. Such, indeed, was the essence of their *Kultur*. Germany was, therefore, something more than an autocratic monarchy with a military background and military ideals. It was also a paternalism.

The moral and material strength of such a nation is evident. Now what about its position in the European family?

Position of Germany in Europe—The Triple Alliance

The policy of Bismarck, who was chancellor from 1871 to 1890, was fundamentally defensive. He had accomplished the great object of his career, and he wanted no more wars. He was unable, single-handed, to restrain Moltke and the militarists when they nearly provoked a new war with France in 1875, and it was only the pressure of the Powers, especially Russia, that saved the situation; but with this exception Bismarck's mastery of his government's policy was unchallenged—at least until 1888—and his chief consideration was the defense of the empire, the conservation

Formation of the Triple Alliance

---

[1] The socialists had also their youth organization, which was naturally pacifist in leanings.

of his handiwork. Assuming as he did the inveterate hostility of France, he made it his business that this power should remain isolated. He accordingly effected an alliance with Austria-Hungary (1879), as well as contracting similar agreements with Russia (the Reinsurance Treaties of 1881 and 1887), and he cultivated friendly relations with England. His crowning diplomatic achievement was the formation in 1882 of the Triple Alliance, composed of Germany, Austria, and Italy.

Formation of the Dual Alliance

An alliance purely defensive and created for defensive purposes, the Triple Alliance nevertheless greatly strengthened Germany's position. The position of France was correspondingly rendered less secure; and a second war-scare in 1887 gave the French much food for thought. Then Bismarck, strange to say, committed a blunder, that gave his old enemy a handle. In spite of having concluded a secret treaty with Russia, providing for mutual amity, he deliberately discouraged the availability of the German money-market for Russian loans. It is probably true that what he wanted was to impress Russia with her dependence (he naturally disapproved of Russia's adoption of a protective tariff), but it was a gratuitous provocation for which there was little if any practical justification. Russia immediately turned to France, who was more than ready to welcome her importunities. French bankers provided Russia with a series of loans, aggregating over 3,000,000,000 francs. The reason was obvious. France saw a chance of ending her isolation by an alliance with Russia. And Russia, on her side, perceived that if she wished to borrow indefinitely in Paris, she would have to agree to a formal alliance, and she believed that meeting in that way her financial needs was eminently worth the price. An understanding was reached in 1891, followed by a military convention in 1892, which became effective in 1894. Defensive like the Triple Alliance, the provisions of the Dual Alliance were also secret. The firstfruit of this alignment was another large loan in 1891. Whether Bismarck could have reclaimed Russia at the last minute is somewhat doubtful, but at any rate he had retired from office in 1890, and no effort was made then to rebuild the bridge.

A disturbance of the balance

We shall notice later on the full import of the Dual Alliance. Suffice it to say here that there was now a division of Europe into two rival systems. Superficially the balance of power had been restored. And yet, in spite of the herculean efforts of France to

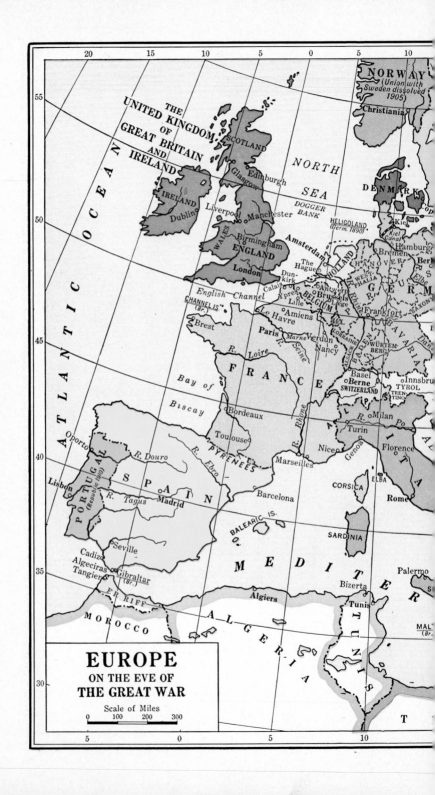

EUROPE
ON THE EVE OF
THE GREAT WAR

Scale of Miles

0   100   200   300

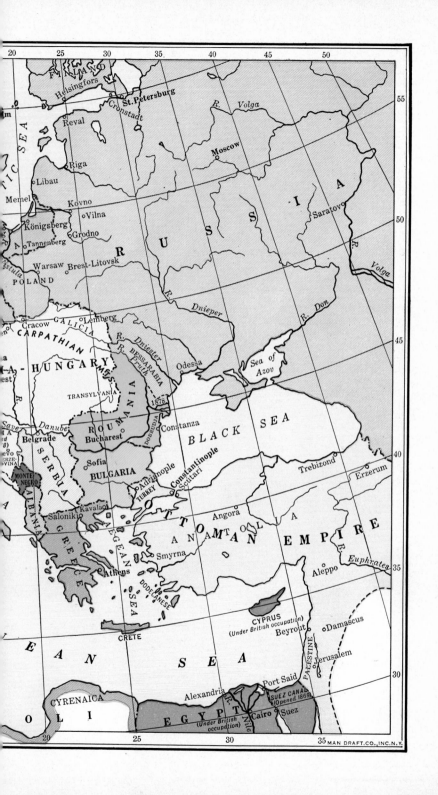

augment her army, there was little doubt that the Triple Alliance was much the stronger of the two combinations. A solid phalanx had been erected across central Europe, and the dominating member of the coalition was Germany. Down to 1904 the hegemony of Germany was still a fact.

It was Germany's position in Europe, coupled with her physical strength, that makes one think of her as a great compressed dynamo. With her growing population (nearly 70,000,000 in 1914), her tremendous industrial growth and commercial expansion, and her dominant position in Europe, she seemed somehow to demand a place in the world more commensurate to her strength. So much stored-up power uncontrolled by an external authority was a standing danger in a world of greed and ambition. Thus any incautious flaunting of her military power was likely to induce other nations of Europe to seek in some way to redress the balance and to assume an obstructive, perhaps an aggressive attitude. The growth of militarism in Europe was, in fact, one of the paths leading to war.

Militarism and the Race of Armaments

Militarism, whether it be armed fear, or that fondness for war and its trappings which lingered on in a world that was becoming more civilized in most respects, was one of the menaces to the world's peace. On the intelligible theory that large standing armies and navies were necessary for national defense armaments were piled on every hand. At the beginning of 1914 conscription was in force in all the great nations except Great Britain, and even in the British Isles there had been a strong agitation to adopt it. Owing to a succession of international crises even neutralized Belgium had so despaired of her safety that she too had adopted the principle of universal service (1913). For reasons which we shall ascertain later armaments had been generally increased during the last two years of the peace; in other words, the race was then accelerated. Since two years in the army were insufficient to bring French man power up to the German level, the service was then lengthened to three years, and Russia lengthened hers to three and a half. Just before the outbreak of war France had a standing army of approximately 800,000, Germany, about 760,000 (with definite plans for 870,000), and Russia, something like 1,500,000; but these figures do not include the much larger

Militarism for defense

numbers which constituted the reserves.   Europe slept on its arms.

The race of naval armaments   One should also remember the naval power of Great Britain. For some time before the Great War naval armaments had been steadily increased.   Great Britain had formulated the doctrine (1889) that for national safety it was necessary that she should have a navy that equaled that of any two powers on the Continent.   The powers she had had in mind were France and Russia,

Underwood & Underwood

BRITISH BATTLE CRUISER

but in 1898 Germany entered the field as a naval power, and in 1900, after a campaign to educate public opinion (since the reichstag had cut down the naval estimates two years earlier) a sensational naval bill was passed, which made the German navy the second in the world.   A memorandum accompanying the bill discussed at length the question of how large a navy would be needed for defense in a war with England.   As this effort was construed as a challenge to British sea power, the British admiralty henceforth looked upon Germany as the potential enemy, and Sir John Fisher, who became active head of the navy in 1903, set to work with such ardor to augment its fighting capacity that he allowed himself to talk of a surprise raid on the German fleets.   When in 1905 the British commenced to construct dreadnoughts, the Germans had, of course, to construct them too, and as most of the older vessels had then to be scrapped, the Germans had almost an even advantage.   A race of naval armaments had commenced, which on one occasion threw the British public into a panic.   Loath to divert the public funds from social insurance to engines of war, the Liberal ministry twice endeavored to persuade Germany to agree to a "naval holiday"— a temporary cessation of battleship-building—but Germany always exacted conditions which made such a truce virtually impossible. On the other hand, Germany was not building as many ships as the British, and there is evidence that the British admiralty quite willfully exaggerated the danger. Perhaps in the last analysis the British and German publics were to blame for this naval feud.

Apart from this baleful frenzy, the feeling of both sides was sound enough in its way. Great Britain felt it to be vitally necessary that she should command the approaches to the British Isles, since, if cut off from the outside world, her people were doomed to starve. On the other hand, the Germans believed it reasonable that they should have a large navy to defend their growing commerce in event of war. Even when they discovered that they could not cope with Great Britain in naval power, they still looked upon their navy as essential to their prestige and useful for their diplomacy. The pity it was that the international anarchy made such instruments seem so necessary.

The futile "peace movement"

There had, it is true, been talk of a general reduction of armaments, and it was for this purpose that the First Hague Conference had been called in 1898 by the czar of Russia, Nicholas II. But there was little sincerity in the movement. Russia herself was suspected of wishing simply to avoid the purchase of guns which would otherwise be necessary to enable her to cope with Austria. France, although quite recently on the verge of war with Great Britain, was frankly opposed to the purpose of the Conference, and even passed the word to Germany to that effect. Even Great Britain was skeptical, and was, of course, quite unwilling that any limitation should be placed on her sea power. When the Conference met in 1899, nothing was done beyond paying homage to a principle. Germany took the position that the heavy burden of taxation entailed for keeping up her army was a patriotic duty which Germans cheerfully bore. Before consenting to the Second Hague Conference of 1907 (instigated by Great Britain in the hope that a reduction of naval armaments would allow her more money for social reforms) she insisted that the subject should not be entered on the agenda, and though it was actually broached at one of the meetings, no serious effort was made to revive the issue.

Even Russia by this time had switched to the opposition, and statesmen on all sides were skeptical or derisive.

There was not much better luck with arbitration. When the question of compulsory arbitration was brought up at the First Hague Conference, not a single power was found to favor it, and Germany was even loath to consent to the establishment of an arbitral court. "To prevent the disgrace of the Czar in the face of Europe," said the Kaiser privately, "I vote for this nonsense. But in my actions now and hereafter I shall trust and invoke only God and my sharp sword." Apart from the establishment of a permanent court of arbitration, the Hague Conferences accomplished little. In truth, none of the European governments (nor the American, either, for that matter) took the "peace movement" very seriously, and it was only a section of public opinion, made up chiefly of intellectuals, that had given it much support.

Militarism for sport

It is no doubt true that militarism of the type we have described, however unnecessary as a basic solution, was at least defensive in intent. But it was a highly dangerous form of preventive medicine, for not all the would-be physicians for Europe's ills were civilian statesmen. In each country where large armies or navies had been developed the general staff had come to exercise an insidious personal influence, and it was they who, watching the activities of one another, did much to arouse the fears of the civil governments. Many commissioned officers were itching to test their mettle against some adversary, and in some countries, like Germany and Russia, the arrogance of the military was sometimes almost insufferable.

Militarism and public opinion

The possession of these weapons was the more dangerous because public opinion was becoming steadily nurtured on fear of war and inflamed by the race of armaments. Injudicious patriots fanned the flame. The famous article in an English journal which solemnly declared that Germany ought to be destroyed was one of the most utterly shameless tirades ever penned. Even in France, where pacifism was strong among the rank and file of the nation, there were occasional noisy exponents of a national war of revenge.

It was Germany, however, where militarism was most "naked and unashamed." A distinguished scholar has shown that German sentiment for war was no greater than that in other countries, but that the Germans were naïvely stupid in showing themselves so frankly opposed to projects of disarmament, for they thus gave world opinion the impression of being the only ones who were bellicose; they should have emulated their rivals who masked their contempt for pacifism. But unfortunately, when Bismarck ceased to be pilot, the ship of state rocked noticeably. Moreover, Germans seemed to delight in parading the paraphernalia of war from the time of the "Sergeant King" down to the reign of the swashbuckling kaiser; and the military tradition, which perhaps goes back to the origins of Prussia, was thoroughly ingrained in the junkers, whom Bismarck called "the pariahs of modern civilization." Anyone who visited Germany in the days before the War will remember how conspicuous was the army on all occasions. There was a veritable cult of the uniform. Emperor William II seldom wore civilian dress, and even the members of the bundesrath met in uniform, giving the appearance of a council of war rather than of a legislative body. Civilians were led to believe that commissioned officers were almost like a privileged caste, to whom they must pay a sort of deference and with whom it was certainly unwise to clash. Added to the undue prominence of the military might be mentioned various utterances of public men extolling the glories of war and its value as purifying the race, or of others, like the Kaiser, bragging of Germany's military strength. "The balance of power," exclaimed William in a public speech, "is me— me and my twenty-five army corps." While it seems fairly evident that this military exuberance was not unlike the behavior of a small boy playing with tin soldiers, it could hardly be wondered that Germany was looked upon by her neighbors as a country that was spoiling for a fight, and especially if one noted the repeated and vociferous clamors for a "greater Germany." Of such wild talk certain intellectuals or army officers, rather than soberminded merchants or peasants, were chiefly guilty; and one may wonder sometimes if it were not a sense of insecurity, almost an inferiority complex, that produced these explosions of megalomania, as when the impetuous kaiser declared, "God has called us to civilize the world; we are the missionaries of human progress." How far the neurotic William reflected a state of mind is no doubt a debatable question, but he was certainly not the only one who indulged in such pronouncements. At all events, such cases of inflated nationalism was naturally enough exaggerated by other powers, and, added to the blatant display of militarism, contributed much to that atmosphere of fear which led public opinion almost unconsciously into war.

But suppose in the meantime Germany promoted an imperialistic policy? It was in this channel that force might prove a tempting weapon. At all events, there were other powers similarly disposed.

THE REVIVAL OF IMPERIALISM AND WORLD POLITICS

The first period of national imperialism had led, as we have seen, to the founding of colonial empires and to struggles between the powers which had led to a repartition of some of the lands acquired. Later additions were made, such as Australia and New Zealand—fruit of British explorations—and a further extension of British power in India, though hardly counterbalancing the loss of the American colonies. French imperialism waned, and even under Napoleon its revival proved abortive; the "nation of shop-keepers" triumphed. In the next sixty years of the nineteenth century—say from 1815 to 1875—the governments of Europe were rather more interested in domestic problems or in dealing with revolution at home or abroad. Great Britain gave some attention to various troublesome problems of imperial administration, and France acquired Algeria—more as the result of accident than of careful premeditation. The British, chastened by the experience of the American Revolution, began to question even the utility of imperialism. Besides, the definite swing in the direction of free trade had much to do with impugning the theoretical value of colonies, and this was true on the Continent as well. Bismarck, for his part, scouted the suggestion that he should demand certain of the French colonies in 1871, and wrote that "all the advantages claimed for the mother country are for the most part illusions. England," he added, "is abandoning her colonial policy; she finds it too costly." Yet if British imperialism slackened, we know that Napoleon III was by no means blind to its lure, and forces were stealthily at work which created a new impetus for colonial expansion. The revival of imperialism was more than anything else a product of the Industrial Revolution, but there were various and sundry causes that we must now consider.

Causes and Significance

Minor factors

First of all, we may mention the scientific impulse. The geographer yearned to know more of the world and its peoples. The work of exploring expeditions opened the way for colonization.

There was also the sporting factor, many delighting in such exploits because of their very novelty and the sense of danger involved. There were also the religious and humanitarian motives which may be conveniently combined into one. Foreign missions were sometimes the forerunners of official penetration in foreign lands, and the need of official protection was often requested by the missionaries themselves. In this activity the Catholic clergy had played an unselfish rôle during the earlier period of world politics; now in the nineteenth century Protestants, as well as Catholics, conducted missions. Moreover, there was undoubtedly a serious desire, albeit often misdirected, to raise the civilization of backward peoples. Demoralizing customs should be done away with; principles of health and sanitation should be introduced among savages; their religions should be displaced by Christianity. When the slave traffic was found to be still flourishing in Africa, the moral sense of Christendom was stirred. But while such considerations as the above are important for their bearing on public opinion, they represent rather the minor motives. The chief factors behind imperialism were (and are) economic and political.

The economic motive was an outgrowth of the Industrial Revolution. Large-scale production had resulted in the turning out of commodities in ever-increasing volume, and the problem was to find more consumers. Henry M. Stanley, the great African explorer, made convincing arguments for colonization when he told the cotton manufacturers how much clothing they would probably sell if the African natives could be shamed into covering their nakedness. Some industries promoted imperialism because its peculiar needs played directly into their hands. Such were the construction companies, the purveyors in railway supplies, the makers of munitions and uniforms, the ship-builders, and the bankers who were ready to underwrite loans to indigent native princes—all of which interests have been aptly termed the "parasites of imperialism." There was also the increasing need of raw materials for the teeming industries at home. Iron for the construction of machinery, oil for the running of engines, raw cotton and raw wool for the production of fabrics might be found in undeveloped countries. With the advent of bicycles and later automobiles the importance of rubber was only too obvious; and the very cheapness of colonial labor—in most cases forced

Economic motives

labor—made such enterprises the more profitable. Then the opening of new countries afforded an opportunity for surplus capital—that is, capital which clamored for greater returns than could be obtained by finding its way into enterprises at home. To get ten per cent and perhaps more on the yield of stock in a coal mine in China or a rubber plantation in central Africa was a tempting lure for the speculator, and, provided his government would stand behind the investment, the risk was not too great. Finally, it may be noticed that the acquisition of colonies helped the mother country to become more self-sustaining. Such countries as Germany and Japan, especially active in promoting industry, and harboring in their towns an ever-growing population, were compelled more and more to look outside for their foodstuffs. It would seem, indeed, that the economic factor was really the most fundamental, and indeed the term, "economic imperialism" has come to convey its salient feature, the exploitation of natural resources. "The controlling agent of the whole process," writes J. A. Hobson, the British economist, "is the pressure of financial and industrial motives, operated for the direct, short-range, material interests of small, able, and well-organized groups in a nation."

Political motives

While it is obvious that such interests involved only a minority of any government's citizens, the political factors were such as to constitute a broad appeal. Among the least conspicuous of such motives, the need of naval bases and coaling stations, were of great importance to empires whose interests were already widely dispersed; and the importance of having an abundant supply of oil was a potent argument with powers possessing navies. There was also the hope of finding a place for surplus population. Even in a country like Germany, not as yet overcrowded, there were enterprising fortune-hunters who looked for new openings which distant lands might give them. A student of imperialism has noted that "from 1871 to 1880 no fewer than 625,968 Germans forsook the fatherland to become inhabitants of the United States, Brazil, and other countries." The acquisition of colonies would mean the securing of places where Germans could remain Germans, and instead of the allegiance of so many of them being lost to the mother country, the man power of Germany could be preserved. Much the same motive came to operate with Italy, who was losing by emigration hundreds of thousands of her subjects. Above all, the hunger for prestige induced powers to seek colonies or other fields of exploitation. France sought to redeem herself for the humiliating results of the Franco-Prussian War by carving out an empire in Africa. Germany and Italy were young nations which felt that their standing in the world demanded following the shining example of the older colonial powers; they must spread over more of the map. Moral motives became closely allied to political when a nation such as France felt that it had a great civilizing mission to perform. Jules Ferry, who had so much to do with reviving French imperialism, talked much in that vein, and eminent French writers supported his view. Similarly the book of the English professor, Seeley, *The Expansion of England*, which appeared in 1883, wrote of the great opportunities presented to England of extending to the backward races the benefits of her civilization. Later on the German professor, Treitschke, warmly championed imperialism as an agency for the spread of German culture; and the Russians had always been impressed with the duty and the glory of civilizing Asia according to Muscovite ideals.

It was these sentimental factors that were most calculated to appeal to public opinion. They were the ones to arouse national vanity, the direct spurs to nationalism. Business interests which needed official backing for their ventures were clever enough to enlist a portion of the press to play up the moral side, such as the boon of civilization to backward peoples and the grandiose political aim of enhancing the national greatness. Since the public was notoriously ignorant of geography, it was the more ready to swallow such arguments. If, moreover, two world powers should happen to clash over the same stakes, the point of honor could be raised, and each of the nations in question would consider its self-respect vitally concerned in winning its point. It has been amply proved that for the larger interest of the nation colonies emphatically do not pay. The trade of France with her colonies has never been more than a small fraction of the entire volume of her external trade, and a still smaller fraction if internal trade is included; and it has been proved by statistics that British manufacturers supply the bulk of their needs from countries outside the British Empire. Moreover the native races of Africa hardly provide a profitable market, for the colonial laborer after buying his food and paying taxes has little left of his pittance with which to buy

Imperialism and the public

European goods. Nor does the consumer at home really profit in the long run. There may be diamonds in South Africa and phosphate in Tunis, but, as Dr. Parker Moon has said, "If an Englishman wants an engagement ring, he pays for the diamond; if a Frenchman wants phosphate to fertilize his farm, he buys it at a price, and at approximately the same price that a Spaniard or Italian would pay." Special interests gain from a policy of imperialism, but the taxpayers who have to bear the cost of naval armaments, military campaigns, ship subsidies, and expensive public works get nothing in return but dramatic food for their patriotism. It is also apparent that imperialism is decidedly to the disadvantage of the industrial worker since much capital that might be utilized at home, and thus provide him with more lucrative employment, is invested in backward countries where labor is relatively cheap. Moreover, colonies have not solved the problem of emigration. Most of those which Germany acquired were either intrinsically unprofitable, or, if potentially valuable, were not habitable by white men. Those which Italy acquired were neither profitable nor habitable, and Italians preferred to seek their fortunes in New York or South America. Indeed, excepting South Africa and the Barbary Coast, Africa is not colonizable territory, and the same is generally true of the South Sea Islands and southern Asia. Perhaps the most potent argument for imperialism has been to provide a supply of wheat that would render the mother country self-contained. Yet, if tariff walls and armaments were abolished, no country would need to worry about its food supply, and until the British were ousted from their naval supremacy, no Continental power at war with Great Britain could hope to reach its colonies. It is obvious enough that even those civilized nations which are under a régime that is supposedly democratic are often lamentably ignorant of their fundamental interests.

Perhaps there has never been a more eloquent example of the folly of public opinion than its backing of imperialism. There have, it is true, been periods of reaction, as in France, England, and Italy (sometimes as the result of some reverse), but some of the leading statesmen of these countries have been the readiest converts to the cause. Imperialism represented a beautiful gamble with extraordinarily high stakes and a never-ending excitement for the players. And the players were the Great Powers, whose mutual suspicions rendered them peculiarly unfitted for so hazardous a game. That imperialism held in itself the germs of war can be readily understood when one contemplates the forces that lay behind it. We must now survey the scenes of its operations.

The Leading World Powers

The weaker powers, whose colonies remained as relics of the earlier period of world politics, may here be omitted from consideration. The great colonial powers of contemporary Europe were Great Britain, France, Germany, Italy, and (in a sense) Russia.

The tremendous size of the British Empire—about a fourth of the earth's surface—is to be accounted for by the immensely successful efforts of the English in earlier days. More than any of their imperial rivals, the English engaged in actual colonization, many of their colonies being particularly well adapted for that purpose; and as the result of practical lessons learned in politics they eventually granted to such colonies self-government. These were the so-called dominions—Canada, Newfoundland, Australia, New Zealand, the Union of South Africa, all of which are bound to the mother country by little more than the sentimental tie of the British crown. There was no more impressive example of statesmanship displayed in empire-building than this phase of British policy. Like most British achievements, it was the product of experience. *Great Britain* *The dominions*

The handling of colonies where the native population was predominant was often fraught with difficulty and in some cases passed through many vicissitudes. Such colonies, known as crown colonies, had sometimes a limited self-government (these being found chiefly in the West Indies); others (chiefly in Africa) were managed by chartered companies who took the full responsibility of administering them until, as in some cases, the government took over their administration; while others were protectorates in which some native prince was nominal ruler though actual authority was in the hands of a resident-general. Egypt was only formally declared a protectorate in 1914, since Great Britain, in occupying Egypt, had always maintained the position that her occupation was only temporary, governing it, however, as a *de facto* protectorate, through a resident "high commissioner." *The crown colonies*

British India has been the most lucrative of all the colonies, as well as the most densely populated, and has proved the greatest test of British imperial statesmanship. Like some of the smaller colonies, its exploitation and control were left for a time in the hands of a chartered company, the East India Company, with whom we have already become acquainted. India proved, however, too vast an undertaking for a body of merchants, who exploited the natives for their own private purposes, while the company itself almost reached a stage of bankruptcy; and the government (toward the close of the eighteenth century) found it necessary to interfere. The result was the experiment of government supervision. While the company had still the unrestricted handling of commercial affairs (its monopoly of the trade with India was not abolished until 1813), the government strictly controlled its action in the political and military spheres through a board at London appointed by the crown; and though the appointment of minor officials (most of the patronage, in fact) was still left to the company, the governor general came in time to be appointed by the crown and exercised large powers. Means were also taken to prevent the exploitation of the natives. The British government was now—since 1784—directly responsible for order and justice in India. But the situation facing successive governors was often too critical to admit of awaiting precise instructions, and their tendency was to assume an immense discretionary power. As a result of troubles with native princes, fomented by the French, the governors embarked on a policy of conquest, and border difficulties finally led to the extension of British power to the Himalayas in the north and to the confines of Persia in the west. Meanwhile in 1857 occurred the Great Mutiny (the mutiny of the Sepoys in the British army) with its accompanying massacres—the result of certain highhanded methods and some thoughtless disregard for native susceptibilities. In 1858, after the rising had been put down with great brutality, the East India Company was deprived of what had been left of its authority, and the government took over completely the administration of India, which was now vested in a viceroy responsible to a "secretary of state for India." In 1877 under Disraeli, the ardent imperialist who had purchased for England the controlling interest in the Suez Canal Company, India became designated as an empire, Victoria assuming the title of "empress of India." In response to some budding nationalism in India some slight con-

cessions in the direction of autonomy were granted the natives
during the first decade of the twentieth century.

The mastery of a country of over 300,000,000 people was indeed
a prodigious feat. It was only possible because of the social and
religious differences among the natives. There is little doubt that
British rule has brought benefits to the population (as had likewise
been the case with the Egyptians), but the work of educating the
natives has not proceeded as rapidly as the construction of railways
and other public works, more important for commercial interests.
Before the Great War only six per cent were literate. But the
proper training for the natives is something of a problem. Even
the educated Hindus do not care as a rule for material prosperity,
their idea of culture being a thing, rather, of the spirit. One can
only speculate what would have been the result if India had not
been under a Western power capable of maintaining order. Generally the oriental mind has little notion of political organization, and deep religious divisions prevent anything like social
solidarity.

The intrinsic importance of India was not relatively as great as *Economic*
it had been in the Middle Ages when it was a repository of all the *importance*
products of the Orient, but apart from the output of its native *of the*
industries, its excellent agricultural land has proved of great value *colonies*
for the production of cotton, rice, tea, opium, and other commodities; and in 1912 the trade with India represented about one
quarter of Great Britain's colonial trade. While South Africa has
been valuable for its minerals, Canada for its wheat, and Australia
for its wool, most of the tropical and subtropical colonies are rich
in the products peculiar to their climate, such as rubber, oils, cocoa,
cottonseed, etc. The West Indies are valued for their fruits. The
Malay Peninsula chiefly exports tin and rubber, and Singapore, its
port, is one of the greatest commercial centers in the Far East.
Egypt, Uganda, and the Sudan are important for cotton; palm
oil is the chief commodity of Nigeria; Ceylon is noted for its tea.
British East Africa or Kenya, after the trade in ivory had largely
disappeared, was developed at great expense as agricultural land.
As far as practicable, the government has utilized the revenues of a
colony for its own development, and has tried to protect the natives from exploitation. Before the Great War the trade of the
British colonies (with the exception of the dominions) was open,
free of tariffs, to all nations, though it was natural that the British

themselves profited most in the long run, and the empire has proved a favorite field for the investment of British capital.

France   Since the British Empire was the only colonial empire with colonies populated to any extent by Europeans, Great Britain has been the only one of the world powers which could wisely grant self-government to its colonies. The French colonies had always been governed very rigidly by governor generals or resident-generals (in the case of protectorates), acting as a rule under instructions from Paris, but often exercising a great deal of personal responsibility. This policy was not appreciably altered by the revival of interest in colonies, though a very slight degree of autonomy was eventually accorded in Algeria, where there was a fairly strong nucleus of French settlers and where native discontent had called for some concessions.

The extension of the French colonial empire has been one of the greatest achievements of the Third Republic. It was foreshadowed, of course, by Napoleon III's extra-European ventures, and its chief individual promoter was Jules Ferry, who was responsible for the acquisition of Tunis, the French Congo, and Madagascar, and for the extension of French holdings in Indo China. With the political and economic motives of this movement we have already become familiar.

On the merits of the French colonial record it is hard to generalize. Only occasionally has imperialism captured the interest of a people whose political and cultural horizons are generally bounded by their European frontiers; and the colonies have been the victims to some extent of indifference, to some extent of unwise theories, and, very noticeably, of the self-interest of minorities. The uprooting of native customs in Indo China and disregard for Moslem law in Algeria have been examples of too much theorizing; the uncontrolled exploitation of native labor and natural resources in the Congo, the despoiling of the Algerians, and the economic subordination of the colonies to the mother country are examples of the pressure of special interests. Taxes on imports from the colonies either to prevent the competition of colonial industries with those at home or for purposes of revenue have greatly hampered the development of the colonies, especially as tariffs had the effect of limiting their market. Where possible, the colonies have tried to send their products to other countries. It has been something like a revival of the old mercantilism without granting the colonies anything in return as that system had usually done. Most of the French colonies are rich in agricultural products (Madagascar and the Congo are chiefly valued for their rubber and the Sudan has great possibilities for cotton); some, like Algeria, produce wool; others such as Tunis have mineral wealth; but on the whole their development has been rather slow, and only a few interests have profited in return for the immense expense which the government has shouldered. On the social side the French have shown their greatest talent. In many cases they have been willing to grant to the natives social equality, and those natives who have become educated have imbibed a large measure of French culture without losing their native traits or discarding their institutions. But when all is said, such success as has attended French colonial policy has been chiefly due to a few brilliant and forceful colonial governors, who have brought the colonies in their charge a régime of order that was the first essential of their prosperity.

Italy

The Italians were late in entering the arena and their empire was an artificial creation, with little regard for meeting national needs. Yearning for prestige was the dominating motive, and Italy possessed neither the experience nor the resources for such a task. The colonies she obtained (Eritrea, Benadir, and Libya) had little potential value, and are still a heavy incubus upon the treasury. For handling the natives the Italians have some of the same facility as the French.

Germany

Germany came into the field also late, and had everything to learn by experience. The colonies she acquired were not very alluring, and they were left to be exploited by chartered companies, which looked at the colonies as nothing but sources of wealth and treated the natives accordingly. After 1908, when the colonies were placed under a secretary for the colonies, their possibilities were much advertised, but the chief purpose of such publicity lay in directing the public attention to imperialism with a view of making it the all-important issue.

Russia

Russia differed from the other powers mentioned in that her penetration of undeveloped country was a case of territorial extention rather than appropriation of lands across the sea. The conquest of Siberia brought Russian power to the Pacific, where she sought—though as yet without success—a port on a warm sea. The Transcaspian region, including several dependent protectorates, brought her within striking distance of India. In the Asiatic empire of Russia there was much potential wealth both mineral and agricultural, but there was little capital to develop it. Russia has had the advantage, however, of gaining a vast domain without having to compete with other powers. In her treatment of conquered peoples she was arrogant and often cruel (the petty bureaucrat was too far from the central government to be under much restraint) and her boasted civilizing mission did little beyond the establishment of order. She raised her Asiatic subjects neither culturally nor materially. In 1862, two years after the cession of Maritime Manchuria by China, the port of Vladivostok was built, and in 1900, after nine years of building, the Trans-Siberian Railroad was completed. Another line was extended from the Caspian Sea to the western wall of the Chinese Empire.

In seeking to extend her influence beyond her political frontiers Russia strove sometimes for trade, sometimes for strategic advantages, but having seldom the means of developing backward lands, her policy was usually to keep them backward and so easier to control. Being semi-Asiatic herself, she showed a natural talent for understanding the people of the Orient, and her rôle as a world power was generally obstructive and unprogressive. This fact will become apparent as we come to deal with the interventions of foreign powers in countries outside their boundaries.

The Areas of Exploitation—Imperialism at Work

Africa

The opening of Africa

Hardly any of the interior of Africa had been penetrated before the middle of the nineteenth century. Apart from the valley of the Nile and the hinterlands of Algeria and the Cape of Good Hope, there had been little attempt to leave the few footholds on the coast—"dots of civilization upon the borders of undeveloped barbarism." Africa was still the "dark continent," a *terra incognita*. Then about the middle of the nineteenth century occurred that wonderful series of explorations in which scientists and sportsmen of many nations participated; and the result was to open the heart of Africa to the world. Educated opinion throughout the world was deeply interested in these feats, and when an American newspaper sent Stanley to find the great explorer, David Livingstone, lost somewhere in the jungles of the Zambesi, the public interest became intense. Other sections of opinion were also interested, and missionaries and merchants followed hard on the trail of

explorers. Among the leaders in the work of financing exploration was Leopold, King of the Belgians, and it was at his instance
that an international conference met at Brussels in 1876. We
shall not relate in full the story of how a movement, at first scientific, humanitarian, and international became rapidly one of cal-
culating self-interest and in its objects purely national. The basin
of the Congo, which Stanley's explorations had opened to the
world, became the subject of an international conference at Berlin
in 1884, and a protocol was signed by plenipotentiaries of the
Powers (1885). Leopold was recognized by the Powers as sovereign
of the "Congo Free State" with limitations designed in the interest
of the natives as well as for free commercial access for the nationals
of all countries— in other words the open door. It was not long,
however, before this rich country was treated as a Belgian preserve; ruthless exploitation of the natives and wanton discrimination against other powers became the principles of its government;
and in 1908, as the result of moral pressure, it was finally deeded
to Belgium with the status of a colony. Though the scandals of
the Congo had roused some indignation, the Powers had not
bothered to enforce the protocol. Internationalism had clearly
shown its hollowness.

Indeed the Powers were too engrossed in their own pursuits to *The
harass the king of the Belgians. Before the Berlin Conference had *partition
met the grabbing of Africa territory had begun. France led off *of Africa*
by seizing Tunis on the gound that Algeria had been endangered by
border raids. Actually the bey of Tunis had borrowed millions
in France on which he could not pay the exorbitant interest, and
his creditors were anxious. It would take too much space to record
the various economic interests that dictated intervention; and the
political motives of French imperialism have already been noted.
As Bismarck and Salisbury had already blessed the enterprise,
there were no international complications, and the natives being
quite helpless, Tunis was easily occupied and turned into a French
protectorate. The following year (as the result of circumstances
to be noticed later) Great Britain settled herself down in Egypt;
and Italy, aggrieved at the seizure of Tunis which she had ear-
marked for herself, procured a foothold on the west shore of the
Red Sea—the future colony of Eritrea. Then France, not disposed to see Leopold grab the whole of equatorial Africa, seized
in 1884 a large block of territory opened by French explorers along

the west coast and skirting the right bank of the Congo. The British even tried to block the outlet of the Free State, but were fortunately prevented by France and Germany.

And already Germany too had entered the field. Bismarck himself was not a champion of imperialism, for, as he had said quite frankly on one occasion, Germany's geographical situation did not fit her to become a maritime power, and having the one thought of rendering her secure in Europe, he was not anxious for complications that might aggravate his problem. But a strong movement for colonies had developed in spite of him, and the shipping interests were pushing it for all they were worth. In 1883 a Bremen merchant acquired a strip of territory in southwest Africa for the price of $300 and 60 guns, and the German flag was raised. This was squarely raising the issue. Yet Bismarck hesitated. Though no protection was then afforded to merchants in that region, there were some British claims to be considered. When, however, the British government (preoccupied just then with Egypt and with Russian designs in Asia) made no formal protest but only growled a little, Bismarck "crossed the Rubicon," and in 1884 Germany founded her first colony, German Southwest Africa. The following year she acquired German East Africa in precisely the same fashion. During the years 1884–6 Germany also gathered in Togoland and the Cameroons on the Guinea Coast of Africa and part of New Guinea and some archipelagoes in the Pacific. The area of the colonial empire totaled more than a million square miles with a population of over ten millions.

The appropriation of so much territory by European powers seemed to suggest the desirability of taking steps to avoid competing claims. It was therefore decided at the Berlin Conference of 1884–5 that in case of a protectorate established over a region along the coast notice should be communicated to other powers and that occupation of such territory should be "effective." Then, in order to prevent an unseemly scramble for the lands still unoccupied, the Powers found it desirable to enter into a series of treaties enabling them to claim the hinterlands of the footholds they occupied on the coast. These zones of potential occupation came to be known as "spheres of influence" (to be distinguished from "spheres of interest," which are purely economic preserves and convey no political rights). Generally these spheres extended to the nearest watershed. While numerous border disputes had, of course, to be adjusted, it is remarkable that the partition of Africa took place without a war. The worst crisis was in 1898 (which we shall consider in another connection), but this was peacefully surmounted. Perhaps it was because Africa was so huge (providing as it did plenty of land for all competitors) that international peace was thus maintained.

In 1898 the only independent states in Africa were the kingdom *The* of Abyssinia, the negro republic of Liberia on the Guinea Coast, *remaining* the sultanate of Morocco, and two little republics in south Africa, *stakes* the Transvaal and the Orange Free State, founded by Dutch peasants, known as the Boers, who, unreconciled to British rule at the Cape,[1] had trekked into the interior. These little inland republics came to be tempting spoil when gold and diamonds were discovered within their boundaries. Morocco was both rich in minerals and good grazing land, and was politically important as holding one of the keys to the Mediterranean. We shall notice that both the Boer republics and Morocco gave rise to international complications.

Asia, though a larger continent than Africa, afforded somewhat *The* less room for the new imperialism. A good third of it was already *Far East* appropriated by Russia and another large section was comprised in British India. There was no question of subjugating Japan, for *Ancient* that power, though only opened to the world in the 'fifties, had *states in* revolutionized itself more or less on a Western model, and was able *Asia* not only to defend herself but to compete with Western imperialism. Siam was also independent—probably because she served as a convenient buffer between the British power in India and the French in Indo China. In the west Afghanistan and Persia (rich in oil) were still independent, and so, of course, was the Ottoman Empire, most of which was now situated in Asia. But the most important stake in Asia was the Chinese Empire, consisting of China (the Eighteen Provinces), and various regions more loosely governed such as Manchuria and Mongolia. Since China was both large and immensely rich in natural resources, the Far East became the scene of the keenest competition.

As a stake in world politics China had no equal. Its anthracite *China as a* coal-fields are, perhaps, the most extensive in the world. Its land *stake* is very fertile, and though the rice grown is chiefly needed to feed

---

[1] Great Britain had acquired the Cape of Good Hope from Holland as a result of the Peace of Amiens in 1802.

the enormous population, extensive sections are devoted to the raising of cotton. Raw silk ranks first among its exports and tea next; there is also a thriving trade in articles of native manufacture. In the nineteenth century China was still a sleepy oriental state, very decentralized and weak, and ruled by an alien and unpopular dynasty, the Manchus. The great mass of the Chinese people, who were said to number 400,000,000, were hard workers but densely ignorant, and most of them, being crowded in the more habitable Eighteen Provinces, were barely able to subsist, and the frequent floods in certain provinces took a terrific toll of lives. The administration was in the hands of the intellectuals, who preserved an ancient culture and were tolerant and pacific by conviction; but these mandarins, as Chinese officials were called, were also exceedingly corrupt, and foreign powers found them as a rule evasive (often a shield for their weakness) and thoroughly untrustworthy. It was because the mandarins saw a chance for graft and extortion that the East India Company was able to trade with China (importing chiefly opium) at a time when the Manchu government was disposed to hold the West (which it despised) at arm's length. Until 1842 trade was admitted only at the port of Canton and was under many restrictions.

The opening of China   China was really opened in 1842 as the result of British success in the Opium War. British historians seem disposed to avoid this name for the struggle; yet it was the Peking government's sudden enforcement of the official ban on opium that constituted the chief cause of the war, though it is probable that a clash would have come anyway sooner or later. By the Treaty of Nanking (1842) six of China's ports were opened without restriction to British trade, and by subsequent agreement a tariff was fixed on Chinese imports and British nationals might be tried for any offenses committed in China in their own consular courts—a privilege known as extraterritoriality. The same rights were then acquired by other powers, who profited by British success. Since, however, the provincial mandarins, who were almost independent of the central government, refused to take the treaties seriously, it was necessary to wage a second war with China (the so-called Second Foreign War) in which France as well as Great Britain was involved; and after a triumphant entry into Peking, the Chinese capital, legations of the powers were established in this city, able henceforth to bring home to the Chinese government any infraction of a treaty. Disturbances were not uncommon, however, for Christian missionaries were not always welcome in China, and both merchants and missionaries often penetrated beyond the treaty ports. For every outrage, no matter what the provocation, China was made to pay indemnities, and usually to open more ports. It was obvious that oriental finesse was no match for the pushful powers of the West, backed by regiments and ironclads.

When a country was as rich as China and at the same time as defenseless, spoliation was inevitable. Already certain outlying countries tributary to the Chinese Empire had been stealthily gobbled up. Taking advantage of disorders in China, Russia had secured the province of Maritime Manchuria (1860); France was able to force a recognition of her protectorate over Annam and Tonkin in Indo China (1885); and the British, after a wanton attack on its native prince, annexed Burma (1886). In both these latter cases China had been forced to renounce her sovereignty, though in the case of Annam and Tonkin, it had cost France a brief war. It may be noted here that France also secured a preferential position in trading with the two border provinces of China as well as favored treatment in the building of possible railroads in these provinces. Once a European power has established itself close to the borders of a weak state, economic imperialism soon begins to bore.

Between the powers themselves rivalry was so far peaceful, and Great Britain had exacted no privileges that she was unwilling to share with others. But it could hardly be expected that the other powers, who were not disciples of free trade, would stand firm for the open door; and two powers in particular, Russia and Japan, had the advantage of readier access to the area of penetration. Japan fought a war with China in 1894-5, and by the Treaty of Shimonoseki (1895) forced her to renounce her suzerainty over Korea, which left that country open to Japanese absorption. She also endeavored to gain the Liaotung Peninsula, which would give her a point within easy striking distance of Peking. But such would have been too threatening to Western imperialism. Hence Russia, with the backing of France and Germany, compelled Japan to hand it back to China, receiving in recompense an additional indemnity. But Russia herself was every bit as menacing. After making an alliance with China she secured the right to build a railway through Manchuria to Port Arthur (on the Liaotung

The partition of China

Peninsula), and her influence was for some years in the ascendant at Peking. The meaning of her recent collusion with France and Germany was soon to be made clear.

In 1897, on the pretext that two missionaries had been murdered, Germany sent a squadron to Chinese waters, and demanded a ninety-nine year lease of the shores of the bay of Kiaochow in the province of Shantung, as well as the right to build railroads in that province and to exploit the mines along their course. The following year, not only was this granted but Russia secured a lease of the Liaotung Peninsula; France got a lease of the shores of Kwangchow Bay, as well as the right to tap some of the resources of two southern provinces; and Great Britain, not to be outdone by her predatory rivals, leased the Kowloon peninsula, as well as the port of Weihaiwei, the latter to be held as long as the Russians kept Port Arthur. When, later, it appeared that a Belgian company, backed by Russia and France, had received the right to construct a railroad from Peking to Hankow, and was planning a network of lines covering much of the country, Great Britain forced China at the threat of war to yield her valuable concessions in the Yangtse valley. It was an interesting example of the British government directly backing British financial interests in China.[1]

It may be observed that in addition to economic rights each power had acquired a naval base on the Pacific. Acquisition of territory in China proper was a new departure in imperialistic policy in the Far East. Great Britain had obtained the island of Hong Kong by the Treaty of Nanking, and later, for its protection, she had secured the tip-end of the Kowloon peninsula but, apart from this latter footing, no power had as yet seized territory on the mainland. Now it appeared that actual dismemberment was under way. Moreover, the Powers were now carving out zones of exploitation, the British being led into the scramble by the fear of the consequences of being left out; and, as usual, got the choicest share. In the following years the several powers marked out by treaties with one another what came to be known as "spheres of interest." Political acquisition was not implied (though China was forced to promise in certain cases not to alienate a province), but a virtual monopoly of the resources of certain regions was understood. It can be judged that the principle of the open door

[1] The same motive had contributed largely to the British occupation of Egypt.

was gravely threatened. Of more immediate import was the blow
to native pride. Hardly strange, then, that a fierce nationalist
reaction commenced in China, culminating (1900) in what was
known as the Boxer Rebellion. After some weeks of peril for the
legations an international army entered Peking, and bankrupt
China was forced to pay heavy indemnities as well as undergo
other humiliations. Russia took advantage of the crisis to occupy
Manchuria, the evacuation of which she postponed on various
excuses. It was now that the course of events took a fresh turn.

The advance of Russia could only be regarded by Japan with
the greatest concern. With a population of over 50,000,000, shut
up in a group of mountainous islands with scanty natural resources,
her growth under modern conditions was painfully dwarfed. She
was like England not only in being a manufacturing country,
compelled to look outside for most of her food and raw materials,
but also in being menaced by any power which should become
formidable on the Continent. Korea was to Japan as Belgium was
to Great Britain; it was an outwork of defense. But, unlike England, she aspired to become a mainland power not only for defensive
reasons but also for purposes of exploitation. Thus Russia, who
was likely to become a menace, was in any case a barrier. After
she (Russia) had occupied Manchuria she soon showed how little
respect she meant to pay to the open door, for with her lagging industries she could only hope to foster her foreign commerce by a
monopolistic policy, enforced by political pressure. Already Japan
saw her virtual exclusion from Manchuria; and when the power
she feared began to edge into Korea, she felt that her national
existence was in jeopardy.

It was hardly the menace of Western imperialism which had
driven Japan into a policy of expansion, for her war with China
had anteceded the scramble for leased ports and spheres of interest,
but she learned a salutary lesson from her diplomatic reverse of
1895 when she had been forced to disgorge the Liaotung Peninsula.
The Western Powers were natural enemies, and it was very necessary that they should not be united against her. Fortunately
Great Britain could always be counted upon as hostile to Russia
and, in principle at least, as the champion of the open door. The
result was the formation of the Anglo-Japanese Alliance in 1902,
by which Japan was, in effect, assured of British assistance in
case a third power (e.g. France) joined Russia against her. Thus

Japanese imperialism and the Russo-Japanese War

the guns of the Dual Alliance were effectually spiked, and Japan had opened a breach in the ranks of her rivals. She may now be said to have entered the family of nations.

Thus strengthened in her defensive position, Japan was now able to face Russia with confidence. Since by 1904 it was clear that Russia was not going to recede but was waiting for the convenient moment to strike, Japan suddenly became the aggressor. Superficially it looked like a one-sided struggle (Russia having three times the man power of Japan), but the Russians had to travel three thousand miles to reach the theater of war, and in addition to her geographical advantage, Japan had a better fighting machine as well as superior naval power. Before the weight of numbers might have told against her she was able to occupy Korea, seize the Liaotung Peninsula, and destroy two Russian fleets. Threatened at home with revolution, Russia finally decided to "call it off." The result was the Peace of Portsmouth (1905), *Hegemony of Japan in the Far East* which acknowledged Japan's paramount interests in Korea, transferred to her the lease of the Liaotung Peninsula, and practically made southern Manchuria into a Japanese sphere of interest. Japan could now fairly claim to be regarded as a Great Power, and in a very real sense the sentinel of the Far East. In this clash of two imperialisms it was the Russian which had been worsted. The Great Bear must look elsewhere for his draught of warm water.

It is obvious, of course, that with both powers the people of Manchuria and Korea were of small concern. Numerous treaties, including that of Portsmouth, affirmed the "independence" and "integrity" of Korea, but Japan had no sooner got from Russia a free hand than she proceeded to reform Korea under what was practically a protectorate. The sleepy and barbarous Koreans preferred to remain sleepy and barbarous—and hated the Japanese. Finally, after constant friction and the murder of the Japanese resident-general, Japan annexed Korea in 1910. The Japanese sphere in Manchuria became meanwhile a bee-hive of industrial activity; and China, the nominal ruler, had but little hold on the country.

Financial imperialism in China In China, in the meantime, European imperialism was fastening its coils about a helpless government. The invasion of China by foreign capital took partly the form of loans as well as extorted concessions. Before the Sino-Japanese War the Chinese government had supported itself entirely from its own sources of revenue, but the heavy indemnity imposed by Japan in the Treaty of Shimonoseki required borrowing from abroad—particularly as the lucrative maritime customs could not be raised without impinging upon foreign treaties. A loan was pressed by Russia, whose ally, France, was willing to provide the capital, and it was by virtue of this aid that both powers had been able to share so profitably in the spoliation of China. Since the Chinese government was quite untrustworthy (and that was why wealthy Chinese would never lend), the security for the loan was found in the maritime customs, which ever since 1863 had been excellently administered ·by an Englishman, Sir Robert Hart. A loan subsequently obtained from an Anglo-German group of bankers mortgaged some of the revenues obtained from internal taxation as well, and it was partly an attempt to augment these taxes that led to the anti-foreign Boxer Rebellion. Then came the crushing indemnities [1] imposed as punishment for this affair, and the maritime customs had to be mortgaged almost to the limit. In 1911 discontent with the Manchu dynasty led to a revolution which ended in its dethronement and the establishment of a republic, but the finances of the country had been thrown into complete disorder by the upheaval, and another large loan was imperative. A "consortium" of banking interests, representing six powers, was formed to float the loan, but the pressure of selfish interests within the group proved so great that China, whose position was rendered acute by long delays, finally borrowed outside of the group notwithstanding British threats. Unhappily she had eventually to come back to the consortium, which now exacted onerous terms without, it may be added, adequate assurance that China's disordered finances would be put on a stable basis. Always a prey to decentralization, China soon lapsed into chronic anarchy under a government that barely lived from hand to mouth. Not until she should be able to effect complete rehabilitation would she free herself from the toils of "financial imperialism."

The Chinese, it is true, had gained something from the impact of Western civilization. Medical science has done much to save life; education of the Western type with emphasis on practical subjects has made considerable headway; superstition has been undermined; and some ancient, barbarous customs have disap-

[1] Amounting in all to about $335,000,000.

peared. But politically and economically, the Chinese had been manipulated by the Powers of the West, who had found their "civilizing mission" highly profitable.

The Near and Middle East

Case of Persia

In the Near and Middle East competition was less intense, but the methods and objects were strikingly similar. The Middle East may be said to consist chiefly of Afghanistan and Persia, and as the former was still immune from foreign capital (so far its value is still unknown), the important stake was Persia. Here, as might be supposed, if one looks at the map, Russian influence was in the ascendant. Russia enjoyed a virtual monopoly of everything in northern Persia, and deliberately used her power to prevent its material development. The Shah had mortgaged most of his resources to procure foreign loans, and his position was so weak that a small standing army, officered by Russians, was all that he could rely on to keep order. It was only in the south, along the Gulf, that British interests predominated, for before 1900 the British had failed to make any great headway in the interior. In that year they got their first oil concession, and Russian dominance began to be slightly threatened. Persia, too, was evidently to become a stake in world politics.

The Ottoman Empire: (1) *its position*

The area of exploitation in the Near East was the Ottoman Empire, most of which was now confined to Asia. Here again one finds a weak oriental potentate whose authority over his dominions was very precarious and east of Asia Minor was hardly recognized at all. His judicial and financial sovereignty had both been invaded by foreign powers. Commercial treaties customarily known as "Capitulations," some of which were very old, insured to foreigners extraterritoriality, and also fixed the tariff, which, in virtue of "most favored nation" clauses in all these treaties was a uniform eight per cent on the value of goods imported. So heavily was Turkey indebted to foreign bankers that the revenues securing such debts were under the control of what was known as the Ottoman Public Debt Administration, a body which represented the bond-holders of several countries. Turkey was capable, however, of much material development. Her Asiatic possessions were practically virgin country, and if capital were expended on irrigation and public works, the region known as Mesopotamia, watered by the two great rivers, the Tigris and the Euphrates, might be made into a fertile plain, as it had been in the days of Babylon. Farther north was the zone of oil, which partly extended into

(2) Its importance

Persia; while Asia Minor, in the west, contained mineral wealth
such as lead, copper, and zinc. The British had some interests
in Mesopotamia, and British and French companies had begun to
construct railroads from the Mediterranean coast, but the Germans
were the ones, as we shall notice, to view Asiatic Turkey as a sphere
of interest, to be traversed by a German railroad from Constantinople to Bagdad and the Persian Gulf. Whether Russia, with her
eye on Constantinople and the Straits, would have a voice in the
future of the Ottoman Empire remained to be seen. At the turn
of the century the Eastern Question was promising to regain its
old importance. We must now enter the latter part of this period
of world politics when imperialistic rivalries came more and more
to spell eventual catastrophe.

The Clash of World Powers

That the scramble for raw materials or for important strategic
positions would sooner or later bring the powers into dangerous
collision would seem to be a foregone conclusion and may be said
to lie in the logic of imperialism. We have so far described but
one clash, and that was between a European and an Asiatic power;
but before that time two European powers had nearly come to
blows. With the revival of imperialism came once more the intense
rivalry of France and Great Britain, the two foremost colonial
powers.

Anglo-French Rivalry—The Egyptian Question

It can hardly be said that Anglo-French rivalry was ever dormant. When the French occupied Algeria, the British took active
steps to prevent the possible extension of French power into
Morocco. British jealousy of the Suez Canal has already been
noted. And even though Salisbury had given France his blessing for any plan to acquire Tunis, the British were very quer-
ulous after the fact had been achieved. But suppose it had been
Egypt!

Premonitions

Of all colonial prizes (if we leave China out of account) there
was perhaps nothing to compare with Egypt. Apart from its
intrinsic value, which was considerable, it commanded the shortest
route to the East, and, provided the old barrier of native hostility
were removed, there would be no question any longer of rounding
the Cape of Good Hope. It is true that unless Turkey were ousted

The importance and plight of Egypt— The Anglo-French condominium

from her nominal sovereignty, no European power, in actual possession of Egypt, was likely to use this door for its own exclusive advantage; yet such an asset, from the point of view of bargaining with other powers was incontestable, and in time of war such a position was of incalculable importance. Egypt, as we have noticed, had been long ear-marked by France. French interest did not cease with the withdrawal of Napoleon Bonaparte, and when an able pasha, Mehemet Ali, made himself practically independent, he was ostentatiously patronized by France. Later on it was the French who had dug the Suez Canal—the project of which Richelieu had dreamed. At this time the pasha, or khedive, as he had come to be called, was Ismail Pasha, who, emulating the more capable Mehemet Ali, had tried to make Egypt a formidable power —an aspiration only possible through foreign loans, since he had wrung the last penny from his poor, oppressed subjects. "There is nothing in the financial history of any country," wrote a British observer, "from the remotest ages to the present time to equal this carnival of extravagance and oppression." But this orgy of dissipation was bound to end, and the Powers were forced to establish a collective control over his finances by way of protection for their bond-holders. He was also obliged, as we have noticed, to sell his shares in the Suez Canal Company, which, thanks to French ineptitude (he had offered them first to France), the British government obtained. British interest was focused not only on bonds but on the security of the canal, through which passed most of the British trade with the East. When it finally became necessary to oust Ismail, his successor proved willing, under pressure, to adapt himself to an Anglo-French condominium, or dual financial control, representing all the powers whose nationals were creditors of Egypt. Then in 1881 a nationalist rising took place against foreign domination, and it looked for a while as if Egypt might break free of all restraint.

The collapse of the condominium and the British occupation of Egypt

The time had come for France and Great Britain to assert their authority, and Gambetta, who was then premier of France, pointed the way to intervention. Unfortunately for French interests, Great Britain did not relish his initiative, and Gladstone, her prime minister, was not at all in sympathy with British imperialists who always thought of Egypt in terms of bonds. While he was hesitating, Gambetta fell from power, and when word came that some Europeans had been killed, the British government resolved

upon intervention—with or without France. Then it appeared
that French opinion was not in favor of strong measures. Jules
Ferry had been recently turned out of office because of his successful seizure of Tunis, and the government and public opinion
were fearful of complications with the other powers. Even the
lure of Egypt as a tradition was not as yet enough to make imperialism a national issue. For the moment France was bewildered
and unable to make up her mind, and, thanks to this fact and a
cabinet crisis, she definitely lost the prize to her erstwhile partner.

But it was not long before she bitterly repented. When Great *Divers*
Britain not only occupied Egypt but seemed likely to make her *quarrels*
occupation permanent despite frequent promises to withdraw as
soon as order was restored, much acrimonious bickering took
place between the two governments. It is true that the Suez
Canal was finally neutralized by international treaty in 1888;
but the French could not forget that they had lost the chief prize,
and their failure naturally rankled. "I believe," Gladstone had
said, "the moment we occupy Egypt it will end the cordial relations between France and England; nations have good memories."

It is hardly to be wondered under the circumstances that the
'eighties and 'nineties were full of friction between the two.
There was trouble over Madagascar, which France had annexed
in 1896, thus depriving the British of the privilege of the open
door; there was more serious trouble over the Niger country,
ended by a settlement (1898) which gave France the control of
the mouth of the river; there was a quarrel over Siam (1893) which
nearly led to war; and these were simply a few of the encounters
that occurred during these troubled years. The British had,
meanwhile, suffered some misfortune. In 1884 occurred the insurrection of the Mahdi, the leader of a sect of dervishes in that portion of the Sudan which constituted the hinterland of Egypt and
which Mehemet Ali had conquered in 1821. Gladstone made up
his mind to abandon the region, and it was only necessary to relieve some beleaguered garrisons. But the force which the Premier
sent, under a gallant leader, "Chinese" [1] Gordon, proved pitifully
inadequate, and after being besieged in Khartum for several
months, Gordon and his men were finally taken and put to death.
This reverse naturally precipitated Gladstone's downfall, but the
Conservatives who succeeded him were not yet keyed up to re-

---

[1] So called from certain exploits in China.

venge, and the Sudan remained abandoned. It was, hence, a question whether Egypt could still rightfully claim it as hers or whether it was "no man's land"—what is known in international law as *res nullius*.

Struggle for the Upper Nile— the Fashoda Crisis

France took the position that it was *res nullius*. Here was a golden chance to revive the Egyptian question. As a British writer expressed it, "Not able . . . to enter the Nile region by the front door, France tried to enter from the rear." She had the plan (conceived by the aggressive colonial party) of connecting the French Sudan with Obok on the Red Sea and thus spanning the Continent from west to east. Such a scheme, however, countered the British dream of an unbroken stretch from Egypt to the Cape of Good Hope; and it will be observed that the point of intersection for the two grandiose projects was the Upper Nile. It was therefore a race for the Upper Nile. Great Britain secured Germany's and Italy's assent to this region as her sphere of influence, and she even offered Leopold a piece of it—a step which she was compelled, however, later to renounce, as it obviously took no account of Turkish suzerainty. The French were, meanwhile, pushing forward their posts into the debatable zone, and, unknown to the British government, had sent what they called a "civilizing mission" (a small exploring force under a certain Captain Marchand) to hack its way through tropical jungles to Fashoda on the Nile. Hearing some rumors of French activity, Sir Edward Grey, who was then undersecretary of foreign affairs, made his famous pronouncement that the occupation of the land in question by an outsider would be deemed "an unfriendly act" —which in diplomatic language was a threat of war. Soon afterward the Salisbury ministry sent General Kitchener with a force to reconquer the Sudan, and the power of the Mahdists was effectually broken.

But meanwhile (1898) Marchand had reached Fashoda. Then shortly afterward Kitchener arrived; and but for the presence of mind of the two commanders an exchange of shots might have occurred, which would have made war inevitable. Fortunately the question of possession was referred to the home governments; and though a very serious crisis ensued, France finally gave way and recalled Marchand. British opinion had been adamant; while French opinion, though at first very firm, was too harassed over the Dreyfus affair to trouble itself for once over a "point of honor."

Théophile Delcassé, the French foreign minister, felt that peace and possible reconciliation was preferable to war, and though Great Britain got the Upper Nile (technically for Egypt), a fairly amicable boundary settlement was reached. The sequel of Delcassé's change of front was soon to appear.

German Imperialism and the Rise of the Triple Entente

A new note in German imperialism seemed to be struck when William II, German emperor since 1888, came to reveal his restless ambition. It was not long before it was demonstrated that this arrogant young monarch could not get along amiably with Bismarck, whose guidance of German policy had never been seriously challenged; and in 1890 Bismarck resigned, to spend his last days in bitterness and seclusion. William was a man of some shrewdness, but superficial, impulsive, and given to theatrical effects. His father [1] had once written, "In view of the unripeness and inexperience of my eldest son, combined with his tendency to bragging and conceit, I consider it positively dangerous to allow him to come into contact with foreign affairs." Yet such was the man to whom Bismarck bequeathed, as it were, the hegemony of Germany in Europe. It may be a matter of doubt whether the Emperor's explosions were the result of excess of self-confidence or the lack of it. But he was a true Prussian in his sublime faith in the army ("the foundation on which the Empire rests," he once declared), and he was determined to enhance the greatness of his Germany—a greatness that must be felt by the rest of the world. It was largely due to him that Germany was to become a great naval power.

And, unlike Bismarck, the new emperor was a convinced imperialist. To William the idea of ruling such a colonial empire as Bismarck had handed down—the left-overs after the older powers had picked what they wanted—may well have been intolerable. Germany must have a colonial empire that properly fitted her greatness. She must have "a place in the sun," as one of her chancellors aptly expressed it. But if William picked up a map and looked over the two hemispheres, he would have found but little opening. In 1898 he got a foothold in China, but only a foothold; there was little chance of wedging into north Africa; and in America the Monroe Doctrine stood as a barrier. There were possibilities, it

The Anglo-German Feud

A new era of German imperialism

---

[1] William's father, the Emperor Frederick, reigned only a few months.

is true, in Asiatic Turkey, and to this problem we shall later give attention. But it must not be supposed that William followed any carefully determined plan or that, in general, he formulated German policy. The idea that he was his own chancellor, as Louis XIV had been his own prime minister, has been pretty well exploded. William was too erratic, too muddle-headed to work out and direct the program of German imperialism. And yet, as he not infrequently influenced policy, and as his chancellors were men of second-rate capacity, German policy showed a marked want of stability; and if William were not the pilot, he at any rate frequently rocked the boat. It should also be stated that for many years an obscure official of the foreign office, a former disciple of Bismarck, Baron von Holstein, had a certain malign influence over his government's foreign policy—unchecked because sometimes it was so insidious and because the higher officials were very often irresolute. The really progressive force in German imperialism was the settled will of a great part of the nation itself, of which emperor and chancellors were to a large extent the expression. And German opinion was very sensitive to the churlish and grudging attitude of British imperialism. One can hardly doubt that Imperial Germany looked with considerable longing at South Africa—a prize that was worth the plucking if only the insatiable British could be held back. Hence, the ostentatious interest in the Boers; and so many decorations were sent to Krüger, president of the Transvaal, that as Holland Rose remarks, "his quaint farmer figure was a very Christmas tree of gewgaws." The prize in question was climatically the choicest spot in all Africa and also valuable country, as we have seen.

Question of South Africa and the Boer War

Slowly and rather unobtrusively the British Empire had been growing in Africa. After the recovery of the Egyptian Sudan it extended to the sources of the Nile, and only the Boer republics and German East Africa prevented a solid block of British territory from Cairo all the way to the Cape of Good Hope. It was the dream of Cecil Rhodes, a great prospector in South Africa, to build a Cape-to-Cairo railroad; he had also important mining interests; and as official of the Cape government, he had long cherished designs on the Boer republics, though he was reasonable enough to wish to put the two peoples (Dutch and British) on a plane of complete equality in such a plan. There had, unfortunately, long been friction between the two. Under Disraeli the

Transvaal had actually been annexed as a prelude to the crushing of the Zulus, but during the ministry of his successor the Boers rose against their masters and won the famous skirmish of Majuba Hill (1881), after which Gladstone, who was more of a liberal than an imperialist, restored them to virtual independence. Rhodes, who owned some newspapers in England to press the cause of British imperialism, had later much to do with the extension of British possessions in South Africa (Bechuanaland, for example, was taken over and thus a barrier erected between the Transvaal and German Southwest Africa), and the Boers were soon completely surrounded by British territory. Meanwhile the discovery of gold resulted in the influx of a great horde of British adventurers whose demands for rights of citizenship in the Transvaal were resisted by the Boers for the simple reason that they were afraid that they themselves would become submerged. For them it was a question of self-defense; they felt naturally that they ought to be left in peace. Seated on their diamonds and their gold, they cherished the illusion that they could resist the attacks of economic imperialism. In the meantime, Germany, as we have seen, had taken them under her patronage, and had put it up to Great Britain that if she annexed the Boer states she would have to reckon with Berlin, which might, however, be satisfied with "some small colonial advantages." [1] The policy of blackmailing a power for the sake of some paltry gains was to be a common maneuver of William's government. For the moment its chief endeavor was to persuade France to join it in resisting British imperialism. Then came the "Jameson raid." In 1896 a henchman of Rhodes attempted without any authorization from the British government to make an armed incursion into the Transvaal, which, however, ended in a fiasco. Although the British government was quick to express its regrets over the incident, the Kaiser, who at first wanted to declare a German protectorate over the Transvaal and insisted that some action should be taken, was finally persuaded to content himself with sending Krüger a telegram, congratulating him on having "repelled" the "small bands" which had "broken into" his country. This "high explosive," as Dr. Gooch has termed it, was explicitly intended to teach Great Britain a lesson. But British resentment was very deep, and from that time on the Kaiser was

---

[1] This feeler was made in response to the British ambassador's boast that Great Britain had the means of satisfying her enemies.

never liked in England. Indeed, dislike seems to have been mutual, for during the Fashoda crisis William tried to persuade the Czar to intervene, and ranted with all his might against "British greed."

*Continuous
discords*
There is little doubt that William's ambitious naval policy was immediately occasioned by the Jameson episode—which had ended in British stiffness and Germany's isolation (for the Kaiser had quite failed to interest other powers). When the naval bill of 1898 fell far short of satisfying the Kaiser, one can well understand how bitter he became when at the final test he lacked the sea power to influence decisions. When in 1899 the British government, inspired by Rhodes and Chamberlain, embarked on war with the Boers, German opinion was vociferously hostile, though William himself now posed as friendly to the British. Anyway Germany had lost her chance. After considerable exertion Great Britain defeated the Boers and annexed the two republics; and then with admirable sagacity she gave her defeated antagonists self-government, and they have become the dominant element in the Union of South Africa, founded in 1910.

But the question had, unfortunately, a wider significance. Neither the Krüger telegram nor the bitter reverberations of the Boer War were soon forgotten, and henceforth British and German opinion were more or less at daggers' points. Official relations were not less prickly. We may note that as far back as 1894, when Salisbury proposed to the Kaiser a partition of the Ottoman Empire, he met with a sharp rebuff. Germany not only distrusted England but seemed to feel that by "treating her rough" at a time when she was quarreling with France she (England) might somehow be forced into joining the Triple Alliance. It is interesting evidence of the stupidity of German methods. When in 1898 Great Britain, tired of her isolation, made overtures to both Germany and Russia, the Kaiser not only refused the advances made to him, but, despite their confidential nature, disclosed
*Underlying
factors*
them to the Czar; and both rulers decided that the British were simply guilty of double-dealing. Under these circumstances, and considering German reaction to the Boer War, was it strange that the British government took precautions that the terminus on the Persian Gulf, desired for the Bagdad Railroad, should not be occupied by the Turks and so possibly become a German naval base? It is true that some agreements were reached on minor

matters, but there were clearly no feelings of amity, and when in 1900 Germany launched her ambitious naval program, the British began to feel renewed distrust. The following year Edward VII [1] ascended the British throne, and German distrust was revived; for William and his "Uncle Bertie" had never been fond of each other, and the latter was always very much at home in Paris. Moreover, one should realize that German commerce was making great advances all this time, and that British merchants were finding that in some places their markets were slipping away.

What we have then to note is that an Anglo-German feud had come to be a phase of world politics. To an overwhelming extent it was a national quarrel—between the British public on the one hand and the German on the other. On the part of the former, commercial rivalry and fear and distrust of German sea power were the dominating factors; on the part of the latter, the jealousy of a young and aspiring colonial nation for a power which had already more of the world in its possession than seemed reasonable or just. Just how much the German government was responsible for German opinion is not clear. It is more certain that Germany's rejection of British friendship at a time when Great Britain and France were on the road to reconciliation (we allude to the fate of a last British overture in 1901) was exceedingly stupid diplomacy. William II and his advisers had none of the sagacity of Bismarck. They had already "cut the wire" to St. Petersburg, and they were soon to reap the fruit of their haughtiness toward England.

The Entente Cordiale and the First Moroccan Crisis

Formation and significance of the Entente Cordiale

What Germany regarded as impossible soon happened. Thanks to Edward VII and to Lord Lansdowne (the British foreign secretary) as well as to numerous others, Great Britain and France signed a convention in April, 1904, which adjusted all existing differences and was, in short, a complete reconciliation. The most important feature of the "Entente Cordiale," as it was called, was that Great Britain should have a free hand in Egypt and that France should be free to "restore order" in Morocco, though she disclaimed all intention of altering its political status, and reservation was made for Spanish interests on the Moorish coast. There were also secret articles but they hardly signified more than was implied in the open clauses. The point is that Great Britain's *quasi*-protectorate over Egypt was recognized by France, and

[1] Son and successor of Victoria. He was succeeded in 1910 by the present king, George V.

*Germany's
intervention
—the
Moroccan
crisis and
settlement*

France was to employ some species of political action in Morocco. Could anyone doubt that Morocco was marked out for a protectorate? A few months later France and Spain secretly entered into an agreement, which, after affirming "the integrity of Morocco under the sovereignty of the Sultan" arranged for the partition of the country between the two powers. But the fate of Morocco was not, perhaps, so important as the relations between France and Great Britain, just established. Not only was British diplomatic support pledged to France in case of difficulties over Morocco, but, as we shall see, a series of understandings was inaugurated for the purpose of defending their common interests from German attack. A common distrust of Germany, whether justified or not, had brought these powers together in what may perhaps be called a conspiracy of defense.

Whatever were France's ultimate intentions regarding Morocco, she had squared Great Britain and Spain, and she had also (one may add) placated Italy by countenancing her designs on Tripoli. But it was evidently felt unnecessary to approach Germany, whose interests in the Mediterranean were relatively slight; and it is interesting to notice that before the Entente Cordiale was actually signed the Kaiser had expressed his gratification to the King of Spain at the rumors of a Franco-Spanish partition of Morocco. But Germany was really much annoyed at being treated as if she were a power of no importance; besides she did not relish the thought that her interests in Morocco, however slight, were now in danger of being ruined by a French protectorate. It was well known that the Sultan was tightly bound to French bankers and that France was already engaged in "reforming" Morocco in the interest of order while she promoted its material development. It was a typical case of economic imperialism, combined with the political object of buttressing Algeria; and Germany must certainly have recognized these facts. Instead, however, of taking the initiative and forcing France into the open, she "blew hot and cold" by turns, and preferred, in general, the more fractious policy of intriguing against French interests in Morocco. Finally, after further discomfiture, and in consideration of the weakness of France's ally, Russia (then embroiled in the Far East), she decided on a bolder stroke—one that would effectually test the strength of the Entente Cordiale. With much reluctance (since he wanted to make friendly overtures to France and draw all the powers into a

combination against England), the Kaiser was persuaded to land
at Tangier in Morocco in March, 1905, and to proclaim his championship of the sovereignty of the Sultan. The maneuver was
rightly regarded in Paris as a challenge, and French opinion became very nervous. Then the issue was made more definite by a
demand from Germany that the whole question be submitted to
an international conference. Such a position was legally sound
since in 1880 various powers had signed a convention upholding
the sovereignty of Morocco and the maintenance of the open door,
and for that reason the Morocco question might be considered
international. Delcassé would have resisted Germany's demand
even at the cost of war, but he was not supported by his colleagues
or by public opinion (remarkably self-possessed under the circumstances) and he consequently resigned. It might have been
possible for Germany by direct negotiation to have got a complete
adjustment of colonial claims (such, in essence, was a French proposal), but her chancellor, Prince Bülow, seems to have preferred
instead to win a diplomatic triumph. We must now hurry over
the course of events. The international conference duly met in
1906 at Algeciras in Spain, but instead of ending in a victory for
Germany all the powers save Austria-Hungary sided with France,
and it was Germany, not France, who was left isolated. France
was now in a stronger position than before; for she and Spain
were accorded a limited right of policing Morocco,[1] and their
position now rested on an international agreement.

We should add, too, that if Germany had some notion of breaking
the Entente Cordiale, she had signally failed. It had been strengthened rather than weakened by German blustering. In 1905 Lansdowne had secretly initiated some "conversations" between the
French and British staffs, both military and naval, and but for
the fall of Delcassé something closely approximating a secret
alliance might have resulted. In any case Lansdowne's policy was
followed and even carried further by Sir Edward Grey, who succeeded him as foreign secretary with the change to a Liberal
ministry in January, 1906. Well-intentioned but shallow-minded,
and lacking the energy to go personally to the bottom of a problem,
Grey entered office with an intense prejudice against Germany,
whose tactless methods had already offended him in the days
when he was an undersecretary. No doubt, too, he was impressed

*The
strengthen-
ing of the
Entente
Cordiale*

[1] Their police rights were limited respectively to certain ports.

by public opinion, and felt that in event of a crisis, he could count on popular support in any policy of combating Germany. To the French ambassador he stated (and he said the same to the German ambassador) that, according to his personal opinion, should France be attacked by Germany as the result of the Morocco agreement, public opinion in England would not permit the government to remain neutral. The danger of such a remark was that it might encourage France to count on British support in the event that she pursued a policy that was calculated to *provoke* attack. But Grey seldom saw beyond his nose.

The Anglo-Prussian Rapprochement and the Impenetrable Wall

The Entente Cordiale may be described as one side of a triangle and the Dual Alliance as another, and it only required a link between England and Russia to complete the triangle which came to be known as the Triple Entente. It is true that there had been nothing more certain or more persistent in world politics than the Anglo-Russian feud. Nevertheless the Salisbury ministry had flirted with Russia, as we have seen, and it had been urged upon Lansdowne that a good way of solving the difficulties in Persia was an economic partition of that land between the two powers. Overtures had come from Russia in 1906, and after long negotiations the Convention of 1907 was signed between England and Russia. All outstanding differences were adjusted, and Persia was divided into two spheres of interest, one Russian, one British, as well as a middle and neutral zone. The sovereignty and integrity of Persia were proclaimed in the preamble, and Persia was explicitly assured by the British minister to Teheran that she need not fear for her independence, which was "forever assured" by the Convention. The hypocrisy of imperialism was never more shamefully exemplified than in Persia.

The Anglo-Russian Convention of 1907

From Economic to political imperialism in Persia

Thus was established the Triple Entente. Grey's object was certainly to bind Great Britain and Russia as forging the third link in the defensive chain he was constructing about Germany, though a secondary object of the Convention had been the safeguarding of India from Russian attack (it is noticeable that the British sphere was chiefly desert and had practically no economic value). Grey wrote at the time that the spheres were not supposed to be areas of exclusive exploitation, but that it was merely intended to exclude the operations of the two powers from each other's spheres; in other words they were not presumed to exclude concessions to a third party. There is also no reason to suppose that he anticipated any harm coming to Persia. But when the Persians, who had reduced the Shah's power by revolution, endeavored to shake off the financial yoke which he had brought upon their country, they found they had to reckon with Great Britain as well as Russia. Thus they were not permitted the luxury of borrowing from the Germans in order to pay off their debts to the British and Russians. In the meantime, as the finances were in a muddle, Great Britain and Russia decided that Persia should have some foreign financial advisers, and a new loan was offered (chiefly for the raising of guards to protect the trade routes), though only on condition that the British and Russian governments should be consulted before the granting of any concessions. Manifestly this was an attack both on the sovereignty of Persia and on the principle of the open door. Germany, mindful of her prestige, feebly protested, then beat a complacent retreat when it appeared that Persia's rejection of the Anglo-Russian terms (thus threatening to aggravate the issue) would not be formally received by the two legations. When Persia, for her part, finally took the bit in her teeth and appointed an American expert to reorganize her finances, Russia thwarted him at every turn and finally, after pouring troops into Persia, forced his dismissal. Grey himself had backed this high-handed action—not, it is true, without misgivings, but fearful that if the Russians were unable to coerce Persia, they might march into Teheran and thus rouse British opinion against the Anglo-Russian entente. Indeed, he told the Russian ambassador that if the Convention were to collapse, he would resign. The Russians frankly believed that Grey's "European policy" (i.e., enmity to Germany) permitted them to do as they pleased in Persia. From 1912 to 1917 the northern part of Persia, including the capital, was practically a Russian province.

In the Persian question Germany had morally something at stake, even if her interests were still slight. But here, as in Turkey, she was singularly cautious—we might say timidly cautious—lest she offend Great Britain or Russia. She wished to do nothing to estrange the British whose capital might be needed to promote the Bagdad Railroad. German consuls, poking around in the Red Sea and Persian Gulf for possible coaling stations, had been told that such projects were impracticable as likely to offend the British. Nor would she risk provoking Russia by accepting a proffered concession from Persia for a railroad. When the Persians had

Imperialistic encirclement

sought a loan from Berlin, she had withheld her official backing, though it is interesting to notice that Great Britain and Russia had been worried over the matter and explicitly feared a "second Morocco." When it was evident that economic imperialism was becoming political, she did not persist in the defense of her legal rights. None the less, it is clear that the door had been shut in her face even more pointedly in Persia than in Morocco. The Triple Entente had become aggressively imperialist and were solid enough to exclude all undesirable competitors. Moreover, Italy was in collusion.

The Equivocal Position of Italy

Italy had long been a very lukewarm member of the Triple Alliance. She had entered into that alliance by force of circumstances, being embittered against France for taking Tunis (which she had coveted), and feeling that she required a stronger international position; but it had always been an essentially unnatural alignment. For Italy hated Austria, first because the latter held all the good harbors on the Adriatic, secondly because she possessed the southern Tyrol, which brought her over the mountains into a position threatening to Italy's security, and thirdly because she ruled some 600,000 Italians most of whom presumably longed to be redeemed. Moreover, Italians were rather drawn by natural affinity to the French, and with their long and exposed coast line they could hardly afford to risk a quarrel with powers, like France or Great Britain, whose naval strength was reasonably to be feared. No doubt it was the part of expediency for Italy to have friends on both sides, and in case of war she could join the side that promised her the most profit. After a succession of agreements with France cordial relations were re-established; and Italy was often so secretive, as far as her own allies were concerned, that they soon—and with good cause—became convinced of her duplicity. In the five-year renewals of the Triple Alliance they had been forced to make concessions that would nominally insure her loyalty, but her open support of France at Algeciras showed clearly the way things stood. Though we can hardly take space to prove it, there is little doubt that Italy had become a mere appendage to the Triple Entente.

By 1908, then, the Triple Alliance was the weaker of the two combinations on whose even balance the peace of Europe was supposed to depend. The hegemony of Germany had been gradually shattered; her legitimate ambitions were being blocked at all

points.   German imperialism seemed faced by an impenetrable
wall.   Only in Asiatic Turkey could Germany hope to make a
breach, though even in that quarter she had come to appreciate
the strength of the coalition that seemed to encircle her.   Yet if she
could reach her goal on the Persian Gulf, she might resume her
old confidence.   We must now shift our attention to the Near East.

The Eastern Question as the Harbinger of War

The clash of world powers over Egypt or Morocco might be
serious enough, but if no one wanted war, some adjustment could
be found that would ease the situation—and it must be insisted
that no power during these years that we have been studying
wanted war.   But in the Eastern Question there were peculiarly
complex factors less susceptible to control.   There were the Balkan
states, whose affiliations were largely a gamble; and there were
stakes in the Near East more worthy of being gambled for.

The Rivalry for Supremacy in the Balkans— the Question of the Straits and the Bosnian Crisis

The efforts of Russia to dominate the Balkans as the result of
the upheaval of the 'seventies ended in her bitter disappointment.
The terms she had dictated in the Treaty of San Stefano as the
victor in her war with Turkey had been revised as the result of
the intervention of the powers, and the Treaty of Berlin (1878)
had given her but little satisfaction beyond the erection of the
state of Bulgaria and the cession of the province of Bessarabia,
which, being wrested from Roumania, who had aided her in the
war, produced bitter feelings at Bucharest.   Later on, the clumsiness of her policy at Sophia had alienated Bulgaria, and it was
actually against her wishes that the prince of Bulgaria had forcibly
annexed Eastern Roumelia [1] in 1885.   Incidentally we may observe that the Treaty of Berlin was breaking down, as had the
Treaty of Paris.   A repetition of the demand that Turkey should
reform (that is, give her Christian subjects adequate protection)
was treated with the same indifference as of old.   Until the Concert
of Europe was willing to come to the point of encroaching on
Turkish sovereignty by supervising directly the institution of
reforms, the Sultan knew that he could profit by the usual rivalries
and do nothing.   Internationalism was just as ineffective in the
Near East as it had been in central Africa and Morocco.

The Treaty of Berlin and the recession of Russia

[1] An autonomous state created by the Congress of Berlin for the purpose of
separating some of the Bulgars from the main body in Bulgaria, thus breaking up
the greater Bulgaria which Russia had extorted from the Turks in the Treaty of
San Stefano.

The Austro-German advance

Parallel with the recoil of Russia from the Balkans we must note the advance of Austria. In order to purchase Austrian neutrality during the Russo-Turkish War of 1877-8 Russia had been obliged to agree that Austria might annex Bosnia and Herzegovina, the two provinces forming the hinterland of Dalmatia. In the Treaty of Berlin Austria obtained only the right to "administer" them, but this was rather a distinction without a difference, as Turkish sovereignty became only nominal as a result. Furthermore Austria had received the right to garrison the Sanjak of Novi Bazar, a Turkish district which separated Serbia and Montenegro, and constituted a kind of corridor for Austrian incursion into the Balkans. It was commonly believed that Vienna had its eye on Saloniki.

Bismarck, the "honest broker," as he had called himself, sought to establish a kind of balance between Austria and Russia, and would like to have seen a division of the peninsula into two spheres of interest, but his wish could never prevail. He had no thought of any direct German interest in the Near East, having once remarked that the Eastern Question was "not worth the bones of a Pomeranian grenadier," and was sufficiently content that Austria had found a direction for her energies which turned her definitely away from German affairs. At the same time he maintained very friendly relations with Russia, and in a secret treaty in 1887 he assented to Russian designs on Constantinople and the Straits.

The "trend eastward," which Bismarck urged upon Austria, was soon conspicuously displayed, though in the form of an economic rather than a political invasion. The Austrian Lloyd Steamship Company opened a coastal service which brought Austrian activity into the whole of the Levant and meant much for the development of closer relations with Turkey's Adriatic littoral. Meanwhile, the construction of a railroad to Constantinople and Saloniki, built by German capital, and loans to Serbia and Bulgaria by German and Austrian capitalists cemented still closer ties. In this policy of peaceful penetration backward Russia could not possibly compete. The fledgling nationalities of the Balkans, who as yet had no industries of their own, got all their needs satisfied from Vienna; and the long and short of it was that the Balkans fell gradually into the economic orbit of Austria-Hungary. Moreover, at this time there were political bonds as well as economic. Roumania, whose king never forgot that he was a Hohenzollern,

secretly joined the Triple Alliance in 1883. Greece, who lay outside of Austria's economic interests, was somewhat drawn toward
the Central Powers by the fact that her heir apparent, the later
King Constantine, had married the Kaiser's sister in 1889. Serbia
under the Obrenoviches was definitely pro-Austrian and in 1881
actually pledged herself to sign no treaty without Austria's previous
approval. When she attacked Bulgaria in 1885 and got badly
whipped, it was Austria that saved her from loss of territory.
Bulgaria as a factor was rather uncertain, since the new prince,
Ferdinand of Saxe-Coburg, the successor of Alexander, whose
abdication Russia had forced, made it his business to play one
of the Great Powers off against the other, but in the main he
leaned toward Austria. In Turkey British influence was predominant until the 'nineties, but Germany had long been a close
second, and by assiduously courting Turkey she was able to oust
the British (more concerned with protesting against Turkish
atrocities) from first place. As early as 1883 a German military
mission had been sent to Turkey, and the Turkish army was
accordingly trained on the German model. In 1897 Germany took
care to be benevolently neutral when Turkey fought Greece; and
the ground was being prepared for Germany's Asiatic venture,
which we shall notice presently. For twenty years there was little
to resist the Austro-German penetration of the Near East.

Yet Russia never wholly took her eye off Constantinople. At *The*
the very least she wanted the exclusive right to send her warships *Recovery*
through the Straits, unreconciled to the various international *of Russia*
treaties which had, in effect, closed them against her.[1] In 1896 she
had even a plan of a forcible seizure of the Straits, though it never
matured; and the following year Austria and Russia agreed to
respect the status quo in the Balkans, the right of Austria to annex
Bosnia and Herzegovina being, however, contemplated under certain circumstances. Since Russia was mainly interested in Manchuria at this time, she was apparently still willing to deal gently
with the Near East, and when Macedonia became the chief sore-
spot in the Balkans (due to Turkish oppression of Christians),
Russia and Austria were able to concur to some extent. But there
was evidence that Russia was really edging back. Her relations

[1] For a brief sketch of technical questions involved see Fay, *The Origins of the
World War*, vol. i, pp. 72-3. The freedom of the Straits for merchantmen was not
at first a matter of concern.

with Bulgaria became gradually improved, and ripened into a
military alliance (1902).[1] Then in 1903 occurred a palace revolution in Serbia and the accession of the Karageogeviches, the
protégés of Russia, to the throne. Distinctly Russia had redressed
the balance.

*The Bosnian
Crisis and
the inter-
vention of
Germany*
Then in 1908–9 occurred the Bosnian Crisis. Disquieted by
Serb intrigues, and taking advantage of a sudden revolution in
Turkey, Baron Aehrenthal, the Austrian foreign minister, an
aggressive and unscrupulous diplomat, made up his mind that
the time had come to turn the occupation of Bosnia and Herzegovina into downright annexation. Strictly speaking, such an
act was a breach of the Treaty of Berlin, but in effect it would
mean no tighter hold on these provinces than Austria had maintained for thirty years. Moreover, Izvolski, the Russian foreign
minister, had, himself, suggested this action, hoping to get for
Russia the coveted use of the Straits; he was even willing that
Austria should annex the Sanjak, though Aehrenthal decided, on
reflection, to evacuate it. We shall not relate the interesting misunderstanding which subsequently developed between the two.
Suffice it to say that the Russian diplomat was duped, and that
anyway there was no chance of Russia getting what she wanted
without the assent of Great Britain, who deliberately strengthened
Turkish obduracy. While Izvolski stormed against Aehrenthal
and tried without success to embroil Austria with the Powers,
the crisis did not really become acute till Serbia threatened war.
Though Russia, it is true, tried earnestly to quiet the Serbs, she
seemed very likely to be forced into supporting them, and when
war seemed eminently probable (for Austria was more than ready
to accept the Serbian challenge), Germany made it plain to Russia
that in such an eventuality she would side with Austria. It was a
very pointed hint that the big Slav brother had better back down;
and Russia, not being encouraged by France and Great Britain,
and not having recovered from the effects of the Japanese War,
had no choice but to do so. In the words of the German chancellor,
"the German sword had been thrown into the scale of European
decision."

But the Bosnian Crisis was a landmark in the Austro-Russian
struggle for preponderance in the Balkans. Izvolski, who smarted

---

[1] A convention for the protection of Bulgaria, explicitly in response to a military
convention in 1900 between Austria and Roumania.

under his personal defeat, and who later went to Paris as am- *Aftermath of the Bosnian Crisis* bassador, bent all his efforts from then on to draw France closer to Russia for a war of common revenge. And Russia herself was bitter over her forced capitulation. However much Isvolski had been to blame for the course of events, the British ambassador noted that Russia felt that she "had never undergone such humiliation." Soon afterward she signed a secret treaty with Bulgaria (whose prince had employed the crisis, with Austrian concurrence, to proclaim his independence of Turkey), declaring that the realization of Slav ideals would be possible only after a Russian victory over the Central Powers. Worse than that, Russia had passed the word to Serbia that she had only to be patient, for Austria-Hungary's reckoning with the Slavs was bound to come. Insofar as Russia preferred war to another humiliation and encouraged Serbia to believe that she would back her in war with Austria, the Bosnian Crisis formed a link in the chain of circumstances which led to the Great War.

In the meantime the vexing Eastern Question had already *The Bagdad Railway Scheme* broadened its range to include Asiatic Turkey. In 1891 Sultan Abdul Hamid had conceived the idea of a railroad to Bagdad and the Persian Gulf as a means of getting a better grip on his ill-organized dominions. Though various projects of the sort had *Inception of the scheme* been in contemplation (primarily for economic reasons), it was a German company which the Sultan plainly favored. In 1898 the Kaiser made a spectacular pilgrimage to the Holy Land, in the course of which he proclaimed himself the protector of the Mohammedan world, and the following year the German company definitely got the concession. The president of the Deutsche Bank (which had most to do with financing the undertaking) has revealed the fact that it cost the Germans $600,000 to bring the Turks around. In any case it was a marvelous scoop, and in 1903 a convention was signed which definitely launched the enterprise. Was Germany to fulfill her dream? The combination of German capital and German engineering was calculated to turn this desert country into one of the most productive lands in the world, and to satisfy in time all the needs of German industry.

But it must not be supposed that Germany's rivals relished the *Attitude of Germany's rivals—difficulties and settlement* project or failed to display their envy. The British could never be quite sure that the railroad was not political in its object (and we cannot be sure that it had not that ultimate object), and it was for that reason that they had been so very nasty about a terminus on the Persian Gulf. As for Russia, she frankly disliked a project which threatened the Russian grain trade with serious competition, seemed also to menace her position in northern Persia, and, above all, promised a regeneration of the Ottoman Empire, which for obvious reasons she wanted to remain weak. In 1900 she had forced a convention upon Turkey, which practically made of Armenia a Russian sphere of interest at a time when it was intended that the railroad should take a northerly and rather less difficult route. The Germans were also embarrassed by the lack of sufficient capital, and hence set out to secure it both in Paris and in London. The British Conservatives, for their part, were ready enough to sponsor co-operation, and Lansdowne sensibly believed that the participation of British capital would prevent the design from becoming exclusively German; but as soon as it was known that British financiers were interested, public opinion forced the government to relinquish its support. Then exactly the same thing happened in France (except that money had been actually subscribed), and the Germans had to scrape together enough to carry on their enterprise alone. So far, so good— but there were still boulders ahead. The chief weakness of the enterprise was still finance. In driving a hard bargain with the Turks the Germans had rather overreached themselves, for Turkey had to furnish a heavy subsidy, which in view of her serious financial embarrassments could not be paid unless the customs were increased. This, however, required the assent of the various powers who traded with Turkey, and the Entente was not greatly disposed to countenance a measure that would hurt their commercial interests. It was the British who were chiefly affected, and it was Great Britain who now held the whip hand. Already she had tried to get the railway concession canceled; then, failing that she extorted from Turkey the right to construct a parallel line— apparently with the object of forcing Germany to concede international management in the last section of the road; and it was only on such a basis that she would grant the customs increase. It was not till three years later—on the eve of the War—that Germany by liberal concessions reached an agreement with France and Great Britain, but in 1911 she had adjusted all her differences with Russia in what was known as the Potsdam Convention. It began to look as if, after all, the road would in time be completed.

In the years following the Bosnian Crisis the tension between *The Growing Tension* the Powers had seemed to relax a little. In July, 1909, the cautious and pacific Bethmann-Hollweg became German chancellor. Not only did relations between Germany and Russia improve but *An illusory calm* Austria was on better terms with Serbia. Finally, France and Germany came to an agreement over Morocco—a curious arrangement which virtually scrapped the Act of Algeciras and left each free to exploit Morocco, while Germany, oddly enough, recognized France's "special political interests" and both paid scant regard for the open door.

And then in 1911 the international sea was ruffled again, the Turco-Italian War, a Russian design on the Straits, and the Agadir Crisis showing that all the old dangers had been lurking beneath the surface.

In spite of some haggling over commercial matters all went *The Agadir Crisis* reasonably well in Morocco till the country fell into serious disorder and France announced that she must send an army into Fez, the Moroccan capital, to protect Europeans. That the danger was sufficient to warrant this decision is perhaps debatable (the Germans persistently belittled it, though experiences in China would certainly suggest avoiding any risk), but anyway Germany had given France *carte blanche* to maintain order. Germany reasoned, however, that once France had entered Fez she would never get out, and that a protectorate was certain to be the outcome. France, of course, insisted that she had no intention of remaining indefinitely in Fez, but her policy in respect to Morocco had been so tricky that one could not hold her assurance as worthy of much confidence. The fact of the matter is, given a country like Morocco, chained by economic bonds to a European power, an eventual protectorate was practically assured, and France must have anticipated this outcome from the first. On the assumption that this was correct, Germany resorted to the familiar tack of requesting "compensation." Such was a possible basis for an understanding.

In the matter of satisfying Germany with some titbit elsewhere France was prepared to accept the principle, but unfortunately the question was postponed by a sudden change of ministry; and, without waiting for the outcome of this temporary crisis, Germany proceeded to send a gunboat to Agadir, a port on the west coast of Morocco, nominally to protect her interests (she had previously scoffed at all danger) but actually to force the French to come to terms. It was a hazardous maneuver, since it took little account of the explosive public, and it was liable to grave misunderstanding in London. Oddly enough, French opinion was for the moment calm notwithstanding the greedy demands of some of the leading German papers, but Great Britain, always ready to block Germany, persuaded herself that the latter cherished designs on a part of Morocco and was resolved to thwart her at all costs. Accordingly on July 21 Lloyd George in a public speech gave a veiled threat of war. This action, as Professor Fay says, "caused an explosion of wrath in Germany, where it was interpreted as a threat and where it was felt that England was interfering in Franco-German negotiations, which were none of her business." Certainly the fact that Great Britain expressed her views in so public a manner instead of resorting to the usual diplomatic channels was a very dangerous experiment—and it nearly precipitated war. Public opinion in both England and Germany was keyed to the highest pitch. Happily the German government managed to keep its temper (William himself had never approved of the dispatch of the gunboat); and Caillaux, the new French premier, was also determined to prevent war, and accordingly welcomed the willingness of the Germans to reduce their demands. In the end France acquired a protectorate over Morocco (except, of course, the part allotted to Spain), and Germany received a slice of the French Congo—a very poor solace for so much pother. As a result of the crisis France and Great Britain were drawn more closely together and Germany nourished considerable rancor over what she regarded as a gratuitous humiliation. It seemed that every time Germany tried to force respect for her prestige, it was diminished rather than increased by her action.

The Turco-Italian War   This crisis was hardly surmounted when Italy broke the peace. Aggrieved over the meager showing of her African adventure (she had been badly beaten by Abyssinia in 1896), Italy had long been laying her plans to possess herself of Tripoli, and hence, in 1911, when Morocco became the focus of attention, she deliberately forced war upon Turkey. Tripoli was eventually conquered, and in order to bring the Turks to terms, Italy occupied the Sporades (the Dodecanese) including Rhodes. Ultimately Tripoli was ceded by the Peace of Ouchy (1912), and Italy was to hand back the Sporades—which, however, she never did. In the meantime,

Russia, seeing that other powers were busily aggrandizing themselves, decided to raise once more the question of the Straits. But such a plan, as always, predicated British assent, and Grey insisted, as he had before, that if the Straits were to be opened to war-vessels, they must be opened to them all. Yet the very project was ominous. Russian restlessness was not likely to be allayed until it finally reached its goal. But there is no wonder that the French were annoyed when they learned of important projects in the Balkans, which their ally had not disclosed to them.

Renewal of Russian designs

It should be added that the reckless strain in Russian policy was due in part to the inefficient organization of the czar's government. Each minister was directly responsible to the czar instead of being subordinated first to the wishes of the premier. Thus in 1912 the Russian premier had to admit to the British ambassador that he had no check whatever upon the foreign office; and it was a subordinate in that office who was able during the temporary absence of the foreign minister to work his will on helpless Persia. Furthermore, Russian agents in the more backward states, like Persia, Turkey, and Serbia were frequently allowed a discretionary authority, their actions being approved if they seemed successful or disavowed if they brought embarrassments to the government. Thus the ambassador to Constantinople in 1911 was represented as exceeding his instructions and recalled when his feelers regarding the Straits had proved a failure. Under such circumstances Russian imperialism was apt to be slippery and very puzzling in its aims; and the word of a Russian diplomat could hardly ever be trusted. No doubt lying is part of the diplomatic game, and even the simple-minded Grey showed strange lapses of memory when driven into a corner, but, with all due disrespect to the Italians, the Russian diplomats, as the documents well show, were quite the most inveterate liars of all.

Though the Straits were still to be seized, yet if Russia could really dominate the Balkans, the prize would probably fall into her lap. As far back as 1908 Grey had ventured the opinion that in another ten years the Triple Entente would be able to dominate the Near East; and such a condition would presumably mean giving Russia a free hand. For some time her diplomacy had been working to the end of forming a league of Balkan states under her auspices—a weapon which might be used against Turkey on the one hand or Austria on the other. It seemed inconceivable that

The Balkan League and the First Balkan War

the little Balkan states, who hated one another even more than they did the Turk, could ever form an alliance, but the lure of Macedonia was very great, and the Tripolitan War together with an uprising in Albania seemed to furnish a promising occasion for aggressive action.   After protracted negotiations, more or less guided by two skillful Russian diplomats, Serbia, Bulgaria, Greece, and Montenegro formed what was known as the Balkan League, and in the fall of 1912 began a war against Turkey. Viewing the episode broadly, it was Russia's countermove in response to the Austrian victory in the Bosnian Crisis.

The Second Balkan War   Yet it is rather amusing to notice that Russia had joined the other powers in forbidding the Balkan states to go to war. When, much to the surprise of everyone, perhaps to the Balkan states themselves, they won an easy victory over Turkey, the Powers were none the less worried, and it looked at one moment as if a general war might break out. While Russia forbade the Bulgarians to take Constantinople, Austria warned Serbia that she was not to keep Albania, which should be formed into an independent state. Since the Serbs, as usual, balked, Austria mobilized a portion of her army, and Russia began to do likewise. But the Triple Entente—even Russia, in fact—was not willing to risk a war over Serbian ambition, and when the terms of peace came to be discussed, they accepted the Austrian solution. Something like the old Concert of Europe was now functioning to preserve the peace. But in any case Russia had reaped considerable satisfaction. Turkey, the satellite of Germany, had been beaten by her protégés, and if only the League would keep from falling to pieces, it was likely to remain an instrument of Russian policy.

Unhappily for Russia, it did fall to pieces. The Balkan states after much controversy had divided the spoils of victory in advance, but they had not reckoned on Austrian interference; and now that Serbia was cheated out of Albania, she expected a larger share of Macedonia than had been stipulated in the Serbo-Bulgarian treaty. Bulgaria would not yield an inch, however, and a crisis soon impended. Vain were Russia's efforts at moderation. Austria had made up her mind to smash the Balkan League, and she deliberately incited Bulgaria against her allies. "We shall let the dogs devour one another," an Austrian official was quoted as saying, "and then *we* shall dominate the Balkans." In July, 1913, Bulgaria made a treacherous attack upon Serbia, and thus

commenced the Second Balkan War. As Greece had likewise been
quarreling with Bulgaria, she formed an alliance with Serbia; then
Roumania and even Turkey fell upon the offender; and Bulgaria
was thus forced, single-handed, to fight four powers. As a result
she was speedily overwhelmed; and she naturally lost some of the

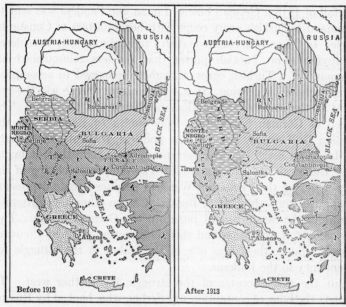

*From McKinley, Howland, and Dann, World History Today,
courtesy of the American Book Company*

THE BALKAN STATES BEFORE AND AFTER THE BALKAN WARS OF 1912-1913

gains she had made in the previous war. The policy of Vienna
had ended in a snare.

By the Treaty of Bucharest (1913), which had closed the Balkan
upheaval, all the Christian Balkan states had become enlarged,
even Roumania gaining some territory at the expense of Bulgaria.
But the results of the Balkan Wars were chiefly important for their
bearing upon Europe. The Austro-Serbien feud, as we shall notice
presently, was greatly aggravated. Apart from the uncertainty of
Bulgaria's attitude, the position of the Central Powers was much
weakened, and Russia's position, despite the collapse of the Balkan
League, was correspondingly improved. She was now measurably
nearer her goal, since Turkey, the tool of German imperialism, lay

*Importance
of the
Balkan
Wars and
the position
of Con-
stantinople*

crushed and broken. It is no wonder that Germany welcomed a Turkish request for another German mission to put the Turkish army in a better state of fitness, though her eagerness seems partly to have been induced by the fear that the Ottoman Empire was now approaching dissolution, coupled with the conviction that she (Germany) must be in a position to bag her share. Hence in the fall of 1913 a German officer, Liman von Sanders was sent to command a Turkish army corps with headquarters at Constantinople. In the end Russia made such a fuss (she secretly considered occupying some Turkish ports) that Sanders relinquished his command of a Turkish corps, though he remained to accomplish the objects of his mission. In a sense Constantinople was the key point in the conflicting ambitions of Russia and Germany. The sweep of German imperialism from Berlin to Bagdad and the Persian Gulf might, if it became political, frustrate the designs of Russia to reach the Mediterranean; more than that, it might close the Straits to Russian trade. The temporary closing of the Straits during the Tripolitan War had produced acute depression among the grain-shippers of Russia. On the other hand, Russian seizure of the Straits would puncture the German dream. Two movements of expansion had their intersecting point at Constantinople. Such, then, was one of the stakes in the struggle for ascendancy in the Balkans.

Serbia, as the storm center of Europe

But the actual center of the struggle lay further west. To Austria the bone of contention was Serbia, who, backed by Russia, seemed to threaten her existence; while to Russia Serbia was always the "guardian of the gate," a sort of outpost of the Balkans, calculated to buttress her supremacy in the Near East. But a clash between Austria and Russia could hardly fail to involve their respective allies. Thus it was Serbia that more and more became the storm center of Europe—the point on which the rivalry of the Powers over the Balkans and the Austro-Serbian feud naturally converged. Since it was Austro-Serbian relations which produced the final crisis, they demand our special attention.

AUSTRIAN DYNASTICISM *vs.* SERB IRREDENTISM

We have already examined the importance of irredentism in undermining the flimsy fabric of Europe. It is not impossible that the hope of recovering Alsace-Lorraine led France into the mood of backing Russia's adventurous Balkan policy. Italian irredentism was also responsible for the breach in the Triple Alliance, though it was not actually contributive to the War. Serb irredentism was infinitely more serious, and to understand its rise we must take another excursion into the affairs of the Dual Monarchy.

Austria-Hungary and the South Slavs

We have already noted the outworn texture of the Dual Mon- *Incongruity and instability of the Dual Monarchy* archy. Held together by the accident of a common sovereign and by the artificial tie of an omnipresent bureaucracy, this state, composed of eleven nationalities, was clearly obsolete in the nineteenth century. The anomaly is all the more glaring when we realize that the Dual Monarchy was a partnership of two actual minorities, the Germans in Austria and the Magyars in Hungary. Yet even the Germans and Magyars were by no means fond of each other, and the stability of the Dual Monarchy is to be accounted for by certain basic factors. In the first place, it had a *Sources of its strength* logical economic unity if not political, for Austria was industrial and Hungary agricultural; they complemented each other to form an economic unit, and the Danube was the artery for both. In the second place, the two nations needed each other to constitute a Great Power, able to defend their common European interests. And in the third place, it was through this combination that they were able to hold the other nationalities down. To be sure, by the Law of Nationalities, passed at Deák's influence as a supplement to the Ausgleich, all nationalities were accorded equal rights, but this act had always remained in Hungary a dead letter. From political and educational advantages as well as in all matters of policy Slovaks and Roumans were excluded for the benefit of the Magyars. In Austria, thanks to universal suffrage (granted in 1907), Czechs, Poles, Ruthenians, Slovenes, Croats, Serbs, and *Position of the Southern Slavs* Italians had a rather better position, and even in Hungary the Croats, as we have seen, enjoyed a limited autonomy, though it was steadily infringed upon by Hungary and was consequently precarious. Taken together, the Slovenes, Croats, and Serbs formed what was known as the Jugoslavs or Southern Slavs. Most of the Serbs were concentrated in Bosnia and Herzegovina (governed jointly by the two states) and it was the Bosniaks who were particularly restive under alien rule. The Slovenes and Croats, being

Catholic, would normally prefer to remain in the Dual Monarchy, but Croat discontent had gained steadily and tended to drive this element into alliance with the Serbs, who were frankly separatist. The most explosive spot in the Dual Monarchy was Bosnia, which at times had to be placed under martial law. Such was one phase of the South Slav problem. The other concerns Serbia, the magnet of these Slavs.

The Evolution of Panserbism

Serbia and Balkan politics

The Serbs outside the Dual Monarchy were either scattered groups in the Ottoman Empire (before 1912) or lived in the two independent states of Serbia and Montenegro. Though they were normally under the patronage of Russia, Serbia under the later Obrenoviches had become pro-Austrian, sacrificing the national independence for relations which brought the country material gain. All this changed when the Obrenovich king was murdered in 1903 and Peter Karageorgevich came to the throne. Henceforth Serbia was to be found in the Russian column.

Underlying causes of the Austro-Serbian feud

But the feud between Austria and Serbia rested on fundamental factors. Serbs, on the one hand, and Germans and Magyars, on the other, were ancient enemies, as border peoples often are, especially if there is territory in dispute; and the appropriation of Bosnia and Herzegovina with their million and a half Serbs had left in Serbia feelings of soreness which even Obrenovich rule could not efface. But the chief clue to the feud was to be found more in geography than in history. Serbia was a land-locked power, and her only practicable outlet lay through Austria-Hungary. This gave her powerful neighbor a lever for extorting economic concessions which were hardly to Serbia's interest. Serbia's chief commodity was pigs; and when in the hope of ending economic dependence she sought to open another route to foreign markets, she at once encountered resistance from Austria-Hungary, who denounced the existing commercial treaty between them, and for a time closed the frontier to Serbia's pigs. This commercial row is historically known as the "Pig War." While it chiefly injured Serbia, it did react in a measure upon Austria-Hungary. As Professor Schmitt says, "The Serbian peasantry was convinced that Austria-Hungary stood in the way of their prosperity and they came to have for the [Dual] Monarchy feelings of the most bitter hatred."

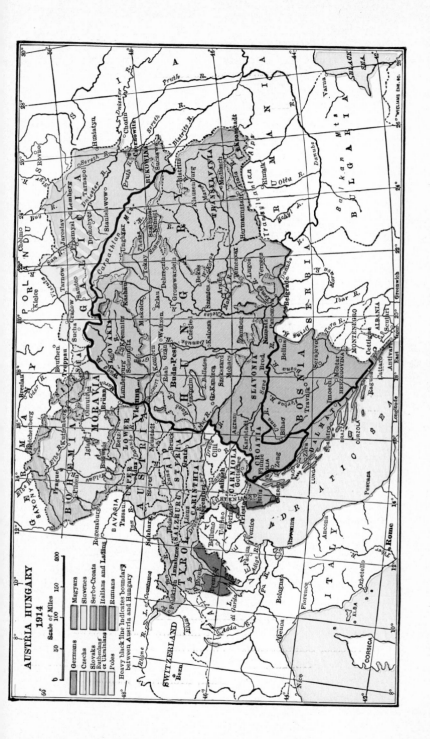

Economic relations were still thorny when Austria annexed Bosnia and Herzegovina in 1908. We have discussed the crisis in its larger aspects, but it is worthy of note here that Aehrenthal had long cherished designs on Serbia, and when the crisis developed, he wrote of it as a "nest of revolution" which he was determined to snuff out. To Serbia the annexation was a bitter blow, for she had somehow hoped that sooner or later she would be able to acquire Bosnia and thus reach the Adriatic. She had no claim to it but that of nationality, but nationalism is generally a law unto itself, and the time had come to raise the issue squarely. The Serbs would gladly have fought their enemy and pinned their hopes on Russian intervention, but Russia could not fight, and when, instead, she counseled them to disarm, they had nothing to do but yield. Then Austria, rubbing it in, forced Serbia to promise formally to treat her in future as a friendly power; and a commercial treaty followed. Then three years later came the First Balkan War and Serbia had new cause for bitterness and hatred. When at last she had the window on the Adriatic actually in hand, Austria forbade her to retain it. But the war left her doubled in size and population, and one might say more than doubled in pride and ambition. Austria's day of reckoning would come, for so Russian diplomats had persistently assured her. When the Russian foreign minister was counseling moderation before the Second Balkan War, he said, "Serbia's promised land lies in the territory of Austria-Hungary. . . . Time is working for Serbia and for the destruction of her enemies, who already show clear signs of disintegration." "The first round is won," the Serbian premier was quoted as saying. "Now we must prepare for the second, against Austria."

Growth of Serbian resentment— the question of the Adriatic

There is no doubt that Austria herself thoroughly appreciated the danger. A danger seemingly routed in a frontal attack often quietly takes to subterranean channels where it soon becomes many times more deadly; and there was plenty of Serb propaganda at work on Austrian territory. There were two alternative ways of meeting the peril. One was to placate the Southern Slavs at home by erecting for them a kingdom of their own on a par with Austria and Hungary. Such a plan was ascribed to the crown prince, the Emperor's nephew, Francis Ferdinand, though it was bound to meet with the opposition of Hungary, who bitterly hated the heir apparent and resented any concessions to the Slavs.

Stress of Austria's problem

The other defensive weapon was a deliberate thrust at Serbia. Urged on by the military clique, Count Berchtold, successor of Aehrenthal (who had died in 1912), planned to launch an attack upon Serbia during the Second Balkan War. Yet as Russia was certain to spring to Serbia's aid, he felt himself obliged to consult his allies, and neither Germany nor Italy would countenance such an act. "Should she [Austria-Hungary] try to do this," warned Bethmann-Hollweg, "it would mean a European war"; and the Italian foreign minister later remarked to an Austrian diplomat, "We shall hold you back by the coat-tails if necessary." So Berchtold gave up the plan. But a few months later when Serbia had occupied a part of Albania (pending an adjustment of the frontier), he dispatched an ultimatum to Belgrade with the full approval of Germany.[1] Fortunately Russia held aloof, and the Serbs backed down, but the maneuver had been risky in the extreme. The only safe way to stop a petty Balkan quarrel was for the Central Powers to act in concert with Russia. In this case, as far as we know, no advances of any sort had been made to St. Petersburg.

The issue of Panserbism

At all events there is no doubt that Austria felt that the integrity of the Empire was at stake. Serbia imagined herself a second Sardinia whose mission it was to unite the South Slav peoples. The Bosniaks were, of course, ready for anything and in 1910 an attempt had been made on the life of the Austrian governor. There were also secret societies with headquarters at Belgrade, spreading the gospel of revolutionary Panserbism to the millions of Jugoslavs in the Dual Monarchy; and it is notable that one of these societies, the so-called "Black Hand" had already employed the weapon of assassination. Thus the dynasticism of the Hapsburgs was challenged by Panserbism. A situation was at hand so combustible that it only required a spark to produce an explosion.

But Europe itself was frantically plunging toward an abyss.

---

[1] "How often have I wondered," wrote the German ambassador to Vienna to his chief, in May, 1914, "whether it is really worth while to tie ourselves up so tightly to this Austro-Hungarian Monarchy, which is creaking and cracking in every joint, and to go on painfully dragging it after us. But, as yet, I can see no other political combination that would compensate us for the loss of the asset we still hold in our alliance with Austria-Hungary." Unhappily for Germany, it was Austria that was doing the "dragging." Germany had allowed herself to be steadily drawn into the fatal Austro-Serbian feud. In October, 1913 the Kaiser had gone so far as to say to Berchtold, "I stand behind you and am ready to draw the sword if necessary."

PREPARATIONS FOR WAR

At the beginning of 1914 there were two defensive systems— *The tightening of the Triple Entente* the Triple Alliance and the Triple Entente. Italy, as we have seen, was only in name a member of the former. Great Britain, on the other hand, while not an ally of the Dual Alliance, had been drawn so close to France that circumstances might very well align her with both these powers in event of war.

A policy begun under Lansdowne and followed by Grey was that of authorizing the British staffs (military and naval) to work out plans of common defense in collaboration with the French staffs, and later similar action was taken between the British and Belgian staffs. In November, 1912—probably as the result of the Agadir Crisis—France and Great Britain went so far as to agree (not through a treaty but by interchange of letters) that if either had reason to expect "an unprovoked attack by a third power," they should "discuss" what measures they should "take in common." More than that, as the result of much discussion the French navy took it upon itself to defend the common cause in the Mediterranean while the British navy assumed a like rôle for the Channel and the North Sea. This plan had originated with the British, since with the failure of Lord Haldane's effort (1912) to secure a naval truce with Germany, the British admiralty felt the need of amassing all its strength in the North Sea. But the significance of the step was not ignored. Since under the circumstances Great Britain could hardly in decency allow the German navy to attack the northern coasts of France (and Grey admitted as much to Russia), one can see that the Entente Cordiale had become *in effect* an alliance—a defensive alliance, it is true, but none the less an alliance.

As far as personal factors go, the tightening of the Triple Entente *Position of Poincaré* was mostly due to Raymond Poincaré, an able and masterful man, who became premier of France in January, 1912. For this reason and owing to the fact that he was a native of Lorraine and an ardent patriot (not to mention the dubious testimony of Izvolski) some writers have striven to prove that Poincaré deliberately plotted to bring about war for the restitution of Alsace-Lorraine.[1] It is true that despite his warning to Russia before

[1] For an incisive treatment of the thesis of Entente guilt, see Barnes, *The Genesis of the World War.*

the Balkan Wars that France would not be drawn into a Balkan imbroglio, he nevertheless took pains to assure her *after* the Balkan Wars that France could be counted upon to fulfill her obligations— an assurance possibly inspired by the fear that Russia might flirt with Germany (for Russia was none too trustworthy!).[1] It is also true that he labored hard to get Russia to increase her military efficiency; that he prompted a Franco-Russian naval agreement; and that he persuaded Russia (to whom he confided the Anglo-French arrangements) to seek by negotiation a naval agreement with England. Yet none of such circumstantial evidence really proves that Poincaré's efforts were more than strictly defensive. He looked for a test of strength between the alliances, and, should such a crisis come, he determined that the Triple Entente should be thoroughly ready to meet it.

The gathering storm

Undoubtedly the Balkan Wars greatly increased the tension. The Austrian ultimatum, the Liman von Sanders mission, the anarchy in Albania were sufficient to make any diplomat jumpy; and in certain government circles the feeling almost amounted to hysteria. The specter of Panslavism, conjured up by the German chancellor, had readily brought the reichstag to vote for greater armaments. In April, 1913, Germany raised her effective forces, and Austria did likewise. France and Russia then answered with similar measures. Statesmen on both sides expected war, and frankly said so. Yet no one seemed to think of any solution but greater armaments. And meanwhile, army maneuvers, naval activity, and an atmosphere of haunting premonition! "The Central Powers," said an Austrian diplomat, "cannot accept the Treaty of Bucharest as a definite settling of the Balkans; and nothing but a general war can bring about a suitable solution." "We will go and fight with joy and confidence in our heart," boasted the Kaiser in a public speech, "if it is necessary to defend what has been conquered." "War with Germany," wrote a Russian professor, "would be a misfortune, but one cannot escape from a bitter necessity when it is really necessary. Only possession of the Straits can end this intolerable situation, in which Russia's

---

[1] There was a strong pro-German faction at the Russian court, which may account for some of the unsteadiness of Russian policy. The Potsdam Agreement of 1910–1 had given France some disquietude, and neither France nor Great Britain was unaware of the instability of the Czar. It is not inconceivable that Poincaré deliberately made the most of Russian exasperation against Germany in order to prevent all possible backsliding.

export trade can be stopped at any moment." The fact that the
French elections (May, 1914) revealed a pacifist reaction in that
country or that France and Great Britain were giving their approval to the Bagdad Railway enterprise could not somehow
counterweigh the feverish drilling, the wild talk, the spasms of

Wide World Photos

THE KAISER INSPECTING BAVARIAN TROOPS

official nerves. "It is militarism run stark mad," observed an
American sojourner in Europe.

If we look back upon the history of the last ten years we find
that France, Russia, and Great Britain begrudged Germany opportunities of expansion, partly because of a natural misunderstanding
of German militarism, partly because of the pressure of their own
economic interests, which they were steadily promoting. On the
other hand, Germany and Austria inspired by wounded vanity
or fear, were rather more ready to play with fire, more guilty
than their rivals of forcing crises. The result of all this was the
division of Europe into two mutually suspicious armed camps,
neither of which was willing to give way to the other, should an
unusually difficult crisis ever arise. For the general public mil-

*The question
of responsi-
bility*

itarism was largely a cover for fear, and even an act of aggression would be viewed by the nation concerned as no more than one of defense. But when diplomats themselves disagreed as to what was "aggression" and talked glibly of "preventive wars," one may wonder whether anything under Heaven could have averted the coming crash. Politically Europe was in anarchy, and it was for that reason that militarism, imperialism, and irredentism could combine to produce the greatest war in history.

FOR FURTHER READING OR STUDY

Robinson, J. H., and Beard, C. A., *Readings in Modern European History*, chaps. xxiii (*passim*), xxvii, xxix, and xxx; Scott, J. F., and Baltzly, A., *Readings in European History since 1814*, chaps. x (*passim*), xii, and xiii; Cooke, W. H. and Stickney, E. P., *Readings in European International Relations since 1879*, part i; Wetterlé, E., *Behind the Scenes in the Reichstag; The Kaiser vs. Bismarck* (long-suppressed third volume of Bismarck's memoirs); Crispi, F., *Memoirs*, 3 vols.; Livingstone, D., *Missionaries' Travels and Researches in South Africa;* Stanley, H. M., *Through the Dark Continent;* Hayashi, T., *Secret Memoirs* (important for the Anglo-Japanese alliance); Blunt, W. S., *My Diaries, 1888–1914* (interesting though not always convincing British observations on foreign relations); Eckardstein, H., *Ten Years at the Court of St. James* (by a secretary to the German embassy); Grey, E., *Twenty-Five Years* (the British foreign secretary's apology); Hammann, O., *The World Policy of Germany, 1890–1912* (by the head of the press bureau of the German foreign office); *German Diplomatic Documents* (ed. Dugdale, E. T. S.), 4 vols. (a selection from the monumental German compilation); Siebert, B. von, and Schreiner, G. A., *Entente Diplomacy and the World* (chiefly translations of Russian dispatches); *The Willy-Nicky Correspondence* (ed. Bernstein, H.); Bülow, B. von, *Imperial Germany* (very misleading longer memoirs have appeared); Tirpitz, A. von, *Memoirs* (by the German sea-lord); Fisher, J., *Memories* (by the British sea lord); Schön, E. E., *Memoirs of an Ambassador;* Asquith, H. H., *Memories and Reflections;* Shuster, W. M., *The Strangling of Persia;* Haldane, R. B., *Before the War;* Beyens, N. E., *Germany before the War;* Churchill, W. S., *The World Crisis*, vol. i; Nekludoff, A., *Diplomatic Reminiscences* (important for the Balkan League); Baernreither, J. M., *Fragments from a Political Diary* (important work by an Austrian official); Jonescu, T., *Some Personal Impressions;* Poincaré, R., *Memoirs*, vols. i–ii.

Hayes, C. J. H., *Political and Social History of Modern Europe,* vol. ii, pp. 397–426, 490–711; Schapiro, J. S., *Modern and Contemporary European History*, chaps. xx (Germany), xxv (the Balkans), xxx–xxxiv; Higby, C. P., *History of Modern Europe*, chaps. xvi (Germany), xvii (Austria), xx–xxv; Fueter, E., *World History, 1815–1920*, chaps. xxviii–xxxi and xxxiv; Palm, F. C., and Graham, F. E., *Europe since 1814*, chaps. xix, xxi–xxv; Slosson, P. W., *Twentieth Century Europe* (good readable text for foreign affairs and imperialism); Gooch, G. P., *History of Modern Europe* (strictly diplomatic, generally fair, but a little pro-British).

Schmitt, B. E., *Triple Alliance and Triple Entente* (brief and lucid sketch);
Sontag, R. J., *European Diplomatic History, 1871–1932* (interesting and discriminating); Swain, J. W., *Beginning the Twentieth Century* (confined to diplomatic history, a brilliant critique, perhaps a little too hard on personalities); Mowat, R. B., *The Concert of Europe* (an important theme not very well handled); Brandenburg, E., *From Bismarck to the World War* (sober German account); Fay, S. B., *The Origins of the World War*, vol. i (clear and judicial though more strictly diplomatic than the title implies); Dickinson, G. L., *The International Anarchy, 1904–14* (convincing indictment of all the powers); Donaldson, J., *International Economic Relations;* Culbertson, W. S., *International Economic Policies;* Feis, H., *Europe, the World's Banker* (shows connection between finance and diplomacy); Howard, B. E., *The German Empire* (detailed study of its political organization); Lichtenberger, H., *Germany and its Evolution in Modern Times;* Howard, E. D., *The Causes and Extent of the Recent Industrial Progress of Germany* (published in 1907); Dawson, W. H., *The Evolution of Modern Germany, Industrial Germany, The German Workman,* and *Municipal Life and Government in Germany;* Gauss, C., *The German Emperor as Shown in His Public Utterances;* Ludwig, E., *Kaiser William II* (popular); Gooch, G. P., "Baron von Holstein, the 'Mystery Man' of the German Foreign Office," *Camb. Hist. Jour.*, i, 61 ff.; Langer, W. L., *European Alliances and Alignments, 1871–90;* Taffs, W., "The War Scare of 1875," *Slav. Rev.*, ix, 335 ff., 632 ff.; Wertheimer, M., *The Pan-German League;* Hausser, H., *Germany's Commercial Grip on the World* (important light on a subject that needs more clarification); Nicolai, H., *The Biology of War;* Playne, C. E., *The Neurosis of the Nations;* Brailsford, H. N., *The War of Steel and Gold: A Study of the Armed Peace;* Smith, M., *Militarism and Statecraft;* Angell, N., *The Great Illusion;* Bakeless, J., *The Economic Causes of War;* Culbertson, W. S., *Raw Materials and Food Stuffs in the Commercial Policies of Nations;* Schuyler, R. L., "The Recall of the Legions: A Phase of the Decentralization of the British Empire," *Amer. Hist. Rev.*, xxvi, 18 ff.; Hobson, J. A., *Imperialism;* Lippmann, W., *The Stakes of Diplomacy;* Muir, R., *The Expansion of Europe,* esp. chaps. v–viii; Moon, P. T., *Imperialism and World Politics* (scholarly and amusingly caustic); Reinsch, P. S., *World Politics at the End of the Nineteenth Century;* Villiate, A., *Economic Imperialism;* Hoskins, H. L., *European Imperialism in Africa* (brief); Johnston, H. H., *History of the Colonization of Africa by Alien Races;* Lucas, C., *The Partition and Colonization of Africa;* Hutchinson, T. W., *Peoples and Problems of India;* Vinacke, H. M., *A History of the Far East in Modern Times;* Dutcher, G. M., *The Political Awakening of the East;* McNair, H. F., and Morse, H. B., *Far Eastern International Relations;* Morse, H. B., *The Trade and Administration of China* and *The International Relations of the Chinese Empire*, 3 vols.; Overlach, T. W., *Foreign Financial Control in China;* Clyde, P. H., *International Rivalries in Manchuria;* Latourette, K. S., *The Development of China* and *The Development of Japan;* Orchard, J. E., and D., *Japan's Economic Position: The Progress of Industrialization;* Asakawa, K., *The Russo-Japanese Conflict: Its Causes and Issues;* Kawakami, K. K., *Japan in World Politics;* Blaisdell, D. C., *European Financial Control in the Ottoman Empire;* Robinson, H., *Development of the British Empire*, chaps. xi–xxiv; Williamson, J. A., *A Short History of British*

Expansion and *Europe Over-seas;* Knowles, L., *The Economic Development of the British Over-Seas Empire;* Hall, W. P., *Empire to Commonwealth;* Jebb, R., *The Britannic Question;* Knaplund, D., *Gladstone and Britain's Imperial Policy;* Roberts, S. H., *History of French Colonial Policy,* 2 vols.; Southworth, C., *The French Colonial Venture;* Girault, A., *The Colonial Tariff Policy of France;* Townsend, M. E., *The Rise and Fall of Germany's Colonial Empire;* Rohrbach, P., *Germany's World Politics;* Seymour, C., *The Diplomatic Background of the War,* chaps. iv and v (Germany's world policy); Schnee, H. von, *German Colonization* (by a former governor of German East Africa); Skrine, F. H., *The Expansion of Russia;* Vámbéry, A., *Western Culture in Eastern Lands;* Leroy-Beaulieu, P., *The Awakening of the East;* Lobanov-Rostovsky, A., *Russia and Asia;* Keller, A. G., *Colonization* (for German and Italian colonization); Halévy, A., *A History of the English People, Epilogue,* vol. i, 1895–1905 (British imperialism) and vol. ii; Ward, A. W., and Gooch, C. P., *The Cambridge History of British Foreign Policy* (by several authors), vol. iii; Hallberg, C. W., *The Suez Canal;* Newton, Lord, *Lord Lansdowne;* Riker, T. W., "A Survey of British Policy in the Fashoda Crisis," *Pol. Sc. Qu.,* xliv, 54 ff.; Sontag, R. J., "The Cowes Interview and the Krüger Telegram," *ibid.,* xl, 217 ff.; Bickford, J. D., and Johnson, E. N., "The Contemplated Anglo-German Alliance, 1890–1901," *ibid.,* xlii, 1 ff.; Williams, B., *Cecil Rhodes;* Sontag, R. J., "German Foreign Policy 1904–1906," *Amer. Hist. Rev.,* xxxiii, 278 ff.; Gooch, G. P., *Studies in Modern History* (esp. for essays on German theories of state and Holstein, as above); Michon, G., *The Franco-Russian Alliance;* Carroll, E. M., *French Public Opinion and Foreign Affairs, 1870–1914* (an important work); Nicholson, H., *Portrait of a Diplomatist* (based on the dispatches of a British undersecretary and an important source as well as delightful reading); Anderson, E. N., *The First Moroccan Crisis;* Hale, O. J., *Germany and the Diplomatic Revolution: A Study of Diplomacy and the Press, 1904–6;* Kantorowicz, H., *The Spirit of British Policy and the Myth of the Encirclement of Germany* (a little too partial to Great Britain); Fay, S. B., "The Kaiser's Secret Negotiations with the Czar," *Amer. Hist. Rev.,* xxiv, 48 ff.; Seton-Watson, R. W., "William II's Balkan Policy," *Slav. Rev.,* vii, 1 ff.; Pears, E., *Turkey and Its People* (interesting and informing) and *Life of Abdul Hamid II;* Forbes, N. *et al., The Balkans;* Earl, E. M., *Turkey, the Powers, and the Bagdad Railroad;* Brailsford, H. N., *Macedonia;* Schmitt, B. E., "The Bosnian Annexation Crisis," *Slav. Rev.,* ix, 312 ff., 650 ff., and x, 161 ff., 408 ff., and xi, 64 ff.; Langer, W. L., "Russia, the Straits, and the European Powers, 1890–4," *Eng. Hist. Rev.,* xliv, 59 ff. and "Russia, the Straits Question, and the Balkan League," *Pol. Sc. Qu.,* xliii, 321 ff.; Kerner, R. J., "The Liman von Sanders Mission," *Slav. Rev.,* vi, 12 ff., 344 ff., 543 ff., vii, 90 ff.; Steed, H. W., *The Hapsburg Monarchy;* Seton-Watson, H. W., *The Southern Slav Question and the Habsburg Monarchy;* Jászi, O., *The Dissolution of the Habsburg Monarchy* (extremely useful); Lutz, H., *Lord Grey and the Great War* (very critical of Grey).

XVI. THE GREAT WAR: ITS OUTBREAK, COURSE, AND CONDUCT

1. THE SARAJEVO CRISIS AND THE OUTBREAK OF WAR

The Sarajevo tragedy; Culpability of Serbia; Attitude of the Central Powers; Question of the immediate responsibility and the outbreak of the general war; Fundamental explanation of the War.

2. THE WIDENING OF THE WAR

A. THE GREAT POWERS DRAWN IN

France; Great Britain; Japan; Italy.

B. THE MINOR POWERS DRAWN IN

Belgium, Montenegro, and Turkey; Bulgaria; Roumania; Greece; Other states.

C. THE INTERVENTION OF THE UNITED STATES

The United States as a world power; Factors making for avoidance of war; Character and position of Wilson; The approach of intervention; The breach; The renascence of American patriotism.

3. PRELIMINARY SURVEY OF THE GREAT WAR

General character of the War; Comparison of the belligerents.

4. THE FIRST SHOCK OF THE WAR—THE GREAT MILITARY CRISIS OF 1914

The German plan of assured victory; Opening of the Marne campaign; First Battle of the Marne; Fate of the Russian offensive.

5. THE PERIOD OF GERMANY'S MILITARY ASCENDANCY

Ypres—the failure of the Germans to reach the Channel; Collapse of Russia; Failure of Allied policy in the Near East; An exhausting deadlock.

6. THE TRIUMPH OF THE ALLIES

Concerted efforts of the Allies; Battle of Picardy; Second Battle of the Marne; Collapse of the Central Powers; Conclusion of the war.

The Great War was the greatest convulsion that has shaken the world since the French Revolution, and in many respects it was a revolution itself, as we shall observe. It was a conflict demanding greater mobilization of human effort and greater demands upon science than any previous European struggle, and was largely a test of endurance. Primarily it was a trial of strength between two rival systems of European powers, but so many nations were drawn in that it became eventually world-wide in scope. Nationalism had done its worst. Europe, as we have seen, had become a tinder-box of hatred and suspicion, and when the Austro-Serbian feud had come to the point of actual war, there was little hope of averting a general conflict. We must first consider the crisis which arose out of the tragedy of Sarajevo and the circumstances which steadily and in spite of the real desires of the powers concerned led straight to a general war.

THE SARAJEVO CRISIS AND THE OUTBREAK OF WAR

The Sarajevo tragedy

On June 28, 1914 the Archduke Francis Ferdinand and his morganatic wife, the Countess of Hohenberg, were shot and killed as they were riding through the streets of Sarajevo, the capital of Bosnia. The murder was the act of a Bosniak who had been furnished arms by a member of the "Black Hand," who was in turn an agent of a high Serbian official who belonged to that society. The Archduke had been warned not to go to Sarajevo at this time, and the date of his official visit had coincided with the Serbian national holiday, but he was a headstrong and fearless man, and he would make no alteration of his plan. It will be recalled that Francis Ferdinand was the statesman credited with the plan of placating the Jugoslavs of the Dual Monarchy, and he was thus, in the event of the aged Emperor's death, a major obstacle in the path of Panserbism.

Culpability of Serbia

The shock which this murder brought to the European governments was terrific. Now at last had come the climax of that bitter neighborhood feud, and no one doubted that Austria would take summary measures. In general, European opinion was sympathetic. So atrocious an act seemed less pardonable even than war, and it was not forgotten that assassination had been all too common as a political instrument in Serbia. There is evidence to show—though it was not known until long afterward—that the Serbian government itself had long known of the plot hatched by the "Black Hand" to kill the Archduke, and had taken insufficient precautions to stop it, the reason probably being that the position of the ministers depended on the result of a coming parliamentary election and to take drastic steps against the "Black Hand" might have turned an inflamed opinion decisively against them. It is true that an unofficial warning was transmitted to Vienna that Bosnia was not at that time a safe place for the Archduke to visit, but nothing whatever was said of an actual plot, and though it might have behooved the Austrian government to follow this leader and insist on fuller particulars, the fact remains that the premier of Serbia and some of his colleagues knew that assassins had crossed the frontier, and that even then the truth was not communicated to Vienna.

In any case Austria believed that Serbia was officially responsible and resolved to act accordingly. That her action was long delayed, that almost a month passed between the murder and the fatal ultimatum was due to a number of causes. The first (though this consumed less than a week) was the necessity of assuring herself that Germany would stand by her in the event that her action should lead to war and that Russia should intervene. Information that the German ambassador to Vienna had counseled moderation drew from the Kaiser the comment, "Now or never! . . . The Serbs must be finished up with, and right soon!" When Berchtold dispatched a special envoy to Berlin on behalf of the Emperor-King, it took Germany little time to show her colors. After assuring themselves that the army and the navy were in readiness for any emergency, the Kaiser and Bethmann-Hollweg declared to Austria that Germany would be ready to fulfill her pledges as an ally even if action against Serbia should lead to war with Russia. In the meantime Austria was investigating the murder—a task which occupied some time—though the evidence collected was not directly incriminating to Serbia. Another difficulty was the reluctance of the Hungarian premier to consent to drastic measures, and he did not give his approval till July 14. A possible fourth reason for Austria's pause was a deliberate plan of waiting until Poincaré, who was then at St. Petersburg, should have departed for home. With the president of France (and the premier, too, for that matter) on the sea for a day or more the Entente would be less able to concert measures for meeting the crisis which Austrian action could be expected to produce.[1] There was, however, little doubt of the character of the coming ultimatum, and Germany —despite the stupid lies of her foreign minister—was well aware

Attitude of the Central Powers

[1] Berchtold himself gave Poincaré's presence in St. Petersburg as a reason for delay, but he put it on the ground that to launch the ultimatum at the time when the President of France was being fêted by the Czar might be viewed as a "political affront." What—if anything—was in the back of Berchtold's mind is purely a matter of conjecture.

of its nature several days before it was sent and knew its exact contents the day after. She could easily have prevented its dispatch seeing that Austria was dependent on German support; but she preferred to let her ally force the issue. Whether she felt that if war must come eventually this was a better moment than some years later when the Entente would perhaps be stronger is a debatable question. She did not, at any rate, mean to let Austria slowly disintegrate from nationalist disorders. Hence she took the position—broadly speaking, indefensible, of course—that the struggle should be localized to Austria and Serbia. But her famous blank check was a fatal move, which none of the subsequent events was able to overcome.

On July 23 Austria issued her ultimatum to Serbia—a communication so sweeping in its demands, so brusquely worded, and allowing so short a time (forty-eight hours) for reply that there could hardly be any doubt that it was meant to provoke war. "Russia cannot accept it," commented Francis Joseph when he read it, "it will be a big war." Serbia's reply was unexpectedly conciliatory, though she balked at one demand that would have compromised her sovereignty, and, rightly sensing Austria's intentions, began to mobilize. Austria, of course, rejected the Serbian reply, withdrew her minister from Belgrade, and on July 28 declared war. But in these intervening days some efforts had been made to avert the storm. Russia tried in vain to get the time allowed Serbia lengthened in order that the matter might be discussed, and Grey made various proposals for composing the quarrel—without getting much support from any of the powers. The Kaiser had expressed himself as gratified with the Serbian reply, and though Grey's maneuvers nettled him ("Grey must be told very sincerely and plainly that I won't stand any nonsense; Grey makes the mistake of putting Serbia on the level with other powers"), this harassed and excited ruler had certainly a genuine horror of the possibility of war. But the issue had already been decided. As Germany had given Austria *carte blanche*, and Austria had made up her mind to smash Panserbism for good, the moments were fast getting beyond the point where peace was possible. With the outbreak of war on the Danube, the crisis became immeasurably more acute.

There is much in the succeeding days that is still the subject of controversy. Had Russia the right to interfere (she made it perfectly clear that she would not allow Serbia to be crushed) just *Question* *of the* *immediate* *responsi-* *bility and* *the outbreak* *of the* *general war*

because her predominance in the Balkans might be forfeited to the Central Powers? And if she had no moral right to meddle, were the Central Powers, nevertheless, justified in acting in a way which they knew would involve her and bring on war? Did Germany's subsequent efforts to hold Austria back impress the latter as sincere? It is evident that a sudden fear that Great Britain might side with their rivals moved Germany to back-step, and even Berchtold finally deigned to parley a little with Russia. But by this time the Russian general mobilization had brought the military party at Berlin into the ascendant. Again, did the Russian mobilization (at first only a partial mobilization and employed as a club on Austria) amount to the beginning of war, or did the German ultimatum of July 31, demanding demobilization within twelve hours force the conflict? With respect to the Russian mobilization, which for tactical reasons became general mobilization on July 30, it is now known that the French and Russian staffs considered this act as "meaning war"; yet the Czar telegraphed to William promising on his word of honor not to move a man across the frontier as long as negotiations with Austria continued. It was Germany who finally took the formal step of declaring war on August 1.

It is impracticable within the proper limits of this book to try *Funda-* *mental* *explanation* *of the War*

to settle these points, but in any case it is rather doubtful if such an exercise is profitable. A few facts stand out clear and make it hardly worth while to try to individualize responsibility. In the first place, while none of the leading powers really wanted a general war, neither the Triple Entente nor the Central Powers were willing, after the Austrian ultimatum, to accept a diplomatic defeat even though to avoid it meant war. Secondly, the strain of these nine or ten days was so overwhelming and the confusion of proposals, counter-proposals, telegrams, and so on was so great that the diplomats who held the fate of Europe in their hands could hardly have avoided some hasty judgments and faulty decisions. Finally, if war had become inevitable, as all the governments came more and more to believe, the question of keeping the peace then languished in importance before the question of what advantages should be snatched before formal hostilities should commence. Hence, the furious pressure of the military staffs at St. Petersburg and Berlin and their final and fatal command of the situation. It seems clear that in Russian circles the Czar alone still hoped for peace on July 30. Bethmann-Hollweg gave up hope the following day. Now if war was bound to come, Germany was anxious to crush France before Russia was completely ready, for it was assumed that the latter's mobilization would occupy several weeks. "We could not," wrote Bethmann-Hollweg on July 31, "wait quietly to see whether counsels of prudence would prevail at St. Petersburg, while Russian mobilization continued in full swing, as this would involve our being completely outstripped in military preparations." Equally well, of course, Russia felt that unless she had a good start on her adversaries, she could not accord sufficient aid to France when the clash of arms commenced. There is, it is true, some ground for suspecting that even Russia's partial mobilization, thoroughly approved by France and Great Britain, was merely a cover from the start to enable Russia to begin the war (provided it came) under less serious disadvantage.

The fundamental factors, are, in fact, much more potent than the immediate considerations. Austria-Hungary, though an obsolete state, was fighting for her life against Serb irredentism. The opposing systems in Europe had staked so much on supremacy in the Balkans, and nationalism in the large had become so intemperate, so suspicious, and so full of frenzied fear that one may doubt if the various diplomats at the helm, second-rate men all of them, had really much chance of averting the crash. Probably no war in history has been so nearly inevitable as this one. And no war has engulfed so many nations.

THE WIDENING OF THE WAR

The Great Powers Drawn in

A war between Russia and the Central Powers was bound to involve France, who had so firmly backed her ally in all these recent events. Assuming this to be true, Germany dispatched an

France

ultimatum to Paris the same day (July 31) that she sent one to Russia, inquiring whether France would remain neutral in event of war, and, if so, demanding that she hand over at once two fortresses as a gauge of her neutrality. This silly demand was properly ignored. There was, at any rate, no hope of averting war. France began to mobilize on August 1 (the day after Germany's mobilization), and two days later Germany declared war.

The enigmatical factor was Great Britain. There was no doubt of Grey's sympathy with the Dual Alliance; but the cabinet was divided, some of them not being at all in favor of war on behalf of *Great Britain* France; and the temper of public opinion was also uncertain. It is possible that Great Britain, by threatening to support her friends in event of war, might in that way have prevented the tragic climax (though obviously at the cost of the Central Powers, who would most likely have sought revenge at the earliest opportunity). But Grey was not a daring soul and not a bluffer either. It was more typical of British character to act in a difficult crisis with circumspection. Meanwhile France had taken the precaution to hold her troops at a certain distance from the frontier in order to avoid a possible "incident" that might be construed as showing the French as the aggressors. On August 2 the British government gave assurance that it would protect the French coasts—this in accordance with the agreement of 1912. Yet the French were still in doubt of the final outcome, and the greatest anxiety prevailed at Paris.

It was not, indeed, France but Belgium that proved the lever which brought Great Britain into the war. It became evident to the British that Germany intended to march through Belgium, and, in fact, on August 2 Germany had sent an ultimatum, demanding of Belgium the right of transit through her territories, making it clear that she would go through in any event. King Albert appealed to Great Britain on the following day, but already London had heard of the ultimatum, and on August 4, in pursuance of a decision of the cabinet the previous evening, the British ambassador to Berlin handed to the German government an ultimatum requesting a promise to respect Belgian neutrality within twelve hours. As the German army had actually entered Belgium on the 3rd, the die had been cast already. Bethmann-Hollweg, greatly excited at being faced with the actual fact of a breach with Great Britain, lamented that the latter should allow a "scrap of paper" (the Belgian neutrality treaty) to come between two kindred nations. The expression was most unfortunate for the Germans, for they never heard the last of this cynical appraisal of a treaty. Recall of the British ambassador on August 4 meant a declaration of war. With public opinion the wanton attack on Belgium had been decisive. With the government the prevailing argument was probably the fact that Germany, once in Belgium, might remain. British policy had never permitted a strong power to hold this position. It was the old question of the balance of power with Belgium as its axis. In Paris the relief which finally came with the end of suspense can well be understood.

Japan

The intervention of Great Britain was a nominal excuse for that of her ally, Japan; and the British government, after some hesitation, appealed to Japan on the basis of that alliance. As a matter of fact, the British, with their supremacy on the sea, were not in any danger from German attack in the Far East; but Japan had nothing to lose and everything to gain by heeding such a request. The memory of Germany's action in 1895 when the latter had joined with the Dual Alliance in preventing her from harvesting the whole fruitage of the war with China was no doubt a factor that had considerable weight at Tokio. Still more important was the chance to fall heir to Germany's possessions in the Far East. On August 15 she delivered an ultimatum to Germany, demanding the leasehold of Kiaochow with a view to its "eventual restoration" to China. As Germany made no reply, Japan declared war on August 23. The War had now extended to the Pacific.

Intervention in the War for the purpose of acquiring some of Germany's holdings in the Far East was one way in which this dexterous and astute power made use of the world crisis. Another way was the coercion of China, to whom Japan presented in 1915 an ultimatum demanding concessions which in effect would have made China little less than a protectorate of her powerful neighbor. Thanks to the pressure of Great Britain and the United States, Japan moderated considerably her demands, but she bagged enormous economic gains; and her attitude toward the War was always something of a puzzle. She plucked her prizes at small cost, and was always suspected of playing a waiting game—not wholly impervious to German influences.[1]

Italy

The case of Italy was markedly different from that of the powers which had first been involved in the War. Her security was not menaced by any act of any power, and though it was no surprise that she declined to regard the War as defensive on the part of her allies and accordingly refused to join them, there was no imperative

---

[1] The mask was somewhat lifted in 1917 when she intimated that her services must receive explicit reward; and accordingly France and Great Britain secretly promised her by treaty Germany's leasehold and economic rights in Shantung, as well as the German islands south of the Equator (Great Britain was to receive the islands north of the Equator). In November of the same year the United States went still further, and acknowledged that Japan because of "geographical propinquity" possessed "special interests" in China. This convention, though later abrogated, was singularly out of harmony with American policy in the Far East.

reason why she should enter the lists against them. Her attitude was fairly stated by her premier who defined his country's policy as one of "sacred egoism" (sacred, of course, according to the holy religion of nationalism!). Nicely covered by her contradictory position in European politics, she was able to adopt the easy rôle of neutrality. Yet Italy readily saw that the chance had come—by skillful bargaining with both sides—to realize her nationalist aspirations, and that if she stayed out of the War, her position might be difficult when it ended, amounting perhaps to isolation. True, she waited nearly nine months before taking the plunge, and in the meantime had the experience of being besieged by both sides— the Central Powers for the purchase of her continued neutrality, the Entente for an alliance and consequent entrance into the War. But there was scarcely any doubt as to the quarter that would promise her the greater loot. Only by joining the Entente could she acquire both the Trentino and Trieste, though Austria, under persistent pressure from Germany, was finally willing to part with part of the former. While the King and some of the socialists were rather disposed to keep out of the War, public opinion, if nothing else, pushed her steadily to the precipice, and on May 30, after driving an excellent bargain with the Entente, she broke with her former allies and entered the war. The action of Italy meant the participation of all the Great Powers of the Old World in the War.

For the attitude of the minor powers we must travel back a little. *The Minor* Belgium had virtually been forced into the War, as has been *Powers* noticed; and Montenegro had voluntarily thrown in her lot with *Drawn in* Serbia. It seemed to be a foregone conclusion that Turkey would enter the War, on the side of the Central Powers. German influence *Belgium,* was predominant at Constantinople, and the Turks were really *Montenegro,* nothing but tools in Germany's hands. On August 2 a secret al- *and Turkey* liance was signed with Berlin and was apparently never discovered by the Entente until Turkey had finally acted. But the Turks were in no hurry. They waited for a while to see how the struggle proceeded and meanwhile ventured to repudiate the Capitulations —which, of course, affected Germany, as well as other foreign states. Finally, after conclusive evidence had been given of its partisanship toward Germany, the Porte came to blows with the Allies late in September, 1914.

The attitude of the other Balkan states was for a time uncertain. *Bulgaria* It was hardly to be supposed that they would keep out of a war in which they might hope for territorial aggrandizement, but the people of the Balkan peninsula are pastmasters in the art of bargaining, and it was practically a question of which of the opposing camps could offer them the more. Much effort was expended by the Allies to secure Bulgaria, and since that power was much cast down by the Treaty of Bucharest, the Allied diplomats strove to induce Serbia and Greece to disgorge some of the gains made at Bulgaria's expense. Serbia was, of course, in too much peril to reject such a proposal entirely, but Greece, for reasons we shall note presently, flatly refused. An Allied expedition to force the Dardanelles was partly designed to influence the wavering Balkan states (so also, the sending of an army to Saloniki later on), but the failure of this attack on Constantinople had naturally the reverse effect. It must be realized, too, that the Central Powers had been promising even greater gains to Bulgaria, and thus the crafty Ferdinand was able to threaten and haggle to his heart's content. Impressed by the collapse of the Russian army and convinced that the Central Powers would triumph in the War, Bulgaria finally made her choice, and joined the Central Powers in October, 1915. Thus the way to the Persian Gulf for German imperialism remained secure.

Roumania   Roumania hesitated much longer. Though secretly in alliance with the Central Powers, the Roumanian ministry on learning of the treaty flatly refused to consider it binding, and neutrality was formally declared on August 4, 1914. Roumania's situation was complicated by the fact that her irredentist aims required the cession of Transylvania from Hungary, on the one hand, and most of Bessarabia from Russia on the other. Yet this very fact that she had grievances against both contestants gave her an excellent chance to bargain. There seemed little doubt that she meant to enter the War as a priceless opportunity of aggrandizement, and that Roumanian opinion was in general on the side of the Allies. But it took some time to gain from these powers the promise of as much of Hungary as she wanted, since, in default of Bessarabia, she expected even territory peopled by Slavs, and another cause for her long hesitation was uncertainty as to the outcome of the War. Finally, in August, 1916, after extorting the promises she wanted, she made her decision and entered the War on the side of the Allies.

The attitude of Greece was for a long time equivocal, and so much pressure was exerted by both sides (amounting at times to *Greece* direct attacks on her neutrality) that it is somewhat difficult to judge of Greek opinion. King Constantine, a brother-in-law of the Kaiser, was apparently pro-German in sympathy, and, believing that the Central Powers would win, he desired to preserve, at least for a time, a cautious neutrality until perhaps a favorable moment should come for action. His prime minister, Venizelos, however, was insistent that the surest way of fulfilling Greek ambition to get the Turkish islands peopled by Greeks as well as the Greek-inhabited coasts of Asia Minor was for Greece to enter the War in the service of the Allies. Apparently Greek opinion was with him (at least at first), and it was on his initiative that the Allies sent their army to Saloniki—an act by which Greece compromised her neutrality. But the King forced Venizelos to resign, and though he could not, of course, get rid of the Allied forces, the uncertainty of his attitude quite paralyzed their action. When the struggle between the belligerents to win Greece became more intense and Greek opinion became hopelessly divided, Venizelos finally headed a revolt against Constantine, and as the result of a wanton attack on the city of Athens by the French fleet the King was forcibly deposed and Greece definitely threw in her lot with the Allies in the summer of 1917.

One more minor European state had meanwhile entered the *Other states* War, and that was Portugal—on the basis of an old treaty alliance with Great Britain. But other belligerents appeared on other continents. An invitation of the United States to all neutrals to break with Germany secured a favorable response from China and Siam in Asia, from Liberia in Africa, and from numerous Latin American states. There were twenty-seven belligerents in all, though China contributed nothing but coolies to work in the Allied trenches, and the hostility of the other minor states outside of Europe was hardly more than formal, except for the confiscation of German property within their borders. The circumstances which brought America into the War must now be treated.

That the leading power of the New World would be drawn into *The Inter-* the struggle was hardly a foregone conclusion. It is true that the *vention of* United States had become a world power—the result, very largely, *States* of the War with Spain, which an inflamed public opinion had forced upon the government. It is also true that under President Theodore Roosevelt the United States had played a conspicuous

The United
States as a
world power

Factors
making for
avoidance
of war

rôle at certain times in world affairs and that imperialistic interests had received additional impetus. But as long as Spain had still owned colonies in the Western Hemisphere she had been viewed by the United States as a neighbor power, whereas the European War seemed to belong to a different world. And fundamentally Americans are an insular people. Comparatively few travel to Europe, and the resources of the country are so boundless that opinion does not look very often beyond its borders. It was just because the struggle seemed so remote that it could be viewed with considerable detachment, as an affair which had no claim on American patriotism. Hence the ordinary observer reacted to it in accordance with his moral sense or according as he happened to feel a strong bond of kinship with one of the belligerents. At the outset of the War the northeastern corner of the United States (New England and some of the Middle Atlantic States) was much inflamed over the occupation of Belgium as a peculiarly wanton example of brute force; yet even in this region the press carefully avoided any suggestion that America should intervene. On the other hand, interest in the struggle was very keen, and partisanship was natural. The large Germanic element in the United States was much embittered by the growing criticism of Germany (due partly to the success of Allied propaganda) and the Irish-Americans constantly voiced their hatred of England. At most, then, it was a nation with a divided heart. In general, it was a nation not willing to be drawn into a distant war. The fact that patriotism, usually so blind and unreasonable, could even suffer the loss of American lives and American ships without a nation-wide explosion of indignation is a very curious paradox of modern history, and possibly proves that the American people are not really nationally minded. The fact that a president of the United States protested to both sides against infractions of her neutrality was apparently sufficient solace for most of her citizens. Moreover, Woodrow Wilson himself, who had been elected in 1912 on a platform of internal reform, was very anxious to avoid external distractions; and though he did get himself involved in a measure with Mexico, this very fact confirmed his resolution to keep his country out of the struggle in Europe. Thus he immediately declared the neutrality of the United States, and counseled his countrymen to "act and speak in the true spirit of neutrality."

Not wanting war, the public looked to Woodrow Wilson to

manage somehow to keep the country at peace, and though this *Character* *and position* *of Wilson* statesman was bitterly criticized by the partisans of both sides, the sense of the nation as a whole was that Wilson should avoid war at almost any cost. Wilson was a man of whose merits as a statesman there is much diversity of opinion. Trained in university circles, his mind was academic in its view of public questions and slow to comprehend the stark realities of a situation. He was at the same time rather stubborn and autocratic, as strong characters are wont to be, and inclined to be unreceptive of the opinions ventured by others. Naturally of a rather retiring temperament, and inclined to distrust the professional politician, he relied greatly on the judgment of a personal friend, E. M. House, to whom he twice confided the mission of visiting Europe in order to gain an understanding of the situation. Such a procedure was somewhat novel and rather contrary to the spirit of the constitution, as House was not an official and consequently not accountable to the senate or even to the department of state; but the experiment perhaps exemplified the scholarly training of Wilson and also his tendency to mental isolation. He was never the good "mixer" that Roosevelt had been, though, possessed of the happy faculty of phrasing his views in attractive language, he was at times able to stir the popular mind. Had he been something of a demagogue, he might perhaps have proved a more effective leader in a country where democracy was largely personal in application. But after all, his policy regarding the War was strictly negative. When Great Britain, extending the blockade, infringed on American rights, he penned a note of protest; when Germany sank American ships, he did likewise. He had too much respect for the dignity of the United States to brook these things in silence. But he meant to have no war if it could be avoided by the pen, and he rested America's case on a strictly legal basis. He was also dispassionate enough to believe that neither side could wisely win decisively— hence his much-criticized plea for a "peace without victory"— and it is probable that he hoped that the United States by remaining neutral would be able to become the arbiter of peace when the War was ended. It is hardly to be denied that Wilson was a man always moved by what he felt to be just and right, and that high moral principles had usually much more weight with him than temporary expediency.

Wilson did not bring his policy to the point of war until he had

*The
approach of
intervention*

exhausted every resource. The struggle was really so desperate that the rights of a neutral power were respected by neither side. The British government, convinced that Wilson would never even in a pinch make war on the Allies, practically cut off all intercourse with Germany and positively refused to consider any of Wilson's reasonable efforts to find a middle ground that would enable the Germans to moderate their submarine warfare. The Germans, on the other hand, while really no more defiant of American neutrality than the British, were responsible for the loss of American lives—a fact of more serious consequence than losses of profits or property. The sinking of the British liner, *Lusitania* (May 7, 1916), though it was carrying munitions of war, and though the act was disavowed by the German government, involved the death of more than a hundred American citizens and reacted very unfavorably on American opinion. Even then, however, there were few who demanded war; and it is to be noted that as late as 1916 Wilson won his re-election to the presidency on the specious plea that he had "kept us out of war." Germany took this as a sign that America was for peace at any price, quite regardless of the fact that Wilson had become convinced—rather tardily, it is true—that his country must be prepared for any emergency, and that important steps had been taken to strengthen the army.

The breach

That war finally came was due to the questionable policy of the German government, which took too little account of the susceptibilities of the American people and drove a peace-loving president into an enemy against his will. All along Germany had chafed under the fact that the Allies alone (having command of the sea) were able to buy munitions of war in America, and it was partly for that reason that her submarines were so active. Efforts were also made to blow up munition factories, and the Austrian ambassador was so involved in these conspiracies that he had to be recalled when the truth became known. In January, 1917, despite a pledge to the contrary (following the *Lusitania* incident) Germany renewed her unrestricted submarine warfare—resulting in the deaths of more Americans—and during the tension that naturally followed a plot of the German government to incite Mexico to attack the United States was unearthed by the British intelligence service. In April, 1917, Wilson requested Congress to support a declaration of war, and it did so without delay. At the last Wilson was much cast down, for he had reached his final decision in a spirit almost of despair. "It is a fearful thing," he said, "to lead this great peaceful people into the most terrible and disastrous of all wars, civilization itself seeming to be in the balance." The submarine warfare was in his opinion "a war against humanity," and though he acquitted the German people of responsibility, he felt that the German government must be humbled.

There was no flinching of American opinion when the crisis came, for nearly everyone seemed now to feel that war was unavoidable. Those bankers who had loaned money to the Allies were probably relieved, since, without an Allied victory, it was questionable whether the debts could ever be paid. But most of the nation were rather in the position of having been dragged into the war by the course of events. Inasmuch as it was now necessary to find a high moral purpose for such action, Wilson trumpeted intervention as a veritable crusade—"The World must be made safe for democracy!" From now on American opinion accepted without question the view that Germany was a menace to civilization and that the struggle was a holy war. But the conflict had been raging for nearly three years before America entered, and we must now go back and ascertain its character.

The renascence of American patriotism

Preliminary Survey of the Great War

It had been anticipated that the progress of invention in all things concerned with the handling and equipment of armies would make a great war in the twentieth century very different from any previous struggle in history. Neither the Russo-Japanese War nor the Turco-Italian War had possessed the complexity or intensity of this conflict; neither had so taxed the faculties of men. An historian of the period, Professor Slosson, has pointed out how much more exacting was this struggle than previous European wars. The recruitment of civilians for auxiliary work—whether as dentists to mend shattered jaws, or artists to design camouflage, or censors to examine civilian correspondence, or writers to make a business of propaganda to influence neutral countries, or the men of the Y.M.C.A. and kindred organizations to relieve with a little joy the grinding drudgery of the trenches—such were some of the various services cheerfully rendered by non-combatants in the War. "Civilian life as such," writes Slosson, "practically dis-

General character of the War

appeared. There were strictly military activities, such as fighting
and nursing the wounded and there were sub-military activities
such as agriculture, manufacturing, transportation, and commerce;
but all were directed by order of the government to definite ends."
In a large number of cases governments directly regulated the economic life and restricted the intellectual and moral freedom of

Wide World Photos

GOING OVER THE TOP

their citizens, though in this respect, of course, the precedent had
been set in earlier struggles. In some respects also science had
done much to facilitate the conduct of a great war. The use of the
field telephone and of wireless telegraphy and the importance of
aircraft for scouting are but a few examples. But also in some
respects science had rendered war considerably more terrible.
Artillery was more devastating in its force and effect than ever
before and the use of poisonous gases and of the submarine contributed new horrors. In the suffering which the Great War brought
upon civilians one needs to liken it more to the wars of the seventeenth century than to those of the eighteenth and nineteenth.
One is also impressed with the fact that armies were not as mobile

as they had been in Napoleon's time. When the struggle was most intense, as on the western front, it was largely a war of sieges. Stretched along in miles upon miles of trenches, armies dug themselves in and protected themselves with barriers such as sandbags and barbed-wire entanglements, then occasionally made a frontal attack under a screen of artillery fire, gaining perhaps a few yards, making a sort of dent in the enemy's lines, and usually at a terrific cost of life. There was little outflanking, as in Napoleon's day. It was more like a terrific but long-drawn-out concussion in which the weightier antagonist would win.

At the outset the advantage clearly lay with the Central Powers. *Comparison of the belligerents* Next to Russia, Germany possessed the largest army, and it is generally conceded that it was also the best equipped. There were no guns in the beginning which equalled those of the Germans in weight, precision, or length of range, and in no other army were the soldiers' numerous needs so completely provided for. While it may be true that the small British army was on the whole the best trained (though the assertion is not unchallenged), it was the German host which possessed most co-ordination, and could move as a great machine, every one of whose parts was in place. Provided the issue could be fought out in a few months, this army would almost certainly win. But if the War were prolonged, then the greater material resources and man power of the Allies would be decisive. For Germany, the loss of her sea-borne trade, and the consequent inability to supply her primary needs after existing reserves had been depleted, due to the fact that superior sea power lay with the Allies, would tend to make such a struggle increasingly exhausting. But it would be long before the Allies would surmount their initial handicaps. Germany had probably the best system of railways for military purposes, and had the opportunity of operating on interior lines; with her central position she could shift troops back and forth from the eastern to the western or the western to the eastern front, as expediency seemed to demand. France and Great Britain could not easily communicate with Russia, and there was little co-operation between them. Germany had also the advantage of greater unity of command. Whereas there was much jealousy between the French and British and a tendency on the part of the governments to enforce their respective conceptions of strategy, Germany was so indisputably the leader of the Central Powers that her plans of co-ordination were practically unquestioned, and, in contrast to France and Great Britain, the high command in Germany was practically immune from civilian interference. In the matter of generalship, as displayed by the opposing staffs, there is probably little choice between them, and if we except a few commanders such as Ferdinand Foch, one is impressed more by the blunders that were committed than with any examples of exceptional brilliance. When it comes to the fighting qualities of the troops comparison is not easy. The German soldier had hardly the initiative of the French, though much more intelligence than the docile and downtrodden Russian. In the French army there was a fine camaraderie between officers and men, the like of which was probably not existent in any other, and the French soldier is always exceptionally daring on the offensive. But the morale of all the armies was generally good. That of the Germans was perhaps more easily sustained because they held a margin of victory for so long and were fighting in the enemy's country. It was for this very reason that the fortitude of the Allies deserves unstinted praise. Under the influence of defeat the Germans showed up less well. As to the spirit of the nations as a whole, there is again little choice to be made between them except that in Austria-Hungary some of the Slavic nationalities were decidedly lukewarm and Great Britain had her troubles with the Irish. But the great goddess, Patriotism, had generally little occasion for complaint. No doubt at the beginning of the War both sides felt keyed up to what they regarded as a struggle for existence. Just as the Germans solemnly believed that they were fighting in self-defense against Russian barbarism and British greed, so the Allies were convinced that Germany had wished to dominate the world and had brought on war deliberately to achieve that end. Such obsessions had been very common since war had ceased to be an affair exclusively of monarchs, and there is nothing that better proves the instability of public opinion. As a rule, of course, the thesis of the enemy's guilt was deliberately taught or fostered by the governments themselves—partly from conviction, partly from the desire to inflame a nation's fighting spirit.

At the outset both sides were confident of victory—a victory that would signify the enemy's complete subjection. But there is always an advantage with the power that takes the offensive. And this is where Germany scored early.

THE FIRST SHOCK OF THE WAR—THE GREAT MILITARY CRISIS OF 1914

Germany's plan of warfare against the Dual Alliance, as we have said, was to deal France a knock-out blow while Russia was still unready, and then, after the former had been successfully disposed of, to concentrate her whole strength upon Russia. It was assumed that only a small force would be needed to guard the eastern frontier, while an Austrian army might take the offensive against the Russian position in Poland. The fact that the execution of the plan involved the violation of Belgium's neutrality which Germany was pledged to respect had no weight with the general staff. For them speed meant everything, for otherwise the War would be long and desperate. Since, however, there was no certainty that Great Britain would have entered the War unless Belgium had been invaded (and it was certainly the invasion of Belgium that clinched British decision), it may be suggested that it would have been better for Germany to have respected Belgian neutrality and risked a long war. After the British intervention, however, a prompt and decisive victory was the more necessary else the greater man power of the Allies would in the end determine the outcome, and there was still, of course, the chance that she might crush France before Great Britain had added materially to her small standing army. *The German plan of assured victory*

But apart from its questionable strategy from the standpoint of general policy, there is no doubt that the invasion of Belgium greatly facilitated the German offensive. In the first place it enabled the Germans to get around France's strongly fortified barrier, whereas the forts on the Belgian frontier, thanks to French reliance on Belgian neutrality, were relatively weak and unlikely to be able to withstand the heavy German guns. In the second place, whereas a direct attack upon France would have involved the launching of troops through narrow river valleys flanked by steep slopes, the march through Belgium meant the traversing of a comparatively level country and where there was also plenty of room for an immense army to spread out. In the third place, instead of having to hazard a frontal attack, an invasion of Belgium offered the chance of an enveloping movement with the object of crunching the French army between the larger force coming down through Belgium and a smaller force operating from the east.   The very rapidity of this offensive, carried out chiefly through Belgium, was expected to catch the French before their full strength was mobilized and so render victory all the more certain.

Opening of the Marne campaign

But the Germans had made two miscalculations.   In the first place, the Russian mobilization had proceeded much more quickly than had been expected, and before this campaign was over, Germany had to detach two army corps to re-enforce her small body of troops in East Prussia.   And secondly the Belgians put up an unexpectedly stiff resistance.   Three days had to be consumed in taking the forts defending Liége; and as most of the Belgian forces were able to elude the invaders and take refuge in Antwerp, it was also necessary to use two corps to protect the rear of the invading army.   The delay entailed in dealing with Belgium (though only a small portion of her army had time to mobilize) was providential to the French whose mobilization had been retarded, as we have noticed, for diplomatic considerations.   It also enabled Great Britain to send a force of 100,000 men across to France, and it was this small but excellent army that held the most critical position—the extreme left wing of the Allied army— in the ensuing campaign.   As far as numbers went, the opposing armies seem to have been nearly equal; and generalship on neither side was brilliant.   General Joffre, the French chief of staff, had certainly not made the best use of his respite.   With insufficient strength he had attempted some counter-offensives, one to assist the Belgians, the other an invasion of Alsace chiefly to satisfy public opinion (and it was then that the famous statue of Strasborg in Paris was stripped of its mourning).   Joffre's attempts to snatch the offensive had only the effect of dissipating his strength, and after some sharp defeats near the Belgian frontier the Allied army was forced to retreat—though in good order, pivoting on the fortress of Verdun; while behind Verdun was the strongly fortified hill, known as the Couronné de Nancy, barring the way to a flank attack from Lorraine.   It is worth noting that the Germans, who tried desperately to dislodge the French from this position, had greatly over-rated their enemy's strength and massed a needlessly large force at this end of the line, but this only enhances the glory of General Castelnau whose gallant holding of this hill contributed powerfully to the outcome of the campaign.

The First
Battle
of the Marne

The German chief of staff, General von Moltke (nephew of the great Moltke) had undoubtedly bungled seriously in the disposition of his forces, but he continued the intended plan [1] of trying to envelop the Allied army, and the tiny British force was hard pressed by General von Kluck, who was entrusted with this maneuver. Joffre's plan was to retire until he had reached the line of the river Marne between Paris and Verdun where he had waiting some reserves ("armies of maneuver," as the French called them) by which he hoped to outflank the enemy's right wing. On September 5 he took his stand, issuing his famous order: "The time has come to advance at all costs and to die where you stand rather than give way." With one of his armies of maneuver he struck at Kluck and bent back the German line. Rallying from this assault and believing that he could pierce the enemy's lines, Kluck thrust at the point between the French and British, hoping to sever them completely and to throw the British as well as the army of maneuver back upon Paris. But the French held fairly firm and Kluck was so badly pommeled that in order to save him the Germans had to leave a breach of some thirty miles in their center, though they hoped that their plight was concealed by a thick swamp that lay between them and the enemy. The hope, however, proved vain. General Ferdinand Foch, who commanded the Allied army at this point, saw the gap in the German lines, and concentrating all available forces, made such a furious attack at this vulnerable point that he drove clear through the enemy's lines. Only by a precipitate retreat did Moltke save his huge army from a very serious disaster. The Battle of the Marne, which had occupied a week's fighting along an extended front, was won chiefly by the heroism of the French soldier and the tactical skill of Foch. It was not so complete a victory as to result in the expulsion of the invaders from France, for the Germans halted on a line which had already been dug for them some fifty miles back from the scene of battle, and there they were able to hold their enemies at bay. But it was none the less a decisive victory. It had saved Paris, the loss of which would have had a depressing effect upon the Allied cause, and it enabled the Western Powers to recover their breath, as it were, and prepare for greater exertions. Above all, it effec-

[1] Moltke followed, in general, the plan which had been drawn up by Count Schlieffen, a former chief of staff, though he altered it in certain particulars to his own disadvantage.

tively frustrated the German plan to win the War by a swift elimination of France.

The Allies hoped, of course, to drive the enemy out of France, and they made a desperate effort to turn his flank. But the Germans were too quick for them; and the result was that parallel lines of trenches were soon extending from Switzerland to the sea. The Germans were fortunate in occupying all the industrial provinces of France with their rich coal mines and the whole of Belgium save the extreme southwest corner where the Allies still held the town of Ypres. It is probable that with a little more effort the British might have saved Antwerp, but on October 8 the Germans took the city, thereby strengthening their hold on Belgium. On the other hand, Moltke had lost a great opportunity of seizing the Channel ports, while they were still undefended.

And whatever the justification of the German occupation of Belgium, it was none the less a boomerang for the occupants. In their haste and exasperation at the delays involved in Belgium's resistance they foolishly destroyed a large part of the city of Louvain (including the ancient university) on the ground that some civilians had had the temerity to fire on them. This tragic blunder did a great deal toward turning neutral opinion against Germany, and when some other atrocious acts were perpetrated (for example, the dropping of bombs on Antwerp from the air) a most effective instrument was put in the hands of the Allied governments. Wholesale tales of German atrocities were spread abroad with the effect of stimulating recruiting in England and embittering an influential section of the American public against Germany. The fact of Germany's subjugating a weaker nation and then maltreating her roused all a sportsman's instinct to protest against such crimes. In general, the German occupation of Belgium, while stern (for there was no doubt that Belgium was systematically bled for trifling offenses) was not as a rule signalized by cruelty. Some outrages no doubt took place early in the period of occupation—how many will probably never be known—but it is no longer contended that German policy, in spite of the theories of the German staff, deliberately sought to break the resolute spirit of the Belgian people by an organized system of terror.[1] The story of Belgium's "agony" was the creation of one of the most efficient

---

[1] It appears, however (since the above was written), that Mr. Cruttwell, in his recently published *History of the Great War*, does hold this view.

propaganda services ever organized. But each belligerent power was similarly served, and lies were deliberately published to influence public opinion. It is probable that never in history has so systematic an effort been made to inculcate hatred in the citizenry as a means of inspiring its energies to the utmost.

We must devote a little space to the Russian offensives in the East. A vigorous attack upon East Prussia from the side of Poland (which, as the map shows, was a huge salient projected between German and Austrian territory) promised so much success that $100,000 was raised in St. Petersburg (from the sale of enemy flags) for the first soldier who entered the German capital. It was intended, of course, to clear the flanks before pushing on to Berlin, and for that reason another Russian army penetrated Galicia, which, being on the Russian side of the Carpathians, was easy to overrun. The Russian objective was Cracow, so situated as to command a line of approach either to Vienna or to Berlin. Possession of Galicia would also rob the Central Powers of most of their oil.

Fate of the Russian offensive

But Germany did not underestimate her danger. General von Hindenburg, an aged and retired officer but one who knew intimately the peculiar terrain of East Prussia with its woods and numerous lakes, was placed in command of the defending army, and re-enforcements, as we have noted, were quickly sent from the western front. With a smaller army but relying on his thorough knowledge of the ground, he completely outmaneuvered the Russians and won the decisive Battle of Tannenberg.[1] The Russian offensive was broken and some 90,000 prisoners were taken as well as an immense number of guns and other equipment. In face of this staggering blow the Russian victory over the Austrians seemed of small avail. Yet if the Russians could completely clear Galicia, there was some chance of an invasion of Germany from that direction; and by the end of the year about half of that province was in their hands. An advance of Hindenburg into Russia had meanwhile failed.

But apart from the success of the Russians against Austria the Allies were thrown almost completely on the defensive. Germany

---

[1] Contrary to the usual accounts, Capt. Liddell Hart explicitly withholds credit for this victory from Hindenburg, whom he seems to regard as pretty much of a figure-head throughout the war. He gives the chief credit for Tannenberg to Ludendorff and especially his staff officer, Hoffmann, though he also thinks that the whole Russian offensive had been too precipitate and ascribes its defeat more to the exhaustion of the Russian army and the bungling of its two commanders than to the strategy or tactics of the Germans.

was strongly entrenched in the northeast corner of France, and was still in a better position than the Allies to take the offensive.

The Period of Germany's Military Ascendancy

Ypres—the failure of the Germans to reach the Channel

After the campaign of the Marne the only offensive effort for some time on the part of Germany in the west was an attempt to take Ypres and break through to the Channel ports—a feat that if successful would have driven a wedge between the French and British and made it difficult for Great Britain to pour any troops into France. It was only with the most heroic tenacity that the British forces, greatly outnumbered, held their position. A second effort was later made to force the lines at Ypres but again the Germans were foiled.

Collapse of Russia

In general, however, Germany was content to rest for a time on the defensive in the west, confident of being able to hold her strong position while she turned to deal with Russia. In October Hindenburg had been appointed commander of the entire Austro-German forces operating on the eastern front, and he was given re-enforcements detached from the army in the west. After some initial failures the Germans won the honors in a hard campaign. The Battle of the Dunajec in April, 1915, resulted in the expulsion of the Russians from Galicia, and the Polish salient was then pinched and Warsaw taken. The Germans carried their lines well into Russia, and by straightening them out as they could do after the conquest of the Polish salient, they managed to defend their position with a smaller number of troops, hence sparing some strength to send back to the western front. The Russian commander, the Grandduke Nicholas, had succeeded in extricating his army without serious disaster, but Russia was none the less soundly beaten, and save for an occasional spurt, was thrown permanently on the defensive. Her defeat was due not only to the superior quality and organization of the German forces but also largely to the fact that her army was inadequately supplied with guns and shells. While it is true that the war ministry was singularly incompetent, much of this shortage was due to the fact that Russia had never possessed munition plants in sufficient numbers to carry on a great war, and, owing to the German blockade of the Baltic and to the closure of the Straits by Turkey, there was no way of getting herself replenished from outside.

It was this fact chiefly which prompted Great Britain and

France (the idea was British) to send an expedition to force the Dardanelles, though a secondary object was the hope of inducing the neutral Balkan states, once Constantinople was captured, to add their strength to the Allied cause. For some reason Russia herself played no part in the affair, though a simultaneous push into the Bosphorus would have greatly increased the prospect of success. As it was, the expedition was hazardous, for the Straits were thoroughly mined and strongly fortified, and battleships are as a rule no proof against forts well furnished with heavy guns. An effort to force the Straits with naval forces alone failed dismally. Then an attempt was made to land soldiers to storm the Turkish batteries in conjunction with the warships in the Straits, but again the result was vain. One historian is reminded of many former efforts of British strategy to attack far distant points without properly estimating the difficulty or even the value of the object immediately sought. "The history of Britain," he writes, "is strewn with the wrecks of divergent operations." Yet, broadly speaking, the strategy of this exploit was not unsound, for success would have done much to put Russia on her feet, and even before the Dunajec Russia was bound to require aid before very long. The objection to the expedition lay in the fact that to succeed it would have required a tremendous concentration of forces. Naval authorities had disapproved of the project, which was inspired by politicians. The same influences accounted for the sending of the Anglo-French army to Saloniki, though it was then too late to save Serbia (already crushed by an Austrian invasion), and, as it turned out, the equivocal attitude of Greece held the army fast to its base for nearly three years. Accordingly such efforts did not avail to keep Bulgaria from entering the War on the side of Germany and did not encourage Roumania or Greece to join forces with the Allies. Whether it was their fault or not, the Allies' policy in the Near East was a total failure. It was not till 1916 that Roumania entered the War—only to be speedily crushed. Meanwhile through Turkey and Bulgaria Germany preserved direct connection with Asia Minor and Mesopotamia, and a British attempt on Bagdad in December, 1915, failed miserably.

Almost the only encouragement that the Allies drew from this period of the war is to be credited to British sea power—the bottling up of the German navy, the driving of Germany's commerce from the seas, and the loss of all her colonies. Italy, it is true, had

Failure of Allied policy in the Near East

An exhausting deadlock

entered the War in May, 1915, but any advance on Austria was exceptionally difficult, as it meant campaigning in the mountains with the Austrians strongly entrenched on higher ground. In May, 1916, an Austrian counter-offensive was attempted, but, thanks to a Russian diversion in Galicia, it failed to do more than recover lost ground.

The year 1916 was simply a continuation of the stalemate.[1] Germany retained her grip on the western front, and attempts to dent her lines were costly and futile. Yet Germany herself was hardly more successful. Partly in order to anticipate an Allied offensive (for the Allied armies had now artillery in abundance), the Germans struck with furious force at Verdun with the hope either of capturing a key point or, by tempting the French to rally all their army in its defense, to deal it so crushing a blow that the Allies could never recover. In this four months' battle the casualties were appalling (the defenders lost even more heavily than the assailants), but the German effort failed, and the Allies breathed again. It is possible that the entry of Roumania into the War (which occupied a large German army) and a British diversion (the Battle of the Somme) were contributive causes of Germany's defeat, but fundamentally it was due to the desperate courage of the French army. That dogged resolve, "They shall not pass" had won for the French soldier eternal glory.

But a heroic defense does not mean winning a war, and 1917, as it turned out, was no more decisive than 1916. It seemed for the Allies the darkest period of the War. It is true that the United States entered the lists, but it was not expected that she would be in a position to render aid for a long time. Then Revolutionary Russia found the task of rehabilitation too great for her capacity, and in the autumn she took steps which portended her withdrawal from the War. This meant, of course, that Germany could now concentrate on the western front. In the meantime, a terrific Austro-German drive had been launched against Italy. After dealing the Italians a crushing defeat at Caporetto (October, 1917), the invaders were able to penetrate the Venetian plain. Not even had the Russians been routed more completely. But with French help the Italians finally managed to rally, and their brave stand

---

[1] It was in May, 1916, that a German fleet attempted to take the British off their guard and to annihilate a part of their fleet in the North Sea. The Battle of Jutland, as it is called, failed of its purpose, however, and the German navy did not again take the offensive.

in the Battle of the Piave may be compared to the Anglo-French resistance on the Marne. The enemy had, in fact, spent his strength. Again had decisive victory eluded the Central Powers.

Much of the ease with which the Austro-German army had mowed its way into Italy was due to what has been called "defeatism"—a spirit of revolt against the War and a willingness to accept at least a compromise rather than struggle on any longer. It was a sort of caving in behind the lines but so insidious that even the lines themselves were partially affected. While the contagion was perhaps most serious in Italy, all nations suffered from it during this trying year. Austria even attempted to make a separate peace with France, and subsequently the new foreign minister, Count Czernin, told the Emperor Charles I (grandnephew and successor of Francis Joseph, who had died in 1916) that "the burdens laid upon the population are assuming proportions that are unbearable." Even in Germany the chancellor under pressure from the reichstag was compelled to make a peace feeler, though his remarks were very general and chiefly significant as a symptom of the strain behind the lines. In France the spirit of defeatism reached the stage of mutiny in certain divisions, and a widespread propaganda seemed to be sowing disloyalty and discontent. It was to curb this tendency that Clemenceau was made premier, for this "tiger of France" was a man of unquenchable spirit and able to meet a danger, however grave, without flinching. Meanwhile Great Britain was facing the gravest crisis of the War. The submarine had so crippled British commerce that the food supply of the nation was imperiled. With time she could build enough destroyers to obtain the upper hand, but the present German assault—another of those stupendous efforts by which Germany sought to eliminate a foe—was painfully near succeeding. Poignant appeals were made to America to send destroyers and other craft without delay. "Destroyers," wrote Balfour to Wilson, " . . . are required now and in as great numbers as possible. There is no time for delay." The British public was never aware of the acuteness of the crisis, but war-weariness in England was very pronounced (a certain element beginning to talk of "peace by negotiation"), and though conscription had been pretty generally enforced, it was not applied to Ireland, which had been seething with revolt throughout the year. The saying that it is always darkest before dawn was certainly borne out by Allied fortunes in 1917.

Yet there were a few glimmers of light on the horizon. America did rouse herself and sent the naval aid the British required. Italy did recover her confidence. And in March, 1917, a British force had entered Bagdad. Such a feat had no effect on the general situation, but it seemed to rob Imperial Germany of her chosen "place in the sun."

THE TRIUMPH OF THE ALLIES

Concerted efforts of the Allies

The summer of 1918 was the turning-point. The Allies had already got a grip on themselves, and encouraged by the arrival of more and more contingents from America, they had started at the beginning of the year to lay their plans for a new offensive. The most important step which they had taken was the constitution of a "supreme war council," representing France, Great Britain, and Italy, and its first act had been the appointment of an "inter-Allied general staff," consisting of the chiefs of staff of the three armies. It was hoped by this means to secure a greater co-operation of effort and a more unified strategy than had formerly been the case. Even yet they had not appointed a supreme commander, but the time was not far distant when the British would humble their pride and make this further expedient possible.

Meanwhile, in anticipation of the military offensive, the Allies began what may be called a diplomatic offensive. Whether with this object in view or not, some of Wilson's speeches were directed against the loyalty of the German people to their government and against their tenacity in a wearing and perhaps hopeless struggle. As far back as the summer of 1917, in commenting on the German peace feeler, Wilson declared that the German government would justify itself to the people if it could secure peace on the basis of what it had gained, but that if it should fail, the people would thrust it aside; "a government accountable to the people will be set up in Germany." In a number of utterances Wilson took the view that an autocracy rather than a people had launched Germany into war and that the German people must inevitably desire now to assert themselves and obtain peace. In January, 1918 (partly in response to Russian demand) he gave further encouragement to those desiring peace by issuing his famous "Fourteen Points" the substance of which might lead Germans to realize that their enemies did not plan their annihilation. Of more immediate moment, perhaps, were some nearly simultaneous declarations of

the British premier, Lloyd George, in which he definitely disavowed
any idea of changing the structure of Germany or of destroying
the Dual Monarchy or even of expelling the Turk from Europe.
The pronouncement was obviously addressed to enemy waverers
who might have feared what an Allied peace would entail.

But the time had not yet come for these arguments to bear *Battle of*
fruit; for Germany was still unbeaten. While it is true that the *Picardy*
submarine had failed to vanquish Great Britain, she had at least
"command of the air," though in the more decisive matter of
artillery she was turning out but half as much as her enemies. In
the meantime she had been searching for the master mind that
would crown her efforts with victory. Falkenhayn, who had succeeded Moltke as chief of staff had, in turn, been relieved of his
command after the Verdun fiasco and succeeded by Hindenburg,
who had become the idol of the nation. Since, however, it came to
be doubted that a man of his years was equal to the test of a
struggle in the west, the active direction of the army was given to
General von Ludendorff, a young officer who had acquitted himself
creditably under Hindenburg in the east. Ludendorff was a capable
though rather reckless commander and a man of great energy and
confidence. It was clear to him that Germany must once again
anticipate her enemies and launch a new offensive.

Thus for the moment Germany—or at least her government and
staff—was still determined to snatch a victory. Since Austria was
on the verge of internal collapse and since with every month the
strength of the American army would increase, there was no time
to be lost. Moreover, there were ominous signs of restiveness
among the German people (especially among the working class
who suffered most from the privations due to the blockade), and
William and his advisers were beginning to feel that only by
decisive victory could the existing régime be saved. Ludendorff
has affirmed in his memoirs that the spirit of the army was excellent, and there seems to be little doubt that he was confident of
success. In any event the time had come for Germany's supreme
effort. So in March, 1918, with an army about equal to that of the
Allies he made his great thrust at the enemy's lines, seeking to
break it at the point of junction between the French and British
forces. His offensives continued until the middle of July; the
British were at one time in deadly fear of invasion; and at one
point the Germans came within forty-five miles of Paris. Three

times Ludendorff broke the enemy's lines, but each time the Allies had rallied, and the strength of the German offensive began gradually to slacken. The British had now an army of over a million men on the western front and by July the total of the American forces in France had reached 1,200,000. It was a proof of the desperate earnestness of the Allies, now chastened by severe defeat, that they at last agreed to the appointment of a supreme commander, and the one to be chosen was Ferdinand Foch. A man of exceptional daring, the hero of the Marne had also the skill to take advantage of every opportunity. No better choice could have been made.

Second Battle of the Marne

After Ludendorff's offensives had begun to peter out Foch launched his counter-offensive, and now at last it was the Germans' turn to retreat. It was noticeable that German morale had at last begun to crack. It was a different matter now when confidence in the issue had ceased to steel the hearts of the Kaiser's troops. At the first Allied advance Ludendorff saw that the game was up and to save his exhausted army a bloody disaster he implored the German government to sue for peace. When he later recovered his nerve, it was too late.

Collapse of the Central Powers

The collapse of the Central Powers was startling in its suddenness, considering the length of time that they had been holding the Allies at bay. But in the end it had been a question of endurance, and whereas the Germans had expended all their reserves, the Allies had fresh troops, as well as inexhaustible artillery, to throw into the breach. Already the strain of the War had become too much for Austria-Hungary. Her subject nationalities, always unwilling participants in the struggle, were on the verge of revolution, some of them secretly plotting their independence. Bulgaria was, however, the first to capitulate. Attacked at last by the army from Saloniki and learning that Germany was powerless to help her, she had succumbed completely to panic and demoralization. The defection of Bulgaria early in October was soon followed by that of Turkey. Meanwhile Austria sustained a smashing defeat on October 29 at the hands of Italy, which, coming on top of the successful revolt of the Czechs and Slovaks, sealed her doom. Emperor Charles had promised autonomy to his subject nationalities but the concession had come too late. On November 3, 1918 Austria-Hungary signed an armistice after what amounted to unconditional surrender.

In the meantime, the German retreat, conducted, it is true, with remarkable skill, was steadily proceeding. The invaders though fighting bravely were pressed back all along the line. All but a small portion of France was cleared, and Germany herself was now threatened with invasion. The French and British governments had hopes of a crushing victory followed by a triumphant entry into Berlin.

But the Germans were in no mood to bear defeat, and if Luden- *Conclusion of the War* dorff had not suggested an armistice public opinion would un- doubtedly have forced the government's hand. On October 3 Germany addressed a note to Wilson, asking for peace on the basis of the Fourteen Points. After some correspondence between the two and some negotiations between the Allies the terms of an armistice were agreed upon, and Germany was assured peace— more or less on the basis of the Fourteen Points. Foch, when asked why he did not press on to an invasion of Germany, made it known that he meant to secure without bloodshed all the results that he could hope to obtain by further war. Of the three chiefs of staff, only the American, General Pershing, wished to continue the War.

The terms of the armistice, drafted by Foch and accepted unconditionally, were severe and left no opening for Germany to renew the War. She had not only to retire from Belgium and what she still held of France but to permit an Allied army to occupy the Rhineland; and in addition she had to renounce what she had gained by her treaties with Russia and Roumania, release pris- oners of war, and surrender a specified amount of war material as well as her entire navy—which was promptly interned at Scapa Flow, a port of the Orkney Islands. The blockade of her coasts was also to continue—an utterly needless infliction of suffer- ing upon the civilian population, dictated not originally by Foch but apparently by the premiers of France, Great Brtain, and Italy. It was a sad beginning for the new German republic, sprung from the crash of the Empire in the last days of the war. Was it the last "atrocity" of the War or the beginning of an "atrocious" peace?

FOR FURTHER READING OR STUDY

Scott, J. F. and Baltzly, J., *Readings in European History*, chap. xiv (*passim*); Cooke, W. H., and Stickney, E. P., *Readings in European International Relations since 1879*, parts ii and iii; Bridge, W. C., *How the War Began: Being the Diary of the Russian Foreign Office;* Steed, W. T., *Through Thirty Years;* Morgenthau, H., *Ambassador Morgenthau's Story;* Repington, C., *The First World War*, 2 vols.;

Salandra, A., *Italy and the Great War; The Secret Treaties and Understandings*
(ed. Cocke, F. S.); Gerard, J. W., *My Four Years in Germany;* Bernstorff, J. H.,
My Three Years in America; French, J., *1914;* Falkenhayn, E.
von, *The German General Staff and Its Decisions;* Hindenburg, P. von, *Out of My Life;* Ludendorff, E. von, *Ludendorff's Own Story;* Burian, S., *Austria in Dissolution;* Whit-
lock, B., *Belgium: A Personal Narrative;* Negulesco, G., *Rumania's Sacrifice;*
Adam, H. P., *Paris Sees It Through;* Gibbs, P., *Now It Can be Told;* Poincaré, R.,
Memoirs, vol. ii; Churchill, W. S., *The World Crisis,* 4 vols.; Seymour, C.,
Letters and Papers of E. M. House, 4 vols.

Hayes, C. J. H., *Political and Social History of Modern Europe,* vol. ii, chap.
xxxi and pp. 711–22; Schapiro, J. S., *Modern and Contemporary European
History,* chaps. xxxiv–xxxv; Higby, C. P., *History of Modern Europe,* chap.
xxvi; Palm, F. C., and Graham, F. E., *Europe since Napoleon,* chaps. xxix and
xxx; Slosson, P. W., *Twentieth Century Europe,* chaps. x–xii, xiv *(passim);*
Benns, F. L., *Europe since 1914* (informing and reliable text, though a trifle
dull), chaps. iii–iv; Langsam, W. C., *The World since 1914* (readable text,
poorly indexed), chaps. ii–iii; Sontag, R. J., *European Diplomatic History,
1871–1932,* chap. vi.

Swain, J. W., *Beginning the Twentieth Century;* Schmitt, B. E., *The Coming
of the War,* 2 vols. (the most exhaustive study of the immediate preliminaries
of the War and the subject of considerable controversy); Renouvin, P., *The
Immediate Origins of the War* (interesting and fairly objective); Fay, S. B.,
The Origins of the World War, vol. ii; Scott, J. F., *Five Weeks: The Surge of
Public Opinion on the Eve of the Great War;* Seton-Watson, R. W., *Sarajevo*
(strongly pro-Serb); Howard, H. N., *The Partition of Turkey: A Diplomatic
History;* Slosson, P. W., *The Great Crusade and After* (on the American inter-
vention); Hayes, C. J. H., *A Brief History of the Great War;* Liddell Hart,
B. H. L., *The Real War;* Cruttwell, C. R. M. F., *A History of the Great War;*
Buchan, S., *History of the Great War,* 4 vols.; Kerner, R. J., "Russia, the Straits,
and Constantinople," *Jour. Mod. Hist.,* v, 400 ff.; Golovine, N. N., *The Russian
Army and the World War;* Recouly, R., *Foch, the Winner of the War;* Lasswell,
H. D., *Propaganda Technique in the World War;* Gretton, R. H., *A Modern
History of the English People,* vol. iii; Bevan, E. R., *German Social Democracy
during the War;* Playne, C. E., *Society at War, 1914–6;* Le Bon, G., *The World
in Revolt* (psychological study); Seymour, C., *American Diplomacy during the
World War* (interesting).

XVII. THE RECONSTRUCTION OF EUROPE

1. THE PRELUDE OF THE PEACE

Rôle of Wilson; British war-aims and the Fourteen Points; Wilson's mission to Europe; Surge of public opinion on the eve of the peace conference.

2. THE CONGRESS OF PARIS AS THE AGENCY OF RECONSTRUCTION

Personnel of the Congress; Setting of the Congress; Opening of the Congress; The Congress in essence; Qualifications of the "Big Four"; Question of publicity; Idealism *vs.* practical politics; Claims of France—Struggle and compromise; Problem of security and Wilson's position; The questions of reparations; Obstacles to an equitable peace: (1) public opinion, (2) the secret treaties; Dissensions in the Congress: (1) claims of Italy, (2) claims of Japan.

3. THE PEACE TREATIES

A. THE TREATY OF VERSAILLES

Preliminary arrangements; Basic principles and terms; Criticism; Significance.

B. THE TREATY OF ST. GERMAIN

Situation of Austria; Provisions of the treaty; Plight of Austria.

C. THE TREATY OF TRIANON

Vicissitudes in Hungary; Terms of the treaty; Position of Hungary.

D. THE TREATY OF NEUILLY

E. THE TREATIES OF SÈVRES AND LAUSANNE

Problem of solving the Eastern Question; Question of Constantinople; Question of Smyrna; Treaty of Sèvres; Insurgence of Anatolia and breakdown of the treaty; Treaty of Lausanne; New position of Turkey.

4. NATIONALIST PROBLEMS AND THEIR SOLUTION

Triumph of nationalism in the War; Difficulties in the way of solution; Compromise decisions: (1) plebiscite zones, (2) case of Upper Silesia, (3) case of Teschen, (4) Danzig and the Polish Corridor; Solutions by *faits accomplis;* A solution by negotiation: Fiume; Problem of the protection of subject nationalities; The mandate system for backward peoples; Neglect of the economic factor.

5. THE LEAGUE OF NATIONS

Origins; Establishment; Machinery; Value; Limitations.

6. THE DEFECTION OF THE UNITED STATES

American reaction against Europe; Eclipse of Wilson; Triumph of isolation.

The Great War, like other great European wars, resulted in much territorial reshaping and in many convulsive changes, political and social. To what extent the work of reconstruction would follow the accustomed dictum that to the victor belongs the right of sitting in judgment upon the vanquished, or in what degree it might reflect a more dispassionate and equitable spirit would depend in great measure upon public opinion, which, now that the dictation of the military leader was at an end, would express itself through the diplomat and the statesman. For the peace-makers of 1919, not being despots like their prototypes of 1814, had always to reckon with the sentiments of the millions whom they represented, and if in their assumption of leadership they should prove to possess the courage to guide or correct or enlighten those teeming millions, they would pass a test of statesmanship almost without precedent in history. But it was those very millions, those generators of public opinion, who had passed the ordeal by fire. Could one hope for better than a compromise peace at best? It is only too obvious that, as nationalism had fought the war, nationalism would try to dictate the peace. If we bear in mind that morality is usually subjective, we shall approach the peace from the correct angle. One need not have been a particularly astute prophet to forecast the general character of the peace, nor a fatalist to say that it was practically inevitable that it would be exactly what it turned out to be. There is a logic of history that not only explains the acts of men but forces us to regard them with a certain measure of charity. Let us, then, approach the peace from the standpoint of the nations and national leaders who were to shape it.

The Prelude of the Peace

The rôle of Wilson

To the belligerents peace had no allurements during the first three years of the War. Each side was only content with a decisive victory, and such was hard to obtain. We have mentioned the efforts of the United States as a neutral power to find a common ground for ending the struggle. From neither side had Wilson found much basis for encouragement. Germany was satisfied that she would ultimately win the War and delighted in thinking of the terrible terms she would wring from her vanquished foes; and the Allies, for their part, fighting mostly on the defensive, knew that they could not expect a victorious peace until they had first expelled the enemy from France. The Pope was no more fortunate than Wilson in bringing the nations to terms. There was little chance of peace until one side or the other had won a decisive victory.

Still Wilson remained as the one great leader who, looking beyond the hatred and carnage of war, hoped to find the basis of a solid and durable peace. An unswerving believer in democracy, he felt that if only the people were to assert themselves and overthrow autocracy everywhere in Europe, peace would be assured and the millenium would come. It was characteristic too of a champion of democracy that he stood outspokenly for nationalist "self-determination"—the right of a nationality to shape its own fortunes, and, if living in subjection, to be free. But contrary to the usual type of nationalism, which viewed even moral questions through narrow lenses, Wilson expressed his firm belief that a durable peace could only be built on broad principles of justice. There must be a "peace without victory," he told congress shortly before the United States entered the War, for "only a peace between equals can last." And again later he declared, "Punitive damages, the dismemberment of empires, the establishment of selfish and exclusive economic leagues we deem inexpedient and in the end worse than futile, no proper basis for a peace of any kind, least of all for an enduring peace." In his broad, catholic outlook Wilson was essentially an internationalist. One is reminded of the analogous rôle of the Czar Alexander I after the Napoleonic wars, but Alexander had proved a flabby leader and his standpoint had been that of a benevolent despot rather than of a man who sought the approval of the people. Yet the creed of internationalism, strained and tempered as it had been through a century of meddling and muddling by the Concert of Europe, could hardly be thought of in 1917 as a sturdy plant. If the World had appreciated Wilson, History would have lost her true character. One cannot span a cycle in a single stride.

The talk of "peace without victory" naturally did not appeal to powers who had sacrificed so much for a cause in which they had staked everything to win. During the year 1917, when the entrance of the United States into the War gave rise to a new confidence, there was at first little thought of peace on the side of the Allies, and there is much reason to doubt if some overtures from Germany were more than a bit of temporizing, prompted solely by pressure

British war-aims and the Fourteen Points

from the reichstag. Yet 1917 proved a dreary year for both sides, as we have noticed, and it was probably the outspoken desire of the labor element for peace, together with the spread of defeatism in England, France, and Italy that moved Lloyd George on January 5, 1918 to announce the position of his government on the subject of peace. We have already noticed the value of these remarks as a diplomatic offensive. He stated emphatically that the British Empire was not fighting to undo the existing organization of Germany or to procure the dissolution of Austria-Hungary or the expulsion of Turkey from Europe, but he declared (though his language was not very explicit) for recognition of the nationalist rights of Czecho-Slovaks, Roumans, Jugoslavs, and Arabs, and he insisted on the restoration of Alsace-Lorraine to France and the liberation of unredeemed Italy. As he had done before in reply to a note of Wilson's in 1916, he demanded full reparation—not indemnities but damages for losses. Such was a charter of justice, which if national or nationalist in viewpoint, was at least not immoderate in its tone. But already Wilson, prompted largely by the demands of Revolutionary Russia for explicit terms of peace, had drafted with the help of House a more comprehensive statement of the conditions which he thought the Allied and Associated Nations should offer the Central Powers as a basis of peace. These terms were the famous "Fourteen Points," and they deserve to be given here in substance:

1. Open covenants openly arrived at. Diplomacy always in the public view.

2. Absolute freedom of navigation outside of territorial waters alike in peace and in war except by international action.

3. Removal as far as possible of all economic barriers.

4. Adequate guarantees that armaments will be reduced to lowest point consistent with national safety.

5. Absolutely impartial adjustment of all colonial claims with strict observance of the principle that the interest of the populations concerned will have equal weight with the claims of the governments.

6. Evacuation of Russia.

7. Evacuation and restoration of Belgium.

8. Evacuation of France and the wrong done to her in the matter of Alsace-Lorraine to be righted.

9. Readjustment of the frontiers of Italy along clearly recognizable lines of nationality.

10. The peoples of Austria-Hungary to have autonomy.

11. Roumania, Serbia, and Montenegro to be evacuated, and Serbia assured access to the sea.

12. The Turkish portions of the Ottoman Empire to be assured sovereignty and the non-Turkish peoples to receive autonomy. The Dardanelles to be internationalized.

13. An independent Poland to be erected with territories inhabited by Poles and assured access to the sea.

14. An association of nations to afford mutual guarantees of political independence and territorial integrity.

In making these proposals Wilson was gratifying his missionary ardor and hoped with all sincerity to found an enduring peace. Such a maneuver had the advantage of giving the Central Powers an idea of what they might expect as the price of peace, and if they were sufficiently pressed, they might prefer it to the possibility of worse. Public opinion in the Allied countries was divided in its impressions. While radical organs praised the document unstintingly, the more conservative papers were disposed to feel suspicious of its indefiniteness, and British opinion, generally, felt uncertain about the "freedom of the seas."

Nevertheless, it was on the basis of the Fourteen Points, imperfect as they were, that Germany sued for peace, and on the understanding that they would be observed that she signed the armistice. The Allies, for their part, may not have relished being committed in advance by the United States on the basic terms of peace, but the only objection seems to have come from the British who feared that "freedom of navigation" might be intended to deprive them of the use of the blockade in time of war. The British government therefore announced its freedom of action on that point and also stipulated that reparations should cover "all damage done to the civilian population of the Allies and their property by the aggression of Germany by land, by sea, and from the air." These reservations were understood by Germany before she surrendered. As a matter of fact, though it was not known to the general public, many of the Fourteen Points had been considerably qualified by an official commentary, which, we are given to understand, received Wilson's own approval. Thus, contrary to the general belief and to the impression given by the President's eulogists, the Fourteen Points were not construed to demand open diplomacy, the general abolition of tariffs, the reduction of armies to the figures required for police purposes, or the preservation of all the German Tyrolese to Austria. As to the matter of the "freedom of the seas," the commentary seems to beg the whole question.

Such compromising before the battle of interests commenced may be criticized from the standpoint of strategy, but one may guess that Wilson had not worked out his ideas very precisely, and his main preoccupation was the desire, above all things, to get established a league of nations to enforce peace. It was probably mainly for this purpose that he planned to attend the peace conference in person as America's leading delegate. He was strongly advised by friends and close associates not to take this step, as it was feared that he would lose in influence by leaving the vantage point of distance and parleying with men who knew the European situation better than he; but having made up his mind, he refused to change it, and apparently flattered himself that he would be chosen president of the conference. When told that his decision met with disapproval in France and England (these powers may well have feared his moral weight with the masses) he was greatly disappointed, but his resolution to go remained unchanged.

That, judging by results, the decision was a blunder has been generally recognized. The effect upon his position in the conference and upon his interests at home will be noticed later. A more immediate effect was to quash the idea of a preliminary peace, which House had urged. Such a peace in broad outlines would very probably have averted many catastrophes in Europe growing out of uncertainties and delays, but Wilson having resolved to take the trip decided first to address congress, and this meant to postpone his departure till December. It must be stated, however, in justice to Wilson, that the armistice had come so suddenly that the Allies had only a very general notion of what they intended to demand, and there was enough room for disagreement to make even a preliminary understanding very difficult. When the French with their usual precision finally drafted a tentative program as a basis for discussion (a program much more definite than the Fourteen Points), it was rejected by both Wilson and Lloyd George, and this failure to get down to business was destined still further to delay the peace. It should be added, too, that neither France nor Great Britain was disposed to accept Wilsonian dictation, and they knew that their hands were tied by secret treaties already made with some of their allies during the War.

The entry of Wilson into the Old World was signalized by a welcome seldom accorded to a public figure. During his journeys in England, France, and Italy he was greeted by tumultuous crowds wherever he showed himself. To those who looked for a new era more favorable to the masses and free from all taint of militarism the President seemed to have come as a new messiah. Superficially one might say that no one has ever had a greater opportunity.

Yet it is undoubtedly true that underneath this effervescence of enthusiasm was a very different feeling. A large proportion of the people in France and England and Italy were now intent upon punishing the guilty and recouping losses. In England in December the premier, Lloyd George, and his colleagues in the government made their fight for re-election on the plea of "Hang the Kaiser and make Germany pay for the war." And in France the uppermost thought was to obtain reparation for the colossal losses sustained. In both countries it was felt that militarism was concentrated in Germany and that for the sake of future peace she must be permanently dismembered and disarmed. It was all a sort of emotional torrent, born of years of patient suffering, and now breaking the dam which long uncertainty of the outcome had held in check. And it was in this vindictive atmosphere—unfortunate but quite intelligible—that the Congress of Paris was to begin its work. That its leading members should reflect this sudden exsurgence was practically inevitable.

Surge of public opinion on the eve of the Peace Conference

The Congress of Paris as the Agency of Reconstruction

The great congress which was to liquidate the War and usher in the reign of peace and justice opened its sessions at Paris on January 18, 1919. The French capital had been selected partly because of convenience but chiefly in order that Germany might obtain her retribution in the very place, even in the very building (that is, the palace of Versailles) where she had celebrated the humiliation of France in 1871. It is manifest that whatever measure of justice would be shown the vanquished nations would depend on the quality of mercy and the degree of foresight present in the victors; for, unlike most treaties which had followed wars, this peace was not to be a subject of negotiation but framed in advance by the victors and handed to prostrate enemies. The Congress was made up of representatives of the twenty-seven Allied

Personnel of the Congress

and Associated Powers. Absent from the list was, of course, Russia, since she had long ago deserted the Allied cause, though the question of what to do with Russia, now the hearth of a revolution of a peculiarly virulent type, had harassed the leading diplomats and even elicited their action before the Congress itself had begun its sittings. Absent also were representatives of the beaten powers, now awaiting anxiously their deserts. The Congress of Paris was never an areopagus of sages, chosen from the world at large to make peace on the basis of a study of the habits of men and nations. And we have already described the atmosphere in which it had its birth.

Setting of the Congress   But this was not all of the setting. There was a spirit of earnestness about the Congress of Paris that had been lacking in the Congress of Vienna. The city teemed with commissions; for some of the delegations, notably that of the United States, had corps of experts working laboriously to sift the topographical, ethnological, and other data which might enable them to suggest to the Congress the fairest drawing of national frontiers. Never, to all appearance, was there to be such a scientific peace. Moreover, the delegates took their rôles far too seriously to waste their time in lavish parties and pageants, as had been the case with that earlier conclave; and it is probable that there was less intriguing in the background than had been the case at Vienna in 1814. But Paris was crowded with outsiders. Besides the delegates and their retinues and the various commissions to assist them (all these amounted to several thousand persons), there were hordes of newspaper men, and any number of persons who flocked to the city in the wake of the more important personages just to be within range of the great show. During the evenings the cafés were full of people who seemed to have plenty of money to spend, and one needed plenty of money, as the cost of living had mounted by leaps and bounds. These pleasure hunters formed a sort of fringe of the Congress, sometimes, indeed, absorbing one of its members, and the favorite pastime seemed to be dancing, for which there was everywhere a rage just after the War. Meanwhile it was a motley crowd that jostled each other in the corridors of the Palais du Quai d'Orsay where the Congress held its sittings—Jews from Palestine, Bolsheviks and Russian reactionaries, Koreans, negroes from Africa, and strange people in stranger dress from the Caucasus and western Asia. Every little potentate of ever so small a country rising out of the fortunes or misfortunes of war seemed to feel that from the Congress the aspirations of his "nationality" would find sympathy. It was the problem of seeing so many deputations that inflicted the heaviest strain on the man who had the misfortune to be regarded as a kind of magician—Woodrow Wilson. Yet already his star was on the wane. For Paris is not conducive to quixotic ideals.

Since the Congress met in Paris, France was in a sense the host, and it was Poincaré, her president, who formally opened it. Portraying the War as a "crusade of humanity" and proclaiming its results "the victory of right," he wound up his address by indicating the direction along which its work should proceed. "This very day," he said, "Forty-eight years ago, on the 18th of January, 1871, the German Empire was proclaimed by an army of invasion in the Château at Versailles. It was consecrated by the theft of two French provinces. It was thus a violation from its origin and by the fault of its founders was born in injustice. It has ended in oblivion. You are assembled in order to repair the evil that has been done and in order to prevent a recurrence of it. You hold in your hands the future of the world. I leave you gentlemen to your grave deliberations and declare the Congress of Paris open." Clemenceau, the French premier, was then nominated for president of the Congress and chosen by acclamation. The following day the assembly began the burden of its labors. *Opening of the Congress*

But it must not be supposed, in spite of Poincaré's exhortation to the men "who held in their hands the future of the world;" that this body, representing twenty-seven nations (from the British Empire down to the little negro republic of Liberia), was really the one to found and shape the new order. Without any mandate from any one, the Great Powers at once usurped the right of determining the settlement. The delegations representing France, Great Britain, Italy, Japan, and the United States quickly assumed an eminence not granted to any of the rest. It was felt that they alone had made the War decisive and that smaller fry like Poland and Roumania must take what they would give them. Besides, so large a body as the Congress of Paris in its entirety would have been much too unwieldy to accomplish this difficult task with tact and expedition. Hence the president of the United States and the premiers of the other Great Powers, together with the ministers or secretaries of foreign affairs formed a Council of Ten, which *The Congress in essence* took upon itself the burden of pointing the way. But not for long. Efforts to preserve secrecy in even as small a group as this proved unavailing, and about the middle of March it was decided that the president of the United States and the premiers of Great Britain, France, and Italy should meet alone and decide all paramount questions. Their decisions, it is true, were supposed to receive the approval of the Congress as a whole, but this formality was seldom taken seriously, and in all the Congress as such held but six plenary sessions. The Congress in essence consisted of Wilson, Lloyd George, Clemenceau, and Orlando. Four old men to build a new world!

Qualifica-
tions of the
"Big Four" None of the four was a diplomat by profession, but three of them at least were exceptional men. Orlando had a legal mind and no one of the four could make a clearer exposition of a problem, but as his country was but little concerned in the fate of Germany and seldom looked beyond its own peculiar interests, he took the least active part in the deliberations. Lloyd George was an exceedingly astute politician who relied on explosive eloquence and a witty and engaging "bluff" to carry his points. He never scrupled to shift his position when expediency seemed to demand it, and was essentially an opportunist. Like Gladstone, he had never given much attention to foreign affairs, and for the most part leaned heavily on Balfour, the British foreign secretary, for information and reasoned judgment. Wilson was even less informed of conditions in Europe, and had the disadvantage of possessing a mind that usually dwelt in the abstract. Whether it is true, as one observer says, that he actively instigated many of the decisions or, as another witness declares, he was inclined to drift and leave the initiative to others can probably not be settled. When vitally interested in a cause, however, he displayed exceptional charm and force in presenting his views and the tenacity of a true Calvinist in fighting for them. And no one at the Congress labored harder. Because of the detachment which clung to the chief magistrate of a non-European power, he had to receive appeals from innumerable nations, deputations, and individuals, and it is remarkable that under such a burden he kept his equanimity. But such a strain may have affected the quickness of his mentality, and Lansing noted a nervous mannerism which the President had never exhibited before. Of the four Clemenceau was easily the most skillful in maneuver. While he could bully an opponent if he chose—and his

treatment of the Congress and particularly the small nations was merciless at times—he had the sagacity to handle his associates of the inner council with the utmost tact and consideration. He was an exceedingly good judge of character and seemed to know just when and to what extent he might hope to win and when he must yield a point. In his judgments there was a precision and definiteness that proved an effective weapon against the superficial meanderings of Lloyd George, the legal subtleties of Orlando, or the euphemistic postulates of Wilson. He had also the advantage of being the one person of the four who spoke both French and English fluently, and he was easily the best informed on European questions. Wilson was at his best when he thundered from Olympus whereas Clemenceau and Lloyd George were in their element when sparring directly with men, and Clemenceau, unlike Wilson, knew exactly what he wanted. And no illusions troubled the processes of his thinking. He was a realist to the core.

It was for that reason that Clemenceau felt no interest in trying *The question of publicity* to found a new order, and clung to the old and well-tried methods of diplomatic bargaining. Had Wilson not explained that his "open covenants openly arrived at" meant nothing but "open covenants," there would doubtless have been contention over whether secrecy should be preserved or abandoned in the proceedings. Neither Clemenceau nor Lloyd George favored publicity in treaty-making, and it was decided to admit the scions of the press merely to the plenary sessions of the Congress. On the proceedings of the Council of Ten only a bald minute was to be issued, though it was found that so many of its papers reached the press and that so much information leaked out through the French foreign office that the smaller body, the Council of Four, soon came to supersede it, as we have said. Of what went on among the Four little was known; and the treaties of peace were brought to completion before any of the terms were transmitted even to the small nations, which in some particulars were vitally concerned. The secrecy of proceedings had the disadvantage that when journalists were forbidden access to deliberations they grasped what snatches of information came their way and often dished up gossip and rumors as the truth. Yet it is easy to see the disadvantage of discussing delicate and controversial points in the open; and a veritable hubbub might have been caused by the opinions, let us say, of Lloyd George on the subject of Poland. In the face of the instability and (in some cases) the self-interest of public opinion "open diplomacy" would have greatly complicated the task before the peace-makers and probably delayed results. Yet it is not too much to say that the secrecy which enshrouded the Congress of Paris made an enemy of the press and weakened to some extent the moral strength of the whole settlement.

Idealism vs. *practical politics*   The one to lose most from lack of publicity was Wilson, whose honest efforts for an enlightened peace might otherwise have won the continuous backing of American opinion and thus averted the future loss of his popularity. But it must not be supposed that the press was predominantly liberal or disinterested, for some of the most influential organs were the most rampant against Germany and in nearly all the European papers national interests had come to the fore, regardless of who was to pay the cost. Moreover, the President's greatest triumph—the Covenant of the League of Nations and its incorporation in the German treaty—had one unfortunate aspect. Out of deference to Wilson the project of a league had been put first on the agenda of the Congress, but the discussion of this intricate innovation, as well as Wilson's trip to America to explain it, naturally postponed considerably the completion of the German treaty (and in consequence the other treaties) with the result that Europe fell into chaos, wracked by currency inflation, communist epidemics, and petty wars. The plight of Germany, still aggravated by the Allied blockade and by the uncertainties involved in "reparations," was worse than it had been during the War.

Whether Wilson's faith in the League was justified is also to be questioned. That it was the finest and most constructive achievement of the Congress may well be conceded. The most fundamental problem before the world was that of security, in other words, the preservation of peace, and Wilson's aim was to provide a means far more efficacious than the readjustment of national frontiers or the disarmament of a single country. But that such an organization as he had in mind would be given sufficient power and support to guarantee eternal peace between the Great Powers one might reasonably have doubted. Its serious limitations we shall later attempt to show. Suffice it to say here that Clemenceau, for his part, was too old and too cynical to find in it the bulwark France so sorely needed. It can thus be seen that on the fundamental question of security there was bound to be divergence from the start.

What, then, did France require to insure her against a future attack from Germany? Before the Congress had begun its meetings Marshal Foch (for he had thus been rewarded for his great services) had addressed a note to Clemenceau, demanding that the Rhine should be the political frontier of Germany. What government should be designed for the German districts on the left bank of the Rhine was, he felt, a matter for the Congress to determine, but he insisted that Germany should be barred from "all military access to or political propaganda in" these territories, and that, further, these lands should be held—he did not say for how long— by an Allied army of occupation. Clemenceau decided to support these proposals, and it came to be assumed that these Rhenish districts would be formed into an independent state. A movement to encourage separation from the German Empire was even tried in the lands in question. As to military occupation Clemenceau wished to set the limit at thirty years.

Apart from the restitution of Alsace-Lorraine (a foregone conclusion), a share in the German colonies, and ample material reparation, France's demands were the Rhine frontier (as above interpreted), the disarming of Germany, and the annexation of the Saar Basin, a region contiguous to Lorraine and once belonging to France but chiefly valued for its coal. On most of these questions there was little disagreement, but Wilson was strenuously opposed to Foch's proposals and to the severance of the Saar region from Germany. These matters were left unsettled while Wilson made a hurried trip to America, but on his return they were at once revived and produced an acute crisis in the Council of Four. Lloyd George supported Wilson against any creation of a "new Alsace-Lorraine" and he was also opposed to the plan of a military occupation. Wilson, for his part, was opposed not only to the transfer of the Saar Basin but even to Lloyd George's proposal that the coal mines be ceded in perpetuity to France. There were some stormy meetings. On one occasion Clemenceau accused Wilson of being pro-German and left the conference. Later Wilson let it be known that he might himself leave the Congress for good and all and return home. House wrote in his diary that "the President was thoroughly discouraged." The result was a compromise. Clemenceau yielded to the objections regarding the Rhineland, but procured the Allied occupation of three bridgeheads on the river, the demilitarization of the left bank, and a promise that

The claims of France— struggle and compromise

Great Britain and the United States would jointly pledge themselves to come to France's assistance in the event of a future German aggression. On the question of the Saar Lloyd George's compromise, as elaborated by a commission of experts, was adopted. The Saar region with its quarter of a million Germans should be placed for fifteen years under the administration of a commission appointed by and responsible to the League of Nations, after which the inhabitants should vote their own disposition, but the coal mines should belong to France with the proviso that Germany might repurchase them if and when the people should vote their return to German rule. The result was thus a compromise and it had the advantage of giving France something definite in the way of reparation.

The problem of security and Wilson's position

Obviously a congress which has to deal with national interests must necessarily be a scene of "give and take." Whereas Wilson's position was broadly objective and international (as was possible on the part of a spokesman of a disinterested power), that of his colleagues was selfishly, perhaps inevitably national. While for the question of security the League of Nations was supposed to be an adequate solution, other devices had more weight with the powers chiefly concerned.[1] The French gains we have mentioned; Italy secured a frontier which more than protected her from attack; and Great Britain was assured the confiscation of Germany's navy while she continued to retain her own traditional weapons. Why, one may ask, did not Wilson insist on defining the "freedom of the seas"? Had he made a cardinal issue of the immunity of private property at sea in time of war, it would no doubt have led to a bitter controversy with London; yet such an innovation would have marked a greater advance toward the general security than keeping the French from annexing the tiny region of the Saar. And why did he, without any investigation, consent to the transfer of the German Tyrolese to Italy, as he was also later to yield to a somewhat questionable demand of Japan? Regarding the sacrifice of the Tyrolese, a competent British observer, Harold Nicolson, declares that the President thereby forfeited the confidence of his admirers, who felt that if he could violate his principles thus easily he was "not a great or potent

---

[1] While the projected guarantees for France were little enough to provide her with adequate protection, they were an obvious blow to the prestige of the League of Nations.

man," and that with this disillusion "demoralization spread through Paris like a disease." But the clue to Wilson's actions seems to resolve itself into this: he wanted to make sure of the League of Nations (later also an amendment to the Covenant to meet American objections which he encountered on a hurried trip to America), and for the success of this major project he felt that he had to pay with certain concessions. Wilson got the League fully established, and France, Italy, Japan, and Great Britain got most of what they wanted. As to the "freedom of the seas" he satisfied his conscience with the thought that if the League were really effective the question would not arise. Wilson was not a political genius, and he took too much on himself. But he liked to think that he had solved the most vital problem—that of security.

The other outstanding problem was that of reparations.[1] It had already been decided that Germany should restore all the countries she had occupied as well as cede Alsace-Lorraine to France. It was likewise assumed that she would make ample reparation for the damages she had inflicted upon France, Great Britain, Belgium, and the United States during the War. After the Congress met, the question of defining reparations as well as that of Germany's capacity to meet them, was referred to commissions for study. On the first question there was much discussion. An earlier notion of expecting Germany to pay the whole cost of the War had happily been abandoned, but the British insisted, since their land had not been devastated, that reparations should also include pensions. The loss of a life was surely more important, Lloyd George contended, than the loss of a chimney; and his position, contrary to the advice of the American experts, was approved by Wilson [2] and finally prevailed. On the question of Germany's capacity no agreement could be reached, though some American engineers had computed the material damage wrought by Germany at $15,000,000,000, and if pensions were added to this sum it was calculated that the figure would have to be doubled. But whatever the value of these estimates, they were far below what public opinion demanded in France and England. In France which shouldered a debt of 150,000,000,000 francs

The question of reparations

---

[1] The term, "reparations" was preferred to "indemnity," because it sounded less invidious.

[2] When the American delegation told Wilson that logic was against the inclusion of pensions, he is reported to have replied, "I don't give a damn for logic. I am going to include pensions."

besides the necessity of restoring the devastated regions the one thought was to make the enemy pay to the uttermost farthing. The vindictive spirit was hardly less strong in England and with less reason because the British losses in shipping were as nothing compared with the material losses in France and the cost of her navy was not nearly so great as that of the army which France had to maintain until the peace of Europe was definitely established. Lloyd George, it is true, had been wise enough to see the folly of immoderate demands and had begun to talk moderation, but, ever the servant of public opinion, he had changed his tune completely when he sensed the mood of the British electorate, and during his campaign for re-election had actually promised as much as $120,000,000,000. For public opinion it was a moral, not a practical question at all.

The result of this explosion of public sentiment was curious. Clemenceau and Lloyd George knew that the French and British people would not be satisfied with what Germany could reasonably pay (the former had even admitted that any sum agreed on would fall below what the French expected) and they feared that if they fixed on a reasonable sum, they would at once be turned out of office—a serious thing to contemplate in view of the unfinished task. They therefore hedged and decided that the total sum should not be fixed. In vain the American delegation pressed Lloyd George not to side with Clemenceau; he was too essentially opportunist to face his own people with the facts. Accordingly, the only definite figure agreed upon was the sum of $5,000,000,000 to be paid in money or in kind [1] by May 1, 1921. Otherwise the question was shelved; and in view of future events it was probably the greatest blunder of the Congress. Since Germany had no idea how much she was eventually to pay, her moral incentive to keep her engagements was naturally vitiated and, worse still, her credit was seriously impaired. That Clemenceau was helpless in the matter is fairly evident. That Lloyd George should have acted according to his own judgment and braved the result is a debatable question. But that public opinion was primarily responsible for this folly is patent enough. It is all too easy to find individual scapegoats. The people of France and England as a whole were not in a mood to allow in some respects a rational peace.

Obstacles to an equitable peace: (1) public opinion

[1] As the Commission on Reparations should determine.

While the questions of security and reparations were the most vital to be dealt with, they were by no means all that taxed the ingenuity of these diplomats. Nationalist problems, the League of Nations, the question of devising punishment for divers enemy nationals—these will be considered presently. To a large extent the Congress leaned on the work of commissions, though often results were achieved in summary fashion, as when Clemenceau drew on a map the "historic frontiers" of Bohemia without any regard for ethnological features. In any question of doubt the enemy had to pay.

It is easy to see that the Congress with all its paraphernalia of learning was by no means minded to shape an equitable peace, and it should be added that even if public opinion had allowed them to view things broadly, the free judgment of the Congress, or rather that of the Council of Four, was somewhat precluded by secret treaties into which the Allies had entered during the War. France and Russia had agreed to stand on the Rhine frontier for France and Russian possession of Constantinople; Italy and Roumania had been promised certain territories in order to make sure of their coming into the War; and Japan had also received promises in order to insure her loyalty to the common cause.[1] Such procedure may be criticized as premature and as not allowing for various factors that would eventually deserve study in a final settlement. Yet the making of such deals was quite in accordance with custom and if we can place ourselves in the position of those who contracted them we may be compelled in all fairness to modify our strictures. When the (now defunct) Franco-Russian agreement was signed, the consensus of opinion in Europe was that the enemy if beaten must pay the victors with ample concessions. Such was the verdict of history, and one does not revolutionize ethics in a moment. Furthermore, a division of spoils in advance helped to preclude any serious wrangle when the time came to make the final settlement at a peace conference. Most of the secret treaties were a matter of practical politics. It was important to keep Japan loyal and the transfer of the German holdings from one power to another did not involve any new encroachment upon China, whose sovereignty had long been a fiction. The promises to Italy and Roumania are the easiest of all to justify since the support of these powers was needed in a critical situation, and,

(2) The secret treaties

[1] See page 650, note.

superficially at least, their gains were to be wrested from an enemy power. Such transactions were typical of the spirit of secret barter which had always characterized international politics, but from the standpoint of France and England they did not denote more than the solution of certain ugly but practical problems. It is manifest, however, that they restricted from the outset Wilson's opportunity of following broader principles. True, they should not have been a shock to him, for it is fairly certain that he had knowledge at least of the treaty with Italy before he came to the Congress; but they unquestionably added to his difficulties, and his efforts to circumvent them threatened the Congress with disruption.

Dissensions in the Congress: (1) the claims of Italy   By the secret Pact of London Italy had been promised all the lands occupied by Italians at the head of the Adriatic, a portion of Dalmatia, the southern Tyrol clear through the Brenner Pass, the port of Valona in Albania, the Dodecanese (which she was then occupying), and territorial acquisitions in Asia and Africa that would approximate such gains as might be made by France and England. Some of these spoils would have involved the incorporation of several hundred thousand non-Italians, but as most of them were subjects of Austria-Hungary and some of them were fighting in her armies, it is doubtful if there were any scruples harbored at the time. The collapse of Russia, however, led Italy to reach an agreement with a committee of Jugoslavs (then looking forward to separation from Austria-Hungary) whereby the boundary between Italians and Jugoslavs should be determined along nationalists lines; this was when Italy, defeated, was glad to clutch at the hope that the Jugoslavs might weaken her powerful neighbor by revolt. Then came the dissolution of Austria-Hungary, the emergence of a new state, Jugoslavia, on the other side of the Adriatic, and the resolution of the Italian government that it would now once and for all possess the mastery of that sea. Flushed with her sudden military triumph in October, 1918, and strong in the pledges which her allies had given her, Italy entered the Congress of Paris, determined to liquidate everything that had been promised her—and more besides.

It is to be noted that the port of Fiume had not been included in the haul assured to Italy by the Pact of London. Fiume was an Italian town with a port that was predominantly Slav and—what was chiefly important—the natural outlet on the sea for both

Hungary and Jugoslavia, commanding a gap between the mountains, and the actual terminal of railways from Hungary and Croatia. Whether there had been any discussion over Fiume in 1915 we do not know; but when at the Congress of Paris Italy presented her claims, they included Fiume.

Now Wilson had declared in his Fourteen Points for readjustment of the Italian frontier along lines of nationality. Yet when he came to Paris he promised the Brenner Pass to Italy, though it involved the surrender of 230,000 sturdy German Tyrolese and despite the fact that a line drawn further south would have sufficed for Italy's protection and, while saving some of the Germans, would have rendered Austria safe from Italian attack. But when it came to Fiume he was adamant. He would not hear of Italy's having it, while Orlando, for his part, rejected a proposal that it be made a free city under the auspices of the League. Wilson also objected with reason to giving Italy as much of Dalmatia as had been promised her, though the line that he proposed would have handed her as many as 360,000 Slavs. But there was no moving Orlando. Clemenceau and Lloyd George, for their part, would gladly have supported Wilson in his contentions, but they felt their hands to be partially tied by the London Treaty, though they welcomed any arrangement that he might make. After several weeks of futile discussion Wilson took the unprecedented step of appealing over the head of the Italian government to public opinion. His language was not offensive and his reasoning seems on the whole to have been sound, but such a maneuver only infuriated the Italians, though it may have turned general opinion against them. Orlando, who was not a skillful political leader, immediately left the Congress to go home and insure his credit with the Italian people. Thus the Council of Four became for a time a Council of Three.

While the row with Italy was troubling the Congress, a rumpus was also threatened with Japan. This power, in token of her secret treaty with France and Great Britain during the War,[1] demanded the transfer of the German interests in Shantung, and though she gave an oral promise that she would eventually restore the leasehold to China, she insisted that it should first be given her by the German treaty. This position may seem illogical, but the Japanese are a sensitive people and they resented the opposition of certain

(2) The claims of Japan

[1] See page 650, note.

sections of American opinion to their appropriation of these prizes. Wilson, who had cherished the hope of seeing all leaseholds abandoned in China, insisted on direct restitution to China, but the Japanese stood firm and after several weeks of discussion began to press—a little ominously—for an immediate decision. In the end Wilson, whom House had been trying to bend to a more conciliatory policy, became genuinely afraid that Japan would bolt the Congress as Italy had done, and with two of the great Allied Powers absent from the roll the League of Nations would have had a rather sorry beginning. Hence he yielded the point. It is extremely doubtful if Japan had any intention of leaving the Congress, though a sudden change of headquarters in Paris lent color to that belief.

It is perhaps remarkable, considering the number of interests involved and the uncertain pressure of public opinion, that the Congress passed off as smoothly as it did. Even Italy came back to the fold when it appeared that her allies were able to get on without her and that without their backing she might lose her share in "reparations"; there was, besides, the problem of peace with Austria which in deference to her had been given consideration simultaneously with the German treaty.

And now what was to be the reckoning of the vanquished?

THE PEACE TREATIES

The Treaty of Versailles

The long suspense imposed on Germany while her fate was being decided was a heavy tax on the endurance of a people already suffering from shortage of food as well as economic depression.

Preliminary arrangements

If the new republic which had emerged from the wreck of the empire had turned in despair to communism, there is no telling what complications might have ensued. Happily by spring this danger was averted; and on May 7 (the anniversary of the sinking of the *Lusitania*) the completed draft of the treaty was read to a German deputation which had been summoned to Versailles for that purpose. Three weeks were than allowed the German government for making any comments they might wish to make in the form of an official statement. Naturally the Germans had plenty of objections, and they were careful to point out that the treaty did not accord with the Fourteen Points. So great, in fact, was the storm of indignation across the Rhine that Lloyd George was afraid that in the end they would not sign, and excitedly urged his colleagues to make concessions. But Wilson was greatly put out by the Germans' allusion to the Fourteen Points, to which he declared the treaty absolutely adhered, and save for allowing a plebiscite in Upper Silesia instead of handing it outright to Poland, the Council of Four stuck to the treaty as it stood.

In very truth the Germans were hesitant about submitting to so abject a surrender, and the existing cabinet resigned rather than

Drawing by Matania, from La Victoire, supplément au Panorama de la Guerre

THE GERMAN DELEGATION AT VERSAILLES, MAY 7, 1919

incur the odium of having done so. But the Congress made it clear that refusal would mean invasion, and it soon became apparent that in spite of the public outcry most Germans had decided that peace—even so humiliating a peace as this—was preferable to the risk of a renewal of war or of a communist revolution. Hence a cabinet was formed that was willing to perform the sacrifice, and two emissaries came to Versailles, where on June 28, 1919 they signed the treaty. The ceremony was performed in the very hall of the palace where France was so humiliated in 1871, and as the Germans left the palace they were hooted and stoned by a Paris mob—perhaps on the whole the most degraded element of humanity. But History will not grudge the Germans a measure of satisfaction. On the eve of the signature the German navy, which had been interned at Scapa Flow under the terms of the armistice, was mysteriously sunk, and some French flags, spoils of the War of 1870–1, which were to have been restored according to the treaty, were burned in Berlin by an excited populace. When Clemenceau, whose sense of humor never extended to the Germans, now urged a punitive invasion of the industrial region east of the Rhine, his colleagues refused assent.

Basic principles and terms   The treaty represented two main ideas: a stern and relentless justice on the basis of the assumption of German guilt and a need of protecting Europe against a revival of German ambition. Some articles of the treaty, such as those connected with reparations, really come under both heads, since they predicated Germany's duty to make good the damage she had wrought and were at the same time expected to weaken her physical power. To begin with, Germany was forced to accept responsibility for the War—a ridiculous provision, since a forced acceptance of any idea can have no weight whatever. On the score of retributive justice, as well as the principle of nationality, she was forced to restore Alsace-Lorraine to France, to give up some small districts in the west (for Belgium to acquire by plebiscite if she could)[1] and to relinquish a large block of territory in the east, most of which was handed to Poland, while certain other areas were left to be disposed of by plebiscite. She was likewise deprived of her colonies, as well as her interests in China and her investment in the Bagdad railroad.[2] She was compelled to grant certain economic privileges to the Allies without reciprocity, and to allow Czechoslovakia to lease a zone in each of two German ports. Similarly, the navigation of certain German rivers was placed under an international commission, and the Kiel Canal was declared to be open to the vessels of any nation with whom she was at peace. She was also obliged to give up (if required) all German property in Allied countries in order to liquidate Allied claims, as well as replace the merchant vessels destroyed (this was reckoned in tonnage), and make certain specified deliveries in coal to indemnify certain powers for the plunder of their mines as well as other payments in kind, all of which was to be credited on her reparation account. She was, besides, to support an army of occupation and pay a further indemnity the amount of which was to be later determined. It was,

[1] Except one little area which was ceded direct to Belgium.
[2] Strictly speaking, the investment of her nationals (condemned under the liquidation provisions), but obviously the railroad was a government interest.

finally, on the basis of an avenging justice, that the Kaiser was supposed to be handed over for trial on the charge of beginning the War, and certain specified officers, alleged to have committed atrocities, were also to be surrendered for a like purpose. It may be said here that no special effort was made to enforce this provision. Some of the minor "criminals" were eventually tried by a German court, and got off with trifling sentences. As for the Kaiser, he was safe in the sanctuary of Holland. Such provisions were an example of the hatred engendered by the War.

On the score of protection against German militarism Germany *Criticism* was limited to an army of 100,000 men including no more than 4,000 officers, and in order to prevent a continuous change in the personnel officers were required to enlist for at least twenty-five years and privates for at least twelve. Universal military service was thus abolished, and the small army allowed was enjoined to devote itself "exclusively to the maintenance of order within the territory and to the control of the frontiers." The navy was similarly reduced and the fortifications of Heligoland dismantled. No submarines for any purpose were permitted. Nor were any air forces or aircraft allowed. There were even restrictions on the manufacture of munitions. Besides all this, Germany was not to have any fortifications on the left bank of the Rhine or on the right bank within a certain distance of the river. In order to see that these measures were enforced the Allies were privileged to keep an army of occupation in the territory west of the Rhine as well as to hold three bridgeheads on the right bank for a period of fifteen years.

Such were the main provisions of the Treaty of Versailles. It was perhaps not more severe than Germany, judging her by the Treaty of Brest Litovsk, would have imposed upon the Allies, had she been successful; but it was the kind of treaty that has too often been inflicted by the conquerors on the conquered because they have had the will and the strength to impose such an instrument, and it was unworthy of an age which in less trying times had shown a real spirit of humanity. Fundamentally it may be criticized on two chief grounds. In the first place, it was, as might be expected under the circumstances, quite at variance with any broad principles of equity or justice. Economic privileges were exacted without any reciprocity. The late German colonies were to be administered theoretically under a new and enlightened régime but no such responsibility was assumed by the victor powers for colonies they already had. The principle of nationalist self-determination was supposed to justify the liberation of Poles, Alsatians, and others, but it was deliberately set at nought when it was a question of allowing German Austria to become a part of the German Republic. Finally in spite of the "absolute guarantees . . . that national armaments will be reduced to the lowest point consistent with national safety," proposed in the Fourteen Points, it may be asserted here that no appreciable progress has been made in that direction by the victor powers and there is grave reason for suspecting their sincerity. Considering that Germany understood that she was to receive a treaty based on the Fourteen Points, there is some ground for feeling that she has been treated with bad faith.

But the moral defects of the treaty are no more glaring than the practical. No great nation like Germany can submit indefinitely to discrimination in the matter of armaments and other things. Assuming also that colonies are of value to their possessors, it is not reasonable that a great people like the Germans should be barred from such advantages. Moreover, the splitting of Germany in two by the territorial cessions to Poland meant to deal her a blow from which her pride could never recover, and there was nothing better calculated to induce her to look forward to another war. Finally, those provisions which materially lessened her natural resources made utterly impossible the idea of collecting a huge indemnity, while the very uncertainty of the amount was a serious obstacle to the national recovery. One cannot starve a goose and expect it to lay golden eggs.

Significance   The Treaty of Versailles was the product of chauvinism or exaggerated national interest, prompted by bitter memories and to some extent by fear. It laid Germany low as a great power had seldom been treated before. She lost in area more than 25,000 square miles and 6,000,000 people in Europe, while her lost colonies totaled 1,000,000 square miles and an estimated population of 12,000,000. She also gave up a large part of her mineral wealth— sixty-five per cent of her iron, for example, and forty per cent of her coal—and the loss of certain of her colonies deprived her of all her rubber. There is no special need of feeling pity for a nation which had been inflated with vanity and over-devoted to its military chiefs, but in the interest of the future welfare of the world it would have behooved the Allied Powers—or more truthfully public opinion in the Allied nations—to have been more merciful.[1] The Treaty of Versailles held the germs of another war.

The treaties with Austria and Hungary (for the Dual Monarchy was split in twain) were a much less complicated affair. The dissolution of the Hapsburg empire and the downfall of the dynasty had led to the creation of two small republics, German Austria and Hungary, corresponding to most of the German and Magyar population, and shorn, of course, of all the subject nationalities. The very weakness of Austria suggested to her a revival of some sort of tariff union with the states which had emerged or become aggrandized at her expense, or, better still, a political union with Germany. But Italy put her foot down on the former proposition —she wanted nothing suggestive of the old Danubian monarchy— and it was learned that France would never approve of annexation to Germany. The Treaty of Saint Germain, signed September 13, 1919, registered Austria's losses of territory to Italy, Poland, Roumania, Jugoslavia, and Czechoslovakia. As in the case of Germany, there was an obligation to pay an unspecified sum in reparations, and certain art treasures long ago taken from Italy were to be restored. Her navy was to be surrendered, her army reduced to 30,000 men, and a list of "war criminals" indicated for trial. She was allowed free access to certain ports on the Adriatic which had formerly belonged to her, and a similar right was accorded to Czechoslovakia. Finally, lest Austria try to better her position by joining Germany, she had to promise to "abstain from any act which might . . . compromise her independence." Even the name, "Republic of Austria" was imposed upon her in place of "German Austria," which she had preferred. To this ludicrous pass had fallen the principle of self-determination!

The Treaty of St. Germain

Situation of Austria

Provisions of the treaty

There was no power more shattered by the war than Austria. Reduced to a population of about 6,000,000 with a capital numbering over 2,000,000, Austria was obviously top-heavy. She was a poor country, mountainous and relatively unproductive, yet bound to support a great metropolis. She had been left no territories on the sea, thus suffering now, like Hungary, the fate which they had once imposed upon Serbia. Much of her former wealth and splendor had been drawn from Czechoslovakia (formerly

Plight of Austria

[1] For a more favorable view of the Treaty of Versailles than taken here see Slosson, *Twentieth Century Europe*, p. 460.

Bohemia) where many of the aristocracy had held lands and which, as before remarked, had been the industrial heart of the Hapsburg realm. Now not only wealth but normal means of subsistence were cut off. Vienna, long the capital of the world of music and perhaps the leading center of medical science, as well as a city of unique charm, was now condemned to progressive decline. Truly Berchtold had put up tremendous stakes when he forced war upon Serbia in July, 1914, and terrible indeed was the cost.

The Treaty of Trianon

The treaty with Hungary was a much longer time in being prepared than that with Austria, chiefly because Hungary became a prey to internal disorders. An amendment to the armistice to the

Vicissitudes in Hungary

end of allowing Czechoslovaks and Roumans to occupy certain zones peopled almost entirely by Magyars had caused grave disquiet, and the premier, Karolyi, being unable to get satisfaction from Paris and therefore become distasteful to a people embittered by defeat, decided at length to resign, though it was evident that he was handing over his country to the communists. During the following three months Hungary passed through a terrible period marked by the communistic experiments of a Jewish adventurer, Bela Kun, and finally by war with Czechoslovakia and Roumania. The Czechoslovaks managed with the aid of the French to repel invasion and stopped at that, but the Roumanians, who were more than ready to do police duty for the Allies, eventually got quite out of hand, and, disregarding an order to halt, continued their march to Budapest, plundering as they went. The communist régime immediately collapsed, and a reactionary government was established. Hungary proclaimed herself a kingdom and was henceforth ruled by a regent, though expediency seemed to forbid the restoration of the Hapsburgs. Meanwhile, the country being pacified, she received her belated reckoning, known as the

Terms of the treaty

Treaty of Trianon, June 4, 1920, signed like the Austrian treaty in a palace near Paris. In most respects it followed the lines of the Austrian treaty. Hungary, like Austria, lost her subject nationalities and even some of her own people. The general effect of the War was not, however, as serious as was the case with her former

Position of Hungary

partner, for Hungary has at least abundant food supply. But thrust back from the sea and robbed of her former greatness, Hungary has never ceased to mourn. Three statues in a garden in Budapest, representing her lost provinces, remind one of the symbol of France's grief over Alsace-Lorraine.

Bulgaria had hoped, like Austria, to get off with an easy sentence by blaming her troubles on a previous régime. Ferdinand had abdicated, and it was insisted that he was the cause of all her woes. But the victors brushed aside her arguments, and she had to be content with a settlement which through force of circumstances was somewhat less ruinous than those which had been handed to her allies. The Treaty of Neuilly, November 27, 1919 (signed before the Treaty of Trianon) trimmed her frontiers to the advantage of Jugoslavia and especially of Greece, who extended her holdings in Thrace. This latter cession cut off Bulgaria from the Ægean—thus depriving her of the window which she had obtained in the Balkan War—though she was guaranteed an economic outlet. In the matter of an indemnity and of the size of the army the treaty followed the lines of the others. From having been the strongest state in the Balkans Bulgaria fell to the position of a third-class power. *The Treaty of Neuilly*

The reckoning with Turkey came last of all, for it had been hoped that Wilson might persuade American opinion to accept a mandate over the Turks, and there were also questions involved on which agreement proved to be difficult. Early in the War the expulsion of the Turk from Europe had been taken for granted. Now, it seemed, had come the time to mete out historic justice and solve the age-old Eastern Question. Just how it was to be solved was a more difficult consideration, but there had been general agreement that Russia should at last possess Constantinople, this object being consecrated in an inter-Allied agreement during the spring of 1915. Later on it was announced that Greece should profit largely by the expected dissolution of the Ottoman Empire, acquiring at least eastern Thrace and the Turkish islands of the Ægean; and the Arabs—who had been encouraged by Great Britain to revolt—were to form an independent state out of Arabia. Even the Armenians had been promised independence after the War. The liquidation of Asiatic Turkey had interested the Great Powers as well. By various agreements Russia, France, and Great Britain had carved out for themselves certain portions of the country as spheres of interest, and subsequently room was made for Italy. But Russia, of course, forfeited all her hopes when she "went Bolshevik" and withdrew from the War. *The Treaties of Sèvres and Lausanne*

The problem of solving the Eastern Question

The defection of Russia reopened the question of the disposition of Constantinople. It would be no solution to give it to Greece,

The question of Constantinople

since Bulgaria's antagonism would then be assured, and this would make the Balkan situation all the more difficult. And, of course, neither Great Britain nor France would allow the other to possess it. But circumstances were apparently playing to the advantage of the Turks. Lloyd George's "diplomatic offensive," as we have seen, had assured the Turks against expulsion from Europe, and Wilson's Fourteen Points had had much the same effect. It is true that after the armistice when a British naval force (much to the disquiet of the French) had taken over Constantinople, Lloyd George turned one of his frequent somersaults and said that "there must be a new porter at the gate"; and subsequently it was hoped that the United States would take a mandate over Turkey, including the Straits. But when it was made certain that American opinion would not countenance this experiment, Lloyd George and Clemenceau definitely decided that the Turks should retain the city. Great Britain had become convinced that dispossession of the Turks might be sharply resented by her eight million Moslems in India, and France felt that it might be well in view of her large holding of Turkish bonds to keep the Sultan in Europe where responsibility could be more easily fixed. Thus the question of Constantinople was to be solved by letting the Turks retain it after all.

The question of Smyrna

Meanwhile the question of the disposal of the rest of the Ottoman Empire had received a good deal of attention. The withdrawal of Russia had canceled the secret agreements, though Lloyd George had thought at one time during the Congress of buying off Italy's designs upon Fiume with something additional in Asia Minor. Unfortunately in a pinch neither France nor Great Britain wanted to part with anything, and though an Italian force had landed at Adalia in Asia Minor, it looked as if Italy, in the thick of the Fiume crisis, might lose out entirely. Then, to make confusion worse confounded, the Greeks, during Orlando's absence from Paris, made a descent upon Smyrna with the connivance of the remaining members of the Council of Four. As Smyrna was the commercial center of Asia Minor and the natural outlet for the Turks of Anatolia, its permanent possession by Greeks would seriously threaten to strangle the prosperity of these regions. It also belonged in the sphere of interest orginally allotted to Italy, who may now have begun to regret her spectacular strike against the Congress. When Orlando returned to Paris, he was assured that this maneuver did not signify anything definite, and haggling went on as before, Lloyd George now leaning toward a cession of Fiume to Italy if she would forgo all gains in Asia Minor, but no agreement could be reached. Meanwhile Balfour had pointed out that the most any of the powers could expect was a sphere of interest under the qualifying influence of a "mandate," and it was perhaps the lowered value of the stock that may account for Italy's failure to resent the intrigue with the Greeks. In any case little headway was made on the Turkish problem before Wilson took his departure and the Council of Four broke up. But it is interesting to observe that on learning of the final decision to keep the Turk in Constantinople Wilson vehemently protested—though, of course, in vain, since by this time the United States had washed her hands of Europe.

Agreement was finally reached between the other three powers in April, 1920, and the Treaty of Sèvres in August was the result. By this settlement Turkey was compelled to relinquish her remaining islands (the Dodecanese went to Italy, Cyprus to Great Britain, and the rest to Greece), cede eastern Thrace (including Adrianople) to Greece, recognize the independence of the Arabs and Armenians, and grant at least autonomy to the Kurds, a nomad people in upper Mesopotamia. Smyrna and its immediate hinterland were given to Greece to administer for five years after which a plebiscite was to be held to determine its ultimate disposition—of which there was little uncertainty, since the Greeks easily predominated. Practically all that was left to Turkey were Anatolia and the city of Constantinople with a hinterland of a few miles. Her population was reduced from twenty-one to five millions. Nor was this all. Besides the usual punitive clauses to be found in the other treaties, Turkey's finances were to be placed under the control of a commission (composed of representatives of France, Italy, and Great Britain), and the Straits (which were to be unfortified) were to be placed under the general charge of an international commission. Nothing was said in the treaty of spheres of interest, but on the same day France, Great Britain, and Italy entered a tripartite agreement, staking off their preserves. The Sultan signed the Treaty of Sèvres, as he saw nothing else to do. But the Turks of Anatolia showed an unexpected resistance under a leader worthy of their trust, Mustapha Kemal. They repudiated the Treaty of Sèvres and the authority of the Sultan who had

The Treaty of Sèvres

The insurgence of Anatolia and the break-down of the treaty

signed it. More than that, they threatened France's position in Syria and they were equally resolved to dislodge the Greeks. While the Greeks, contrary to the Treaty of Sèvres, had extended their sphere of operations in Asia Minor, they were the only ones who could be depended upon to defend the Treaty of Sèvres, and it was not long before the Powers saw that its revision was inevitable.

But the plot soon thickened instead of abated. Counting on British approval and now receiving orders from Constantine, who had just recovered his throne, the Greeks pressed far into the interior, even threatening Angora, the new capital of the revived Turkey. Fortunately for Turkey neither France nor Italy approved of the turn of affairs. Italy had never wanted the Greeks in Asia Minor since they were treading on a sphere she had wanted herself. France had a special antipathy to Constantine and was highly indignant with England, whom she blamed for her difficulties in Syria, suspected of stealing a march on her in Constantinople (Great Britain headed the financial commission, though the French held sixty-five per cent of the Turkish bonds), and accused of intrigues with the Germans on the question of reparations. To make matters worse, French forces had been beaten back by the Turks from the region to the north of Syria, a part of France's "sphere." The result was that France compounded with Kemal, accepting a narrower zone of influence, and supplied him with ammunition to use against the Greeks. The tide of fortune then turned. The Greeks were badly defeated and even driven from Smyrna, which in the course of the mêlée was almost totally destroyed. Flushed with triumph, Kemal then directed his course toward Constantinople, which was defended by only a small British force. It was a most serious crisis for British prestige, and it led to the downfall of Lloyd George, who for once had overreached himself; but with French mediation an armistice was signed, and an understanding reached. By the Treaty of Lausanne, July 24, 1923, all the Turks' demands were met. They recovered eastern Thrace, the Smyrna region, Armenia, and Kurdistan; and both the hated Capitulations and the more recent financial encroachments on their sovereignty were formally abolished. By the Convention of the Straits, signed the same day, the Dardanelles and Bosphorus were to be unfortified, opened to neutral vessels during peace or war, and placed under the supervision of an international commission responsible to the League of Nations.

Treaty of Lausanne

Thus the efforts of the Allies to solve the Eastern Question had *New position of Turkey* ended in a ridiculous f.asco. True, the Greeks had acquired some islands and the Arabs their independence, but the poor Armenians were once more thrust back on the mercy of the Turk, and, save for the new status of the Straits, the new Turkey was sovereign in the fullest sense of the word. The most that Italy was able to secure in Asia Minor were some voluntary concessions; while some very extensive grants to an American syndicate showed that Kemal meant to avoid at least the more dangerous promoters of economic imperialism. But if the Eastern Question was not precisely at an end, Turkey may be now regarded as an Asiatic power, and there is ground for believing that her influence in the Balkans is at an end. To a large extent the Turks themselves have solved the Eastern Question.

It was nationalism which had played its part in the dissolution of the Ottoman Empire—a fact recognized by the Turks themselves in their cry, "The Ottoman Empire is dead. Long live Turkey!" And it is time now to give some attention to the principle of nationality insofar as it directly inspired the work of the Congress.

Nationalist Problems and Their Solution

The Great War was to a great extent a triumph of the principle *Triumph of nationalism in the War* of nationality. Nations like Italy and Roumania had redeemed their lost brethren; new nations like Czechoslovakia and Poland had arisen; and even semi-civilized people like the Arabs had won a degree of recognition.[1] The collapse of empires had involved a tremendous nationalist upheaval.

It might at first be thought that the map of Europe could very *Difficulties in the way of solution* well be drawn on the basis of nationality. Since this principle had come to possess a peculiar sanctity, and since the forces behind it were powerful enough in most cases to liquidate their claims, why not slip each nationality into its compartment and thus dispose of the ugly problem for all time? But there were several considerations which influenced the Congress in a contrary direction. These considerations or factors were four in number.

In the first place there was the balance of power. Ever anxious over the problem of her security, France refused to allow Germany to acquire the Austrian Germans, since to do so would have strengthened her territorially. For the same fundamental reason

[1] In the so-called kingdom of the Hedjaz.

she supported Polish claims to territory occupied by Russians and Lithuanians, since she looked upon Poland as her outpost in the east. To balance Europe against Germany—not the present but a potential Germany—was the constant aim of Paris.

In the second place historic claims were advanced as a counterweight to the principle of nationality. Since Venice had once possessed Dalmatia, Italy, the heir of Venice, should now possess it. France's possession of the Saar basin was urged partly on the ground that it had belonged to France in 1814. The Poles, on their side, wished to revive their ancient state to its former extent, though this would have meant the incorporation of millions of non-Poles, and even as it was, they were allowed to take Galicia, which in population was more than two thirds Ruthenian. But the historical factor, being purely romantic, had consciously little importance with the peace-makers, though it undoubtedly whetted the ardor of the acquisitive power in question.

In the third place, there were geographical considerations which challenged the nationalist principle. In the case of Fiume, which was perhaps three-fifths Italian and Smyrna, which was predominantly Greek, such ports were needed by the hinterland for commercial purposes. Czechoslovakia needed or thought she needed an outlet on the Danube, though such a reach would gather in a goodly number of Magyars; and to get valleys offering intercommunication for her Slovaks she required the accession of additional Magyar districts. Sometimes it was a case of a mountain boundary desired for strategic reasons. Thus Italy demanded the Brenner Pass as security against a Germany which might some time acquire Austria; and also for strategic reasons she wished to dominate the Adriatic. Czechoslovakia desired to fill her historic semicircle, the inner rim of which was German, because thus she could assure herself of a mountain barrier against Germany.

In the fourth place there were nationalities badly situated or so intermingled with one another that it was difficult if not impossible to draw satisfactory lines of demarcation. A large block of Magyars in the Carpathians was inevitably cut off from the rest of this ethnic group, simply because they formed a sort of island in a Roumanian sea. In the so-called Banat of Temesvar, a very rich region, watered by the river Theiss and its tributaries, Roumans and Serbs were so mixed up that any clean line of division was quite impossible, and the result of partition was to award the eastern third to

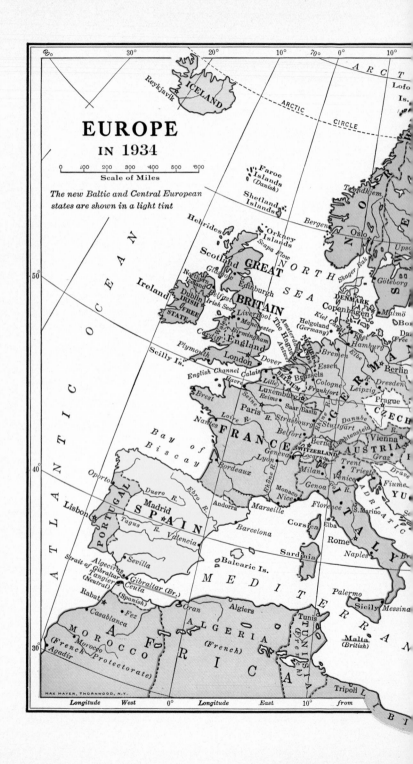

EUROPE
IN 1934

0 100 200 300 400 500 600
Scale of Miles

*The new Baltic and Central European
states are shown in a light tint*

60° 30° 20° 10° 70° 0° 10°

ARCT

Reykjavik ICELAND Lofo Is.

ARCTIC CIRCLE

Faroe Islands (Danish)

Shetland Islands

Hebrides Orkney Islands Scapa Flow Bergen Oslo Upsa

Scotland GREAT NORTH SEA Skager Rak Göteborg

Ireland Northern Ireland Glasgow Edinburgh DENMARK Copenhagen Malmö Bor

Dublin IRISH Belfast Irish Sea Liverpool Amsterdam Kiel Canal Helgoland (Germany) Hamburg Da (Free

FREE STATE Manchester The Hague Kiel Elbe

Cardiff England Birmingham Bremen Berlin

Scilly Is. Plymouth London Dover Essen Leipzig Dresden

English Channel Calais Brussels Cologne Prague CZECH

Havre Lille BELGIUM Frankfort G E R M A N

Brest Seine Luxemburg Reims Saar Basin Vienna

Paris Strasbourg Stuttgart Liechtenstein AUSTRIA Graz

Nantes Loire R. Belfort Danube R.

Bay of FRANCE Berne SWITZERLAND Trent Drave

Biscay Geneva Locarno Milan Venice Trieste Fiume YU

Bordeaux Lyon Rhône R. Genoa Florence Adriatic

Oporto Monaco Nice Elba S.Marino

Lisbon Duero R. Andorra Marseille Corsica Rome ITALY Br

PORTUGAL Madrid SPAIN Ebro R. Barcelona Naples

Tagus R. Valencia Sardinia

Sevilla Balearic Is. Palermo Sicily Messina

Algeciras MEDITERRAN

Strait of Gibraltar Gibraltar (Br.) Tangier (Neutral) Ceuta Oran Algiers Tunis (French) Malta (British)

Rabat (Spanish)

Casablanca Fez ALGERIA

MOROCCO A (French) TUNISIA

Morocco F Tripoli LIB

(French Protectorate) R

Agadir I C A

Longitude West 0° Longitude East 10° from

MAX MAYER, THORNWOOD, N.Y.

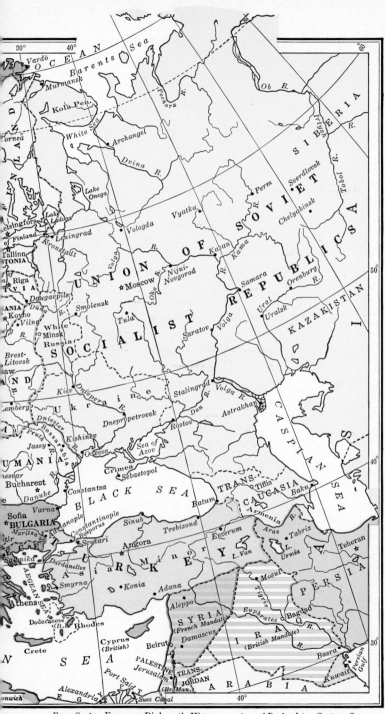

Roumania and the western two thirds to Jugoslavia. In Macedonia, "the witch's cauldron," there was a medley of nationalities, and even to experts it is a puzzle how to classify its people. There were Greeks who belonged to the religious jurisdiction of the Bulgarian Church, and people of Bulgarian extraction who talked Greek. Such cases could be decided only roughly, and it would be impossible not to avoid subjecting people of one nationality to the authority of another.

Finally there were backward peoples—outside of Europe—who were not culturally ready for independence, and would seem to require the rule or at least the guiding hand of a more civilized power. What of them?

The Congress, equipped with its score or more of experts, worked hard on solving these problems. In some particulars, as we have intimated, consideration for the balance of power or for the geographical interests of some power on the winning side was allowed to have precedence over the principle of nationality. It was on such grounds that Italy and Czechoslovakia acquired Germans. In some cases plebiscites were held—usually in the hope of detaching more people from the German Empire. Two districts in the west, after a badly conducted plebiscite, voted for union with Belgium. Of two areas near the Danish frontier one (in north Schleswig) voted for union with Denmark, while the other voted to remain with Germany. Two areas in East Prussia voted also in favor of Germany. The case of Upper Silesia was long undecided. The plebiscite resulted in a large majority for Germany, though certain sections had voted overwhelmingly Polish. The Poles, therefore, demanded a division, and it was highly significant that the Polish section held most of the coal mines. After a great deal of controversy, in which France and Great Britain were ranged on opposite sides, a division was made by an agreement in 1922, following the recommendations of the League of Nations, as far as possible along the lines suggested by the recent vote, but since the whole of Upper Silesia was an economic unit, a special régime was established which should preserve it as such for a period of fifteen years. In the case of the little region of Teschen claimed by both Poland and Czechoslovakia a division was arranged which awarded to Czechoslovakia most of its coal, while the city itself was divided. "The larger and western portion of the town," wrote Dr. Bowman, the American geographer, "goes to Poland,

Compromise decisions: (1) plebiscite zones

(2) Case of Upper Silesia

(3) Case of Teschen

but the western part with the railway station goes to the Czechs; the electric light plant goes to the one state but the gas works to the other, and I do not recall what has become of the municipal water works. This judgment of Solomon is a curious monument of the wisdom of diplomats."

(4) Danzig and the Polish Corridor There was, however, one spot which seemed to defy absolute possession by any power or any practicable mode of division, and that was Danzig. The population of the city was overwhelmingly German; yet, situated as it was at the mouth of Vistula, it was Poland's natural port. The commission which studied the Polish question for the Congress recommended that Danzig be given to Poland outright, and this view had the backing of Wilson and Clemenceau, but Lloyd George's bargaining propensities were thereby offended, and the result was a curious compromise. Danzig with some territory around it was erected as a free state under the guardianship of the League, which should appoint a high commissioner as the chief of its government. To Poland, however, special rights were granted—free use of the harbor, untrammeled trade with the city, and the charge of its foreign relations. It is the irony of history or diplomacy that Poland has since founded a new port on the Baltic, and the prosperity of Danzig has consequently declined. But the whole problem of trying to do justice to both Poles and Germans was one of the thorniest of the Congress. Geographical considerations were arrayed against each other. It seemed to be a case of giving Poland her natural access to the sea through a belt indisputably Polish (the so-called "Polish Corridor") and thus of dividing Germany into two, or of sacrificing some Poles to Germany and giving Poland the awkwardly situated port of Memel, far to the east (also, incidentally, a German town). In the present juncture the rights of the numerically superior Poles, who were also protégés of the Allies, were preferred to those of the Germans. Considering the greater size and importance of Germany and the fact that a territorial unity, more than a century old, was thus disrupted, it was not, perhaps, a very practical settlement.

Solutions by faits accomplis While the questions of Danzig and the Polish Corridor were settled without serious friction because one of the interested parties, Germany, was helpless to put up a fight, it was otherwise sometimes with some of the smaller nations which had arisen out of the War. Lithuania, a state which had emerged from the wreck of Russia, demanded the port of Memel, which had been taken from Germany and held by some French troops in the name of the Congress of Paris while its disposition was still unsettled. When the matter dragged on without decision Lithuania suddenly expelled the French and seized possession of the town, and this *fait accompli* actually received, under certain conditions, the approval of the Allied Powers. In the case of Vilna, the object of a long dispute between Poland and Lithuania the League of Nations failed lamentably to settle the question, and Polish possession of the town rests on force pure and simple.

The disposal of Fiume was also settled outside the Congress and without the intervention of the Allied Powers. We shall not enter into the numerous efforts made to solve this vexing question. Italy returned to the Congress when she saw that it could get along without her and that she was liable to lose her share in reparations. Since, however, no amount of parleying could satisfy public opinion, Orlando was overthrown, and his successor, Nitti, sought by various subterfuges to get what Italy wanted. Among other things the poet, d'Annunzio, with the connivance of the Italian government, crossed the Adriatic with a band of volunteers and seized Fiume, where he proceeded to set up a provisional government. Finally, Wilson having departed for America for good, Clemenceau and Lloyd George washed their hands of the whole matter. The question was, in fact, left entirely to negotiation between Italy and Jugoslavia. In 1924 Fiume with some territory around was constituted a free state, but this settlement broke down for various reasons, and finally by the Treaty of Rome in 1928 the little state was divided between the rivals, Italy obtaining the city itself. The margin of advantage which Italy obtained was a testimony of the strength of a great power rather than an example of the collective wisdom of the appointed peace-makers of Europe.

A solution by negotia- tion: Fiume

But while investigations or compromises might settle many of the disputes, there was still the case of nationalities who were forced through the factors we have discussed to remain under alien rule. What should be done with them to insure their happiness and protection? There were three expedients tried. In the first place, the method of migration was encouraged where possible. This was not, of course, practicable in the case of the Magyar population in Roumania, but arrangements were made by the

Problem of the protection of subject nationalities

Treaty of Neuilly for the migrations of Greeks and Bulgars to their respective countries, and later some plans were carried through by the League of Nations to further the transfer of Greeks to Turkey and Turks to Greece, ample means being taken to see that neither suffered materially by the change of abode. Such procedure was purely voluntary on the part of the peoples concerned, but insofar as it is practicable, it is probably the best approach to a solution of the problem.

A second device was one sponsored by President Wilson, and that was the incorporation in the treaties with Austria, Hungary, Bulgaria, and Turkey, as well as in special treaties with Poland, Czechoslovakia, Jugoslavia, and Roumania special guarantees that subject nationalities should possess full religious freedom, unrestricted use of their language (which meant also instruction in that language in the schools where they were in the majority), and political rights equal to those of other citizens. Such a principle had in a measure been adopted by the Congress of Berlin in the case of some of the Balkan states, but there had been no machinery to enforce it, and it had remained a dead letter. Now, however, the League of Nations was empowered to take cognizance of all cases of violation of the agreements conferring these guarantees. While such provisions could hardly be forced on the nations which had freed themselves from Russia, the Baltic states were admitted to membership in the League itself only on condition of giving satisfactory evidence of treating well their ethnic minorities, though there are unfortunately no safeguards for the future. It is an interesting fact that some of the new nations protested against the compulsion to adopt these guarantees on the ground that they were a derogation of sovereignty, and it was inconveniently pointed out by Roumania that the Great Powers themselves should just as fairly take this obligation upon themselves. What about the Germans in the Tyrol, or Mexican communities in the United States? It was eloquent of the fact that the victorious Allies imposed their righteous experiments on the weaker powers alone.

Considering the inflammable material involved in any nationalist question, it would seem that, at first at least, the new guarantees worked fairly well. There was trouble, it is true, in Poland over her attempted eviction of the Germans who had acquired land in Prussia's colonization schemes, but the matter was finally settled with a fair amount of justice; there was much discrimination against the Jews in various countries, and some serious cases of friction in the Balkans; but the vigilant eye of the League usually ferreted out abuses, and the publicity which naturally attended the more flagrant examples were an aid in securing redress. In 1920 the Council of the League decided that petitions might be received from minorities having grievances, and it subsequently refused to rescind this action, as demanded by Czechoslovakia and Poland. But it is said that in recent years the Council has been less serious in its obligations. What is everybody's business is nobody's business, and the Great Powers (one of whom has been oppressing a nationalist minority) are interested rather in questions more vital to themselves. Thus, states with "protected" minorities have been free to try a policy of assimilation—the very thing forbidden by public law. Perhaps the most flagrant abuses have been in Roumania, where the Magyars have constantly complained of discrimination against their interests, and in Jugoslavia where all Macedonians are looked upon as Serb despite Bulgarian sympathies. No doubt the permanent value of the guarantees for nationalist minorities depends somewhat on the prestige which the League itself may possess, and that, of course, depends on the "Great Powers."

The same may be said of the scheme concocted for the protection of backward peoples. The mandate system was devised for certain peoples whose stage of civilization did not seem to warrant independence, and who therefore needed the guidance of a more civilized power; or to put it from another standpoint it was devised to prevent certain backward peoples from becoming subjects, without restriction, of some colonizing power who might readily seek to exploit them. The origins of the scheme are not entirely clear. There had, however, been cases where Great Britain and the United States had respectively exercised a temporary protectorate for the good of the peoples concerned, and theoretically Leopold of Belgium had administered the Congo Free State under conditions (laid down by an international congress) which safeguarded the interests of both the natives and the other powers. Lloyd George, before the opening of the Congress of Paris, had announced apropos of the German colonies that the wishes and interests of the natives should receive first consideration, and General Smuts, the premier of South Africa, had worked out a scheme which to a large extent

The mandate system for backward peoples

was ultimately adopted. When the Congress met, however, it was Wilson who became the sponsor for the proposed innovation. Instead of allowing the German colonies and certain regions of the Ottoman Empire to be handed over as spoils to the victor powers, who in most cases had already occupied them, he proposed that these lands, inhabited by "backward peoples" should be placed under the tutelage of powers who should be regarded as trustees under the League of Nations. It was assumed that such people were potential if not actual nationalities and that it was the duty of the tutelary power to prepare them for ultimate independence.

The proposal was not received with much enthusiasm, and, but for Wilson's persistence, might have died an early death. Some of these lands had already been allocated by secret treaties negotiated during the War; others had at least been occupied and in some cases the occupant had incurred considerable expense in establishing a semblance of order. In spite of the pronouncement of Lloyd George it developed that some of the dominions—notably Australia and New Zealand—were vehement in demanding downright annexation of the German colonies, and now Lloyd George, much impressed by dominion opinion as well as habitually prone to change his mind, gave some support to their views. France and Japan also preferred annexation, though they did not make it an issue, Clemenceau only insisting that France should have the right of raising native armies in any land under her mandate. After Lloyd George had paraded the dominion premiers before a meeting of the Council of Ten, it was decided to accept a compromise proposed by General Smuts, which would enable the recalcitrant powers to obtain what they wanted under a system closely approximating annexation. The territories to be disposed of were divided into three categories "A," "B," and "C." In every case the power acquiring one of these regions was supposed to hold a "mandate" from the League of Nations, which implied that the "mandatory" power accepted "the principle that the well-being and development of such peoples form a sacred trust of civilization, securities for the performance of this trust being embodied in the Covenant." But whereas in the case of the A group the mandatory power was merely to "assist with advice" the native government, in respect to the B group it should take full responsibility of administration, subject only to certain guarantees like the maintenance of the open door and the prohibition of certain prac-

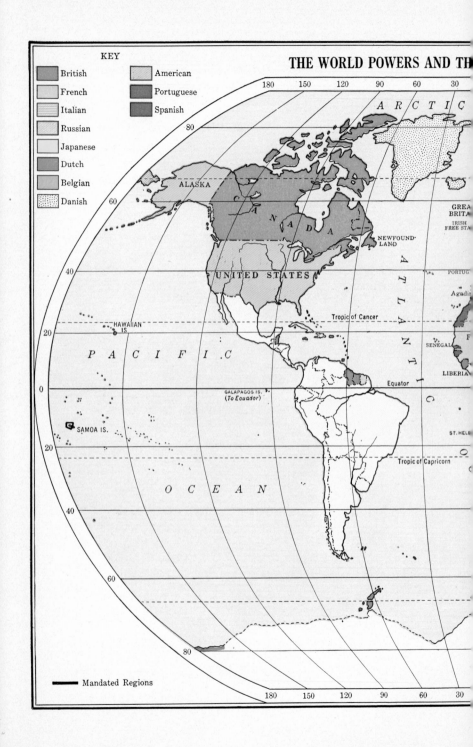

KEY

British	American
French	Portuguese
Italian	Spanish
Russian	
Japanese	
Dutch	
Belgian	
Danish	

THE WORLD POWERS AND TH

ARCTIC

ALASKA

C A N A D A

NEWFOUND-LAND

UNITED STATES

Tropic of Cancer

HAWAIIAN IS

PACIFIC

GALAPAGOS IS.
(To Ecuador)

Equator

SAMOA IS.

OCEAN

Tropic of Capricorn

ATLANTIC

GREAT BRITA
IRISH FREE STA

PORTUG

Agadir

SENEGAL

LIBERIA

ST. HELE

—— Mandated Regions

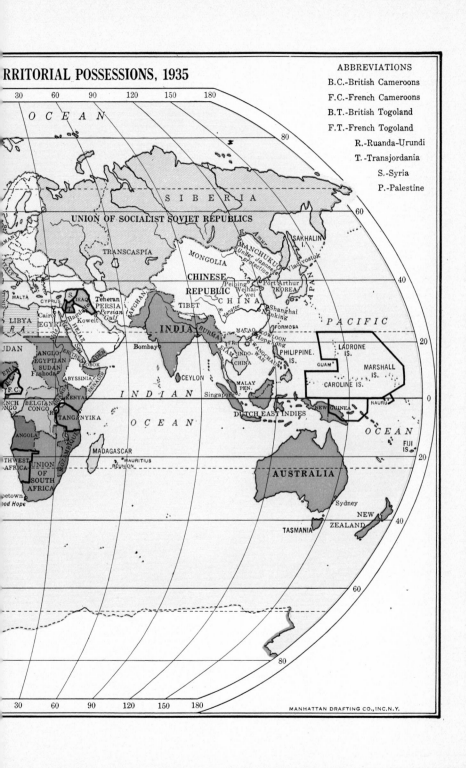

RRITORIAL POSSESSIONS, 1935

O C E A N

S I B E R I A

UNION OF SOCIALIST SOVIET REPUBLICS

TRANSCASPIA

MONGOLIA

CHINESE
REPUBLIC

MANCHUKUO
Under Japanese
protection

SAKHALIN
I.

Vladivostok

Peibing
Welhai-
wei
CHINA
TIBET
Port Arthur
KOREA

JAPAN

MALTA
CYPRUS
IRAQ
Teheran
PERSIA
Persian
Gulf
AFGHAN.
Shanghai
Nanking

Cairo
Bayda
Koweit
HEJAZ

LIBYA
EGYPT
INDIA
BURMA
FORMOSA

PACIFIC

UDAN
Bombay
SIAM
FR.
INDO-
CHINA
MACAO
KOWLOON
Hongkong
WANGCHAI

LADRONE
IS.

ANGLO
EGYPTIAN
SUDAN
Fashoda
ERITREA
JOBOK
CEYLON
PHLIPPINE.
IS.
GUAM

MARSHALL
IS.

ABYSSINIA

MALAY
PEN.
Singapore
CAROLINE IS.

F.C.
KENYA
I N D I A N

BELGIAN
CONGO
TANGANYIKA
O C E A N
DUTCH EAST INDIES
NEW GUINEA
NAURU

ANGOLA

THWEST
AFRICA
UNION
OF
SOUTH
AFRICA

MADAGASCAR
MAURITIUS
REUNION

O C E A N

FIJI
IS.

petown
ood Hope

AUSTRALIA

Sydney

NEW
ZEALAND

TASMANIA

MANHATTAN DRAFTING CO., INC.N.Y.

tices to the detriment of the natives, and in the case of the C group because of such circumstances as "the sparseness of their population" or "their small size" or "their remoteness from the centers of civilization" or "their geographical contiguity to the territory of the mandatory" the mandatory might rule them as part of its own territory. In each and every case, however, the mandatory power should present an annual report to the Council of the League of Nations; and a "permanent mandates commission," appointed by that body, was subsequently established to exercise a general supervision over the work. Special mandates were drafted in the case of each mandated region, but except for the privilege which France secured in two instances of recruiting natives for service outside of Africa in the event of a general war, the mandates in each group were fairly uniform. Many indeed of the original arrangements had been decided by the Powers themselves before the League of Nations began to function.

It was so in respect to the distribution of mandates. The power exercising this tutelary privilege might well have been chosen finally by the League or at least by the Congress itself after careful consideration. But in some cases agreements had already been reached between the powers most interested, and the disposition of the Ottoman mandates were left to be finally settled along with the Turkish treaty. France secured Syria and the Lebanon in Class A and the greater part of the Cameroons and Togoland in Class B. Great Britain obtained Palestine, Transjordania, and Mesopotamia (or Iraq) in Class A and most of German East Africa (rechristened Tanganyika) and small portions of the Cameroons and Togoland in Class B. Belgium also received a small slice of German East Africa, known as Ruanda-Urundi in Class B. In the C group Australia acquired German New Guinea; New Zealand, German Samoa; The Union of South Africa, German Southwest Africa; and Japan, the German islands north of the Equator (save the little island of Nauru, which went to Great Britain).

It is perhaps too early to decide whether the system is a success. When the Union of South Africa came under criticism for her handling of Southwest Africa, the intervention of the League produced salutary results. Experience with the territories taken from Turkey (all in Class A) has greatly varied, for France was severely censured in 1926 for her handling of Syria, whereas Great Britain has, in general, got on pretty well, though it is evident that the

Arabs resent the term, "mandate" and those in Iraq welcomed the idea of a treaty governing their relations with Great Britain. Such a treaty—giving the mandatory substantial control over military, financial, and foreign affairs—was signed in 1922 and renewed in 1925, but terminated in 1932, when Iraq was admitted to membership in the League of Nations. Perhaps Iraq may be considered the first of the mandated states to have "grown up." [1] A palpable weakness of the system is the fact that complaints from a "mandated" region can be presented only through the medium of the mandatory. In the aforesaid case of Southwest Africa the mandates commission took the initiative and conducted an investigation. Though logically, of course, the whole system should have been applied to the colonies of a similar character already governed by a European power, the very fact that mandatory powers have to watch their steps should naturally have the effect of making these same powers more considerate of the natives who are elsewhere in their charge. And it is undoubtedly true that many real improvements have been introduced in the mandated regions. Both France and Great Britain have done much for the health and education of their charges, and both have expended large sums in public works in these lands, and apart from some of the Arabs, who are a warlike and difficult people bitten with the idea of independence, and the Druses of Syria whom France needlessly offended, there seems to be no great evidence of discontent among the mandated peoples, even if there is no more than the customary passivity. It may be, of course, that restiveness under a foreign administrator will increase in proportion as the people of the mandated regions become civilized—a fact which would not prove the incompetence of the mandatory power. "The [mandate] commission has urged "writes Quincy Wright," and the mandatories have agreed that native customs and institutions be utilized as much as possible and developed to meet new conditions rather than destroyed. This is obviously the sane way of meeting the native problem." On the whole, the system seems to be working better with time and experience. Certainly, the principle that the more advanced powers holding these regions are stewards who

---

[1] Though supposed now to be independent, Iraq nevertheless agreed to allow transit facilities for British armies and also to engage British subjects as military instructors. While the British have honestly observed the spirit of their mandate, it may be questioned whether the freedom of action which they assumed was permissible under the Covenant.

are supposed to give primary consideration to the welfare of the natives and give a regular account of such stewardship is a new note in imperialism.

The policy of the Congress of Paris in dealing with nationalism may be subjected to much criticism, and in some cases its attempted solutions have given rise to fresh problems. Yet, if we grant that, in allowing new nations to form, it was simply surrendering to natural forces, it did succeed in a measure in finding some healing processes that would prevent an unnatural condition from becoming an open sore. The most serious criticism which may be brought against its work—in this sphere as in the treatment of enemy countries—was its failure to give adequate attention to economic factors. It could not be helped that the new national frontiers cut across long established economic units, but the same wisdom which prescribed guarantees for nationalist minorities should have prevented the erection of tariff barriers. In this wise much of the economic distress of central and eastern Europe could have been averted. In the meantime, how much nationalism would really be held in check for its own and the general good must depend on the actual strength of an incipient internationalism. On the value of the League of Nations would the greatness of the Congress of Paris chiefly rest. *Neglect of the economic factor*

THE LEAGUE OF NATIONS

The idea of a league of nations to watch over the peace of Europe had been attempted, as we have noticed, after the Congress of Vienna, but the failure of the Concert of Europe to effectuate anything practical put the idea into abeyance for almost a century. Yet international co-operation for disposing of certain problems was frequently manifested at different times, and the Hague Tribunal was the result of efforts to solve the problem of peace. When the Great War showed the inadequacy of such efforts, it was natural for a new movement to arise to lessen the dangers inherent in the political fabric, which under the strain of international rivalries had proved to be nothing less than world anarchy. *Origins*

The movement which led to the formation of the League of Nations did not emanate originally from Wilson's imagination. In the last years of the War there was much talk both in America and England about the advisability of forming all the powers into some sort of organization designed to insure peace. The calamity of 1914 must never again be allowed to happen. The idea of preventing such catastrophes in future was born of the horror which the Great War had brought to the hearts of men. In America there was a society formed, called the League to Enforce Peace, which carried on an extensive propaganda. The idea naturally appealed to Wilson; and the more he thought of it, the more he determined to give it the foremost place in the program he hoped to put through at the peace. He first made this clear in a speech during May, 1916, before the League to Enforce Peace, and the idea was, after all, but an elaboration and extension of the plans he had long been harboring for North and South America. Then, too, he had been encouraged by a letter from Grey to House, which had looked forward to some species of international organization. Inevitably such a plan took its place as one of the Fourteen Points, and it was stressed in the speech in which he presented the Points to Congress. But oddly enough, Wilson himself did not contribute anything original to the organization of the League, and the tentative scheme he brought to Paris was that of his friend, House, who had read and carefully digested the plans of others. Then in Paris he became acquainted with a project of General Smut's, and revised his scheme, while still another plan emanated from Lord Robert Cecil, a member of the British delegation; and eventually the Hurst-Miller draft (Hurst and Miller were legal advisers of the British and American legations respectively) was grounded on these various schemes and became the basis of discussion at the Congress.

Establish-
ment

The question was bound, of course, to cause considerable speculation, and both its importance and its scope, as well as its attendant details were matters to be determined. France had welcomed the idea of a league before the War was ended, but wanted it restricted to the Allied Powers and their friends—something like the old Chaumont organization of 1814.[1] House was apparently in favor of restricting it to the Great Powers. But Wilson was firm in his determination that it should be open to all nations, and as soon as practicable he wished that Germany herself should be included. In any event, by the time the Congress opened, it seemed generally assumed that a league of nations was to be established, and it was so ordered at the opening session. At the next session, January 25, the principle was formerly adopted by

[1] Page 386.

the Congress as a whole. A commission then went to work on the Hurst-Miller Plan, and with little alteration it was submitted on February 14 to a plenary assembly of the Congress. The public reception of this "valentine" was generally favorable except that certain emendations seemed desirable in response to American criticism, especially a recognition of the Monroe Doctrine as being in no way invalidated by the scheme. Finally, on April 28 the revised "Covenant" was adopted by the Congress as a whole. Wilson's principal triumph was the decision of the Council of Four to make the Covenant an integral part of the Treaty of Versailles, for by so doing he made sure that the question would not be shelved after territorial adjustments had been made.

The League was composed of all sovereign states (including the *Machinery* British dominions) with a few exceptions, and ultimately all the defeated nations were added. The machinery provided by the Covenant consisted of (1) an assembly, in which all member powers (including the British dominions and India) were equally represented, (2) a council, in which France, Great Britain, Italy, and Japan were accorded permanent seats, while four non-permanent places were to be allotted to powers selected at the first meeting of the assembly,[1] (3) an international court of justice, and (4) a secretariat. The assembly is chiefly important as giving every nation, however small, the feeling that it has a contributive part in the progress of the League. It is a place where dangers to the peace can be brought up and discussed, and is largely a clearing house of ideas. It controls the budget (levied on member states according to the apportionment applied in the international postal union), votes on applications for membership in the League, appoints the non-permanent members of the council, and shares with the council the right of choosing judges on the international court. Though the council and the assembly have in some respects a concurrent jurisdiction (since they both consider prevalent dangers to the peace), the council is much the more active body (it meets at least four times a year whereas the assembly meets but once) and upon it rests the task of mediating in international disputes as well as advising what action should be taken in a crisis. The permanent court of international justice passes judgment on

[1] Germany was granted a permanent seat when she entered the League in 1926, and the number of non-permanent seats was subsequently increased to nine. Since then the withdrawal of Germany and Japan and the accession of Russia have had the net effect of making the total membership thirteen.

questions submitted, and its action is based on public law; thus, as distinguished from the Hague tribunal, it adjudicates rather than arbitrates. It also acts in general as the legal adviser of the council. The secretariat comprises the administrative machinery of the League and in its archives are supposed to be deposited all international treaties. The spirit of the League is opposed to secret articles and secret treaties.

The League of Nations was not so constituted as to guarantee the peace of the world, but it was provided with the means of handling a crisis in such a manner as to lessen the chances of war. In the first place, member states are pledged to submit their differences to arbitration or mediation and not to go to war until at least three months after the arbitrators or the council (as the case may be) has announced its decision. This would at least give two quarreling nations an interval to cool down. The council has the presumptive right of deciding which of two states is the aggressor, though if a legal question is involved it will first refer the question to the international court. In case either of the disputants resorts to war in face of the decision made, the council is empowered to advise the members of the League to cut off all economic relations with the offender and to specify such forces as it may see fit to recommend each member to contribute for bringing her to terms. But the council does not monopolize the initiative in intervening in a dispute, since any member state may bring before it a case that it deems liable to lead to war. A state which is not a member of the League is invited, and even expected, to bring a dispute before the council in the same manner as a member state, and is held equally accountable to the council's judgment.

Value   The greatest value of the League of Nations lies in its primary purpose of lessening the chances of war. Small disputes which might easily become large ones may be robbed of their danger to the peace. The council successfully adjusted a dispute between Sweden and Finland, another between Germany and Poland, and a third between Serbia and Albania; and while the machinery of force has never yet been applied in any case, the threat of subjecting Serbia to a boycott was sufficient in the last-named case to bring her to terms. The League has also performed an immensely important service in its tutelary capacity regarding nationalist minorities, mandated territories, and certain special régimes like those of Danzig, the Saar Basin, and the Straits. Finally, under

its ægis a great many international conferences have been held
dealing directly with such matters as transport questions, opium,
the white slave traffic, labor problems, matters of health and so on;
and it has even acted as a means of co-ordinating scientific work
in different countries. It has likewise served as a very effectual
medium for furnishing relief where national interests might have
prevented such action. One of its greatest services was to rescue
Austria from economic ruin.

Yet the League has several patent defects which are due to its *Limitations*
experimental character and partly and mainly the result of the
strength of national interests. The rule that except in certain
specified cases the council must be unanimous (and the same is
true of the assembly) tends to block effective action in an emergency and is painfully reminiscent of the Polish *liberum veto*. The
exemption of regional understandings from the jurisdiction of the
League (the result of the United States' insistence on the priority
of the Monroe Doctrine) may give other nations, notably Japan,
the excuse for obstructing the jurisdiction of the League. Finally,
it is clear that the League lacks the legal power to enforce peace.
Members are free to reject if they wish the recommendations of the
council. They may or may not be willing to combine in coercive
measures. The French, whose realistic turn of mind saw the
fundamental flaw in the institution, had suggested at the Congress
the establishment of an international army to execute the council's
punitive decisions, but though Wilson would have assented, Lloyd
George declared that such a device would be opposed by British
opinion, and it is, of course, abundantly clear that American
opinion would have equally withheld approval. Generally speaking, the Powers do not want the League of Nations to possess
teeth; they are too afraid of an invasion of their sovereignty. The
time has yet to come when the League will be strong enough to
prevent a war between two of the Great Powers whenever they
should happen to think their vital interests involved. On some
occasions already the League's prestige has become considerably
impaired. Its decisions were flouted by Italy in a quarrel with
Greece in 1923 and likewise by Japan in her recent encroachments
upon Manchuria. In the last analysis it must be realized that the
strength of the League lies solely in the moral support which its
members are willing to give it. It is, unhappily, much too easy in a
crisis for national selfishness to paralyze its action.

It is perhaps fitting to close our account of the Congress of Paris and its most ambitious experiment by a few appended words on the failure of the United States to fulfill the hope that she would remain a continuous force in world affairs.

THE DEFECTION OF THE UNITED STATES

The War over and the army demobilized, the United States began to have her misgivings about an active participation in European affairs. Wilson, of course, felt otherwise, but Wilson—alas!—was in Europe, and public opinion needed a voice to hold it staunch in the beaten track. The very fact that the date of the armistice came to be celebrated as a holiday seemed to show that Americans were only relieved that the War was over; the peace could take care of itself. That feeling of insularity which the War had rudely interrupted but not essentially modified now returned in full force.

For this reaction against Europe and against the high idealism with which America had entered the War Wilson himself was partly responsible. Party rivalry is very intense in the United States, and when the nation is not actually at war, the party out of power seeks every possible occasion for knifing the administration. In the present case the general ignorance of Europe which characterizes American opinion gave the Republicans an easy handle—all the easier, too, because since the elections of 1920 they controlled both houses of congress. All this, however, Wilson might conceivably have averted. He had been shortsighted enough to make the War a partisan affair, a responsibility of the Democratic Party, rather than to seek a non-political co-operation. Thus he had appealed to the public to elect a Democratic congress in 1920; he had not felt called upon to take into his confidence any of the chiefs of the Republican Party; and he had picked a delegation to the Congress of Paris in which no Republican save an ex-diplomat was included. Apart from the moral justification, it would have been a shrewd political move to have selected ex-President Taft or Elihu Root, both of whom had been strongly in favor of a league of nations. But Wilson seems to have been averse to conferring with men of the highest caliber whose views might sometimes differ from his own. Again, it might have been expedient to have chosen a Republican from the senate in order to insure its ratification of the Covenant; but Wilson appears to have lacked the capacity to understand practical politics, and trusted rather to his ability to sway public opinion. Unfortunately even here he was signally at a disadvantage, for in going to Paris he had left his country to be "converted" by his enemies.

When Wilson returned, he found the senate decidedly caustic *Eclipse of Wilson* in its reaction to the Covenant. Under the leadership of Senator Lodge a sheaf of reservations was insisted upon as conditional of its acceptance. None of these reservations would have materially enhanced the weakness of the League, since in the last analysis every member retained the power to adhere or not, as it chose, to the various expedients devised to avert war. But Wilson felt that the moral obligation of a power must not be weakened by reservations, and he refused all efforts at compromise, preferring to put his case before the people of the United States. In the course of a vigorous campaign to enlighten public opinion he was suddenly stricken with paralysis—due no doubt to the long strain which he had undergone—and it was his misfortune to live just long enough to see the utter ruin of his hopes. Into the discard with the League of Nations had gone the project of an American mandate over Armenia and the proposed three-cornered alliance for the protection of France. Internationalism had capitulated to nationalism.

The cessation of American participation in the work of recon- *Triumph of isolation* struction was, in fact, rather abrupt. Under the administration of Wilson's successor the Treaty of Versailles was repudiated and separate treaties signed with Germany and Austria. With the withdrawal of the United States all Americans who sat on various commissions were speedily recalled, and early in 1923 the American contingent in the Rhineland was ordered home. When later American officials were sent to sit on special commissions to study reparations or questions which touched her interests closely, they were supposed to be "unofficial" or sometimes "observers" who did not vote. As far as she could, the United States stood aloof, and while willing to discuss such questions as a reduction of armaments or the traffic in opium, she steadily refused even to sanction the new court of international justice on the assumption that it was a mere adjunct of the League of Nations. So forgetful were Republican congresses of American participation in the Hague conferences and Roosevelt's active interest in European politics! Instead of working with war-torn Europe, the United States basked in the prosperity which she won as the result of the War, and contented herself with raising her tariff walls, while she demanded the payment of debts which could only be met with goods. For all this reaction against Europe public opinion was largely responsible. It was no longer a party question, for the Democrats were as afraid of internationalism as their opponents. Not until she had wallowed in several years of depression did the United States begin to see that at least her foreign investments had a bearing on the question of international co-operation.[1] But her policy is rather hesitant at best, and national self-sufficiency is thus far (1935) the keynote of the present administration (1932).

FOR FURTHER READING OR STUDY

Scott, J. F., and Baltzly, A., *Readings in European History since 1814*, chap. xiv; Cooke, J. H., and Stickney, E. P., *Readings in European International Relations since 1879*, part iii (*passim* for peace parleys), iv and v; Poincaré, R., *Memoirs* (in process of translation); Lansing, R., *The Peace Negotiations: A Personal Narrative* and *The Big Four and Others of the Peace Conference;* Baker, R. S., *Woodrow Wilson and World Settlement*, vol. iii (some useful documents); *The Intimate Papers of Colonel House* (ed. Seymour, C.), 4 vols.; Beadon, R. H., *Some Memories of the Peace Conference* (by a British military adviser, largely on the Russian problem); Clemenceau, G., *The Grandeur and Misery of Victory* (reflections); Marburg, T., *Development of the League of Nations Idea* (mostly source material); Steed, W. W., *Through Thirty Years;* Karolyi, M., *Fighting the World;* Tormay, C., *An Outlaw's Diary*, 2 vols.; Burian, S., *Austria in Dissolution;* Andrassy, G., *Diplomacy and War;* Bandholtz, H. H., *An Undiplomatic Diary* (affairs in Hungary); Masaryk, T. G., *The Making of a State;* Benes, E., *My War Memories.*

Hayes, C. J. H., *Political and Social History of Modern Europe*, vol. ii, chap. xxiii; Schapiro, J. S., *Modern and Contemporary European History*, chap. xxxvi; Higby, C. P., *History of Modern Europe*, pp. 413–27, 442–72; Palm, F. C., and Graham, F. E., *Europe since Napoleon*, chaps. xxxi–xxxii; Benns, F. L., *Europe since 1914*, chaps. vii–ix; Langsam, W. C., *The World since 1914*, chaps. iv–vi; Slosson, P. W., *Twentieth Century Europe*, chaps. xv, xvi, and xviii (succinct and good).

Swain, J. W., *Beginning the Twentieth Century*, chap. xxxviii; Sontag, R., *European Diplomatic History, 1871–1932*, chap. vii; Dahlin, E., *French and German Public Opinion on Declared War Aims;* Seymour, C., *American Diplomacy during the World War;* Beales, A. C. F., *The History of Peace;* Thompson, C. T., *The Peace Conference Day by Day;* Baker, R. S., *Woodrow Wilson and World Settlement*, vols. i and ii (informing but idealistic in tone); Tardieu, A., *The Truth about the Treaty;* Nicolson, H., *Peacemaking, 1919* (interesting reflections by a keen observer); Satow, E., "Peacemaking, Old and New,"

---

[1] It is worthy of note that an official American "observer" attended one of the meetings of the council of the League of Nations dealing with Japan's quarrel with China in 1932.

Camb. Hist. Jour., ii, 23 ff.; Nevins, A., *Henry White: Thirty Years of American Diplomacy;* Keynes, J. M., *The Economic Consequences of the Peace* (a powerful though perhaps one-sided arraignment); House, E. M., and Seymour, C., *What Really Happened at Paris* (valuable contributions by different writers); Baruch, B. M., *The Making of the Reparation and Economic Sections of the Treaty;* Miller, D. H., *The Drafting of the Covenant,* 2 vols.; Churchill, W. S., *The Aftermath;* Lloyd George, D., *Whither Europe?* (not very profound); Bowman, I., *The New World* (useful for geographical background); Glaise von Horstenau, E., *The Collapse of the Austro-Hungarian Empire;* Burian, S., *Austria in Dissolution;* Abbott, G. F., *Greece and the Allies, 1914–22;* Mair, L. P., *The Protection of Minorities;* Junghann, O., *National Minorities in Europe;* Ladar, S. P., *The Exchange of Minorities;* Gerig, B., *The Open Door and the Mandate System;* Buell, R. E., *International Relations;* Hicks, F. C., *The New World Order;* Margolith, A. M., *The International Mandates;* Bassett, J. S., *The League of Nations* (one of the earlier works); Webster, C. K., *The League of Nations: Theory and Practice* (a useful brief study); Eagleton, C., *International Government;* Simonds, C. H., *How Europe Made Peace without America;* Slosson, P. W., *The Great Crusade and After.*

XVIII. THE OUTSTANDING RESULTS OF THE GREAT WAR

1. IMMEDIATE RESULTS: COLOSSAL LOSSES, ECONOMIC CHAOS, MORAL AND POLITICAL INSTABILITY

Loss of life; Material losses; The problem of readjustment; Economic prostration in central Europe; Political disorders: (1) from communism, (2) from nationalism; Immediate triumph of democracy.

2. THE PROMOTION OF NATIONALISM

The War as a nationalist revolution; Gains of the victorious Allies; Status of imperialism; Triumph of repressed nationalism; Nationalism outside of Europe; Case of the Irish.

3. IMPROVED POSITION OF THE PROLETARIAT AND THE PEASANTRY

The War as a social revolution; Conditions favorable to the proletariat: (1) in victor countries, and economic advantages gained, (2) in defeated countries; International importance of the labor problem; Influence of the "lower classes" in politics; Progress of social reform; Position of socialism; Abasement of the aristocracy.

4. THE REVOLT OF WOMAN

Woman's historic dependence and its causes; Woman's disabilities and progress in the nineteenth century; Woman's position as affected by the War: (1) legal, (2) moral.

5. THE REVOLT OF YOUTH

Before the War; Disillusion; Self-reliance and restlessness.

The Great War, as we have stated before, was more than an international conflict; it was a revolution. It is impossible as yet to determine all of its results or to measure fully its historical significance. We do not know how many of the changes that have been wrought are merely transitory, and one needs to be careful about marking historical tendencies in a period as short as seventeen years. Thus the new internationalism—an immediate result of the War—may possibly advance with the passage of time, or, instead, be wholly undone by the counteracting influence of nationalism. For the present, indeed, we cannot be sure that the world is any better off as the result of the War, while, conversely, we know but too well its immediate cost as well as the scourge of fear and hatred which it engendered. But whatever its place in history, there are some upheavals born of the War, such as the Russian Revolution, which have at least a considerable importance for the nations concerned, and have had a certain reaction on the outside world. There are also certain social results of the War, which have the appearance of being permanent, and consequently seem to justify our classing it as a revolution. But, whatever the abiding effects, we can discern the immediate results of the War with some precision, for the evidence of what Europe had to pass through from 1918 to 1920 is sufficiently abundant and illuminating to enable us to point out certain facts that are beyond dispute. It is to the immediate results of the War that we shall first give our attention.

Immediate Results: Colossal Losses, Economic Chaos, Moral and Political Instability

The cost of the War in lives and property was nothing less than *Loss of life* appalling. Estimates vary, but it seems fairly clear that the number of men engaged who lost their lives totaled somewhere between eight and twelve millions, and that quite as many civilians perished through one cause or another, attributable to the War. Even these figures, however, do not include the more than two million lives lost in Russia during a famine, which being due to the Revolution, was at least an indirect result of the War. Nor do they include the number of soldiers who died after the War as the result of injuries they had sustained or the number of persons who died afterward of diseases traceable to the struggle. Nor do they include the casualties yet to come that are due to the hardships of the War or of the period immediately following it. In France, where population had become almost stationary, it will presumably take many decades for her losses to be made good by natural population increase,[1] hence has come about, incidentally, her recent campaign against birth control. The number of French soldiers (or sailors) killed approximated 1,360,000 or about sixteen per cent of her total fighting strength; Germany lost over 1,750,000 or about

---

[1] France received, however, an addition to her population of approximately 1,500,000 people in Alsace-Lorraine, and there has been a considerable immigration of Italians in recent years. Her population, according to the census of 1931 is 41,894,932, as compared with 39,604,922 in 1911 and 39,252,245 in 1906.

seventeen per cent,[1] though this loss was much less than the French if considered in proportion to total population. It is worth noting that Roumania lost almost half her army. While American losses were negligible in comparison with those of other countries, the British military dead numbered more than 800,000. It should be noted also that death took its toll from the strongest males in the population, and that the casualties among officers during the War and among the professional classes after the War (as the result of hardships and privations) meant for the world an appreciable loss of mental power.

Material losses

The material losses were likewise stupendous. The countries which suffered most were Serbia, Roumania, Belgium, France, and the lands which came to form the republic of Poland. "Our country," lamented the Polish writer, Sienkiewicz, "has been made the cockpit of Europe and been devastated from end to end." Little, indeed, of Poland escaped the ravages of war. Mines were ruined, crops destroyed, railroads cut, and machinery broken or confiscated. "Of all the helpless, unearned suffering, of lonely, uncourted death, of the pitiless clutch of circumstance which this war has produced," wrote a Red Cross worker, "no desolation unless it be that of the Armenians, equals that of Poland." But the destruction and looting in Serbia was equally appalling; and the property loss to Belgium was estimated at $7,000,000,000. In France about 8,000 square miles of agricultural land were laid waste, acres and acres of orchards destroyed, and 500,000 buildings damaged of which half were completely demolished; bridges, railways, waterworks, and other public utilities similarly suffered. The region occupied was the chief industrial part of France, and the Germans had systematically ruined its mines and wrecked its factories. Mr. William McDonald states that "the number of industrial establishments partially or totally destroyed was about 20,000." Much of the destruction, however, was the result of artillery fire, and even the soil itself was seriously damaged, so far as its fertility was concerned, for many years. There was also a terrific waste of timber. Anyone visiting this region after the War might have viewed from the ridge of Craonne miles and miles of country covered with bristling stumps, with an occasional barren spot where a village had once stood. It was the havoc wrought in

[1] Next to the Roumanian this was the highest per cent of mortality among the forces mobilized.

France that partly explains her fixed determination to bleed her enemy as well as to prevent by all possible means another invasion. But even the Germans themselves suffered some losses at the hands of the Russians—though the area of devastation was relatively small. Professor Bogart estimates the property loss in Europe as amounting to nearly $30,000,000,000. When there is added the

Wide World Photos

A GLIMPSE OF PÉRONNE AFTER THE GERMAN EVACUATION

cost of waging the War itself, which he computes at $186,333,637,-897, and certain indirect costs in addition to property loss, he reaches the staggering figure of $337,946,179,657. It should be realized, moreover, that in a great part of the world for four years industry had been organized primarily in order to destroy. For ordinary constructive purposes little had been done. The productive power of the world had been deliberately diverted into activities artificial and abnormal, with the result that the world's economy suffered serious disorganization.

Thus the immediate result of the War was a painful readjustment to the ways of peace. Millions of soldiers had to be rapidly absorbed into civilian life. Employment had to be found, and, if

*The problem
of read-
justment* possible, found immediately. Yet industries, as we have said, had
subordinated everything else to the one purpose of equipping
armies, and could not easily or quickly go back to normal conditions. When manufacturers looked for their former markets, perchance they were gone. And in countries still shut off by the blockade there was such a dearth of raw materials that most factories
had to close. Conditions, it is true, became for a time very favorable in England, which being highly industrialized (and not, like
Germany, ruined by the armistice and blockade), was able to supply the needs of many of the Continental countries; yet even here
the boom was only temporary, as we shall later note and explain.
Elsewhere, about 1920, business began to pick up, and some fortunes were made from the greatly increased prices of industrial products, but as Mr. G. D. H. Cole has pointed out, it was an utterly
false prosperity, based on scarcity rather than plenty, and the bub-
ble soon burst.   Meanwhile all the late belligerents carried a heavy
load of debt, which though soon made very much lighter in most
cases by currency inflation, was for that very reason bound to
bring serious losses to thousands of bond-holders,[1] not to mention
the heavier taxes that would be needed in the interval. In France
there was the special task of restoring the devastated regions, and
as this involved the question of reparations, which affected Germany most vitally, and as the amount was for long undetermined,
there was a lack of that public confidence which is always at the
basis of credit and so vital to the commercial relations of nations.
It was partly this uncertainty that upset foreign exchange, though
a more serious cause was monetary inflation, practiced in central
Europe as a desperate means of obtaining ready money. Since the
value of the franc or the lira or the mark was constantly changing,
prices were in a constant state of flux, thus making the revival
of business all the more difficult. Europe suffered not only from the
War but from the shock of a sudden peace.

*Economic
prostration
in central
Europe*   But the plight of some of the nations of central and eastern
Europe was far worse in the beginning than anything western
Europe had to bear. To the dislocation accompanying war had
been added the rigors of the blockade, which for a time made the
import of raw materials impossible; and hence factories could not
reopen. It was necessary for the German consumer to exist as
best he could on what stocks were still available. In most of

---

[1] When the monetary unit, as in France, became stabilized on a lower basis.

these countries, moreover, the currency was disorganized by over-issuance of paper money. Statesmen who could not extract money by taxes or did not dare to try found it only too easy to manufacture money, and once the process started, it seemed impossible to stop. Prices rose with such rapidity that salaried people were rapidly impoverished. There was at times an orgy of spending, since no one knew on the morrow how much his money would be worth. Under such conditions it was well nigh impossible to re-vamp the industries ravaged by the War. There was need of raw materials and machinery in order to produce; yet these could only be paid for by commodities (hence, a vicious circle), and credit, which should normally have afforded some escape from such an *impasse*, was all but blocked by the chronic instability of exchange. The result in central Europe was widespread unemployment sim-ply because the machinery of production had almost stopped. Work would have been the salvation of a people like the Germans, whose nerves had been so frazzled by disasters and privations; yet work was denied to most of them by the inexorable play of events. Economic prostration was also partly due to lethargy, the lack of the will to work. Undernourishment, due to the food shortage, had much to do with the depleted spirits and energies of the working class, and in Germany this famine continued for more than a year after the War. Also in Germany the sense of hopelessness in having to pay large indemnities acted as a deterrent to industrial recovery. "It is far worse than the War," was the comment of a Bavarian lady. "During the War we had hope. We knew it would end some day. Now there is no hope."

Then to make matters worse, nationalism dictated the raising of artificial barriers. Trade stopped at the frontiers because of tariffs; often, indeed, transportation itself was stopped, and there was no knowing whether a train from Prague to Vienna would ever get there. Perhaps the worse sufferer was Austria, which normally had had few industries, and without her lost provinces could not possibly feed herself. The British journalist, Philip Gibbs, visiting Vienna in November, 1919, wrote that eighty-three per cent of Vienna's children were stricken with rickets—the result of undernourishment. There was no milk for children over a year old, and the bread rations for each individual (adult or child) was two pounds a week. "More than lack of food," wrote an Austrian lady, once a member of the Metropolitan Opera Company of

New York, "we suffer from the cold. There is no wood or coal to be got, and the temperature of the houses is 43 or 45 degrees Fahrenheit." Yet an Austrian writer tells us of quantities of coal in Czechoslovakia, much of which went to waste, while people in Vienna, clad in their threadbare garments, were freezing to death.

The suffering in central Europe (and Austria got no relief until some food at last came through the American Food Commission) was a ghastly chapter in human history. Insofar as the Allied blockade prolonged the agony, one can hardly find expressions sufficiently scathing to denounce it, for Germany was disarmed and Austria a pitiful wreck. As an eminent British publicist declared, "We too sank Lusitanias. We too for some cold political end plunged the unarmed, the weak, the helpless children, the suffering women to agonizing death and torture—without a tremor." The food which Germans ate for a year after the War was in quantity and quality barely life-sustaining. Such was the dearth of fabrics that new-born children in hospitals were often wrapped in paper, and the shoes of most of the population were made of paper and wood. Childhood and old age contributed, of course, the heaviest mortality. Underfeeding naturally gave the fullest play to disease. Tuberculosis and other maladies carried off hundreds of thousands, and in Poland for a time typhus fever raged unchecked, for the supply of doctors and drugs as well as hospital equipment was hopelessly unequal to the demand. The class which probably suffered the most was the small group of intellectuals, such as artists and musicians, who, not having ever learned to do manual labor and finding no longer any professional work to do, were reduced to the direst straits. The suffering of the cities was, of course, more intense than that of the countryside, but misery was fairly universal. Conditions in Hungary were generally less appalling than in Austria; yet such was the extent of the pillage by the Roumanians that the transportation system was paralyzed for a time, and famine conditions prevailed in much of the land. The Poles secured relief before their former oppressors, the Germans, but Poland had been ravaged by both sides during the War, and the mortality among the civilian population had been staggering. Even those children who survived in these wasted countries must ever bear the mark of this terrible period—a condition which must affect the future of a generation. And the effect of so much privation was moral as well as physical. "Hunger and want of work," wrote an observer, "in these lies the chief cause of human misery and the chief cause of human rebellion."

Thus in many cases the woes of Europe were aggravated by the sufferers themselves. The political unrest which followed immediately after the War was on their part in many cases the groping for a panacea which always seemed to elude them. Monarchies fell in Germany, Austria, Russia, Turkey, and Greece as a direct result of the War, and ultimately that of Spain was swept into the current as well. Moderate parties tried to stem the course of revolution in most of these countries, but they led an uneasy existence between reactionaries on the one hand and communists on the other. Russia succumbed to communism, and it looked as if this movement would sweep, like a veritable pestilence,[1] over the stricken continent. Hungary did go under for a time; Austria barely escaped; Poland faced a struggle for her existence; and Germany had to pass through two crises before the contagion was arrested. Largely these inroads of communism were due to sheer despair. People thought of it as a possible escape from an agonizing existence that seemed to promise nothing. It was perhaps due to the solid qualities of the German people as a whole that Europe finally struggled through this crisis.

Political disorders: (1) from communism

But if states were menaced from within by communist propaganda, they were also in many cases threatened from without by another form of popular restlessness—inordinate nationalism, feeding on jealousy and hatred. Just as after a great conflagration has been put out, there are still smoldering embers, so a score of petty wars followed in the train of the Great War. Some, of course, are too small to deserve attention, but the war between Roumania and Hungary, that between Russia and Poland, and the one between Turkey and Greece were vexing affairs and produced additional hardships. It seemed as if every people felt free to attack its neighbor. Nationalism, ever ready to exude its poison, was now the more dangerous because of the general demoralization.

(2) From nationalism

---

[1] Communism, unlike socialism, as the latter was usually interpreted, though perhaps equally the child of Marx, signified the establishment of a socialist régime by violence under a proletarian dictatorship. It tended to take the form of a strict regimentation in the life of the community. In Hungary, where it was tried out for a few months in 1919 all homes became the property of the state, and a determined effort was made to put all persons on the same economic level. A drastic recasting of the social order through violence would have been a doubtful experiment for central Europe, already weakened and demoralized by war. It proved unworkable in Hungary even before it was suppressed from outside.

Had the Allies delayed demobilization until the peace was made and rendered secure, much of this discord would have been spared. But the British and American publics dictated an immediate demobilization, and as Italy cared for nothing but her own frontier, it devolved upon the French to do what policing had to be done. It was the French who saved Poland in 1920 and aided in the pacification of Turkey, but France was too exhausted to carry the load alone. The fickleness of democracies, struggling for a durable peace and then shirking its responsibilities, is painfully apparent. Yet in justice to the British it may be noted that they were sharing with the French the custody of certain former possessions of the Ottoman Empire. It was frenzied central Europe that was left to its sorry devices. For the Continent one can feel only pity in these days. One is reminded of a deep gash that will not heal.

Immediate triumph of democracy   Would popular government heal it? Certainly an immediate result of the War was a spread of democracy. We have mentioned the toppling of thrones, which included the passing of three of the oldest dynasties in history, the Romanovs, the Hapsburgs, and the Hohenzollerns, and all the constitutions of the new nations, as well as of Germany and Austria, were markedly democratic. We may also recall that the electorate had been greatly extended in England during the War. But as time went on, there was some reaction, and the experiment of dictatorship has been tried in various nations. Greece and Spain resorted to it temporarily; Hungary, Turkey, and Jugoslavia with some promise of permanency; Italy erected her Fascist régime; Poland found autocracy more suited to her capacity than constitutional government; and the Germans have recently shown that democracy does not appeal to their national temperament. Regardless of Wilson's exalted ideal of "making the world safe for democracy," each nation has sought to apply its own particular solution, but the prevalence of dictatorships has seemed to show that democracy was not capable of coping with conditions so abnormal as those confronting post-war Europe. Whether the general trend can be considered as toward democracy or away from it is perhaps too early to decide. But as to the progress of nationalism there is no doubt.

THE PROMOTION OF NATIONALISM

That voracious goddess, Nationalism, drew new strength from the War, for many were the triumphs she could record as its result.

We have noted the familiar types, patriotism, striving to gratify *The War as* *a nationalist* its instincts of fear, greed, or hatred, and the yearning of national- *revolution* ities, long subjected, to obtain their liberation; in this fact of liberation and in the triumph of irredentism we see the War once again in the light of a revolution. The beaten nations, as we have seen, received short shrift, but the victors reaped a harvest.

France emerged the strongest nation of Europe. She had *Gains of the* recovered her lost provinces, increased her mineral wealth, ex- *victorious* *Allies* tended her colonial interests (through the medium of the mandate system), and was able by husbanding her gold reserve to loan money to the new nations and build up a coalition of powers attached to her leadership. Nationalism to her meant thenceforth self-defense—the protection of her frontiers.

Italy completed her nationalist unification, gained a strong frontier to the north, and, thanks to the possession of Trieste and Fiume and a species of protectorate over Albania (imposed in 1926), she became unquestionably mistress of the Adriatic. Though she failed to obtain her expected sphere of interest in Asia Minor, she received, as the result of agreements with France and Great Britain large extensions of territory in Africa.

Great Britain also extended her colonial interests under the ægis of the mandate system, and her supremacy of the sea was propor- tionally greater with the extinction of the German navy. But it is noticeable that in general the War left Great Britain rather weaker as a power. We shall dwell later on the depletion of her economic strength. We may note here the progressive decentralization of the British Empire. Loyal as they are to the motherland, the dominions have become more self-assertive since the War. In certain cases their influence has actually determined British policy, and some at least have refused to be bound by the commitments of such policy as applied to Europe. The feeling that each must follow its own peculiar interests and that imperial policy is second- ary is now more pronounced than ever. Canada has even her sep- arate ambassador to the United States, and so has Ireland, the youngest cf the dominions. It is noticeable also that Great Britain had to relinquish her hold on Egypt (only safeguarding the Suez Canal), and has had to make important political concessions to India. The British Empire was, in short, profoundly shaken by the War.

The United States acquired no territory as the result of the War, but it brought her more than a decade of unprecedented prosperity. She obtained much of the market which had formerly been enjoyed by Germany and Great Britain, and her export trade almost doubled. Above all, she became Europe's leading creditor. It is sometimes asserted that New York, much more than London, is now the financial center of the world.

The status of imperialism

Is imperialism dead? One would like to think so; but while there are still lands to exploit, the old forces are likely to operate. Perhaps the chief reasons for an abatement of imperialism are the preoccupation of France and Great Britain with their mandated possessions, the exclusion of Germany from over-seas activities, and the fact that industry in general has yet (1935) to recover the levels it reached before the War. Yet even so we must observe that concession-hunting has far from disappeared. The oil fields of Persia proved still a tempting bait for Great Britain, who, after Communist Russia had renounced the sphere of interest she had inherited from the czarist régime, endeavored in 1919 to get the whole of the kingdom as her own sphere of interest through the imposition of a sort of protectorate over Persia. But Persia had recovered her independence when the Russians withdrew and she did not propose to jeopardize it again. While it is true that her capacious oil fields are largely in the hands of foreign companies, it may be that the awakened nationalism of backward countries like Persia will serve as something of a safeguard, now that imperialism has come to be contemned by public opinion. At least we may hazard the view that exploitation of weaker races may be less easy than it was before the War. Only the poor, distracted Chinese Republic seems unable to guard its treasures, and it is here—more than anywhere else outside of Europe—that dangerous complications are likely to happen. And the danger lurks in Japanese policy. In fact, the one power whose imperialism has moved forward steadily is Japan—a subject we shall discuss in a later chapter.

The triumph of repressed nationalism

Despite the flouting of the nationalist principle in the interest of Poland and Italy, the liberative type of nationalism, including irredentism, won signal triumphs through the War. Empires which had peoples in subjection against their will dissolved into their component elements. The liberation of the Roumans and Jugoslavs of Austria-Hungary brought about a greater Roumania and a greater Serbia (now called Jugoslavia). There was even some protection accorded, as we have noted, to some of those nationalist minorities which had to remain in subjection—those islets within nations. But this multiplication of nations may not be an unmixed blessing; and some have observed that central Europe has become "Balkanized." The arrogance of nationalism was shown after the War in the intermittent friction and in the raising of tariff walls and other forms of economic obstruction. There is little doubt that most of the people of the Danube lands were materially better off in the days of the Dual Monarchy. That antiquated state was at all events an economic unit. Now business is impeded by a multitude of currencies and commercial regulations. But nationalism, as we have noticed, demands its primal gratification regardless of the cost to material interests.

More alarming perhaps is the extent to which the idea of "self-determination" has penetrated Africa and Asia. Unrest among the Arabs greatly complicated the task for France and Great Britain; and the latter power has felt obliged to yield to Egyptian nationalism and grant to the land of the Pharaohs nominal independence (1922).[1] Even far-off India has become a scene of constant agitation, and none of the concessions which the British have been forced to make give much promise of solving the problem.[2] How safe it may be to accord independence to people with no experience in self-government is no doubt a matter of opinion. In any case the East has awakened, with results that cannot possibly be foreseen.

Nationalism outside of Europe

But there was one triumph of nationalism (an example of the liberative type), which, apart from occasional economic difficulties, has so far given no ground for apprehension, and that was the case of the Irish. We have noticed the increasing unrest and irritation

The case of the Irish

---

[1] During the War Great Britain formally declared a protectorate over Egypt, but after the War she had to encounter so much lawless resistance that after an investigation by a commission, and following its recommendations, she recognized Egypt as "an independent, sovereign state"—not, however, as part of a treaty, since the Egyptians would not consider the safeguards which Great Britain demanded for foreign interests. Intermittent and sometimes serious friction continued, and no final settlement has been reached. In the meantime a small British force defends the canal.

[2] The agitation has been led by a remarkable Hindu, Mahatma Gandhi, who, while counseling against violence, has imbued his people, regardless of caste or religion, with an intense spiritual fervor. While there has been some rioting, economic boycott and refusal to pay taxes have been the usual weapons of the nationalists. In general, the British government has shown considerable patience with the movement, and has greatly extended Indian self-government, though still denying full dominion status, which the nationalists demand.

of the Irish and the rapid development of the Sinn Fein movement, looking not to home rule but to complete separation from Great Britain. This movement, as we saw, resulted in a Sinn Fein landslide in the elections of 1918, after which it may be stated that the political aspect of the Irish question had entered upon a new phase: the demand for independence. It is an interesting fact that at this time the Irish were enjoying a material prosperity they had never known before.

The Irish now commenced a definite campaign to secure their ends. As Wilson refused to listen to their case in Paris (seeing that the British government obviously regarded the question as strictly domestic), they decided that revolution was their only practicable course. The newly elected members of parliament resolved not to take their seats, but, instead, set up a provisional government at Dublin. A professor of mathematics, Eamon de Valera, was chosen provisional president. The Irish Republican Association was formed to carry on a guerilla warfare against British rule. Boycott and murder were its weapons. Naturally the British government would not tolerate such disorder, and replied by placing Ireland under martial law.

At the same time, with their usual spirit of compromise, the British statesmen sought a basis for conciliation. An effort of Lloyd George to bring about peace by the creation of two parliaments, one for Ireland, one for Ulster, with a common executive (this was the fourth home rule bill) was rejected by the "government" at Dublin. Dominion status, which Asquith would have preferred, was equally unacceptable to the British parliament. The shooting of police and soldiers continued, and in the following year (1921) disorder reached its height. By this time the British government had sent over some auxiliaries, and these forces met the terror with counter-terror. Ulster alone remained quiet, and having decided to accept the new home rule bill, she organized her own parliament and ministry. This, meant, of course, a divided Ireland, which was contrary to the principles and hopes of the Catholic Irish, but they were powerless to prevent it.

Finally Great Britain came to the point of offering dominion status, and after much hesitation the Irish leaders were persuaded to parley with the government on that basis. To make a long story short, the negotiation ended in a treaty (December 6, 1921), which created the Irish Free State. The essence of this settlement was the establishment of dominion status for Ireland. At the same time Ireland remained in allegiance to the British crown; she was to allow the British navy to utilize some of her ports; and her army was to be no larger in proportion to population than that of Great Britain. This settlement was ratified in a close vote [1] by the Irish parliament (the *dail eirann*) and by a very substantial majority [2] in the British parliament; and the Irish then proceeded to make a constitution for themselves and to organize a government. The result had been a compromise, though one so favorable to the Irish would scarcely have been thought possible in 1918. Ireland became an added pillar of the British Empire, and was now at last free to conduct her own affairs. At the same time Ulster's separate status (it is now known as "Northern Ireland") was assured; and by the military and naval safeguards mentioned Great Britain was relieved of anxiety lest Ireland become the instrument of some foreign enemy.[3]

But political changes, whether organic or territorial, were hardly more important than social changes produced by the War. While mass production, as we have shown, had had something to do with lessening social differences, the upheaval produced by the War had even more noticeable effects.

The Improved Position of the Proletariat and the Peasantry

In the enhanced importance of the so-called lower classes the War promoted a process which, as we have noticed, had been going on for some time. In accentuating class consciousness and making the proletariat (or in some cases the peasantry) a powerful factor in politics the War seemed to mark the beginning of a revolution. But only in Russia was the movement completely destructive of the old social order. And it was only in Russia that efforts were made to nationalize the land. Elsewhere individualism was strengthened among the peasants. While the proletariat usually aspired to the nationalization of industry in some form of workers' control, more and more peasants became individual proprietors.

The War as a social revolution

---

[1] 64 to 57. But in the elections for the constituent assembly which was to draft a constitution, the adherents of the Free State polled a large majority.

[2] 302 to 60.

[3] Ireland was for a while rent by civil war, as de Valera would have none of the settlement and still demanded complete separation. In the end, however, he gave up the struggle.

This change was especially notable in Roumania and Czechoslovakia, where the large estates were systematically dismembered after the War.

Conditions favorable to the proletariat: (1) in victor countries

The strengthened position of the proletariat in society, as a result of the War was due to two factors, which operated in varying intensity in different quarters. Never had the working class been of such practical importance as during the War. They had had to make munitions for the army and transport them. On moral grounds it might perhaps have been just to conscript them for such tasks and to expect a spirit of self-sacrifice such as the man in the trenches was called upon to display. But governments could not but recognize that the working class had still but meager earnings while at the same time it possessed a power to push its interests in a way that might have been fatally embarrassing. Hence governments tacitly admitted the strategic advantage of the proletariat, and readily enough dictated an increase of wages. In several countries representatives of the workers were also given posts of responsibility.

And economic advantages procured

It was nevertheless true that, apart from employment for everyone, the working class in general had not been really better off during the War, but rather the contrary; for if wages had risen materially, so also had prices, and in England wages failed to catch up with prices until after the War. The workers themselves, however, are not apt to take this fact into consideration, and wage-increases certainly produced a stimulating effect as well as optimism for the future. In 1920 when England enjoyed a temporary boom and the workers had then attained a ratio between wages and prices better than at any time in their history, they were determined to resist to the utmost any lowering of their improved standard of living. It is no doubt a proof of their newly acquired strength that, if we leave out of account those who were unemployed, their financial position in virtue of the purchasing power of their wages was better in 1932 (as an official report shows) than it had been in 1914. It was, rather, the army of unemployed that came to reflect the depleted strength of Great Britain after the war.

While the period subsequent to the boom was to show that all classes had to share in a certain way the painful cost of readjustment, the workers did secure a shorter day, and this promises to be permanent. In 1920 the English miners won a seven-hour day, and in most other industries eight hours or thereabouts became the standard. To the maintenance of this benefit the workers fought with the utmost determination, and though the miners had to return to an eight-hour day (by reason of the desperate plight of the coal industry), the gain as a whole has so far been maintained.

In the matter of unemployment, which had resulted from the after-war depression, the English working class received striking consideration. In 1920 unemployment insurance was applied to all workmen except those engaged in agriculture and domestic service, in other words about 12,000,000 persons, including even those women who had been drawn into industry during the War. The measure was, in fact, so liberal that a worker came under its provisions if he could not find work that paid him as much as he had customarily received. In 1927 it was amended to the extent of applying to a workman who could not find work in the line in which he had been trained; and in 1930 he was actually assured the benefits of the measure unless he refused work offered him by a labor exchange—being thus excused from the need of hunting a job. In the meantime, by legislation in 1924,[1] no time limit had been placed on the enjoyment of the benefits provided, and thus had been inaugurated what was commonly known as the "dole"— assuming that unemployment was a more or less permanent condition, and that a worker could not be expected to return to a job in twenty-six weeks, as heretofore assumed. Since, as a matter of fact, unemployment had aggregated anywhere from 1,000,000 to 2,000,000 workers each year, reaching in 1932 twenty per cent of the total working class, it can be judged that the dole could hardly have been avoided. The immense cost of supporting so large a number of people was borne by a weight of taxation so heavy that in case of the wealthy it was almost confiscatory. Yet it was not merely a matter of social justice. If people were to be left to starve, they would of necessity have recourse to revolution. The British workman would suffer long before he dabbled in revolution (communism has little appeal for him), yet the right of self-preservation might force him into that path against his will. On the other hand, we must note that while sporadic strikes had something of a moral importance (though the solidarity of the

---

[1] This reform was rescinded in 1925 but re-enacted in 1927 and is still (1935) in force.

workers was hardly as great as supposed), the British government refused to yield to direct pressure of that sort. It is well known that a Britisher does not like to be coerced, and on the occasion of a railroad strike the general public sided against the strikers, and trains were run by voluntary aid. After the so-called "general strike" of 1926 the government got a bill passed by parliament which made sympathetic strikes illegal. Trade-unionism in England has shown a lessened strength in recent years.

In France labor conditions were less acute after the War for there was little unemployment thanks to the work of reconstruction, and France was less industrialized than Great Britain. Yet class unity had been furthered among the workmen during the War; the "C.G.T." had enormously extended its membership; and there were also some formidable strikes, fomented, of course, by the syndicalists. As in England, however, the workers secured redress more from a general appreciation of their claims to social justice than as the result of a resort to violence. In Italy the strikes which followed in the train of demobilization kept that country in a turmoil for several years and led ultimately to a system which, as we shall later observe, brought conditions affecting the workman under the direct control of the government.

(2) In defeated countries

In the defeated countries, notably Germany and Austria, the heightened importance of the proletariat was chiefly due to revolution. Socialist parties were able to get control of the government and to some extent pursued a class policy. Wages, of course, were variable, for the economic condition of central Europe was often grave, but wage standardization was at length attempted, and much was done in the way of improving housing conditions, as well as providing some insurance against unemployment. The city of Vienna until recently was dominated by the interests of the proletariat.

The international importance of the labor problem

The importance of the working class was also recognized at the Congress of Paris. Attached to the Covenant of the League of Nations was a provision for an International Bureau of Labor, whose duty is to compile and preserve data bearing upon working conditions throughout the civilized world. Labor congresses have been held, and some of its recommendations, such as the elimination of child labor, an equal scale of remuneration for men and women, and the eight-hour day have been widely accepted.

The new importance of both the working class and peasantry

has been interestingly reflected in politics. In Great Britain recog- *Influence of the "lower classes" in politics* nition of the growing importance of the labor problem led to a remarkable growth of the Labor Party, which recruited so much of its strength from the Liberal Party that it came to supplant the latter as the "Opposition" in parliament, and twice was called upon to constitute a cabinet. Though it has not yet possessed a majority in the house of commons, it is a strong and aggressive factor in British politics. Even in France the strength of the socialists grew measurably, and the radical ministries since the War have been composed of important elements from this group. In Italy, after a period of much disorder, the trend took, rather, the opposite direction, but in Germany and Austria as well as in some of the new nations the socialists wielded an important in- fluence for many years, though from the time of the "world de- pression," which set in 1929, they seem to have steadily lost ground. Even so the proletariat is more of a political factor than it was before the War. It is also noticeable that in agricultural states like Roumania, Jugoslavia, and Bulgaria the peasants have been pretty generally in control, and that in Russia a proletarian dic- tatorship still rules.

If we take a general view of the economic position of the pro- *Progress of social reform* letariat since the War, we may note that the relative position of unskilled labor has improved, and for labor skilled and unskilled there has been somewhat greater security attempted against poverty and unemployment. There is also a growing recognition of the principle that a shorter working day need not necessarily mean decreased production, for a scientific study of the workers' capacity has led to the conclusion that the element of fatigue has not been given due weight, and that shortening the working day by an hour or two would have little effect on industrial produc- tivity. The eight-hour day is generally accepted as a standard, to which Europe adapts itself as far as actual conditions permit. Meanwhile the increasing displacement of workers through the rationalization of industry seems likely to result in even shorter hours as a means of keeping labor forces intact; but so far such a principle has not, in general, found its way into legislation. In the matter of unemployment insurance there has, however, been notable progress, and the principle of the minimum wage has been given a wide application both in England and in France. There has even been some experimenting in the direction of what we may call "industrial democracy"—the idea, as one authority has put it, that workers are "co-workers with the employers and not merely living tools." Recognition of unions and the compulsion of employers to yield to the principle of collective bargaining had been a step in that direction in the nineteenth century. During the War the experiment of workers' committees through which the employees could voice their complaints on questions of management and working conditions was tried out in England in a number of trades, though the plan was not continued after the War. In certain other countries the institution gained ground. In Germany, for example, the new constitution of the republic, established a system of economic councils, with a federal council at the top, to make proposals on economic questions. Subsequently, by the Works Councils Act of 1920 every business establishment employing as many as twenty men was required to have a "works-council" to safeguard the interests of employees. While this meant in no wise workers' control, the question of discharging a workman was left to the judgment of these bodies and the right of appeal to a board of conciliation acted as a guarantee against arbitrary dismissal. But the general attitude of labor toward these committees was one of skepticism and moderate disapproval; it was felt that the employers were no more ready than ever to give the workers a voice in the actual management of a business and that minor concessions were liable to ennervate class feeling. For the same reason systems of profit-sharing have usually encountered resistance from trade unions. One of the most successful schemes in Germany (as long as it lasted) was the adoption in 1923 of a systematic plan of compulsory arbitration in wage disputes. Whether class differences will be bridged by the corporative scheme, recently adopted in Italy and Germany (adjustment of common interests within two parallel federations or "corporations" under the ægis of the State) has yet to be demonstrated.

The position of socialism   Much, of course, of the social reform which we have noted above was due to the influence of the proletariat in politics. But it is an interesting fact that outside of Russia socialism itself has made but little headway. Even many socialists have become a little wary of the idea of nationalizing industry on the ground that it would involve too elaborate a bureaucracy to give sufficient assurance of social justice, and the moderates who were in control after the War preferred, in general, to stick to capitalism until there was much more evidence of economic recovery. Moreover, as conditions improve, it has been found again and again that a good many socialists look with decidedly increasing favor on private enterprise. While the British Labor Party still stands for nationalization at least as applied to mining and transportation, most Continental socialists (excluding, of course, the communists) have become but little more than social reformers in practice. It was the very indefiniteness of their program that weakened the socialist parties in Germany and Austria, just as extremism had ruined them in Italy; and during the last four years it is perfectly plain that the power of the proletariat in most countries has been decidedly on the wane. Yet even so the enhanced prestige of this class as the result of the War seems much too stable to encounter more than a temporary reaction. We must also be mindful of the condition of the workers in relation to other classes. The fact that they are not better off than before the War is due to post-war conditions; the significant fact is that in a period of disorders and depression their economic position in relation to other classes has improved.

Parallel with the enhanced importance of the proletariat and the peasantry has come the abasement of the aristocracy. Social and political revolutions had, of course, long ago disposed of the French and Italian nobility, and the culture of those countries is rather the common possession of the bourgeoisie. Prussia, of course, kept her powerful junkers after the War, though they have had to share their prestige with the rich industrialists. The British aristocracy also remained, though so cramped by heavy taxation that its fine estates are passing and its famous London "season" is but a faint replica of what it once was in the prosperous Victorian days. To revel in the world of culture one must be fairly sure of one's income; one must have the wherewithal to enjoy one's leisure. Above all, one must have a home. Russian *émigrés* are scattered throughout Europe—a restless and intriguing element without means and without hope. Some of them run cafés or wait on tables in Parisian restaurants or invade the realm of business in humble rôles; some are mere adventurers, gambling at Monte Carlo or selling their empty titles for American heiresses. Europe is full of dispossessed nobles from Russia, Roumania, Czechoslovakia, the Baltic countries, and Poland. But the most staggering blow, dealt to that old culture which seemed to cling

The abasement of the aristocracy

to aristocracy, was in Austria. Unique among cities for its peculiarly native charm, its blending of the East and West, its glory in all the arts and some of the sciences, was Vienna. It had an atmosphere all its own, and was more like the eighteenth century at its best than a center of an industrialized Europe. The Austrians are, in general, neither military nor practical; they have the same

Underwood & Underwood

THE HEART OF VIENNA

artistic skill as the French, but, as a people, far more genial, more expansive, more romantic. Perhaps the best expression of Old Vienna was the waltz; its rhythm, its haunting melody, its vivacity seemed to express a perennial mood. The aristocracy of Vienna, who possessed estates all over the empire, were, of course, the patrons of that culture and of the brilliant display which made their city seem the center of a world of romance. But the dream was entirely shattered by the War and the miseries which followed. Light-hearted the Viennese may always be, but the great days are gone, and in very truth Vienna has passed into romance. No doubt aristocracy was doomed in any case; its political influence was challenged before the War; but until the War it ruled the social and cultural life of most of central Europe. Its passing means that Europe is somewhat less interesting than it was.

In these changing times the position of woman was also profoundly affected.

The Revolt of Woman

If the right of individual man to self-expression had been slow to win recognition through the ages, delay has been doubly true in the case of woman. Socially her place under the Old Régime had normally been restricted to the family circle, where her rôle as wife and mother was too vital to call for question. Economically she had been primarily a housewife, though if she belonged to the peasant class, she might also have toiled in the fields or worked with spindle and distaff for the family support. Even when woman began to play an active part in high society, her function was chiefly to amuse men, though, as her charms might often be used as political capital, she frequently became a channel of intrigue, and had sometimes considerable power; hence the rôle of a Pompadour. Now and then a woman became a monarch and had a chance to sharpen her intellect and vie with men, as was the case with Catherine the Great. But such cases were exceptional. Yet with the Renaissance and afterward one finds a few titled ladies who expended some of their time in developing a talent for letters, and the rise of the salon in the seventeenth century gave woman a certain position in the intellectual world. Few women, of course, had really the education to compete with men, and those of the upper classes who did not marry were apt to look to a convent for their solace. In the eighteenth century young gentlewomen were commonly taught to read and write, to dance and to play some musical instrument, and possibly to learn one foreign language—all of which training was designed to enable them to please and hence to capture some worthy gentleman for a husband. Napoleon declared that by reason of the "weakness of women's brains" he would prescribe for them needle-work and other innocent pursuits. Even in our own day Kaiser William II marked out woman's sphere as "church, children, cooking." In nothing did habit operate more firmly than in the traditional conception of woman.

Woman's historic dependence and its causes

To balance the intellect of woman against that of man or to fix the relative place of the emotions in shaping her conduct is far too controversial a subject to justify discussion in these pages. As compared with man she has seemed to show rather less creative ability, but she was able sometimes to discern talent in men and to give them a welcome patronage in her salon. The very fact that she was practically divorced from politics and that she left war and business to the other sex gave her at least an opportunity, as time went on, to cultivate an interest in the arts. But it was still a man's world, and remained so until comparatively recent times. The reason was twofold. Women were the weaker sex, and since for a long period of time politics was accompanied by occasional violence and not infrequently involved war, a woman was hardly considered fitted for public life. If violence decreased in time with the growing respect for law, habit still operated to exclude women from politics. In the second place, woman was needed to rear the family and to hold the home together. It was a social function that had to be performed and Nature had seemed to decree that woman should perform it. It was because of the duty of perpetuating the line that woman's moral position was of necessity hedged in. Men could be promiscuous, but for a man's wife there must be no question of the legitimacy of the heir. It is true, of course, that there were in all periods women of easy morals, but, generally speaking, they were known as such, and did not alter the general conception of woman as a creature that must be sheltered from the temptations of the world and whose morals must be always "above suspicion."

Woman's disabilities and progress in the nineteenth century The French Revolution, apart from its stress on lofty abstractions, liberty and equality, did nothing for the advancement of woman. The Industrial Revolution achieved a little in that direction, for it made her a wage-earner, and as wage-scales rose, she came to achieve some measure of economic independence. Yet the fact remained that most women were still dependents and their sphere was still the home. The law did not recognize her as a separate personality (her property being her husband's), and even to get release from a cruel husband was very difficult, for in most countries the Church stood as a barrier against divorce. She was debarred from most of the professions (teaching school was sometimes the exception) and she could not, of course, hold office or cast a ballot. One of the few professions opened to her was nursing, and here is where Florence Nightingale displayed her singular courage and ability, founding the first base hospital for the care of the wounded in the Crimean War—an institution which had doubtless an influence in creating the Red Cross (authorized by the Geneva convention in 1864). Perhaps it was the thought of Florence Nightingale that inspired John Stuart Mill to put in his plea for woman suffrage. At any rate with the growing trend toward democracy more and more freedom was extended to woman. We cannot describe this progress in detail. Suffice it to say that by the end of the nineteenth century her separate property rights were generally recognized; divorce was made easier; she began to fill positions of executive importance and in some countries to be admitted to the professions of medicine and law. There was also in several countries an organization of women battling ceaselessly for the suffrage. In England in 1869 they had already acquired the right to vote in municipal elections and in 1888 they were permitted to vote for members of county councils. The full right of suffrage was first extended in New Zealand in 1893 and in Australia in 1902. The Scandinavian countries followed, and England in 1918, as we have noticed. In the latter case appreciation of woman's work during the War had probably quite as much to do with this result as the campaigning of the "suffragettes," though the activities of the latter had prepared the public mind for such an issue. "Feminism," as the movement for "equal rights" has been called, had thus made considerable progress before the close of the Great War. Much ground remained to be gained. Yet to the names of Marie Curie, the scientist, Josephine Butler, the social worker, Suzanne Lenglen, the tennis player, Marie Corelli, the writer, Maria Montessori, the educator, Sarah Bernhardt, the actress, Maud Royden, the evangelist, and Selma Lagerlöf, Nobel prize-winner, might be added those of so many other illustrious women at the close of the century that one cannot but notice the expanding influence of woman in human society. It was a "sign of the times."

But the Great War has had, perhaps, a greater effect on woman —her position and her outlook on life—than any other chapter in modern history. The fact that she acquired equal rights with men in all the countries of central Europe, as well as in Poland, Russia, and the Baltic states, gave her at least a legal position that was all that she could wish. This did not mean, of course, that she would

Woman's position as affected by the War: (1) legal

hold as many offices as men, for a large proportion of her sex were not at all interested in politics, and the horizon of many women was still entirely bounded by their homes. But it gave woman a chance to aspire to power if she chose. Though in the course of subsequent events she lost her political rights in Germany, it was an incalculable gain that by the standards of democracy universal suffrage meant also votes for women. France, as we have noted, still refused to grant her the suffrage, but here, as in other Latin countries, the difficulty has been a fear of the influence of the Church, for Frenchwomen are thought to be deeply religious and France is always on her guard against the return of its insidious influence in public affairs. Yet it is probably true that Frenchwomen, in general, care little to obtain the suffrage. The Frenchwoman is primarily a home-maker and if she happens to belong to the lower middle class she is apt to hold the purse-strings as well, and not infrequently manages her husband's business.

(2) Moral But woman's chief emancipation as the result of the War has been moral. Woman has gained in self-respect and self-confidence. It is that feeling of independence (sometimes perhaps a distortion of social values) that has tended to draw the woman worker away from domestic service—a fact which no doubt has made it increasingly harder for the housewife. It is also that spirit of independence which has made the young girl of today less apt to jump into marriage as the only practicable solution for her economic needs. And again, it is that yearning for a broader life that has drawn so many matrons from their homes (though far fewer in Europe than in America), with sometimes unfortunate effects on family life. Thousands of women who during the War had enjoyed their first experience of making their own way were anxious to continue in industry and many if not most of them were able to find a permanent place for themselves. Also the educational advantages, offered to an increasing extent to women, have given them added poise and confidence in themselves and in many cases have fitted them to compete with men. But the woman of post-war Europe has also more disposition to enjoy herself. She refuses to be hemmed in by man-made conventions. She adopts the sports of men and dresses to fit the occasion. She goes about more freely, comes in contact with a wider circle of men, and tends to emulate their free and easy ways. She may not be less moral in the conventional sense, but she considers herself mistress of her conscience and tends

to shape her own ethical standards. While it may be true that the great majority of women are still but gradually throwing off old habits (perhaps their protective instinct toward the young has made them the more conservative of the sexes), yet the fact remains that woman as a class has been profoundly affected by the War. She is more prone to face realities, more ready to think for herself, more apt to weigh conventions and to alter them as she pleases.

The bursting of woman's fetters was somewhat paralleled by the experience of youth.

THE REVOLT OF YOUTH

The War perhaps intensified but certainly did not originate the European youth's interest in politics. As a sharp contrast to conditions in America, university students in Europe had taken throughout the nineteenth century the keenest interest in politics, as well as in other serious things. They were the young intelligentsia—material from which professors, pamphleteers, and politicians were made. They furnished some of the explosiveness to nihilism, and in many of the revolutionary upheavals of the century they played a striking rôle—at any rate at the beginning. In the British universities they solemnly discoursed on public questions, and in Oxford's debating society, the Union, men like Gladstone gained a certain preliminary training in debate. As a rule, youth was intensely patriotic. His emotional fervor, his romantic attachment to an ideal, and his expansive energies aroused his fighting instincts and made him eager and ready to support his country's cause whenever challenged. In its demand for heroism and self-sacrifice the Great War levied a heavy toll on youth. It was "theirs not to reason why." But from the very fact of their youth, such young men went to the colors with buoyancy of heart and a pathetic confidence. *Before the War*

To anyone as susceptible as the young the shock of this cataclysm was necessarily terrific. Perhaps it affected them in two principal ways. To some it brought disillusion. When it appeared that the several governments had not been as innocent as they had alleged and that the struggle was not the "holy war" at first supposed; when, moreover, the young soldiers of opposite camps came to appreciate that all were fighting in the same romantic spirit for what they believed a righteous cause, there was something of a revulsion against war as an instrument as barbarous as it was futile. *Disillusion*

In Germany the rôle of the *Wandervögel* ("Wanderbirds") is of special interest. Originating before the War [1] as a protest against the over-standardization of German life, this organization, while non-political in character, seems to have gained fresh momentum after the struggle. Bands of these youths tramped the country as though to see what there was to be seen in a world which the War and the Peace had so sadly altered. They worked their way as they went, and lived pretty much for the present, as though the morrow had little to offer. Among the English youth there was a distinct note of pacifism in the days following the War. It was perhaps of no little significance that the Oxford Union resolved in 1933 by a large vote that under no circumstances was one justified in "fighting for king or country." In a gathering of students from all the belligerent countries in Switzerland in 1922 all but the German contingent admitted that responsibility for the War should be shared by all sides. With the German youth also disillusionment gradually came about, but it was of quite another sort. To him the idea that the victors could trample on the fallen—for such was his impression—was a fact not in keeping with his idea of honest sport or social justice. In the heart of the German youth the fire of revenge was kindled. To raise his fallen country to her former height became in time an obsession. Some-what the same spirit permeated the younger generation in Russia, *Self-reliance and restlessness* though the enemy there was not a foreign nation but an oppressive and decaying order of society. These sentiments struggling for expression in many lands were paralleled in Germany and Russia by something like a renascence of belligerent intolerance. To the Italian youth also the martial spirit was quickened, but rather by a government which knew so well how to touch those inner springs of emotion that can always produce a patriot.

In the second place, youth was swept by a feeling of restlessness after the War. Apart from the possible shattering of ideals, the natural reaction from a régime of stern discipline as well as the effect on the nervous system of constant exposure to danger made the young soldier little adapted for quietly settling back into the normal ways of life. The difficulty was doubly great in countries like Germany and Austria which went through a period of depleted rations and unemployment. Much of the energy of youth in all

[1] In Germany, as we have noticed (page 579), the "youth movement" had been much fostered by the Prussian government.

countries was displayed in organizing societies for sport or political purposes, but such a movement was particularly manifest in Germany. The *Studentschaft*, a German student society, designed to bring students together from different universities (even those outside of Germany) into an organization for the discussion of student problems and to furnish mutual assistance whenever needed, was for a long time directly encouraged by the German government, though its democratic principles and organization hardly fitted it for a part in present-day Germany and they have consequently passed into oblivion. Czechoslovakia is said to have become the student's Mecca because of the government's tolerant attitude toward alien nationalities. It is not, of course, alleged that these student associations are a mere reflex of restless energy, but they do show a greater spirit of self-reliance and a disposition on the part of youth to solve its own problems. Those organizations of youth which were patriotic in character—notably in China, Ireland, Germany, and Russia—were perhaps no less sincere than the non-political associations, but they were clamorous and emotional and illustrate better the lawless side of the restlessness which emanated from the War. But there were other, less striking ways in which this unharnessed spirit displayed itself. In Germany the *Wandervögel*, already mentioned, seemed to show a craving for freedom—freedom from the conventional—that affected at least a section of German youth; and the coming of jazz from America, while by no means a respecter of age, seemed to appeal to youth abroad as a sort of welcome reflex of its mood. How generally youth has undergone a change is hard to determine. Canons of conduct vary in different countries, and in France parental influence is very strong. In Latin countries formality still shields the young girl of the middle class from chance acquaintances, but in England since the War a freer association between young men and young women has been very noticeable. Perhaps the most that we can say is that among a great many of Europe's younger generation a freer spirit is now displayed than was the case before the War, as well as an eager desire to know the truth, whatever road may lead to that end. With youth, as also with woman, the shock of that great upheaval tended to rouse a spirit of revolt against the sanctity of convention. Whether such changes are permanent is, of course, too early to judge.

FOR FURTHER READING OR STUDY

Hayes, C. J. H., *Political and Social History of Modern Europe*, vol. ii, chap. xxxii; Schapiro, J. S., *Modern and Contemporary European History*, pp. 754–8; Slosson, P. W., *Twentieth Century Europe*, pp. 429–34 (losses in the War) and chap. xx; Palm, F. C., and Graham, F. E., *Europe since Napoleon*, chaps. xxxvi (triumph of nationalism) and xxxix (unrest outside Europe) and xl; Ogg, F. A., and Sharp, W. C., *Economic Development of Modern Europe*, chaps. xxvi, xxix–xxx; Eisenmenger, A., *Blockade: the Diary of an Austrian Middle Class Woman*.

Bogart, E. L., *Direct and Indirect Cost of the War;* Folks, H., *The Human Costs of the War;* Kohn, S., and Meyendorff, A. F., *The Cost of the War to Russia;* Beard, C. A., *Cross Currents in Europe Today* (published in 1922); Périgord, P., *The International Labor Organization;* Kautsky, K., *The Labor Revolution;* Armstrong, B. N., *Insuring the Essentials* (a valuable survey of social reform up to 1932); Beveridge, W. H., *Unemployment;* Lorwin, L. L., *Labor and Internationalism;* Saposs, D. J., *The Labor Movement in Post-War France;* Shadwell, A. S., *The Socialist Movement*, 2 vols., and *The Breakdown of Socialism;* Evans, I., *The Agrarian Revolution in Roumania;* Cohen-Portheim, P., *The Discovery of Europe* (exceptionally entertaining); Phillips, W. A., *The Revolution in Ireland;* Kohn, H., *A History of Nationalism in the East* and *Nationalism and Imperialism in the Hither East;* Muir, R., *The Expansion of Europe* (new edition), chap. xi; Elliott, W. Y., *The New British Empire;* Millspaugh, A. C., *The American Task in Persia;* Tramerye, P. l'E., *The World's Struggle for Oil;* George, H. L., *The Story of Woman;* Finot, J., *The Problem of the Sexes;* Anthony, K., *Feminism in Germany and Scandinavia* (published in 1915); Shreiner, O., *Women and Labor;* "The New Woman" (A symposium), *Cur. Hist.*, xxvii, 1 ff.; High, S., *The Revolt of Youth;* Kosok, P., *Modern Germany* (for youth movement).

For informing articles on current European affairs the student is referred to *Foreign Affairs* (N. Y.); *Current History; Reports of the Foreign Policy Association;* and the *Annals* (American Academy of Political and Social Science).

XIX. THREE NATIONS IN UPHEAVAL—THE EXPERIMENT OF REVOLUTIONARY DICTATORSHIP

1. THE RISE OF FASCISM IN ITALY

Origins of Fascism; Mussolini and the organization of Fascism; The Fascist coup d'état; Fascism and public opinion; Fascism in theory and practice; Strength and weakness of Fascism.

2. THE RUSSIAN REVOLUTION

A. ORIGINS OF THE REVOLUTION

Fundamental causes of the Revolution; Foundations of the Old Régime: (1) political, (2) social; Abolition of serfdom; Beginning of a revolutionary movement: (1) assault from above, (2) assault from below; Coming of the Industrial Revolution and its significance.

B. THE PRELIMINARY STORM

The occasion; The revolutionary crisis of 1905–6; Reaction under Stolypin; Stolypin's agrarian reform.

C. THE COMING OF THE REVOLUTION

Failure of autocracy in the Great War as a paramount cause of the Revolution; The gathering storm; Outbreak of the Revolution.

D. THE PERIOD OF TRANSITION—THE PROVISIONAL GOVERNMENT AND ITS COLLAPSE

The dyarchy; Weakness of the Provisional Government and causes of its failure; Collapse of Russia; Coming of Lenin and the Bolsheviks; The Bolshevik triumph—the coup d'état of November, 1917.

E. THE COMMUNIST RÉGIME—THE DICTATORSHIP OF THE PROLETARIAT

Consolidation of Bolshevik or Communist power—the Reign of Terror; Basic platform of Communism; Structure of the Communist state; Position of the Communist Party; Economic policy of Lenin and its failure; Temporary reaction—The " Nep "; Death of Lenin; Return to pure communism under Stalin; A planned economy in operation; Communist society; Explanation of the stability of the Communist Régime.

F. RELATIONS WITH EUROPE

Attitude of the Allies; The Allied intervention and the civil war; Triumph of the Soviet government; The Communist offensive; Passing of a crisis; Admission of Communist Russia into the family of nations; Dismemberment of Russia; Question of a world revolution.

3. REVOLUTION AND REACTION IN GERMANY

A. CAUSES AND OUTBREAK OF THE GERMAN REVOLUTION

Popular restlessness during the War; A preliminary revolution "from above"; Downfall of the Empire and its causes.

B. Germany in Transition—The Liberal and Experimental Republic

> Revolution "from below"; Establishment of the Republic; Question of the limitation of the Revolution—repression of communism; Triumph of a middle-of-the-road policy; The Weimar constitution; Character and vicissitudes of the Weimar régime; The causes of reaction.

C. The Triumph of Reaction and the Founding of a New Autocracy

> Elements of support for "National Socialism"; The lengthening shadow; A divided opposition; Triumph of "National Socialism"; Inauguration and foundations of the new régime; Policy of repression; Organization and constructive policy; Outlook on the world; Signs of inner weakness.

Much has been said, in general, of the social and political unrest that followed the War. In three countries, Italy, Russia, and Germany, the overturning of principles and institutions has been especially pronounced; and both for the effects on these countries themselves and for the bearing which it may have on Europe as a whole, the subject must be treated with some fullness. We shall begin with the movement in Italy.

The Rise of Fascism in Italy

The origins of Fascism

We have already demonstrated the difficulties of democratic government in Italy. The individualistic and highly mercurial temperament of the Italians, the large proportion of illiterates, and the comparative newness of democratic institutions had combined to prevent the parliamentary régime from functioning efficiently or winning the public confidence. Such represents the general background of the rise of Fascism and the principal cause of its success. But the more definite and immediate cause is to be found in the state of Italy following the War.

The difficulties attending demobilization and the problem of readjustment to peace conditions seemed too great for a people that were not at best distinguished for their discipline and patience. In many quarters, especially the industrial region of the north, the socialists got on a rampage; there were incessant strikes, and in some cases the workmen took over the factories—hypnotized, it seemed, by the red glare of the sky over Moscow. It looked for some years as if Italy might go communist. Even the peasantry was affected, for in some of the rural communities tenant farmers or hired hands ousted the landlords and seized their property. Famine conditions were threatened. There was also, apparently, a kind of pacifist reaction against the War, for soldiers were frequently insulted. Sometimes the railway force would stop a train if there were uniformed men on board. In all this period the ministries which successively governed Italy showed lamentable want of nerve, and one of them (that of Giolitti) was noticeably submissive to the workers. The prestige of the government was badly shaken.

Parallel with these disorders one might note another sort of moral upheaval—a resentment against the treatment which Italy had been accorded by the Congress of Paris. The strike against the Congress and d'Annunzio's raid on Fiume were examples of that glow of nationalism, sensitive and acquisitive, which spurred the nation to action. Obviously this feeling was not as a rule manifested by the lower classes, who were inclined rather toward pacifism, and whose objects, if they had any, were strictly economic; it was more the attitude of the liberal elements, which were fervently patriotic and also shocked by the prevalence of disorder. Great resentment was felt when Giolitti recalled the troops from Albania, which Italy had occupied during the War. One might say that the more stable elements in the population yearned for a restoration of order and a rehabilitation of Italy's position in Europe.

It was to these two sentiments that Fascism appealed. As far back as Caporetto some patriotic societies had been formed to revive the national morale, and when coherence was necessary for organizing a movement, the required man to essay this task was ready to hand—one, Benito Mussolini. A man of humble parentage, but, thanks to his stolid ambition, well educated, Mussolini had been the editor of a newspaper before the War; then, after an honorable record in the service, he resumed his editorial position when the War was over. He had been a socialist and even something of a pacifist until 1915 (just before Italy's entry into the struggle), and then he went to the opposite extreme and became a militant patriot. In 1919 he became head of the movement we have described, and the organization over which he presided was known as the "Fascists" (from the *fasces* which the Roman consul had carried as part of his symbol of office). The Fascists were zealous patriots and they were also staunch champions of law and order. If the government was unable to put down disorders, the Fascists were ready enough to do so on their own responsibility. Violence was met with violence. Socialist agitators were pretty

Mussolini and the organization of Fascism

roughly handled, and some towns were completely terrorized by Mussolini's blackshirts. Going beyond the mere matter of "pacifying" Italy, the Fascists even broke up workers' industrial organizations. The government meanwhile, seemed no more able to put down this form of lawlessness than the other.

It is still a matter of controversy whether the Fascists saved Italy from communism or lifted her out of anarchy, as they proudly boast. During the year 1919 when the country was most in danger the Fascists made little headway, and none of their number, not even Mussolini himself, was elected to the parliament chosen in that year. Much of this disorder seemed to collapse of its own weight, as neither the working class nor the peasants were efficiently organized, and the attempt of ignorant men to operate factories had ended up as might have been expected. Mussolini himself was very wary, and his platform far from clear; he was not at first disposed to break with the socialists, and it was, indeed, the socialists who first broke with him, and forced him to resign his editorship. But there is little doubt that the efforts of the Fascisti to repress disorder made a generally favorable impression, and after convincing himself that the moment had come to take a more definite stand, he openly denounced the cowardice of the government. In 1921 thirty-five Fascists, including Mussolini himself, were elected to the chamber, and their leader then pronounced himself in favor of three things: a strong foreign policy, the protection of private enterprise, and the reassertion of authority. Of Mussolini's sincerity as a statesman one can hardly speak with certainty. He has shown no scruple whatever in changing his principles; once a republican, socialist, and free-thinker, he was to become an upholder of monarchy and capitalism, and the ally of the Church. But the position of a statesman in power is often very different from that which he has shown in opposition, and Mussolini is an astute politician. Much of his bluff and bluster, which has irritated foreign governments, is probably for home consumption, understanding as he does the emotional nature of his countrymen and the psychology of nationalism. Though far inferior to Napoleon, to whom he likes to be compared, he is like him in both his nervous intensity and his organizing skill. While undoubtedly vain and imperious, he has proved himself a man of uncommon force and determination.

In the autumn of 1922 Mussolini reached the cross-roads. If he did not act with vigor, the movement which he captained might *The Fascist coup d'état* rapidly lose ground. He had been shrewd enough to refuse a seat in the cabinet. He was now determined to overthrow the government itself. On October 28 some two thousand "blackshirts" marched on Rome, presumably in order to pave the way for their chief, who quickly followed. As the army could not be counted on to resist this demonstration, and as civil war was certainly to be avoided, Mussolini was at once welcomed by the King with open arms, and immediately made premier. Since the parliament as a whole was certainly hostile, this action was a coup d'état. Fascism had conquered the government and Mussolini had now become its *de facto* head.

It is fairly evident that Fascism would not have succeeded if it *Fascism and public opinion* had not enjoyed the passive approval of a large and perhaps preponderant section of public opinion. The middle class, as a whole, tired of labor troubles and a weak government, looked upon the Fascists as likely to maintain order and protect its interests. Even most of the liberals after some hesitation decided to support the change. Ex-service men were as a rule favorable also, since Fascism upheld the national dignity. The People's Party, which represented the Church, was somewhat lukewarm, though not openly antagonistic. Whatever, in fact, may be thought of Fascism in theory or practice, it can at least be conceded that it had a steadying effect, restored the nation's confidence in itself, gave it at last a government for which it could feel respect.

But such advantages were gained only at a price. No longer *Fascism in theory and practice* was there any semblance of democracy. Mussolini has been frank in his denunciations of popular sovereignty, which he has declared a "tragic jest"; he professes to believe that it never existed and that it never could work if it did. His ideal is a state in which as in Germany before the War (and again lately under Hitler) the individual must subordinate himself to the collective interest, as interpreted by the government. The masses have no inherent rights; "their welfare is a concession, not a right." It was not, of course, a socialist state which he established—far from it. Private enterprise was to remain the basic feature of the economic order;[1] there was to be no proletarian régime, and hence any resort to a strike—

---

[1] Though always under strict governmental control, which is avowedly favorable to "big business." Every merchant must have a license, and his business is subject to inspection and restriction. Moreover, the professional classes can practice only after demonstrating their loyalty to Fascism.

indeed, every species of class war was strictly prohibited. Labor and capital should act as partners, not as enemies; and by organizing each and bringing the two together in a common body under the ægis of the State he has arranged to adjust their differences and to attain, as far as practicable, their common ends. Equally in the interest of unity was his religious policy. Mussolini's relations with the Church were sometimes difficult, but he made up his mind to win her favor and he succeeded. It was no small feather in his cap that in 1929 he settled the long controversy with the papacy. Italy accorded to the Church certain privileges, slightly extended the pope's territorial jurisdiction (which was guaranteed as inviolate), and indemnified him for the loss of his temporal power; in return, the pope recognized the king of Italy. The result of this pact has been a virtual dissolution of the People's Party, and a fairly hearty backing of the government by the partisans of the Church. Meanwhile, the spirit of unity (as well as loyalty to the new dictatorship) has been carefully conserved by whetting the national ambition and pressing Italy's claims as a great power. Mussolini acquired Fiume, as we have noted, and enlarged Italy's African possessions. But unity is fundamentally due to the military power of the dictator and the strength of the party machine. Very early in the new régime the Fascists gained complete control of parliament, and in 1933 the chamber was abolished altogether, being replaced by a smaller body, composed of representatives of the corporations—the organization of capital and labor—under the leadership and control of the central government. Mussolini, the premier—"Il Duce," as he is called—is theoretically responsible to the crown, but in fact is a dictator,[1] actually occupies several portfolios, and completely controls the legislature. But the actual organs of government are of comparative unimportance. All decisions are made by the grand council of the Fascist Party under the presidency of Mussolini, and the functions of the legislature are merely those of sanctioning them and putting them into legal shape. The Fascist Party—the only party allowed in the State—numbers several millions, and there are also organizations of young Fascists, which serve as sort of training-schools or nurseries of Fascism. Side by side with the army are the Blackshirts—a sort of unofficial police who stifle opposition when it appears. When the liberals

---

[1] Even the command of the army and navy has been transferred from the King to Mussolini, and it is the latter alone who issues orders to the Blackshirts.

broke away after the murder of a socialist leader (perhaps the most scandalous crime that has stained the Fascist record), there was a good deal of petty persecution, and men of doubtful views were subjected to heavy penalties. Hundreds of thousands fled to foreign lands. But even these voluntary exiles were liable to lose their citizenship and property if they committed any acts "likely to foment disorder or to damage the prestige of Italy." Meanwhile a strict censorship was established, and every unbeliever was open to suspicion and subject to surveillance. "Fascism," said Mussolini, "tolerates no differences of opinion."

Therein, of course, lies the moral weakness of Fascism. Policy is ground out from the top and is not susceptible to criticism. It is true that some of the best intellects in Italy are partisans of the government, and that in the sphere of education—where a selective process has been adopted by which a youth is pushed only to his proper mental level—some excellent experiments are being tried. It is true also that government in Italy has been more efficiently and economically managed than ever had been the case under the parliamentary régime. It is further true that some relief has been given the peasants with the reclamation of marshlands and other aids to agriculture, that the middle and working classes seem content under the régime of the corporations, and that the clericals are rejoiced at the stress which has been placed on the importance of religion. Probably the national unity has been materially promoted by the constant stimulation of an intense national spirit, and it is typical of the new régime that, despite foreign criticism, the Germans in the Trentino are being rapidly and thoroughly Italianized. Meanwhile, Italy seems to have won a stronger position in the family of nations than she has ever before enjoyed. But there are hundreds of thousands of Italians in exile who feel that even a benevolent autocracy is not a moral advance for the Italian people, and that violating as it does their ancient individualism, it holds, in effect, the national soul in fetters. Moreover, Fascism is not always admitted to be "benevolent," and its organized system of violence cannot appeal to the really enlightened men of today. With a less capable man than Mussolini at the helm one might find that the Italian temperament had not materially changed. But where public opinion is cowed there is no opportunity of self-expression; and hence no opportunity of knowing the public mind. It is probable that Fascism, having to share

Strength and weakness of Fascism

honors with Catholicism, has never possessed the religious hold
on the nation that is true of Communism in Russia or National
Socialism in Germany.

To the transformation in Russia we shall next give our attention—a movement that brings us back to the period before
the War.

The Russian Revolution

The Russian Revolution is a movement the full importance of
which is as yet to be determined. Whether the principles for which
it stands will, like those of the French Revolution, come in time
to have general approval lies still in the womb of the future. But
it is important at least in the transformation it has wrought in
Russia itself, and it has altered in some respects Russia's position
as a great power. This alone is sufficient reason for giving it careful
consideration. Taking into account the number of people involved,
it has proved to be the greatest social upheaval since the French
and Industrial Revolutions.

*Origins of
the
Revolution*

Of the Russian Revolution there were two fundamental and
paramount causes: the negative cause, the failure of autocracy,
and the positive cause, the enlightenment which filtered into
Russia from the West and produced a movement ultimately subversive of the existing order. These two causes were so interrelated
that we cannot conveniently deal with them separately, but the
student can gather his material for the study of each one when we
have finished our survey.

*The
fundamental
causes of the
Revolution*

*The
foundations
of the
Old Régime:
(1) political*

In the middle of the nineteenth century Russia was still a land
of the Old Régime. Her government was still an autocracy; her
social order still rested on an agrarian economy. Despotism, it is
true, had sometimes been "benevolent"; but more often it had
been stupid and capricious. Nominally the czar was the supreme
ruler of Russia, a sovereign by divine right, head of the State and
head of the Church, and looked up to by the masses with a reverence almost amounting to idolatry. But actually the dominant
power was the landed aristocracy, who filled all the higher posts
in the government, and constituted the bulk of the far-flung
bureaucracy. A czar like Nicholas I often initiated policy, particularly in foreign relations; but few of the czars were men of
force, and fewer still were capable—they were, in the main, either
timid idealists or stubborn reactionaries—and for the governance

of the State they leaned on their aristocratic advisers, most of whom were opposed to all change. No state in Europe, not even Austria before 1848, was more addicted to its habits, more embedded in routine. And these habits to which we refer were totally out of accord with nineteenth century Europe. Partly because the empire was so vast that centralized authority was difficult, partly because the masses of the people were inarticulate, the bureaucrats and police were pretty apt to be petty tyrants. Though there were, of course, many cases of real devotion to the czar and to "Holy Russia," the average bureaucrat was more than likely a time-server who lived to line his pockets as he could. It was a harsh government, indeed, without even the merit of efficiency, though it managed to hold the empire together, and the masses were at least thoroughly used to it. The czars and their ministers did not want the people educated, and even most of the sons of the nobility saw little of the outer world. Catherine the Great and later Alexander I had played with Western liberalism, and their efforts did result in the creation of a small nucleus of the nobility who looked toward the West for inspiration. But the strongest element in Russia belonged to a school, known as the Slavophils, which exalted the self-sufficiency of Russia, deprecated any departure from her indigenous institutions, and looked upon Western culture as a demoralizing influence. Typical of the Slavophils was Nicholas I (1825–53), who made it difficult for his subjects even to travel, established the strictest censorship for publications (especially those from the West), muzzled the faculties of the universities, and with the aid of his secret police, the *okhrana*, sent all political offenders to Siberia. That Russia should stay pure and undefiled, she must be hermetically sealed against ideas from outside her borders. It was evident that the Russian people were not intended to do much thinking.

Such a régime was politically less progressive than that of Peter the Great. Indeed, some Slavophils looked upon bureaucracy itself with abhorrence, as a noxious importation from the West and imagined that they would like to go back to the world of Muscovy. In any case the social, as well as the political, order dated from as early as the seventeenth century. A middle class, save in a few of the large towns, hardly existed; for the few industries in Russia were either government-supported factories (drawing on the countryside for their labor) or factories established by certain of the

(2) Social

nobles on their estates (with serfs as workmen) [1] or the cruder manufacturing by hand in which most of the peasants engaged during the long winter period—mainly in order to supply their personal needs, but partly in many cases in order to make enough profit to pay their quota of taxes. In the middle of the nineteenth century there were just two strata, of society: the nobles and the serfs. The greater proportion of the land was owned by the nobility, who, as we have said, filled most of the offices of state, including, of course, the commissions in the army and the navy. Many of them came to court, like the French nobles of the eighteenth century, and some of them were really enlightened, having traveled to the West or learned to think for themselves in one of the Russian universities. There were some very cultured minds in Russia and a few brilliant figures, as the names of Tchaikowsky, the composer, and Tolstoy, Turgeniev, and Dostoievsky in the field of letters will attest. But most of the nobility were country squires, who lived on their estates the year round, led a simple and very monotonous existence, and were hardly distinguishable in habits and dress from the peasants who did their work. Yet however small a noble he might be, he possessed almost the power of life and death over his serfs. He was the censor of their conduct; he was responsible for the payment of their taxes; his consent was necessary to their marriage. He could send a serf to Siberia, and in fact, could mete out any punishment short of killing him or maiming him for life. The peasants were known as "souls" ("dead souls," one writer called them), and could be sold with the land itself like so much merchandise.

The peasants were still under the communal system of land tenure. Each tilled on his own account some strips of land (so scattered that it sometimes meant traveling nineteen miles to cover them all, with the result that labor was wasted and much land was left uncultivated), while all the peasants shared in common the use of the meadows, pastures, and woodlands. Some of the strips were left fallow each year to recover their former fertility, for agricultural methods were generally the most primitive, and the plow used was simply a long pole with a hook on the end. The serf was also required to work three days a week for his lord on the portion of the estate set aside for the latter's use, and some of his family might be employed in the lord's household, for any service

[1] These rapidly decayed after the emancipation of the serfs.

could be required of a serf. Collectively the peasants formed, as we have noticed, the *mir* or village community, where a certain rudimentary autonomy still survived in the government of elders or heads of families. It was the *mir* itself which conducted the periodic redistribution of lots, since every adult male was entitled to his share; and the tendency in consequence was for each man's portion to become smaller. Obviously there was little incentive for the peasant to improve his lot, which might be lost at the next redistribution, and the progressive diminution of the peasant's farm, while the population increased and methods of tillage remained unchanged, was a cause of the frequent famines. Naturally, too, the system deadened initiative, giving the peasant fixed habits of dependence. He would have been a pathetic figure, had he known any other existence. His religion (a mystical and highly emotional religion), his superstitions, and his drink were almost his only diversions. Economically and morally he was degraded in the extreme.

But even in a country as backward as Russia there had been *Abolition of serfdom* misgivings about the perpetuation of serfdom. Alexander I had freed the serfs of the Baltic provinces, though as no land was provided for them, they fell to the level of hired hands, and their condition was actually worse than it had been before. Even Nicholas I had talked of emancipation, and in failing to bring it about he got his retribution. It was the disastrous Crimean War that convinced the Russian aristocrats—or at least many of them— that a country with an economy based on serfdom could not cope with the Western Powers. Serfs made poor soldiers, and would so continue. Hence the lesson of this war plus the accession of a liberal czar give us the immediate causes of emancipation. By the decrees of Alexander II in 1861 serfdom was abolished. This reform in itself placed Russia on a higher moral level, and by releasing the peasants' sons to go to the towns gave her eventually a more flexible economy. But the economic condition of the peasant was little relieved. In the first place, since the nobles had the making of the reform, the lots assigned to the peasants in the division of the estate were generally the poorest land and too small to provide for the normal growth of families; hence, congestion and growing poverty. In the second place, the peasants, while no longer obliged to furnish their labor free to a lord, were forced to pay the price of their redemption (so much a year for forty-nine years), for the government had agreed to compensate the nobles and the amount of the compensation was, accordingly, charged to the peasants. This financial burden (which, of course, was additional to ordinary taxes) was greater than the *corvées* had been. Hence it was in order to meet his taxes that the peasant was obliged often to sell his grain at the very time when he needed to store it for his winter's food—a condition which explains the large export trade in wheat while the peasants were sometimes starving.[1] In the third place, while technically delivered from the soil, the peasants were not free to go elsewhere, since the *mir* was now collectively responsible for the payment of taxes (including, of course, the redemption money) and without its permission none of its members might leave. It was only some of their sons who were able to go to the towns, but in any case it was the government's policy to keep the mass of peasants where they were, as a fixed and stable element in society. In such a system it is quite obvious that the more energetic peasant had to carry his shiftless neighbor. Yet it has recently been ascertained that the nobles themselves were not materially helped by this reform. Impractical and accustomed to free labor, they found it hard to adapt themselves to the change, and they soon discovered that the bonds which the government issued to them as compensation money were not readily convertible into cash. It has been found that a good many of them sold or leased their lands to the more enterprising peasants, and thus peasant proprietorship, already made possible by an edict of Nicholas I,[2] had secured what seemed to be fairly solid foundations. But the average peasant, of course, was not enterprising; he was submissive, resigned to his fate, and inclined to be lazy. Perhaps there was a little oriental fatalism somehow present in his character, though centuries of oppression were enough to make him listless. Given the form of government, a social order with a wide cleavage between upper and lower classes and the character of the people—easy-going, emotional, superstitious, and rather innately harsh (however stoical), and we have the explanation of Russia's backwardness.

Yet, as we have seen already, no part of the world in the nineteenth century could long remain immune from outside influence.

[1] When, later, a protective tariff was adopted in order to foster Russian industries, the brunt of the increased prices of most merchandise was also borne by the peasants who constituted the bulk of Russia's consumers.

[2] Allowing the serf to make private contracts with his lord.

Even Nicholas began to construct railroads (greatest of all devices for the promotion of internal trade), and it was only a question of time when Russia would be linked by rail with the West. From the time of the French Revolution there were liberals even in Russia, and some of those at court nearly coaxed Alexander I into granting a constitution. This group had as their object a revolution from above. They hoped to get the czars to grant reforms, such as a parliament and local self-government, and whenever the press was free (which was not often) they strove to create a public opinion among the nobility favorable to these ideas. These were the "Westerners," whom the Slavophils cordially detested. It was through their influence with Alexander II (1853–81) that the Russian judiciary was purged of its worst abuses, that provincial councils, known as the *zemstvos*, were established,[1] and that the emancipation of the serfs had been accomplished. Possibly Alexander II (who was a little less panicky than Alexander I) would finally have granted a constitution (already considered), and certainly he would have emancipated the Jews, who lived under the most onerous disabilities; but it is one of the paradoxes of history that the most humane and enlightened among the czars was struck down by a revolutionist, and his death was the signal for a reaction. Such was the end of the "Czar Liberator." "Revolution from above" was apparently discredited.

The beginning of a revolutionary movement: (1) the assault from above

It is evident that a more violent revolutionary movement was in process. Certain intellectuals, gaining their inspiration from Marx rather than from the French and English liberals, organized in Russia the movement known as "nihilism." The nihilists were anarchists. They wished to destroy almost everything in the existing order. The struggle with autocracy seemed so hopeless that at first they were not concerned with a constructive program. Their method was terrorism. Through assassination plots, carefully worked out in secret societies, they hoped to terrorize autocracy into submission. Each official was a marked man, even the czar himself; while agents of the police were the commonest victims. Such was a policy of repaying violence with violence. Obviously each nihilist took his life in his own hands; but there was no flinching in their devotion, and it would be hard to find in history a more

(2) The assault from below

---

[1] Though under the control of the landlords and possessed of only limited jurisdiction in local matters (such as education, public hygiene, famine relief, etc.), they nevertheless represented a relaxation of the customarily rigid centralization. Later, under Alexander III, their authority became more and more restricted.

earnest and self-sacrificing group than these men and women who struggled to free Russia by the bomb. They were obviously not patriots (as the term is commonly used), for Russia of the czars was not *their* Russia, and it was during a foreign war or any other national crisis that they were usually most active; they had only one thought: the subversion of autocracy. But they soon came to the conclusion that in order to win the masses it was necessary to arrive at some really constructive ideal, and to this end they adopted socialism. With the true fervor of missionaries they conducted during the 'seventies what was known as the "going to the people." They went to the peasant villages, sometimes lived the life of the peasant, and conducted a secret propaganda. But it was an utterly hopeless task, however heroic. There was nothing much more isolated than a peasant village, and the police were only too ready to pounce on any stranger. Moreover, the peasant was too thick-headed to get much inspiration from Karl Marx. Manifestly some likelier material must be found.

The coming of the Industrial Revolution and its significance

Fortunately, during the 'eighties and 'nineties the industrialization of Russia had begun to make great progress. One of the ministers of Alexander III (1881–94) was a man of exceptional energy and vision, Count Sergius Witte, and it was largely through his efforts that foreign capital came into Russia,[1] attracted by the vast untapped resources and the quantity of cheap labor now made readily available by the emancipation of the serfs. The result was the rapid construction of railways, the opening of mines, the multiplication of banks, and above all the coming of large-scale production. Witte even adopted a high protective tariff to foster this new development. Towns now multiplied, and St. Petersburg and Moscow became large cities. Thus emerged for the first time a well-developed middle class. And naturally we find its counterpart, an urban proletariat.

It was this group of factory workers that was now to be relied on as the cohorts of revolution. And it was not unpromising material. Conditions in Russian factories were as bad as anything in the worst days of the Industrial Revolution; and while anything might have been tolerable to the peasant who had been a serf, a younger generation was springing up, less contented with its place in the crowded towns in which it toiled. From this class the message of socialism was bound to receive a response. In 1883

---

[1] The alliance with France proved of great service in obtaining loans at Paris.

the Social Democratic Party was founded for pushing the workers' interests. Terrorism seemed cowed under the harsh rule of Alexander III, and even incipient unions had been crushed;[1] but the effort of the party for a time was to give the factory workers a greater sense of solidarity and the strength of a common creed. In 1901 a rural socialist party was also founded, known as the Social Revolutionary Party, which, unlike the other party, believed in terrorism as a weapon, though they kept it for the present in reserve. In 1903 a more radical element in the Social Democratic Party split off from the main body on the ground of favoring a stricter party discipline. This body, which came to be known as the Bolsheviks,[2] followed a young nobleman, Nicholas Ulianov, alias Lenin, who was destined in course of time to become the leader of the Revolution. In any case, a revolutionary movement had come into being, and, as we have noticed, there were two main streams,

Underwood & Underwood

LENIN

the liberal and the socialist, the aristocratic-bourgeois and the proletarian. It was under one of the most autocratic of the czars, Alexander III, that the government's own policy had actually, though unwittingly, given new strength to the forces of revolution.

The two streams of revolution, flowing together, became a torrent in the reign of Nicholas II. This ruler, the last of the czars had come to the throne in 1894. He was a man of small mentality and weak will, and by temperament so volatile that he was apt to

The Preliminary Storm

---

[1] Efforts were made to revive them after his death, and there were numerous strikes, though contrary to law. The government was afraid of trade-unionism as liable to become political in its activities; but, in 1897, in an effort to pacify the workers it restricted the working day to eleven and a half hours!

[2] The name signifies "majority men," for the Bolsheviks were in a majority on the question which caused their secession, though as a party they remained far inferior in numbers to the Mensheviks ("minority men").

The occasion follow the opinions of the last person who had been with him. He was also very Russian in his fatalism, and disposed to let things drift, feeling that somehow autocracy was part of the divine order of things and that it mattered very little who were its agents. Nicholas retained all the ministers of his father (whom he greatly revered), and under the weaker monarch autocracy became exceptionally oppressive. It was also quite as incompetent as ever. The war with Japan was badly conducted, and was thoroughly unpopular. When the news poured in of a succession of disasters, the murmuring grew louder. At the tidings of the fall of Port Arthur students paraded the streets, crying, "Down with autocracy!" and "End the war!"

The revolutionary crisis of 1905-6 It was the plight of the government that inspired a revival of the revolutionary movement. For some time there had been widespread agrarian unrest, but this had been due rather to the misery of the peasantry. It was in the urban centers that the influence of the government's failures had most effect. In July, 1904, a particularly unpopular minister was assassinated, and soon afterward the Czar's uncle, the governor of Moscow, suffered the same fate. Yet, in general, the revolutionary movement of 1905-6 was not distinguished by terrorism, but came right out into the open, as it were. Nothing could have been more innocent than the demonstration of January 22, 1905 when a huge concourse of workers marched to the Winter Palace to hand the Czar a petition. This episode, which ended in the petitioners being fired upon by Cossacks, is known as "Bloody Sunday." It sent a thrill of horror throughout Russia, and there was pretty general unrest, especially in the countryside, where the peasants began to pillage the great landlords. But there were even mutinies in the army, and though the war was practically over, it was decided to delay demobilization. The very foundation of czarism seemed to be crumbling. Hence the government, thoroughly frightened, felt forced to announce the coming of a duma or national assembly to be consulted in the matter of reforms. This Russian "estates general" was, of course, too slight a concession to please the public. The liberals at once agitated for a legislative body, to be elected on a really broad suffrage. With much more effect the socialists attempted a general strike; and the movement was so far successful that transportation ceased, most of the factories closed, and the nation's economic life was almost paralyzed. The Czar consulted Witte, who was for a short time premier, and decided as a result to make further concessions (for, after all, concessions could be revoked); so in October, 1905, he issued what was known as the October Manifesto —the nearest approach Russia had had to a constitution. Certain fundamental rights, like inviolability of person and freedom of conscience, press, and association were granted. Legislative power was also accorded the duma, which was to be elected on a very broad suffrage.

There was great exultation, but it proved to be premature. The government soon created a second chamber of the national parliament, so constituted as to make it essentially conservative, and issued the Organic Laws, which vested in the Czar an absolute veto in legislation. There were also violations of the newly granted civic rights. When the duma met (May, 1906), it was helpless to achieve anything and was soon dissolved. The revolutionary leaders were the Constitutional Democratic Party, popularly known as the "Cadets," led by Miliukov, a professor in the University of St. Petersburg. After the passing of the duma, they issued from Finland the so-called "Viborg Manifesto," exhorting the Russian people to refuse to pay taxes till another duma was called. But the revolution had spent itself, and reaction was already in full swing. Moreover, an instrument was found who was able to deal effectively with what was left of it.

The day that he dismissed the duma the Czar appointed as premier the man who had been serving as minister of the interior and who had represented the government in its relations with the duma. Stolypin was a man of great courage and devotion, and far more practical and intelligent than the usual Russian bureaucrat. Faced with the problem of disposing of the "revolution," he was willing to tolerate the duma as an institution (in fact, he even felt it to be a useful check on the government), but he wished it to be composed exclusively of the landed gentry—"men with roots in the country," as he expressed it. When he failed to alter the complexion of the second duma by manipulating the elections (and accordingly had it quickly dissolved), he got the Czar on his own authority to amend the electoral law, with the result that but 135,000 voters were allowed out of a total population of about 175,000,000. Thus the third duma proved to be the kind of instrument he wanted—no longer a nucleus for revolution but an auxiliary of the government. Then, while he sought to conciliate the

Reaction under Stolypin

working class [1] and peasantry by certain reforms, he put down
lawlessness with a heavy hand. There were so many executions
that the hang-man's rope came to be called "Stolypin's necktie."

Stolypin's
agrarian
reform

The chief concession to the peasants, the Agrarian Law of 1906,
deserves some special attention. It allowed a peasant to detach
himself from the *mir* and become the owner of the lands he tilled.
(By a subsequent act he was also entitled to a share in full ownership of the meadows, pasture, and woodland.) At the same time,
if two thirds of the elders in the *mir* voted for a transfer to private
ownership, the *mir* was forthwith dissolved. One of the most
interesting of Stolypin's measures was the ending of the fixed
social status of the peasant, who was now free to go wherever he
saw fit, and even to enter the public service. Land banks were
meanwhile established to facilitate sales of land, and some effort
was made to provide the peasant with instruction in more modern
methods of farming. [2] Of course, the peasants who readily availed
themselves of the agrarian reform were those of the *kulak* type,
the more energetic and enterprising members of the class, or else
those who liked the lots they happened to be tilling, or those who
wished to sell out and move to the towns; there was, in fact, a
notable influx to the towns after the reform. With the great
majority of peasants, however, the old policy of dependence was
too strong to induce them to break at once with the communal
system, not to mention the force of habit, which produced the
argument, "Our forefather lived in the commune—why should we
leave it?" Moreover, for one of the peasants to become materially
better off than the rest was at variance with the communal spirit
of equality. Yet the consolidated farm under private ownership
was clearly the one demanded by the acquisitive spirit of the age
and the very existence of the *kulaks* showed that even the Russian
peasant was not impervious to new ideas. By further legislation
the government not only forebade all redistribution of lots and
did what it could to facilitate concentration but arbitrarily established hereditary holding where no redistribution of land had

[1] Trade unions were legalized, though under official supervision, and strikes were
still prohibited.
[2] If peasant proprietorship were finally to become universal, as the government
hoped, cultivation would have to be more intensive, as the available land for extensive cultivation would by that time be exhausted. The liberality of these reforms is
shown by the fact that the Czar turned over for cheap sale as much as five million
acres of land at his personal disposal. The government also encouraged immigration
to Siberia by expending large sums on making it attractive to settlers.

taken place. At the time of Stolypin's death in 1911 some 19,000,-000 acres had passed into private ownership.

In spite of Witte's claim that the basic idea was really his (it was Witte who in 1903 had canceled the rest of the redemption money due for emancipation), Stolypin's reforms reflect credit on his statesmanship. He seems to have realized that the export trade in grain inevitably impoverished the peasants as long as communal tenure remained in force, and that impoverishment could only mean periodic unrest (already the *mir* had frequently been used as an instrument of revolt). To shift to individual proprietorship would, on the contrary, open the way to more intensive cultivation. While it is evident that more land was still required to relieve congestion (and to this end the czar was persuaded to offer for cheap sale as much as 5,000,000 acres from the crown estates), Stolypin was thinking rather of the peasants who had the capacity to become independent. His wager was on the strong, as one scholar has aptly put it. No doubt he reasoned that there was hardly a stronger bulwark for autocracy than a prosperous and contented peasantry. Had not the coming Revolution taken an entirely different course, it is probable that Russia today would be a nation of peasant proprietors.

But Stolypin's days were numbered. He had plenty of enemies —the Finns, whose constitution he abrogated (in his nationalism he was something of a Slavophil), the more liberal elements because of his mangling of the duma, the reactionaries because he would have a duma at all, and the more rabid revolutionaries because of his harsh measures against sedition. He narrowly escaped being murdered in 1910. In 1911 he was assassinated in the imperial theater at Kiev in the presence of the Czar, who displayed scant regret at the loss of a devoted servant. With the passing of Stolypin, autocracy lost its last great instrument and champion. Except for an economic revival, domestic history returned to its usual humdrum routine, and ministers apparently took no thought of the morrow. And the morrow—to Russia's misfortune—was another and more terrible war.

It was the Great War which proved autocracy's undoing and in a broad sense constituted the immediate cause of its downfall. There was no little enthusiasm and patriotism at the outset and hardly a dissentient voice; all Russia looked upon the War as a "holy war," requiring the fullest and staunchest effort. But

The Coming of the Revolution

*The failure
of autocracy
in the Great
War as a
paramount
cause of the
Revolution*
Russia was not equal to a struggle such as this. She was still too
backward a nation to vie with the technical efficiency of the
West; her railways were unsuited to the transportation of large
armies; her munition factories were unable to produce the volume
of armaments required. Moreover, there was graft in high places.
The minister of war gave contracts to men who cheated the government while they lined their own pockets. In the campaign of 1915
the supply of rifles failed; there were insufficient shells; and Russia
was badly beaten. There was naturally a public outcry. Pressed
by the duma, which came to be the mouthpiece of the discontent,
the Czar dismissed the incompetent minister of war and allowed
the duma itself some measure of co-operation in trying to augment
the nation's military capacity.

But the patriots reckoned without those covert influences which
in Russia played so often a fatal part in shaping her destinies.
The old reactionary element came to dislike the War, fearing lest
its disasters might lead to revolution, and detesting Russia's
liberal ally, France. This group found a champion in the Czarina
Alexandra, a beautiful and queenly woman, of strong will but of a
morbid and superstitious nature, as well as a haughtiness and
reserve which had the effect of isolating the dynasty at a time when
it sorely needed the public affection. It was she who generally
swayed the weak-willed Czar, whom she was constantly admonish-
ing "Be firm! Be master!" It is probably untrue that she lent
herself to secret intrigues with Germany, but her one idea was to see
autocracy handed down unimpaired to the little Czarevitch, and
she dreaded lest the War should let loose some liberal forces. "For
baby's sake we must be firm," she told the Czar; otherwise his
heritage will be awful." And the Czar too often listened to this
neurotic and consulted her on all political matters. This fact
was the more serious because the Czarina in turn was influenced
by a man of the basest character—one of the most sinister figures
that ever polluted the pages of history.

Gregory Rasputin was a Siberian peasant who after thirty years
of obscurity became a wandering mystic, and ultimately acquired
the prestige of a saint. He was a huge, ungainly, uncouth, and
filthy profligate with an overmastering ambition to exercise power.
His avenue of approach to the imperial family lay in the fact that
he had a reputation for healing (probably he did possess some
therapeutic powers), and on one occasion when the little Czarevitch

suffered a terrific attack of his strange malady (he was what is commonly known as a "bleeder"), Rasputin was called in, and the attack was soon allayed. He came frequently to the palace, and was said to have declared that the fate of the Czar and his family was interwoven with his own. In any case Rasputin was not content simply to play the rôle of "court physician." He dabbled in politics, and through the influence of the Czarina he made and unmade ministers. That he was in traitorous relations with Germany is not yet proved, but he was certainly an avowed pacifist, and his influence was defeatist and corrosive as far as it touched the conduct of the War. It was through Rasputin that Stürmer became premier ("a soapy-mannered man with an overdone smile," a British observer called him), whose ingratiating manner won the confidence of the Czarina. Disliking Sazonov as a "parliamentarian" (for she hated the duma), she had him ousted, and the portfolio of foreign affairs was then also given to Stürmer. For minister of the interior, thanks again to Rasputin, a certain Protopopov was chosen, reputed to be an excellent dinner companion (and as such a favorite of the Czar) but a traitor in disguise and undoubtedly somewhat insane. Such were the leading figures who guided Russia during the most trying years of the War.

This state of affairs was only too well known to the men of the duma. The chief of staff, the Grandduke Nicholas, had been removed because he had offended Rasputin and was reputed to have said that the Czarina should be committed to a madhouse. As the Czar himself took active command and left for the front, the Czarina was now the freer to dictate policy with the aid of her spiritual counselor. But the patriots knew full well where the source of misgovernment lay, and in the fall of 1916 there was an explosion of wrath in the duma. Rumors of a separate peace were in the air, and the government was bitterly attacked. An impassioned speech of Miliukov in the duma portended the downfall of Stürmer, who was succeeded by a man, just as incompetent perhaps, but at least not suspected of being a traitor. The storm then raged about Rasputin; and even staunch conservatives clamored for his head. "I will say this," wrote Felix Yousoupov, "There reigned at court a sort of nightmare. Each day fewer and fewer people remained. If the Revolution had not broken out from the bottom, it would have broken out from the top." In December, 1916, the "holy man" was murdered by the youth who had uttered these words, and his

The gathering storm

body was thrown into the Neva. Of the Czarina's foul trinity only Protopopov now remained, and he was claiming to have communion with the spirit of Rasputin. One might expect almost anything of a régime so obsessed. Meanwhile, the government was blind to its fate and even hampered the work of carrying on the War. Like an animal at bay, with her back against the wall, the Czarina defied her enemies and brooded over the loss of her chosen counselor.

The outbreak of the Revolution   But the storm finally broke, when in March, 1917, the capital suddenly suffered from a shortage of food; and when rioting broke out, neither the imperial nor the city government could put it down, for the garrison itself was mutinous. Every day the situation grew worse, and on March 14, a *soviet* or committee of workmen was constituted in the city to direct the rising. Before long the red flag waved over the Winter Palace, and a mob had taken possession of the fortress of Saints Peter and Paul, the Russian "Bastille."

On March 15 the duma, despite the Czar's attempt to dissolve it, set up a provisional government; and two days later, at its request, the Czar abdicated. Finding that his personal guard had finally deserted, Nicholas had had no other course. He said that he would go to one of his palaces in the country— "I love flowers," he added. As a matter of fact, he and his family were imprisoned in a palace close by, where they remained until they were later removed to Siberia. Meanwhile, no one seemed to want to occupy the vacant throne; so Russia became—in fact at least—a republic.

The Period of Transition —the Provisional Government and its Collapse   But it was a very curious republic. The Provisional Government, composed mostly of Cadets, and chosen from the duma, was the *de facto* government; but the real power (though without responsibility) was wielded by the soviet, composed of the more moderate socialists, known as Mensheviks, and looking for their power to

The dyarchy   the masses. While the provisional government was naturally aristocratic and bourgeois, the soviet was proletarian; and the only personal connection between the two was the man who was minister of justice and vice president of the soviet, Alexander Kerensky. The soviet claimed to be a sort of watch-dog of the Revolution. It acted as a kind of censor of the government and came in time to overshadow it. Resembling the Jacobin Club in the French Revolution and extending its branches over the country, it was that sinister force which speedily engulfed the Revolution.

This dual leadership, this anarchy at the top, was one of the reasons for the collapse of the Revolution as a liberal and democratic movement. But there were other reasons (beside the rise of an extremist party to be noticed later). The Cadets, though they granted all the liberties which were current in the West, were really much too "Western" in their models, too exotic to the soil, to understand Russia, a country that was far too backward and at the same time too wracked by misery and exhaustion to adjust itself readily to a sane and liberal leadership. The masses wanted peace, bread, and land; they were not prepared to wait for the coming of a constituent assembly or for a scientific solution of the agrarian problem; they wanted no law, no discipline, no further sacrifices. With the downfall of the Czar ("the little father," as he had been called) the moral tie which had always united them had suddenly snapped. And material unity had crumbled under the stress of a disastrous war, followed in turn by revolution.

Weakness of the Provisional Government and causes of its failure

The result was very rapid disintegration. Perhaps the first to feel demoralization were the factories, where the workmen refused to apply themselves, struck for higher wages and fewer hours, and wasted their time in long political discussions. The habit of discipline was broken, and without discipline the Russian worker was worse than useless. The natural result was a continuous falling off of production, which inevitably reacted upon the entire country. Already the peasants had become infected with the revolutionary spirit, inspired no doubt by the soviets which had by this time permeated the countryside. In many cases they seized the large estates of the nobility, and more and more of the land dropped out of cultivation. And when the government tried to requisition grain at a fixed price, they balked at being paid in paper money that was rapidly depreciating. Thus the whole economy of Russia was upset. Merchandise from the towns no longer flowed into the country; the country no longer sent its food to the towns, which in consequence were seriously threatened with famine. Confusion was made still worse by the crumbling of the military front, hundreds of thousands of peasants now deserting in haste to the villages before all the available land had been seized. In addition to the anarchy in the government, in the country, and in the towns we should note the anarchy in the army. The common soldiers refused to obey their officers, many of whom were murdered, and

The collapse of Russia

in some cases fraternized with the Germans across the trenches. As soldiers had been admitted to the soviets, the army had been drawn into politics, and as an instrument of war was wholly useless. Finally, the subject nationalities, like the Finns, were beginning to assert their freedom and break away. The empire was in a process of rapid disintegration. The whole existing order, material and moral, was in a state of dissolution. And in the prevailing anarchy a party sought to make capital—a party whose avowed aim was the instant and complete destruction of the existing order.

The coming of Lenin and the Bolsheviks   The Bolsheviks, as we have noted, had been the seceders from the Social Democratic Party. Unlike the Mensheviks (the remainder of that group), who were willing to come to socialism by gentler methods and easy stages, the Bolsheviks would scrap the existing order at once and enthrone the proletariat, however small an element in the population. During the early years of the War practically all of them had been in exile or in prison, but the Revolution gave them their opportunity. And they had an extraordinary leader in Nicholas Lenin.

Lenin was one of the most remarkable men in modern history. He was a nobleman who had espoused revolutionary doctrines and had suffered a term of imprisonment in Siberia as a consequence. Escaping from prison, he had settled for a time in Switzerland where he edited a paper known as *The Spark*, and kept alive the flicker of hope among his followers. Later, as we have noticed, he headed the group known as the Bolsheviks, and he took a somewhat inconspicuous part in the revolutionary movement of 1905. At the outbreak of the War he happened to be in Austria where he was interned as a Russian subject. But he was soon released in order to sow his subversive propaganda, especially in order, it was hoped, to start a revolution in Russia. He went immediately to Switzerland, where he tried in vain to dominate the Second International, a group of socialists from various countries, now assembled to seek a common basis for bringing the War to an end. Most of them had still too much of their patriotism left to follow this Russian agitator, who only cared for the interests of the proletariat, and Lenin eventually bolted to set up a rival organization. When the Revolution broke out, the German government gave him welcome transport across Germany, well knowing that such a firebrand was worth as much as an army in compassing the overthrow of Russia. Lenin was hardly an original thinker. He accepted the doctrines of Marx as he understood them without any appreciable modification, though, unlike Marx, he proposed to establish the dictatorship of the proletariat without waiting for any period of transition. He was not an effective speaker but, like Robespierre, he impressed the masses with his absolute sincerity; he was their "veiled oracle," as someone expressed it. He had certainly a genius for organization and a tenacity that never knew defeat. Yet the man is something of a mystery, and we are still without the evidence for gauging his character or the rôle that he has played in history. Fanatic, adventurer, or prophet—who shall say? He was at all events the most dynamic force in the revolutionary upheaval that proceeded from the War, and he was undoubtedly one of the greatest political leaders of his day.

Led by Lenin, the Bolsheviks sought to scuttle the Provisional Government and become the leaders of a people engulfed in revolution and groping for an ideology. It was gratifying to Lenin that a system of soviets had come about from the Revolution, for he saw them as the basis of the order he meant to erect. With his adjutant, Leo Bronstein, alias Trotsky, he established his headquarters in the capital, founded a paper, called *The Truth*, and at once engaged in propaganda especially among the army. Success, however, was not very tangible at first, for the people were rather dazed by the Revolution, and the Mensheviks were still the chosen leaders. Thus he failed repeatedly to capture the soviets and after talking violent pacifism, he was finally moved to deny that he was advocating a separate peace. But he had only to dig in and wait, for Russia was fast collapsing and the Mensheviks of the soviet were steadily though unconsciously accelerating her ruin.

At this moment Russia fell under the leadership of a man who resembled a comet flashing across a sky of utter blackness. With the downfall of the liberal members of the Provisional Government (chiefly owning to their efforts to push the War in collaboration with Russia's allies) Alexander Kerensky became minister of war and ultimately premier. He seems to have been a vain man who found great enjoyment in his personal popularity and relied on his remarkable gift of eloquence for swaying his emotional fellow-countrymen; but his ardent patriotism was probably sincere, and he cherished the impossible hope of rehabilitating Russia and enabling her somehow to continue the War. Firing a portion of the army with his enthusiasm, he was responsible for a sensational

The Bolshevik triumph— the coup d'état of November, 1917

offensive against the enemy, which, taken by surprise, sustained a temporary defeat; but it was, of course, quite impossible for Russia to continue fighting, and disaster speedily followed. Taking advantage of the crisis, some of the Bolshevik elements in the capital tried to pull off an insurrection, but it proved to be premature; and it was only because Kerensky was a trimmer that the Bolsheviks were not effectually crushed. While Trotsky suffered a few weeks of imprisonment, Lenin, who had gone into hiding, succeeded in making his escape to Finland, whence he continued to direct the activities of his party. It became more and more evident, as time went on that Kerensky and the moderates were steadily losing ground, and that the Bolsheviks, who alone promised peace, were gradually gaining a hold on the population. They soon emerged from retirement and raised the cry, "All power to the soviets!" for they knew that the soviet (that is, the Petrograd[1] soviet) had reduced the power of the government to a cipher, and they felt confident that they would soon be able to control this principal organ. In October by skillful tactics they finally attained this end. And on November 9 by a coup d'état they overthrew the Provisional Government. Kerensky, after putting up a hopeless fight, fled into exile. The Bolsheviks had triumphed.

The Communist Régime— "the Dictatorship of the Proletariat"

And now what use were they to make of their victory? "He is no socialist," Lenin had written, "who does not understand that a victory over the bourgeoisie may require losses of territory and defeats. He is no socialist who will not sacrifice his fatherland for the triumph of the social revolution." To Lenin the world was not divided into nations but into classes, and he intended, in the spirit of Marx, to wage the class war until he had thoroughly consolidated the rule of the proletariat. But he must first end foreign war, not only because the masses demanded it but because he needed external peace in order to amass the strength which he required for the destruction of his enemies—that is, all who did not fully adopt his policy. Thus after the soviet had been reorganized as a body of "commissars" (the bourgeois term, "minister," being avoided), Trotsky at once opened negotiations with the Powers. Naturally Russia's allies studiously ignored him, but the Germans were more than ready to accept his overtures, with the result that the army was speedily disbanded, and Russia signed with Germany the Treaty of Brest Litovsk (March 6, 1918).

The consolidation of Bolshevik or Communist power—the Reign of Terror

[1] St. Petersburg was re-named Petrograd during the War.

Perhaps no more humiliating treaty has ever been signed by a national government. Russia gave up large portions of her territory and opened what was left to German exploitation. But Lenin probably knew that Germany would find Russia much too hot an iron to tamper with—a fact which proved to be true—and, as for the loss of territory, he was willing to pay the price. Ultimately he might hope to get it back through revolution. So he spoke of the peace as a "respite"—not, of course, a final reckoning with the capitalistic world. And he secured his immediate ends.

He had meanwhile given his attention to capturing the country. A strict censorship, which allowed only Bolshevik sheets to appear, and the general prohibition of public meetings were preliminary measures designed to do away with a free public opinion and enable the Bosheviks alone to spread their doctrines. It was, in fact, Lenin's purpose to break the Revolution as a popular or democratic movement, not only on grounds of principle (democracy was "bourgeois," so the Bolsheviks considered) but also because the masses, as far as they professed any politics, were still affiliated to the Menshevik and Social Revolutionary Parties, and he knew that if the latter expressed their will, they would oust him from his leadership. The chance to do this lay in the coming of the Constituent Assembly, which, put off from time to time, was at last to meet in January, 1918. Lenin tried to control the elections but in vain; hence after the assembly had met and when he discovered that it was controlled by the Social Revolutionaries and that it could not be compelled to follow his lead, he sent a contingent of sailors to disperse it by armed force. When he heard how quickly the peasant deputies had scattered, he was said to have laughed so hard that some of his followers almost feared that he might hurt himself. But the passing of the Constituent Assembly was only another step in the class war. During the following months Lenin and Trotsky organized a reign of terror, following somewhat the methods of the French Revolutionary Terror, with a tribunal, known as the *tcheka* to mete out summary justice. It is interesting to observe that the man who came to dominate this organ, Dzerzhinsky, was an intellectual of Polish noble extraction, thoroughly disinterested and in private life a man of gentle manners and disposition, but that so absolutely dehumanizing was the movement he represented that as an official he has been charged with homicidal mania. Just how many aristocrats, men of the middle class, and peasants were slaughtered during this period will probably never be known. A German scholar has estimated the number as at least eight hundred thousand. Among the victims were the ex-Czar and his family, who had been in confinement in different places ever since the outbreak of the Revolution. Hundreds of thousands of Russians, not only reactionaries but liberals and moderate socialists, sought shelter in exile; others were not able to leave in time and suffered the consequences; still others, in order to save themselves, remained as far as possible in obscurity and eventually passed into the service of the Bolsheviks. The only serious resistance was encountered in the Ukraine, where various elements with the aid of foreign powers plunged Russia into civil war; but Lenin's government triumphed in the end—though this period of civil war had its effect on Bolshevik policy, as we shall notice in another connection.

Some of the disorders and destruction of life and property at this time were doubtless due to the anarchy that prevailed before Lenin had a complete grip on things. Then some of his own followers were the dregs of humanity, and they felt themselves privileged to rob and murder as they pleased. Moreover, being a practical politician, he found it necessary, while he destroyed the brains of the resistance, to make certain concessions to the masses. Thus he granted the eight-hour day and even left the management of factories in the hands of the turbulent workmen, though he was, of course, well aware that economic restoration would be impossible by such means. Similarly, after proclaiming the nationalization of the land, he left it undisturbed in the possession of the peasants. But such were merely temporizing measures while he mobilized his strength. He had already raised a large army—the Red Army —which, under Trotsky's organizing skill, was battling in the civil war, enforcing the Reign of Terror, and constituted the cornerstone of the new despotism. Before long Lenin could begin to erect his system. He had chiefly been engaged in a work of destruction. But his great underlying purpose was to establish a new order. We have now to ask: what did bolshevism intend? Just what was the transformation which Lenin hoped to achieve.

The basic platform of communism   Bolshevism, or communism, as developed by Lenin, involved four things. In the first place, it signified the complete overthrow of the capitalistic order and its displacement by a socialist régime. All private capital was abolished; all profits whether from interest,

rent, or any other source, and all foreign debts were repudiated.
Though the proletariat numbered at this time not much more than
ten per cent of the population it was eventually to comprise everyone. There should be no entrepreneurs and no privately hired
labor. There should be none but wage-earners, employed by the
State. In the second place, communism signified a social revolution,
the elevation of the lowest stratum of society, the proletariat, to
the top, all other classes being outcasts, until with the complete
triumph of the class war, there would be none but the proletariat
surviving. In the third place, communism, as it developed, aimed
to destroy the existing religion, as dispensed by the Orthodox
Church, and became in itself a religion with its own peculiar
tenets and its own code of morality. What is considered good or
bad must depend upon its relation to communist aims. It was also
a religion that had no concern beyond this material world—in
short, a materialistic atheism. And fourthly and finally, communism implied a discarding of the State in the form which it had
developed in the West, based on a more or less territorial representation in accordance with the distribution of population, and the
erection, instead, of a state on a vocational basis, following the
syndicalist plan. Thus a political body, or in other words, a soviet,
should be composed of representatives of industrial units, the
various villages, shops, and factories, instead of a body elected by
all adult citizens with an equal voice. Lenin liked to speak of
doing away with the State altogether, substituting an agglomeration of self-managing industries (the syndicalist ideal), but obviously he could not dispense with a central organization, directing
human relationships and co-ordinating the life of the entire community. If these four objects taken together were to succeed,
Russia would pass through an economic, social, religious, and political revolution the like of which the world had never seen.

We may begin with the work of political reconstruction, which *The*
was obviously of first importance, since nothing could be achieved *structure*
until authority had been organized and everywhere enforced. *communist*
"Our first watchword," Lenin had said, "is centralization." The *state*
political structure of Russia was determined by a constitution
promulgated in 1918 and later somewhat altered and amplified.
To begin with, all adults of eighteen or over were termed active
citizens and might vote provided they belonged to one of four
categories: those who were engaged in useful labor, those who

kept house for those who were so engaged, those who had lost the
capacity for work, and those who served in the army and
navy. To these proletarians were accorded equal rights and
freedom of conscience, opinion, and association. The constitution obviously created a privileged class, the proletariat,
though it must be remembered that all were ultimately to belong
to that category. All the instruments of production were declared to be national property; thus was socialism consecrated
in the constitution. The organization of the State was exceedingly
complicated. The local soviets (urban or rural) chose delegates
to larger bodies, which in turn chose bodies above them until at
the apex was an organ known as the presidium, which carried on
most of the work of legislation. There was also an executive body,
the council of people's commissars, which was, however, amenable
to the control of the presidium and of a larger committee of which
it (the presidium) was a part. In 1922, after Russia had become
enlarged by the recovery of certain regions which had seceded, a
federal system was established, the Union of Socialist, Soviet
Republics (U.S.S.R.), each one being modeled after that of
Russia proper, as was also the federal government itself. At the
head of the latter was also a presidium (composed of twenty-seven
members) and a council of commissars (composed of ten), which
constituted the executive. The rôle of the federal presidium was
mainly supervisory, and it could quash any decisions of any body,
executive or legislative. It was the most important organ of the
machinery of government.

The position
of the
Communist
Party

Yet the intrinsic importance of all these bodies is really very
slight. Sovereignty lies not in the visible organism but in a body
invisible and extra-constitutional—the so-called political bureau,
composed of the élite of the Communist Party. As in the case of
the Fascists, the Communist Party has a compact and efficient
organization, dominated by its leaders who compose the political
bureau, a small segment of the central executive committee. These
nine men are communists tried and true, and they fill the key
positions in the State, as well as control the presidium of the federation. It is they who finally determine what legislation is to be
passed by the various legislative organs, and it is they who shape
government policy; and through the presidium of the federal state
they have their hands on the whole machinery of government.
Chief of them today is Joseph Stalin, who, unlike Lenin (and

Mussolini), holds no office in the government but is simply a member of the political bureau and secretary general of the executive committee of the Communist Party. While it is true that none but convinced communists can hold office (in fact, no other party has any legal existence), membership in the party itself is not necessary to eligibility, though naturally, of course, the most responsible posts are held only by members. To be enrolled in the party one must pass a severe test, and one may lose one's membership by deviating from the path of the official policy. Every year there is a "purging," conducted by an important organ of the party, known as the organization bureau. The active Communists, very like Jesuits in the rigidity of their training and their staunch devotion, form the very framework on which Russia rests today. There are small groups of them ("cells," as they are called) in every factory; they are the high-ups in the army and in the State; and they are both a corps of vigilance, observing the conduct of the masses, and the missionaries of the faith. They get small remuneration but are repaid by the sense of power and, above all, by the consciousness of pursuing a holy cause.

It was in its economic policy that the worth of communism had to pass its chief test, and we may judge the avidity with which Lenin proceeded to put it into operation. The nationalizing of industry seemed also particularly imperative by reason of the civil war. By the summer of 1918 the policy of taking over plants and factories had proceeded at a considerable pace. The more basic industries like textiles, oil, coal, and transportation were among the first to be seized, control in each case being centralized in a directing board at the top; while over all was placed the "supreme council of public economy" as a means of co-ordinating the economic life of the country as well as the sole medium through which foreign trade could be carried on. At the same time many smaller factories and plants were appropriated by the State. In the meantime, the land was nationalized, though in actual practice the State was content with requisitioning grain at a fixed price.[1] Since the ruble had lost all value, the use of money practically ceased, and a socialistic economy had apparently come into being. But the whole system broke down, because the factories were badly managed, because the workers refused to speed up (in many cases they were

The economic policy of Lenin and its failure

----

[1] These forced requisitions were largely instigated by the need of feeding the Red Army while it was engaged in the civil war.

underfed and deserted to the country, causing an acute shortage of labor), because the means of production and transportation were in bad shape, and because the peasants resisted the demands upon their produce. In fact, the whole national economy was dislocated. The workers would not work, largely because they could not get food, and in consequence production rapidly fell off (in 1919–20 it was fourteen per cent of what it had been in 1913); the peasants, on their side, would not deliver their grain because they could not get the manufactured products they required, and flatly refused to take paper money (which, owing to wild inflation, was practically worthless). Since the food problem seemed the most fundamental of all, Lenin formed committees in every village, composed of the poorer (and sometimes shiftless) peasants to plunder the thrifty ones and make them give up their surplus grain. "There can be but one outcome," Lenin had said, "the dictatorship of the proletariat—the power of the pitiless iron hand, which will complete the work of the social revolution. The new difficulties that are coming we shall meet by calling to our aid the millions of poverty-stricken peasant folk." At the same time, coercion was employed in the shop. The workers were compelled to work longer and were subjected to severe discipline. But the results of such a policy were far from satisfactory. The peasants met this campaign by a passive but stolid resistance; they refused to raise more than enough grain to feed themselves; and the result was the worst famine that Russia had ever known. At the same time the discontent of the workers was so great that strikes and riots were frequent, and in 1921 occurred a mutiny of sailors at Kronstadt, which made it appear that even the military might ultimately fail the government.

Temporary reaction— the "Nep"   Lenin came unwillingly to the conclusion that his system would not work, though he was comforted, perhaps, by the thought that he had prophesied a period of transition before the workers would have the experience to operate industry successfully. Technical skill and knowledge were chief among the needs. "Without the direction of specialists in different branches of knowledge, technique, and experience," he said, "the transformation toward socialism is impossible." So experts were employed to run the industries, even when it was necessary to pay them high salaries; foreigners were given concessions as a means of enhancing productive capacity; and the monetary system was at last stabilized. But the essence of the change was a reversion to capitalism, permitted and even for a time encouraged though always subjected to official interference. The private capitalist was tolerated on paying for a government license. The smaller plants were returned to their owners, the larger ones, leased to individuals; while the key industries were organized into trusts, privately managed and even allowed a margin of profit, though shaping of general policy was still reserved to the government. It was a policy of compromise with capitalism, and was popularly known as the "Nep." Lenin enforced it upon his party, and several thousand Communists were struck from the party rolls for their opposition. The Nep also invaded agriculture. The peasant was allowed to pay a moderate tax in money and to enjoy the usufruct of his land, and subsequently was allowed to lease land and even to employ a certain number of hired hands. Although there were still many difficulties —particularly when the peasants produced too great a surplus, and it was necessary to scale down industrial prices and find means of raising the price of grain—yet by 1925 production as a whole was only thirty per cent below that of 1913, and by 1927 the industrial output was supposed actually to have reached that earlier level.[1] It was as a result of this improvement that the government was able once more to encroach on private trade. By compromise Lenin had saved his government, and in the meantime he had insured a greater technical efficiency in all State-owned or State-controlled industries. But it was only a stategic retreat, and though Lenin did not live to resume his settled policy (he died in January, 1924), there is no doubt that it was his intention as soon as possible to resume it. *Death of Lenin*

The passing of so strong a personality made some foreigners believe that the system which he had founded could not endure without him. But the foundations had been laid too strong for that. There was a struggle over his mantle between the explosive egoist, Trotsky, and the gruff, cold, flintlike Stalin. Both agreed that the time had come for a return to pure communism (in fact, a communistic reaction had begun, as we have seen, before Lenin's death); but Trotsky felt that it was also time to go back to the old idea of a world revolution, which had been proclaimed in the days of the civil war. Stalin, on the other hand, believed that Russia *Return to pure communism under Stalin*

[1] Agricultural production is now (1934) believed to have reached the 1913 level; industrial production is far beyond it.

must first apply communism herself and that the class war had still much to accomplish within Russia. It was Stalin who triumphed within the party. Trotsky was degraded from all his positions and exiled, and later others who offered resistance to the official policy were consigned to a similar fate. The dictatorship of Stalin has apparently been impregnable ever since. A rather enigmatical character, like so many reserved men (he

Underwood & Underwood

A GLIMPSE OF THE NEW RUSSIA
Giant Furnace of the Stalin Metal Works on the Lower Don

learned to be secretive through a long career of conspiracy), Stalin is the embodiment of quiet force and political acumen. Not a Russian at all, but a Georgian from the Caucasus, and rather poorly educated, he is not an intellectual like Trotsky and some of the earlier revolutionists. To him the romance of the Revolution is over and its ideology settled. It was enough that Lenin had formulated its platform. Stalin has merely to defend and consolidate the movement. Thus his rôle is that of a practical politician, patient, forceful, and, when necessary, ruthless.

Under Stalin, then, the Communist Régime resumed its policy of nationalization. The "nepmen," as the capitalists were called,

were strangled by heavy taxation, and deprived of most of the
necessities of life, until at last they became communists—passive
communists at least; and privately owned enterprises ceased to
exist. But the chief struggle was with the *kulaks*, the thrifty,
industrious peasants whom Stolypin had made individualists and
whom the Revolution had enriched. Deportation or death was to
be the fate of countless thousands of this class. Yet to have allowed
peasant proprietorship in a country whose population is overwhelmingly agrarian was perhaps too great a danger to a communist régime.

A sharp turning point came in 1928, ending a period wherein
the general standard of living had appreciably risen. Having
disposed of Trotsky in that year, Stalin placed his unflagging
energy and his somewhat fatalistic confidence in the task of making
communism successful. It was in 1928 that he inaugurated the
famous "Five-Year Plan," by which under careful planning the
whole economic life was to be driven with such a momentum that
industrial output should be more than doubled and agricultural
production immensely increased. There should be more than
enough to supply the domestic need; there must be a surplus
(especially of grain) for exportation, since the magnitude of the
plan demanded large supplies of machinery from abroad. Such a
policy entailed tremendous hardships for the people, partly because
consumption needs were deliberately sacrificed to the providing
of capital equipment, and partly because the attack on the *kulaks*
(whom the government was unwilling to assist as the quickest
means of stimulating production) produced for some years a
shortage of foodstuffs. It was, however, the peasantry in particular
—the great mass of the population—which bore the most crushing
burden. To provide this immense volume of exports as well as to
furnish food for the rapidly growing industrial centers, the government practiced exploitation to a degree never experienced even
in the worse of czarist days; while at the same time it proceeded
to drive the peasants willy-nilly into the collective farms and to
uproot the *kulaks*. When a second great famine occurred—in
1932—chiefly as the result of the pitiless requisitions, the government denied its existence (it could easily, of course, have averted
it), and apparently made no effort to relieve conditions, since the
calamity was simply regarded as a means of forcing the peasants
to knuckle under. "Famine," as a competent observer has re-

A planned economy in operation

marked, "was quite deliberately employed as an instrument of national policy." [1] But the war for the nationalization of the land has been won, and it seems now only a question of time when all peasants will be wage-earners, like ordinary proletarians, working "collective" farms with agricultural machinery under (theoretically) skilled official direction. As to the work of the Five-Year Plan (quite apart from any moral considerations), it is generally felt that the transition was too rapid. The transportation system did not keep pace with expanding industry; there has not yet developed the technical skill necessary to insure proper qualitative standards for the enormous volume of production; even the problem of housing the immense army of workers has not been adequately met. But efforts are being made to correct mistakes; and already a second, and similar, five-year plan has come into being. As far as bulk is concerned, the output of the first plan had been astounding. Official estimates had generally been exceeded.

But, in the meantime, for this vast population to find employment at a living wage (and the population rapidly increases) and for industries to expand at ferocious speed, while ordinary needs such as clothes are barely satisfied, tremendous sacrifices and hardships must be endured; and despite the promise of a more comfortable living as the result of the second plan, there is little sign as yet that this is coming. At the beginning of the first plan—that is, in 1928—it was decided that with such a slender volume of production for private needs, a careful system of rationing was indispensable; and it is hoped that current methods of distribution will become so deeply embedded in the national habits that all money exchanges can ultimately be done away with. In similar wise private property has no standing, and may at any time be confiscated, though it is generally respected. Even so, one has little to call one's own. Not until Russia's economy has been thoroughly set in order can the standard of living rise to a decent

---

[1] Mr. W. H. Chamberlain informs us that the famine area included some of the most fertile regions in Russia, including the Ukraine. "The excess of deaths," he writes "over a normal mortality rate can scarcely have been less than three or four million." This would indicate a much greater mortality than in the famine of 1921, when, as a matter of fact, the government was less sensitive about its prestige, and foreign aid was welcomed. Thousands of *kulaks* were also deported from different parts of Russia for forced labor on construction projects such as the Baltic-White Sea canal. It may be wondered whether the crushing of the *kulaks* will not react disadvantageously on agricultural productivity.

level—even for Russians. It is because so much patience is required that communism is preached as a religion, and that the "Promised Land" is always kept in view. As Calvin Hoover, the American economist, wrote in 1930, "The future of the Soviet Régime depends upon whether or not the Communist Party has miscalculated the breaking point of the Russian people." This statement was of course, made, before the crushing of the *kulaks*.

If it depends on the soul of the people, there seems little doubt *Communist* that the policy is so far meeting the test. In many respects the *society* Russian people have undergone a considerable change. The fact that the rationing system prevails and that industrial production has been insufficient to meet even the most elemental needs, added to the fact that no one is permitted to work for profit, has tended to keep the Russian from longing for material things. After all, he has still the out-of-doors for reveling in sport, as well as an abundance of cheap amusements, such as music and the cinema, and even a chance to read—a diversion hardly to be dreamed of in earlier days. Everyone is also sure of a job, however little it may pay and however distant from his home; and if we except the political offenders engaged in forced labor, there is much more leisure time to enjoy the things that do not minister to material comfort. For the natural desire to get ahead in the world (always stunted in a country of communal tenures) is sometimes substituted the desire to serve society. Instead of competition for gain one is encouraged to harry the *kulak* or some person whose bourgeois extraction renders suspect; the class war must go on if for no other reason than it furnished an emotional outlet for the people. "Communism," writes Professor Hoover, "has brought not peace to Russia but the sword." The old Church is dying, for the government has restricted its operations and undermined its influence; meanwhile most of the population unconsciously look upon communism itself as a religion. Anyone visiting the Red Square in Moscow may see on a public building the inscription: "Religion is opium for the people." Hard by is the mausoleum of Lenin, where his embalmed body may be viewed by all his worshipers— the shrine of the new Russia. Orthodox morality, like orthodox religion, has gone into the discard. Under the Communist Régime sentiment is much opposed to moral restrictions, whether imposed by the laws of the State or by tradition; and as such matters are left entirely to the individual, what are spoken of as "irregular unions" in other countries are in Russia considered normal (only promiscuity being discouraged); for though it is true that matters of sex are rather ignored than overemphasized in Russian society, the idea that marriage is a condition fundamental to mating is rapidly becoming exploded. Marriages are easily dissolved, and illegitimate children have exactly the same status as legitimate. Women, whether married or unmarried, have equal rights with men as well as duties, and, whether married or unmarried, are encouraged to become active workers in the industrial life of the community. Hence a beginning has been made in providing State nurseries for small children, and it is expected that these will ultimately become so numerous that mothers will be dispensed from the care of the young. The older children have little parental control. Some of them are novices, as it were, in the service of the Communist Party; and there are organizations of youths who do much to spread the gospel of the new religion, though their bumptiousness has frequently made them a nuisance. There is a life and bustle in the new Russia that was never present in the old. Far-reaching schemes of social insurance, electrification of the peasant villages, and instruction in hygiene have been inaugurated, though they are still greatly handicapped for lack of funds. One of the greatest achievements of the new régime has been the marked diminution of illiteracy. There has also been scientific research, and the necessities of the Five-Year Plan has led to considerable stress on vocational training; but history and economics must always be approached from a strictly communist angle, and, in fact, the science of economics is supposed to have done its work. The creed of communism permeates everything—the schools, the press, literature, the cinema, and theater. Its alleged truths are regarded as axiomatic; they are not susceptible to question, but are regarded with the same sublime faith as the fundamentalist or Christian Scientist regards his religion. It is this faith that sustains a people whose standard of living is lower than it was in czarist days, who are virtually forced to remain on the same dead level, who are fed under a rationing system of the narrowest range, and who are kept under careful watch lest someone happens to display a little luxury that would convict him of individualism. From the standpoint of the West, it is a weird and unenchanting experiment— this molding of a communist community. Yet much of what is revolting is simply a means to an end. And when one considers the constructive achievements of the men who are driving this vast untutored herd from age-old darkness into the light of the twentieth century, one is moved to feel a measure of admiration. Once again is a Peter the Great striving to raise a backward nation to the material standards of the West. It is the Russian people themselves who may wonder if the goal is worth the price.

Why, then, has the Communist Régime grown stronger rather than weaker, and, in spite of the sacrifices entailed, secured a firm grip on the people? In the earlier years the organizing skill and fighting spirit of Lenin, the weakness of the elements of opposition, the passive acquiescence of the peasants, who, in order to insure possession of their stolen land, preferred communism to czarism as the French peasants had preferred Napoleon to a return of the Bourbons—these factors enabled the dictatorship of the proletariat to become consolidated. Then, in course of time, the superb discipline of the Communist Party, with its periodic "cleasings," its searching examination of its members, has signified the existence of a great machine (to belong to which is the highest temporal reward), which buttresses the power of the proletarian dictatorship. Moreover, restrictions on freedom of opinion (in spite of the rights guaranteed by the constitution), the creation of a mind sealed against the West (a sort of revived slavophilism), the virtual ban on emigration and the nurturing of the rising generation by communist propaganda still further consolidated the new régime. Then the fact that communism has become a religion gives it that spiritual power that enables the individual to rise above his hardships. A god he knows not, but to the Revolution he has willingly given his soul. Also, in order to hearten him, the class war goes on relentlessly. Sometimes people are deliberately branded as bourgeois in order to give the mob the delicious excitement of tormenting them. There is also the *ogpu*, the historic successor of the *tcheka*, which deals with every suspicion of counter-revolution, and even on occasions invents it, and keeps the population in an atmosphere of fear. Then, too, if life is humdrum and at times painful, one must not forget that spirit of resignation, which has at all times and all periods enabled the Russian people to endure oppression of all sorts. And finally, the Russian people know that a dictatorship of the proletariat, false as the term may be (since government is autocratic) is at least a dictatorship *for* the proletariat. Russia is no longer exploited by an extravagant court, by

Explanation of the stability of the Communist Régime

the aristocratic landlord or by the rich industrialist. She exists
for the material well-being and improvement of the masses. Faith
and force have made a people united in soul. In November, 1917,
hardly three per cent of the population were communists; now in
1935 it is fair to say that almost as few are avowedly anything else.

Relations with Europe

The position of a great nation which has come under a socialistic
régime in a capitalistic world naturally calls for some attention.
The relations of Bolshevik Russia with foreign powers have often
been stormy, and for a long time she was an outcast among nations.

Attitude of the Allies

The Western Powers could not believe—at least for some years—
that a small minority of extreme revolutionists would be able to
stay in power. They studiously ignored the Soviet government,
and their ambassadors withdrew as soon as they could—not
without some difficulty. Opposition of the Western Powers
was based largely on fear of a communist régime, which might
incite the working class within their own borders to revolt. They
were also alienated by the Soviet government's renunciation
of the foreign debts contracted under the Old Régime—
an act which particularly concerned the French, who held
$3,000,000,000 in Russian bonds. Finally, it was feared that
Germany, with or without Russia's consent, would get possession of some arms which had been sent by Russia's allies and
were at present deposited at Murmansk (on the Murman coast),
Archangel, and Vladivostok. In the spring of 1918, after the Germans had apparently got Finland under their sway, a small international force was landed at Murmansk and Archangel; and later a
similar force, composed of British, Americans, and Japanese,
landed at Vladivostok. In the meantime, all the Baltic nationalities, aided by the Germans, had succeeded in repelling Bolshevik
interference, and by the terms of the Armistice the Germans were
required to hold these lands in temporary occupation. It was a
strange device for combating Bolshevik Russia.

The Allied intervention and the civil war

When the Allied representatives finally gathered at Paris in
December, 1918, there was much anxiety over Russia, though it
was difficult to come to any decision. The Bolsheviks themselves
were anxious for recognition and Lloyd George seems to have
leaned in that direction. Clemenceau, on the other hand, would
have welcomed war with Russia, provided the United States,
whose forces were the least exhausted, would be willing to bear
the brunt of the intervention. Wilson knew, of course, that such

a policy would be impossible to justify in America (where the outcry was for immediate demobilization), though he was willing
that American troops should remain for the present with the other
forces cantoned at Vladivostok and Archangel. The final decision
was a sort of half-intervention. The small international armies remained in Russia; British forces occupied positions in the Caucasus
and the French some points in southern Russia as bases for helping
the anti-Bolshevik forces to whom munitions were also sent; and
the Allied blockade was extended to Russia. The chief reliance lay
in the counter-revolutionary elements within Russia, and there
were a number of these scattered groups, under whose auspices
various armies were launched at Moscow or Petrograd. There
was also a force of some 70,000 Czechoslovaks, who, released from
Russian prisons, had beaten their way to the Urals *en route* to the
Pacific whence they expected to embark for their homes in central
Europe. This body would have made a likely nucleus for an armed
uprising of all enemies of the Communist Régime. But the Reign
of Terror had been sufficient to prevent widespread opposition from
developing, and the country was so vast that any united resistance
seemed improbable.

The civil war lasted for over two years, and we have already
noted its reaction on the domestic affairs of Russia. At one time
Wilson persuaded his colleagues of the Congress of Paris to agree
to a peace conference on the Isle of Prinkipo in the Sea of Marmora,
to which all the warring factions, including the liberated nationalities, should send envoys, with a view of settling their differences.
But the counter-revolutionary elements would not hear of "sitting
with assassins," and the Communists, who were then holding their
own, refused to assent to a truce, which was one of the prerequisites
of the conference. The whole scheme was no doubt chimerical.
Then one after the other, the various drives against the Soviet
government failed. In 1919 Poland, encouraged by France, and
anxious to extend her frontier as well as to defend herself against
Bolshevik meddling in her affairs, commenced a war against
Russia, but success was only temporary, and the Poles, as we shall
note again, narrowly escaped annihilation.

For various reasons Soviet Russia pulled through the civil war
and triumphed over its enemies. In the first place, there was a
great deal of dissension in the ranks of the counter-revolutionists
—royalists at odds with republicans, the military leaders quar-

Triumph of the Soviet government

reling with the politicians. In the second place, the peasants feared the return of the old landlords, and numerous cruelties perpetrated by the "White" armies rather deepened the prejudice against them. In the third place, foreign support was half-hearted and inadequate. Interference in Russia was far from popular in the Allied countries, the Labor Party in England being especially vehement in its opposition. In the end, the Allied forces withdrew, and the blockade was terminated.

The Communist offensive

No doubt the successful resistance of the Soviet government strengthened its moral position—in Europe as well as at home. But it viewed itself as continually at war with the rest of the world and meant to carry out its dream of a world revolution.[1] In 1919 had been organized originally as an act of self-defense, the so-called Third International, to which communists from all over the world were invited to send delegates, but which was mainly, and is now entirely, a Russian institution. The purpose of this body, which was not a part of the government but worked in close harmony with it, was to engineer communist propaganda in foreign lands. It was even intended to spread communism in Asia, and there is no doubt that "Red" agents have been active in India and China. In the years immediately following the War there was a good deal of trepidation in the West that the Russian Revolution, now in its communist phase, would submerge the rest of the world.

There was also fear of the Red Army, which, if successful against Poland, might press into Germany and win conquests by the sword just as the armies of Revolutionary France had done. Hence, the importance of the Russo-Polish War of 1919–20. As there were a good many communists in Poland, the Russians had every hope of winning the conflict, and British labor objected to any relief being sent from England. It is not astonishing that when a Russian army had beaten back the Poles and beleaguered Warsaw, a brilliant French officer, General Weygand, hurried to Poland, and it was he who rallied the Poles in what Winston Churchill has called the "miracle of the Vistula." Perhaps the Battle of Warsaw

The passing of a crisis

may be regarded as one of the decisive battles of history, though of course one cannot be sure that Russian armies would have done more than conquer Poland. At any rate the Russians were beaten,

---

[1] It has been suggested quite plausibly that Lenin's eagerness to spread the Revolution before it was even well consolidated in Russia was due to the fact that Marx had taught that a proletarian revolution in a single country was impossible.

and the Peace of Riga (1920) settled the issues between the two nations.

As the fear of Revolutionary Russia subsided, and as the Communists themselves became more conciliatory with the inauguration of the Nep, there seemed no reason why some conditions of relationship could not be worked out that would enable outside powers to recover the Russian market and Russia herself to supply her numerous needs from abroad. In 1921 a trade agreement was signed with Great Britain—an act which signified at least *de facto* recognition, though there were not as yet formal diplomatic relations. Much of the difficulty in the way of recognition lay in the question of foreign debts, and at Lloyd George's instance a Russian request to be represented at an international conference to consider reparations and other matters was granted by the Powers. No decision was reached on the Russian question, but during the sessions—to the dismay of some of the Powers—Germany and Russia signed a treaty, by which, among other things, Germany granted recognition to the Soviet government. In February, 1924, Great Britain, under a Labor government, followed suit, and likewise Italy and even France soon afterward. Most of the lesser states followed; but the United States withheld her recognition till 1934. There was, however, some friction at times in the relations of Russia with other powers. Owing to financial aid, sent by certain Russian trade unions to striking workmen in England, diplomatic relations were severed between Moscow and London for a time; and once a Russian ambassador was recalled from Paris at France's request. But more and more the avowed principle of Stalin is that Russians should limit their energies to achieving success at home and that socialism (contrary to Lenin's teachings) may succeed in a single country. Moreover, the rise of the new Germany with its hopes of eastward expansion was viewed by Stalin as liable to become a menace. Hence Russia has come to display even a spirit of co-operation with other powers. In 1932 she was represented at a disarmament conference and made some drastic proposals. And finally in 1934, so completely had her policy become opportunist, she accepted membership (with, of course, a seat on the council) in the once-dispised and "capitalistic" League of Nations. Europe had not only forgiven Russia but had restored her to the family of nations.

One result of the Revolution has been the dismemberment of

Admission of Communist Russia into the family of nations

*Dismem-
berment of
Russia* Russia. Her Poles were liberated to become a part of the new Poland. Finland, Esthonia, Latvia, and Lithuania, aided at first by
the Germans, became independent states, and since the civil war
there has been no effort to subdue them. Russia seems content
with her ethnic frontiers. Russian nationalism, according to Communist theory, has broadened into a world-wide cosmopolitanism,
which, based on the dictatorship of the proletariat, knows no
national frontiers, but the effort to attain this ideal, which would
*The question
of a world
revolution* obviously entail a world revolution, must at present give place to
the task of internal regeneration. Meanwhile Russia hopes to
captivate the world by the force of her example.

Germany, her enemy, had been one of the nations whose condition, in Russian eyes, seemed most ripe for regeneration.

REVOLUTION AND REACTION IN GERMANY

**Causes and
Outbreak of
the German
Revolution** It is not hard to understand why Germany also should have
been a scene of revolution. In a struggle as intense as the Great
War the credit of every government must needs have hung in the
balance. Had it been successful, the imperial régime would probably have emerged stronger than ever. Its failure was bound to
have a converse effect. But why it was not merely shaken but
utterly demolished demands a closer investigation.

*Popular
restlessness
during the
War* Dissentient voices were negligible when Germany had begun to
wage her "war of defense." Though there were a few reluctant
hearts, the Social Democratic Party (which was then the strongest
party in the reichstag) voted unanimously for the needed appropriations for the War. Subsequent success at the front easily
persuaded these socialists to forget that they were supposed to be
pacifist internationalists. But in 1916, as the War dragged on
without results, there were innumerable murmurs, and after the
unusually hard winter of 1916-7 (due chiefly to the British blockade), the official boasts of Germany's coming conquests fell on
rather dull ears. Weariness with a war that would seemingly never
end led to a bloc of all the relatively liberal parties in the reichstag,
and a peace resolution was the result, which, however, failed of its
purpose, as the military authorities were in the ascendant. Perhaps these dissentients would have been wiser to have insisted first
of all on parliamentary government.

But the working class had meanwhile become increasingly restive. The Russian Revolution, with the enhanced prominence of

socialist doctrines, had had an undoubted effect on the German proletariat. At the same time the entrance of the United States into the War seemed to promise a prolongation of the struggle. There had been sporadic strikes in 1916 and 1917; in January, 1918, there was a really formidable one, and the strikers, some half a million in all, demanded not only peace without indemnities or annexations (the Russian formula) but a complete democratization of the Empire. Yet the demonstration ended in complete failure. Ludendorff assumed full responsibility for suppressing the strike, and he did it thoroughly. It was proved a great mistake, however, to punish some of the offenders by impressing them into the army, for they naturally spread the virus of discontent to the men at the front.

All these incidents were premonitory symptoms of a new temper, but the fate of the imperial government really hinged on the outcome of the struggle in the West. When it was finally clear that Germany had lost the War, its days were numbered. After the resolution was taken to sue for peace, Ludendorff who, more than the Kaiser or his chancellor, had become the real ruler of Germany, deliberately transferred his power to the reichstag. The leading historian of these events has called it a "kind of revolution . . . without a parallel in the whole history of the world." He also points out that the imperial reichstag, still politically a child, was utterly incompetent to rise to the emergency. It only goes to show that when autocracy breaks down, there is nothing immediately strong enough to replace it. For the present, William chose the liberal Prince Max of Baden to be chancellor at the head of a ministry responsible to the reichstag, and it was hoped that by creating a really parliamentary monarchy the dynasty might be saved. *A preliminary revolution "from above"*

But the fall of the Empire came, and was due to three circumstances: the strategy of Wilson, the pusillanimity of the Kaiser, and the bewilderment of a nation which had suffered not only defeat but complete moral collapse. Germany's overtures of peace, addressed, as we saw, to Wilson, met with a guarded response. In an interchange of notes which then ensued Wilson questioned the German statement that request for an armistice had been made "in the name of the German people," and demanded the degradation of that "power which had hitherto controlled the German nation," adding that it was "within the choice of the German nation to alter it." In his final note he declared that if *Downfall of the Empire and its causes*

he had to deal with an autocrat, he "must demand not peace negotiations but surrender." Such suspicions were wholly unjust to the existing government, but Wilson had no trust in any state of which William II was even nominal head, and he grasped at the opportunity of forcing the German people to take the cure-all tonic of democracy.[1] At all events, it was borne home to the German government and also surmised by the people that the Kaiser was the chief obstacle to peace.

Throughout this crisis William himself played a very sorry rôle. He might have surrendered his power graciously and in that way might possibly (despite the shame of defeat) have retained the loyalty of a people who stood in dire need of gallant leadership. But, instead, after committing his fortunes to Max, he retired hurriedly to army headquarters, as if he could only get protection from the military. Throughout the War he had played a curiously passive rôle, never making an effort to sustain the national morale, and latterly he had virtually surrendered his power to Ludendorff. He was persuaded, it is true, that he had to give up his autocratic powers, but when it came to the question of abdication—which began to be demanded during the latter part of October—he was adamant. It was not until he learned that not only was the navy in a state of mutiny but that he could not even rely upon the army to support him, and not until he became convinced that if he did not go willingly he would certainly be deposed, that he consented to abdication. On November 9 Prince Max, hearing that the step was decided upon (actually it was not till November 28 that William formally abdicated), handed over his authority to Friedrich Ebert, the leader of the Social Democratic Party. On the following day, without more ado, William took his departure for Holland. Had William loved Germany more than himself he would have remained quietly in Berlin. Had he not feared for his life, he would have shown a greater dignity even at the risk of his life. Like many of his dynasty before him, the Kaiser seems to have been a coward.

One can never know, of course, whether William could have evoked any loyalty from his people if he had comported himself differently. If a peace could be got more cheaply by scrapping their ruler, then many felt that the price was little to pay. In

[1] Professor Charles Seymour thinks that Wilson was following an ideal rather than consciously employing tactics likely to undermine the Kaiser.

any case the nation seemed for the moment almost stunned by its decisive reverse of fortune. Since it is always possible to be wiser after the fact, the question easily arises: could Germany, with her army intact, and a strong line of fortresses, have put up a desperate resistance, and thereby have avoided the harsh terms of the Armistice—terms which left her disarmed and powerless? [1] Assuming the victors to be merciless, could she, even in the face of ultimate and certain defeat, have won at least the right to negotiate as an equal and thus have avoided the devastating Treaty of Versailles? Doubtless it must be left for some future historian to pass an impartial judgment on her surrender. The members of the high command did show a genuine reluctance to quit the struggle (so also did Prince Max before his downfall), but in the face of the public apathy and the beginning not only of actual revolution but of mutiny in the back lines of the army both staff and civil government felt that further resistance was hopeless and that the most impending problem was the danger at their doors—namely bolshevism. In any event the morale of the nation had obviously collapsed.

But there is a reason which goes far toward exculpating the German people from a charge of want of courage. The point needs to be emphasized that virtually the whole nation had been suffering from undernourishment—a fact which largely accounted for the strikes we have already noted. Since Germany in the matter of food was far from self-sufficient, and since the British blockade prevented shipments from neutral countries, there had long been a shortage of everything, and particularly of fats. From 1916 on food had been systematically rationed to the whole population, but even so there was never enough. The winter of 1916-7 is remembered as the "turnip winter," for even the stock of potatoes had run short, and it hardly needs to be said that meat was rarely tasted. During 1917 some relief had come from Roumania after the German occupation of that country, but the supply was still inadequate to the demand, especially as the army must be fed even if citizens went hungry. Such privations were usually fatal to the weaker members of society and it is probable that some quarter of a million perished

---

[1] This question was actually investigated by the Constituent Assembly. See *The Causes of the German Collapse* (ed. Lutz), esp. pp. 81-8. A weakening of the military morale through the depression due to defeat and as a result of revolutionary propaganda was brought to light in the investigation. It would seem that revolution reacted fatally against the national cause.

as the result of various diseases that attack the underfed. Those who survived succumbed to a sort of lethargy. The will to struggle and endure had been sapped as the result of depleted strength. Such is probably the chief explanation of the moral collapse. Finally it should be added as a contributive factor to this condition that the country for several months had been bombarded by Allied propaganda from the air, blaming the War on the Kaiser and portraying a peace-loving people as having been hoodwinked by its government. It is probably true that by this time most Germans had become heartily sick of monarchy, which they associated only too painfully with the War; and they seemed not even to be troubled by the ignominy of surrender. Life would only be tolerable when the past could be forgotten.

Germany in Transition— the Liberal and Experimental Republic

In the meantime, while the army was greatly relieved that peace was impending, the high command of the navy planned a dash at the British coasts as an attempt to show that Germany could still "pass out with honor." But the plan seemed only ridiculous to the sailors, who simply resorted to mutiny in order to make its execution impossible. As the navy had been substantially inactive during the War, it had had little to do but watch the swaggering of its officers, and it did not propose now to be sacrificed for a gesture. But the mutiny, because of fear of capital punishment if it were quelled, soon developed into a real revolution. In Kiel workers' and sailors' councils were formed after the model of the Russian soviets (proving, it would seem, the influence of Bolshevik propaganda), and the movement (supported, it appears, by army reservists) soon spread to other towns. Eventually councils of workmen and soldiers sprang up throughout Germany, including, of course, Berlin. It was this threatened domestic upheaval which had partly accounted for Germany's surrender to the Allies. But the present movement was only in its beginnings. Much depended on the conduct of the new government.

Revolution "from below"

Establishment of the Republic

On November 9, the day of the supposed abdication of the emperor, a republic was proclaimed in Berlin, and the following day a provisional government was set up by the Socialist leaders. Three of the six "commissars" (as they were called) were Majority Socialists (the more conservative wing of the Social Democratic Party) and three were Independent Socialists, the two parties forming a bloc against the communists, popularly known as the

"Spartacides." [1] The split into the first two groups had taken place during the War, when the Independents had insisted upon a peace without indemnities or annexations, while the Majority Socialists refused at that time to hamper the government. With the establishment of the Republic divergence became more marked. The Majority Socialists were opportunists and ready to shelve their socialist doctrines until a democratic state had been erected on firm foundations. The Independents, on the other hand, clamored for a social revolution without delay. Their hopes lay chiefly in the workers' councils, though for the present fear of the communists stayed their hand. The workers' council of Berlin formally recognized the new government, though at first on the understanding that the latter derived its authority from the council; and later it was agreed that the government should function at least until a meeting of representatives of all the councils. All this seemed to smack somehow of "bolshevism." Was Germany to be driven irresistibly into that current?

How far and how deep the German Revolution would go was a question soon to be decided. The question of the fate of the various monarchies within the Empire was not long in being settled. "It was easy for you Frenchmen to bring about your revolution," a German socialist had once said to a French friend. "You had only one head to cut off. We shall be obliged to cut off twenty-five." Yet history had quite belied him, for all these thrones had toppled very quickly, the King of Bavaria having actually anticipated the Kaiser in flight; and there was not only no resistance but in a few cases these princelings had retired with the blessings of their subjects. Much more serious was the question whether Germany would go communist. The disorganization attendant upon the conclusion of the War and the effects of the British blockade (which, now extended to the Baltic, cut off all supplies from Sweden), together with the difficulty for lack of railway cars of distributing what food there was, had produced increasing misery, and the temptation to turn to communism as a kind of emotional outlet was no doubt very great. Besides, the communists, backed by emissaries from Moscow, were trying to make capital out of the distress. Yet the bulk of the working class remained passive in spite of all. Forced, at length, to make their choice, the Inde-

Question of the limitation of the Revolution —repression of communism

---

[1] From Spartacus, a leader of a revolt of slaves during the Roman Republic. The Spartacides were offered representation in the government but refused.

pendents reluctantly agreed to the calling of a constituent assembly; and when a congress of all the councils met in December, it was controlled by the Majority Socialists, and accordingly was persuaded to support the government. Probably its action was also prompted by the feeling that if Germany went communist, the War might be renewed, the country invaded, and even much harder terms of peace imposed. One of the leaders of the Majority Socialists had begged the congress not to give the Allies any excuse for delaying the conclusion of peace. The congress also fixed the date for the election of the Constituent Assembly, much to the disgust of the Independents who had wanted a socialist régime erected first. As a matter of fact, the workers' councils had demonstrated already their incompetence, and anarchy and economic collapse were seriously threatened.[1] Evidently the Independents were definitely losing their tactical advantage. Soon afterward three of the party resigned from the government, their places being taken by Majority Socialists, who, now holding all six places, engrossed responsibility for its policy.

But while the Independents were trying without much success to find a middle position, the Spartacides were determined to overthrow the government by violence and establish without delay the dictatorship of the proletariat. They had tried to paralyze the work of the workers' congress but without success. In January, 1920 they pulled off a formidable riot in Berlin, and in March they were able to set up a kind of communist republic at Munich in Bavaria. But Germany in the end repudiated communism for several reasons. In the first place, most Germans, unless they reach the point of despair, are disinclined to violence or radical measures; the lack of a vengeful spirit toward the junkers had demonstrated that. In the second place, the public, in general, was apparently persuaded that the peace might be delayed (or be even more severe than was anticipated) if Germany went communist, and the greatest immediate need was the raising of the blockade. And in the third place, the commissar of defense in the provisional government, Gustav Noske, was a man who by long training as a labor agitator had come to know how to handle workmen and did not hesitate when necessary to be ruthless. Both the Berlin riot and the Bavarian rebellion were put down

---

[1] See Lutz, *The German Revolution* (Stanford University Publications in History, Economics and Political Science), p. 81.

with a heavy hand. Meanwhile, elections to the Constituent Assembly had resulted in a sweeping victory for the moderates, even the Independents winning only twenty-two seats. An attempt of the Spartacides to hamper its work was speedily quashed. The government had, of course, to face the reactionaries on the right as well as the communists on the left, but it managed to hold its own. The middle course of the Majority Socialists seemed likely to give Germany a régime that would be both solid and enlightened. *Triumph of a middle-of-the-road policy*

The elections had, in short, resulted in a triumph for the Majority Socialists, who would form the largest party (though not a majority) in the assembly. The place of meeting was Weimar, a town with liberal traditions and preferred to Berlin because of the danger from extremists in that city. When the assembly met, it proceeded to frame a provisional constitution under which Ebert and Scheidemann, the Majority Socialist leaders, were respectively chosen president and chancellor. The permanent constitution was finally drafted, submitted, and passed by the assembly by a vote of 242 to 76.

By the constitution of the German Republic the federal character of the State was retained and the upper house continued to be composed of deputies from the various states, though no state was to have more than two fifths of the representation. Autonomy, though slightly less than under the Empire, was granted to each of the states. In most respects the new régime was markedly different from the old. There was a declaration of fundamental rights of the individual, and women were to have the same status as men. The supremacy of the popular chamber, the reichstag (elected by universal suffrage), was clearly established, while cases were even provided for allowing a referendum to the people. Laws which did not emanate from the government usually originated in the reichstag, and the reichsrath (the federal chamber) had only a suspensive veto. The chancellor, the active head of the government like the premier in other countries, was directly responsible to the reichstag. The position of the president was peculiar and showed a lurking apprehension of possible dangers to the Republic. In many respects (the length of his term, his irresponsibility for ordinary public acts, and his right of selecting a chancellor likely to control the reichstag) his position closely resembled that of the president of France; but there were two *The Weimar constitution*

important exceptions: he was elected by the direct vote of the
people and not by the legislature; and to him was entrusted the
application of article 48, the "emergency clause" of the constitution. This meant the very special right, at any time when
public order was disturbed, of taking any measures necessary
to restore it—even the use of the armed forces—and of suspending
wholly or in part the fundamental rights established in the constitution. This right, as a learned authority has declared, gave
the president "a constitutionally more important position than
that which was held by the Kaiser." A plan of proportional representation and the determination of the number of deputies in
the reichstag in accordance with the number of votes cast were
interesting experiments; also the establishment of an economic
council, recruited from workers' and employers' councils, to advise
the reichstag on social legislation. Thus, in a limited sense, was
safely embedded the conciliar system in the framework of the
government. Socialism itself was not put into practice, though
the constitution explicitly opened the way to the nationalization
of industry.

*Character
and
vicissitudes
of the
Weimar
Régime*

But this democratic republic was never what could be called
socialistic, and even its "socialization" of the coal and steel industries was nothing more than a measure of government control.
It did, however, show at first great favor to the proletariat, as
might be expected. The eight-hour day, promised as early as
November, 1918 for a date not later than January 1, 1920, was
duly put into force; payment of wages by the hour was generally
substituted for payment by the piece; the wages of the unskilled
were raised almost to the level of that of the skilled; and certain
measures were taken to safeguard the workers' interests in factory
and shop. The new régime also stood for a degree of social equality
never hitherto known in Germany. Workmen's sons could now
obtain a university education, enter a profession, or obtain a
government post. But with the exception of the eight-hour day,
the severe economic stress of the next few years ended or at least
vitiated most concessions to the proletariat; and even the national
economic council was pretty generally ignored. Apart from their
ingrained moderation and, perhaps, timidity, the Majority Socialists were forced by political weakness to tolerate capitalism, and
all that they could hope for were occasional social reforms. Though
the Independents and Majority Socialists were finally reunited

in 1922 to form the United Social Democratic Party, it never enjoyed a majority in the reichstag, and the chancellor, who was rarely a member of that party, owed his position as a rule to a *bloc* of moderate groups. Added to this difficulty of coalition ministries, frequently changing, the royalists twice attempted to overthrow the government—once in 1920 when only a general strike of the Berlin workmen, which cut off water and light in the city prevented its success, and again in 1923 when Ludendorff tried what was known as his "beer-hall" *putsch;* and though they seemed to fear the communists more than the royalists, the republican statesmen probably never felt very secure. Perhaps they would have staved off trouble if they had set up a semi-dictatorship, but such an act would have been contrary to their principles.

But the greatest difficulties of the Republic were economic. The financial position of the state was precarious, partly owing to the fact that food and raw materials for German industries were needed at a time when productivity was necessarily lowered, partly owing to unwise expenditures in the interest of the working class, and partly due to the compulsion to make reparation payments. As a means of paying its debts the government resorted to inflation, and though it is true that in respect to taxes it was much too lenient toward the rich, it is not at all certain that printing-press money could have been avoided. The government had also the problem of trying to placate the Allies without losing all respect for itself at home. When these efforts failed and the French and Belgians took possession of the mining region, known as the Ruhr, the government's policy of passive resistance—ordering a general strike in the Ruhr and supporting the strikers in the meantime—produced still wilder inflation. Prices came to be quoted in billions of marks, and often a person of means who hoarded his money instead of spending it was quickly reduced to indigence. The sufferings of the workmen and the middle class (especially the salaried people) were probably as bad as during the worst period of the War; and when at last, in October, 1923, the currency was stabilized and the budget balanced, new sacrifices were demanded, as economy forced the dismissal of some 700,000 persons from public employments, a moratorium was declared on public loans (thus depriving the government's creditors of their interest), and even taxes were increased. Yet the government did not allow people to starve, and as business picked up, conditions became generally better. By the middle of 1924 German industries were well on the way to recovery. Then, during the following year, were signed the Treaties of Locarno, which promised to safeguard the country from another invasion. So bright indeed seemed the future that the government plunged into new and reckless expenditures on welfare projects, aiming to meet the growing deficit by foreign loans instead of raising additional revenues from taxation. Yet in spite of its many misfortunes and mistakes and a tendency to live from hand to mouth (which was to be expected) it can hardly be said that the Republic was an utter failure.

We have mentioned business recovery. Under the benevolent protection of the government a real industrial renascence had set in—a phenomenon we shall consider more fully in another place, and which, suffice it to say here, lifted Germany economically above all the rest of Europe. Though the sweeping introduction of rationalization involved for a time some unemployment, the government happily intervened by a thoroughgoing measure of unemployment insurance, and by 1929 the problem seemed to be solved by the simple fact that the workers were now being reabsorbed into these rapidly growing industries. Moreover, wages steadily increased. Since the national credit had been greatly enhanced (especially after the second reparation settlement, the "Young Plan"), an abundance of foreign capital poured into Germany, though usually in the form of short-term loans, and it obviously behooved the Germans to watch their step.

If only the political situation had remained tranquil, it is probable that Germany would have faced the world-wide depression, which began in 1929, with much less prospect of suffering than would have been the case with any other country. Unhappily, as we have observed, she had been trading on a long-continued boom, and her finances were on very shaky foundations. Unhappily, too, the government had from the first been forced to meet much adverse criticism for its approval of the Young Plan, and in the elections of 1930 the Communists,[1] together with a new party of the right, the National Socialists, captured nearly a third of the vote. It was evident that the moderates had lost ground to the extremists on both sides. The Communists could never forgive

---

[1] The earlier party designation, "Spartacides," seemed to pass out of use.

the Social Democrats for not having put socialism into practice, and the National Socialists were opposed to the least gesture of conciliation to the Allies. The result of these symptoms of unrest was a withdrawal of foreign capital, and the recently thriving industries were forced into rapid retrenchments with the result that more and more workers were turned out of employment. With unity and patience the crisis might conceivably have been surmounted, but only confusion prevailed. Efforts of the chancellor, Brüning, to balance the budget by retrenching on welfare projects and raising the level of taxation lost him at times the support of the reichstag, and it was only by the president's intervention that he was able on such occasions to stay in power. The bitterest enemies of the government were the Nationalists (the junkers' party), incensed at the Chancellor's project of breaking up their estates in the interest of the peasantry and as a means of providing relief for unemployment, and it was Hindenburg's final decision to oppose this measure that finally forced Brüning into retirement. It has also been alleged that Fritz Thyssen, the great steel magnate, was helping with his money to finance the opposition because Brüning had favored a rival in the steel trust. With the fall of Brüning in 1932 the constitutional régime was practically doomed. We must now ascertain the various causes of the fall of the Weimar Republic.

The failure of the German people to sustain the liberal achievements of their revolution and their resort to a government much more autocratic than any they had ever experienced seems at first sight one of the most curious twists of history. Writing as late as 1929, a careful student of the new Germany had declared, "The Republic has been consolidating itself from year to year until now it is impregnable . . . . Political democracy has been achieved brilliantly in Germany." It was felt in the outside world that with the adoption of the Young Plan and the astounding revival of German industry the worst days of the Republic were over. And even after some unexpected disasters had taken place (the economic slump and the rise of the National Socialists) one might suppose that the definite collapse of the hated reparations issue (as became evident in 1932) would operate as a stimulant and fortify the intelligence of the German people. But a good many things in history are explained by national character, and in this we may perhaps discern one fundamental clue to the failure and

The causes of reaction

collapse of the Republic. The Germans as a people are patient under hardships but they also possess an immense reserve of emotion, which, if it finally breaks forth, is liable somehow to sweep them off their feet and seems to dull their intelligence. This trait was illustrated by the National Socialists, whose objects we shall presently discuss, and to some extent it came to be noticeable in the nation as a whole. Perhaps also we may agree with Sombart's crisp characterization of Germans as "the most subservient to authority of any people on the globe." The Republic did not change that habit of subservience, as was proved when it had to meet its hardest test. Moreover, democracy was still new to the German people, and they had had to shoulder the experiment under conditions often abnormal and very discouraging.

As the factor which profoundly affected the temper of the German people, we must note as the second cause a strong and fundamental discontent, which was partly political in its inspiration, partly economic. As to the former, there was a deep-seated resentment over the humiliations imposed upon Germany by the Treaty of Versailles—a resentment which was not much allayed by the security Germany obtained against further invasions of her territory or the concessions which were made in respect to reparations. The trials which the German people had had to bear were too great to be forgotten, and in their eyes the Weimar régime had failed to protect the national honor. While it is true that reparations had constituted a relatively small part of the taxpayer's burden [1] and that social welfare work accounted for much of the load, nevertheless the current belief was that reparation payments were chiefly responsible for the heavy taxation, and there was, as we shall see, a party interested in strengthening this conviction. The Republic had been compromised from the beginning by its acceptance of the Treaty of Versailles, and the Allies, who had every reason from the standpoint of the general interest to make its position as easy as their own interests would allow had rendered it more difficult by failing so long to fix the amount to be paid as reparations and the unrelenting tenacity with which they had pressed the whole question. When finally the reparation question died, it was not lost on the German people that the reactionary government which followed Brüning had procured more

---

[1] But, as pointed out by Professor James W. Angell, this money went abroad, and therefore could not be used in the productive life of the country.

concessions from the Allies than any previous government had succeeded in obtaining since 1918.[1]

It should be noted also that economic discontent had other causes unrelated to reparations, and that this discontent deepened as the result of new circumstances. While it is true that in 1928 the national income reached a level twelve per cent higher than that of 1913 (the increase per capita being fifteen and a half per cent), it must be realized that the distribution of wealth was very uneven. The American economist, J. W. Angell, has pointed out that while the large business interests had made considerable profit and the economic position of employed workers had slightly improved, the peasantry had rather lost ground since the War, while the lower middle class had become impoverished during the period of wild inflation. It is also true that there were a million and a half workers unemployed (though most of them, it seems, leaned to the left rather than to the right). As for the lower middle class, if it had bettered itself a little during the boom, the recession from industrial activity, which, of course, affected everyone, was for this class all the harder to endure, since its savings had been lost and, unlike the proletariat, no system of insurance had been designed for its relief. A large proportion of this class had indeed been driven into the ranks of the proletariat—a fact which meant a lowering of social prestige. It was the lower middle class that felt the greatest bitterness toward the constitutional régime.

One should also add as a phase of this second cause that an important factor in the moral revolt against the consequences of the War was German youth. The young men who had fought in the War found in the period which followed, when they were groping, as it were, for some ideals, that they still had a cause to serve— at least in their hearts. They yearned for a chance to defend their beleaguered country from the "oppression" of the Allies. There were millions, who, too young to fight in the War, had come to look upon that struggle as a catastrophic blunder of the older generation. In a vague, romantic way they looked to a new Germany that would arise out of the ruins of the old. Many of them, moreover, were unable to obtain employment and they threw their surplus energy into various organizations in which self-discipline

---

[1] As a matter of fact, Brüning deserved most of the credit for convincing the Powers that the reparation question was dead, and the Conference of Lausanne was indirectly due to him rather than to his successor.

and devotion to the fatherland were the keynotes. It was this element which came to form the principal driving power in the cataclysm to come.

A third and negative cause of the fall of the Weimar régime may be found in certain mistakes of the republican statesmen. We have alluded to questionable handling of financial problems, and we shall presently notice the bland indifference to the strength of the reactionary elements. Above all, the constitution itself had certain weaknesses that proved to be very serious. The scheme for proportional representation, so admirable in principle, made it all the more difficult for any single party to control the reichstag, and accordingly the Social Democrats, compelled to share their power with other groups, were forced to adhere to a rather negative policy, which made them lose their identity and gave the Republic itself a somewhat colorless character. It is true, of course, that all the coalition parties were loyal to the Republic, and that even in the reichstag of 1930 they commanded a majority, but the chancellor failed at a critical moment to control it, and the political bickering of the next two years was fatal to the Republic. A more serious feature of the constitution, however, was the provision which permitted the president to decide when a situation was an emergency and on such an occasion to exercise discretionary power —a clause that made it possible and easy for a president to end the Republic by some sort of coup d'état. As long as Ebert was president, all was well, but the danger of subjecting this office to the popular choice is obvious enough—especially if democratic sentiment should wane. It was an evidence of the decline of the Social Democrats that they won not even a plurality in the presidential election of 1925; and the place was finally won by Marshal von Hindenburg, put forth as a candidate of the right because of his personal popularity. Hindenburg, as a monarchist, was hardly expected to be loyal to the Republic, though until the junker intrigue against Chancellor Brüning it cannot be positively stated that he used his influence for anything but harmony. He was unfortunately the instrument by which Brüning was forced out of office, and the two following chancellors whom he chose had neither of them the backing of the reichstag. By such action he was obviously stretching his right under the constitution to "take such measures as are necessary to restore public safety and order." Yet it may be said in defense of this dull but honest statesman that being very old he was hardly in a position to view so serious a crisis broadly, and it is quite possible that by putting the junkers into power he hoped to be able at least to head off the more formidable National Socialists.

A fourth cause of the disaster to the Republic was the strength of the royalist elements and the *quasi*-privileged position which they enjoyed. Whether through lack of nerve or simply sublime optimism the Social Democrats had treated with great mildness those implicated in the drives on the Republic in 1920 and 1923; and respect for the law (so natural to the German people) was apparently fast ceasing to be a virtue. For many years the country had been infested with irregular bands, who meted out punishment to communists as though they were special police, duly commissioned for that purpose. From the same nefarious sources is to be accounted the murder of two men[1] who, next to Stresemann, were probably the ablest statesmen of the Republic. It is, indeed, a strong evidence that the Republic was always living in a fools' paradise that the junkers still remained as the kernel of the army and that they still held the chief posts in the judiciary—a fact which explains its fixed bias against communists when the aforesaid armed rascals were haled into court. The awe with which the moderates regarded this element may also be judged from the fact that the large estates in East Prussia, which had long been heavily mortgaged, had received direct assistance from the government. Very influential were the "Steel Helmets," an organization of junkers, which in military training was only second in importance to the army. Professor Hoover considers that the army, which was the instrument of its capable organizer, General von Schleicher, had enjoyed as early as 1923 "a power of veto over Germany's political destinies."

A fifth and more immediate cause of the débâcle was the worldwide depression, which definitely brought to an end the industrial boom (already affected, as we have seen by political unrest) and then produced a slump, resulting in a great increase of unemployment. It was this slump that made the industrialists so deter-

---

[1] Rathenau and Erzberger, both moderates. Rathenau, a wealthy industrialist but disliked as a Jew and a moderate, had been indispensable during the War for his organizing talent and had contributed powerfully to Germany's industrial recovery. A conciliatory attitude toward the Allies in the matter of reparations was largely his undoing. Erzberger, leader of the Centrist (i.e. Catholic) party, not only had signed the Armistice but had dared while in office to recommend heavy taxation to meet Germany's obligations.

mined to control the government, though most of them were not as yet National Socialist and they hoped through the medium of a strong and conservative chancellor to ward off radical experiments from either direction. How the depression affected the middle and working classes we have already said. It must be realized that the depression, as well as the national hatred of the Allies, formed part of the fuel for the fire which the National Socialists had kindled.

And thus finally we come to Hitler and the following which he recruited from royalists and malcontents—a movement which determined to capture the government of Germany and set up an entirely new régime. Adolf Hitler was a German Austrian of the lower middle class, a native of Braunau, close to the border of Bavaria, and as a recent writer has said, "There are few people more typically German than those Austrians near the German border among whom abstract and fanatical ideas of pan-Germanism have always flourished." Whether from delicate health or indolence, Hitler failed in his studies at school, and consequently, in spite of artistic talent, was unable to get admission to an academy of art or to an architectural school. He was eventually forced by penury to ply the trade of a mason, but as a member of the middle class who had sunk to the level of the proletariat, he thoroughly hated his work and the men with whom he had been forced to cast his lot. It was in Vienna, where he worked, that he became a bitter enemy of socialism and also of the Jews, of whom there were a great many in the ranks of the proletariat. Those who knew him accounted him "queer." He liked to talk at random, but did not seem somehow to "fit in," and he lived, in fact, a rather isolated life. As he had moved to Munich in 1912, he fought in the German army during the War, was promoted to a corporalship, and even awarded the iron cross, though he never gained a commission. After the War, his health impaired by gas poisoning, he devoted most of his time and leisure to politics, and helped to organize a little group which eventually became the National Socialist Party. In 1923 he took part in the abortive Ludendorff plot, and suffered a brief imprisonment as a result—during which he commenced his memoirs, later the gospel of National Socialism, *My Battle*. Both from his writings and his utterances one can infer that he was not a man of any intellectual depth. His mentality seemed rather to pivot on relatively simple abstractions—

HEIL HITLER!

anti-socialism, anti-semitism, and nationalism—but he succeeded in finding anchorage while others were still groping for some hard and fixed idealism. Hitler is an example of the power of eloquence over the multitude—especially in a time of discontent. He was always ready to talk, and he knew how to sway his audience. With his apparent inability to see any qualifications and his zeal in driving straight to his main objective he may perhaps be justly considered a fanatic.[1] But it was just this ardent nationalism which he consciously personified that made him the patron saint of German youth; and it was this element which formed the nucleus of the party which he captained and which party took the name of "National Socialists" or, in briefer form, "Nazis." The name itself seems at once a paradox, for nationalism and socialism are logically on different bases, but actually Hitler stood not for socialism but social reform,[2] and this part of the party label was doubtless designed to appeal to the workers. In any case the movement became more powerful than its leader, though Hitler is its spiritual focus and without this hero-worship the party itself might easily have broken up.

The Triumph of Reaction and the Founding of a New Autocracy

The elements of support for "National Socialism"

National Socialism provided the banner under which the various elements of discontent could coalesce. It appealed to the army because of its fervid patriotism—though for some time the Steel Helmets were a possible rival and only gradually absorbed. It appealed to the lower middle class because no other party had come to its relief. It could not, of course, convert the rabid Communist, but thousands of the workmen who had filled the Communist ranks simply as an experiment of despair were ready enough to swing to a new movement promising redress, and of the millions of unemployed Hitler certainly got his share. Finally, National Socialism attracted—always had attracted—German youth, and it was this element that furnished much of its moral and physical power. But, above all, National Socialism appealed to countless millions who longed for some sort of miracle to restore the national prestige. Hitler's curious theory that Germany was undefeated in the War and that only her betrayal by the Republic had caused

---

[1] In certain qualities, such as his sincerity, his doctrinairism, and his ruthlessness in pursuit of his ideals, he bears a close resemblance to Robespierre—also, by the way, a bachelor and of blameless private life, in contrast to some of his colleagues.

[2] A series of twenty-five points, drawn up by one of his intimates had shown, it is true, a certain hostility to the moneyed interests, but they could hardly be called an exhibition of socialism. Hitler felt it necessary, in fact, to invent a new meaning for socialism.

her present plight had a wonderful appeal to a people trying to regain their self-respect.

The first significant proof of the growth of National Socialism was afforded by the elections of 1924 when it polled a vote of nearly 2,000,000, and hence won thirty-two seats in the popular chamber. The elections of 1928 registered a set-back for the party, but in those of 1930, after the first effects of the depression had begun to be felt, the National Socialists polled 6,406,397 votes, which made them in numerical strength second only to the Social Democrats. With a view of getting some needed political strength (in the event that this strange new force might possibly be tamed), Brüning in 1932 offered Hitler a place in his cabinet; but the Nazi leader refused it, having the political shrewdness to wait until he was strong enough to force his way into power on his own terms. In 1932 he challenged Hindenburg for the presidency and his vote in round numbers was 11,400,000 against the marshal's 13,400,000. There was no doubt that Hitler's movement had grown to the point where it would be difficult very much longer to keep it from swamping the government itself. And what that victory might mean must long have been evident. For uniformed bands of Nazis had frequently displayed already that sinister union of emotionalism with force. Hitler himself had sounded the warning that if he ever came into power, "heads would roll in the sand."

The lengthening shadow

There were still, however, three elements of opposition to this movement, though they could hardly be expected to coalesce. The Social Democrats largely controlled the government of Prussia and that meant the Prussian police, though, as events were soon to show, the police was not a unit, and its loyalty was uncertain. The Communists were, of course, bitterly hostile to National Socialism, but they were lacking in capable leadership, and having exhausted themselves by intermittent strikes at the bidding of Moscow, they always failed to act promptly at critical moments. It should be noted, too, that the hatred of the Communists for the Social Democrats was far too deep to make it possible for these two elements to combine. Finally, there were the junkers, the so-called "Nationalist Party," who disliked "National Socialism" as republican and possibly socialistic, and were somewhat uncertain of its attitude toward their agricultural interests. As for the magnates of business, the industrialists, they played a cautious rôle, still watching the course of events. Some of them, like Thys-

A divided opposition

sen, had helped to finance Hitler in the belief that his rise was inevitable and that in consequence they should try to win his favor. Though they expected to manage the Nazis as they had managed the Social Democrats, it was doubtful whether so turbulent a torrent could be controlled.

The triumph of "National Socialism"

We shall pass rather hastily over the period of confusion in government circles which preceded the National Socialists' advent to power. When Brüning continued in office against an adverse vote of the reichstag, parliamentary government had been flouted and the ministry rested on the power of the president. When the royalists ousted Brüning, the president selected in his place a staunch conservative, Colonel von Papen, who was expected to find the means of restoring monarchy. Papen began vigorously enough, making almost a complete sweep of the Social Democrats in office, and even ousting the existing government of Prussia by a coup d'état; and it was evident that he intended soon to have done with the constitution. Apparently he counted on an alliance with the Nazis, but again Hitler studiously held aloof, and the industrialists, distrusting the government's support of the junkers' agrarian interests, decided finally to knife it, with the result that Papen resigned. As Hitler, when approached by Hindenburg, had refused to accept the chancellorship unless he were given what practically amounted to a dictatorship, the president chose instead the defense minister, Schleicher, who had been prominent in undermining Brüning, and was supposed to have the strength of the army behind him. But Schleicher, while much broader in general outlook than his predecessor and really anxious to relieve economic distress, soon found himself without any political backing on which he could count, and both Hindenburg and the Nationalists came to distrust him. It is possible that if he had not been suffering from ill health he might have attempted a coup d'état. As it was, the president was easily persuaded to dump him, and there was now no alternative but Hitler. It was then, of course, that the Communists missed their opportunity. But the Nationalists were not to gain either. Though Hitler readily accepted an alliance with this group and even gave their leader a prominent position in his cabinet, it did not take him long, after consolidating his position, to repudiate his bargain and turn them out. National Socialism, for all its reactionary character, was not (as yet) in favor of either monarchy or junkerdom.

The rule of the National Socialists commenced on January 30, 1933 when Hitler accepted the position of chancellor on terms of his own making. There was never any doubt that he intended to overthrow the existing republic. When elections were announced for the reichstag, his followers made it clear that even if they were defeated they meant to remain in office. As a matter of fact, the National Socialists, together with their recent allies, the Nationalists, won by a clear majority,[1] for none of the other parties had been allowed to electioneer, while they themselves had conducted a feverish canvass. Perhaps in any case they would have won, for Germans were tired of fiddling, and demanded action—some action, no matter what. Yet there could be no doubt in anyone's mind that the triumph of Hitler meant the establishment of an autocracy. The leader (*der Führer*) was head of a militant party in which obedience was the keynote. Neither Papen nor Schleicher, it is true, had held a mandate from the people, and the "presidential dictatorship" had been tolerated if not openly approved. Now, however, more than fifty per cent of a nation by its vote registered its willingness for autocratic rule.

And it most assuredly got it. In March the reichstag passed the Enabling Act, which empowered the chancellor for four years to make laws as he saw fit without its consent and without regard to the constitution. Later, when Hindenburg died (August, 1934), Hitler usurped the president's functions, no longer admitting a rival in the national leadership, though, strangely enough, he submitted his act to the people in a plebiscite. The fundamental rights of the citizen, as defined in the constitution, were, of course, a thing of the past, and even the censorship in Russia was hardly more drastic than that which was adopted in Germany. Public opinion was to be molded from above and molded in one pattern. Also the autonomy of the different states was greatly reduced, for a *statthalter* over each was appointed by the government; and the federal chamber, the reichsrath, was abolished. Germany became

Inauguration and foundations of the new régime

---

[1] As far as the vote itself was concerned, the two parties polled only fifty-two per cent, and they secured only 341 out of 648 seats in the reichstag. But the Enabling Act, which set up the new dictatorship, was passed by a vote of 441 to 94. The Communists being forcibly excluded, only the Social Democrats had voted against the measure. Thus the moderate parties evidently accepted Hitler's rule. It has been suggested that fear of communism had something to do with achieving this result, as the burning of the reichstag building on the eve of the election was officially attributed to the Communists. There are some who believe that the Nazis had perpetrated the act themselves as shrewd political capital.

a political unit as never before. Like all despotisms, Germany's rests on force. The army is behind it; the Steel Helmets have been won over; and there are, besides, the so-called "Storm Troops," the "Brownshirts," who play a rôle analogous to that of the Fascist bands in Italy, terrorizing opponents, while the black-shirted "Defense Squads" form a sort of modern pretorian guard for the party leaders. But the "Third Régime" (*das dritte Reich*), as Hitler calls this new government, rests not only on brute force but on the enthusiastic approval of a large section of the German nation. When military and moral factors contribute to lay the foundations of a new order, its strength is quite phenomenal.

Policy of repression

Naturally enough with a movement that was inspired by so much hatred, the first activities of the new régime were devoted to the work of destruction (in some measure important as con-solidating its power). The trade unions were systematically destroyed and even their funds confiscated. As in Fascist Italy and Communist Russia, no party but that of the Nazis was allowed to exist, and the Social Democrats fared almost as ill as the Com-munists, both being subjected to petty persecution and intermit-tent violence. But the Jewish population was made the especial scapegoat of Germany's past woes. The fact that most of them were believed to be communistic was the capital point against them; the fact that by reason of sheer ability they had come to a place in the professions out of all proportion to their numbers was a cause of petty jealousy; the fact that some of them had made fortunes when most of the population had been badly pinched aroused a feeling of passionate hatred. They were now debarred from most professions and from chairs in the university, and an effort was made to ruin such as were engaged in business by a decree forbidding anyone to enter a Jewish shop. As, however, some Jewish proprietors of large stores threatened to close and thus turn out their employees, the boycott was given up after an experiment of one day. How many Jews have been the victims of organized terror is at present impossible to say. The instru-ments of violence were usually Storm Troopers, who were recog-nized as auxiliaries of the police, and of course, upheld by the courts. As the Jews were less than one per cent of the population, and in no sense a military danger, there was no possible excuse of political necessity. But the atmosphere of terror which such vio-lence produced had a notable effect in strengthening an attitude of subservience toward the Nazis. It would seem that conscience itself (as Professor Hoover has noted) had been paralyzed along with political freedom.

Some of Hitler's anti-semitism was due to his conviction that Jewish financiers were actually engaged in a plot to secure world domination. But hatred of the Powers was chiefly, of course, due to the Treaty of Versailles and its results. Hitler had always said that that treaty must be renounced. When, however, he found that the treatment of the Jews had caused a revulsion of horror abroad and had brought Germany into a position of moral isolation, he was sensible enough to try to reassure foreign opinion by announcing that he would hold to the Treaty of Versailles. It can hardly be supposed that his assurances carried credence, but they did serve for a time to relax the tension. There was at the same time an abatement of measures against the Jews.

It is time now to turn to constructive policy and inquire what National Socialism seeks to do with Germany. The reorganization of the government under a permanent dictatorship may be said to represent the essence of its political policy. There are indications that even a subservient reichstag will have no place in the new constitution. As with Fascism in Italy, the National Socialists assumed control of every department of the public life; and the establishment of party "cells" in every office, factory, and shop is an interesting imitation of the Communist methods in Russia. The consolidation of the State and the repression of public opinion have already been noted. As to the administration of justice, loyalty to the State, as in Italy and Russia, must be enforced at all costs. "The guilt or innocence of a man," declared the president of one of the tribunals in 1934 "is to be determined by whether he is dangerous to the existence of the State." Hardly less important than political reconstruction was the need of a reasoned economic program. As a means of preventing political unrest it was particularly necessary to deal with the serious problem of unemployment. The larger industries have been generally forced— sometimes with the aid of subsidies—to add more men to their pay-rolls (though this change has usually meant simply a spreading of the work more thinly, with a consequent lowering of wages); the increased production of armaments has meanwhile provided jobs for a good many thousands; and since women workers have been largely displaced by men (for the Nazis believe that woman's

Organization and constructive policy

sphere is the home), still further places have been found for the unemployed. Much, however, of the re-employment is artificial, such as a year of compulsory labor for German youths on public works, and the maintenance of the Storm Troops and similar organizations. At first the long-mooted project of breaking up the large estates was heralded as a benefit for the unemployed, but so far (1935) it has yet to be carried out. Probably Hitler is not quite ready to offend the junkers, who are the backbone of the army. The peasants, for their part, have been won to the new régime by the government's fixing of agricultural prices; and reduction of interest rates are supposed to aid the lower middle class. Meanwhile, in order to preclude class war and to promote the welfare of industry as a whole, the government devised a corporative plan,[1] on the model of that of Italy, bringing employers and employees into a common organization under the beneficent control of the State. As with Fascism and to a certain extent with the old imperial régime, the interest of the community was deemed to be paramount. This might mean control of prices, as well as wages, and even production, through official action. Much more tangibly than in the days of imperial rule, the government keeps its thumb on the economic structure of Germany. The large industries were not nationalized, for that would be too much like socialism, but they were none the less controlled by the appointment or at least ratification of their directorates by the government. Chastened by her war experience, Germany resolved at all costs to be self-sufficient. Apparently she did not welcome foreign capital, and for a time was not even anxious for foreign markets for German products except to balance the commodities which Germans themselves were for the present forced to import. As long as there was no balance in Germany's favor, she could continue to talk poor and disregard her foreign debts—a procedure less tactically imprudent then stark repudiation.

Outlook on the world   But it was not the economic side of German idealism, as worked out by Hitler and his associates, that constituted a challenge to the world. In the van of the new nationalism was the idea that all Germans must be united—a revival of the old pan-Germanism—which means not only the incorporation of Austria but of all the Germanic elements outside Germany. It was an insistence upon the purity of the German stock that formed some of the case

[1] To some extent it was an outgrowth of the economic councils, page 804.

against the Jews, who were held to be non-German. But, apart from this ideal, there seemed no question but that Germany was fully resolved to have done with the hated trammels of the Treaty of Versailles. Her eventual repudiation of its military provisions will be discussed in the next chapter; but it may be noted here that the actual number of Germans who had been getting military training since the War had long exceeded the limits prescribed by treaty. The number had been further increased by the plan, finally inaugurated in January, 1934, that 600,000 youths should be called each year to serve for a year's time in a "labor camp" where they were to "pass through labor service and then military service as soon as compulsory military service has been introduced." And it may be asserted that this was more than the application of conscription; it was, on the part of the conscripts themselves, an act of faith. Much is made of the fact that the spirit of the new Germany is one of intense self-abnegation and unflinching devotion to the State—something like that reverence for the State that the German philosopher, Hegel, had once invoked for Prussia.[1] Something of the asceticism which we noted in the case of Communist Russia is also true of Germany. The young Nazis are encouraged to despise material objects and cleave to the things of the spirit—though not so much for the public welfare as for the grandeur of the German branch of the Aryan race. The German schools are nurseries of patriotism, just as those of Communist Russia are analogous agencies of communism. A ceaseless propaganda is organized [2] through the schools, the universities, the press, the radio, the cinema, and even in art and literature. There are loud laudations of war, and the supreme virtue that is taught is courage in battle. Just as Moscow sustains the class war, so Germany of the "Third Régime" embodies the flavor of a crusade. Such is the very essence of the spirit, not unmixed with hate, that Adolf Hitler inculcated into the movement which created her. What befell the German nation in 1933 was an autocratic and militant reaction, a return to the ideals of Prussia, but resting on a much broader spiritual foundation than was true in the days of Frederick the Great, or of Bismarck, or of William II.

[1] Hegel was accused of "confusing the kingdom of Prussia with the kingdom of Heaven."

[2] There is even a minister of propaganda.

Yet emotionalism might prove very unsatisfying if the millions who had voted for National Socialism should discover that their hopes of material betterment were not fulfilled. In the course of the year 1934 Germany's foreign trade fell off to an alarming degree (the greatest blow being dealt by Russia, who deliberately switched to other markets), and the government came to the decision that it was necessary not only to restrict imports in the hope of restoring the balance but also to proclaim arbitrarily a moratorium on foreign debts. But if contraction rather than expansion were the policy, there might be reason to believe that Germany was in the throes of a new crisis, especially as German industry had shown but slight recovery. During the fall of 1934 there was a general fixing of prices by the government. And while the number of unemployed has been somewhat reduced, a decline in the general wage-scale has been noticeable since the middle of 1933. That, at least at one time, there was some plotting among the junkers and even within the ranks of the Nazis themselves was indicated by the "military executions" of prominent men (a conspicuous example of terrorism!) in the summer of 1934.[1] No doubt Hitler's recent defiance of the Powers has greatly enhanced the moral prestige of the government—despite the additional taxes to pay for armaments. At present (1935) the chief reliance is on regimentation, a specially constituted dictator having a strict control of the whole economic mechanism. Whether so weak an economic structure can be adequately repaired by isolated action, and whether, if not repaired, it can be held together by force—only the future can disclose. The supreme test appears to be at hand. For economic distress is the one pre-eminent evil that a revolutionary dictatorship has to fear.

FOR FURTHER READING OR STUDY

Robinson, J. H., and Beard, C. A., *Readings in Modern European History*, vol. ii, chap. xviii (old Russia through 1906); Scott, J. F., and Baltzly, A., *Readings in European History since 1814*, chaps. viii (old Russia), xv (the Revolution), and xvi, secs. ii (Fascism) and v (Bolshevism); Mussolini, B., *Autobiography* (only important for a study of character); *Mussolini as Revealed in His Public Speeches* (ed. Quaranta, B. B.); Nitti, F. F., *Escape* (experiences of a political prisoner under the Fascist Régime); "Stepniak," *Underground Russia;* Gogol, *Dead Souls;* Kropotkin, P., *Memoirs of a Revolutionist*, 2 vols.; Figner, V., *Memoirs of a Revolutionist* (experiences of a nihilist); Pobyedonostseff, K. P.,

---

[1] Hitler's predecessor, Schleicher, was "shot while resisting arrest."

Reflections of a Russian Minister; Novikoff, O., *Russian Memories;* Witte, S., *Memoirs;* Pares, B., *My Russian Memories; Letters of the Tsaritsa to the Tsar; Letters of the Tsar to the Tsaritsa;* Radzianko, M. V., *The Reign of Rasputin;* Yousoupoff, F., *Rasputin;* Gilliard, F., *Thirteen Years at the Russian Court* (by the Czarevitch's tutor); Botkin, G., *The Real Romanovs* (by a son of the Czar's physician); Marie (Grandduchess), *The Education of a Princess;* Paléologue, M., *Memoirs of an Ambassador,* 4 vols.; Buchanan, G., *My Mission to Russia and Other Diplomatic Memories,* 2 vols.; Cantacouzène, J., *Revolutionary Days, 1914-7;* Price, M. P., *My Reminiscences of the Russian Revolution;* Breshkovskaia, K., *Hidden Springs of the Russian Revolution;* Kerensky, A., *The Catastrophe* (Kerensky's apology); Francis, D. R., *Russia from the American Embassy;* Lenin, N., *The Revolution of 1917, The State and Revolution, Soviets at Work,* etc.; Trotsky, L., *Our Revolution* and *History of the Russian Revolution to Brest Litovsk: Documents of Russian History* (ed. Golder, F. A.); Sorokin, P., *Leaves from a Russian Diary;* Kalpashnikov, A., *A Prisoner of Trotsky;* Cederholm, P., *In the Clutches of the Tcheka;* Tchernavin, M., *Escape from the Soviets;* Ludendorff, E. von., *Ludendorff's Own Story,* 2 vols.; Maximilian (of Baden), *Memoirs,* 2 vols.; Scheidermann, P., *The Making of New Germany,* 2 vols.; Lutz, R. H., *The Fall of the German Empire,* 2 vols. (a collection of documents); Hitler, A., *My Battle;* "The Hitlerites on Hitlerism: Quotations from the Nazi Press," *The Nation,* cxl. 149-50.

Hayes, C. J. H., *A Political and Social History of Modern Europe,* vol. ii, chap. xv (old Russia) and xxiv (the Revolution); Schapiro, J. S., *Modern and Contemporary European History,* chaps. xi and xiii (both on old Russia), xxxvii (the Revolution), and xxxix *(passim)*; Higby, C. P., *History of Modern Europe,* chaps. xxviii, sec. 2 (Italy), xxix (Germany), and xxx (Russia); Palm, F. C., and Graham, F. E., *Europe since Napoleon,* chaps. xx (old Russia), xxxiii (the Revolution), xxxiv (Italy), and xxxv (Germany); Munro, W. B., *The Governments of Europe* (chapters on Italy, Germany, and Russia); Ogg, F. A., *European Governments and Politics,* part ii and *The Economic Development of Modern Europe,* chap. xv (old Russia); Day, C., *Economic Development in Modern Europe;* Benns, E. L., *Europe since 1914,* chaps. xii (Italy), xiii (Germany), and xviii-xix (Russia); Langsam, W. C., *The World since 1914,* chaps. xiii (Italy), xv (Germany), and xviii (Russia); Slosson, P. W., *Twentieth Century Europe* (chiefly for Russia); Dean, V. M., and others, *New Governments in Europe: The Trend toward Dictatorship* (very useful little book, though it needs an index).

Villari, L., *Italy* and *The Expansion of Italy* (pro-Fascist); Salvemini, G., *The Fascist Dictatorship in Italy* (bitterly anti-Fascist); Bonomi, I. *From Socialism to Fascism;* Matteotti, G., *The Fascisti Exposed;* Sturzo, L., *Italy and Fascismo* (from the clerical standpoint); King, B., *Fascism in Italy* (brief critical survey); Schneider, H. W., *Making the Fascist State;* Goad, H. E., *The Making of the Corporate State;* Spencer, H. R., *The Government and Politics of Italy;* Reut-Nicolussi, E., *The Tyrol under the Axe of Italian Fascism;* Pares, B., *A History of Russia (passim)*; Kovalewski, M., *Russian Political Institutions (passim)*; Knowles, L., *Economic Development in the Nineteenth Century* (excellent chapters on Russia); Mirski, D., *Russia: A Social History* (from a communist standpoint); Leroy-Beaulieu, P., *The Empire of the Czars and the Rus-*

sians, 3 vols. (exceedingly readable and informing); Wallace, D. M., *Russia* (another classic survey during the Old Régime); Alexinski, G., *Modern Russia* (written before the Revolution); Miliukov, P., *Russia and its Crisis* (written before the Revolution); Baring, M., *The Russian People;* Masaryk, T. G., *The Spirit of Russia*, 2 vols. (largely on currents of thought); Miller, M. S., *The Economic Development of Russia, 1905–14;* Robinson, G. T., *Rural Russia under the Old Régime* (a useful study); Vasil'ev, A. T., *The Okhrana;* Florinsky, M. T., *The End of the Russian Empire* (excellent); Gronsky, P. P., and Astrov, N. J., *The War and the Russian Government,* Mavor, J., *An Economic History of Russia* and *The Russian Revolution* (conservative); Sack, A. V., *The Birth of Russian Democracy;* Meyendorff, A. F., *The Background of the Russian Revolution* (a short essay); Spinka, C., *The Church and the Russian Revolution;* Tyrkova-Williams, A., *From Liberty to Brest-Litovsk* (from the liberal standpoint); Mel'gunov, S. P., *The Red Terror in Russia;* Vernadsky, G., *Lenin, Red Dictator* (unsympathetic); Marcu, V., *Lenin* (a vivid essay); Rosenberg, A., *A History of Bolshevism* (somewhat abstract); Pasvolsy, L., *The Economics of Communism* (excellent on the first years of the experiment); Dobb, M., *Russian Economic Development since the Revolution* (published in 1928); Gorian, W., *Bolshevism: Theory and Practice* (highly critical from the social standpoint); Karlgren, A., *Bolshevist Russia* (not very favorable observations of a Danish scholar during the early period); Hindus, M., *Humanity Uprooted, Red Bread,* and *The Great Offensive* (all very readable and impartial); Colton, E. T., *The X.Y.Z. of Communism* (highly entertaining); Batsell, W. R., *Soviet Rule in Russia* (good on political structure); Maxwell, B. W., *The Soviet State;* Hoover, C. B., *The Economic Life of Soviet Russia* (outstanding); Chamberlain, W. H., *Russia's Iron Age* (a most revealing survey by a journalist long resident in Russia); Dillon, E. J., *Russia Today and Yesterday* (impressions on the return of a former resident); Miliukov, P. N., *Bolshevism* (on early propaganda) and *Russia Today and Tomorrow* (illuminating on the Whites); Rosenberg, A., *The Birth of the German Republic* (admirable); Greenwood, H. P., *The German Revolution* (sympathetic); Luehr, E., *The New German Republic* (published in 1929); Kraus, H., *The Crisis of German Democracy;* Hoover, C. B., *Germany Enters the Third Reich* (thorough and penetrating); Heiden, K., *A History of National Socialism* (gossipy but often suggestive); Diesel, E., *Germany and the Germans* (delightful reading); Anon., *Germany: Twilight or New Dawn?;* Lengyel, E., *Hitler;* Lewis, W., *Hitler;* Wertheimer, M. S., "Facts underlying the Nazi Revolution," *Foreign Policy Reports*, vol. x, no. 10; Schumann, F. L., "The Political Theory of German Fascism," *Amer. Pol. Sc. Rev.*, xxviii, 210 ff.; Spearman, P., "The Psychological Background of Dictatorship," *Sociological Review*, xxvi, 158 ff.

XX. THE PROBLEM OF STABILIZING
EUROPE

1. THE PROBLEM OF RECOVERY

Situation of Great Britain; Situation of France; A lost opportunity;
Situation of Germany; The reparations tangle; The invasion of the Ruhr
and the Dawes Plan; Temporary recovery of Germany; The Young Plan;
Collapse of the reparations issue; The general slump in Europe; Problem of
recovery in Great Britain.

2. THE PROBLEM OF SECURITY

Inadequacy of the League of Nations; The hegemony of France and fresh
methods to solve the problem of security; The Treaties of Locarno; Feeble
efforts of the powers; Elements of danger: (1) Japan, (2) Germany; The
crisis of 1935; A peace of circumstance.

3. THE CRISIS FOR WESTERN CIVILIZATION

The testing of capitalism; The testing of "democracy"; The testing of
nationalism.

The two prime issues since the War have been recovery and
security. By "recovery" we mean the return of Europe to something like that economic health and stability that she had enjoyed
before the War. By "security" we mean the devising of some
means of insuring Europe against another great war. Since the
same powers were concerned in both these problems and since
financial exigencies produced warlike moods as truly as fear tended
to preclude financial concessions, the two issues interacted and
cannot be considered as entirely separate, but for convenience we
shall concentrate first upon one of these problems and then upon
the other. Of their importance there can be no question. They
formed two deep, dark stripes through international relations from
1918 on. And until these two problems can be solved, there can be
no settled order of things in Europe. Whether, indeed, the very
bases of our present society are not shaking under the stress of this
troubled period is a question upon which to ponder.

The Problem of Recovery

We have already dwelt upon the ghastly material losses caused
by the War. Devastation and disorganization wrought untold

825

havoc, and even the victor powers suffered severely. Recovery at best would be slow.

Situation of Great Britain

Great Britain after a short-lived boom, due chiefly to the opportunity of supplying those nations of Europe whose industries had been prostrated, found in 1921 that her services were no longer needed. The efforts of the Continent to start on the slow road to recovery, the raising of new tariff walls, and the competition of oil with coal were among the factors that caused a relapse. Great Britain's foreign trade became reduced to an alarming degree, and as the extent of her exports was inextricably bound up with the problem of her food supply, the question was vital in the extreme. The need to get back her markets had an important bearing on British policy toward Germany, as we shall see.

Situation of France

France was superficially better off only because she had sacrificed the stability of her national credit to the immediate question of relief. The losses incurred by French nationals as the result of damage to industry and agriculture were calculated at about 35,000,000,000 francs, but the government made it clear from the first that it would assume responsibility for these damages, meaning, of course, to repay itself eventually from reparations. The French government, therefore, undertook an extensive work of rehabilitation. The trenches were effaced, roads repaired, towns rebuilt, new orchards planted, the mines restored to their former efficiency, individuals reimbursed, and so on. At the same time, France, like Great Britain, had a heavy load of foreign debt, and was compelled for lack of other guarantees to maintain a large army. The expense of all this was prodigious, and for many years the government was quite unable to balance its budget. Financial collapse seemed only a question of time.

A lost opportunity

It was for this reason and also because of their feeling that on moral grounds the enemy should pay for the misery he had caused that France determined to extract from Germany as much as she could in reparations. The idea of enforcing collection by the mere presence of an army of occupation—the plan applied by Germany to France on two occasions—seemed to occur to none of the diplomats, or else it was felt that this method would entail too long an agony, since the amount to be exacted was prodigious. Another alternative, that of rebuilding the damaged regions in France with German materials and German labor, was suggested by the Germans themselves, but whether because of opposition

from French workmen or because of the influence of French building interests, the French government vetoed the plan. It is obvious
that the German plan would have saved billions besides giving the
French the satisfaction of seeing the Germans themselves engaged
in this work, but the French mind does not readily turn from an
objective once pursued, and the one thought was reparations in
money or kind to extend for countless years.

But Germany too was suffering, for, excepting a certain group *Situation* *of Germany*
of profiteers, most of her people had speedily lost all chance of
recovery in the quagmire of inflation—an expedient begun by
the imperial government (which refrained from raising taxes
during the War) and continued by the Republic because it was
the line of least resistance. Yet if reparations could have been put
at a reasonable figure and Germany's credit re-established, a rapid
recovery might have been possible. Indeed, if the reparation bill
had been really moderate and an Allied army quartered in Germany until it was paid, it is not improbable that this vexing problem would have been solved in a few years. Unfortunately, as
we have noticed, the public hysteria had prevented any definite
settlement of the question. To the suggestion of the American
experts that a reasonable figure might be found after patient
study, Clemenceau had replied that no sum suggestible would
satisfy French opinion. The only thing definitely agreed upon
had been the sum of $5,000,000,000 for Germany to pay by
May 1, 1921. Since, however, precedence was given to the
claims of Belgium and to the expenses of the army of occupation, and since Germany's payments by the date set were
far below the stipulated amount, France received only a very
small proportion of what she had expected. Thus the problem of meeting the expense of reconstruction had not been
solved.

In the meantime it was decided to let the Germans propose *The* *reparations* *tangle*
what they themselves thought they could pay, but when this failed
to produce satisfactory results, the Allies demanded the enormous
figure of $56,500,000,000. Germany, invited to reply, proposed
$7,500,000,000 as an immediate cash payment under certain con-
ditions; and this proposal was, of course, discountenanced. The
reparation commission (which had come to be regarded as a permanent institution, though it had lost its American members
when the United States withdrew from Europe) finally decided

on the sum of $33,000,000,000,[1] whereupon the Powers, adopting the new figure, transmitted it to Germany in an ultimatum, with the threat of an occupation of the Ruhr. Germany, of course, submitted, but this did not really mean that payments would be accelerated.

In fact, the situation was really approaching a deadlock. While it is perfectly true that the German finances were in a mess and that the government's fallen credit made a foreign loan impossible, the inflation orgy had resulted in a shifting of wealth, not in its disappearance, and there were rich industrialists who might have been heavily taxed, had the government possessed the courage. Moreover, a great amount of capital had been invested in foreign lands in order to escape the expected taxes for reparations. After all, it is hard to criticize evasion of obligations which had taken so little account of material capacity. Doubtless, too, the Germans were trading on a change in the international situation. Great Britian had come to realize that it was not to her advantage for the Germans to pay heavy reparations. Insofar as those damages were paid in goods, they would obviously compete with the output of British industries. But, above all, British interests demanded that Germany get on her feet, since she had formerly been one of Great Britain's best customers, and the question of recovering its lost markets had become for British industry a very real problem. For this reason, when the question of reparations came to be aired at various international conferences, Great Britain was as much for leniency as France was for putting on the screws. Anglo-French relations came to be much embittered. The two powers were on opposite sides over the Upper Silesia question and over affairs in the Near East. It would have considerably eased the situation if the United States had shown a generous attitude regarding the debts which the Allies owed her [2] (mainly credits for munitions bought in America during the War), and Balfour, the British foreign secretary, offered the proposal that Great Britain would cancel as much of the debt owed to her by foreign powers as the debt which she still owed the United

---

[1] Plus a billion dollars more for the Belgian war debt.

[2] This originally amounted to over $10,000,000,000, and with accrued interest came to total about $11,500,000,000. By various agreements with the debtor powers after the War the United States was to receive repayment together with interest over a period of sixty-two years. Interest was lowered from the original five per cent to a figure supposed to accord with the debtor's capacity to pay. This placed Great Britain, for example, at a distinct disadvantage in relation to Italy.

States, provided the latter would cancel this obligation. Since this proposal, however, met with a chilly reception in the United States, the hard fact remained that France was convinced that she could get on her feet only by collecting reparations.

In 1923, therefore, France prepared to act. She would either *The invasion* make Germany pay or at least make her erstwhile ally see that *of the Ruhr and the* she was terribly in earnest. As Poincaré, who had become prime *Dawes Plan* minister early in 1922, was a man who dared to try extraordinary measures, the result was that with Belgium's concurrence a Franco-Belgian army was sent into the Ruhr. The act was immediately denounced by the British as illegal, since enforcement of any proposals of the reparation commission concerned all the powers there represented and not simply France and Belgium. The Germans, for their part, retaliated by carrying on a "passive resistance," all industry being suspended in the occupied region, while the government undertook to support the workmen who had thus been forced into idleness. But a bankrupt state was in no position to try an economic war, and with the total collapse of the German currency through inflation the government saw and tacitly admitted that further resistance was out of the question.

If acts are to be judged by their results, the Franco-Belgian action may be variously interpreted. It was in one sense a costly adventure, for the expense of maintaining the army of occupation far exceeded the meager sums it managed to extract from the Ruhr itself. Moreover, the conduct of the troops in the occupied district showed a callousness that brought them general obloquy. And, viewing the question broadly, the Germans had certainly not merited all the misery that they suffered as a result. Yet, in one respect, Poincaré's strategy was successful, for he forced both Germany and Great Britain to take the reparation question more seriously. Germany now proposed an international conference to study and form an opinion of her capacity to pay, and Great Britain readily welcomed such an experiment. A commission of experts, headed by the American banker, Charles G. Dawes, was accordingly appointed, and this body undertook to devise means by which Germany could meet her obligations. They worked out a plan by which Germany should pay so much each year (how long was, of course, reserved for the Allied governments); and in the meantime Germany had managed to stabilize her currency. In 1924, the Franco-Belgian forces having evacuated the Ruhr and Germany having begun to pay regularly under the new scheme, it looked as if some real headway had been made. And even though the inflation debauch [1] had beggared thousands of Germans, the government itself had disposed of its floating debt and could now be considered solvent.

Temporary recovery of Germany   The fact is, the ease with which Germany appeared to meet her obligations is to be ascribed in a measure to the industrial renascence mentioned in the previous chapter which was a feature of the general recovery of Europe; more specifically it was due partly to the sale to foreign speculators of paper currency which was afterwards repudiated (it is said that this added $2,000,000,000 to the real wealth of Germany), partly to the influx of foreign capital as the result of currency stabilization, and partly to the adoption of rationalization by all the important industries. Deprived of most of their iron and a large part of their coal as the result of the War, the German industrialists had turned to lignite and electricity for power, concentrated their energies by forming new trusts and cartels, lowered costs by closing less efficient mines and plants and dispensing for a time with some of their workmen as machine production developed, and made a concerted (and on the whole successful) effort to capture foreign markets. The adaptability of these magnates is well illustrated by the Krupps, who, not finding the manufacture of munitions very profitable for an army of 100,000, turned their plants into the production of such things as locomotives, motor trucks, and agricultural machinery. The dye trust amassed enormous profits in making nitrates for use in fertilization of the soil, and chemists even studied to devise methods of making oil. By 1928 industrial production was twelve per cent higher in the aggregate than it had been before the War, and far exceeded that of England. The very fact that so much equipment had been lost by the Treaty of Versailles meant that its displacement gave German industry a mechanical organization that by its very newness promised continuous progress. Yet it has to be admitted that the position of the ordinary consumer did not as yet reflect this sudden prosperity. Prices had generally risen, and taxes—thanks largely to the heavy cost of social insurance and expenditures on public works—were (in spite of some reduction in 1927) considerably higher than in 1913, though pro-

---

[1] For an interesting account of the decline of the mark see Langsam, *The World Since 1914*, pp. 383–4.

vided prosperity should continue, the burden was likely to be lightened in the near future. What was needed was a period of domestic peace and public confidence during which rationalization could go on to greater completeness and readjustments made that would gradually ease the burden on the middle class and peasantry. The former would gain through the steady advance of industry; the latter might hope to receive more direct governmental assistance. But German industry still required capital to advance, and much depended on its facility for obtaining it.

For four years Germany kept rigorously to the terms of the *The* Dawes Plan, but the fifth year required under the scheme the *Young Plan* beginning of heavier payments, and as the total amount, fixed in 1923, had never been revised, Germany persistently demanded a revision downward. After a study of the problem by a new corps of experts a substitute plan (the Young Plan) was adopted in 1926 by the powers. Germany got a rather easier deal. The total of reparations was fixed (payable, of course, over a long period of years), but was reducible in proportion as inter-Allied debts might be reduced; at the same time the Allies agreed to withdraw their forces from the Rhineland. Once again it seemed that this vexing problem had been solved. Belief in Germany's ultimate recovery, as well as the new security provided by the Locarno Pacts,[1] led to heavy American investing in German securities, and with the loans thus obtained Germany met her reparation payments. An American publicist, Frank H. Simonds, has noted with amusement that whereas Americans had steadily refused to reduce war debts and insisted that they had no connection with reparations, the American investor was now lending money to Germany who was turning part of it over to the Allies, who in turn were paying installments of their debt to the United States. "Thus what was actually taking place was that the American investor was paying the Allied debts to his own government."

But again the financial and political worlds were disappointed, *The collapse* for Germany was not able to keep the pace. It was certainly not *of the* her fault that Americans, carried higher up on that wave of pros- *reparations* perity which had come to them after the War, began to prefer to *issue* put their money into domestic projects, with the result that the long-term credits practically ceased (thus bringing rationalization quickly to an end) and that Germany had to look to neighboring

[1] See page 840.

countries for short-term loans as the only possible alternative. Again, it was not her fault that the depression began to reach her toward the end of 1929, making it necessary to cut drastically the prices of exports in order to hold the foreign market, thus putting an added burden on the consumer (forced to buy at a higher price than the foreign purchaser), while a necessary slackening of production brought an ever-increasing unemployment. Yet had her government been patriotically supported by public opinion, the

Wide World Photos

A BREAD LINE IN BERLIN

crisis might perhaps have been surmounted. Unfortunately discontent sought stormier outlets. Germany therefore rapidly drifted into political unrest;[1] there were consequently heavy withdrawals of foreign investments; and thus, left without credit, Germany began again to default. At this juncture President Hoover, who would have been glad to see a revision of all the debt and reparation settlements, persuaded the Powers to agree to a year's moratorium on both debts and reparations. It was the first suggestion from America that there was any connection between the two, and many observers felt that both were now painlessly put to rest. At all events, after the expiration of the respite, Germany still affirmed, as was expected, that she could no longer pay reparations—a situation now due to the general depression. In 1932 the leading powers together with Belgium held a conference

[1] Foreign bankers feared that the Young Plan was in danger. A proposed economic union of Austria and Germany (the *Anschluss*) was also an upsetting factor. See page 833.

at Lausanne, which tentatively agreed on reducing the total amount of reparations to $714,000,000—much less than was required to reimburse the United States for her war loans to the Allies. But the question failed of final solution, though it seemed to be generally felt that reparations at any figure would never be collected. Meanwhile Germany continued to mark time, and France defaulted in the payment of her debt-installment to the United States. Inasmuch as the whole European economic situation had greatly darkened since the world depression had set in, there seemed nothing to do but wait for the definite beginnings of a general recovery. In the meantime reparations and inter-Allied debts are slumbering peacefully together in spite of the American theory that they have never become acquainted.

No one doubts any longer that Germany is entirely free of the economic fetters which the Treaty of Versailles had placed upon her. It is now the task of her new régime, established in 1933, to carry through some program that will lift her out of her present economic straits.

Though a faint beginning has been made, the real solution is still ahead. And so it is with all the other European nations; for all, after experiencing a period of recovery, suffered a diminution of trade and an ever-swelling number of unemployed, France suffering perhaps less than most, because she was less industrialized. The withdrawal of American capital had shown the essential hollowness of Europe's promising revival after the War, and the banks of central Europe were unequal to the strain of filling the gap. Also with America's plunge into the depression, the market for Europe's goods had materially shrunk; and industry was reduced to a bare existence. Yet, apart from unavoidable moratoria, little was done to ease the general situation. The problem of some relief for the Danubian lands (whose currency had no longer any standing in foreign exchange) unhappily foundered on the mutual distrust of the Great Powers. When in 1931 Austria discussed with Germany the feasibility of the so-called *Anschluss*, a customs-union between the two, France was able to frustrate the plan on the score that political union would inevitably follow. An alternative project of France was to bring Austria and Hungary as well as Jugoslavia, Czechoslovakia, and Roumania, into a giant customs-union, thus restoring one of the benefits of the Dual Monarchy, but Germany and Italy, with some backing from

The general slump in Europe

Great Britain, balked the scheme on the ground that it might strengthen France politically on the Danube. When Austria came to realize that Germany—under Nazi rule—was planning her annexation, she herself turned against the *Anschluss*. Yet Austria can have no future without some access to foreign markets, and the question of her relations with Germany continues one of the most vexing problems of international politics. In the meantime the severity of the depression has enhanced political unrest throughout Europe, and popularized dictatorships as better able to function in a crisis than democracies.

The problem of recovery in Great Britain

In no country has the problem of economic recovery been more poignant than in Great Britain, even though here there is no danger as yet to liberal institutions. The loss of much of their foreign market, the heavy taxation national and local, and the generally undiminished totals on their pay-rolls kept manufacturers' profits down to a minimum and threatened many with bankruptcy. How was Great Britain to come out of the *impasse?* Most politicians, more especially in the ranks of Labor, took the view that disorders on the Continent were largely responsible for the loss of British markets, and that hence it was necessary not only to ease the load on Germany but also to support all measures leading to international security. Such a policy was, however, of little avail, since the Russian market was in large part lost (owing to the Revolution); most Continental countries were striving for self-sufficiency; and Germany, whenever supplied with sufficient credits, proved a serious industrial competitor. The Conservatives after some hesitation espoused as a second method that of tariff reform, coupled, as before, with imperial preference.[1] It was argued that Great Britain could not hope to get back her Continental markets and should rely on her dominions and colonies for food and raw materials; meanwhile, home industries should be strengthened by protective tariffs. Adopted at first in limited form, this policy was greatly extended in 1931; and while it is too early as yet to appraise it fully (and policies during a depression are not necessarily applicable to normal times), a protective tariff has at least enabled the government to bargain with other powers for reciprocal concessions. A third and principal method by which British industry might conceivably get on its feet was through a greater application of rationalization. It was proved by investi-

[1] See page 560.

gation that the coal mines had been "living off their surface," that there was coal to be got from below but that such a task required more equipment, and that during the boom immediately following the War the mine-owners had made no effort to safeguard the future. What was true of the coal industry was frequently true of others. Some of the British industrialists were so hide-bound to custom that they looked with much suspicion upon such features of rationalization as concentrated effort, scientific management, and mass production. During the War the government had instituted an organization to promote industrial research and through that means had arranged to pay half the expenses of such investigations provided the industries concerned would pay the remaining half. This policy met with a fairly ready response, though some of the leading industries have so far held aloof. In some cases bankers to whom manufacturers had turned for loans have insisted on a measure of rationalization, but even apart from the national habits of conservatism, the problem has been a difficult one, for during a period of depression there is little capital available for expensive equipment. Another aspect of the whole industrial problem was the working capacity of labor. It was generally conceded that unemployment and the dole, unavoidable as they may be, had tended to make the jobless worker less efficient, and even less willing to work. Also the strain of carrying the masses of unemployed was terrific for the rest of the nation. One needed but to visit England to appreciate the hardships that country was forced to endure.

Yet if appearances are not deceptive, Great Britain has turned the corner and is now on the highroad to recovery. Unemployment, which had reached the staggering figure of over 3,000,000 in June, 1932, was reduced by more than a third by June, 1934; and though in April, 1935 the number was slightly in excess of 2,000,000, this figure is largely explained by the natural increase of population, for the actual figures for employment were the highest yet on record. There had obviously been a striking industrial revival. The serious decline in the export trade (which, by the way, has been more than arrested) had had at least the effect of greatly stimulating the home market, and the tariff has noticeably aided a number of industries. The general improvement in conditions was reflected in a lowering of taxes on smaller incomes. While even a budgetary surplus has been shown, it is necessary, of course, to realize that the debt to the United States has only been temporarily suspended, pending the return of more settled conditions.

In general, though economic recovery has been retarded by the present slump, Europe had managed to survive the bitter years immediately following the War, and had shown a much greater recuperative capacity than at one time had been expected. By dint of *concerted effort* one might feel that the Great Depression would be ultimately surmounted. Will nationalism permit this? Much, of course, depends on the problem of external peace.

THE PROBLEM OF SECURITY

Inadequacy of the League of Nations

The problem of security, while not so pressing as the problem of recovery, was hardly less important, for unless men were at peace they could not work and civilization itself would be threatened again with ruin. We have already discussed the rise of the League of Nations and the experiment of internationalism as a means of solving the problem. We have also noted that this body was not in itself sufficient to guarantee the maintenance of peace. Until the world should finally grow to appreciate it, some alternative devices seemed absolutely essential.

The hegemony of France and fresh methods to solve the problem of security

All alternative schemes have proceeded quite definitely from nationalism or national interest of the familiar type. It was assumed, as we have noticed, that Germany was the great potential menace to the peace, and it was but natural that France should take the lead in grappling with the problem of security. Generally speaking, she cared but little for peace as a universal need; she was thinking of her own security. Yet by so doing she hoped to avert all chance of another great war, the dread of which has been the most cogent factor behind her policy.

We have noticed that the demilitarization of the Rhine and the promise of a three-cornered alliance had been an outcome of Clemenceau's policy to obtain security against Germany. The three-cornered alliance had come to nothing because of the refusal of American opinion to countenance it and the fact that Great Britain's part had been made conditional on that of the United States. Since, however, France was not disposed to risk her whole fate on the hope of a permanently crippled Germany, there were two other safeguards that appealed to her as necessary. She must maintain a large army and she must build up a system of alliances

—the old idea of a balance of power. Ultimately, as we shall see, she even came to regard the League of Nations itself as an instrument that might be effectively employed for keeping the peace.

Of the French army little need be said. Since 1927 its size on a peace footing has been over 700,000. Much had been done to sustain its accustomed efficiency and it is today (1935) not only the largest (with the possible exception of the Russian) but probably the best-equipped standing army in Europe.

Meanwhile French diplomacy has been active. With the elimination of Russia from present consideration and the unwillingness of Great Britain to accept commitments on the Continent there seemed no other alternative than to look to some of the smaller nations of Europe for the necessary co-operation in maintaining the status quo. There was at least the tie of a common benefit from such treaties. Thus Belgium, who had renounced in 1919 [1] her neutrality as a useless derogation of her sovereignty, formed in 1920 an alliance with France presumably because some slight accessions of territory at Germany's expense together with the endless problem of reparations linked her logically with France against the power which they had humbled. Yet the chief reliance of France must rest on powers which could supply a greater man-power. Such nations being unable to make much progress by themselves must be helped by French loans to be put in proper fitness for co-operation. It was an expensive policy, but the French investor would bear the burden, quite confident that his government was bound to succeed because, in truth, it must succeed. Foremost among these arrangements was the alliance with Poland in 1921—a country so situated as to be a buttress against Germany in the east and to some extent holding the position formerly occupied by Russia. It was, however, a risky experiment, since there is no feature of the Versailles Treaty that Germany more bitterly resented than the projection of the Polish Corridor between the dissevered portions of her former empire. Few if any Germans regard this settlement as final. Obviously, then, it was quite imaginable that Poland might sometime actually drag France into war, as Russia had done in 1914. Incidentally we may remark—looking ahead a few years—that Poland eventually came into Germany's orbit, and she is now (1935) more dominated by

[1] The abrogation of Belgian neutrality was incorporated in the Treaty of Versailles.

Germany than by France.[1] How the lion and the lamb may get along together is an amusing puzzle of international politics.

But even back in 1921 France could not, of course, depend entirely on Poland, and did not do so. Out of the wreckage of the Dual Monarchy had arisen a new congeries of powers, Czechoslovakia, Jugoslavia, and Roumania, the so-called Little Entente, bound by a common interest in preserving the treaty-settlements with Austria and Hungary and in preventing any revival of a central European bloc dominated by Germany. It was but natural that France should gravitate toward such a stabilizing influence in eastern Europe, and the result has been her patronage of the Little Entente. But the interest of these three powers in drawing toward France was hardly less cogent. Jugoslavia needed a strong power to counterweigh the rivalry of Italy; Czechoslovakia, partly surrounded by Germany and menaced by the frequently recurring idea of a union of Austria with Germany, needed the support of the power most able to defend her; and Roumania, threatened by war at any moment with Russia because of the Roumanian seizure of Bessarabia, had found it expedient to ally herself with Poland in 1921—for Poland, if not herself a strong power, was an ally of France. So the Little Entente and Poland formed the chief pillar of France's strength and altogether they represented a population of seventy millions.

Yet the policy of security was so vital to France that even yet she was not content. An Anglo-French alliance of some sort was not wholly despaired of—not, it is true, in the form which Clemenceau had planned, since an agreement to help without a reciprocal obligation seemed rather humiliating, but an alliance to guarantee the status quo. Since, however, this project failed to win British approval on the ground that eastern Europe was too remote from British interest, French diplomacy sought another means of achieving the desired end. It seems that a commission of the League of Nations had been working on the problem of disarmament, and two of its members, a Frenchman and a Britisher, developed a scheme of combining the reduction of armaments with some devices for strengthening the League itself as an instrument of peace. The failure of the League in the Greek-Italian and Polish-Lithuanian incidents had seemed to show the need of

---

[1] French support of Russia's admission to the League of Nations in 1934 is to be explained by uncertainty of Polish policy.

making its members come to feel a greater responsibility. The new plan, known as the "Draft Treaty of Mutual Assistance," besides making room for existing military alliances, was to pledge the members of the League to support any power that was the victim of aggression (the manner of support being determined by the council), and also contemplated a general reduction of armaments. Unfortunately, the British government felt indisposed to tighten its responsibilities under the League, and, largely for that reason, the proposal failed of general acceptance. France persisted, however, in trying to bolster up the League, and she knew that she could at least count on most of the lesser nations. So in 1924 under the inspiration of the French and British premiers the assembly of the League passed what was known as the Geneva Protocol, the main features of which were compulsory arbitration of disputes and a definition of what was meant by the "aggressor," together with the pledging of all members to go to war with the one so named, and finally a renewed plan for a general reduction of armaments. "We in France," said the French premier, "regard these terms, arbitration, security, and disarmament, as inseparable." Very auspicious for the fate of the Protocol was the hearty co-operation of the two premiers, and it is to be observed that it was unanimously passed by the forty-eight states represented in the assembly, being then referred to the member-governments for approval. But the weakness of the Protocol, as also of its predecessor, the Draft Treaty of Mutual Assistance, was the fact that the territorial status quo was considered sacrosanct. It is indeed curious that the nations defeated in the Great War were practically silent on the subject,[1] seeming to believe that the security afforded by the Protocol was worth the price, and that the power which again prevented settlement was Great Britain, in general, an enthusiastic adherent of the League. The explanation seems to be that the dominions were opposed to the Protocol, and the British government did not care to take up a position in opposition to their wishes. As the attitude of the dominions was based on a misconception,[2] and as they were not themselves in

[1] Austria, Hungary, and Bulgaria.
[2] They believed that one of the amendments would have allowed a domestic problem to enter into the question of the merits of two disputants in a quarrel. Some of the dominions were afraid that Japan, the proposer of the amendment, was seeking to undermine their immigration laws. As a matter of fact, the sovereignty of the members of the League was too well protected to make that possible.

danger as long as the mother country was mistress of the seas, we have the spectacle of a narrow regionalism blocking Europe's hope of permanent peace. The political hollowness of the British Empire and the growing influence of the dominions had thus wrecked the Protocol. Yet it is also probably true that the English themselves had come to weary of the Continent and to relapse into that feeling that they must not risk being drawn into new complications. It was in vain that the French pointed out that the science of aviation had had the effect of making Great Britain no longer an island. The British Isles hugged the delusion that they were safe under the protection of their navy. Furthermore, frequent squabbles with France had irritated British opinion and made for jealousy of French hegemony on the Continent. The British were not sure that France was not succeeding to the place once occupied by Germany.

The Treaties of Locarno   On the other hand, there was a powerful element in British politics, which, while welcoming the thought of Germany's economic recovery, was fearful of the possibility of a future war of revenge. If she got into trouble with Poland, she might at once attack France and Belgium, and then there would be the situation of 1914 all over again. It was felt that perhaps, instead of trying to solve the problem through the cumbersome machinery of the League, a regional pact might be devised that would give both Germany and France security in the west. This idea happily co-incided with the opinions of a new minister of foreign affairs in Germany, Gustav Stresemann. This statesman felt the need of an agreement with France. With the experience of the Ruhr fresh in German minds there was a fear of France almost as great as the French fear of Germany. Why not some sort of mutual pact that would afford security to both? France, for her part, would be well satisfied if Great Britain would become a guarantor of such a pact, thus giving her the assurance of support in the event of a German attack. After much negotiation the so-called Pacts or Treaties of Locarno were duly signed, late in 1925. Germany, on the one side, and France and Belgium on the other, agreed to respect the frontiers that then divided them,[1] and Great Britain and Italy added their guarantees to this arrangement. Germany had therefore made a significant renunciation of Alsace-Lorraine. When it came to the eastern frontier, however, she would not

[1] As well as a line of demilitarization fifty kilometers east of the Rhine.

regard the Versailles arrangements as final, though she entered into treaties with both Poland and Czechoslovakia whereby each side promised to refer to arbitration all disputes that might occur between them. Another feature of the pacts was the admission of Germany to the League of Nations (a plan executed the following year) and (at her urgent insistence) the allotment of a place to her on its council. In the meantime the Allies withdrew a proportion of their troops from the occupied area, as they had planned to do much earlier, but which action had been deferred owing to Germany's failing to respect some of her military obligations. The Pacts of Locarno were mainly due to the diplomatic skill of Gustav Stresemann and of Aristide Briand, the French minister of foreign affairs. Stresemann's chief object in the next few years was the complete withdrawal of the army of occupation, but it was not till June 30, 1930 (more than six months after his death) that the last of the Allied troops left German soil.

Whatever the ultimate fruits of Locarno, it had an obvious immediate significance. The isolation of Germany was, for the present at least, ended. She was now restored to the family of nations and even protected against French aggression. For France, too, it seemed to mean a fair security. She could still, of course, be drawn into war over the Polish question, but the chance seemed at least remote. And Great Britain was back once more at her old game of trying to keep a balance on the Continent. According to the wording of the recent settlement, it was to remain in force "until such time as the council [of the League of Nations] should decide by a two-thirds majority that the League insured sufficient protection to the high contracting parties." It was an eloquent admission of the inadequacy of the League.

The Great Powers, indeed, preferred their ancient methods. *Feeble efforts of the powers* Apparently the most hopeful experiment in the direction of a stabilized Europe has been a series of non-aggression pacts. Russia has signed such pacts with all her neighbors in Europe, including Roumania. While so far (1935) an "eastern Locarno" has proved impracticable (owing to Germany's unwillingness to accept these frontiers as final), Germany and Poland have entered into a non-aggression pact (January, 1934) to last for ten years; and shortly afterward four Balkan states (the exceptions were Bulgaria and Albania) reached an agreement guaranteeing the status quo in the Balkan Peninsula. Meanwhile Russia, already bound to France by a non-aggression pact (1932), has been drawing steadily closer to the Little Entente. Whether the change to more friendly relations between France and Italy may also prove a stabilizing influence is hard to predict, for Mussolini is crafty and has no mind to subject himself to the leadership of France. Perchance a fully-armed Germany may lead to a cleavage of Europe, similar to that of 1914. Certainly the policy of keeping Germany weak—the policy inaugurated by the Congress of Paris—has already proved its futility.

One is constantly impressed with the shallowness of most endeavors to provide for permanent peace. The Pact of Paris, or Kellogg Pact [1] (a contribution of the United States to the problem of security) was merely a formal "out-lawing" of war, and by careful reservations this ban was not to apply to defensive wars—the only sort that powers admit waging! Meanwhile instruments of warfare continued to be conspicuous. Efforts to agree on a substantial reduction of armaments have been made repeatedly and failed. In the matter of naval armaments Great Britain with some reluctance accepted parity with the United States, but France has refused to grant this boon to Italy, feeling that her Mediterranean interests are threatened by Fascist chauvinism. It may be observed that neither Great Britain nor the United States had really yielded much, since each retained supremacy over any other power and because of their insular position could easily talk of military reductions. It may be noted that France revived in 1932 her proposal that the League should have an international force at its disposal but again it proved abortive. There is hardly any question but that France herself is to be blamed for her uncompromising attitude toward the harassed Weimar Republic—an attitude which partly explains the rise of the Nazis to power; there is also some reason to feel that her stubborn defense of the status quo with all its territorial defects is evidence of a narrow approach to the problem of security; yet all her regrettable intransigence was due to an explicable fear (amounting almost to an obsession) of German recovery. In wishing to strengthen the League, she was at least intelligently constructive. But the Powers as a whole were suspicious of any experiment that might impede their freedom of action. The scales were heavily weighted against internationalism.

[1] Named after the Secretary of State.

And there are two powers who do not seem to want permanent *The elements of danger* peace, or at least not until they have got the things they want. While Russia, whatever her motives, has shown in recent years a growing spirit of co-operation, the same can hardly be said of Japan and Germany. In 1931 after wrestling for years with a Chinese boy- *(1) Japan* cott which threatened to cut her off from her main sources of food supply, Japan invaded Manchuria on the pretext that the Chinese had seized a stretch of Japanese railroad. Actually she wanted Manchuria because it was a rich country, in which almost $1,000,-000,000 in Japanese capital had been invested, and there was also plenty of room for immigration. Somewhat after the example of the United States in Panama, she proceeded to erect a puppet state, the kingdom of Manchukuo, under her sway. China, helpless of course to make her resistance effective, promptly appealed to the League of Nations; and never had a less welcome task been assumed by that impotent body. Since Japan would not countenance action by the League, probably nothing but turning its whole interventive machinery against her would have availed to bring her to terms, but inasmuch as the Great Powers, caught already in the toils of the depression as well as worried over European problems, were unwilling to face the issue, the council of the League floundered and seemed unable to reach any decision. When at last a commission of inquiry, appointed at Japan's instance, issued a lengthy report condemning her action, she repudiated its judgment and announced her intended withdrawal from the League of Nations. As a belated American protest was equally futile, the Japanese steadily advanced even to the neighborhood of Peking.[1] The episode clearly showed that Japan (who for some years had been dominated by the militarist element) was ready as usual to capitalize any crisis that arose in Europe. In 1933 she proclaimed herself "responsible for the maintenance of peace and order in the Far East," and significantly referred to the exemption of so-called "regional understandings" from the jurisdiction of the League.[2] What Japan explicitly claims is a "Monroe Doctrine" of the Far East. As long, however, as China remains in her present state of impotence and the interests of other powers are not affected, it would seem unlikely that Europe will interfere. Minded to strengthen her hegemony in Asia, she has an-

[1] Now called Peiping.
[2] See page 719.

nounced her intention of building a navy second to none in the
world.

The case of Germany looms largest. With the generally aggressive attitude of the new Germany we have already become acquainted. How real is the pan-German dream has been fully
enough exemplified in her attitude toward Austria. At one time
it seemed that propaganda and force would bring this neighboring
republic into subjection, and whether, indeed, the dictatorship
established at Vienna (as the price of Mussolini's gracious protection!) will suffice to save that power from union with Germany
is a matter of grave concern. Much impetus was certainly given
the pan-German movement when, as the result of the plebiscite
in January, 1935, the Saar Basin returned to Germany, and it is
evident that by "boring from within" (as in the case of Austria)
Germany hopes to recover Danzig and possibly Memel. Hitler
has even revealed the hope of eastward expansion, which would
include not only several Baltic states but also the bulk of the
Ukraine. It is just this outspoken menace (for the Nazis are not
subtle) that persuaded Soviet Russia to line up with the Western
Powers.

All such grandiose objects were, of course, contingent on military power, such as the old Germany had possessed. But in any
case the new Germany determined to suffer no longer the humiliating position imposed upon her by the Treaty of Versailles. Already
reparations were a thing of the past, but the Polish Corridor remained, as the outward visible sign of the *Reich's* dismemberment.
Moreover, Germany needed colonies to provide her with raw
materials, and the recovery of these possessions has already entered
the domain of Hitler's demands. But at the very least Germany
insisted upon military parity—in other words an army that would
be at least as large as that of any of her neighbors, not to mention
a respectable navy, and all the necessary equipment. As a matter
of fact, such a formula (that is, military parity) had been accepted
in principle by the Powers themselves in December, 1933 shortly
before Hitler had attained to power, and the question became the
subject of a long controversy at an international conference over
disarmament. But unfortunately any practical application of
the idea eventually foundered on the suspicion which Nazi
activities in Austria had incurred; hence France and her allies
insisted that Germany was not to receive the privilege in full for

a period of five years. This decision naturally wounded German pride, and Germany accordingly left the conference in high dudgeon.[1] Hitler then appealed to Germans to endorse his policy in a plebiscite—a result which was naturally attained. Thereafter there could be hardly any doubt that Germany would seek her end by unilateral action; indeed, she had already threatened such a step if she should fail to get equality through negotiation. But undoubtedly the greatest blow to the cause of security was her brusque announcement that she intended definitely to withdraw from the League of Nations.[2] Clearly Germany had entered a new phase in the history of her relations with other powers since the War. From 1919 to 1925 she had been an outcast among the powers, occupying a position of compulsory isolation. From the Treaties of Locarno in 1925 to her definite breach with the League in 1933 she had been once more a member of the family of nations and, at least until Hitler's coming, had co-operated more or less cordially with the other powers. Now, succeeding to the policy of conciliation by which Stresemann had sought to obtain concessions for Germany, there had emerged a policy of voluntary isolation and defiance of the rest of Europe. Perhaps on the whole it was singular that nationalism had kept its temper so long.

Whatever the shock to the public, professional diplomats were hardly unprepared for the action which Hitler took on March 16, 1935. In a proclamation to the German people he announced the renunciation of the military provisions of the Treaty of Versailles. This decision, as he went on to show, signified the reinstitution of conscription, the construction of a strong navy, and the raising of an army which was apparently to total about 600,000 men. The decision was based on the need of security and justified by the fact that a general program of disarmament, proposed by the Fourteen Points and definitely promised by the Treaty of Versailles had failed in sixteen years to reach a semblance of realization. The manifesto closed with the words: "For in this hour

The crisis of 1935

---

[1] In order to justify his action Hitler publicly declared (October, 1933) that Germany was ready to disarm if other powers would do likewise. "If the World decides that all weapons are to be abolished down to the last machine gun, we are ready" he said "to join at once in such a convention. But if the World grants to each nation certain weapons, we are not prepared to let ourselves be excluded from this concession as a nation with inferior rights." He also took occasion to say that France and Germany no longer had anything to fight about—a sort of implied recognition of the Pacts of Locarno.

[2] According to the Covenant two years must elapse between a power's announcement of intention to withdraw and actual withdrawal.

the German government renews before the German people, before the entire world, its assurance of its determination never to proceed beyond the safeguarding of the German honor and the safeguarding of the *Reich*, and especially does it not intend in rearming Germany to create any instrument for warlike attack but, on the contrary, exclusively for defense and thereby for the maintenance of peace."

Historically it is hard to resist the feeling that Germany's action was at least humanly natural and was perhaps to some extent justified. Looking back over sixteen years, the Powers had made but half-hearted efforts to promote the cause of peace through a general reduction of armaments; and during all this period Germany had lacked the means of repelling any punitive attack (such as the invasion of the Ruhr) from the self-appointed judges of her conduct. Even the admirable Treaties of Locarno might break down, as the treaty of Belgian neutrality had done. And while it is true that the German nation would most likely have attained its end, military parity, through negotiation (provided, of course, it avoided provocation), the pride of a great nation seemed to demand that it should now free itself. Hardly a German, whether Nazi, socialist, or liberal, could have done otherwise than rejoice that Germany, on her own initiative, was breaking the moral servitude imposed by the Congress of Paris. Even Hitler's exasperation when it was proposed by France and Great Britain that Germany should guarantee her eastern frontier in return for the right to rearm without delay seems not to have been wholly unjustified, and this proposal may, indeed, have been the immediate cause of his action. Germany should show the world that her sovereignty was restored in the fullest sense.

At the moment this book goes to press it is too early to determine the results of this ominous action. Naturally there was much communing among the Powers; the culprit was formally condemned by the League of Nations; and (what is more important) France and Russia signed a pact of mutual assistance, May 2, 1935—an alliance by another name!—for a period of five years.[1] But the crowning fact is that Germany is arming; and in view of the well-known temper of her present régime, one cannot feel greatly encouraged by Hitler's assurance of harmless intent. Cer-

---

[1] This may conceivably weaken the Locarno Pacts since Great Britain would not want to protect a France drawn into war by a German attack on Russia.

tainly her neighbors are all taking renewed precautions, and the
outcome is gray with doubt. With all the Great Powers (including
the United States) now piling up armaments again, one is painfully reminded of those years which immediately preceded the
Great War.

True, if positive provocation can be avoided, Germany may *A peace of circumstance*
keep the world guessing for an indefinite period. There are still
millions of unemployed; the economic structure has yet to be
rebuilt; and there is much needed in the way of equipment for
the army—unless, of course, the chief reliance will be placed on
poisonous gases. It is not at all improbable that a Germany, so
cramped in a material way, may find it much less easy to wrestle
with depression, may more easily succumb to economic collapse.
There is also the fact of her moral isolation. She is at present alone
in a hostile and suspicious world. This is, perhaps, the best safeguard of Europe's peace. But it is a peace based on circumstances,
not on solid foundations. Neither the League of Nations nor the
efforts of separate powers through numerous pacts have availed
to solve the problem of security, and Europe has returned once
more to an armed peace. With the League's declining prestige
the situation is ominous indeed.

It is manifest that neither the problem of security nor that of
economic recovery has been solved. The Treaties of Locarno and
the four-year boom in production had proved a ghastly illusion.
With the recrudescence of German nationalism and the overpowering weight of the world-wide depression Europe has sunk into a
morass from which there is as yet no apparent deliverance in sight.
Especially acute at present is the economic crisis, which appears
to be more widespread and more serious than Europe has ever
experienced. Are these merely fortuitous circumstances or is there
something fundamentally at fault with civilization as evolved by
the Enlightened West?

THE CRISIS FOR WESTERN CIVILIZATION

Western civilization, as we have watched it develop in the
modern world, has seemed to rest on three main pedestals: capitalism, democracy, and nationalism. To all three the individual
has contributed, and by all three, in large measure, has he been
subjected, thus demonstrating, in fact, that to various "systems"
of the Middle Ages, discussed in our introduction, other "systems"

have succeeded. Capitalism and democracy were natural out-growths of the progressive freedom of the individual, but all three have often proved a negation of individualism, and nationalism, in dividing up humanity into a multitude of group minds has prevented both capitalism and democracy from bringing about a coherent world order.

The testing of capitalism

Capitalism, as representing fundamentally the individual's right to personal profit, is so faithfully indicative of human nature that the part which it has played in history hardly needs any eluci-dation. Carried, however, to the extreme of endangering the life and health of society, it required some restriction; and hence the idea of laissez-faire had to give way to a certain measure of social control. Thus, the rise of the "social state" in the nineteenth century. The working class at least must be protected against excessive exploitation. For the protection of the consumer—who represents all society—little indeed was done, for it is much more the interests of the producers than those of the consumers that have controlled modern society.

And even with respect to the workers, it is still pretty generally recognized that they have not yet been granted their proper share in the profits accruing from industry. Hence has come the in-centive, on the part of many of this class, to turn for a remedy to socialism as a system which seems to promise in its application a more equitable distribution of wealth. That it is impossible for the workers to be justly and rationally remunerated under a capitalistic economy is rather too much to assert, but the fact needs to be faced that under the present economy this end has not been attained.

In any case human patience is so long-suffering that if the av-erage worker can really satisfy his elemental wants, he is not likely to raise the moral question whether he ought by right to receive a greater remuneration for his labor. Social legislation, especially various forms of insurance, has helped as a rule to keep him from falling below the level of subsistence. It is only when the evil of unemployment seems not only to have become chronic but to embrace millions of his kind (with the result that the social state cannot stagger under the load) that the whole economic sys-tem under which such things could happen challenges analysis. Moreover, it is clear, as has been intimated, that not only the workers suffer in a depression but most of the rest of humanity.

who become forced with lessened resources to relieve the privations
of the impoverished.

As to the riddle of what has really produced the Great Depression, opinions are so divergent that it would be folly for the historian to venture any opinion. Alternating periods of prosperity and depression, each with increasing intensity as time went on, have occurred ever since the expansion of industry greatly increased the diffusion of capital and made all nations economically interdependent. The world, viewed from this angle, is a delicate economic structure, and any serious misjudgment of the market, overestimating or underestimating existing consumption power, or any over-expansion of credit may produce a sudden crisis, which, if serious enough, is felt throughout the world. As a cause of the present slump, it has been suggested by various scholars that the great corporations, intent upon future profits, had expended their surplus capital too lavishly on equipment, with the result that their goods placed on the market could not be readily consumed at the prices necessary to meet the expenses of this outlay and insure a profit; the result was a recession of prices, a slackening of production, a consequent lowering of wages, and the throwing of more and more persons out of employment. In other words speculative ardor had outrun consumption power. The banks, which are able to create credit and bolster up production power, did not dare, when the crisis came, to make further loans, and those who had capital to invest waited naturally for better times. If less of the accumulated profits were to go into saving and more into the hands of the workers, it is alleged that the rate of consumption power would be less variable. Whether this theory is correct or not, it seems to be clear that at times there is overproduction or (if one likes) underconsumption, and that when production slackens as a consequence, the consumer, whether a workman or a merchant or an investor, is impoverished in the process. Obviously once a depression begins, it tends rapidly to become worse; for just as rising prices (up to a certain point) may stimulate buying for fear of a greater rise, so a lowering of prices leads to an interval of waiting in hope of a greater drop; and the lower the scale of prices, the less profit can be derived from production, and the less can be paid in wages to the workers or to the peasants in return for the products of the soil. Only indeed when prices have fallen very low (one cannot say how low) will demand become revived and the

PAYING HOMAGE AT THE SHRINE OF LENIN

trend back to prosperity begin. The protraction of a depression is, of course, often due to conscious hoarding, based upon fear, and the revival of public confidence is one of the most difficult of all phases of the problem. And in the meantime has come a lowering of the standard of living for almost all. Yet it is a curious anomaly that at no time in the history of the world has the productive power of man been so enhanced as it has been in the twentieth century. Can no means be found of making it adequately serve the need of humanity—not merely on occasions but continuously? Mr. G. D. H. Cole insists that it is human folly alone that prevents the world from fully enjoying the fruits of its technical skill and organizing genius. Overproduction, he says, might be viewed as impossible; it is only the maldistribution of wealth that prevents the enjoyment of the productive power that science has created. And this, of course, invites the challenge of an entirely different system, that of socialism—a system based on service rather than individual profit. The ills of capitalism are to be cured by killing the victim.

With the moral possibilities of socialism we shall not here deal. On the economic side we are well aware that not only would it involve a much less wide divergence of income; there would be a concentrated management of all economic life. Provided intelligent leadership were found, there would be no social waste, no sacrificing of the future to the present, no permission for one industry to become inflated and another depressed; there would be planning for the whole economic unit. Whether the idea is humanly sound and whether if really sound there is enough intelligence to apply it, Russia is giving the world the benefit of her experience. If she finally succeeds and if capitalism is still in a shaken condition, socialism will certainly constitute a formidable appeal. Paul Einzig puts it tersely when he writes, "If within the next few decades it becomes evident that the communist experience in Soviet Russia is successful and that it is capable of providing the large masses of the population with a higher standard of living than that of capitalist countries, then our present political, social, and economic system is doomed." Yet even the success of communism—and success is, after all, a relative term—does not necessarily mean that capitalism could not achieve still better results if modified in certain of its characteristics. Capitalism is simply put to a greater test than ever before in its history.

One thing which seems to be generally admitted at this time is that individuals working for profit (as always under capitalism) cannot safely be allowed to exercise their judgment without some social restraint. To allow them to do so leaves the matter of everyone's income or profit peculiarly liable to periodic fluctuations and to an absence of that security which is essential to human happiness. Some social planning seems essential to the recovery and then afterward to the conservation of the capitalistic order. Another thing less readily admitted is that economically the world forms a unit. Huge political debts (like "reparations"), tariff walls, and currency-manipulating are all so many obstacles to the free opening of the world's markets and the development of consumption power that will in turn insure a high level of production. But nationalism refuses to bow to this fact, and to this we shall refer again. Perhaps a more immediate consideration is whether that degree of governmental control needed for the purpose of a planned economy is practicable under a democratic régime. Must democracy finally abdicate in order that the world may be rescued from the present chaos? Is the only alternative to communism an equally autocratic control of capitalism—what is commonly known as "fascism"?

The testing of "democracy"   A capitalistic economy has in the past found democracy well suited to its development because of the spirit of individualism that is common to both and in spite of the fact that "the total number of economic agents is small [to quote Sombart] as compared with the total number of persons participating in economic life with the result that a large majority is subject to the power of a few economic agents." Democracy is not, however, necessary to capitalism, for it was in the period of absolute monarchies that modern capitalism got its first great impetus. In those days it was submitted more or less to State control and regulation. When the middle class became strong enough, they ended this régime, and the idea of laissez-faire, as we have noticed, became triumphant. Then finally democracy tempered laissez-faire, but still left capitalism most of its former power. Government regulation, though applied in the case of the tariff (as an example of defensive nationalism), was hardly felt to be applicable to a democratic society. The individual producer was free to make his blunders to the detriment of his own and of other peoples' interests. Only in time of war was it deemed necessary for the State to step in and mobilize the resources of a country for a common end. The Great

War—a great military crisis—resulted in a species of temporary dictatorship in all the democratic nations which participated. It was not so very different, except in some of its methods, from the historic Reign of Terror. It was an eloquent indication of the supposed limitations of democracy.

The economic crisis, which followed in the train of the Great War, came to present the same problem. To end capitalism or regulate it—such has seemed to be the inevitable choice. Russia chose the former alternative; Italy and Germany, the latter; but all have proceeded on the same assumption that only an autocracy was fitted to grapple with vital economic problems. We hold no brief for communism or fascism; their success is still uncertain. But can the remaining democracies prove that they themselves are better adapted for the task? Shall they be able to make the choice between—let us say—socialism and a regulated capitalism without confiding their fortunes to a rigorous dictatorship?

One cannot give a categorical answer. But it may not be amiss to seek some light on democracy and how it seems to work. If statesmanship has seemed so barren and futile in a crisis, may it not be that the system which underlies it is at fault? Do the best brains enter politics? Are the people able to discover them, and, if so, do they really want them? We are not concerned with Germany or Italy, where liberal institutions had failed to take adequate root, but rather with France and Great Britain—and one is tempted also to add the United States. Not without some profit have political scientists and social psychologists been turning a veritable searchlight on democracy, and some have raised some ugly but pertinent questions. How, after all, is it to be expected that the masses in any country will choose competent persons to run their governments? In the first place, if psychological tests are to be trusted—a good deal more than half of the adult population of any country is of very limited intelligence. In the second place, the art of government has become such a complex affair that only a small proportion of the most intelligent can have a rational view on most public questions. How many persons could readily demonstrate that nationalization of the railroads would be socially beneficial? To be able to plumb the depths of some of the problems of the day requires intellectual capacity and equipment. And that is not all; it requires much time and patience. But as even the very intelligent fraction is occupied as a rule with the problem of making a living and may feel that in its leisure time it needs a much more stimulating form of diversion than studying the tariff or some form of social control, one can easily deduce that there is a very small proportion of voters who really possess an intelligent opinion on public questions. It was once true that politics furnished a measure of entertainment if for no other reason than it afforded a fund for argument, but in the twentieth century the automobile, the moving picture, and the radio supply amusement with which politics can hardly be expected to compete. Democracy thus breaks up into myriads of individuals too sluggish or too preoccupied to study their common interests.

Since the masses, then, are not well informed and are not mentally acute, they tend to cling to traditional institutions or if compelled to face an issue, they vote either yes or no on the general idea, or if no question in particular forces their attention, they vote more or less blindly for a party or a personality. In fact, it is all that they are fitted to do. Moreover, hundreds of thousands do not bother to register any opinion at all. While it is true that in Europe there is no such apathy as is normal in the United States, the proportion of citizens who do not vote at all is certainly disquieting to those who believe in democracy. Lord Bryce, one of the greatest champions of democracy, was sufficiently disillusioned as to write in 1920, "The lapse of years has given us a fuller knowledge. . . . The proportion of citizens who take a lively and constant interest in politics is so small, and likely to remain so small, that the direction of affairs inevitably passes into the hands of the few."

Such a deduction signifies that democracy, properly speaking, does not really function at all. It is difficult to resist the conclusion that régimes supposedly democratic are in reality oligarchies. The idea of the omnipotent citizen is, as Lippmann says, a false ideal. The men who constitute governments are largely politicians who enjoy perhaps the backing of a machine which knows only too well how to twist the public mind. Issues can often be over-simplified or sentimentalized; candidates, ready with slogans or catch phrases, can sway an audience with empty eloquence; the radical can capitalize latent discontent and offer his platform as a prescription for any malady, while the conservative can deliberately play upon fear or upon that ingrained hatred of change which people with enough to live on generally display. If the masses do not think, it is to their emotions that the shrewd politician generally appeals. The greatest lever for the development of public opinion has been the press. There the voter gets his opinions ready-made. The facts may be false as presented to him, and they are bound to be one-sided, but as few can afford to take two newspapers of opposite opinions (even if they are so disposed), the masses are usually influenced by the nearest or perhaps the cheapest sensational journal. Few editors, indeed, are concerned with the solemn business of enlightening the public; they are business men who are scheming for as large a circulation as they can create, since a large circulation means plenty of advertising, and it is advertising that makes the paper pay; hence they give the reading public the kind of reading matter that it wants. It is patent therefore that democracy has opened the way to a science of practical psychology. Parties and politicians study the popular mind, note its trends and aberrations, twist it to believe this or that, and compete with one another for its approval at the polls. Only on certain occasions does the tail wag the dog. Only, perhaps, in times of great stress, when popular emotions are worked up to a fever heat by sudden resentment or long-stored-up hatred does public opinion really stampede the politician. The French and English had but one opinion on the proper treatment of Germany in 1918, though it is worth noting that in England the activities of the Northcliffe press had a great deal to do with promoting this spirit of revenge. Generally speaking, one finds it hard to resist the conclusion that power is generated from the top much more than from the bottom.

Much, in any case, rests on the responsibility of the men who get themselves chosen to represent the people. Many, if not most of them, are fairly alive to popular needs, as such needs come to be construed by a people badly informed and often deliberately misled. Many of them, indeed, are estimable gentlemen, who give a good deal of attention to public problems. But they are not necessarily persons whose previous records have proved their fitness for responsibility. Politics does not breed experts. Such persons would have little time to play the demagogue and the public would be unlikely to understand them. Moreover, the trend of things in Europe has had the general effect of hardening economic lines. Just as the labor and socialist parties represent the interests of the proletariat, so the more conservative parties form the vanguard of organized capital. In the light of these "pressure groups," [1] as they have been called, the broader interests of society as a whole become obscured. It is not here implied that politicians as a rule are deliberately corrupt, and there is not in Europe the domination of the lobbies, which is the curse of American politics; how common, indeed, are cases of indirect bribery through conscious appeals to a lawmaker's cupidity or social ambition is hard to determine, though examples of such have been known. Nor can one really prove that in Europe the moneyed interests bind the politician by finding him ways of adding to his income—another prevalent abuse in the United States. If he serves the world of capital, it is more probably because he regards it as fundamental to the social order. And possibly he is right. But generally it is true that neither training nor outlook equip him for the responsibility of discerning his country's needs and the way to meet them.

Yet an analysis of democracy and a realization of what it is and what it is not does not necessarily prove that the system cannot be modified to work better in the long run than any other polity that history has contributed. Freedom of opinion has never flourished under autocracy, and it is hard to believe that civilization would really advance without the right of the individual to speak or write his thoughts. One may even hazard the opinion that the right to be misgoverned is more precious than all the efficiency of a government that fetters the spirit. Perhaps it may be possible in time to educate the masses up to the point of choosing as their rulers persons of recognized character and breadth. Such persons, wise in their ignorance, might be expected to consult the men who have given the most careful and thorough study to public questions. In British politics there was once a tradition of service, whose exponents often managed to stand above all petty interests, and though the social status of such men had the undoubted tendency to make them ultra-conservative, the sense of responsibility which they developed was comparable to the spirit of the judiciary. Humanity is not devoid of persons of intelligence and character, as any of the trades and professions amply attest. But until the

---

[1] The influence of regionalism is much less powerful in Europe than in the United States, partly because European countries (excepting, of course, Russia) have populations less widely scattered, and partly because the members of popular chambers are not required to be residents of the constituencies they represent. There are also fewer pressure groups representing religious, moral, or military organizations.

world is brought to see that the business of running a government requires as fine a mental equipment as the handling of a great corporation, democracies are liable to function in a sorry and haphazard fashion. Only time can rectify the faults of such a system. Today democracy, like capitalism, is put to a crucial test.

One of the arguments for democracy is that only under such a régime can nationalism be tempered. Autocrats will almost inevitably look to their own country as the limit of their concern. *The testing of nationalism* Worse still, they are always liable to precipitate a war for national glory if they think their position at home is becoming weaker. But nationalism, when wholly spontaneous, might possibly be susceptible to higher motives; or, to put it squarely, nationalism might possibly disappear if the people who gave it force were to take a larger view of the world they lived in. Such a hope may perhaps be quixotic; yet even enlightened self-interest demands a broader outlook; further, it demands a world at peace. And there can be no durable peace until the world has learned the lesson of international co-operation. Moreover, the interdependence of nations should make it evident enough that bitter national rivalries are basically artificial—the product of the narrowest self-interest or of utterly blind emotionalism. A well-known scholar, Dr. Krehbiel, has pointed out that nationalism is simply the historical product of a world that has overemphasized political divisions, and he declares that it is logically an anachronism. But, whatever the historian's logic, the fact remains that nationalism is stronger today than in any period of history. Fear and hatred seem deeper in Europe than ever they have been before. Nations are heavily armed, and look to another war as a likely eventuality. And a narrow and strictly self-protective attitude in dealing with the Great Depression has led to a display of economic nationalism, more intense than the world has witnessed since the bygone days of mercantilism. Nationalism has proved but a sorry means of giving Europe her needed stability.

And what of the new internationalism—hopeful offspring of Wilson's vision? Alas, it was soon shattered by the products of a stupid peace. "Modern man," writes the French publicist, Delaisi, "is in truth a citizen of the World. But he is completely unaware of the fact. and herein lies the tragedy of our time."

FOR FURTHER READING OR STUDY

Scott, J. F., and Baltzly, A., *Readings in European History since 1814*, chap. xvi, secs. iv, vii–ix; Cooke, W. H., and Stickney, E. P., *Readings in European International Relations since 1879*, nos. 162–83; Tiltman, H. H., *Slump; A Study of Stricken Europe;* D'Abernon, *An Ambassador of Peace*, 2 vols. Schapiro, J. S., *Modern and Contemporary European History*, chap. xxxviii; Higby, C. P., *History of Modern Europe*, pp. 427–42; Palm, F. C. and Graham, F. E., *Europe since Napoleon*, chaps. xxxvi–xxxviii; Ogg, F. A., and Sharp, W. R., *Economic Development of Modern Europe*, chap. xxxi; Day, C., *Economic Development in Modern Europe*, chaps. v–vi, x, xiii; Benns, E. L., *The World since 1914* (extremely useful), chaps. x, xi, xiv, and xv; Langsam, W. C., *The World since 1914*, chap. vii (reparations); Sontag, R. J., *European Diplomatic History*, chaps. viii–ix; Cole, G. D. H., and M. I., *The Intelligent Man's Review of Europe Today*.

Siegfried, A., *Post-War Britain;* McDonald, W., *Reconstruction in France;* Angell, J. W., *The Recovery of Germany;* Meakin, W., *The New Industrial Revolution* (on the temporary boom in Germany); McFadyean, A., *Reparations Reviewed;* Schacht, H., *The End of Reparations* (by an eminent German); Wheeler-Bennett, J., *The Wreck of Reparations* (easy reading); Moulton, H. G., and Pasvolsky, L., *War Debts and World Prosperity* (published in 1932); Salter, A., and others, *The World Economic Crisis* (a sheaf of lectures); Salter, A., *Recovery: Second Effort;* Toynbee, A. J., *Survey of International Affairs* (an annual, useful for reference); Simonds, F. H., *Can Europe Keep the Peace?* and *America Faces the Next War;* Stephens, C. S., *Danger Zones of Europe: A Study of National Minorities;* Withers, H., *The Case for Capitalism;* Cole, G. D. H., *A Guide through World Chaos* and (editor) *What Everybody Wants to Know about Money;* Schlichter, S. H., *Modern Economic Society;* Tawney, R. H., *The Sickness of an Acquisitive Society;* Webb, S., and B., *The Decay of Capitalist Civilization;* Shaw, G. B., *The Intelligent Woman's Guide to Socialism and Capitalism;* Denis, L., *Is Capitalism Doomed?;* Barnes, H. E., *Living in the Twentieth Century* (for helpful analyses of democracy and nationalism); Cooley, C. H., *Social Organization;* Bryce, J., *Modern Democracies*, 2 vols.; Burns, C. D., *Democracy;* Le Bon, G., *The Crowd: A Study of the Popular Mind;* Wallas, G., *Human Nature in Politics* and *The Great Society;* Bryce, J., *Modern Democracies*, vol. ii (for conclusions); Lippmann, W., *A Preface to Politics, Public Opinion, The Phantom Public,* and *Methods of Freedom* (decidedly worth reading); Sait, E. M., *Democracy* (admirable summary of current views); Laski, H. J., *Democracy in Crisis* (penetrating but rather verbose); Bonn, M., *The Crisis in European Democracy;* Herbert, S., *Nationality and its Problems;* Delaisi, F., *Political Myths and Economic Realities;* Laski, H. J., *Nationalism and the Future of Civilization* (an interesting lecture); Cohen-Portheim, P., *The Discovery of Europe* (on the cultural outlook); Wilde, J. C. de, "Germany's Trend toward Economic Isolation," *Foreign Policy Reports*, vol. x, no. 18; Dean, V. M., "The Soviet Union as a European Power," *ibid.*, no. 11; Salter, A., "The Future of Economic Nationalism," *Foreign Affairs*, xi, 8 ff.; see also references following chap. xviii.

INDEX

East Prussia, 108–9, 116, 665

Ebert, Friedrich, 798, 803, 810

Ebro River, 79, 363

Ecclesiastical Reservation, 59, n.

Economists (or Physiocrats), 257–8

Edinburgh, 194

Edward I, king of England, 51, 172

Edward III, king of England, 173

Edward VI, king of England, 21

Edward VII, king of England, 615

Egypt, as gateway to East, 30, 45, 677; early French interest in, 167, 230–1, 343, 357, 608; British relations with, 591, 597, 608–9, 733, 735

Elba, 371

Elbe River, 109

Electricity, 512–3

Elizabeth, czarina of Russia, 115

Elizabeth, queen of England, reformation under, 21, 176; and Catholic Reaction, 57, 175, 195; penalizes Catholics, 177; as a mercantilist, 207

Émigrés, beginning of, 286; influence of, 296; measures against, 318, 325; return of, 346, 371

Ems, 496

Enabling Act, 817

Encyclopedists, 257

Engels, Friedrich, 443, 447

England, reformation in, 20–2; wage regulation in, 33, 423, 433; as a modern state, 42–3, 170; as a national state, 50–4; allies with France, 82; struggle of, with Louis XIV, 98–100; aids Frederick II, 115; treats with Moscow, 138; constitutional development of, 171–93; progress of, in 18th century, 193–4; acquires Scotland, 194–5; exploits Ireland, 195–6; mercantilism in, 205, n. 2, 206–8; commercial growth of, 209; capitalism in, 210–1; social changes in, 212–3, 249; relations of, with Dutch, 214, 218–9; colonial policy of, 224; rationalism in, 257; commercial treaty of, with France, 279; threatened with invasion, 343; post-Napoleonic conditions in, 393–5, 432; as home of Industrial Revolution, 413–4, 416; trade-unionism in, 428, 433–4, 547–8; proletarian agitation in, 435–7;

socialism in, 437, 547; as a social state, 448–50; depression in, 516; public opinion in, 526–7, 535; political reform in, 528–32; agriculture in, 547; gets Suez shares, 592; post-War economic conditions in, 739–40; see also Great Britain

English, traits of, 171, 177, 393, 535, 567; as colonists, 223–5

Enlightenment, meaning of, 254; spread of, 257, 265; triumph of, 378; see also Rationalism

Entente Cordiale, formation of, 615, 618; testing of, 616–7; approximates an alliance, 637

Equality, social, sought by French bourgeoisie, 251, 280; attitude of Voltaire toward, 259; attitude of Rousseau toward, 263–4; legal, in France achieved, 293; practical interpretation of, 334, 346; as result of French Revolution, 377–9, 396, n.; problem of, in 19th century, 555; among Russian peasants, 770

Erasmus, Desiderius, 12–13

Eritrea, 595, 597

Estates general, complexion and rôle of, 39; weakness of, 39–40, 92; called by Marie de' Medici, 74; exalted by writers, 256; agitation for, 269–70; called by Louis XVI, 271; significance of the calling of, 277; opening of, 280–1; becomes "National Assembly," 282

Erzberger, Mathias, 811, n.

Esthonia, 105, 145, 156, 796; see also Baltic states

Euphrates River, 606

Europe, as a continent, 2–3

Extraterritoriality, 600, 606

Factory Acts, 449–50

Falkenhayn, General von, 671

Family Compact, 101, 317

Faraday, Michael, 512

Far East, produce of, 30–1; Napoleon's interest in, 357; as scene of world politics, 599

Farther Pomerania, 106

Fascism, 754–60

Fashoda, 610, 614

Feminism, meaning of, 747; see also Woman